W9-AAD-412

CANADIAN BUSINESS AND THE LAW

SIXTH EDITION

CANADIAN BUSINESS AND THE LAW

SIXTH EDITION

Dorothy DuPlessis

University of New Brunswick

Shannon O'Byrne

University of Alberta

Philip King

Western University

Lorrie Adams

MacEwan University

Steven Enman

Acadia University

Canadian Business and the Law, Sixth Edition
by Dorothy DuPlessis, Shannon O'Byrne, Philip King, Lorrie Adams, and Steven Enman

VP, Product and Partnership Solutions:
Anne Williams

Publisher, Digital and Print Content:
Anne-Marie Taylor

Senior Marketing Manager:
Alexis Hood

Content Development Manager:
Suzanne Simpson Millar

Permissions Coordinator and Photo Researcher:
MRM Associates (Derek Capitaine)

Production Project Manager:
Jaime Smith

Production Service:
MPS Limited

Copy Editor:
Laurel Sparrow, Top Copy Communications/Sparrow and Associates

Proofreader:
MPS Limited

Indexer:
May Hasso

Design Director:
Ken Phipps

Managing Designer:
Franca Amore

Interior Design:
Trinh Truong

Cover Design:
Courtney Hellam

Cover Image:
Seamartini Graphics/Shutterstock

Compositor:
MPS Limited

Library and Archives Canada Cataloguing in Publication

DuPlessis, Dorothy, 1955-[Canadian business & the law]
    Canadian business and the law / Dorothy DuPlessis (University of New Brunswick), Steven Enman (Acadia University), Shannon O'Byrne (University of Alberta), Philip King (Western University).—Sixth edition.

Revision of: DuPlessis, Dorothy, 1955-. Canadian business & the law. Includes bibliographical references and index. ISBN 978-0-17-657032-3 (bound)

    1. Commercial law—Canada—Textbooks. I. Enman, Steven R. (Steven Robert), 1951-, author II. O'Byrne, Shannon, 1958-, author III. King, Philip, author IV. Title. V. Title: Canadian business & the law.

KE919.D86 2017
346.7107   C2015-904795-1
KF889.D86 2017

ISBN-13: 978-0-17-657032-3
ISBN-10: 0-17-657032-2

IMPORTANT DISCLAIMER: This book provides legal information of interest to those studying business law. It neither offers nor contains legal advice of any kind. If you have a personal legal question that requires legal advice, please consult a lawyer.

ABOUT THE AUTHORS

Dorothy Roberta Ruth DuPlessis, B.Com., LL.B., M.B.A. (Dalhousie University), LL.M. (University of London), is a professor in the Faculty of Business Administration, University of New Brunswick (Fredericton). She is a member of the Canadian Academy of Legal Studies in Business and a past member of the Nova Scotia Barristers' Society. Professor DuPlessis has taught courses in business law, administrative law, international law, and Internet law at both the undergraduate and the graduate levels. She has also lectured at the Czech Management School and at the Institute of Professional Management. Professor DuPlessis has published articles on auditor's and director's liability, copyright, and university administration. She is also the past law examiner for the Certified General Accountants Association of Canada.

Shannon Kathleen O'Byrne, B.A. (University of Regina), M.A., LL.B., LL.M. (University of Alberta), is a professor in the Faculty of Law, University of Alberta, and a former Associate Dean of Graduate Studies and Research. She was admitted to the Law Society of Alberta in 1987 and is a past member of the board of directors of the Edmonton Bar Association. Her law review articles are influential, with several having been cited with approval by courts across the country, including the Supreme Court of Canada. Professor O'Byrne is the recipient of the University of Alberta's highest teaching honour, the Rutherford Award for Excellence in Undergraduate Teaching, as well as the Faculty of Law's Teaching Excellence Award, named after the Hon. Mr. Justice Tevie Miller. Professor O'Byrne has also received the Distinguished Service Award for Contributions to Legal Scholarship, awarded by the Law Society of Alberta and the Canadian Bar Association (Alberta branch), and the University of Alberta Alumni Award of Excellence.

Philip King, B.A. Philosophy (Western University), LL.B. (Western University), M.B.A. (Ivey Business School, Western University), teaches at Western Law, the Ivey Business School, and the Dan Program in Management and Organizational Studies, and practises corporate and commercial law in London, Ontario. Philip has practised law since 1992, helping businesspeople achieve their goals by managing legal issues effectively. During that time, he has had the privilege of working with some of Canada's finest lawyers and businesspeople. While a student at Western, Philip was awarded the gold medal in the combined Law and M.B.A. program.

Lorrie Adams, B.Comm., LL.B., LL.M. (University of Alberta), is an assistant professor in the School of Business at MacEwan University (Edmonton) where she is a member of the department of International Business, Marketing, Strategy and Law. At MacEwan University she has chaired two School of Business programs and has taught courses in business law, employment law, international business transactions, and civil procedures. She has been a presenter for Alberta's bar admission program and is an evaluator and facilitator for the Canadian Centre for Professional Legal Education (the organization that administers the bar admission program in Alberta, Saskatchewan, and Manitoba). Lorrie has been a member of the Law Society of Alberta since 1993 and practised law in Edmonton for 17 years, advising insurers on a range of tort liability, litigation, and contract matters.

Steven Robert Enman, B.B.A. (Acadia University), LL.B. (Dalhousie University), LL.M. (Bristol University), was an associate professor in the Fred C. Manning School of Business Administration, Acadia University, when he retired in 2011. He was admitted to the bar of Nova Scotia in 1978, taught business law at Acadia for 32 years, and was director of the school for four years. Professor Enman is a retired member of the Nova Scotia Barristers' Society and a member of the Academy of Legal Studies in Business. He was the editor of two editions of *Canadian Business Law Cases*. He has presented papers at conferences dealing with privacy, unconscionable contracts, and commercial morality.

BRIEF CONTENTS

CONTENTS

PREFACE

In *Canadian Business and the Law,* Sixth Edition, legal knowledge is regarded as a business asset that builds competitive advantage for the individual and the organization alike. This text demonstrates how the law can protect persons and their property as well as resolve disputes. The text also shows that the law facilitates personal and commercial interactions. In short, the law provides both opportunities to be capitalized on and risks to be managed.

Canadian Business and the Law is written from the perspective that the law plays an integral role in all business decisions. Furthermore, it systematically advocates a risk management approach as the optimum way of dealing with legal considerations in the business world. A risk management model is introduced in Part 1 and applied in every subsequent part of the book. Topical coverage is organized as follows:

- **Part 1** establishes the rationale for students' study of business law. It accounts for what the law is, where it comes from, and how the law regulates business. It also establishes risk management as the recurring theme of the book and the study of business law.

- **Parts 2** and **3** recognize that the legal issues a businessperson is most likely to face are in the areas of contract law and tort law. Part 2, Contracts, and Part 3, Business Torts, provide a practical and contextualized analysis of these important areas. Here students acquire not only an essential legal grounding in contract and tort principles, but also the basic background for the specialized topics discussed later in the book. These two essential parts of the book are carefully written so that contracts and torts can be read and taught in whichever sequence is preferable to the user.

  The fundamentals of contract law are examined in depth in Part 2 to allow for application in context in later parts, which deal with topics such as agency, partnership, employment, and insurance. By applying the law to particular relationships, students gain insight into the kinds of contracts that will figure prominently in their professional lives.

In our experience, students best understand the law when it is related to core subject areas in the business curriculum, including finance, human resources, sales, and marketing. For this reason, the remaining parts of the book look at the functional areas of business and consider legal issues in relation to those activities.

- **Part 4** concerns the selection and use of the form of business.
- **Part 5** examines the creation, acquisition, use, and protection of property.
- **Part 6** analyzes the acquisition and use of human resources.
- **Part 7** focuses on the selling and marketing of goods and services.
- **Part 8** addresses financing the business activity.
- **Part 9** explores the transference of risk through the use of insurance.

Our work in *Canadian Business and the Law* focuses on meeting a number of objectives:

- Our most important aim is to explain the basic legal principles and concepts in a business context that is engaging and relevant for all readers.
- The second objective is to reinforce that all aspects of the legal environment necessitate active management. We offer a model for identifying, evaluating, and managing legal risk in Chapter 3. Examples of the model's

application to business enterprises and a risk management orientation are reflected in the treatment of legal subjects throughout the text.

- The third objective is to convey legal information in contexts geared to the practical application of knowledge. A **Business Law in Practice** scenario opens each chapter with a business situation containing both legal and managerial implications. Questions posed by the opening scenario give students direction and purpose and encourage critical thinking as they read the chapter. As a means of testing the students' comprehension and analytical skills, the scenario is revisited later in the chapter with suggested responses to the opening questions.

  The practical application of legal knowledge is reinforced through boxes provided throughout the text entitled **Business Application of the Law**. These provide examples of the impact of the law on business enterprises. By illustrating how legal issues arise in the business environment and how these issues are managed, this feature helps students develop a concrete understanding of why the law matters in a business context.

- The fourth goal of the text is to recognize the importance of legal considerations inherent in the emergence of new technologies, internationalization and globalization of the economy, as well as ethical and environmental concerns, all of which cut across traditional legal subjects. Based on our contextualized approach to teaching and learning, these topics or unifying themes are integrated throughout the body of the text and through features entitled **Technology and the Law**, **International Perspective**, **Ethical Considerations**, and **Environmental Perspective**.

- The fifth goal is to provide a pedagogically effective framework for the presentation of judicial decisions. Our special Case format begins with a description of the business context surrounding the legal dispute in question, followed by a concise statement of the relevant facts that led to the legal conflict. Next, a statement of the legal issues is provided as a summary of how the court resolved the conflict. The feature concludes with several questions that students are asked to consider to deepen their understanding of the case under study. This feature focuses on context and relevance. Judicial rulings are summarized and supplemented with brief excerpts of judicial language.

  The **Landmark Case** and **Business and Legislation** features provide an account of pivotal case law and historical legislative initiatives, which can be essential to grasping contemporary law.

Finally, an **Ethical Considerations** feature assists the student in assessing the sometimes uncomfortable compromises that the law forges between competing interests. As demonstrated in the chart on the inside front cover, the textbook organizes coverage of the international, environmental, ethics, and technology themes because of their importance to the modern business world. We have increased both the depth and the breadth of these four themes according to strands, or markers, to illustrate the range of topics that the text covers. The comprehensive chart is also designed to assist instructors in creating their lectures. At a glance, instructors can access the textbook's nearly 50 themed boxes and locate material according to the subject they wish to address, such as ethics in consumer relations or ethics in relation to employees.

What's New in This Edition

In this edition, we continue to build on the strengths of the textbook. The content is Canadian, current, business oriented, and focused on risk management. In addition to enhancing the thematic approach as noted above, we present students with new, real-world examples of the application of the law as well as the latest Canadian cases and legislation. We have also crafted several new Business Law in Practice chapter openers that explore legal issues in different contexts and have rewritten sections to promote student learning and reflect the ongoing changes in the law. For example, some of the major additions and changes to this edition are:

- New cases. Many new cases have been added. Examples include: *Bhasin v Hrynew* 2014 SCC 71 (Chapter 7); *Fullowka v Pinkerton's of Canada Ltd* [2010] 1 SCR 132; *Resurfice Corp v Hanke* [2007] 1 SCR (Chapter 11); *Mainstream Canada v Staniford* 2013 BCCA 341 (Chapter 12); *TMS Lighting Ltd v KJS Transport Inc* 2014 ONCA 1; *Piljak Estate v. Abraham*, 2014 ONSC 2893 (Chapter 17); *Scotia Mortgage Corporation v. Gutierrez*, 2012 ABQB 683; *Fairview Donut Inc. v The TDL Group* 2012 ONCA 867; (Chapter 14); *Chan v City Commercial Realty* 2011 ONSC 2854 (Chapter 16); *Teva Canada Ltd v Pfizer Canada Inc.* 2012 SCC 60; *Cinar Corporation v Robinson* 2013 SCC 73; *Canada (Attorney General) v Johnstone* 2014 FCA 110 (Chapter 20); *Communications, Energy and Paperworkers Union v Irving*, 2013 SCC 34 (Chapter 20); *Potter v New Brunswick Legal Aid Services Commission*, 2015 SCC 10 (CanLII) (Chapter 21); *Royal Bank of Canada v Samson Management & Solutions Ltd.*, 2013 ONCA 313 (CanLII) (Chapter 26); and *McRudden (Re)*, 2014 BCSC 217 (CanLII) (Chapter 27).

- New legislation. We have highlighted new and amended existing legislation relevant to business, including legislation concerning protecting the health of animals (Chapter 1); franchises (Chapter 14); securities regulation (Chapter 15); copyright and trademarks (Chapter 18); workplace bullying (Chapter 20); the transition of accountants in Canada to the new Chartered Professional Accountant (CPA) designation (Chapter 22); and reducing email spam (Chapter 24).

- New real-world examples. This new edition discusses, for example, the inhumane treatment of animals by an Ontario poultry farm (Chapter 1); the collapse of a Bangladeshi factory that produced clothing for Canadian fashion brand Joe Fresh (Chapter 1); faulty ignition switches at General Motors (Chapter 3); violations of Canada's new anti-spam legislation by Plentyoffish Media Inc and Compu-Finder (Chapter 6); a customer's liability for a stolen rental car (Chapter 9); the criminal and civil liability of an NHL player for attacking on opponent on-ice (Chapter 10); Scotiabank's dispute over the Tangerine name (Chapter 15); the advent of crowdfunding for raising equity capital (Chapter 15); the push for women on corporate boards (Chapter 16); a hospital's claim of ownership over its patient's excised tissue (Chapter 17); ownership and regulation of water rights (Chapter 17); Canada Goose's action against Sears for trademark infringement (Chapter 18); director, corporate, and taxpayer liability for environmentally contaminated land (Chapter 19); the liability of auditors to misled creditors (Chapter 22); convictions for price fixing and other anti-competitive behaviour (Chapter 24); and the failure of Target Canada (Chapter 27).

- Updated and revised real-world examples from previous editions. Examples include liability of a store owner for failing to comply with Nova Scotia's *Tobacco Access Act* (Chapter 2); the result of a class action law suit against Bell Mobility regarding 911 access (Chapter 7); new convictions under Canada's anti-bribery legislation (Chapter 8); the settlement of the claim of a lottery partnership (Chapter 14); the continuing saga of Lord Black (Chapter 15); an update on Canadian securities class actions (Chapter 15); penalties in the death and injury of workers falling from scaffolding (Chapter 16); an update on the unpaid overtime class actions (Chapter 20); and bitcoins and other new methods of electronic payment (Chapter 25).
- New and updated chapter openings (**Business Law in Practice**) for Chapters 1, 10, 14, 15, 16, 23, and 24.
- New and revised end-of-chapter material. We have added or replaced questions in the **Questions for Review, Questions for Critical Thinking,** and **Situations for Discussion** features.

Canadian Business and the Law, Sixth Edition, is offered as a modern resource for learning the fundamentals of business law from a business perspective. Rather than simply providing a summary of the law, it presents traditional business law topics in a manner that resonates with commercial reality. If you have any suggestions for improvements, additions, or clarifications, please let us know:

Dorothy DuPlessis	ddupless@unb.ca
Shannon O'Byrne	sobyrne@ualberta.ca
Philip King	king@pklaw.ca
Lorrie Adams	adamsl14@macewan.ca

INTEGRATED PEDAGOGICAL SYSTEM

Basic legal principles and concepts are explained and reinforced through the use of extensive pedagogy designed to help students proceed and learn the material.

Chapter Objectives outline the learning goals of each chapter.

1

OBJECTIVES
After studying this chapter you should have an understanding of

- the role of law in guiding conduct
- the importance of legal knowledge in the business environment
- the challenges posed by business ethics and their relationship to legal requirements

KNOWLEDGE OF LAW AS A BUSINESS ASSET

BUSINESS LAW IN PRACTICE

Lionel Garfield, who grew up on a large farm in Ontario, decided to go into the chicken processing business for himself. When a local Ontario poultry producer decided to retire, Lionel jumped at the opportunity to purchase the business—including buildings and equipment. Lionel looked forward to a prosperous future.

First on his list of things to do was to rebrand the operation with the hope of increasing sales over what the vendor had managed to achieve. The previous owner had been winding his business down over the last number of years and barely had a presence in the industry anymore. Lionel thought it best to start fresh with a new name. Having an unusual sense of humour and wishing to come up with something unique, Lionel decided to carry on business under the name of "Chelsea Chickens." Because he was most emphatically *not* a fan of the English football team called Chelsea, Lionel thought that calling his business the "Chelsea Chickens" was therefore clever and funny, *and* gave him a distinctive business name to boot. Delighted with this analysis, Lionel began to advertise in the industry under the name "Chelsea Chickens" and erected a large sign outside his poultry farm with big, bold letters stating "Home of the Famous Chelsea Chickens." He also ordered letterhead and related office supplies with the name "Chelsea Chickens" being prominently displayed throughout.

The success of Lionel's business was slow but sure. He received an increasing number of orders for broiler (male meat) chickens because of his growing reputation for quality and reliability. And then, suddenly, everything seemed to go downhill.

- a lawyer for a chicken processing corporation in northern Canada, Chelsee Eggs and Poultry Ltd., has demanded that Lionel stop doing business under the name of "Chelsea Chickens" because it is misleading customers into thinking that Chelsea Chickens is somehow associated with Chelsee Eggs and Poultry Ltd. This includes removing his large and expensive "Home of the Famous Chelsea Chickens" sign. Lionel is aghast since he had no intention of confusing anyone. He simply wanted a catchy business name that had a humorous story behind it.
- a client of Lionel's business is angry because Lionel, uncharacteristically, has failed to deliver an order of processed chicken. Though this was a breach of contract, Lionel has concluded that the deficiency was not his fault. He had done

A **Business Law in Practice** scenario opens each chapter with a business situation containing both legal and managerial implications. A special section before the Chapter Summary called **Business Law in Practice Revisited** reviews the questions posed in the scenario with suggested responses.

The real-world application of legal knowledge is reinforced through the **Business Application of the Law** feature, which provides examples that illustrate how the law affects a business enterprise—such as the issues to consider when determining whether to pursue a legal conflict.

BUSINESS APPLICATION OF THE LAW

CONCERT HALL CANCELS ALLEGED CONTRACT WITH MAXIMUM FIGHTING INC.

The Francis Winspear Centre for Music (Winspear), through its Foundation, is alleged to have entered into a contract to lease its premises to Maximum Fighting Inc. (MFI), a mixed martial arts promoter, for three Maximum Fighting Championship (MFC) events in exchange for a rental fee. According to press accounts, the concert hall then cancelled the arrangement, saying that the booking had been made in error.

Ryan Jimmo, pictured above, won the MFC light heavyweight title in 2011 at the River Cree Resort and Casino in Alberta.

New technologies, globalization, and the environment all have implications for many aspects of business law. Learn how in the **Technology and the Law**, **International Perspective**, and **Environmental Perspective** features.

TECHNOLOGY AND THE LAW

PRIVACY OF PERSONAL INFORMATION ON WORK COMPUTERS

It is not uncommon for employees to store personal data on computers, laptops, and other devices that are supplied and owned by employers. Are employers entitled to monitor and access the personal content on these devices or do employees have a reasonable expectation of privacy?

The Supreme Court of Canada in *R v Cole*[66] provides valuable guidance in answering this question. The Court found that a high school teacher had a reasonable expectation of privacy in the information contained on his work-issued computer, particularly as the employer's policy and procedures allowed incidental personal use of the computer. The expectation of privacy, however, is not absolute. It is diminished by the fact that the employer owned the computer and

Do employees have a right to privacy on workplace computers?

the totality of the circumstances. An employer that expressly allows personal use implies an increased expectation of privacy. A policy limiting or excluding personal use diminishes but

Tal v Ontario Lottery Corporation/Lotto 6/49 OLG, 2011 ONSC 644

BUSINESS CONTEXT: Lottery sales are big business in Canada, with over $10 billion in sales over 2014 alone.[1] This volume makes it particularly essential that clear rules governing the payout process are in place and contractually enforceable. Disappointed lottery ticket purchasers have sued lottery agencies, alleging breach of these rules, though not always with success, as this case illustrates.

FACTUAL BACKGROUND: The plaintiff, David Tal, is a 74-year-old retired businessman. He held a winning 4/6 ticket in the October 1, 2008, draw of the Lotto 6/49 game in that he matched four out of the six numbers selected. The applicable prize pool for 4/6 winners was over $1.3 million but because 20 000 other players held a winning ticket, the amount was divided equally among them all, with a per-person payout of $66.90.

Mr. Tal, however, read the rules differently and took the position that he was entitled to the full amount of the prize pool. He sued for $3 182 667.81 in damages—the amount he claims the pool to be—plus $35.3 million in punitive damages. (Note that the law governing

> regional and provincial lottery organizations would lose billions of dollars in virtually every Lotto 6/49 draw, making this lottery game completely unsustainable.

punitive damages in contract is discussed in detail in Chapter 9.)

THE LEGAL QUESTION: What are the contractual rules governing the Lotto 6/49 game in this case? Which party has interpreted those rules correctly?

RESOLUTION: The court decided in favour of the lottery organization. It confirmed that the parties were in a contract that was formed as follows: the lottery organization made an offer to the public to play a lottery game governed by written rules that the plaintiff accepted by purchasing the ticket. The written rules therefore were part of the contract and governed this dispute.

The court went on to note that the lottery organization had properly applied those rules:

> Pursuant to the Winning Selections Reports prepared by the regional and provincial lottery organizations, there were 20 120 4/6 Winners nation-wide for the October 1 Draw, of whom 8353 were located in Ontario. Pursuant to ss. 6 and 8 of the . . . Game Conditions, each of these 4/6 Winners was entitled to a share of the 4/6 Pool, which was calculated by dividing the dollar amount of the 4/6 Pool ($1 347 143.10) by the total number of 4/6

CRITICAL ANALYSIS: Do you think this case could have been settled out of court? Why or why not?

CHAPTER STUDY

Key Terms and Concepts

alternative dispute resolution (ADR) (p. 70)
appeal (p. 86)
appellant (p. 87)
arbitrator (p. 75)
binding (p. 77)
burden of proof (p. 84)
claim (p. 81)
class action (p. 79)
contingency fee (p. 88)
costs (p. 84)
counterclaim (p. 82)
decision (p. 84)
defence (p. 82)
defendant (p. 78)
discovery (p. 82)
evidence (p. 84)
judgment debtor (p. 86)
limitation period (p. 78)
mediator (p. 74)
negotiation (p. 70)
plaintiff (p. 78)
pleadings (p. 81)
release (p. 72)
respondent (p. 87)
trial (p. 83)

Questions for Review

1. What are some business law disputes that could arise from the operation of a fast-food restaurant?

2. What is the goal of negotiation in resolving legal problems?

3. What happens when negotiations fail?

4. What is the process for attempting to resolve disputes informally?

5. What issues should a business consider before deciding to proceed with a legal dispute rather than abandon it?

6. What is mediation? What are the advantages of mediation as a method of resolving a dispute?

7. What are the differences between mediation and arbitration?

8. Why is arbitration particularly attractive in international disputes?

9. What are the advantages of arbitration in comparison to litigation?

10. What are the major steps in the litigation process?

11. What happens during the "discovery" stage of litigation?

12. Why is settlement out of court more common than and preferable to going to trial?

13. How does a class action differ from a normal lawsuit?

The **Special Case format** follows a standard analysis for every featured case and landmark case, beginning with an explanation of the BUSINESS CONTEXT that is at issue. Readers are then given the FACTUAL BACKGROUND of the case and presented with the LEGAL QUESTIONS before they read the court's actual RESOLUTION. Each case ends with questions for CRITICAL ANALYSIS. Each of these sections is clearly labelled for easy reference.

End-of-chapter materials include **Key Terms and Concepts** with page references, **Questions for Review**, **Questions for Critical Thinking**, and **Situations for Discussion**. **Questions for Review** will help students to check their understanding of chapter topics; **Questions for Critical Thinking** and **Situations for Discussion** will let them apply the concepts they have learned to other business situations.

The **Ethical Considerations** feature assists the student in assessing the sometimes uncomfortable compromises that the law forges between competing interests.

ETHICAL CONSIDERATIONS

IS IT UNETHICAL TO BREACH A CONTRACT?

Contract law generally does not punish a contract breaker but rather compensates the innocent party for any loss associated with the breach. According to famous jurist Oliver Wendell Holmes:

The duty to keep a contract at common law means a prediction that you must pay damages if you do not keep it—and nothing else . . . . If you commit [to] a contract, you are liable to pay a compensatory sum unless the promised event comes to pass, and that is all the difference. But such a mode of looking at the matter stinks in the nostrils of those who

---

Dickinson v Dodds, [1876] 2 Ch D 463 (CA)

THE HISTORICAL CONTEXT: This case is the leading decision—valid even today—on whether an offeror can renege on a commitment to hold an offer open for a specified period of time.

FACTUAL BACKGROUND: On Wednesday, June 10, Dodds delivered to Dickinson a written offer to sell his property to Dickinson for £800. The offer stated that it would be open for acceptance until 9 A.M. on Friday, June 12. On Thursday, Dickinson heard that Dodds had been offering or was agreeing to sell the property to Mr. Allan. That evening, Dickinson delivered an acceptance to the place where Dodds was staying, and at 7 A.M. on Friday morning—a full two hours before the deadline—he personally delivered an acceptance to Dodds. Dodds declined the acceptance, stating: "You are too late. I have sold the property." Dickinson sued Dodds, alleging there was a contract between them.

THE LEGAL QUESTION: To determine whether Dickinson's action should succeed, the court had to decide whether Dodds was entitled to revoke his offer prior to the deadline he had set. This decision was necessary because if the offer had been properly revoked, it was not capable of being accepted, and, accordingly, there could be no contract between the two men.

RESOLUTION: The court decided that what Dodds did was permissible: "[I]t is a perfectly clear rule of law . . . that, although it is said that the offer is to be left open until Friday morning at 9 o'clock, that did not bind Dodds. He was not in point of law bound to hold the offer over until 9 o'clock on Friday morning."

On this footing, a firm offer can be revoked at any time before acceptance because the offeree has not provided any consideration to support the offeror's implicit promise not to revoke before the deadline. More controversially, the court also held that Dodds's offer had been effectively revoked prior to acceptance because Dickinson learned in advance—from a presumably reliable source—that Dodds was selling the property to someone else.

CRITICAL ANALYSIS: Being guided primarily by legal principles is certainly an acceptable way of doing business. However, what might be the impact on your business reputation of going back on your word and revoking an offer sooner than you had promised you would? Do you think that the method used by Dodds for revocation (i.e., relying on the fact that Dickinson had learned that Dodds was selling to someone else) is the usual way of revoking an offer? What would be a more certain and reliable way of effecting revocation?

Source: *Dickinson v Dodds*, [1876] 2 Ch D 463 (CA).

BUSINESS AND LEGISLATION

EVIDENCE OF ELECTRONIC CONTRACTS

Those who seek to enforce a contract must be able to prove that the contract was formed and that its terms support the claim that is made. Traditionally, that proof takes the form of witness testimony and documents that are submitted to the court as evidence. Of course, in proving the contract, the parties will have to respect the parol evidence rule and other rules of evidence.

With the growth of electronic business, contracts are increasingly negotiated online and the terms are recorded electronically, without a paper version. This method of doing business creates difficulty if it becomes necessary to produce the "original" contract in court. In response, governments across Canada have begun to enact legislation addressing this point.

In 1997, the Uniform Law Conference of Canada proposed draft legislation—called the *Uniform Electronic Evidence Act*, or *UEEA* for short—to make the proof of electronic contracts subject to a uniform set of rules. This draft legislation has since been implemented in a number of jurisdictions. For example, Ontario implemented the *UEEA* by amending

its *Evidence Act*. Section 34.1 of that Act, as amended, provides

Authentication:

> (4) The person seeking to introduce an electronic record has the burden of proving its authenticity by evidence capable of supporting a finding that the electronic record is what the person claims it to be.

Application of Best Evidence Rule:

> (5) Subject to subsection (6) where the best evidence rule is applicable in respect of an electronic record, it is satisfied on proof of the integrity of the electronic records system by or in which the data was recorded or stored.

Beyond Ontario, other provinces and territories (including Alberta, Manitoba, Nova Scotia, PEI, Saskatchewan, and the Yukon), as well as the federal government, have enacted legislation which mirrors, in whole or in part, the Uniform Conference of Canada's draft act.[14]

Critical Analysis: Are these kinds of amendments to *Evidence Act* legislation necessary to deal with electronic contracts? Could judges not be entrusted with the task of providing rules on a case by case basis?

The **Landmark Case** and **Business and Legislation** features provide accounts of pivotal case law and historical legislative initiatives.

Instructor Resources

The **Nelson Education Teaching Advantage (NETA)** program delivers research-based instructor resources that promote student engagement and higher-order thinking to enable the success of Canadian students and educators. Visit Nelson Education's **Inspired Instruction** website at http://www.nelson.com/inspired/ to find out more about NETA.

The following instructor resources have been created for *Canadian Business and the Law,* Sixth Edition. Access these ultimate tools for customizing lectures and presentations at www.nelson.com/instructor.

NETA Test Bank

This resource was written by Lorrie Adams, MacEwan University. It includes more than 1,200 multiple-choice questions written according to NETA guidelines for effective construction and development of higher-order questions. Also included are an average of 20 true/false questions and 10 short answer questions in each chapter.

The NETA Test Bank is available in a new, cloud-based platform. **Nelson Testing Powered by Cognero®** is a secure online testing system that allows instructors to author, edit, and manage test bank content from anywhere Internet access is available. No special installations or downloads are needed, and the desktop-inspired interface, with its drop-down menus and familiar, intuitive tools, allows instructors to create and manage tests with ease. Multiple test versions can be created in an instant, and content can be imported or exported into other systems. Tests can be delivered from a learning management system, the classroom, or wherever an instructor chooses. Testing Powered by Cognero for *Canadian Business and the Law,* Sixth Edition, can be accessed through www.nelson.com/instructor.

NETA PowerPoint

Microsoft® PowerPoint® lecture slides present an average of 30 slides per chapter, many featuring key figures, tables, and photographs from *Canadian Business and the Law.* Extensive additional content, such as teaching suggestions, discussion questions, activities, and references, are provided in the "Notes" section of slides to help instructors encourage student engagement. (Versions of these PPTs with the notes removed are available for students.) NETA principles of clear design and engaging content have been incorporated throughout, making it simple for instructors to customize the deck for their courses.

Image Library

This resource consists of digital copies of figures, short tables, and photographs used in the book. Instructors may use these jpegs to customize the NETA PowerPoint or create their own PowerPoint presentations.

Videos

Instructors can enhance the classroom experience with the exciting and relevant videos provided online and on DVD. These videos have been selected to accompany *Canadian Business and the Law.* Also incorporated into MindTap, they include video questions for students.

NETA Instructor Guide

This resource was written by the authors of the text. It is organized according to the textbook chapters and addresses key educational concerns, such as typical stumbling blocks students face and how to address them. Other features include teaching objectives, teaching strategies, student activities, and detailed explanations of features in the text (such as boxes and photos).

Instructor's Solutions Manual

This manual, prepared by the authors of the text, includes suggested answers to the Questions for Review, Questions for Critical Thinking, and Situation for Discussion questions in the text.

MindTap

MindTap®

Offering personalized paths of dynamic assignments and applications, **MindTap** is a digital learning solution that turns cookie-cutter into cutting-edge, apathy into engagement, and memorizers into higher-level thinkers. MindTap enables students to analyze and apply chapter concepts within relevant assignments, and allows instructors to measure skills and promote better outcomes with ease. A fully online learning solution, MindTap combines all student learning tools—readings, multimedia, activities, and assessments—into a single Learning Path that guides students through the curriculum. Instructors personalize the experience by customizing the presentation of these learning tools to their students, even seamlessly introducing their own content into the Learning Path.

Student Ancillaries

MindTap

MindTap®

Stay organized and efficient with *MindTap*—a single destination with all the course material and study aids you need to succeed. Built-in apps leverage social media and the latest learning technology. For example:

- ReadSpeaker will read the text to you.
- Flashcards are pre-populated to provide you with a jump start for review—or you can create your own.
- You can highlight text and make notes in your MindTap Reader. Your notes will flow into Evernote, the electronic notebook app that you can access anywhere when it's time to study for the exam.
- Self-quizzing allows you to assess your understanding.

Visit http://www.nelson.com/student to start using **MindTap**. Enter the Online Access Code from the card included with your text. If a code card is *not* provided, you can purchase instant access at NELSONbrain.com.

ACKNOWLEDGMENTS

Canadian Business and the Law, Sixth Edition, is a team effort, and credit for the text must be widely shared.

In addition to the valued educators noted below, we extend our appreciation to our colleagues who made an important contribution by commenting on draft chapters in this or earlier editions. They include James McGinnis of Parlee McLaws; Tamara Buckwold, Ronald Hopp, Wayne Renke, David Percy, Gerald Gall, Lewis Klar, Moe Litman, Linda Reif, Barbara Billingsley, Erin Nelson, and Kathryn Arbuckle of the Faculty of Law, University of Alberta; James Gaa of the School of Business, University of Alberta; Michael Pratt of the Faculty of Law, Queen's University; Dion Legge of Macleod Dixon; and Darren Charters of the University of Waterloo.

We would like to acknowledge administrative support from the Faculty of Law at the University of Alberta, as well as research and administrative support from the University of New Brunswick.

We are grateful to Nelson Education's editorial, sales, and marketing team, including Anne-Marie Taylor, Suzanne Simpson Millar, and Dave Stratton for their insights and support throughout the development of this project.

Finally, our deep appreciation goes to those who were instrumental in the preparation of this text by providing direction through their insightful reviews provided for the Sixth Edition. They include

Ani Abdalyan	*Durham College of Applied Arts and Technology*
Connie Gullage	*College of the North Atlantic*
Darragh McManamon	*Memorial University of Newfoundland*
Douglas Peterson	*University of Alberta*
George Allen	*Red River College*
Heidi Walsh Sampson	*Saint Mary's University*
Paul Ebbs	*Algonquin College of Applied Arts and Technology*
Lorrie M. Adams	*MacEwan University*
Murray Kernaghan	*Brandon University*
Susan Robson	*Red River College*

By dedication of this book we thank our families for their sacrifice and support.

Dorothy's dedication is to Neil, Andrea, and Charles.

Shannon's dedication is to Jamie, Kerry, and Sean.

Philip's dedication is to Monica, Daniel, and Josh.

Lorrie's dedication is to Rick, Olivia, and Sandy.

Steven's dedication is to Jennie, Michael, and Edward.

TABLE OF CASES

TABLE OF CASES

TABLE OF STATUTES

THE LEGAL ENVIRONMENT OF BUSINESS

This text deals with the importance of the law to business and, in Parts Two to Nine, it presents fundamental legal principles in their relevant business contexts. The text contends that those engaged in business need to manage the legal environment as much as any other aspect of their business. Part One provides the basis for that management by introducing the foundations of business law and the concept of legal risk management. It emphasizes the importance of knowing the law, complying with the law, avoiding unexpected legal problems, and regarding law not as an obstacle but as a way to facilitate commercial activity.

1

OBJECTIVES

After studying this chapter, you should have an understanding of

- the role of law in guiding conduct
- the importance of legal knowledge in the business environment
- the challenges posed by business ethics and their relationship to legal requirements

David Chasey/Photodisc

KNOWLEDGE OF LAW AS A BUSINESS ASSET

BUSINESS LAW IN PRACTICE

Lionel Garfield, who grew up on a large farm in Ontario, decided to go into the chicken processing business for himself. When a local Ontario poultry producer decided to retire, Lionel jumped at the opportunity to purchase the business—including buildings and equipment. Lionel looked forward to a prosperous future.

First on his list of things to do was to rebrand the operation with the hope of increasing sales over what the vendor had managed to achieve. The previous owner had been winding his business down over the last number of years and barely had a presence in the industry anymore. Lionel thought it best to start fresh with a new name. Having an unusual sense of humour and wishing to come up with something unique, Lionel decided to carry on business under the name of "Chelsea Chickens." Because he was most emphatically *not* a fan of the English football team called Chelsea, Lionel thought that calling his business the "Chelsea Chickens" was therefore clever and funny, *and* gave him a distinctive business name to boot. Delighted with this analysis, Lionel began to advertise in the industry under the name "Chelsea Chickens" and erected a large sign outside his poultry farm with big, bold letters stating "Home of the Famous Chelsea Chickens." He also ordered letterhead and related office supplies with the name "Chelsea Chickens" being prominently displayed throughout.

The success of Lionel's business was slow but sure. He received an increasing number of orders for broiler (male meat) chickens because of his growing reputation for quality and reliability. And then, suddenly, everything seemed to go downhill:

- a lawyer for a chicken processing corporation in northern Canada, Chelsee Eggs and Poultry Ltd., has demanded that Lionel stop doing business under the name of "Chelsea Chickens" because it is misleading customers into thinking that Chelsea Chickens is somehow associated with Chelsee Eggs and Poultry Ltd. This includes removing his large and expensive "Home of the Famous Chelsea Chickens" sign. Lionel is aghast since he had no intention of confusing anyone. He simply wanted a catchy business name that had a humorous story behind it.

- a client of Lionel's business is angry because Lionel, uncharacteristically, has failed to deliver an order of processed chicken. Though this was a breach of contract, Lionel has concluded that the deficiency was not his fault. He had done everything possible to deliver but an unavoidable mechanical breakdown in his production facility meant that a few orders could not be processed on time.

- a potential customer was touring Lionel's production facility when she slipped and fell on the freshly mopped floor in the holding barn. The customer suffered a serious concussion and will be off work for at least half a year.
- about 100 chickens froze to death when Lionel transported them on a flatbed trailer from the holding barn to a farm customer about two hours away in very cold conditions. Lionel has been charged under the *Health of Animals Act*[1] for causing undue suffering to birds.

Given these mounting problems, Lionel does not know which way to turn.

1. How does the law affect Lionel's business?
2. What are the purposes of the laws that affect Lionel's business?
3. What has gone wrong with Lionel's business and why?

Law in the Business Environment

The law impacts virtually every aspect of society, including the business environment. It affects most business decisions—from development of the basic business idea through to its implementation, and all the attendant matters in between, including financing, hiring, production, marketing, and sales. As Lionel starts his business, for example, he will be involved in a number of transactions and events with significant legal implications. For instance, to advance his chicken processing business, Lionel has to decide whether to form a corporation, operate as a sole proprietor, or find partners. He also has financing decisions to make: should he borrow money, use his own funds, or perhaps sell shares in his venture? While his operation is starting out small, he may ultimately have to hire many employees. Lionel also has to market his business in order to build and maintain a customer base. All of these decisions have legal aspects, whether Lionel recognizes that or not.

By understanding the role of law in the multitude of business decisions that people like Lionel must make, an entrepreneur can maximize the protection that the law extends while avoiding its pitfalls. Put another way, knowledge of the law is a business asset that can assist owners and managers in reaching their goals and objectives. This is because **business law**:

Business law

A set of established rules governing commercial relationships, including the enforcement of rights.

- defines general rules of commerce.
- protects business ideas and more tangible forms of property.
- provides mechanisms that permit businesspeople to select their desired degree of participation and exposure to risk in business ventures.
- seeks to ensure that losses are borne by those who are responsible for them.
- facilitates planning by ensuring compliance with commitments.

Of course, a businessperson can function with little or no understanding of the law. This lack of knowledge, however, may result in failure to maximize opportunities or in losing out on them altogether. For example, a business that neglects to protect its intellectual property may have its ideas taken with impunity by a competitor; a business that ignores employment and human rights laws may be forced to reverse human resource decisions or pay compensation to wronged

---

1 SC 1990, c 21. For more discussion about legislation, see Chapter 2.

employees; and a business that fails to explore different modes of carrying out business may suffer unnecessary losses. Perhaps even more seriously, legal ignorance or intentional defiance of the law may result in the business or its owner being subjected to regulatory and judicial sanctions, including being fined, forced to pay penalties, or closed down altogether.

FACEBOOK SEEKS JUSTICE AGAINST A NOTORIOUS CANADIAN SPAMMER

Canadian Adam Guerbuez, pictured, scammed Facebook users into giving him their user names and passwords through 'phishing' schemes. That is, Guerbuez fraudulently sent out what looked to be a legitimate email so as to entice recipients to reveal this personal information to him. He then inundated these Facebook users with more than 4 million unsolicited advertising messages for marijuana and 'adult' products. In 2008, a California court determined that Guerbuez was in violation of American anti-spamming legislation, known as *Controlling the Assault of Non-Solicited Pornography and Marketing Act of 2003*.[2] This legislation closely regulates the sending of non-solicited commercial emails ("spam") and includes a prohibition against misleading headers (e.g., the email's "To" and "From" information). The California court ordered Guerbuez to pay $873 million (US) to Facebook in damages. In 2010, Justice Lucie Fournier of the Quebec Superior Court agreed to Facebook's request that its US judgment be recognized as valid in Quebec, noting that: "[I]t was after the repeated and intentional actions of Guerbuez that the [American] judgment was rendered. It was not an arbitrary award." The judge also considered how Guerbuez would be treated under Canada's then-proposed anti-spamming legislation ("Bill C-27") and concluded that the outcome could be similar.[3] Beyond this, both pieces of legislation shared the goal of deterring reprehensible online behaviour. She therefore rejected Guerbuez's argument that the award was so large and punitive that to enforce it in Quebec would be against "public order." Guerbuez applied to the Quebec Court of

Canadian spammer Adam Guerbuez

Paul Chiasson/The Canadian Press

Appeal in 2011 for leave to appeal this ruling but his application was denied. Accordingly, Facebook can pursue Guerbuez's assets in Quebec so as to help collect on its nearly billion-dollar judgment.

As Paul Taylor writes for *Canadian Lawyer* magazine, Facebook has to sue spammers like Guerbuez in order to protect the positive experience of its users, retain customer loyalty, and protect legitimate ad revenue. As Taylor writes:

> . . . [I]n a time when increasing value is placed on individuals' privacy, that is the nature of statutory damages. The 4 366 386 messages Guerbuez sent infringed upon the privacy of users of the site and made it appear as though one's friends sent these messages. . . . [D]eleting the message and moving on does not take away the feeling, and the fact, that one's privacy has been violated.*

Guerbuez has also declared bankruptcy, started his own website, and appears to be enjoying the

---

* *Canadian Lawyer*. "This far and no further: Facebook ruling shows courts are putting a high price on privacy" by Paul W. Taylor. October 25, 2010. Copyright © 2015 Thomson Reuters Canada Ltd.

---

2 *Controlling the Assault of Non-Solicited Pornography and Marketing Act of 2003*, 15 USC §§ 7701-7713 (2003), online: Cornell Legal Information Institute <http://www.law.cornell.edu/uscode/html/uscode15/usc_sup_01_15_10_103.html> ["*CAN-SPAM Act*"].

3 For discussion of Canada's new anti-spamming legislation, see Chapter 6.

limelight, at least for the time being. In a CBC interview with Mark Kelley, Guerbuez welcomed all the publicity surrounding his case, stating:

> This gets me out there. People know my name. People know what I do because I'm telling them what I do and they know I can get across to millions of people without paying a cent to do so. This is free publicity for me . . . . This is wonderful . . . . I don't know anybody who could afford this kind of publicity if they were paying for it . . . . I'm everywhere . . . . If you type in the word 'Adam' [Guerbuez's first name], I'm the third suggested result on Google right now in the world. That is something that is amazing.

In the meantime, Facebook is being realistic about what it can recover from Guerbuez, noting on its blog:

> Does Facebook expect to quickly collect $873 million and share the proceeds in some way with our users? Alas, no. It's unlikely that Guerbuez . . . could ever honour the judgment . . . (though we will certainly collect everything we can). But we are confident that this award represents a powerful deterrent to anyone and everyone who would seek to abuse Facebook and its users.

Critical Analysis: What is objectionable about spamming? How is it different from marketing? Should American judgments be enforceable in Canada? Why or why not?

Sources: *Facebook Inc v Guerbuez*, 2010 QCCS 4649, aff'd 2011 QCCA 268; YouTube, "Adam Guerbuez on primetime TV show 'Connect'", online: YouTube <http://www.youtube.com/watch?v=_unvC5jP-5M>; Chloe Albanesius, "Judge Awards $873M Fine for Spamming Facebook" *PCMag* (24 November 2008), online: PCMag <http://www.pcmag.com/article2/0,2817,2335375,00.asp>; CBC News Staff, "Quebec spammer must pay Facebook $873M" *CBC News* (5 October 2010), online: CBC News <http://www.cbc.ca/news/canada/montreal/story/2010/10/05/quebec-court-upholds-facebook-spammer-ruling.html>; and Max Kelly, "Making Facebook Safe Against Spam" (24 November 2008), online: The Facebook Blog <http://blog.facebook.com/blog.php?post=40218392130>.

Rules and Principles

Broadly defined, the **law** is a set of rules and principles intended to guide conduct in society, primarily by protecting persons and their property, facilitating personal and commercial interactions, and providing mechanisms for dispute resolution.

Law

The set of rules and principles guiding conduct in society.

Protecting Persons and Their Property

Probably the most familiar purpose of the law is to provide protection. Those who violate the *Criminal Code of Canada*—such as by breaking into another person's house, assaulting someone, or committing a commercial fraud—are subject to criminal sanctions, such as fines or imprisonment.

As another example, businesses are legally required to adequately protect their customers' personal information due to the regime established by Canada's *Personal Information Protection and Electronic Documents Act*.[4] This is discussed in the following box.

BUSINESS AND LEGISLATION

BREACH OF PRIVACY FOR HOTEL TO REVEAL CHECK-IN/CHECK-OUT INFORMATION

A disgruntled hotel guest—who regularly stayed at the same hotel for his work—filed a complaint with the Office of the Privacy Commissioner of Canada against a hotel for revealing his personal information. In response to an enquiry from the hotel guest's employer, a front desk clerk disclosed that guest's check-in and departure dates. The guest/employee believed that this check-in and departure information was

---

4 S.C. 2000, c. 5.

requested by the employer as part of its investigation into whether employees were claiming overtime "unnecessarily" and, further, that the information provided by the hotel contributed to the guest/employee being dismissed from his employment. The guest/employee claimed that the hotel violated Canada's *Personal Information Protection and Electronic Documents Act* (*PIPEDA*) by revealing information about his hotel stays.

PIPEDA is a legislation passed by the federal government. It has a number of objectives, including the regulation of how the private business sector collects, uses, and discards personal information acquired from its customers. Such customer protection is essential because, as the Office of the Privacy Commissioner of Canada's website notes:

> When you do business with a company, you do more than simply exchange money for a product or service: Unless you pay in cash, you also leave behind a trail of personal information about yourself. Your name, address, credit card number, and spending habits are all information of great value to somebody, whether that's a legitimate marketer or an identity thief.

PIPEDA sets national privacy standards that apply in most Canadian provinces, though provinces such as Alberta,[5] British Columbia,[6] and Quebec[7] have enacted their own largely comparable provincial regimes, with Manitoba poised to do the same.[8] However, even in these provinces, *PIPEDA* applies to industries governed by the federal government, such as banking. For more discussion on legislation in general, see Chapter 2.

A website maintained by the Office of the Privacy Commissioner of Canada (OPC) describes the obligations that commercial organizations owe to their customers under *PIPEDA*. In short, such organizations can only collect, use, or disclose personal information "by fair and lawful means" and only with the consumer's consent, and only for the purposes "that are stated and reasonable." The website also notes that the private sector must protect this personal information "through appropriate security measures and to destroy it when it's no longer needed for the original purposes."[9]

PIPEDA gives consumers the option of making a complaint to the Privacy Commissioner. The Privacy Commissioner is independent from government and is mandated to try to resolve such complaints. When the OPC looked into allegations by the terminated employee against the hotel, it determined that the complaint was well founded. The OPC concluded that check-in and check-out times constituted personal information and that disclosing it without consent was a contravention of PIPEDA. It also declared the matter resolved, offering no further details.

Note that PIPEDA also permits a complainant to make a claim for damages against the perpetrator, which is what Rabi Chitrakar did when Bell TV conducted a credit check without his permission. What transpired was that Bell TV—not

Rabi Chitrakar won his battle against Bell TV.

© CBC

---

5   *Personal Information Protection Act*, SA 2003, c P-6.5. Note that the Supreme Court of Canada in *Alberta (Information and Privacy Commissioner) v United Food and Commercial Workers, Local 401*, [2013] 3 SCR 733, 2013 SCC 62 (CanLII) held the Act to be unconstitutional but suspended the declaration for 12 months.

6   *Personal Information Protection Act*, SBC 2003, c 63.

7   *An Act Respecting the Protection of Personal Information in the Private Sector*, RSQ c P-39.1.

8   *Personal Information Protection and Identity Theft Prevention Act*, SM 2013, c.17. Assented to September 13, 2013 but not yet in force.

9   For further discussion, see Office of the Privacy Commissioner of Canada, "A Guide for Business and Organizations, Privacy Toolkit: Canada's *Personal Information Protection and Electronic Documents Act*" (updated March 2014), online: Office of the Privacy Commissioner of Canada <http://www.priv.gc.ca/information/pub/guide_org_e.asp>.

having dealt with Chitrakar before—decided to do a credit check on him and then, presumably satisfied, delivered a satellite dish that Chitrakar had ordered. At time of delivery, Chitrakar was required to provide an electronic signature on a POD Machine—or Proof of Delivery Device. Bell then embedded Chitrakar's signature on its Bell TV Rental Agreement which, in turn, contained a clause permitting Bell to conduct credit checks. The court called this conduct "reprehensible" and noted that credit checks can have adverse effects on a person's credit score. In fact, Chitrakar let the court know that after the unauthorized credit check, he had been denied a student loan—the first time he had been denied a loan in 10 years—but the court ruled there was no direct evidence that Bell's credit check was the cause.

The court agreed that Bell had given Chitrakar the "royal run around" and, moreover, had not taken the proceedings seriously. It ordered that Bell pay Chitrakar $21 000. Chitrakar was satisfied with the ruling and gave the following statement to the CBC: "I was right, Bell was wrong. What they did is illegal, unlawful and unauthorized."

Critical Analysis: In what way does *PIPEDA* protect people and their property? Do you think that the legislation puts too much responsibility on business?

Sources: Office of the Privacy Commissioner of Canada, PIPEDA Report of Findings #2013-07 "Report of Findings: Hotel check in check out times are personal information and must not be disclosed without consent" (7 August 2013), online: Office of the Privacy Commissioner of Canada <https://www.priv.gc.ca/cf-dc/2013/2013_007_0807_e.asp>; *Chitrakar v Bell TV* 2013 FC 1103; Lynn Desjardin, CBC News Online "Court awards damages for unauthorized credit check" (9 January 2014), online: CBC News <http://www.rcinet.ca/en/2014/01/09/court-awards-damages-for-unauthorized-credit-check/>; Office of the Privacy Commission of Canada, "A Guide for Individuals: Protecting Your Privacy," online: Office of the Privacy Commissioner of Canada, <https://www.priv.gc.ca/information/pub/guide_ind_e.asp> and <https://www.priv.gc.ca/information/pub/guide_ind_e.pdf>.

The law protects members of society in two ways: (1) it sets rules with penalties in order to encourage compliance, and (2) it seeks to hold those who break the law accountable for their misconduct.

The law also protects businesses by setting penalties and ensuring accountability. For example, if one business misappropriates another business's legally protected commercial idea, the law can censure that conduct. As well, the law ensures that losses are paid for by the parties responsible for creating them. For example, if a law firm gives negligent advice to a client, that client can sue the firm for associated losses.

Lionel's business intersects with the law in both of these ways. First, the law guards his business interests. For example, should a supplier fail to deliver a product to Lionel, this is a **breach of contract** and Lionel can sue for damages. If a competitor wrongfully injures Lionel's business reputation, he can sue for defamation.[10] However, the law also protects those who deal with Lionel's business. Lionel must perform his contracts on time. He must not discriminate in hiring practices. He must not disregard health and safety regulations or animal welfare legislation governing his operation. He must pay his creditors. In sum, Lionel is obliged to abide by the law on a variety of fronts, since failure to comply can have severe consequences, including financial penalties and legal prosecution.

The government must also be responsive to emerging hazards in the marketplace and seek to regulate in the public interest, as the box on page 9 illustrates.

Breach of contract

Failure to comply with a contractual promise.

---

10 Defamation is the public utterance of a false statement of fact or opinion that harms another's reputation. For further discussion, see Chapter 12.

MAPLE LODGE FARMS'S CONVICTION

Maple Lodge Farms, one of the largest chicken producers in Canada, was recently sentenced by an Ontario court for violating the *Health of Animals Act*.[11] Maple Lodge Farms had inhumanely transported chickens and many died from exposure to cold weather. According to the court in relation to some of the deaths:

> Although Maple Lodge Farms took some steps to protect the birds from the elements by tarping which was standard at the time, they failed to take reasonable steps to leave some outer crates empty [of birds] to defray the frigid air intake venting into the trailer. They also failed to adequately monitor the trailer in the holding barns, while the birds were still on the trailer, to ensure they did not suffer unduly pending their processing on the [slaughter] line.[12]

In relation to other chicken deaths, the court summarized the matter as follows: "Regrettably, Maple Lodge Farms . . . decided that commercial imperatives trumped animal welfare . . . ."[13] And by way of general comment, the court relied on a quote frequently attributed to Gandhi: "The greatness of a nation and its moral progress can be judged by the way its animals are treated."[14]

In sentencing the corporation, the court observed that for those offences to which Maple Lodge Farms admitted guilt or on which it was found guilty, "twenty-five thousand four hundred and fifty chickens (25 450) died inhumanely by undue exposure to weather or inadequate ventilation during transport."[15] The court went on to fine Maple Lodge Farms $80 000 and placed the corporation on probation for three years. A condition of the probation requires the company to spend at least $1 million to make substantial improvements to its vehicles and facilities. The court's stated goal was that Maple Lodge Farms would set the model

What are the reputational costs to Maple Lodge Farms for its recent convictions and how can those be managed?

for the industry via anticipated innovations in how birds would be transported in the future.[16]

On its website, Maple Lodge Farms has expressed concern: "We acknowledge the seriousness of these charges [under the *Health of Animals Act*] and the moral obligation we have to better the conditions for the chickens we process."[17]

Two animal rights groups—the Canadian Coalition for Farm Animals (CCFA) and Animal Alliance of Canada (AAC)—have spoken out against Maple Lodge Farms, noting as follows: "Economics over animal welfare was a clear theme which emerged from the trial. Maple Lodge Farms failed to ensure proper animal welfare for the birds, including not properly training its drivers, and not following Canada's voluntary Codes of Practice or the company's Standard Operating Procedures for bird welfare."[18]

Critical Analysis: What is the role of businesses to ensure the humane and ethical treatment of animals in their care? What is the role of government to ensure the humane and ethical treatment of animals by businesses?

Sources: Maple Lodge Farms, "Our Journey to Improved Bird Welfare" (undated) at <http://www.maplelodgefarms.com/files/Our%20Journey%20to%20Improved%20Bird%20Welfare%20%28with%20Probationary%20and%20Conviction%20links%29.pdf>, and quote from *R v Maple Lodge Farms*, 2013 ONCJ 535 at para. 456.

Age of majority

The age at which a person becomes an adult for legal purposes. In Canada, this ranges from 18 to 19 years of age, depending on the province.

11 *Supra* note 1.
12 *R v Maple Lodge Farms*, 2013 ONCJ 535 at para. 456.
13 *Ibid* at para 468.
14 *Ibid* at para 1.
15 *R v Maple Lodge Farms*, 2014 ONCJ 212 at para 13.
16 *Ibid* at paras 54 to 57.
17 Maple Lodge Farms, "Our Journey to Improved Bird Welfare" (undated), online: Maple Lodge Farms <http://www.maplelodgefarms.com/files/Our%20Journey%20to%20Improved%20Bird%20Welfare%20%28with%20Probationary%20and%20Conviction%20links%29.pdf>.
18 See CCFA-AAC, "Economics over Animal Welfare: Production, Transport, and Slaughter of Chickens in Canada (2014)" (27 March 2014), online CCFA-AAC <http://www.humanefood.ca/pdf%20links/Maple%20Lodge%20Farm%20report.pdf>.

REGULATING THE TANNING INDUSTRY

A 2014 report from the Canadian Cancer Society indicates a sharp rise in the incidence of melanoma or skin cancer—the most commonly diagnosed cancer in the country. One cause is the increased use of tanning beds. As the Canadian Cancer Society notes:

> Tanning beds are high-output UV machines that deliver intense doses of radiation designed to produce rapid and deeply coloured tans. The amount of radiation emitted has been documented to be many times more than natural sun at midday in summer. The World Health Organization classifies tanning beds as a known factor that causes cancer in humans. According to research, people who first started using indoor tanning equipment before the age of 35 have a 59% increased risk of melanoma.

Most Canadian provinces have legislation regulating the use of tanning beds. The approach to the problem is not uniform, however. A majority of jurisdictions (such as British Columbia, Nova Scotia, New Brunswick, Quebec, Newfoundland, Ontario, and Prince Edward Island) require warning signs on the tanning salon premises and prohibit those under the **age of majority** from using tanning beds altogether. In British Columbia, the fine for permitting underage tanning is $345, while in Nova Scotia, tanning salon owners face business closure for up to two years and fines of up to $10 000. The other approach, taken in Manitoba at least as recently as 2015, mandates warning signs but does not outright ban underage tanning. Instead, written parental consent is required.

Manitoba's approach has been subject to serious criticism, including by the Canadian Cancer Society. In a letter to Teresa Oswald (Manitoba's then Minister of Health), obtained by CBC News,

Katie Donnar, 18, shows her scars from surgery to remove a melanoma. Katie used to use tanning beds frequently.

the Canadian Cancer Society stated, in part: "The only position that can reasonably be taken is that tanning for minors must be banned, just as the sale of tobacco to minors is banned." Manitoba has since shifted direction and tabled legislation which would prohibit underage tanning.

Critical Analysis: Should the government try to protect young people from the dangers of tanning or should the matter be left up to the individual consumer?

Sources: CBC News, "Manitoba's Tanning Bed Rules for Teens Criticized" (07 June 2012), at <http://www.cbc.ca/news/canada/manitoba/manitoba-s-tanning-bed-rules-for-teens-criticized-1.1253559>; Tom Henderson, "Tanning Teens Run High Risk of Skin Cancer, FDA Warns" *Parentdish* (19 July 2010), at <http://www.parentdish.com/2010/01/19/tanning-teens-run-high-risk-of-skin-cancer-fda-warns/>; Canadian Cancer Society. "Melanoma: deadliest type of skin cancer is on the rise", 28 May 2014. © Canadian Cancer Society. <www.cancer.ca>; 2014 at <http://www.cancer.ca/~/media/cancer.ca/CW/cancer%20information/cancer%20101/Canadian%20cancer%20statistics/Canadian-Cancer-Statistics-2014-EN.pdf>; BC Ministry of Health, "BC Ban on Tanning Bed Use by Youth under 18" (undated document) at <http://www.health.gov.bc.ca/protect/tanning-bed-ban.html>.

Facilitating Interactions

The law facilitates personal interactions by providing rules concerning marriage, adoption, and the disposal of property upon the owner's death, to name a few examples. The law also facilitates commercial activity by providing rules governing the marketplace. The law of contract, for example, provides a way for parties to enter into binding agreements, thereby creating a measure of security and certainty in their business operations. **Contract law** allows business enterprises to plan for the future and to enforce their expectations.

Contract law

Rules that make agreements binding and, therefore, facilitate planning and the enforcement of expectations.

Although the law addresses failed relations—as when one party does not meet its contractual obligations or gives negligent legal advice—it is not primarily about conflict. Rather, the law functions to prevent disputes and to facilitate relationships. It provides certainty for Lionel's commercial agreements and enables him to engage in transactions that might otherwise be unstructured and unpredictable.

Nor is the law primarily about rules that constrain commerce. Though the law does forbid certain activities—such as false advertising and operating without a business licence—its more significant role is facilitative. Legal rules provide definition and context to doing business. For example, assume that Lionel wants to enter into a long-term relationship with a particularly reliable local supplier. Contract law allows him to accomplish this end by providing a mechanism through which Lionel and the supplier can describe—and enforce—their commitments to each other. Therefore, Lionel can agree in advance with his supplier on what kind of product is to be provided, how much, at what price, over what period of time, and when.

The creation of certainty in business relationships is one of the most important contributions that law can make to the commercial arena. While the necessity of creating certainty means that some anticipated contracts founder when it comes to formalizing their content, the law has not necessarily failed. It more likely means that the businesspeople involved were not as close to being in agreement as they had initially assumed. Further discussions, perhaps through lawyers, have simply identified problems that, although hidden, were always there.

No contract can recite and provide for all contingencies; there will be some issues left unstated, but often the parties themselves find ways of overcoming these omissions. Generally, they will be guided by the need to achieve the original intent behind the contractual relationship, with the objective of dealing fairly with the unexpected or unaddressed event that has just occurred. In this way, the business relationship "fills in the blanks" in the contractual arrangement. If one or both of the parties involve the legal system, a judge will apply established rules governing contracts to resolve the issue. The influence of the law on the business environment does not have to be exacting and literal. In fact, parties to a business contract do not always observe their agreement to the letter, preferring to maintain their relationship rather than sue for breach of contract. For example, assume that Lionel has a five-year contract with a reputable supplier of chicken feed. Owing to poor planning, the supplier will be unable to make its delivery on time and has advised Lionel of a three-day delay. Although he may be annoyed at the default, Lionel stands to lose more than he would gain from suing, particularly if the supplier is otherwise reliable and the two have a solid working relationship. There is no good reason to risk this relationship and devote resources to **litigation**, that is, the process involved in suing someone. In this way, the contract between Lionel and the supplier provides the legal backdrop to their relationship—by defining rights and obligations—but it is the business relationship that determines whether strict legal rights will be insisted upon. This is an important reality that affects how the law actually operates in the business environment.

Providing Mechanisms for Dispute Resolution

Whether a conflict can or even should be resolved outside the formal legal system depends on the circumstances. If Lionel hires an on-site manager who proves to be incompetent, it is in the interests of his enterprise to terminate the person's employment. While Lionel may have a case to fire the employee outright, he might also consider offering a small severance package to reduce the possibility of being

Litigation

The process involved when one person sues another.

Vincent Besnault/Photolibrary/Getty Images

How can parties resolve a business dispute without going to court?

sued for wrongful dismissal.[19] This is a judgment call, but the time and money saved in avoiding a court battle may more than offset the cost of the severance package. Conversely, it may be that the employee has had his hand in the till and has stolen from the business. Lionel is in a different situation now. He not only must ensure that the employee leaves the company immediately but also will probably want to involve the police and try to recover what the employee has taken. In these kinds of circumstances, a full-blown legal conflict is much more likely and appropriate.

When one party fails to keep a contractual commitment, suing that person may seem to be the best and only response. This is particularly true when someone feels badly treated and believes that an essential principle is at stake in the conflict. However, the desire to stand up for this principle at all costs is a short-term way of thinking that should be resisted. Maintaining a good business relationship with the party in breach—or at least minimizing the financial costs of the dispute—is often much more important than proving yourself to be right in a court of law. Questions to ask include:

- are legal proceedings absolutely necessary, at least right now?
- is there a way to resolve the problem from a larger, relationship-preserving perspective, rather than from a strictly legal viewpoint?

Solutions to a legal dispute exist at various levels of formality. The first logical step is for the parties to try to come to a resolution between themselves and produce, if necessary, a formalized settlement agreement. If this solution does not work, the legal system offers **mediation** and **arbitration** as ways of avoiding litigation. Thus, the law provides a number of mechanisms for settling disputes short of a courtroom battle.

Sometimes, however, one business will commence legal action against another and take the matter to court. Perhaps there had been no previous agreement between the parties to refer disputes to arbitration and they have no desire to do so now; perhaps one of the parties refuses to accept mediation; perhaps one of the parties is tremendously unfair and cannot be reasoned with; or perhaps the dispute has reached the point at which a court ruling is the only way to end the matter once and for all. It is essential to a workable business environment that

Mediation

A process through which the parties to a dispute endeavour to reach a resolution with the assistance of a neutral person.

Arbitration

A process through which a neutral party makes a decision (usually binding) that resolves a dispute.

---

19 For a discussion of wrongful dismissal, see Chapter 21.

Liability

Legal responsibility for the event or loss that has occurred.

the last-resort solution provided by the litigation process be available to the disputants. In this way, the **liability** of one business to another can be established.

How and Why the Law Works

There are any number of ways to resolve a dispute, including trial by ordeal (as in the notorious Salem witch trials of seventeenth century America); pistol duel (prevalent in France and England until the nineteenth century); and even modern-day drive-by shootings. What these methods lack, however, is accordance with modern ideas of what is just, fair, and reasonable.

Canada's legal system stands in opposition to such inequitable, arbitrary, and violent alternatives. While our legal system is far from perfect, it possesses essential improvements over its predecessors because it determines liability in accordance with certain principles and processes that are regarded as just.

For example, assume that Lionel is sued by his customer for breach of contract because he failed to deliver product on time and the matter has now come before a judge. The Canadian legal system demands that both the process for determining liability and the rules or laws that are applied in that process are fair and free from bias. Though it is impossible for our legal system to completely reach such a standard, these are its laudable goals. Lionel's customer, as the party who has initiated the complaint of breach of contract, is obligated to prove his case. The judge, in turn, is obligated to be as objective as possible in determining whether the customer has proven his case. Part of the judge's job is to determine what the agreement between the parties actually was, as well as the law governing the matter. The judge must then apply this law as impartially as possible to the situation. In order that the outcome of the customer's dispute with Lionel be seen as just, the law that the judge ultimately relies on must also be fair and reasonable.

For instance, it is a rule of law that a party who suffers a breach of contract is entitled to be put in the position that he or she would have been in had the contract been fulfilled. If the customer can prove that, as a result of Lionel's breach, he lost business, for example, a court may well award damages for loss of profit. The rationale behind the rule is simple: Lionel has broken his contractual promise, albeit unintentionally. Lionel must therefore assume responsibility for any direct and foreseeable financial consequences that his customer experiences as a result.

The goals of the Canadian justice system are ambitious and often difficult to achieve. There are also obvious limitations to what the law can actually accomplish, even when it is most successful. Employment equity law will not end discrimination. Reform of bankruptcy law will not prevent business failures. More restrictive copyright laws will not stop unauthorized copying in everyday life. As noted earlier, the law can, however, offer itself as a mechanism for achieving the goals of protection, facilitation, and dispute resolution. For example, bankruptcy law is the vehicle for ensuring that all those affected by a failed business are treated fairly, reasonably, and according to a set of agreed-upon rules. The law is prepared to confront bigotry by providing remedies to those who are the targets. It provides rules for contract formation. And it provides a vast machinery for resolving conflict.

Global News Edmonton

This man claimed to have been locked in a car trunk over a debt owed to his attackers. He was freed from the trunk by firefighters. How is this method of dispute resolution inconsistent with the values informing the Canadian justice system?

Knowledge of the Law as a Business Asset

Entrepreneurs like Lionel can use the law to protect and advance their business interests. Conversely, they can cause themselves much anxiety, grief, and financial loss by ignoring the law.

For example, the law of occupiers' liability holds Lionel responsible for the head injuries suffered and income lost by his potential customer who slipped on a wet floor on his premises.[20] Likewise, the law forbids Lionel from using a business name similar to that of the northern Canadian company ("Chelsee Eggs and Poultry") if that misleads the public into thinking that the two businesses are somehow related. Though Lionel did not intend to mislead the public, this is no defence to any action launched by Chelsee Eggs and Poultry.[21]

Lionel's negative experience with the law illustrates the point that knowledge of the law is a business asset. Had Lionel taken more time to inform himself about the laws governing his operations—as well as about the consequences for failing to abide by them—his business experience presumably would have been much more positive and profitable.

An effective way to avoid Lionel's mistakes is to implement a **legal risk management plan**. This means identifying the legal risks associated with a business and implementing concrete measures for managing those risks. The objective is to identify and plan for risks *before* they occur.[22]

Legal risk management plan

A comprehensive action plan for dealing with the legal risks involved in operating a business.

Law and Business Ethics

From the perspective of reputation and profitability, it is not enough for a commercial enterprise simply to comply with the law. **Business ethics** also provide an increasingly important overlay. Business ethics concern moral principles and values that seek to determine right and wrong in the business world. On this basis, while it is ethical for a business to comply with the law, ethics may demand even more. Business ethics require entrepreneurs to conform to principles of commercial morality, fairness, and honesty. Entire books have been written about the ethical problems or dilemmas that a business might face.[23] However, from an introductory perspective, it is useful to consider how ethics impacts on business decisions from a number of vantage points:[24]

Business ethics

Moral principles and values that seek to determine right and wrong in the business world.

- *Business to Consumer:* How far should a company go in extolling the virtues of its product? When does sales talk become deception?
- *Business to Society:* To what lengths should a company go to enhance shareholder return? To reduce costs, should a business employ child labour in those countries where it is legal to do so? What if the child's income is essential to the family's survival?
- *Business to Employee:* Should a business monitor employee emails and Internet use on company computers?
- *Business to Business:* Short of lying or fraud, is it ethical to bluff during business negotiations? When does bluffing become a form of corruption?

---

20 For discussion of occupiers' liability, see Chapter 12.
21 For discussion of passing off, see Chapter 12.
22 See Chapter 3 for a risk management model.
23 See, for example, Robert Sexty, *Canadian Business and Society: Ethics and Responsibility,* 2d ed (Whitby, ON: McGraw-Hill Ryerson, 2011); Robert Larmer, *Ethics in the Workplace: Selected Readings in Business Ethics,* 2d ed (Belmont, CA: Wadsworth Thomson Learning, 2002).
24 These vantage points are derived from the work of Larmer, *supra* note 23.

Indeed, skirting ethical norms can lead to lost revenue, bad publicity, public demonstrations, and condemnation for contributing to social injustice, as the following box illustrates.

BANGLADESHI FACTORY COLLAPSE

A recent Bangladeshi factory collapse killed more than 1100 workers and injured another 2500. It has been described as the "worst garment industry accident in history."[25] The senseless devastation visited upon victims and their families brought criticism to the international garment industry for not paying sufficient attention to how their orders for clothing were outsourced through middlemen and the conditions at the factories where the outsourcing occurred.[26]

Canadian company Loblaw, whose Joe Fresh line of clothing was made in the Bangladeshi factory, has paid into a fund offering compensation to those affected and also signed an agreement whose purpose is to improve the "substandard fire and building safety in Bangladesh."[27] As summarized by Howard Husock, a *Forbes* online contributor, anti-sweatshop organizations such as Clean Clothes Campaign have already independently observed that compensation for victims and financial support for local improve-

Jason Burke for The Guardian

Though Shima, 25, pictured above, survived the Bangladeshi factory collapse, her best friend died.

ments in workplace safety by international brand name retailers would be both appropriate and morally required. In short, firms should subscribe to such a code of conduct, "even if they are not legally required to do so."[28]

Critical Analysis: In what way can ethical standards be higher than legal ones? Do you think it should be sufficient for business simply to meet legal standards or is more required?

BUSINESS LAW IN PRACTICE REVISITED

1. How does the law affect Lionel's business?

As Lionel starts his business, he will be involved in a number of transactions and events with significant legal implications, including the following:

- **Business form.** Does Lionel want to operate his business alone as a sole proprietor, would he prefer to work with partners, or is he interested in incorporating? Each business vehicle has its own set of

25 Amber Hildebrant, "Bangladesh's Rana Plaza factory collapse spurs change, finger-pointing: Only $15 million of a promised $40 million fund committed" *CBC News* (24 April 2014), online: CBC <http://www.cbc.ca/m/touch/news/story/1.2619524>.

26 Marina Strauss and Bertrand Marotte, "Loblaw outlines Bangladesh compensation plan" *Globe and Mail* (24 October 2013 and 25 October 2013), online: Globe and Mail <http://www.theglobeandmail.com/report-on-business/international-business/loblaw-to-compensate-victims-of-bangladesh-factory-collapse/article15041964/>.

27 *Ibid.* CBC News, "Joe Fresh continuing garment business in Bangladesh in year after tragedy" (11 April 2014), online: CBC News <http://www.cbc.ca/news/world/joe-fresh-continuing-garment-business-in-bangladesh-in-year-after-tragedy-1.2606120>.

28 Howard Husock, "The Bangladesh Example and Corporate Social Responsibility," *Forbes* online (5 February 2013), online: Forbes <http://www.forbes.com/sites/howardhusock/2013/05/02/the-bangladesh-fire-and-corporate-social-responsibility/>.

rules, which Lionel must find out about. For instance, the incorporation process is strictly dictated by federal and provincial law.[29]

- **Business name.** Lionel must be sure to choose a name that is not confusingly similar to the name of another business. Even if he chooses such a name inadvertently, he will be subject to legal consequences, including being sued for damages by the individual or company that has built up goodwill in the name in question.[30]
- **Financing considerations.** If Lionel decides to borrow his operating capital from the bank, he must enter into a specialized form of contract known as a promissory note. In this contract, he promises to repay the loan, with interest, according to a schedule.[31] If Lionel decides that he wants to raise money by selling shares, he will definitely have to incorporate a company. As well, should Lionel's company end up selling shares to the public, it will have disclosure obligations under securities legislation.[32]
- **Property.** If Lionel decides to expand, he must determine whether to buy, build, or lease additional premises for his business operation. Each option involves a unique set of laws.[33] Furthermore, many aspects of the property used in Lionel's business are regulated through health legislation and fire regulations, to name two examples. Additionally, if customers are injured on his premises, Lionel may be held liable and be required to pay damages.[34]
- **Services.** Lionel may ultimately hire staff to run his business. He must become aware of the laws concerning unjust dismissal and employment equity, as well as human rights legislation that prohibits discrimination.[35]
- **Marketing.** In promoting his business to the public, Lionel must be sure to abide by laws prohibiting false and misleading advertising,[36] as well as trademark and copyright law, to name two examples.
- **Selling.** Lionel must be sure to provide a reasonable level of service to his customers.

Just as Lionel must devote resources to monitoring any staff that he might have, attending to proper bookkeeping, and keeping his loans in good standing, he also must spend time managing the legal elements of his business environment. Since the law affects Lionel's business from a variety of perspectives, he is much better off accepting this responsibility from the outset, rather than fighting a rear-guard action. Once he understands the law, Lionel can take simple, proactive steps to ensure that he complies with it; just as importantly, he can plan for the future. A properly devised risk management plan is an invaluable tool to achieving this end.

2. What are the purposes of the laws that affect Lionel's business?

One of the most important functions of law in the business environment is to facilitate planning, particularly—though not exclusively—through contract law. Business law also has a protective function in that it seeks to ensure that those who cause a loss are held financially responsible and otherwise accountable for their actions, including through the criminal justice system. Finally, the law

---

29 For a discussion of the incorporation process, see Chapter 15.
30 *Ibid.*
31 For a discussion of credit, see Chapter 26.
32 For a discussion of securities law, see Chapter 15.
33 For a discussion of real estate law, see Chapter 19.
34 For discussion of occupier's liability law, see Chapter 12.
35 For a discussion of employment law, see Chapters 20 and 21.
36 For a discussion of marketing law, see Chapters 23 and 24.

provides a series of mechanisms and rules for dispute resolution, thereby making an essential contribution to certainty in the marketplace.

3. What has gone wrong in Lionel's business and why?

The Business Law in Practice scenario provides a lengthy illustration of the kinds of penalties and liabilities Lionel faces for neglecting the legal rules that govern his enterprise and failing to manage against their violation.

CHAPTER SUMMARY

Law is involved in all aspects of business, whether the entrepreneur is aware of it or not. The law protects persons and their property, facilitates commercial interactions, particularly through contract law, and provides mechanisms for dispute resolution.

Though not perfect, the Canadian legal system has much to recommend it. The system strives for just outcomes by demanding that both the process for determining liability and the rules or laws that are applied in that process are fair, objective, and free from bias. No justice system, of course, can consistently accomplish all these goals.

Indeed, there are serious limitations to what the law can realistically achieve when a legal problem arises; thus, it is imperative that a business adopt a proactive approach in managing the legal aspects of its environment through a legal risk management plan. This chapter has emphasized the idea that knowledge of the law is an essential business asset. Informed owners and managers can protect their businesses by ensuring compliance with legal requirements. They can capitalize on the planning function of law to ensure the future of their business by entering into contracts. They also can seek enforcement of legal rules against those who do business or have other interactions with the enterprise. In this way, the property, contractual expectations, and profitability of the business are made more secure. Business ethics—while sometimes but not always coextensive with legal requirements—are also increasingly important to running a successful business.

CHAPTER STUDY

Key Terms and Concepts

age of majority (p. 8)

arbitration (p. 11)

breach of contract (p. 7)

business ethics (p. 13)

business law (p. 3)

contract law (p. 9)

law (p. 5)

legal risk management plan (p. 13)

liability (p. 12)

litigation (p. 10)

mediation (p. 11)

Questions for Review

1. What is the function of law?

2. How does the law protect members of society?

3. How does the law facilitate business activity?

4. In what ways does the law facilitate certainty in the marketplace?

5. Does the nature of the business relationship affect the enforcement of legal rights?

6. How does the law resolve disputes?

7. Does dispute resolution always involve going to court?

8. In what way is knowledge of the law a business asset?

9. How might a lack of knowledge of the law negatively impact a business?

10. Why should a business put a legal risk management plan in place?

11. What is the role of business ethics?

12. Why are business ethics important?

13. What is spam?

14. What is the purpose of regulating spam?

Questions for Critical Thinking

1. The law is sometimes made subject to the criticism that it does not necessarily forbid unethical behaviour and is therefore too narrow in scope. What is the relationship between ethics and law? Are ethical responsibilities the same as legal responsibilities?

2. When is a lawsuit the best response to a legal dispute? What is at risk?

3. Knowledge of the law is a business asset. How can you acquire this asset short of becoming a lawyer? How is ignorance of the law a liability?

4. There has been considerable concern about the safety of Tasers (electroshock weapons) and their possible role in the death of hundreds of people in North America. For example, the danger associated with Tasers was brought to light because of the death of Robert Dziekanski, a Polish immigrant who died at the Vancouver International Airport immediately after being tased by RCMP officers. According to the CEO of Taser International, however, there is "no other device with as much accountability" as a Taser and he maintains that Tasers actually save lives.[37] What is the role of the law in regulating the products sold in the marketplace and ensuring their safety or relative safety?

5. Adam Guerbuez, the spammer described in this chapter, was made subject to a judgment of almost $1 billion by an American court. Do you think this judgment is unreasonably large? Should the defendant's ability to pay be taken into consideration by the court? Why or why not?

6. Was it a good idea for Maple Lodge Farms (discussed in the Ethical Perspectives Box in this chapter) to fight charges under the *Health of Animals Act* for failing to prevent undue suffering by exposing chickens to the cold during transport? What are the risks of doing so? What are the risks of admitting guilt?

Situations for Discussion

1. Louella Lambast has decided to open a gift store. She intends to offer a wide selection of ever-changing, low-priced giftware, including T-shirts, novelty toys, costume jewellery, and video games. She is tremendously excited about her new venture but cash poor. For this reason, Louella decides to do a lot of the work of setting up the store herself, including assembling a large glass display case. Louella also imports some small table lamps for sale in her shop. When the lamps arrive, she notices that they do not contain labels identifying them as certified by Underwriters Laboratories of Canada or another approved group. (Underwriters Laboratories (UL) is an international, independent, not-for-profit organization whose mandate is to evaluate product safety. The UL mark means that the organization has tested samples of the product in question and concluded that requisite safety requirements have been met.) Because Louella is completely satisfied that the lamps pose no risk, she decides to attach some counterfeit labels on the lamps to reassure customers. A few months later, Louella's world is falling apart. A customer suffers a head injury when the glass display case that Louella had improperly assembled suddenly collapses. A group of demonstrators has begun picketing Louella's business premises, protesting the violent kind of video games she sells. UL has learned that lamps in Louella's store contain counterfeit UL labels. Louella's lawyer has explained that she will likely face prosecution for counterfeiting those UL labels. What has gone wrong in Louella's business and why?

2. The Privacy Commissioner's Annual Report (2011) criticized Staples Business Depot for not taking better steps to protect the privacy of customers who returned computers and USB hard drives. These returned items had undergone a "wipe and restore" process prior to resale but the Privacy Commission's audit found that sensitive data such as social insurance numbers and tax records had not been erased in all cases. What should Staples Business Depot do to ensure better

---

37 Omar El Akkad, "Taser CEO grilled by public safety committee" *The Globe and Mail* (31 January 2008), online: The Globe and Mail <http://portal.sre.gob.mx/canada/pdf/taserceo31.pdf>.

compliance with privacy legislation? Would it be sufficient, for example, to ask customers to sign a form saying that they have wiped the returned electronic device clean prior to its return?

3. Peter is a fudge maker of some renown and obviously requires a reliable supplier of sugar. His current sugar supplier has been very dependable but recently, is delivering late— sometimes days at time. Peter is concerned that the supplier has entered into too many supply contracts with a variety of businesses and cannot fill his orders on a timely basis. Peter knows the sugar supplier is in breach of his contract for delivering late but wants to avoid a full-blown legal battle. What alternative approaches might address Peter's problem more effectively?

4. Several provinces across Canada, including Ontario, Manitoba, and Saskatchewan, have proposed or passed legislation that prevents children from buying or renting video games that are expressly violent or sexual, as determined by a ratings board. Businesses found selling these games to minors face penalties that range from fines to having their business licences revoked.[38] How effective do you think government regulation is in limiting children's access to violent video games? Are there better ways of achieving these types of goals? Is it the role of government to provide legal consequences for the underage renting or purchase of violent video games?

5. Olivia owns a convenience store and has invested a lot of money in gambling machines for the store. Recently, the government passed a law banning the machines from the store immediately, although pubs are allowed to continue operating these machines. Is this law fair? Does it violate any of the common values associated with the law? Would it make a difference if the law applied only to new businesses? Would it make a difference if the government provided compensation to the convenience stores affected, or phased in the law to allow for a period of adjustment?

6. When her husband died of a heart attack in 2001 after taking the painkiller Vioxx, Carol Ernst sued the pharmaceutical manufacturer, Merck & Company (Merck). In 2005, a Texas jury awarded her $253.5 million after concluding that Vioxx had caused Mr. Ernst's death. In 2008, a Texas appeals court reversed Mrs. Ernst's victory. The court concluded that there was no evidence that Vioxx had in fact caused the death of Mr. Ernst[39] and, as a result, Mrs. Ernst has been left with no compensation whatsoever for her husband's death.

According to news reports, Merck has taken an aggressive stance on lawsuits against it and has spent more than $1 billion on legal fees to date.[40] Merck has observed that the plaintiffs are required to prove that Vioxx caused the heart attack in question. Given that heart attacks are the most common cause of death in the United States, Merck would have faced "an essentially unlimited pool of plaintiffs" without taking such a hard line, according to an American law professor.[41] Merck has also taken steps to resolve some of the cases brought against it, however. In 2007, it funded a $4.85 billion settlement, the goal of which is to bring to a conclusion a majority of the remaining Vioxx lawsuits.[42] According to press accounts, more than 97% of eligible claimants (48 550 out of 49 960) have enrolled in the proposed settlement. Payments are to be made according to a complex formula that factors in the seriousness of the individual claimant's injury, how much Vioxx that individual took, and other risk factors associated with that individual.[43] Beyond this, a $37 million settlement of a Canadian class action has recently been approved and will be enforced across the country.[44]

Do you agree with Merck's approach to the lawsuits that have been brought against it?

38 Based, in part, on Steve Lambert, "Manitoba video-game legislation remains in limbo" *The Globe and Mail* (6 January 2005) at A9; and CBC News, "Manitoba moves to rate violent video games" *CBC News* (29 April 2004), online: CBC News <http://www.cbc.ca/canada/story/2004/04/29/vids040429.html>.

39 Eric Strauss, "Merck wins Vioxx appeals in Texas, New Jersey" *The Star -Ledger* (30 May 2008), online: NJ.com <http://www.nj.com/business/index.ssf/2008/05/merck_wins_vioxx_appeals_in_te.html>.

40 Alex Berenson, "Plaintiffs Find Payday Elusive in Vioxx suits" *The New York Times* (21 August 2007), online: New York Times <http://www.nytimes.com/2007/08/21/business/21merck.html?_r51&scp51&sq5plaintiffs%20find%20payday%20elusive%20in%20Vioxx%20suits&st5cse&oref5slogin>.

41 *Ibid*.

42 Strauss, *supra* note 39.

43 Associated Press, "Merck to begin paying $4. 85B in Vioxx Settlements" (updated 17 July 2008), online: NJ.com <http://www.nj.com/news/index.ssf/2008/07/merck_to_begin_paying_485b_in.html>.

44 Tom Blackwell, "Vioxx Suit Settled for $37M", *National Post* (19 January 2012), online: National Post <http://news.nationalpost.com/2012/01/19/blackwell-on-health-vioxx-suit-settled-for-37-million/>.

THE CANADIAN LEGAL SYSTEM

BUSINESS LAW IN PRACTICE

James McCrae owns a small convenience store in Nova Scotia which sells a variety of items, including cigarettes and other tobacco products. On what he regards to be a point of principle, McCrae refuses to comply with recent regulations passed under Nova Scotia's *Tobacco Access Act*.[1] These regulations prohibit the display of tobacco or tobacco products in retail outlets and specify how such products are to be stored. The law requires that tobacco not be visible to the public except at the moment of sale at the till.

McCrae is also aware that the tobacco industry pays retailers to display their goods and this is part of his income stream. Retailers subject to display bans lose preferred shelf space revenue which ranges from $3 000 to $6 000 per store.[2] Legislation like that of Nova Scotia is found in jurisdictions across the country.[3] The idea behind such enactments is that the retail display of tobacco products (called power walls) 'normalizes' the consumption of tobacco and encourages smoking. As noted on the government of Nova Scotia's website:

> Power walls, or point-of-sale advertising, are large, visually appealing displays, located in most gas stations and local stores. Research has indicated these displays are particularly appealing to children and young adults. The legislation will force store owners to conceal cigarettes, and any other tobacco product. The removal of power walls will further restrict the advertising reach of tobacco companies.[4]

There is also evidence that anti-power wall legislation has helped reduce the number of young people who smoke or take up smoking. As the *Guardian* notes for example, "Those countries that have removed displays of tobacco have experienced falls in smoking prevalence among young people. In Iceland, there was a fall of 7.5% among

1 *Tobacco Access Act*, SNS 1993 c 14.
2 Randy Ray, "Bloodied but Unbowed" YCM [Your Convenience Manager] Magazine (2006) 11:1 Jan/Feb.38 at 39, online: YCM <http://magazine.ycmonline.ca/i/78046-january-2006>.
3 As noted in a report by the Propel Centre for Population Health Impact at the University of Waterloo, entitled "Tobacco Use in Canada: Patterns and Trends, Supplement: Tobacco Control Policies in Canada" (2014 edition), all provinces and territories have bans on the display of tobacco products at point of sale as of January 1, 2010, at page 23. See online: Propel Centre <http://www.tobaccoreport.ca/2014/>.
4 See Government of Nova Scotia, News Release, "Government Pulls the Plug on Tobacco Power Walls" (31 October 2006), online: Government of Nova Scotia News Releases <http://www.gov.ns.ca/news/details.asp?id=20061031002>.

The Right Honourable Beverley McLachlin, Chief Justice of the Supreme Court of Canada

OBJECTIVES

After studying this chapter, you should have an understanding of

- the impact of the Canadian legal system on business
- the role of constitutional law in protecting commercial rights and freedoms
- the government's law-making powers under sections 91 and 92 of the *Constitution Act, 1867*
- the executive's formal and political functions in regulating business
- the judiciary's role in assessing the constitutionality of legislation
- the classifications of law
- how administrative law affects business

Blair Gable/Reuters/Landov

people aged 15–16, while Canada saw a fall of 10% over five years among those aged 15–19."[5] From McCrae's perspective, Nova Scotia's legislation interferes with freedom of expression, as protected under section 2(b) of the *Canadian Charter of Rights and Freedoms*, which states:

> 2. Everyone has the following fundamental freedoms...
>
> (b) freedom of thought, belief, opinion and expression, including freedom of
>
> the press and other media of communication;[6]

McCrae's view is that displaying tobacco products is a protected form of expression.

McCrae is eventually charged under the *Tobacco Access Act* for displaying tobacco products out in the open. He wants his lawyer to have the charges thrown out on the basis that the *Tobacco Access Act* is unconstitutional, as contrary to section 2 of the *Canadian Charter of Rights and Freedoms*, quoted above.

1. Is Nova Scotia's *Tobacco Access Act* constitutional and hence enforceable?
2. Who assesses whether the legislation is permissible?
3. Are there any moral or ethical questions that arise from this scenario?

Introduction

The Canadian legal system is the machinery that comprises and regulates government. Government, in turn, is divided into three branches:

- the legislative branch creates law in the form of statutes and regulations.
- the executive branch formulates and implements **government policy** and law.
- the judicial branch adjudicates on disputes.

Constitutional law—which is the supreme law of Canada—is charged with ascertaining and enforcing limits on the exercise of power by the branches of government. It is also charged with upholding "the values of a nation."[7] These values are tied to the political philosophy known as **liberalism**. Briefly put, liberalism emphasizes individual freedom as its key organizing value. A related aspect is that any interference with freedom—including the freedom to display a legal product in one's business premises—must be justified according to the principles of constitutional law.

The **Canadian legal system**—along with the constitutional law that governs it—can be an overwhelming and sometimes very technical area. Even so, some basic knowledge is essential for business owners and managers because:

- the legislative branch of government passes laws that impact on business operations. For example, when government enacts a law, failure to comply can result in fines and other penalties, including closure of the business. Ignorance of a law also means that business loses out on opportunities to influence government policy and to take advantage of favourable laws; failure to challenge laws that are unconstitutional means that business is needlessly constrained.

Government policy

The central ideas or principles that guide government in its work, including the kind of laws it passes.

Constitutional law

The supreme law of Canada that constrains and controls how the branches of government exercise power.

Liberalism

A political philosophy that emphasizes individual freedom as its key organizing value.

Canadian legal system

The machinery that comprises and governs the legislative, executive, and judicial branches of government.

---

5 Janet Atherton, "Keep it hidden", *The Guardian* (4 February 2009), online: *The Guardian* <http://www.guardian.co.uk/society/joepublic/2009/feb/04/children-smoking>.

6 *Canadian Charter of Rights and Freedoms*, section 2(b), Part I of the *Constitution Act, 1982*, being Schedule B to the *Canada Act 1982* (UK), 1982, c 11 [*Charter*].

7 Peter Hogg, *Constitutional Law of Canada*, vol. 1, loose-leaf (Scarborough, ON: Carswell, 2007) at 1–1.

Bob Jordan/AP Photo/The Canadian Press

Some customers are unhappy with display bans, including Rene LaPointe. "It's just another law for the government to throw at us," says LaPointe. "They're treating the adults like children." Do you agree with his analysis?[8]

- the executive branch implements and generates policy that may be directed at business. For this reason, companies such as General Motors of Canada Ltd. have a corporate and environmental affairs department that is charged with monitoring government policy as well as tracking and contributing to debates over public policy that could affect GM operations.[9] Smaller businesses may work to influence government on a more modest scale by monitoring issues in-house, hiring lobbyists, and working through industry associations.

- the judicial branch provides rulings that not only resolve existing legal conflicts but also impact on future disputes. For example, the Supreme Court of Canada's determination of whether commercial expression is protected speech under the *Canadian Charter of Rights and Freedoms* has an impact on any number of industries, from cigarette producers to toy manufacturers.

McCrae's challenge to the *Tobacco Access Act*, mentioned in the chapter opener, involves all three of these branches. The legislative branch passed the law to which McCrae objects. The executive branch formulated and advanced the government policy that led to the legislation being enacted. And the judicial branch—by applying constitutional law—will determine whether McCrae's objections to the law are valid or not.

The Canadian Constitution

The Canadian Constitution is not contained in one document. Rather, it is located in a variety of places, both legislative and political, written and unwritten. While this means that the Constitution may sometimes not be specific, it also means

---

8 "Smokers fume over tobacco display ban" *The Edmonton Journal* (1 June 2008) A8, online: *The Edmonton Journal* <http://www.canada.com/edmontonjournal/news/story.html?id=cb2b5095-4506-495a-8650-207f27169acb>.

9 Interview of Ms. Miriam Christie, Manager of Government Relations, Corporate and Environmental Affairs Department, General Motors of Canada Ltd. (10 March 2000).

that the Constitution can more easily grow to resolve questions or issues related to government.

The written elements of the Constitution include the *Constitution Act, 1867* (part of which divides legislative power between the federal and provincial governments) and the *Canadian Charter of Rights and Freedoms* (which identifies the rights and freedoms that are guaranteed in Canada). Additionally, relevant decisions by judges concerning constitutional law—discussed later in this chapter— also form part of the Constitution. Though these documents provide some of the framework and values informing Canada's system of government, other important constitutional features (known as constitutional conventions) are not mentioned at all.

Constitutional conventions are a "code of ethics that governs our political processes."[10] They are not binding the way that constitutional rules contained in legislation would be; they cannot be enforced in a court of law. Rather, they are in place because politicians historically have agreed to abide by them. One example relates to the office of prime minister; nowhere in Canada's written Constitution is this important office even mentioned, yet no one doubts that the federal government is to be headed by such an officer. In this way, constitutional conventions come to the fore and provide some of the detail of governance.

The Canadian Constitution also attends to a number of other matters, including the admission of new provinces and territories to Canada,[11] provisions for amending the Constitution,[12] and autonomy from the United Kingdom Parliament.[13] Most significantly for our purposes, however, the Canadian Constitution provides for the three branches of government: legislative, executive, and judicial, discussed below.

The Legislative Branch of Government

The **legislative branch** of government creates a form of law known as **statute law** or legislation. A familiar example of statute law is the *Criminal Code of Canada*, which prohibits a variety of offences, such as assault, theft, and fraud. The *Tobacco Access Act* was also created by the legislative branch, this time at the provincial level.

In fact, three levels of government—the federal, provincial, and municipal levels—make legislation in Canada. Parliament, the federal legislative branch, is composed of the House of Commons and the Senate. For legislation to become law, it must first be passed by the House of Commons and then be approved by the Senate. Because the Senate assesses the work of the House of Commons, it has been called "the chamber of sober second thought."

Each province also has a law-making body. In British Columbia, for example, this is called the Legislative Assembly, while in Nova Scotia this is called the House of Assembly. At the provincial level, there is no Senate, or upper house.

Municipalities, which are created by provincial legislation, have legislative bodies often called city councils. Their powers are delegated to them by the province in which they are located. (See Figure 2.1.)

Constitutional conventions

Important rules that are not enforceable by a court of law but that practically determine how a given power is exercised by government.

Legislative branch

The branch of government that creates statute law.

Statute law

Formal, written laws created or enacted by the legislative branch of government.

---

10 Bernard Funston & Eugene Meehan, *Canada's Constitutional Law in a Nutshell*, 4th ed. (Toronto: Carswell, 2013) at 6.
11 As Hogg observes, *supra* note 7 at 2-12, section 146 of the *Constitution Act, 1867* governs this matter. For a link to constitutional documents, including legislation creating provinces as they are admitted to Canada, see online: Government of Canada <http://laws.justice.gc.ca/en/Const/index.html>.
12 See Part V of the *Constitution Act, 1982*, being Schedule B to the *Canada Act 1982* (UK), 1982, c 11, and Hogg, *supra* note 7 at 4–12 and 4–15.
13 For further discussion of this point, see Hogg, *ibid* at 3–1 to 3–15.

FIGURE 2.1 Law-Making Jurisdiction

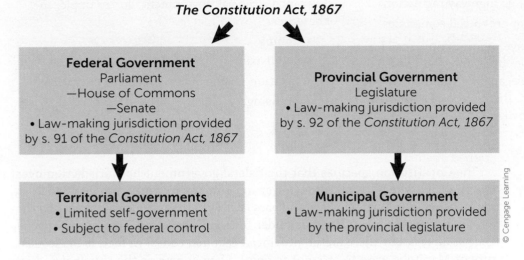

Statute Law and Jurisdiction

As already noted, the Constitution—through the *Constitution Act, 1867*—dictates whether each level of government can make a given law or not. Expressed in legal language, each level of government has the **jurisdiction** to pass laws within its proper authority or sphere. Jurisdiction is divided in this way because Canada is a federal state, which means that governmental power is split between the central, national authority (the federal government), and regional authorities (the provincial governments). Additionally, the federal government empowers territorial governments to engage in a form of limited self-government. The provincial governments, in turn, empower municipal governments to legislate in specifically defined areas.

Jurisdiction

The power that a given level of government has to enact laws.

BUSINESS AND LEGISLATION

CONSTITUTION ACT, 1867

The federal government has the power, or the jurisdiction, to make laws in those areas set out in section 91 of the *Constitution Act, 1867* (formerly known as the *British North America Act* or the *BNA Act*). Areas in which the federal government may enact laws include the following:

- interprovincial/international trade and commerce
- trade as a whole
- postal service
- navigation and shipping
- seacoast and inland fisheries
- currency
- national defence
- criminal law

- banking
- all legislative areas not given to the provinces (Note: This is a residual category in the sense that the federal government has all the law-making power not expressly given to the provinces. For example, it is the residual power that justifies federal legislation that creates federally incorporated companies.)

The provincial governments have jurisdiction to make laws in those areas set out in section 92 of the *Constitution Act, 1867*, including the following:

- hospitals
- property and civil rights within the province (e.g., the regulation of contracts)
- administration of justice (e.g., the court system)

- local matters (e.g., highway regulation)
- incorporation of provincial companies

Municipalities have no constitutionally recognized powers. They have only the law-making authority that is delegated to them by the provincial governments. The municipal governments have jurisdiction to make laws as permitted by the relevant provincial government, for example, in these areas:

- zoning
- subdivision
- taxation for the benefit of the municipality
- licensing

The Constitution specifies that the federal government has jurisdiction over criminal law, which includes the power to define new crimes, provide penalties for breaches of the criminal law, and pass laws with the purpose of protecting the public. Because criminal law falls under federal jurisdiction, there is a *Criminal Code of Canada* but there are no provincial criminal codes. In fact, if the legislature of Manitoba were to attempt to enact a law known as the *Criminal Code of Manitoba*, for example, this law would be unconstitutional because a provincial government does not have the power to pass such a law. No court would enforce the code because it would be contrary to the Constitution to do so. In short, the federal government has **exclusive jurisdiction** over criminal law.

Sometimes, the federal and provincial governments have shared or **concurrent jurisdiction**. This means that the area being regulated does not fall neatly into the federal or provincial jurisdiction but straddles them both. Public health is one such area, with both federal and provincial governments legislating in the area. The environment is another, as discussed in the following box.

Exclusive jurisdiction

Jurisdiction that one level of government holds entirely on its own and not on a shared basis with another level.

Concurrent jurisdiction

Jurisdiction that is shared between levels of government.

ENVIRONMENTAL PERSPECTIVE

CONCURRENT JURISDICTION OVER THE ENVIRONMENT

From a business perspective, one tremendously significant area of concurrent jurisdiction relates to the environment. Both the federal and provincial governments share jurisdiction but, perhaps surprisingly, so do municipalities. This is because, as Shawn Denstedt and Daniel Kirby observe, municipalities are

> traditionally responsible for water and sewage systems and noise issues, [and] in some cases now restrict or prohibit the use of pesticides

and herbicides (even after their use has been approved by the federal or applicable provincial government), require public disclosure regarding the use of toxic substances and often try to control the impact of development on the environment through their role as the primary authority for land-use planning.[14]

Federal jurisdiction over the environment centres on (a) protection of oceans and inland waterways; (b) fisheries protection; (c) the import and export of hazardous products; and (d) the interprovincial/international transportation of dangerous goods.[15] For example, the federally enacted

---

14 Daniel Kirby and Shawn Denstedt, "Environmental Law in Canada" at 68 in Shawn Denstedt and Daniel Kirby with contributions by Rahda Curpen *Doing Business in Canada* (March 2009) at 68, online: Osler, Hoskin & Harcourt <http://www.google.ca/url?sa=t&rct=j&q=&esrc=s&source=web&cd=1&ved=0CCEQFjAA&url=http%3A%2F%2Fwww.osler.com%2FuploadedFiles%2FNews_and_Resources%2FPublications%2FGuides%2FDoing_Business_in_Canada_-_2011%2FDBIC-Chapter14.pdf&ei=6RCmU_nllMmZyAT904C4Bw&usg=AFQjCNEaNaoF8eAODUBTAG46kDsc0NsFSg&bvm=bv.69411363,d.aWw>.

15 Robert Warren, John Buhlman & Carole McAffee Wallace, "Environmental Protection Law in Ontario" (Spring 2009), online: WeirFoulds <http://www.weirfoulds.com/files/4130_WeirFoulds%20LLP-EnvironmentalLawProtectionOntario.pdf> at 3.

legislation called the *Canadian Environmental Protection Act*[16] (CEPA) sets out comprehensive rules governing toxic substances as they relate, from a business perspective, to "research and development through to production, marketing, use and disposal."[17] The goal of the legislation is to protect human health and the environment from the dangers of harmful and toxic substances.[18] On a related front, *CEPA* is important because, as Environment Canada notes, it "manages environmental and human health impacts of products of biotechnology, marine pollution, disposal at sea, vehicle, engine and equipment emissions, fuels, hazardous wastes, environmental emergencies, and other sources of pollution."[19]

CEPA provides strong penalties for violation, including fines of up to $1 million a day for each day the offence continues, imprisonment for up to three years, or both. Those convicted are also subject to paying clean-up costs, as relevant, or forfeiting any profit earned as a result of failing to comply with the Act.[20]

The *Criminal Code of Canada* is another example of federal law concerning the environment.[21] Charges can be laid under the *Criminal Code* when, for example, an environmental discharge causes bodily injury or death.[22]

Every province and territory in Canada has extensive environmental protection legislative regimes. In Ontario, for example, the most significant legislation on point is the *Environmental Protection Act*.[23] For example, section 14 (1) of the Act states as follows: "a person shall not discharge a contaminant or cause or permit the discharge of a contaminant into the natural environment, if the discharge causes or may cause an adverse effect."

If a spill occurs, the legislation requires that it be reported pursuant to section 15 and, pursuant to section 17, that the person responsible remediate the problem (i.e., clean up).

The court can impose fines and even jail time for violation of the Act with penalties varying according to the kind of offence committed as well as whether the violation was a first offence or not.[24]

Directors and officers also face personal liability for non-compliance with environmental protection legislation and are thereby exposed to potentially heavy fines and, in the extreme case, even imprisonment. For further discussion on this point, see Chapter 16.

Regulation and protection of the environment is complex, in part, because jurisdiction is spread among three levels of government. This makes it particularly important for businesses to know what legislation applies to the situation in question, to deploy risk management strategies to ensure that such legislation sees compliance, and to acquire environmental insurance as a backstop should the organization fail in its statutory obligations.

Critical Analysis: What are the advantages of concurrent jurisdiction over the environment? What are the disadvantages?

In areas of concurrent jurisdiction, what the provincial government cannot do is enact legislation that would create a conflict with federal legislation. That is, in an area of concurrent jurisdiction—such as health or the environment—the doctrine of **paramountcy** applies. This doctrine makes the federal legislation

Paramountcy

A doctrine that provides that federal laws prevail when there are conflicting or inconsistent federal and provincial laws.

16 *Canadian Environmental Protection Act*, 1999 SC c 33 ["*CEPA*"].
17 Kirby and Denstedt, *supra* note 14 at 68.
18 Environment Canada, "A Guide to Understanding the *Canadian Environmental Protection Act, 1999*" (December 2004; modified December 2013), online: Environment Canada <http://www.ec.gc.ca/lcpe-cepa/default.asp?lang=En&n=E00B5BD8-1> [Environment Canada] at 2.
19 *Ibid*.
20 *Ibid* at 14.
21 *Criminal Code*, RSC 1985, c C-46.
22 *Supra* note 14 at 70.
23 *Environmental Protection Act*, RSO 1990, c E 19.
24 Warren, *supra* note 15.

Ratify

To authorize or approve.

Treaty

An agreement between two or more states that is governed by international law.

paramount or supreme and the provincial law inoperative, but only to the extent of the conflict. Though a significant doctrine, it is also a limited one. The judiciary has held that paramountcy generally applies only if there is an express contradiction between the two laws. If a person could simply obey the stricter law—and thereby comply with both pieces of legislation—then paramountcy would not apply; both laws would operate fully.

ANTI-SMOKING TREATY

In response to the millions of deaths caused by tobacco every year numerous countries, including Canada, have **ratified** a **treaty** known as the "Framework Convention on Tobacco Control." According to the World Health Organization:

> … the treaty requires countries to impose restrictions on tobacco advertising, sponsorship, and promotion; establish new packaging and labelling of tobacco products; establish clean indoor air controls; and strengthen legislation to clamp down on tobacco smuggling.

For example, countries would be required to adopt and implement rotating health warnings and messages on tobacco products, occupying at least 30 percent of the display areas. Canada ratified this treaty in 2004.

As reported in the *Globe and Mail*, research confirms that appropriate health warnings are effective in tobacco control strategies and that picture warnings have more impact and encourage more smokers to quit as compared to text warnings alone.

Given that tobacco is highly addictive and often marketed to young people, Canada's failure to legally require appropriate warnings on *all* tobacco products concerns people like Rob Cunningham, senior policy analyst with the Canadian Cancer Society, as the *Globe and Mail* reports. For example, individual packaged cigars are generally sold with no health warnings at all; chewing tobacco is sold with a text warning only; and water pipe or shisha tobacco is sold with no health warnings at all.

Because the federal government has decided *not* to require appropriate warnings on these kinds of products, Canada is in violation of the

Shisha tobacco is at least as dangerous as cigarette tobacco. Should it be exempt from appropriate health warnings in Canada?

Istvan Csak/Shutterstock

Framework Convention discussed above. For Cunningham, this hurts Canada's reputation as a "leader in the field of tobacco control."

The *Globe and Mail* reports that in 2011, the federal government said it would be phasing in warnings on these exempt products but has not done so to date.

Critical Analysis: Should Canada ensure it is compliant with the anti-smoking treaty? How might a treaty ratified and implemented by multiple countries be more effective in reducing tobacco consumption than if each country simply worked in isolation? What are the advantages of global cooperation? What are the disadvantages?

Sources: Carly Weeks, "The double standards of Canada's tobacco control," *Globe and Mail* (17 June 2014) online <http://www.theglobeandmail.com/life/health-and-fitness/health/the-double-standards-of-canadas-tobacco-control/article19202446/>; World Health Organization, "An international treaty for tobacco control" (12 August 2003), online: World Health Organization <http://www.who.int/features/2003/08/en>; and FCTC, "Parties to the WHO Framework Convention on Tobacco Control," online: World Health Organization online <http://www.who.int/fctc/signatories_parties/en/>.

Business is affected by all levels of government, but it is most affected by the provincial and municipal governments. An important exception relates to businesses in banking, international or interprovincial transport, and communication (e.g., telephone and cable). These are areas of federal jurisdiction and, accordingly, such businesses are subject to federal law concerning licensing, labour, and occupational health and safety, to name several examples.

The regulation of business is generally a provincial matter because the provinces have jurisdiction over property and civil rights.[25] Municipalities have jurisdiction to legislate in a broad variety of matters, from levying appropriate taxes and regulating local zoning, parking, and subdivision, to requiring the licensing of businesses and dogs. Municipal legislation takes the form of **bylaws**.

The Executive Branch of Government

The executive branch of government has a formal, ceremonial function, as well as a political one. From a formal or ceremonial perspective, for example, the executive branch supplies the head of the Canadian state, the Queen. The **formal executive** also has a significant role in the legislative process, since the executive branch of government, represented by the governor general (the Queen's federal representative) or lieutenant governor (the Queen's provincial representative), issues approval as the final step in creating statute law.

The **political executive** is of great relevance to businesses because it performs the day-to-day operations of government by formulating and executing government policy and administering all departments of government. It is also the level of government that businesses typically lobby in order to secure favourable or improved treatment under legislation or with respect to policy formation.

The chief executive of the federal government is the prime minister, while the chief executive of the provincial government is the premier. Other members of

Bylaws

Laws made by the municipal level of government.

Formal executive

The branch of government responsible for the ceremonial features of government.

Political executive

The branch of government responsible for day-to-day operations, including formulating and executing government policy, as well as administering all departments of government.

BUSINESS AND LEGISLATION

TOBACCO REGULATION BY THE FEDERAL GOVERNMENT

Regulations are a form of legislation that is more precisely referred to as subordinate legislation. This is because regulations can be passed only if that power is accorded by the statute in question. That said, such power is routinely given. For example, the *Tobacco Act (Canada)* permits the Governor (General) in Council (i.e., the federal cabinet) to make regulations respecting information that must appear on cigarette packages. Cabinet exercised this power through the *Tobacco Products Information Regulations* which require that graphic health warnings and other information be placed on cigarette packages.

In 2011, new federal regulations came into force governing warnings to be placed on cigarette packages. Important features include:

- "new graphic health warning messages covering 75 percent of the front and back of cigarette and little cigar packages;
- new health information messages that are enhanced with the use of colour and graphic elements;
- a pan-Canadian toll-free quitline number and web portal to inform tobacco users about the availability of smoking cessation services, subject to provincial/territorial agreement; and

---

25 Hogg, *supra* note 7 at 21–3.

Licensed under Health Canada copyright. Photo © Greg Southam/Edmonton Journal.

This image depicts Barb Tarbox, who died of lung cancer caused by smoking. She was so addicted to cigarettes that she continued smoking until her death. One of her final wishes was that her dying image appear on cigarette packages as a warning to others.[26] *Are such images effective?*

- easier-to-understand toxic emissions statements."

These regulations also provide a set of images to be included on cigarette packages, including the one depicted here.

Sources: *Tobacco Act, SC 1997*, c 13; Health Canada "Tobacco Products Labelling" Regulations," Public Health Agency of Canada http://www.hc-sc.gc.ca/hc-ps/tobac-tabac/legislation/label-etiquette/index-eng.php

the political executive—both provincial and federal—include cabinet ministers, civil servants, and the agencies, commissions, and tribunals that perform governmental functions.

The **cabinet**—made up of all the ministers of the various government departments, as well as the prime minister or premier—also has a very significant law-making function. It is often the cabinet that passes **regulations** providing detail to what the statute in question has enacted. When the cabinet enacts regulations, it is known by its formal name: the lieutenant governor in council (provincially) and the governor general in council (federally).

The Judicial Branch of Government

It may seem surprising that the **judiciary** is a branch of government, given that the judiciary is supposed to be independent of government. Expressed more completely, however, the concept is this: the judiciary is to be independent from the legislative and executive branches of government.

The judiciary is composed of **judges** who are appointed by both federal and provincial governments. These judges are required to adjudicate on a variety of matters, including divorce and the custody of children, civil disputes such as those arising from a will, breach of contract, car accidents, wrongful dismissal, and other wrongful acts causing damage or injury. Judges also preside over criminal proceedings. Businesses, however, predominantly rely on the courts to settle commercial disputes.

The System of Courts

Judges operate within a system of courts that vary somewhat from province to province. Despite these variations, each provincial and territorial system of courts has three basic levels: trial, intermediate appeal, and final appeal. Figure 2.2 indicates the hierarchy of courts relevant to commercial disputes.

Trial courts are of two types: inferior and superior. An **inferior court** is presided over by a judge appointed by the provincial government. These courts are organized by type of case, such as criminal, family, and civil. The civil court—sometimes

Cabinet

A body composed of all ministers heading government departments, as well as the prime minister or premier.

Regulations

Rules created by the political executive that have the force of law.

Judiciary

A collective reference to judges.

Judges

Those appointed by federal or provincial governments to adjudicate on a variety of disputes, as well as to preside over criminal proceedings.

Inferior court

A court with limited financial jurisdiction whose judges are appointed by the provincial government.

---

26 "Family of Tarbox wants her deathbed image on cigarette packs" (08 December 2010), online: Calgary CTV <http://calgary.ctv.ca/servlet/an/local/CTVNews/20101207/CGY_smoke_warnings_101207/20101208/?hub=CalgaryHome>.

FIGURE 2.2 Courts Dealing with Commercial Disputes

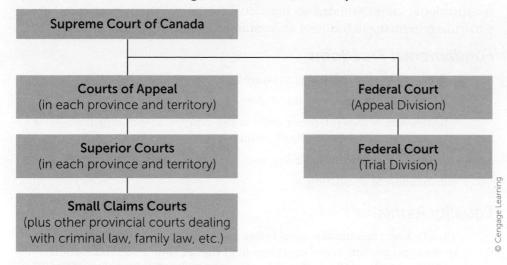

© Cengage Learning

called **small claims court**—handles disputes involving smaller amounts of money. The amount varies from province to province: $50 000 is the limit in Alberta;[27] $25 000 is the limit in British Columbia, Nova Scotia, and Ontario;[28] and $20 000 is the limit in Saskatchewan.[29] The small claims process is designed to be simpler, quicker, and less expensive than mainstream litigation. Parties often appear in this court without a lawyer. **Superior courts**—whose judges are appointed by the federal government—have the jurisdiction to handle claims involving an unlimited monetary amount. In addition, they are the entry level for the more serious criminal matters. Here, the procedure is much more formal and technical, with parties usually being represented by lawyers.

Provincial courts of appeal hear appeals from these lower courts, and from there cases go to the **Supreme Court of Canada**. In most commercial cases, litigation tends to end in provincial courts of appeal because appeal to the Supreme Court of Canada is available only after permission or "leave" to appeal is granted by the Supreme Court itself. Ordinarily, the Supreme Court of Canada will hear only appeals that involve questions of national concern or significance.

The **Federal Court of Canada** has special authority to deal with certain cases in which one of the parties is the federal government or one of its agencies.

The Canadian Charter of Rights and Freedoms

An important responsibility for judges is determining whether a given law meets the requirements of the Canadian Constitution, including the *Canadian Charter of Rights and Freedoms* (*Charter*). Created in 1982, the *Charter* is intended as a judicially enforceable guarantee that the government will act consistently with the values associated with a liberal democratic state. The right to freedom of expression and of religion, the right to a fair and speedy trial, equality rights,

Small claims court

A court that deals with claims up to a specified amount.

Superior courts

Courts with unlimited financial jurisdiction whose judges are appointed by the federal government.

Supreme Court of Canada

The final court for appeals in the country.

Federal Court of Canada

The court that deals with some types of litigation involving the federal government.

Canadian Charter of Rights and Freedoms

A guarantee of specific rights and freedoms enshrined in the Constitution and enforceable by the judiciary.

---

27 *Provincial Civil Ct Division Regulation* Alta Reg 329/89, consolidated up to 139/2014. See too Alberta Government, "Higher small claims court limit increases access to justice" (21 July 2014), online: Government of Alberta <http://alberta.ca/release.cfm?xID=36856F648A53F-BA5B-A6D3-942144FBE5372212>.

28 See the Courts of Nova Scotia, "The Small Claims Court" online: Government of Nova Scotia <http://courts .ns.ca/Small_Claims_Court/NSSCC_home.htm> and The Ministry of the Attorney General of Ontario, "Guide to Making a Claim", online: <http://www.attorneygeneral.jus.gov.on.ca/english/courts/scc/b4aClaim.asp>; and Ministry of Justice [British Columbia], Small Claims, online: <http://www.ag.gov.bc.ca/courts/small_claims/>.

29 See Courts of Saskatchewan, "Small Claims Court", online: <http://www.sasklawcourts.ca/index.php/home/ provincial-court-small-claims-court>.

and the right to vote are all examples of *Charter* protections that reflect a set of constitutional values founded on individual freedom. Two protections that are particularly germane to business are contained in sections 2 and 15.

Fundamental Freedoms

2. Everyone has the following fundamental freedoms:

   a. freedom of conscience and religion;

   b. freedom of thought, belief, opinion and expression, including freedom of the press and other media of communication;

   c. freedom of peaceful assembly; and

   d. freedom of association.

Equality Rights

15. (1) Every individual is equal before and under the law and has the right to the equal protection and equal benefit of the law without discrimination and, in particular, without discrimination based on race, national or ethnic origin, colour, religion, sex, age, or mental or physical disability.

The *Charter* is a powerful constitutional document because it provides protection from improper or oppressive government conduct—conduct that most often takes the form of legislation or policy. In short, section 32 of the *Charter* prohibits government and government alone from violating any of the rights or freedoms recited. By way of contrast, violation of rights in the private sector, such as through employment discrimination, is a matter for provincial and federal human rights codes and thus is addressed according to a separate set of rules.[30]

In order to determine whether legislation such as Nova Scotia's *Tobacco Control Act* is unconstitutional, the court must first determine whether it violates a *Charter* right, in this case freedom of expression. Note that even though the expression restricted under the Act is commercial expression, it too receives constitutional protection. As the Supreme Court notes:

> . . . [o]ver and above its intrinsic value as expression, commercial expression which, as has been pointed out, protects listeners as well as speakers, plays a significant role in enabling individuals to make informed economic choices, an important aspect of individual self-fulfillment and personal autonomy. The Court accordingly rejects the view that commercial expression serves no individual or societal value in a free and democratic society and for this reason is undeserving of any constitutional protection.[31]

But demonstrating a violation of section 2 does not automatically render legislation unconstitutional because the rights and freedoms guaranteed by the *Charter* are not absolute. On the contrary, the *Charter* acknowledges that the government is entitled to restrict freedom of expression—as well as any other right recited in the *Charter*—but only if it has balanced all relevant interests carefully and reasonably, as required by the very first section of the *Charter*.

1. The *Canadian Charter of Rights and Freedoms* guarantees the rights and freedoms set out in it subject only to such reasonable limits prescribed by law as can be demonstrably justified in a free and democratic society.

Section 1 requires the government to justify why it is infringing a right, as well as to demonstrate that, in doing so, it is restricting the right in question in

---

30 For a discussion of human rights codes in an employment context, see Chapter 20.
31 *Ford v Quebec (Attorney General)*, [1988] 2 SCR 712 at 767.

a reasonably measured, controlled, and appropriate way. If the government is unable to do so, the legislation is struck down by the court, that is, it is declared to be of no force or effect. In essence, the legislation is thrown out because it is unconstitutional. The court's authority to order such a powerful remedy is set out in sections 24 and 52 of the *Charter*.

The following box concerns an individual store owner who brought a *Charter* challenge against Nova Scotia's *Tobacco Access Act* and provides a very helpful example of how the courts will approach such matters.

BUSINESS AND LEGISLATION

STORE OWNER CHALLENGES NOVA SCOTIA'S TOBACCO ACCESS ACT

Robert Gee owns a store in Kentville, Nova Scotia, that focuses on tobacco sales. He was charged with displaying tobacco products contrary to the *Tobacco Access Act*. Though Gee had been complying with some provisions in the Act, he had been refusing to cover up his tobacco products. Gee expressed his position to the press in this way: "I find it troubling that government is coming into my business and telling me what I can and can't do selling a legal product. It's to the point we can't show the product. If they [governmental authorities] don't want it, they should make it illegal."[32]

In response to being charged, Gee challenged the constitutionality of the *Tobacco Access Act*. In short, if the legislation were unconstitutional, he could not be convicted under it and, moreover, he would be free to display his tobacco products out in the open.

Gee's lawyer was successful in convincing a court that Gee's freedom of expression had been violated. That is, the judge ruled that the *Tobacco Access Act* constituted an infringement of a protected form of freedom of expression—namely product display.[33] Indeed, the legislation restricted "communicative activity" with respect to the sale of tobacco products,[34] thus running afoul of a *Charter* guarantee. In short and as already noted, commercial expression is protected expression under the *Charter*.

However, the Crown was successful in showing that the legislation should be saved under the section 1 analysis—that the violation of freedom of expression caused by the legislation was "demonstrably justified in a free and democratic society" as previously discussed. Though the court's section 1 analysis was technical and lengthy,[35] the gist of the judges' analysis was as follows:

- the purpose of the legislation under attack was to protect the health of Nova Scotians, particularly that of youth. Its goal was to reduce tobacco consumption by reducing the public's access to it.
- the purpose of the legislation was important (i.e., pressing and substantial) given the danger of tobacco products.
- the ban on display was a rational means of achieving the legislative goal of protecting health. As the court observed, a display of tobacco products could, for example, cause a former smoker to lose his or her resolve and also make it difficult for the smoker who wanted to quit.
- the legislation was careful not to impair Gee's rights to operate a business any more than was necessary to achieve the purpose of the legislation. Gee could still offer information about the products he sold and show the product at time of purchase, for example. As well, the detrimental effect on store owners like Gee was minimal while the

---

32 Kirk Starratt, "Won't Give Up: Tobacco store owner vows to see legal battle through to bitter end" *Kings County News* (9 July 2009), online: Kings County News <http://www.kingscountynews.ca/Business/Retail-%26amp%3B-services/2009-07-09/article-590703/Wont-give-up/1>.

33 *R v Mader's Tobacco Store Ltd*, 2010 NSPC 52.

34 *Ibid* at para 59.

35 The court's section 1 analysis is contained in a separate judgment. See *R v Mader's Tobacco Store Ltd*, 2013 NSPC 29.

legislation could potentially reduce tobacco related disease and death.

All these factors meant that the legislation survived Gee's constitutional challenge.

The court went on to find Gee guilty on charges of violating the *Tobacco Access Act* and fined him $430.[36] Gee's legal expenses in challenging the legislation amounted to $60 000.[37]

Jeff Gee, the store owner's son, told the local press[38] that the store now complies with the legislation: tobacco displays located behind the counter and elsewhere in the store have been removed. Referring to the tobacco products now hidden away, Jeff Gee stated: "You can't see a thing.... We're just trying to transform the store now to make it what they want it to be.... The government won this battle against tobacco, but they will never win the war.... [The store is] here to stay."[39] Jeff Gee also commented that customers are disappointed by the decision and find it ridiculous.

Note that a challenge recently brought in Alberta to that province's legislation prohibiting point of sale display of tobacco products was also dismissed, on highly similar grounds.[40]

Robert Gee

Critical Analysis: With whom do you side in this conflict: Mr. Gee or the Nova Scotia legislature in passing the law it did? Why?

Sources: Kirk Starratt, "Won't Give Up: Tobacco store owner vows to see legal battlethrough to bitter end", *Kings County News* (9 July 2009).

Judges have the power to strike down legislation if it proves to be unconstitutional but not all Canadians agree that such a power is appropriate. Some believe that it is undemocratic for the courts to have the right to eliminate or amend a law duly enacted by elected representatives. However, those who support the *Charter* argue that even a majority (the elected representatives who enacted the legislation) should not have the power to infringe on the rights of others. Put another way, a liberal democratic system of government is not just about majority rule, as reflected in the following statement from Madam Justice Wilson of the Supreme Court of Canada:

> The *Charter* is predicated on a particular conception of the place of the individual in society. An individual is not a totally independent entity disconnected from the society in which he or she lives. Neither, however, is the individual a mere cog in an impersonal machine in which his or her values, goals and aspirations are subordinated to those of the collectivity. The individual is a bit of both. The *Charter* reflects this reality by leaving a wide range of activities and decisions open to legitimate government control while at the same time placing limits on the proper scope of

36 Gordon Delaney, "Tobacco vendor quits battle" *Herald News* (28 May 2013; updated 29 May 2013), online *Herald News*: <http://thechronicleherald.ca/novascotia/1131811-tobacco-vendor-quits-battle>.
37 *Ibid.*
38 *Ibid.*
39 *Ibid.*
40 *R v 712098 Alberta Ltd. (c.o.b. River City Cigar)* 2012 ABPC 313.

that control. Thus, the rights guaranteed in the *Charter* erect around each individual, metaphorically speaking, an invisible fence over which the state will not be allowed to trespass. The role of the courts is to map out, piece by piece, the parameters of the fence.[41]

Though the court has the power to assess the constitutionality of legislation—and to strike down the law, if need be—it is the legislative branch of government which has the last word in many cases. (See Figure 2.3.) That is, the *Charter* permits the government to override or disregard a judicial decision that a given piece of legislation is unconstitutional or to pre-empt judicial involvement at the start. Section 33 of the *Charter* allows the government to enact legislation "notwithstanding" its unconstitutionality. While the government does not have this option with respect to all rights and freedoms guaranteed by the *Charter*, it does have this option for a great many of them, including the right to freedom of expression.[42]

There are, of course, political consequences to using section 33, as when the government of Alberta invoked this provision when it introduced **Bill** 26 on 10 March 1998. This bill would limit the right of recovery to $150 000 for those wrongfully sterilized under that province's *Sexual Sterilization Act*, which was repealed in 1972. As a result of public outcry that the government would deny sterilization victims their right to establish in court that they had suffered damages exceeding $150 000, the government quickly withdrew its proposed legislation.[43]

Bill
Proposed legislation.

The *Charter* governs the relationship between the person and the state, restraining government action that is, for example, discriminatory. By way of contrast, certain kinds of discrimination in the marketplace by one person against another are made illegal primarily by human rights codes as well as by related forms of legislation.[44]

Because of its foundational importance, it is intentionally very difficult to amend Canada's Constitution. For example, the general amending formula (section 38) requires resolutions of the Senate and House of Commons and "resolutions of the legislative assemblies of at least two-thirds of the provinces that have, in the aggregate... at least fifty percent of the population of all the provinces."[45]

Sources of Law

There are four sources of law in Canada: constitutional convention (discussed earlier), statute law (outlined in the preceding section), the royal prerogative, and the common law. (See Figure 2.4.)

The **royal prerogative** has diminishing influence in the modern Canadian legal system. Briefly put, the royal prerogative refers to the historical rights and privileges of the Crown, including the right to conduct foreign affairs and to declare war.[46]

Common law, unlike statute law, is judge-made law. Common law is the end product of disputes that come before the judiciary. That is, when a judge gives

Royal prerogative
Historical rights and privileges of the Crown, including the right to conduct foreign affairs and to declare war.

Common law
Rules that are formulated in judgments.

41 *R. v Morgentaler*, [1988] 1 SCR 30 at 164.
42 Section 33 of the *Charter* permits government to violate a large number of rights and freedoms, including: freedom of conscience and religion; freedom of thought, belief, opinion, expression, and peaceful assembly; freedom of association; the right to life, liberty, and security of the person; the right to be free from unreasonable search and seizure; the right to be free from arbitrary detention and imprisonment; the right not to be subject to cruel or unusual punishment; the right against self-incrimination; and the right to equality.
43 Eoin Kenny, "Klein Government Drops Bill to Compensate Victims" (11 March 1998) online: QL (CP98). Eugenics is a discredited belief that, through selective breeding, the "quality" of the human race can be improved.
44 For a discussion of human rights codes in relation to employment, see Chapter 20.
45 See Hogg, *supra* note 7 at 4-15 to 4-16.
46 *Ibid* at 1-20.

FIGURE 2.3 Sampling of Constitutional Challenges Brought by Business

Case	Nature of Alleged *Charter* Violation	Result
Siemens v Manitoba (Attorney General), [2003] 1 SCR 6	Provincial law permitting a ban on lottery terminals based on a local plebiscite is contrary to the right to life, liberty, and security of the person. Local businesses rely on such terminals as a source of revenue.	Action failed. The Supreme Court of Canada ruled that purely economic interests—such as being able to retain business income—are not encompassed in the *Charter*'s protection of life, liberty, and security of the person.
R v Big M Drug Mart, [1985] 1 SCR 295	Federal law that prohibited most commercial activity on Sunday is contrary to the right to freedom of religion.	Action succeeded. The Supreme Court of Canada ruled that the law was unconstitutional since its purpose was "to compel the observance of the Christian Sabbath."
R v Edwards Books and Art, [1986] 2 SCR 713	Provincial law prohibiting retail stores from opening on Sunday is contrary to the right to freedom of religion.	Action failed. The Supreme Court of Canada held that the law was valid. Though the law did violate freedom of religion (i.e., its *effect* placed a burden on those who observed a non-Sunday sabbath), the law was saved under section 1. The court held that the valid secular purpose of the law—to provide a common day off for retail workers—was sufficiently important to justify limiting the right of freedom of religion.
Little Sisters Book and Art Emporium v Canada, [2000] 2 SCR 1120	The federal *Customs Tariff Act* that prohibits importation of "obscene" books and magazines violates the right to freedom of expression.	Mixed result. The Supreme Court of Canada held that the standard of obscenity was valid. However, the court identified discrimination in how the legislation was implemented since homosexual literature was disproportionately and without justification targeted by customs officials.
Ford v Quebec, [1988] 2 SCR 712	A Quebec law requiring advertisements and signage to be in French violates the right to freedom of expression.	Action succeeded. The Supreme Court of Canada ruled that freedom of expression includes "the freedom to express oneself in the language of one's choice." *(Note: This law was reenacted using section 33.)*
Irwin Toy v Quebec, [1989] 1 SCR 927	A Quebec law prohibiting advertising directed at children under 13 years of age violates the right to freedom of expression.	Action failed. Though the law violated freedom of expression, it was saved under s. 1. The Supreme Court of Canada ruled that protection of children is important, hence justifying the limitation. As well, since the law permitted the advertisement of toys and breakfast cereals, provided cartoons were not used, the ban was only partial in any event.
Rocket v Royal College of Dental Surgeons, [1990] 1 SCR 232	Ontario's *Health Disciplines Act* violates freedom of expression since it prohibits dentists from advertising their services, including office hours or languages spoken.	Action succeeded. The Supreme Court of Canada held that while maintaining high standards of professional conduct justified some kind of regulation, the Act went too far in banning all advertising.
Slaight Communications v Davidson, [1989] 1 SCR 1038	Labour board order that an employer provide a reference letter to an unjustly dismissed employee violates the right to freedom of expression.	Mixed result. The Supreme Court of Canada held that if the letter were ordered to contain an opinion that the employer did not hold, that would be unconstitutional. Where the letter had only to contain "objective facts that are not in dispute," the order can be justified under section 1.
Hunter v Southam, [1984] 2 SCR 145	Powers of search and seizure permitted by the *Combines Investigation Act* violates the right to be free from unreasonable search and seizure.	Action succeeded. The Supreme Court of Canada held that the Act did not contain enough safeguards to determine when documents can be seized.
McKinney v University of Guelph, [1990] 3 SCR 229	Mandatory retirement policy of the university violates prohibition of discrimination on the basis of age.	Action failed. The *Charter* applies only to government or bodies that are not independent from government. Here, the university was classified as a private body. Additionally, the university could rely on the Ontario *Human Rights Code* (which applies to the private sector), which permitted mandatory retirement. Though this provision of the code contravened s. 15, the discrimination was demonstrably justified under s. 1.

FIGURE 2.4 The Sources of Law

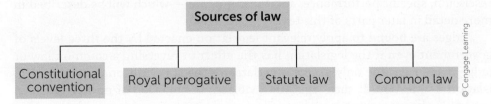

a decision in determining the outcome of a given legal conflict, it is known as a judgment; judgments referred to cumulatively are called the common law.

Ordinarily, a judge does not just give a bald resolution to the dispute in question. Rather, the judge seeks to explain, justify, and account for whatever decision she has reached. In doing so, the court relies on decisions made by other judges in other cases that are relevant to the matter at hand. These cases are known as **precedent**.

The key principle of precedent can be summarized as "like cases should be treated alike." This means that judges should rule in a given case in a manner consistent with the way judges have adjudicated on or dealt with similar matters in the past. In short, the judge looks to the common law in order to resolve the matter at hand.

A number of rules govern the application of precedent, including the following:

- a lower court must follow a relevant precedent created by a higher court within the same jurisdiction.
- not all precedents are of equal value—the higher the court that created the precedent, the more valued the decision is.
- the Supreme Court of Canada—the highest court in Canada—is entitled to decide a case in any way it sees fit.

While the process of applying precedent is reasonably easy to describe, it is inevitably riddled with some ambiguity, uncertainty, and subjectivity. Although judges endeavour to be impartial, unbiased, and objective, such a standard is probably impossible to consistently achieve. Further, even reasonable people may differ in interpreting whether a given case from the common law applies to the dispute in question. This is not to imply that the study of law is futile or that the judicial application of precedent is without rhyme or reason. It is merely to suggest that the outcome in any case cannot be fully predicted.

Judges sometimes choose to apply another set of rules, known as rules of **equity**. Like common law, equity originated in England. The role of equity is to provide assistance to the deserving person who otherwise would not receive adequate help under the rules of common law. Equity focuses on what would be fair given the specific circumstances of the case, as opposed to what the strict rules of common law might dictate. In this way, equity seeks to soften the harsh or unfair result that the common law might otherwise cause. This is not to suggest that "anything goes, as long as it's fair." Equity itself is constrained by principles that limit when it can render assistance. For example, assume that a businessperson has transferred some real estate to her spouse in order to hide that asset from creditors. If the spouse later refuses to transfer that property back, the businessperson may be in some difficulty. Should the businessperson seek help from a judge on equitable grounds to get her property back, a court would have the discretion to refuse. This is because—according to an important equitable principle—equity assists only those with "clean hands." There is a good argument that the businessperson fails to meet this description.

Precedent

An earlier case used to resolve a current case because of its similarity.

Equity

Rules that focus on what would be fair given the specific circumstances of the case, as opposed to what the strict rules of common law might dictate.

CHAPTER 2: THE CANADIAN LEGAL SYSTEM

Equity also provides its own set of remedies—rectification, *quantum meruit*, rescission, specific performance, and the injunction—which will be described in more detail in later parts of this text.

Judges are bound to apply relevant legislation enacted by the three levels of government even if the legislation has the effect of reversing a common law or judge-made rule. The only exception relates to the constitutionality of the legislation in question. If such legislation violates the division of powers between the levels of government or violates *Charter* provisions, a court may declare that it has no force or effect. Otherwise, statute law trumps or has priority over the common law. Note too that the courts can make common law about statutes and how to interpret them.

Classifications of Law

The law can be organized according to various categories. It is important for a businessperson to have a basic understanding of these classifications in order to better grasp the nature of the legal problem at issue. Such an understanding will also assist the businessperson to better communicate with legal counsel.

Domestic versus International Law

Domestic law is the internal law of a given country and includes both statute and common law. Domestic law deals primarily with individuals and corporations and, to a lesser extent, the state.

International law governs relations between states and other entities with international legal status, such as the United Nations and the World Trade Organization. An important source of international law is treaty law. International law focuses mainly on states and international organizations.

Substantive versus Procedural Law

Substantive law refers to law that defines rights, duties, and liabilities. Substantive law was at issue in all the cases described in Figure 2.3. They concerned the duty of the government to legislate in accordance with the *Charter* as well as the right of the plaintiff to challenge the government for failing to meet that standard.

Procedural law refers to the law governing the procedure to enforce rights, duties, and liabilities. For example, the fact that a trial judge's decision can be appealed to a higher court is a procedural matter.

Public versus Private Law

Public law describes all those areas of the law that relate to or regulate the relationship between persons and government at all levels. An important aspect of public law is its ability to constrain governmental power according to rules of fairness. Examples of public law are criminal law, tax law, constitutional law, and administrative law (see Figure 2.5).

Private law concerns dealings between persons. Many of the major topics in this text fall within private law, including contract law, tort law, property law, and company law (see Figure 2.6).

The distinction between public and private law is not absolute. Most of the law of property is private, even if the government is buying, selling, or leasing. However, should the government choose to exercise its executive right to expropriate land, for example, issues of public law would be involved.

Domestic law

The internal law of a given country, which includes both statute and common law.

International law

Law that governs relations between states and other entities with international legal status.

Substantive law

Law that defines rights, duties, and liabilities.

Procedural law

The law governing the procedure to enforce rights, duties, and liabilities.

Public law

Areas of the law that relate to or regulate the relationship between persons and government at all levels.

Private law

Areas of law that concern dealings between persons.

FIGURE 2.5 Examples of Public Law

Criminal law	Identifies behaviour that is seriously unacceptable. In the interest of maintaining order and security in relations between citizens, the government prosecutes those who transgress basic standards of conduct, and the courts enforce sanctions for that conduct, including fines and imprisonment.
Tax law	Sets the rules for the collection of revenue for governmental operation.
Constitutional law	Sets the parameters on the exercise of power by government.
Administrative law	Governs all regulatory activity of the state.

© Cengage Learning

FIGURE 2.6 Examples of Private Law

Contract law	Provides rules that make agreements between parties binding.
Tort law	Includes rules that address legal wrongs committed by one person against another, apart from a breach of contract. The wrongs may be intentional (as in an assault) or unintentional (as in a case of negligent driving).
Property law	Sets rules that define and protect property in all forms.
Company law	Provides rules concerning the rights, liabilities, and obligations of companies and other business vehicles.

© Cengage Learning

Furthermore, a single set of circumstances can have two sets of consequences, one involving private law and the other involving public law. For example, where a personal injury arises from an assault, the Crown may decide to prosecute the perpetrator of the assault under the *Criminal Code*. This is the domain of public law. The victim, however, also has civil rights that can be enforced through tort law, which is in the area of private law. Specifically, the victim of the assault can initiate an action in the courts to seek financial compensation for damages from the perpetrator.

Common Law versus Civil Law

While common law refers to judge-made law, it is also used in a totally different sense to describe the system of private law in place in all provinces except Quebec. A common law system is one that bases its private law on judicial decisions that—if relevant and binding—must be applied to the case at issue. The private law in nine Canadian provinces, as well as the territories, is governed by common law in this sense of the word.

The province of Quebec is, of course, bound by federal law such as the *Criminal Code*, but it has its own system of private law, which is governed by the **Civil Code of Quebec** (*Civil Code*). Although there are many similarities between common law principles and what would be found in the *Civil Code*, conceptually there are significant differences between the two systems. One key difference is that judges in Quebec look to the *Civil Code* for general principles to be applied to the case at hand. They are not bound by how other judges have interpreted the *Civil Code*, though practically speaking, these interpretations would be helpful and relevant.[47] Nor is a judge in a civil code system bound to apply a relevant provision of the *Civil Code* if to do so would produce an unjust outcome.[48]

Civil Code of Quebec

The rules of private law that govern Quebec.

---

47 Gerald L Gall, *The Canadian Legal System*, 5th ed (Toronto: Carswell, 2004) at 31.
48 *Ibid*.

FIGURE 2.7 Divisions/Classifications of the Law

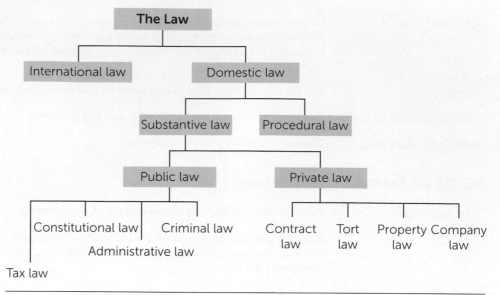

Source: From Gerald G. Gall, *The Canadian Legal System, 5th edition* (Toronto: Carswell, 2004). Figure 2.7, p. 29. Adapted by permission of Carswell, a division of Thomson Reuters Canada Limited.

Figure 2.7 shows the various classifications of law and how they are related. These various classifications can be applied to the legal problem faced by the retailer in the chapter opener. The question of the validity of Nova Scotia's *Tobacco Access Act* concerns

- domestic law (not international law) because the *Tobacco Access Act* was passed by the government of Nova Scotia and does not in any way involve a foreign jurisdiction.
- substantive law (not procedural law) because at issue is whether the law violates the right to freedom of expression under the *Charter*.
- public law (not private law) because at issue is a law that regulates the relationship between tobacco retailers and the government. More specifically, it involves constitutional law because the challenge concerns whether the government has exercised its law-making power appropriately.
- common law (not Quebec civil law) because the dispute will be resolved by applying Nova Scotia's common law system, not the *Civil Code of Quebec*.

The elements of constitutional law are summarized in Figure 2.8.

Administrative Law and Business

Administrative law Rules created and applied by those having governmental powers.

Administrative law is one of the primary legal areas in which government and business interact. This area of law refers to rules created and applied by the various boards, agencies, commissions, tribunals, and individuals who exercise a governmental function as a result of legislation giving them that power. It also refers to rules of fairness that constrain how administrative bodies exercise their authority.

Administrative bodies have often been established on a needs basis to deal with particular problems or difficulties as they have arisen, rather than pursuant to some overall regulatory plan. This piecemeal nature can make the area somewhat perplexing at times.

FIGURE 2.8 A Summary of Constitutional Law

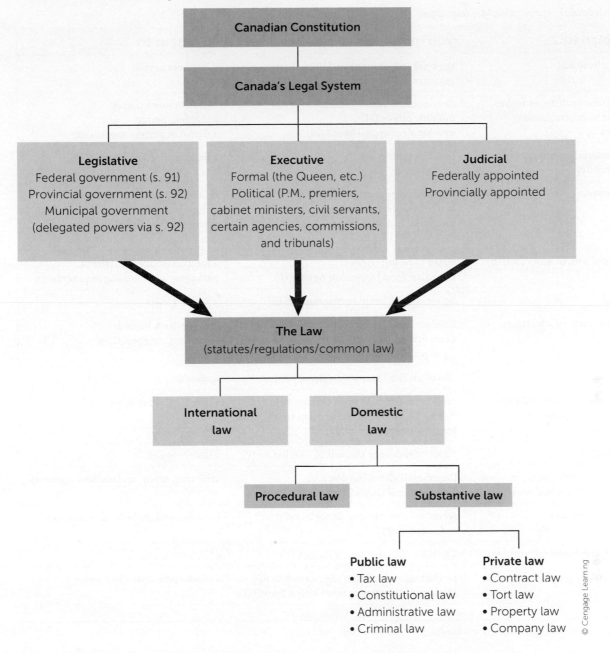

The functions of administrative bodies and officials often vary. In some instances, the body or individual carries out purely administrative functions, as when the Canada Employment Insurance Commission processes a claim for benefits; sometimes the body also has judicial functions, such as when the Labour Relations Board settles a dispute between an employer and employee; sometimes the body exercises legislative functions, as when the Canadian Radio-television and Telecommunications Commission (CRTC) passes regulations concerning the amount of Canadian content on radio and television; and sometimes the body has some combination of these functions. As a result, it is often difficult to summarize how businesses are subject to administrative regulation.

FIGURE 2.9 Administrative Bodies and Officials Affecting Business

Legend: F = federal; P = provincial; M = municipal

If you plan to ...	you may interact with ...	in regard to ...
establish a business	regional and/or municipal licensing tribunal, minister, agency, or officer (M)	a business permit
construct new facilities or make exceptions to existing zoning regulations	development officer zoning board (M) building officer (M) development appeal board (M)	a development permit a building permit a denial of permit application
alter the interior or exterior of an existing building	building officer (M)	a building permit
hire employees	workers' compensation board (P) labour relations board (P) provincial human rights tribunal (P)	an accident or injury unions, collective agreements discriminatory practices in the workplace
manufacture, sell, or store food or drink	board of health (P, M) Canadian Food Inspection Agency (F)	a food establishment permit packaging and labelling requirements
sell alcohol	liquor control board or commission (P)	a liquor licence
manufacture, sell, or advertise products	Consumer Product Safety Commission (F) Competition Bureau (F) trade practices legislation (P)	product/item hazards fair advertising practices
import products	Canadian Food Inspection Agency (F)	approval
practise in architecture, pharmacy, law, dentistry, medicine, or accountancy	professional society (e.g., Law Society of British Columbia; Public Accountants Council for the Province of Ontario) (P)	a licence to practise the profession
sell real estate	Superintendent or Council of Real Estate (P)	a licence to sell
carry on a radio, television, or telecommunications business	Canadian Radio-television and Telecommunications Commission (F)	structure, scope, and content approval
sell financial products	securities commission, financial services commission (P)	licensing and procedural requirements
engage in interprovincial trucking	Canadian Transportation Agency (F)	a business licence
sell a particular agricultural product	product agency or board (e.g., Canadian Egg Marketing Agency; Canadian Wheat Board) (F)	a production and sales licence

Source: Researched and written by Catherine Bradley.

Nonetheless, this area of law has a significant impact on business because so much commercial activity is regulated by these bodies—from licensing requests to zoning and subdivision applications and human rights complaints. (See Figure 2.9 for a summary of the administrative bodies and officials that affect business.)

BUSINESS LAW IN PRACTICE REVISITED

1. Is Nova Scotia's *Tobacco Access Act* constitutional and hence enforceable?

R v Mader's Tobacco Store, discussed on page 31 of this chapter, demonstrates that the legislation violates section 2 of the *Charter* by forbidding the public display of tobacco products. However, since the purpose of the Act is to reduce smoking in young people and for other reasons given by the court discussed earlier, the legislation is demonstrably justified in a free and democratic society and is saved by section 1.

2. Who assesses whether the legislation is permissible?

Judges are mandated to hear challenges to the legal foundation of laws passed by all levels of government.

3. Are there any moral or ethical questions that arise from this scenario?

While cigarettes are a legal product, cigarettes cause death and serious illness. For this reason, there are moral and ethical issues for anyone associated with the tobacco industry. It would seem, in particular, that retailers would not want to do anything to encourage children or young people to smoke.

CHAPTER SUMMARY

Canadian society is bound by a set of constitutional values, many of which insist on the importance of the individual and the right to freedom from unreasonable government interference. These values restrain how government operates at all levels—federally, provincially, and municipally. Constitutional law plays an important role in how government does its job by constraining how the three branches of government exercise power.

Each branch of government has its own work to do. The legislative branch creates statutes. The executive branch is responsible for the ceremonial features of government and for day-to-day operations, including formulating and executing government policy, as well as administering all departments of government. The judiciary has a significant role in scrutinizing the legislative and executive branches of government and can be an important resource for those who believe they have been unreasonably limited, such as in how they are permitted to carry out business, or unfairly treated by a governmental officer, board, or tribunal. The judiciary also adjudicates on private disputes.

The Constitution places mandatory limits on the power of the legislature to pass any law it sees fit. The court, as required by the Constitution, insists that the power of government be exercised in a manner that is

- within that body's "jurisdiction," as defined by the *Constitution Act, 1867*.
- consistent with the values and principles contained within the *Charter*.

The judiciary itself is bound by the rules of precedent to help ensure that any given legal dispute is resolved in a manner that is consistent with decisions in previous similar disputes. An important part of precedent involves the court system since only a higher court can bind a lower court. Judges also have discretion, accorded to them by the rules of equity, to ensure that each matter before them is justly resolved.

Canadian law is organized according to classifications reflecting the nature of the legal problem at issue: domestic/international; substantive/procedural; public/private; and common law/civil law. Administrative law provides protection by ensuring that a fair process accompanies any regulatory decision that affects a business or any other activity.

CHAPTER STUDY

Key Terms and Concepts

administrative law (p. 38)

bill (p. 33)

bylaws (p. 27)

cabinet (p. 28)

Canadian Charter of Rights and Freedoms (p. 29)

Canadian legal system (p. 20)

Civil Code of Quebec (p. 37)

common law (p. 33)

concurrent jurisdiction (p. 24)

constitutional conventions (p. 22)

constitutional law (p. 20)

domestic law (p. 36)

equity (p. 35)

exclusive jurisdiction (p. 24)

Federal Court of Canada (p. 29)

formal executive (p. 27)

government policy (p. 20)

inferior court (p. 28)

international law (p. 36)

judges (p. 28)

judiciary (p. 28)

jurisdiction (p. 23)

legislative branch (p. 22)

liberalism (p. 20)

paramountcy (p. 25)

political executive (p. 27)

precedent (p. 35)

private law (p. 36)

procedural law (p. 36)

public law (p. 36)

ratify (p. 26)

regulations (p. 28)

royal prerogative (p. 33)

small claims court (p. 29)

statute law (p. 22)

substantive law (p. 36)

superior courts (p. 29)

Supreme Court of Canada (p. 29)

treaty (p. 26)

Questions for Review

1. What is the key idea upon which the Canadian Constitution is based?

2. What does "jurisdiction" mean?

3. What is an example of a constitutional convention?

4. Which document determines whether a government has the jurisdiction to pass a law or not?

5. What is the doctrine of paramountcy?

6. Which level of government does paramountcy seem to favour?

7. How does the authority of a municipal government come into existence?

8. What is the difference between a regulation and a bylaw?

9. What is the executive branch of government?

10. How is the executive branch different from the legislative branch?

11. What is precedent? Why is a system of courts essential to its creation?

12. What are the two types of trial courts?

13. What is the common law? Who creates it?

14. What is the *Canadian Charter of Rights and Freedoms*?

15. What can a judge do if he determines that a piece of legislation is unconstitutional?

16. If a law is found to violate a person's freedom of expression pursuant to the *Charter*, is it automatically struck down? Is there something in the *Charter* that might allow the government to justify violating that person's freedom of expression?

17. What is the difference between public law and private law?

18. Which Canadian province operates under a civil law system?

19. What is the role of equity?

20. What is one important function of administrative law?

Questions for Critical Thinking

1. Women pay higher prices for certain products and services compared to what men are charged—from dry-cleaning to haircuts. This is known as gender-based pricing. Is gender-based pricing objectionable? Should government regulate price when it is discriminatory or should that be left to the free market?

2. The Supreme Court of Canada in *Saskatchewan Federation of Labour v Saskatchewan*, 2015 SCC 4, ruled that public sector employees (i.e., employees who work for government) have a constitutionally protected right to strike. More specifically, it ruled that labour reform legislation from Saskatchewan was unconstitutional because it interfered with the right to strike in a way that went beyond what was reasonably required. For example, the legislation prohibited government employees who performed essential services from participating in a strike but provided that the public sector employer alone had the right to determine who those employees would be. Do you think the employer should have the absolute right to decide who provides essential service? What would such absolute power do to the right to strike?

3. Under a common law system, judges follow precedent when making decisions or resolving disputes. What are the advantages of following precedent? Describe a situation where it might be inappropriate to follow precedent.

4. Review Figure 2.3 on page 34. In your opinion, how has the *Charter* affected business activity?

5. Do you think that the *Charter* strikes a good balance between protecting the rights of individual citizens and allowing governments to legislate for the benefit of larger groups, or even all members of society? Is section 1 of the *Charter* necessary, or should an individual's fundamental rights and freedoms be absolute?

6. Dozens of administrative tribunals—such as the Labour Relations Board, the Canadian Radio-television and Telecommunications Commission, various human rights tribunals, and the Occupational Health and Safety Commission—have been established by both the federal and provincial governments. Why do you think administrative tribunals are such a predominant feature in Canada? Why have they been established?

Situations for Discussion

1. The government of Alberta has passed regulations that include requirements that home inspection businesses be provincially licensed and carry $1 million in errors and omissions insurance. Beyond this, the province has mandated educational standards for home inspectors with the goal of improving the quality of work done by the home inspection industry. Then-Opposition Liberal MLA Hugh MacDonald endorsed the regulations as a means of clamping down on fly-by-night home inspectors, observing: "If I'm making an important decision to purchase a home based on information I'm getting from a home inspector, that person should be licensed and have minimum credentials."[49] Do you agree that government should regulate such an industry? What are the costs and benefits of such regulation to the consumer?

2. A brawl at a popular Halifax nightclub called the Dome resulted in 38 arrests and the suspension of the Dome's liquor licence. Government officials believe that one-dollar drinks offered by the Dome are one factor contributing to such violence. "This has blown into a cultural problem, and one of the issues we have identified is low-price, deep-discount drinks," said Barry Barnet, then Nova Scotia's Minister of Health Promotion and Protection.[50] The Nova Scotia government expressed its hopes to develop recommendations to address problems associated with excess alcohol consumption.[51] From a risk management perspective, how

49 Karen Kleiss, "Home buyers get more protection," *The Edmonton Journal* (14 May 2011).

50 Dakshana Bascaramurty, "Officials blame $1 drinks for Halifax brawl" *The Globe and Mail* (20 December 2007) A12.

51 *Ibid*. Note that Nova Scotia now mandates minimum drink prices by regulation. See NS Reg 365/2007, as amended up to O.I.C. 2014-28 (January 28, 2014), N.S. Reg. 15/2014. Section 50A states as follows: 50A(1) Except for the off-premises sale of beer under Section 58B, a licensee must not offer for sale or supply a serving of liquor for less than a total purchase price of $2.50, including any applicable taxes.

should local bar owners approach governmental concern over bar violence?

3. With the goal of reducing childhood obesity, the Ontario government in 2014 introduced a bill to require restaurants to post calorie counts beside menu items so consumers would know, for example, that a "raisin bran muffin from Tim Hortons has more calories than a cheeseburger" in the words of then Health Minister Deb Matthews.[52] The Canadian Restaurant and Foodservices Association (CRFA) has dismissed the initiative as too simplistic as well as confusing. "There could be 10 000 ways to make a pizza. How do you put that out there?" said James Rilett, the CRFA's vice-president for Ontario. "It's not simply just stick a number up there and people will understand it."[53] Do you agree with the proposed legislation? Why or why not?

4. Liberal leader Justin Trudeau is in favour of ending the prohibition on marijuana, noting that it costs $500 million a year in law enforcement, has caused 475 000 Canadians to have criminal records since 2006 and pumps money into organized crime and crime gangs.[54] The Conservative government is on the record as being opposed to decriminalization but is considering a softening in the current laws so that police could simply ticket those found with small amounts of marijuana instead of laying charges.[55] Should marijuana be decriminalized? Why or why not? If a province wanted to legalize marijuana, would it have the power to do so?

5. An accounting student is researching the deductibility of business expenses. She has found an amendment to the federal *Income Tax Act* that states that certain expenses are not deductible. However, she has also found case law that states that the expenses are deductible. Which law prevails? What additional information do you require to answer this question?

6. Several provinces have passed legislation that restricts the sale of violent video games to children.[56] How could this legislation be challenged under the *Charter*? Explain. Are there any ethical considerations when contemplating such a challenge?

52 Robert Benzie, "Ontario moves ahead with calorie counts on restaurant menus" *The Star* (24 February 2014), online: *The Star* <http://www.thestar.com/news/queenspark/2014/02/24/ontario_moving_ahead_with_calorie_counts_on_restaurant_menus.html>.

53 Kelly Grant, "Ontario to require chain restaurants to serve up calorie counts" *Globe and Mail* (24 February 2014), online: *The Globe and Mail* <http://www.theglobeandmail.com/news/national/ontario-to-move-ahead-with-calorie-counts-on-fast-food-chain-menus/article17063860/>.

54 Bill Graveland, "Justin Trudeau says Canada should draw on 'best practices' from marijuana legalization in Colorado, Washington" *National Post* (23 January 2014), online: National Post <http://news.nationalpost.com/2014/01/23/justin-trudeau-says-canada-should-draw-on-best-practices-from-marijuana-legalization-in-colorado-washington/>.

55 Josh Wingrove, "Ottawa considers softening marijuana laws" *Globe and Mail* (05 March 2014), online: *Globe and Mail* <http://www.theglobeandmail.com/news/politics/mackay-hints-at-loosening-of-marijuana-laws/article17317503/>.

56 Chris Metcalfe & Chris Bennett, "Commentary: Anti-violence legislation on video games passes easily under *Charter*" *The Lawyers Weekly* (9 March 2007) 8.

MANAGING LEGAL RISKS

3

BUSINESS LAW IN PRACTICE

Northland Mining Inc. ("Northland") is a nickel mining company located in northern Manitoba. With all its operations situated adjacent to a town of 10 000, Northland extracts 3000 tons of ore per day from underground mines. In addition to several mines, the Northland property contains an on-site processing facility, a large maintenance shop, a building devoted exclusively to office space, and a lake which is used to hold "tailings" or mining waste after nickel has been extracted. Northland discards about half of its tailings back into the ground with the remainder being deposited into this lake on a regular basis.

Most of the company's underground extraction process relies on a continuous mining machine which cuts ore from the mine walls. Upon extraction, the ore is hoisted to the surface where it is crushed, washed, and conveyed to the processing plant which, in turn, produces a nickel concentrate. Northland employees transport this concentrate by truck to the railway so that it can reach customers in eastern Canada and the United States. Most of the customers are stainless steel manufacturers.

Alex Tanguay, president of Northland, is pleased with the company's success to date and wonders if Northland should begin pursuing opportunities to operate mines in South America, including Peru. To help deliberations on this point, Alex asks Marie Gagnon, the Director of Insurance and Security for Northland, to undertake two related investigations. First, he requires a review of Northland's entire legal risk management plan. Second, he wants an assessment of the kinds of new legal risks Northland faces should it take some of its operations global. Alex wants an assurance that Northland has identified and managed all the major legal risks associated with its Canadian operations before it undertakes any new projects in foreign countries.

1. What is a legal risk management plan and how is it developed?

2. What are Northland's major legal risks from its Canadian operations? How should Northland manage these risks?

3. What are Northland's legal risks should it decide to operate in a foreign jurisdiction such as Peru? How should it manage these risks?

OBJECTIVES

After studying this chapter, you should have an understanding of

- methods of managing the legal environment of business

- the development of a legal risk management plan

- the importance of anticipating and reacting to developments in the legal environment

- how to access and manage legal services

STRINGER/CANADA/Reuters/Landov

Assessing the Legal Environment

Many factors determine the success of a business organization. It must be able to analyze and evaluate its activities, forecast changes in the business environment, and react effectively to unexpected developments. Of central importance is the ability to strike the right balance between managing the present and planning for the future.

To meet its goal of producing a product or delivering a service at a profit, the business enterprise must have a set of functions and systems in place, including finance, marketing, and human resources. To ensure the smoothest possible operation of these systems, the business also needs to deal effectively with the legal environment. By doing so, the business will reduce the likelihood and impact of mistakes that are

- costly in terms of the expense of legal services and damage claims.
- distracting in terms of time and effort.
- harmful in terms of relationships and reputation in the industry.

This chapter explores how a business can manage its interaction with the law and legal issues. It considers two basic approaches—preventive and reactive. The preventive approach requires a thorough evaluation of the risks associated with the business's activities in order to minimize their impact. The emphasis is on compliance with legal requirements and anticipation of changes in the legal environment. The reactive approach recognizes that legal problems may still materialize, so the firm needs a strategy in place to deal with such developments. These two approaches are combined in a management plan that reduces the impact of **legal risk** on the organization.

Legal Risk Management Plan

Managing the intersection of law with an organization's activities requires completing a comprehensive assessment of legal risk exposure and developing a legal risk management plan. This process is often part of a broader exercise—called **enterprise risk management**—in which *all* risks within an organization, including those with legal implications, are assessed and managed. In essence, legal risk management attempts to identify and then manage threats that could generate negative legal consequences such as fines, penalties, compliance orders, licence suspensions, and liability for the payment of money. This requires an understanding of what could happen, how it could happen, and how its impact could be most effectively managed.

Large businesses like Northland may have a department headed by a senior manager with a title such as risk officer or compliance officer (or as in Marie's case, Director of Insurance and Security) to organize and oversee this process. In smaller organizations, the risk management function may be performed by the chief executive or delegate or even by someone outside the organization, such as an insurance agent or a risk management consultant. Lawyers may also be involved in the process in a variety of roles as determined by their familiarity with the legal risks of the business.

Regardless of where primary responsibility lies, risk management is not a task for any one individual since no single person within an organization has complete knowledge. Risk management involves the cooperation of managers and employees at every level. The challenge for those responsible for this function is to identify the players inside and outside the business who can help in the development of a useful plan. Those involved may use a variety of methods and

Legal risk

A business risk with legal implications.

Enterprise risk management

The process of identifying and managing all business risks.

approaches, such as surveying or interviewing managers and employees, forming workplace committees, or convening a panel of experts.

Creating a legal risk management plan is a four-step process:

- **Step One:** Identify the legal risks.
- **Step Two:** Evaluate the risks.
- **Step Three:** Devise a risk management plan.
- **Step Four:** Implement the plan.

Applying the Four-Step Process

Identify the Legal Risks

The most critical step in the development of a legal risk management plan is the identification of risk, because a risk which is not identified cannot be managed. That said, it is probably not possible to identify all possible risks. The goal is to be reasonably certain that no significant risks have been overlooked. There are many methods that a business can use to identify its potential exposure to legal risks. For example, in applying Step One, a business may assess its functional areas, that is, the areas traditionally recognized in business school curricula (such as marketing and sales, human resources, finance and accounting, and information systems). It could also approach the problem by assessing its business decisions, its business relationships, or its operations and transactions. The approach or approaches used will vary depending on the nature of the business and the industry. A highly departmentalized company might choose to focus on evaluating the risks associated with its functional areas because relevant information is organized in this manner. A small consulting firm would not be organized by functional areas and therefore it, by way of contrast, would more likely focus on legal risks arising from its business relations, that is, client relationships. A utility company with varied sources of power generation (hydro, coal, oil, nuclear, and wind) and a transmission and distribution system would concentrate on its operations. This is because its major risks arise from operating procedures and systems relating to the production and delivery of power. There is no single method which is the correct one for any particular situation. The key is to be systematic so that major risks and threats are not overlooked.

Step One: Identify the Legal Risks

- ✓ Assess the organization's functional areas.
- ✓ Review the organization's business decisions.
- ✓ Examine the organization's business relationships.
- ✓ Analyze the organization's operations and transactions.

In reviewing how her predecessor identified legal risks at Northland, Marie concluded that his focus had been on the functional areas of business only. What follows is the list he assembled of activities and events that have possible legal consequences:

- *Marketing and sales:* aggressive marketing programs by Northland could result in fines and penalties under the *Competition Act*; the improper transportation of mine waste could result in prosecution under *The Dangerous Goods Handling and Transportation Act* of Manitoba; the sale of inferior nickel or the late delivery of nickel could result in customers suing for breach of contract;

- *Production:* processes used by Northland could harm the environment and result in prosecution under environmental legislation or civil actions by affected people; machine breakdown could result in a loss of production and an inability to fulfill contracts resulting in lawsuits for breach of contract; members of the public could be injured on the property, resulting in liability under occupier's liability legislation;
- *Human resources:* injury to Northland workers could result in prosecution under occupational health and safety legislation; employee harassment could result in human rights investigations and penalties; improper terminations could result in actions for wrongful dismissal;
- *Finance and accounting:* harsh credit terms from suppliers may result in Northland being unable to pay debts as they fall due, thereby triggering legal action by creditors; aggressive accounting practices could result in an investigation by the securities commission.

Marie's predecessor correctly identified several important risks relating to production and human resources. Northland production processes do pose environmental hazards and, most certainly, Northland workers could be injured, harass others, and be wrongfully dismissed. However, the predecessor did not take his analysis far enough. For example, he failed to consider possible changes in the law that could negatively affect Northland's operations and he failed to identify risks that crossed functional lines. Most significant was a failure to identify technology-related risks, including those posed by hackers. This is a particularly important risk to identify since a successful breach by hackers might result in not only a disruption of Northland's operations but also a loss of customer and employee data. Such losses could result in lawsuits as well as penalties under privacy legislation. The following Technology and the Law box provides examples of the risks and costs associated with technology.

TECHNOLOGY AND THE LAW

THE RISK AND COSTS OF A BREACH OF PRIVACY

Privacy breaches continue to occur at an alarming rate at many companies and agencies. In some instances, the breach is the result of a sophisticated computer hacker infiltrating systems to collect data. For example, in 2014, a hacking attack on retailer Home Depot may have affected 56 million credit and debit cards in the United States and Canada. The hackers used custom-built malware to steal the numbers from Home Depot's point-of-sale systems. Also in 2014, cyberattackers broke into eBay's database and affected 145 million users. The database included customers' names, encrypted passwords, email addresses, physical addresses, phone numbers, and dates of birth. In the 2013 Christmas holiday season, hackers stole the credit and debit account information of 40 million Target customers, and compromised 1.1 million customer payment cards at Neiman Marcus and hundreds of customer cards at the craft store, Michaels. Also in 2013, Bell Canada suffered a breach of more than 22 000 usernames and passwords. In the Bell case, a hacker group, NullCrew, took credit for the attack and posted five valid credit card numbers to the Internet. Bell was also the victim of an attack in 2008, when a thief stole the personal information of 3.3 million Bell customers.

Privacy breaches, however, are not limited to criminal behaviour by hackers. Many breaches are due to carelessness and security system flaws. In 2013, Human Resources and Skills Development Canada (HRSDC) lost a portable hard drive containing unencrypted personal and financial information, including Social Insurance Numbers and birth dates of 583 000 people who were clients of the Canada Students Loans program. Also in 2013, the Investment Industry Regulatory Organization of Canada revealed the loss of a mobile device containing the personal financial information of about 52 000 brokerage firm clients.

The costs associated with security breaches can be huge; in the case of HRSDC, the costs may exceed $1 billion. In addition to mailing letters to the affected people, the department will provide credit and identity protection services for up to six years at a cost of about $15 per month for a total of more than $600 million. Costs associated with a privacy breach include:

- direct damage costs (e.g., decline in revenue related to the breach, extra expenses to restore assets).

- liability to others (e.g., compensation to affected clients from unauthorized access to personal information; third-party costs, such as credit card issuers' charges to reissue credit cards).

- the cost of preparing a response plan (e.g., costs of public disclosure to clients, including letters and advertisements;[1] regulatory costs and fines; crisis management costs, including costs of establishing a call centre to handle inquiries; the cost of advice from legal and public relations professionals).

Critical Analysis: Most businesses depend on computer and network systems to conduct their businesses. While there are enormous benefits to conducting business over network systems,

What steps can a business take to protect its sensitive data from hackers?

there is a downside. The loss or theft of data is one risk associated with computer technology. What are other computer technology or cyber risks faced by business? How can these risks be effectively managed?

Sources: "Home Depot admits 56 million cards hit by security breaches," *CBC News* (18 September 2014) at: *CBC News* http://www .cbc.ca/news/business/home-depot-admits-56-million-cards-hit-by -security-breach-1.2770827; Rita Trichur, "Cyber-attack on Bell supplier highlights rising hacker threat" *The Globe and Mail* (2 February 2014) at: http://www.theglobeandmail.com/report-on-business/bell-small -business-customer-information-breached-in-hacking-attack/ article16653395/; Jonathan Stoller, "Data breaches: It's more expensive to react than prevent" *The Globe and Mail* (23 May 2013) B13; Jennifer Brown, "Companies will live and die on data breach policies: experts" *In House* (24 February 2014) at: http://www.canadianlawyermag.com/ 5024/Companies-will-live-and-die-on-data-breach-policies-experts .html; Michael Partridge, "ISS recommends ouster of Target directors after data breach" *Goodmans LLP* (6 June 2014) at: Mondaq http://www .mondaq.com/canada/x/318912/Securities/ISS+Recommends +Ouster+Of+Target+Directors+After+Data+Breach; Jacqueline Nelson, "The true cost of cybersecurity" *The Globe and Mail* (23 May 2014) B4; "Federal agency loses data on 583,000 Canadians" *CBC News* (11 January 2013) at: http://www.cbc.ca/news/canada/federal-agency-loses -data-on-583-000-canadians-1.1327172; Donalee Moulton, "Cyberstorm" *Forensic Accounting and Fraud* Vol 3 No. 1 (2013) 11.

At the same time, Marie also noted that risks that were not particularly relevant to Northland had somehow been put on the list. For example, the risk of an aggressive marketing campaign was identified yet Northland, as a miner of nickel, has no need to market its product at all, let alone aggressively.

Marie decided to use a combination of risk management approaches based on consultation with a broad spectrum of people in Northland, several risk

---

1 Both Alberta and Manitoba's privacy legislation contains mandatory privacy breach notification requirements for private sector organizations subject to the legislation. The federal government has passed Bill S-4, the *Digital Privacy Act*, which contains mandatory breach notification provisions. Once these provisions are in force, organizations will be required to notify the Privacy Commissioner and potentially affected individuals of a privacy breach if there is a real risk of significant harm..

management consultants in the mining industry, and the global mining and metals group of an international law firm. As a result of this better process, Marie developed a list of legal risks that was much more reflective of the mining industry at large and included challenges posed by technology, the regulatory environment, and operating in a foreign country. This list is contained in Figure 3.1.

The approach taken by Marie in identifying risk is superior to what her predecessor had devised. This is because, rather than identifying and treating each risk individually, she has utilized a combination of approaches that assesses and addresses the risks from all sources. The focus is on the

FIGURE 3.1 Legal Risks at Northland

Whether Northland continues to operate only domestically or decides to expand internationally, it faces a number of legal risks, including:

Environmental: damage to the environment (including wildlife and fisheries) by tailings waste; harm to the property of adjacent landowners and contribution to climate change by plant emissions; impact on land surface and the water table by drilling and extraction; liability triggered by improper closure or remediation of mines;

Human resources: injury to workers due to pit failure, underground collapse, or large equipment failure; health risk to workers (noise-induced hearing loss, dermatitis due to contact with solutions containing nickel); injury to employees when transporting product; harassment and termination of employees;

Operational: breakdown of machinery and equipment; production of inferior or defective product; injury to visitors on property; damage to property or vehicles when product is in transit; injury to employees or members of the public when the product is in transit;

Regulatory: changes to regulatory, legislative, or compliance regimes (i.e., occupational health and safety, environmental, licensing requirements) impacting on operations; changes to laws in foreign jurisdictions affecting the viability of company; operations in foreign countries resulting in liability under Canadian law;

Financial: inability to meet obligations as they become due; incomplete or poorly performed contracts; extending credit to customers who do not pay their bills; errors in financial statements that mislead the public;

Technological: lack of security in electronic transaction; failure of computer systems and networks.

What are the legal risks from mining operations?

Greg Taylor/GetStock.com

© Cengage Learning

corporation's entire risk profile rather than risks emerging from individual departments.

This first step in developing a legal risk management program may seem to be unduly negative because it seeks to identify everything that could possibly go wrong in a business operation. The purpose of Step One, however, is to provide a realistic assessment of the potential legal dangers of doing business, with a view toward minimizing loss.

Evaluate the Risks

The techniques used in Step Two vary from a simple, subjective evaluation to a complex, statistical approach involving actuaries and other professionals. These techniques involve assessing both the probability and the severity of loss.

Step Two: Evaluate the Risks

✓ Assess the probability of loss.

✓ Assess the severity of loss.

Most organizations have a wealth of information to assist in performing such assessments, including the organization's loss history, industry statistics on losses, and expert opinions from both within and outside the organization.

A high probability that a particular event will occur can be offset by a relatively low level of loss should the event actually occur. Events that are unlikely to occur also deserve close attention if the potential loss is high. In the Northland situation, employees may occasionally come into contact with solutions that contain nickel, despite the use of protective clothing and precautionary measures. However, the contact is unlikely to result in serious injuries that could jeopardize Northland's operations. However, if an employee is seriously injured or dies in a workplace accident, this can result in severe penalties. Other risks, such as environmental impairment or breach of contract, may have varying consequences depending on their severity. The expansion of Northland's operations into a foreign country such as Peru also poses risks. Although there are many multinational corporations operating in South America and there is the potential for profits, there are considerable risks for a company like Northland. The International Perspective box on the next page explores risks that arise from international mining operations.

The international law firm advising Marie indicates that expansion into South America poses the risk of expropriation. Bolivia and Argentina have nationalized foreign operations and Peru could do likewise. Also, because mining has a tremendous impact on the natural environment, Northland—because of its inexperience in operating abroad—could run afoul of local legislation. Even if Northland obeys Peruvian laws, there is the risk that it could become the target of legal action by environmental activists in the Americas and beyond.

The point in evaluating risks is to recognize that not all risks are alike, nor should they be treated alike. Some risks crystallize into liability fairly often, but their financial and legal impact is relatively small. Other risks materialize infrequently, but when they do, their impact is severe. A business can use this assessment to determine priorities for risk management and as guidance in choosing how to manage a particular risk in Step Three.

RISKS IN MINING ABROAD

Canada is a leader in mining development and Canadians have a long history of participating in mining at home and abroad. However, environmental concerns and sensitivities about foreign ownership have made mining abroad a very risky business. Consider the following examples of legal difficulties encountered by Canadian mining companies:

- HudBay Minerals Inc., a Canadian mining company, is facing three lawsuits in Ontario over the actions of its subsidiary in Guatemala. The lawsuits are seeking $55 million for alleged human rights abuses committed by security personnel at the Finex nickel mine in 2007 and 2009. HudBay has since sold the mine.

- Caledonia Mining Corp, a Toronto-based company that operates the Blanket gold mine in Zimbabwe, has been subject to government action affecting its operations. In 2012, Caledonia reached an agreement to turn over a 51 percent interest in the mine to native Zimbabweans to comply with foreign ownership rules that came into effect in 2010. Since then, President Robert Mugabe has threatened to expropriate the assets of Canadian gold mining and other companies.

- Vancouver-based Eldorado Gold's project in northeastern Greece has attracted widespread protest from opponents concerned about the effect of the project on the environment and the region's tourism. In February 2013 about 50 people stormed the mine site, assaulted two guards, and torched construction offices, trucks, and equipment.

- Barrick Gold Corp., the world's largest gold mining company, has suspended construction of its Pascua-Lama gold mine on the border of Chile and Argentina.

Protest in Thessaloniki, Greece against Eldorado's planned gold mine

Chile's environmental regulator stopped construction, citing violations of Barrick's environmental permit. Also, an indigenous community has a court order blocking the construction of the mine until all environmental promises are kept. Meanwhile, in Ontario, Barrick has been named in a shareholder class action lawsuit that seeks $6 billion in damages because the company allegedly failed to make timely disclosures of problems at the mine.

Critical Analysis: What steps should Canadian mining companies take to manage the risks of operating abroad?

Sources: Douglas Mason, "One area where we are not risk adverse" *The Globe and Mail* (22 November 2012) B8; Jodie Wolkoff, "Expanding abroad? Proceed with caution" *The Lawyers Weekly* (14 December 2012) 21; Paul Luke, "B.C. miners dig up rage abroad" *Edmonton Journal* (24 August 2013) B4; Jeff Gray, "Lawyers clash over HudBay case" *The Globe and Mail* (6 March 2013) B3; Geoffrey York, "Zimbabwe threatens expropriation of foreign assets" *The Globe and Mail* (25 April 2013) B10; Eva Vergara, "Chilean court sides with Indians, blocks Barrick mine" *The Telegram* (16 July 2013) D3; Drew Hasselback, "Barrick Gold Corp shareholders file class action suit over Pascua-Lama Mine" *The Financial Post* (24 April 2014) online: Financial Post <http://business.financialpost.com/2014/04/24/barrick-gold-corp-shareholders-file-class-action-suit-over-pascua-lama-mine/>.

Devise a Risk Management Plan

A business can follow a number of methods to manage its legal risk, including risk avoidance, risk reduction, risk transference, and risk retention. Choosing one or more approaches involves evaluating the risk matched with the organization's resources, financial or otherwise—in other words, doing a cost–benefit analysis.

Step Three: Devise a Risk Management Plan

- ✓ Avoid or eliminate the risk.
- ✓ Reduce the risk.
- ✓ Transfer the risk.
- ✓ Retain the risk.

Risk Avoidance

Eliminating risk, or **risk avoidance**, is appropriate when the risk is simply too great or when the undesirable result of the activity, product, or service is greater than the advantages. In the Northland context, Marie has determined that the legal risks associated with expanding to a foreign jurisdiction like Peru are too high relative to the benefits. As indicated above, although there is potential for profits, there is considerable risk that the operations will result in liability.

Another example of risk avoidance relates to Northland's Canadian operations. The company can avoid potential liability under legislation that protects endangered species, such as the boreal woodland caribou, by operating in areas away from where these animals herd and graze. Similarly they can avoid First Nations' hunting and burial grounds by not locating operations near them.

Businesses often eliminate products and product lines, discontinue programs such as tours and job-shadowing, and stop activities as a way to avoid the associated risk.

Risk avoidance

Ceasing a business activity because the legal risk is too great.

Risk Reduction

A business can undertake **risk reduction** in relation to most risks that cannot be avoided. This strategy involves introducing policies, practices, and procedures to reduce the probability of an event happening. For example, Northland cannot do business without extending credit to customers. The provision of credit inevitably involves the risk that some customers will not pay their accounts. To minimize that risk, Northland should have procedures in place (such as regular credit checks and taking collateral) for evaluating and periodically reassessing the creditworthiness of customers.

As another example, Northland can reduce potential liability under environmental legislation by improving its environmental performance. It can improve air quality by installing and upgrading equipment to voluntarily reduce emissions. It can construct facilities to treat all mine water to reduce the risk of contamination. It can also monitor and manage the tailings pond to ensure that waterfowl and other birds that nest in the grasses on the shores are protected.

To address the health and safety of employees, Northland could introduce a system that includes the reporting and auditing of workplace accidents as well as encouraging a culture of safety. A tracking system provides the information needed to determine the root cause of accidents and the appropriate corrective measures. The company may also provide personal protection equipment such as custom-molded hearing devices, and provide education on hygiene practices and their importance in reducing exposure to harmful chemicals.

To minimize the chance that members of the public will injure themselves by falling, Northland can pay extra attention to keeping its grounds clear of possible hazards. It can also limit access to its property through fencing and other barriers.

Risk reduction

Implementing practices in a business to lower the probability of loss and its severity.

Risk Transference

This approach complements risk reduction by transferring the remaining risk to another by contract. Insurance, which is an integral part of most risk management plans, is discussed in detail in Chapter 28. Insurance is likely the best response to many of the risks faced by Northland. Injuries to members of the public will be covered by a comprehensive general liability policy. Motor vehicles owned by Northland will be covered by vehicle insurance. Damage to plant and equipment through events such as fires will be covered by property insurance. Northland may also consider environmental insurance policies to cover clean-up costs and impairment of the environment and cyber insurance to cover the costs associated with technology failures. However, insurance can be costly, some risks (such as potential environmental liability) are difficult to insure against, and insurance provides coverage only to the extent and in the amount actually purchased. As well, insurance does not prevent loss or the adverse publicity resulting from a high-profile case, even if the insurance company honours the policy.

Risk transference

Shifting the risk to someone else through a contract.

Although **risk transference** is usually thought of in terms of insurance, it can also involve protection such as limited or excluded responsibility that can be provided by contract (see Chapter 7).

Northland produces a product and delivers it by truck to the railway. Many things can go wrong that may cause loss to the customer, resulting in a claim against the business. The product may be delivered late, it may fail to meet the customer's expectations, or it may be defective. One common approach to such risks is to negotiate for terms in the contract that limit the liability of the business for such claims. For example, Northland might negotiate for a clause in its customer contracts providing that, in the event of a defect, Northland is only liable to pay the customer a specified portion of the purchase price in damages.

The challenge in such a contract is to create terms and conditions that achieve the business objective of risk transference that are acceptable to customers, clearly written, and legally enforceable if a dispute arises.

Risk Retention

Risk retention

Absorbing the loss if a legal risk materializes.

Keeping or absorbing all or part of the risk within the organization is known as **risk retention**. This approach is appropriate when the cost of avoiding or transferring a risk is greater than the impact on the business if the risk materializes. In effect, the organization pays losses out of its own resources. The organization can do this in several ways:

- **Self-insurance**. The organization can establish a funded reserve.
- **Insurance policy deductibles**. The organization can retain risks to a certain dollar amount.
- **Noninsurance**. The organization can charge losses as an expense item.

There has been a marked increase recently in the use of risk retention, owing in part to significant increases in insurance premiums in many industry sectors or even the refusal of insurance companies to cover certain risks such as terrorism or sexual abuse in volunteer organizations. There are also some risks that cannot be avoided or reduced to zero; these risks must be absorbed by the business. For example, Northland cannot avoid regulations relating to its operations. If occupational health and safety or waste disposal rules change, Northland may face significant expense, despite its best efforts to anticipate and adapt to the changes.

Another example concerns equipment; despite training and instruction, accidents involving Northland's vehicles occur. Rather than fully insuring the vehicles, Northland may insure subject to a deductible of $2000 per vehicle. This means that Northland has accepted the first $2000 in risk of damage to vehicles and has transferred the remainder to the insurance company. The same concept applies to injuries on its property. Claims to the insurance company for injuries suffered by members of the public are subject to a deductible, meaning Northland is absorbing part of the risk.

Any plan devised in Step Three must be reasonable in terms of its cost and complexity; no plan can eliminate all risk. The goal is to be aware of risks and to make conscious decisions about dealing with them. To assist in this process, managers may turn to legal professionals for balanced advice, either on a lawyer–client basis or through in-house counsel. However, the lawyer must know the business and the industry in which it functions in order to provide useful input.

ETHICAL CONSIDERATIONS

FAULTY IGNITION SWITCHES AT GENERAL MOTORS

In March 2010, 29-year-old nurse Brooke Melton was killed in an automobile accident near Atlanta, Georgia. Melton's 2005 Cobalt went into a spin on the highway and was hit by another car, knocking it off the road and into a creek. It was subsequently determined that the ignition switch was faulty. Sensors in the car showed the ignition switch had slipped out of the "run" position into "accessory," thereby shutting off the power steering, the power brakes, and the air bags. Apparently the ignition switch could easily slip out of the run position if the keys are jostled by the driver or stressed by a heavy key chain.

The faulty ignition in its compact cars has become a major scandal for General Motors (GM), the manufacturer of the car. The faulty ignition has been linked to numerous deaths;[2] has led to the recall of millions of cars;[3] has prompted an avalanche of government investigations including one by the National Traffic Safety Administration (the agency that regulates U.S. auto safety) that has resulted in a $35 million fine for delay in reporting the switch problem; has led to the establishment by GM of a fund to compensate victims and apologies by GM chief executive, Mary Barra; and has spawned a raft of lawsuits, including in Canada.

The faulty switch problem dates to the early 2000s when GM's chief switch engineer approved the switch for use in GM compact cars even though it fell below GM specifications as related to torque. The engineer, who had encountered an array of other problems with the switch, did not believe that the torque problem would have any impact on the car's performance. Apparently, he did not want to further delay production by fixing what was viewed as a minor problem. After the cars went into production, there were complaints about the ignition switch but a "business decision" was made not to fix the problem. The faulty switches were viewed, at that time, as a customer satisfaction issue, not a safety issue. In 2006, the switch engineer provided a fix for

2 The exact number of deaths is unknown; GM's initial estimate was 13. However, GM's compensation fund has approved more than 100 death claims related to the ignition switch. Victim advocates estimate the death toll to be much higher. See: Rishi Iyengar, "General Motors says 100 people have now died from faulty ignition switches" *Time Magazine* (12 May 2015) online: Time Magazine <http://time.com/3855017/general-motors-ignition-switch-death-toll-100/>.

3 The initial recall by GM was 2.6 million compact cars with ignition switch problems. Later recalls brought GM's total recall in 2014 to 39 million vehicles. Not all of these recalls, however, relate to ignition problems. See: "GM Recall" *NBC News* (assessed 20 January 2015) online: NBC News <http://www.nbcnews.com/storyline/gm-recall>.

Mary Barra, CEO of General Motors

$5 million, the family is looking to reopen its case based on allegations that GM acted fraudulently by concealing the switch problems. In Ken Melton's words: "We hope someone during our case will be helped, maybe a life will be saved somewhere."

Critical Analysis: Do you think there can be any justification for the "business decision" not to fix the faulty ignition switch? Why do you think information about the fixed switch was withheld? Why do you think the cars with the faulty switches were not recalled until 2014?

Sources: Anton Valukas, "Report to board of directors of General Motors Company regarding ignition switch recalls" *Beasley Allen* (29 May 2014) online: Beasley Allen <http://www.beasleyallen.com/webfiles/valukas -report-on-gm-redacted.pdf>; Adam L. Penenberg, "GM's hit and run: How a lawyer, mechanic, and engineer blew open the worst auto scandal in history" *Pando Daily* (18 October 2014) online: *Pando Daily* <http:// pando.com/2014/10/18/gms-hit-and-run-how-a-lawyer-mechanic -and-engineer-blew-the-lid-off-the-worst-auto-scandal-in-history/>; Tom Krisher, "Initial lawsuit could limit GM's legal liabilities" *Herald Business* (1 July 2014) online: *Herald Business* <http://thechronicleherald .ca/business/1219707-initial-lawsuit-could-limit-gm-s-legal-liabilities>; David Friend, "GM faces barrage of lawsuits" *The Edmonton Journal* (21 March 2014) B3; Jeff Green, "GM CEO apologizes for stalled recall" *The Globe and Mail* (19 March 2014) B9; Matthew Goldstein & Barry Meier, "G.M. calls the lawyers" *The New York Times* (16 March 2014) 1.

the problem by making a change in the specifications but he did not change the part number or notify the rest of the organization about the fix. From 2007 to 2013, a number of car crashes including Brooke Melton's were linked to the ignition switch. GM began a formal recall of vehicles in January 2014. Though Brooke Melton's family settled its claim against GM for

Implement the Plan

Once a business has devised a risk management plan, it must put the plan into action and assess its effectiveness on an ongoing basis.

Step Four: Implement the Plan

✓ Carry out the plan.

✓ Monitor and revise the plan.

Responsibility for implementing the risk management plan must be clearly assigned. Much of this allocation may be obvious. For example, if the analysis has suggested a quality-control problem, the plan must identify those responsible for both monitoring quality and delivering the service or producing the product. It will not be enough, however, to simply advise the appropriate personnel of the problem. The employees must be educated as to why the problem requires correction and what techniques should be adopted to ensure that the problem is corrected. In addition, guidelines for carrying out the procedures should be collected in a manual for immediate reference. The document should include, as appropriate, a schedule of inspections of facilities, a formal system of ensuring that those inspections take place as scheduled, an accident-reporting system, and information on any insurance coverage in place. Such a manual can be a two-edged sword, however. If Northland is sued for injury or loss and it is shown that Northland neglected to follow its own policy on the matter, the claimant may have grounds for establishing liability.

The plan must be continually monitored and revised as necessary. Management should have a regular review process in place to determine whether the plan is working, and, if not, why. The frequency and severity of events anticipated in the plan will provide feedback on the plan's effectiveness. For example, as a result of the faulty ignition switches, GM will presumably reconsider its retention of the risk in relation to its vehicles.

The nature of the business conducted by a firm may change, requiring major reconsideration of the plan. For example, a meat packing company might decide on a major strategic shift from fresh meat and poultry products to a broader range of processed and packaged meat products. The latter involve greater value added and higher profit margins. The company would need to determine that its previously sound risk management approach is appropriate for the changed business or ensure that it was adequately adapted and altered. Risks may frequently change and practices will need to be adapted, but a routine review process can help to ensure that the requisite adjustments are made.

The legal risk management model is summarized in Figure 3.2.

FIGURE 3.2 Summary of the Legal Risk Management Model

Step One: Identify the legal risks.

- Assess the organization's functional areas.
- Review the organization's business decisions.
- Examine the organization's business relationships.
- Analyze the organization's operations and transactions.

Step Two: Evaluate the risks.

- Assess the probability of loss.
- Assess the severity of loss.

Step Three: Devise a risk management plan.

- Avoid or eliminate the risk.
- Reduce the risk.
- Transfer the risk.
- Retain the risk.

Step Four: Implement the plan.

- Carry out the plan.
- Monitor and revise the plan.

© Cengage Learning

A risk management plan need not be a lengthy or complicated document. The key is for managers like Marie to identify and evaluate legal risks and then rely on a cost–benefit analysis to devise an action plan in response. For example, the cost of installing fencing around Northland's mine site may outweigh the possible cost of members of the public falling and injuring themselves there. The cost of prevention is a certainty, while risks and the resulting losses may never materialize. Proper signage throughout the property may be a legally effective response, including "No Trespassing" signs and signs warning of dangers such as open pits. Figure 3.3 outlines a summary of

FIGURE 3.3 Summary of Northland's Risk Management Plan

Environmental risks:

Reduce: introduce practices to minimize impact of operations on the environment; install a new scrubber (a piece of equipment that captures and removes large particles like heavy metals from exhaust) to prevent pollutants from entering the atmosphere; upgrade waste water filtration system for tailings pond; ensure the clay liner in tailings pond remains intact;

Avoid: decide not to expand operations into environmentally sensitive areas; decide not to operate in a foreign country;

Transfer: secure comprehensive general liability insurance that includes coverage for damage to third parties; purchase an all risks[4] property insurance policy with environmental coverage for mine site;

Retain: agree to a deductible on all insurance policies based on cost of insurance, frequency of events, and ability to absorb losses.

Human resources risks:

Reduce: work toward establishing a culture of safety; establish a workplace health and safety management system including a safety committee; establish a reporting and audit system for workplace injuries; ensure that the mine safe room is equipped with first aid materials and water; review human resource policies relating to termination and harassment;

Transfer: ensure registration under provincial workers' compensation program; maintain the company in good standing under the program.

Operational risks:

Reduce: train operators on equipment; introduce enhanced product control measures; permit visitors on property only under supervision; install fencing and other barriers to prevent access to dangerous areas;

Transfer: purchase comprehensive general liability insurance for injuries to third parties, all risks property insurance for equipment and machinery breakdown and loss of inventory, business interruption for losses from a temporary shutdown, and auto insurance to cover injuries and damage to vehicle;

Retain: agree to a deductible on all insurance policies based on cost of insurance, frequency of events, and ability to absorb losses.

Regulatory risks:

Reduce: monitor political environment for potential changes to regulations; lobby and provide input to potential changes;

Retain: ensure that Northland adheres to Canadian regulatory, legislative, and compliance regimes;

Avoid: decide against operating in a foreign country.

Financial risks:

Reduce: institute quality control measures to ensure full and complete performance of contracts; ensure compliance with accounting and reporting requirements through internal and external audit functions; conduct credit checks of customers prior to issuing credit;

Transfer: negotiate for contractual provisions in contracts with customers reducing potential liability.

Technological risks:

Reduce: hire an information technology firm specializing in security to install firewalls (software that protects against unauthorized access to computers and networks); store data off-site on a daily basis;

Transfer: purchase all risks property insurance to cover damage to computers and cost of data recovery.

© Cengage Learning

---

4 All risks insurance is a type of insurance coverage where any risk not specifically excluded is covered. For example, if a policy does not exclude flood coverage, then the property is covered in the event of a flood.

a possible plan for Northland that Marie might develop with the management team by applying the risk management model. It addresses the risks identified in Figure 3.1.

To create this kind of plan, management needs to analyze business activities, develop practices to minimize risks, and know when to seek assistance outside the business, whether by securing insurance or retaining professionals for advice. All risks are generally dealt with through some combination of risk avoidance, reduction, transference, and retention.

Interacting With the Legal Environment

Reacting When Prevention Fails

Prevention of loss is the primary goal of a risk management plan, but some risks cannot be avoided. Disputes inevitably arise; products and services sometimes fail; the business climate, the attitude of government toward business, or the marketplace can change. The value of a risk management plan is that when a risk does materialize, the business already has in place an effective way of addressing it and can more readily assess when legal advice may be necessary.

In the case of Northland, despite measures to protect workers, an employee may be injured on the job site. In such a situation, the details of the risk management plan should include guidelines as to how the employee is to be treated; what kind of investigation should take place; what kind of record is to be made of the incident; what follow-up is to be done to ensure that this type of incident does not reoccur; and the process for accessing income from the workers' compensation plan.

In other situations, however, an event may occur that is not contemplated by the risk management plan, or the consequences of an event are much greater than anticipated. For example, despite its best efforts, one of Northland's mines could cave in and result in the loss of life. In this situation, the company would be in crisis management.

BUSINESS APPLICATION OF THE LAW

THE MANAGEMENT OF A CRISIS

A crisis can come in many forms. Sometimes it is a minor or expected event that spirals out of control, or sometimes it is an unforeseen and unexpected event that an organization is ill-prepared to handle. One of the more famous crises affecting a company occurred in 1982 when seven people died after taking extra-strength Tylenol that was laced with cyanide. The manufacturer of Tylenol, Johnson & Johnson, responded quickly by pulling 31 million bottles of Tylenol off the shelves and stopping all production and advertising. The culprit was never found. Other more recent examples of the management of a crisis are British Petroleum dealing with the spilling of roughly 4.9 million barrels of oil from a blown-out well into the Gulf of Mexico, Maple Leaf Foods responding to a wide-spread outbreak of listeriosis linked to the company's plant in Toronto, which resulted in 22 deaths, and Toyota Motor Corp. recalling 8.8 million cars because of unintended acceleration problems. The recall was precipitated by a single horrific car crash in California. The improper installation of all-weather floor mats from a sports utility vehicle into a loaner Lexus sedan by a dealer led to the vehicle's accelerator getting stuck. An off-duty highway patrol officer and three members of his family were killed in the ensuing crash.

Although these events are very different, all of the companies involved were able to effectively manage the crisis and restore their reputations. They were able to do so because of their reaction to the event and their communication strategy. The latter is particularly important for public companies in that statements made by company representatives have an impact on the market for their shares. The lessons from these events include:

- react quickly and in a positive fashion: Toyota, Maple Leaf Foods, and Johnson & Johnson immediately recalled products.
- use a prominent spokesperson to tell the company's side of the story and, as appropriate, publicly apologize for the tragic event:[5] both Toyota's and Maple Leaf Foods' presidents publicly apologized for the situation.
- explain how the problem occurred and what the company is doing to fix it: Johnson & Johnson introduced tamper-resistant bottles; Maple Leaf Foods improved its cleaning processes and inspection systems.
- use appropriate messages in different media: the companies expressed concern for the victims and did not argue whether the companies were responsible; they used both traditional media such as television,

Akio Toyoda of Toyota Motors Corp.: "I am deeply sorry"

radio, and newspaper advertisements, and social media.

- be open and consistent in acknowledging the problem and the company's role in the problem: the companies did not remain quiet or complacent, nor did they offer vague, content-free, public statements.

Critical Analysis: How can the lessons learned from a crisis be incorporated into an organization's risk management plan?

Sources: Kim Bhasin, "9 PR Fiascos That Were Handled Brilliantly By Management" *Business Insider* (26 May 2011) online: *Business Insider* <http://www.businessinsider.com/pr-disasters-crisis-management-2011-5?op=1>; "7 lessons from Maple Leaf Foods' crisis communication" *Dave Fleet* (25 August 2008) online: Dave Fleet <http://davefleet.com/2008/08/7-lessons-from-maple-leaf-foods-crisis-communications/>; Christopher Guly, "Dealing with the storms" *In-House Counsel* (Spring 2010) 24.

Managing Legal Services

The development of a risk management plan, the operationalization of the plan, and crisis management can involve accessing legal services. Lawyers may be part of the risk management team or consulted by the team at various stages of the process. They can help in identifying and assessing legal risks, suggesting options for the risk management plan, and managing a crisis (see Business Application of the Law: The Role of Lawyers in Legal Risk Management, on page 62). Legal services may be provided in-house, as when the organization employs a lawyer or lawyers on a full-time basis, or they can be provided by outside legal counsel. The following sections provide an account of the issues involved in hiring outside legal counsel.

---

5 For discussion of the legal consequences of an apology in the context of apology legislation, see Chapter 4.

When to Seek Legal Advice

Knowing when to seek legal advice is central to successful management of legal services. Consulting lawyers too soon and too often is expensive and cumbersome. Consulting them infrequently to save money may be more expensive in the long run. Seeking advice at the appropriate time is preferable to waiting for problems to develop.

In Northland's case, legal advice is necessary to assess the legal risks associated with operating in a foreign jurisdiction. It may also be necessary to understand regulatory matters. It may be more efficient for a lawyer to assess environmental requirements, waste disposal guidelines, occupational health and safety rules, and the like than for a business to explore such issues on its own. Beyond this, even if a dispute is unlikely to go to court or a crisis is unlikely to materialize, legal advice is important in negotiations and exploring options.

It is important to clarify within the organization who should decide when a matter requires legal advice. If there is an internal law department, it is likely that those in that department will make the decision, otherwise there must be clear guidelines as to who has the authority to seek outside counsel and when.

How to Choose a Lawyer

A **lawyer** provides legal services, and the business should manage this service in the same way as any other service. The first step is to find the lawyer or **law firm** appropriate to the business's needs in terms of expertise, approach to dealing with clients, and cost.

There are many sources available for identifying lawyers such as friends, relatives, and business associates. Local and provincial bar associations maintain lists of members by geographical area and preferred type of practice. *The Canadian Law List*[6] is a publication available in libraries and online that includes basic biographical information about most lawyers in private practice.

Some advice follows for choosing from among a group of lawyers or firms:

- consult with business associates with similar legal problems and needs about the service they have received from any of the prospects.
- consider meeting with each lawyer or with a representative of each firm to discuss the needs of the business for legal advice in general or in relation to a particular legal problem. Lawyers have a strict professional duty to maintain the confidentiality of client affairs.
- discuss alternative fee structures with the prospects. Lawyers are increasingly willing to provide a fee structure that suits the client, such as billing at an hourly rate, setting a standard fee for routine work, working on an annual retainer, or accepting a percentage fee. The client should expect itemized billing on a schedule that suits the business's financial cycle.
- evaluate the prospects according to a predetermined list of criteria such as expertise, availability, willingness to understand the business, and willingness to communicate.

Lawyer

A person who is legally qualified to practise law.

Law firm

A partnership formed by lawyers.

6 See <http://www.canadianlawlist.com>.

CHAPTER 3: MANAGING LEGAL RISKS

The object of the exercise is to develop a productive, long-term relationship between the business and the legal advisor. For this reason, there is also a need to continually monitor and evaluate the relationship, primarily to ensure that the business is receiving the advice and assistance it needs at a cost it can afford.

BUSINESS APPLICATION OF THE LAW

THE ROLE OF LAWYERS IN LEGAL RISK MANAGEMENT

Legal risk management is the identification and management of risks that have or could have legal consequences for an organization. Lawyers can play a huge role in this function by offering:

- an understanding of the organization derived from providing advice on various aspects of the organization's functions.
- an expertise in law and legal analysis.
- an independence that comes from membership in a professional body.[7]

The specific role a lawyer plays depends, to a large extent, on whether the lawyer is outside or in-house legal counsel. Traditionally, outside counsel's role is more circumscribed as she is often only called when an event has occurred. In this situation the outside counsel's role is reactive as she is providing advice on a known event or transaction. The narrow, reactive role for outside counsel, however, is changing and increasingly outside counsel is moving into a preventative role in managing legal risk. For example, Simon A. Fish, general counsel of BMO Financial Group, states that managing risk is no longer an internal exercise; BMO is now bringing in outside counsel as part of the process. According to Fish: "In representing BMO, the firms are required to be mindful of the legal,

regulatory, and reputational risks involved in any transaction or matter, and involve the senior members of the legal group in the assessment and management of such risks."

The role of in-house legal counsel in legal risk management has always been broad because an awareness of risks has always been central to the job. But this role too is changing as in-house legal counsel is increasingly seen as an integral part of the management team. Rather than simply being responsible for keeping an eye on legal matters and supervising the work of outside counsel, in-house counsel is often taking part in corporate strategic decision making. Sanjeeve Dhawan, senior counsel at Hydro One, states that ". . . companies are discovering that in-house counsel can transcend their traditional legal roles." By being part of the team that makes the organization's strategic decisions, in-house counsel is in an excellent position to ensure that legal risks are recognized and managed as part of the organization's overall strategy.

Critical Analysis: What skills and techniques do lawyers need to contribute effectively to the risk management process?

Sources: Christine Dobby, "A Game of Risk" *The Financial Post* (28 May 2011) FP7; Jeremy Hainsworth, "A novel risk-management plan" *Canadian Lawyer Magazine* (October 2012) online: *Canadian Lawyer Magazine* <http://www.canadianlawyermag.com/A-novel-risk-management-plan.html>.

BUSINESS LAW IN PRACTICE REVISITED

1. What is a legal risk management plan and how is it developed?

A legal risk management plan is a plan that identifies the major legal risks of an organization; evaluates the probability of the risk materializing and the impact of the risks; develops strategies for managing the risks; and implements and

---

7   Andrew M Whittaker, "Lawyers as Risk Managers" *Butterworths Journal of International Banking and Financial Law* (January 2003) 5.

monitors the strategies. The plan is developed by the appropriate executive or manager in consultation with internal and external personnel familiar with the legal risks of the organization.

2. What are Northland's major legal risks from its Canadian operations? How should Northland manage these risks?

Northland's major legal risks from its Canadian operations are identified in Figure 3.1 on page 50. Once the major legal risks are identified, Marie and her team need to evaluate them by assessing the probability and the severity of each potential loss. They must then develop a risk management plan by deciding how to address each risk—by avoiding, reducing, transferring, retaining, or through some combination of those options. Figure 3.3 on page 58 presents the outline of a plan that Marie might produce. Risk management is a continuous process, so Marie or others must monitor the plan to measure its effectiveness in dealing with risks and be prepared to recommend any necessary adjustments.

3. What are Northland's major legal risks should it decide to operate in a foreign jurisdiction such as Peru? How should it manage these risks?

The major legal risks to going global are identified in Figure 3.1 and are also discussed in the International Perspective box on page 52. Risks include the possibility that Northland will commit environmental transgressions in Peru. Should this risk ensue, Northland will face adverse publicity, prosecution under environmental legislation, and civil suits by environmental activists and local residents affected by the breach. Also, there is a possibility that the Peruvian government prohibitively tightens legal rules thereby affecting the viability of Northland's operation or even nationalizes it. As noted in the risk management plan in Figure 3.3, Marie recommended that Northland not expand operations to outside of Canada because the current risks are simply too large.

CHAPTER SUMMARY

A business can manage its legal environment by assessing that environment, developing a risk management plan, reacting to changes in the legal environment, and managing its legal services.

It is crucial for a business to actively manage the legal risks arising from its activities in order to avoid and minimize legal claims and expenses. Legal risk management involves a four-step process: identifying legal risks, assessing those risks, devising a risk management plan, and implementing the plan. Risks can be identified through assessment of the functional areas of the business, the decisions made within the organization, the internal and external relationships maintained by the business, and its operations and transactions. However, it is important to also identify risks that might cross categories and maintain a flexible approach. The risks are then assessed in terms of how likely they are to occur and how severe the losses might be. There must be an action plan for dealing with each risk. Should the risk be avoided? If not, how can it be reduced or transferred to someone else? To what extent must the risk be retained? These strategies are not usually mutually exclusive and the management of most risks will involve some combination of them.

Management must assemble a knowledgeable team of employees and experts in order to make the plan work. A business must also monitor and revise its plan to ensure that it is current and effective. No risk management plan can anticipate and deal with all possible developments. A business must, therefore, be prepared to react in a coordinated and timely fashion to a crisis.

A business also needs to actively manage its legal services, whether it is employing outside lawyers or in-house counsel. This management involves identifying the legal services that are needed, carefully searching out an appropriate lawyer or law firm, and maintaining a stable relationship with legal advisors.

CHAPTER STUDY

Key Terms and Concepts

enterprise risk management (p. 46)

law firm (p. 61)

lawyer (p. 61)

legal risk (p. 46)

risk avoidance (p. 53)

risk reduction (p. 53)

risk retention (p. 54)

risk transference (p. 54)

Questions for Review

1. What is meant by the preventive and reactive approaches to legal issues in a business?

2. What is the primary goal of a legal risk management plan?

3. How does a legal risk management plan relate to enterprise risk management?

4. What is the value of a legal risk management plan?

5. What steps are involved in the legal risk management model?

6. How can a business identify its legal risks?

7. What legal risks are posed by technology?

8. How is breach of privacy a legal risk? What are the costs associated with a privacy breach?

9. How can a business evaluate its legal risks? What is the purpose of evaluating legal risks?

10. What is the best strategy for managing legal risks?

11. What is an example of risk retention? When is this strategy most appropriate?

12. What is an example of risk avoidance? When is this strategy most appropriate?

13. What procedures are necessary to implement a risk management plan?

14. How can a business keep its risk management plan current and relevant?

15. What are some of the legal risks in doing business internationally? How can these risks be managed?

16. How does the management of a legal crisis differ from managing legal risks?

17. When should a business seek legal advice?

18. What is the role of lawyers in legal risk management?

Questions for Critical Thinking

1. The International Perspective box on page 52 illustrates some of the risks of doing business abroad. How should the legal risk management model be adapted for conducting international business? Which of the four steps of the model are the most important?

2. Risk reduction is a strategy for managing risk. When is it the most appropriate strategy for managing a risk? What are some examples of risk reduction?

3. The pharmaceutical industry involves inherent risks. The drugs developed by corporations

in the industry may not be as effective as research indicated and over time may produce unexpected, unintended, and serious side effects. How can pharmaceutical corporations use risk avoidance, risk reduction, risk transference, and risk retention in managing these risks?

4. Risk management is a continuous process that requires commitment, time, and expense. However, the benefits are often difficult to identify because they arise largely from prevention. How can a business decide whether the benefits of a risk management plan compensate for the time and expense involved in its design and implementation?

5. A common method of controlling the cost of legal services is to refrain from consulting a lawyer until a serious legal problem absolutely requires it. Another approach is to hire or retain lawyers on an ongoing basis to provide advice as business decisions are made. Which approach is the most expensive? What should a business consider in making that choice?

6. An article in *The Lawyers Weekly*, a leading legal publication, is entitled "Corporate counsel key to risk management."[8] Do you agree with that statement? How can lawyers contribute to risk management? Do you see any problems with outside or in-house lawyer involvement in risk management?

Situations for Discussion

1. Johann is the comptroller of Super Tech Inc., a highly aggressive firm in the high-tech industry that specializes in software development. Sarah, the CEO, prides herself on her ability to make fast decisions and doesn't worry about documenting her actions. Her favourite sayings are, "We can't spend all of our time writing things down," and "Why worry? That's why we have insurance and lawyers." This approach appears to have served her well, at least in the initial years of the business. Johann is concerned, however, because he is often faced with legal bills without having any knowledge of the issues involved. The firm's legal costs are steadily increasing. How should Johann present

a recommendation to Sarah that Super Tech should develop a legal risk management plan?

2. If Sarah accepts Johann's recommendation, whom should he recruit for the risk management team? Should he be the leader of the team? How should he go about identifying the legal risks in the firm's business? Whom should he consult?

3. Johann's review has identified a particular problem with Super Tech's software designers. When used by customers, their designs are failing at a higher rate than the industry norm. The designers are unwilling to go back and correct problems because they prefer to develop new products and are under pressure to do so. Super Tech is faced with legal claims and lost customers. How should Johann evaluate and address this problem in the context of his risk management plan, taking into consideration the software designers and the company's profitability? Which of the four risk management strategies are appropriate?

4. Vancouver-based retailer Lululemon experienced a problem with its $100 black luon yoga pants. They were too sheer, pilled easily, and customers were returning them. Chip Wilson, founder of the company, in an interview with Bloomberg TV stated, "Quite frankly, some women's bodies just actually don't work. It's really about the rubbing through the thighs, how much pressure there is over a period of time." Numerous media outlets picked up the story and a firestorm of negative comments on social media ensued. Four days later, Wilson apologized on Lululemon's Facebook page stating, "I'm sad for the repercussions of my actions. I'm sad for the people of Lululemon who I care so much about, who have really had to face the brunt of my actions...I'm sorry to have put you all through this."[9] What mistakes did Lululemon make in handling this situation? What lessons can be learned?

5. Drake International, a Canadian job placement firm, has been a victim of a hacking scheme.

8 Luigi Benetton, "Corporate Counsel Key to Risk Management" *The Lawyers Weekly* (20 February 2009) 20.

9 Rebecca Harris, "Lululemon founder Chip Wilson plunges company into PR crisis" *Marketing Magazine* (12 November 2013) online: Marketing Magazine <http://www.marketingmag.ca/advertising/lululemon-founder -chip-wilson-plunges-company-into-pr-crisis-93637>.

The hackers stole a database containing the names, email addresses, phone numbers, and passwords of over 300 000 clients in Canada, Australia, the United Kingdom, and New Zealand. They demanded $50 000 to keep the stolen information private and not publish it on the Internet. The database that was compromised was an old database built under outdated security practices that included unencrypted passwords.[10] What is the risk to Drake of threats from a group of hackers after a security breach? How could Drake have identified and addressed this risk in advance? How should Drake respond to the hackers?

6. Siena Foods Ltd., located in Toronto, Ontario, is a manufacturer and distributor of prepared meat products. In 2010, the Canadian Food Inspection Agency (CFIA) and Siena Foods issued a health hazard alert warning the public not to consume certain Siena brand ham as it may be contaminated with *Listeria monocytogenes*.[11] Food contamination is a major risk in the food processing business with potentially disastrous consequences for the company and its customers. How should Siena manage this risk? What preventive and reactive action plans should be in place? To what extent can Siena rely on the CFIA to manage the risk?

7. Anna, a customer in a Wendy's restaurant, claimed that she bit into a piece of a human finger while eating a bowl of chili. Anna filed a claim for damages. The event attracted wide media attention. Anna gave several interviews in which she graphically described the trauma that she experienced. The volume of business at all Wendy's outlets in the region plummeted. After several weeks, Wendy's accused the customer of deliberately placing the finger fragment in the chili. When the finger was examined, it proved to be uncooked. Anna and her husband were eventually charged and convicted of several criminal offences. The finger came from a co-worker of Anna's husband, who had lost it in a workplace accident. Apparently Anna and her husband have a history of filing false injury claims.[12] Apply the legal risk management model to this situation. What plan should businesses such as Wendy's have in place to deal with this risk?

8. JetBlue is an American low-fare airline. In 2007, its operations collapsed after an ice storm hit the East Coast of the United States. The storm led to the cancellation of over 1000 flights in five days. Other airlines were affected by the storm but were able to rebound within a day or two. JetBlue's problems dragged on for days. The main problem was JetBlue's communication system. A large portion of its pilots and flight attendants were not where they were needed and JetBlue lacked the means to locate them and direct them to where they were needed.[13] How could a risk management plan have addressed JetBlue's problems? How should JetBlue's crisis have been handled? Are there opportunities for an organization in responding to a crisis?

10 Christine Dobby, "Hackers blackmail Canadian company" *The Financial Post* (10 January 2013) A1.

11 Canadian Food Inspection Agency, *Health Hazard Alert: Certain Siena brand prosciutto cooked ham may contain* Listeria monocytogenes, (11 March 2010) online: Canadian Food Inspection Agency <http://www .inspection.gc.ca/english/corpaffr/recarapp/2010/20100311be.shtml>.

12 Based, in part, on The Associated Press, "Finger-in-chili caper nets wife 9 years, hubby 12" *The Edmonton Journal* (19 January 2006) A3.

13 Jeff Bailey, "JetBlue's C.E.O. is 'mortified' after fliers are stranded" *The New York Times* (19 February 2007) online: NY Times <http://www .nytimes.com/2007/02/19/business/19jetblue.html?pagewanted=all>.

DISPUTE RESOLUTION

BUSINESS LAW IN PRACTICE

Marie Gagnon, referred to throughout Chapter 3, is the Director of Insurance and Security of Northland Mining Inc., a nickel mining company located in northern Manitoba. She has just returned from a well-deserved holiday in Mexico. For several weeks prior to her holiday, Marie was involved in revising Northland's legal risk management plan using the approach outlined in Chapter 3. The basic elements of the plan are presented in Figure 3.3 on page 58. During Marie's absence, several events occurred that related to Northland's plan. Marie is reviewing the following incident reports:

- **The delinquent customer**. A customer failed to pay its account within the usual 30 days. When Northland investigated, it discovered that the customer was in serious financial difficulty.

- **The hacking attempt**. An environmental activist group opposed to mining attempted to "hack" into Northland's computer system. Although there was no loss of data, there was some minor damage to Northland's network and it had to be shut down for several hours.

- **The pollution incident**. A small amount of ash-laden dust from Northland's processing mill was blown onto a neighbouring farmer's land causing some damage to his crops and buildings. The farmer is irate and is threatening to bring legal action. He has told Northland that he intends to contact the media and environmental protection groups to let them know about what has happened to him.

- **The machine breakdown**. The conveyor belt on the continuous mining machine that cuts ore from the mine walls caught on fire. It will take at least three weeks for it to be fixed. Although Northland has insurance covering its losses, the insurance company is denying coverage.

1. How well does Northland's risk management plan deal with these incidents and how could its performance have improved?

2. How well does Northland deploy the various methods of dispute resolution in relation to the legal risks that materialized?

OBJECTIVES

After studying this chapter, you should have an understanding of

- how business activities may lead to legal disputes
- the options for resolving a legal dispute
- alternative dispute resolution methods
- the litigation process

Introduction

As emphasized in Chapter 3, business organizations require a risk management plan to minimize the potentially adverse impact of the legal environment through prevention and a planned reaction to adverse events when they arise. Legal problems cannot always be avoided even when sound management practices are in place. This chapter focuses on the reactive aspect of risk management.

It is not in the best interest of a business to avoid all legal conflict at all costs. For example, if Northland is not being paid on a large account, it must risk a legal dispute or face the unpalatable alternative of a substantial writeoff. It could spell the end of Northland if management were simply to concede defeat any time a legal problem seemed to be developing. Businesses like Northland should seek, instead, to manage such disputes with the express goals of

- avoiding time-consuming and expensive litigation.
- preserving desirable long-term commercial relationships.

Business Activities and Legal Disputes

Business operations—both internal and external—involve numerous interactions that have potential legal consequences. Consider the following analysis of how the legal risk management plan anticipated and dealt with the events in the Business Law in Practice scenario.

The Delinquent Customer

The customer's refusal to pay its account may indicate that Northland has failed in its procedures for extending credit. Management should explore this possibility to prevent recurrences. In the meantime, Northland must decide if it should: give the customer an opportunity to recover financially before demanding payment; offer to accept less than the full amount; write off the debt altogether; or take steps to be paid on its account, such as selling the debt to a collection agency at a discount, suing for the debt, or filing a claim if the customer is involved in bankruptcy proceedings.

Setting guidelines for granting credit to customers does not guarantee that every debt will be collectable. If this debt is not large and the customer is in serious financial difficulty, coming up with a negotiated repayment plan or writing it off may be more practical than spending money to try to collect it. The debtor is certain to welcome such a compromise, and therefore no legal dispute will arise from this event.

The Hacking Attempt

The hacking attempt by an outside party—an environmental activist group—was anticipated by the plan. Northland, as part of its risk reduction strategy, had engaged the services of an information technology security firm to install firewalls. As a result, the damage to Northland's computer systems was minimal and there was no loss of data. The incident does highlight that hacking incidents can potentially be quite costly. If future hackers are able to breach the firewalls, Northland could incur extra expense associated with the recovery of data, liability for the loss of sensitive customer and employee data, and a loss of revenue resulting from an interruption of the computer system. Northland's investigation of the incident reveals that while it has an insurance program in place, it does not cover all of the possible costs associated with a breach of its computer system. Northland will analyze the costs of obtaining additional, specialized insurance coverage and, if it is warranted, revise its risk management plan accordingly.

The hacking attempt by the environmental activist group is unlikely to result in a legal dispute. Although Northland could potentially sue the group for trespass to its property, this course of action is premature in that Northland does not know the identity of any of the group members. Even if their identity were known, it is still unlikely that Northland would pursue a lawsuit as the damage to its system was minimal and the publicity associated with such an action may be unwelcome.

The Pollution Incident

Northland's operations have resulted in the discharge of a small amount of pollutants into the environment. Northland must report the pollution incident to the relevant environmental regulatory agency. The agency may impose a fine, clean-up order, or some other administrative penalty depending on the nature, cause, and severity of the incident. This possibility was anticipated by the risk management plan and is unlikely to result in a legal dispute, providing the penalty is in accordance with the applicable environmental protection legislation. Northland has no viable option but to comply with properly enacted legislation.

Northland must also report the incident to its insurer. The insurance policy covering this event will require reporting within a short period of time—usually 5 to 10 days—otherwise the insurance coverage for the event is invalidated. An investigation by Northland reveals that the discharge of pollutants was due to a malfunction in the scrubber (a piece of equipment that captures and removes large particles like heavy metals from exhaust). When a new scrubber was being installed, the exhaust fan controlling the intake and discharge of exhaust stopped working. This, in turn, caused a build-up of ash and dust particles. The build-up was not noticed by the operator so when the scrubber was re-started, a huge dust cloud was released into the atmosphere. Luckily, the wind was blowing away from the adjacent town, but it blew the ash and dust particles onto a farmer's land. Although the pollution incident was anticipated by the risk management plan and Northland has insurance in place to cover the damage to the farmer, this incident may result in a legal dispute. The insurance company has indicated that the damage to the farmer—including the cost of washing his buildings and replacing a barn roof, as well as a reduced crop yield—comes in at less than $50 000. The farmer, however, insists that his damages amount to over $100 000. This matter is a legal dispute, since the farmer is refusing to accept compensation and is threatening to contact the media and environmental protection groups. The dispute with the farmer goes beyond the payment of money as Northland's relationship with a neighbour and its reputation in the community are also in jeopardy.

The pollution discharge incident highlights to Northland that any pollution into the environment can be problematic. In this particular incident, Northland was "lucky" in that the wind was not blowing toward the nearby town. Even though insurance coverage may cover all of the claims, Northland is likely to suffer the loss of goodwill and damage to its reputation. Northland's risk management plan may need revision to further reduce the possibility of a future discharge. For example, Northland may need to purchase a back-up fan or it may need enhanced operator training and restart procedures.

The Equipment Breakdown

An investigation into the machine breakdown reveals that a bearing in the machine failed, causing the ore conveyor belt to catch on fire. It will take at least three weeks to get and install a replacement belt. Northland's chief financial officer estimates that the breakdown will result in lost profits of $3 million. The insurer has been notified of the event, but it is denying coverage. It is arguing that the bearing failure and the resultant losses were not due to a sudden and accidental event covered by the insurance policy, but were due to Northland's failure to properly maintain the equipment. Ordinary wear and tear and failure to maintain the equipment are not covered by the insurance policy. Beyond this, the insurance policy contained a provision requiring Northland to keep complete maintenance records on the machine's bearing or else coverage would be voided. The insurer is demanding those records. For its part, Northland argues that it properly maintained the equipment in accordance with the manufacturer's original specifications.

Although machine breakdown and resulting loss of profit was anticipated and managed by the purchase of insurance, this incident will result in a legal dispute. The amount of money involved is simply too large for Northland to write off.

As the foregoing analysis suggests, Northland's risk management plan predicted and planned for several events that did in fact occur. For various reasons, a legal dispute is unlikely to arise from them. Some events will not develop into legal disputes because the company has no other viable option but to live with what has happened. That is, Northland will likely write off the delinquent customer's bad debt as an anticipated cost of doing business; Northland will not throw away its resources on a lost cause. Similarly, Northland cannot launch a legal action over the hacking attempt because it does not know the identity of the hackers and, besides, there is little point in launching an action where the damage is minor and the resulting publicity is unwelcome. However, other events may result in legal conflict, including the problems with the disgruntled farmer and the intransigent insurance company.

Northland's challenge with these latter issues is to actively and effectively manage them—just as it would any other aspect of the business's environment. Managing disputes does not mean simply proceeding to court. There are many ways to resolve a dispute that do not involve litigation. See Figure 4.2 on page 89 for a summary of **alternative dispute resolution (ADR)** methods. The most common are negotiation, mediation, and arbitration.[1]

Alternative Dispute Resolution

Negotiation

Negotiation is a problem-solving process in which parties discuss their differences and attempt to reach a mutually agreeable resolution. It is the most common alternative dispute resolution method because it is cost effective, is usually quick,

---

Alternative dispute resolution (ADR)

A range of options for resolving disputes as an alternative to litigation.

Negotiation

A process of deliberation and discussion intended to reach a mutually acceptable resolution to a dispute.

---

1   Another method is mediation/ arbitration (med/arb). This is a hybrid dispute resolution process that begins with mediation using a neutral person as mediator. If necessary, the parties proceed to arbitration with the same neutral person acting as arbitrator.

and allows parties to craft a solution that is suitable for their particular situation as opposed to having another party, such as a judge, impose a resolution. It also helps to preserve the relationship between the parties because it does not tend to be as confrontational as more formal methods of dispute resolution.

When to Negotiate

Negotiation can be used to resolve virtually any type of dispute. It can, for example, be used to resolve Northland's dispute with the farmer and the insurance company, provided they are willing to negotiate. In addition to situations where the parties agree to negotiate once a dispute arises, a provision in a contract may require the parties to attempt negotiation. It is increasingly common for parties to include in their contract a clause whereby they agree that during and after the conclusion of the contract, they will make efforts to resolve any disputes by negotiation. When negotiation is used, it can be employed at any stage of a dispute, even on the eve of or midway through a trial.

Even though negotiation may be used to resolve most types of disputes, there are some situations where negotiation is not the proper way to proceed, even as a first step, such as when insurance covers the risk that is the subject of the dispute. In such circumstances, the business is required to allow the insurer to conduct settlement negotiations. Any attempt by the business to negotiate privately may jeopardize the coverage. In Northland's dispute with the farmer, insurance potentially covers the farmer's damage and the insurance company would normally negotiate a settlement. However, in this situation, the insurance company agreed to allow Northland to attempt to resolve the dispute because of its sensitive nature and its potential impact on Northland's reputation.

How to Negotiate

Negotiations are most often carried out by the parties to the dispute. However, in some cases it may be preferable to hire a lawyer, advocate, or counselor who has the expertise to help in the negotiations or who can negotiate on behalf of the parties. In Northland's case, because both disputes involve insurance issues, negotiations will most likely be carried out by the person responsible for acquiring the insurance, that is, Marie Gagnon, Director of Insurance and Security.

Regardless of who does the actual negotiating, the first step is to investigate the situation to determine the nature and extent of the dispute. The person responsible should contact the individuals involved in her own organization and the appropriate people on the other side of the dispute to clarify the situation. The process of negotiation is not governed by technical rules; it can operate in whatever way the parties wish to solve their problem.[2] It is important to get the negotiations off on the right foot, however. For example, Northland—in negotiating with the disgruntled farmer—should contact him immediately and assure him that it is concerned with his situation and will make every effort to remedy his loss. Northland may also decide to apologize to him for the damage. As the box on page 72 explains in more detail, several provinces including Manitoba[3] have passed "apology legislation" to permit an individual to show remorse without triggering adverse legal consequences.

---

2 For principles of effective negotiation, see: Roger Fisher & William Ury, *Getting to Yes: Negotiating Agreement Without Giving In* (New York: Penguin Books, 1983).

3 *Apology Act*, SM 2007, c 25, CCSM c A98.

SAYING SORRY

Research in the area of apologies suggests that they facilitate personal reconciliation and can assist in resolving legal disputes.[4] According to the Uniform Law Conference of Canada (ULCC), however, the traditional concern was that an apology in a legal context could prove dangerous. An apology might amount to an admission of liability that "could void an insurance policy, encourage a lawsuit, or result in a court holding the apologizer liable."[5] In response, several jurisdictions in Canada have passed broad apology legislation. As summarized by the ULCC, the apology legislation in British Columbia—which covers statements admitting or implying wrongdoing as well as expressions of regret or sympathy—provides that an apology:

- is not an admission of liability.
- is not relevant when a judge makes a determination of liability.
- cannot be used as evidence establishing liability.
- cannot be used to void an insurance policy.[6]

Businesses, however, should be careful in issuing apologies. As noted, some jurisdictions do not

Saying "sorry"

Why do apologies de-escalate legal disputes?

have apology legislation and, even in jurisdictions that do have legislation, it may not provide the protection expected. For example, Alberta's Court of Queen's Bench has held that factual statements that accompany an apology are not part of the apology and are admissible in court.[7] As Mary Paterson of Osler, Hoskin & Harcourt observes: "In short, you can say you are sorry, but you cannot say what you are sorry for without risking making an admission."[8]

Critical Analysis: What are the pros and cons of an apology in the face of a legal dispute? What should an apology contain?

With negotiation, the goal is to reach a resolution that is agreeable to all parties. That said, there is no guarantee that a settlement will be reached. Whether negotiations do succeed will depend on a number of factors, including the following:

- the willingness of the parties to compromise and negotiate in good faith.
- the nature and significance of the dispute.
- the priority the parties give to its resolution.
- the effectiveness of those involved in the negotiations.

If negotiations are successful and the parties reach a settlement, it is usual for them to enter into a settlement agreement or **release**[9] so that the dispute is unlikely to be resurrected or litigated in the future. It is also common to have

Release

An agreement where a party agrees to relinquish past, present, and future claims arising from a certain event.

---

4 Russell J Getz, "Uniform Apology Act" Uniform Law Conference of Canada (Civil Law Section), 2007 at 2.
5 *Ibid* at 3–4.
6 *Ibid* at 13.
7 *Robinson v Cragg,* 2010 ABQB 743, 41 Alta L R (5th) 214.
8 Mary Paterson, "Apologies as dispute resolution," *Osler, Hoskin & Harcourt, LLP* (May 2012) online: Association of Corporate Counsel <http://www.lexology.com/library/detail.aspx?g=f7badccb-1ab6-42ee-939a-4483722ffee4>.
9 Releases in an employment context are discussed in Chapter 21.

a confidentiality clause as a part of the settlement or release. This prohibits the parties from revealing the terms of the settlement and prevents other persons from using the settlement to advance claims against the parties.

Northland entered into negotiations with the disgruntled farmer who was willing to talk once he understood that Northland was concerned about his situation. He agreed not to call the media or environmentalists pending a resolution of the dispute. As part of the negotiations, Northland explained how and why the pollution occurred and what it was doing to prevent a future incident. The farmer was adamant that his damage was over $100 000. However, included in his estimate was structural improvement to his facilities (he wanted new siding on all buildings as opposed to having the siding cleaned) as well as depreciation on the barn's roof. After further discussion, the farmer agreed to abandon his claim for new siding when Northland agreed to pay for a new roof without consideration of depreciation. The parties settled for $75 000 and the farmer signed a release with a confidentiality clause. A release is binding on the parties unless it is grossly unfair or unconscionable.

When Negotiations End

In the majority of cases, such as the dispute with the farmer, parties reach settlement. Other times, an impasse is reached where neither party is prepared to compromise further.

Northland also negotiated with its insurance company, but the results were disappointing. The insurance company was not willing to compensate Northland for any losses. It continued to argue that the losses were due to poor maintenance, which was an exclusion (a provision that eliminates coverage for certain events or named perils) under the insurance policy.

When an impasse such as this occurs, the business is faced with a difficult choice: concede and cut its losses or risk the expenditure of more time and money. Whether Northland should continue or abandon the legal conflict depends on its analysis of what is in the best interests of the organization in the long term (see Figure 4.1).

If Northland decides to continue its dispute with the insurance company, it may end up having to sue. Alternatively, the parties may agree to either mediation or arbitration as a method to resolve the dispute.

FIGURE 4.1 In Deciding Whether to Proceed or Not to Proceed with a Legal Dispute Consider the Following Questions

- What further steps are available and how long will they take?
- Can the business devote the resources necessary to proceed with the dispute, in terms of both the commitment and the time of business personnel?
- Will a lengthy dispute affect the public profile and reputation of the business?
- Is the relationship with the other side valuable?
- Will that relationship be harmed, whatever the outcome?
- What is the likely cost in terms of legal fees and company time?
- Are there worthwhile principles at stake that go beyond the particular dispute?
- If the dispute goes to court, what are the chances of winning?
- If the court decides in favour of the business, does the other side have the assets to pay the claim?

Mediation

Mediator

A person who helps the parties resolve their dispute.

Mediation is an ADR process whereby a neutral person, called a **mediator**, assists the parties in reaching a settlement of their dispute. It is a popular method for resolving disputes because, like negotiation, it:

- is less expensive and quicker than more formal dispute resolution methods.
- is private and confidential if the parties choose.[10]
- helps to preserve the relationship between the parties.
- can result in a resolution tailored to the needs of the parties.

When Mediation Is Used

Mediation, like negotiation, can be used to resolve most disputes. Whereas, historically, mediation was mainly used in family disputes and divorce issues, it is now commonly used to settle commercial disputes. It has been successfully used to resolve a wide range of business conflicts involving contract matters, personal injuries, employment matters, environmental protection, and the like. That said, some disputes are more amenable to mediation than others. Success is more likely if the parties are interested in considering each other's position with the goal of compromising and settling the dispute, and if they value the advantages of mediation. Northland and its insurer could agree to mediation to resolve their dispute over insurance coverage.

In addition to situations where the parties voluntarily agree to mediation, or where it is required pursuant to a clause in a contract, there are cases where it is imposed. For example, Ontario has a mandatory mediation program that requires many civil (non-criminal) cases[11] to be referred to mediation before a trial can be scheduled.

How Mediation Works

Once the parties have agreed to mediation, they choose a neutral third party to act as mediator. There are no mandatory qualifications for ADR practitioners, but there are many training programs available through universities and the private sector. Mediators are often lawyers or retired judges, but anyone is eligible to become a full-time or part-time practitioner. The ADR Institute of Canada, a self-regulatory body for ADR professionals, maintains a national roster of mediators. Usually the mediation will happen with the parties meeting face-to face, but it can also be conducted through videoconferencing and online[12] if it is appropriate for the parties and the type of dispute. Once the mediator has been chosen, she helps the parties clarify their interests and overcome obstacles to communication. The mediator does not work for either party and instead manages the process, organizes the discussion, clears up misunderstandings, and helps reduce tensions between the parties. The mediator does not, however, make or impose a solution on the parties—it is the parties that must reach a resolution voluntarily.

In the case of mandated mediation programs, the parties may choose a mediator, but if they are unable to agree, a mediator will be assigned to them from a

---

10 To ensure confidentiality in ADR proceedings, the parties should include a clause to that effect. Parties should not automatically assume that their deliberations and settlement are confidential. See: Anthony Daimsis, "Confidentiality in ADR" *The Lawyers Weekly* (11 February 2011) 9.

11 The mandated mediation program applies in Toronto, Ottawa, and Windsor to most non-family civil actions where the claim exceeds $50 000. See: Ontario, Rules of Civil Procedure, RRO 1990, Reg 194, r 24.1.

12 See: Luigi Benetton, "The benefits of video mediation" *The Lawyers Weekly* (10 December 2010) 9; Garry Oakes, "Your virtual day in court: How online dispute resolution is transforming the practice of ADR" *The Lawyers Weekly* (15 August 2008) 23.

roster of mediators. In mandated mediation, like voluntary mediation, the mediator does not impose a solution but merely assists the parties.

When Mediation Ends

Mediation, like negotiation, has a very high success rate. For example, it is considered to be successful in settling approximately 80 percent of the cases where it is used even after litigation has begun.[13] At the end of a successful mediation, the parties normally enter into a settlement agreement setting out the essential terms of their agreement. This will bring closure to the dispute and help prevent future litigation concerning the same matter. The settlement agreement is a contract and can be enforced in the same manner as any other contract. Ontario[14] and Nova Scotia[15] have also enacted legislation that allows parties who have settled a commercial dispute through mediation to register their agreement and have it enforced like a court judgment.

Mediation, however, is not uniformly successful. It does not always produce a resolution, so time and money may be invested only to have the matter proceed to litigation. Northland and its insurer initially agreed to mediation, but quickly realized that their dispute was not amenable to this resolution approach. This was because both parties were unwilling to compromise and both wanted a definitive decision on whether the insurance covered Northland's losses.

Arbitration

Arbitration is a method for resolving a dispute whereby a third person (or persons), called an **arbitrator**, appointed by the parties makes a decision. It is similar to litigation in that it usually involves a hearing where the parties or their representatives make submissions, and the resolution is outside the control of the parties. Arbitration has advantages in comparison to litigation. The parties control the process in that they choose the rules for conducting the arbitration including the degree of formality, privacy, and finality of the decision, the timing, and the decision-maker or arbitrator. Arbitration is advantageous because the parties have an opportunity to review the arbitrator's background prior to ceding decision-making power and can choose an arbitrator who has knowledge and expertise in their particular dispute. This option is not available in a court action. Arbitration is usually cheaper and faster than litigation and can lead to an overall sense of satisfaction. However, if the parties choose a process that has the same degree of formality as the litigation process, or if a party uses an absence of rules to engage in delay tactics, the arbitration can lead to costs and time periods similar to, or greater than, those experienced in a court action.

Arbitrator

A person who listens to the parties to a dispute and makes a ruling that is usually binding on the parties.

When Arbitration Is Used

Arbitration, like other forms of ADR, is theoretically capable of resolving any dispute. It works particularly well for most commercial and business disputes[16] because the parties can select an arbitrator with relevant experience and keep commercially sensitive information private.

---

13 Paul Jacobs, "Deal mediation: settling disputes before they arise" *The Lawyers Weekly* (18 September 2009) 10.
14 *Commercial Mediation Act, 2010*, SO 2010, c 16, Schedule 3.
15 *Commercial Mediation Act*, SNS 2005, c 36.
16 For example, the Canadian Motor Vehicle Arbitration Plan (CAMVAP) funded by the auto industry resolves some disputes between customers and auto manufacturers. See: <www.camvap.ca>.

Arbitration is often chosen by the parties before a dispute arises through a term in a contract providing that disagreements arising from the contract are to proceed to arbitration. Most significant commercial contracts, whether domestic or international, have an arbitration clause. Increasingly, many contracts between providers (particularly online providers of goods) and consumers contain arbitration clauses.

ARBITRATION CLAUSES IN CONSUMER CONTRACTS

Dell Computer published the wrong prices on its online order pages. Two models of handheld computers indicated prices of $89 and $118 rather than $379 and $549, respectively. Several hundred consumers attempted to buy computers at the erroneous prices but were unable to so. The consumers attempted a class action to force Dell to sell them the computers at the lower advertised prices. Dell argued that the consumers were not able to take the matter to court because of a clause in the online contract requiring all disputes to proceed to arbitration. The Supreme Court of Canada upheld Dell's argument. The consumers were left with their individual remedy of going to arbitration—presumably a very much inferior option. Since then, Alberta,[17] Quebec, and Ontario have passed legislation explicitly prohibiting arbitration clauses in consumer contracts. In other provinces without such legislation, arbitration clauses are likely enforceable with a few exceptions.[18]

What are the advantages and disadvantages of arbitration clauses in consumer contracts?

Critical Analysis: Should arbitration clauses be prohibited in consumer contracts? Why or why not?

Sources: Luis Millan, "Customers can sue despite ADR clause" *The Lawyers Weekly* (1 April 2011) 1; *Dell Computer Corp v Union des consommateurs*, 2007 SCC 34, [2007] 2 SCR 801.

In the absence of a clause, arbitration can be adopted at any point in a dispute if the parties agree. Northland and its insurer did not have an arbitration clause in their contract. They initially considered arbitration as a method of resolving their dispute but could not agree on an arbitrator. But more importantly, the insurance company wanted to establish a legal precedent. It wanted a judge's interpretation of the scope of the exclusion clauses in its insurance policy, a result not available with arbitration.

How Arbitration Is Used

Agreements to settle a dispute by arbitration are subject to arbitration legislation[19] in the relevant jurisdictions. These statutes oust the jurisdiction of

---

17 In Alberta, an agreement requiring a consumer to submit a dispute to arbitration is upheld only if the arbitration agreement is approved by the Minister. See: *Fair Trading Act* RSA 2000, c F-2, s16.

18 See *Seidel v Telus Communications Inc*, 2011 SCC 15, [2011] 1 SCR 531, where the Supreme Court of Canada held that in some cases, consumer protection legislation provisions may override an arbitration clause.

19 See for example, *The Arbitration Act*, SM 1997, c 4, CCSM c A120. The general arbitration acts do not govern certain types of arbitration, most notably, arbitrations in labour relations are governed by specific legislation.

the courts and provide general guidelines for the conduct of the arbitration. The agreement between the parties to submit their dispute to arbitration will normally specify the process for choosing an arbitrator and the rules of procedure.

The parties may agree on an arbitrator or they may have a third party choose an arbitrator. As mentioned above, there are no mandatory qualifications for ADR practitioners. Many of the same people who provide mediation services also provide arbitration services. The ADR Institute of Canada maintains a roster of arbitrators. The key is to retain the services of a qualified and skilled professional experienced in both the type of dispute and the dispute resolution process.

The parties decide on the rules for conducting the arbitration. They may establish their own rules, or incorporate rules set out in the arbitration statutes or developed by a recognized body such as the ADR Institute of Canada. The parties have great flexibility in specifying the degree of formality in the procedures. The rules, for example, will specify how the hearing is conducted, when and where it is conducted, how evidence can be presented, and timelines for its presentation.

When Arbitration Ends

At the end of the arbitration, the arbitrator renders a decision. The finality of the decision depends on what the parties have agreed to in their agreement to submit the dispute to arbitration. Usually the decision will be a final decision with little or no right of appeal. Alternatively, the parties may agree to preserve rights of appeal and may provide for an appeal process.

The arbitration award, unless it is overturned or varied on appeal, is **binding**, that is, it is enforceable by the courts. The arbitration acts provide for the enforcement of the arbitral decision in much the same manner as a judgment of the court.

Binding

Final and enforceable in the courts.

INTERNATIONAL PERSPECTIVE

ARBITRATION IS THE NORM IN INTERNATIONAL TRANSACTIONS

Litigation of a business dispute in a domestic transaction can be time-consuming, damaging, and expensive. If the dispute arises in an international transaction, problems are compounded by questions of which country's law applies, which country's courts will hear the case, and whether the courts of one country will recognize and enforce a judgment obtained in another country. There is no international court for the resolution of commercial disputes, nor is there a comprehensive international system for the enforcement of awards obtained in domestic courts of other countries.

For these reasons, ADR mechanisms are extremely popular for settling international commercial disagreements. In international commercial contracts, arbitration has emerged as the favoured form of settlement, and arbitration clauses are the norm. In fact, it would be a rare situation where a significant international commercial contract did not have an arbitration clause in it. The arbitration process has been greatly enhanced by the adoption in many countries of standardized rules as well as by procedures and provisions for the reciprocal recognition and enforcement of the arbitral award. Canada, for example, has adopted the *New York Convention on the Recognition and Enforcement of Foreign Arbitral Awards*. This convention ensures international arbitration awards are enforceable in the over 140 countries that are signatories to it. Also, all jurisdictions in Canada have enacted international commercial arbitration legislation based on the United Nations Commission on International Trade Law (UNCITRAL) *Model Law on International Commercial Arbitration*. The legislation sets out the process for an international commercial arbitration as well as its review and enforcement.

Critical Analysis: Is arbitration of international disputes a positive development?

Source: Mary Jo Nicholson, *Legal Aspects of International Business: A Canadian Perspective*, 2d ed (Toronto: Emond Montgomery, 2007) at 361–71.

The Litigation Process

As already discussed, most of the legal risks that materialized for Northland—including the delinquent customer situation and the pollution incident—are likely to be resolved out of court. However, Northland's conflict with its insurer over the equipment failure may end up in litigation because alternative dispute resolution methods have failed. As the parties have been unable to find a compromise, they will now seek a court's answer to whether the continuous mining machine broke down because of an accidental event (which means Northland's losses would be covered by the insurance policy) or due to improper maintenance by Northland (which would not be covered).

Litigation arises when one party brings a legal action against another. In this case, Northland would be the **plaintiff** or claimant. It would sue (that is, initiate legal action, known as a lawsuit or litigation) the insurer (as **defendant**), claiming that the defendant breached the insurance contract when it refused to pay out Northland's loss under the policy.

Litigation should be deployed only when all other feasible methods have failed and the claim cannot realistically be abandoned. This is not just because litigation can harm commercial relationships and bring unwelcome publicity. Complicated litigation, in particular, is a drain on corporate resources, diverts operations from profitable business activities, and causes stress for those involved in the process. Beyond this, there is no guarantee of success in obtaining a favourable decision from the court or in collecting a judgment from the defendant. In short, litigation is generally slow, expensive, and unpredictable.

While litigation often involves just a single plaintiff against a single defendant, class actions are also possible, as the Business and Legislation box below discusses.

The legal foundation and outcome of a lawsuit are governed by legal rules contained in common law and statute law. Some of these rules are substantive because they address, in part, who should win the action and why. *How* the claim is carried through the civil justice system is dictated by the procedural rules—that is, the rules that mandate such matters as what documents are to be filed with the court, what the process leading up to the trial will be, and in what manner the trial will proceed.

There are crucial rules in each province which set specific time periods within which to commence legal action. The **limitation period** can vary widely, depending on the nature of the lawsuit and the province in which the litigation will occur. Alberta, for example, has a general limitation period of two years (meaning that the action must be commenced within two years of when the cause of action is discovered) and an ultimate limitation period of 10 years

Plaintiff

The party that initiates a lawsuit against another party.

Defendant

The party being sued.

Limitation period

The time period specified by legislation for commencing legal action.

(commencing when the cause of action arises), whichever period expires first.[20] Ontario has a general limitation period of two years and an ultimate limitation period of 15 years,[21] as do New Brunswick,[22] and British Columbia.[23] Provinces do provide some exceptions to the limitation periods such as for minors and disabled persons, but otherwise the rule is that the right to sue is lost after the applicable period of time ends.

Class action

A lawsuit launched by one person who represents a class of persons having similar claims against the same defendant.

BUSINESS AND LEGISLATION

CLASS ACTION LAWSUITS

A **class action** is a proceeding brought by a representative plaintiff on behalf of, or for the benefit of, a class of persons having similar claims against the same defendant. The purpose of a class action is to improve access to justice by enabling claimants to combine their resources in a single action, and to efficiently address cases of alleged mass wrong by eliminating the need for a large number of individual actions.

Until the 1990s, class actions were uncommon in Canada because of precedents that made it difficult to use this process. Beginning in 1992, all of the jurisdictions in Canada,[24] with the exception of Prince Edward Island and the territories,[25] passed legislation to broaden the availability of class actions. Generally, the legislation enables a class action to be certified or approved by the court if

- the pleadings disclose a cause of action.
- there is an identifiable class of two or more persons.
- the claims of the class raise issues that are common to all class members.
- the class proceeding is the preferable procedure for the resolution of the common issues.
- there is a representative plaintiff who fairly and adequately represents the interests of the class and who does not have a conflicting interest with other class members.

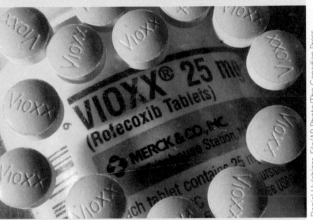

Daniel Hulshizer, File/AP Photo/The Canadian Press

When is a class action the preferable method of settling a claim?

The result of the legislation has been a complete transformation of the class action landscape in Canada. There has been a tremendous increase not only in the number of lawsuits launched and certified, but also in the amounts of money involved. The actions have been commenced in a wide variety of areas such as product liability, environmental contamination, securities, financial services, employment disputes, consumer protection, franchises, and pension plans. The actions have involved every conceivable claim.

Some recent examples of settled class actions are:

- a class action alleging a price-fixing conspiracy among international manufacturers of dynamic random access

---

20 *Limitations Act*, RSA 2000, c L-12, s 3.
21 *Limitations Act*, SO 2002, c 24, Schedule B, ss 4, 15.
22 *Limitation of Actions Act*, SNB 2009, c L-8.5, s 5.
23 *Limitation Act*, SBC 2012, c13, ss6.
24 See, for example, *Class Proceedings Act*, 1992, SO 1992, c 6; and *Class Proceedings Act*, SNS 2007, c 28.
25 These jurisdictions may still certify class actions under the common law.

memory (DRAM), a semiconductor memory product that provides high speed storage and retrieval information found in computers and other electronic equipment, was settled for $80 million.[26]

- a class action against the manufacturer of VIOXX by individuals who used the drug and suffered myocardial infarction, ischemic stroke, or sudden cardiac death was settled for $37 million.[27]

- a class action against chocolate producers Cadbury Adams Canada Inc., Hershey Canada Inc., Nestlé Canada Inc., Mars Canada Inc., and distributor, ITWAL Limited for conspiring to fix or maintain prices for chocolate products in Canada was settled for $23.2 million.[28]

- a class action against Hyundai Auto Canada Corp. and Kia Canada Inc. involving the fuel economy ratings of some of their vehicles was settled for $69.7 million.[29]

The advent of the class action in Canada has not been without controversy. Some applaud class actions not only for making it less onerous for individuals to seek redress against large companies, but also for forcing companies to change behaviour in a positive way. Others complain the courts have been too lenient in allowing class actions to proceed and that it is usually just the lawyers who benefit.

Critical Analysis: Class action legislation has significantly increased the risk of a class action for business. How can a business address this risk in its legal risk management plan?

Sources: Luis Millan, "Class action conundrum" *The Lawyers Weekly* (23 April 2010) 24; Jacob Ziegel, "Class actions: the consumer's best friend?" *The Lawyers Weekly* (20 February 2009) 5; David Weiner, "Class action communications: the era of the public lawsuit has arrived" *The Lawyers Weekly* (2 May 2008) 27.

The rationales for strict limitation periods include:

- providing a very strong incentive for plaintiffs to advance their claims within a reasonable period of time.

- preventing plaintiffs from advancing old claims in which evidence has been lost because time has passed.

- providing defendants with a time after which the threat or possibility of litigation comes to an end.[30]

Limitation period rules are an important reason why legal advice should be sought at an early stage in disputes, particularly where there are significant financial consequences. Lawyers in such cases must be aware of the relevant limitation period and ensure that litigation is commenced if settlement does not occur within that period.

Commercial litigation (which involves businesses suing businesses) is also known as private (or civil) litigation. The litigants bear the costs of bringing a matter through the judicial system and any recovery of compensation comes

---

26 DRAM Class Action, online: Sutts, Strosberg <http://www.dramclassaction.com/>.

27 VIOXX National Class Action Canada (20 April 2013) online: VIOXX <http://vioxxnationalclassaction.ca/ 013>.

28 Chocolate Products Price-Fixing Class Action, online: <http://www.chocolateclassaction.com/>.

29 "Hyundai, Kia fuel-efficiency class-action settlements total $70M" *CBC News* (27 January 2014) online: CBC News <http://www.cbc.ca/news/hyundai-kia-fuel-efficiency-class-action-settlements-total -70m-1.2513465>.

30 Pamela Pengelley, "Limitation Periods for Property Damage Losses in Canada" *Subrogation & Recovery Law Blog* (15 August 2011) online: Subrogation & Recovery Law Blog <http://www.subrogationrecoverylawblog .com/2011/08/articles/international-1/limitation-periods-for-property-damage-losses-in-canada/>.

from the losing party. Government's only involvement in the process is through the provision of the administrative structure, the court facilities, the judges, and other court officials. There is no government funding for the private litigants themselves, with the limited exception of legal aid programs which assist in certain civil matters, such as divorce and custody lawsuits, but not in commercial disputes.

Every province and territory has its own system of courts and rules for civil litigation. In some cases, the amount of the claim determines the court in which the action would be commenced. When the plaintiff is suing for a relatively small amount of money, for example, the lawsuit can be processed in the local equivalent of a small claims court. The name of the court varies from province to province, with the monetary limit ranging from $10 000 all the way up to $50 000. The small claims process is designed to be simpler, quicker, and less expensive than mainstream litigation. Litigants do not need to hire a lawyer to assist them, though some choose to do so, especially if the matter is complex.

Claims in excess of small claims limits must be pursued in the local equivalent of the superior court, which has unlimited monetary jurisdiction. Litigation in superior courts is governed by complicated rules of court determined by each province. Such litigation is ordinarily conducted by a lawyer in consultation with the client. While it is technically permissible for a business to attempt to meet the many formal requirements of superior court litigation without the benefit of legal advice, this is generally inadvisable. A litigant's need for what can often be costly legal advice raises the issue of accessibility to the justice system for those who cannot afford the services of a lawyer.

Stages of a Lawsuit

In superior courts, a lawsuit that goes through the full court process comprises four stages.

Pleadings

The first stage is known as **pleadings** and involves the exchange of the formal documents outlining the basis of the suit. The plaintiff initiates the action by preparing a document that contains the allegations supporting the **claim**. For example, in Northland's action against its insurer, the initial document would, among other matters, identify the insurance contract and the coverage provided. The claim would indicate that the equipment was insured under that contract of insurance, identify the accident that caused the loss, and state the dollar amount of the loss. The claim would then also state that the insured had made demand for payment of the loss from the insurer under the policy and that the insurer had refused to do so, in breach of the policy. This initial document is a notice of the claim and is registered, or "filed," with the appropriate court office. It is then formally delivered to the party being sued (the defendant), through a process known as service. If the defendant has retained a lawyer, that lawyer may accept service of the documents on the defendant's behalf.

This first stage does not include evidence, but instead outlines the key points that the plaintiff needs to prove at trial in order to succeed. The defendant then has a short period of time (e.g., 20 days in Ontario) in which to respond to the allegations. Failure by the defendant to respond within the allowed time is

Pleadings

The formal documents concerning the basis for a lawsuit.

Claim

The formal document that initiates litigation by setting out the plaintiff's allegations against the defendant.

equivalent to admitting the claim. If the defendant has no defence to the claim, he or she may choose to allow the plaintiff to "win" the case. The plaintiff, in turn, simply explains to the judge that the defendant has conceded the case. The court gives a default judgment to the plaintiff, who is then free to move to the enforcement stage.

If there are matters in dispute, the defendant will likely seek legal advice and prepare a formal response to the claim, known as a **defence**. The lawyers may agree to allow the defendant longer than the minimum period in which to prepare the defence. In Northland's example, the insurer would assert in its statement of defence that Northland's loss was not an insured loss. The statement of defence would state that the loss did not arise as a result of accident but as a result of poor maintenance.

Speaking more generally, the defendant also has the option of filing a **counterclaim** against the plaintiff in the appropriate case. For example, when a defendant is sued for allegedly causing a motor vehicle accident resulting in injury to the plaintiff, the defendant may turn the tables and file a counterclaim, alleging that it was actually the plaintiff who caused the accident and injury to the defendant.

Discovery

Once the basic claims and allegations have been made and clarified, the suit proceeds to the second stage, commonly known as **discovery**. Both parties must now reveal and demonstrate the facts that support their allegations. These facts are found in documents, in the oral testimony of those directly involved in the situation, and in expert reports. In this context, documents include electronic data (such as email archives and the contents of hard drives) and give rise to complicated issues of preservation and access. Electronic data is easier to access, organize, and distribute, but can be challenging to find and control. It has become important for firms to have comprehensive data retention policies in anticipation of e-discovery. Computer technology can help track the numerous documents in complicated cases. In its litigation with the insurer, Northland would produce, among other documents, the maintenance records it kept regarding the continuous mining machine. Unfortunately for Northland, it was unable to locate some of the relevant maintenance records on the bearing.

The time frame for this stage is undefined and depends largely on the degree of complexity of the case. The purpose of this stage is to test the strength of the opposing positions, so that, based on a greater appreciation of the strengths and weaknesses of both sides of the case, the parties will be encouraged to reach a compromise. At this stage, initiatives in various provinces come into play for the purpose of clearing the backlogs in the courts and streamlining the litigation process. Generally, these initiatives require the parties involved in litigation to engage in a formal attempt to resolve their dispute before it actually goes to court. These attempts may require the parties to engage in a process of mediation, whereby a facilitator, who may be a judge, helps them reach a compromise and avoid a trial. In many jurisdictions, the parties can proceed to trial only when the mediation phase is completed. Besides these mandatory dispute resolution methods, the parties are required to participate in a settlement and pre-trial conference, the purpose of which is to narrow the issues in dispute and make the actual trial as short as possible in the event that it does occur.

Defence

The defendant's formal response to the plaintiff's allegations.

Counterclaim

A claim by the defendant against the plaintiff.

Discovery

The process of disclosing evidence to support the claims in a lawsuit.

ETHICAL CONSIDERATIONS

FREEMEN-ON-THE-LAND

Calgary pensioner Rebekah Caverhill has been in a two-year dispute with her tenant over a duplex. Andrea Pirelli, also known as Mario Antonacci, allegedly refused to pay rent, changed the locks, removed interior doors, and gutted the kitchen. He claimed the pensioner owed him for the work and placed a $17 000 lien on the house. Pirelli also declared the property a sovereign embassy and refused to vacate. He was eventually arrested and evicted.

Pirelli is a member of the loosely organized Freemen-on-the Land group. Members who also sometimes call themselves Sovereign Citizens, Living Souls, or Natural Persons do not have a specific manifesto but attempt to avoid legal obligations by rejecting the authority of the state. They believe that all statute law is contractual and therefore, the law only applies to them if they choose or consent to be governed. As a consequence, they refuse to pay taxes or mortgages or to register cars, and do not use birth certificates, social insurance numbers, or other government-issued identification. One of the main tactics of this group that may number up to 30 000 in Canada and hundreds of thousands in the United States is "paper terrorism." They file private prosecutions and claims in courts typically seeking costs and orders against public officials, peace officers, and others. In support of their litigation, they file copious amounts of incomprehensible documents and spend hours of court time with baffling and outlandish arguments.

Fed up with the antics of the Freemen-on-the-Land group, Alberta's associate chief justice John Rooke in *Meads v Meads*[31] issued a scathing rebuke of "Organized Pseudolegal Commercial Arguments" litigants, as he called them. He strongly condemned their schemes, concepts, and arguments

Rebekah Caverhill's tenant, a member of the Freemen-on-the-Land group, claimed her rental property as an embassy.

that disrupt court operations and "attempt to frustrate the legal rights of governments, corporations, and individuals." He recommended that courts, when dealing with vexatious litigants, use all the tools in their arsenals including striking actions immediately, awarding punitive damages, elevating costs, and issuing fines. In the year following his decision, Justice Rooke has been cited in at least 23 court decisions, including an income tax case in Pictou, Nova Scotia. and the dismissal of a $108 quadrillion case filed in Vancouver.

Critical Analysis: What is the threat to the Canadian justice system of the group, Freemen-on-the-Land? What is the danger of turning away members of the Freemen-on-the-Land movement from the judicial system?

Sources: Brent Wittmeier, "Judge shuts down 'pseudolegal' ploys" *Edmonton Journal* (28 September 2013); Chansra Lye, "Officials say government familiar with Freeman tactics" *CTV Edmonton* (28 September 2013) online: CTV Edmonton <http://edmonton.ctvnews .ca/officials-say-government-familiar-with-freeman-tactics-1.1474934>; Dave Bilinsky, "The Freeman-on-the-Land Movement" *The Law Society of British Columbia Benchers Bulletin* (2012) online: Law Society of British Columbia <http://www.lawsociety.bc.ca/page.cfm?cid=2627>.

Trial and Decision

If no settlement is reached at the discovery stage, the plaintiff can proceed to **trial**. The timing will depend on the availability of the courts and on how long it

Trial

A formal hearing before a judge that results in a binding decision.

31   2012 ABQB 571, [2013] 3 WWR 419.

CHAPTER 4: DISPUTE RESOLUTION

takes the parties to prepare for the formalities of the trial. Most trials proceed with a single judge and no jury. Jury trials are available for commercial matters, but a jury trial can be opposed if, for example, the case is deemed too complex for a jury to understand.

At trial, the **burden of proof** falls on the plaintiff. The plaintiff must formally introduce **evidence**, according to established rules, to prove that its version of events is more likely true than not, known as "proving the case on the balance of probabilities." Expressed numerically, the plaintiff must prove that there is a better than 50 percent chance that the circumstances of the dispute are as it contends they are and that, furthermore, these circumstances entitle it to receive the remedy that it seeks. The defendant has the opportunity to challenge the plaintiff's witnesses and documents and to introduce its own account of events to oppose the claim. The judge must decide what happened between the parties and whether their claims are justified. This is not generally a straightforward task, as the parties typically have widely differing versions of events. Once the facts have been established, the judge is then in a position to consider and apply the relevant law.

The parties make submissions about the legal rules and precedents that support their desired conclusion. The judge then identifies and applies relevant legal rules to those factual findings to produce a decision. The decision may be given by the judge immediately at the end of the trial or reserved until a later time, to allow the judge some time for deliberation.

The trial between Northland and its insurer is likely to proceed before a judge without a jury unless one side feels that a jury might be more sympathetic to its position than a judge. In a commercial matter such as this, that is unlikely to be the case. Northland, as plaintiff, will present its evidence to support its claim that its insurer is bound to honour the insurance policy and more specifically, that the machine in question failed as a result of an accident. The insurer will produce evidence in opposition to the Northland claim, suggesting that deficient maintenance procedures were the cause. In this case, a crucial issue is what caused the Northland equipment to fail. Both sides will likely rely on experts' reports to support their opposing versions of events.

The judge's **decision** contains the judge's resolution of the case—who must pay how much to whom—supported by the appropriate justification based on the evidence and legal rules. Though most plaintiffs seek a monetary award, other remedies are available in exceptional circumstances, such as when the successful party requests an order from the court for the losing party to perform a specific act (e.g., transfer a piece of land) or cease some activity (e.g., trespassing on property).

In the Northland litigation, the pivotal issue of what caused the machinery to fail would be determined by the judge, in part, on the basis of his or her assessment of expert reports on point. Also important would be the judge's assessment of the credibility of the witnesses who, for example, had responsibility to maintain the machinery in question. As previously noted, Northland, as plaintiff, has the onus of proof and must demonstrate to the judge, on the balance of probabilities, that the machinery failed due to an accidental fire and not improper maintenance.

Any monetary award includes the basic amount of the claim plus interest, and, in the usual case, the legal costs of the successful party. **Costs** are awarded by the judge based on a predetermined scale, combined with the judge's view of the complexity of the case. An award of costs usually falls well short of fully compensating the winning party for all its legal expenses, providing only a partial recovery for the successful litigant. In Alberta, for example, costs typically only cover up to about one third of the successful party's actual legal costs. In short,

Burden of proof

The obligation of the plaintiff to prove its case.

Evidence

Proof presented in court to support a claim.

Decision

The judgment of the court that specifies which party is successful and why.

Costs

Legal expenses that a judge orders the loser to pay the winner.

even successful litigation involves expense. The downside for the losing party is significant: in addition to the amount of the judgment and interest, it is likely to be required to pay "costs" to the winner, as well as pay its own legal expenses.

In exceptional cases where the conduct of the losing party has been seriously objectionable, the court may award what are known as *solicitor and client costs*. This award reflects the actual legal expenses incurred by the successful party so that they are fully indemnified for their litigation expenses.

The dispute between Northland and its insurer was resolved by litigation, with Northland being mainly successful. To obtain coverage on the bearing, the policy required that Northland produce complete maintenance records. It was unable to do so and, therefore, the judge disallowed that portion of the claim. Fortunately for Northland, the requirement to produce complete maintenance records did not apply to the conveyor belt and attendant losses. The court awarded damages for these losses because it was satisfied that the fire was triggered by an accident, as claimed by Northland. Beyond this, Northland was awarded its costs.

THE RISKS OF ENVIRONMENTAL LITIGATION

Businesses that emit toxins on a large scale—such as chemical manufacturing plants, petroleum processors, and metal refineries—face an increased risk of class actions in relation to the release of pollutants. As already noted, class actions permit affected individuals to advance a claim on a group basis, thereby accessing legal resources, including representation by lawyers, that they almost certainly could never afford as individuals working alone.

For example, in 2000, Ellen Smith became alarmed upon learning of high levels of nickel contamination in the soil on her property in Port Colborne, Ontario. The nickel particles had come from Inco Ltd.'s nickel refinery, which had operated in the area starting in 1918 and ending in 1984. She was not alone; residents were concerned about possible health risks and decreased property values accompanying such contamination. In response, a class action against Inco was eventually certified, meaning that a judge approved of a claim against Inco going to trial, where the full matter concerning Inco's liability could be adjudicated upon. The class of claimants approved to proceed in this action included those who owned residential property in most of Port Colborne; approximately 7000 properties were involved.

How does the risk of litigation make industry more accountable for the pollution it may cause?

Deborah Baic/The Globe and Mail/The Canadian Press

CHAPTER 4: DISPUTE RESOLUTION

Among other matters, the trial judge ruled that the nickel particles which Inco operations deposited in the surrounding soil constituted physical damage to the properties in question. He also ruled that potential public health concerns surrounding such deposits meant that the properties in question failed to appreciate in value as much as they otherwise would have. On this basis, the trial judge went on to award the plaintiffs $36 million in damages.

In October of 2011, however, the Ontario Court of Appeal overturned this award.[32] Among this court's conclusions was that the nickel deposits did not cause physical harm to the properties in question, but merely changed the chemical composition of the soil—like fertilizer would, for example. For the plaintiffs to win their case, according to the Court of Appeal, they would also have to show some detrimental effect either on the land itself or on its use by the owners. Harm to the land could be demonstrated if there was evidence of harm to the claimant's health or that the nickel "at least posed some realistic risk of actual harm to their health and wellbeing."[33] The fact that nickel particles in the land raised public concerns about potential health risk was not enough. And in a fatal blow, the Court of Appeal concluded that the plaintiff had failed to show that there was insufficient appreciation in the value of the property affected by the nickel deposits. The Court of Appeal dismissed the plaintiffs' action in its entirety and awarded Inco costs of $100 000.

The Supreme Court of Canada has ruled that it will not hear an appeal.

Critical Analysis: What are the risks that litigants take in commencing an action of this kind? Are these risks outweighed by the possible benefits?

Source: Tracy Glynn, "Canada's Largest Environmental Lawsuit" *The Dominion* (12 July 2010) online: *The Dominion* <http://www.dominionpaper.ca/articles/3545>.

Enforcement

Judgment debtor

The party ordered by the court to pay a specified amount to the winner of a lawsuit.

The fourth and final stage of the litigation process is enforcement of the judgment awarded to the winning party. The winner of the suit must enforce the judgment with the assistance of the court. The judge issues a judgment for a certain amount of money which, in turn, can be enforced against the loser, now known as the **judgment debtor**. If the judgment debtor fails to voluntarily pay the judgment, court officials or other designated persons will assist in seizing and selling the assets of that debtor, which may include land, vehicles, equipment, inventory, accounts receivable, and other assets. Laws in every jurisdiction limit the extent to which the winning party can take assets when the losing party is a human being rather than a corporation, the point being to ensure that the individual is not left destitute.

The winner recovers the judgment only to the extent that the loser's assets provide; there is no public fund from which these judgments are paid. Therefore, it is advisable for a prospective plaintiff to investigate the defendant's ability to pay before commencing the suit. A judgment in any amount is generally of little value if the proposed defendant has insufficient assets to pay, has a large number of other unpaid creditors, or is in bankruptcy proceedings.

A judgment is valid for a long period (up to 20 years depending on the jurisdiction) and can be extended.

Appeals

Appeal

The process of arguing to a higher court that a court decision is wrong.

A party who does not wish to accept the trial decision may consider an **appeal** to the next court in the hierarchy. An appeal must be initiated within a specific

32 *Smith v Inco Ltd*, 2011 ONCA 628, 107 OR (3d) 321.
33 *Ibid* at para 57.

PART ONE: THE LEGAL ENVIRONMENT OF BUSINESS

period of time (such as 30 days). There are several reasons an appeal should be undertaken only after careful consideration. In addition to the time and commitment required to pursue an appeal, the chances of success are limited. An appeal is not a rehearing of the case, but merely an opportunity to argue that the trial decision contains significant errors in how the law was applied. It is normally not possible to dispute the conclusions regarding what events actually transpired between the parties (i.e., what the trial judge found the "facts" to be), but only to dispute the judge's understanding and application of the law. Appeal courts tend to confirm trial decisions unless serious errors have been demonstrated.

Appeals at higher levels are normally conducted by a panel of at least three judges. Generally, no new evidence is presented. The lawyers representing the **appellant** (who makes the appeal) and the **respondent** (who defends the appeal) make written and oral submissions to the appeal judges, who then decide whether to confirm the original decision, vary it in some way, reverse the decision, or, in exceptional cases, order that another trial be conducted.

After the court of appeal rules, the unsuccessful party can consider a further appeal to the Supreme Court of Canada. The appellant must obtain leave from the Supreme Court to proceed with that appeal. The leave application is only successful if the case involves a matter of "public importance" or involves an "important issue of law."[34] As a result, the chance of an appeal making it all the way to the Supreme Court of Canada is very slight.

Developments in litigation (in particular, contingency fees, punitive damages, and class actions) are addressed in the following comparison of the systems in Canada and the United States.

Appellant

The party who begins or files an appeal.

Respondent

The party against whom an appeal is filed.

INTERNATIONAL PERSPECTIVE

THE RISKS OF LITIGATION IN THE UNITED STATES

A significant risk for Canadian companies doing business in the United States marketplace is litigation with competitors, partners, suppliers, customers, and governments. The incidence and costs of litigation in the United States are significant[35] and high in relation to Canada. Differences between the American and Canadian civil ligation systems contribute to the greater litigation risks in the United States. The key differences are as follows:

- **Costs:** In Canada, the losing party in civil litigation pays a portion of the winner's legal costs. In the United States, there is no general rule[36] that the losing party pays any of the winner's legal costs. The "loser pay" rule in Canada increases risk and discourages weak and questionable cases. In the United States, there is no such disincentive.

---

34 Role of the Court: Leave to Appeal, online: Supreme Court of Canada: <http://www.scc-csc.gc.ca/court-cour/role-eng.aspx>.

35 The United States has a uniquely costly civil justice system with costs as a percentage of gross domestic product far higher than those in the rest of the developed world. See Marie Gryphon, "Greater Justice, Lower Cost: How a 'Loser Pays' Rule Would Improve the American Legal System" (2008) 11 *Civil Justice Report, Manhattan Institute for Policy Research* online: Manhattan Institute for Policy Research <http://www.manhattan-institute.org/html/cjr_11.htm>.

36 In the United States, costs are generally not recoverable unless specifically permitted by statute or contract. However, many states are moving toward a 'loser pay' system. See Adele Nicholas, "Texas' 'loser pay' law mixed bag for business" *Inside Counsel* (1 August 2011) online: Inside Counsel <http://www.insidecounsel.com/2011/08/01/texas-loser-pays-law-mixed-bag-for-business>.

- *Jury Trials:* In the United States, litigants have a constitutional right to a jury trial. In Canada, jury trials, except for defamation and personal injury cases, are rare. Some cases are prohibited by statute from being tried by a jury and, even where juries are permissible, courts have a broad discretion to deny a jury if the legal or factual issues are complex or if the defendant may be prejudiced. The use of juries increases costs such as the costs of retaining jury consultants and increases risk because of the unpredictability of juries. Juries are often unsympathetic to business and may award large damages against such defendants. This poses a significant risk for business.

- *Damage Awards:* Damage awards in the United States are much larger than in Canada, thus the incentives to sue are greater. In the United States, punitive damages (to punish the loser) are generally available whereas in Canada they are rarely awarded and, when they are, they are much lower than in the United States[37] Although many states have passed legislation capping punitive damage awards, the awards can still be 10 times the compensatory damages. Also, in Canada damages for pain and suffering in personal injury cases are capped;[38] there are no similar caps in the United States. A further factor contributing to large damage awards in the United States are statutes in areas such as antitrust that provide triple damages.

- *Class Actions:* Class action lawsuits are widely available in the United States and create incentives to sue. A single individual with a small claim is not a great risk, but when many individuals with small claims unite and pursue their claims as a group, the risk for business is huge. In Canada, as described earlier, class actions are becoming more accessible and widely used so the distinction between the two systems on this basis may be decreasing.

- *Contingency Fees:* The use of contingency fees is more widespread in the United States. A **contingency fee** is an arrangement between the lawyer and the client where the lawyer receives a percentage of the judgment if the case is won and receives nothing (or disbursements only) if the case is lost. Such arrangements increase risk for business because they improve accessibility to the legal system for claimants who might otherwise lack the resources to sue.

- *Discovery:* In the United States, discovery rules are far-reaching. This results in more time-consuming and expensive litigation. U.S. litigants have broad powers to obtain oral and documentary evidence, whereas in Canada oral discovery can be restricted in the number of persons who can be examined and time limits for examination.

Critical Analysis: How can Canadian businesses manage the litigation risks of doing business in the United States?

Sources: Berkley Sells, "Litigation: Civil Litigation in Canada and in the United States—Part 1" *Inside Counsel* (14 April 2011) online: *Inside Counsel* <http://www.insidecounsel.com/2011/04/14/litigation-civil-litigation-in-canada-and-the-united-states->; Berkley Sells, "Litigation: Some Key Differences between Civil Litigation in Canada and the United States—Part 2" *Inside Counsel* (28 April 2011) online: *Inside Counsel* <http://www.insidecounsel.com/2011/04/28/litigation-some-key-differences-between-civil-litigation-in-canada-and-the-united-states-part-2->; Berkley Sells, "Litigation: Some Key Differences between Civil Litigation in Canada and the United States—Part 3" *Inside Counsel* (12 May 2011) online: *Inside Counsel* <http://www.insidecounsel.com/2011/05/12/litigation-some-key-differences-between-civil-liti>; Richard S Sanders, "Litigation is a risk of doing business in the United States" *The Lawyers Weekly* (6 February 2004) 15.

Contingency fee

A fee based on a percentage of the judgment awarded, and paid by the client to the lawyer only if the action is successful.

The methods of dispute resolution are summarized in Figure 4.2.

---

37 For additional discussion of punitive damages awards in the United States, see Chapter 10.

38 The cap in 2015 was approximately $360 000 and is indexed to inflation.

FIGURE 4.2 Forms of Dispute Resolution

	Negotiation	Mediation	Arbitration	Litigation
Who is involved	Parties and/or their representatives	Parties and a mediator	Parties, their lawyers (usually), and arbitrator(s)	Parties, lawyers, a judge and, occasionally, a jury
When it is used	By consent or contract	By consent or contract or by statute	By consent or contract or by statute	By one party suing the other
How it works	Parties decide	Mediator assists the parties	Arbitrator makes decision after submissions	Judge makes decision after trial
When it ends	If successful, settlement	If successful, settlement	Binding decision (usually)	Judgment by the court
Advantages	Quick, cheap, controllable, private, helps preserve relationships, may produce final decision	Quick, cheaper than arbitration and litigation, controllable, private, helps preserve relationships, may produce final decision	Can be quicker and less costly than litigation, can be private, choice of process and arbitrator, decision may be binding	No agreement to proceed required, sets precedent, final decision
Disadvantages	Requires agreement to proceed, no precedent, may fail	May require agreement to proceed, no precedent, may fail	May require agreement, can be as slow and expensive as litigation, imposed decision, no precedent, may destroy relationships	Slow, expensive, stressful, imposed decision, no choice over process and decision maker, public, usually destroys relationships

BUSINESS LAW IN PRACTICE REVISITED

1. How well does Northland's risk management plan deal with these incidents and how could its performance have improved?

Marie prepared a comprehensive risk management plan for Northland which is found in Chapter 3 at Figure 3.3. The plan was largely successful because it anticipated numerous events that might give rise to legal consequences and offered solutions on how and when to reduce, transfer, or accept the risks associated with those events. Four risks materialized and the effectiveness of the plan in relation to these incidents is recounted in more detail in this chapter. To recap:

- the delinquent customer situation was anticipated, but not avoided. Northland should have properly investigated the customer's credit worthiness in advance, particularly given the size of the account. Northland requires an improved system for deciding when to grant credit to customers and must ensure that the new system is properly deployed by its staff going forward.

- the hacking attempt was particularly well anticipated by the risk management plan. Firewalls helped prevent data loss and even though the attack caused a temporary shutdown of Northland's network, there was no lasting damage. Northland also had obtained insurance to cover off legal risks associated with such attacks, but the insurance proved to be underinclusive. Northland should investigate purchasing a more comprehensive policy to cover additional costs associated with breaches of its computer system. Its insurance program requires enhancement.

- the risk management plan anticipated the pollution incident, but did not adequately prevent its occurrence. Northland must improve procedures for replacing scrubbers to prevent a future incident, a matter its insurance company will certainly require in any event. Fortunately, the dispute with the farmer whose land was impacted by the pollution was nicely resolved. The farmer was compensated to his relative satisfaction and he signed a confidentiality agreement. Insurance covered the cost of the settlement.

- the equipment breakdown proved to be the most intractable problem for Northland and highlighted a problem with the implementation of the risk management plan. Even though the plan called for maintenance records on all equipment, the records were incomplete. As a result, Northland was unsuccessful in recovering all of its losses. Setting aside this deficiency, it is hard to see how the dispute with the insurer over the interpretation of the insurance policy could have been avoided. Northland worked hard to resolve the dispute through negotiation and mediation, but a compromise was unattainable. Some disputes—albeit the tiny minority—can only be resolved by litigation.

2. How well does Northland deploy the various methods of dispute resolution in relation to the legal risks that materialized?

Northland accessed a variety of dispute resolution methods as it sought to manage the legal risks that materialized. With the exception of the hacking attempt, each one of the incidents required negotiation. Negotiation alone solved the problem with the disgruntled farmer, likely propelled by Northland's open approach and willingness to offer an apology. Also through negotiation, Northland learned that the delinquent customer could not pay its bill and has simply decided to write the debt off. This outcome, though perhaps disappointing, is based on facts surrounding the customer's financial status and is therefore realistic. There is no sense spending money needlessly by launching what would almost certainly be a pointless lawsuit. In both of these instances, therefore, ADR proved highly effective for Northland.

Northland's dispute with its insurer over coverage related to the equipment breakdown went through the phases of negotiation and mediation. Because the parties became unwilling to compromise, these phases failed to produce a resolution. Arbitration was not required by the contract between Northland and its insurer, but the parties considered the possibility in any event. This option was ultimately rejected, however, when the insurer decided it wanted a judge's interpretation concerning a clause in the insurance policy. Only litigation could produce the result the insurer wanted. As noted, not every dispute can be effectively resolved through ADR.

All in, Marie's risk management plan and Northland's willingness to access ADR proved to be a highly successful combination. The risk management plan reduced a great many legal risks or prevented them from occurring, but when they did occur, Northland's response was largely effective. As a result, only one of the disputes discussed in this chapter will be resolved through the slow, costly, and uncertain process of litigation.

CHAPTER SUMMARY

This chapter has explored a range of disputes in which a business such as Northland might become involved. A risk management plan that is well developed and carefully implemented can minimize the number of disputes that arise and provide guidance for dealing with those that do. Legal disputes should be approached with a view to achieving an acceptable resolution, rather than winning at all costs.

There are a wide variety of techniques for resolving disputes that avoid litigation altogether or enable the parties to minimize damage to the businesses and their commercial relationships. The parties can negotiate their own resolution, or, if that is not possible, they can involve another person as a mediator to assist them or as an arbitrator to make a decision for them. If the parties resort to litigation, they are involving themselves in a lengthy, costly, public, and risky process with strict procedural rules. The process has four stages—pleadings, discovery, trial, and decision. The winner must collect the amount awarded by the court. That amount usually does not include full recovery of the legal expenses incurred to win the lawsuit.

CHAPTER STUDY

Key Terms and Concepts

alternative dispute resolution (ADR) (p. 70)

appeal (p. 86)

appellant (p. 87)

arbitrator (p. 75)

binding (p. 77)

burden of proof (p. 84)

claim (p. 81)

class action (p. 79)

contingency fee (p. 88)

costs (p. 84)

counterclaim (p. 82)

decision (p. 84)

defence (p. 82)

defendant (p. 78)

discovery (p. 82)

evidence (p. 84)

judgment debtor (p. 86)

limitation period (p. 78)

mediator (p. 74)

negotiation (p. 70)

plaintiff (p. 78)

pleadings (p. 81)

release (p. 72)

respondent (p. 87)

trial (p. 83)

Questions for Review

1. What are some business law disputes that could arise from the operation of a fast-food restaurant?

2. What is the goal of negotiation in resolving legal problems?

3. What happens when negotiations fail?

4. What is the process for attempting to resolve disputes informally?

5. What issues should a business consider before deciding to proceed with a legal dispute rather than abandon it?

6. What is mediation? What are the advantages of mediation as a method of resolving a dispute?

7. What are the differences between mediation and arbitration?

8. Why is arbitration particularly attractive in international disputes?

9. What are the advantages of arbitration in comparison to litigation?

10. What are the major steps in the litigation process?

11. What happens during the "discovery" stage of litigation?

12. Why is settlement out of court more common than and preferable to going to trial?

13. How does a class action differ from a normal lawsuit?

14. What is a limitation period?

15. To what extent does the winner of a lawsuit recover the expenses of the litigation?

16. How does the winner of a lawsuit enforce the judgment?

17. What factors should be considered before appealing a court decision?

18. What is a contingency fee?

Questions for Critical Thinking

1. Dr. Julie Macfarlane, a professor in the Faculty of Law at the University of Windsor and author of *The New Lawyer: How Settlement Is Transforming the Practice of Law*, notes that figures out of the United States indicate that 98.2 percent of civil matters are settled before court. The rate is almost as high in Ontario at approximately 95 to 96 percent.[39] Why is settling out of court replacing going to court? Is this a good trend?

2. The Canadian system of litigation partially compensates the winning party for its legal expenses through an award of "costs," to be paid by the loser in addition to any damages awarded by the court. In the United States, it is usual for the parties to bear their own costs. Which rule is more fair? Does the awarding of costs encourage or discourage litigation?

3. Class actions are a popular way for a large number of small consumer claims that might otherwise have been ignored to be brought against a corporation. For example, ticket purchasers brought a class action against Ticketmaster alleging that it conspired to have Canadians pay inflated prices for tickets by directing them away from its lower-priced website to its premium-priced website. Ticketmaster settled and concert goers received $36 per ticket for a projected payout of $5 million. Lawyers received 25 percent of each payout for a projected $1.26 million.[40] Who benefits from a successful class action lawsuit? Who loses from a successful class action lawsuit?

4. Most jurisdictions in Canada now have an element of mandatory ADR in their systems of litigation. For example, in British Columbia all civil litigation with a few exceptions is subject to mandatory mediation. What is the purpose of requiring ADR prior to litigation? Is it logical to make ADR mandatory rather than consensual? Are weaker litigants at the mercy of stronger parties?

5. Alternative dispute resolution has many positive features. It can be faster and cheaper than litigation. And unlike litigation, the process can be confidential and the parties can control the process, the timing, and the selection of the facilitator. Are there any downsides to the avoidance of litigation in favour of ADR in the resolution of disputes? When is litigation the most appropriate method of resolving a dispute?

6. Should a mediation clause be included in all commercial contracts? Why or why not?

Situations for Discussion

1. General Mills, one of North America's largest food companies, updated the legal terms on its website. The new terms provided that any dispute related to the purchase or use of any General Mills product or service would be resolved through binding arbitration. If consumers "liked" General Mills's social media pages, downloaded coupons from its website, or entered any company-sponsored contests, they were agreeing to have any dispute with General Mills referred to arbitration and could not sue or join a class action. After a public outcry on social media, the company revised its position and sent an email stating that it was reverting to the old terms, which made no mention of binding arbitration.[41] Why do you think the public was upset by a clause requiring disputes to be settled by binding arbitration? Would Canadian courts enforce General Mills' rescinded legal terms?

2. Cameron and Tyler Winklevoss entered into a settlement with Facebook over their

---

39. Donalee Moulton, "Vanishing trials: Out-of-court settlements on the rise" *The Lawyers Weekly* (17 October 2008) 22.

40. Adrian Humphreys, "Lawyers get best seats in Ticketmaster class-action as court approves $5M payout" *National Post* (10 July 2012) online: National Post <http://news.nationalpost.com/2012/07/10/lawyers-get-best-seats-in-ticketmaster-class-action-2-4m-payout-for-legal-team/>.

41. Jeff Gray, "General Mills abandons controversial legal policy to strip consumers of rights" *The Globe and Mail* (19 April 2014) online: Globe and Mail <http://www.theglobeandmail.com/report-on-business/industry-news/the-law-page/general-mills-abandons-controversial-legal-policy-to-strip-consumers-of-rights/article18070962/>.

allegations against Mark Zuckerberg, the founder of Facebook. They alleged that they had hired Zuckerberg, their classmate at Harvard University, to work on their social networking site, ConnectU, but instead, he stole their idea and launched his own site. The dispute was settled for $20 million cash and $45 million in Facebook shares. Three years later, the Winklevoss twins attempted to have the settlement overturned on the basis that they had been misled during negotiations about the value of the shares they would receive as part of the settlement. They lost their attempt at both the U.S. Circuit Court and the U.S. Court of Appeals. The result illustrates that courts are generally very reluctant to reopen settlements.[42] Why are courts reluctant to reopen settlements? What steps can be taken to reduce the possibility of litigation after a settlement?

3. York University launched a lawsuit against its former assistant vice-president, Michael Markicevic, accusing him of masterminding a $1.2 million fraud. The case was a year and a half old and not close to trial when Ontario Superior Court Justice D.M. Brown ruled on a preliminary matter and speculated that the final legal bills for the defendants might be more than $800 000. He wrote: " If we have reached the point where $800 000 cannot buy you a defence to a $1.2 million fraud claim, then we may as well throw up our collective hands and concede that our public courts have failed and are now open to the rich."[13] What factors contribute to the high cost of justice? How could access to justice be improved?

4. The Loewen Group, based in Burnaby, B.C., was one of the largest owners of funeral homes in North America. Throughout the 1980s and 1990s, the company pursued a strategy of growth through the aggressive acquisition of U.S. funeral homes. In 1990, Loewen purchased Wright & Ferguson, the largest funeral operation in Jackson, Mississippi. Shortly after

the purchase, a dispute arose concerning an earlier contract involving Gulf Insurance. Gulf alleged that Loewen had breached this earlier contract and sued Loewen for damages of $107 million. In 1995, a Jackson jury awarded the plaintiff $100 million in compensation and $400 million in punitive damages. The award equalled almost half the value of Loewen's assets and almost 13 times its 1994 profit of $38.5 million. Loewen vowed to appeal. However, under Mississippi law, Loewen was required to post a bond of 125 percent of the award—$625 million—while appeals were pending. Rather than face several years of uncertainty, the company agreed to a settlement worth about $175 million.[44] Despite the settlement, the litigation seriously undermined Loewen's equity value and credit rating. The company eventually went bankrupt. Shareholders who lost their equity filed claims under the North American Free Trade Agreement (NAFTA), but were unsuccessful. What does this case illustrate about the risks of doing business internationally and the uncertainties of litigation? How could Loewen have tried to avoid these uncertainties?

5. A woman from British Columbia, Saliha Alnoor, recently sued Colgate-Palmolive, alleging that she was injured by a defective toothbrush. She stated that the toothbrush snapped as she was brushing her teeth, which injured her gums and caused them to bleed profusely. Alnoor claimed that she had endured permanent injury and sought damages, including $94 000 in anticipated treatments. Colgate denied any wrongdoing. Soon after the trial began, the judge made several rulings against Alnoor, who was self-represented. Alnoor later agreed to drop her claim in response to Colgate's offer to waive legal costs against her (estimated at about $30 000) if she did so. According to the National Post, Alnoor's brother stated as follows: "We spent $21 000 on lawyers and experts, but we have no regrets. Now we know how justice works.

42 Guynn, "Twins gamble $160M on Facebook suit" *Edmonton Journal* (1 March 2011) D1; Nina Mandell, "Winklevoss twins, who claim Mark Zuckerberg stole their idea, lose appeal in federal court" *The Daily News* (11 April 2011) online: NY Daily News.com <http://articles .nydailynews.com/2011-04-11/news/29426547_1_winklevoss-twins -mark-zuckerberg-cameron-and-tyler-winklevoss>.

43 James Bradshaw, "Ontario courts 'only open to the rich'" *The Globe and Mail* (3 July 2013) A4.

44 Based, in part, on Adam Liptak, "Review of US Rulings by NAFTA Tribunals Stir Worries" *The New York Times* (18 April 2004) online: *The New York Times* <http://www.nytimes.com/2004/04/18/politics/ 18COUR.html?ex=1397620800&en=13814425a12bc791&ei=5007 &partner=USERLAND>.

CHAPTER 4: DISPUTE RESOLUTION

Now we are much wiser."[45] Do you agree with Colgate's approach to Alnoor's litigation? What are the risks Colgate faced from the litigation? What are Alnoor's risks?

6. In 1959, the Canadian-born Lord Beaverbrook, a newspaper baron and member of Sir Winston Churchill's World War II war cabinet, established an art gallery in Fredericton, New Brunswick. The Beaverbrook Art Gallery houses an impressive collection of over 3 000 pieces of Canadian and British art as well as unique samples of works from international artists.

   In 2004, two charitable foundations founded by Lord Beaverbrook claimed ownership of over 200 paintings and sculptures, arguing that the paintings had not been gifts to the gallery but were merely on loan. The United Kingdom Beaverbrook Foundation (Foundation "A") claimed ownership of 133 paintings valued at more than $200 million. The Canada Beaverbrook Foundation (Foundation "B") claimed ownership of another 83 pieces of art. Both foundations launched lawsuits against the gallery and its board of directors in Great Britain.

   In 2006, the gallery and Foundation A agreed to arbitration. Lawsuits by Foundation B were set aside pending the outcome of the arbitration with Foundation A. In 2007, after public hearings, the arbitrator ruled that 85 works including the core of the collection belonged to the gallery and the other 48 belonged to Foundation A. Cory also ordered Foundation A to pay $2.4 million in compensation for several paintings it removed from the gallery over the years and costs of $4.8 million. Foundation A appealed, as under the terms of the arbitration a disputant could appeal if it felt that the arbitrator's ruling contained legal errors or disregarded important rules of evidence.[46]

   In 2009, an appeal panel upheld the ruling in its entirety. In 2010, Foundation A filed an application in the Court of Queen's Bench of New Brunswick to appeal the panel's results on a point of law. Before a hearing on the application was held, the parties reached a confidential settlement. Each side is estimated to have spent more than $10 million in legal fees.[47] The dispute between Foundation B and the gallery settled in 2014, with the foundation receiving 43 and the gallery receiving 35 of the 78 works in dispute.[48] Why do you think Foundation A (the UK Foundation) and the gallery chose arbitration for their dispute? What were the advantages of arbitration for the parties? How well did the dispute resolution methods work for the gallery and the foundations?

7. In 2007, the Flynns hired Applewood Construction to build them an environmentally friendly home. The house was erected on a concrete slab. The Flynns moved into their new home and discovered within the first year that the concrete slab had cracked, causing considerable damage to the structure. The Flynns successfully sued Applewood for damages, but before they could collect, Applewood went out of business. In 2015, the Flynns sued Superior Foundations, the company hired by Applewood to pour the concrete slab.[49] What defence might Superior have against the Flynns' claim?

8. In 2008, several hundred people became ill and a number of them died as the result of an outbreak of listeria bacteria. The illnesses were traced to the consumption of deli meats that were produced from a single processing plant operated by MegaMeats Inc. Those most affected by the bacteria were the elderly, the very young, and those who were already ill. Is this an appropriate situation for a class action lawsuit? What do the victims have in common? How are their claims different? What process must be followed? How should MegaMeats deal with these claims?

45   Brian Hutchinson, "BC woman walks away smiling from foolish 'killer toothbrush' lawsuit" *National Post* (5 January 2012) online: National Post <http://news.nationalpost.com/full-comment/brian-hutchinson-b-c-woman-walks-away-smiling-from-foolish-killer-toothbrush-lawsuit>.

46   James Adams, "Beaverbrook foes go at it again in $100-million battle" *The Globe and Mail* (20 September 2008) R4.

47   Marty Klinberg, "Lengthy Beaverbrook art dispute has drawn to a close" *New Brunswick Telegraph-Journal* (15 September 2010) online: New Brunswick Telegraph-Journal <http://www.globalnews.ca/lengthy+beaverbrook+art+dispute+has+drawn+to+a+close/83952/story.html>.

48   James Adams, "Beaverbrook art groups settle feud" *The Globe and Mail* (1 March 2014) A3.

49   Based, in part, on *Flynn v Superior Foundations Ltd*, 2008 NSSC 296, 269 NSR (2d) 279.

PART TWO

CONTRACTS

Business relies on contract law—more than any other area of law—to facilitate commerce. Contract law provides a structure through which individuals and organizations are able to create legally binding, commercial commitments. Essentially, parties must keep their contractual promises or pay damages to the other side for breach.

A working knowledge of contract law is essential to anyone involved in business. This knowledge is crucial because the law advances commercial activities and can be used to build productive and cooperative business relationships. In fact, contract law forms the basis of many commercial relationships, including employment, credit, property, and insurance dealings, as well as the sale of goods and services.

5

AN INTRODUCTION TO CONTRACTS

OBJECTIVES

After studying this chapter, you should have an understanding of

- the general concept of a contract
- the business context of contract formation
- the business context of contractual performance

iStockphoto/Thinkstock

BUSINESS LAW IN PRACTICE

Amritha Singh is a middle manager with Coasters Plus Ltd. (Coasters), a company that designs and manufactures roller coasters for amusement parks across North America. She has been appointed one of the project managers for the design and delivery of a special roller coaster for the Ultimate Park Ltd., an American customer. A major component of the project is the steel tracking, and one possible source is Trackers Canada Ltd. (Trackers). Amritha's supervisor has asked her to negotiate the necessary contract. This task causes Amritha some concern, since she has never been solely responsible for contractual negotiations before. She does know, however, that Coasters needs a reliable supplier that can deliver high-quality tracking for under $2 million, and in good time for installation at the Ultimate Park site.

1. How should Amritha approach her task of securing the necessary tracking?

2. How can the law facilitate Amritha's acquisition task?

3. What rules apply to a commercial relationship between a manufacturer (such as Coasters) and a supplier (such as Trackers), and how are disputes resolved?

4. What are the legal consequences to Coasters of assigning the negotiation task to Amritha?

5. What are the non-legal factors contributing to the proposed legal agreement?

David Toase/Photodisc

Introduction to Contract Law

This chapter offers a general introduction to contract law and its business context. It also helps prepare the ground for topics that are covered over the course of Chapter 6 (Forming Contractual Relationships), Chapter 7 (The Terms of a Contract), Chapter 8 (Non-Enforcement of Contracts) and Chapter 9 (Termination and Enforcement of Contracts).

Amritha needs to extract a firm commitment from Trackers to ensure that Coasters receives the necessary tracking in a timely fashion at the agreed-upon price (see Figure 5.1). The flip side of her task is to ensure that—should Trackers renege—Coasters can sue Trackers to recover any related financial loss. Simply put, Amritha needs to negotiate and secure a contract with Trackers on behalf of her company.

A **contract** is a deliberate and complete agreement between two or more competent persons, not necessarily in writing, supported by mutual consideration, to do some act voluntarily. By definition, a contract is enforceable in a court of law.

What follows is a brief synopsis of these elements, which are analyzed more comprehensively in subsequent chapters.

- **An agreement.** An agreement is composed of an offer to enter into a contract and an acceptance of that offer; this is a matter explored in Chapter 6. The promises contained in the agreement are known as terms; these are discussed in Chapter 7. The informing idea behind a contract is that there has been a "meeting of the minds"—that the parties have agreed on what their essential obligations are to each other.

- **Complete.** The agreement must be complete, that is, certain. Certainty is explored in Chapter 6.

- **Deliberate.** The agreement must be deliberate, that is, both parties must want to enter into a contractual relationship. This matter—formally known as an intention to create legal relations—is discussed in Chapter 6.

- **Voluntary.** The agreement must be freely chosen and not involve coercion or other forms of serious unfairness; this is explored in Chapter 8.

- **Between two or more competent persons.** Those who enter into a contract are known as parties to the contract. There must be at least two parties to any contract, who must have legal capacity—a matter discussed in Chapter 8. As a general rule, only parties to a contract can sue and be sued on it; this matter is discussed in Chapter 9.

Contract

An agreement between two parties that is enforceable in a court of law.

FIGURE 5.1 A Contract Contains Binding Promises

Through a contract:

Trackers
makes binding promises concerning price, quantity, and delivery of tracking to
➡ **Coasters**

Coasters
makes a binding promise to pay the purchase price to
➡ **Trackers**

- **Supported by mutual consideration.** A contract involves a bargain or exchange between the parties. This means that each party must give something of value in exchange for receiving something of value from the other party. Expressed in legal terminology, a contract must be supported by mutual consideration; this is discussed in Chapter 6.
- **Not necessarily in writing.** As a general rule, even oral contracts are enforceable, though it is preferable for negotiators to get the contract in writing. That said, in most Canadian jurisdictions there are certain kinds of contracts—such as those involving an interest in land—that must be in writing in order to be enforceable. These exceptions are discussed in Chapter 8.

The genius of contract law is that, once a contract is created, it permits both parties to rely on the terms they have negotiated and plan their business affairs accordingly. If a dispute arises between the two parties, there are various options for dispute resolution, as outlined in Chapter 4. This includes taking the matter to court and suing for losses sustained. In short, contract law ensures that each party gets what it bargained for—namely, performance of the promises made to it or monetary compensation in its place. Chapter 9 discusses the termination and enforcement of contracts.

For the most part, the rules governing contracts are based on common law. The common law, as discussed in Chapter 2, refers to judge-made laws, as opposed to laws made by elected governments. This means that a judge resolving a contractual conflict is usually relying not on statute law to guide deliberations, but rather on what other judges have said in past cases that resemble the current case. As noted in Part One, these past cases are known as precedents because they contain a legal principle found in a past situation similar to the one being litigated. The judge will hear evidence from the two parties in support of their respective positions and then determine which common law rules of contract are applicable to the situation and what the outcome should be. Depending on the nature of the contract, legislation such as the *Sale of Goods Act* may also be relevant.

Contracts are the legal cornerstone of any commercial operation. Through a contract, the business enterprise can sell a product or service, hire employees, rent office space, borrow money, purchase supplies, and enter into any other kind of binding agreement it chooses. In this way, contract law is facilitative: it allows participants to create their own rights and duties within a framework of rules that a judge will later enforce, if called upon to do so.

Contracts come in a wide variety. A contract for the purchase and sale of a box of pens from the corner store, for example, is casually conducted and instantly completed. The only document that will be produced is the sales receipt. Other contracts, such as for the purchase and sale of high-quality tracking for a commercial project, will require lengthy negotiations, considerable documentation, and time to perform. Some contracts are one-shot deals, in that the parties are unlikely to do business with each other again. Other contracts are part of a long-standing and valued commercial relationship, as one might find between supplier and retailer. Regardless of the context, however, every contract is subject to the same set of mandatory legal rules. This means that contract law principles will be applied by a judge to resolve a contractual dispute between the parties, whether the parties were aware of those principles or not.

Amritha's attention is currently focused on one transaction: her company's acquisition of tracking from a suitable supplier. Her goal should be to enter into a contract with a supplier like Trackers, because Coasters requires legally enforceable assurances that its supplier will fulfill its commitments. The alternative to a contract—in the form of a casual understanding—makes little business sense, even if Trackers is highly reputable and trustworthy, because cooperation and goodwill between parties can suddenly evaporate when an unforeseen conflict or problem arises. Personnel can change, memories may become selective and self-serving, and genuine differences of opinion may arise. At this point, Amritha's company needs the protection of a well-constructed contract—including the right to commence a lawsuit based upon it—not the vague assurances she may have received from Trackers personnel sometime in the past.

This is not to say that informal business arrangements never succeed, but only that there is no remedy in contract law should one of the parties fail to keep its word. This is a risk that a business should ordinarily not be prepared to run.

CASE

Tal v Ontario Lottery Corporation/ Lotto 6/49 OLG, 2011 ONSC 644

BUSINESS CONTEXT: Lottery sales are big business in Canada, with over $10 billion in sales over 2014 alone.[1] This volume makes it particularly essential that clear rules governing the payout process are in place and contractually enforceable. Disappointed lottery ticket purchasers have sued lottery agencies, alleging breach of these rules, though not always with success, as this case illustrates.

FACTUAL BACKGROUND: The plaintiff, David Tal, is a 74-year-old retired businessman. He held a winning 4/6 ticket in the October 1, 2008, draw of the Lotto 6/49 game in that he matched four out of the six numbers selected. The applicable prize pool for 4/6 winners was over $1.3 million but because 20 000 other players held a winning ticket, the amount was divided equally among them all, with a per-person payout of $66.90.

Mr. Tal, however, read the rules differently and took the position that he was entitled to the full amount of the prize pool. He sued for $3 182 667.81 in damages—the amount he claims the pool to be—plus $35.3 million in punitive damages. (Note: The law governing

punitive damages in contract is discussed in detail in Chapter 9.)

THE LEGAL QUESTION: What are the contractual rules governing the Lotto 6/49 game in this case? Which party has interpreted those rules correctly?

RESOLUTION: The court decided in favour of the lottery organization. It confirmed that the parties were in a contract that was formed as follows: the lottery organization made an offer to the public to play a lottery game governed by written rules that the plaintiff accepted by purchasing the ticket. The written rules therefore were part of the contract and governed this dispute.

The court went on to note that the lottery organization had properly applied those rules:

Pursuant to the Winning Selections Reports prepared by the regional and provincial lottery organizations, there were 20 120 4/6 Winners nation-wide for the October 1 Draw, of whom 8353 were located in Ontario. Pursuant to ss. 6 and 8 of the . . . Game Conditions, each of these 4/6 Winners was entitled to a share of the 4/6 Pool, which was calculated by dividing the dollar amount of the 4/6 Pool ($1 347 143.10) by the total number of 4/6

(Continued)

---

1 Statista, "Sales of provincial lotteries in Canada from 2009-2014 (in billion Canadian dollars)"(undated document), online: Statista <http://www.statista.com/statistics/215284/sales-of-canadian-state-and-provincial-lotteries/>.

CHAPTER 5: AN INTRODUCTION TO CONTRACTS

Winners (20 120). This amounted to a prize of $66.90 per 4/6 Winner (after being rounded down from $66.96 pursuant to s. 8 of the ILC Game Conditions).

The court rejected all the plaintiff's arguments to the contrary. For example, the plaintiff asserted an interpretation of the rules such that *every* 4/6 winner was entitled to the entire pool as opposed to merely sharing in it. This was rejected as contrary to the plain meaning of the rule in question as well as being commercially absurd. As the court stated:

> If all 20 120 of the 4/6 Winners were entitled to a prize of $1 347 143.10, over $26 <u>billion</u> in prizes would have to be paid out to just the 4/6 Winners in that one Draw. This amount is more than 600 times higher than the total national ticket sales of approximately $42 million for the October 1 Draw . . . [T]he regional and provincial lottery organizations would lose billions of dollars in virtually every Lotto 6/49 draw, making this lottery game completely unsustainable.

Steve White

CRITICAL ANALYSIS: Do you think this case could have been settled out of court? Why or why not?

This chapter has thus far introduced the *legal* elements to a contract, but *business* factors also figure prominently in contractual relationships. The next section locates important legal factors in their business context. Without this context, the legal ingredients of a contract cannot be properly understood.

BUSINESS APPLICATION OF THE LAW

CONCERT HALL CANCELS ALLEGED CONTRACT WITH MAXIMUM FIGHTING INC.

The Francis Winspear Centre for Music (Winspear), through its Foundation, is alleged to have entered into a contract to lease its premises to Maximum Fighting Inc. (MFI), a mixed martial arts promoter, for three Maximum Fighting Championship (MFC) events in exchange for a rental fee. According to press accounts, the concert hall then cancelled the arrangement, saying that the booking had been made in error.

Perry Nelson/Sun Media

Ryan Jimmo, pictured above, won the MFC light heavyweight title in 2011 at the River Cree Resort and Casino in Alberta.

By way of explanation, a Winspear spokesperson said that the facility was designed for concerts and was not a "suitable venue" for MFC events, and offered an apology: "It is regrettable that this unfortunate situation has occurred and the Winspear Centre has taken steps to ensure that it never happens again. The Winspear has extended its apology to representatives of MFC for what has transpired."

Mark Pavelich, president of MFC, responded by filing a $500 000 lawsuit against the Foundation responsible for operating the Winspear, alleging breach of contract. The claim seeks compensation for loss of profit, loss of sponsorship funds, out of pocket expenses—such as printing and advertising—as well as for embarrassment and damage to reputation.

Critical Analysis: Is there a contract between the Winspear Foundation and MFI and, if so, what are the terms? Do you think that the Winspear Foundation has a successful defence, namely that the booking itself was a "mistake" and the music hall was not suitable for sporting events? How can these kinds of disputes best be resolved?

Sources: Elizabeth Withey, "No more fight night at Winspear Centre" *Edmonton Journal* (23 January 2010) D1; Tony Blais, "MMA promoter sues over cancelled match" *Edmonton Sun* (9 August 2010), online: *Edmonton Sun* <http://www.edmontonsun.com/news/edmonton/2010/08/09/14972086.html>.

Legal Factors in Their Business Context: Creating the Contract

Communication

Most contractual relationships begin with communication, which may originate in a number of ways—through informal contact between individuals in different businesses who recognize mutual needs, or perhaps through a general inquiry made to a supplier concerning price and availability of materials. Amritha may initiate contact with potential suppliers based on recommendations from others in her company who have purchasing experience, from colleagues in the industry, or from industry organizations. And, of course, Coasters may be approached periodically by tracking suppliers. Regardless of who makes the first move, Amritha will likely communicate with a number of businesses in order to determine who can give her company the most favourable terms.

Communication is not just about discussing possibilities with the other side, however. Communication—in the form of contractual negotiations—is automatically laden with legal meaning. It is therefore important for the businessperson to know when simple business communications crystallize into legal obligations.

ETHICAL CONSIDERATIONS

IS IT ETHICAL TO BLUFF DURING BUSINESS NEGOTIATIONS?

Albert Carr, in a well-known article published in the *Harvard Business Review*, argues that business is a game and therefore is not subject to the same ethical standards that govern one's private life. On this footing, it is perfectly acceptable for a businessperson to bluff during negotiations since it is merely strategic—just as it is in poker—and does not reflect on the morality of the bluffer. According to Carr,

Most executives from time to time are almost compelled, in the interests of their companies or themselves, to practice some form of deception when negotiating with customers, dealers,

CHAPTER 5: AN INTRODUCTION TO CONTRACTS

labor unions, government officials, or even other departments of their companies. By conscious misstatements, concealment of pertinent facts, or exaggeration—in short, by bluffing—they seek to persuade others to agree with them. I think it is fair to say that if the individual executive refuses to bluff from time to time—if he feels obligated to tell the truth, the whole truth, and nothing but the truth—he is ignoring opportunities permitted under the rules and is at heavy disadvantages in his business dealings.

Carr goes on to argue that, like every poker player, a businessperson can be faced with a choice between certain loss and "bluffing within the legal rules of the game." The individual who wants to win and have a successful career "will bluff—and bluff hard."

Carr is not suggesting that businesspeople break the law to seek an advantage in business negotiations. He is, however, claiming that the morality of the businessperson who conceals, exaggerates, or misstates is simply not in question. Short of fraud or actionable misrepresentation, bending the truth a little is simply playing the game of business. For analysis of contractual misrepresentation, fraud, and disclosure duties in contract, see Chapter 8.

Critical Analysis: What are the dangers of Carr's approach to business ethics? What are the possible benefits?

Source: Albert Z Carr, "Is Business Bluffing Ethical?" (1968) 46: 1 *Harvard Business Review* 143.

First and foremost, contract law concerns itself with what the negotiators say and do, not with what they think or imagine. For example, if Amritha makes what looks like an offer to purchase tracking, the other side is entitled to accept that offer whether it was intended as one or not. This is because contract law is governed by the **objective standard test**. This test asks whether a reasonable person, observing the communication that has occurred between the negotiators, would conclude that an offer and acceptance had occurred. Assuming that all the other ingredients of a contract are in place, the parties are completely bound.

Bargaining Power

The kind of contract a businessperson ends up creating is very much influenced by her bargaining power. The business reality is that negotiating parties rarely have **equal bargaining power**. It is almost invariably the case that one side will have more experience, knowledge, market leverage, or other advantages. The greater one's bargaining power, of course, the more favourable terms one will be able to secure.

The law, however, does not recognize or attach legal significance to this business reality. On the contrary, contract law is constructed on the basic assumption

Objective standard test

A test based on how a "reasonable person" would view the matter.

Equal bargaining power

The legal assumption that parties to a contract are able to look out for their own interests.

that those who negotiate and enter into contracts have equal bargaining power, meaning that they are capable of looking out for themselves and will work to maximize their own self-interest. As a result, courts are normally not entitled to assess the fairness or reasonableness of the contractual terms the business parties have chosen. Courts will generally assume that the parties had their eyes open, considered all the relevant factors, evaluated the risks, and were prepared to accept both the costs and benefits of the contract.

The law applies the principle of equality of bargaining power even though, in almost every situation, one party will have some distinct advantage over the other. The rationale is that parties should be able to rely on contractual commitments. Though one party may have agreed to a price she now considers too high or, in fact, may have made a bad deal, none of this is justification for securing the court's assistance and intervention. People are simply expected to take care of themselves.

Occasionally, however, circumstances favour one party over the other to such an extent that the court will come to the assistance of the weaker party and set the contract aside. Such judicial assistance is very much the exception, not the rule, as discussed in Chapter 8.

The fact that Amritha may have less bargaining power than the tracking supplier she contracts with does not generally affect the enforceability of their concluded contract. On the contrary, Amritha must be careful to protect her company's position and not enter into a bad bargain. Coasters is unlikely to succeed in having any contract set aside because Amritha was an inexperienced negotiator or because the supplier was a relatively bigger, more powerful company.

Business Context: Performing or Enforcing the Contract

Business Relationships

Businesspeople regularly breach contracts. For example, a purchaser may fail to pay invoices on a timely basis; a supplier may deliver the wrong product, or the wrong amount of product, or a defective product. All these amount to breaches of contract. Whether the other side sues for breach of contract, however, is as much a business decision as it is a legal one.

Contract law is narrow in scope: its emphasis is often on a specific transaction, such as a single sale, and is not traditionally concerned with longer-term business relationships. Because contract law does not focus on the longer-term relationship, one may be misled into thinking that when faced with a legal wrong, the best response is a lawsuit. When the business context is considered, however, this approach reveals itself to be counterproductive in many circumstances. For example, if Coasters' supplier is late in delivering its tracking, the supplier is in breach of contract, and Coasters will be entitled to compensation for any resulting loss, such as that caused by late completion of the project for the Ultimate Park. However, if Coasters insists on that compensation, the relationship with that supplier may be irreparably harmed. Absorbing the loss in this instance—or splitting the difference—may be a small price to pay in the long term, particularly if the supplier is otherwise reliable and Coasters is not interested in investing time and money in finding a replacement. Put another way, insisting on one's strict legal rights may not be the best business option.

The expense and uncertainty of litigation are also reasons to avoid a full-blown legal conflict.

GETTING IT IN WRITING

Even when businesses have worked together in the past and built up mutual trust, a written contract between them helps to avoid misunderstandings, legal conflicts, associated litigation expenses, and the destruction of business relationships.

This is the lesson from *1004964 Ontario Inc v Aviya Technologies Inc*, 2013 ONSC 51, where the plaintiff contracted with the defendant without ever putting a written contract in place. In short, because the parties had an established and positive ongoing business relationship, they did not think it was important to document their mutual obligations. When a conflict over the scope of work arose, the parties ultimately ended up in court. The court's exasperation with the conflict is clear in the following statement: "It is nearly impossible . . . to repeat each of the factual disputes between the parties. They agree on very little. In fact, this case illustrates the need for a written agreement to be in place as opposed to relying upon an oral agreement . . ." at para 21. In relation to one dispute, the court ruled that a key term which the defendant said was part of the agreement—the installation of a 'real time' computer—was *not* in fact part of the original scope of work and had to be paid for as an extra. Commenting on the case in the *Lawyers Weekly*, James Kosa accurately observes that business-people should get their contracts in writing and thereby "treat the contracting process as a business process that can save money and mitigate real risk. The . . . *[Aviya Technologies]* case does not turn on abstract legal theories—it was entirely about getting the business basics right."

Critical Analysis: Why is an oral agreement sometimes worse than having no agreement at all?

Economic Reality

Though contract law exists to create legally binding commitments, it is not always the best economic decision for a party to keep that commitment. The law has some built-in flexibility, since it requires contractual obligations to be performed or compensation to be paid for non-performance. Accordingly, there may be situations where the cost of compensation is a perfectly acceptable price to pay for release from obligations. For example, a business whose production is committed to a one-year contract may be quite willing to pay what is necessary to be relieved of the one-year obligation if a more profitable, long-term deal becomes available for the same production. This idea is explained further in the Business Application of the Law box below.

ECONOMIC BREACH

An economic breach occurs when one party calculates that it is more financially rewarding to breach the contract in question than to perform it. For instance, suppose hypothetically that Trackers signs a contract to deliver tracking to Coasters for $2 million in two equal installments. After Trackers has delivered the first installment, another business contacts Trackers and explains that, owing to an emergency, it desperately needs tracking to complete a major project. This new business offers Trackers $2 million to supply the same amount of tracking still owed to Coasters—double the price that Trackers would receive from Coasters. Trackers has several options in response to this new request:

- *Option 1:* Complete delivery to Coasters as agreed and decline the new business request.
- *Option 2:* Try to persuade Coasters to accept late delivery of the remainder of its order and offer a price break as an incentive.
- *Option 3:* Abandon the balance of Coasters' contract and fill the new business order.

Each option has its own economic and legal consequences:

- *Option 1* respects the Coasters contract and maintains good relations with Coasters but concedes the extra profit and the potential relationship to be gained from filling the new business order.
- *Option 2* has the potential to satisfy both customers and to gain from the new business (less some portion for Coasters as compensation).
- *Option 3* generates extra profit and a potential long-term relationship with the new business, but it destroys any relationship with Coasters and likely will lead to a claim for compensation from Coasters for its extra tracking cost and potential losses from late completion

of the project. Before accepting the competitor's order, Trackers needs to assure itself that the extra profit generated from the new business will offset the damages it will have to pay to Coasters for breach of contract. Those damages could be quite high, depending on the circumstances, and difficult for Trackers to assess.

There is no question that Trackers has a legal obligation to Coasters, but that does not preclude Trackers from considering other opportunities. If Trackers chooses to breach the contract, there are also non-financial factors to be considered, such as future relations with Coasters, but in legal terms, a business that is prepared to pay damages for breach of contract can always refuse to perform its contractual obligations. Contract law provides compensation for breach, rather than punishment. There are no criminal consequences to breach of contract, and the law has traditionally refrained from making moral judgments about business activities.

Critical Analysis: Is Option 3 the least desirable option when one is considering economic breach? Discuss.

Note: For further discussion of economic breach, see Richard Posner, *Economic Analysis of Law* 9th ed (New York: Wolters Kluwer, 2014).

Reputation Management

A business that makes a practice of breaching contracts due to bad planning or in order to pursue an apparently more lucrative business opportunity will certainly be within its legal rights to breach and pay damages in lieu of performance. Such a business is also likely to acquire a reputation in the industry as an unreliable and undependable company. The long-term viability of a business organization is undoubtedly compromised if customers, suppliers, and employees grow reluctant to deal with it.

Similarly, a business that insists on strict observance of its legal rights may damage its reputation in the marketplace. Although a manufacturer may have a valid defence for having produced a defective product, for example, it may be better in the end to compensate the customer voluntarily rather than fight out a lawsuit. A lawsuit in the circumstances of this example may result in a serious blow to reputation and a public relations disaster.

BUSINESS LAW IN PRACTICE REVISITED

1. How should Amritha approach her task of securing the necessary tracking?

Given the size and expense of the proposed acquisition of tracking, Amritha should make it a priority to enter into a contract with a supplier such as Trackers. Nothing less than a contract will do, since Coasters must be able to exercise its legal right to sue, should Trackers fail to perform as promised.

2. How can the law facilitate Amritha's acquisition task?

Legal knowledge will help Amritha ensure that her negotiations produce an enforceable contract that meets her employer's needs and protects its interests. If Amritha does not know what a contract is, how it is formed, and what its legal significance might be, she is not competent to accomplish the task her employer has set for her.

3. What rules apply to a commercial relationship between a manufacturer (such as Coasters) and a supplier (such as Trackers), and how are disputes resolved?

The rules governing contracts are found in the common law (which develops through the decisions of the courts on a case-by-case basis), and to a lesser extent, in statute law. If a dispute arises between Coasters and Trackers, there are several options available for attempting to resolve the dispute, including mediation and arbitration. Litigation is a last resort and will bring the matter to court. A judge will evaluate the terms of the contract and the conduct of the parties, apply the relevant law, and then come to a determination.

4. What are the legal consequences to Coasters of assigning the negotiation task to Amritha?

Amritha is representing her employer in negotiations and therefore will need to appreciate at what point legal commitments are being made by both sides. Coasters should consider its relative bargaining position with available suppliers and ensure that Amritha has adequate support in her negotiations. Her inexperience and Coasters' size and expertise in contract negotiations will not relieve Coasters of its obligations. The contract itself will be between Coasters and the supplier (as the parties to the contract). They are the only parties able to enforce rights and the only parties that are subject to the obligations in the contract.

5. What are the non-legal factors contributing to the proposed legal agreement?

If Coasters has a good working relationship with companies that can supply the required tracking, those suppliers are the logical candidates for Amritha's project. Their business practices and reliability will be known to Coasters and negotiating a contract with them is likely to be more efficient than with a new supplier. Even a significant price advantage from a new supplier may not justify endangering long-term relationships with others.

Although both parties are obligated by the terms of any contract they make, there may be developments in the market or in the situation relating to the operations of Coasters or Trackers. The request to Trackers from a competitor of Coasters for the supply of tracking is only one example of an event that may cause these companies to reconsider their business and legal relationship. They must weigh all factors, including long-term business dealings and their reputation in the industry, when faced with a decision about whether to honour the contract, seek adjustment, or consider breaching the contract.

CHAPTER SUMMARY

Through an awareness of contract law, business organizations are better able to protect themselves when forming and enforcing contracts. Contracts generally are not required to be in a particular form, but clear agreement on all essential terms is necessary. Those involved in negotiating contracts should be aware of the legal impact of their communication with each other, and they should realize that they are largely responsible for protecting their own interests before agreeing to terms. Contract rules are understood best when assessed in the broader business context, which includes the impact that any given legal decision by a business may have on its reputation with other businesses, with its customers, and in the community at large. A business must also assess its legal options in light of the business relationship at issue, the need to generate a profit, the uncertainty of the marketplace, and the importance of conducting operations with a sense of commercial morality, honesty, and good faith.

CHAPTER STUDY

Key Terms and Concepts

contract (p. 97)

equal bargaining power (p. 102)

objective standard test (p. 102)

Questions for Review

1. What is a contract?

2. What are the elements of a contract, according to the common law?

3. Must all contracts be in writing in order for them to be legally binding?

4. What are the purposes of contract law?

5. Is the matter of whether a contract exists judged according to a subjective standard or an objective one? Explain.

6. Contract law assumes that parties have equal bargaining power. What is the effect of this assumption?

7. How does the presence of a written contract assist in dispute resolution?

8. What is the role of public relations in contracts?

9. What is an economic breach?

10. Why might a business elect not to perform on a contract, and what are some of the consequences that may arise from this decision?

Questions for Critical Thinking

1. What are the dangers of taking a highly legalistic, inflexible approach to contractual disputes?

2. Are there any circumstances in which parties might rightly decide that an oral contract is appropriate? Discuss.

3. Why are the non-legal factors in a contractual relationship so important? Why is it important to place contract law in a business context?

4. Should negotiators follow a course of strict and absolute honesty in contractual negotiations? Why or why not?

5. How important is it to be aware of the law when negotiating a contract? Does it depend on whom you negotiate with? Does it depend on the size and complexity of the contract in question?

6. How could relying on the notion of economic breach prove disastrous to a business?

Situations for Discussion

1. June is a hair stylist who wants to open her own business. Though June has absolutely no experience in the business world, she is determined to succeed. June begins negotiations with a landlord to lease appropriate space for her new salon. The landlord insists that he will only enter into a lease with June if June's parents also agree to co-sign the lease, making them responsible should June default on her rent obligations. June and her parents agree, thinking that such a provision must be a standard requirement of leases. June has since learned that the newest tenant in the building has secured a lease with the landlord but did not have to produce a co-signer. June is certain that the landlord has taken advantage of her naivety. What are the pros and cons of June's inexperience being a legal basis for getting the contract set aside?

2. Frank did some home renovations for a homeowner who has refused to pay Frank's final account, based on some alleged deficiencies in the quality of Frank's work. Frank is thinking of suing in order to recover what he is owed. What factors should he take into account before making his final decision on whether to sue or not?

3. Melissa, an accounting student, interviews for a job with two firms. She really wants to work for Firm X but gets an offer of employment from Firm Y first and accepts it. A week later she receives an offer from Firm X, which she also accepts. She does so because she believes she is economically better off with Firm X and will be able to "cancel" her acceptance with Firm Y.

   a. What is Melissa's legal situation now?

   b. Even assuming that she is better off economically by joining Firm X, what other costs does she face?

   c. Do you think that Firm Y will sue Melissa for breach of contract because she has accepted an employment offer elsewhere?

   d. What could Melissa have done to prevent this situation from occurring in the first place?

   e. What should Melissa do now?

4. Samantha Jones entered into a contract with Jason Black to act as a contractor for a new house she is having built. She was anxious to have the house built as soon as possible and, upon receiving Jason's estimate that the work, including labour and materials, will cost $250 000, she immediately paid a $50 000 deposit. However, since receiving Samantha's deposit, Jason has been contacted by a developer who is willing to pay him a significant amount more to work on a new housing development, provided that he begins immediately. Jason does some calculations based on the current market. He decides that the amount the developer is offering is enough that he can afford to return the deposit, compensate Samantha for breaching the original contract, and still come out ahead on the development contract. He lets Samantha know that she will have to find a new contractor and begins work on the housing development. When he calls Samantha a few months later to offer her compensation, she informs him that she has finally been able to hire a new contractor, but that the estimate for the work has now doubled. In the intervening months, the costs of labour and materials have skyrocketed. The house that originally would have cost $250 000 will now cost her $500 000. Do you think that Jason should be responsible for the additional costs of building Samantha's house, even though they very much exceed his original estimates?

5. Leopold applied to his provincial government for a student loan and was advanced $13 500. The loan agreement obligated the government to advance further funds midway through the school year. Leopold stopped attending classes in September for medical reasons but did not advise his university's Student Services Office of this, contrary to a term in his loan agreement. He also used the funds for living expenses instead of for tuition, contrary to the

loan agreement. The university determined that Leopold was not eligible for the second installment of his loan, and the government therefore refused to advance it. Leopold sued the government for breach of contract and sought damages in the amount of $1.5 million. Do you think Leopold's action should be successful? Why or why not?[2]

6. In 2007, a 22-year-old Grande Prairie man was shocked to receive an $85 000 cell phone bill from Bell Canada. The reason for the high cost was that the customer had been using his cell phone as a modem for almost two months. In one month alone, he downloaded what amounted to 10 high-resolution movies, according to Bell. The customer contended that he did not realize what the cost would be to use the modem system and that Bell should have alerted him as his cell phone bill began to climb precipitously. Bell acknowledged that accessing the modem services is costly but also emphasized that to do so, customers are required to register online and must agree to contractual terms that show the higher fees. It also admitted that its newly implemented data-usage monitoring system failed to pick up the customer's high usage. In the meantime, Bell has offered to reduce the bill to approximately $4000, but the customer is refusing to pay even that sum. Who is right in this dispute and why? What additional information do you require to answer this question?[3]

2 See *Wang v HMTQ (British Columbia)*, 2006 BCCA 566, leave to appeal to SCC refused, [2007] SCCA No 82.

3 See Jorge Barrera, "Grande Prairie cellphone user racks up $85 000 bill in 2 months" *The Edmonton Journal* (13 December 2007) at A1–2.

6

OBJECTIVES

After studying this chapter, you should have an understanding of

- how negotiations lead to a contractual relationship
- how negotiations can be terminated
- the legal ingredients of a contract
- how contracts can be amended or changed

Arthur Tilley/Taxi/Getty Images

FORMING CONTRACTUAL RELATIONSHIPS

BUSINESS LAW IN PRACTICE

Amritha, introduced in Chapter 5, began negotiations with Jason Hughes. Jason is a representative of Trackers, the steel tracking manufacturer willing to supply tracking to Coasters, Amritha's employer. Amritha provided Jason with the plans and specifications for the roller coaster, and they negotiated a number of points, including price, delivery dates, and tracking quality. A short time later, Jason offered to sell Coasters a total of 900 metres of track in accordance with the plans and specifications provided. Jason's offer contained, among other matters, the purchase price ($1.5 million), delivery date, terms of payment, insurance obligations concerning the track, and a series of warranties related to the quality and performance of the tracking to be supplied. There was also a clause, inserted at Amritha's express request, which required Trackers to pay $5000 to Coasters for every day it was late in delivering the tracking.

After reviewing the offer for several days, Amritha contacted Jason and said, "You drive a hard bargain, and there are aspects of your offer that I'm not entirely happy with. However, I accept your offer on behalf of my company. I'm looking forward to doing business with you."

Within a month, Trackers faced a 20 percent increase in manufacturing costs owing to an unexpected shortage in steel. Jason contacted Amritha to explain this development and worried aloud that without an agreement from Coasters to pay 20 percent more for the tracking, Trackers would be unable to make its delivery date. Amritha received instructions from her supervisor to agree to the increased purchase price in order to ensure timely delivery. Amritha communicated this news to Jason, who thanked her profusely for being so cooperative and understanding.

Jason kept his word and the tracking was delivered on time. However, Coasters has now determined that its profit margin on the American deal is lower than expected, and it is looking for ways to cut costs. Amritha is told by her boss to let Jason know that Coasters will not be paying the 20 percent price increase and will remit payment only in the amount set out in the contract. Jason and Trackers are stunned by this development.

1. At what point did the negotiations between Jason and Amritha begin to have legal consequences?

2. In what ways could negotiations have been terminated prior to the formation of the contract?

3. Can Coasters commit itself to the price increase and then change its mind with no adverse consequences?

4. How could Trackers have avoided from the outset this situation related to cost increases?

The Contract

Chapter 5 emphasized that Coasters must enter into a contract with Trackers in order to secure the product that Coasters needs. This chapter accounts for several of the basic elements of a contract, namely that it is:

- an agreement (i.e., composed of offer and acceptance).
- complete (i.e., certain).
- deliberate (i.e., intention to create legal relations is present).
- supported by mutual consideration.

In short, this chapter sets out the legal ingredients that transform a simple agreement—which can be broken without legal consequences—into an enforceable contract.

An Agreement

Before a contract can be in place, the parties must be in agreement, that is, they have reached a consensus as to their rights and obligations. This agreement takes the form of offer and acceptance.

Offer

Definition of Offer

An **offer** is a promise to enter into a contract, on specified terms, as soon as the offer is accepted. This happened in negotiations between Amritha and Jason when Jason committed to provide tracking to Coasters in the concrete terms noted; he named his price, terms of payments, delivery date, and other essential matters. At this point, negotiations have taken an important turn because Amritha is entitled to accept that offer and, upon her doing so, Trackers is obligated to supply its product exactly as Jason proposed, assuming that the other ingredients of a contract are established.

Offer

A promise to perform specified acts on certain terms.

Certainty of Offer

Only a complete offer can form the basis of a contract. This means that all essential terms must be set out or the contract will fail for uncertainty. An offer does not, however, have to meet the standard of perfect clarity and precision in how it is expressed. If the parties intend to have a contract, the courts will endeavour to interpret the alleged offer in as reasonable a fashion as possible and thereby resolve ambiguities.

An offer can achieve the requisite standard of certainty even if it leaves certain matters to be decided in the future. For example, Jason's offer could have made the final price for the tracking contingent on the market price, as determined by a given formula (e.g., cost plus 15 percent). Though the price would not be set out in the offer, a workable way of determining price would have been established, and a contract could be entered into on that basis. A court will not speculate, however, on what the parties would have agreed to had they completed their negotiations.

Invitation to Treat

An offer is different from a communication that merely expresses a wish to do business. In law, the latter form of communication is called an invitation to treat and has no legal consequences. Whether a communication is an offer or an **invitation to treat** depends on the speaker's intention, objectively assessed. Subjective intent is of no legal relevance.

When Amritha provided Jason with plans for the roller coaster, she was not offering to buy tracking from Jason at that point but merely indicating her interest in receiving an offer from him. This was an invitation to treat. Similarly, if Jason had offered to sell tracking to Coasters during negotiations but provided no other detail, he would simply be demonstrating his wish to do business with Coasters. Such expressions of interest have no legal repercussions because they essentially have no content. Vague commitments to buy or sell tracking are invitations to treat and not offers because they fail to specify the terms or scope of the proposed arrangement.

To assist in the sometimes difficult task of classifying whether a communication is an offer or an invitation to treat, the common law has devised a number of rules. A rule of particular significance to business relates to the advertising and display of goods for sale in a store.

Enterprises such as retail outlets prosper by attracting customers to their premises. They do this through advertising their existence, as well as describing the products they sell and prices they charge, especially when those prices have been reduced. For practical reasons, these advertisements are generally not classified as offers.[1] If advertisements were offers, the store owner would be potentially liable for breach of contract if the store ran out of an advertised item that a customer wished to purchase. By classifying the advertisement as an invitation to treat, the law ensures that it is the customer who makes the offer to purchase the advertised goods. The owner is then in a position to simply refuse the offer if the product is no longer in supply. As a result of this refusal, no contract could arise.[2] In this way, the law seeks to facilitate commercial activity by permitting a businessperson to advertise goods or services without ordinarily running the risk of incurring unwanted contractual obligations.

Similarly, the display of a product in the store is not an offer by the store to sell. The display is simply an indication that a product is available and can be purchased. In short, it is an invitation to treat and, by definition, is not capable of being accepted. In this way, the store maintains the option of refusing to complete the transaction at the cash register (see Figure 6.1).[3]

Invitation to treat

An expression of willingness to do business.

---

1 An exception to this general rule occurs when the advertisement is so clear and definite that there is nothing left to negotiate. See *Lefkowitz v Great Minneapolis Surplus Store, Inc*, 86 NW 2d 689 (1957).

2 Store owners may have other legal problems if they run out of an advertised sale product; for example, see the "bait and switch selling" provision of the *Competition Act*, RSC 1985, c C-34, s 74.04(2).

3 Note, however, that human rights legislation across the country prohibits a business owner from refusing to serve a customer on the basis of race, gender, and other discriminatory grounds.

Some contracts are only formed after protracted discussions. Other contracts, like the purchase of photocopying paper from an office supply store, are formed without any negotiations whatsoever. The customer simply takes the purchase to the cashier—thereby offering to purchase the item at its sticker price—and the cashier accepts the offer by receiving payment. Similarly, the **standard form contract** is entered into without any negotiations. Sales and rental businesses frequently require their customers (consumer and commercial) to consent to a standard set of terms that have been developed by the business over years of operation. Such contracts often heavily favour the business that created them and, because they are not usually subject to bargaining, are known colloquially as "take it or leave it" contracts. Examples include renting a car and borrowing money from the bank. Standard form contracts are not inherently objectionable, however, since they help reduce transaction costs and increase business volume, thereby potentially lowering price.[4]

Regardless of whether bargaining precedes the contract or not, the law expects people to take care of themselves. While there is provincial consumer protection legislation that may be of assistance in certain consumer transactions, the better course—particularly in a contract of some importance—is to read and understand the contract before signing it.

When negotiations are complicated, it is important for the parties to know when an offer has been made, since at that moment significant legal consequences arise, whether the parties intend them to or not. A fundamental rule is that a contract is formed only when a complete offer is unconditionally accepted by the other side. The key factor in deciding whether an offer has been made is this: if the purported offer is sufficiently comprehensive that it can be accepted without further elaboration or clarification, it is an offer in law. Jason's proposal to Amritha, outlined in the opening scenario, contains the requisite certainty and completeness. On this basis, the first building block to a contract between Trackers and Coasters is in place.

FIGURE 6.1 Legal Analysis of the Retail Purchase

Display of Goods
(invitation to treat)

↓

Customer Takes Item to Cash Register
(offer to purchase at sticker price)

↓

Clerk Takes Payment
(acceptance of offer)

Standard form contract

A "take it or leave it" contract, where the customer agrees to a standard set of terms that favours the other side.

BUSINESS APPLICATION OF THE LAW

SPAMMING

Unsolicited commercial email (sometimes called spam) is an annoyingly common way of advertising goods and services. But, more seriously, spam is a major detriment to the global marketplace. As the government of Canada notes in a regulatory impact analysis statement, such electronic messages:

> . . . have become a significant social and economic issue, and a drain on the business and personal productivity of Canadians. Spam now makes up over 80% of global

---

4   For a discussion of the benefits of the standard form contract, see, for example, M J Trebilcock & D N Dewees, "Judicial Control of Standard Form Contracts" in Paul Burrows & Cento G Veljanovski, eds, *The Economic Approach to Law* (London: Butterworths, 1981).

email traffic, imposing significant costs on businesses and consumers. Spam impedes the efficient use of electronic messages for personal and business communications and threatens the growth and acceptance of legitimate e-commerce. In addition, related electronic threats such as phishing, malware, botnets, identity theft, and online scams have become more sophisticated and widespread, giving rise to a new generation of electronic threats that engage activities such as the installation of computer programs and altering transmission data.[5]

In response, the federal government passed legislation addressing these threats, by the lengthy title of *An Act to promote the efficiency and adaptability of the Canadian economy by regulating certain activities that discourage reliance on electronic means of carrying out commercial activities, and to amend the Canadian Radio-television and Telecommunications Commission Act, the Competition Act, the Personal Information Protection and Electronic Documents Act and the Telecommunications Act.* For short, the legislation is known as CASL (Canada's Anti-Spam Legislation). Most of the legislation came into effect in July 2014.[6] According to the government, CASL's purpose is " . . . to encourage the growth of electronic commerce by ensuring confidence and trust in the online marketplace. To do so, the *Act* prohibits damaging and deceptive spam, spyware, malicious code, botnets, and other related network threats."[7]

For example, CASL tightly regulates the usage of commercial electronic messages (CEMs) without the prior opt-in consent of the recipient. CEMs are any electronic message delivered to an electronic address (including by email, text message, and social media) whose contents would cause one to conclude that its purpose or one of its purposes was to encourage the participation in commercial activity. Examples include offers to purchase or sell goods and services or to provide investment or gaming opportunities—with even a single email to a single recipient amounting to a CEM under the Act.[8] Consent to receiving CEMs can be implied—as strictly defined by the Act—or consent can be express, again, as strictly defined by the Act. For example, the person, when seeking express consent to send CEMs, must state the purpose for which consent is being requested, state that consent may be withdrawn, and provide contact information, among other requirements. Note that seeking consent by email to send CEMs is also considered to be a CEM.[9]

Once consent is in place, the CEM must be in the prescribed form and described by the Government of Canada in the following way:

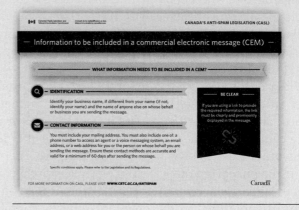

Source: Information to be included in a commercial electronic message (CEM), www.crtc.gc.ca/eng/com500/CASL_Infograph5_PDF.pdf. Reproduced with the permission of the Canadian Radio-television and Telecommunications Commission on behalf of Her Majesty in Right of Canada, 2015.

Beyond this, the legislation also requires an "unsubscribe" mechanism in the CEM that must be simple and easy to use.

5   Industry Canada, "Regulatory Impact Analysis Statement" (4 December 2013, date modified), online: Government of Canada <http://fightspam.gc.ca/eic/site/030.nsf/eng/00271.html>.
6   CRTC, "Frequently Asked Questions about Canada's Anti-Spam Legislation" (8 August 2014, date modified), online: Government of Canada <http://www.crtc.gc.ca/eng/com500/faq500.htm>.
7   *Supra* note 5.
8   Barry Sookman, "CASL: The unofficial FAQ, regulatory impact statement, and compliance guideline" (14 January 2015), online: Barry Sookman <http://www.barrysookman.com/2015/01/14/casl-the-unofficial-faq-regulatory -impact-statement-and-compliance-guideline>.
9   Government of Canada, "Canada's Anti-spam Legislation and Regulations" online: Government of Canada <http://fightspam.gc.ca/eic/site/030.nsf/eng/00285.html>.

While the law targets a legitimate problem, many in the business community are critical of the law. Some, such as the Information Technology Association of Canada, are worried that the law's opt-in approach will put local businesses at a disadvantage in the global marketplace by creating more bureaucratic hurdles.[10] It argues that companies in countries that have adopted an opt-out approach (i.e., spam is permitted until the consumer requests that no further spam be sent by the business in question), such as the United States, will therefore have a competitive advantage.[11] However, Professor Michael Geist, Canada Research Chair of Internet and E-commerce Law, argues that Canada is merely following in the footsteps of Australia, the United Kingdom, and European Union countries which have all implemented an opt-in approach and that there is no cause for concern.[12]

Enforcement of the anti-spam legislation has begun. In 2015, the Canadian Radio-television and Telecommunications Communications' Chief of Compliance and Enforcement, Manon Bombardier, issued a notice of violation to Compu-Finder which included a fine of $1.1 million. In a statement, Bombardier noted that Compu-Finder had "flagrantly violated the basic principles of the law" which included sending CEMs without recipient consent and without properly functioning unsubscribe features.[13] And Plentyoffish Media Inc. has recently paid $48 000 for sending email to members of its online dating service that did not have a proper unsubscribe mechanism.[14] Plentyoffish has since updated that mechanism to make it legislatively compliant.[15]

Why is spam objectionable?

It should be noted that, to avoid harshness, the Act permits the defence of due diligence to protect the person who is trying to comply but nonetheless makes a mistake and runs afoul of the rules.[16]

Penalties for non-compliance are up to $1 million for individuals and up to $10 million for corporations or organizations, per violation. Beyond this, the legislation gives a private right of action, as of July 1, 2017, to any spam victim, which will most usually be used to target major spammers, perhaps by way of class action. For more analysis of CASL, see Chapter 24.

Critical Analysis: Do you believe that the anti-spam legislation imposes provisions that are proportionate to the problems caused by spam? Why not leave the problem of spam to the marketplace to resolve?

Source: Industry Canada, "Regulatory Impact Analysis Statement" (4 December 2013 date modified) online: Government of Canada <http://fightspam.gc.ca/eic/site/030.nsf/eng/00271.html>.

10 Barry Sookman, "Delete this anti-spam law" *National Post* (February 28, 2013), online: National Post <http://opinion.financialpost.com/2013/02/28/delete-this-anti-spam-law/>.

11 *Ibid.*

12 Michael Geist, "Canadian Chamber of Commerce Attacks Spam Law" (February 8, 2013), online: Michael Geist <http://www.michaelgeist.ca/2013/02/chamber-on-casl-opt-in/>.

13 Government of Canada News Release, "CRTC Compliance and Enforcement Officer issues $1.1 million penalty to Compu-Finder for Spamming Canadians" (5 March 2015), online: CRTC <http://news.gc.ca/web/article-en.do?nid=944159>.

14 Government of Canada News Release, "Plentyoffish Media Inc. pays $48 000 for alleged violation of Canada's anti-spam law" (25 March 2015), online: CRTC <http://news.gc.ca/web/article-en.do?nid=954949>.

15 *Ibid.*

16 See section 33 of the CASL and Peter Murphy, "Preparing Your Organization for CASL's Commercial Electronic Message Requirements" Gowlings (April 2014), online: Gowlings <http://www.gowlings.com/KnowledgeCentre/article.asp?pubID=3252>.

Offeror

The person who makes an offer.

Offeree

The person to whom an offer is made.

The person who makes an offer is known as the **offeror**. The person to whom an offer is made is known as the **offeree**. In the Business Law in Practice scenario, Jason is the offeror, and Amritha is the offeree.

Termination of Offer

An offer can be accepted only if it is "alive," meaning that it is available to be accepted. If the offer has been legally terminated, no contract can come into existence, since one of its essential ingredients—the offer itself—is missing.

An offer can be terminated or "taken off the table" by any of the following events:

- revocation.
- lapse.
- rejection.
- counteroffer.
- death or insanity.

Revocation

Revocation

The withdrawal of an offer.

Revocation of an offer can take place at any time before acceptance simply by the offeror notifying the offeree of its withdrawal. An offer that has been revoked does not exist anymore and therefore cannot be accepted.

In the opening scenario, there were several days between the communication of Trackers's offer and Amritha's acceptance of that offer. During this time, Jason would have been legally entitled to revoke his offer by simply advising Amritha of that fact. Amritha's alternatives would then be reduced, since she cannot accept an offer that has been revoked, nor can she make Trackers do business with her if it is no longer interested.

What factors will determine whether a contract will be the result of lengthy negotiations or will be easily and quickly concluded?

Bigg v Boyd Gibbins Ltd, [1971] 2 All ER 183 (CA)

THE BUSINESS CONTEXT: For the purpose of entering into a contract, parties may negotiate considerably. Difficulties arise when one party believes that a contract has been concluded while the other party disputes that conclusion.

FACTUAL BACKGROUND: Plaintiff and defendant negotiated extensively for the purchase and sale of real estate by the plaintiff to the defendant. The negotiation over this property—known as Shortgrove Hall—took the form of correspondence that the plaintiff/vendor claims culminated in a contract. The first legally important letter from the plaintiff stated:

> Thank you for your letter received last week . . . . As you are aware that I paid £25 000 for this property, your offer of £20 000 would appear to be at least a little optimistic. For a quick sale I would accept £26 000, so that my expense may be covered.

In response, the defendant wrote:

> I have just recently returned from my winter holiday and, turning this matter over in my mind now, would advise you that I accept your offer.

The plaintiff replied:

> I thank you for your letter . . . accepting my price of £26 000 for the sale of Shortgrove Hall. I am putting the matter in the hands of my solicitors . . . . My wife and I are both pleased that you are purchasing the property.

The defendant denies a contract was formed, asserting that the parties had merely agreed on price.

THE LEGAL QUESTION: Is there a contract between the parties?

RESOLUTION: The court found for the plaintiff. There was a contract for the purchase and sale of Shortgrove Hall. To reach this conclusion, the court carefully analyzed the correspondence provided and acknowledged the defendant's argument that agreement on price does not necessarily mean that the parties have reached a full agreement. On these facts, however, a contract did exist. As the court concluded:

> The impression conveyed to my mind by these letters, and indeed the plain impression, is that the language used was intended to and did achieve the formation of . . . [a] contract. As I have indicated, in the last letter stress was laid on the phrase "accepting my *price* [emphasis added] of £26 000 for the sale of Shortgrove Hall." I think, in the context of the letters that preceded that, it is to be read, as I have said, as "accepted my *offer* [emphasis added] to sell Shortgrove Hall" at that price."

CRITICAL ANALYSIS: Who is the offeror and who is the offeree in this case? Do you agree with the court that a contract was in place? Should courts hold parties to the meaning of the exact words they use, or should words be interpreted in their larger context?

Revocation in the Context of a Firm Offer As the following landmark case illustrates, the law permits offerors to revoke their offers despite a promise to leave the offer open for a set period of time (called a firm offer). In short, such a promise is enforceable only if the other party has purchased it or otherwise has given the offeror something in return for the commitment. Accordingly, if Jason had promised to leave his offer to sell tracking open for 30 days, but Amritha did not provide something in return for this promise—like the payment of a sum of money—she would have no legal recourse if Jason were to break his word and revoke his offer the next day.

Dickinson v Dodds, [1876] 2 Ch D 463 (CA)

THE HISTORICAL CONTEXT: This case is the leading decision—valid even today—on whether an offeror can renege on a commitment to hold an offer open for a specified period of time.

FACTUAL BACKGROUND: On Wednesday, June 10, Dodds delivered to Dickinson a written offer to sell his property to Dickinson for £800. The offer stated that it would be open for acceptance until 9 A.M. on Friday, June 12. On Thursday, Dickinson heard that Dodds had been offering or was agreeing to sell the property to Mr. Allan. That evening, Dickinson delivered an acceptance to the place where Dodds was staying, and at 7 A.M. on Friday morning—a full two hours before the deadline—he personally delivered an acceptance to Dodds. Dodds declined the acceptance, stating: "You are too late. I have sold the property." Dickinson sued Dodds, alleging there was a contract between them.

THE LEGAL QUESTION: To determine whether Dickinson's action should succeed, the court had to decide whether Dodds was entitled to revoke his offer prior to the deadline he had set. This decision was necessary because if the offer had been properly revoked, it was not capable of being accepted, and, accordingly, there could be no contract between the two men.

RESOLUTION: The court decided that what Dodds did was permissible: "[I]t is a perfectly clear rule of law . . . that, although it is said that the offer is to be left open until Friday morning at 9 o'clock, that did not bind Dodds. He was not in point of law bound to hold the offer over until 9 o'clock on Friday morning."

On this footing, a firm offer can be revoked at any time before acceptance because the offeree has not provided any consideration to support the offeror's implicit promise not to revoke before the deadline. More controversially, the court also held that Dodds's offer had been effectively revoked prior to acceptance because Dickinson learned in advance—from a presumably reliable source—that Dodds was selling the property to someone else.

CRITICAL ANALYSIS: Being guided primarily by legal principles is certainly an acceptable way of doing business. However, what might be the impact on your business reputation of going back on your word and revoking an offer sooner than you had promised you would? Do you think that the method used by Dodds for revocation (i.e., relying on the fact that Dickinson had learned that Dodds was selling to someone else) is the usual way of revoking an offer? What would be a more certain and reliable way of effecting revocation?

Option agreement

An agreement where, in exchange for payment, an offeror is obligated to keep an offer open for a specified time.

One way to avoid application of the rule in *Dickinson v Dodds* that firm offers can be revoked prior to their deadlines is for the parties to form an **option agreement**, whereby the offeree pays the offeror to keep the offer open for the specified time. An option agreement is a separate contract that may or may not lead to the acceptance of the offer and a resulting agreement of purchase and sale. Its purpose is simply to give the offeree a guaranteed period of time within which to deliberate whether to accept the offer or not. If the offeror withdraws the offer before the option agreement permits, he has committed a breach of contract, and the offeree can sue for damages.

Option agreements are commonly found in real estate developments—the developer will buy a number of options to purchase land from owners in the development area. The developer can choose whether to exercise the options and knows that during the option period, the owners are contractually bound not to withdraw their offers to sell at the specified price.

Dickinson v Dodds also demonstrates that an offer does not have to be directly revoked by the offeror—that revocation can take place through a reliable third-party source. This method of revocation, however, is both unusual and unreliable.

Prudent business practice would have the offeror expressly revoking offers as necessary.

Revocation in the Context of a Tendering Contract A specialized set of rules governs the tendering process. When an owner wishes to secure competitive bids to build a large project, for example, it typically calls for tenders. In response, contractors (also known as tenderers) submit tenders (or offers) that set out a price for the work to be done. If the ordinary rule of revocation applied, a contractor could simply withdraw its tender at any time prior to acceptance and thus be positioned to avoid any commitments it would ultimately rather not pursue. However, such latitude would undermine the tendering process and so the Supreme Court of Canada, in *R v Ron Engineering & Construction Ltd*,[17] devised a new legal structure for how tenders are to be understood. Instead of regarding the call for tenders as an invitation to treat, the Supreme Court of Canada said that the call for tenders could be construed as an offer of a preliminary contract known as Contract A. While this is a fact-specific matter, Contract A typically requires the tenderer and the owner to follow the rules governing the tender selection process, including a promise by the tenderer not to revoke its tender for a specified period of time. Everyone who submits a tender is accepting the offer of a Contract A to govern the relationship as well as offering to enter into Contract B, if chosen to do so. Contract B refers to the larger contract to perform the work in question. While there would be as many Contract A's as there were tenderers, only the successful tenderer would enter into a Contract B with the owner.

Should the tenderer seek to revoke its tender before the specified period of time has elapsed, it is likely a breach of Contract A and subject to legal action by the owner. As well, if the tenderer refuses to enter into Contract B when chosen to do so, it has committed another breach of Contract A.

Lapse

An offer can **lapse** in one of two ways. It may contain a date upon which it expires; after this date, it is no longer "alive" and therefore cannot be accepted. If the offer contains no expiry date, it will remain open for a reasonable period of time, which, in turn, will depend on all the circumstances of the case, including the nature of the transaction at issue. For example, an offer to sell a piece of woodland that is sitting idle would probably remain open longer than an offer to sell a piece of property that is about to be commercially developed. A judge will bring as much precision as possible to the question of when an offer lapses, but the whole exercise is inherently speculative.

With this in mind, an offeror should consider specifying an expiry date for the offer and thereby avoid the debate altogether. For his part, the offeree should act promptly, because of the principle in *Dickinson v Dodds* permitting revocation prior to the expiry date, or at least keep in contact with the offeror to ensure that the status of the offer is known.

Rejection

It is important for those involved in contractual negotiations to know that an offer is automatically terminated upon **rejection** by the offeree. The offer can be accepted only if the offeror revives it by offering it anew or if the offeree presents it as his own offer, which can then be accepted or rejected by the original offeror. The risk in rejecting an offer is that it may never be renewed by the other side.

Lapse

The expiration of an offer after a specified or reasonable period.

Rejection

The refusal to accept an offer.

---

17 [1981] 1 SCR 111.

Counteroffer

A **counteroffer** is a form of rejection. Through a counteroffer, the offeree is turning down the offer and proposing a new offer in its place. The distinction between an acceptance and a counteroffer is not always readily apparent. For example, suppose that a seller offers 100 widgets to the buyer at $10 per widget, and the buyer responds, "Great, I'll take 800." Or suppose a seller offers a car for $10 000, and the buyer says, "I'll take it. I'll give you $5000 today and the balance next week." In both situations, it looks like the buyer has accepted, but in law she has made a counteroffer. Any change to a term of an offer—including to price, quantity, time of delivery, or method of payment—is a counteroffer. Because a counteroffer is a rejection, the original offer is automatically terminated and can be accepted only if it is renewed by one of the parties. Whenever a party makes a counteroffer, she jeopardizes the chance of being able to accept the original offer.

Death or Insanity

While the matter is not free from controversy, it would seem that an offer generally dies if the offeror or offeree dies. However, if the offer concerns a contract that would not require the affected party to personally perform it, a court may decide that the offer could be accepted notwithstanding that party's death.

Someone who makes an offer and then, subsequently, becomes insane would not be bound, as a general rule.

Acceptance

Definition of Acceptance

When an offer made by one party is unconditionally and unequivocally accepted by the other party, a contract is formed. To be effective, the **acceptance** must demonstrate an unqualified and complete willingness to enter into the contract on the precise terms proposed. If the purported acceptance does not mirror the offer by agreeing to all its content, it is a counteroffer and no contract has been formed.

In the opening scenario, Amritha clearly accepted Jason's offer—she did not propose modifications or alterations to his proposal. While she expressed some reservations, saying that she was not entirely happy with the offer, this was not a rejection. Rather, she went on to fully and completely accept his offer. At this point, two of the building blocks of a contract between Coasters and Trackers are in place—namely, offer and acceptance.

Communication of Acceptance

In order to effect legal acceptance, the offeree must communicate—by words or by conduct—an unconditional assent to the offer in its entirety. This message of acceptance can be conveyed in any number of ways: in person, in writing, by mail, by fax, by email, by telephone, and by other actions. In fact, any manner of communication that is reasonable in the circumstances ordinarily will do. However, the offer must be scrutinized to determine if it requires a specific method of communicating an acceptance. If it does, and by the terms of the offer that method of communication is mandatory, then the offeree must follow that method of communication in order to ensure legal acceptance. For example, if a company offers, by telephone, to sell a given item but specifies that acceptance must be in writing, then the offeree's calling back with a purported acceptance will be ineffective. In this case the offeror is entitled to insist on written acceptance before it is bound.

Why might a business decide to accept an offer by conduct instead of formally communicating acceptance to the other side? What are the risks of doing so?

Ron Levine/Photographer's Choice/Getty Images

C A S E

Lowe (DJ) (1980) Ltd v Upper Clements Family Theme Park Ltd (1990), 95 NSR (2d) 397 (SCTD)

THE BUSINESS CONTEXT: Businesses often have to act quickly to address a problem that has developed. In such circumstances, proper attention may not be given to the legal requirements of contract formation. This lack of focus can lead to disappointed expectations.

FACTUAL BACKGROUND: Mr. Bougie, construction manager of Upper Clements Family

Theme Park, was under a tight construction schedule and needed a crane quickly to complete construction of a theme park. He discussed leasing a crane from Mr. Lowe's company, but the two men could not come to an agreement. Lowe insisted that the crane be leased for a minimum period of two months, whereas Bougie did not want to commit to that length of a term, preferring to prorate[18] charges based on a monthly rental. The next day, however, Bougie delivered a letter to Lowe from Mr. Buxton, the general manager of the

(Continued)

18 When a sum is prorated, it means that what is charged is determined in relation to a certain rate. In this example, the monthly rate is $10 000. Based on a 30-day month, the prorated daily charge would be $10 000 divided by 30, or $333.

CHAPTER 6: FORMING CONTRACTUAL RELATIONSHIPS

theme park, dated November 24, 1988. The letter summarized the parties' agreement and included this statement: "The Upper Clements Family Theme Park Limited agrees to pay the sum of $10 000 (ten thousand dollars) per month, prorated for partial months for crane hire." The letter concluded by asking Lowe to sign a copy of the letter if he was in agreement with this condition.

This letter did not, in fact, reflect the parties' agreement and was never signed by Lowe, but he did send a crane to the construction site. Lowe apparently believed that he and the theme park personnel could come to an agreement on price, and within two days of delivering the crane, approached Bougie with a draft agreement setting out a monthly rate for a two-month term. Bougie said that he had no authority to deal with the document, and it would have to wait for Buxton's return from an out-of-town trip. In the end, the theme park had the crane on-site for four days and then immediately returned it, along with payment of $1250. Lowe's company sued for the balance, claiming that it was owed a total of $20 000.

THE LEGAL QUESTION: Is there a contract between the parties? If so, did Buxton's terms on price prevail or did Lowe's?

RESOLUTION: The trial judge determined that there was a contract between the parties for the rental of the crane. Whether Buxton's letter was classified as an acceptance or a counter-offer, said the judge,

> . . . it was the serious expression of an intention by the Theme Park to enter into a contract

with the Lowe company . . . Having received that letter, Mr. Lowe had his company go ahead with delivery of the crane, knowing it was essential that the Theme Park have it at the earliest possible moment. Rather than risk losing the contract, Lowe accepted the offer by delivering the crane and acquiescing in the Theme Park's use of it.

In doing so Mr. Lowe was not intentionally capitulating to an unfavourable counteroffer. Based upon his experience in the industry and his previous dealings with the Theme Park, Mr. Lowe was taking a calculated risk that even though his company was entering into a contract, he could later negotiate more satisfactory terms . . . . His expectations were not unreasonable. However they were frustrated first by Mr. Buxton's absence and then by his own . . . . The two-month term [set forth in the draft lease that Lowe subsequently presented to Bougie] was not part of the contract that was entered into. The governing provision is in Mr. Buxton's letter of November 24th . . . . That is the provision of the counter-offer Mr. Lowe wished to avoid, but it is the one that governs. The Theme Park is entitled to return the crane for the monthly rental prorated for the partial month when it had possession of the crane . . . . The amount to be paid was calculated at $1 250.00 by the Theme Park and previously tendered to the Plaintiff. I accept that calculation and award the Plaintiff damages.

CRITICAL ANALYSIS: How can a business avoid unwanted obligations when there is insufficient time to properly negotiate a contract? Is it reasonable for the judge to decide the case based on the terms of one letter?

Since entering a contract is about assent, the law determines that the offer is effective only when it has been communicated to the offeree. In this way, the offeree becomes aware of its terms and can respond. Similarly, the acceptance, if any, must be communicated to the offeror so that the offeror is aware of the unqualified acceptance. Acceptance is achieved expressly, as when the offeree accepts in person or sends a message through some medium to the offeror. Occasionally, however, acceptance can be indicated by conduct, as the case just above demonstrates.

It is also possible—though less than usual—for the offer to be expressed in such a way that no communication of acceptance is needed.

Carlill v Carbolic Smoke Ball Co, [1893] 1 QB 256 (Eng CA)

THE HISTORICAL CONTEXT: This case was decided at a time when Victorian England was being inundated with quack cures. Examples of "miracle" cures included Epps Glycerine Jube Jubes and a product called Pepsolic, which claimed to prevent marriage breakups because it prevented indigestion. The ad for this product noted that indigestion "Causes Bad Temper, Irritability, Peppery Disposition, Domestic Quarrels, Separation and—the Divorce Court."[19]

FACTUAL BACKGROUND: This case considers the legal obligations that resulted from the advertisement placed by the Carbolic Smoke Ball Company in a London newspaper at the turn of the 19th century (see Figure 6.2).

FIGURE 6.2 Carbolic Smoke Ball Advertisement

£100 REWARD

WILL BE PAID BY THE

CARBOLIC SMOKE BALL CO.

To any person who contracts the increasing Epidemic,

INFLUENZA

Colds, or any diseases caused by taking cold,

AFTER HAVING USED the BALL

3 times daily for two weeks according to the printed directions supplied with each Ball.

£1000

Is deposited with the ALLIANCE BANK, REGENT STREET,

showing our sincerity in the matter.

During the last epidemic of Influenza many of our CARBOLIC SMOKE BALLS were sold as Preventives against this Disease, and in no ascertained case was the disease contracted by those using the CARBOLIC SMOKE BALL.

Carlill v Carbolic Smoke Ball Co, [1893] 1 QB 256 (Eng CA)

Mrs. Carlill used the smoke ball as directed for two weeks but caught influenza anyway. When the company refused to pay her the advertised reward, she commenced an action for breach of contract.

THE LEGAL QUESTION: Was there a contract between the parties, even though Mrs. Carlill did not communicate her acceptance of the Carbolic Smoke Ball Company's offer?

RESOLUTION: While communication of acceptance is generally required, this is not always the case. Because the Carbolic Smoke Ball Company—the offeror—had chosen to dispense with the necessity of notice, it could not complain about Mrs. Carlill's failure to communicate acceptance now. In the end, the court found that Mrs. Carlill had accepted the company's offer of a reward by using the smoke ball as requested and that, upon becoming sick, she was contractually entitled to the £100.

CRITICAL ANALYSIS: This case is an example of an offer of a unilateral contract, though the court did not identify it as such. Through such an offer, the offeror promises to pay the offeree a sum of money if the offeree performs the requested act. For example, a company might offer a $200 reward to anyone who finds a missing laptop computer. Unlike the ordinary business contract, where both parties have obligations, in the unilateral contract only the offeror is bound because the offeree can perform the requested act—find the laptop—or not. He has no obligation even to try. If he does find the computer and returns it, the contract is complete, and the offeror is contractually required to pay. For obvious reasons, this kind of offer typically does not require people who decide to look for the computer to advise the company of their intention to do so. From the company's perspective, it is enough to hear from the person who actually finds the computer.

---

19 AWB Simpson, "Quackery and Contract Law: The Case of the Carbolic Smoke Ball" (June 1985) 14:2 J Legal Stud 345 at 355-56. The historical information contained in this box draws heavily on Simpson's analysis.

Ordinarily, however, communication of acceptance is expected and required. In practical terms, the offeror needs to be aware of the acceptance in order to appreciate that the contract exists and that performance of the obligations in it should proceed.

A problem arises when the offeree sends an acceptance that for some reason never reaches the offeror. Perhaps a letter gets lost in the mail, an email message goes astray, or a fax gets sent to the wrong number. Has there been acceptance or not? Normally, the answer would be that no acceptance has occurred until actually received. Put another way, acceptance is effective only when communicated—it is at this moment that a contract comes into existence.

A specific exception to this general rule is the "postbox rule," also called the "postal rule." If it is clear that the offeror intends the postbox rule to apply to her offer, then acceptance is effective at the time of mailing the acceptance, rather than the time of delivery. Even if the letter containing the acceptance is never delivered to the offeror, a contract has been formed. Since application of the postbox rule means that an offeror could end up being in a contract without even knowing it, that person is best advised to avoid application of the postbox rule by making it clear in the offer that actual communication or notice of acceptance is absolutely required.

When a court will apply the ordinary rule (which requires communication of acceptance) and when it will apply the postbox rule depends on the facts of the case. As Lord Wilberforce states, "No universal rule can cover all such cases; they must be resolved by reference to the intentions of the parties, by sound business practice, and in some cases by a judgment, where the risks should lie . . . ."[20] Courts have applied the postbox rule to telegrams,[21] presumably on the basis that the offeror had impliedly constituted the telegraph company as his agent for the purpose of receiving the acceptance. Otherwise, the ordinary rule applies and the acceptance by telegram is effective only upon receipt.[22] The postbox rule has also been applied where the acceptance was delivered by courier.[23]

That said, it is much more common for the courts to apply the ordinary rule—that acceptance is effective only when communicated. They have done so with respect to many forms of instantaneous communication, including the telephone, the telex, and the fax.[24]

The practical application of the rules governing offer and acceptance is affected by the requirement of proof that the necessary events occurred. Someone who seeks to enforce a contract that the other party denies exists must be able to prove that offer and acceptance occurred. While, ideally, this proof is created through documentary evidence, documents are not always available. In such circumstances, the individual seeking to rely on the contract must convince the court of its existence without the benefit of extraneous proof. Oral agreements are very difficult to prove without some independent verification or corroboration—by a witness to the negotiations, for example—of what was said. Beyond this, some contracts must be evidenced in writing to be enforceable.[25]

---

20 *Brinkibon Ltd v Stahag Stahl Und Stahlwarenhandelsgesellschaft mbH*, [1983] 2 AC 34 (HL) [*Brinkibon*]; the rule in *Brinkibon* was adopted in Canada by *Eastern Power Ltd v Azienda Comunale Energia & Ambiente* 1999, 178 DLR (4th) 409 (Ont CA).

21 John McCamus, *The Law of Contract* 2nd (Toronto: Irwin Law, 2012) at 74.

22 *Società Gei A Responsabilità Limitata v Piscitelli*, [1988] CLD 679 (Ont Dist Ct).

23 *Nova Scotia v Weymouth Sea Products Ltd*, (1983) 4 DLR (4th) 314 (NSCA) and *Fp Bourgault Ind. Cultivator Division Ltd v Nichols Tillage Tools Inc* 1988, 63 Sask R 204 (QB).

24 *Eastern Power Ltd v Azienda Communale Energia*, (1999) 178 DLR (4th) 409 (Ont CA), leave to appeal to SCC refused, [1999] SCCA No 542.

25 See Chapter 8 for further discussion.

ELECTRONIC CONTRACTING

Electronic business—such as the sale of goods and services, the exchange of commercial information, and the payment of debts conducted over public and private computer networks—has grown tremendously over the last decade.

In an effort to facilitate the growth of electronic business, the Uniform Law Conference of Canada has adopted the *Uniform Electronic Commerce Act (UECA)*[26] based on the United Nations Commission on International Trade Law's (UNCITRAL) Model Law on Electronic Commerce.[27] The *UECA*, which is designed to remove barriers to electronic commerce, is intended to serve as the basis for provincial and federal electronic commerce legislation. The model law has three parts. Part 1 sets out basic functional equivalency rules; to remove any doubts pertaining to the legal recognition of electronic contracts, the model legislation provides that a contract shall not be denied effect on the sole ground that it was entered into electronically.[28] Part 2 deals with special rules for the formation and operation of contracts, the effect of using automated transactions, corrections of errors when dealing with a computer, and the sending and receipt of computer messages. Part 3 makes special provision for the carriage of goods. Electronic commerce legislation—in place across the country—is based on or influenced by this model.[29]

The *UECA* and the legislation that it has spawned do not modify or change the general rules

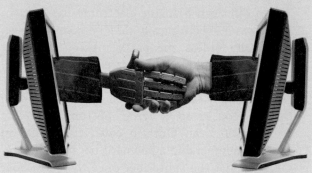

How does electronic business benefit from a standardized set of legislative rules?

applicable to contracts. The formation of electronic contracts is governed by the same general rules as other contracts. There must be an offer, acceptance, and communication of the acceptance.

Offer: The *UECA* provides that an offer may be expressed electronically. The legislation does not, however, specify whether communication displayed on a website is an offer or an invitation to do business. Generally, advertisements in catalogues and goods displayed in a store are not viewed as offers on the basis that merchants have only a limited supply and therefore could not reasonably be making offers to everyone. Presumably, electronic catalogues, advertisements, and price lists would be subject to the same rule. However, if the website displaying goods or services for sale not only indicates the price but also indicates that the item is in stock then the online advertisement could conceivably be considered an offer, without clear wording to the contrary.[30]

---

26 Uniform Law Conference of Canada, "*Uniform Electronic Commerce Act (1999)*", (no date), online: ULCC<http://www.ulcc.ca/en/1999-winnipeg-mb/359-civil-section-documents/1138-1999-electronic-commerce-act-annotated>.

27 United Nations Commission on International Trade Law,"1996—UNCITRAL Model Law on Electronic Commerce with Guide to Enactment" (no date), online: UNCITRAL <http://www.uncitral.org/uncitral/en/uncitral_texts/electronic_commerce/1996Model.html>.

28 Uniform Law Conference of Canada, *supra* note 26, section 5.

29 Teresa Scassa and Michael Deturbide, *Electronic Commerce and Internet Law in Canada* 2nd ed (Toronto: CCH, 2012) at 2-3. E-commerce legislation in Canada includes the *Electronic Transactions Act*, SA 2001, c E-5.5 (Alberta); the *Electronic Transactions Act*, SBC 2001, c 10 (British Columbia); the *Electronic Commerce and Information Act*, CCSM 2000 c E55 plus other related legislative amendments (Manitoba); the *Electronic Transactions Act*, RSNB 2011, c 145 (New Brunswick); the *Electronic Commerce Act*, SNL 2001, c E-5.2 (Newfoundland); the *Electronic Commerce Act*, SNS 2000, c 26 (Nova Scotia); *the Electronic Commerce Act*, SO 2000, c17 (Ontario); the *Electronic Commerce Act*, RSPEI 1988, c E-4.1 (Prince Edward Island); the *Electronic Information and Documents Act*, SS 2000, c E-7.22 (Saskatchewan); *the Electronic Commerce Act*, RSY 2002, c 66 (Yukon); and the *Electronic Commerce Act*, SNu 2004, c 7 (Nunavut).

30 Barry Sookman, Chapter 10 in *Computer, Internet and Electronic Commerce Law* online: WestlawNextCanada at footnotes 60.1 to 62 and surrounding text (accessed 30 March 2015).

Acceptance: The *UECA* provides that acceptance of an offer can be made electronically. Thus an offer made electronically may be accepted electronically unless the party making the offer insists on some other means of communication. Case law has recognized that an offer made electronically can be accepted by clicking on an online icon or an "I agree" button. In *Rudder v Microsoft*,[31] an Ontario court held that an online membership agreement became enforceable against the subscriber once the subscriber clicked on the "I agree" button.[32] The *UECA* also recognizes that an acceptance (as well as an offer) can be affected by an electronic agent.[33]

Communication of Acceptance: An acceptance of the offer must be communicated to the offeror to take effect. Where the acceptance is effective usually determines where the contract is formed and consequently what law applies to the transaction. In the absence of an agreement, an acceptance using an instantaneous means of communication (telephone, telex, facsimile) takes effect where the offeror receives the communication, whereas, generally speaking, acceptance using a non-instantaneous means of communication (such as the mail) can be effective on sending, that is, where the offeree is located. What then of communication by electronic means? Is this an instantaneous means of communication? Electronic mail is not quite like ordinary mail because, generally, it is significantly faster and it is often dependent on the actions of the recipient for arrival; it is not quite like a telephone because there is no direct line of communication between the parties and it is not always possible to verify whether the intended recipient has received the message. Internet communication can be interactive and in real time, however, therefore exhibiting characteristics of instantaneous means of communication.[34] The *UECA* has provisions specifying when a message is sent and when it is received, but it does not specify where an acceptance becomes effective. While still a matter to be decided on a fact-specific basis, several courts have applied the instantaneous rule of communication to email acceptances, including *Christmas v Fort McKay*, 2014 ONSC 373.

Critical Analysis: Legislation has removed some of the uncertainty about online contracting. However, questions still remain concerning whether communications on a website are an offer or invitation to do business and whether an electronic acceptance is effective on sending or receipt. What risks do these uncertainties pose for business? What steps can a business take to minimize these risks and avoid contractual disputes?

Developments in technology have created new methods of doing business that test the relevance and applicability of the older common law rules regarding offer and acceptance to which this chapter has already alluded.

BUSINESS AND LEGISLATION

LOTTERY TICKET WITH WINNING NUMBERS PURCHASED TOO LATE

On May 23, 2008, at 8:59:47 P.M., Joel Ifergan asked for two lottery tickets at a convenience store in Quebec. The deadline for the May 23 draw was 9:00 P.M. The first ticket printed out before this deadline and expressly showed it was eligible for the May 23 draw. The second ticket was registered on Loto Quebec's central

---

31 (1999), 2 CPR (4th) 474 (Ont SCJ).
32 The enforceability of these types of contracts—known as click-wrap agreements—is discussed in Chapter 7.
33 According to the *UECA, supra* note 26, section 19, an electronic agent is a computer program or electronic means used to initiate an action or to respond to electronic documents in whole or in part without review by an actual person at the time of the response or action. Electronic agents are discussed in Chapter 13.
34 Sookman, *supra* note 30 at footnotes 93.1 to 95 and surrounding text.

computer at 9:00:07 P.M. and therefore printed out in the store after the deadline. This second ticket showed that it was eligible for the May 30 draw. Ifergan was offered the chance by the convenience store owner to reject the second ticket since it was not for the draw he had wanted but Ifergan declined that opportunity and retained the ticket. When the numbers on the second ticket turned out to be the winning numbers for the May 23 draw, Ifergan took the position that he was entitled to share in the jackpot. Loto Quebec refused to pay, however, because his ticket said it was for the May 30 draw. Ifergan sued on the basis that he had purchased the ticket before the 9:00 P.M. deadline. Canadian Press offers this summary of Ifergan's argument:

> Ifergan alleged the transaction was concluded on time and that both tickets were in the system at 8:59:47. What cost him, he says, is the 10 seconds it takes for a ticket to emerge. "The contract was crystallized at 8:59 P.M.," he said. "How they process their thing, that's their problem, not me, and I end up being penalized."

Ifergan lost his case at trial and on appeal where, in both instances, the issue was *when* Ifergan's contract with Loto Quebec was formed: before or after the 9:00 P.M. deadline. In *Ifergan c. Société des loteries du Québec*, 2014 QCCA 1114, the Quebec Court of Appeal determined as follows: Loto Quebec made the offer to sell the lottery ticket through its advertisement in the store (at para 33). Note that though the lower court had ruled that the Loto advertisement was an invitation to treat, the Court of Appeal held that the advertisement was in fact an offer because all the essential elements were determinable or in place. Continuing its analysis, the Court of Appeal held that Ifergan's acceptance of that offer was complete when it was registered on or received by Loto Quebec's main computer (at para 67). Since

Joel Ifergan

Ryan Remiorz/The Canadian Press

this occurred *after* the 9:00 P.M. deadline, the contract itself was formed after the deadline and Ifergan's ticket was ineligible to win the May 23 draw. Note that while this case was decided under the Civil Code of Quebec, the outcome in common law Canada would likely not be dissimilar.

The Supreme Court of Canada has refused to hear Ifergan's appeal. His seven-year legal fight, which cost $100 000 in legal fees, is over. As Ifergan told Canadian Press: "My crusade is up, I've done all I can, I spent enough money going to the Supreme Court."

Critical Analysis: Do you agree with the Court of Appeal's analysis of when the contract was formed? Is it relevant to the case that the store owner offered Ifergan the chance to reject the second ticket because it was not for the draw that he had wanted?

Sources: Sidhartha Banerjee, "7 second delay costs Quebec man a $13.5M lotto jackpot" Canadian Press *Metro* (29 January 2015), online: Metro <http://metronews.ca/news/canada/1274458/seven-second-delay-costs-quebec-man-a-13-5m-lotto-jackpot/>; Josh Elliott, "7 seconds too late: SCC won't hear $27M lotto appeal" CTV News (29 January 2015), online: CTV News <http://www.ctvnews.ca/canada/7-seconds-too-late-scc-won-t-hear-27m-lotto-appeal-1.2211516>

Formalization

Even though the parties may have reached an agreement through offer and acceptance, this will not always produce an enforceable agreement. In fact, it is common that businesses may not wish to be bound in any way until the contract's formal language is agreed to and the formal contract signed. The question, should a dispute arise on point, is whether the parties intend further documentation as a precondition of a contract existing *at all* or simply as "an indication or expression of desire as to the manner in which the contract already made will be implemented."[35] Though the court will take into account all the facts of a given case, the words "this agreement is subject to formal contract" can indeed signal that there is no concluded contract[36] unless and until the formal contract comes into existence. In such circumstances, there are generally no enforceable obligations between the parties.

Consideration

The Nature of Consideration

A contract is a set of commitments or promises. It therefore entails a bargain or an exchange between the parties. Each party must give up something of value in exchange for receiving something of value from the other contracting party. In the example of the agreement between Jason and Amritha, it is clear that there is **consideration** on both sides of the transaction: the buyer promises to pay the purchase price in exchange for the seller's promise to provide tracking of the specified quality and quantity. Seen from the other perspective, the seller promises to provide tracking of the specified quality and quantity in exchange for the buyer's promise to pay the purchase price (see Figure 6.3). This bargain, or exchange of promises, is a classic example of the legal requirement of consideration.

Consideration is a key ingredient that distinguishes a legally enforceable promise from one that is not legally enforceable. If Trackers promises to provide tracking to Coasters at no charge and later changes its mind, Coasters cannot successfully sue for breach of contract. Coasters has not given something back to Trackers in order to purchase Trackers's promise; accordingly, there is no contract in place, and any lawsuit by Coasters will fail. In law, Trackers has made a **gratuitous promise**—that is, a promise unsupported by consideration. Classically, the law has concluded that such a promise can be broken with legal impunity because it has not been "purchased," though, as discussed below, another view on the matter is emerging.[37] Certainly, if the parties have exchanged promises or something else of value, their obligations are contractual and, therefore, undoubtedly enforceable.

As the above examples illustrate, a "price" must be paid for a promise before a party can sue when it is broken. Most commonly, the price for a promise to supply goods or services takes the form of another promise—including a promise to pay an agreed-upon sum in the future—or immediate payment of money. However, the consideration need not be monetary. The only requirement is that something

Consideration

The price paid for a promise.

Gratuitous promise

A promise for which no consideration is given.

FIGURE 6.3 Consideration as an Exchange of Promises

Coasters

➡ promises to pay in consideration for Trackers's promise to supply

Trackers

➡ promises to supply in consideration for Coasters's promise to pay

---

35 *Klemke Mining Corp v Shell Canada Ltd*, 2007 ABQB 176 at para. 183.
36 *Holly Downs Developments Inc v 1428508 Ontario Ltd*, 2014 ONSC 1628 at para 41.
37 See discussion at notes 38-43 and surrounding text.

of value be given up by the party seeking to purchase the promise of another. Furthermore, that item of value may be conferred on a third party and still amount to consideration, provided it was conferred at the request of the other side. For example, if Jason requested that the purchase price of the tracking be paid to a creditor of Trackers, Coasters's agreement to do so would support Trackers's promise to supply the tracking.

The requirement for consideration is strongly linked to the idea of freedom of bargaining. Although the law requires that consideration be present on both sides of the transaction, it is up to the parties to negotiate a deal that is mutually acceptable. They, not a judge, decide what constitutes a fair and reasonable price. Therefore, the adequacy of consideration is normally not open to challenge. If Amritha has agreed to pay a price for the tracking that turns out to be well above its market value, that is her choice. She cannot later go to a judge and ask that the price be lowered on that basis alone. The law will generally enforce a contract even where one party has agreed to pay too much because the parties are responsible for being fully informed of all aspects of the transaction and for evaluating the risks involved. If Amritha is concerned that she may end up paying too much for tracking, she should consult experts in the field and seek competing bids to help her establish a fair market price before accepting Jason's offer. Similarly, if one or both of the parties is concerned that the value of the goods or services contracted for may change between the time of agreement and the time of performance, a clause allowing the contract price to be adjusted for market fluctuations should be included in the contract. In short, parties are expected to take care of themselves and plan for contingencies.

Pre-Existing Legal Duty

Just as a contract can be viewed as a set of promises, it can also be viewed as a set of duties. The consideration for each party's duties is the other party's duties. Once those duties or promises have been finalized, the contract is concluded. If the parties agree to alter the contract in a way that benefits only one of them, the traditional perspective says that the alteration is unenforceable. In other words, a new promise needs new or fresh consideration. For example, if a contract provides that a project is to be completed on a particular date, a promise by the owner to pay an additional sum of money—say, $2000—to ensure completion on that date is unenforceable. The promise to pay an additional $2000 is not supported by fresh consideration because completion on a particular date is already required under a contract. In short, it is a **pre-existing legal duty**. This is the view taken in the following case.

Pre-existing legal duty

A legal obligation that a person already owes.

(Continued)

C A S E	**Gilbert Steel Ltd v University Construction Ltd, [1976] 12 OR (2d) 19 (CA)**

THE BUSINESS CONTEXT: A business may enter into a contract that suddenly becomes unfavourable because of changes in the market. If it secures a concession from the other side in response to these changes, without regard to legal requirements, the concession may prove to be unenforceable.

FACTUAL BACKGROUND: Gilbert Steel (Gilbert) and University Construction (University) were in a contract that required Gilbert to supply a set amount of fabricated steel at an agreed-upon price. When steel prices rose dramatically, Gilbert asked University if it would pay more for the steel. University agreed but later refused to pay the increase and sent only payment for the originally agreed-upon price. Gilbert sued for breach of contract.

THE LEGAL QUESTION: Is there consideration supporting University's promise (i.e., what is Gilbert doing in return for University's promise to pay more for the steel)?

RESOLUTION: There is no consideration from Gilbert for University's promise, and it is therefore unenforceable. Gilbert is doing only what it is already contractually obliged to do—namely, supply steel to University. Put another way, Gilbert has a pre-existing legal duty to provide the steel and, accordingly, is giving nothing "extra" to University to support University's promise to pay more. The promise is therefore unenforceable, even though University made the second promise in good faith, possibly with a full intention to pay the higher price. Gilbert's action for breach of contract therefore fails.

Gilbert should have contemplated a rise in the cost of steel when setting the original price and built into the contract a formula permitting an increase in the contract price. Alternatively, it could have provided something in return for the higher price, such as earlier delivery or any other benefit that University requested. A final option would have been to get University's promise under seal (see below).

CRITICAL ANALYSIS: Does this rule concerning performance of a pre-existing legal duty reflect the reasonable expectations of both the parties involved and the broader business community?

Variation of Contracts

The rule that performance of a pre-existing legal duty is not good consideration for a new promise also finds expression in the traditional rule that all variations of a contract must be supported by "fresh" consideration. As *Gilbert Steel Ltd v University Construction Ltd* illustrates, just as a contract needs to reflect a two-sided bargain, so must variations or changes to that contract. This is why University's promise to pay more for the steel is, under this traditional analysis, considered to be worthless without some corresponding concession from Gilbert.

More recently, however, the New Brunswick Court of Appeal (in *Greater Fredericton Airport Authority Inc v NAV Canada*[38]) has ruled that a contractual variation unsupported by consideration is enforceable—provided it is not otherwise procured by economic duress. As the court notes, among other matters:

> The reality is that existing contracts are frequently varied and modified by tacit agreement in order to respond to contingencies not anticipated or identified at the time the initial contract was negotiated. As a matter of commercial efficacy, it becomes necessary at times to adjust the parties' respective contractual obligations and the law must then protect their legitimate expectations that the modifications or variations will be adhered to and regarded as enforceable.[39]

The court expressed the view that the doctrine of consideration should not be frozen in time and that incremental change to the common law is important in order to advance modern policy objectives.[40] Provided that the party who agrees to a gratuitous variation did not do so because of pressure that left no practical alternative and that the party therefore essentially "consented" to the variation,

---

38 2008 NBCA 28. For further discussion of duress, see Chapter 8.
39 *Supra* note 38 at para 28.
40 *Ibid* at paras 30–31, relying on *Williams v Roffey Bros & Nicholls (Contractors) Ltd,* [1990] 1 All ER 512 (CA).

it is enforceable.[41] The idea is to respect the parties' legitimate expectations that the contractual modifications would be adhered to.[42]

This means that there are now two lines of authority in Canada regarding the enforceability of gratuitous contractual variations. In Ontario and jurisdictions following the *Gilbert Steel* approach, they are not enforceable. In New Brunswick and jurisdictions that choose to follow the *Greater Fredericton Airport Authority* case, they can be.[43] When consideration *is* present, of course, the difference between the two jurisdictions is no longer relevant—the variation is most certainly enforceable.

Note that when parties to a contract decide to terminate it and replace it with a new contract, there is no doubt that consideration is present in that both parties have given something back to the other. If only one side has given something up, however, then the contract has been varied (as opposed to being replaced) and the enforceability of the variation depends on what authority the court in question relies on—*Gilbert Steel* or *Greater Fredericton Airport Authority*.

When Trackers, through Jason, asked Amritha's company to pay more for the tracking, it was seeking a variation of the contract. Because Trackers did not provide anything new to Coasters in return, Coasters' commitment to pay an increased price was a gratuitous promise. On the traditional analysis, the fact that Trackers supplied the tracking on time does not count as consideration because Trackers had a pre-existing duty to do just that. On this basis, Coasters is not bound by its promise to pay more. Its only obligation is to pay the price recited in the contract that Amritha first negotiated. From a business perspective, however, its refusal to abide by its own promise will almost certainly destroy any possibility of Coasters and Trackers ever doing business together again. On the new analysis offered by the New Brunswick Court of Appeal in *Greater Fredericton Airport Authority*, it would seem that Coasters' commitment to pay an increased price *is* enforceable. This is because Trackers did not put Coasters under economic duress—there seems to be little doubt that the agreement to pay more was entirely voluntary and something to which Coasters consented.

Promises Enforceable Without Consideration

Consideration is not always necessary for a contract or contractual variation to be enforceable. Important exceptions to the consideration requirement are promises under seal, promissory estoppel, and, in some jurisdictions, partial payment of a debt.

Promise Under Seal

Before commercial negotiations became as commonplace and sophisticated as they are today, and before the rules of contract were fully developed, a practice originated to authenticate written agreements by putting hot wax beside the signature on a document and placing an imprint in the wax, unique to the person who signed. The use of a seal has evolved so that today the seal takes the form

---

41   *Supra* note 38 at para 55.
42   *Ibid* at para 28.
43   For example, NAV has been followed in Newfoundland and Labrador in *Burin Peninsula Community Business Development Corp v Grandy*, 2010 NLCA 69 as well as in New Brunswick. See *Bonne Bay Fish Farms Inc v Nutreco Canada Inc*, 2010 NBQB 108.

CHAPTER 6: FORMING CONTRACTUAL RELATIONSHIPS

What is the purpose of placing a seal on a document?

of a red gummed circle or wafer attached to the document beside the signature of the party making the promise. The legal effect is the same, however. If the document containing the promise is signed and the seal affixed, the fact that there may not be consideration for the promise is irrelevant. The seal is taken as evidence of serious intent by the promisor and amounts to an acknowledgment that the promise is enforceable, even if it is gratuitous. Contracts of guarantee, for example, typically have seals attached.[44]

Promissory Estoppel

Without a seal, a gratuitous promise is traditionally not enforceable at common law, even if made with great deliberation, and regardless of the adverse consequences to the person who relied on the promise. In response to the harshness that this common law rule could sometimes generate, courts began to assist parties through the equitable doctrine of **promissory estoppel**.

Promissory estoppel focuses on the idea of fairness, but since fairness is relatively subjective and courts are reluctant to stray too far from the doctrine of consideration, the party seeking to rely on the doctrine (Party A) must show that a number of distinct factors also exist in relation to the promise made by Party B, as listed below:

- Party B has, by words or conduct, made a promise or an assurance to Party A that was intended to affect their legal relationship and to be acted on.
- in reliance on the representation, Party A acted on it or in some way changed its position.[45]
- Party A's own conduct has been above reproach and, in this way, Party A is deserving of the court's assistance.

Promissory estoppel

A doctrine whereby someone who relies on a gratuitous promise may be able to enforce it.

---

44 Guarantees are discussed in detail in Chapter 26.
45 *Maracle v Travellers Indemnity Co of Canada*, [1991] 2 SCR 50.

A final requirement is that promissory estoppel can be used only as a defence to legal claims made by the promise-breaker.[46]

Assume, for example, that Jason contacts Amritha one month before the delivery date specified in their contract. Jason tells her that Trackers is having minor production difficulties and there is a chance that the tracking will be delivered three days late. He asks Amritha if this will be a problem for Coasters. He also wants to know if Coasters will insist on enforcing the late delivery clause in their contract obligating Trackers to pay $5000 per day for every day it is late. After securing instructions from her supervisor, Amritha gets back to Jason and tells him not to worry: "Jason, it poses no problem for us if you are up to one week late, and no, we won't come after you for late charges. We just want our tracking in good time." In the end, the tracking is delivered three days late, and Coasters suddenly takes the position that it is owed $15 000.

Subject to the reach of *Greater Fredericton Airport Authority*, Coasters's promise not to rely on the late charges clause is unenforceable at common law because there is no consideration supporting it. Trackers is giving nothing back to Coasters in exchange for Coasters's promise to accept late delivery without complaint. For this reason, the common law would allow Coasters to go back on its word and collect the $15 000. However, there is an excellent chance that the doctrine of promissory estoppel would be applied by a judge to prevent this outcome because

- Coasters promised not to rely on its contractual right to collect late charges.
- Trackers relied on this promise and changed its position by scheduling production accordingly and taking no additional steps to speed up its schedule.
- Trackers's conduct throughout has been beyond reproach—it did not threaten Coasters or otherwise place undue pressure on it to accept late delivery.
- Trackers is using the doctrine to defend itself from a claim by Coasters for the late charges.

For these kinds of reasons, Coasters would be estopped from relying on the late charges clause, and its action for $15 000 would fail.

Promissory estoppel is a relatively complicated doctrine and cannot be fully detailed here. The foregoing analysis is offered only as an introductory account of how the doctrine might arise in a business context.

Partial Payment of a Debt

A common difficulty encountered by a business arises when the customer cannot pay its account but offers a smaller amount to settle the debt in full. Can the business agree to the customer's proposal, accept the smaller amount, and then sue for the balance? Put another way, does the compromise on a bill amount to a binding contract, or is it simply a gratuitous promise by the creditor to accept a lesser amount? The discussion under promissory estoppel illustrates that equity may provide assistance to the debtor and enforce the creditor's promise. As well, the debtor may have recourse because she has provided consideration or because

---

46 Most Canadian courts insist that promissory estoppel can be used only as a defence, though there is some case law to the contrary. See, for example, *Robichaud c Caisse Populaire de Pokemouche ltée*, (1990) 69 DLR (4th) 589 (NBCA). See too, criticism of that rule offered in *Greater Fredericton Airport Authority, supra* note 38 at para 29. Based on the traditional doctrine, promissory estoppel cannot be used by Trackers to enforce Coasters's promise to pay more for the tracking. Trackers cannot sue on the promise—it can use it only as a defence.

the new agreement is under seal. Finally, there may be a statute that makes the creditor's promise binding.

The common law rule that a creditor can go back on a promise to accept a lesser sum in full satisfaction of the debt has been reversed by legislation in several jurisdictions, including Ontario. Section 16 of Ontario's *Mercantile Law Amendment Act*, for example, essentially provides that once the lesser amount has been freely agreed upon and paid, the creditor cannot later claim the full amount.[47] A policy rationale for the legislation is to promote settlement of debts on a final basis.

For example, assume that Coasters has fallen on hard times and has been able to pay only $1 million on its account with Trackers. Therefore, $500 000 is outstanding. Trackers agrees to accept $300 000 from Coasters and write off the balance. At common law, Trackers can go back on its word and sue for the remaining $200 000 because its promise to accept a smaller sum is gratuitous. There is no consideration from Coasters supporting Trackers's promise to accept less than what is owed. Since Coasters has a pre-existing legal duty to pay $500 000, paying $300 000 is not consideration for Trackers's promise to forgive the balance. Put another way, Coasters is not giving Trackers anything in return for Trackers's promise, except a $300 000 payment that it was obligated to make in any event.

In jurisdictions that have legislation making such agreements binding, the creditor cannot sue for the balance once she has received from the debtor the smaller amount promised. In jurisdictions without such legislation, the creditor's promise is not enforceable, under traditional analysis. The consideration rule remains in force so that, in order for the promise to be enforced, the creditor must give the promise under seal or receive something in return for her promise to accept less (such as payment earlier than required).[48] Another alternative for the debtor seeking to enforce the creditor's promise is to rely on promissory estoppel, if circumstances permit.

The varying status of how partially paid debts are handled across Canada illustrates two important aspects of contract law. First, provincial legislatures may intervene at any time to alter or override a common law rule governing contracts. Second, though largely uniform across the country, contract law is under provincial control and is therefore subject to important provincial variations.

Intention to Contract

The last important ingredient in a contract is the intention to contract. In order for one party to enforce the promise of another, the promise at issue must have been intended to be a contractual one, that is, one that would be enforceable by a court of law. Absent such an intention, there is no contract between the parties.

---

47 The *Mercantile Law Amendment Act*, RSO 1990, c M.10, section 16 states, "Part performance of an obligation either before or after breach thereof when expressly accepted by the creditor or rendered in pursuance of an agreement for that purpose, though without any new consideration, shall be held to extinguish the obligation." Similar provisions are in effect in jurisdictions such as British Columbia (*Law and Equity Act*, RSBC 1996, c 253, section 43); Manitoba (*Mercantile Law Amendment Act*, CCSM c M120, section 6; Saskatchewan (*Queen's Bench Act*, SS 1998, c Q-1.01, section 64); and Alberta (*Judicature Act*, RSA 2000, c J-2, section 13).

48 The debtor in New Brunswick (where there is no legislation binding the creditor to a gratuitous promise to accept a lesser sum) may now have a new argument that the creditor is bound notwithstanding, due to the *Greater Fredericton Airport Authority* case, *supra* note 38. The conclusion would be that, absent duress, the creditor's gratuitous promise to accept a lesser sum should be enforceable, for the policy reasons given in that case. Note that such a parallel argument was unsuccessful in England (which likewise has no such legislation binding the creditor). The English Court of Appeal in *Selectmove* stated that the common law rule (which says that a promise to take a lesser sum is unenforceable absent consideration) should not be judicially reversed. It was up to Parliament to enact legislation to effect such a result, if it were so inclined. See *Re: Selectmove Ltd*, [1955] 2 All ER 531 (CA).

Business Agreements

Most agreements in the commercial world, such as the one between Trackers and Coasters, are quite obviously intended to be contractual. The common law recognizes this reality through the rule stating that in the marketplace, the intention to contract is *presumed*. Therefore, if Trackers ends up suing Coasters for breach of contract, it will not have to prove that the agreement between them was intended to be a contractual one. The law gives Trackers a presumption to this effect; it is a **rebuttable presumption**, however. This means that while the court will assume that intention was present, Coasters can try to displace that presumption by proving a lack of intent to contract, judged objectively. Given the circumstances of its relationship with Trackers, Coasters faces an uphill battle on this point.

Family Agreements

Agreements between family members are regarded differently in law because of the personal nature of the underlying relationship. In fact, the common law presumes that promises between family members are non-contractual. Therefore, people who want to enforce an alleged contract against their parents or siblings, for example, must demonstrate to a court that there was an intention to contract. If they cannot positively prove that intent, their action will fail.

Managing the Risks in Contract Formation

Negotiators such as Jason and Amritha face two main risks. The first is the risk of misunderstanding when statements and conduct have legal consequences. For example, if Amritha makes what objectively looks like an offer to Jason, he is entitled to accept it and a contract is thus formed. Amritha cannot then go back and unilaterally amend the terms of her offer. The second risk is failing to anticipate and plan for contingencies that might occur after the contract has been formed. For example, if Jason agrees to supply tracking at a set price and later faces a substantial increase in production costs, Trackers still must provide the tracking as agreed, even though this will cause enormous financial hardship to Trackers. Customizing contractual terms in order to accommodate future contingencies such as these is discussed further in Chapter 7.

BUSINESS LAW IN PRACTICE REVISITED

1. At what point did the negotiations between Jason and Amritha begin to have legal consequences?

When Jason made an offer to sell tracking on specific terms, his negotiations with Amritha took a legal turn. At this point, Amritha was in a position to accept Jason's offer and, if she did, Trackers would be obligated to supply tracking on precisely those terms.

2. In what ways could negotiations have been terminated prior to the formation of the contract?

Amritha could have ended her negotiations by rejecting Jason's offer and telling him that Coasters would be looking elsewhere for its tracking. Though Amritha is not legally obligated to reject an offer, it is helpful to do so to ensure clarity and to avoid misunderstandings and disappointed expectations later on. Amritha

Rebuttable presumption

A legal presumption in favour of one party that the other side can seek to rebut or dislodge by leading evidence to the contrary.

should also withdraw any offer she may have made on behalf of Coasters to prevent Jason from accepting it sometime down the road. While the doctrine of lapse will prevent Jason from accepting after a certain point in time, it is difficult to predict how long a court would consider the offer to be open. It is preferable to simply withdraw the offer and avoid the debate altogether.

3. Can Coasters commit itself to the price increase and then change its mind with no adverse consequences?

Trackers has a pre-existing legal duty to supply the tracking at the price stated in the contract. Since it has given Coasters nothing in return for Coasters's promise to pay more, the traditional view is that Coasters has no legal obligation to pay the increase. Put another way, the promise is gratuitous. Any change to a contract—known in law as a "variation"—must be supported by consideration or be under seal in order to be enforceable. There is, however, a significant consequence to Coasters's decision from a business perspective; its relationship with Trackers will be seriously harmed and possibly destroyed. If Coasters ever needs tracking again, it is unlikely that Trackers will agree to be its supplier.

A competing analysis is offered by the New Brunswick Court of Appeal: provided the variation is not the product of duress, a contractual variation is enforceable due to principles of commercial or business efficacy—the goal is to protect the parties' legitimate expectations that such a contractual variation would be respected and adhered to.

4. How could Trackers have avoided from the outset this situation related to cost increases?

Trackers should have negotiated a clause in the contract that included a formula for varying the price according to prevailing market conditions, as established by a third party, trade journal, or other source. Other possibilities include negotiating a "cost plus contract," meaning the contract price would comprise the tracking manufacturer's actual costs, plus a set percentage of profit. Another alternative would have been to charge a higher price to begin with to cover unexpected cost escalations.

If Trackers were unsuccessful in getting such price adjustment mechanisms into the contract, it would assume the full risk of unanticipated cost increases. If Coasters did subsequently agree to pay more for the steel, Trackers should provide consideration for that promise or get it under seal.

CHAPTER SUMMARY

A contract comprises four essential elements: offer, acceptance, consideration, and intention to contract. Before a contract can be formed, one party must make an offer on a complete set of certain terms. An offer can be terminated in a number of ways, including by revocation, lapse, rejection, counteroffer, death, or insanity. Assuming that an offer is on the table, the other party must unconditionally accept all the terms of the offer for the offer to be considered accepted. Each party must give something (called consideration) in exchange for the promise or performance of the other. The parties must intend their bargain to be a contractual one. If any one of these elements is missing, the relationship is non-contractual by definition.

There are occasions, however, when the law will enforce a promise that is not supported by consideration. In short, if the promise is under seal, meets the requirements of promissory estoppel, or is subject to a specialized statutory scheme, such as the partial payment of debt, it will be enforceable. As well, the New Brunswick Court of Appeal is willing to enforce gratuitous contractual variations provided there is no economic duress. Aside from these exceptions, a gratuitous promise is not binding, no matter how seriously it was intended and no matter how much the other party may have relied on it. This legal reality is particularly important when varying a term in an existing contract.

While the conditions for creating a legal agreement may seem stringent, they serve an important purpose. Contract law is about creating voluntary agreements and is therefore facilitative. In sum, it helps those in the marketplace to determine—in advance of litigation—the legal enforceability of commitments they have received, and thereby lets them do business more effectively.

CHAPTER STUDY

Key Terms and Concepts

acceptance (p. 120)

consideration (p. 128)

counteroffer (p. 120)

gratuitous promise (p. 128)

invitation to treat (p. 112)

lapse (p. 119)

offer (p. 111)

offeree (p. 116)

offeror (p. 116)

option agreement (p. 118)

pre-existing legal duty (p. 129)

promissory estoppel (p. 132)

rebuttable presumption (p. 135)

rejection (p. 119)

revocation (p. 116)

standard form contract (p. 113)

Questions for Review

1. What must an offer contain?

2. Is an advertisement an offer or an invitation to treat? Why?

3. Are oral contracts enforceable?

4. What is a standard form contract?

5. Explain why it might be a good idea to get a contract in writing.

6. Does the acceptance of an offer have to mirror it exactly, or are slight variations permissible?

7. What is the "postal rule"?

8. How is the postal rule different from the "ordinary rule" for acceptance?

9. When must an offeree communicate acceptance to the offeror in a specific form?

10. Why is a counteroffer a form of rejecting an offer?

11. When can an offeror revoke or withdraw an offer?

12. What is consideration?

13. What is an option agreement? How is the concept of consideration related to the enforceability of such an agreement?

14. What is a pre-existing legal duty?

15. Is a promise to pay more for performance of a pre-existing legal duty generally enforceable?

16. What is a gratuitous promise? Give an example.

17. Are the rules governing the formation of electronic contracts different from those for written or oral contracts?

18. How does the relationship between the parties affect presumptions concerning their contractual intent?

19. What does Contract A refer to in a tendering context?

20. What does Contract B refer to in a tendering context?

Questions for Critical Thinking

1. The Ontario Court of Appeal in *Gilbert Steel* and the New Brunswick Court of Appeal in *Greater Fredericton Airport Authority* take opposite views on the enforceability of contractual variations unsupported by consideration. Which view do you prefer and why?

2. Which approach to controlling spam do think makes more business sense: an "opt-out" approach so that a businessperson can send an initial unsolicited email but that message must contain an opt-out or unsubscribe mechanism which the sender must respect; or Canada's "opt-in" approach described in this chapter?

3. Family members are presumed not to intend legal relations, while businesspeople are subject to the opposite presumption, namely that an intention to create legal relations is present. Why should the relationship between the parties affect the enforceability of their promises?

4. Was legislation necessary to make the determination that offer and acceptance can be expressed electronically? Why not simply leave such matters up to a judge?

5. What risks do negotiators face if they lack knowledge of the rules of contract?

6. Do you think that the doctrine of promissory estoppel serves a useful purpose? Would it not be easier if the law simply insisted that all contractual variations be supported by consideration?

Situations for Discussion

1. Daniel owned some out-of-town real estate which Paul had been eyeing for some time. On June 1, Daniel's real estate agent passed along an offer to Paul, whereby Daniel offered to sell Paul that land for $590 000. The offer was expressly to be "open" until June 8 and acceptance had to be in writing. Paul was delighted and even more pleased to learn from the realtor that there was plenty of time to consider the offer and that no one else was "dealing on the property." On June 3, the real estate agent gave Paul some bad news: Daniel had unexpectedly sold the property to someone else. Paul replied, "Well I accepted last night by initialing Daniel's offer so Daniel is clearly already in a contract with me. And I'll hold him to it." After hanging up, Paul wrote out a formal acceptance and delivered it, along with the initialed offer, to Daniel. Is Paul in a contract with Daniel?[49]

2. An advertisement similar to the following appeared in a popular Canadian business magazine. What legal obligations does it create for Star?

At ★ Star ★ We try harder!!

Any car rental company will reserve you a car. Only ★ Star ★ tries harder to get you where you're going.

3. Jack and his sister Lisa inherited their parents' commercial building. Jack suggested to Lisa that he would be willing to buy her out for $50 000. Lisa thought about it for a minute and then quickly agreed. "A deal is a deal," said Lisa and shook hands with her brother. "There is no need for us to go to a lawyer and get a big fancy contract written up."

   If Lisa ever has to prove this contract in a court of law, what are the problems she faces?

4. On October 30, Casgrain offered to purchase some farmland from Butler for $14 500, with possession in January. On November 15, Butler made a counteroffer, by telegram, at $15 000. The telegram was delivered to Casgrain's home on November 20 but Casgrain was absent on a hunting trip. Casgrain's wife read the telegram and wrote back to Butler saying that her husband was away for 10 days and asking that he hold the deal open until Casgrain could consider the matter. Butler did not respond. On December 10, Casgrain returned home and

---

49 Based, in part, on *Hughes v Gyratron Developments Ltd*, [1988] B.C.J. No. 1598.

immediately wired Butler, purporting to accept Butler's offer of $15 000. The wire was received on December 12. By this time, Butler had already sold the land to someone else. Has Casgrain accepted the offer in time or has it lapsed?[50]

5. Mr. and Mrs. Smith were regular participants in a lottery pool with their friends. Each Friday, the group would meet at the local pub and contribute to a pool of cash which would then be used to purchase lottery tickets. The group agreed that if a winning ticket were purchased, the amount would be shared among the participants. There was also discussion that if someone in the group did not come to the pub on the day in question, another person present would contribute on the missing person's behalf and get paid back later. On one Friday, the Smiths did not attend the pub and therefore did not contribute to the pool of lottery cash, but they trusted that their friends would contribute on their behalf. This did not happen. One of the tickets purchased turned out to be a winner and Mr. and Mrs. Smith say they are entitled to a share. The others in the group say that only those who actually paid into the pool for that winning ticket are entitled to a share of the prize. Which view do you think is correct and why?[51]

6. ABC Ltd. is owed $10 000 from Mr. Smith for home repair. Mr. Abbott, a senior officer with ABC Ltd., went to Smith's home to secure payment and spoke with Smith. Abbott explained that, without payment, ABC faced bankruptcy. In response, Smith began complaining about the poor quality of the work done (even though he knew the work was perfectly fine) and that he would only pay $4 000. "Take it or leave it, buster," he said. Abbott took his cheque and cashed it, feeling that he had no choice in the matter. He would now like to go after Smith for the balance. Can he do so?[52]

7. April manufactures leather chairs and sofas, and she is happy because she has just negotiated a contract with Bob's Fine Furnishings Ltd. to supply them with her handmade furniture. The terms of the contract are that, on the first Monday of every month, April is to send over 10 chairs and two sofas, and Bob's Fine Furnishings will pay her $7000. She is excited to learn that her furniture is so popular that Bob's Fine Furnishings has a waiting list of customers who have prepaid for their chairs, as her last shipment sold out in only a week. April is a little worried, however, as she has just received a phone call saying that her leather supplier will not be able to send her any leather for the next three months, due to a local shortage. Without the leather, she knows she cannot fill her order for Bob's Fine Furnishings by the first Monday of next month, much less for the two months after that. What could April have done when negotiating the contract with Bob's Fine Furnishings to help manage the risk of a situation like this? What should she do now that the contract is already in place?

8. Jack was in a lease with Douglas for the rental of a farm, including a large barn. In order to secure a lower monthly lease payment, Jack agreed to be responsible for all necessary repairs to the barn, repairs which had to be completed within six months of Douglas giving notice of those repairs being required. Failure to complete those repairs within six months of that notice gave Douglas the right to evict Jack. In January, Douglas gave Jack notice that some of the hand-built trusses in the barn roof needed replacement. Jack started the repairs but then had the idea that perhaps he could purchase the farm outright from Douglas. To Douglas's knowledge, he stopped doing repairs on the roof. "Why would I do repairs on Douglas's timelines when I may just become the owner of the place?" Jack observed to a friend. Jack and Douglas discussed a possible sale of the property for five months at which point negotiations broke down irretrievably. Jack then resumed doing repairs but still had not completed them by the next month. At that point, Douglas served Jack with an eviction notice for failure to make repairs in the six-month notice period. Can Jack rely on the doctrine of promissory estoppel to prevent the running of time this way? Explain.[53]

---

50 Based, in part, on *Barrick v Clark*, [1951] SCR 177.
51 Based, in part, on *Clancy v Gough*, 2011 ABQB 439.
52 Based, in part, on *D & C Builders v Rees*, [1965] 3 All ER 837 (CA).

53 Based, in part, on *Hughes v Metropolitan Railway*, (1877) 2 App Cas 439 (HL).

7

THE TERMS OF A CONTRACT

OBJECTIVES

After studying this chapter, you should have an understanding of

- the difference between implied and express terms

- how judges determine and interpret the content of a contract

- how a party can use terms as a business tool to protect itself from liability

BUSINESS LAW IN PRACTICE

The dispute discussed in Chapter 6 between Coasters and Trackers over the purchase price was resolved reasonably amicably—the parties agreed to split the increased cost of the steel required to manufacture the tracking and thereby avoid the expense and disruption of litigation. All the tracking has been delivered, and the new purchase price has been paid. Jason not only is tremendously relieved but also wants to improve his performance as a negotiator, since matters did not proceed entirely smoothly. He is reviewing the Coasters–Trackers contract to determine whether it did, in fact, contain the terms Trackers needed to protect itself.

The contract between Coasters and Trackers covered a number of terms already discussed in the previous chapter, including: price ($1.5 million); quantity (900 metres); delivery dates; and late-delivery charges ($5000 a day). Other significant clauses are excerpted below.

> Excerpt from the contract between Trackers (the "Seller") and Coasters (the "Buyer") for the purchase and sale of tracking (the "Goods")
>
> …
>
> **12. Warranties—Guarantees.**
>
> Seller warrants that the Goods shall be free from defect in material, workmanship, and title and shall conform in all respects to the design specifications provided by Buyer and attached as Schedule A to this contract. Where no quality is specified, the quality shall be of the best quality.
>
> If it appears within one year from the date of placing the Goods into service for the purpose for which they were purchased that the Goods, or any part thereof, do not conform to these warranties, Buyer, at its election and within a reasonable time after its discovery, may notify Seller. If notified, Seller shall thereupon promptly correct such nonconformity at its sole expense.
>
> …
>
> **13. Limitation of Seller's Liability.**
>
> Except as otherwise provided in this contract, Seller's liability shall extend to all damages proximately caused by the breach of any of the foregoing warranties or guarantees, but such

(Continued on the next page)

Feng Yu/Shutterstock

liability shall in no event exceed unit price of defective Goods and in no event include loss of profit or loss of use.

...

14. **Exemption of Seller's Liability.**

   Seller is exempted from all liability in respect to losses, damages, costs, or claims relating to design of Goods.

...

20. **Entire Contract.**

   This is the entire agreement between the parties, covering everything agreed upon or understood in connection with the subject matter of this transaction. There are no oral promises, conditions, representations, understandings, interpretations, or terms of any nature or kind, statutory or otherwise, as conditions or inducements to the execution hereof or in effect between the parties or upon which the parties are relying relating to this agreement or otherwise.

1. How is the scope of Trackers's and Coasters's obligations determined?

2. Are there any ambiguous or unclear terms in the contract?

3. Are there any additional terms that Jason should have tried to include?

4. Does the contract relieve the parties from responsibility for inadequate performance?

The Content of a Contract

This chapter is about the content—or terms—of a contract and how the courts interpret those terms. The terms of a contract simply refer to promises made by one party to another by virtue of offer and acceptance. From a risk management perspective, a contract is a business tool that can be used to manage a business's exposure to liability—also the subject matter of this chapter.

Terms

Contractual terms can be express or implied.

Express Terms

An **express term** is a provision of the contract that states or makes explicit one party's promise to another. In the Coasters–Trackers contract, for example, a number of terms are express, including the price, quantity, and warranties associated with the tracking. It is important that the essential terms of a contract be expressed so that each party knows its obligations and the obligations of the other side. Parties negotiating a contract should be very careful not to make assumptions about any aspect of the transaction, as only terms, not assumptions, have legal weight.

Express term

A provision of a contract that states a promise explicitly.

Judicial Interpretation of Express Terms

Vague or Ambiguous Language Even when a term is express, there may be problems interpreting what it means because the language is vague or ambiguous. Assuming that the existence of the contract is not in doubt, the court assigns as reasonable a meaning as possible to vague or ambiguous terms.[1] As well, if the contract has been drafted by one of the parties, any ambiguity in language will likely be construed against that party in favour of the other.[2] The policy rationale for this rule is that the drafter should bear the risk of unclear language.

The reference to "best quality" in clause 12 of the Coasters–Trackers contract is somewhat nebulous, as it introduces an express element of subjectivity: what, exactly, is "best quality"? If faced with such a question, a court would conclude that "best quality" refers to the highest quality available, which, in turn, is a matter that expert evidence would establish. A court would not set the contract aside for uncertainty because some meaning can be assigned to the phrase "best quality."

There is a point, however, at which language is so ambiguous that the contract cannot be understood. In such cases, the contract will fail for uncertainty, and none of the promises it contains will be enforceable.

It can be very difficult to predict how a court will interpret any given contract because **rules of construction**—that is, guiding principles for interpreting or "constructing" the terms of a contract—are often conflicting. For example, on the one hand, courts are required to enforce the contract as it is written and to rely primarily on the plain, ordinary meaning of the words that the parties have chosen. The court simply asks how a reasonable person would regard the term in question and can refer to dictionaries, legal reference materials, and cases that have considered such terms in the past. On the other hand, courts are to give effect to the parties' intentions. Both of these rules make sense standing alone, but they do not provide a solution to the situation in which the parties' intentions may be inadequately reflected in the written contract itself. Should the court apply the plain-meaning rule or give effect to the parties' intentions? Which rule should prevail?

In the Coasters–Trackers contract, Trackers promised to pay $5000 to Coasters for every day it was late in delivering the tracking. The intent of the parties, objectively assessed, may have been to motivate Trackers to do everything in its power to provide the tracking by the contractual delivery date. On this basis, if Trackers were late in delivering because of a mechanical problem in its plant, the clause would apply. It would be more contentious to apply the clause if late delivery were caused by an event completely outside Trackers' control—such as a severe lightning strike disrupting electricity to its plant for several days. Trackers might advance the position that to apply the clause in such circumstances would be contrary to the parties' intentions.

In response, Coasters would ask that the court apply the plain-meaning rule and disregard evidence of the parties' intentions. On the basis of the plain-meaning rule, a court could easily conclude that the late-delivery clause speaks for itself and is unconditional: if Trackers delivers late, it has to pay $5000 per day. Whether a court would use the plain-meaning rule standing alone or allow the clause's plain meaning to be tempered with evidence of what the parties intended the term to mean is impossible to predict—another inherent risk of litigation.

Trackers could face further problems in convincing a court of its interpretation of the late-delivery clause based on the parties' intentions. Two possible sources

---

Rules of construction

Guiding principles for interpreting or "constructing" the terms of a contract.

---

1 Stephanie Ben-Ishai & David R Percy, eds, *Contracts: Cases and Commentaries*, 9th ed (Toronto ON: Carswell, 2014) at 111.
2 *Ibid* at 509.

of problems are the parol evidence rule and the fact that the Coasters–Trackers contract contains what is known as an entire contract clause. Both matters are discussed later in this chapter.

When parties fail to address an important aspect of their contractual relationship, the law may help to "fill in the blanks" through implied terms, discussed below. The assistance that implied terms can provide, however, is sporadic and cannot be relied on with any certainty.

Implied Terms

When an event arises that is not addressed in the contract through express terms, courts may be asked to imply a term in order to give effect to the parties' intentions. A judge will do so if he is satisfied that not all of the terms that the parties intended to include in the contract were, in fact, included. In the classic scenario, the plaintiff argues to include an **implied term** but the defendant asserts that no such term was intended. Since the plaintiff carries the burden of proof, she will lose unless she can demonstrate that the term exists based on the balance of probabilities (i.e., she needs to prove that it is more likely than not that the parties intended such a term to be included).

Implied term

A provision that is not expressly included in a contract but that is necessary to give effect to the parties' intention.

BUSINESS APPLICATION OF THE LAW

911 EMERGENCY ACCESS

In 2014, James Anderson and his son Samuel Anderson of Yellowknife won a lengthy class action battle against Bell Mobility Inc. (Bell), a Canadian cellular phone service provider at the trial level.[3] As quoted in the *Globe and Mail*, Keith Landy (a lawyer for the plaintiffs) stated as follows: "It was a David and Goliath struggle in which the consumers have won an important victory."

For years, Bell had been charging the Andersons 75 cents a month for live 911 emergency access even though there actually is no live 911 emergency access service in the Northwest Territories (NWT). Calling 911 anywhere in the NWT simply triggers a generic recording, directing the caller to hang up and dial the local police or fire station for assistance. Among other arguments, the Andersons contended that Bell was in breach of contract for charging a fee for live 911 service when no such service was available or provided.

The Supreme Court of the Northwest Territories agreed that the words "911 emergency

service" in the service contract with Bell meant "911 live operator service." Furthermore, the court ruled, though the contract did not *require* Bell to actually provide live 911 operator service, neither did the contract permit Bell to *charge* for such a service when no such service was in place. As the court states:

> The Bell Mobility Service Agreement begins with the wording ". . . The Agreement is binding on you and us for each device that you connect to our network and for service we provide to you for your device." I conclude that Bell Mobility did not provide a 911 live operator service and therefore, under the terms of its agreement cannot bill for "911 emergency service fees."

The trial judge's ruling was upheld on appeal.[4]

According to the appellate court: "In my respectful view, connecting someone to nothing is still nothing. A right to charge a door-to-door delivery fee for milk cannot be triggered by delivering empty bottles."

For similar reasons, the Court of Appeal rejected Bell's argument that the customer still

---

3 *Anderson v Bell Mobility Inc* 2013 NWTSC 25.
4 *Bell Mobility Inc. v Anderson* 2015 NWTCA 3.

James Anderson

plaintiffs' counsel was anticipating a claim "for between $3 million and $5 million."

That Bell even appealed the trial decision puzzles James Anderson—whose $338 000 costs award was also largely upheld on appeal.[5] As Anderson told the Northern News Service in 2014: "It's perplexing in that the costs that Bell would have incurred for their legal representation, plus the costs that they're compelled to pay our legal team . . . to me it would have far exceeded the illegitimate 911 fees that Northern consumers paid."

Since then, Bell's application for leave to appeal to the Supreme Court of Canada was dismissed.[6]

Critical Analysis: Do you agree with how the trial judge and appeal court interpreted the contract with Bell?

receives a benefit when he or she dials 911 since this will connect the caller to someone else's recorded message advising that there is no service and instructing the caller to use local emergency numbers. The court was entirely unconvinced, noting that ". . . to seek to charge for that by calling it 911 service, seems to me very unreasonable. It is like delivering to a starving person a photograph of a turkey dinner, and then charging him or her for a turkey dinner (or delivery of one)."

The *Globe and Mail* reports that the defendant is "very disappointed with the decision" and that the matter of damages will proceed by way of separate trial. As of the date of the *Globe*'s report,

Sources: Christine Dobby, "Bell loses appeal of class-action suit over non-existent 911 services" *Globe and Mail* (8 January 2015), online: *Globe and Mail:* <<http://www.theglobeandmail.com/report-on -business/bell-loses-appeal-of-class-action-suit-over-non-existent -911-services/article22370425/>>; Daniel Campbell, "Bell forced to pay costs in 911 fee case: Judge orders provider to dole out $338,000 in legal fees after losing last May" *Northern News Service* (22 March 2014), online: *Northern News Service* online <http://www.nnsl.com/ frames/newspapers/2014-03/mar24_14bell.html> Jeff Gray, "Bell loses class-action case over 911 fees in North" *Globe and Mail* (17 May 2013), online: *Globe and Mail* << http://www.theglobeandmail.com/ report-on-business/industry-news/the-law-page/bell-loses-class -action-case-over-911-fees-in-north/article12003832/>> CBC News, "Bell Mobility to appeal ruling in 911 lawsuit" (18 May 2013), online: CBC News << http://www.cbc.ca/news/canada/north/bell-mobility-to -appeal-ruling-in-911-lawsuit-1.1338101. Grant Robertson "Frustrated with no 911 services, customers fight back", Globe and Mail (11 April 2010), online: Globe and Mail <http://m.theglobeandmail.com/report -on-business/frustrated-with-no-911-service-customers-fight-back/ article1530801/?service=mobile>

Courts will imply terms based on a number of grounds, such as those listed below.

Business Efficacy The doctrine of business efficacy permits judges to imply terms necessary to make the contract workable. For example, if Trackers promised to use a certain grade of tracking, "providing it is available," a court will almost certainly imply a promise by Trackers to put reasonable effort into trying to find that grade of tracking. Though Trackers has not expressly committed itself to make systematic efforts in this regard, business efficacy makes the obligation implicit.[7]

---

5 *Ibid* at para 128.
6 [2015] SCCA No 92.
7 For a case that follows this analysis, see *Dawson v Helicopter Exploration Co,* [1955] SCR 868.

Were it otherwise, the express term in relation to the quality of tracking would mean next to nothing.

The following case illustrates how a term of good faith can be implied.

PART TWO

LANDMARK CASE

Gateway Realty Ltd v Arton Holdings Ltd 1991, 106 NSR (2d) 180 (SC), aff'd (1992), 112 NSR (2d) 180 (CA)

THE BUSINESS CONTEXT: Businesspeople might assume that the only obligations they owe the other party are those recited in the contract between them. This assumption may prove to be unfounded, particularly in the situation where one party is in a position to adversely affect the interests of the other.

FACTUAL BACKGROUND: Gateway owned a shopping mall in which Zellers was the anchor tenant. The lease permitted Zellers to occupy the premises, leave them vacant, or assign them to a third party without any obligation to secure the consent of the landlord. After being approached by Arton, a competitor of Gateway, Zellers agreed to locate in Arton's mall. As part of this arrangement, Arton agreed to take an assignment of Zellers' lease with Gateway. As a result, a large part of Gateway's mall had been assigned to its competitor. Pursuant to a subsequent contract between Gateway and Arton, the companies agreed to use their best efforts to get a tenant for the space formerly occupied by Zellers. Arton, however, rejected all prospective tenants. Gateway then sued, alleging that Arton was in breach of contract for declining prospective tenants. From Gateway's perspective, Arton was simply trying to undermine the economic viability of the mall by letting a large portion of it remain unoccupied.

THE LEGAL QUESTION: Is there an implied obligation of good faith on Arton's part to take reasonable steps to sublet the premises?

RESOLUTION: The court found that Arton breached the express obligation to use its "best efforts" to find a tenant, as well as an implied term to act in good faith.

According to the court:

> The law requires that parties to a contract exercise their rights under that agreement honestly, fairly and in good faith. This standard is breached when a party acts in a bad faith manner in the performance of its rights and obligations under the contract. "Good faith" conduct is the guide to the manner in which the parties should pursue their mutual contractual objectives. Such conduct is breached when a party acts in "bad faith"—a conduct that is contrary to community standards of honesty, reasonableness or fairness.

The court went on to say:

> In most cases, bad faith can be said to occur when one party, without reasonable justification, acts in relation to the contract in a manner where the result would be to substantially nullify the bargained objective or benefit contracted for by the other, or to cause significant harm to the other, contrary to the original purpose and expectation of the parties.

CRITICAL ANALYSIS: The *Gateway* case has been followed or cited with approval by numerous Canadian courts. Do you think the court was correct to imply a term of good faith in the contract between the parties?

Customs in the Trade of the Transaction

Relying on trade customs to imply a term is rarely successful, since it must be proved that the custom is so notorious that the contract in question must be presumed to contain such an implied term.[8] Though a party is occasionally successful in relying on custom in a trade, the more prudent course is to ensure that all important terms in a contract are expressly recited.

---

8   GHL Fridman, *The Law of Contract in Canada*, 6th ed (Toronto: Carswell, 2011) at 474.

Glenko Enterprises Ltd v Ernie Keller Contractors Ltd, [1994] 10 WWR 641 (Man QB), aff'd [1996] 5 WWR 135 (Man CA)

THE BUSINESS CONTEXT: Unpaid accounts are an unfortunate reality of the business world. Even when the customer admits that the account is owed, disputes can arise on the rate of interest payable if the contract does not expressly address this matter.

FACTUAL BACKGROUND: Though a number of factual and legal matters were at play in this case, it is most germane to note that the subcontractor, Glenko Enterprises Ltd., worked on a project but was not paid by the project contractor (Ernie Keller Contractors Ltd.). The contractor admitted that it owed $123 862.75 but insisted that since no interest had been stipulated in the contract, no interest on the overdue account should be payable. The plaintiff stated that interest was owed at the rate of 1.5 percent per month or 18 percent per annum on accounts over 30 days for three reasons:

- there was an implied agreement that such interest was payable based on the term being contained in the invoices sent to the contractor.

- the contractor did not object to the term regarding interest and, on the contrary, continued to deal with the subcontractor.

- it is a common trade practice to be charged, and to pay, interest on overdue accounts. The contractor itself included such an interest provision in its own invoices.

THE LEGAL QUESTION: Since the contract between the contractor and subcontractor was silent on the point of interest, what interest, if any, would be payable? Could a term be implied based on trade custom?

RESOLUTION: Even though this matter was not extensively discussed at trial, the judge ruled that the contractor was aware of and followed an industry practice of charging interest on overdue accounts. This was largely because the contractor had itself included a provision for interest in its own invoices. The plaintiffs were therefore entitled to the interest as claimed.

CRITICAL ANALYSIS: Why should industry or trade practice be relevant to understanding the parties' contractual obligations? Would it not be simpler for a court to apply the contractual terms as stated and refuse to look outside that document? What are the risks of relying on industry practices as a way of implying terms into a contract?

Previous Dealings Between the Parties If parties have contracted in the past, it may be possible to imply that their current contract contains the same terms.[9] A risk management perspective would suggest, however, that the parties clarify the basis of their contractual relationship each time they do business with each other.

Statutory Requirements An important source of terms implied by statute[10] is found in provincial sale-of-goods legislation, which is largely uniform across the country. This legislation provides that certain terms are a mandatory part of every contract for the sale of goods unless specifically excluded by the parties.[11] Specialized rules governing the sale of goods and the extent to which consumer transactions can exclude their application are discussed in more detail in Chapter 23.

---

9 *Ibid* at 472.
10 For discussion, *ibid* at 475 and following.
11 For a discussion of sale of goods legislation, see Chapter 23 as well as GHL Fridman, *Sale of Goods in Canada*, 6th ed (Toronto: Carswell, 2013).

If Trackers delivers too much tracking to Coasters under its contract, the Ontario *Sale of Goods Act*,[12] for example, would resolve the situation according to the following rule:

29. (2) Where the seller delivers to the buyer a quantity of goods larger than the seller contracted to sell, the buyer may accept the goods included in the contract and reject the rest, or may reject the whole, and if the buyer accepts the whole of the goods so delivered, the buyer shall pay for them at the contract rate.

How can a business avoid having terms implied into a contract?

---

12 *RSO* 1990, c S1.

Entire contract clause

A term in a contract in which the parties agree that their contract is complete as written.

Contractual quantum meruit

Awarding one party a reasonable sum for the goods or services provided under a contract.

In general, terms are not easily implied except in routine transactions or unless the *Sale of Goods Act* applies. It must be clear that both parties would have included the term in question, had they addressed the matter.

Similarly, courts ordinarily will not imply terms when the parties have agreed that their contract is complete as written. The clearest way parties can signal this intention is through an **entire contract clause** like the one in the Coasters–Trackers contract excerpted earlier in this chapter. The function of this clause is to require a court to determine the parties' obligations based only on what is recited in the contract itself.

BUSINESS APPLICATION OF THE LAW

A REQUEST FOR GOODS OR SERVICES: IMPLYING A PROMISE TO PAY

When someone requests the supply of goods or services, the law—be it through common law or by applicable legislation such as the *Sale of Goods Act*—will imply a promise to pay a reasonable price for those goods or services. The law draws this conclusion because, in a business situation, it is the intention of the parties that goods or services are not to be provided for free, but rather are to be purchased. Implying such a term reflects what can only be the reasonable expectation of the parties and is needed to give purpose and effect to the rest of the contract. If the goods or services have already been provided but there has been no agreement on price, a term must be implied to require payment. The obligation on the customer is not to pay whatever the supplier chooses to charge or whatever the customer is willing to pay, but to pay a reasonable amount, as determined by the judge. This is known as a **contractual quantum meruit**, which is Latin for "as much as is merited or deserved." Given the expense and uncertainty of judicial proceedings, it is in the interests of both parties to agree on the price, in advance, as an express term. The objective is to avoid the surprises and misunderstandings that may lead to a legal dispute.

Critical Analysis: Does the law's willingness to imply a promise to pay lead to uncertainty? Why should someone have liability on a promise that she has not expressly made?

Bhasin v Hrynew 2014 SCC 71

THE BUSINESS CONTEXT: Parties to a contract are generally entitled to put self-interest first but there is a point at which such conduct can cross a legal line. In the face of such conduct, courts may interpret the contract so as ensure that such a party cannot take the benefit of its dishonesty.

FACTUAL BACKGROUND: The defendant, Canadian American Financial Corp. (Can-Am), was a marketer of education savings plans to investors. Can-Am's product sales were made by enrollment directors—small business owners—who would earn compensation and bonuses by building their own sales teams. The plaintiff, Mr. Bhasin, was just such an enrollment director with Can-Am. The agreement between Bhasin and Can-Am essentially permitted either side to decide not to renew the contract on six months' notice. The contract did not require that there be a reason for non-renewal. It simply called for notice.

As found by the trial judge, Can-Am was either untruthful or equivocated about its intention not to renew under the clause and its desire to merge Bhasin's agency with that of his competitor when asked about these matters by Bhasin. When Can-Am did finally provide the six months' notice, Bhasin learned

---

about these earlier misrepresentations and sued for breach of contract including for loss of income and loss of value of his business.

THE LEGAL QUESTION: Is Can-Am in breach of contract?

RESOLUTION: Bhasin was successful at trial, with the judge ruling that the defendant exercised its option not to renew the contract in bad faith. The Court of Appeal reversed, ruling that—by the plain words of the contract—Can-Am was entitled not to renew on giving the requisite notice. Having good faith reasons was not required and should not be implied as a prerequisite, particularly as the contract here contained an entire contract clause.

The Supreme Court of Canada rejected both these approaches and found for Bhasin according to its own analysis. First, the Supreme Court stated that contract law is infused by a good faith principle in contractual performance, which insists that parties act "honestly and reasonably, not capriciously or arbitrarily." Second, and based on this principle, the Supreme Court concluded that common law contains a newly recognized duty of honesty, which means as follows:

> …parties must not lie or otherwise knowingly mislead each other about matters directly linked to the performance of the contract. This does not impose a duty of loyalty or of disclosure or require a party to forego advantages flowing from the contract; it is a simple requirement not to lie or mislead the other party about one's contractual performance.

The court went on to note that parties might be free to modify this duty by contract in the

Neil Finkelstein was co-counsel to Bhasin before before the Supreme Court of Canada.

Courtesy of Neil Finkelstein

right circumstances but could not eliminate the duty's "core requirements."

The Supreme Court found that Can-Am had breached its duty of honesty on multiple occasions by being untruthful or equivocating with Bhasin about the renewal and merger. It also ruled that, if Bhasin had known the truth, he could have taken steps to retain the value of his agency prior to notice being given. On this basis, Bhasin was awarded the value of the agency at the time of non-renewal: $87 000.

CRITICAL ANALYSIS: If Can-Am had simply avoided all communication with Bhasin about its intention not to renew, would it be in breach of the new duty of honesty? Why or why not?

The Parol Evidence Rule

Contracts can take three possible forms:

- entirely oral (i.e., the terms of the contract are based on a conversation).
- entirely written (i.e., the terms of the contract are contained in a written contract).
- both oral and written (i.e., some of the agreement is written down and other assurances are not). For example, if Jason gave Amritha an oral assurance that Trackers would provide expert advice on how to install the

tracking as a service included in the contract price, their contract would be both oral and written.

Except in a few specialized instances, discussed in Chapter 8, the form a contract takes does not affect its enforceability. So long as the party claiming that there is a contract can prove it—through witnesses, for example—the fact that the parties only "shook hands" on the deal is not an impediment. Nevertheless, from the perspective of proving the contract, a written contract is always best.

Parol evidence rule

A rule that limits the evidence a party can introduce concerning the contents of the contract.

There is an important consequence to having a written contract. Such contracts may trigger the **parol evidence rule** when a court is asked to determine—according to the parties' intentions—what a contract means and includes. "Parol" means "oral" or "spoken" but in this context refers to any kind of evidence that is extrinsic to the written agreement. The rule forbids outside evidence as to the terms of a contract when the language of the written contract is clear and the document is intended to be the sole source of contractual content. In the example above, the parol evidence rule may prohibit Amritha from bringing forward evidence of Jason's oral promise to provide expert installation advice. For this reason, a businessperson must be careful not to rely on oral assurances made by the other party, because if the assurance is not in the contract, a court may decline to enforce it as a contractual term.

Entire contract clauses are used to ensure application of the parol evidence rule to the contract in question. As noted earlier, such clauses generally operate to prevent a party from arguing that the terms of the agreement were found not just in the written document, but also in oral form. Clause 20 of the Coasters–Trackers contract is an entire contract clause. Such a clause is intended to ensure that any oral commitment made by one side to the other that is not ultimately written into the contract simply dies.

The parol evidence rule emphasizes the sanctity of the written agreement and means that the parties should, before agreeing to a written contract, ensure provision of all terms important to them. Failure to do so may mean that the rule is invoked against the party that cannot support its interpretation of the contract without leading evidence "outside" the contract.

The parol evidence rule has itself become the subject of judicial consideration which, in turn, has justifiably limited its operation. Indeed, there are several situations where evidence outside the contract is important and is considered

- if there is an alleged problem going to the formation of the contract—because one party alleges fraud at the hands of the other or asserts that there has been a mistake, for example—a party may bring to the court evidence to establish that allegation. Chapter 8 considers problems going to the formation of a contract in more detail.

- if the contract is *intended* to be partly oral and partly in writing, the rule has no application. The rule applies only when the parties intended the document to be the whole contract.

- if the promise to be enforced is contained in a separate (collateral) agreement that happens to be oral, the rule does not apply. For example, an agreement to sell (for a set price) a building with all the equipment in it may not actually include the equipment if the written agreement fails to mention it. If there is a separate agreement and a separate price for the equipment, however, the fact that the agreement for the building says nothing about the equipment is likely not a concern. The difference in the two situations is in the matter of there being separate consideration for the building and the equipment. If there is only one agreement and one price, the rule likely applies to the detriment of the party seeking to enforce the purchase and sale of the equipment.

- if the language in the contract is ambiguous, evidence outside the written contract can be used to resolve the ambiguity.

The following case demonstrates how even an entire contract clause may not prevent a court from considering parol evidence.

CASE

Corey Developments Inc v Eastbridge Developments (Waterloo) Ltd (1997), 34 OR (3d) 73, aff'd (1999), 44 OR (3d) 95 (CA)

THE BUSINESS CONTEXT: The parol evidence rule in its absolute form may cause manifest injustice and defeat the true intentions of the parties. Thus, almost from its inception, it has been subject to many exceptions. In recent times, the rule has also received disapproval from various law reform commissions. As well, several provinces have abolished the rule altogether in consumer situations. Consumer protection legislation in these provinces means that oral pre-contractual statements are not necessarily superseded by written terms.

In commercial transactions, the parol evidence rule has generally prevented the introduction of extrinsic evidence in challenging the written document and establishing the existence of oral promises. This treatment of the parol evidence rule as an absolute bar in commercial transactions has come under attack, however.

FACTUAL BACKGROUND: Corey Developments Inc. signed an agreement of purchase and sale with Eastbridge Developments Ltd., which was controlled by Mr. Ghermezian, a well-known Alberta developer. Corey gave a deposit of $201 500 to Eastbridge. According to Corey, as the money was to be used by Eastbridge to fund the costs of obtaining subdivision approval, Ghermezian said he would give his personal guarantee for the return of the deposit if the agreement did not close. The agreement of purchase and sale, however,

made no mention of the personal guarantee, and Ghermezian denied ever having made such a promise. Evidence, including various letters between the parties, established the existence of the promise. The agreement of purchase and sale, however, contained an entire contract clause indicating that the agreement was intended to be the whole agreement. Therefore, by strict application of the parol evidence rule, the judge could not admit the oral evidence of Corey or the other documentary evidence.

THE LEGAL QUESTION: Was Ghermezian's personal guarantee to return the deposit a part of the contract?

RESOLUTION: Justice MacDonald referred to *Gallen v Allstate Grain Ltd,*[13] in which Justice Lambert found that the parol evidence rule provided only a presumption that the written terms should govern and allowed the extrinsic evidence. Justice MacDonald went on to state, "The court must not allow the rule to be used to cause obvious injustice by providing a tool for one party to dupe another."

Applying the principle from *Gallen,* Justice MacDonald ruled that Ghermezian's personal guarantee was part of the contract between the parties, notwithstanding the entire contract clause and the parol evidence rule.

CRITICAL ANALYSIS: Is the *Corey* decision a welcome development? What are the justifications, if any, for abolishing the parol evidence rule in a commercial context?

Source: Jan Weir, "The death of the absolute parol rule" *The Lawyers Weekly* (6 February 1998) 3.

---

13 (1984), 9 DLR (4th) 496 (BCCA).

EVIDENCE OF ELECTRONIC CONTRACTS

Those who seek to enforce a contract must be able to prove that the contract was formed and that its terms support the claim that is made. Traditionally, that proof takes the form of witness testimony and documents that are submitted to the court as evidence. Of course, in proving the contract, the parties will have to respect the parol evidence rule and other rules of evidence.

With the growth of electronic business, contracts are increasingly negotiated online and the terms are recorded electronically, without a paper version. This method of doing business creates difficulty if it becomes necessary to produce the "original" contract in court. In response, governments across Canada have begun to enact legislation addressing this point.

In 1997, the Uniform Law Conference of Canada proposed draft legislation—called the *Uniform Electronic Evidence Act, or UEEA* for short—to make the proof of electronic contracts subject to a uniform set of rules. This draft legislation has since been implemented in a number of jurisdictions. For example, Ontario implemented the *UEEA* by amending

its *Evidence Act*. Section 34.1 of that Act, as amended, provides

Authentication:

(4) The person seeking to introduce an electronic record has the burden of proving its authenticity by evidence capable of supporting a finding that the electronic record is what the person claims it to be.

Application of Best Evidence Rule:

(5) Subject to subsection (6) where the best evidence rule is applicable in respect of an electronic record, it is satisfied on proof of the integrity of the electronic records system by or in which the data was recorded or stored.

Beyond Ontario, other provinces and territories (including Alberta, Manitoba, Nova Scotia, PEI, Saskatchewan, and the Yukon), as well as the federal government, have enacted legislation which mirrors, in whole or in part, the Uniform Conference of Canada's draft act.[14]

Critical Analysis: Are these kinds of amendments to *Evidence Act* legislation necessary to deal with electronic contracts? Could judges not be entrusted with the task of providing rules on a case by case basis?

Using Contractual Terms to Manage Risk

The planning function of law permits a businessperson to use contractual terms as a buffer against future, uncertain events as well as a way of limiting liability.

Changed Circumstances

Numerous circumstances may arise that prevent a party from performing its contractual obligations or that make performance much more expensive than anticipated. The rule, however, is that the terms of a contract are settled at the time of acceptance. Therefore, if disaster strikes—such as when a plant burns, railways go on strike or are closed, trade regulations change, or an entire manufacturing process becomes obsolete—the obligations in a contract are enforceable, unless a clause to the contrary is included. Though the legal doctrine of "frustration" occasionally

---

14 See, for example *Alberta Evidence Act*, RSA 2000, c A-18 ss 41.1-41.8; *Evidence Act*, RSNS 1989, c 154 ss 23A-23H (Nova Scotia); *Evidence Act*, RSO 1990, c E.23 ss 34.1(1)-34.1(11) (Ontario); *Electronic Evidence Act*, RSPEI, c E-4.3 (Prince Edward Island) and Manitoba *Evidence Act*, CCSM c E150 ss 51.1-51.8. For discussion of UEEA legislation in Canada, see Charles Morgan & Julien Saulgrain, *E-Mail Law* (Markham: LexisNexis, 2008) at 130–132.

relieves parties from their obligations (see Chapter 9), it operates in very limited circumstances and cannot be counted on to provide an avenue of escape.

It is therefore particularly important in longer-term contracts that negotiators evaluate risks, speculate on possible changes in the business environment, and be wary of making inflexible commitments. Taking these precautions is essential because changed circumstances may render a contract extremely disadvantageous to one party. For example, the price for the tracking that Trackers needed to fill Coasters' order dramatically increased, making it very expensive for Trackers to complete its end of the bargain. Rather than run such a risk, Trackers could have negotiated for a term that would permit the contract price for the tracking to rise should the price of tracking increase. A contractual term could

- provide a formula setting the price of the goods supplied, in a manner that is tied to market value.
- set the price according to the cost of materials, plus a specific percentage for profit.
- allow the parties to reopen negotiations or terminate the contract altogether if specified events occur, such as a commodity price reaching a certain level.

Instead of having to go to Coasters for some kind of accommodation, Trackers could have included a clause protecting its interests. Though the approach of voluntarily altering the agreement as the need arises can be successful, legally there is no obligation on either party to reach agreement. Furthermore, as discussed in Chapter 6, the voluntary agreement is unenforceable unless fresh consideration is given, a court is willing to apply *Greater Fredericton Airport Authority Inc v NAV Canada*,[15] promissory estoppel applies, or the document is put under seal.

Parties must try to build some flexibility into their agreements, while avoiding creating a document that is so vague that they run the risk of having no contract at all. If in negotiations a customer such as Coasters refuses to accept a price-variation clause of any description, the supplier must then choose to risk an adverse change in market conditions, try to negotiate a higher price to compensate for possible market changes, or lose the order altogether.

Why do well-drafted contracts anticipate events that can affect performance?

Steve Russell/GetStock.com

---

15 2008 NBCA 28.

Conditional Agreements

Conditional agreements are essential when one party wants to incur contractual obligations but only under certain circumstances. For example, a business enterprise may be interested in buying a warehouse, but only if it is able to secure financing from the bank. If the business simply agrees to purchase the warehouse without making its agreement conditional on securing financing, it will be obligated to complete the transaction even if the bank refuses the request for a loan. This outcome could have devastating financial consequences for the business in question. Conversely, if the business makes an offer to purchase the property subject to financing,[16] and that offer is accepted by the vendor, the business is obligated to complete only if and when the financing is approved.

From a risk management perspective, it is important that the law provide a mechanism not only for making the contractual obligation conditional on a certain event happening, but also for binding the parties in some way during the time set aside for that condition to occur. If the vendor of the warehouse was entitled to sell to someone else while the business enterprise was trying to secure necessary financing, the whole arrangement would be somewhat futile.

To bind the other side during the time set aside for the condition's fulfillment, the law provides two mechanisms: the condition subsequent and the condition precedent. A **condition subsequent** will always bind the parties to a contract pending the fulfillment of the condition. The occurrence of a condition subsequent operates to terminate the contract between the parties—that is, it must, by definition, relate to an existing contract. For example, parties to an employment contract may agree that an employee is to work for an organization unless the employee's sales drop below a certain amount. This is a contract subject to a condition subsequent. If the condition occurs—that is, if the employee's sales fall below the threshold—the contract automatically comes to an end.

For the most part, a **condition precedent** works in the same way—that is, there is a contract between the parties.[17] However, unlike the condition subsequent situation, where parties perform their contractual obligations until the condition occurs, the condition precedent situation means that the parties' obligations to perform are not triggered pending fulfillment of the condition. That is, a contract exists between the parties, but the obligation to perform the contract is held in abeyance pending the occurrence of the event. Because there is a contract between the parties, the law is able to imply certain terms binding on the parties in the meantime. In the real estate situation, for example, a court would imply a term that the vendor must wait until the time for fulfilling the condition has passed before it can sell to someone else. Similarly, a court would imply a term on the purchaser to make good faith efforts to secure the necessary financing. Without a contract between the parties, these kinds of terms could not be implied because, without a contract, there are no terms whatsoever.[18]

---

16 Such a clause must contain sufficient detail; otherwise, it will be unenforceable owing to uncertainty. For discussion of such clauses, see Gwilym Davies, "Some Thoughts on the Drafting of Conditions in Contracts for the Sale of Land" (1977) 15:2 Alta L Rev 422.

17 Not all conditions precedent operate within the context of a contract, however, and this is where the law can become somewhat confusing. As a rule, conditions precedent will bind the parties to a contract if the condition itself is reasonably certain and objective. Conditions that are tied to whim, fancy, or extreme subjectivity as in "I'll buy your house if I decide that I like it" do not bind the parties because they essentially have no objective content. These are known as illusory conditions precedent and leave the parties free to do as they please, since there is no contract between them. For obvious reasons, illusory conditions precedents are rare. For discussion and case law on this point, see Ben-Ishai & Percy, *supra* note 1 at 329 and following.

18 It is beyond the scope of this text to discuss the issue of waiver of conditions precedent. For an assessment of this particularly thorny problem, see Gwilym Davies, "Conditional Contracts for the Sale of Land in Canada" (1977) 55:2 Can Bar Rev 289.

Condition subsequent

An event or circumstance that, when it occurs, brings an existing contract to an end.

Condition precedent

An event or circumstance that, until it occurs, suspends the parties' obligations to perform their contractual obligations.

Purchasers of real estate, for example, frequently rely on the conditional agreement by making the contractual obligation to buy and sell subject to

- rezoning.
- subdivision approval.
- annexation of the property by a municipality.
- mortgage financing.
- provision of adequate water and sanitary sewer services to the property.

Conditional agreements might also arise in other contexts. For example, a business may be willing to commit to perform a contract provided it can

- access a certain source of supply.
- engage people with the necessary expertise.
- obtain a licence to use certain intellectual property.

Conditional agreements would permit such an enterprise to contract with the other side but would provide an established reason to escape the obligation to perform.

CASE

Wiebe v Bobsien (1984), 14 DLR (4th) 754 (BCSC), aff'd (1985), 20 DLR (4th) 475 (CA), leave to appeal to SCC refused (1985), 64 NR 394 (SCC)

THE BUSINESS CONTEXT: Because the purchase of real estate can involve a large expense, businesses and individuals alike often require time to either borrow the money necessary to make the purchase or divest themselves of an existing property, the proceeds of which can be applied to the contemplated purchase. Such a process can take weeks or months, during which time the freedom of the vendor to deal with other buyers or back out of the arrangement altogether can become an issue.

FACTUAL BACKGROUND: Dr. Wiebe made an offer to purchase a house owned by Mr. Bobsien. This offer was made conditional on Wiebe being able to sell his current residence on or before August 18, 1984. Wiebe's offer was accepted by Bobsien. However, on July 22, 1984, Bobsien changed his mind and informed Wiebe that their agreement was "cancelled." Wiebe did not accept this cancellation and on August 18 he informed Bobsien that he had obtained a buyer for his current house and that, since the condition had been fulfilled, the main transaction had to go through. Bobsien refused to complete the sale, saying that he had no contractual obligation to do so.

THE LEGAL QUESTION: Was there a contract between Wiebe and Bobsien such that Bobsien was obligated to wait until August 18 to see whether Wiebe could fulfill the condition?

RESOLUTION: According to the court, the condition precedent that Wiebe be able to sell his current residence merely suspended the obligation to perform the contract pending occurrence of that event. On this basis, Wiebe had a contractual obligation to take all reasonable steps to sell his house, and if he failed to take those reasonable steps, he would be in breach of contract and liable in damages to Bobsien. As for Bobsien, he was contractually bound to wait and see if Wiebe would be successful in selling his current residence and did not have the legal right to "cancel" the contract on July 22. Since Wiebe fulfilled the condition within the time provided in the contract, Bobsien was contractually bound to sell to him. Bobsien's failure to do so was a breach of contract.

CRITICAL ANALYSIS: Do conditions precedent introduce too much uncertainty into contracts?

Limitation of Liability Clause

When a party fails to meet its contractual obligations, it is liable for breach of contract and is responsible to the other side for any reasonably foreseeable damages the breach may have caused.[19] For example, in the Coasters–Trackers contract, a failure by Trackers to deliver adequate tracking may result in Coasters losing its contract with the American amusement park, the ultimate purchaser of the roller coaster (see Figure 7.1).

FIGURE 7.1 Trackers' Liability to Coasters

1. **Trackers ➡ ➡ ➡ ➡ Coasters**
    breaches contract by
    supplying substandard tracking

2. **Coasters➡ ➡ ➡ ➡ American customer**
    breaches contract by
    failing to deliver tracking

3. **American customer finds an alternative supplier and terminates contract with Coasters.**

4. **Coasters loses $1 million in profit on contract with American customer.**

On the basis of this scenario, Coasters could recover from Trackers its loss of profit, particularly since Trackers knew very well that Coasters needed the tracking to fulfill contractual obligations to an American amusement park. However, since contracts are about consensus and choice, parties can agree to limit liability for breach to something less than would otherwise be recoverable. This is precisely what the parties to the Coasters–Trackers contract accomplished. Clause 13 of the contract (set out in the opening scenario) is a **limitation of liability clause**. It provides that Trackers's liability shall in no event exceed the unit price of the tracking, and in no event shall it include loss of profit. Therefore, by the clear words of the contract, any loss of profit that Coasters may suffer from Trackers's breach is not recoverable. Since the parties agreed to place such a limit on damages when they entered into the contract, Coasters is bound.

Exemption Clause (or Exclusion Clause)

Through an **exemption clause**, a party to a contract can identify events or circumstances causing loss for which it has no liability whatsoever. Clause 14 in the Coasters–Trackers contract achieves such an end, since it exempts Trackers from all liability with respect to losses, damages, costs, or claims relating to design of tracking. This means that if there is a problem with the design, Coasters cannot sue Trackers for any loss it might sustain to replace or alter the tracking, for example.

Limitation of liability clause

A term of a contract that limits liability for breach to something less than would otherwise be recoverable.

Exemption clause

A term of a contract that identifies events causing loss for which there is no liability.

---

19 The classic test for foreseeability in contract, discussed further in Chapter 9, is stated in *Hadley v Baxendale* (1854), 9 Ex Ch 341: Where two parties have made a contract which one of them has broken, the damages which the other party ought to receive in respect of such breach of contract should be such as may fairly and reasonably be considered either arising naturally, i.e., . . . such as may reasonably be supposed to have been in the contemplation of both parties, at the time they made the contract, as the probable result of the breach of it. Now, if the special circumstances under which the contract was made were communicated by the plaintiffs to the defendants, and thus known to both parties, the damages resulting from the breach of such a contract, which they would reasonably contemplate, would be the amount of injury which would ordinarily follow from a breach of contract under these special circumstances so known and communicated.

Tilden Rent-A-Car Co v Clendenning (1978), 83 DLR (3D) 400 (Ont CA)

THE BUSINESS CONTEXT: A business may decide to use a standard form contract with its customers in order to save money. However, this may prove to be a false economy should the business fail to properly explain to the customer the consequences of the standard form contract in question. Such a business runs the risk of a court taking the customer's side and disallowing a term that would otherwise protect the business.

FACTUAL BACKGROUND: Mr. Clendenning rented a car from Tilden at the Vancouver airport. At the time of entering into the agreement, he was asked if he wanted additional insurance, which involved a higher fee but did provide full, non-deductible coverage. Thinking that this would protect him if the car were damaged in his possession, he agreed. As he was in a hurry, he signed the long and complicated rental agreement without reading it. An exemption clause, on the back of the agreement and in very small type, provided that the insurance would be inoperative if the driver had consumed any alcohol whatsoever at the time the damage occurred. Clendenning was unaware of the clause. When the car was damaged—Clendenning drove into a pole after consuming some alcohol—Tilden sued to recover the full cost of repairing the vehicle.

THE LEGAL QUESTION: Can Clendenning rely on the clause providing him with full, non-deductible coverage, or is that clause inoperative because Clendenning had consumed some alcohol?

RESOLUTION: The Ontario Court of Appeal held that Clendenning's signature on the contract was not a true assent to the terms of the contract and, therefore, Tilden could not rely on the exemption clause denying insurance coverage to Clendenning. The clerk who had

What risks do lengthy contracts—as found in the car rental industry—pose to the consumer and to the business supplying the vehicle?

Suzanne Plunkett/Bloomberg via Getty Photos

Clendenning sign knew that he had not read the contract and knew, therefore, that the contract did not represent his true intention. Given that the contract contained "stringent and onerous provisions," it was incumbent on Tilden to show that it took reasonable measures to draw these terms to Clendenning's attention. This did not occur and therefore Tilden could not rely on the exemption clause. The court went on to observe that since the trial judge had accepted that Clendenning was capable of proper control of a motor vehicle at the time of the accident, and since Clendenning had paid the premium, he was not liable for any damage to the vehicle.

CRITICAL ANALYSIS: Courts may be less helpful to the customer in a non-consumer context, since parties are expected to look after their own interests. In a 1997 decision from the Ontario Court of Appeal, for example, the court emphasized that inadequate notice of the kind complained of in the *Tilden* case will not ordinarily be grounds for attacking an exemption clause in a commercial situation. The court affirmed the rule that a person will be assumed to have read and understood any contract that he signs.[20] Should consumer and commercial contracts be treated differently?

---

20 See *Fraser Jewellers (1982) Ltd v Dominion Electric Protection Co et al* (1997), 34 OR (3d) 1 (CA). Note that *Abrams v Sprott Securities Ltd* (2003), 67 OR (3d) 368 (CA) distinguished *Fraser Jewellers* by narrowing the proposition in three ways: first, the *Fraser* proposition depends on the absence of misrepresentation by the party seeking to rely on the written agreement (the party seeking to rely on the clause had no legal obligation to draw it to the other party's attention); second, it depends on there being no special relationship between the parties; and finally, a person cannot rely by way of estoppel on a statement induced by his or her own misrepresentation.

CLICK-WRAP AND BROWSE-WRAP AGREEMENTS

Even when terms are written down, one party may claim not to have known that certain terms were actually part of the contract. As noted above, this can arise in the standard form contract, for example, when a customer of a car rental company signs a lengthy agreement without having read it. Questions of enforceability of terms also arise in the more modern context of click-wrap, and browse-wrap contracting practices.

Click-Wrap Agreements: A click-wrap is an agreement that appears on a user's computer screen when a user attempts to download software or purchase goods or services online. The user is instructed to review the terms prior to assenting by clicking an "I accept" button, a hyperlink, or an icon. Usually the user cannot proceed any further without agreeing to the terms.

In Canada, the validity of this method of contracting has been upheld. In *Rudder v Microsoft Corp*,[21] the plaintiffs brought a class action suit against Microsoft (MSN), alleging that MSN had breached the member service agreement. MSN applied for a permanent stay of proceedings based on a clause in the click-wrap agreement that indicated that all MSN service agreements are governed by the laws of the state of Washington and that all disputes arising out of the agreement would occur in that state's courts. The Ontario Superior Court granted the application. In response to the plaintiffs' argument that they did not receive adequate notice of the term, Mr. Justice Winkler said,

> All of the terms of the Agreement are the same format. Although there are certain terms of the Agreement that are displayed entirely in upper-case letters, there are no physical differences which make a particular term of the

agreement more difficult to read than any other term. In other words, there is no fine print as the term would be defined in a written document. The terms are set out in plain language, absent words that are commonly referred to as "legalese." Admittedly, the entire Agreement cannot be displayed at once on the computer screen, but that is not materially different from a multi-page written document which requires a party to turn the pages.[22]

Browse-Wrap Agreements: Also of recent interest has been the validity of browse-wrap agreements. Browse-wrap agreements are said to be formed on this basis: the user agrees that—by virtue of simply using the website—he or she is bound by the terms of use associated with the website and agrees that those terms are part of a binding contract between the parties. In short, a browse-wrap agreement is formed not because the user has clicked on an "I accept" button. Rather, the webpage presents a link or button that takes the user to the terms and conditions that apply to the transaction or the terms are found at the bottom of the website in question. This would seem to be a potentially risky way of attempting to create a contract, particularly as the common law requires that the person purporting to accept an offer do something affirmative or positive to signal assent.[23]

That said, the Quebec decision in *Canadian Real Estate Association ("CREA") v Sutton (Quebec) Real Estate Services*[24] recognized a browse-wrap form of acceptance. In this case, the realtor (Sutton) had been downloading listings from the Multiple Listing Service website of the Canadian Real Estate Association (CREA), which was expressly contrary to the terms of use posted on the website. Sutton argued that any such breach was not actionable because it had done nothing to expressly consent to these terms of use, such as clicking on an "I agree" button. The Court

---

21 (1999), 47 CCLT (2d) 168 (Ont SCJ).
22 *Ibid* at 173.
23 Morgan & Saulgrain, *supra* note 14 at 10. In the U.S. decision of *Ticketmaster Corp v Tickets.com*, 2000 U.S. Dist Lexis 4553 (Dist Ct, CD Cal 2000) for example, a California court found that without a positive gesture, such as clicking on an "I accept" button, there was no contract between the parties. Mere use was insufficient."
24 *Canadian Real Estate Association v Sutton (Quebec) Real Estate Services Inc*, [2003] JQ no 3606 (CS).

disagreed, noting that the terms were posted on the MLS website and could be accessed via hyperlink. Moreover, as Charles Morgan *et al.* point out, Sutton itself had similar terms of use on its own website and therefore "should have known" that such terms would also govern CREA's MLS site.[25] Relying in part on the *CREA* case, the British Columbia Supreme Court also recently enforced a browse-wrap agreement, concluding that a contract had been formed between the plaintiff and defendant.[26] The court noted that the defendant had a clear opportunity to review the terms of use of the website and knew that acceptance would be deemed by continued use.

Note too that browse-wrap agreements have been deemed enforceable as they relate to *amending* an existing contract, but not consistently so. In *Kanitz v Rogers Cable Inc.*,[27] for example, a click-wrap agreement expressly allowed telecommunications company Rogers to amend its online service agreement with customers by simply posting such amendments on its website. The court agreed that the customer's continued use of the service after such amendments were posted amounted to acceptance of Rogers's unilateral amendments. In short, the parties had agreed to a means of amending their contract which did not require an act of positive acceptance by the consumer.[28] By way of contrast, a court in Quebec held in 2005 that continued use of an online system (here, myPaySystems Services) was not good acceptance of a contractual amendment requiring arbitration.[29] To side-step such controversy regarding enforceability, e-vendors should consider avoiding browse-wrap agreements altogether and require their customers to do something affirmative to signify assent—such as clicking on an icon[30] which says "I accept" or "I assent." This is particularly important in a consumer context where courts are more likely to be solicitous of the customer than in a business-to-business scenario.[31]

Hyperlinked terms: The Supreme Court of Canada in *Dell Computer Corp v Union des consommateurs*[32] has upheld the enforceability of contract terms introduced via hyperlink. The court decided that contractual terms are enforceable provided they are "reasonably accessible" and this accessibility can be provided by a hyperlinked document. That is, even though the terms may not be on the ordering page itself, it is sufficient that the terms are accessible via a hyperlink.[33]

Critical Analysis: The enforceability of terms in click-wrap agreements depends on notification prior to assent. What steps can a business take in preparing and presenting an agreement to ensure that the terms will be found to be enforceable? Do you think that browse-wrap agreements should be enforceable? Why or why not? As a businessperson, how confident would you be at this point concerning the enforceability of a browse-wrap contract in Canada?

Liquidated Damages Clause

A **liquidated damages clause** sets out—in advance—what one party must pay to the other in the event of breach. Through such clauses, the parties themselves decide before a breach has even happened what that breach would be worth by way of compensation. Provided that the clause is a genuine pre-estimate of the

Liquidated damages clause

A term of a contract that specifies how much one party must pay to the other in the event of breach.

---

25 Morgan & Saulgrain, *supra* note 14 at 15.
26 *Century 21 Canada Ltd Partnership v Rogers Communications Inc*, 2011 BCSC 1196.
27 *Kanitz v Rogers Cable Inc*, (2002) 58 OR (3d) 299 (Sup Ct).
28 Morgan & Saulgrain, *supra* note 14 at 10–11.
29 *Aspencer1.com Inc v Paysystems Corporation*, [2005] JQ no 1573 (CS).
30 For further discussion, see Derek Hill, "'Click-wrap' online contracts generally considered enforceable" *Law Times* (4 August 2008) 12.
31 *Ibid.*
32 2007 SCC 34.
33 Michael Geist, "*Dell* Case Sets Standard for Online Contracts" (31 July 2007), online: Michael Geist <http://www.michaelgeist.ca/content/view/2141/1/>.

Penalty clause

A term which is not enforceable because it sets an exorbitant amount that one party must pay to the other in event of breach.

damages that the innocent party will suffer, it is enforceable.[34] The clause will not be enforceable, however, if it sets an exorbitant amount as a remedy for the innocent party. If so, the clause is a **penalty clause**—it intends to punish, not compensate—and a court will simply disregard it in assessing damages for the breach in question. As a general rule, contract law is only interested in compensating the innocent party, not punishing the party in breach. As noted in Chapter 6, Amritha had insisted on a contractual clause that Trackers pay $5000 to Coasters for every day it was late in delivering the tracking. Such a clause is enforceable only if it fits the definition of a liquidated damages clause. If it is simply a clause meant to scare or terrorize Trackers into timely performance because of the financial punishment it would face in the event of delay, the court will simply not enforce it.

These three kinds of clauses—the limitation of liability clause, the exemption clause, and the liquidated damages clause—illustrate the planning function of the law. Through such clauses, a business can manage the kind and extent of liability it faces.

BUSINESS LAW IN PRACTICE REVISITED

1. How is the scope of Trackers's and Coasters's obligations determined?

If the parties cannot resolve a dispute concerning obligations by themselves, a judge will determine whether there is a contract between the parties and, if so, what its content is. Every contract must cover certain essentials in order to be enforceable. If key terms are missing, the court may conclude that the parties were still at the point of negotiating and had not actually entered into a contract yet. The other possibility is that the court will imply a term that one or the other party finds unsatisfactory or contrary to expectations.

The Coasters–Trackers contract was complete because it contained all the terms that the circumstances of the case would identify to be essential, as well as some clauses that defined the relationship in more detail. For example, the contract identified the following terms:

- Parties: Coasters and Trackers
- Price: $1.5 million
- Delivery dates: as specified
- Product: tracking
- Quantity: 900 metres
- Quality: as per specifications and, where no specifications, of the best quality
- Guarantees: tracking to be free from defect for one year
- Limitations on/exemptions of liability: liability not to exceed unit price; no liability for design defects; no liability for defects after one year
- Insurance: vendor to insure tracking

2. Are there any ambiguous or unclear terms in the contract?

While certain aspects of the contract were somewhat ambiguous, such as the term specifying that the quality was to be of the best quality, a court would have

---

34 See John McCamus, *The Law of Contracts* 2nd (Toronto: Irwin Law, 2012) at 966.

been able to assign meaning to the term because there was a contract between the parties and expert evidence would have been available to establish what the phrase meant.

3. Are there any additional terms that Jason should have tried to include?

Jason managed to negotiate a reasonably complete contract, as noted above. He included a number of clauses to limit the liability of Trackers, which was prudent, but he should have gone further and included a clause expressly eliminating application of the *Sale of Goods Act*. This term would have ensured that the Act would have no application in a contractual dispute with Coasters sometime down the road. It was wise from Trackers' perspective to include, as it did, an entire contract clause, as this would have helped forestall any arguments from Coasters that there were additional warranties or guarantees not expressly recited in the contract.

Jason probably should have included a price-variation clause to deal with the problems that arose when the price of steel rose dramatically. In addition, an arbitration or mediation clause might have proven useful to deal with conflicts, although, as it turns out, the parties negotiated their own resolution to the pricing dispute that arose.

4. Does the contract relieve the parties from responsibility for inadequate performance?

The contract limited Trackers's liability for defective tracking for one year and to an amount not exceeding the unit price. Trackers had no liability for problems in the design of the tracking.

Coasters's obligation to pay the purchase price was not qualified by the express terms of the contract. Of course, if Trackers had failed to deliver, Coasters would not have had to pay. If Trackers had delivered seriously defective goods, Coasters would have had the option to refuse delivery. If the defect had been less significant, Coasters probably would have remitted payment in a reduced amount, to reflect the track's lesser value or the cost of repairing the defects in the tracking. Clauses to this effect are not necessary and probably do not help in establishing certainty, in any event. Whether the tracking was seriously defective or only somewhat so would have been not a question of fact but a matter for debate, which no clause in a contract can resolve. If the parties cannot resolve that question informally, it will be determined by a judge in an action by Trackers against Coasters for the purchase price set out in the contract.

CHAPTER SUMMARY

The nature, scope, and extent of the obligations of the parties to a contract are known as the terms of the contract. The terms may be express, as when they have been specifically mentioned and agreed upon by the parties, or they may be implied. Since the court has considerable discretion to imply a term or not, parties are best advised to make their agreement as clear and as explicit as possible.

How courts will resolve a contractual dispute over terms is an open question, as is any matter that proceeds to litigation. An important evidential rule that guides a judge is known as the parol evidence rule. It prevents the introduction of evidence that varies or adds to the terms of a written contract when the contract is clear and intended to be the sole source of the parties' obligations. Entire contract clauses are used to propel a court to apply the parol evidence rule in any given case.

An important planning function of contract law lies in the fact that it permits parties to manage the risk of future uncertainties. Additionally, it permits them to establish, in advance, the extent of responsibility for breach through limitation clauses and exemption clauses. Furthermore, parties can bargain for what will be payable in the event of breach. Such a term will be enforceable, provided the amount is a genuine pre-estimate of damages and not a penalty.

Courts may refuse to apply a clause that disadvantages a consumer if the business in question failed to take reasonable steps to ensure that the consumer was alerted to the clause in question in circumstances where it appears the consumer has not assented. Courts are less likely to assist the commercial or industrial customer, however, on the basis that sophisticated business interests should be left to take care of themselves.

CHAPTER STUDY

Key Terms and Concepts

condition precedent (p. 154)

condition subsequent (p. 154)

contractual quantum meruit (p. 148)

entire contract clause (p. 148)

exemption clause (p. 156)

express term (p. 141)

implied term (p. 143)

limitation of liability clause (p. 156)

liquidated damages clause (p. 159)

parol evidence rule (p. 150)

penalty clause (p. 160)

rules of construction (p. 142)

Questions for Review

1. What is the difference between an express and an implied term?

2. What are two major rules of construction used by the courts in interpreting a contract?

3. Who decides the content of a contract and on what basis?

4. What are four sources that the court can rely on to imply terms?

5. Why are express terms preferable to implied terms?

6. How does the doctrine of business efficacy affect the interpretation of implied terms?

7. How do the courts deal with ambiguities in the contract?

8. What is the expression used to describe an implied legal promise to pay a reasonable price for goods or services?

9. What are three ways that a party can control its exposure to liability for breach of contract?

10. What is a limitation of liability clause?

11. How is a limitation of liability clause different from an exemption clause?

12. Why are conditional agreements important?

13. What is the parol evidence rule?

14. What is a separate or collateral agreement?

15. What is an entire contract clause?

16. What assumptions do the courts make about how contract terms relate to changing circumstances?

17. What is the difference between a click-wrap agreement and a browse-wrap agreement?

18. What is a liquidated damages clause?

Questions for Critical Thinking

1. Entering a contract can create a great deal of risk for the parties. What are examples of these risks, and how can they be managed?

2. Discuss how the law seeks to analogize electronic contracts to hard-copy, paper contracts. Are these efforts successful?

3. The Supreme Court of Canada in *Bhasin* stated that there is a new duty of honesty in contractual performance. What is this duty and how might it interfere with freedom of contract?

4. Why does contract law refuse to enforce a penalty clause? Why are penalty clauses inherently objectionable?

5. Do you agree that contracts should be interpreted based on an objective assessment of the parties' intentions? What would be the advantages and disadvantages of interpreting contacts based on evidence of what the parties subjectively intended?

6. Do you think the law is unreasonable to require business owners to point out to consumers any unexpected clauses in a standard form contract if it appears that the consumer has not assented? Should customers simply be required to take care of themselves and read the contract before signing it?

Situations for Discussion

1. Former U.S. administrative law judge Roy Pearson famously sued a local dry cleaner over a lost pair of pants. Among other things, he sought $2 million for mental distress and discomfort as well as $15 000 for a rental car he said he would need in order to drive to another dry cleaner outside his neighbourhood. Pearson claimed, for example, that the dry cleaner owners committed fraud by not living up to the sign in their window that stated "Satisfaction guaranteed." According to Pearson, this guarantee was unconditional, he was by no means satisfied, and the defendants had thereby committed an unfair trade practice. How should a judge interpret the "satisfaction guaranteed" sign?[35]

---

35 There are multiple Internet stories on point. See, for example, Dan Slater, "The Great American Pants Suit, R.I.P." *The Wall Street Journal* (18 December 2008), online: Wall Street Journal Law Blog <http://blogs.wsj.com/law/2008/12/18/the-great-american-pants-suit-rip/>. For a basic statement of the facts of the claim, see Manning Sossamon, "The Facts of *Pearson v Chung*" online: Manning Sossamon <http://www.manning-sossamon.com/pantfacts/>. For the trial judge's decision, see *Pearson v Chung*, 644 F Supp (2d) 23 (Dist Ct DC 2009), online: DC Courts <http://www.dccourts.gov/dccourts/docs/05CA4302PearsonFindings.pdf>. Following an unsuccessful appeal, it appears that Pearson has now abandoned his lawsuit, see Manning Sossamon, "The Facts of *Pearson v Chung*" online: Manning Sossamon <http://www.manning-sossamon.com/pantfacts/>.

2. Louise purchased land from Reggie subject to the condition that subdivision approval be secured. Unfortunately, the contract between them does not specify who is to try to get the subdivision approval. Louise begged Reggie to seek the approval, noting that only the vendor has the information necessary to make the application successfully. Reggie, who had changed his mind about selling the property altogether, is triumphant: "Where does it say in the contract that I have to do anything about making an application for subdivision? Next time, try to be more clear. And in the meantime, our contract is off." Is Reggie obligated to try to secure the subdivision approval? If so, on what basis?[36]

3. Kristin signed a user agreement with Hagel's Cable Inc. (Hagel's), upon installation of high-speed Internet service in her home. Included in the agreement was a provision that the agreement could be amended at any time, and that customers would be notified of changes on Hagel's website, by email, or through regular mail. Hagel's later added a clause to the agreement that any right to commence or participate in a class action suit was waived. The agreement, including the new clause, was posted on its customer support website, and a notice was posted on the main website that the agreement had been amended. Kristin has continued using the service since this time. However, she now wants to join a class action suit that is alleging a number of breaches of the agreement.[37] Will the clause in the amended user's agreement prevent her from bringing such an action? Did she receive adequate notice of the amended term? Does the fact that the user agreement relates to Internet services make a difference in whether the notice was adequate? How is this situation similar to the *Rudder v Microsoft Corp.* case discussed in this chapter?

4. Jason and Floë booked a two-week vacation in the Caribbean with The Nation's Vacations Inc. (Nation), having reviewed Nation's brochure regarding destinations there. The brochure also

---

36 Based, in part, on *Dynamic Transport Ltd v OK Detailing Ltd* (1978), 85 DLR 3rd 19 (SCC).

37 Based, in part, on *Kanitz v Rogers Cable Inc*, (2002) 58 OR (3d) 299 (SC).

contained an exclusion of liability clause, which stated:

> Please review with care the terms and conditions below as they govern your purchase of travel services from Nation. Your booking with Nation constitutes acceptance of these Terms & Conditions.

> ...

> **LIABILITY**

> **Liability for suppliers:** Nation makes arrangements with third-party suppliers who provide travel services such as flights, accommodation, and car rentals. Nation endeavours to choose the most reputable suppliers but is not responsible for their acts and omissions. Disappointed customers must sue those third party suppliers directly for any loss or damages.

> ...

> Nation assumes no responsibility for any claim, loss, damage, cost, or expense arising out of personal injury, accident or death, loss, damage, inconvenience, loss of enjoyment, or upset caused by Nation's third party suppliers.

The brochure itself was designed to open to the page quoted above when flipping through the brochure from back to front. It was in easy-to-read font and with the emphasis indicated above. Though Jason and Floë had spent about 90 minutes reading over the brochure before booking their vacation package, they say that they did not know about the exclusion clause. Moreover, Jason, a construction firm manager, says that he does not even know what an exclusion clause is, so reading it would have been pointless in any event.

When Jason and Floë arrived at the Caribbean resort, they were immediately disappointed. Though the resort was a four-star resort as advertised by Nation, Jason and Floë say that when they went to eat dinner in the resort buffet restaurant, they found the conditions to be unhygienic because, among other matters, several small, tropical birds were walking around on the floor of the restaurant, having gained access through

open doors. At a later point, a cat strolled into the restaurant and, they say, defecated in the corner—though the resort disputes this. Jason and Floë also claim that the bathroom in their suite was unhygienic and the staff were uniformly unfriendly, even hostile. Jason and Floë hotly refused management's offer of a free room upgrade and demanded to be flown home immediately. The resort made those arrangements. Jason and Floë left the next day. Jason and Floë have now sued Nation for breach of contract, seeking, among other matters, reimbursement for their flight to and from the resort as well as ground transportation and accommodation costs.[38] Nation says it delivered the requested travel services contracted for and in any event has successfully limited its liability through the exclusion clause. What do you think a judge will say?

5. Lunar Inc. had developed a mechanism that harnessed heat from the sun. What the company lacked, however, was a method for storing the heat until it was needed. Trays-R-Us (Trays) had developed a unique tray that appeared to solve this problem, so the parties entered into negotiations. It was agreed that Trays would sell the trays to Lunar at a set unit price per tray for a term of one year. No particular sales volume for the year was agreed upon or guaranteed. After the trays were produced, however, Trays discovered that they leaked and were unable to hold any solar heat owing to a design flaw that could not be fixed. As a result, Trays refused to fill any orders for the trays placed by Lunar. Lunar sued for breach of contract, alleging that there was an implied term in the contract that Trays would make trays available to Lunar as required.[39] Does the business efficacy rule require that such a term be implied in the contract between Trays and Lunar? Do you think that such a term might have been left out on purpose? How can a business avoid having terms implied into a contract?

6. The decision of *Wiebe v Bobsien*, discussed earlier in this chapter, went on to appeal and at that level, the dissenting judge would have

---

38 Based, in part, on *Eltaib v Touram Ltd Partnership*, 2010 ONSC 834.
39 Based, in part, on *Solar U.S.A. Inc v Saskatchewan Minerals*, [1992] 3 WWR 15 (Sask QB).

found for the vendor. According to the dissent, the conditional agreement was unenforceable because its scope was too uncertain. The dissent stated:

> I think this case falls in that category of incurable uncertainty. What term should be implied? A term requiring the purchaser to make all reasonable efforts to sell his house sounds alright... [but] it leaves unresolved the question of whether he must sell at the price he can get, on the market, in the time allotted, or whether he is entitled to insist that the sale can only take place at a price he considers reasonable and is willing to accept.

> I think that what the parties usually intend by this type of clause is the second alternative. That is, that the purchaser is only committed to sell his own house if he gets the price he has in mind. The reason is that in the residential housing market the purchaser is likely to be unfamiliar with the market, but he is almost sure to know how much cash he has and what size of mortgage he can count on being able to service.

> ... The way to deal with this problem in the real estate market is for the form of subject clause to state the price and the essential terms upon which the purchaser must sell his own house. Then a court would have no trouble in implying a term that the purchaser must make all reasonable efforts to sell at that price and on those terms. And the court could assess whether the purchaser had made reasonable efforts to do so.

Do you think that the dissent is asking for too much precision and detail in a subject to clause. Why or why not?

7. Lucy Smith became interested in enrolling as a member in Trident Ltd's online discount service for goods and services in exchange for a monthly membership fee. She decided to join up and linked to the enrolment page. The message on the enrolment page promised "up to" $20 off on select purchases including "10% to 40% savings at over 10 000 Participating Restaurants." The form required Lucy to enter her city of birth, credit card number, and contact information, as well as to create a password. Text on the enrolment page also stated that by entering one's "City of Birth" and password and clicking the "Yes" button, the purchaser acknowledges that he or she agrees to Trident's "Terms & Conditions." Lucy filled in the form completely and then clicked on the "YES" button. Within a few minutes, Lucy received an email from Trident outlining additional terms and conditions of her agreement with Trident, including a provision which prohibited Lucy from joining any class actions against Trident. Is Lucy bound by this new clause? When was her contract with Trident Ltd. complete?[40]

8. Trackers is three days late in delivering the tracking to Coasters. Amritha now wants to rely on the clause in the contract that Trackers will pay $5 000 for each day that the tracking is late, and she is claiming that Trackers owes Coasters $15 000. However, Trackers points out that Amritha has not been inconvenienced by the late delivery, because construction on the roller coaster had already been delayed by two weeks. It has been a week and a half since Trackers was able to deliver the tracking, and Coasters has still been unable to use it. Is Amritha entitled to rely on the clause and collect the $15 000? Do you need any additional information to make your decision?

---

40 Based, in part, on *Schnabel v Trilegiant Corp.*, 2012 WL 3871366 (2d Cir. Sept. 7, 2012)

DAJ/Getty Images

8

OBJECTIVES

After studying this chapter, you should have an understanding of

- why enforcement of contracts is the norm

- the exceptional circumstances in which contracts are not enforced

- which contracts must be in writing and why

NON-ENFORCEMENT OF CONTRACTS

BUSINESS LAW IN PRACTICE

Martha Smith bought a fitness club in downtown Toronto and renamed it "Martha's Gym." She invested $50 000 of her own money and financed the remainder through a business loan from the local bank. Martha tried to attract a large clientele to the facility, but the volume of business failed to meet her expectations. She began to run short of cash and fell behind in her monthly loan payments to the bank. Eventually, the bank called the loan, which had an outstanding balance of $20 000. The bank told Martha that unless she paid off the entire balance in two weeks, it would start seizing assets from the fitness club.

Martha convinced her elderly parents, Mr. and Mrs. Smith, to help her by borrowing $40 000 from the same bank. She explained that through such a cash infusion, she would be able to retire her own loan with the bank and use the balance as operating capital for her business. Martha assured her parents that the problems at the fitness club were temporary and that by hiring a new trainer, she would be able to quickly turn the business around.

Martha and her parents went to meet Kevin Jones, the branch manager, who had handled Mr. and Mrs. Smith's banking for over 35 years. Kevin said that he would give the Smiths an acceptable interest rate on the loan—namely, 8 percent—but insisted that the loan be secured by a mortgage on their home. Since the Smiths had no other means of paying back the loan and the house was their only asset, they were nervous about the proposal, which they did not fully understand. However, they did not want Martha to go through the humiliation of having her fitness equipment seized and sold at auction.

For his part, Kevin was tremendously relieved that the Smiths had come in to see him. Kevin was the one who had approved Martha's ill-fated business loan in the first place, and he had failed to ensure that it was properly secured. He saw this as an opportunity to correct his own error and get Martha's loan off his books altogether.

Kevin had the mortgage documents prepared and strongly encouraged the Smiths to sign, saying that this would protect Martha's assets from seizure. He also told them that to a large extent, signing the mortgage was just a formality and that he was confident that nothing would come of it.

In the end, the Smiths decided to put their trust in Kevin that he would not let them enter into a contract that could bring about their financial ruin. They simply signed the mortgage. Immediately,

$20 000 went to the bank to pay the outstanding balance on Martha's loan. The remaining $20 000 was paid directly to Martha (see Figure 8.1 below).

Martha's business continued to operate until the additional capital was completely expended. Its prospects failed to improve, as Martha was still unable to attract customers and the new trainer quit. Eventually, neither Martha nor her parents could make the payments on the mortgage, and the bank began to foreclose on the Smiths's home. Mr. and Mrs. Smith are in shock—they never believed that it would come to this.[1]

FIGURE 8.1 Martha's and Her Parents' Financial Arrangements With the Bank

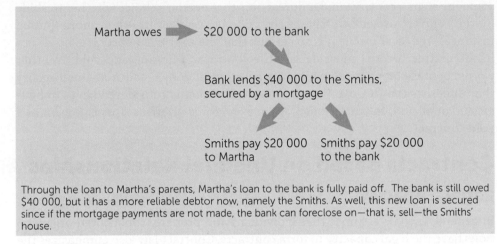

Martha owes → $20 000 to the bank

Bank lends $40 000 to the Smiths, secured by a mortgage

Smiths pay $20 000 to Martha   Smiths pay $20 000 to the bank

Through the loan to Martha's parents, Martha's loan to the bank is fully paid off. The bank is still owed $40 000, but it has a more reliable debtor now, namely the Smiths. As well, this new loan is secured since if the mortgage payments are not made, the bank can foreclose on—that is, sell—the Smiths' house.

1. Did Kevin manipulate or pressure the Smiths into signing the mortgage? If so, what legal remedies do the Smiths have?

2. Did Mr. and Mrs. Smith enter into the contract on the basis of mistake or misrepresentation? If so, what legal remedies do they have?

3. How could Kevin have managed this transaction better?

The Importance of Enforcing Contracts

Once negotiators reach an agreement that appears to contain their consensus on the essential elements of a bargain, a contract is formed. The law then focuses on enforcing that agreement in order to preserve the integrity, reliability, and predictability of contractual relationships. Were it otherwise, the business world would be unable to predict with any certainty which agreements would be binding.

At the same time, the Canadian legal system recognizes the injustice of enforcing contracts without any provision for exceptional circumstances. Accordingly, the law endeavours to achieve a balance between two competing goals. On the one hand, it must prevent people from pulling out of deals because they have found better opportunities elsewhere or have failed to conduct diligent negotiations. On the other hand, it must remedy situations where an apparently valid contract fails to reflect the real agreement of both parties or is fundamentally unjust.

---

1 This Business Law in Practice scenario is based on *Morrison v Coast Finance Ltd* (1965), 55 WWR 257 (BCCA); and *Lloyds Bank v Bundy,* [1974] 3 All ER 757 (CA).

Voidable contract

A contract that, in certain circumstances, an aggrieved party can choose to keep in force or bring to an end.

Void contract

A contract involving a defect so substantial that it is of no force or effect.

Legal capacity

The ability to make binding contracts.

This chapter presents a number of legal doctrines—developed through common law and statute—that are exceptions to the general rule that a contract, once formed, is enforceable. It categorizes these doctrines on the basis of there being

- an unequal relationship between the two parties.
- misrepresentation or important mistakes concerning the contract.
- a defect within the contract itself.

If the aggrieved party can bring itself within one of the doctrines discussed in this chapter, there are two possible outcomes. In certain circumstances, he may elect whether to keep the contract in force or have it brought to an end. Where this option is available, it is said to be a **voidable contract**. For example, when someone signs a contract under duress, it is that person's choice whether to abide by the contract or seek to have it set aside by a judge. In other, more limited instances, the legal problem is so serious that the aggrieved party has no choice in the matter: a court must declare the contract to be null and void. In other words, because of some tremendously substantial defect—such as the illegality that underlies the "hit man" contract—the contract is considered never to have existed at all and, for that reason, to be of no force or effect. This is known as a **void contract**.

Contracts Based on Unequal Relationships

Legal Capacity

In general, the law assumes that individuals and properly constituted organizations have the **legal capacity** to form contracts. Contract law also emphasizes the importance of consent and voluntariness. Because they may be unable to give true consent to their agreements, certain kinds of people—namely, children and those with mental incapacities—are given the benefit of special legal protection.

Minors

The age of majority is the age at which a person is recognized as an adult for legal purposes. Those under the age of majority (minors or infants) are in a very different position concerning their ability to enter contracts than are those who have attained the age of majority. To protect minors from the enforcement of contracts that may not be in their best interests, the general rule is that minors are not obligated by the contracts they make.

However, since the goal of the law in this area is to protect the underaged, minors have the option to fulfill their contractual commitments and can enforce a contract against the other party should that party be in breach. In this way, contracts with a minor are usually voidable, at the option of the minor alone.[2]

The age of majority—which defines who is not a minor—is within provincial control and is set at 18 or 19 years of age, depending on the province.[3] For example, Ontario's *Age of Majority and Accountability Act*[4] sets the age of majority at 18.

Because minors may have to provide for their own welfare in certain circumstances, there are exceptions to the general common law rule of immunity from

---

2 It is beyond the scope of this chapter to discuss whether there is a category of void minors' contracts. For discussion see GHL Fridman, *The Law of Contract in Canada*, 6th ed (Toronto: Thomson Carswell, 2011) at 150 and following.
3 *Ibid* at 140.
4 RSO 1990, c A7.

liability. Minors are obligated by contracts for essentials, known in law as "necessaries," and are required to pay a reasonable price for them. What amounts to a necessary in a given case is legally determined in relation to two questions:

1. Is the item being acquired necessary to this minor?[5]
2. Does this minor already have an adequate supply of the item?[6]

BUSINESS APPLICATION OF THE LAW

DEALING WITH MINORS

Although there may be sound business reasons for entering into a contract with a minor, there is considerably more risk of non-performance and unenforceability than when contracting with an adult. If the contract is for any significant value, a contractor should consider either contracting with the parent or guardian instead of the minor, or requiring an adult to cosign or guarantee the performance of the minor.

In the employment context, in order for the employment contract to be enforceable against the minor, the employer must be able to prove that the minor is receiving a significant benefit. Otherwise, the minor can simply abandon the contract, at the minor's sole option.

Critical Analysis: What are the justifications for treating infants differently in the contractual arena than adults?

While food, shelter, and clothing are the most common categories of necessaries, the two-step test must still be satisfied in order for the supplier to be able to enforce the specific contract. Suppliers should also be aware that even when the contract is one for necessaries, problems of enforcement can arise. Suppliers may be faced with the presumption that a minor who lives with a parent or guardian is already adequately provided for and has no outstanding needs.[7]

Contracts known as beneficial contracts of service are also binding if they are considered largely for the benefit of the minor. For example, an employment contract with a minor is enforceable if the employer can show that the contract involves a significant element of training and career development, such as one would expect in a program required to enter or progress through a trade or profession. Enforceability in this context means that the employer can be awarded damages for breach of contract.

The common law generally provides that when a minor reaches the age of majority, there is no impact on contracts formed when underage. They remain unenforceable against the minor unless they involve necessaries or beneficial service contracts. Only if the person—now of legal age—expressly adopts or ratifies the agreement does it become enforceable. The one exception to this rule is where the agreement is of a permanent or continuous nature, such as a partnership

---

5 Courts are entitled to consider the infant's socioeconomic status in determining the answer to this question. See, for example, *Ottenbreit v Daniels*, [1975] SJ No 98 (Dist Ct).

6 Fridman, *supra* note 2 at 143. This common law rule has been codified in sale of goods legislation in Canada. For example, section 4 of the Alberta legislation, RSA 2000, c S-2 states,

   4(2) When necessaries are sold and delivered to a minor or to a person who by reason of mental incapacity or drunkenness is incompetent to contract, the minor or person must pay a reasonable price for them. (3) In this section, "necessaries" means goods suitable to the condition in life of the minor or other person and to the minor's or person's actual requirements at the time of the sale and delivery.

7 See David Percy, "The Present Law of Infants' Contracts" (Edmonton: Institute of Law Research and Reform, 1975) at 5.

agreement. In such a case, the minor, upon attaining the age of majority, must reject (repudiate) this obligation, even if it is for non-necessaries. If he fails to do so, liability will be imposed from the time the minor becomes of age.[8]

In all Canadian jurisdictions except British Columbia, the common law governs the contractual capacity of minors.[9] In British Columbia, a different set of rules applies, as set out in the *Infants Act*.[10] This legislation provides even more protection for the infant than is present at common law, since generally, even contracts for necessities and beneficial contracts of service are unenforceable at the election of the minor pursuant to this Act.[11] However, a court has a number of powers under the legislation and can order, for example, that compensation be paid by or to any of the parties to the contract.

Mental Incapacity

In order for a contract to be formed freely and voluntarily by both parties, both must be able to understand the nature and consequences of their agreement. If people were mentally impaired through illness or intoxication by alcohol or drugs, such that they were unable to understand the consequences of their actions, and the other party was aware of their state, they may be able to avoid the contract[12] at their option.[13] To the extent that the other party has unfairly exploited the party who is lacking capacity, there are additional grounds for attacking the contract's validity—namely, duress, undue influence, and unconscionability. All three are considered below.

The fact that Martha's parents are elderly does not, of itself, mean that they lack mental capacity to enter into financial transactions. Rather, before Martha's parents can avoid paying the mortgage on this ground, a court will have to be satisfied that their advanced age has affected their sanity or mental competence—an unlikely outcome on the facts of this scenario. They may be old and overly trusting, but not legally incompetent.

Duress

Contracts that are made as a result of one of the parties being threatened with physical harm are obviously not enforceable. The presence of this extreme form of duress indicates that the threatened party did not freely consent to the terms of the contract and, in fact, was the victim of a crime. Duress is now a broader concept and includes **economic duress**.

In the more difficult cases—those more likely to arise in commercial dealings—economic duress takes the form of one party financially pressuring the other. For example, a company might threaten to break a contract that it knows is crucial to the other side unless the other side gives certain financial concessions

Economic duress

The threat of economic harm that coerces the will of the other party and results in a contract.

---

8 Fridman, *supra* note 2 at 147 and following.

9 *Ibid* at 140–141 and following.

10 See Part 3 of the *Infants Act*, RSBC 1996, c 223.

11 Fridman, *supra* note 2 at 157 describes the operation of BC's *Infants Act* in the following terms:

   A contract by a minor, i.e., someone who was an infant at the time the contract was made, is unenforceable against him unless: (a) the contract is enforceable against him by some statute; (b) the minor affirms the contract on attaining majority; (c) it is wholly or partially performed by the minor after majority; or (d) was not repudiated by the minor within a year after majority. However, the minor can enforce the contract against the adult party as if the minor had been an adult at the time of contracting. In the case of an unenforceable contract, the minor or another party (if the minor has repudiated the contract or is in breach) can apply to a court for relief.

12 *Ibid* at 159; and Edwin Peel, *Treitel: The Law of Contract*, 13th ed (London: Sweet & Maxwell, 2011) at 588 and following.

13 Fridman, *supra* note 2 at 159.

or payments in return.[14] Under the traditional test, these concessions will be unenforceable if it is shown that the coercion went beyond ordinary commercial pressure to a force or a coercion of will that prevented the other side from giving true consent to the proposal.[15] Courts have more recently suggested that a party's lack of a "practical"[16] or "realistic"[17] alternative can count as evidence of economic duress in the proper case.

When duress is established, the contract is voidable at the option of the party who was subject to the duress.

There is no possibility that Martha's parents can rely on the doctrine of duress to avoid their obligations under the mortgage. Though the bank was going to seize Martha's fitness club equipment and offer it for public sale, this "threat" did not amount to duress. Certainly, her parents may have been very upset and worried by the situation, but this would not force them to borrow $40 000 from the bank. Furthermore, the bank is fully within its legal rights to seize property when a loan has fallen into arrears.

Undue Influence

Since the basic premise of contract formation is that both parties have chosen to enter into the contract, surrounding circumstances that put in question the ability of one of the parties to exercise free will or choice[18] are of great concern. If these factors are sufficiently strong, then the contract is voidable at the option of the party whose free will was lost because of the **undue influence** of the other contracting party.

Undue influence traditionally operates in two circumstances:

- *actual pressure.* Sometimes a transaction—commercial or otherwise—arises because one party has exerted unfair influence on the other. In such a case, the party who seeks relief from the contract must show that the influence existed, was exercised, and resulted in the agreement in question.[19] If an elderly person is pressured into signing over an estate to caregivers in return for care, such a transaction could be set aside for undue influence.

- *presumed pressure based on a special relationship.* Sometimes the relationship that already exists between the parties gives rise to a presumption that the ensuing agreement was brought about by one party's unfair manipulation of the other. For example, when the contract is formed between family members or between a lawyer and client or a doctor and patient, for example, the court is entitled to assume that undue influence has been exerted. Other kinds of relationships—as between a banker and a customer, for example—do not import this presumption. When the presumption is in place, however, it then falls to the more powerful party to prove that no undue influence was present.[20]

There is a chance that the elderly Mr. and Mrs. Smith would succeed in having the $40,000 mortgage set aside as having been procured by undue influence,

Undue influence

Unfair manipulation that compromises someone's free will or choice.

---

14 This was held to amount to duress in *North Ocean Shipping Co Ltd v Hyundai Construction Co Ltd*, [1978] 3 All ER 1170 (QB).
15 The traditional case in the area is *Pao On v Lau Yiu Long*, [1979] 3 All ER 65 (PC).
16 *NAV Canada v Greater Fredericton Airport Authority Inc*, 2008 NBCA 28.
17 *Stott v Merit Investment Corp* (1988), 63 OR (2d) 545 (CA).
18 Stephanie Ben-Ishai and David Percy, *Contracts: Cases and Materials* 9th ed (Toronto: Carswell, 2014) at 700-701.
19 Peel, *supra* note 12 at 449.
20 For recent discussion of undue influence, see *Buccilli v Pillitteri* 2012 ONSC 6624 at para 139 and following.

either actual or presumed. The Smiths could argue that they entered into the mortgage with the bank only because the bank manager insistently preyed on their overwhelming need to help their daughter. If so, they could then win on the grounds of actual pressure. An argument could also be advanced on the grounds of presumed pressure. Though courts will not ordinarily presume that a bank has undue influence over its customers, the Smiths may succeed by proving that they placed themselves entirely in the hands of their long-standing bank manager and had received no qualified outside guidance.[21] It would then fall to the bank to show that the mortgage was freely and independently entered into by the Smiths.[22]

One way of proving that the contract was freely chosen is to arrange for the weaker party—such as the Smiths—to get independent legal advice concerning the transaction before it is entered into. The lawyer providing that advice will also produce what is called a "certificate of independent legal advice," which is then appended to the mortgage or other document in question. In the certificate, the lawyer attests to a number of matters, including that:

- he or she has explained the proposed transaction to the weaker party.
- the weaker party appears to understand the proposed transaction.
- the weaker party is proceeding with the transaction on a free and informed basis.

CASE

Bank of Montreal v Duguid (2000), 47 OR (3d) 737 (CA), leave to appeal to SCC granted, (2000) SCCB 2238; notice of discontinuance filed (2001) SCCB 1416

THE BUSINESS CONTEXT: When a bank lends money to a customer, it wants to ensure that, in the event of default, the customer has provided sufficient collateral to cover any shortfall. If the customer does not have satisfactory collateral, the bank may refuse to make the loan unless a third party either cosigns or guarantees the loan. This situation can pose serious risks for the third party, given its responsibility that loan payments must be made.

FACTUAL BACKGROUND: In 1989 Mr. Duguid and a business partner applied to the Bank of Montreal for a loan to finance their investment in a condominium project. The bank said that it would make the loan only if Mrs. Duguid would cosign it.

Mr. Duguid approached his wife, a real estate agent, who did sign the loan. Contrary to the bank's usual policy in such matters, its representative failed to recommend to Mrs. Duguid that she secure independent legal advice prior to signing. In short order, the loan went into default, Mr. Duguid declared bankruptcy, and the bank sued Mrs. Duguid for the amount outstanding on the loan, namely $87 000 plus interest.

THE LEGAL QUESTION: Did Mrs. Duguid cosign the loan as a result of her husband's undue influence?

RESOLUTION: Though the bank itself did not exert undue influence, any undue influence exerted by the husband would release the wife from her obligation under the loan if the bank knew or should have known about the undue influence and did nothing about it. Because Mr. Duguid was in a close, personal relationship with the other debtor—namely, his wife—the bank had a duty to make inquiries since the

---

21 This argument is based on *Lloyds Bank Ltd v Bundy, supra* note 1.
22 Peel, *supra* note 12 at 457 and following.

loan was clearly to the wife's disadvantage. If there was any undue influence, this failure by the bank would lead to the wife's loan being set aside.

A majority of the Ontario Court of Appeal said, however, that there was no undue influence. Only if the wife could demonstrate that she reposed "trust and confidence" in her husband concerning financial matters would there be a presumption of undue influence. As a real estate agent, she knew the risks of her husband's investment, and there was no potential for domination. On this basis, undue influence could not be presumed. Even if it could be presumed, the bank had rebutted that presumption, given Mrs. Duguid's knowledgeable background. On this basis, the loan was enforceable against her.

The dissenting judge would have set the loan aside based on undue influence. The dissent said that while Mrs. Duguid did not repose trust and confidence in her husband in the classic sense, she did fear "destroying the relationship between herself and her husband" should she refuse to cosign. Her background as a real estate agent was simply irrelevant to this more emotional question. Given that Mrs. Duguid agreed to the loan during a low ebb in her marriage and that she signed in order to maintain "some level of tranquility" in the household, a presumption of undue influence had been established. This presumption was not rebutted by the bank since it knew that the transaction was to the wife's disadvantage and that there was a substantial risk that her husband would pressure her to sign. Since the bank failed to advise her to get independent legal advice, Mrs. Duguid's loan should be set aside due to undue influence.

CRITICAL ANALYSIS: Do you think that the dissent was correct to assess Mrs. Duguid's emotional reasons for cosigning the loan? Or do you prefer the majority's focus on Mrs. Duguid's relatively sophisticated background as a real estate agent?

Unconscionability

Where one party stands in a position of being able to take advantage of someone and causes that person to enter into an unfair or improvident agreement, an **unconscionable contract** is the result. According to the Supreme Court of Canada, proof of unconscionability involves a two-step process:

- proof of inequality between the parties.
- proof of an improvident bargain or proof of exploitation.[23]

If the transaction is sufficiently divergent from community standards of commercial morality, this is a "strong indication of exploitation."[24] At this point, the

Unconscionable contract

An unfair contract formed when one party takes advantage of the weakness of another.

---

23 *Norberg v Wynrib*, [1992] 2 SCR 226 at 228 [*Norberg*]. Though this case involved non-commercial facts, courts have considered *Norberg*'s analysis of unconscionability in a commercial, albeit familial context. See, for example, *Buccilli, supra* note 20 at para 153 and *Waxman v Waxman* (2002), 25 BLR (3d) 1 (Ont Sup Ct Jus), varied as to damages (2004), 44 BLR (3d) 165 (CA), leave to appeal refused, [2004] SCCA No 291, reconsideration allowed (2004), 6 BLR (4th) 167 (CA); as well as *Ellis v Friedland*, [2001] 2 WWR 130 (Alta QB), aff'd 2003 ABCA 60. Note too that certain appellate courts have regarded unconscionability as involving a four-step test—see *Cain v Clarica Life Insurance Co.* 2005 ABCA 437 and *Titus v William F Cooke Enterprises*, 2007 ONCA 573 at para 38—and have adopted a four-step test as follows: 1. a grossly unfair and improvident transaction; 2. victim's lack of independent legal advice or other suitable advice; 3. overwhelming imbalance in bargaining power caused by victim's ignorance of business, illiteracy, ignorance of the language of the bargain, blindness, deafness, illness, senility, or similar disability; and 4. other party's knowingly taking advantage of this vulnerability. This test has been criticised in *Pitcher v Downer*, 2013 NLTD (G)82 as too strict.

24 *Norberg, supra* note 23.

court will presume unconscionability. It then falls to the stronger party to show that the contract was, in fact, fair.

Inequality Between the Parties

The required inequality may result because one party is unsophisticated, is poorly educated, lacks language facility, or has lower economic standing than the stronger party. Parties to a contract are never on strictly equal bargaining terms; therefore, disparity between them is, on its own, insufficient to upset a contract.

Since the Smiths are inexperienced and unsophisticated senior citizens who received no independent legal advice prior to signing the mortgage, this element could arguably be established, particularly if a court were sympathetic to their plight.

An Improvident Bargain

The party seeking to have the contract set aside must also be able to demonstrate that its terms greatly advantaged one party over the other. In short, there must be proof of substantial unfairness.

In the case of the Smiths' mortgage to the bank, the rate of interest was set at 8 percent and, from that perspective, was reasonable. However, there is a strong argument that the transaction was nonetheless a very unfair bargain for them. Through the mortgage, the Smiths put at risk their only substantial asset, for a loan they could never repay from their own resources. In fact, while the bank and Martha stood to gain enormously from the transaction, the Smiths stood to lose some of their assets for absolutely no return.

People seeking to avoid a contract owing to mental incapacity, duress, undue influence, or unconscionability must do so as promptly as possible or risk losing their case.

Why should contracts that appear normal on the surface be subject to challenge on the basis of the relations between the parties or the surrounding circumstances?

Atlas Supply Co of Canada v Yarmouth Equipment (1991), 103 NSR (2d) 1 (CA), leave to appeal to SCC granted (1991) SCCB 3035; notice of discontinuance filed (1992) SCCB 897

THE BUSINESS CONTEXT: Businesses are expected to obtain necessary information and not agree to terms until they have an agreement they can live with. Sometimes, however, one party takes such extreme advantage of the other that the court agrees to intervene.

FACTUAL BACKGROUND: Atlas was a subsidiary of Esso that supplied parts and accessories to Esso auto service stations. Atlas decided to franchise its operations because its profits were declining. Mr. Murphy's company, Yarmouth Equipment, was interested in purchasing the franchise for a particular area. Atlas prepared two sets of financial projections for the business in that area. The projections given to Murphy portrayed a viable operation. The other set showed that the franchise was not viable at all. Yarmouth bought the franchise in reliance on the optimistic written projections supplied to him as well as on other oral assurances. The contract Murphy signed with Atlas, however, contained an "entire contract" clause stating, "Except as provided herein, there are no conditions, representations, warranties, undertakings, inducements, promises, or agreements." This would mean that the written projections and other oral assurances were not to form part of the contract. Another clause recited, "The Franchisee [Murphy] further acknowledges that it has had an adequate opportunity to be advised by advisors of its own choosing regarding all pertinent aspects of the franchise business, Atlas, and this agreement."

Murphy's operation failed and closed in less than a year. Murphy was called upon to pay a substantial sum under his personal guarantee of Yarmouth's debt to Atlas. In defence, Murphy argued that Atlas's positive income projection was a term of the contract and that Atlas was in breach of that term. On a related front, he argued that the exclusion clauses—which would suggest that Atlas's income projection formed no part of the contract—should not apply, given Atlas's unconscionable conduct. The trial judge found in Murphy's favour; Atlas appealed.

THE LEGAL QUESTION: Do Atlas's income projections constitute a contractual warranty or do the exclusion clauses prevent this conclusion? Is Murphy liable on his guarantee to Atlas?

RESOLUTION: The appeal court ruled 2 to 1 in favour of Murphy. Justice Matthews found that the agreement was entered into on the one hand by a national company with international connections through its parent, Imperial Oil, and on the other by a small businessman who, though no neophyte, had little or no retail experience.

He concluded that it was unconscionable for Atlas to give Murphy misleading information while withholding contrary information. On this footing, he refused to allow Atlas to rely on the exclusion clauses. This meant that Atlas was in breach of its contractual warranty. The court also partially released Murphy from his guarantee to Atlas, given all the circumstances, including Atlas's unconscionable conduct.

The dissenting judge found that Murphy was a very experienced businessperson who was aware of the basis for the financial projections and was not compelled to agree to the terms, which were clearly expressed. He cautioned that the courts should be very reluctant to set aside business deals such as this one.

CRITICAL ANALYSIS: Should a large business with the advantage in information (such as Atlas) be allowed to take advantage of a small, relatively uninformed one (such as Yarmouth)? Which of the judges do you find to be the most persuasive?

Note that some provinces have enacted consumer protection legislation which includes unconscionability as a standard against which to assess the fairness of a consumer transaction.[25]

---

25 See, for example, Ontario's *Consumer Protection Act*, 2002, SO 2002, c30. For discussion of consumer protection legislation generally, see Chapter 23.

Misrepresentations and Important Mistakes
Misrepresentation of Relevant Facts

Parties involved in negotiating a contract are usually not obligated to volunteer information. The basic principle or rule is that both parties are to look out for their own interests and if they want information, they should ask for it.

Sometimes parties do owe a duty to disclose information without being prompted, however. Consider the follow scenarios:

- *one party provides only partial information to the other side*. This may amount to a misrepresentation, since once information is offered, it must not be misleading or incomplete.
- *one party actively conceals the truth*. For example, if the vendor of a building takes steps to conceal a crack in the foundation, this must be disclosed or it will amount to a misrepresentation.
- *one party neglects to correct an earlier assertion that, when stated, was correct but now no longer is so*. If a physician selling his practice gives initial information regarding its value that later becomes inaccurate, the physician must go back and disclose this new fact to the prospective purchaser.
- *the parties are in a relationship requiring utmost good faith*. Insurance law provides an example of this. The person applying for insurance coverage has a duty to disclose all information that would be relevant to the insurer who is assessing the risk of accepting the application.[26]
- *a statute imposes a positive obligation to disclose information*. For example, and as discussed in Chapter 16, legislation requires directors of a corporation to disclose their interest in certain kinds of contracts involving the corporation they serve.[27]

The difference between a statement made in the contract and one that is made prior to entering into the contract is crucial in this area of law.[28] If the statement is made in the contract, it is a promise or a term of the contract. If it proves to be untrue, a breach of contract has occurred. However, if the statement is made prior to entering into the contract but is not a term, it still can have legal consequences. A statement that meets the conditions set out below is known in law as an actionable **misrepresentation**.

Contract law allows the party who has relied on a misrepresentation to have the contract cancelled. This cancellation is called **rescission** and involves putting the parties back into their pre-contractual positions. Because rescission is an equitable remedy, the court requires the person seeking such assistance to act promptly in bringing the complaint forward.

Where rescission is not possible, such as when one party has substantially altered the subject matter of the contract, the courts will endeavour to do what is

Misrepresentation

A false statement of fact that causes someone to enter a contract.

Rescission

The remedy that results in the parties being returned to their pre-contractual positions.

---

26 The first four examples in this part of the text are based in case law and are taken from John McCamus, *The Law of Contracts* 2nd ed (Toronto: Irwin Law, 2012) at 342–343. For discussion of the insurance contract scenario, see Peel, *supra* note 12 at 430. Note that the common law duty to disclose information is also repeated in legislation governing insurance contracts. See for example, *Insurance Act*, RSO 1990, c I.8, s 148.

27 See, for example, discussion of the self-dealing contract in Chapter 16. Directors must disclose their interest in certain kinds of corporate contracts.

28 Consumer protection legislation in some jurisdictions, however, specifies that pre-contractual representations are part of the contract. The distinction between pre-contractual representations and terms of the contract, while important in the commercial context, is less important when a business deals with a consumer.

practically just so that the innocent party receives some redress, including monetary compensation.[29]

Ingredients of an Actionable Misrepresentation

The law provides that a negotiating party must answer inquiries accurately and that any information volunteered must be correct. Whether or not a statement is a misrepresentation that allows the other party a remedy depends on its nature and effect. To count as a misrepresentation, it must be proven that the statement is

- false.
- clear and unambiguous.
- material to the contract; that is, it must be significant to the decision of whether or not to enter into the contract.
- one that actually induces the aggrieved party to enter into the contract.
- concerned with a fact and not an opinion, unless the speaker claims to have special knowledge or expertise in relation to an opinion.

Categories of Actionable Misrepresentations

The law further divides misrepresentations into three categories:

- *fraudulent misrepresentation.* The speaker has a deliberate intent to mislead or makes the statement recklessly without knowing or believing that it is true.
- *negligent misrepresentation.* The speaker makes the statement carelessly or negligently.
- *innocent misrepresentation.* The speaker has not been fraudulent or negligent, but has misrepresented a fact. By process of elimination, the misrepresentation is merely innocent.

When Kevin told the Smiths that signing the mortgage was a formality, this statement amounted to a misrepresentation, since a mortgage is in fact a legal instrument with far-reaching consequences, the most serious being that the bank could foreclose on the Smiths's house. If the Smiths can prove that they relied on that representation in deciding to sign the mortgage, they will probably succeed in establishing an actionable misrepresentation. Minimally, this statement was negligent, but, given the likely state of Kevin's banking knowledge, the statement might even be fraudulent.

When Kevin told the Smiths he was confident that nothing would come of their signing the mortgage, this was arguably an expression of opinion—not a statement of fact—and therefore not actionable. A court might find, however, that since Kevin is an expert in the area of mortgages and other banking matters, his statement was one of fact, and order a remedy on that basis. While a court would be unlikely to find this statement to be a fraudulent misrepresentation, given the sparse facts, it may well find it to be negligent.

Remedies for Misrepresentation

Besides entitling courts to rescind or set aside a contract, certain kinds of misrepresentations are torts, which provide for a remedy in damages. If the misrepresentation is fraudulent or negligently made, damages in tort can be awarded in

---

29 See, for example, *Kupchak v Dayson Holdings Ltd*, [1965] 53 WWR 65 (BCCA).

FIGURE 8.2 Remedies for Misrepresentation

	Type of Misrepresentation		
	Fraudulent	**Negligent**	**Innocent**
Remedy	Rescission in contract Damages in tort	Rescission in contract Damages in tort	Rescission in contract

addition to the remedy of rescission provided by contract law. Where the misrepresentation is neither fraudulent nor negligent, an action is still available to set the contract aside based on innocent misrepresentation (see Figure 8.2 above). Negligence and fraud (or deceit) are discussed further in Chapter 12.

Upon the Smiths demonstrating an innocent misrepresentation, the court can order that their contract with the bank be set aside. If the Smiths can go on to prove that the bank—through Kevin—is responsible for the tort of negligence or fraud, they are entitled to damages as well.

Given the cost of litigation—and the fact that the innocent party may fail to prove her case on the balance of probabilities that an actionable misrepresentation had been made—prevention is the best medicine. It is prudent to insist that important terms be an express part of a written contract, so as to achieve the goal of clarity between the parties. It is generally easier to prove breach of a written term than to establish that an oral statement made during contractual negotiations amounts to a misrepresentation in law. If the other party balks at reciting an important representation as an express, written term, the customer would be best advised to do business elsewhere.

Mistake

Mistake

An error made by one or both parties that seriously undermines a contract.

The doctrine of legal **mistake** is one of the most difficult aspects of contract law. In the course of its development by the courts, the law of mistake has become so complex and confusing that it presents a major challenge even to seasoned lawyers and judges. In practice, legal mistake is rarely proven, but when it is, the court is entitled to set the contract aside as a remedy.

The central point is that legal mistake is much narrower than the everyday idea of a mistake. A simple oversight or error by one negotiating party does not constitute a legal mistake and provides no basis for voiding a contract. As previously noted, negotiators are expected to look after themselves and to exercise appropriate caution before making legal commitments. Compare the following two examples.

- **Example 1:** Kerry intends to make an offer to sell her car for $11 000 and in error sends a written offer to Sean for $10 000. Sean accepts her offer.
- **Example 2:** Kerry makes a written offer to sell her car for $1 100 rather than $11 000, and Sean promptly accepts. There is no reason to believe that the car, worth approximately $11 000, should be sold at a substantially lower price. Moreover, there is nothing in the relationship that would suggest that Kerry would give Sean a break in price.

In both cases, Kerry has made a mistake according to the common understanding of that word. However, in all likelihood, only in Example 2 would this be interpreted at law as a mistake worthy of a remedy. The error Kerry has made in Example 1 is not one that would surprise or otherwise alert Sean. This could be exactly the price for which Kerry intends to sell her car. In contrast, in Example 2, Sean could not reasonably expect that the price would be so low, especially if Kerry and Sean have had earlier discussions about the possible price range. Kerry has made an error, and any reasonable person in Sean's position would realize that. In the latter example, there can be no true agreement for $1 100. The law will not permit Sean to "snap up" Kerry's offer in this way.

A legal mistake may also occur if both parties have made the same error (known as **common mistake**). If Kerry's car appears to be old and relatively worthless, and she and Sean negotiate on that basis for a relatively low price, their agreement is based on a common mistake if the car turns out to be a valuable antique. Only if the error is such that the car purchased is a totally different thing from what the parties thought it was will the contract be set aside on the basis of mistake. For example, if the difference is between low-grade transportation (what the parties thought the car was) and a classic car to be displayed and never driven (what the car actually is), a mistake in law could possibly be established. To the extent that the error is simply a mistaken assumption about the quality of the car (i.e., in terms of value), however, no legal mistake has occurred, and the purchaser is entitled to retain what may appear to be a windfall. Needless to say, such distinctions can be subtle.

Under the Business Law in Practice scenario, Martha's parents may have signed the mortgage under the mistaken belief that Martha's business problems were temporary and reversible. This is not a legal mistake, however, and there is no possibility that the mortgage would be set aside on the basis of this misapprehension.

Common mistake

Both parties to the agreement share the same fundamental mistake.

C A S E

R v Ron Engineering & Construction Ltd, [1981] 1 SCR 111

THE BUSINESS CONTEXT: As noted in Chapter 6, owners commonly secure competitive bids to build large projects through a call for tenders. In response, contractors (also known as tenderers) submit tenders that set out a price for the work to be done. Though this is a fact-specific matter, the tendering rules can require the contractors to submit a tender deposit that is forfeited by the contractor who is chosen if he refuses to undertake the job. It is therefore important that the tender price be accurately tabulated before the tender is submitted to the owner since it can be difficult to withdraw after the fact, at least not without risking the deposit.

FACTUAL BACKGROUND: Ron Engineering submitted a tender on a project for a price of $2 748 000 along with a certified deposit cheque for $150 000 as the tendering rules required. The tendering rules—contained in the Information for Tenderers—stipulated that

tenders could be withdrawn up to the official closing time, after which they would be irrevocable. The rules also provided that the deposit was forfeited by the successful contractor if the successful contractor refused to proceed with the project.

Tenders closed at 3:00 P.M. and soon thereafter, Ron Engineering realized that, due to a simple miscalculation, it had submitted a bid that was $750 000 less than it had intended to submit. Though this error was detected by Ron Engineering and explained to the owner within 72 minutes of closing, the owner insisted that Ron Engineering proceed with the project or forfeit its deposit.

THE LEGAL QUESTION: Does the law of mistake provide Ron Engineering with a route of escape, or is the company obligated to either perform or forfeit its deposit? Is it too late for Ron Engineering to withdraw its tender?

RESOLUTION: The Supreme Court of Canada ruled that tenderers in the position of Ron

(Cotinued)

CHAPTER 8: NON-ENFORCEMENT OF CONTRACTS

Engineering could not withdraw tenders after the official closing time. Upon submission of its tender, Ron was in a preliminary contract with the owner. This preliminary contract (known as Contract A) required the owner to respect the rules on how to evaluate tenders and required tenderers not to withdraw their tenders after the official closing time. Only the successful tenderer would enter into the larger contract to perform the work in question (known as Contract B).

Ron Engineering unsuccessfully argued that the law of mistake prevented Contract A from ever coming into existence. According to the court, since Ron Engineering intended to submit the very tender submitted, including the named price, there was no mistake in any legal sense. Furthermore, even though the tender was $750 000 less than it should have been, this error was not so large as to suggest to the other side that there had been a miscalculation. Unless there was something seriously amiss with the tender—such as an entire page missing—Contract A would come into existence. Since no such circumstances existed here, Ron Engineering lost its deposit. The court insisted that such strictness was essential to protecting the integrity of the tendering process.

CRITICAL ANALYSIS: Is the law of mistake too harsh? What would the consequences be if a party could escape its contractual obligations simply because it had made a mathematical error?

An argument that is often made, though seldom successfully, concerns signed documents. The signer may misunderstand the type or nature of the document. Perhaps the signer thinks he is signing a guarantee of a debt, but the document is actually a mortgage on his residence. Or the document is a transfer of land, and the signer thought he was signing an option to sell the property. The argument is "I never intended to sign this type of contract." In practice, this argument tends to succeed only when there is a good reason for the signer's failure to more closely examine the document before signing—as when the signer is poorly educated, illiterate, or otherwise dependent on the creator of the document (the other party) for an explanation of what it is. Simple carelessness in signing a document without attention to what it is or to what its consequences might be is not enough to avoid enforceability.[30]

Contracts Based on Defects

Illegality

Under the classical model of illegality, even a freely chosen contract will be unenforceable if it

- is contrary to a specific statute.
- violates public policy.

These contracts are void and of no effect unless the court decides that the offending portions of the contract can be deleted, or severed, and the remaining portions saved. In such a case, only some of the contract will remain in effect and be enforceable. What a court will not do, however, is re-draft the offending portions to make them comply with the law.

Contracts that are illegal may or may not be criminal. In this context, an **illegal contract** is simply one that violates statute law or public policy.[31]

Illegal contract

A contract that cannot be enforced because it is contrary to legislation or public policy.

---

30 For an exception to this statement see the discussion in Chapter 7 concerning *Tilden Rent-A-Car Co v Clendenning* (1978), 83 DLR (3d) 400 (Ont CA).
31 See Stephanie Ben-Ishai & David R Percy, *supra* note 18 at 751.

Illegal by Statute

Numerous kinds of contracts are made illegal by legislation. Examples include the following:

- the *Criminal Code*[32] forbids loans at a rate of interest considered "criminal"—defined as a rate exceeding 60 percent per year. The courts may or may not invalidate the entire transaction, depending on whether it is possible to sever the clauses dealing with the criminal rate of interest from the rest of the contract.
- the federal *Competition Act*[33] invalidates a range of commercial transactions that unduly restrict competition. For example, resale price maintenance contracts are prohibited because, through them, manufacturers attempt to influence retail prices in the stores by keeping them high. Entering into such contracts can lead to criminal sanctions.
- Ontario's *Real Estate and Business Brokers Act*[34] provides that an unlicensed realtor cannot maintain an action for services rendered.

Business enterprises should take care to meet their statutory and regulatory obligations lest they be faced with a challenge to the legality of a contract they have entered into. Increasingly, however, the consequences of statutory illegality depend on all the circumstances of the case.[35] As one leading text in this area of law states, "If every statutory illegality, however trivial in the course of performance of a contract, invalidated the agreement, the result would be an unjust and haphazard allocation of loss without regard to any rational principles."[36] This statement signals a more flexible perspective, which may fully eclipse the strict, traditional approach that says that illegal contracts are automatically unenforceable.

Contrary to Public Policy

At common law, contracts are contrary to **public policy** when they injure the public interest. For example, an employer may wish to restrict the activities of employees to prevent them from joining the competition or becoming the competition. Or someone wishing to acquire a business may want to ensure that the vendor cannot simply set up shop down the street and immediately begin competing with the new owner. The motivation for such clauses is understandable since both the employer and business acquirer, as the case may be, want to protect their own best interests. Clauses which restrict someone's business activities in this way are known as restrictive covenants or covenants in restraint of trade. If drafted too broadly, they are unenforceable as being contrary to public policy. In short, restrictive covenants may unduly interfere with the other side's ability to earn a livelihood, and they reduce competition within a sector.[37] In 2009, the Supreme Court of Canada in *Shafron v KRG Insurance Brokers* expressly reaffirmed that restrictive covenants in the sale of a business are subject to less scrutiny

Public policy

The community's common sense and common conscience.

---

32 *Criminal Code*, RSC 1985, c C-46, s 347.
33 *Competition Act*, RSC 1985, c C-34.
34 *Real Estate and Business Brokers Act, 2002*, SO 2002, c 30, Sch C, s 9.
35 See *Still v Minister of National Revenue*, [1998] 1 FC 549 (CA) at para 43 and 48 whose historical analysis was approved by the Supreme Court of Canada in *Transport North American Express Inc v New Solutions Financial Corp*, 2004 SCC 7.
36 SM Waddams, *The Law of Contracts*, 6th ed (Toronto: Canada Law Book, 2010) at 420.
37 *Doerner v Bliss and Laughlin Industries Inc*, [1980] 2 SCR 865 at 873.

Non-solicitation clause

A clause forbidding contact with the business's customers.

Non-competition clause

A clause forbidding competition for a certain period of time.

because the business owner is typically paid for goodwill.[38] In the employment context, by way of contrast, the employee receives no such recompense, and there is typically a power imbalance between employee and employer.[39]

There are two main kinds of restrictive covenants that are found in this area. A **non-solicitation clause** simply forbids the employee (or business vendor) from contacting the business's customers. A **non-competition clause** forbids competition outright for a certain period of time and is therefore much more intrusive.

The following case explains how non-competition clauses should be assessed by the judiciary.

CASE

Elsley v J G Collins Insurance Agencies Limited, [1978] 2 SCR 916

THE BUSINESS CONTEXT: The purchaser of a business often wants to prevent the vendor from competing against him for a specified period of time in order to prevent the vendor from setting up a similar business across the street. If the purchaser hires the vendor to work at the business, the employment contract may also contain a non-competition covenant for a related reason.

FACTUAL BACKGROUND: Elsley and Collins entered into a purchase and sale agreement whereby Collins purchased Elsley's general insurance business. This agreement contained a non-competition covenant, which stipulated that Elsley was restricted from carrying on or engaging in the business of a general insurance company within a certain geographic area for a period of 10 years. By a separate employment agreement, Elsley worked as a manager for Collins. This agreement also contained a non-competition covenant covering the same geographic area, whereby Elsley could not compete with Collins for a period of five years after he ceased to work for Collins. After 17 years, Elsley resigned and opened his own general insurance business, which took some of Collins's customers.

THE LEGAL QUESTION: Is the non-competition covenant in Elsley's employment contract valid?

RESOLUTION: In finding the non-competition covenant to be valid, the court stated:

A covenant in restraint of trade is enforceable only if it is reasonable between the parties and with reference to the public interest. As with many of the cases which come before the Courts, competing demands must be weighed. There is an important public interest in discouraging restraints of trade, and maintaining free and open competition unencumbered by the fetters of restrictive covenants. On the other hand, the courts have been disinclined to restrict the rights to contract, particularly when the right has been exercised by knowledgeable persons of equal bargaining power. In assessing the opposing interests the word one finds repeated throughout the cases is the word "reasonable." The test of reasonableness can be applied, however, only in the peculiar circumstances of the particular case.

According to the court, the assessment of non-competition clauses involves considering whether

- the employer has a proprietary interest that he is entitled to protect.
- the temporal and geographic restrictions are reasonable.
- the restrictions are reasonably necessary to protect the employer, given the nature of the business and the nature and character of the employment.

Once the reasonableness of a restrictive covenant has been established, it is enforceable unless it runs contrary to the public interest.

In this case, the clause was reasonable and therefore fully enforceable. The plaintiff was

---

38 *Shafron v KRG Insurance Brokers*, [2009] 1 SCR 157 at paras 20–21. For a recent Supreme Court of Canada endorsing this analysis, see *Payette v Guay* 2013 SCC 45.

39 *Shafron, ibid* at paras 22–23.

entitled to an injunction and damages for breach of the clause.[40]

CRITICAL ANALYSIS: Do you agree that non-competition clauses in employment contracts should be less likely to be enforced than similar clauses in sale-of-business agreements? What are an employer's "proprietary interests"?

INTERNATIONAL PERSPECTIVE

PAYING BRIBES TO FOREIGN OFFICIALS

Canadian businesses may feel compelled to pay bribes in order to facilitate business overseas but they also face serious liability for doing so, not to mention damage to corporate reputation. This is because Canada's *Corruption of Foreign Public Officials Act*, SC 1998 c 34 (*CFPOA*) criminalizes the offering of bribes to foreign public officials in the course of business. Canada has been criticized for its lax enforcement of anti-bribery legislation in the past (including by Transparency International in 2009) but several recent high profile cases may help to change that reputation.

In *R v Griffiths Energy International Inc* [2013] AJ No. 412 (QB), for example, the Alberta Court of Queen's Bench fined Calgary-based Griffiths Energy International Inc (Griffiths), an oil and gas firm, $10.35 million. This represents the highest penalty ever assessed by a Canadian court in relation to corporate bribery of a foreign official then to date. As recited in an agreed statement of facts, Griffiths acknowledged that in anticipated exchange for securing two oil and gas exploration blocks, the company's previous management and representatives bribed the wife of a Chad official in the amount of $2 million and an allotment of corporate shares.

In accepting Griffiths's guilty plea, the Court observed, at para 8:

> The bribing of a foreign official by a Canadian company is a serious matter . . . . [S]uch bribes, besides being an embarrassment to all Canadians, prejudice Canada's efforts to foster and promote effective governmental and commercial relations with other countries; and where, as here, the bribe is to an official of a developing

nation, it undermines the bureaucratic or governmental infrastructure for which the bribed official works.

The major aggravating factor of the case was the bribe's large size but significantly, the Court also listed mitigating factors. Most important was the fact that it was Griffiths's own *new* management team who discovered the bribe and who then acted "quickly and decisively to fully investigate the matter" at para 14. Further, Griffiths entered a guilty plea and fully cooperated with authorities, thereby dramatically reducing the cost of prosecution.

The second recent case, *R v Karigar*, 2014 ONSC 3093, represents the first time that an individual has been sentenced to jail under the *CFPOA*. Here, the accused, a businessman from Ottawa, received three years in prison for offering bribes in the amount of US $450 000 and an allotment of corporate shares both to Air India and the Indian Minister of Civil Aviation. The money was to help secure a bid to win a $100 million contract to supply facial recognition software and related equipment to Air India. During sentencing, the Court stressed the severity of crime, highlighting that white-collar crime is neither harmless nor victimless. In the court's words, at para 18:

> . . . the corruption of foreign public officials, particularly in developing countries, is enormously harmful and is likely to undermine the rule of law. The idea that bribery is simply a cost of doing business in many countries, and should be treated as such by Canadian firms competing for business in those countries, must be disavowed. The need for sentences reflecting principles of general deterrence is clear.

---

40 For examples of how lower courts have relied on both *Shafron* and *Elsley*, see *Payette, supra* note 38, *Mason v Chem-Trend Limited Partnership*, [2011] ONCA 344 and *Belron Canada Incorporated v TCG International Inc*, [2009] BCSC 596, aff'd 2009 BCCA 577.

Recent amendments to Canada's anti-bribery legislation (under Bill S-14) have also recently won praise from Janet Keeping, Chair and President of anti-corruption watchdog Transparency International Canada (TI-Canada) as follows:

> For many years TI-Canada has been recommending improvements to Canada's anti-corruption legislation and we are pleased that the government has taken our recommendations and started the process to turn them into law. These amendments send a powerful message to the Canadian business community.

The amendments (which have received royal assent) include increasing the imprisonment penalty to a maximum of 14 years.

Critical Analysis: Do you agree with the penalty assessed in *Griffiths*? Should it matter how Griffiths conducted itself after the offence had been committed?

Nazir Karigar

Enforcement" (14 February 2013) (McCarthy Tetrault), online: McCarthy Tetrault:<http://www.mccarthy.ca/article_detail.aspx?id=6176>; Jennifer Brown "Karigar could be made example of in first conviction under CFPOA," Lawyers Weekly (10 March 2014), online: Lawyers Weekly <http://canadianlawyermag.com/5048/Karigar-could-be-made-example-of-in-first-conviction-under-CFPOA.html?print=1&tmpl=component>; Transparency International Canada, Press Release: "Transparency International Canada says Ottawa's move to strengthen anti-corruption legislation sends a powerful message to the Canadian business community" (05 February 2013), online: Transparency International Canada <http://www.transparency.org/news/pressrelease/05022012_transparency_international_canada_says_ottawas_move_to_strengthen>. Researched and written by Sean McGinnis.

Sources: Paul Blyschak and John Boscariol "A Closer Look at the Griffiths Energy Case: Lessons and Insights on Canadian Anti-Corruption

The Supreme Court of Canada in *Shafron* has also confirmed that courts are not to re-draft overly broad non-competition clauses by "reading them down" until they become reasonable—that is, legal and enforceable.[41] Rather, such clauses are simply and utterly unenforceable. A central policy objective is to prevent employers from intentionally drafting broad clauses with the promise that the courts will simply reduce their scope as appropriate. This could lead to employees who never make it to court, being bound by an unreasonable non-competition clause.[42] The Court also agreed that judges may remove part of an impugned provision to "cure" it, but only sparingly and "only in cases where the part being removed is clearly severable, trivial and not part of the main purport of the restrictive covenant."[43] Finally, the Supreme Court also ruled that vaguely or ambiguously drafted clauses are also unenforceable, generally speaking, because it is difficult to prove that the clause is reasonable when its meaning is in fact unclear.[44]

The Supreme Court of Canada in *Payette v Guay*[45] recently offered analysis on non-solicitation clauses. Like non-competition clauses, they too must be reasonable but beyond this, a "determination that a non-solicitation clause is reasonable and lawful does not generally require a territorial limitation."[46] This is, in

---

41 *Supra* note 38 at paras 33, 36.
42 *Ibid* at para 40.
43 *Ibid* at para 36.
44 *Ibid*.
45 *Supra* note 38.
46 *Ibid* at para 72.

part, because "in the context of the modern economy, and in particular of new technologies, customers are no longer limited geographically, which means that territorial limitations in non-solicitation have generally become obsolete."[47]

Writing as a Requirement

As a general rule, contracts do not have to be in writing in order to be enforceable. A party to an oral contract must find other means to prove its existence, such as the calling of witnesses. Sometimes, however, a contract must be evidenced in writing due to the *Statute of Frauds*.

The *Statute of Frauds* was imported to Canada from England. Except in Manitoba, where it has been completely repealed,[48] it applies to differing extents in all common law provinces.

The purpose of the *Statute of Frauds* is to prevent fraud and perjury by requiring written proof of certain kinds of contracts. The categories discussed below are the most relevant to business. A contract falling into these categories must have its essential terms contained in a document or documents signed by the party against whom the contract is to be enforced. Several documents can be combined to meet the requirement if each of the documents can be connected with the others. If the writing requirement cannot be met, however, the contract is generally unenforceable.

Contracts of Guarantee

A guarantee is a promise to pay the debt of someone else, should that person default on the obligation. A guarantee must generally be evidenced in writing.[49]

The province of Alberta has gone even further than the *Statute of Frauds* by requiring additional formalities from non-corporate guarantors, including the requirement that the written guarantee be accompanied by a lawyer's certificate. In this certificate, the lawyer attests that the guarantor is aware of the contents of the guarantee and understands it.[50]

Contracts Not to Be Performed Within a Year

The rationale for requiring a written record for these kinds of contracts is the difficulty of proving promises that were possibly made in the distant past. Since the arbitrary cutoff of one year is bound to be unfair in some cases, the courts have been known to interpret the *Statute of Frauds* in such a way as to avoid an injustice.

The requirement of writing for this kind of contract has been repealed in several jurisdictions, such as Ontario,[51] British Columbia, and Manitoba.

Contracts Dealing With Land

Contracts concerning land—including leases and sales—generally must be evidenced in writing in order to be enforceable.[52] Nevertheless, in the interest of

---

47 *Ibid* at para 73.
48 *An Act to Repeal the Statute of Frauds*, CCSM c F158.
49 This rule does not apply in Manitoba.
50 See the *Guarantees Acknowledgment Act*, RSA 2000, c G-11, as amended. British Columbia has extended the writing requirement to indemnities owing to the *Law and Equity Act*, RSBC 1996, c 253, s 59(6).
51 *Statute of Frauds*, RSO 1990, c S-19, s 4, amended by *Statute Law Amendment Act*, SO 1994, c 27, s 55.
52 Even in Manitoba—where the *Statute of Frauds* has been repealed—courts have been known to insist that contracts dealing with land be in writing, particularly when the offer is made in writing, as in *Jen-Den Investments Ltd v Northwest Farms Ltd*, [1978] 1 WWR 290 (Man CA). See too *Megill-Stephenson Co Ltd v Woo* (1989), 59 DLR (4th) 146 (Man CA).

fairness, the courts have also created an exception to the absolute requirement for writing in the case of "part performance." If the person attempting to enforce an oral agreement for purchase and sale of land has performed acts in relation to the land that could be explained by the existence of an agreement, that performance may be accepted in place of a written agreement.[53]

TECHNOLOGY AND THE LAW

ELECTRONIC SIGNATURES

Contracts are generally enforceable, no matter what form they take, but there are important exceptions. For example, signature requirements exist in statutes such as the *Statute of Frauds*.

As noted by the New Brunswick Court of Appeal in *Girouard v Druet* 2012 NBCA 40, it is generally accepted that the purpose of a signature is (1) "to identify the person who is signing; that is to say, to identify the source and authenticity of the document" and (2) "to establish the signatory's approval of the document's contents" at para 27. In the context of written contracts, courts have avoided being unduly technical. As Stephanie Ben-Ishai and David Percy summarize the matter, a mark made by the person signing is sufficient if intended as authentication of the document; as well, mere initialling of the document can suffice.[54]

In relation to electronic contracts, legislators across the country have offered guidance as to what fulfills a signature requirement. Ontario's *Electronic Commerce Act*, 2000, for example, provides that, with some significant exceptions, "a legal requirement that a document be signed is satisfied by an electronic signature." Section 1(1) defines an "electronic signature" as "electronic information that a person creates or adopts in order to sign a document and that is in, attached to, or associated with the document." Most Canadian jurisdictions have accepted electronic signatures according to statutory rules of varying strictness.

While case law in the area is still limited, there are nonetheless several helpful cases in

How does legislation governing electronic signatures help create certainty in the marketplace?

place. For example, in *Leoppky v Meston* (2008) 40 BLR (4th) 69 at para 46 (Alta QB), the Court concluded that an email with the sender's name typed at the bottom counted as a signature required by the *Statute of Frauds*. By way of contrast, in *Pereira Fernandes v Mehta* [2006] 1 WLR 1543, the Court ruled that an email in which the sender's email address was automatically inserted into the header of the email by an Internet services provider after the document had been transmitted was not a signature within the meaning of the *Statute of Frauds* because no signature was intended. According to the court, at para 26:

> [A] party can sign a document . . . by using his full name or his last name prefixed by some or all of his initials or using his initials, and possibly by using a pseudonym or a combination of letters and numbers . . . providing always that whatever was used was inserted into the document to give, and with the intention of giving,

---

53 It is beyond the scope of this text to discuss the varying tests for part performance that exist at common law.
54 Ben-Ishai and Percy, *supra* note 18 at 269-270.

authenticity to it. Its inclusion must have been intended as a signature for these purposes.

Given that intention of the signatory is of paramount concern, questions surrounding the validity of a signature will almost certainly have to be decided on a case by case basis.

Critical Analysis: Are electronic signatures more or less reliable than the handwritten variety?

Sources: Teresa Scassa and Michael Deturbide, *Electronic Commerce and Internet Law in Canada*, 2nd ed (Toronto: CCH, 2012); Donalee Moulton "E-signatures are fast, but manage the risk" *Lawyers Weekly* (31 May 2013) 13.

The mortgage given by the Smiths to the bank must comply with the *Statute of Frauds*, since it concerns an interest in land. That is, through the mortgage, the bank acquires the right to sell the land and apply the proceeds against the Smiths's loan, should they default on payments. The mortgage prepared by the bank appears to meet the requirements of the *Statute of Frauds* because the agreement is a written contract and has been signed by the Smiths.

Contracts for the Sale of Goods

All provinces have a version of the *Sale of Goods* Act, and most[55] contain a provision that contracts for the sale of goods above a specified amount must be in writing to be enforceable by the courts. The amount is generally set at between $30 and $50, not adjusted to reflect inflation. Thus, it would appear that most sales of goods are caught by the Act. Since written contracts are generally not produced for routine transactions, it is fortunate that sale of goods legislation also contains very broad exceptions that limit the application of the rule. For example, if partial payment is made by the buyer, or if the buyer accepts all or part of the goods, no written evidence is required for the contract to be enforceable.

BUSINESS AND LEGISLATION

INTERNET CONTRACTS

Even where a contract is not caught by *Statute of Frauds* requirements such that it must be in writing, other legislation may nonetheless require the business in question to produce a written copy of the contract. That is, governments may decide it is in the best interests of consumers to give them additional protection and safeguards when entering into certain kinds of transactions.

As Scassa and Deturbide note, provinces including Manitoba, Alberta, Saskatchewan, Nova Scotia, Newfoundland and Labrador, Ontario, and British Columbia have passed legislation reflecting, in varying degrees, the consumer protection measures of the *Internet Sales* *Contract Harmonization Template*. The template was released by a group called the Consumer Measures Committee, and endorsed by all federal, provincial, and territorial ministers responsible for consumer affairs. The template and its various counterparts apply to consumer purchases of goods and services over the Internet and require sellers to clearly disclose certain information to the buyer before an online contract is formed. The information to be disclosed includes the seller's business name and address (including email address), a fair and accurate description of the goods and services, all costs (including taxes and shipping), delivery arrangements, and return policies. All of this information must be accessible such that it can

---

55 The exceptions include New Brunswick, Manitoba, Ontario, and British Columbia. See too GHL Fridman, *Sale of Goods in Canada*, 6th ed (Toronto: Carswell, 2013) at 41.

be printed and retained by the consumer, and it must be clearly and prominently displayed. Consumers must also be given an opportunity to accept or decline the terms of the agreement and to correct errors before the contract is formed.

Legislation across the country is not always consistent with the template—some have fewer requirements while provinces like Ontario have more. Ontario's *Consumer Protection Act*, for example, requires a supplier to deliver to a consumer who has entered into an Internet agreement a copy of that agreement. If the supplier fails to do so within a specified time, the consumer may cancel the agreement and it becomes unenforceable.

By requiring that the supplier provide a written contract to the consumer, the consumer is better able to confirm what rights and liabilities exist under the contract. The consumer is also able to confirm whether the written agreement reflects the consumer's understanding of the contract.

Sources: Teresa Scassa and Michael Deturbide, *Electronic Commerce and Internet Law in Canada* 2nd ed (Toronto: CCH, 2012) at 42. See also s 39(1) and s 40(2) of the *Consumer Protection Act, 2002*, SO 2002, c 30, Sch A. Researched and written by Meredith Hagel.

Even without *Statute of Frauds* requirements, creating a record of an agreement is generally a prudent business decision. Personnel may change and memories may fade, and genuine disagreement as to the terms of a contract can result. Through a well recorded written document, such disagreements—and perhaps the expense of litigation—can be avoided.

That said, businesses and individuals must strike a reasonable balance between the comfort of complete records and the time and effort required to produce them, particularly in small transactions.

Managing the Risks of Unenforceability

When contracts are entered into, a business runs the risk that they may ultimately be unenforceable. Since a contract is only as good as the process leading up to its formation, businesses should train their employees carefully in how to negotiate contracts. Matters to be concerned about include:

- are the parties to the contract under any legal incapacities?
- has one party taken unfair advantage of the other?
- has one party misled the other?
- has a substantial mistake been made?
- is the contract contrary to legislation or in violation of public policy?
- is the contract required to be in writing?

An affirmative response to any of the foregoing may signal a possible problem if suing becomes necessary. Securing a deal at any cost may end up producing no deal at all.

BUSINESS LAW IN PRACTICE REVISITED

1. Did Kevin manipulate or pressure the Smiths into signing the mortgage? If so, what legal remedies do the Smiths have?

While the Smiths have the capacity to contract and were not subject to duress by Kevin, the mortgage transaction is probably unconscionable. There was inequality between the parties—namely the bank and the Smiths—because the Smiths were inexperienced senior citizens who had received no prior independent legal advice. As well, the transaction was very unfair, since the Smiths were risking their only substantial asset for a loan they could never repay on their own. In short, only the bank and Martha would benefit from the transaction, while the Smiths stood to lose everything. On this basis, both of the steps necessary to establish unconscionability have been met, and a court will set the mortgage aside unless the bank can somehow show that the transaction was fair.

The mortgage transaction is also liable to be set aside at common law on the grounds that it was signed on the basis of undue influence. There is a good argument that the Smiths did not freely enter into the mortgage but did so only because Kevin preyed on their deep need to help their daughter. As well, it appears that the Smiths put their entire trust in Kevin, which is another basis for a court to find undue influence.

2. Did Mr. and Mrs. Smith enter into the contract on the basis of mistake or misrepresentation? If so, what legal remedies do they have?

The Smiths could argue that they did not understand what they were signing and that the whole thing was a "mistake." This may be true from their point of view, but they did sign the mortgage document. The law ordinarily expects people not to sign documents unless they understand them. Accordingly, the mortgage is unlikely to be set aside on the grounds of mistake.

There is a very strong argument, however, that Kevin misrepresented the nature of the transaction by telling the Smiths that signing the mortgage was just a formality and that likely nothing would come of it. While it could be argued that this statement was merely an opinion, this defence is unlikely to succeed since the words were spoken by a banker who should know better. While it also could be argued that the Smiths did not rely on Kevin's statement—in other words, that they knew very well that their house could be foreclosed upon if Martha failed to make the payments—a judge is much more likely to take the Smiths's side. There is an excellent chance that the mortgage would be set aside on the basis of Kevin's misrepresentation.

3. How could Kevin have managed this transaction better?

Since the essence of a contract is the free and voluntary adoption of obligations, Kevin should never have asked the Smiths to sign the mortgage until they had secured independent legal advice.

Furthermore, it would probably have been better for Kevin not to have been involved in the transaction at all, and instead to have sent the Smiths elsewhere. Most of the legal problems in this scenario arose because Kevin was trying to get a bad loan he had given to Martha off his books. This motivation may have interfered with his judgment in how to handle the Smiths from the outset.

CHAPTER SUMMARY

There is a broad range of doctrines available to cancel all or part of a contract, but they apply only in relatively unusual or extreme circumstances. Moreover, courts are justifiably demanding in what parties must prove in order to be released from their obligations. Courts expect parties to negotiate carefully and deliberately to ensure that any commitment they make accurately reflects their intentions. If the deal merely turns out to be less desirable than expected, the doctrines in this chapter are unlikely to apply.

With limited exceptions, contracts made by minors are not enforceable against them. At common law, unless the contract is for a necessary, or amounts to a beneficial contract of service, it is unenforceable at the election of the minor. In British Columbia, minors have even more protection through legislation. Persons suffering from a mental impairment also do not generally have the capacity to contract when they are incapable of understanding the transaction.

The doctrine of duress permits a court to set aside a contract when one of the parties was subjected to such coercion that true consent to the contract was never given. The doctrine of undue influence permits the same outcome if one party, short of issuing threats, has unfairly influenced or manipulated someone else into entering into a contract. Unconscionability also considers the unequal relationship between the two contracting parties. If both inequality between the parties and an improvident bargain can be established, the contract can be rescinded by the court. If the transaction is sufficiently divergent from community standards of conduct, this may signal the presence of exploitation and lead to a finding of unconscionability.

Misrepresentation concerns the parties' knowledge of the circumstances underlying a contract. If one party misrepresents a relevant fact and thereby induces the other side to enter into the contract, the innocent party can seek to have the contract set aside or rescinded. If the misrepresentation also counts as a tort, the innocent party is entitled to damages as well.

A party who has entered into a contract based on wrong information can try to have the contract set aside on the basis of mistake, but this strategy will rarely be successful because mistake is an exceedingly narrow legal doctrine.

Contracts that are illegal because they violate a statute or are at odds with public policy can also be rescinded. Courts are increasingly looking at all of the circumstances surrounding contracts and will not automatically set them aside.

The *Statute of Frauds*, in its various forms, seeks to prevent fraud and perjury by requiring written proof of certain kinds of contracts. With the use of electronic and Internet contracts becoming more and more common, modern legislation also seeks to address the same types of problems in the new environment of technological commerce.

CHAPTER STUDY

Key Terms and Concepts

common mistake (p. 179)

economic duress (p. 170)

illegal contract (p. 180)

legal capacity (p. 168)

misrepresentation (p. 176)

mistake (p. 178)

non-competition clause (p. 182)

non-solicitation clause (p. 182)

public policy (p. 181)

rescission (p. 176)

unconscionable contract (p. 173)

undue influence (p. 171)

void contract (p. 168)

voidable contract (p. 168)

Questions for Review

1. Explain the difference between a void contract and a voidable contract.

2. Who has the legal capacity to form contracts?

3. What must be proven by someone seeking to avoid a contract based on mental impairment?

4. Describe the doctrine of undue influence.

5. What is duress? How does it relate to the idea of consent?

6. What is an unconscionable transaction?

7. Give an example of economic duress.

8. What is a misrepresentation?

9. How does the concept of a legal mistake differ from its ordinary meaning?

10. Name one statute that makes certain kinds of contracts illegal.

11. What is the role of public policy in contract enforcement?

12. How are non-competition covenants used in employment contracts?

13. How does the *Statute of Frauds* affect contracts?

14. What four types of contracts relevant to business law are required to be in writing?

15. How might the fact that a contract is electronic affect its enforceability?

16. Is an electronic contract subject to the same basic principles as a traditional contract?

17. Who is a minor?

18. Are contracts with minors binding?

Questions for Critical Thinking

1. Courts have decided that restrictive covenants must be reasonable between the parties with reference to the public interest to be enforceable. Is this a justifiable limitation on freedom of contract?

2. What factors should a business consider in developing a policy on documentation of commercial relationships? Should it insist that all contracts be in writing, or is more flexibility in order?

3. Which doctrines discussed in this chapter would be unlikely to arise in an online transaction? Why?

4. How can a business use a risk management plan in order to reduce the chances that it will enter into an unenforceable contract?

5. The law of mistake will rarely provide a defence for someone seeking to avoid a contract. Is the law of mistake too strict and inflexible? Why or why not?

6. Before the weaker party can rely on a defence of mental incapacity through illness or intoxication, he or she must prove that the other party was aware of such an impairment. Is this requirement a reasonable one? If a person does not have the capacity to contract, should that not be the end of the matter?

Situations for Discussion

1. Through her lawyer, Ms. Tanya, a commercial landlord, sent a letter to her tenant, Ms. Desie, who ran a bridal shop out of the premises. Tanya's lawyer demanded all back rent and stated that if the rent owed was not received by the deadline specified, Tanya would lock her tenant out of the business premises. Desie had no money to pay the back rent and therefore did not make the specified deadline. In fact Desie sent in no money at all. The landlord changed the locks. Soon thereafter, the parties later came together in settlement whereby Desie agreed to provide a promissory note in the amount owed in addition to Tanya's legal fees in relation to this matter.

   Subsequently, Desie alleged that Tanya's lawyer had forced her to settle and sign the promissory note in question. Desie said that she felt that she had no choice but to sign because otherwise, she would not have been allowed back onto the rental premises. Desie says that the agreement should be unenforceable due to the lawyer's duress.[56] Did the conduct of the lawyer amount to duress? What constitutes duress?

2. Madeline was 35 years old when she was seriously injured in car accident caused by the other driver. She was hospitalized for over a month. An insurance adjuster (an employee of the insurer of the culpable driver) visited

---

56 Based on *Taber v Paris Boutique & Bridal Inc (cob Paris Boutique)*, 2010 ONCA 157.

Madeline at her home upon her release from hospital with the hope of getting her to agree to settle her case out of court for a set amount of money. Though the adjuster knew Madeline would almost certainly win her case in court and be awarded damages at least in the amount of $250 000, he offered only $50 000, assuring her that he had her best interests at heart and it was time to "wrap things up." Madeline felt confused during the conversation as she was on strong painkillers to help deal with the terrible headaches she suffered as a result of the accident. She really was not quite sure what was going on. Madeline asked for a minute to think about what he had said because she was feeling unwell but the adjuster was adamant. Madeline then took the pen that the adjuster handed her and signed the agreement. Madeline now realizes that she has made a terrible deal.

What doctrines in this chapter are relevant to the situation? Do you think Madeline is bound?

3. Ms. Stewart bought a business operating in rented space in a shopping mall. Shortly after she took over the business, the landlord pressured her to sign a lease that made her responsible for the arrears in rent of the previous tenant. The landlord secured Ms. Stewart's agreement by exerting tremendous pressure on her. For example, he called in the sheriff to execute a distress for rent when, at that time, she was in arrears only for the month of January. The landlord told Ms. Stewart that if she did not pay the former tenant's arrears, "she would be the one to suffer." The landlord knew that Ms. Stewart was unsophisticated in business dealings and that she had signed the lease without seeking advice.[57] Is she obligated by the lease?

4. Leona was interested in purchasing property that she intended to use for her family's expanding brickyard business. She spoke with the owner, who had recently inherited the property from his elderly aunt. Leona asked if there were any restrictions on the land preventing it from being used as a brickyard. The owner replied, "Not that I am aware of." Though this was literally true, the owner failed to explain that he had never checked whether the land was subject to any restrictions. Leona purchased the land and has found out that it cannot be used as a brickyard. Can she have the contract rescinded based on misrepresentation? Why or why not?[58]

5. Derek was a minority shareholder and employee of Bridge Decks Ltd. (Bridge), a corporation that provided concrete work on new bridges. When Bridge sold all its assets to Concrete-Works-R-Us Ltd, Derek and Bridge agreed to a non-competition clause with the purchasers which, among other matters, restricted them from competing with Concrete-Works-R-Us Ltd in any jurisdiction in Canada. This meant that the covenant's geographical restriction even included Manitoba—a province that neither Derek nor Bridge had ever worked in—though they had provided bridge work in a town very close to the border between Saskatchewan and Manitoba. The restrictive covenant also prohibited competition by Derek and Bridge in the area of concrete work or "bridge construction or rehabilitation of any kind."

Is the non-competition clause Derek agreed to enforceable when measured against the factors identified by the Supreme Court of Canada in *Elsley* (discussed earlier in this chapter)? Does it make any difference that the non-competition clause in this Derek's case is related to an asset-sale transaction as opposed to an employment contract?[59]

6. Symphony & Rose was a developer and builder of high-rise condominium projects. A Symphony & Rose sales rep told Wendy and Sam that a penthouse apartment was still available in their current project. Wendy and Sam provided Symphony & Rose's real estate agent with information relevant to the purchase and delivered cheques for the various deposits. The agent told them that in a few days they would be required to sign an offer on Symphony & Rose's standard form; they thought they had a deal. A few days later, a senior representative of Symphony & Rose contacted Wendy and Sam

---

57 Based, in part, on *Stewart v Canada Life Assurance Co* (1994), 132 NSR (2d) 324 (CA).

58 Based on *Nottingham Patent Brick and Tile Co v Butler* (1886), 16 QBD 778 (CA).

59 Based on *Martin v ConCreate USL Limited Partnership*, 2013 ONCA 72.

to tell them that the penthouse had already been sold but 40 other units were currently still available.[60] Do Wendy and Sam have an enforceable agreement? Should they have done anything differently?

7. John Tonelli was an exceptionally talented young hockey player who, in 1973 at the age of 16, entered into a two-year contract with the Toronto Marlboros Major Junior A hockey club, a team in the Ontario Major Junior A Hockey League. The league had an agreement with the National Hockey League (NHL) that prevented the drafting of underage players and that called for the payment of certain fees once a player was drafted at the end of his junior career. However, a similar agreement could not be reached with the World Hockey Association (WHA). John—like all other junior hockey players of his time—was forced to sign a new contract as a condition of continuing to play in the junior league. This new contract essentially bound him to play three years longer than his earlier contract with the Toronto Marlboros; in addition, it imposed monetary penalties if he signed with a professional team within that time frame or within a period of three years after he ceased to be eligible to play in the junior league. As soon as he turned 18 (the age of majority), John abandoned the contract with the Toronto Marlboros and signed with the Houston Aeros, a professional team. The Marlboros sued him for breach of contract.[61] Is John's contract enforceable against him? If yes, does this seem fair, and from whose point of view? If no, is it fair that John can sign a contract and then ignore his obligations under it?

8. Sam Moore, an alert and intelligent 52-year-old businessman, tried without success to purchase a piece of farmland from Louis Wells. When he heard that Louis's brother, James, was willing to sell his nearby farm, he went to see him at his nursing home to make an offer to purchase it. James was 62 years old and, unbeknownst to Sam, was suffering from brain damage. Sam offered to purchase the land for $7000. James signed an acceptance to the offer and received a deposit of $100, without receiving any independent advice on the transaction. The land in question was worth quite a bit more than $7000—in fact, the farmer who was leasing James's land at the time had offered to pay $14 000 to $15 000 for it just the year before. Since then, a trust company had been appointed under the *Mentally Incapacitated Persons Act* and had taken over the management of James's affairs. The trust company refused to transfer the farm to Sam, who decided to sue in order to enforce the contract he entered into with James.[62] Is the contract for the sale of the farm enforceable? If yes, does that seem like a just result? If not, what legal doctrine would likely be used to rescind it? If the contract is not enforceable, do you think that it is fair to Sam? What factors ought Sam to have taken into account?

60 Based, in part, on *Bay Tower Homes v St Andrew's Land Corp* (1990), 10 RPR (2d) 193 (Ont HCJ).

61 Based, in part, on *Toronto Marlboro Major Junior 'A' Hockey Club v Tonelli* (1979), 96 DLR (3d) 135 (Ont CA).

62 Based, in part, on *Marshall v Canada Permanent Trust Co* (1968), 69 DLR (2d) 260 (Alta SC).

9

TERMINATION AND ENFORCEMENT OF CONTRACTS

OBJECTIVES

After studying this chapter, you should have an understanding of

- the termination of a contract by performance
- the termination of a contract by agreement
- the termination of a contract by frustration
- the methods of enforcing contracts
- the concept of privity
- remedies for breach of contract

Lindsay Upson/Image Source/Getty Image

BUSINESS LAW IN PRACTICE

Janet and Alphonso Owen entered into a contract with Charles Conlin to construct their family home in Vancouver, B.C. Conlin inspired a lot of confidence. He told the Owens that he understood the importance of building the family home with great care and attention. "It's where you're going to live, for goodness sake," he stated. "Your home is an extension of you. Don't worry about anything. My work is second to none." For her part, Janet was particularly excited about a see-through fireplace that would be installed in the centre portion of the proposed house. A see-through fireplace opens onto two rooms: in this case, the living room and dining room.

Pursuant to the contract, Conlin, known as the "Contractor," had a number of obligations, including the following:

…

12. The Contractor covenants to construct in accordance with the relevant sections of the British Columbia *Building Code*.

13. The Contractor covenants to construct in accordance with plans and specifications attached to this Contract.

…

20. The Contractor covenants to complete construction on or before 30 June 2009.

The plans and specifications were duly attached to the contract and included a provision for the see-through fireplace that Janet loved so much.

The Owens covenanted to pay a total of $500 000 and provide advances on a regular basis. Over time, the Owens advanced $300 000 to Conlin and looked forward to the day when they would be able to move in. Their excitement about their new home construction eventually turned to disappointment when Conlin failed to complete construction according to schedule. The Owens gave several extensions, but when Conlin missed the last deadline, the Owens went to talk to him at the job site. Upon arrival at the site, Alphonso noted that the house was only half-built and did not even look structurally sound (the centre of the living room ceiling drooped in an alarming fashion). He asked Conlin for an explanation and a progress report. Conlin became absolutely enraged, stating, "You're complaining about things here just to grind me down on my price. Well, at least my wife isn't ugly like yours is." This was the last straw. The Owens ordered Conlin and his crew to leave the property. They took possession of the house and promptly changed the locks.

What kinds of issues can a construction contract raise in relation to the termination and enforcement of contracts?

About two weeks later, the Owens's luck changed for the better. A well-known house-building expert, Mr. Holmstead, agreed to assist the Owens. The Owens hired Holmstead to fix the problems and finish the house.

In addition to creating structural problems, Conlin's employees had defectively constructed the see-through fireplace. When in use, it filled the entire living area with smoke due to the failure of the chimney to draw. Holmstead took the view that, in order for it to properly function as a fireplace, parts of it would have to be dismantled and rebuilt. When consulted on this, Conlin took the position that the problem could easily be solved by simply bricking in one side of the fireplace, since this would create the draw needed to carry the smoke up and out of the chimney. "My solution will cost about $200," said Conlin. "Your so-called solution will cost at least $5000. It's insane." Notwithstanding, the Owens decided to have Holmstead rebuild the fireplace and deal with Conlin later.

All in all, the Owens paid $300 000 to Holmstead, who fixed and completed the house to high standards.

In the meantime, Janet has been suffering considerable distress. Her disappointment in Conlin's work became overwhelming, and every day seemed to get harder. Though not clinically depressed, Janet found herself bursting into tears and waking up in the middle of the night, worrying about the house.

1. Can the Owens demonstrate all the steps in an action for breach of contract against Conlin?
2. Are the Owens themselves in breach of contract for refusing to permit Conlin to complete the contract?
3. Did the Owens properly mitigate their damages?
4. What damages can the Owens receive?

Termination of Contracts: An Overview

When parties enter into a contract, there are several ways in which it can be brought to an end—known, in law, as "termination":

- *through performance*. When both parties fulfill their contractual obligations to each other, they have performed the contract. This is generally the ideal way of concluding a contractual relationship.
- *through agreement*. Parties are always free to voluntarily bring their contract to an end. Both parties could agree to simply walk away from their agreement, or one party could pay a sum to the other side by way of settlement in exchange for agreeing to end the contract.
- *through frustration*. The doctrine of frustration applies when, after the formation of a contract, an important, unforeseen event occurs—such as the destruction of the subject matter of the contract or the death/incapacity of one of the contracting parties. When a contract is frustrated, it is brought to an end.
- *through breach*. A breach of contract, when it is particularly serious, can release the innocent party from having to continue with the contract if that is his wish. Less significant breaches generally entitle such a party to damages only.

What follows is a discussion of these four methods of termination and an outline of the remedies available for breach of contract.

Termination Through Performance

What amounts to termination by performance depends on the nature of the contract, as in the following examples:

- a contract to provide an audit of a corporation is performed when the audit is competently completed and the auditor's account for service rendered is paid in full.
- a contract to buy and sell a house is performed when the purchase price is paid and title to the property is transferred to the buyer.
- a contract to provide a custom-designed generator is complete when a generator conforming to contract specifications is delivered and the purchase price is paid.

In short, a contract is performed when all of its implied and express promises have been fulfilled. When a contract is terminated through performance, this does not necessarily mean the end of the commercial relationship between the parties, however. They may continue to do business with each other by means of new, continuing, and overlapping contracts.

Performance by Others

The law easily distinguishes between those who have the contractual obligation to perform and those who may actually do the necessary work. When a corporation enters into a contract to provide goods or services, for example, it must by necessity work through employees/agents. Even when the contracting party is an individual, employees may still have an important role. In both cases, the employee/agent is ordinarily not a party to the contract. Expressed in legal terms, such an employee/agent lacks privity of contract and therefore cannot sue or be sued on the contract, though there may be liability in tort. Privity is discussed in more detail later in this chapter. Agency is discussed in Chapter 13.

It is permissible to use employees to vicariously perform a contract in question, as long as personal performance by the particular contracting individual is not an express or implied term of a contract. For example, if a client engages an accountant and makes it clear that only that particular accountant is to do the work, **vicarious performance** through other accountants is not permitted. If there is no such term, the accountant is free to delegate the work to others in the firm while remaining contractually responsible for the timing and quality of the work.

Vicarious performance

Performance of contractual obligations through others.

In the case of Conlin and the Owens, there was nothing in the contract requiring Conlin to perform the contract unassisted. In fact, it would appear that the Owens fully understood that Conlin would use staff members to help him. For this reason, Conlin is not in breach of contract simply because he did not perform every aspect of the contract himself. He is, however, in breach of contract because his employees failed to properly perform aspects of the contract: the structural defects mean that the house was not built to Code and the fireplace was not constructed in accordance with plans and specifications since it could not draw air properly. The law holds Conlin responsible for his employees' incompetence. This is known as vicarious liability and is discussed further in Chapters 10 and 20.

Termination by Agreement
By Agreement Between Parties

Parties may enter into an agreement that becomes unfavourable for one or both of them. In response, they may decide to

- *enter into a whole new contract*. This is known as **novation**. Provided both parties benefit from this arrangement, the agreement will be enforceable by the court as a new contract. For example, if the Owens subsequently decide that they want to buy an entirely more luxurious home than they have contracted for from Conlin, they and Conlin are free to negotiate a new contract and cancel the old one.

Novation

The substitution of parties in a contract or the replacement of one contract with another.

- *vary certain terms of the contract*. If the Owens decide that they would like upgraded bathroom fixtures installed instead of the ones provided for in the plans and specifications, they can seek a variation of contract. Traditionally, as discussed in Chapter 6, the party benefiting from the variation (the Owens) must provide consideration to the other side (Conlin). In a case like this, the typical consideration would be an increase in the contract price, reflecting the additional cost of acquiring and installing the upgraded bathroom fixtures. Note, however, as discussed in Chapter 6, that the New Brunswick Court of Appeal,[1] for example, has shown a willingness to enforce contractual variations that are not supported by consideration in certain circumstances.

- *end the contract*. The parties may decide to simply terminate the contract, with both parties agreeing not to enforce their rights or with one party paying the other to bring his obligations to an end.

- *substitute a party*. The law permits a more limited form of novation whereby one party's rights and obligations are transferred to someone else. In short, a new party is substituted, and the old party simply drops out of the contract

---

1   *NAV Canada v Greater Fredericton Airport Authority Inc*, 2008 NBCA 28.

altogether. For example, if Conlin discovered that he had double-booked himself and could not in fact build the Owens' house, he might be able to recommend someone else who would "step into his contractual shoes." This new contractor would not only assume all of Conlin's obligations but also be entitled to payment by the Owens. However, everyone—the Owens, Conlin, and the new proposed contractor—must agree to this substitution in order for it to be effective. Of course, if the Owens are unhappy with Conlin's proposal, they are free to insist on performance by him and sue for breach of contract if he fails to perform.[2]

An agreement between the parties is almost always the best way of dealing with events that make the contract disadvantageous in some respect. By taking such a route, the parties are able to avoid the expense and uncertainty of litigation.

Transfer of Contractual Rights

A party who wants to end his involvement in a particular contract has the option—in certain circumstances—to transfer it to someone else. This transfer does not terminate the contract but does have the effect of eliminating the transferor's role in it. In short, while contractual duties or obligations cannot be transferred to someone else without agreement by the other side, contractual rights can be transferred without any such permission being required.

This means that Conlin cannot unilaterally transfer to another contractor his obligation to build the Owens' home. The Owens have contracted for performance by Conlin and his employees. They cannot be forced to deal with a new contractor altogether. However, Conlin can transfer his right to be paid for the building job to someone else.

In law, when one party transfers a contractual right to someone else, this is known as an **assignment** (see Figure 9.1). The person who is now or will be entitled to payment from a contract is known as a creditor. The party who is obligated to make the payment is known as a debtor.

The law of assignment of rights permits the creditor (the assignor) to assign the right to collect to another person (the assignee) without the agreement of the debtor.

Assignment

The transfer of a right by an assignor to an assignee.

FIGURE 9.1 The Steps in Assignment

Step One: Creditor–Debtor Relationship
C (creditor) ⟷ D (debtor)
Contract is entered between C and D, whereby D owes money to C for services rendered.

Step Two: Assignor–Assignee Relationship
C (assignor) ⟷ A (assignee)
Contract is entered between C and A, whereby C assigns the debt he is owed by D.

Step Three: Assignee–Debtor Relationship
A (assignee) ⟷ D (debtor)
A gives notice to D.
D is now obligated to pay debt directly to A.

2 If they choose this route, the Owens still have a duty to mitigate, as discussed later in this chapter.

However, to be effective, the debtor must have notice of the assignment so that she knows to pay the assignee rather than the creditor. The assignee is entitled to collect the debt despite not being involved in the creation of the contract that produced the debt. Conversely, after receiving notice of the assignment, the debtor can perform her obligation only by paying the assignee. If the same debt is assigned to more than one assignee, normally the assignee who first notifies the debtor is entitled to payment.[3] Expressed in legal language, the rule is that the assignees who take in good faith rank in the order that they have given notice to the debtor. This means that a later assignee may end up collecting from the debtor ahead of an earlier assignee simply by being the first to give notice to the debtor. In the meantime, the disappointed assignees can sue the assignor for breach of the contract of assignment; however, doing so is usually pointless if the assignor has disappeared or has no resources to pay damages.

The advantage of an assignment for a creditor such as Conlin is that he can "sell" rights for cash now and let the assignee worry about collecting from the Owens. Of course, Conlin will pay a price for this advantage by accepting less than the face value of the debt from the assignee. This discount will reflect the cost of early receipt, as well as the risk that the debtor cannot or will not pay.

Additionally, the assignee's right to payment is no greater than the right possessed by the assignor. This means, for example, that if Conlin breaches his contract with the Owens and becomes entitled to less than the full contract price, Conlin's assignee is likewise entitled to less. The objective is to ensure that the debtor—in this case, the Owens—is not disadvantaged by the assignment.[4]

Termination by Frustration

The doctrine of frustration considers whether events subsequent to creation of the contract provide a legal excuse for non-performance. That is, **frustration** terminates a contract upon the occurrence of an "unforeseen catastrophic event that makes the contract impossible, or prevents the contract from being performed in a manner at all similar" to what the parties envisioned when they entered the contract.[5] Unlike the doctrine of mistake—which relates to severely erroneous assumptions concerning existing or past circumstances surrounding a contract at its formation frustration deals with events that occur after the contract has been formed.[6] Like mistake, however, the defence of frustration is intentionally difficult to establish, given that the purpose of contract law is to enforce voluntarily chosen agreements.

There are at least four factors that govern whether an event frustrates the contract in question or not. The event must:

- be unforeseen;[7]
- not arise due to the fault of the parties;[8]
- make the purpose of the contract either "impossible or drastically more difficult to achieve";[9] and
- not be a risk the occurrence of which was contractually allocated to either of the parties.[10]

Frustration

Termination of a contract upon the occurrence of an unforeseen catastrophic event which makes contractual performance impossible or prevents the contract from being performed in a manner at all similar to what the parties envisioned when they entered the contract.

---

3 GHL Fridman, *The Law of Contract in Canada*, 6th ed (Toronto: Thomson Reuters Canada Ltd, 2011) at 649.
4 *Ibid* at 650. Note that in certain jurisdictions, there is also legislation related to assignments. These are discussed by Fridman, *ibid* at 652 and following.
5 Bruce MacDougall, *Introduction to Contracts* 2nd ed (Markham: LexisNexis: 2012) at 261.
6 For discussion of mistake, see Chapter 8.
7 MacDougall, *supra* note 5 at 262.
8 *Ibid.*
9 *Ibid.*
10 John McCamus, *The Law of Contracts*, 2nd ed (Toronto: Irwin Law, 20121) at 612–613.

In such circumstances, both parties are excused from the contract and it comes to an end. Neither side is liable to the other for breach.

Case law establishes that the death of an employee terminates the contract of employment by frustration.[11] Likewise, the enactment of legislation which prohibits performance also terminates the contract in question.[12] The case of *Taylor v Caldwell*, discussed below, provides another example of the doctrine of frustration.

Taylor v Caldwell (1863), 122 ER 309 (CA)

THE BUSINESS CONTEXT: A common situation that gives rise to frustration occurs when the subject matter of the contract is destroyed, as discussed below.

FACTUAL BACKGROUND: Taylor rented from Caldwell the Surrey Gardens and Music Hall for four days to be used for a series of concerts. Prior to the scheduled concerts, the music hall was destroyed by a fire for which neither party could be faulted, and all of the concerts had to be cancelled. Taylor sued for his expenses related to advertising and other preparations, which were now wasted.

THE LEGAL QUESTION: Was Caldwell in breach of contract for failing to supply the music hall as promised?

RESOLUTION: Since the parties had not expressly or implicitly dealt with who would bear the risk of the music hall being destroyed by fire, the court had to decide whether the contract had been frustrated or not. It reasoned that the existence of the music hall was essential to performance of the contract, or, put another way, its destruction defeated the main purpose of the contract. On this basis, the contract had been frustrated, and Taylor's action failed.

CRITICAL ANALYSIS: Why did the court not simply decide that the owner of the music hall was liable when he failed to supply the promised venue, no matter how extenuating the circumstances?

Sometimes events that would disrupt contractual performance are expressly dealt with in the contract through a *force majeure* or other clause.[13] That is, rather than leaving it to a judge to decide whether the occurrence of a given event amounts to frustration, the parties contractually define for themselves—in advance—what events would frustrate the contract or otherwise bring it to an end.

FORCE MAJEURE CLAUSES

The commercial objective of parties to a contract sometimes can be defeated by circumstances beyond their control. Unforeseen events, both natural and human-made, may occur that make performance onerous or even impossible. The risk of unforeseen events is particularly great in international transactions. Storms, earthquakes, and fires may destroy the subject matter of the contract. Wars, blockades, and embargoes may prevent the performance of the contract. Hyperinflation, currency devaluation, and changes in government regulation may create hardship for the parties to the contract.

---

11 *Ibid* at 606.
12 *Ibid* at 606–607.
13 *Ibid* at 633.

Legal systems, for the most part, recognize that the occurrence of some unforeseen events may be a valid excuse for non-performance. This notion finds expression in various doctrines, such as commercial impracticality, impossibility, and frustration. The challenge for traders is that, although legal systems recognize this kind of defence, there are varying rules governing when non-performance is excused without liability on the part of the non-performing party. It is difficult to predict precisely which events will release a party from contractual obligations. Additionally, exemption from performance is normally restricted to situations where it is impossible to perform—hardship or additional expense involved in performance is usually not an excuse. For these reasons, it is common business practice both in domestic and international contracts to include *force majeure* clauses.

A *force majeure* clause deals with the risk of unforeseen events. It allows a party to delay or terminate a contract in the event of unexpected, disruptive events such as the following:

- fire, flood, tornado, or other natural disaster.
- war, invasion, blockade, or other military action.
- strike, labour slowdown, walkout, or other labour problems.
- inconvertibility of currency, hyperinflation, currency devaluation, or other monetary changes.
- rationing of raw materials, denial of import or export licences, or other governmental action.

Critical Analysis: What is the problem with drafting a clause that is very simple, such as, "In the event of a *force majeure*, the affected party may terminate its obligations under the contract"? Similarly, what is the problem with drafting a very specific clause that lists the events that allow a party to terminate the contract?

Source: Mary Jo Nicholson, *Legal Aspects of International Business,* 2d ed (Toronto: Edmond Montgomery Publications, 2007) at 226–27.

Many circumstances that may appear to frustrate a contract do not amount to frustration in law. For example, if Conlin finds that construction material has unexpectedly tripled in price, and thus he will suffer a substantial loss on the contract, this circumstance would not amount to frustration. It has become financially disadvantageous to perform the contract, but it is still possible to do so. Similarly, if Conlin contracts to provide a certain kind of building material and no other, and that material proves to be unavailable at any price, that part of the contract has not been frustrated either. Conlin has simply made a promise that he cannot keep and is in breach. As a final example, if Conlin is unable to perform the contract because he has fired all his employees at the last minute, the contract may have become impossible to perform, but owing only to Conlin's own conduct. Self-induced impossibility does not count as frustration in law.

In those rare cases in which a contract is terminated by frustration—as when the contract expressly states that the goods to be supplied must come from a particular source, which fails[14]—the consequences for the parties are often unsatisfactory. At the moment frustration occurs, any further obligations under the contract cease. If neither party has performed, they are left where they were before the contract was formed. If one party has begun to perform and incurred costs, there is no easy way to compensate that party, the reason being that, by definition, the contract has ended through the fault of neither party. Shifting the loss to the other would be no more just than leaving it where it lies. There are

---

14 *Howell v Coupland* (1876), 1 QBD 258 (CA).

CHAPTER 9: TERMINATION AND ENFORCEMENT OF CONTRACTS

complicated and uneven developments in the common law and in the statutes of some provinces that attempt to address these problems, but these are beyond the scope of this book.[15]

Enforcement of Contracts

When one party fails to perform its contractual obligations, it is in breach of contract and subject to a lawsuit. To succeed in its action for breach of contract, the plaintiff (the person who initiates the lawsuit) is obligated to demonstrate the following elements to the court's satisfaction, that is, on the **balance of probabilities**:

Balance of probabilities

Proof that there is a better than 50 percent chance that the circumstances of the contract are as the plaintiff contends.

- *privity of contract*. The plaintiff has to establish that there is a contract between the parties.
- *breach of contract*. The plaintiff must prove that the other party (the defendant) has failed to keep one or more promises or terms of the contract.
- *entitlement to a remedy*. The plaintiff must demonstrate that it is entitled to the remedy claimed or is otherwise deserving of the court's assistance.

As noted in Chapter 4, the balance of probabilities means that the plaintiff must prove there is a better than 50 percent chance that the circumstances of the contract are as it contends they are and, furthermore, that these circumstances entitle it to receive what is claimed.

Privity of Contract

Privity is a critical ingredient to enforcing a contract. It means that, generally speaking, only those who are parties to a contract can enforce the rights and obligations it contains.[16]

Because a strict application of the doctrine of privity can lead to serious injustices, courts have recently shown a willingness to allow third parties to rely on contractual clauses placed in the contract for their benefit. For example, a contract between a business and a customer may have an exclusion clause protecting employees from liability in the event that the customer suffers a loss. Under a classical approach to privity, employees would not be permitted to rely on such clauses as a defence to any action brought by a disgruntled customer because they are not parties to the contract—only their employer and the customer are. In the following case, however, the Supreme Court of Canada refused to apply privity in this way, choosing instead to create a limited exception to its application.

CASE

London Drugs Ltd v Kuehne & Nagel International Ltd, [1992] 3 SCR 299

THE BUSINESS CONTEXT: Businesses may try to protect their employees from being successfully sued by including clauses in their contracts with customers that shelter employees from liability.

FACTUAL BACKGROUND: Kuehne & Nagel International Ltd. (K&N) stored a variety of merchandise for London Drugs, including a large transformer. A term in the storage agreement limited K&N's liability on any one item to $40. Owing to the negligence of two K&N employees, the transformer was dropped while

---

15 For a discussion of statute law applying to frustration, see McCamus, *supra* note 10 at 637 and following.
16 There are a number of ways in which someone who is not a party to a contract (called a third party) may acquire an enforceable benefit, but this chapter discusses only one of them, in the employment context.

it was being moved and sustained over $33 000 of damage. London Drugs brought an action for the full amount of damages against both the employees and K&N. It was acknowledged that K&N's liability was limited to $40.

THE LEGAL QUESTION: Can the employees rely on the clause limiting liability to $40?

RESOLUTION: The trial judge agreed that the negligent employees could be sued by the customer. Expressed in more technical legal language, the court applied the rule that employees are liable for torts they commit in the course of carrying out the services their employer has contracted to provide. Because the K&N employees were negligent in their attempt to lift the transformer, they were liable for the full extent of London Drugs' damages. The employees could not rely on the clause limiting recovery to $40 because this clause was found in a contract to which they were not a party. Put another way, the employees lacked privity to the contract between London Drugs and K&N.

In response to the harshness that the strict doctrine of privity creates in this kind of situation, the Supreme Court of Canada created an exception to its application. As Justice Iacobucci explains,

> This court has recognized . . . that in appropriate circumstances, courts have not only the power but the duty to make incremental changes to the common law to see that it reflects the emerging needs and values of

our society . . . . It is my view that the present appeal is an appropriate situation for making such an incremental change to the doctrine of privity of contract in order to allow the . . . [employees] to benefit from the limitation of liability clause . . . . I am of the view that employees may obtain such a benefit if the following requirements are satisfied: (1) the limitation of liability clause must, either expressly or impliedly, extend its benefit to the employees (or employee) seeking to rely on it; and (2) the employees (or employee) seeking the benefit of the limitation of liability clause must have been acting in the course of their employment and must have been performing the very services provided for in the contract between their employer and the plaintiff (customer) when the loss occurred.

The court went on to hold that the employees could rely on the limitation of liability clause. This is because the clause in question did extend its protection to the employees and, when the transformer was damaged, it was due to the negligence of the employees while doing the very thing contracted for, as employees. Though the negligence of the employees caused London Drugs' damages in the amount of $33 955.41, it was entitled to recover only $40 from the employees.[17]

CRITICAL ANALYSIS: Do you agree with Justice Iacobucci's decision? Should employees be able to rely on a clause in a contract to which they are not parties? How could employees protect themselves if they were not permitted to rely on such a clause?

The Owens could easily establish a critical step in a successful breach of contract action against Conlin—namely, privity of contract. Conlin and the Owens entered into a contract whereby Conlin would supply certain goods and services to the Owens in exchange for payment.

The Owens may well have an action against Conlin's employees, but only for the tort of negligence (discussed in detail in Chapter 11). There is no action in contract against the employees, however, because there is no contract between them and the Owens. The contract is between only the Owens and Conlin.

---

17 Those who are not party to a contract containing exclusion clauses should not automatically assume that they can rely on those clauses notwithstanding the outcome in *London Drugs*. In *Haldane Products Inc v United Parcel Service* (1999), 103 OTC 306 (Sup Ct Jus), for example, the plaintiff contracted with UPS to deliver industrial sewing needles to British Columbia. The contract contained a limitation of liability clause but there was no stipulation that anyone other than UPS employees would discharge UPS contractual obligations. UPS's subcontractor—who was transporting a UPS trailer containing the package—failed to deliver due to a fire in the trailer. The subcontractor was found liable for over $40,000 because the court refused to allow it to shelter under the exclusion clause in the UPS–Haldane contract.

Statutory Modifications of the Doctrine

The common law of privity has also been modified by statute in two important areas, consumer purchases and insurance. In certain jurisdictions such as Saskatchewan, consumer protection legislation provides that a lack of privity is no defence to an action brought under the act for breach of warranty brought against a manufacturer, for example.[18] Similarly, insurance legislation across the country permits the beneficiary under a life insurance contract to sue the insurer even though the beneficiary is not a party to the contract (i.e., even though the beneficiary lacks privity).

Breach of Contract

Classification of the Breach

Virtually every breach of contract gives the innocent party the right to a remedy. When determining what that remedy should be, the courts will first consider whether the term breached can be classified as a condition or a warranty.

A contractual term will be classified as a condition or warranty only if that is the parties' contractual intention. Courts will consider all the circumstances surrounding the contract, including the language chosen by the parties in the contract itself, in making this determination.

A **condition** is an important term that, if breached, gives the innocent party the right not only to sue for damages, but also to treat the contract as ended. This latter right means that, if she so chooses, the non-defaulting party can consider herself to be freed from the balance of the contract and to have no further obligations under it. For example, it is an implied term of the contract between the Owens and Conlin that Conlin will be reliable. His multiple breaches of contract and insulting behaviour strongly suggest that he will not properly perform the contract in the future. On this basis, it could be argued that Conlin has breached a condition of the agreement and the Owens are not obligated to continue in the contract with him.[19]

A term classified as a **warranty** is a promise of less significance or importance. When a warranty is breached, the innocent party is entitled to damages only. Viewed in isolation, Conlin's failure to build the fireplace properly is likely to be regarded as a breach of warranty, entitling the Owens to damages only.

Even after the parties' intentions have been assessed, some terms cannot easily be classified as warranties or conditions; this is known in law as an **innominate term**. In such circumstances, the court must look at exactly what has happened in light of the breach before deciding whether the innocent party is entitled to repudiate the contract. For example, it is a term of the contract that the house be built to Code. It would be difficult to classify such a term as either a condition or a warranty of the contract. The contract is unclear on this point and the term is one that could be breached in large and small ways. If Conlin failed to install shingles on the roof that were Code approved, this is likely a breach of a warranty-like term, giving rise to a claim for damages only. On the other extreme, Conlin's failure to provide a structurally sound home would be a breach of a condition-like term, allowing the Owens to end the contract on the spot, as they have done. Provided that the plaintiffs can establish just one breach of condition or condition-like innominate term, they are entitled to end the contract.

Condition

An important term that, if breached, gives the innocent party the right to terminate the contract and claim damages.

Warranty

A minor term that, if breached, gives the innocent party the right to claim damages only.

Innominate term

A term that cannot easily be classified as either a condition or a warranty.

---

18 The *Consumer Protection Act*, SS 1996, c C-30.1, s 55. See too *Consumer Product Warranty and Liability Act*, SNB 1978, c C-18.1, s 23.
19 This analysis is based on McCamus, *supra* note 10 at 672 and cases cited therein.

Note, however, that if the Owens end the contract on the erroneous assumption that such a serious form of breach has occurred, they themselves will be in breach of contract and subject to a lawsuit by Conlin.

Parties are free to classify a term in advance within the contract itself by setting out the consequences of breach. The court will generally respect this classification if it has been done clearly.[20]

Exemption and Limitation of Liability Clause

As already noted, parties are free to include a clause in their contract that limits or excludes liability for breach. This is what the storage company did in the *London Drugs* case discussed earlier. Historically, courts have been reluctant to allow the party in breach to rely on such a clause when that party's breach was severe and undermined the whole foundation of the contract. This is known as a **fundamental breach**. The argument is that such a breach automatically renders the entire contract (including the exclusion clauses) inoperative, and therefore the innocent party should be compensated. While such judicial concern might be helpful in a consumer contract, it is less welcome in a commercial context. The Supreme Court of Canada has finally resolved the issue by ruling in 2010 that the doctrine of fundamental breach in relation to exclusion clauses no longer forms any part of the law in Canada, as discussed in the box below.

Fundamental breach

A breach of contract that affects the foundation of the contract.

C A S E

Tercon Contractors Ltd v British Columbia (Transportation and Highways), 2010 SCC 4

THE BUSINESS CONTEXT: Owners who put a project out to tender often include a contractual term to limit or even exclude liability so as to permit wide latitude in decision making and provide a defence in any action for breach of contract. Whether the clause will have its intended effect depends very much on the facts of the case.

FACTUAL BACKGROUND: Tercon, an unsuccessful bidder on a large highway project, sued the government of British Columbia because it chose an ineligible bidder for the job and even tried to hide that ineligiblity, contrary to the terms of Contract A.[21] Tercon also said that this breach of Contract A entitled it to damages in the amount of profit it would have earned had it been awarded Contract B.

By way of defence, the government relied on an exclusion clause (specifically called a 'no claims clause') that stated:

> Except as expressly permitted . . . no Proponent [bidder] shall have any claim for any compensation of any kind whatsoever, as a result of participating . . . and by submitting a proposal each proponent shall be deemed to have agreed that it has no claim.

According to the government, the effect of the exclusion clause was to make any breach of the contract not actionable. Note that, unlike in *Tilden Rent-a-Car v Glendenning*[22] (discussed in Chapter 7), which went to whether the exclusion clause was even part of the contract, the concern in *Tercon* was the effectiveness of an exclusion clause which was otherwise an uncontested part of the contract.

THE LEGAL QUESTION: Does the exclusion clause provide the government with a defence to Tercon's action?

(Continued)

---

20 *Wickman Machine Tool Sales Ltd v Schuler*, [1974] AC 235 (HL).
21 For discussion in this text regarding the difference between Contract A and Contract B, see discussion of *R v Ron Engineering & Construction Ltd*, [1981] 1 SCR 111 in Chapter 6.
22 (1978), 83 DLR (3d) 400 (Ont CA).

RESOLUTION: The court was unanimous in holding that the concept of fundamental breach should no longer have any role to play when a plaintiff seeks to escape the effect of an exclusion of liability clause. Instead, the outcome is determined by considering the answers to three issues or enquiries. As the court states:

> The **first** issue . . . is whether as a matter of interpretation the exclusion clause even applies to the circumstances established in evidence. This will depend on the Court's assessment of the intention of the parties as expressed in the contract. If the exclusion clause does not apply, there is obviously no need to proceed further with this analysis. If the exclusion clause applies, the **second** issue is whether the exclusion clause was unconscionable at the time the contract was made, "as might arise from situations of unequal bargaining power between the parties" (Hunter, at p. 462). This second issue has to do with contract formation, not breach.

> If the exclusion clause is held to be valid and applicable, the Court may undertake a **third** enquiry, namely whether the Court should nevertheless refuse to enforce the valid exclusion clause because of the existence of an overriding public policy, proof of which lies on the party seeking to avoid enforcement of the clause, that outweighs the very strong public interest in the enforcement of contracts. [emphasis added]

The court also confirmed that:

> Conduct approaching serious criminality or egregious fraud are but examples of well-accepted and "substantially incontestable" considerations of public policy that may override the countervailing public policy that favours freedom of contract. Where this type of misconduct is reflected in the breach of contract, all of the circumstances should be examined very carefully by the court.

On these facts, the Supreme Court of Canada agreed that that the government breached Contract A by choosing an ineligible bidder. A slim majority found in favour of the plaintiff because it concluded that the exclusion clause did not apply to the facts at hand. As the majority stated, clear language would be necessary to exclude damages resulting from the government permitting an ineligible bidder to participate and to exclude the government's implied duty to conduct itself fairly in relation to all bidders. As the majority stated: "I cannot conclude that the parties, through the words found in this exclusion clause, intended to waive compensation for conduct like that of the Province in this case that strikes at the heart of the integrity and business efficacy of the tendering process which it undertook."

Because the clause did not apply to the breach in question, Tercon had won and it was not necessary for the majority to consider the other two issues. Instead, it affirmed the trial judge's decision awarding Tercon over $3 million for loss of profit.

CRITICAL ANALYSIS: Do you think that the Supreme Court of Canada's three-issue analysis injects too much uncertainty into contract law? Should parties be bound by whatever clause they agree to?

ETHICAL CONSIDERATIONS

IS IT UNETHICAL TO BREACH A CONTRACT?

Contract law generally does not punish a contract breaker but rather compensates the innocent party for any loss associated with the breach. According to famous jurist Oliver Wendell Holmes:

> The duty to keep a contract at common law means a prediction that you must pay damages if you do not keep it—and nothing else . . . . If you commit [to] a contract, you are liable to pay a compensatory sum unless the promised event comes to pass, and that is all the difference. But such a mode of looking at the matter stinks in the nostrils of those who

think it advantageous to get as much ethics into the law as they can.

This is known as the "bad man" theory of breach and coincides with the concept of economic breach already discussed in Chapter 5. Economic breach means that the potential contract breaker measures the cost of breach against the anticipated gains. If the projected benefits exceed the probable costs, the breach is efficient. The difficulty with this strictly economic perspective on the question of breach is that it purposely ignores or marginalizes the ethical implications of breaking a promise.

What, then, is the role of ethics in the realm of contract law? It must have at least a limited role, according to Robert Larmer, since morality is essential for a functioning business environment:

> [U]nless those in business recognize the obligation to keep promises and honour contracts, business could not exist. This is not to suggest that business people never break contracts, but

if such behaviour ever became general, business would be impossible. Just as telling a lie is advantageous only if most people generally tell the truth, shady business practices are advantageous only if most business people recognize the existence of moral obligations. Immorality in business is essentially parasitic because it tends to destroy the moral environment which makes its very existence possible.

Critical Analysis: Should contract law start punishing those who breach contracts more regularly because such conduct amounts to a betrayal of trust and may lead to the market being undermined? Is it practical to ask the law to enforce a moral code or is Holmes's approach preferable? What non-legal penalties might a contract breaker face?

Sources: Robert Larmer, *Ethics in the Workplace: Selected Readings in Business Ethics*, 2d ed (Belmont, CA: Wadsworth Thomson Learning, 2002); and Oliver Wendell Holmes, "The Path of the Law" (1897) 10 Harv L Rev 457.

Timing of the Breach

A breach of contract can occur at the time specified for performance—as, for example, when one party fails to deliver machinery on the date recited in the contract. A breach can also occur in advance of the date named for performance—as, for example, when one party advises the other, in advance of the delivery date, that no delivery with be forthcoming. This is known as an **anticipatory breach**. Anticipatory breaches are actionable because each party to a contract is entitled to a continuous expectation that the other will perform during the entire period between the date the contract is formed and the time for performance. This means that the innocent party can sue immediately for breach of contract and is not required to wait and see if the other party has a change of heart.

When the anticipatory breach is sufficiently serious, the innocent party is not just entitled to damages. She can also treat the contract as at an end. This option puts the innocent party in somewhat of a dilemma, since she will not know for sure whether the contract can legally be treated as at an end unless and until the matter is litigated—an event that will occur months or, more likely, years later.

Anticipatory breach

A breach that occurs before the date for performance.

Entitlement to a Remedy

The final step in an action for breach of contract is for the plaintiff to satisfy a court that he is entitled to a remedy. In the usual case, **damages**—or monetary compensation—are awarded, but in specialized circumstances, a plaintiff is entitled to an equitable remedy.

Damages

Monetary compensation for breach of contract or other actionable wrong.

The Measure of Damages

Expectation damages

Damages which provide the plaintiff with the monetary equivalent of contractual performance.

There are several ways of measuring the plaintiff's loss. The most common way is to award **expectation damages**, which provide the plaintiff with the monetary equivalent of performance.

Expressed in legal language, the plaintiffs, in this case the Owens, are entitled to compensation that puts them, as much as possible, in the financial position they would have been in had the defendant, Conlin, performed his obligations under the contract. Subject to the principles discussed in this chapter, the Owens should at least be able to recover from Conlin any amount to complete the house over and above what they had committed to pay Conlin. Though they paid Holmstead $300 000 to complete the job, they cannot recover that whole sum. Had the contract been properly performed by Conlin, the Owens would have spent $500 000 on their home. As it is, they had to spend $600 000. They are only entitled to recover the difference (i.e., $100 000) because the house promised by Conlin would not have come to them for free. The costs the Owens would have had to pay to Conlin for the house must be deducted in this case.

Whether the context is a claim for pecuniary (tangible) or non-pecuniary (intangible) loss, the purpose of damages in contract law is to *compensate* a plaintiff. As the Supreme Court of Canada confirms in *Whiten v Pilot Insurance Co*, **punitive damages** are exceptional and are only awarded against the defendant for "malicious, oppressive and high-handed" misconduct that "offends the court's sense of decency."[23] In addition, the plaintiff must show that the defendant has committed an independent actionable wrong—for example, *two* breaches of contract. Though this requirement is long established, its rationale is less than clear.

Punitive damages

An award to the plaintiff to punish the defendant for malicious, oppressive, and high-handed conduct.

Pecuniary and Non-Pecuniary Damages

As they will be discussed in detail in Chapter 10, damages in tort can be pecuniary (for financial loss) and non-pecuniary (for loss of enjoyment, mental distress, and other emotional consequences). The same holds true in contract law, except that recovery for non-pecuniary damages is historically unusual. In law, a defendant is responsible only for the reasonably foreseeable damages sustained by the plaintiff and not for absolutely every adverse consequence experienced by the innocent party after the contract has been breached.[24] While pain and suffering or other emotional distress is reasonably foreseeable when one person negligently injures another in a car accident, it is not generally anticipated as being the consequence of a breach of contract.

Test for Remoteness The kinds of damages recoverable in contract law are determined by the test for remoteness, which was established in the still-leading decision of *Hadley v Baxendale*.[25] That test states that the damages claimed are recoverable provided

- the damages could have been anticipated, having "arisen naturally" from the breach, or
- the damages—although perhaps difficult to anticipate in the ordinary case—are reasonably foreseeable because the unusual circumstances were communicated to the defendant at the time the contract was being formed.

---

23 *Whiten v Pilot Insurance Co*, 2002 SCC 18 at para 36. For further discussion of the *Whiten* case, see Chapter 28.

24 It is beyond the scope of this book to discuss whether the test for remoteness is stricter in contract than it is in tort.

25 (1854), 9 Exch 341.

Any claim for damages in contract must pass one of the remoteness tests set out above; otherwise, it is simply not recoverable. The policy rationale of such a rule is the need to ensure that defendants do not face unlimited liability for the consequences of a breach and to allow them, by being informed of special circumstances, the option of turning down the job, charging a higher price to compensate for the increased risk, or perhaps, purchasing the necessary insurance.

BUSINESS APPLICATION OF THE LAW

BREACH OF CONTRACT AND REASONABLE FORESEEABILITY

Gabriella Nagy of Toronto is suing Rogers Wireless for $600 000 for breach of contract. She alleges that Rogers, at her husband's request, terminated her personal cell phone account and rebundled it with the family's TV, home phone, and Internet bill. The bill was then listed in her husband's name. Nagy's husband discovered that Nagy was having an extramarital affair after reviewing her cell phone records, which showed that she had been calling one number with particular frequency. When the husband called that number, the man who answered said that he had recently ended a three-week affair with Gabriella Nagy. Nagy's husband immediately left her, and she fell into a depression and lost her job.

Critical Analysis: Has Rogers breached its contract with Nagy by bundling her cell phone account without her permission? Assuming this is breach of contract, is the nature of Nagy's

Gabriella Nagy, shown in disguise, is suing Rogers Wireless.

damages reasonably foreseeable? What other problems might Nagy have in proving all the elements of her action for breach of contract?

Source: Linda Nguyen, "Woman sues Rogers for exposing her affair" *Edmonton Journal* (18 May 2010), online: *Edmonton Journal* <http://www2.canada.com/edmontonjournal/news/story.html?id=38f9f276-5c87-4ce3-8ebc-a1040907fd10>.

Recovery of Non-Pecuniary Damages

As already noted, recovery for non-pecuniary damages—such as for mental distress—is traditionally viewed with suspicion in contract law. This traditional approach has been challenged, however, by the Supreme Court of Canada in the case discussed just below.

CASE

Fidler v Sun Life Assurance Company of Canada, 2006 SCC 30

THE BUSINESS CONTEXT: When a supplier of goods or services fails to meet contractual obligations, the customer may experience frustration and distress. Depending on the kind of

contract involved, the customer may be entitled to damages for enduring such upset, thereby driving up the size of the damage award.

FACTUAL BACKGROUND: Ms. Fidler worked as a receptionist at a bank in British Columbia. She was covered by a long-term disability policy

(Continued)

CHAPTER 9: TERMINATION AND ENFORCEMENT OF CONTRACTS

that would provide her with an assured income should she become ill and unable to work. Ms. Fidler began to receive benefits when she was diagnosed with chronic fatigue syndrome and fibromyalgia. The insurer later cut her off from payments, citing video surveillance that detailed activity proving that she could work. In the face of medical evidence that Fidler could not, in fact, work, the insurer refused to reinstate her benefits. Fidler sued the insurer for breach of contract. Just before trial, the insurer agreed to reinstate benefits, leaving only a few issues to be determined at trial, including the one described below.

THE LEGAL QUESTION: Was the plaintiff entitled to recover damages for mental distress caused by the defendant's wrongful denial of benefits?

RESOLUTION: The Supreme Court of Canada rejected the traditional notion that damages for mental distress should be tightly controlled and exceptional. On the contrary, the court should simply ask, "What did the contract promise?" and provide damages on that basis. More specifically, the plaintiff seeking recovery for mental distress must show:

1. that the object of the contract was to secure a psychological benefit that brings mental distress upon breach within the reasonable contemplation of the parties [i.e., the test in *Hadley v Baxendale* cited above]; and

2. that the degree of mental suffering caused by the breach was of a degree sufficient to warrant compensation.

The court ruled that—as disability insurance contracts are to protect the holder from financial and emotional stress and insecurity—mental distress damages should be recoverable. On this basis, Fidler was able to bring herself within the first step of the test above. And because Fidler's distress was of a sufficient degree, she met the second part of the test. The court affirmed the trial judge's award of $20 000 for mental distress.

CRITICAL ANALYSIS: Do you agree that damages for mental distress should be recoverable? Do you think that a plaintiff who is left feeling angry or frustrated by a breach would pass the test for recovery stated in *Sun Life,* or is something more pronounced required?

Based on this case, it would seem that Janet Owen has a particularly strong claim for mental distress damages. A contract to construct a home—given its personal nature—has as one of its objects the provision of a psychological benefit that brings mental distress upon breach within the reasonable contemplation of the parties. Second, since Janet has been very upset because of Conlin's breach and is even having trouble sleeping, it would seem that the degree of mental suffering caused by the breach is of a degree sufficient to warrant compensation.

Recovery of Pecuniary Damages Those who have suffered a breach of contract can recover all their resulting pecuniary (or monetary) losses unless a clause is included that limits, excludes, or fixes liability at a set amount.[26] Recovery of pecuniary damages is possible in situations such as the following:

- a purchaser of a warehouse with a leaky roof can recover the cost of repairing the roof provided the roof was warranted to be sound.
- a client who suffers a financial loss owing to negligent legal advice can recover those losses from the lawyer in question.
- a person whose goods are stolen while they are in storage can recover the cost of those items from the warehouse owner.

---

26 Liquidated damages clauses are discussed in Chapter 7.

Similarly, because Conlin did not construct and complete the house properly, the Owens are entitled to recover additional damages that flow from that breach. This is discussed in the next section of the text.

LIABILITY FOR A STOLEN FORD MUSTANG

Kristen Cockerill entered into a weekend car rental contract with an Enterprise Rent-a-Car (Enterprise) outlet in Dartmouth, Nova Scotia, for a Ford Mustang. At the end of the rental period, Cockerill returned the Mustang but because it was a Sunday, the Enterprise outlet was closed. Those who return vehicles on Sunday are instructed by Enterprise to park the car on the lot and then leave the car keys in a secure drop-box provided by Enterprise. This is what Cockerill did.

Cockerill was contacted by Enterprise the next day: it had the keys, but where was the Mustang? Police soon established that the car had been stolen from Enterprise's lot sometime before the rental company opened for business on the Monday.

Soon thereafter, Cockerill received a bill from Enterprise for $47 000, which was the replacement cost of the vehicle. Needless to say, Cockerill was taken aback and very worried about receiving a bill of this size. She checked with her insurance company which said that neither she nor it should have any legal responsibility for the loss because the car was not in her control when it was stolen. Enterprise took another view, relying on a contractual term which Cockerill described as follows: "It is in the fine print of the contract that I am responsible for the vehicle until they receive it."

Enterprise also said that if Cockerill's insurer did not pay the $47 000, it would charge that amount to her credit card.

After CBC contacted Enterprise for further response, Ned Maniscalco of Enterprise emailed CBC noting as follows: "Sometimes customers mistakenly believe if they didn't personally cause or witness any damage that they are not responsible. This is one of the most common misconceptions," he said. "In fact, customers are financially responsible for any damage or theft that occurs during a rental transaction, regardless of fault or negligence—just as if they owned the rental vehicle themselves." He also pointed

Kristen Cockerill

out that the drop-box where Kristen left her keys has a prominent sign reminding customers that "the vehicle remains their responsibility until it can be checked in by an employee."

Soon after this, Cockerill learned that Enterprise would not be forcing her to pay the $47 000. She was also offered an apology by the company. Cockerill told CBC that "It's been extremely stressful, actually, just not knowing where things are going to go, the financial piece hanging over my family. It's been quite stressful. But I'm happy to see it come to an end."

Critical Analysis: Enterprise's legal analysis may well be correct that the rental contract made Kristen responsible for the car when it was stolen and on that basis, was entitled to $47 000 as its contractual remedy. But what price did Enterprise pay by insisting on its strict contractual rights? What should it have done differently in handling this dispute with Cockerill?

Sources: Blair Rhodes, *CBC News* (3 January 2014), "Enterprise willing to 'work' with woman on hook for $47K Mustang" online: CBC <http://www.cbc.ca/news/canada/nova-scotia/enterprise-willing-to-work-with-woman-on-hook-for-47k-mustang-1.2483207>; *CBC News* "Stolen Enterprise rental Mustang has woman facing $47K bill" (3 January 2014), online CBC: <http://www.cbc.ca/news/canada/nova-scotia/stolen-enterprise-rental-mustang-has-woman-facing-47k-bill-1.2482273>; *CBC News* "Kristen Cockerill Won't Have To Pay For Stolen $47K Rental Car" (updated 09 March 2014), online: CBC <www.huffingtonpost.ca/2014/01/07/kristen-cockerill-enterprise-mustang-rental_n_4557465.html>.

Duty to Mitigate Everyone who suffers a breach of contract has a **duty to mitigate**. This means that they must take reasonable steps to minimize losses that might arise from the breach, as in the following examples:

- a person who is fired from his job, in breach of contract, has a duty to mitigate by trying to find replacement employment.
- a landlord whose tenant breaches a lease by moving out before the expiry of its term has a duty to mitigate by trying to find a replacement tenant.
- a disappointed vendor whose purchaser fails to complete a real estate transaction has a duty to mitigate by trying to find a replacement purchaser.

If the plaintiff fails to mitigate, its damage award will be reduced accordingly. For example, if the employee making $100 000 a year had one year left on his contract before he was wrongfully terminated, his damages would be $100 000. However, his duty to mitigate requires him to look for comparable employment. If he immediately does so and secures a job at $80 000, there is authority for the view that his damages drop to $20 000.[27] If he fails to mitigate—by, for example, refusing such a job—a court will reduce his damages by $80 000, since that loss is more attributable to him than to his former employer.

By the same token, any reasonable costs associated with the mitigation are recoverable from the party in breach. An employee could, in addition to damages related to salary loss, also recover reasonable expenses related to the job search.

In the Owens' case, mitigation took the form of hiring Holmstead to finish and repair the house for $300 000. Assuming that this is reasonable, the Owens will be able to recover $100 000 from Conlin. This is because the Owens have had to pay an extra $100 000 for their house over and above what they had committed to pay Conlin. The calculation is based on the following analysis: The Owens were going to spend $500 000 on the house but have paid Conlin $300 000 and Holmstead $300 000 for a total of $600 000. Since this extra cost of $100 000 to obtain their bargain flows from Conlin's breach of contract, it is recoverable. Note that even the $5000 to rebuild the see-through fireplace (which is included in Holmstead's $300 000 bill) is recoverable. A court will almost certainly agree that the Owens are entitled to the price of rebuilding the fireplace even though this amount is much higher than Conlin's solution of simply bricking in one of the fireplace walls. In short, the Owens had contracted for a see-through fireplace and are entitled to it.

Equitable Remedies

In those relatively rare situations in which damages would be an inadequate remedy for breach of contract, the court may exercise its discretion to grant one of the equitable remedies discussed below.

Specific Performance An order by the court for the equitable remedy of specific performance means that instead of awarding compensation for failing to perform, the court orders the party who breached to do exactly what the contract obligated him to do. This remedy is available only when the item in question is unique and cannot be replaced by money. The classic situation for specific performance is a contract for the sale of land, where the particular piece of land covered by the contract is essential to the buyer's plans, perhaps as part of a major

---

27   For discussion of conflicting case law on this point, see Anna Wong, "Explicit language needed for fixed-term contract" *Lawyers Weekly* (11 July 2014) at 11.

Should the court enforce contracts as they relate to aesthetics and matters of taste or should contractors be given the discretion to follow cheaper alternatives?

development project. Without the remaining piece, the project cannot proceed, so damages would fail to provide a complete remedy.

Because specific performance is an equitable remedy, a court can refuse to order it, at its discretion, as in the following circumstances:

- *improper behaviour by the plaintiff.* Any improper motive or conduct on the part of the plaintiff may disqualify them from being granted such special assistance. Rules governing equity, like "he who seeks equity must do equity" or "she who comes to equity must come with clean hands," mean that only the deserving plaintiff will succeed.
- *delay.* Failure by the plaintiff to bring a claim promptly can be grounds for denying the plaintiff an equitable remedy.[28]
- *impossibility.* A court will not order a defendant to do something that is impossible, such as convey land that the defendant does not own.[29]
- *severe hardship.* If specific performance would cause a severe hardship to the parties, or to a third party, a court may refuse to order it.
- *employment contracts.* A court will not, ordinarily, order specific performance of an employment contract, because being forced to work for someone else against the employee's wishes would interfere too much with the employee's personal freedom.

Injunction If a contract contains promises not to engage in specified activities, disregarding those promises by engaging in the prohibited acts is a breach of contract. While an award of damages is of some help, additionally, the plaintiff would want a court order requiring the offender to refrain from continued violation of the contract. For example, if the vendor of a business agrees not to compete with the new owner and the relevant clauses are reasonable restrictions

---

28 For a discussion and excerpts of relevant case law concerning equitable remedies and defences thereto, see Stephanie Ben-Ishai and David R Percy, eds, *Contracts: Cases and Commentaries*, 9th ed (Toronto: Carswell, 2014) at 937 and following.

29 See *Castle v Wilkinson* (1870), 5 LR Ch App 534.

(see Chapter 8), damages alone are an inadequate remedy for breach because they fail to prevent the vendor from competing. Only an order to cease doing business will provide the buyer with a complete remedy.

Like an order of specific performance, an injunction is an equitable remedy and is subject to the court's discretion. However, it is commonly ordered to restrain a party from breaching a promise not to do something, as noted above. There are occasions where a court will not order an injunction, however, as when the plaintiff does not have "clean hands" (i.e., is undeserving) or delays in bringing the matter before the court.

Courts also have the jurisdiction to order an injunction for a limited period of time. This type of injunction, known as an **interlocutory injunction**, requires someone to stop doing something until the whole dispute can be resolved through a trial.

Rescission It may be appropriate, in some cases, to restore the parties to the situation they were in before the contract was formed, rather than use compensation to put the innocent party in the position it would have been in had the contract been completed. For example, many of the doctrines in Chapter 8 for avoiding contracts provide rescission as the contractual remedy.

As with other equitable remedies, there are bars to receiving rescission of a contract. For example, where parties cannot restore each other to their pre-contractual positions—because, perhaps, the subject matter of the contract has been altered—the court has the power to do what is practically just, including the power to order that the innocent party be compensated. Another bar to rescission is delay by the plaintiff in seeking the court's assistance.

Restitutionary Remedies

Sometimes a contractual claim fails not because the plaintiff is undeserving but because he cannot prove that an enforceable contract is in place. The law of restitution gives recourse to a plaintiff who has conferred benefits on the defendant in reliance on a contract that cannot be enforced due, for example, to noncompliance with the *Statute of Frauds*.[30] For example, if the plaintiff has done work for the defendant pursuant to an unenforceable contract for the purchase of land, the plaintiff may end up being recompensed by the defendant, not under contract but pursuant to the law of restitution.

Restitution is a complex area of law but its main objective is clear—to remedy **unjust enrichment**. Unjust enrichment occurs when the defendant has undeservedly or unjustly secured a benefit at the plaintiff's expense. In such circumstances, the court will ordinarily order that the benefit be restored to the plaintiff or otherwise be accounted for by the defendant.

In response to an unjust enrichment, the court has several options, including ordering the defendant to:

- pay a **restitutionary *quantum meruit***; that is, an amount that is reasonable given the benefit that the plaintiff has conferred.[31]

- pay compensation; that is, an allowance of money to put the plaintiff in as good a position as the plaintiff was in prior to conferring the benefit.[32]

Interlocutory injunction

An order to refrain from doing something for a limited period of time.

Unjust enrichment

Occurs when one party has undeservedly or unjustly secured a benefit at the other party's expense.

Restitutionary *quantum meruit*

An amount that is reasonable given the benefit the plaintiff has conferred.

---

30 See Chapter 8.
31 Contractual *quantum meruit* has already been discussed in Chapter 7.
32 GHL Fridman, "*Quantum Meruit*" (1999) 37 Alta L Rev 38.

PART TWO: CONTRACTS

Managing Risk

There are several risks that a business faces when the time comes to perform a contract. It may be that the business cannot perform at all or that when it does perform, it does so deficiently. A business can attend to these possibilities proactively or reactively. From a proactive perspective, the business can negotiate for clauses to limit or exclude liability as well as for a *force majeure* clause, as appropriate. It may be, however, that the other side is unwilling to agree to such clauses. Another proactive strategy is to ensure that employees are competent and properly trained, since any mistakes they make in performance of the contract are attributable to the employer. The better the employees do, the more likely the contract will be performed without incident. Securing proper insurance can also be effective, a matter will be discussed in more detail in Chapter 28.

Once the business is in breach of contract, however, matters are now in a reactive mode. The contract breaker is in an unenviable position, since it faces liability for all reasonable costs associated with its default. To reduce financial exposure and litigation expenses, the business should consider seeking mediation, arbitration, and other forms of compromise, including settlement offers, as alternatives to going to trial. Depending on the nature of the breach, the loss may be covered by insurance.

Those who contract for the provision of a product or service should undertake to ensure that the supplier is reputable and reliable. This way, legal conflict is perhaps avoided altogether.

When faced with a breach of contract, the innocent party must make a business decision—as much as a legal one—and decide how it should treat that failure. This decision involves evaluating the risks of losing in court; the remedies available, including the amount of damages; the likelihood of being able to negotiate a settlement; and whether there is a valuable business relationship to preserve.

BUSINESS LAW IN PRACTICE REVISITED

1. Can the Owens demonstrate all the steps in an action for breach of contract against Conlin?

The Owens can meet all the steps to succeed in an action for breach of contract. They can show privity of contract between themselves and Conlin. They can show that Conlin breached the contract in multiple ways, including by failing to build the house according to Code and not providing the fireplace contracted for. Finally, the Owens can show that they are entitled to a remedy. Both have suffered pecuniary loss and, in addition, Janet has suffered non-pecuniary damages in the form of mental distress.

2. Are the Owens themselves in breach of contract for refusing to permit Conlin to complete the contract?

Conlin's multiple breaches of contract and insulting behaviour strongly suggest that he will not properly perform the contract in the future. A court may well conclude that this amounts to a breach of a condition of the contract—namely that he will be reliable. If the Owens can prove a breach of condition, they have the right to end the contract. They are therefore not in breach of contract for refusing to permit him to complete.

The term that the house be built to Code may be hard to classify as a condition or warranty up front since the parties' intentions are not clear and the term itself can be breached in both large ways and small. On this basis, the court will look to how serious the structural defects are. If they are serious, the breach will be of a condition-like innominate term, also bringing with it the right to treat the contract as at an end.

3. Did the Owens properly mitigate their damages?

Assuming that there has been a breach of condition or condition-like innominate term, the Owens properly mitigated their loss in hiring Holmstead to repair and complete the home. This is also based on the assumption that the extra cost was reasonable.

4. What damages can the Owens receive?

The Owens stand a good chance of receiving considerable pecuniary and non-pecuniary damages.

Pecuniary Damages Because the Owens had to hire Holmstead to finish and repair the house for $300 000, they paid an extra $100 000 for their home. That is, the contract price with Conlin was $500 000. They have already paid Conlin $300 000 and will be paying Holmstead another $300 000. Assuming that Holmstead's fees were reasonable, the Owens will be able to recover $100 000 in pecuniary damages from Conlin.

Note that even the $5000 to rebuild the see-through fireplace (which is included in Holmstead's $300 000 bill) is probably recoverable even though a cheaper "solution" was offered by Conlin. The Owens contracted for a see-through fireplace and therefore Conlin's idea of simply bricking in one of the fireplace walls is not acceptable. Note that the recovery of $5000 is already included in the $100 000 discussed above. It cannot be claimed and recovered twice.

Non-Pecuniary Damages Janet Owen may also be able to recover damages for mental distress and suffering because Conlin's breach of contract caused her mental distress. A contract for home construction arguably has, as one of its objects, the provision of a psychological benefit, so the first step in *Fidler* is met. The second step is also met since Janet has suffered mental distress to a degree sufficient to warrant compensation. She has experienced great upset and even has had trouble sleeping.

It is difficult to predict how much a court will award for non-pecuniary damages but, based on existing case law, it is unlikely to be a large sum given the extent of her upset.

CHAPTER SUMMARY

In the vast majority of situations, a contract terminates or ends when the parties fully perform their obligations. Less common are situations where the contract ends because the parties find it impossible or tremendously difficult to perform their obligations. In such cases, prudent business parties will have addressed such a possibility through a *force majeure* clause or equivalent.

A more usual and complicated situation, from a business perspective, occurs when one party breaches the contract by failing to perform or by performing inadequately.

There are several ways that a contract is terminated: by performance, by agreement, through frustration, and through breach.

When a contract is terminated by performance, the parties have fulfilled all their implied and express promises. The work necessary to achieve performance may be done by the parties personally or through their agents/employees, unless a term to the contrary is included.

Sometimes, parties terminate a contract by agreement. For example, the parties may agree to end the contract entirely or to replace it with a new one. Alternatively, the parties may vary certain terms of the contract or substitute a new party who, in turn, assumes rights and duties under the contract.

Contract law allows one party to assign his rights under a contract but not the liabilities. The law of assignment permits the creditor to assign his right to collect under a contract to another (the assignee) without the agreement of the debtor. Once the assignee has given notice of the assignment to the debtor, the latter can perform the obligation only by paying the assignee.

The doctrine of frustration terminates a contract, but only in very limited circumstances. It must be shown that an unanticipated event or change in circumstances is so substantial that performance has become functionally impossible or illegal. Provided the risk of such an event has not been allocated to one party or the other, and provided the event did not arise through either party's fault, the contract has been frustrated.

When one party fails to perform its contractual obligations, it is in breach of contract and subject to a lawsuit. To succeed in its action for breach of contract, the innocent party must establish the existence of a contract, breach of contract, and entitlement to a remedy.

Privity means that, with limited exceptions, only those who are parties to a contract can enforce the rights and obligations it contains.

When a party to a contract fails to keep his promise, he has committed a breach of contract and is liable for such damages as would restore the innocent party to the position she would have been in had the contract been performed. These are known as expectation damages. If there is an exclusion or limitation of liability clause in the contract, the defendant's liability will be reduced or eliminated, depending on the circumstances.

Damages in contract are ordinarily pecuniary, but in some circumstances, the innocent party is entitled to non-pecuniary damages for mental suffering and distress. As well, punitive damages are exceptionally available.

When one party suffers a breach of contract, he must take reasonable steps to mitigate. If the party fails to do so, the damage award will be reduced accordingly. By the same token, any reasonable costs associated with mitigation are also recoverable from the party in breach.

Contract law also offers equitable remedies, such as specific performance and injunction, when damages are an inadequate remedy. On occasion, the best solution is to rescind the contract—that is, return the parties to their pre-contractual positions.

The law of restitution also provides remedies in a contractual context because its main objective is to remedy unjust enrichment. Unjust enrichment occurs when the defendant has undeservedly or unjustly secured a benefit at the plaintiff's expense.

Whether the innocent party takes the contract breaker to court is as much a business decision as it is a legal one.

CHAPTER STUDY

Key Terms and Concepts

anticipatory breach (p. 207)

assignment (p. 198)

balance of probabilities (p. 202)

condition (p. 204)

damages (p. 207)

duty to mitigate (p. 212)

expectation damages (p. 208)

frustration (p. 199)

fundamental breach (p. 205)

innominate term (p. 204)

interlocutory injunction (p. 214)

novation (p. 197)

punitive damages (p. 208)

restitutionary *quantum meruit* (p. 214)

unjust enrichment (p. 214)

vicarious performance (p. 197)

warranty (p. 204)

Questions for Review

1. What are the four major ways that a contract can be terminated?

2. What is an assignment? What risks does the assignee of a contractual right assume?

3. What is privity of contract?

4. How is vicarious performance used by business?

5. How is a new contract created through novation?

6. When is a contract frustrated?

7. What is a *force majeure* clause?

8. What elements need to be established in a successful action for breach of contract?

9. How is the severity of a breach of contract evaluated?

10. What is the difference between a warranty and a condition?

11. What is the purpose of awarding damages for breach of contract?

12. When will a court award punitive damages for breach of contract?

13. When is a plaintiff entitled to damages for mental distress?

14. What is unjust enrichment?

15. What is restitutionary *quantum meruit*?

16. What is specific performance?

17. When will a court grant an injunction?

18. What is the remedy of rescission?

19. When can the innocent party treat the contract as at an end?

20. How can a plaintiff avoid the application of an exclusion of liability clause?

Questions for Critical Thinking

1. A contract is considered frustrated only in very unusual situations; should the doctrine of frustration be applied more often? Would a broader application produce fairer results? What is the downside of such a change in commercial contracts?

2. Breach of a condition can signify the end of the contract while breach of warranty does not. Should courts be allowed to exercise discretionary power in determining whether an innominate term should have this same result? What should parties do if they wish to reduce the uncertainty as to how a given term will be classified?

3. The privity rule is one of the basic elements of contract law. Is it too restrictive? On the other hand, is there a danger in creating too many exceptions to the rule?

4. Contract law is intended to facilitate commercial activities and to enable businesses to conduct their affairs so that their legal obligations are certain. Do you think, after considering the material in the last five chapters, that contract law achieves its goals? Can you think of ways to improve the effectiveness of contract law?

5. The Canadian Radio-television and Telecommunications Commission (the CRTC)

has put in place the *Wireless Code* (the *Code*) in order to deal with a number of cell phone issues, including customers receiving extremely high bills for data roaming charges. In response to this perceived unfairness, the *Code* places a cap on a customer's national and international data roaming charges in certain cases unless the customer expressly agrees to pay such additional charges. Is it the role of a public authority to interfere with contractual freedom in this way? If a wireless customer fails to keep proper track of her data roaming usage and then ends up with a bill in the thousands of dollars, is that simply not the fault of the customer? Why should the CRTC interfere with the market in this way?

6. Historically, it was difficult to receive damages for mental distress in a breach of contract action. To cite two objections, some courts concluded that mental distress simply was not a reasonably foreseeable consequence of breach or were concerned that permitting such recovery would encourage plaintiffs to exaggerate the extent of their upset. How does modern contract law permitting recovery of mental distress respond to these concerns?

Situations for Discussion

1. Leonard purchased an unconstructed condominium in a large development. The contract stated that delivery of the completed condo was to be on a date set by the developer before February 1, 2010. Construction proceeded on schedule except, on April 25, 2009, the whole development burned to the ground. After spending some time looking for the cause of the fire, the developer started the process of rebuilding in October 2009. It looks like the condo will be delivered about a year later than originally anticipated. Is Leonard bound by the contract under these circumstances? Does it matter if the fire was caused by the developer's negligence?[33]

2. Mr. White woke up one morning to find that the interior of his car had been consumed in a fire, rendering the vehicle a total write-off. He promptly made a claim under his car insurance

policy. Soon after that, the insurance company accused White of starting his own car on fire and refused to pay out the claim. When White asked the insurance company to explain on what basis it was alleging arson, the company refused to provide an answer. Since that first refusal, the local fire chief has said there was no evidence of arson but still the insurance company refuses to pay. White believes that the insurance company is in breach of contract on several fronts including: failing to pay out on the policy and failing to answer his questions regarding refusal of his claim when he first posed them. Assuming this analysis is correct, do you think White will be successful in claiming punitive damages?[34]

3. In 2007, Susan, a law professor, was in Israel when her cell phone was stolen from her home in Toronto. Upon her return, Rogers, the cell phone service provider, advised that $12 000 in calls had been made from that phone and she was responsible for payment. Susan replied that she would not pay, since those calls were unauthorized and had been made from her phone after it had been stolen. In response, Rogers, among other actions, cut off her young son's cell phone service. The son's phone had been acquired by Susan for safety reasons since he would be taking the subway, alone, to school for the first time starting in September. Susan was responsible for bills associated with her son's cell phone, but the cell phone was held under a separate contract.

   A judge ultimately determined that Rogers was in breach of contract when it cut off her son's phone service, since it had no legal reason to do so. Among other heads of damage, the judge awarded Susan $612 in damages for "lost wages" because she had to drive her son to school while his cell phone was blocked. Do you think Susan's mitigation was reasonable? What else could she have done? Do you think that Rogers should appeal this decision? Why or why not?[35]

4. Atlantic Fertilizer (AF) operates a fertilizer plant in New Brunswick. AF made a major

---

33 Based, in part, on *Fishman v Wilderness Ridge at Stewart Creek Inc*, 2010 ABCA 345.

34 Based, in part, on *Whiten, supra* note 23.

35 Based, in part, on *Drummond v Rogers Wireless*, [2007] OJ No 1407; and John Jaffey, "Law prof wins punitive damages against Rogers in small claims" *The Lawyers Weekly* (27 April 2007) 7.

sale to the government of Togo in Africa and engaged Pearl Shipping (PS) to transport the fertilizer to Togo for a fee of $60 000. The contract between AF and PS specified that AF would deliver the cargo to PS for loading on its ship between March 25 and 31 and that AF would pay $1 000 (in addition to the shipping charges) for each day after March 31 that the cargo was delayed. AF had difficulty in filling the large order in its plant and notified PS that delivery would be sometime after March 31.[36]

PS is contemplating AF's message and deciding how it should react. Options under consideration are to wait for AF to deliver and add the $1 000 daily charge to the bill, give AF a firm date by which it must deliver, or terminate the contract with AF and seek another cargo for its ship. Which options are legally available to PS? Which should PS choose?

5. Peter Pan Equestrian Ltd (Peter Pan) wanted to increase the amount of natural light in its horse-riding arena. It decided to purchase a skylight system from Skylights-R-Us Ltd (Skylights) which duly supplied and installed metal frame acrylic skylights on the north and south sides of the riding arena. Unfortunately, the skylights soon began to experience problems with humidity, condensation, and leaking. As well, the acrylic itself began to crack. In response to complaints by Peter Pan, Skylights suggested that Peter Pan add supplemental heat to the building as well as install a proper ventilation system. They had previously made this suggestion to Peter Pan when negotiating the contract but Peter Pan refused. Peter Pan refused, again saying that it had been supplied with defective skylights. Now the skylights are riddled with cracks and are beyond repair. Peter Pan has now sued Skylights for breach of contract and is seeking damages to replace the skylights as well as undertake mould remediation work in the riding arena. What is the argument that Peter Pan has failed to properly mitigate? If that argument is successful, what impact does this have on Peter Pan's damage claim? What other weaknesses do you detect in Peter Pan's case.[37]

6. XYZ Ltd. entered into a contract with ABC Ltd. for the supply of resin, which XYZ Ltd. needed in order to produce pipe necessary for a large pipeline. ABC Ltd. made the business decision to supply defective resin to XYZ Ltd. and drafted the contract between the parties to protect itself from liability in relation to that defect as follows:

> XYZ Ltd. assumes all responsibility and liability for loss or damage arising from the use of the resin supplied under this contract herein and acknowledges that ABC Ltd.'s liability is limited to the selling price of the resin.

Another clause stated:

> XYZ Ltd. to notify ABC Ltd. of any objection to the resin supplied within 30 days. Failure to provide such notice constitutes unqualified acceptance and waiver of all claims.

ABC Ltd. knew that the resin was dangerous and would allow natural gas to escape. In fact, this is exactly what happened. There was an explosion in the pipeline for which XYZ Ltd. supplied pipe and which XYZ Ltd. fixed at great cost. When it asked ABC Ltd. for help, ABC Ltd. refused to take any responsibility, pointing to the exclusion clauses. Due to negative publicity surrounding the gas pipe leaks, XYZ Ltd. lost both its reputation and financial viability. Assuming that the supply of defective resin was a breach of contract, do you think ABC Ltd. will be able to rely on the exclusion clauses above? If so, on what basis?[38]

7. Imperial Brass Ltd. wanted to computerize all of its systems. Jacob Electric Systems Ltd. presented Imperial with a proposal that met Imperial's needs. In August, Imperial accepted the proposal, along with Jacob's "tentative" schedule for implementation, which led Imperial to expect a total computerized operation by mid-January, with the possibility of a 30-day extension. In October, it became clear that there were problems with the software being developed, and Imperial asked for corrections

---

36 Based, in part, on *Armada Lines Ltd v Chaleur Fertilizers Ltd* (1994), 170 NR 372 (FCA), rev'd [1997] 2 SCR 617.
37 Based, in part, on *Epstein Equestrian Enterprises Inc v Frank Jonkman and Sons Limited*, 2013 ONSC 78 (CanLII)

38 Based, in part, on *Plas Tex Canada Ltd v Dow Chemical of Canada Ltd*, 2004 ABCA 309.

to be made. At the end of October, the hardware and two software programs were delivered to Imperial, and Imperial's employees attempted to begin to use the programs. Very little training was provided, however, and there were major problems with the computer screens freezing and data being lost. More programs were delivered in January, along with some operating instructions, but Imperial's employees were still unable to make any use of the programs they had. The programmer whom Jacob assigned to Imperial's contract, Mr. Sharma, continued to work on the remaining programs. In May, however, Jacob informed Imperial that Sharma would be leaving the company, and Imperial informed Jacob that if that were to happen, given the problems and delays the company had already experienced, Imperial would be forced to end the contract with Jacob's company.[39] Is the breach by Jacob's company serious enough to permit the innocent party, Imperial, to treat the contract as at an end?

8. Canadian Pacific Airlines (CP) agreed to safely transport the Newells' two pet dogs on a flight from Toronto to Mexico City. The Newells were concerned about the safety and welfare of their dogs, but CP's employees reassured them that the dogs would be safe in the cargo compartment of the aircraft and reported to them before they boarded that their dogs had been safely placed in the cargo area. When the flight arrived in Mexico City, one dog was dead and the other was comatose. The Newells sued CP for general damages to compensate them for "anguish, loss of enjoyment of life, and sadness" that they allege resulted from the breach of contract.[40] Are the Newells entitled to anything other than compensation for their direct financial loss (i.e., the monetary value of the dogs)? If so, what would be an adequate amount to compensate for the mental distress suffered by the Newells?

39 Based, in part, on *Imperial Brass Ltd v Jacob Electric Systems Ltd (1989)*, 72 OR (2d) 17 (HCtJ).

40 Based, in part, on *Newell et al v Canadian Pacific Airlines Ltd* (1977), 14 OR (2d) 752 (Co Ct J).

PART THREE

BUSINESS TORTS

Tort law provides remedies to persons who have suffered physical harm and/or economic loss because of the intentional or careless actions of another.

Business is exposed to tort risks on a variety of fronts. A paper mill may release toxins into a nearby river and ruin the water downstream. A customer may slip on the floor of a store and suffer serious injury. One business may intentionally seek to drive a competitor out of business by spreading lies concerning the quality of products sold. An accountant or lawyer may provide negligent advice that causes the client to lose money. In response, tort law provides a set of rules through which the innocent party can recover financial compensation for the loss sustained. The next three chapters consider the risk exposure of business in the context of tort law.

10

INTRODUCTION TO TORT LAW

OBJECTIVES

After studying this chapter, you should have an understanding of

- the broad scope of tort law
- the differences between a civil action and a criminal action
- the purpose of tort remedies
- how business can manage its potential liability in tort

BUSINESS LAW IN PRACTICE

Gretchen Grenada works on the installation crew for Tour-Allure Ltd. (Tour-Allure). Tour-Allure provides sound, lighting, and audio-visual services to night clubs, restaurants, theatres, and retail spaces throughout Alberta. Sixteen-hour shifts were not uncommon but in such circumstances, Gretchen's boss—Ross Dirk—would provide beer to his crew-members once the install was close to completion. Gretchen decided to partake because the venue was particularly hot and sipping beer seemed to help her cool off. Dirk placed no restrictions on how much employees could drink. In the end, Gretchen drank a substantial amount of beer between 10:00 P.M. and 11:30 P.M., while on the job. After that, she stayed behind at the installation site, drinking with Dirk and her co-workers until 1:00 A.M. At this point, Gretchen insisted on driving herself home though Dirk unsuccessfully tried to convince her to take a cab as he knew that she had been drinking. Because Gretchen was seriously impaired, she could not maintain control of her vehicle. She collided with another car, causing catastrophic injury to its 25-year-old driver in the form of paraplegia. Gretchen was less seriously hurt, suffering a broken leg and a concussion. Following correct legal procedure in every way, the police secured a blood sample from Gretchen which showed that her alcohol level was three times the legal limit and so she has been charged under the *Criminal Code* with impaired driving causing bodily harm.[1]

1. What legal actions against Gretchen arise from this scenario?
2. What legal actions arise against Tour-Allure?
3. What kinds of risk management actions could Tour-Allure have taken to prevent Gretchen's accident in the first place?

Defining Tort Law

The word **tort**[2] describes any harm or injury caused by one person to another—other than through breach of contract—and for which the law provides a remedy.[3] According to the Supreme Court of

© Bill Stormont/Corbis

---

1   Portions of this Business Law in Practice scenario are based on *Jacobsen v Nike Canada Ltd* (1996), 133 DLR (4th) 377 (BCSC) and *Hunt v Sutton Group Incentive Realty Inc* (2001) 52 OR (3d) 425 (Sup Ct Jus) rev'd on other grounds (2002), 215 DLR (4th) 193 (CA).
2   The word "tort" is derived from the Latin word meaning "crooked" and the French word meaning "wrong." See Lewis Klar, *Tort Law*, 5th ed (Toronto: Thomson Carswell, 2012) at 1.
3   *Ibid.*

Canada, tort law provides a means whereby compensation, usually in the form of damages, may be paid for:

> . . . injuries suffered by a party as a result of the wrongful conduct of others. It may encompass damages for personal injury suffered, for example, in a motor vehicle accident or as a result of falling in dangerous premises. It can cover damages occasioned to property. It may include compensation for injury caused to the reputation of a business or a product. It may provide damages for injury to honour in cases of defamation and libel. A primary object of the law of tort is to provide compensation to persons who are injured as a result of the actions of others.[4]

Given this diversity, the law historically evolved so as to break torts down into distinct categories, each with its own discrete definition. What follows is a brief sampling:

- *trespass to land*. **Trespass to land** involves wrongful interference with someone's possession of land.[5] Parking garage operators might rely on the tort of trespass when drivers leave their cars in the lot but fail to purchase the required ticket from the automated ticket dispenser. The driver is responsible for the tort of trespass because he has left the vehicle on the property without permission.

- *deceit or fraud*. This tort is based on a false representation intentionally or recklessly made by one person to another that causes damage.[6] The tort of **deceit or fraud** occurs when, for example, a customer purchases a vehicle based on the vendor's intentional representation that the vehicle has a new engine when, in fact, it does not. The vendor has committed the tort of deceit because he made an untrue statement, which the purchaser relied on in deciding to make the purchase.

- *negligence*. The tort of **negligence** compensates someone who has suffered loss or injury due to the unreasonable conduct of another.[7] It is one of the most common torts to arise in a business context. For example,

  - when a taxi driver is injured due to an unsafe lane change by another driver, she is the victim of the tort of negligence. The driver causing the injury is responsible for the tort of negligence because he has made the unsafe lane change and failed to show the care and attention that the circumstances required.

  - when lawyers, accountants, or other professionals give their clients incompetent advice that causes loss, they have committed not only a breach of contract but also the tort of negligence, more specifically known as professional negligence.

  - when consumers purchase a defective product, they may have an action against the manufacturer for negligence if the product was improperly designed and/or produced. This area of law is known more specifically as product liability, but its foundations are in negligence.

  - when a bar overserves a customer, it may be found negligent if that intoxicated customer is injured or causes injury to others.

Tort

A harm caused by one person to another, other than through breach of contract, and for which the law provides a remedy.

Trespass to land

Wrongful interference with someone's possession of land.

Deceit or fraud

A false representation intentionally or recklessly made by one person to another that causes damage.

Negligence

Unreasonable conduct, including a careless act or omission, that causes harm to another.

---

4 *Hall v Hebert*, [1993] 2 SCR 159 at para 58, per Cory J.
5 *Supra* note 2 at 110.
6 *Ibid* at 696 and following.
7 *Ibid* at 167.

The law of torts will not automatically provide a remedy when someone has been physically or economically injured. One of the key objectives of tort law is to distinguish between a situation in which the loss suffered by an injured individual should remain uncompensated and one in which responsibility for the loss should be "shifted" to the person considered responsible for causing the loss. Tort law provides an evolving set of rules for making that determination.

To a large extent, tort law seeks to impose liability based on fault, as the following two examples illustrate:

Example 1 A truck driver falls asleep at the wheel. As a result, his rig crashes into a parked car, causing substantial property damage.

- The driver has committed the tort of negligence. His careless acts or omissions have caused harm or loss to another, namely the owner of the parked car. The owner can successfully sue in tort.

Example 2 A truck driver—with no previous history of health problems—suffers a heart attack while at the wheel. As a result, his rig crashes into a parked car, causing substantial property damage.

- Assuming that the driver's heart attack was not reasonably foreseeable or reasonably preventable, no tort has been committed by the driver. Though his rig caused property damage, it was not due to a careless act or omission.

It is important to note that liability in these examples will vary from province to province depending on the no-fault elements of the provincial *Insurance Act* as relating to auto insurance that may be in place. A pure no-fault system eliminates the ability to claim in tort. No-fault insurance is discussed further in Chapter 28.

A central function of tort law is to compensate an injured party when the injury is the result of someone else's blameworthy conduct. While one may feel sympathy for anyone who suffers damages, tort law does not provide a remedy in all circumstances.

CASE

Fullowka v Pinkerton's of Canada Ltd, [2010] 1 S.C.R. 132

THE BUSINESS CONTEXT: During a labour strike, owners may decide to hire a security guard company in order to protect replacement workers and employees willing to cross the picket line since strike-breaking predictably makes strikers angry. In the event of violence by the strikers, the security company may face a lawsuit arguing that it was negligent in the provision of services and that it is therefore responsible for the loss or injury that follows.

FACTUAL BACKGROUND: A tremendously bitter strike by miners at the Giant Mine in Yellowknife—an underground gold mine—soon became violent. The owner hired Pinkerton's Canada Ltd. (Pinkerton's) to provide security but, unfortunately, the violence only escalated. At one point, a large number of strikers even started to riot during which time they damaged property and injured both security guards and replacement workers. In response, the owner fired approximately 40 strikers. Eventually, the atmosphere grew calmer though some violence and property damage continued. A horrible tragedy and crime then ensued when Roger

Warren, a striker, evaded Pinkerton's security, gained access to the mine, and planted an explosive device there. The device was detonated by trip wire, killing nine miners. The widows of the dead miners sued Pinkerton's, among others, in negligence for failing to prevent the murders.[8]

THE LEGAL QUESTION: Did Pinkerton's commit the tort of negligence?

RESOLUTION: The Supreme Court of Canada rejected the argument that Pinkerton's had been negligent even though Roger Warren did gain unlawful access to the mine. This is because Pinkerton's legal obligation had not been to *ensure* that mine entrances were properly guarded to stop intrusions. Instead, Pinkerton's obligation was to use *reasonable care* to prevent such intrusions. As Canada's highest court observed, the law does not require Pinkerton's to guarantee success in its security mission, particularly given "Mr. Warren's determination to commit an intentional, criminal act."[9] The Supreme Court of Canada therefore dismissed the claim against Pinkerton's in its entirety.

Note that the bomber, Roger Warren, was convicted of nine counts of second degree murder in 1995 and sentenced to life. In 2014, he was granted parole.

CRITICAL ANALYSIS: Do you agree with the Supreme Court of Canada's analysis?

As noted in Chapter 2, courts are governed by precedent when determining the law in any particular case. The nature of precedent is inherently historical, meaning that judges can reach back and rely on old cases as well as more recently decided ones.

How Torts Are Categorized

Torts can generally be categorized as falling into two main groups: torts committed intentionally and torts committed through negligence. The first, called an **intentional tort**, is a harmful act that is deliberate or committed on purpose. For example, if store security personnel prevent a customer from leaving the premises because they mistakenly believe she has shoplifted, the security guards have committed the tort of **false imprisonment**. They have *intentionally* prevented the customer from going where she has a lawful right to be[10]—namely out of the store. False imprisonment is discussed further in Chapter 12 but is defined as unlawful detention or physical restraint or coercion by psychological means. If the guards physically restrain or punch the suspected shoplifter,

© Ian Lishman/Juice Images/Corbis

The law requires employers to keep the workplace safe. How can the risks of a workplace accident be managed?

---

8   It is beyond the scope of this text to analyze the Workers' Compensation Board aspect of this litigation. Suffice it to say that because their husbands had been killed on the job, the widows were receiving ongoing compensation from the Workers Compensation Board of the North West Territories (WCB), now called the Workers' Safety and Compensation Commission. The purpose of the widows' subsequent action against Pinkerton's et al. was at least twofold: first, if successful, it would permit the WCB to recoup its costs in paying benefits to the widows from the culpable defendants; and second, it would permit the widows to potentially secure additional compensation. See later in this chapter for brief consideration of WCB legislation. See too CBC News, "Giant Mine widows' claim rejected by top court" (18 February 2010), online: CBC <http://www .cbc.ca/m/touch/canada/story/1.871230>. For discussion of the insurer's right of subrogation, see Chapter 28.

9   *Fullowka v Pinkerton's of Canada Ltd,* [2010] 1 S.C.R. 132 at para 80.

10 Klar, *supra* note 2 at 59.

Intentional tort

A harmful act that is committed deliberately or on purpose.

False imprisonment

Unlawful detention or physical restraint or coercion by psychological means.

Battery

Battery
Intentional infliction of harmful or offensive physical contact.

for example, they have committed the tort of **battery** because they have intentionally inflicted harmful or offensive physical contact.[11] The fact that the guards have made an innocent mistake as to her criminality is no defence. Chapter 12 also examines this and other kinds of business-related torts, most of which are intentional.

Torts committed through negligence comprise another large group. When someone is negligent, he is liable for damages even though he did not intentionally cause the event in question. For example, Tour-Allure (through its manager Dirk) is obligated by the law of negligence to take reasonable care to see that Gretchen, who has consumed alcohol at work, is not harmed.[12] Though her employer did not intend for Gretchen to be injured, this is not a defence. Courts have found that employers owe an "overriding managerial responsibility" to protect employees like Gretchen and "safeguard her from an unreasonable risk of personal injury while on duty"[13] so as not to interfere with her ability to drive home safely. In short, the employer must provide a safe workplace.[14] Dirk should never have permitted drinking in the workplace nor allowed Gretchen to drive. He should have taken away her keys, if necessary. The law even goes so far as to require Dirk to call the police, failing all else, if someone like Gretchen insists on driving.[15] Based on the case law, a court likely will find Tour-Allure liable in negligence because it provided alcohol in the workplace, did not monitor Gretchen's consumption, and then permitted her to drive.[16] The tort of negligence is assessed in more detail in Chapter 11.

This chapter discusses tort law from a more general perspective in order to lay the foundation for subsequent discussion.

Tort Law and Criminal Law

The same event can give rise to two distinct legal consequences: one in tort law and one in criminal law. From the perspective of criminal law, Gretchen has been charged under the *Criminal Code* with impaired driving causing bodily harm. What follows are the relevant provisions of the *Criminal Code*:

> **253.** (1) Every one commits an offence who operates a motor vehicle or vessel or operates or assists in the operation of an aircraft or of railway equipment or has the care or control of a motor vehicle, vessel, aircraft or railway equipment, whether it is in motion or not,
>
> (a) while the person's ability to operate the vehicle, vessel, aircraft, or railway equipment is impaired by alcohol or a drug; or
>
> (b) having consumed alcohol in such a quantity that the concentration in the person's blood exceeds eighty milligrams of alcohol in one hundred millilitres of blood.
>
> . . . .
>
> **s. 255.** (2) Everyone who commits an offence under paragraph 253(1) (a) and causes bodily harm to another person as a result is guilty of an indictable offence and liable to imprisonment for a term of not more than 10 years.

---

11 *Ibid* at 46–47. Note that *Norberg v Wynrib* (1992), 12 CCLT (2d) 1 SCC) at 16 defines battery as the "intentional infliction of unlawful force on another person."
12 *Hunt, supra* note 1 at para 55.
13 *Ibid* at para 55, citing *Rice v Chan Estate* (1998) 62 BCLR (3d) 113 (SC).
14 *Hunt, supra* note 1.
15 *Ibid* at para 56.
16 See *Nike, supra* note 1 at para 53.

But not only has Gretchen been charged with a criminal offence, she faces tort liability too. This is because the driver who was seriously injured can bring an action in negligence against her. Put another way, Gretchen's behaviour and its consequences give rise to two separate legal actions. This is because, in addition to tort law, the *Criminal Code* prohibits one from driving while impaired.

Purposes of the Actions

The purpose of a criminal prosecution is to censure behaviour—such as impaired driving causing bodily harm—and secure the sanction of a fine, imprisonment, or both. The action is brought because the Parliament of Canada has determined that anyone who violates the *Criminal Code* should be *punished* and deterred from such conduct in the future. Prosecution is considered to be critical to maintaining a rights-respecting society. Criminal law does not compensate the victim of a crime, leaving compensation to other areas of law.

In tort law, on the other hand, the objective is to *compensate* the victim for the harm suffered due to the culpability of another. It enforces the victim's private right to extract compensation from the party who has caused the loss.[17]

Commencing the Actions

In criminal law, the legal action is called a prosecution and is brought most often by Crown prosecutors employed by the federal or provincial governments. Rarely do the injured parties bring the prosecution, though it is technically possible for them to do so.[18] In a criminal action, Gretchen would be known as the "accused" or "defendant" and the injured driver is known as the "complainant."

In tort law, the injured party brings the legal action. This means that the injured driver would sue in order to enforce his personal or private right to secure compensation for the injuries caused by Gretchen's negligent driving. His action is called a civil action because it is enforcing a right belonging to an individual. In a civil action, the injured driver is known as the "plaintiff" and Gretchen as the "defendant."

Proving the Actions

To secure a conviction under section 253 of the *Criminal Code*, the Crown must show that Gretchen was using the vehicle and that she was impaired when doing so.

The Crown has the burden of proof in a criminal action. This means that the prosecutor must prove all the elements of the offence beyond a reasonable doubt based on "reason and common sense,"[19] not on "sympathy or prejudice."[20] Guilt must be a logical deduction from the evidence, and it is not sufficient that the jury or judge believed the accused "probably" committed the act.[21]

Gretchen acknowledges that she was driving and the results of her legally obtained blood sample demonstrate a blood alcohol content well above the

---

17 Note that in Ontario, as one example, victims of crime also have access to a fund that allows some compensation for their loss or suffering. See, for example, *Compensation for Victims of Crime Act*, RSO 1990, c C-24, and the *Victims' Bill of Rights*, 1995, SO 1995, c 6 and the *Prohibiting Profiting from Recounting Crimes Act*, SO 2002, c 2.

18 Private prosecutions—that is, those brought by the victim or anyone else who is not an agent of the Crown—are uncommon but permissible. See Law Reform Commission of Canada, *Private Prosecutions, Working Paper No. 52* (Ottawa: Law Reform Commission of Canada, 1986) at 51–59.

19 *R v Lifchus*, [1997] 3 SCR 320 at para 30.

20 *Ibid* at para 31.

21 *Ibid* at para 39. See too Arbour J's decision in *R v Rhee*, [2001] 3 SCR 364 at para 20.

FIGURE 10.1 Differences Between Civil and Criminal Actions

Type of Action	Commencing the Action	Proving the Action	Outcome
Negligence (a tort action)	The injured driver files a claim against Gretchen based on the tort of negligence.	The injured driver must prove his case on the balance of probabilities.	A court orders Gretchen to pay the injured driver compensation for his injuries.
Impaired driving causing bodily harm (a criminal action)	The Crown prosecutes Gretchen based on section 253 of the *Criminal Code*.	The Crown must prove its case beyond a reasonable doubt.	A court orders Gretchen to be imprisoned, fined, or both.

legal limit. On this basis, Gretchen almost certainly faces conviction and will be subject to sentencing under section 255 of the *Criminal Code*.

In tort, by way of contrast, the injured driver must prove that Gretchen is liable for negligence, on the balance of probabilities. Put another way, the injured driver must establish that it is more likely than not that Gretchen was negligent. Represented in numerical terms, the injured must convince the judge that there is a better than 50 percent chance that Gretchen was negligent.

Given the different burdens, it is obviously easier to prove a civil case than a criminal case, and for good reason (see Figure 10.1). Criminal convictions can result in depriving persons of their liberty. This has always been considered to be far more serious than requiring them to pay damages in a civil action. While the odds are high that the plaintiff will succeed in tort if the defendant has already been convicted under criminal law, this is not a certainty since the definitions of the individual torts and crimes are not always exactly the same. However, some courts have agreed that evidence of a conviction for conduct constituting a crime is relevant to establishing the existence of a related tort.[22]

Liability in Tort

Primary and Vicarious Liability

There are two kinds of liability in tort law: primary and vicarious. Primary liability arises due to one's own personal wrongdoing. Gretchen has primary liability for injuring the other driver. **Vicarious liability**, by way of contrast, arises due to the relationship that someone has to the person who actually commits the tort. For example, the doctrine of vicarious liability makes an employer liable for the torts committed by its employees acting in the ordinary course or scope of employment. For example, if retail employees commit the tort of false imprisonment by wrongfully restraining a customer, the retail employer will be vicariously liable for that tort.

See too, the Business Application of the Law box (re: Steve Moore) later in this chapter.

Traditionally regarded, an employee's wrongful conduct is within the ordinary course or scope of employment if it is

- authorized by the employer; or
- an unauthorized mode of doing something that is, in fact, authorized by the employer.

Vicarious liability

The liability that an employer has for the tortious acts of an employee committed in the ordinary course or scope of employment.

---

22 *Simpson v Geswein*, [1995] 6 WWR 233 (Man. Q.B.). For a further discussion of this point, including relevant statute law, see Klar, *supra* note 2 at 41.

It can be particularly difficult to distinguish between an unauthorized "mode" of performing an authorized act that attracts liability and an entirely independent "act" that does not. This problem is illustrated in the application of vicarious liability to sexual assaults and other intentional, as opposed to negligent, acts committed by employees.[23] To provide further context, the Supreme Court of Canada states in *Blackwater v Plint*:

> Vicarious liability may be imposed where there is a significant connection between the conduct authorized by the employer. . . and the wrong. Having created or enhanced the risk of the wrongful conduct, it is appropriate that the employer or operator of the enterprise be held responsible, even though the wrongful act may be contrary to its desires. . . . The fact that wrongful acts may occur is a cost of business.[24]

Note that there is no vicarious liability for *crimes* committed by employees even if there is arguably a significant connection between the conduct authorized by the employer and the wrong committed by the employee.

Vicarious liability is discussed further in Chapter 20.

Liability and Joint Tort-Feasors

A person who commits a tort is called a **tort-feasor**. Those who commit a tort with others are known as **joint tort-feasors**. For example, if a Tour-Allure customer is injured by a ceiling-mounted loudspeaker which fell onto him due to improper installation by two Tour-Allure employees, those two co-workers would have joint liability for those injuries (and Tour-Allure itself would have vicarious liability). Legislation passed across Canada states that if the negligence of more than one person is responsible for the loss, the victim or plaintiff can sue any or all of them, with recovery apportioned between the joint tort-feasors according to their level of responsibility. Notwithstanding the apportionment of liability *between* the joint tortfeasors, the plaintiff can recover 100 percent of the judgment from any of those defendants whom a court has held to be jointly responsible for the loss or injuries.[25]

Liability and Contributory Negligence

Tort victims may be at least partially responsible for their own injuries. If the defendant successfully argues that the plaintiff was responsible for at least a part of the loss—that is, the defendant uses the defence of **contributory negligence**—the amount of damages that the plaintiff is awarded is reduced by the proportion for which the plaintiff is responsible. Contributory negligence is a common defence used in lawsuits involving car accidents. For example, if the driver injured by Gretchen's negligence was not wearing a seatbelt at the time of the accident, Gretchen's lawyer may well be able to establish that the injuries he sustained were worse than they otherwise would have been. At this point, the court will decrease the injured driver's damages award in proportion to the plaintiff's degree of contributory negligence. For example, if the plaintiff's damages are set at $2 million and the court finds the plaintiff to have been 20 percent contributorily negligent—that is, responsible for 20 percent of the loss—the plaintiff's damages award will be reduced to $1 600 000.

Tort-feasor

Person who commits a tort.

Joint tort-feasors

Two or more persons whom a court has held to be jointly responsible for the plaintiff's loss or injuries.

Contributory negligence

A defence claiming that the plaintiff is at least partially responsible for the harm that has occurred.

---

23 See, for example, the Supreme Court of Canada's analysis in *Bazley v Curry*, [1999] 2 SCR 534.
24 *Blackwater v Plint*, [2005] 3 SCR 3 at para 20, per McLachlin CJ.
25 For example, *Negligence Act*, RSO 1990, c N-1; *Contributory Negligence Act*, RSNB 2011, c C-131; *Contributory Negligence Act*, RSNS 1989, c 95; *Negligence Act*, RSBC 1996, c 333.

Damages in Tort
The Purpose of Damages

The primary goal of a tort remedy is to compensate the victim for loss caused by the defendant. Generally, this is a monetary judgment. Less common alternatives are equitable remedies, such as an injunction—a court order requiring or prohibiting certain conduct. An injunction would be ordered if money would not suffice—for example, in the case of a recurring trespass where there is little economic harm, but the plaintiff simply wants the trespasser to stop coming onto the land in question. Financial compensation means the defendant is ordered by the court to pay a sum of money to the successful plaintiff. Such a remedy has obvious limitations. For example, where the plaintiff has suffered serious physical injuries, how can money truly compensate someone for the permanent loss of health? However, in personal injury cases there are no ready alternatives to financial compensation.

BUSINESS AND LEGISLATION

WORKERS' COMPENSATION

Although tort law remains primarily a common law matter, it has also been modified by statute law. **Workers' compensation legislation**, for example, provides monetary compensation to employees for work-related injuries and illnesses. At the same time, it prohibits the employee from suing the employer for any negligence or other tort that might have caused the loss. In this way, the statute takes away the employee's common law right to sue but provides compensation no matter who is at fault.

Critical Analysis: Should employees be deprived of their right to sue their employer when that employer has been in the wrong and caused the employee's injury?

Workers' compensation legislation

Legislation that provides no-fault compensation for injured employees in lieu of their right to sue in tort.

Tort law compensates not only for physical injury or loss but also for mental pain and suffering and other forms of emotional distress. These latter areas are approached with more caution by the judiciary, but are compensable if proven through psychiatric and other expert evidence.

Because any award or out-of-court settlement is final, a plaintiff's lawyer will not usually settle or bring the case to court until the full extent of damages is known.

Pecuniary and Non-Pecuniary Damages

Under Canadian law, the losses for which damages are awarded are categorized as being either pecuniary (i.e., monetary) or non-pecuniary.

Non-pecuniary damages—sometimes called general damages—are damages that are awarded to compensate the plaintiff for:

Non-pecuniary damages

Compensation for pain and suffering, loss of enjoyment of life, and loss of life expectancy.

- pain and suffering.
- loss of enjoyment of life.
- loss of life expectancy.

Because Gretchen's negligence caused the other driver to suffer from paraplegia, that driver has undoubtedly suffered a considerable amount of general damages. These damages are non-pecuniary in the sense that they are not out-of-pocket, monetary losses, but they are nonetheless both real and devastating.

The quality of the injured driver's life has been seriously diminished due to a loss of mobility and independence; his life expectancy has likely been reduced. A judge will award damages based on these facts, as well as on expert testimony as to how badly he has been injured. The more serious and permanent the injury is, the higher the general damages will be. Courts have developed precedents to assist in this process, and the Supreme Court of Canada has set a clear upper limit on what can be awarded for general damages.[26]

Pecuniary damages fall into three main categories:

- cost of future care.
- loss of future income.
- special damages (out-of-pocket expenses).

Cost of Future Care

The injured driver is entitled to an award sufficient to provide him with all the care and assistance his injury will necessitate. This can include the cost of a personal care attendant for the rest of his life, modifications to his living accommodations to increase accessibility, and the costs related to equipment and treatment of his condition. As in other areas of damages, what he is ultimately awarded will be based on the testimony of experts, including occupation, rehabilitation, and medical experts.

Loss of Future Income

A judge will value the injured driver's diminished earning capacity resulting from the injury. This calculation can be complex, involving the input of vocational experts, labour economists, accountants, and actuaries. Since he has suffered a serious injury as a result of Gretchen's negligence and he is a young person, his loss of future income will likely be considerable.

Special Damages

Special damages relate to out-of-pocket expenses resulting from the injury-causing event. These expenses may include any number of items, including ambulance costs, medication costs, housekeeping, and yard work. The injured driver should keep records and receipts of such costs and expenses in order to prove them in court. In some provinces medical costs must be claimed as special damages, although these will be repaid to the provincial health insurer under the insurance principle of subrogation.[27]

Punitive or Exemplary Damages

Punitive damages—also known as exemplary damages—are an exception to the general rule that damages are intended only to

Pecuniary damages

Compensation for out-of-pocket expenses, loss of future income, and cost of future care.

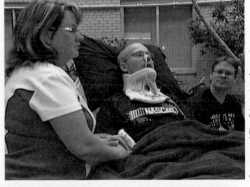

Courtesy of The Edmonton Journal

Dennis Schulz was catastrophically injured at a Bon Jovi concert. Schulz alleges that several people started fighting in the stands and one of them ended up falling on him from above, breaking his neck and resulting in quadriplegia. What kinds of damages should Schulz seek and why?[28]

---

26 *Andrews v Grand & Toy Alberta Ltd*, [1978] 2 SCR 299; *Arnold v Teno*, [1978] 2 SCR 287; and *Thornton v School Dist No 57 Bd of School Trustees*, [1978] 2 SCR 267. In *Andrews*, the Supreme Court of Canada placed a ceiling on recovery for general pain and suffering at $100 000. In 2015 dollars, this amounts to approximately $360 000.

27 It is beyond the scope of this text to discuss the law governing health care expense subrogation.

28 Based on Ryan Cormier, "Man seeks $13M for injuries at Bon Jovi concert" *The Edmonton Journal* (23 November 2007) at B7.

compensate the plaintiff. Punitive damages are awarded to punish the defendant for malicious, oppressive, and high-handed conduct or where the defendant might otherwise profit from the behaviour.[29] For example, if Gretchen had *intentionally* driven her car into the path of the oncoming car, causing injury to the driver, punitive damages would almost certainly be awarded. The court would seek to punish such offensive conduct.

BUSINESS APPLICATION OF THE LAW

PUNITIVE DAMAGES IN THE UNITED STATES AND CANADA

The Canadian Press regularly reports instances of high punitive awards given by American juries to sympathetic plaintiffs in the United States. Most famously, Stella Liebeck of Albuquerque, New Mexico, was awarded nearly $3 million in punitive damages against McDonald's when she suffered serious burns upon opening a cup of coffee that she had placed between her legs while in a vehicle. Due to severe scalding, she remained hospitalized for eight days. According to *The New York Times*, the jury was influenced by McDonald's prior knowledge that at least 700 of its customers had also been burned. *The Times* also reports what is less commonly known, namely that the plaintiff was found 20 percent contributorily negligent and that an out-of-court settlement reduced her damages award significantly.[30]

Jury trials are much less common in Canada than they are in the United States. This is at least one factor that keeps punitive damages lower, since judges may be less easily influenced to make large awards than members of the public who compose juries. Second, the spectre of "uncontrolled and uncontrollable awards of punitive damages in civil actions"[31] is a matter that the Supreme Court of Canada guards

Should the defendant's ability to pay be a consideration in the awarding of punitive damages?

© Ratmandude/Dreamstime.com

against by insisting on "proportionality" as the measure for punitive damages. Any punitive award must be rationally related to and be no more than necessary to punish the defendant, deter wrongdoers, or convey denunciation of the defendant's conduct. Moreover, the court has insisted that punitive damages should be exceptional, leaving criminal law as the main venue of punishment.

Significantly, the U.S. Supreme Court in *Exxon v Baker*[32] reviewed the history of punitive damages in the United States. At issue was the appropriate amount of punitive damages the plaintiffs should receive as a result of damage

---

29   *Klart, supra* note 2 at 122.

30   Anthony Ramirez, "For McDonald's, British justice is a different cup of tea" *The New York Times* (7 April 2002) at 7. In *Bogle v McDonald's Restaurants Ltd*, [2002] EWHC 490 (QB), an English court was much less sympathetic to a similar claim by plaintiffs who had been burnt by hot beverages at McDonald's outlets in the United Kingdom. According to that judge, "Persons generally expect tea or coffee purchased to be consumed on the premises to be hot. . . . Persons generally know that if a hot drink is spilled onto someone, a serious scalding injury can result. . . . [T]he allegations. . . that McDonald's are legally liable for these unfortunate injuries have not been made out".

31   *Whiten v Pilot Insurance Co* (2002), 209 DLR (4th) 257 (SCC). This case is summarized in Chapter 28.

32   554 US (2008).

caused by an Exxon supertanker grounding on a reef and spilling millions of gallons of oil into Prince William Sound, Alaska. The plaintiffs were commercial fishers, seafood producers, and others who relied on Prince William Sound to make their livings. What made the circumstances of the accident particularly egregious was that the captain, who had a history of drinking problems, "inexplicably left the bridge, leaving a tricky course correction to unlicensed subordinates."[33] Expert evidence indicated that the captain was legally impaired at the time of the accident. At trial, the jury awarded $5 billion in punitive damages against Exxon, which was lowered to $2.5 billion by the appeals court. The U.S. Supreme Court lowered that amount even further, based on its view that punitive damages, in federal maritime law, should be limited to the same amount as the compensatory damages. Compensatory damages in this case were set at $507.5 million, and therefore an equivalent amount was awarded by way of punitive damages. In bolstering its analysis, the U.S. Supreme Court noted that some states have regulated punitive damages by legislation, such as, for example, limiting them to a 3:1 ratio of punitive damages to compensatory damages,[34] with Nebraska going so far as to ban punitive awards altogether.[35] The Supreme Court's view was that, contrary to myth, there have been no "mass-produced runaway awards" in the United States.[36] However, the court acknowledged that "punitive damages overall are higher and more frequent in the U.S. than anywhere else"[37] and, more importantly, expressed concern about the

How can businesses avoid being ordered to pay punitive damages?

"stark unpredictability of punitive awards"[38] in the United States. Setting a 1:1 ratio would alleviate that problem. The court was fortified in its selection of a 1:1 ratio by studies indicating that most awards of punitive damages put the median ratio at less than 1:1. In the court's words, "we consider that a 1:1 ratio, which is above the median award, is a fair upper limit in such maritime cases."[39]

Critical Analysis: Do you think that Canada should follow the approach taken by the U.S. Supreme Court or do you prefer the flexibility of the Canadian approach? Would it be a good idea just to set a fixed dollar amount as a maximum and not worry about ratios or word descriptors?

Aggravated Damages

Aggravated damages compensate the plaintiff for intangible injuries such as distress and humiliation caused by the defendant's reprehensible conduct.[40] For example, when store detectives unlawfully restrain a customer, they have

Aggravated damages

Compensation for intangible injuries such as distress and humiliation caused by the defendant's reprehensible conduct.

---

33 *Ibid* at 1 per headnote summary.
34 *Ibid* at 37.
35 *Ibid* at 21.
36 *Ibid* at 24.
37 *Ibid* at 22.
38 *Ibid* at 26.
39 *Ibid* at 40.
40 *Vorvis v Insurance Corporation of British Columbia*, [1989] 1 SCR 1085.

committed the tort of false imprisonment. If, in restraining the customer, they treat the person in a humiliating or degrading fashion, a court may well award aggravated damages to compensate the plaintiff for the mental distress the whole experience caused.

STEVE MOORE'S TORT ACTION AGAINST TODD BERTUZZI

In response to an on-ice attack, Steve Moore sought tort damages against Todd Bertuzzi, among others, in compensation for serious injuries he suffered when he was sucker-punched by Bertuzzi during an NHL game. The attack—which is called battery in tort law because it involved actual physical contact or violation of bodily security—ended Moore's NHL career.

One court described the circumstances as follows:

> During a National Hockey League (NHL) game on March 8, 2004, the defendant Todd Bertuzzi, then with the Vancouver Canucks Hockey Club (Canucks), allegedly struck the plaintiff Steve Moore, then a hockey player with the Colorado Avalanche Hockey Club, from behind and drove his face onto the ice causing Moore serious injury and allegedly ending his career in the NHL. It is alleged that the action was taken as a payback for an incident in an earlier game between Moore and another Canucks player, Markus Näslund. The Canucks are owned by the Orca Bay defendants. The incident was highly publicized, has been the subject of ongoing media attention and was described as one of the most violent attacks in the NHL, tarnishing the image of Canada's national sport. Bertuzzi pleaded guilty to a charge of assault causing bodily harm on December 22, 2004, and was disciplined for his conduct by the NHL with a multi-game suspension.[41]

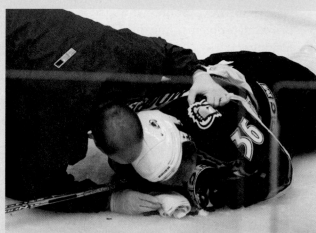

An injured Steve Moore

Chuck Stoody/The Canadian Press

Moore's injuries are lasting and devastating, according to his lawyer who stated to the press:

> "We have the top neurosurgeons in the world on this case and we have reached the point where we can say Steve's brain injury is permanent," Timothy Danson said Monday. "Unfortunately for Steve Moore, he's not only dealing with the loss of his NHL career, he has to deal with the serious damage to his post-NHL career as a result of the brain injury."[42]

Moore also sued the Vancouver Canucks hockey team.[43] Claims against the team included vicarious liability as Bertuzzi's employer and because, allegedly, its personnel encouraged Bertuzzi's attack and failed to take reasonable measures to prevent violence against Moore.

---

41 *Moore v Bertuzzi,* 2012 ONSC 597 at para 4. According to Colin Perkel, "Canucks ex-owner has to testify" *Edmonton Journal* (25 March 2014) page C5, Bertuzzi was sentenced on the criminal charges to one year's probation and 80 hours of community service.

42 Allan Maki, "Seven years later, Steve Moore still haunted by hit" *Globe and Mail* (7 March 2011; last updated 23 August 2012), online: *Globe and Mail* <http://www.theglobeandmail.com/sports/hockey/seven-years-later-steve-moore-still-haunted-by-hit/article1933045/>.

43 More technically speaking, the statement of claim names, as defendants: Orca Bay Hockey Limited Partnership and Orca Bay Hockey, Inc., doing business as the Vancouver Canucks Hockey Club, as well as the Vancouver Canucks Limited Partnership and Vancouver Hockey General Partner Inc.

More specifically, the amended statement of claims sought:

- $35 million for pecuniary and non-pecuniary damages, including loss of income. The amended statement of claim asserts that the defendants' actions caused Moore severe emotional distress "including but not limited to stress, fear, anger, shock mental anguish, and pain and suffering."
- $1 000 000 in aggravated damages because Moore suffered a "loss to his dignity"
- $2 000 000 for punitive damages on the basis that Bertuzzi's attack, for example, amounted to conduct that was "high handed, malicious, contumelious, insolent and vindictive."[44]

Both Bertuzzi and the Canucks filed statements of defence, disputing Moore's claims.

In a victim impact statement submitted in the sentencing portion of Bertuzzi's criminal trial, Moore described his life in these terms:

As I reflect on the impact this attack has had on me, both on my health and on my life as a whole, I am overwhelmed. There is not one single piece of my life where I do not find myself severely and profoundly affected. Everything has changed. The toll that all of these cumulative effects have had on my health and my life, and in my relationships with family and friends, cannot be measured. I think back to anxiously looking forward to being a part of the greatest championship in sports, the Stanley Cup play-offs; thrilled at embarking on such a monumental journey, with such special teammates. Those experiences were taken away from me, and I can never get them back. So many extraordinary experiences that I so unfairly missed out on, are now gone forever. My whole career, built upon the hard work, discipline and commitment of my entire life, and fuelled by a persistent dream, has been halted in its tracks.[45]

In the end, the civil trial never proceeded because the matter was settled out of court for an undisclosed sum. Responding to the settlement news, *Globe and Mail* sportswriter Gary Mason stated: "The best that can be said is the NHL can now officially close one of the ugliest chapters in its history. But the stain left on the game will never come out."[46]

Critical Analysis: In what way do the criminal and civil actions against Bertuzzi overlap? In what way are they distinct?

Source: Allan Maki, "Seven years later, Steve Moore still haunted by hit", *Globe and Mail* (7 March 2011; last updated 23 August 2012) online: *Globe and Mail* <http://www.theglobeandmail.com/sports/hockey/seven-years-later-steve-moore-still-haunted-by-hit/article1933045/>.

Tort Law and Contract

Sometimes the same set of facts can give rise to liability in tort and in contract. For example, assume that a nightclub bouncer punches a patron, mistakenly thinking that the patron is about to start a fight. The bouncer's tortious conduct is attributed to his employer, the nightclub, by way of vicarious liability and, on the same facts, *also* places the nightclub in breach of its contract with the patron. That is, it would be an implied term in the contract for the purchase of beverages that the nightclub would provide a reasonably safe environment for their consumption. When the patron was attacked by the bouncer, this term was breached.

Overlapping liability in contract and tort is also common when a professional—such as an accountant, lawyer, or banker—gives advice to a client. If that

---

44 Amended Statement of Claim in *Moore v Bertuzzi* Court file No: 06-CV-306081PD3.

45 "Moore's Victim Impact Statement" TSN (22 December 2004), online: TSN <http://www.tsn.ca/story/print?id=109008>.

46 Gary Mason, "Lessons unlearned" *Globe & Mail* (20 August 2014), S1 at S4.

advice is incompetent, the professional is in breach of contract *and* has committed the tort of negligence. This matter is explored further in Chapters 11 and 22.[47]

Managing Tort Risk

Chapters 3 and 4 extensively discussed the issues of risk management and dispute resolution. Businesses are exposed to a wide variety of risks related to tort actions, particularly in the area of negligence. In addition, they are vulnerable because of the doctrine of vicarious liability.

No business can eliminate all risk. It must, however, assume active measures to minimize it. This is because ignoring tort risk can result in

- incurring the costs of a tort that could have been avoided, including lawyers' fees, management time devoted to defending the claim, and the amount of the actual judgment awarded to the successful plaintiff.
- losing insurance coverage because of a poor claims history.
- losing a hard-earned business reputation.

Risk management strategies that business operations such as Tour-Allure might deploy are set out in Business Law in Practice Revisited.

BUSINESS LAW IN PRACTICE REVISITED

1. What legal actions against Gretchen arise from this scenario?

Gretchen faces a civil action by the injured driver for the tort of negligence. The driver has suffered loss and injury due to Gretchen's unreasonable conduct of driving while impaired. The tort of negligence is assessed in more detail in Chapter 11.

Gretchen also faces a criminal action and conviction for impaired driving under the *Criminal Code*. This is because she was driving the vehicle in question and the results of her blood sample placed her above the legal limit.

2. What legal actions arise against Tour-Allure?

The young injured driver—in addition to his action against Gretchen—could sue Tour-Allure in negligence because Tour-Allure could reasonably have foreseen that Gretchen would be a danger to other drivers on the roads and failed to take proper steps to stop her from driving home. In this case, the employer is directly liable for the tort it committed against the young driver.

It is unlikely that Tour-Allure would be found vicariously liable for Gretchen's tort of negligence against the injured driver because the accident did not occur while Gretchen was on the job. This is not, of course, a problem for the young driver since his action in negligence against the employer covers the same general terrain.

Note too, that the employer has no vicarious liability for Gretchen's crime as the law does not impose vicarious liability in the realm of criminal law. Corporate employers can be found directly liable in criminal law on other grounds, however, which is a matter discussed in Chapter 16.

---

47 Note that torts may not be just committed when the contract is being performed, as when a lawyer provides negligent legal advice. As discussed in Chapter 6, the torts of negligent and fraudulent misrepresentation can be committed when the contract is being *formed*.

Gretchen can sue her employer for the tort of negligence. Her employer failed to safeguard her and should not have permitted alcohol in the workplace let alone permit her to attempt to drive home.

3. What kind of risk management actions could Tour-Allure have taken to prevent Gretchen's accident in the first place?

Tour-Allure requires a better understanding of how to keep the workplace safe and the legal duties it owes to its employees. The best risk management strategy is to avoid such tragedies from happening. According to David P. Church and Sharon D. Matthews, employers should not supply alcohol during working hours or, if they choose to do so, ensure that the amount available for consumption is strictly limited and that how much each employee drinks is strictly monitored. If the employee is visibly impaired or has consumed enough alcohol to be impaired, the employer must provide transportation and/or accommodation to that employee. Church and Matthews add that the employee must be required to accept the transportation and/or accommodation offered.[48] Other steps include warning employees not to drink and drive and having proper liability insurance in place should prevention attempts fail.[49] Calling the police is also an important option.

CHAPTER SUMMARY

Tort law has a significant impact on business enterprises, particularly in the area of negligence. Tort law permits someone who has been injured or suffered a loss to sue the responsible person for damages. The objective of a damages award is to compensate the plaintiff, though punitive damages are sometimes available if the defendant's conduct has been particularly egregious. Aggravated damages are also available to compensate the person who suffers intangible injuries such as distress or humiliation caused by the defendant's reprehensible conduct. Less commonly, the injured party will seek an injunction or other form of equitable remedy, as in a trespass-to-land scenario.

Criminal law also affects a business, though to a lesser degree. As the purpose of a criminal law is to punish the offender—through fines and imprisonment—distinct procedures are in place to help ensure that only guilty people are convicted. For example, in a criminal prosecution the Crown must prove its case beyond a reasonable doubt. By way of contrast, the plaintiff in a tort action need only demonstrate his case on the balance of probabilities.

Liability in tort can be primary and vicarious. Primary liability arises due to one's own personal wrongdoing. Vicarious liability arises due to the relationship one has with the actual tort-feasor, as in an employer–employee context. Since a business may have several employees, its exposure in this area can be considerable.

When a person is injured due to the tortious conduct of more than one person, those culpable are known as joint tort-feasors. A court can apportion liability between them, but the victim or plaintiff can recover 100 percent of the judgment from any one of them.

---

48 See David P. Church and Sharon Matthews, "Alcohol in the Workplace" (1996) OHS, online: OHS <http://www.ohscanada.com/LawFile/alcowork.aspx?&er=NA>.

49 Howard Levitt "Keep Control of Party Cheer" *National Post* (November 16, 2005), online: Levitt & Grosman <http://levittgrosman.com/readarticle.php?article=23>.

When a tort victim is partially responsible for his own injuries, he has been contributorily negligent. The amount that the plaintiff is awarded will be reduced by the proportion for which he is responsible.

Sometimes, the same set of facts can give rise to liability in tort and in contract, particularly in the context of a professional advice giver such as a lawyer or an accountant.

The best response a business can have to its potential liability in tort is to establish a risk management plan that reduces, eliminates, or transfers risk.

CHAPTER STUDY

Key Terms and Concepts

aggravated damages (p. 235)

battery (p. 228)

contributory negligence (p. 231)

false imprisonment (p. 227)

deceit or fraud (p. 225)

intentional tort (p. 227)

joint tort-feasors (p. 231)

negligence (p. 225)

non-pecuniary damages (p. 232)

pecuniary damages (p. 233)

tort (p. 225)

tort-feasor (p. 231)

trespass to land (p. 225)

vicarious liability (p. 230)

workers' compensation legislation (p. 232)

Questions for Review

1. What does the term "tort" mean?

2. Give an example of a tort.

3. What are the two main categories into which torts are organized?

4. Why does the law require employers to maintain a safe workplace?

5. The goals of tort and criminal law are quite distinct, even when they stem from the same event. Explain the differences.

6. What is a joint tort-feasor?

7. What does *burden of proof* mean?

8. How does the burden of proof differ between a criminal case and a tort action?

9. What is the difference in the way tort and criminal actions are initiated?

10. What is the purpose of damages in tort?

11. Under what circumstances might an injunction be awarded in tort?

12. Vicarious liability is an essential feature of modern tort law. What is it?

13. What might be a defence to a claim for vicarious liability?

14. How does contributory negligence affect the amount of damages a plaintiff may receive?

15. Explain the difference between pecuniary and non-pecuniary damages.

16. How are pecuniary damages typically calculated?

17. What are punitive damages? How are they different from aggravated damages?

18. When is overlapping liability in tort law and contract law common?

Questions for Critical Thinking

1. What are the justifications for the basic legal principle that the standard of proof is higher in a criminal matter than in a civil one?

2. Punitive damages are somewhat controversial even in jurisdictions where they are relatively common. At the same time, there are circumstances in which a person's tortious actions have been particularly callous and

calculating, yet the actual loss suffered by the plaintiff is not extensive in monetary terms. In these latter cases, what are the compelling reasons for allowing the plaintiff additional recovery over and above the actual loss? Should the compensation principle of tort law be compromised in this way?

3. The concept of vicarious liability developed in the business world, where the company is out to make a profit and its activities are for the most part directed to generating profit. Is it appropriate to apply a test developed in this context to a charitable organization? What are the pros and cons for holding organizations liable for the conduct of their employees?

4. Does the idea of contributory negligence reflect the major aims and purposes of tort law? Does it make sense to reduce the amount of damages available to a plaintiff, when he may not have suffered the loss to the same extent, or at all, but for the negligence of someone else?

5. Do you think that a tort action like Steve Moore's (discussed in this chapter on page 236) helps to make the game of hockey safer? How?

6. Negligence law requires a security company like Pinkerton's to show reasonable care in the provision of services (as discussed in this chapter on page 226). Is this standard too low, particularly in the context of a violent workplace strike?

Situations for Discussion

1. Jason attended a beach party with his friends. At the end of the evening, he and his friends started walking back to their cars when Jason realized he had left his sandals behind at the beach. He went back to retrieve them but unfortunately, was randomly attacked by a group of young men who encircled him and beat him viciously. Jason lost consciousness and awoke again in the hospital. As a result of the vicious, unprovoked attack, Jason suffered serious physical injury and great emotional trauma. Jason is now suing the men who attacked him for the tort of battery, which is defined as the intentional infliction of harmful or offensive physical contact. Assume that Jason can prove that the tort of battery took

place. Do you think a court will award Jason aggravated damages given the circumstances of his attack? What about punitive damages? Explain.[50]

2. Reginald Smith, an employee of UR Safe Ltd., a security company, broke into a branch of a bank that was a customer of UR Safe Ltd. Smith did so when he was not on shift with UR Safe Ltd., and by using keys he had stolen from his employer. Using these keys, Smith gained access to the ATM room in the bank, but could not figure out how to open the ATM combination lock. He was close to giving up when he noticed that the bank kept an ATM instruction manual on a shelf right beside the ATM in the ATM room. Smith read the manual and on that basis was able to open the safe. Is UR Safe Ltd. vicariously liable for Smith's tortious conduct?[51]

3. Albert was walking home from his night shift at 3:30 A.M. The road was very dark, and Albert was wearing a red jacket, blue pants, black shoes, and green cap. Albert walked along the edge of the road but on the wrong side, such that his back was to oncoming traffic. Albert heard a vehicle approaching behind him, but decided not to look or even move. Unfortunately, Albert was hit by the vehicle, a delivery van; the driver was taking newspapers to a local drop-off point so that carriers could then deliver them to homes on their routes. Albert was seriously injured.

Albert has two witnesses. The first is a police officer who arrived on the scene and administered a breathalyzer test to the van driver. The van driver was not impaired. Albert's second witness is an individual who lives in a house directly across the road from the accident scene. This witness heard the impact of the accident and ran outside to help. This witness's evidence only related to the position of the plaintiff's body and the location of the defendant's delivery van.

Will Albert be able to establish negligence as against the driver of the van? Why or why not?[52]

---

50 Based, in part, on *Merrick v Guilbeault*, 2009 NSSC 60.
51 Based, in part, on *Royal Bank of Canada v Intercon Security Ltd* (2005), 143 ACWS (3d) 608 (Ont SJ).
52 Based on *Anderson v Short*, (1986), 62 Nfld & PEIR 232 (Nfld. S.C. T.D.).

4. The plaintiff hired the defendant to renovate the wooden wharf that the plaintiff owned in British Columbia. The wharf was part of the plaintiff's grain-loading facility in Vancouver Harbour. During this renovation process, the wharf was seriously damaged by fire. The fire was started by molten slag from an oxyacetylene torch operated by the defendant's employee. The defendant's employee did not minimize the fire hazard created by the torch. Among other deficiencies, the defendant's employee failed to wet the combustible surfaces before using the torch and failed to keep a proper fire watch during cutting operations so that any slag that landed could then be doused with water. When it came time to fight the fire, the defendant's employee ran into difficulties because the plaintiff had not provided a fire-protection system anywhere near the wharf in question, not even a fire extinguisher. The plaintiff claims damages in the amount of $1 million. Assuming that the defendant's employee has been negligent in how he used the torch, what would a possible defence of the defendant be? Should the plaintiff recover all its damages or only a portion thereof? Is the defendant responsible for the tort of its employee? Why or why not?[53]

5. Louise arrived for a two-week vacation at a Mexican resort. She spent the day at the beach and, upon returning to her room, found a bottle in the fridge containing a clear liquid. Louise assumed the liquid was water and started to drink from the bottle. It turns out that a member of the cleaning staff had inadvertently left a bottle of caustic cleaning solution in the fridge in Louise's room and this is what Louise had drunk. Louise suffered extensive injury and required emergency surgery to remove some of her esophagus. Louise wants to sue the cleaning staff member who left cleaning solution in Louise's fridge. Will this action be successful? Does the cleaning staff member have any defences?[54]

6. Archie became drunk at the office Christmas party. When he was leaving the event, his employer grew concerned and offered to drive him home, particularly as the winter weather was getting bad. Archie declined, notwithstanding a snowstorm and his own impairment. Archie was in a serious car accident, resulting in his suffering brain injuries and multiple fractures. Is the employer responsible to Archie for negligence? Will a court find Archie contributorily negligent?[55]

---

53 Based, in part, on *Alberta Wheat Pool v Northwest Pile Driving Ltd* (1998), 80 ACWS (3d) 692. (B.C.S.C.), reversed in part (2000), 80 BCLR (3d) 153 (CA).

54 Based on news story by Elise Stolte, "Woman sues Mexican resort over caustic cleaning fluid left in fridge" *Edmonton Journal* (20 February 2011) at A5.

55 Based, in part, on *Hunt v Sutton, supra* note 1.

THE TORT OF NEGLIGENCE

BUSINESS LAW IN PRACTICE

Meat Products Ltd. (Meat) is an Ontario-based food-processing and distribution company. It supplies deli meat and related products throughout Canada and parts of the United States. It seems that several consumers have recently died or been sickened as a result of consuming products manufactured by Meat. A bacterium known as *Listeria monocytogenes* has somehow infected meat processed there.

The CEO quickly instituted a recall of all Meat products, closed the production plant, and ordered that it be tested for *Listeria*. This was a crucial step, since technicians found *Listeria* deep inside the machinery of several meat-slicing machines. These germs somehow survived the company's cleaning and sanitizing protocols.

The CEO's worst fears were confirmed when tests demonstrated that several of Meat's products had tested positive for *Listeria monocytogenes*.

Prior to the recall, Jennifer Jones consumed a deli product made by Meat and became seriously ill with listeriosis. Jennifer missed several months of work, and as soon as she felt better, she spoke to a lawyer. As a result, Meat has now been made the subject of a class action. The firm Jennifer contacted is acting on her behalf as well as on behalf of other members of that class of persons who contracted listeriosis after having consumed contaminated food produced by Meat. The claim for damages is in the amount of $100 million.[1]

1. What tort may Meat have committed and what do the plaintiffs have to prove in order to establish that tort?

2. What defences does Meat have to this action?

3. What additional risks does a class action create for Meat?

4. How could Meat have better managed its risk of tort liability in this case?

OBJECTIVES

After studying this chapter, you should have an understanding of

- the conduct that the law of negligence addresses

- the principles of the law of negligence

- the defences in a negligence action

- the common kinds of negligence actions that businesses face

- the difference between negligence and strict liability

David Buffington/Photodisc

---

1 Based, in part, on press accounts of the *Listeria* outbreak at Maple Leaf Foods Inc's Bartor Road plant. For stories on point, see CBC News Staff, "Class action lawsuit launched over *listeria* outbreak," *CBC News Canada* (26 August 2008), online: CBC News <http://www.cbc.ca/news/canada/british-columbia/story/2008/08/26/bc-listeria-class-action-lawsuit.html>; CBC News Staff, "$27 M settlement reached in Maple Leaf listeriosis suits," *CBC News Canada* (2 February 2009), online: CBC News <http://www.cbc.ca/news/story/2009/02/02/maple.html>.

The Law of Negligence

What Is Negligence?

Reasonable care

The care that a reasonable person would exhibit in a similar situation.

Chapter 10 defined the tort of negligence as a careless act that causes harm to another. The law understands carelessness as a failure to show **reasonable care**, that is, the care that a reasonable person would have shown in a similar situation.

Negligence is a very common tort action in the commercial world because it covers a broad range of harmful conduct. For example, a negligence action can be brought by someone

- who has been injured by the dangerous driving of a delivery truck driver.
- who has suffered loss by relying on poor advice provided by an accountant, lawyer, architect, or engineer.
- whose furniture has been damaged in transit by a moving company.

The plaintiff need not show that the defendant intended to cause the damage or that there were deliberate acts that gave rise to the damage. Instead, the tort of negligence makes the defendant liable for failing to act reasonably—for driving too fast, for giving unprofessional advice, or for not taking proper care of furniture entrusted to it.

In the Business Law in Practice scenario above, the class action plaintiff, Jennifer, can only succeed in her action in negligence against Meat if she can show that Meat failed to use reasonable care in the manufacture of the meat product she consumed and that it caused her illness.

Negligence law—like tort law in general—seeks to compensate victims for their loss or injury. It provides this compensation after applying rules that determine who is liable to compensate another, on what basis, and for how much. Without such limiting rules, business and professional people might be reluctant to produce goods and services because the risk of liability in negligence would be unknowable. Those goods and services that did reach the market would be relatively more expensive since the price would need to reflect the increased risk flowing from widespread liability. With these kinds of factors in mind, the courts have the task of balancing competing interests. They must compensate victims of negligence, but without discouraging legitimate activity and without making the legal standards that a business must meet unreasonably exacting.

The roots of the modern negligence action are found in the following case.

LANDMARK CASE

Donoghue v Stevenson, [1932] AC 562 (HL)

THE BUSINESS CONTEXT: Before large-scale production, most goods were sold directly from producer/artisan to consumer. By the 20th century, a multistage distribution chain was the norm, comprising several distinct transactions or contracts—from manufacturer, to supplier, to retailer, to the ultimate consumer.

FACTUAL BACKGROUND: A customer bought some ice cream and an opaque bottle of ginger beer for her friend, Donoghue. Some of the ginger beer was poured over the ice cream and some was drunk by Donoghue. When the remainder of the beer was being poured into a tumbler, a decomposed snail was discovered in the contents. Donoghue became ill and subsequently sued the manufacturer for damages, based on negligence.

THE LEGAL QUESTION: At this time, the extent of the manufacturer's duty of care was severely constricted; the manufacturer was responsible

---

only to those with whom it had a contractual arrangement. Most consumer "victims" were prevented by this limited responsibility from recovering from the manufacturer. There was almost certainly a retailer in the transaction and no direct contractual relationship between the manufacturer and consumer.

RESOLUTION: Lord Atkin, for the majority, wrote the following classic statement when discussing how to determine to whom a duty of care is owed in negligence:

> The rule that you are to love your neighbour becomes in law, you must not injure your neighbour, and the lawyer's question, Who is my neighbour? receives a restricted reply. You must take reasonable care to avoid acts or omissions which you can reasonably foresee would be likely to injure your neighbour. Who, then, in law, is my neighbour? The answer seems to be—persons who are so closely and directly affected by my act that I ought reasonably to have them in contemplation as being so affected when I am directing my mind to the acts or omissions which are called in question.

Carbolic Smoke-Ball Co., www.carbolicsmokeball.com

Why is the consumer of ginger beer the neighbour of the beer's manufacturer?

CRITICAL ANALYSIS: Is it reasonable to make manufacturers liable for their products to end users? Would it be enough, simply, to make the retailer liable for breach of contract and leave the manufacturer out of the equation?

Establishing a Negligence Action

The rules that govern when a plaintiff like Jennifer will succeed in a negligence action are set out in a series of classic elements, as summarized in Figure 11.1.

The elements in a tort action, by design, lack a certain specificity. Their purpose is to describe general standards or markers that help a court assess whether the defendant in any given case has been negligent.

FIGURE 11.1 Elements in a Negligence Action

1. Does the defendant owe the plaintiff a duty of care? If yes, proceed to the next element.

2. Did the defendant breach the standard of care? If yes, proceed to the next element.

3. Did the defendant's careless act (or omission) cause the plaintiff's injury? If yes, proceed to the next element.

4. Was the injury suffered by the plaintiff too remote? If not, the plaintiff has proven negligence.

1: Does the Defendant Owe the Plaintiff a Duty of Care? The defendant, Meat, will be liable to Jennifer if it owes Jennifer what is known in law as a **duty of care**. A defendant owes a duty of care to anyone who might reasonably be affected by the defendant's conduct. This is known as the **neighbour** principle, as discussed in *Donoghue v Stevenson*, just above.

Duty of care

The responsibility owed to avoid carelessness that causes harm to others.

Neighbour

Anyone who might reasonably be affected by the defendant's conduct.

CHAPTER 11: THE TORT OF NEGLIGENCE

Since *Donoghue*, courts have continued to refine the test for whether a duty of care is owed. As formulated by the Supreme Court of Canada, a court must first ask whether the case at bar presents a novel situation or not. If the case is comparable to an already-decided case in which a duty of care was recognized, then Stage 1 described immediately below can be skipped and the plaintiff can proceed directly to Stage 2. If the case at issue is novel, then the court is required to assess the issue of duty by asking as follows: [2]

Stage 1: In the relationship between the plaintiff and defendant, is there a prima facie duty of care?

To fulfill Stage 1, the plaintiff must demonstrate two things:

> **Reasonable Foreseeability:** That the harm that occurred was a reasonably foreseeable consequence of the defendant's act.
>
> Reasonable foreseeability considers whether the defendant should objectively have anticipated that his or her act or omission would cause harm to the plaintiff.

AND

> **Proximity:** That there is a relationship of sufficient proximity between the parties such that it would not be unjust or unfair to impose a duty of care on the defendant.
>
> Proximity considers whether the specific circumstances of the parties' relationship are such that the defendant is under an obligation to be mindful of the plaintiff's "legitimate interests" in conducting his or her affairs.

If the plaintiff can establish foreseeability and proximity, he or she proceeds to Stage 2.

Stage 2: Are there residual policy considerations outside the relationship of the parties that may negate the imposition of a duty of care?

This stage of the inquiry no longer considers the relationship between the parties but asks the question more generally, to determine whether imposing a duty in these kinds of circumstances "would [be] unwise"[3] because it would extend liability too far.

There is no doubt that a business like Meat owes a duty of care to the consumer.[4] Under Stage 1, it is reasonably foreseeable that careless acts or omissions by a manufacturer of food products could cause harm to the consumer due to food contamination, including contamination by *Listeria*. It is also clear that the relationship between the manufacturer and the end user is a relationship of sufficient proximity to establish a duty of care. There is nothing in the specific relationship between Meat and the plaintiff-consumers to negate or reduce that duty.

On this basis, a *prima facie* duty of care is established. Under Stage 2, it is necessary to determine whether there are any more general considerations that ought to eliminate or reduce that duty. The objective of this is to ensure that businesses and other defendants are not made liable to an unreasonably broad, unknowable, and indeterminate extent. In practice, considerations that eliminate or reduce a defendant's duty of care are more likely to arise in the area of pure economic loss—such as loss of profit—than in cases of physical harm such as Jennifer has

---

Prima facie

At first sight or on first appearances.

---

2   The approach is based, in part, on *Odhavji Estate v Woodhouse*, 2003 SCC 69 at paras 47–51.
3   *Ibid* at para 51.
4   See, for example, *376599 Alberta Inc v Tanshaw Products Inc*, 2005 ABQB 300 at para 146.

suffered. Concerns regarding economic loss recovery are prevalent in the context of negligent misstatement, a tort that is discussed later in this chapter.

In Meat's case, a judge would almost certainly not find any reason under Stage 2 that would eliminate or reduce Meat's duty of care to consumers. This conclusion flows from the nature of Meat's business—manufacturers like Meat want people like Jennifer to purchase its product. If consumers are sickened or even die as a result of the product being contaminated, what possible reason could there be to suggest that Meat should not owe a duty of care to them? Though Meat stands to be liable to a great number of consumers, this is the nature of its chosen business and the fact that its product is intended to reach a large number of the public. Furthermore, the class of those who could successfully sue Meat will be composed of those who have consumed product from the contaminated plant only and hence is not an unlimited or indeterminate class.

Having established that Meat owes a duty of care to the ultimate consumer of its product, it is necessary to move to the next elements in establishing a successful action in negligence.

2: Did the Defendant Breach the Standard of Care?
In general, the defendant's conduct is judged according to the standards of behaviour that would be observed by the reasonable person in society. In law, a **reasonable person** is regarded as being an ordinary person of normal intelligence who uses ordinary prudence to guide his conduct. The law does not demand that the reasonable person be perfect.

Where the defendant exercises specialized skills, the standard of the reasonable person described above is not applied. Professionals such as doctors, accountants, engineers, and lawyers must meet a higher or specialized standard of care because the level of expertise of the average member of society is simply inadequate as a measure of competence. In cases involving specialized tasks, courts introduce the standard of the "reasonable" person with that specialized training—the reasonable electronics engineer, or the reasonable heart surgeon, for example. To determine just what the standard is on the facts before it, the court will hear from expert witnesses who, in turn, will present evidence of what that standard is.

Where the activity or product poses a high risk, the law imposes a higher standard of care. The policy reason for this higher standard is to encourage competence and caution in light of the very serious harm that could result if the task were poorly performed.

In assessing whether Meat breached its duty of care, a court will apply a higher standard because of the dire consequences should Meat's products be contaminated and the specialized knowledge that goes into their production. Of crucial relevance would be how sanitation at the defendant's plant measured up to standards in the industry and whether there were any failures in Meat's hygiene protocol. Practically speaking, Meat will be held to a very high standard given the nature of its products and the tremendous amount of harm those products might cause were something to go wrong in the manufacturing process.

3: Did the Defendant's Careless Act (or Omission) Cause the Plaintiff's Injury?
While the legal test for **causation** is sometimes debated, courts generally ask the following question: Would the harm not have occurred *but for* the defendant's actions?[5]

Reasonable person

The standard used to judge whether a person's conduct in a particular situation is negligent.

Causation

The relationship that exists between the defendant's conduct and the plaintiff's loss or injury.

---

5   Lewis Klar, *Tort Law*, 5th ed (Toronto: Thomson Carswell, 2012) at 448. See, too, *Clements v Clements* 2012 SCC 32.

Whether any failure by Meat to use reasonable care in the production process caused Jennifer and others in the plaintiff class to sicken and even die is a matter to be established through expert evidence. Given that *Listeria* was found in Meat's premises and in some of its products, including the kind consumed by Jennifer, causation appears to be in place.

Resurfice Corp v Hanke, [2007] 1 S.C.R. 333

THE BUSINESS CONTEXT: Every day, people are injured by using potentially dangerous products and then bring lawsuits against the manufacturer to recover compensation. However, if the user's injury was not caused by the manufacturer but by the user's own carelessness, the manufacturer has a complete defence to the claim.

FACTUAL BACKGROUND: The plaintiff, Mr. Hanke, was the operator of an ice-resurfacing machine which he was using to groom the ice in a local arena. Unfortunately, Hanke was badly burned because he mistakenly placed hot water in the gasoline tank portion of the machine rather than in the hot water tank portion, where it belonged. As a result, vapourized gasoline was released into the air, which was then ignited by an overhead heater. This created an explosion and fire resulting in devastating injuries to Hanke. Hanke sued the manufacturer of the machine, Resurfice Corp., among others, for damages on the basis that the gasoline and water tanks were similar in appearance and placed close together on the machine. He argued that this design was negligent because it made it easy for someone to confuse one tank for the other.[6]

THE LEGAL QUESTION: Did the manufacturer cause Hanke's loss?

RESOLUTION: The plaintiff must show that "but for" the defendant's alleged negligent act—here in the design of the machine—the disfiguring

Ralph Hanke since sustaining injuries from the fire and explosion

accident would not have happened. The Supreme Court of Canada restored the trial judge's ruling that the alleged design defects did not cause the accident; Hanke's *own* carelessness caused his injuries. According to the trial judge:

> [44] I agree with the argument of Counsel for Resurfice Corp. [the manufacturer and defendant] that Hanke knew precisely which was the water tank and which was the gasoline tank on the machine that day. His evidence of having "noticed" that the machine did not have a propane tank and that it had a gasoline tank and his evidence of his discussion with Binette [another employee] about looking at the machine and seeing the gasoline tank and asking Binette if the machine had to be filled with gas, lead to the conclusion that he knew the difference between the tanks. He further testified that when he looked at Unit 4059, a similar machine, a photograph of which was Exhibit #21, that "he knew precisely which was the water tank and which was the gasoline

---

6   Note that because the accident occurred when Hanke was at work, he received benefits under provincial workers' compensation legislation (discussed in Chapter 10) and the outcome of this litigation would not affect his entitlement to do so. Rather, this action was brought by the Workers' Compensation Board (WCB) in Hanke's name. The WCB hoped to prove negligence and thereby recover from the defendant the amount of compensation paid to Hanke by showing the defendant was negligent and collecting from that defendant. This is called a subrogated claim, which is discussed in more detail in Chapter 28.

tank." He testified that he was fully familiar with the fact that hot water should not be introduced into the gasoline tank.

[43] In my opinion it is also significant that Hanke was never asked and did not say whether he was confused or distracted, although his answers to other question leave the impression that clearly he was not.

. . .

[45] My conclusion on the facts is that if Mr. Hanke did not put the hose in the gasoline tank, he did see it there. His training and experience was such that he should have known that it was in the wrong place and he carelessly and unthinkingly or absent mindedly, turned hot water into the gasoline tank. . . .

In short, the accident did not happen because the machine had a confusing design. Hanke understood how the machine worked and, tragically, was simply not paying proper attention to what he was doing.

CRITICAL ANALYSIS: Do you agree with the court's analysis that Hanke entirely caused his own loss through carelessness? Do you think that the machine could have been better designed by, for example, making it impossible for the water hose to fit into the gas tank portion? Should the court have required more from the manufacturer so that an operator's momentary inattention could not create such catastrophic consequences?

4: Was the Injury Suffered by the Plaintiff Too Remote?

At this point in the test for negligence, a court asks, "Even if there is an obligation to take reasonable care and it was breached, how far will the legal liability of the defendant stretch?"[7] The idea is that there must be some limit on the defendant's responsibility for the consequences of his negligence.

Jennifer was sickened by listeriosis due to bacterial contamination in the meat she consumed. This injury is not too remote and is clearly a reasonably foreseeable consequence of Meat's negligence.

By way of contrast, consider the following case, where the concept of **remoteness of damage**—that is, the absence of a sufficiently close relationship between the defendant's action and the plaintiff's loss—is illustrated.

Remoteness of damage

The absence of a sufficiently close relationship between the defendant's action and the plaintiff's injury.

CASE

Spagnolo v Margesson's Sports Ltd (1983), 145 DLR (3d) 381 (Ont CA)

THE BUSINESS CONTEXT: A business owner's negligence can have very broad consequences in that not just immediate customers may suffer loss or injury.

FACTUAL BACKGROUND: A customer's car was stolen from a parking lot due to the negligence of the parking lot owner in keeping the keys safely secured. Six days later, the thief was in an accident with the plaintiff while driving the stolen car.

THE LEGAL QUESTION: Is the parking lot owner responsible for the plaintiff's injury, or is the loss too remote?

RESOLUTION: The court held that damage to the plaintiff was not a reasonably foreseeable consequence of the parking lot owner's negligence, particularly given that the accident occurred so long after the theft. The court also noted that the term "reasonably foreseeable" lacks a precise meaning and that it contains "more policy than fact."

CRITICAL ANALYSIS: What if the plaintiff were injured as the thief was fleeing the parking lot in the stolen vehicle? Would this change the outcome?

---

7 Klar, *supra* note 5 at 487.

In assessing Meat's responsibility, a court need only be satisfied that the injury Jennifer suffered was foreseeable. It is not necessary, in addition, to foresee the full extent of the injury of any given type.

The principle that only the type of the injury must be foreseeable also finds expression in the **thin skull rule**. This rule protects the plaintiff who has an inherent weakness or "thin skull" that makes a given injury more serious than one might otherwise reasonably anticipate. The rule states that such a plaintiff is still entitled to recovery for the full extent of the injury. For example, if Jennifer's recovery from listeriosis takes a longer period of time than would normally be anticipated because she has an impaired immune system, her damages will not be reduced for that reason. Though the condition impairing the immune system is reasonably rare, Meat cannot use this fact to escape liability to fully compensate Jennifer.

Thin skull rule

The principle that a defendant is liable for the full extent of a plaintiff's injury even where a prior vulnerability makes the harm more serious than it otherwise might be.

CASE

Mustapha v Culligan of Canada Ltd **2008 SCC 27**

THE BUSINESS CONTEXT: Manufacturers and suppliers who provide a product to the consumer are responsible for the quality of that product. Even with the best quality-control measures in place, a defective product can slip through the system.

FACTUAL BACKGROUND: Mustapha was a customer of Culligan, a manufacturer and supplier of drinking water. Mustapha used Culligan's services because cleanliness and proper sanitation were tremendously important to him. As Mustapha was replacing a large, empty water bottle with a new, unopened one, he noticed that the new bottle contained a dead fly. Mustapha became obsessed with the dead fly and its "revolting implications" for his family's health and well-being. At trial, Justice Brockenshire awarded $80 000 for Mustapha's emotional upset although he found the claim to be "objectively bizarre." He also awarded $237 600 for past and future economic loss. According to the trial judge, it was clearly foreseeable that supplying contaminated water would cause the plaintiff and others like him to suffer nervous shock. The Court of Appeal reversed the decision, and leave to appeal to the Supreme Court was granted.

THE LEGAL QUESTION: Was Mustapha's reaction a reasonably foreseeable consequence?

RESOLUTION: The Supreme Court of Canada agreed that Culligan owed a duty of care to Mustapha to provide clean water and that it breached the standard of care by supplying

Mr. Mustapha, shown above, had his case litigated all the way to the Supreme Court of Canada.

water containing a dead fly. As well, this breach was the factual cause of the serious psychological damages Mustapha suffered, which included a major depressive disorder. The problem with Mustapha's case was that his extreme reaction to a relatively insignificant event was not a reasonably foreseeable consequence of the fly incident. Only if mental injury would occur in a person of ordinary mental fortitude could recovery for such damages flow. Here, the plaintiff could not show that mental injury would occur in the ordinary person faced with a dead fly in an unopened bottle of water. On this basis, the plaintiff's action failed. Note that if mental injury would occur in a person of ordinary mental fortitude, the thin skull rule applies and the defendant must take the plaintiff as it finds him. In such a case, even an extreme reaction would be compensable.

CRITICAL ANALYSIS: Do you agree with the Supreme Court of Canada's resolution of this case? Do you think that Mustapha's action in contract might succeed even though the tort action failed?

Based on analysis in this chapter thus far, Jennifer should be entitled to recover for damages related to consuming Meat's contaminated product. This would include the right to recover loss of income during her convalescence and, if her ability to work in the future is compromised, the amount of lost future income attributable to her reduced ability. These damages are recoverable because Jennifer is entitled, therefore, to be put in the position she would have been in had the tort not occurred.

What tort law traditionally is reluctant to permit is recovery for **pure economic loss**, that is, loss that is only financial and involves no personal injury or property damage to the plaintiff. When a person not in a contractual relationship causes someone else to suffer a financial detriment only, such a loss is generally not recoverable. One explanation is that the rule prevents defendants from being overwhelmed with liability.[8] A related explanation is that to permit recovery of damages in such cases would cause too much litigation in the courts. It is only in a relatively few areas, such as negligent misstatement (discussed later in this chapter), that a plaintiff can recover for pure economic loss.

The law requires the plaintiff to prove *each and every element* in a negligence action. It is not enough to establish some of the elements or even most of them. In short, the plaintiff must show that the defendant owed a duty of care and breached the standard of care associated with that duty. Provided that the breach in question caused the plaintiff's loss and that the loss was not too remote, the plaintiff has won the negligence action.

Pure economic loss

Financial loss that results from a negligent act where there has been no accompanying property or personal injury damage to the person claiming the loss.

Defences to a Negligence Action

Though a court may find the defendant to have been negligent, the plaintiff is not automatically entitled to recover all of her damages. The defendant may raise defences against the plaintiff in order to place at least some of the responsibility for the loss on that party. This section explores two such defences: the defence of contributory negligence and the defence of *volenti non fit injuria*—that the plaintiff has voluntarily agreed to assume the risk in question.

Contributory Negligence

The defence of contributory negligence was introduced in Chapter 10. It refers to unreasonable conduct by the plaintiff that contributed—or partially caused—the injuries that were suffered.[9] This defence recognizes that, in many instances, both the defendant and the plaintiff may have been negligent. If the plaintiff is found to have been part author of her own misfortune, then, as noted in Chapter 10, provincial legislation[10] will come into play. It provides that

---

8   For a general discussion of these points, see Klar, *supra* note 5 at 230 and following.
9   *Ibid* at 531.
10 *Ibid* at 534. Each common law province has contributory negligence legislation, which has replaced the common law.

responsibility for the tortious event must be apportioned between or among the respective parties. Through this mechanism, the plaintiff's damages award is then reduced in proportion to her own negligence.

Kralik v Mount Seymour Resorts 2008 BCCA 97

BUSINESS CONTEXT: When providing services to the public, business owners face liability in negligence if they fail to provide a reasonable standard of customer safety. However, should the customer *also* fail to pay proper attention to his own safety, such failure can provide the foundation for the defence of contributory negligence.

FACTUAL BACKGROUND: Kralik, an experienced skier, was trying to clear some snow and ice from the chair of a chairlift as it moved toward him from the boarding ramp. Too focussed on this task, he failed to seat himself in time. Instead of moving away and waiting for the next chair, Kralik instinctively grabbed onto the chair he had been cleaning and dangled from it as the chair began to ascend. Kralik realized that the longer he hung from the chair, the higher the fall would be. He therefore let go and fell about 3 metres to an embankment below. His right shoulder sustained injury, causing him loss of future earning capacity.

THE LEGAL QUESTION: Was Kralik contributorily negligent for failing to pay attention as the chairlift approached him and grabbing onto it at the last second?

RESOLUTION: The trial judge found the lift operator liable in negligence and the ski resort vicariously liable for its employee failing to notice that there was a problem with how Kralik had loaded. She should have stopped the chair immediately. But beyond this, the court found

Is the law too harsh for deducting from a plaintiff's damages award because he made a mistake?

that Kralik had *not* been contributorily negligent. On appeal, the British Columbia Court of Appeal reversed the finding on contributory negligence for these reasons:

> . . . Mr. Kralik did not only suffer a "momentary lapse" [quoting from the trial judge]. He did not simply stand to the side and let the chair continue on without him. Instead, he grabbed onto the seat in some fashion (not explored in the evidence which I have read), with the inevitable result that he was soon high in the air, being transported up the mountain. With all due deference to the trial judge's findings of fact, I conclude that Mr. Kralik was 50% at fault for failing to take reasonable care for his own safety. Pursuant to s. 1(1) of the *Negligence Act*. . . I would apportion 50% of the responsibility for Mr. Kralik's injuries to himself.

CRITICAL ANALYSIS: Do you agree with the Court of Appeal's decision that Kralik was contributorily negligent?

Voluntary Assumption of Risk

Voluntary assumption of risk

The defence that no liability exists as the plaintiff agreed to accept the risk inherent in the activity.

When the court makes a finding of *volenti non fit injuria* or **voluntary assumption of risk**, it is concluding that the plaintiff consented to accept the risk inherent in the event that gave rise to the loss. *Volenti non fit injuria* is therefore a complete defence to the lawsuit, and the plaintiff will be awarded nothing by a judge even though the defendant had been negligent.

To succeed on this defence, the defendant must show that the plaintiff—knowing of the virtually certain risk of harm—released his right to sue for injuries incurred as a result of any negligence on the defendant's part.[11] In short, both parties must understand that the defendant has assumed no legal responsibility to take care of the plaintiff and that the plaintiff does not expect him to.[12] Since this test is not easy to meet, *volenti non fit injuria* is a very rare defence.

CASE

Crocker v Sundance Northwest Resorts Ltd [1988] 1 SCR 1186

THE BUSINESS CONTEXT: When a business sponsors promotional events, it runs the risk of being held legally responsible for any injuries that might occur.

FACTUAL BACKGROUND: Crocker entered an inner-tube race at an event put on by Sundance, the operators of a ski slope. He decided to do so having seen a video of the event held in the previous year. Like other participants, Crocker was required to sign a waiver—that is, a commitment not to sue the promoters for any loss or injury associated with participating in the event. Crocker signed the waiver without reading it or knowing what it involved.

It was obvious to the manager of the facility that Crocker had been drinking. In fact, on Crocker's second trip down the hill, the manager advised him not to proceed with the race. Crocker did not listen. On his way down the hill, Crocker fell off the tube, broke his neck, and was rendered quadriplegic. Crocker sued.

THE LEGAL QUESTION: Was Sundance negligent? Did Crocker voluntarily assume the risk (i.e., could Sundance rely on the defence of *volenti non fit injuria*)? Was Crocker contributorily negligent?

RESOLUTION: The Supreme Court of Canada ruled that Sundance owed a duty of care to the participants because it had set up an "inherently dangerous competition in order to promote its resort and improve its financial future." It was therefore obligated to take all reasonable care to prevent Crocker—who was clearly drunk—from competing in the event at all. Management's suggestion to Crocker that he not continue with the race was insufficient to meet the standard of care associated with the duty. On the contrary, Sundance allowed and even assisted a visibly intoxicated person to participate in a dangerous event it had organized. Sundance was therefore liable for the resulting damages.

The court rejected Sundance's defence of *volenti non fit injuria*. The court stated that while Crocker's participation in the event could be regarded as an assumption of the *physical* risks involved, even this was a questionable conclusion given that Crocker was inebriated. But, leaving this aside, Crocker had certainly not consented to the *legal* risk. As the court observed, "Sliding down a hill in an oversized inner tube cannot be viewed as constituting per se a waiver of Crocker's legal rights against Sundance." Even though Crocker had signed a waiver, this had no legal effect since he had not read the waiver nor did Sundance have any reasonable grounds for concluding that the signed waiver expressed Crocker's true intention. The defence of *volenti non fit injuria* therefore failed.

The trial judge's finding that Crocker was 25 percent contributorily negligent for his own injuries had not been appealed to the Supreme Court and therefore was not disturbed. Crocker was awarded 75 percent of his damages because his voluntary intoxication had contributed to the accident.[13]

CRITICAL ANALYSIS: Was Crocker treated too harshly by the court in deducting 25 percent from his award for contributory negligence? Was Crocker treated too leniently given that Sundance's defence of *volenti non fit injuria* failed?

---

11 *Dubé v Labar*, [1986] 1 SCR 649 at 658.

12 *Ibid*.

13 In following up on the Crocker case in 2013, Peter Bowal and Daniel Lalonde noted as follows: "Crocker spoke to the *Globe and Mail* after the judgment of the Supreme Court. He sighed, "I put my faith in the system, and the system worked for me. It's been a long time, eight years, three months, and five days but I feel as if 10,000 pounds have been lifted off my shoulders." Crocker was able to leave the care of a nursing home, but he is still restricted by his injuries and must use a wheelchair [footnotes deleted]." See Peter Bowal and Daniel Lalonde, "Whatever happened to. . .Crocker vs Sundance" *Law Now* (30 August 2013), online: Law Now <http://www.lawnow.org/whatever-happened-to-crocker-vs-sundance/>.

Negligent Misstatement (or Negligent Misrepresentation)

Negligent misstatement or negligent misrepresentation

An incorrect statement made carelessly.

When negligence takes the form of words, the tort is known as a **negligent misstatement or negligent misrepresentation**. The plaintiff's loss does not arise due to the defendant's physical actions but due to the defendant's careless oral or written statements. If the plaintiff relied in a reasonable manner on those careless words and suffered damages as a result, those losses are recoverable subject to one large proviso. The plaintiff must first show that the defendant owed a duty of care based on there being a special relationship between the parties.[14] In the box below, the Supreme Court of Canada demonstrates how courts are to analyze the "duty" question in relation to negligent misstatement.

Professional

Someone engaged in an occupation requiring the exercise of special knowledge, education, and skill.

From a business perspective, it is a **professional**—such as an accountant, a lawyer, or an engineer—who is most likely to commit the tort of negligent misstatement by giving bad advice or providing the client with an incompetent report. The professional who gives poor advice to his client not only faces liability for the tort of negligent misstatement but also is in breach of his contract with the client. That is, providing incompetent advice is both a tort and a breach of contract. This is a matter discussed more fully in Chapter 22.[15]

Third party

One who is not a party to an agreement.

When professionals are sued by their clients, they are clearly not faced with an unduly broad scope of liability. If a professional takes someone on as a client and performs her service negligently, a lawsuit is perfectly justifiable. The justification is considerably less strong when the professional gives incompetent advice or provides a negligent report that is relied upon by a **third party** (i.e., someone other than the client). Should that third party have an action in negligence? Keep in mind that in many cases, the professional has had no dealings with that third party and may not even know that third party exists until she is sued. Courts are concerned that the professional could face an unreasonable level of liability. In fact, they have stated that such defendants should not be exposed to liability "in an indeterminate amount for an indeterminate time to an indeterminate class."[16]

Also tied up in the analysis of professional liability is the idea that, generally speaking, professionals cause pure economic loss as opposed to physical loss or injury. When the loss is merely economic—that is, purely monetary—the law is simply less solicitous of the victim. From tort law's perspective, monetary loss is simply not as worthy of compensation as is property damage or personal injury.

For more discussion on professional liability, see Chapter 22.

CASE

Hercules Managements Ltd v Ernst & Young [1997] 2 SCR 165

THE BUSINESS CONTEXT: Accountants are regularly hired by corporations to prepare the audited financial statements that many corporations are required to present to shareholders at their annual general meeting. The audit reports—though prepared for the corporate client—are in fact reviewed by a variety of people from directors and officers, to shareholders, to prospective investors around the world.

---

14 See *Queen v Cognos Inc,* [1993] 1 SCR 87 at 109–110.
15 As Chapter 22 discusses, such conduct can also be a breach of fiduciary duty.
16 *Ultramares Corp v Touche Niven & Co,* (1931), 255 NY 170.

FACTUAL BACKGROUND: Ernst & Young prepared audited financial statements for two companies. These financial statements were the result of incompetent work by the auditors. Shareholders in the two companies claimed that they relied on the financial statements in deciding to invest further in the companies. These shareholders lost hundreds of thousands of dollars when the companies failed to perform.

THE LEGAL QUESTION: Do the auditors owe a duty of care to the shareholders such that they are responsible to the shareholders for negligent misstatement?

RESOLUTION: The court agreed that the defendants owed the shareholders a *prima facie* duty of care because there existed between them a neighbour relationship (or relationship of proximity). The auditors would have realized that the shareholders would look at the audited financial statements and, furthermore, such reliance by the shareholders would be reasonable. However, the court ruled that there were policy reasons that limited or eliminated the *prima facie* duty of care the accountants otherwise owed. While there were no concerns about indeterminate liability in the sense that the defendants had knowledge of the plaintiffs, the concern arose in another context. That is, the accountants prepared the financial statements for the corporate client to be used at the annual general meeting of the shareholders. The financial statements were not prepared for the purpose of helping shareholders decide whether or not to invest further in the companies. As soon as the plaintiffs used the financial statements for other than their intended purpose, they put the accountants at risk of indeterminate liability. On this policy basis, the *prima facie* duty of care owed by the accountants to the shareholders was eliminated; the shareholders' action failed.

CRITICAL ANALYSIS: Do you agree with the court's formulation that the *sole* purpose for which financial statements are produced is for the annual general meeting? Are accountants being too sheltered by the courts? Why did the shareholders simply not sue the accountants for breach of contract?

Negligence and Product Liability

The law imposes a standard of care on manufacturers in relation to the design, manufacture, or sale of their products. This area of law is known generically as **product liability**. The Business Law in Practice scenario under discussion at the beginning of this chapter is a product liability case because Meat breached the standard of care it owed consumers by producing contaminated meat.

Product liability cases often involve contract law as well. Besides being able to sue Meat in negligence, Jennifer has an action for breach of contract against the retailer who provided her with the contaminated product. The retailer is in breach of contract because it supplied Jennifer with a product that was not fit to be sold. Jennifer does not, of course, have a contract action against the manufacturer, since there is no contract between them.

Jennifer's contract action against the retailer will probably be more straightforward than her negligence action against Meat. This is because liability for breaching a contractual term is strict. Since the retailer's promise to supply a non-contaminated product is not qualified in any way, there is no defence for breaching that promise. It is no defence to the contract action for the retailer to prove that it purchased from a reputable supplier, for example, or that there was no way of telling that the product was contaminated. To succeed in negligence against the manufacturer, however, Jennifer has to demonstrate all the elements in the action, as outlined earlier in this chapter.

Product liability

Liability relating to the design, manufacture, or sale of the product.

Why should retailers be responsible for defective products?

Because of the nature of product liability, Jennifer has two defendants she can sue and would be well advised to proceed against both of them. Having two defendants increases the chances that Jennifer will be able to collect at least something on any judgment in her favour. For example, if the retailer is out of business by the time the matter goes to trial, Jennifer will still have the manufacturer left as a source of payment of damages and *vice versa*.

The nature of product liability in foreign jurisdictions is discussed at the end of this chapter. Chapters 23 and 24 offer further discussion of liability relating to the manufacture, distribution, and sale of products.

Negligence and the Service of Alcohol

Commercial establishments serving alcohol owe a duty of care to impaired patrons to assist them or prevent them from being injured.[17] Similarly, these

---

17   See Klar, *supra* note 5 at 200.

establishments can be liable to members of the public who are injured by the conduct of one of their drunken customers,[18] most notably through drunk driving. An important rationale for this duty is that clubs, bars, and taverns benefit economically from serving drinks to their patrons. It stands to reason that such commercial establishments should also have some positive obligation to the inebriated patron and to others put at risk by that patron.[19] This economic relationship between the commercial host and patron provides an important rationale for extending the law of negligence in this way.

CASE

McIntyre v Grigg (2006), 274 DLR (4th) 28 (Ont CA)

BUSINESS CONTEXT: Owners of nightclubs and other drinking establishments must actively manage the risk that a patron will become impaired and then drive a vehicle. Not only might patrons injure themselves or others, but also the owner may be found liable for those injuries and be subject to a large damages claim.

FACTUAL CONTEXT: Andrea McIntyre, a McMaster University student, was walking with several friends, on her way back home from "The Downstairs John," owned and operated by commercial host, McMaster Students Union. As McIntyre was walking along the side of the curb of the sidewalk, she was struck by the defendant's vehicle. The defendant—a Hamilton Tiger-Cats football player named Andrew Grigg—had run a stop sign, and then made a wide right-hand turn while speeding. Next, his vehicle sheared off a lamp post and struck McIntyre, causing severe physical and psychological injury. Just previous to the accident, Grigg had been drinking at The Downstairs John as well as at other venues earlier that evening.

McIntyre sued Grigg as well as the McMaster Students Union.

THE LEGAL QUESTION: Does the McMaster Students Union—a commercial host—have any liability for the injuries suffered by McIntyre?

RESOLUTION: The Court of Appeal quoted the following portion of the trial judge's charge to the jury as properly stating the law regarding commercial host liability:

> At common law commercial vendors of alcohol owe a general duty of care to persons who might reasonably be expected to come into contact with an intoxicated person and to whom the patron may pose some risk. That duty of care arises if there is some foreseeable risk of harm to the patron or to the third party. . . .
>
> Common law and statutory law therefore impose a duty on taverns to its patrons and others to ensure that the tavern does not serve alcohol which would either intoxicate or increase the patron's intoxication. They do not escape liability simply because a patron does not exhibit any visible signs of intoxication if in the circumstances the tavern knew or ought to have known that the patron was becoming intoxicated.

The jury accepted that Grigg was showing signs of intoxication. Even though the majority of witnesses said that Grigg did not appear to be drunk at The Downstairs John, one witness at the accident scene said he did exhibit such signs. As well, Grigg's blood alcohol level two hours after the accident measured nearly three times the legal limit. Expert evidence established that, on this basis alone, he may have been served up to eighteen drinks at The Downstairs John. Accordingly, there was sufficient evidence that Grigg would have been visibly impaired.

(Continued)

---

18 See, for example, the discussion in *Stewart v Pettie*, [1995] 1 SCR 131.
19 See Klar, *supra* note 5 at 200.

CHAPTER 11: THE TORT OF NEGLIGENCE

The Court of Appeal rejected McMaster Students Union's appeal of the jury's findings. In the result, McIntyre received $250 000 for pain and suffering as well as a sizeable amount representing loss of future income. Grigg was held 70 percent liable and the Students Union held 30 percent liable. Grigg was also ordered to pay an additional sum in punitive damages.

CRITICAL ANALYSIS: Do you agree that bars should be held responsible when their patrons cause injury to themselves or others?

The Negligence Standard versus Strict Liability

Strict liability

The principle that liability will be imposed irrespective of proof of negligence.

Strict liability in tort makes the defendant liable for the plaintiff's loss even though the defendant was not negligent and, by definition, had exercised reasonable care.[20] Given that Canadian tort law is founded on a fault-based system, the scope of strict liability is necessarily limited.[21] These exceptions are largely confined to liability for fires, for dangerous animals, and for the escape of dangerous substances.[22]

Another reason strict liability is so unusual is because the law of negligence has expanded to provide a remedy to most victims of accidents who merit compensation.[23]

Though strict liability[24] makes only rare appearances in the law of torts, it would be wrong to conclude that businesses rarely face strict liability. As already noted, there are significant areas where liability is strict, including:

- *liability in contract*. When a business makes a contractual promise that it breaches or fails to perform, that business is liable for breach of contract. The absence of negligence is no defence.

- *vicarious liability*. As already discussed in Chapter 10, vicarious liability is a form of strict liability. An employer is *automatically responsible* for the torts of his employee when, for example, there is a significant connection between what the employer was asking the employee to do and the employee's tort.

A third relevant instance of strict liability is described in the following box.

---

20 *Ibid* at 643.

21 *Ibid*.

22 *Ibid* at 644. This is the *Rylands v Fletcher* tort. The tort is "no fault," and the mere fact that the dangerous substance escapes from one's non-natural use of land is enough to make the defendant tortiously liable, even if the escape was not due to negligence/lack of due care. What constitutes non-natural use is a matter of debate beyond the scope of this text. For discussion, see Klar, *ibid* at 646 and following. Strict liability is further discussed in Chapter 12.

23 Klar, *supra* note 5 at 643–644.

24 Note that strict liability in the context of tort law is different from strict liability in the context of regulatory offences. Governments enact regulatory statutes—creating regulatory offences—in order to protect the public interest. According to the leading case of *R v City of Sault Ste Marie*, [1978] 2 SCR 1299, regulatory statutes such as environmental protection legislation contemplate three classes of offences, one of which is known as a *strict liability offence*. In this context, strict liability does not mean that an offence is created to which there is no defence. For strict liability offences in the regulatory context, a person charged can raise the defence of due diligence. That is, if such a person can show that he took all reasonable care, there will be no liability.

STRICT LIABILITY

Some of Canada's major trading partners, such as members of the European Union (EU) and areas in the United States, use a strict liability rather than a fault-based standard in defective-product liability cases.

For example, all EU member states are subject to a directive requiring that manufacturers be strictly liable for their defective products. The directive provides that a product is defective when it does not provide the safety that a person is entitled to expect, taking into consideration all the circumstances. Relevant considerations include the presentation of the product, expectation of use, and the time the product was put into circulation. The directive also provides for a "state of the art" defence by stating that a product will not be considered defective for the sole reason that a better product is subsequently put on the market.

The effect of a strict liability standard is that manufacturers can be held liable for unsafe products even if they were not negligent in any way and exercised due care. This is markedly different from the result under a fault-based standard. In the latter case, if the manufacturer takes due care at all stages of product production—in designing the product, in selecting a production process, in assembling and testing, and in packaging and labelling—there is no liability regardless of defects. Strict liability, on the other hand, is imposed irrespective of fault.[25]

Critical Analysis: Which approach to liability do you prefer and why?

BUSINESS LAW IN PRACTICE REVISITED

1. What tort may Meat have committed and what do the plaintiffs have to prove in order to establish that tort?

Meat may have committed the tort of negligence. Jennifer must establish that she is owed a duty of care by Meat. This will be straightforward, as manufacturers like Meat owe a duty of care to consumers of their product. That is, Jennifer is clearly Meat's neighbour because it is reasonably foreseeable that a negligent act or omission by Meat in the manufacturing process would cause harm to Jennifer and there is a relationship of sufficient proximity between them. Jennifer is thereby owed a *prima facie* duty of care under Stage 1 as discussed in this chapter. There are no policy considerations under Stage 2 to reduce or eliminate this duty. Next, Jennifer will have to establish that Meat breached the standard of care by failing to have an adequate sanitation and hygiene system such that *Listeria* could not be introduced into the meat via the manufacturing process. In terms of causation, Jennifer must prove that "but for" eating the contaminated meat she would not have become sick. Finally, Jennifer will have to establish that her injury is not too remote. This will also be straightforward, as it is entirely foreseeable that someone who consumes meat contaminated by the bacteria *Listeria monocytogenes* would contract listeriosis.

---

25 EC, Council Directive 85/374/EEC of 25 July 1985 on the approximation of the laws, regulations, and administrative provisions of the Member States concerning liability for defective products, as amended, [1985] OJ. 210/29. For further discussion, see, for example, Helen Delaney & Rene van de Zande, eds. *A Guide to the EU Directive Concerning Liability for Defective Products (Product Liability Directive)* (Gaithersburg, MD: U.S. Department of Commerce, 2001), online: NIST Global Standards Information Europe <http://gsi.nist.gov/global/docs/EUGuide_ProductLiability.pdf>; Europa, "Summaries of EU Legislation: Defective Products: Liability," online: Europa <http://europa.eu/legislation_summaries/consumers/consumer_safety/l32012_en.ht>.

2. What defences does Meat have to this action?

Meat will have difficulty establishing a defence given the facts as recited. It can insist that the plaintiff prove her case, since not everyone who becomes ill after having eaten deli meat has necessarily contracted listeriosis. There could be other reasons why someone has fallen ill, such as viruses. However, if Jennifer's lawyer has done a proper job preparing her case, it may prove difficult to defend.

3. What additional risks does a class action create for Meat?

As noted in Chapter 4, a class action is a lawsuit launched by one or more persons representing a larger group whose members have similar claims against the same defendant. Class actions allow a group of people to bring a claim that someone acting alone might be unable to afford. This means that individuals who otherwise would not have sued can join the class action and receive their fair portion of the damages awarded.

4. How could Meat have better managed its risk of tort liability in this case?

Meat is producing a consumer good that can pose a serious risk to health should the product be contaminated. In the unlikely case that Meat did not have a risk management plan, then devising one according to the principles discussed in Chapter 3 would be very important. Meat almost certainly maintains third-party liability insurance so that, in the event of Jennifer succeeding in her action, Meat can use insurance proceeds to pay out on any damage award. Insurance, which is discussed further in Chapter 28, is a central element in any risk management plan. Meat has already instituted a review process to see why the *Listeria* outbreak occurred. This is an essential step and one which Meat's insurer will insist upon in any event.

There is no doubt that once the contamination problem at Meat's manufacturing plant became known, Meat did an excellent job of managing the risk of future illness and death by initiating a recall and taking immediate steps to determine the cause of the outbreak.[26]

Maple Leaf Foods, which was involved in a situation not unlike that of Meat Ltd., took several steps to continuously improve its operation. These can be seen as forming the basis of its risk management plan going forward. For example, Maple Leaf announced the establishment of a Food Safety Advisory Council. This council, which will guide Maple Leaf, is made up of leading experts in the area of food safety, microbiology, and public health. As well, Maple Leaf created the position of Chief Food Safety Officer, who will establish best practices to enhance food safety. The Maple Leaf plant that was the source of the *Listeria* outbreak has undergone six complete sanitization cycles; the slicing equipment has been torn apart, deep cleaned, tested, and reassembled. More stringent sanitation systems are now in place as well as other operational improvements. For a detailed account, see Maple Leaf's

---

26 Maple Leaf Foods, which was faced with a situation similar to Meat's, has been praised for its response. See Robert Todd, "A 'case study' in effective crisis management" *Law Times* (29 September 2008) at 5 but see Steve Rennie, "More hygiene issues cited at Maple Leaf plant" *Globe and Mail* (9 November 2009) at A10.

website.[27] And beyond this, the class actions against Maple Leaf Foods have been settled.[28]

CHAPTER SUMMARY

Donoghue v Stevenson is the foundation of modern negligence law. Negligence law is an inherently flexible, growing legal area. It seeks to provide a remedy to the plaintiff who has suffered a loss or injury due to the culpable though unintentional conduct of the defendant.

The four elements in a negligence action describe general standards or markers that help a court assess whether the defendant in any given case has been negligent.

One of the most common defences to a negligence claim is that of contributory negligence. The plaintiff's damages award will be reduced in proportion to her own culpability in causing the loss, for example, by failing to wear a seat belt or drinking to the point of impairment.

A less common defence is to allege that the plaintiff voluntarily assumed the risk. This defence is rarely established since the defendant must prove that the plaintiff consented not only to the *physical risk* of harm but also agreed to accept the *legal* risk of not being able to sue the defendant for resulting loss or injury.

Negligent misstatement or negligent misrepresentation holds the defendant responsible for negligence taking written or oral form. Professionals such as accountants and lawyers are most likely to commit this kind of tort. Courts guard against the professional facing liability in "an indeterminate amount for an indeterminate time to an indeterminate class." This sheltering of the professional is also partially justifiable in light of the fact that a professional's negligent misstatement is likely to cause only pure economic loss as opposed to personal injury or property loss. Tort law has been historically less concerned when the plaintiff's loss is purely monetary.

Business is also affected by product liability. Product liability involves both negligence law and the law of contract. The manufacturer of a poorly produced or designed product will face an action in negligence by the disappointed purchaser. The retailer will face a breach of contract action by that same person and—if the retailer was also negligent—an action in negligence as well.

Another area of liability for business relates to the service of alcohol. Commercial servers of alcohol, such as bars, taverns, and restaurants, owe a duty of care to protect against the foreseeable risks of intoxication.

Strict liability is a liability imposed even where the defendant has not been negligent. This is a rare phenomenon in tort law, but there are other areas of law in which strict liability is common. The two most important areas relate to liability for breach of contract and vicarious liability for the torts of one's employees. As well, some of Canada's major trading partners, including the EU and parts of the United States, use strict liability rather than a fault-based standard in defective-product liability cases.

---

27 Maple Leaf Foods, "Food Safety" (undated), online: Maple Leaf Foods <http://www.mapleleaffoods.com/food-safety/food-safety-at-maple-leaf-pledge/>.

28 Maple Leaf's settlement with the plaintiffs "provides that the defendants will pay between $25 and 27 million in full and final settlement of all claims, applicable taxes, class counsel fees and expenses, subrogation claims by provincial health insurers, trustee fees and expenses, arbitration fees and expenses, and claim administration fees and expenses." See International Irradiation Association (iia) news archive "Maple Leaf Foods Reaches a Settlement in Deli Meat Recall" iia (28 May 2009), online: iia <http://iiaglobal.com/index.php?mact=News,cntnt01,detail,0&cntnt01articleid=652&cntnt01origid=15&cntnt01returnid=161>.

CHAPTER STUDY

Key Terms and Concepts

causation (p. 247)

duty of care (p. 245)

negligent misstatement or negligent misrepresentation (p. 254)

neighbour (p. 245)

prima facie (p. 246)

product liability (p. 255)

professional (p. 254)

pure economic loss (p. 251)

reasonable care (p. 244)

reasonable person (p. 247)

remoteness of damage (p. 249)

strict liability (p. 258)

thin skull rule (p. 250)

third party (p. 254)

voluntary assumption of risk (p. 252)

Questions for Review

1. What competing interests must a court balance in deciding a negligence action?

2. What are the four elements in a negligence action?

3. Before *Donoghue v Stevenson*, what defence could most manufacturers of goods raise when faced with a claim for negligence brought by an injured user of those goods?

4. How does the foreseeability test help in defining the neighbour principle in negligence?

5. What is the standard of care in negligence?

6. How is causation usually determined in negligence?

7. Does the normal standard of care vary in any specific circumstances? Explain.

8. Does tort law generally allow recovery for pure economic loss?

9. What does contributory negligence mean and what are the consequences of it being found to exist?

10. What is the consequence of a *volenti non fit injuria* finding?

11. Give an example of when the defence of *volenti non fit injuria* might be applied.

12. What kinds of plaintiffs will be likely to succeed in an action for negligent misstatement against a professional?

13. Why was there no duty of care owed in *Hercules Managements v Ernst & Young?*

14. What area of law other than tort law do product liability actions often involve? Why are actions in that area often more straightforward than in tort law?

15. What is the thin skull rule? Give an example of when it would apply. How does the thin skull rule protect the plaintiff?

16. Is the commercial host liable if one of its patrons is injured because of the patron's own impaired driving? Explain.

17. Why is strict liability rare in Canada's tort regime?

18. Name two areas where strict liability is common.

Questions for Critical Thinking

1. The principles of *volenti non fit injuria* have been restricted to allow the defence to apply only in limited circumstances. Are these circumstances too limited? For example, should the person getting into the car with an impaired driver still be allowed to recover in negligence? Is there not sufficient public knowledge of the dangers of impaired driving for people to understand the risk they assume? What about those who deliberately choose not to wear a seat belt? Why should they potentially recover?

2. From time to time, it has been proposed that the principles of strict liability be applied to product liability in Canada as they are in certain other jurisdictions. What are the pros and cons of applying this concept in Canada? What changes would result for producers of goods and services, as well as for consumers? Are

there inherent risks that might arise for society as a whole if strict liability were imposed in certain industries?

3. Contributory negligence and causation are important doctrines in tort law. How are the two doctrines the same? How are they different?

4. It is relatively new for courts to allow recovery for pure economic loss in negligence, that is, loss unrelated to any physical loss. Some would argue that extending negligence in this regard potentially places an unfair burden on some occupations and service providers. In our society, people should accept that there are some losses for which recovery cannot be obtained. What are the pros and cons of allowing recovery for pure economic loss?

5. The application of the "thin skull rule" often places a considerable burden on a defendant who is found liable in negligence, above and beyond what would normally be "reasonably foreseeable." Is it fair that the negligent party should assume the burden of these extra costs? Does the thin skull rule make sense when considered alongside the rule about remoteness of damage?

6. The court in *Mustapha* had no doubt that the plaintiff suffered extreme mental distress caused by seeing a fly in the sealed bottle of water and that he was not exaggerating his response. As long as the plaintiff is being truthful about his reaction to the defendant's negligence and the court believes him, why should that not be sufficient to permit recovery for emotional upset? Discuss.

Situations for Discussion

1. Mrs. Kauffman was riding up the escalator owned by the Toronto Transit Commission (TTC). The escalator was equipped with a metal-clad handrail instead of the rubber type, which presumably would have been less slippery. Three young men, riding the same escalator just above Kauffman, began pushing each other around. They ultimately fell on Kauffman, knocking her over and severely injuring her. Kauffman sued the TTC for damages, claiming that it had been negligent in installing an untested handrail made of metal which offered less support and that is why she

fell. Will Kauffman succeed in showing that TTC caused her loss?[29]

2. In 2007, hackers attacked Sony Corporation (Sony) causing an outage of its online game service, PlayStation Network and cloud-music service. All told, the attack resulted in up to 100 million accounts being compromised, including the theft of names, passwords, and credit card information. To help alleviate the stress and worry of some of it users, Sony offered free identity theft insurance as well as access to fraud investigators. To date, though, there appears to be no instance of the information stolen from Sony having been sold or resulting in the identity theft of any Sony customer.

   Because of the hacking incident, Sony became the subject of a class action in the United States which alleges, among other matters, that the impugned "breach of security was caused by SONY's negligence in data security, including its failure to maintain a proper firewall and computer security system, failure to properly encrypt data, [and] its unauthorized storage and retention of data...." Furthermore, the statement of claim alleges that Sony was in breach of contract for failing to "properly maintain Plaintiffs'... data and provide uninterrupted PSN [PlayStation Network]."[30]

   Assume for now that the plaintiffs' allegations are true and that, for the purposes of this exercise, Canadian and US laws are largely the same. What will the plaintiffs have to show to succeed in a tort action against Sony? What will the plaintiffs have to show to succeed in a contract action? What are Sony's defences? Assuming that no case of identity theft or other fraud comes to light, do the plaintiffs have any damages? If so, what are these damages?[31]

3. Klutz won a contest sponsored by a radio station, entitling him to play in a twilight golf

---

29 Based on *Kauffman v Toronto Transit Commission* [1960] SCR 251.
30 For the entire statement of claim in this matter, see: <http://www.techfirm.com/storage/JohnsvSony-Complaint-FINAL.pdf>.
31 Note that the class action against Sony has settled. See Jeffrey Roman, "Sony Settles Data Breach Lawsuit" *Data Breach Today* (16 June 2014) online: DBT <http://www.databreachtoday.asia/sony-settles-data-breach-lawsuit-a-6960>.

tournament. He went to the radio station and signed a form releasing the station from any liability connected with the tournament. The event was held at the Dark Side Country Club, beginning at 11 p.m. Klutz attended a pre-tournament instructional meeting and was told that his team was to tee off on the second hole. While the team headed for that spot, Klutz hurried to his car to get his clubs and golf shoes. As he sprinted down the path to the parking lot, he ran into one of a series of black iron posts embedded in the asphalt path at the point where the walkway and parking lot met. Klutz somersaulted several times, ending up on the driveway with banged knees and a badly bruised elbow. He played seven holes of golf, but could not carry on. Prior to the accident, he was a self-employed upholsterer. Following the accident, he was unable to work for three months. After that his production was down 20 percent. His ability to participate in household and leisure activities was also reduced.[32]

Apply the principles of tort law to this situation. Suggest a result. What further information would be useful?

4. Burger Heaven (BH) is a large chain of restaurants specializing in burgers and fries. In response to customer demand, BH added coffee to its menu. The temperature of the coffee and the style of container and lids were part of BH operating standards to be followed by all restaurant operators and staff. BH restaurants provide counter and drive-through service. Sandra bought coffee at the drive-through for herself and her husband, Morley. Sandra passed both cups of coffee to Morley. The car hit a big bump and the coffee spilled in Morley's lap, burning him severely.

What should BH do about this particular incident? Is Morley likely to be successful in any claim for negligence? What defences might BH raise? How can BH manage the risk of a similar incident occurring in the future? Can any preventive steps be taken?

5. Mr. Worton purchased a slide for the family's four-foot-deep aboveground backyard pool from Jacuzzi Canada Inc. A Jacuzzi Canada employee told Mr. Worton that installing this kind of slide with his pool would be "ok" and "not a problem." He was not advised that there was any risk at all in doing so. Worton installed the slide according to the instructions. Unfortunately, Carla, his 15-year-old, was seriously injured when she went down the slide headfirst and as a result is now paralyzed.[33] Carla had been instructed by her parents only to go down the slide feet first, but on this occasion, she failed to follow this rule. Carla's parents have sued Jacuzzi on her behalf. Is there negligence? Did this negligence cause Carla's accident?

6. Ellen attended a skin care clinic to receive laser removal of unwanted hair. The technician performed the entire treatment without first conducting a full patch test and failed to stop the treatment when Ellen complained of pain. As a result, Ellen sustained facial and neck scarring. She was left with permanently lighter skin below the lasered skin and was very concerned that others would think she had leprosy. She was very traumatized and unable to work for at least a month. She also requires ongoing psychological care.[34] What elements must Ellen establish in order to demonstrate a negligence claim? What kind of damages should she seek and on what basis?

7. Big Pizza, a province-wide pizza chain, has a new promotional campaign. The chain guarantees that all pizzas will be delivered within 30 minutes or they will be free. While this promise is readily kept in small cities and towns, it places considerable stress on franchises in large urban areas. Franchisees are required by their franchise agreement to pass on this stress to drivers by fining them half of the cost of any pizza not delivered within the requisite time. To overcome this threat, drivers often decide to drive well above the speed limit. One driver, attempting to meet the deadline, fails to notice another vehicle in its path and collides with it, seriously injuring the passengers in that vehicle.

32 Based, in part, on *Poluk v City of Edmonton* (1996), 191 AR 301 (QB).

33 Based, in part, on *Walford (Litigation guardian of) v Jacuzzi Canada Inc*, 2007 ONCA 729.

34 Based, in part, on *Ayana v Skin Klinic*, (2009) 68 CCLT (3d) 21.

Assuming that the issue of negligence by the driver is clear-cut and that the driver is an employee, can the injured persons claim damages from the franchisee for the actions of the employee? Why or why not? Is there any argument that Big Pizza has itself been negligent? Present arguments for both sides of the case, and determine whether liability will be upheld.[35]

8. The Bridge Engineering Company contracted to build a bridge between a suburb and the downtown of a medium-sized town. For years the two communities were joined by a one-lane bridge, and this new four-lane bridge was a major improvement. Indeed, as a result of the new bridge, a local contractor began building a new housing project of 30 homes. Just before the first home sales were made, a major defect was discovered in the bridge design that meant that the bridge would be unusable for at least two years. Residents would be forced to use a lengthy detour that added approximately 30 minutes to the average drive between the suburb and downtown, where the majority of the residents worked. The market for the new housing project immediately collapsed, and the contractor was unable to sell any houses. The contractor is considering litigation but realizes that he has no claim in contract against the engineering company. Are there any alternatives? Explain.

35 Based on Michael Friscolanti, "Pizza Pizza sued for big money money" Macleans.ca (28 November 2007), online: Macleans <http://www.macleans.ca/canada/national/article.jsp?content=20071128_73882_73882>.

12

© Francis Dean/Dean Pictures/The Image Works

OTHER TORTS

BUSINESS LAW IN PRACTICE

Ron Smithson owns and operates a small manufacturing business in St. John's, Newfoundland and Labrador. The business supplies specially crafted items for gift stores, specialty boutiques, and craft shops. Ron sells mostly through trade shows, although online sales are beginning to account for a sizable part of his business. He also has a small factory outlet. Ron conducts business in a two-storey building that he owns, in a historic part of the city. The basement houses a manufacturing facility consisting of pottery wheels, kilns, and a decorating and glazing studio. The main floor is used for warehousing and storage, packing, and shipping. The second floor, with the exception of a small unit devoted to the factory outlet, is leased to a number of other small businesses.

Ron has had a successful year, although there are two situations that have the potential to jeopardize the bottom line:

- Julie Osbourne, a local resident, suffered serious injuries on Ron's premises. Julie had planned to visit the factory outlet to purchase some gifts for visitors. To access the store, she had to use the elevator. As she travelled between floors, the steel plate covering the indicator lights above the elevator door became unhinged and fell, hitting her on the head, neck, and shoulders. Apparently, the plate fell off because the elevator maintenance company, Elevator XL Services, which had been hired by Ron to maintain all features of the elevator, had run out of plate clips to keep the plate itself in place. It instructed its employee to use a broken clip for the time being rather than leave the steel plate off altogether. Ron knew that a broken clip had been used on the steel plate but had also been assured by the elevator maintenance company that a proper clip would be installed on the very next business day.

- while visiting a trade show on the mainland, Ron saw a replica of his best-selling figurine, "Old Man of the Sea." The replica was dressed in the same fisher garb as Ron's figurine, was decorated with the same colours, and had the same style of packaging and labelling. The only differences were that the replica was made with cheap plastic and that it was named "Man of the Sea." Ron is concerned about the impact that sales of this competing figurine will have on his business.[1]

---

1   Based, in part, on *Sawler v Franklyn Enterprises Ltd* (1992), 117 NSR (2d) 316, 324 APR 316 (TD).

1. What potential legal actions does Julie have against Ron's business?

2. What is the responsibility of Elevator XL Services?

3. Does Ron have any recourse against the manufacturer of the replica figurine?

4. How can Ron manage the risk his business faces of potential tort liabilities?

Introduction

Business activity—whether it involves generating electricity, cutting hair, filing tax returns, or selling automobiles—involves interactions that may ultimately have a negative impact on others and their property. Consider the following examples:

- a customer in a grocery store slips on a lettuce leaf and falls, breaking his ankle.
- a store detective detains a shopper assuming, incorrectly, that the shopper has stolen merchandise.
- a salesperson intentionally overstates an important quality of a product because she wants to close a sale.
- a golf course adversely affects an adjacent landowner because players continually drive balls into her yard.

In each of these examples, the business may have interfered with a legitimate interest of another and could, as a result, be subject to a tort action.

The laws that make a business liable for its tortious conduct also operate to protect that same business when it is the victim of a tort. Consider the following examples:

- a newspaper columnist maligns the environmental record of a business.
- vandals continually spray-paint graffiti on factory walls.
- a competitor entices a skilled employee to break his employment contract and join the competitor's business.
- a new business creates a logo that is remarkably similar to that of an existing business in the same market.

Tort actions relevant to businesses can be conveniently divided between those that arise because a business occupies a property and those that arise because of actual business operations.

Torts and Property Use

Tort actions may arise in relation to property in a number of ways, most commonly when the occupier of the property harms others. An **occupier** is generally defined as someone who has some degree of control over land or buildings on that land.[2] An enterprise conducting business on property is an occupier, whether it is the owner, a tenant, or a temporary provider of a service. Following from this definition, it is entirely possible to have more than one occupier of land or a building.

Occupier

Someone who has some degree of control over land or buildings on that land.

---

2   Lewis Klar, *Tort Law*, 5th ed (Toronto: Thomson Reuters, 2012) at 610 [Klar].

Ron, as owner and user of the building, is an occupier. His tenants on the second floor are occupiers of that space. Elevator XL Services Ltd. was hired to service and maintain the elevator. As such, Elevator XL Services had control of the elevator at a critical time and can also be classified as an occupier, although for a much more fleeting moment. The main tort actions in relation to occupation of property relate to occupiers' liability, nuisance, and trespass.

Occupiers' Liability

Occupiers' liability describes the liability that occupiers have to anyone who enters onto their land or property. This area of the law varies by jurisdiction. For example, jurisdictions such as Newfoundland, Quebec, and Saskatchewan retain the common law while other provinces have occupiers' liability legislation.[3] In New Brunswick, statute has abolished occupiers' liability as a specialized category altogether.[4]

Liability at Common Law

The liability of the occupier for mishaps on property is not determined by the ordinary principles of negligence. Rather, liability is determined by classifying the visitor as a trespasser, licensee, invitee, or contractual entrant. Each class is owed a different standard of care, with the trespasser being owed the lowest standard and the contractual entrant being owed the highest. This area of law is often criticized for the difficult distinctions between the different classes of visitors, the blurring of duties owed between the various classes, and the severity of the result when the visitor is classified as a trespasser.

A **contractual entrant** is someone who has contracted and paid for the right to enter the premises.[5] Visitors to the premises who have bought tickets to see a pottery exhibit would be contractual entrants. The duty owed to this class (in the absence of a contract specifying the duty) is a warranty that "the premises are as safe as reasonable care and skill on the part of anyone can make them."[6]

An **invitee** is someone whose presence on the property is of benefit to the occupier, such as store customers and delivery or service personnel. The occupier owes a slightly lower duty to the invitee than to the contractual entrant. He must warn the invitee of any "unusual danger, [of] which he knows or ought to know."[7] There is no requirement to warn of usual or common danger that "ordinary reasonable persons can be expected to know and appreciate."[8]

Julie is clearly an invitee, and the improperly fastened steel plate would be classified as an "unusual danger." She is therefore entitled to hold the owner and elevator maintenance company liable for injuries suffered as a result of that unusual danger.

A **licensee** is someone who has been permitted by the occupier to enter for the benefit of the licensee.[9] If Ron allowed people accessing an adjacent business to

Contractual entrant

Any person who has paid (contracted) for the right to enter the premises.

Invitee

Any person who comes onto the property to provide the occupier with a benefit.

Licensee

Any person whose presence is not a benefit to the occupier but to which the occupier has no objection.

---

3   *Occupiers' Liability* Act, RSA 2000, c O-4; *Occupiers' Liability Act*, RSBC 1996, c 337; *Occupiers' Liability Act*, CCSM c O8 ; *Occupiers' Liability Act*, RSO 1990, c O-2; *Occupiers' Liability Act*, SNS 1996, c 27; and *Occupiers' Liability Act*, RSPEI 1988, c O-2. See also Klar, *ibid* at 610.

4   See Law *Reform Act*, RSNB 2011, c 184, s 2.

5   Klar, *supra* note 2 at 616.

6   *Ibid* at 624, footnotes omitted.

7   *Indermaur v Dames* (1866), LR 1 CP 274 at 288; aff'd (1867), LR CP 314 (Ex Ch) cited by Klar, *ibid* at 622.

8   *McErlean v Sarel* (1987), 61 OR (2d) 396 at 418, 22 OAC 186 (CA), leave to appeal to SCC refused (1988), 63 OR (2d) x (note) (SCC) cited by Klar, *ibid* at 623.

9   Klar, *supra* note 2 at 614.

take a shortcut through his building, those users would be licensees. A licensee might also include guests invited to someone's property for a social occasion.

The general rule is that occupiers are responsible to licensees for any unusual danger of which they are aware or that they have reason to know about. The latter part of the rule is a recent addition and tends to blur the distinction between the duty owed an invitee and the duty owed a licensee.[10] Since there is no strong rationale for distinguishing between a licensee and an invitee to begin with, this blurring is entirely justifiable.

A **trespasser** is someone who "goes on the land without invitation of any sort and whose presence is either unknown to the occupier, or if known, is practically objected to."[11] A burglar clearly fits the definition of a trespasser.

An occupier still owes some responsibility to a trespasser. In particular, the occupier will be liable for any act done with the deliberate intention of doing harm to the trespasser, or an act done with reckless disregard for the presence of the trespasser.[12] Though the trespasser is not owed a common law duty of care as described in *Donoghue v Stevenson*,[13] the occupier does owe him "at least the duty of acting with common humanity towards him."[14]

Though a trespasser is owed a very low duty, courts have often mitigated the harshness of this result, particularly when the trespasser is a child. For example, courts have at times reclassified the trespasser as a licensee, interpreted the duty owed the trespasser very generously, and even brought the children's claims under the ordinary law of negligence.[15]

Trespasser

Any person who is not invited onto the property and whose presence is either unknown to the occupier or is objected to by the occupier.

PART THREE

Liability under Occupiers' Liability Legislation

With the goal of simplifying the common law, provinces such as Alberta, British Columbia, Manitoba, Nova Scotia, Ontario, and Prince Edward Island have enacted occupiers' liability legislation.[16] Although there are differences in the legislation from one jurisdiction to the next, there is also considerable common ground because of a united legislative purpose. As the Supreme Court of Canada confirmed in the context of Ontario's *Occupiers' Liability Act*, the legislative purpose was "to replace the somewhat obtuse common law of occupiers' liability by a generalized duty of care based on the 'neighbour' principle set down in *Donoghue v Stevenson*."[17]

Indeed, legislation across the country provides for a high duty of care—equivalent to the negligence standard—to be owed to entrants who are on the property with express or implied permission (at common law, contractual entrants, invitees, and licensees). Responsibility to trespassers differs among the various statutes. In general, however, an occupier must not create deliberate harm or danger,[18] and, in Alberta, the responsibilities increase where the trespassers are children.[19]

---

10 *Mitchell v Canadian National Railway Co*, [1975] 1 SCR 592, [1974] SCJ No 67.

11 *Robert Addie & Sons v Dumbreck*, [1929] AC 358 at 371 (HL), cited by Klar, *supra* note 2 at 591.

12 *Robert Addie*, *ibid* at 365.

13 [1932] AC 562 (HL).

14 *British Railways Board v Herrington*, [1972] AC 877 (HL), quoted with approval by the Supreme Court of Canada in *Veinot v Kerr-Addison Mines Ltd*, [1975] 2 SCR 311, 51 DLR (3d) 533.

15 Klar, *supra* note 2 at 618–621.

16 *Supra* note 3.

17 *Waldick v Malcolm*, [1991] 2 SCR 456 at 466, 83 DLR (4th) 144 [*Waldick*] quoting with approval the appellate judge from (1989), 70 OR (2d) 717 (CA). Note however that in Alberta, for example, separate categories for trespassers and child trespassers are retained. As well, in some jurisdictions, snowmobilers are treated according to specialized rules. See Klar, *supra* note 2 at 606.

18 Klar, *ibid* at 639.

19 Klar, *ibid* at 638.

If Ron's business were located in Ontario, where occupiers' liability legislation is in place, the court would likely still find both the elevator company and Ron liable to Julie. This is because under section 3 of the Act, an occupier owes a statutory duty of care as "in all the circumstances of the case is reasonable to see that persons entering on the premises, and the property brought on the premises by those persons are reasonably safe while on the premises." Specifically, a court would find that the elevator company ought to have foreseen that harm could occur as a result of a defective clip. Likewise, since Ron was aware of the use of the defective clip and was prepared to allow the elevator to remain in service, he too is liable.

In the context of Ron's business, the outcomes using either statutory or common law applications are, for all intents and purposes, the same. Nonetheless, it remains important to apply the correct principles to the specific provincial context, as responsibilities can vary at times.

BUSINESS APPLICATION OF THE LAW

SLIP AND FALL

Businesses face liability for the tort of negligence as well as under occupiers' liability legislation (as applicable) for what is known by lawyers as a "slip and fall." *In Swagar v Loblaws Inc,*[20] for example, the plaintiff was awarded damages for injuries he sustained when he slipped on a broken egg in Superstore. According to the court:

> Superstore employees did not adequately adhere to the Defendants' floor maintenance system or its customer incident procedures. I therefore find that although the Defendants had a reasonably adequate floor maintenance system in effect, the Defendants failed to discharge the onus on them to prove that there was proper compliance with those policies by its Superstore employees on the day of the Accident.[21]

On this basis, the store had failed to take reasonable care for the safety of the plaintiff, contrary to Alberta's *Occupiers' Liability Act*, RSA 2000 c O-4. The plaintiff was awarded special damages of $2571.74 and general damages (including past loss of housekeeping capacity due to his injury) of $45 000.

More dramatically, the Ontario Superior Court recently awarded 26-year-old Michelle Botosh the sum of $330 000 (including $65 000

What main defences does a retailer have should a customer sue for a slip and fall?

for general pain and suffering as well as over $150 000 for loss of future income) for damages arising from her fall on an Ottawa sidewalk which had been under construction.[22] The court found liability on the City of Ottawa as well as the general contractor and paving subcontractor. In short, there had been a failure to erect a properly constructed ramp over the curb or place sufficient warning to pedestrians of the construction hazard.

Critical Analysis: What risk management strategies can a business put in place to reduce the chances of a slip and fall?

---

20 2014 ABQB 58
21 *Ibid* at para 84.
22 *Botosh v City (Ottawa),* 2013 ONSC 5418

Henrik Sorensen/The Image Bank/Getty Images

The Tort of Nuisance

The tort of **nuisance**[23] addresses conflicts between neighbours stemming from land use. It concerns intentional or unintentional actions taken on one neighbour's land that cause harm of some sort on another's, as in these examples:

- noise from a steel fabricator's 800-ton press seriously interrupts the neighbours' sleep.
- ashes and unpleasant odours[24] escaping from a rendering company are carried onto neighbouring properties because of dated technology.

The focus of nuisance is on one's right to enjoy the benefits of land/property uninterrupted by the actions of neighbours. The general test is whether the impugned activity has resulted in "an unreasonable and substantial interference with the use and enjoyment of land."[25] For example, Ron may vent his kilns and the decorating and glazing operation in the direction of the window his neighbour must routinely leave open in the summer for cool air. Conversely, the restaurant/bar in the building next door may begin hiring bands that play so loudly that Ron's tenants are threatening to leave.

In striking a balance between the respective parties, courts have developed the following guidelines:

- interference must be substantial and unreasonable.
- nuisance typically does not arise where the interference is only temporary. For example, construction and demolition may be unpleasant, but are likely to be considered temporary and will not lead to a remedy in nuisance.

Nuisance

Any activity on an occupier's property that unreasonably and substantially interferes with the neighbour's rights to enjoyment of the neighbour's own property.

How can locating houses and factories adjacent to each other lead to claims in nuisance?

Dick Hemingway

---

23 As Klar, *supra* note 2 at 747, indicates, there are two distinct causes of actions in nuisance: public nuisance and private nuisance. Since public nuisance plays only a "peripheral role in contemporary law," this text will focus only on private nuisance.

24 Note that Manitoba has legislation limiting liability for nuisance in the context of a business causing or creating an odour. See *Nuisance Act* CCSM c N120.

25 Klar, *supra* note 2 at 759.

CHAPTER 12: OTHER TORTS

- not all interests are protected by the tort of nuisance. For example, the right to sunlight is an unprotected interest as far as the law of nuisance is concerned.
- in nuisance actions, courts will consider tradeoffs in interest. For example, when the noise in question is reasonable and for the public good, the action in nuisance will fail.[26]

Some of these principles are illustrated in the following case.

TMS Lighting Ltd v KJS Transport Inc 2014 ONCA 1, varying 2012 ONSC 5907

BUSINESS CONTEXT: Businesses operating in close proximity can come into conflict when the activity of one business interferes with that of the other. Litigation can result.

FACTUAL CONTEXT: TMS Lighting Ltd (TMS) manufactured high-end commercial lighting fixtures in a prestigious industrial/commercial area of Brampton, Ontario. TMS purchased this location because it required clean premises for its lighting fixture manufacturing facility. KJS Transport Inc. (KJS), which operated a long-haul trucking service, moved in next door some time later. Unfortunately for TMS, KJS's operations interfered with its manufacturing operations. KJS did not pave its parking lot. As a result, over the next four years, dust particles raised by KJS trucks driving on its unpaved parking lot caused damage as dust blew into TMS's factory and settled on the lighting products manufactured on site. Even if TMS closed all its windows and doors, factory fans would draw in dust. And the heat inside the factory created intolerable working conditions. Production would then have to slow down or halt altogether. When KJS failed to remedy the dust problem, the plaintiff sued.

LEGAL ISSUE: Has KJS committed the tort of nuisance?

LEGAL RESULT: The Court of Appeal and trial judge found for the plaintiff, relying on the Supreme Court of Canada's recent case on nuisance[27] to reach that conclusion. The Supreme Court directs that nuisance involves an interference with the plaintiff's use or enjoyment of land that is both (1) substantial and (2) unreasonable. As the Supreme Court explained:

> A substantial interference with property is one that is non-trivial. Where this threshold is met, the inquiry proceeds to the reasonableness analysis, which is concerned with whether the non-trivial interference was also unreasonable in all of the circumstances.[28]

Unreasonableness in turn is to be assessed by, in the Supreme Court of Canada's words, "balancing the gravity of the harm [caused by the defendant] against the utility of the defendant's conduct in all of the circumstances."[29] In assessing the gravity of harm caused by the defendant, courts are to consider such factors as "[1] the severity of the interference, [2] the character of the neighbourhood, [3] the sensitivity of the plaintiff to the harm caused, and [4] the frequency and duration of the interference...."[30]

The Court of Appeal quoted with approval the trial judge's findings that "the frequency, duration, degree and impact of the dust generated by the KJS trucks, among other factors, caused a continuing and substantial interference with TMS's manufacturing operations."[31] Beyond this, the Court of Appeal agreed that the interference was unreasonable given that the dust problems began in 2007 and were not resolved until 2011 when KJS finally paved its parking lot. In particular, and quoting from the trial judge, the Court of Appeal rejected TMS's

---

26 *Mandrake Management Consultants Ltd v Toronto Transit Commission,* [1993] OJ No 995, 62 OAC 202.
27 *Antrim Truck Centre Ltd v Ontario (Transportation),* 2013 SCC 13
28 *Ibid* at para 19, quoted in *TMS Lighting* at para 14.
29 *Ibid* at para 26, quoted in *TMS Lighting* at para 15.
30 *Ibid* at paras 26 and 53–54, quoted in *TMS Lighting* at para 15.
31 *TMS Lighting* at para 16.

argument that the plaintiff's manufacturing operations made it uniquely sensitive to dust and therefore not able to establish nuisance:

> [W]hile TMS's manufacturing process was sensitive to dust, its sensitivity was not unique in the area. Its use of its property was consistent with the use that its neighbours made of their properties, including retail warehouses, small manufacturing concerns, and professional offices. TMS's sensitivity to dust is not what made KJS's failure to pave its [parking] lot for four years unreasonable, although it contributed to the extent of damages TMS suffered because of it.[32]

This conclusion, combined with other factors, including that KJS's business was not of special utility to the community, led to a finding of nuisance.

Though the Court of Appeal agreed with the trial judge on most matters, it did reverse on *how* the lower court assessed TMS's damages for loss of productivity associated with having to divert company resources to deal the nuisance, however. The Court of Appeal ruled that the judge's methodology in awarding $266 500.00 lacked a proper evidentiary foundation and therefore ordered a new hearing on this quantification issue.

CRITICAL ANALYSIS: Could TMS and KJS have come to some kind of compromise on the nuisance issue instead of litigating?

Trespass

The tort of **trespass to land** protects a person's possession of land from "wrongful interference."[33]

Trespass arises in several ways:

- a person comes onto the property without the occupier's express or implied permission.
- a person comes onto the property with the occupier's express or implied consent but is subsequently asked to leave.[34] Any person who refuses to leave becomes a trespasser.
- a person leaves an object on the property without the occupier's express or implied permission.

The tort of trespass is important for resolving boundary/title disputes and, more generally, for protecting property rights. It also protects privacy rights and the right to "peaceful use of land."[35] For these kinds of reasons, trespass is actionable without proof of harm or damage. In the exceptional case where the occupier suffers monetary damages due to another's trespass (as in the case below), those damages are recoverable. More commonly or in addition to damages, the plaintiff will seek an injunction requiring the trespasser to stop trespassing. Provincial legislation in several jurisdictions also provides for fines against the trespasser.[36]

Trespass to land

Wrongful interference with someone's possession of land.

---

32 *TMS Lighting* at para 23.
33 *Supra* note 2 at 110.
34 It should be noted that there are statutory restrictions on a businessperson's common law right to do business with whom she or he sees fit. Alberta human rights legislation (the *Alberta Human Rights Act*, RSA 2000, c A-25.5), for example, prohibits discrimination by those who offer goods or services that are customarily available to the public. This means that if a businessperson refused to serve a customer because of that customer's ethnicity or gender, for example, and that customer refused to leave, a trespass has occurred. However, the businessperson would also be subject to a penalty for violating human rights legislation.
35 *Supra* note 2 at 110.
36 Several jurisdictions have enacted legislation that permits trespassers to be fined. See, for example, *Trespass to Premises Act*, RSA 2000, c T-7 and *Petty Trespass Act*, RSA 2000, c P-11, *Trespass Act*, RSBC 1996, c 462; *Petty Trespass Act*, RSNL 1990, c P-11, *Trespass Act*, SNB 2012, c 117, *Petty Trespass Act*, CCSM c P-50; *Trespass to Property Act*, RSO 1990, c T.21. Note too that the Ontario legislation, for example, also provides for damages to be awarded against the trespasser.

TMS Lighting Ltd v KJS Transport Inc 2014 ONCA 1, varying 2012 ONSC 5907 (continued from above)

BUSINESS CONTEXT: See the case box just above.

FACTUAL CONTEXT: TMS's legal complaint against KJS was not just in nuisance, described above. Beyond this, some of the very large trucks owned by KJS (the eighteen wheelers) would frequently pull onto TMS's driveway because there was an insufficient turning radius on KJS premises. To prevent the trespass from continuing, TMS first installed 6-inch-high concrete curb stones along the edge of its factory driveway but KJS trucks simply drove over those stones, ultimately destroying them. In response, TMS installed 3-foot-high concrete blocks which KJS trucks continued to strike and often ended up pushing them right onto TMS's driveway. This blocked TMS's driveway, requiring TMS to send employees out with forklifts to reposition the blocks on a regular basis.

LEGAL ISSUE: Has KJS committed the tort of trespass?

LEGAL RESULT: The Court of Appeal agreed with the trial judge who stated as follows:

"I find in the present case that the trespass by KJS's trucks over TMS's driveway is a substantial interference with TMS's rights and that KJS was or should have been aware, when it bought the KJS property, that it would not provide a sufficient turning radius for its trucks without their trespassing on TMS's driveway."[37] The Court of Appeal also agreed with much of what the trial judge ordered as a remedy, including an injunction to prohibit future trespass by KJS and compensation for the destroyed barriers.

The Court of Appeal set aside the trial judge's award of $23 400.00, however, for loss of productivity related to costs TMS sustained in having to regularly reposition the barrier stones that KJS trucks knocked over. A new trial was ordered on the issue of how to assess lost productivity damages because, as with the nuisance matter discussed in the previous box, the trial judge's method lacked an evidential foundation.

CRITICAL ANALYSIS: KJS began trespassing on TMS's property in 2007 yet it was not until 2012 that TMS's matter finally went to trial and it was able to secure an injunction. Do you think the civil justice system served TMS well? Why or why not?

ENVIRONMENTAL PERSPECTIVE

TORT ACTIONS RELATING TO THE ENVIRONMENT

At common law, there are four main torts that may provide remedies for environmental damage: (1) the tort of negligence; (2) the tort of trespass; (3) actions based on *Rylands v Fletcher;*[38] and (4) the tort of nuisance. These avenues of redress are all somewhat hit and miss given their highly specific requirements.

To successfully sue in negligence, the plaintiff must establish all the elements of a tort action (discussed in Chapter 11), including that the environmental damage was caused by the defendant's *carelessness*. To succeed in trespass, the plaintiff must show direct intrusion of pollutants generated by the defendant and which came onto the plaintiff's land without permission or authorization.[39] The tort in *Rylands v Fletcher* does not require the plaintiff to show that the defendant was careless but rather that something from the defendant's land (such as water or gas) escaped onto the plaintiff's land due to the defendant's dangerous and non-natural use of his land. Much less drastically, the tort

---

37   *TMS Lighting Ltd v KJS Transport Inc* 2012 ONSC 5907 at para 270.
38   [1868] UKHL 1, (1868) LR 3 HL.
39   *Smith v Inco Ltd,* 2010 ONSC 3790 at para 37, [2010] OJ No 2864, rev'd on other grounds 2011 ONCA 628, [2011] OJ No 4386. For discussion of *Smith,* see Chapter 4.

of nuisance requires proof that the defendant's pollutants amounted to an unreasonable and substantial interference with the plaintiff's rights to enjoyment of his or her own property. The plaintiff in all these kinds of actions would seek damages for associated losses and, in the right circumstances, an injunction to prevent future occurrences.

In response to the limitations of an exclusively private law response to environmental degradation as well as to facilitate tradeoffs in land use, governments began to enact environmental legislation of an increasingly sophisticated and complex nature. Such legislation seeks to balance economic development with a degree of "acceptable" environmental damage. In addition, municipal and land-use planning laws have put further constraints on the kind of activity that can occur on the land affected. (For discussion of environmental legislation in Canada, see Chapter 2.)

Though legislation has therefore displaced some of the importance of common law actions from an environmental perspective, nuisance and other tort actions can be nonetheless regarded as Canada's original environmental law. Until the advent of legislation, they were the only way of controlling adverse neighbouring land use.

Michael Mihin/Shutterstock

In what ways could storing chemical waste in oil drums generate torts in relation to adjoining landowners?

Critical Analysis: What are the advantages of regulation of the environment via environmental protection legislation as opposed to by private action?

Sources: Klar, *supra* note 2; Chris Watson, "Using Nuisance and Other Common Law Torts to Protect Water, Land, and Air," (Vancouver: Pacific Business & Law Institute, 2007); interview of Professor Elaine Hughes, Faculty of Law, University of Alberta (2002).

Torts from Business Operations

Business operations involve a broad range of activities from which tort actions can arise. A useful way of categorizing these torts is to consider separately torts involving customers or clients and those more likely to involve competitors.

Torts Involving Customers

Chapter 11 considered the most important tort arising in this context: negligence. Product liability, motor vehicle accidents, alcohol-related liability, and negligent misrepresentations are all examples of negligence affecting the business/consumer relationship.

In this section additional torts beyond negligence will be considered.

Assault and Battery

The torts of assault and battery are not common in a business or professional context, although they may occur. For example, security personnel may commit the torts of assault and battery when seeking to apprehend a suspected shoplifter or eject a patron. An **assault** is the threat of imminent physical harm by disturbing someone's sense of security. **Battery** (introduced in Chapter 10) is the

Assault

Threat of imminent physical harm by disturbing someone's sense of security.

Battery

Intentional infliction of harmful or offensive physical contact.

intentional infliction of harmful or offensive physical contact. The contact need not cause actual harm.[40] Where the torts of assault or battery are proven, the most common remedy is damages.

Note that sections 494 and 25 of Canada's *Criminal Code* (RSC 1985, c C-46) can sometimes provide a defence to these kind of torts. For discussion, see the next section below.

False Imprisonment

False imprisonment

Unlawful detention, physical restraint, or coercion by psychological means.

False imprisonment occurs most often in retail selling. It arises where any person detains another without lawful justification through physical restraint or coercion by psychological means.

False imprisonment occurs when the victim is prevented from going where he has a lawful right to be.[41] The tort includes physically restraining that person or coercing him to stay by psychological means.

The tort of false imprisonment presents retailers in particular with a significant challenge. To defend against the tort of false imprisonment, the retailer and/or its employees must show legal authority to detain under section 494 of Canada's *Criminal Code*, which provides as follows:

> 494(1) Anyone may arrest without warrant
>
> (a) a person whom he finds committing an indictable offence; or
>
> (b) a person who, on reasonable grounds he believes
>
> (i) has committed a criminal offence, and
>
> (ii) is escaping from and freshly pursued by persons who have lawful authority to arrest that person.

Legal authority

The authority by law to detain under section 494 of the *Criminal Code*.

This provision is called the defence of **legal authority** (or citizen's arrest).

A suspicion or mistaken belief by the person claiming legal authority that he has seen someone commit a crime is not sufficient under section 494(1)(a). The suspect must have actually committed the crime. Furthermore, when store personnel detain a customer in reliance on section 494, the *Criminal Code* requires them to "forthwith deliver the person to a police officer." This means that they must immediately call the police. Beyond this, the store owner or his employees can only use as much force as is necessary given the circumstances under s 25 of the *Criminal Code*. Otherwise, they face liability in tort for assault and battery as well as liability under the *Criminal Code*. *Criminal Code* liability is discussed in the box below.

CASE

R v Chen, 2010 ONCJ 641, [2010] OJ No 5741

BUSINESS CONTEXT: The retail industry loses a considerable amount of inventory to shoplifters every year. In its latest report, the Retail Council of Canada (in 2012) estimated that "shrink rates" in Canada (i.e., retail theft

rates) translated to approximately $4 billion in annual losses to retailers. Though the problem of inventory shrinkage is therefore rampant, store owners and employees who encounter shoplifters must be careful not to violate the *Criminal Code* or commit the torts of false imprisonment, assault, and battery (discussed in the previous section of this chapter.)

---

40 Klar, *supra* note 2 at 60.
41 *Ibid* at 60.

FACTS: David Chen, owner of Lucky Moose Food Mart in Toronto, and some of his employees were charged with assault and forcible confinement (under the *Criminal Code*) after they chased down a shoplifter, tied him up, and held him in a delivery van to await the arrival of the police. The shoplifter, convicted thief Anthony Bennett, had arrived at Chen's store earlier that same day. Surveillance cameras showed him loading up his bicycle with product and then leaving without paying. As reported in the press, Bennett testified during Chen's trial that he had stolen plants from Chen's store and decided to return to the store one hour later to steal more product from Chen. This same media account notes that, during that return trip to the store, Chen asked Bennett to pay for the plants he had previously taken. Bennett refused, cursed Chen with a racist epithet, and then ran away. It was at this point that Chen and his employees gave chase, eventually confining Bennett to a van.

According to Crown prosecutor Eugene McDermott, in a statement to the media:

> Of course shopkeepers are entitled to protect their property. Of course they are entitled to arrest people in the terms of Article 494 [the justification or citizen's arrest provisions of the *Criminal Code*]. But that's not what happened in this case. He [Chen] seized a person off the streets, tied him up, and threw him in the back of a van. Once again, nobody calls the police. There are a number of points that beggar belief.

By way of contrast, Chen's lawyer argued that tying up the shoplifter, Bennett, and holding him in the van was similar to department store personnel bringing a shoplifter to a back room to wait for the police.

LEGAL QUESTION: Are Chen and his employees guilty of forcible confinement and assault?

RESOLUTION: The court concluded that Chen was entitled to make a citizen's arrest under s 494 because he had found Bennett committing a theft on the video tape. Section 494 of the *Criminal Code* states: "Anyone may arrest without warrant: A person whom he finds committing an indictable offense." That Chen

Then Prime Minister Harper visited Mr. Chen at his store several months after Chen's acquittal.

purported to arrest Bennett one hour later—when Bennett brazenly returned to steal more product from the Lucky Moose—was perfectly fine, said the court, because he regarded the original theft and Bennett's subsequent return as "one transaction."

An important related issue was whether Chen had brought himself within section 25 of the *Criminal Code* which provides that, in making a citizen's arrest, one is only entitled to use "much force as is necessary" for that purpose. According to Chen's evidence, he had to tie up Bennett because Bennett was kicking and punching. He did not want to let Bennett go, but instead wanted to get back to his store so he could call the police. Bennett gave an entirely different account of events, suggesting, in the court's words, that "he stood by meekly as they [Chen and his employees] laid a beating on him." Based on this and other incongruities, the court expressed concern about the credibility of the evidence offered by Mr. Bennett, Mr. Chen, and his employees.

The court ultimately entered a verdict of not guilty against the accuseds because, according to the judge:

> It is impossible for me to say that I am satisfied on the material evidence before me that I know what happened that day. It follows therefore that the only conclusion that I can come to is that I have a reasonable doubt. All such doubts must always be resolved in the favour of the defence.

(Continued)

In the meantime, Chen has advised the media that he will no longer attempt a citizen's arrest: "I [will] just take the picture and call the police," he said.

CRITICAL ANALYSIS: Do *you* think the *Criminal Code* provides enough protection to a business owner trying to deal with a shoplifter? Note that the government of Canada recently enacted an amendment to the citizen's arrest provisions under 494(2) of the *Criminal Code* that states: "The owner or a person in lawful possession of property… may arrest a person without a warrant if they find them committing a criminal offence on or in relation to that property and (a) they make the arrest at that time or (b) they make the arrest **within a reasonable time after the offence** is committed and they believe on reasonable grounds that it is not feasible in the circumstances for a peace officer to make the arrest" [emphasis added]. Is this amendment to the *Criminal Code* necessary?

Sources: Retail Council of Canada, *Canadian Retail Security Survey* (2012) at 6, online: RCC <http://www.google.ca/url?sa=t&rct=j&q=&esrc=s&source=web&cd=3&ved=0CC0QFjAC&url=http%3A%2F%2Fwww.pwc.com%2Fen_CA%2Fca%2Fretail-consumer%2Fpublications%2Fpwc-security-survey-2012-10-29-en.pdf&ei=R_K1U92DDIuGqgaR94KABQ&usg=AFQjCNF1s3oJJL6BwePVzY4nVLhVAGAbeA&bvm=bv.70138588,d.b2k>; Peter Kuitenbrouwer, "Grocers to the defence" *National Post* (26 October 2010) A3 and Peter Kuitenbrouwer, "Steven Harper Pays a Visit to Lucky Moose, David Chen" *National Post* (17 February 2011), online: *National Post* <http://news.nationalpost.com/2011/02/17/stephen-harper-pays-a-visit-to-david-chen/>.

Deceit

Deceit

A false representation intentionally or recklessly made by one person to another that causes damage.

The tort of **deceit** arises out of misrepresentations, causing loss, that are made either fraudulently or with reckless disregard for their truth. When deceit arises in a contractual context, one of the remedies available is release from the contract (see Chapter 8) in addition to any other damages in tort that the plaintiff can establish. Though the tort of deceit is not confined to the contractual area, this is where it is most commonly found from a business perspective.

Business-to-Business Torts

Passing Off

Passing off

Presenting another's goods or services as one's own.

The tort of **passing off** occurs when one person represents her goods or services as being those of another. While it may be common to think of the tort in terms of the "dirty tricks" some businesses might adopt to compete unfairly with others, the tort can also be committed inadvertently or innocently.

The tort of passing off arises, for example, when a business name is used that is so similar to an existing business name that the public is misled into thinking that the businesses are somehow related. It also may occur where a competing company markets a product that is similar in presentation or overall look to a product already established on the market.

CASE

Ciba-Geigy Canada Ltd v Apotex Inc, [1992] 3 SCR 120, [1992] SCJ No 83

BUSINESS CONTEXT: Manufacturers of a product generally become concerned if a competitor starts to copy the look or "getup" of their product. This is because consumers will assume that the goods of the competitor are actually those of the original manufacturer.

FACTS: The plaintiff, Ciba-Geigy Canada Ltd., manufactured and sold the drug metoprolol tartrate in Canada. The defendants later began to manufacture and sell the same drug in Canada. The parties' products were officially

---

designated as "interchangeable," meaning that the pharmacist could, in filling a prescription, give the defendant's product in place of the plaintiff's product provided the prescription did not contain a "no substitution" notation.

The plaintiff brought an action in passing off against the defendants (Apotex and Novopharm) on the basis that the defendants were copying the plaintiff's "getup" in relation to the size, shape, and colour of the pills. The plaintiff claimed that this was creating confusion that the Apotex/Novopharm product was actually a Ciba-Geigy product and sued for passing off.

THE LEGAL QUESTION: What must the plaintiff prove in order to succeed in its action for passing off? More specifically, the issue in this aspect of the litigation was as follows: in seeking to prove that there is confusion caused by the defendants, is the plaintiff limited to showing confusion in the mind of professionals (such as doctors and pharmacists) or can it also rely on confusion in the mind of the ultimate consumer (i.e., the patient)?

RESOLUTION: The Supreme Court of Canada confirmed "that competing laboratories must avoid manufacturing and marketing drugs with such a similar getup that it sows confusion in the customer's mind." The court also confirmed that there are three steps to proving the tort of passing off:

1. the existence of goodwill[42] (e.g., in this case, the plaintiff must show that there is goodwill in respect of the "look" or distinctiveness of the product).[43]

2. deception of the public due to a misrepresentation by the defendant (the misrepresentation may be intentional but it also includes negligent or careless misrepresentation).

3. actual or potential damage to the plaintiff.

Under step two, the plaintiff must show that the competing product is likely to create a risk of confusion in the public mind. On this latter point, the Supreme Court was clear that the plaintiff is not limited to showing confusion in the mind of professionals. Confusion in the mind of the patient who uses the product may also be included. The trial judge's ruling on a point of law was ordered to be adjusted accordingly.

CRITICAL ANALYSIS: Do you think it is right that a manufacturer should receive legal protection for the features of its product, including colour?

Based on the Supreme Court of Canada's analysis above, Ron will need to establish the following in order to prove passing off:

1. *goodwill or a reputation is attached to his product*. Ron's "Old Man of the Sea" product already has a well-established and valuable reputation among the relevant buying public. In other words, he holds goodwill in the product, and that goodwill, or ability to attract buyers, flows either from the look of the product or from its name, or from both.

2. *a misrepresentation—express or implied—by the maker of the cheap replica has led or is likely to lead members of the public into believing that it is Ron's product or a product authorized by Ron*. Whether the competitor actually intended to confuse the public does not matter. Given the similarity in appearance and name of the two figurines, the competitor will make many of its sales by falsely associating itself with the established reputation of Ron's "Old Man of the Sea" product.

---

42 Goodwill refers to the reputation of the business and its expectation of patronage in the future.
43 This means that the product has a "secondary meaning" in the mind of the public.

Ron could prove his point by commissioning a survey of the relevant sector of the buying public.

3. *he has or will likely suffer damages*. Ron must show that he has lost sales, or is likely to lose sales, because of the replica product.

While the award of damages is one remedy for a passing-off action, businesses claiming they are being harmed in this way will often seek an injunction forbidding the defendant from continuing the deceptive copying. In the case of *Walt Disney Productions v Triple Five Corp*,[44] for example, Walt Disney Productions secured a permanent injunction prohibiting the use of the name Fantasyland at West Edmonton Mall's amusement park.[45]

The *Trademarks Act*[46] contains a statutory form of action that bears a strong resemblance to the tort of passing off. Such legislation will be considered more thoroughly in Chapter 18.

Interference with Contractual Relations

The tort of **interference with contractual relations** is known by a variety of names, including interference with contract, inducement of breach of contract, and procuring a breach of contract.[47] It has its origins in the relationship of master and servant. The common law made it actionable if one master attempted to "poach" the servant of another. In legal terms, the "poacher" was seen as enticing the servant to break his existing contract of employment, which, in turn, caused economic harm to the master. Over time, this tort extended beyond master–servant relations to any form of contractual relationship.

The tort prohibits a variety of conduct, including conduct whereby the defendant directly induces another to breach her contract with the plaintiff.

In Ron's business, the tort of interference with contractual relations could be important in at least two different contexts:

- Ron employs a skilled potter who makes the "Old Man of the Sea" product. The potter has a three-year employment contract. A competitor approaches the potter in the second year of the contract and convinces the potter to work for him with promises of higher wages and better conditions. The competitor's conduct is tortious because he knew about the contract and acted with the objective of convincing the potter to join him. Since this could happen only if the potter were to breach his contract with Ron, the tort has been made out.

- Ron's largest and most lucrative supply contract is with one of the leading tourism organizations in Nova Scotia. The owner of the competing business making "Man of the Sea" products approaches the tourism organization and suggests that if it breaks the contract with Ron and buys from her, she can offer them a much better deal.

In both cases, then, Ron could likely make out the tort of interference with contractual relations. While he will sue for damages, he may also seek an injunction to prevent a breach of contract occurring if he finds out in time. A court would never order the potter to work for Ron—courts will not award specific

---

44 *Walt Disney Productions v Triple Five Corp* (1994), 17 Alta LR (3d) 225, 149 AR 112 (CA).
45 *Ibid*.
46 RSC 1985, c T-13, s 7, as amended.
47 P Burns, "Tort Injury to Economic Interests: Some Facets of Legal Response" (1980) 58 Can Bar Rev 103 cited by Klar, *supra* note 2 at 708, his note 80.

performance with contracts of personal service—but it can order damages against the potter for breach of contract and damages and/or an injunction against the competitor for the tort of interference with contractual relations.

An example of a successful tort action is *Ernst & Young v Stuart*.[48] A partner left the accounting firm of Ernst & Young to join the firm of Arthur Andersen. In so doing, the partner violated a term of the partnership agreement requiring one year's notice of intention to retire from the partnership. Ernst & Young sued both the partner and the new firm, the latter for interfering with contractual relations. Both actions were successful.

Defamation

The tort of **defamation** seeks to "protect the reputation of individuals against unfounded and unjustified attacks."[49] Though all jurisdictions in Canada have legislation modifying the common law of defamation to some extent, the fundamentals of the common law action remain.[50]

Common terms for defamation are *slander* (typically for the oral form) and *libel* (usually the print form). These terms are not always consistently applied but regardless, both slander and libel can simply be called defamation.[51] The key ingredients to the tort, as recently confirmed by the Supreme Court of Canada, are as follows:

- the defendant's words were defamatory in that they would "tend to lower the plaintiff's reputation in the eyes of a reasonable person."
- the statement did in fact refer to the plaintiff.
- the words were communicated to at least one other person beyond the plaintiff.[52]

The plaintiff will then succeed if the defendant is unable to establish a defence to the action. For example, if the defendant can show that the impugned statement is substantially true, he has a complete defence of **justification**.[53]

From a business perspective, a potential defamation scenario occurs when an employer provides a reference for an ex-employee. If the letter contains a defamatory statement that is true, the employer may have the defence of justification described above. Other defences in this scenario include **qualified privilege**. That is, if the employer's statement is relevant, made without malice, and communicated only to a party who has a legitimate interest in receiving it, the defence is established.

Another defence is **fair comment**. This defence permits a person to offer commentary on "matters of public interest" despite the commentary being defamatory.[54] The defence of fair comment requires the defendant to show that the comment (a) concerned a matter of public interest, (b) was factually based, and (c) expressed a view that could honestly be held by anyone.[55] The defence will then succeed unless the plaintiff can show the defendant was motivated by express malice.[56] In *Sara's Pyrohy Hut v Brooker*,[57] for example, a broadcast journalist raised

Defamation

The public utterance of a false statement of fact or opinion that harms another's reputation.

Justification

A defence to defamation based on the defamatory statement being substantially true.

Qualified privilege

A defence to defamation based on the defamatory statement being relevant, without malice, and communicated only to a party who has a legitimate interest in receiving it.

Fair comment

A defence to defamation that is established when the plaintiff cannot show malice and the defendant can show that the comment concerned a matter of public interest, was factually based, and expressed a view that could honestly be held by anyone.

48 (1997) 144 DLR (4th) 328 (BCCA).
49 *Supra* note 2 at 781.
50 *Ibid* at 782.
51 The distinction between libel and slander has been abolished by statute in a number of provinces.
52 *Grant v Torstar Corp*, 2009 SCC 61 at para 28, [2009] 3 SCR 640 [*Grant*].
53 *Ibid* at para 32
54 Klar, *supra* note 2 at 824 and *Grant* supra note 52 at para 31.
55 Klar, *supra* note 2 at 825.
56 *Ibid*.
57 *Sara's Pyrohy Hut v Brooker* (1993), 141 AR 42, 8 Alta LR (3d) 113 (CA).

fair comment as a defence to a restaurant review containing defamatory content. The court agreed that the defence had been made out, noting that "opinions, even if adverse, may be expressed so long as the facts are not distorted or invented. Here... the review was an expression of opinion without malice, even though some of [the] opinions were unfavourable."[58]

Responsible communication on matters of public interest is a defence recently recognized by the Supreme Court of Canada. It will apply to members of the traditional media where (1) the publication is on a matter of "public interest" and (2) the publisher was diligent in trying to verify the allegation.[59] The defence can also presumably be invoked by bloggers, Twitterers, and others who publish on the Web[60] because the Supreme Court agreed that the defence should be available to anyone "who publishes material of public interest in any medium."[61]

The Supreme Court of Canada offered an extensive list of factors which help determine whether the defence is available, including whether the publication sought the plaintiff's reaction or input, the steps taken by the publisher verify the story, and the importance of the subject matter from a public perspective.

If the plaintiff in a defamation action can prove actual monetary loss as a result of the defendant's defamation, this loss is recoverable. The law recognizes, however, that much of the damage suffered is intangible. Therefore, the court is permitted to assess damages from an alternative perspective. This includes considering the seriousness of the defamation, how widely the defamation was published, the malice of the defendant, and the extent of the damages that have been caused.[62] Where the defendant's conduct has been particularly reprehensible and oppressive, a court is entitled to award punitive damages, as the box below illustrates.

Absolute privilege is another defence to defamation which applies in the very limited context of parliamentary or judicial proceedings.[63] The notion is that freedom of expression is so vital in such venues that no successful defamation action can be brought.[64]

Responsible communication on matters of public interest

Defence that applies where some facts are incorrectly reported but (1) the publication is on a matter of "public interest" and (2) the publisher was diligent in trying to verify the allegation.

Absolute privilege

A defence to defamation in relation to parliamentary or judicial proceedings.

TECHNOLOGY AND THE LAW

E-TORTS: DEFAMATION ON THE INTERNET

A growing objective for business is to guard against defamation via electronic media. The danger of emails, for example, is that once they are sent they cannot be retrieved, yet they can be instantaneously transmitted to an enormous audience. There is likely no email user who has not hit the "Send" key and then realized too late he was transmitting to unintended recipients.

Since the legal process allows for the discovery or tracing of electronic words to their author, electronic defamation can most certainly be established even long after a defamatory message has apparently been deleted.

Defamation can also occur on websites. In *Mainstream Canada v Staniford*,[65] for example, the British Columbia Court of Appeal awarded judgment to Mainstream Canada (a Norwegian owned company) in its defamation action against

---

58 *Ibid.*
59 *Grant, supra* note 52 at para 126.
60 Jeffrey Vicq, "New defamation defences benefit the Twitiverse," *Lawyers Weekly* (12 February 2010)(QL).
61 *Grant, supra* note 52 at para 96.
62 Klar, *supra* note 2 at 835.
63 *Ibid* at 804.
64 *Ibid.*
65 2013 BCCA 341

Don Staniford. Mainstream Canada's BC fish farming operation of 27 salmon farm sites along the coasts of Vancouver Island became the subject of intense critique by Staniford including on his website called Global Alliance Against Industrial Aquaculture ("GAAIA") and in a press release posted there. The Court of Appeal noted that the press release was titled "Salmon Farming Kills—Global Health Warning Issued on Farmed Salmon," and stated as follows:

> The newly-formed Global Alliance Against Industrial Aquaculture (GAAIA) this week launched a smoking hot international campaign against Big Aquaculture. 'Salmon Farming Kills' employs similar graphic imagery to the 'Smoking Kills' campaigns against Big Tobacco and warns of the dangers of salmon farming... [underlining indicates hyperlinks on website].

The Court of Appeal continued its description:

> Following that introduction were mock cigarette packages, each with the words "Norwegian Owned" and bearing Norway's coat of arms. The packages included words such as "Salmon Farming is Poison," "Salmon Farming is Toxic," "Salmon Farming Kills," and "Salmon Farming Seriously Damages Health."[66]

The Court of Appeal agreed with the trial judge that the press release was defamatory because it fit the three traditional steps: (1) the words used would "tend to lower Mainstream's reputation in the eyes of a reasonable person" because it suggested Mainstream's business kills people and makes them sick, for example; (2) the words referred to Mainstream; and (3) the words were published.[67]

However, the Court of Appeal disagreed with the trial judge's conclusion that Staniford could use the defence of fair comment. Relying on *Torstar*, discussed above, the court found that there was inadequate linkage between his defamatory comment and the factual material it was purporting to rely on. The Court of Appeal held that the necessary linkage can be established if the defamatory material sets out the factual

Don Staniford and media lawyer David F. Sutherland

material or refers to the factual material by a clear reference or because the factual material is notorious or widely known.[68] In this way, people could decide for themselves as to the merit of someone's comment. Since no such linkages existed on the facts under consideration, Staniford had no defence against the defamation action.

The Court of Appeal ordered Staniford to pay $75 000 in damages to Mainstream including $50 000 in punitive damages because Staniford's unremitting conduct was judged as malicious and highhanded.[69] Relying on the trial judge's assessment, the Court of Appeal stated: "For example, the trial judge said Mr. Staniford was 'akin to a zealot' and '[v]irtually anything that conflicts with his view and vision is wrong, bad, disgraceful, and worse'" (para. 186); "Mr. Staniford seems incapable of conceding he might be wrong on some things" (para. 187); and "he cruelly and publicly mocks people who have a different point of view" (para. 188).[70] The Court of Appeal also issued a permanent injunction restraining Staniford from publishing similar words or images in the future.

Staniford pledged to appeal to the Supreme Court of Canada, saying to the media: "This is a

---

66 *Ibid* at para 6.
67 *Ibid* at para 10.
68 *Ibid* at para 48.
69 *Ibid* at para 58.
70 *Ibid*.

kick in the teeth for me personally but also to all activists and campaigners on not just environmental issues but social-justice issues." Note, however, that Staniford's appeal for leave to the Supreme Court of Canada was dismissed in 2014.[71]

According to a media report, Staniford believes that he has complied with the B.C. Court of Appeal's injunction by taking down his websites and stopping his blog. He has since moved to Scotland where he intends to continue his fight against fish farming.

Note that the Supreme Court of Canada has held,[72] in a separate case, that merely providing a hyperlink to a site which contains defamatory material is not actionable. While someone who repeats defamatory words first uttered by someone else is liable for defamation because the second speaker has "published" the words of the first, the Supreme Court concluded that

supplying hyperlinks does not amount to publication. As the court noted:

> Only when a hyperlinker presents content from the hyperlinked material in a way that actually repeats the defamatory content, should that content be considered to be "published" by the hyperlinker. Such an approach promotes expression and respects the realities of the Internet, while creating little or no limitations to a plaintiff's ability to vindicate his or her reputation.[73]

Critical Analysis: How can a business protect its reputation from attack on the Internet?

Sources: Keven Drews "Fish-farm firm awarded $75 000 in defamation ruling" *Globe and Mail* (22 July 2013), online: *Globe and Mail* <http://www.theglobeandmail.com/news/british-columbia/activist-must-pay-fish-farm-75000-bc-court-rules/article13348016/>; *CBC News*, "B.C. fish-farm foe takes fight against industry to Scotland: Don Staniford now leads an organization known as Protect Wild Scotland" *CBC News* (24 December 2013), online: CBC <http://www.cbc.ca/news/canada/british-columbia/b-c-fish-farm-foe-takes-fight-against-industry-to-scotland-1.2475380>.

Injurious Falsehood or Product Defamation

Injurious or malicious falsehood

The utterance of a false statement about another's goods or services that is harmful to the reputation of those goods or services.

Injurious or malicious falsehood concerns false statements made not about a person but about the goods or services provided by that person. Sometimes the distinction between injurious falsehood and defamation is subtle; for example, if the statement is made that a particular company routinely provides shoddy maintenance, is this a negative reflection on the quality of the people doing the work or on the company's services? In such a situation, the complainant would sue for both defamation and injurious falsehood.

Injurious falsehood requires the plaintiff to establish that the statement about the goods or services was false and was published (or uttered) with malice or improper motive. It is not necessary to prove that the defendant intended to injure the plaintiff. A reckless disregard for the truth or falsity of the statement is sufficient.

BUSINESS APPLICATION OF THE LAW

PROTECTION OF PRIVACY

The common law protects privacy interests in a variety of ways. The tort of defamation protects reputation. The torts of trespass and nuisance protect the right to enjoy one's property.

The torts of assault, battery, and false imprisonment protect the person's right to dignity.[74]

Beyond this, the Ontario Court of Appeal has recognized a new tort which permits a person to sue for invasion of privacy. In *Jones v Tsige*,[75] the

---

71 [2013] SCCA No. 372.
72 *Crookes v Newton*, 2011 SCC 47, [2011] SCJ No 47
73 *Ibid* at para 42.
74 For more analysis, see Klar, *supra* note 2 at 86 and following.

appellate court ruled that when the defendant electronically accessed the plaintiff's personal banking records (on at least 174 occasions), she had also committed a tort. This new tort helps to recognize that technological change, in the judge's words, "poses a novel threat to a right of privacy that has been protected for hundreds of years by the common law under various guises and that, since 1982 and the *Charter*, has been recognized as a right that is integral to our social and political order."[76] Most importantly, such a tort responds to "facts that cry out for a remedy" given that the defendant's actions were "deliberate, prolonged and shocking."[77]

To succeed in establishing this new tort—also called the **intrusion upon seclusion** tort—the plaintiff must prove as follows: (1) that the defendant's conduct was intentional; (2) that the defendant invaded the plaintiff's private affairs without lawful justification; and (3) that a reasonable person would regard such conduct as "highly offensive causing distress, humiliation or anguish."[78] More specifically, victims will have a legal remedy when someone wrongfully accesses their "financial or health records, sexual practices and orientation, employment, diary or private correspondence."[79] In *Tsige*, the plaintiff was awarded $10 000 in damages,[80] with the court suggesting a ceiling in this kind of case of $20 000.[81]

Note that more recently, an Ontario judge certified a class action against the defendants—the Bank of Nova Scotia and Richard Wilson—based, in part, on breach of privacy through the intrusion upon seclusion tort. In this case, a mortgage administrator with the bank, one Mr. Wilson, allegedly provided to his girlfriend the confidential information of bank clients. It is also alleged that the girlfriend went on to pass this sensitive data to third parties who used it for fraudulent purposes. In fact, many bank clients became victims of identity theft and fraud, adversely affecting their credit ratings, though the bank has already compensated all affected customers for financial loss.

The court concluded that the bank may well have vicarious liability for Mr. Wilson's 'intrusion upon seclusion' tort. In the court's words, the bank had granted Wilson "complete power in relation to the victim's (customers) confidential information, because of his unsupervised access to their confidential information. Bank customers are entirely vulnerable to an employee releasing their confidential information. Finally, there is a significant connection between the risk created by the employer in this situation and the wrongful conduct of the employee."[82] Because it has been certified, the action is now eligible to proceed to trial for a full hearing.

Government has also sought to protect privacy through legislation that deals with the collection, use, and disclosure of personal information by organizations in the course of commercial activities.[83] For example, in *Chitrakar v Bell TV* 2013 FC 1103 (discussed in Chapter 1) the court ordered Bell Canada under federal privacy legislation to pay Mr. Chitrakar damages for failing to secure his permission to do a credit check.

In addition, certain provincial governments have passed legislation that creates the tort of breach of privacy.[84] British Columbia's *Privacy Act*,[85] for example, states:

1. (1) It is a tort, actionable without proof of damage, for a person, willfully and without a claim of right, to violate the privacy of another.

---

75 2012 ONCA 32.
76 *Ibid* at para 68.
77 *Ibid* at para 69.
78 *Ibid* at para 71.
79 *Ibid* at para 73.
80 *Ibid* at para 92.
81 *Ibid* at 87. Note that the common law 'intrusion upon seclusion' tort has not been recognized in all provinces. For example, in British Columbia, *Demcak v Vo* 2013 BCSC 899 directs that invasion of privacy allegations be pursued under the *Privacy Act* of British Columbia rather than as a common law action.
82 See *Evans v Bank of Nova Scotia* 2014 ONSC 2135 at para 22, leave to appeal refused 2014 ONSC 7259.
83 For discussion of the *Personal Information Protection and Electronic Documents Act*, 2000 SC 2000, c 5 ("PIPEDA"), see Chapters 1, 8, 12, and 20.

Intrusion upon seclusion

Intentional, offensive invasion of another's personal affairs without lawful justification.

CHAPTER 12: OTHER TORTS

(2) The nature and degree of privacy to which a person is entitled in a situation or in relation to a matter is that which is reasonable in the circumstances, giving due regard to the lawful interests of others.

(3) In determining whether the act or conduct of a person is a violation of another's privacy, regard must be given to the nature, incidence, and occasion of the act or conduct and to any domestic or other relationship between the parties.

(4) Without limiting subsections (1) to (3), privacy may be violated by eavesdropping or surveillance, whether or not accomplished by trespass.

In *Hollinsworth v BCTV*,[86] the plaintiff successfully relied on this statute to bring his action against Look International Enterprises for releasing to BCTV a videotape showing the plaintiff undergoing an operation to have a hairpiece surgically attached to his head. Since Look International Enterprises had done so without the plaintiff's knowledge and consent, this amounted to a willful invasion of privacy, a clear violation of the statute. In response, the court awarded the plaintiff $15 000 in damages. Likewise, when a landlord secretly set up a video camera which captured on film everyone who entered the plaintiff's apartment, the court found that the *Privacy Act* had been violated and awarded $3 500 to the plaintiff. See *Heckert v 5470 Investments Ltd*.[87]

Critical Analysis: Does the tort of intrusion upon seclusion improve the law? Do you think that the $20 000 ceiling on damage awards set by the court in *Tsige* is too low?

See Figure 12.1 for a summary of the torts discussed in this chapter.

Managing the Risk of Diverse Commercial Torts

Each of the torts discussed in this chapter exposes a business to liability. A risk management analysis should address the fundamental problems that may arise, always taking into account that business activities are usually engaged in by employees in the course of employment. As discussed in Chapter 10, an employer is responsible, under the doctrine of vicarious liability, for the torts of its employees.

An occupier's liability risk management plan would include the following questions:

- are there dangers on the property? Are adequate warnings and protections given to visitors?
- are there known trespassers, in particular children, who come onto the property?
- what could be done to eliminate or reduce the risk flowing from the dangers?
- has the occupier complied with all legislative obligations? Examples include provincial legislation concerning workers' health and safety, as well as municipal bylaws providing for snow and ice removal.
- is adequate insurance in place?

---

84 See, for example, *Privacy Act*, RSBC 1996, c 373; *Privacy Act*, RSS 1978, c P-24; *Privacy Act*, CCSM c P-125; and *Privacy Act* RSNL 1990, c P-22. See too Quebec's *Charter of Human Rights and Freedoms*, RSQ c C-12, s 5, which provides that "[e]very person has a right to respect for his private life." See also Klar, *supra* note 2 at 87 and following.
85 *Privacy Act*, RSBC 1996, c 373.
86 113 BCAC 304, [1998] BCJ No 2451.
87 2008 BCSC 1298, [2008] BCJ No 1854.

FIGURE 12.1 Summary of Chapter 12 Business Torts

I. Torts and Property

Occupiers' Liability: liability that occupiers have to those who enter onto their land or property.

Nuisance: liability for interference with someone's use or enjoyment of land that is both substantial and unreasonable.

Tort of *Rylands v Fletcher*: liability because something from the defendant's land escaped onto the plaintiff's land due to the defendant's dangerous and non-natural use of her land.

Trespass: liability for wrongful interference with someone's possession of land.

II. Torts from Business Operations

Torts Involving Customers:

Assault: liability for threatening imminent physical harm.

Battery: liability for intentional infliction of harmful or offensive physical contact.

False Imprisonment: liability for unlawful detention or physical restraint or coercion by psychological means.

Deceit: liability for a false representation intentionally or recklessly made by one person to another that causes damage.

Intrusion Upon Seclusion: intentional, offensive invasion of another's personal affairs without lawful justification.

Business-to-Business Torts

Passing Off: liability for presenting another's goods or services as one's own.

Interference with Contractual Relations: liability for inciting someone to break his or her contractual obligation.

Defamation: liability for a publicly made, false statement of fact or opinion that harms another's reputation.

Injurious Falsehood: liability for a false statement about another's goods or services that is harmful to the reputation of those goods or services.

Although the classification of entrants under the common law of occupiers' liability may be a useful exercise after an incident occurs (it helps determine liability), from a risk management perspective the process is not particularly helpful since the business that occupies property cannot easily predict what class of entrant will be injured on its property. Maintaining safe premises as a preventive measure is much better than having to debate, after the fact, what class of entrant the injured plaintiff is and what standard is owed.

For each additional tort discussed in this chapter, a similar list of questions could be generated. For example, if the business designs and creates consumer goods:

- do the staff understand that they cannot innovate by copying others?
- is a program in place to review new product ideas, including all aspects of design, to ensure there is no passing off?
- is a climate in place that allows a manager to step in and say, "This cannot be done because I believe we have crossed the line"?

CHAPTER 12: OTHER TORTS

Tort law evolves to reflect changing social values. What once might have been acceptable behaviour may no longer be considered appropriate. This can be seen, for example, in the changing approach to the environmental effects of commercial activities. When a business is assessing its tort exposure, it cannot assume that existing legal rules will apply in perpetuity. Also, it must consider how it can influence public opinion and social values, as those will determine the bounds of future tort liability.

BUSINESS LAW IN PRACTICE REVISITED

1. What potential legal actions does Julie have against Ron's business?

Ron is an occupier of the building. As such, he is responsible to different classes of people who come onto his property both lawfully and unlawfully. The extent of the responsibility varies depending on why the person is on the premises and whether the premises are in a common law or statutory jurisdiction.

In Newfoundland and Labrador, common law principles apply. Julie is clearly an invitee and, as such, Ron owes a duty to warn of "any unusual danger [of] which he knows or ought to know." In this case, it appears he was aware of the inadequate, temporary repair job on the elevator, and therefore had the requisite knowledge.

If these events occurred in a jurisdiction where statute law has replaced the common law of occupier's liability, the responsibility to Julie, a person on the property legitimately, would be very similar to that of the tort of negligence. In all likelihood Ron would still be liable.

2. What is the responsibility of Elevator XL Services?

Elevator XL Services is an occupier, since it had control over the elevator in order to conduct the repairs. This was also the time when the harm occurred. Following the same analysis as used in Question 1 above, Elevator XL Services will be liable to Julie under both common and statute law. Julie was on the property lawfully and, at common law, was an invitee.

3. Does Ron have any recourse against the manufacturer of the replica figurine?

Ron can take action based on the tort of passing off. He can claim that the actions of the competitor meet the conditions of the tort of passing off, and as such he will either seek an injunction to stop any further action by the competitor, or damages, or both. He will need to prove that his "Old Man of the Sea" figurine existed prior to the "Man of the Sea" product, that it had an established reputation that was of value, that the products's names and appearances are similar enough to result in confusion in the minds of the potential purchasers, and that the confusion has resulted or will result in loss of sales or harm to Ron's business. It is sufficient that the defendant's conduct compromises Ron's control over his own business reputation.

4. How can Ron manage the risk his business faces of potential tort liabilities?

Ron, as owner/occupier of the premises, should do a safety audit of all parts of the building to ensure that neither his tenants nor his visitors (lawful or otherwise) could be harmed by any hazards. Ron should consider all aspects of his business operations, including the building itself, obvious hazards such as the kiln, maintenance of elevators, clearing of sidewalks, hiring and training of all employees, and insurance coverage.

In terms of Ron's products, Ron should

- monitor the activity of competitors and potential competitors to ensure that there is no inappropriate copying of his designs.
- ensure that the glazes and materials he uses are lead-free and otherwise harmless.
- hire staff who know how to treat customers well and are trained as to their obligations should they have to handle shoplifters.

CHAPTER SUMMARY

While negligence is the most common tort a business will encounter, various other commercially relevant torts merit analysis. These torts can be categorized and assessed according to whether they would arise because the business is an occupier of property or because it provides a product or service. Furthermore, torts that could be committed against a competitor can be grouped separately from those more likely to involve a consumer. Though these distinctions are not definitive, they provide a useful way of organizing the variety of torts that affect the commercial world.

As an occupier, a business must be sure to keep its property safe so that people coming on-site are not injured, otherwise it faces occupiers' liability according to a regime that classifies the entrant in question under common law or by statute. To avoid committing the tort of nuisance, a business must not unreasonably and substantially interfere with the right of its neighbours to enjoy their property. The law governing trespass gives occupiers a right to exert control over who comes onto their premises, subject to human rights codes.

Torts arising from business operations in relation to customers are false imprisonment, assault and battery, deceit, and intrusion on seclusion. Through these torts, the law seeks to ensure people's right to move about as they please, to have their bodily integrity respected, not to be misled about the quality of a product or service, and to be free from offensive invasion of their personal affairs.

Torts more likely to be committed against a competitor include passing off, interference with contractual relations, defamation, and injurious falsehood or product defamation. These torts endeavour to protect a business's property and its own reputation.

Given the diverse and wide-ranging nature of a business's potential liability in tort, preventing torts from ever occurring should be one of management's top priorities.

CHAPTER STUDY

Key Terms and Concepts

absolute privilege (p. 282)

assault (p. 275)

battery (p. 275)

contractual entrant (p. 268)

deceit (p. 278)

defamation (p. 281)

fair comment (p. 281)

Questions for Review

1. How does the law define the occupier of a property?

2. Who is an occupier?

3. What are the four different classes of visitors in the law of occupiers' liability?

4. What is the standard of care owed to each of the four classes of visitors?

5. What is the major change made by legislation in many provinces of Canada to the common law of occupiers' liability?

6. What is nuisance in tort law?

7. The courts have developed pragmatic rules for resolving inherent conflicts that arise in applying the tort of nuisance. Give two examples of these rules.

8. Under what conditions can trespass arise?

9. What are the limitations to the ability of a store detective to detain a customer who is suspected of shoplifting?

10. Describe how a false imprisonment claim might arise, other than by a person being physically restrained.

11. How can a business manage the risk of retail theft and fraud?

12. Identify what must be established to prove deceit.

13. What is "passing off," and what practices was this tort created to prevent?

14. Describe a situation that might amount to the tort of interference with contractual relations.

15. What is defamation, and what are the defences to this tort?

16. When is a court entitled to award punitive damages for the tort of defamation?

17. What is injurious falsehood?

18. What is the tort of intrusion upon seclusion?

Questions for Critical Thinking

1. One of the controversial aspects of occupiers' liability and its more recent statutory form arises out of the rights afforded trespassers. One possible change to the law would be to eliminate all rights. What would be the consequences of this approach? Are there some trespassers that you would feel uncomfortable leaving without protection?

2. What can businesses do to manage the risk of slip-and-fall incidents?

3. The tort of false imprisonment places serious limitations on any action the retailer can take to detain suspected shoplifters. What are the pros and cons of these limitations? Are they fair? What are the countervailing interests at stake? How can retailers reduce the risks associated with apprehending suspected shoplifters?

4. The common law states that someone is liable for defamation just for repeating or passing on defamatory words he or she heard from someone else. This is called publication. Do you think that publication should be actionable? Why or why not?

5. The tort of interference with contractual relations means that a prospective employer is liable if he induces an employee to breach her employment contract with a third party and start working for him. Does this tort interfere too much with recruitment efforts in the marketplace? Why or why not?

6. Do you agree that the intrusion upon seclusion tort should permit damages for distress, humiliation, or anguish, or should the tort be limited to financial loss, if any, that arises from the tort?

Situations for Discussion

1. Jason owns and operates a company, ABC Ltd., which he wanted to position to bid successfully on a contract to supply security in federal prisons. In its call for tenders, the Department of Supply and Services included a condition that tenderers such as ABC Ltd. were to provide the names and qualifications of at least 25 senior security personnel who would service the contract. (The government's goal with this condition was to ensure that the bidding company had the resources to deliver on the contract should it prove successful.) ABC Ltd. had no such employees but a leading company in the field, Prison Security Services Ltd., had 45 highly qualified security personnel on staff. On the side, Jason convinced these employees of Prison Security Services Ltd. to permit their names to be included in his company's tender and to come to work for ABC Ltd. immediately if the tender were successful. When Jason's company proved to be the successful bidder, these 45 employees promptly joined his company. What tort has Jason committed? Explain.[88]

2. Mr. Favo slipped and fell on a small patch of ice outside a popular car wash. Mr. Favo was late for an appointment and was walking somewhat faster than usual just prior to taking the tumble. Ms. Daby, owner of the car wash, was proud of the 10-year safety record she had established up until this point. She attributes this safety record to being acutely aware of the problems ice causes in winter when wet vehicles exit the car wash, leaving puddles in their wake. On a related front, Daby also held frequent staff meetings in order to emphasize how important it was to prevent ice formation and to salt the sidewalk according to a very strict schedule. The supervisor on shift when Favo fell was adamant that the area had been salted prior to the incident. He also conducted an inspection of the area immediately after the fall and found only a very small patch of ice had been missed. Is Daby liable? Is Favo contributorily negligent?[89]

3. Great Food Restaurant serves a very popular buffet style menu in central Saskatchewan. During one dinner service, a patron became ill and vomited on one of the buffet tables. A supervisor and employee tended to the situation by removing most of the food from the buffet itself, wiping up with a cloth soaked in a weak bleach solution, and mopping the floor. They then replaced the food in the buffet and carried on business. Several people who subsequently ate at the restaurant became ill with the Norwalk virus, a highly contagious pathogen that is easily spread if not deactivated with a sufficiently strong disinfecting solution. A small local newspaper ran a story about the incident, with the headline "Vomit serves up virus at buffet." The article suggested that the illnesses were caused by "eating from a buffet that a customer had vomited on." However, it also quoted a health officer who said the virus was likely spread by contact with contaminated surfaces and "may not have involved the buffet food at all." There was no time to speak to Great Food Restaurant before the story had to go to press. Had the newspaper done so, it would have learned from the manager his view that the illnesses were not caused by the restaurant food. Great Food Restaurant has since suffered a large drop in business and wants to sue the newspaper for defamation. Will its action be successful?[90]

4. Jamie and Shannon live adjacent to a golf course. Portions of their backyard are unfenced so that they can enjoy an unobstructed view of the ninth hole. Several matters are causing them increasing concern. First, the golf course is refusing to take steps to prevent golfers from driving golf balls into Jamie and Shannon's yard. Numerous golf balls crash into their garden and house every day, causing damage to the house and making it impossible for the couple to sit outside in their backyard during golf season. Beyond this, some golf cart drivers are taking short cuts over Jamie and Shannon's property to get to the next hole. The golf club has refused to stop its patrons from doing so. You may assume

---

88 Based, in part, on *ADGA Systems International Ltd. v. Valcom Ltd.* (1999) 43 O.R. (3d) 101 (CA).

89 Based on *Foley v Imperial Oil Ltd*, 2010 BCSC 797, 11 BCLR (5th) 125 aff'd 2011 BCCA 262, 307 BCAC 34.

90 Based in part on *PG Restaurant Ltd (COB Mama Panda Restaurant) v Northern Interior Regional Health Board*, 2005 BCCA 210, 211 BCAC 219; rehearing refused (2005), 41 BCLR (4th) 55 (CA); leave to appeal to SCC refused [2005] SCCA No 270.

13

OBJECTIVES

After studying this chapter, you should have an understanding of

- the agency relationship and its relevance to business

- how an agency relationship comes into being

- agency duties and liabilities

- how the agency relationship ends

THE AGENCY RELATIONSHIP

BUSINESS LAW IN PRACTICE

Sonny Chu is a university student majoring in entrepreneurship and international business. Two years ago, while on a student exchange program in China, Sonny came up with an idea for an Internet business. In China, Sonny had been able to purchase tailor-made silk suits for $250 to $400. The equivalent suits cost $1500 to $1800 in Canada. Sonny believed that he could offer the tailor-made silk suits to Canadians at close to the same price that he had paid for the suits if he could solve the difficulty of having customers take their own suit measurements.

Back in Canada, Sonny worked with a design student, and together they were able to develop a simplified method of taking suit measurements. With this problem solved, Sonny set up a website for his business called "This Suits Me." The website featured several suit styles, a range of silk fabric swatches, and instructions for taking measurements. Customers could easily order suits by clicking on the style and fabric and sending in their measurements by following the simplified instructions provided.[1]

To handle the Chinese end of the business, Sonny employed Dong Lee, a student he had met on the exchange trip. Dong had been born in China and is very familiar with the fabric industry, as both his mother and father are dressmakers. His job for Sonny involves purchasing silk fabric, engaging the services of Chinese tailors, and delivering the customers' selections and measurements to the tailors. The arrangement proved to be very profitable, and, within six months of establishing the website, Sonny was meeting all of his sales targets. However, a couple of recent developments threaten the success of Sonny's business:

- Dong agreed to pay $100 000 to a Chinese supplier for several bolts of silk fabric. Although the fabric is beautiful and will make wonderful suits, Sonny believes that Dong has agreed to pay too much for the fabric and, further, he does not think that his business can afford the purchase at this time. Sonny wants to cancel or renegotiate the contract. He is also very angry with Dong because Sonny had expressly told Dong that he could not enter into any contracts on his behalf in excess of $25 000 without getting his permission first.

---

1   The idea for this business is based on Canwest News Service, "Suit Yourself: Expert Offers Tips for Men" *Canada.com* (5 March 2008), online: Canada.com <http://www.canada.com/story_print.html?id=8353c3a9-7552-4bb9-a689-0f9b53d8d0208>.

- Sonny has also discovered that Dong has been purchasing fabric and engaging tailors on behalf of some of Sonny's competitors. When confronted with this information, Dong stated that he did not see any problem with his actions as he had not signed any exclusive representation contract with Sonny.

1. What is the nature of the legal relationship between Sonny and Dong?
2. Is Sonny bound by the expensive fabric contract Dong entered into with the Chinese supplier?
3. Has Dong breached any duty owed to Sonny by representing other businesses in China?

The Nature of Agency

Agency is the relationship between two persons that permits one person, the **agent**, to affect the legal relationships of another, known in law as the **principal**.[2]

These legal relationships are as binding on the principal as if that person had directly entered them herself.

Agency is about one person representing another in such a way as to affect the latter's relationships with the outside world. In business, agency is a common relationship, as is shown in the following examples:

- a sports agent negotiates a multimillion-dollar deal on behalf of a hockey player.
- an insurance agent sells fire and theft insurance on behalf of several insurance companies.
- a travel agent sells tickets, cruises, and vacation packages on behalf of carriers and hotels.
- a booking agent negotiates fees and dates on behalf of entertainers.
- a stockbroker buys and sells shares on behalf of individuals and companies.

In each case, the agent is acting for someone else (the principal) and is doing business on that person's behalf. This kind of relationship is essential to the success of the principal, who may not necessarily have the expertise to handle the given matter—as may be the case with an athlete or an investor—or who cannot manage and promote his business single-handedly. For this latter reason, insurance companies, hotels, carriers, and entertainers rely on agents regularly.

In the Business Law in Practice scenario at the beginning of this chapter, Dong was needed for just these kinds of reasons. He was familiar with China and had connections in that part of the world. Sonny also required his assistance because Sonny could not run his business alone. Consequently, Dong became Sonny's agent.

Many of the examples of agency given so far are familiar because they involve businesses engaging external specialists or experts to act on their behalf in various transactions. The scope of agency, however, is considerably broader than these examples would suggest.

In fact, in almost every business transaction, at least one of the parties is acting as an agent. A corporation enters into a contract through the agency

Agency

A relationship that exists when one party represents another party in the formation of legal relations.

Agent

A person who is authorized to act on behalf of another.

Principal

A person who has permitted another to act on her behalf.

2 GHL Fridman, *Canadian Agency Law* 2d ed (Markham, ON: LexisNexis, 2012) at 4.

of one of its directors or employees. A partnership is likewise bound to a contract through the agency of one of its partners or a firm employee. Even in a sole proprietorship, the owner may hire others, such as office managers and sales clerks, to carry out critical tasks on the owner's behalf. In short, the agency relationship—which formally recognizes the delegation of authority from one party to another—is a cornerstone of business activity. It is a relationship that makes it possible for businesses to conduct a wide array of transactions.

Agency Defined

Agency relationships, like contractual relationships in general, operate for the most part with few difficulties—agents simply represent principals in transactions with others. This is not to say, however, that problems cannot occur. The fact that parties use agents instead of dealing with each other face to face can result in complications and questions. There are two key relationships at play in an agency situation. The first is the relationship between the agent and the principal (see Figure 13.1).

FIGURE 13.1 The Agent–Principal Relationship

This aspect of agency raises numerous questions, such as the following:

- how does A become an agent? When is one person considered to be an agent for another?
- what is the authority of A? What types of transactions can A enter on behalf of P?
- what are A's duties?
- what are P's obligations?

The second relationship in agency is between the principal and the party with whom the agent does business (see Figure 13.2). Such a party is known as an **outsider** because she is "outside" the agency relationship between principal and agent. The outsider is also sometimes called the third party.[3]

FIGURE 13.2 The Outsider–Principal Relationship

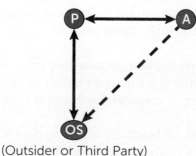

(Outsider or Third Party)

Outsider

The party with whom the agent does business on behalf of the principal.

---

3 The principal and agent are the first and second parties.

This relationship raises questions, including:

- when is the principal liable to the outsider?
- when is the agent himself liable to the outsider?

The complications resulting from these relationships have necessitated rules of law to regulate and resolve them. These rules are known as the **law of agency**, which, in turn, is derived largely from tort and contract law. There is very little legislation pertaining to agency as such, other than special statutes that govern the duties and responsibilities of specific kinds of agents.[4]

The remainder of this chapter will explore how the common law of agency has dealt with the kinds of questions and problems posed above.

Creation of Agency

Agency relationships are created in a variety of ways. Most often, particularly in a business context, the relationship arises by contract between the parties. At other times, the relationship arises by conduct. The parties do not specifically agree to an agency relationship but, by words or actions, outsiders are led to believe the relationship is one of agency.

Agency by Agreement

An agency relationship created by contract normally involves the principal authorizing an agent to act on her behalf and the agent agreeing to do so in return for some fee or other remuneration. This often occurs through a contract created expressly and only for that single purpose, as illustrated in this example:

- a retired public figure who wishes to earn income by speaking about his experiences in office may engage an agent to contact organizations, negotiate fees, and book engagements on his behalf. In return, the public figure will pay the agent a certain sum, perhaps a percentage of his fee. Similarly, Sonny hired Dong to purchase fabric and employ tailors in China.

In other situations, the agency relationship may arise as part of another, broader contract:

- an employment contract may provide for a person to be paid a salary in return for carrying out certain duties, including entering into contracts on behalf of the employer. For example, a sales clerk, besides greeting and assisting customers and stocking shelves, would have the authority to enter into sales transactions—at least at the sticker price—on behalf of his employer.

Of course, not all employees are agents for the businesses that employ them. A clerk/typist is not normally an agent, but, if asked to take money from petty cash and purchase a gift for a departing employee, then in this situation and for this purpose, the clerk/typist is an agent for the employer.

The agency agreement may be express or implied, oral, in writing, or in writing under seal. If the agent is to issue promissory notes or sign cheques in the name of the principal, then the agency agreement should be in writing.[5] A special type

Law of agency

The law governing the relationship where one party, the agent, acts on behalf of another, the principal.

---

4 For example, insurance brokers, mortgage brokers, and mercantile and real estate agents are regulated by legislation that provides for their registration, their training, the regulation of their conduct, and so forth. See, for example, *Real Estate and Business Brokers Act, 2002*, SO 2002, c 30, Schedule C.

5 *Bills of Exchange Act*, RSC 1985, c B-4

Power of attorney

An agency agreement in writing and under seal.

of express agency agreement is the **power of attorney**. It is a grant of authority under seal and it permits the agent to sign documents on behalf of the principal under seal.

The Concept of Authority

The authority of the agent is a key aspect of the agency relationship. It determines whether there is a contract between the principal and the outsider. When an agent acts within the scope of the agent's authority and negotiates a contract for the principal, the principal is bound by the contract, whether the principal likes it or not. However, even when the agent has acted outside the scope of her authority in entering into the contract—that is, by exceeding the powers she has been given—the contract may still bind the principal.

The principal will be obligated by the contract when the agent has actual authority or when the agent has apparent authority.

Actual Authority

Actual authority

The power of an agent that derives from either express or implied agreement.

An agent's **actual authority** can be both express and implied. Express authority is the written or oral authority granted by the principal to the agent and is an authority that the agent actually has. Implied authority is also an authority that the agent actually has, but it is present by implication only. An agent will have implied authority when that authority

- is inferred from the position the agent occupies.
- is reasonably necessary to carry out or otherwise implement the agent's express authority.
- arises by virtue of a well-recognized custom in a particular trade, industry, or profession.

Like other contracts, then, the agency contract can contain implied terms concerning the nature and extent of the agent's authority. It is important to remember that these terms are not any less "real" than express terms. They just exist in another, less tangible form.

In the Business Law in Practice scenario, it is clear that Sonny's agent, Dong, has the actual authority to engage tailors and to buy fabric up to $25 000 per contract. Above that amount, he is required to secure Sonny's approval before proceeding. What kind of implied authority might Dong have? This is always a fact-specific inquiry, but since Dong is empowered to purchase fabric and engage tailors, he almost certainly has the power to arrange for the transportation of the finished product to Canada. This, in turn, would also include the power to acquire insurance to cover any loss or damage to the suits while in transit. For this reason, transportation and insurance contracts will be binding on Sonny.

In a similar vein, the manager of a business may have aspects of his authority expressly recited in his employment contract or job description. To the extent that these documents are not exhaustive on the subject, other components of his authority exist due to the nature of his position and as a result of what is reasonably necessary to manage the business. For example, if he were the general manager of an automotive dealership, he presumably would have the implied power to purchase merchandise, order office supplies, arrange for appropriate advertising of the business, and hire and fire employees. A manager of another kind of business—a fast-food outlet or a convenience store—would have less implied power.

The nature of the authority given to the agent is inherently flexible and easily customized. For example, it can be:

- very broad or very narrow.
- for only one transaction or for several.
- for a short, long, or indefinite period of time.
- very formal, as in the case of a power of attorney, or very informal, in that it is included in the job description of an employee or merely consists of oral instructions.

Dong has entered into a contract on behalf of Sonny. Was the contract binding on Sonny? This contract was not concluded within Dong's actual authority, as Sonny had limited Dong's authority to contracts of $25 000. Dong acted outside his actual authority, but nevertheless, Sonny will be bound by the contract if Dong has the apparent authority to enter into contracts over that monetary limit.

Apparent Authority

Sometimes called ostensible authority, **apparent authority** is the authority that a third party or outsider would reasonably believe the agent has, given the conduct of the principal. For example, as Dong is acting as Sonny's purchasing agent, it would be reasonable for the outsider to infer that he had the usual authority of someone in such a position. It would not be reasonable to expect fabric suppliers to guess that Dong's authority to contract on Sonny's behalf had been limited to contracts for less than $25 000. Sonny is using Dong's services as his buying agent without telling outsiders that his authority is in any way limited. He must bear the risk of Dong exceeding the monetary limit he has privately set for him.

In sum, so long as an agent is acting within his apparent authority, the principal will be bound by the transaction unless the third party knew or ought reasonably to have known of the limitation on the agent's authority.

Purchasing agents are often part of the fashion scene. What is the authority of a purchasing agent?

Apparent authority

The power that an agent appears to have to an outsider because of conduct or statements of the principal.

CASE

Doiron v Devon Capital Corp, 2003 ABCA 336, 20 Alta LR (4th) 11

THE BUSINESS CONTEXT: Actual authority exists when a principal expressly confers authority on the agent. Apparent or ostensible authority arises when the principal represents that an "agent" is authorized to act on his behalf or allows a third party to believe that the "agent" has been authorized to act on his behalf. The doctrine of apparent authority is particularly relevant when an investment adviser, financial planner, insurance broker, or the like, misappropriates client funds, leaving the client looking for a solvent defendant.

FACTUAL BACKGROUND: In 1998, Glennis and Elliot Doiron sold their home in Calgary and decided to invest the net proceeds of $60 000 for a short term until they required the money for a down payment on their new home. They contacted William Demmers for investment advice, as he had previously placed their life insurance and RRSPs with Manulife Financial and was known to them as a Manulife investment advisor. The Doirons were unaware that Demmers had a non-exclusive agency agreement (called a producer's agreement) with Manulife, which provided that he could not bind Manulife without written authorization.

(Continued)

The Doirons gave Demmers a cheque for $60 000 and Demmers filled in the payee as Devon Capital Corporation. The Doirons believed that they were investing in a Manulife product or one guaranteed by Manulife because they believed that Demmers was a Manulife employee and sold only Manulife products. When the investment became due, the Doirons received a cheque from Devon, which was dishonoured. It turned out that Devon was a sham, and the Doirons lost their entire investment.

THE LEGAL QUESTION: Is Manulife liable for the investment losses of the Doirons?

RESOLUTION: A principal is liable for the acts of an agent as long as the agent is acting within the scope of his or her actual or ostensible (apparent) authority. Demmers was not an agent of Manulife in the transaction with the Doirons and had no actual authority to bind Manulife as the guarantor of investments in Devon. However, the doctrine of ostensible authority gives an agent authority to bind a principal to agreements made with third parties when the principal represents to the third party that the agent has authority to enter into a contract and the third party relies on the representation. The representation may be express or implied. Manulife had cloaked Demmers with ostensible authority by providing him with business cards, stationery, and other Manulife paraphernalia and encouraging him to use it, and by allowing him to be contacted through the Manulife main switchboard. Also, Manulife had a co-op advertising program in which it ran advertisements in newspapers that included photographs of "producers" (i.e., salespeople like Demmers) and the Manulife logo.

Although Demmers did not represent that the Devon investment was a Manulife product, the Doirons were entitled to assume that they were investing in Manulife because they had instructed Demmers to invest in a low-risk Manulife product, Demmers provided no written information regarding the investment before accepting their money, and Demmers did not tell them that Devon was not a Manulife product or was unconnected with Manulife. Therefore, given that Demmers purported to contract on behalf of Manulife and the ostensible authority conveyed by Manulife to Demmers, Manulife was bound by the contract.

CRITICAL ANALYSIS: How can companies like Manulife minimize the risk of liability for the actions of their "producers" (i.e., salespeople)? How can companies gain the benefits that accrue from representation without incurring the risk of liability?

Agency by Estoppel

In the preceding section, one of the risks of agency was illustrated: an agent may exceed his actual authority but act within his apparent authority and thereby bind a principal to a contract against his wishes. Sonny is bound to pay for the expensive fabric even though the contract is for an amount above Dong's authority. This is because the contract was within Dong's apparent authority and the fabric supplier was unaware of the limitation on Dong's authority. This is an application of what is known in law as **agency by estoppel**. The relationship between Sonny and Dong has been broadened or extended, not through their mutual consent but by conduct. Sonny is not entitled to deny Dong's apparent authority unless he actually informs the outsider in advance that Dong's authority is limited.

A less common situation in which an agency relationship can be created by estoppel involves one in which the principal indicates that another is his agent when, in fact, no agency relationship exists. For example, suppose that the owner of a business—in a burst of effusiveness—introduces a prospective employee to a customer, saying, "I want you to meet Terrence, my new vice president of

Agency by estoppel

An agency relationship created when the principal acts such that third parties reasonably conclude that an agency relationship exists.

marketing." It would be usual and reasonable for the customer to infer that Terrence has the authority to act on behalf of the owner with respect to selling, promotions, and advertising. Suppose, however, that ultimately Terrence is not hired and, unfortunately, the owner forgets all about having introduced him as the new vice president of marketing. Terrence—now sorely disappointed and wishing to exact some revenge—contacts the customer and enters into a transaction with him, pretending to act on behalf of the owner. Is the owner liable? Assuming the contract is marketing or sales-related and assuming the customer was unaware of the truth, then the owner probably will be liable. In such a situation, the principal's actions (introducing his "new vice president of marketing") created the appearance of an agency relationship. The principal will therefore be estopped from denying the relationship and be bound by the contract with the customer. Put another way, the principal is not permitted to avoid the contract by claiming—albeit truthfully—that no agency relationship existed, because the principal gave every appearance that one did.

Is it fair to place all responsibility on the owner like this? The difficulty is that someone—either the owner of the business or the customer—will end up being adversely affected by Terrence's conduct. That is, either the owner will be stuck with a contract that she never wanted or the customer will be denied the benefit of a contract that he negotiated in good faith. Between these two competing claims, the law sides with the customer through estoppel. In theory, at least, the owner can sue Terrence for misrepresenting himself as an agent, but this can be of little value if Terrence has few assets.

A third situation in which agency by estoppel may operate to bind a principal is that in which an agency relationship has been terminated or an agent's authority has been curtailed. In both situations, the agent had at one time the actual authority to bind the principal, but now the authority has been taken away or reduced.

PART FOUR

CASE

Rockland Industries Inc v Amerada Minerals Corporation of Canada, [1980] 2 SCR 2, rev'g (1978), 14 AR 97 (Alta CA)

THE BUSINESS CONTEXT: This case concerns an agent whose authority has been reduced. The same general principles will apply where the agency relationship has been completely severed.

FACTUAL BACKGROUND: Rockland was a textile manufacturer that also engaged in the purchase and resale of sulphur. Amerada was a producer of natural gas. One of the byproducts of the gas-processing procedure is sulphur. Mr. Kurtz was the manager of Amerada's petrochemical products with responsibility for domestic and foreign sales and the marketing of petrochemicals, including sulphur. He reported to Mr. Deverin, a senior vice president and a member of the executive operating committee.

After protracted negotiations between Amerada, represented by Kurtz, and representatives of Rockland, an agreement was reached for the sale by Amerada to Rockland of 50 000 tons of sulphur at $8 per ton. This agreement was concluded by telephone on 5 September 1974. In the meantime, on 3 September 1974, Deverin had informed Kurtz that he would need to get the approval of the executive operating committee for the sale to Rockland. In other words, Kurtz no longer had the authority to conclude the sale on behalf of Amerada.

The agreement, concluded on 5 September, was not performed by Amerada, and Rockland sued for breach of contract. Amerada argued that there was no contract between the parties,

(Continued)

---

as Kurtz did not have the authority to act on Amerada's behalf.

THE LEGAL QUESTION: Was Amerada bound by the contract negotiated by Kurtz?

RESOLUTION: The court determined that Kurtz had actual authority to act on behalf of Amerada in negotiating and entering the contract with Rockland up until 3 September. At that time his actual authority was curtailed. This limitation on Kurtz's authority, however, was not communicated to Rockland. The court held that the onus was on Amerada to notify Rockland of the limitation—it was not up to Rockland to inquire as to Kurtz's authority. Amerada, by permitting Kurtz to act in its business by conducting negotiations, had represented to Rockland that he had permission to act. In short, there was a representation of authority by Amerada on which Rockland relied.

CRITICAL ANALYSIS: How could Amerada have prevented this situation?

The situations described in this section illustrate several of the risks associated with agency. The onus is on the principals to inform outsiders when a person ceases to be their agent; otherwise the principals continue to be liable for the agent's actions. Similarly, the principals have a responsibility to inform outsiders of any limitation on their agent's usual authority; otherwise the principals run the risk of being bound if the agent exceeds his actual authority but acts within his apparent authority. A principal can inform outsiders by contacting them by letter, telephone, or other means; by taking out advertisements in trade publications and newspapers; by clearly indicating on company forms what constitutes necessary approvals; and by otherwise indicating that only properly documented transactions will be binding.

Agency by Ratification

Agency by ratification

An agency relationship created when one party adopts a contract entered into on his behalf by another who at the time acted without authority.

Agency by ratification occurs when a person represents himself as another's agent even though he is not, and when the purported principal adopts the acts of the agent. For example, suppose Ahmed is keenly interested in obtaining a franchise for a certain fast-food restaurant, and his friend Frank is aware of this interest. An opportunity comes on the market, but Frank cannot reach Ahmed to tell him about it. Feeling pretty sure of himself, Frank goes ahead and purchases the franchise on Ahmed's behalf although he does not have any authority to do so. Though Frank acted with good intentions, Ahmed has no responsibilities unless he chooses to adopt the contract. When and if he does adopt the transaction, an agency relationship will be created between Frank and him. The result is that Ahmed's rights and duties under the franchise contract are identical to what they would have been had Frank been properly authorized to act as Ahmed's agent all along.

In both agency by estoppel and agency by ratification, the agent has no authority to do what he does. What distinguishes the two doctrines is whether the principal has conducted himself in a misleading way. Agency by estoppel forces the principal to be bound by the unauthorized contract because the principal has represented someone as his agent and must live with the consequences when that agent purports to act on his behalf. Under agency by ratification, the agent is perhaps equally out of line but not due to any fault of or misrepresentation by the principal. For this reason, the law does not force the principal to adopt the contract, but rather permits him to make that decision for himself, according to his own best interests.

REAL ESTATE AGENTS

The real estate agent is one of the most familiar and common types of agents. Most sales of property, especially those involving residential property, involve the services of a real estate agent. The real estate agent, however, is somewhat of an anomaly in agency law. Unlike most other agents, usually a real estate agent has no authority to make a binding contract of sale on behalf of his principal, the homeowner. Normally the agreement between the owner of property and the real estate agent—often taking the form of a standard listing agreement—does not confer any authority on the agent to enter a contract on behalf of the property owner. The real estate agent's role is usually limited to listing and advertising the property, showing the property to prospective purchasers, and introducing and bringing together the parties. In short, a real estate agent usually does not have the actual authority to contract on behalf of the principal. As well, a real estate agent does not have the apparent authority to enter a contract on behalf of a homeowner. A principal could, of course, grant actual authority to a real estate agent to enter a contract on her behalf. However, such a grant of authority, to be effective, would need to be conferred by very clear, express, and unequivocal language.[6]

The case of real estate agents illustrates an important point. The term "agent" is often used very loosely to refer to anyone who represents another, and it is not always restricted to relationships where the agent enters into contracts on behalf of the principal. It is always necessary to look at the essence of a relationship rather

Does a real estate agent act for the vendor or the purchaser of property?

than merely relying on what the parties call themselves. Just as agents are not always agents in the strict legal sense, so too, there may be an agency relationship even though the parties have not labelled it as such.

Critical Analysis: How is the authority of a real-estate agent determined?

It should be noted that a principal cannot ratify every contract that his "agent" enters. A principal can only ratify a contract if

- he does so within a reasonable time,
- the principal had the capacity to create the contract at the time the agent entered into it and at the time of ratification, and
- the agent identified the principal at the time of entering the contract.

---

6   William F Foster, *Real Estate Agency Law in Canada*, 2d ed (Toronto: Carswell, 1994) at 99.

A principal's ratification may be express or implied. For example, if a principal accepts a benefit under the contract, the principal will be bound by the contract.

Figure 13.3 summarizes the points contained in the preceding sections.

FIGURE 13.3 Summary of Creation of Agency and Agent's Authority

	How It Is Created	Agent's Authority
Agency by Agreement	P, expressly or impliedly, appoints X as an A	Actual: Express and/or Implied Apparent
Agency by Estoppel	*Representation of Authority* P represents to OS that X has authority to act as an A even though no actual authority given	Apparent
	Extension of Existing Authority P represents to OS that A has authority in excess of actual authority given	Actual Apparent
	Termination or Reduction of Authority P terminates or reduces A's authority but does not give notice to OS	Apparent
Agency by Ratification	P adopts actions of X, and X retroactively becomes an A	No authority until P adopts X's actions

Duties in the Agency Relationship

Duties of the Agent

An agency relationship created by contract imposes on an agent certain duties to perform. If the agent fails to perform these duties, he is in breach of the contract. An agent is required to perform in accordance with the principal's instructions. In the event that the principal has not given any instructions as to how the performance is to be carried out, performance must meet the standard of the particular trade or industry. For example, a real estate agent's duties would normally include appraising property, estimating the revenue and expenses of property the principal wishes to acquire, checking the dimensions of property, advising the principal of the financial implications of transactions, and ensuring that properties the principal wishes to acquire do not contravene bylaws or other municipal regulations, among other matters.[7]

Normally, it is expected that the agent will personally perform the obligations. However, there may be an express or implied provision for delegation—that is, the agent may be permitted to "download" responsibility for performance onto someone else. For example, it may be that Sonny and Dong have an understanding that Dong can have members of his extended family contact fabric suppliers in remote regions of China.

An agent also owes a **fiduciary duty** to the principal. This duty requires the agent to show what the law describes as "utmost good faith to the principal." This duty is often expressed as a "profit rule"—a **fiduciary** must not personally profit by virtue of her position—and a "conflict rule"—a fiduciary must not place

---

7 *Ibid* at 218–19.

herself in a position where her own interests conflict with the interests of the principal. It is a breach of his fiduciary duty for Dong to act as a buyer for both Sonny and his competitors. This is because Dong may be tempted to put the interests of the competitors above the interests of Sonny.

AN INSURANCE AGENT'S DUTY OF CARE

An insurance agent acting on behalf of an insurance company owes a duty of care to the insurance company. The insurance agent also owes a duty of care to a client who relies on her to access insurance products. The content of the duty of care varies according to the agreement between the agent and the client, and the surrounding circumstances.

In the leading case[8] on an agent's duties, the court identified two types of situations to consider in determining an agent's duty of care to a client:

- *specific request:* Where a client asks for specific coverage, the agent is obligated to exercise reasonable care and skill to get the coverage requested. If the coverage is not available or the agent cannot obtain it, the agent must inform the client so that he can take appropriate steps.

- *full coverage:* Where a client asks an agent what insurance he should buy to be protected, the agent must inform herself about the client's business, assess the

What are the duties of an insurance agent?

foreseeable risks, and insure the client against all foreseeable risks. If there is available coverage which would have protected the client and the agent failed to obtain the insurance, the agent would be responsible for any loss that ensued.

Critical Analysis: What steps should an insurance agent take to reduce the risk of liability for breaching the duty of care?

The content of the fiduciary duty will vary with the circumstances. However, as a general rule, an agent has the duty to

- make full disclosure of all material information that may affect the principal's position (e.g., Dong must disclose to Sonny any good deals or bargains on fabrics that he discovers).

- avoid any conflict of interest that affects the interests of the principal (e.g., Dong must not go on a buying trip for Sonny and acquire clothes for a store that he is secretly running on the side).

- avoid acting for two principals in the same transaction (e.g., Dong must not represent both Sonny and a fabric seller in a sales transaction).

- avoid using the principal's property, money, or information to secure personal gain (e.g., Dong must avoid using contacts that he has gained

---

8 *Fine's Flowers Ltd v General Accident Assurance Co of Canada* (1977), 17 OR (2d) 529, 81 DLR (3d) 139 (Ont CA).

through acting as Sonny's agent to set up his own business, and he must not sell or use Sonny's customer lists and records for personal gain).

- avoid accepting or making a secret commission or profit (e.g., Dong must avoid taking payments from fabric suppliers for doing business with them).

There is not, however, an absolute prohibition against conflicts such as acting for two principals or using the principal's property. The agent simply must not do any of these activities secretly, and he must obtain the fully informed consent of the principal prior to the event.

A fiduciary duty is not unique to the relationship between a principal and an agent. This duty is present, as a matter of course, in many other relationships found in business such as the relationships between

- lawyers and their clients.
- accountants and their clients.
- partners.
- directors and senior officers of a corporation and the corporation.
- senior employees and employers.

The categories of fiduciary relationships are not closed. A fiduciary relationship can exist outside the settled categories and has been found to exist, in some circumstances, in other relationships such as the relationship between financial advisors (e.g., bankers, stockbrokers, and investment counsellors) and their clients. A fiduciary duty can arise in any relationship where the facts indicate sufficient elements of power and influence on the part of one party and reliance, vulnerability, and trust on the part of the other.[9] This is not to say that all "power-dependency" relationships are fiduciary. In addition to the discretionary power to unilaterally affect the vulnerable party's legal or practical interests, there must be an express or implied undertaking to act with loyalty.[10] For example, the relationship between an investor and a broker will not normally give rise to a fiduciary duty where the broker is simply a conduit of information and merely takes orders. However, where the client reposes trust and confidence in the broker and relies on the broker's advice in making business decisions, and the broker has undertaken to act in the client's best interests, the relationship may be elevated to a fiduciary relationship.

CASE

Raso v Dionigi (1993), 12 OR (3d) 580, 100 DLR (4th) 459 (Ont CA)

THE BUSINESS CONTEXT: As a general rule, an agent is precluded from acting for both the vendor and the purchaser in the same transaction. There is, however, an exception to the rule. An agent may act for both and not be in breach of fiduciary duties if full and fair disclosure of all material facts has been made to the principals prior to any transaction.

FACTUAL BACKGROUND: Raffaela Sirianni and her husband wanted to invest in income-producing property. They informed her brother-in-law, Guerino Sirianni, who was a real estate agent, that they were prepared to invest $250 000 to $300 000. He located a sixplex

---

9 *Hodgkinson v Simms,* [1994] 3 SCR 377, 117 DLR (4th) 161. For a summary of this case, see Chapter 22.
10 *Galambos v Perez,* 2009 SCC 48, [2009] 3 SCR 247.

owned by Mr. and Mrs. Dionigi. The sixplex was not for sale; however, Sirianni actively prevailed upon the Dionigis to sign a listing agreement. Eventually they did sign an agreement with Sirianni's employer, a real estate agency. The listing price was $299 900. Sirianni presented an offer of $270 000 on behalf of "R. Raso in trust." Raso is the maiden name of Raffaela Sirianni. Sirianni never told the Dionigis that the purchasers were his brother and sister-in-law. The Dionigis made a counteroffer of $290 000, but this was not accepted. Sirianni persisted, and the Dionigis ultimately accepted an offer of $285 000. A few days later, the Dionigis became aware of the purchasers' relationship with the agent, and they refused to complete the action. Raffaela Sirianni sued for specific performance of the contract, and Sirianni and the real estate agency sued for their commission.

THE LEGAL QUESTION: Did Sirianni owe a fiduciary duty to the Dionigis? If so, did he breach the duty? Would a breach preclude him from claiming a commission?

RESOLUTION: Sirianni was not a mere middleman in the sense of introducing the parties; rather, he took an active role in the transaction. A real estate agent who acts for both sides of a transaction has a fiduciary duty to both his principals to disclose all material facts with respect to the transaction. Sirianni breached his fiduciary duty to the Dionigis by failing to disclose that the purchasers were his brother and sister-in-law and by failing to advise of the amount of money that the purchasers had available to purchase the property. A fiduciary who breaches his duty of disclosure of material facts is not entitled to prove that the transaction would have concluded had disclosure been made. In other words, it is immaterial whether the transaction is fair, and it is irrelevant whether the principal would still have entered the transaction if disclosure had been made.

Where an agent has breached a fiduciary duty in this manner, the agent is precluded from claiming any commission. It also follows that the purchasers are not entitled to specific performance, as they not only had knowledge of the agent's breach but also actively participated in the scheme.

CRITICAL ANALYSIS: What are the distinguishing features of a fiduciary relationship? What consequences flow from the designation of a relationship as a fiduciary one? If Guerino Sirianni had disclosed to the Dionigis just how much money Mr. and Mrs. Sirianni had available to purchase the property, would this disclosure have been a breach of his fiduciary duty to the Siriannis? What does this tell you about the perils of acting for both parties to a transaction?

Because professional relationships can be easily categorized as fiduciary, it is incumbent on those who offer their services to others to understand the indicia of the fiduciary relationship. In addition, it is noteworthy that where fiduciary duties are found to exist, the innocent party can look to a wider range of remedies than found in contract or tort. The whole range of equitable remedies is available, and with the spectre of these remedies, it is important for businesspeople to comprehend not only when a fiduciary relationship exists but also the full scope of the duties.

Duties of the Principal

A principal's duties usually are not as onerous as an agent's and normally are set out in the contract creating the agency relationship. Such contracts usually obligate the principal to

- pay the agent a specified fee or percentage for services rendered unless the parties have agreed that the agent would work for free.
- assist the agent in the manner described in the contract.

- reimburse the agent for reasonable expenses associated with carrying out his agency duties.
- indemnify against losses incurred in carrying out the agency business.

In the example involving Sonny and his buying agent, Dong, it may be that Dong has had to travel to various parts of China to make necessary purchases. In the absence of any agreement to the contrary, Sonny would be required to reimburse Dong for his travel expenses. This is a cost that rightfully belongs to Sonny since Dong incurred it on a buying trip that Sonny instigated and sent him on. Similarly, Sonny has an obligation—either express or implied—to reimburse Dong for meals, hotel, and other reasonable expenses associated with the buying trip.

Insurance broker

An independent business that deals with several insurance companies and advises clients on the appropriate insurance coverage.

ETHICAL CONSIDERATIONS

COMPENSATION OF LIFE INSURANCE BROKERS

Until the early 1990s, most major life insurance companies sold their products through in-house sales agents. Now the majority of life insurance policies are sold through independent insurance brokers.[11] An **insurance broker** is an intermediary who represents several insurance companies and at the same time, provides clients with advice on the best insurance product for their needs.

Insurance companies provide a number of incentives to get brokers to direct business to them. An upfront commission is paid when the sale is made. The commission is a percentage of the cost of the insurance and can vary depending on the type of life insurance, company policy, and the province. Life insurance has always been considered a tough sell, therefore the upfront commission is high, often amounting to 30–70 percent of the price paid for the insurance. This commission may be the only compensation received by the insurance broker. However, the broker may also receive a contingent commission based on the volume of business done with the insurance company, or based on the loyalty of the customer directed to the insurance

Do you see any problems with the incentives provided to insurance brokers by insurance companies?

company. The greater the profitability and size of the business directed to the insurance company and the longer the retention of the broker's entire portfolio of business with the insurance company, the more likely the broker receives a contingency commission. Finally, the insurance company may reward brokers with perks such as deluxe trips to exotic locales for themselves and their spouses. These perks are often characterized as "educational" as they are an opportunity

---

11 The terms *insurance agent* and *broker* are often used interchangeably. An insurance agent, however is generally an employee or representative of an insurance company and solicits business on behalf of the company. A broker is an independent business that deals with several insurance companies and advises its clients on appropriate insurance coverage.

for insurance companies to provide brokers with information about insurance products, but usually only a few hours during a week-long trip are set aside for this purpose.

Critical Analysis: Should there be limits or caps on compensation for brokers? Why or why not?

Sources: Grant Robertson & Tara Perkins, "What your insurance broker doesn't want you to know" *The Globe and Mail* (21 December 2010) online: *The Globe and Mail* <http://www.theglobeandmail.com/report-on-business/what-your-insurance-broker-doesnt-want-you-to-know/article1846513/>; Craig Harris, "Commission controversy calling for clarity on broker compensation" *Canadian Underwriter* (October 2004) online: *Canadian Underwriter* <http://www.canadianunderwriter.ca/news/commission-controversy-calling-for-clarity-on-broker-compensation/1000190679/?&er=NA>.

Contract Liability in the Agency Relationship

Liability of the Principal to the Outsider

The most significant result of an agency relationship is that, when an agent enters into a contract on behalf of a principal with a third party, it is the principal, not the agent, who ordinarily is liable on the contract. To a large extent, discussion of this point is simply the flip side of a discussion regarding an agent's actual and apparent authority. Put another way, the principal's liability to the third party depends on the nature of the agent's authority.

As we have already seen under the discussion of an agent's authority above, Sonny is liable on the expensive fabric contract even though Dong exceeded his actual authority. Dong went over the monetary limit his principal had placed on him, but the doctrine of apparent authority applies. The outsider did not know about the limitation on Dong's authority so, on this basis, Sonny is bound.

Liability of the Agent to the Outsider

An agent who acts without authority and contracts with an outsider is liable to the third party for breach of **warranty of authority**. In this situation, there is no contract between either the principal and the outsider or the agent and the outsider.[12]

For example, Sonny would not be bound by a contract Dong enters into on his behalf to purchase a private jet. He could adopt—that is, ratify—such a contract, but otherwise he is not bound because such a contract is not within Dong's actual or apparent authority. Dong may be sued by the vendor of the jet because he wrongly claimed to have the authority to act on Sonny's behalf in the purchase of a jet.

An agent may also be bound when he contracts on his own behalf to be a party to the contract along with his principal.[13]

For example, if Dong negotiated the contract such that both he and his principal were ordering the fabric and promising to pay for it, then he has as much liability to the outsider as Sonny. They are both parties to the contract—Dong is contracting on his own behalf as well as on Sonny's behalf.

Warranty of authority

A representation of authority by a person who purports to be an agent.

---

12 *Supra* note 2 at 159–62.
13 Peter Watts & FMB Reynolds, *Bowstead & Reynolds on Agency*, 19th ed (London: Sweet & Maxwell, 2010) at 546.

Liability of an Undisclosed Principal

An agent may incur liability when he contracts on behalf of an **undisclosed principal**. A principal is said to be "undisclosed" when the third party does not know that she is dealing with an agent at all and assumes that the party she is dealing with is acting only on his own behalf. From the perspective of the outsider, there is no principal waiting in the background.

When the agent is acting for an undisclosed principal, the general rule is that the principal is still liable on the contract so long as the agent is acting within his authority.[14] The agent has no liability, however.

For example, assume that, in negotiations with outsiders, Dong represents himself neither as an agent nor as a principal and that he could be acting in either capacity. In such circumstances, Sonny will generally be liable on the contract, but not Dong. This is a simple application of the general rule stated above.

The general rule, however, has been subject to qualification that may operate to render the agent liable on the contract in certain circumstances.[15] One such qualification relates to representations made by the agent.

Suppose that for the purposes of buying some special fabric, Sonny wishes to keep his identity a secret. He thinks that Dong, his purchasing agent, will get a better price if the seller (the outsider) is unaware of his identity.[16]

If Dong pretends to be the principal—representing to the outsider that he is actually the owner or proprietor of the suit business—and does not disclose the existence of Sonny, his principal, then Dong runs the risk of being personally liable on the contract that is concluded. For example, if the written contract expressly indicates that Dong is the principal, the parol evidence rule[17] may operate to prevent the admission of evidence of an undisclosed principal.[18] In such circumstances, Dong is liable.

A variation on the undisclosed principal is the unnamed principal.[19] If Dong tells the seller that he is acting for a principal but that he is not at liberty to reveal that person's identity, Sonny will be liable on any contract he enters into with the seller. In such circumstances, Dong himself has no liability on the contract because the outsider was fully aware of his status. The outsider did not know the identity of his principal but decided to enter into a contract anyway. If the outsider did not want to deal with an unnamed principal, the outsider could simply have refused to enter the contract in the first place.

Liability of the Agent to the Principal

When an agent exceeds his authority, the principal can sue the agent for breach of their contract—assuming that there is such a contract in place.

Because Dong exceeded his authority in purchasing the fabric, Sonny could sue him for breach of their agency or employment agreement.

Figure 13.4 summarizes the points contained in the preceding sections.

---

14 *Supra* note 2 at 164–65. This rule has been subject to heavy criticism as being inconsistent with the general principles of contract law.
15 *Supra* note 2 at 166–68.
16 This is a not uncommon practice in the real estate industry, particularly when a developer wishes to purchase several tracts of land.
17 The parol evidence rule is discussed in Chapter 7.
18 *Supra* note 2 at 166–68. The law is unsettled in this area: it is unclear when the law will permit evidence of an undisclosed principal.
19 *Supra* note 13 at 33. As Bowstead notes, terminology in this area is not consistently employed by the judiciary and legal writers.

FIGURE 13.4 Summary of Contract Liability in Agency

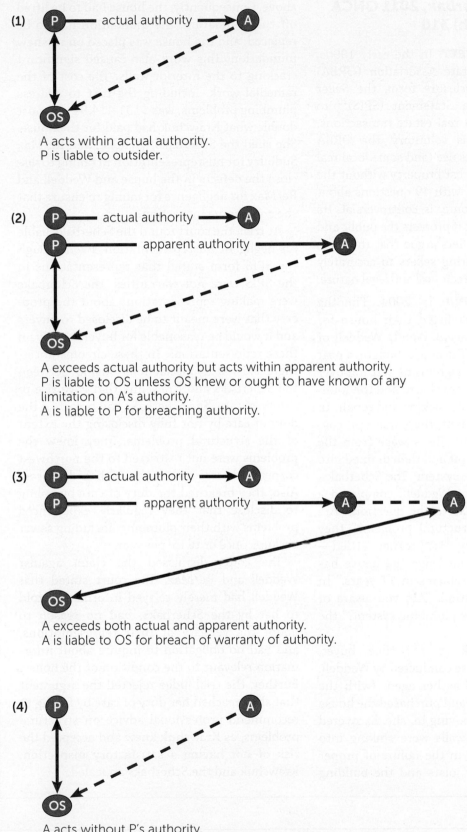

(1)

A acts within actual authority.
P is liable to outsider.

(2)

A exceeds actual authority but acts within apparent authority.
P is liable to OS unless OS knew or ought to have known of any
limitation on A's authority.
A is liable to P for breaching authority.

(3)

A exceeds both actual and apparent authority.
A is liable to OS for breach of warranty of authority.

(4)

A acts without P's authority.
P is liable to OS if P adopts contract.

Krawchuk v Scherbak, 2011 ONCA 352, 332 DLR (4th) 310

CASE

THE BUSINESS CONTEXT: In the early 1990s, the Ontario Real Estate Association (OREA) created a seller's disclosure form, the Seller Property Information Statement (SPIS)[20] to be used in residential real estate transactions. Although the form is voluntary, the OREA strongly encourages its use (and some local real estate boards will not list property without the SPIS form). The form, with 49 questions about the condition of a home, is controversial. Its proponents argue that it protects the public and real estate agents. Others argue that the form is too complex, requiring sellers to accurately answer questions of a technical and legal nature.

FACTUAL BACKGROUND: In 2004, Timothy and Cherese Scherbak listed their house for sale with real estate agent Wendy Weddell of Re/Max Sudbury Inc. The house, built on a peat bog, had experienced significant settling over the years. The floors were sloped and the foundation showed signs of cracking and repair. In addition, in the basement, there was a pit covered with a steel plate. The sewage from the house flowed into the pit and then drained into the municipal sewage system. The Scherbaks, with the assistance of Weddell, completed a SPIS form. In response to the question: "Are you aware of any structural problem?" they disclosed the following: "NW corner settled—to the best of our knowledge the house has settled. No further problems in 17 years." In response to the question, "Are you aware of any problems with the plumbing system?" the answer was, "No."

Zoriana Krawchuk, a first-time buyer, attended an open house conducted by Weddell. She retained Weddell as her agent (with the consent of all parties) and purchased the house for $110 100. After moving in, she discovered that the foundation walls were sinking into the ground, resulting in the failure of proper support for the floor joists and the building

above. Consequently, the house had to be lifted off the foundation, the foundation had to be replaced, and the house was placed on the new foundation. This work also caused significant cracking to the interior walls. The cost of the remedial work, including the cost to address plumbing problems, was $191 414.94—almost double what Krawchuk had paid for the house. She sued the Scherbaks, Weddell, and Re/Max Sudbury for misrepresentation in failing to disclose the defects in the house and Weddell and Re/Max for negligence for failing to ensure that she got a home inspection.

At trial, the court found the Scherbaks liable for negligent misrepresentation. Even though the SPIS form stated that representations in the SPIS were not warranties, the Scherbaks were making representations about the property that were meant to be disclosed to buyers and it would be reasonable for buyers to rely on these representations. In these circumstances, there existed a special relationship between the Scherbaks and Krawchuk that gave rise to a duty of care. The Scherbaks had breached the duty of care by not fully disclosing the extent of the structural problems. They knew the problems were not restricted to the northwest corner and were more serious than disclosed. Also, they breached the duty of care by failing to disclose that they regularly experienced problems with their plumbing, including sewer backups once or twice per year.

The court dismissed the claim against Weddell and Re/Max. The court stated that Weddell had merely relayed information told to her by the Scherbaks, had no reason to doubt the veracity of their representations, and had no obligation to inquire about information relevant to the condition of the house. Further, the trial judge rejected the argument that she breached her duty of care by failing to recommend professional advice on structural problems, as Krawchuk knew and accepted the risk of not having a satisfactory inspection. Krawchuk and the Scherbaks appealed.

---

20 A copy of the SPIS may be obtained from local real estate boards. It is also available at <www.michaelbate.com/SPIS.pdf>.

THE LEGAL QUESTIONS: Are the Scherbaks liable for negligent misrepresentation? Are Weddell and Re/Max liable for negligent misrepresentation and were they negligent in their representation of Krawchuk?

RESOLUTION: The Court of Appeal upheld the trial court decision with respect to the liability of the Scherbaks for negligent misrepresentation. However, it reversed the trial judge's decision on the liability of the real estate agents and held them equally liable with the Scherbaks for Krawchuk's damages. The Court of Appeal referred to the Real Estate Council of Ontario's Code of Ethics, which states that an agent is required to "discover and verify the pertinent facts relating to the property . . ." and an agent "shall encourage the parties to a transaction to seek appropriate outside professional advice when appropriate." Applying these principles, the court held that Weddell had breached her duty of care in that she should have done more to protect her client. Given her awareness of the settling problems, she should have inquired into the sellers' disclosure that the foundation issues were resolved years earlier. She also should have recommended, in the strongest terms, that Krawchuk get an

What are the risks for the agent in a real estate transaction?

independent inspection either before submitting an offer, or by making the offer conditional on a satisfactory inspection. "The failure to do either was an egregious lapse."

CRITICAL ANALYSIS: Do you think this case creates any new duties of real estate agents?

Tort Liability in the Agency Relationship

As a general rule, an agent is personally liable for any torts that she commits. The fact that she may have been acting on behalf of another is no defence in a tort action.[21]

The principal is liable for any tort committed by the agent while the agent is acting within the scope of the agent's authority.[22] Put another way, a principal is vicariously liable for an agent's actions so long as the agent is acting within express, implied, or apparent authority.[23]

For example, assume that Dong is given the responsibility for selling Sonny's inventory of returned suits to discount outlets. Suppose that Dong represents to a discount house that some of these suits are from a famous designer's latest collection and, based on this representation, the discount house purchases a large

---

21 *Supra* note 2 at 202.
22 *Supra* note 2 at 195–96.
23 The question of vicarious liability arising from agency principles overlaps with the application of the doctrine in relation to the acts of employees and independent contractors. For example, a principal is liable for the acts of an agent only if the agent was acting within his actual and apparent authority; however, if the agent has the status of an employee, the employer is liable if the act was committed in the course of employment. Although a principal may not be liable for the agent's acts because they were outside the agent's authority, the employer may be liable for the agent's acts if the agent was an employee acting within the scope of his employment. The liability of employers for the actions of employees and independent contractors is explored in Chapter 20.

number of suits. In this situation, Dong has committed the tort of deceit by representing the suits as suits from a famous designer when in fact they are Sonny's old stock. Dong is personally liable for committing a tort. Sonny is also liable for Dong's actions since they were committed within the scope of his authority.

MANAGING THE RISK OF USING AN AGENT

The agency relationship creates considerable risks for the principal in both contract and tort law. As illustrated in the Business Law in Practice (p. 294) featuring the owner of an Internet tailoring business, a principal may be liable on contracts that are unwanted. This may occur when an agent acts within his actual authority but the principal does not like the resulting contract and when the agent exceeds his actual authority but acts within his apparent authority. A principal is also liable for torts committed while the agent is acting within actual or apparent authority.

While it is impossible to totally eliminate the risk associated with using an agent, a principal may manage the risk by understanding the nature of the agency relationship and how it exposes the principal to risk. The principal can reduce the risk to which she is exposed by doing the following:

- act with care in engaging an agent: check the background of prospective agents and only hire those who can be trusted to act within their authority.
- clarify the agent's authority: spell out the agent's authority in the agency agreement so that the agent understands what he can and cannot do on behalf of the principal.
- monitor the activities of the agent: require the agent to report on her activities to help

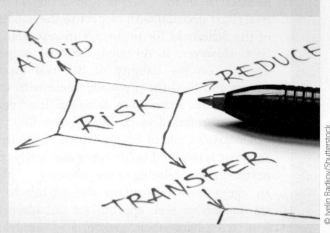

What is the best way of managing the risk of using an agent?

ensure that she stays within the limits of her authority.

- review communications with third parties: make sure both direct and indirect interactions with third parties do not create apparent authority for the agent.
- inform third parties of the termination of an agency relationship: ensure third parties know that an agency relationship no longer exists so that the ex-agent cannot bind the principal.

CRITICAL ANALYSIS: Since the agency relationship creates considerable risk for the principal, why not simply forgo the use of an agent? In other words, why not eliminate the risk by not engaging the services of an agent?

Termination of Agency Agreements

An agency agreement can come to an end in a number of ways:

- the parties may agree to bring their relationship to an end. For example, Sonny and Dong may simply agree to end their relationship.
- one party may give notice of termination to the other.[24]

---

24 As Dong is Sonny's employee, the rules of notice in employment relationships are applicable. These rules are discussed in Chapter 21.

- an agency relationship can cease by operation of the law. Most commonly this occurs due to the death, dissolution (in the case of a corporate agent and/or principal), insanity, or bankruptcy of one of the parties.

When an agency agreement is terminated by the parties, the principal should give notice to third parties so that customers do not assume that the relationship is continuing. In the absence of such notice, the principal may face liability to outsiders, based on his agent's apparent authority.

BUSINESS LAW IN PRACTICE REVISITED

1. What is the nature of the legal relationship between Sonny and Dong?

Dong is an employee of Sonny's business. He was granted the power to purchase fabric and engage tailors in China on Sonny's behalf. Therefore, he is considered in law to be an agent, and the relationship between Sonny and Dong comprises both employment and agency.

2. Is Sonny bound by the expensive fabric contract Dong entered into with the Chinese supplier?

Much of this chapter has been devoted to Sonny's liability on the contracts Dong made on his behalf. Agency law states that the principal, Sonny, is one party to the contract, and that the other party is the outsider, the fabric supplier. The agent, Dong, is merely the means by which the parties enter the contract. Sonny would not be liable for Dong's purchase if the supplier knew or ought to have known that Dong was not authorized to make the purchases he did. But a manufacturer is not expected to know or suspect that Dong was limited to entering into contracts not exceeding $25 000. Sonny is bound, but he can hold Dong liable for breaching his agency agreement in that he exceeded his authority. As noted, however, this will not relieve Sonny of his liability to the fabric supplier, and it is probably not an attractive course of action, as Dong may not have the means of satisfying the debt. As well, suing one's agent can create a lot of adverse publicity.

3. Has Dong breached any duty owed to Sonny by representing other businesses in China?

Dong is an agent for Sonny, the principal. An agent automatically owes a fiduciary duty to his principal. There is no requirement that the duty be specified in the agency agreement or in an exclusive representation contract. The fiduciary duty requires Dong to avoid conflicts of interest unless he has fully disclosed his conflict to Sonny and Sonny has agreed to the conflict. By acting for competitors without Sonny's consent, Dong is in a conflict of interest and in breach of his fiduciary duty.

CHAPTER SUMMARY

This chapter introduced one of the cornerstone relationships in business. Agency is a relationship that allows one person's actions to be attributable to another. In this way, agency permits one party to represent and bind another in contractual matters. Thus a business may use agents in many facets of its operations, such as buying, selling, leasing, and hiring. As a practical matter, without the advantage of agency relationships, business could not be conducted on any significant scale.

The agency relationship most commonly comes into existence when a principal grants authority to the agent to act on her behalf. The law, however, recognizes an agency relationship when the principal represents to another that she is represented by an agent—agency by estoppel—or when the principal adopts a contract made on her behalf by someone who is not her agent—agency by ratification. In this area, it is the substance of the relationship that is important, not what parties call their relationship. An agent's authority to act on behalf of a principal varies. An agent may have actual authority. This is the authority that he is actually given by the principal or that is implied from his position. Alternatively, an agent may have apparent authority. This is the authority that a third party would reasonably believe the agent to have based on the principal's representations. The scope of an agent's apparent authority is fact-specific and therefore varies with the circumstances.

An agent has both express and implied duties to his principal. Most importantly, an agent has a fiduciary duty to act in the best interests of the principal. The principal also has express and implied duties, particularly the duty to compensate the agent for services rendered and for costs associated with the agency relationship.

Agency operates in such a way that the principal is generally liable on contracts entered into by the agent on her behalf. A contract is formed between the principal and the outsider, and the agent drops out of the transaction. Though there are a number of potential problems, the agency relationship generally functions well and according to plan. However, it is possible that agency can operate in ways not desired. For example, the principal may be liable on contracts not desired, as when the agent negotiates a poor contract or exceeds his actual authority but not his apparent authority. So too, a principal may be liable for torts committed by an agent. Thus, ironically, the same person who can help a business grow and prosper can lead that same enterprise to financial loss. The key point is that agency, like other aspects of a business, needs to be managed and monitored: businesspeople must choose an agent wisely, instruct him carefully, and review his work regularly.

CHAPTER STUDY

Key Terms and Concepts

actual authority (p. 298)

agency (p. 295)

agency by estoppel (p. 300)

agency by ratification (p. 302)

agent (p. 295)

apparent authority (p. 299)

fiduciary (p. 304)

fiduciary duty (p. 304)

insurance broker (p. 308)

law of agency (p. 297)

outsider (p. 296)

power of attorney (p. 298)

principal (p. 295)

undisclosed principal (p. 310)

warranty of authority (p. 309)

Questions for Review

1. What is agency? Give an example.

2. Why would a business use an agent to act on its behalf?

3. How is an agency relationship entered into?

4. What is the difference between the actual and apparent authority of an agent?

5. When will an agent have implied authority?

6. What is meant by agency by estoppel? How does agency by estoppel arise?

7. How is an agency by ratification created?

8. Is a principal permitted to ratify any contract entered into by an "agent?" Explain.

9. Is a real estate agent a typical agent? Explain.

10. What are the duties of the agent?

11. What are the duties of the principal?

12. Do all business advisors owe fiduciary duties? Explain.

13. When can an agent be personally liable on a contract entered into on behalf of a principal?

14. Describe how an agent can be liable to the principal.

15. When is a principal liable for torts committed by an agent?

16. How can a principal manage the risk of using an agent?

17. What is an undisclosed principal?

18. How may an agency relationship be terminated?

Questions for Critical Thinking

1. In the insurance industry, the agent acts primarily for the insurance company, which is the principal. Typically, the insurance agent also advises the client on the needed coverage and the meaning of the insurance policy. Do you see any potential problems with this situation?

2. Is it reasonable to hold principals responsible for contracts formed with only apparent authority? What are the tradeoffs?

3. Is a "real estate agent" an agent in law? Explain.

4. In the Ethical Considerations box (pages 308–309), it was noted that life insurance brokers may receive a variety of compensation from insurance companies for the business that they direct to them. In the standard disclosure letter given to consumers at the time of purchasing a life insurance policy, there is usually a line stating that some companies may provide compensation to the insurance broker such as travel incentives or educational opportunities, in addition to commissions. Does disclosure in this manner address the criticism that such travel incentives and educational opportunities amount to a conflict of interest?

5. It is critical to a fiduciary relationship that there was some undertaking on the part of the fiduciary to act with loyalty. The undertaking may be express or implied. What factors do you think are important in determining whether there has been an implied undertaking to act as a fiduciary?

6. The agency relationship creates considerable risks for the principal. What is the nature of these risks in both contract and tort? How can these risks be managed? Does the agency relationship create risks for the agent? Explain.

Situations for Discussion

1. Perry Logan owned a small office building in suburban Halifax. As he was nearing retirement, Perry listed his building for sale with Alice Marshall, a real estate agent. While Perry was on an extended visit to Florida looking for a retirement property, he authorized Alice to sell the building on his behalf provided the offer was for at least $600 000. Alice showed the property to Dee Shannahan during the term of the listing agreement but Dee did not make an offer.

   Two weeks after the listing agreement between Perry and Alice expired, Dee made an offer to purchase the property for $625 000. Alice accepted the offer on behalf of Perry. Is there a contract between Perry and Dee? Explain.

2. RCD Ltd. sells household appliances, including washers, dryers, dishwashers, stoves, and refrigerators. Most of RCD's customers are developers of apartment buildings and condominium complexes. RCD's sales representative is Alastair Du. He is authorized

to make contracts with buyers provided the value of each contract does not exceed $100 000. Alastair ignored the restriction on his authority and concluded a contract to sell 50 sets of washers and dryers to BES Developers at a price of $500 000. BES placed its order on RCD's application form, which states that contracts over $100 000 require written approval of RCD's vice president of sales, and Alastair on behalf of RCD accepted the order. RCD delivered the 50 sets of washer and dryers, and received payment from BES. Within a month of delivery of the washers and dryers, BES complained that the washers vibrate excessively and the dryers overheat, and they have caused damage to the apartments in which they were installed. RCD claimed to be protected from any liability for the faulty machines because Alastair had no authority to bind RCD to this contract. Does RCD's argument constitute a valid legal defence to a claim against RCD by BES? Explain.

3. Atlantic Life Ltd. is a life insurance company. The corporation hired Toby Ryan as its representative in Newfoundland. Toby was provided with Atlantic Life business cards and brochures, along with a company car with the Atlantic Life logo on it. A clause in the contract between the parties provided:

> The representative will not without the prior approval of the Company incur any liability or debt on behalf of the Company, accept insurance or other risks, revive policies, waive forfeitures, extend the time of payment of any premium or waive premium payment in cash, or make, alter, or discharge any contract, and will not make any expenditure on behalf of the Company.

Toby negotiated on behalf of Atlantic Life the sale of a life insurance policy to Sadie Clements, insuring her life for $500 000. Shortly thereafter, Sadie died and her beneficiaries claimed benefits under the policy. Atlantic Life refuses to pay on the basis that Toby did not obtain approval of Atlantic Life for the sale of the insurance policy.[25]

Does Atlantic Life have to pay the benefits? If it does, how could it have prevented this situation?

4. Imam Daud Malik, a community organizer, had connections and influence with Sudanese politicians and government officials. He was interested in using these connections to promote relations between Islamic states and American Muslims. Through mutual acquaintances, Malik met Khan, the president of State Petroleum Corp. Khan, along with other investors, had incorporated State Petroleum to pursue the acquisition of oil concessions in Sudan. At the request of Khan, Malik assisted State in its efforts. There was no contract in place regarding Malik's services. A short time later, State entered into an agreement with the government of Sudan for the acquisition of oil concessions valued at $18 million. Malik claimed compensation from State for his services, but State refused to pay.[26]

Is Malik entitled to compensation from State? Explain. If he is entitled, what factors are important in determining the amount of compensation?

5. Mollie Morrow was a real estate agent working for Commercial Properties. She was approached by Shane Jacobs to find a commercial building in downtown Halifax. She did some investigating and found a suitable property owned by Haldane Properties (HP). She approached the owners about selling, and they agreed to pay a commission of 2 percent if she acted as their agent in the sale of the building. After considerable negotiations, the sale was concluded for $6 million. Unknown to HP, Mollie had agreed to pay half of her commission to Shane. When HP learned about this, it refused to pay the commission. Mollie argued that HP had received what it wanted out of the deal; she had made a sacrifice by giving up part of her commission; and her sacrifice ensured that the deal went through. In short, her actions helped, not harmed, HP.[27] Is Mollie entitled to the commission?

25 Based on *Schwartz v Maritime Life Assurance Co* (1997), 149 Nfld & PEIR 234, [1997] NJ 77 (Nfld CA), leave to appeal to SCC refused, [1997] SCCA 362.

26 Based on *Malik (Representative Ad litem of) v State Petroleum Corp*, 2009 BCCA 505, 98 BCLR (4th) 92.

27 Based on *Ocean City Realty Ltd v A & M Holdings Ltd et al*, 36 DLR (4th) 94, [1987] BCJ 593 (BCCA).

6. Hamilton Utility Inc. appointed Juan Abrams as one of its corporate officers. Juan rented cars from Quality Cars Ltd., a car rental business. The rental agreements named Juan as renter, and he signed the agreements describing himself as company secretary of Hamilton Utility. Juan, however, used the cars for personal purposes and not for company business. Hamilton refused to pay the charges, as Juan had not been given any authority to enter contracts on its behalf.[28]

   Is Hamilton liable to pay the car rental charges? Explain. What would be the result if Hamilton appointed Juan to a secretarial position?

7. Srini Nair owns and operates a grocery store in Fort McMurray. He has a number of employees including Ragini Sharma, who is his assistant manager. Ragini has very limited authority to act on Srini's behalf. One day while Srini is out of town, a distributor of produce offers Ragini a great deal on fiddleheads, a delicacy from New Brunswick. Due to the perishable nature of fiddleheads, the deal is only available for one day. As Srini's grocery store caters to many transplanted New Brunswickers, Ragini places an order. When Srini returns the next day and the fiddleheads arrive, he rejects them on the basis that he has never heard of anyone ever eating fiddleheads. Is Srini bound to accept and pay for the fiddleheads? How should businesses like Srini's deal with the risk of employees exceeding their authority to act on behalf of the business?

8. Ty Sharim has been employed as an agent for Farley's Game and Fishing Lodge Inc. for the past 10 years. Farley's runs an exclusive hunting and fishing camp in northern Ontario. Ty's contractual duties include advertising the camp and soliciting customers at fish and gun shows and conventions in North America and elsewhere. One weekend while on a fishing trip with his family, Ty came across a small fishing camp that was for sale. As Ty has always dreamed of owning and operating his own business, he is thinking of putting in an offer on the camp. Is Ty entitled to put in an offer to purchase the camp, or must he inform Farley's of the camp? Would the answer differ if Ty terminated his relationship with Farley's before offering to buy the camp?

---

28 *Panorama Developments (Guildford) Ltd v Fidelis Furnishing Fabrics Ltd*, [1971] 2 QB 711 (CA).

14

OBJECTIVES

After studying this chapter, you should have an understanding of

- the characteristics of the major forms of business organizations

- the advantages and disadvantages of the major forms of business organizations

- the legal consequences of a partnership

- methods of arranging business activity

BUSINESS FORMS AND ARRANGEMENTS

BUSINESS LAW IN PRACTICE

Luke Bailey grew up in rural Saskatchewan and dreamed of playing in the National Hockey League (NHL). Unfortunately, after a few years of playing semi-professional hockey in the southern United States, Luke was forced to give up on his NHL aspirations because of a chronic injury. He returned to Canada and settled in Calgary. Luke maintained his love for the game but it was now channelled into playing with a very active pick-up league that was populated by a wide circle of friends, colleagues, and other like-minded individuals. Luke was soon prevailed upon to also manage the league but quickly became overwhelmed by organizational headaches and financial stresses associated with the job. Aside from the time commitment required to contact people in advance and at the last minute (to see if they were going to show up) and the financial cost of no-shows, Luke noticed that confusion over ice times led to spotty attendance and the folding of teams. Luke thought there had to be a better way. Not being technologically savvy, Luke contacted a friend of his, Raina El Khoury, a computer engineering graduate, to help devise a solution to the problems he had observed.

For the next 18 months, Luke and Raina worked on the scheduling issues facing pick-up hockey leagues in general and came up with a very promising solution.[1] Their program design permitted the contact information of league players, as well as each team's schedule and roster, to be uploaded on a web platform—otherwise known as a content management system. Once the data was uploaded, managers, organizers, and coaches could essentially put their team on autopilot. Contacting players became easy, including by text messaging. Collecting registration and drop-in fees also went more smoothly. And since the system also integrated with mobile devices and desktop calendars, players had ready access to their schedules at all times. Excited by their innovation, Luke and Raina began marketing their product by word-of-mouth to various pick-up leagues in western Canada. The results were amazing. They soon had several dozen hockey leagues' teams interested and paying for the service. But most encouraging was that teams in other sports were also interested, as well as organizations as diverse as church groups and poker players. For the next

---

1 The idea for this business is based on Rosterbot at <www.rosterbot.com>. See also Anwar Ali, "Hockey jocks join forces to kickstart Rosterbot" *The Financial Post* (6 May 2014) online *Financial Post* <http://business.financialpost.com/2014/05/06/hockey-jocks-join-forces-to-kickstart-rosterbot/>.

six months, Luke and Raina ran the team management system out of Luke's basement. Raina handled the technical side of the service, and Luke handled the cash from the subscriptions and did a bit of marketing. The business grew rapidly with inquiries from other parts of Canada, the United States, and overseas for the service. It actually became more business than Luke and Raina could handle.

Believing that they had a hit, Luke and Raina contacted a business incubator for advice on further developing and marketing their product. Sandra Higgins, of Envision Business Labs, met with Luke and Raina and introduced them to Roger Wiley, a retired businessperson who was willing to invest a maximum of $200 000 from his retirement fund. He was also willing to help out in the business as he had considerable contacts with various organizations that might be interested in the product. Within this context, Sandra observed to Luke and Raina that they were apparently running their business as a partnership but such a business vehicle was unlikely to be the best form for an expansion, especially given Roger's requirements. She suggested that they evaluate together how best to proceed.

1. What business forms are available for carrying on Luke and Raina's business?

2. What are the major considerations in choosing a particular form?

3. What form is best for Luke and Raina's business?

Forms of Business Organization

Choosing how to own a business is a critical decision because it determines in large part who

- is financially liable for the business.
- shares in business profits and other assets.
- makes and is accountable for management decisions.

The Sole Proprietorship

The **sole proprietorship** is the oldest form of business organization and the one most often used by small businesses. It is a particularly popular choice for the home-based enterprise. From a legal perspective, it also represents the simplest form of business organization because there is no legislation pertaining to the sole proprietorship as such. A discussion of the legal consequences of this form of business is a discussion of the rights and liabilities of an individual. Luke, Raina, and Roger could run their business as a sole proprietorship with one being the sole proprietor and the others being employees and/or creditors. The following considers the implications of a sole proprietorship (and assumes Luke to be the sole proprietor).

Sole proprietorship

An unincorporated business organization that has only one owner.

Financial Liability

The financial consequences to Luke should he conduct his business as a sole proprietorship are both straightforward and significant: any obligation of the business is Luke's personal obligation. Consider the following examples.

- *The bank loan.* If Luke decides to borrow money from the bank, it is Luke who promises to repay the loan, not his business. This is because a sole proprietorship, unlike a corporation, is not legally capable of borrowing money on its own. Luke *is* the business; Luke is the debtor and is responsible for the debt.

Suppose that the business begins to falter and the loan cannot be repaid. The bank will take the appropriate legal steps—discussed in more detail in Chapter 26—to recover as much as it can on the loan. All of Luke's business and personal assets are subject to the debts of the business. Also, any judgment against him can be kept alive indefinitely unless he declares bankruptcy, in which case, most judgments against him will be discharged. However, Luke's personal credit rating will be adversely affected, now and in the future. This may make it next to impossible ever to start another venture that would depend on Luke's creditworthiness.

- *The breach of contract.* If at some point the business supplies a defective system to a customer, Luke is in breach of contract. This is because, as noted above, the business cannot enter into a contract. As in the preceding example, Luke is the one who will be sued, and it is Luke's assets that are at risk.

Unlimited liability

Unrestricted legal responsibility for obligations.

In short, a sole proprietor has what is known in law as **unlimited liability**. Regardless of what the owner has invested in his business, his personal assets—and not just the business assets—may be seized to pay the outstanding debts of the business. Unfortunately, these debts can far exceed anything anticipated when the business was started.

Profit Sharing

The sole proprietor not only bears the risk of failure, but also enjoys this advantage: all the profits after taxes accrue to the sole proprietor alone. If the business is a runaway success, Luke reaps all the benefits. The profit motive can be a strong incentive for the sole proprietor to seek to ensure the success of the business.

Decision Making

The sole proprietor, having no partners and no board of directors to report to, can make business decisions very quickly and independently. She has a lot of personal freedom to do exactly as she pleases concerning all aspects of the business, even if it means deciding to discontinue business activities altogether. Should the owner die, the business is terminated—in other words, the sole proprietorship has a limited life span.

There are, of course, disadvantages to working alone in this way: few people are good at everything, yet the sole proprietor is responsible for every aspect of the business, from buying and selling to financing and advertising. Another serious consideration is that the sole proprietor's absence through illness or incapacity can adversely affect the business because so much of the enterprise revolves around this one individual. Though the sole proprietor may hire employees, such as Raina or Roger, he has limited opportunities for advancement, since by definition a sole proprietorship is a one-person show. As a result, these workers may not be particularly motivated or able to provide a high level of commitment.

MJTH/Shutterstock

What are the advantages of a sole proprietorship?

Sources of Capital

A major difficulty with "going it alone" is that the sole proprietor has limited access to capital. Since the proprietor has no business partners, he is limited to his own assets and whatever credit he can draw on to finance the operation. Usually this is less than what would be available if more than one person was involved, as in a partnership, for example.

Taxation

Because a sole proprietorship is not a legal entity separate from the owner, there are no formal or specialized tax rules governing it. Profits and losses are simply reported on the owner's personal income tax return. This may be favourable or unfavourable depending on the taxpayer's circumstances, including whether the owner's marginal tax rate is higher or lower than the applicable corporate tax rate.

Transferability

A sole proprietorship cannot be transferred or sold to another because it has no legal status. There is, in effect, nothing to transfer. However, the assets associated with the proprietorship—such as inventory—are transferable.

Regulations

The legal requirements for establishing and conducting this form of business organization are minimal—one simply commences business activity. There is no general need to incur legal fees to create the business vehicle. In short, doing business through the sole proprietorship is simple and inexpensive.

This is not to say that sole proprietorships are unregulated. They are subject to the same general legislation as any other business form. One important requirement is the registration or licensing of the business. Requirements vary from province to province but, generally, persons who offer specialized services to the public must be licensed to practise their particular skill. Thus, lawyers, doctors, dentists, and electricians, for example, are required to follow provincial legislation governing their activity before providing services. Some businesses, such as those involving interprovincial trucking, require a federal licence to operate. Other types of business, such as door-to-door selling and the transportation of goods, are subject to specialized rules. The fees associated with licensing and registration are generally not substantial.

In addition to the regulations put in place by the federal and provincial governments, municipalities often impose their own registration or licensing requirements. For example, taxi businesses frequently require municipal licences to operate within municipal boundaries.

A sole proprietor who wishes to use a name other than her own for conducting the business must register the name at the local registry office or other government office designated by the province, where such records are kept and made available to the public.[2] The objective is to enable a person who deals with such a business to determine the identity of the proprietor of the business. Failure to register may result in a fine or other penalty and the inability to sue for an obligation incurred in connection with the business except with leave of the court.[3]

---

2 The use of trade or business names is discussed in Chapter 18.
3 See, for example, *Business Names Act*, RSO 1990, c B-17, s 7.

FIGURE 14.1 Pros and Cons of the Sole Proprietorship

Pros	Cons
Simplicity: There are few licensing and registration requirements. The sole proprietor just starts doing business and is free to discontinue business activities at any time.	**Unlimited personal liability:** The sole proprietor carries the risk of the business failing and losing both business and personal assets.
Speed and independence: Since the sole proprietor has no partners and is not answerable to a board of directors, he can make decisions quickly and independently.	**Working alone:** The sole proprietor is responsible for all aspects of the business operation. Though a sole proprietor can hire employees, it is difficult to retain high-calibre people because of the limited opportunities available to them in a sole proprietorship.
Profit motive: Any after-tax profit or other assets that accrue go entirely to the sole proprietor.	**Limited access to capital:** The capital available to the business is limited to the assets of the proprietor and the extent of her credit.
Lower costs: The fees for provincial and municipal licences are relatively small, varying according to the nature and size of the business and the municipality in which it is located. Generally, there is no need to incur legal fees.	**Limited life span:** The owner's death terminates the business. The proprietorship cannot be transferred.
Tax benefits: Profits and losses are reported on the owner's personal income tax return. This may be favourable or unfavourable, depending on the taxpayer's circumstances.	**Tax disadvantages:** See tax benefits.

Aside from these requirements, the sole proprietor is subject to laws of general application. Local zoning bylaws may require sole proprietors to locate in certain areas, provincial tax laws may require them to obtain a permit to act as a collector of sales tax, and health legislation may require them to maintain a high degree of cleanliness where food service or processing is involved. As well, a sole proprietor who hires employees must comply with all applicable legislation, such as that regulating employment standards, employment insurance, workers' compensation, and occupational health and safety.

A sole proprietor (unlike a public corporation) is not required to publish the business's financial statements. Success or failure in the business is a private matter, restricted to the proprietor, the business's accountant, the Canada Revenue Agency, and perhaps the local bank manager.

The pros and cons of the sole proprietorship are summarized in Figure 14.1.

The Partnership

Partnership

A business carried on by two or more persons with the intention of making a profit.

When two or more persons want to pool their resources and carry on business together, one of the most common options is to form a **partnership** (a second common option is to create a corporation as discussed below[4]). A partnership is much like a sole proprietorship in that neither has a legal personality—or legal existence—separate from the people who comprise them. There are no special steps to create a partnership. It is simply the legal relationship that automatically arises when two or more people do business together with the objective of making a profit. Luke and Raina are carrying on their business as partners; an option for them is for Roger to join them as a partner.

The rules governing partnerships come from three sources: partnership legislation (in place in every province), contract law, and agency law. Later in the

---

4   There can be restrictions on professionals, such as accountants and lawyers, incorporating companies. See Chapter 22 for detail.

chapter, these sources will be analyzed in some depth. What follows is a general account of the basic principles that govern partnerships.

Financial Liability

If Luke, Raina, and Roger join forces to market the time management system through a partnership, each has unlimited liability for partnership debts and other obligations. Consider the following examples.

- *The bank loan*. If the partners borrow money from the bank (say $100 000 plus interest) and fail to repay it Luke, Raina, and Roger are liable for the full amount outstanding. This is because—like a sole proprietorship but unlike a corporation—a partnership is not legally capable of borrowing money on its own. The partners are the partnership. The partners are the debtors and are responsible for the debt.

A very important feature of partnership law is that each partner is fully responsible for all the debts and obligations of the partnership and not just for some appropriate proportion. Accordingly, the bank can proceed against the partner with the most assets—perhaps Roger—and collect from that one individual the entire amount owing on the debt. In law, this is known as **joint liability**.[5] The liability is considered to be joint because responsibility is not in relation to the partner's share in the partnership; rather, each one of the partners has full and complete exposure on each and every obligation incurred. However, if the bank proceeds only against Roger for repayment of the bank loan, Roger is entitled to be reimbursed by his partners for their share of the debt. Of course, if the other partners have no assets, Roger will end up bearing the partnership debts himself.

- *The breach of contract*. If the partnership supplies a defective system to a customer, each of the partners is liable for the entire amount of the damages. The contract is between the customer, on the one hand, and all the partners, on the other.

The key point from a liability perspective is that each partner's personal assets can be seized and sold through the judicial process if the partnership assets are insufficient to satisfy partnership obligations. This legal reality should give Roger particular cause for concern. Since Roger wants to limit his financial exposure to $200 000 because the money is from his retirement fund, he will probably not find the partnership to be a feasible business vehicle through which to market the team management system. This is because a partnership, like a sole proprietorship, puts all of Roger's assets at risk, not just his capital contribution. Luke and Raina also have cause for concern. Although they may have less at risk, they still need to consider the impact of a judgment on their assets and their future.

Profit Sharing

It is the partners themselves who decide how profits and other firm assets are to be divided. If they fail to agree on this point, partnership legislation requires them to share profits equally.[6]

Joint liability

Liability shared by two or more parties where each is personally liable for the full amount of the obligation.

PART FOUR

---

5 See, for example, *Partnership Act*, RSNB 1973, c P-4, s 10: "Every partner in a firm is liable jointly with the other partners for all debts and obligations of the firm while he is a partner. . . ."

6 *Ibid*, s 25(a): "The interests of partners in the partnership property and their rights and duties in relation to the partnership shall be determined, subject to any agreement express or implied between the partners, by the following rules: all partners are entitled to share equally in the capital and profits of the business, and must contribute equally towards the losses whether of capital or otherwise sustained by the firm."

Luke, Raina, and Roger may decide to divide the partnership into unequal interests because the contribution of each partner varies. Since Luke and Raina have been developing and marketing the product, they may have a majority interest, for example 40 percent each. Since Roger may only be helping out and be unlikely to have much involvement in the day-to-day operations but contributing considerable capital, his interest in the firm may be set at 20 percent. The point is that the relationship among the partners themselves—including profit sharing—is something they are free to define in any way they see fit.

Decision Making

Because a partnership comprises two or more persons pooling their resources, the management base is potentially strong. Luke's ideas and vision, Raina's technical expertise, and Roger's business experience will all assist in making the business a viable operation. If one of the partners becomes sick or otherwise unable to devote sufficient attention to the business, the other partners are in place to carry on.

The downside is that managing the business will require consultation among the partners, and they may not always achieve consensus. A dispute or disagreement between the partners can be extremely disruptive. Even though the partners may have agreed in advance—through a partnership agreement—on a method of dispute resolution, such clauses can be subject to varying interpretations and can be the source of ill feeling among the partners.

Just as there is the danger of disagreement, there is also the danger of divided authority, which may impede decision making. Although the partners may have determined that they will have authority in different areas, instances are bound to arise in which responsibility overlaps. This too can result in conflict and delayed decision making.

Sources of Capital

Because a partnership is composed of two or more persons, it provides more sources of capital than a sole proprietorship. The partnership looks to each partner for a capital contribution and can rely on the creditworthiness of each one to secure financing from other sources, including the bank.

Taxation

The partnership is not a separate legal entity, and therefore any income from the partnership business is allocated to the partners—on the basis of their interest in the partnership—and they must, in turn, include it on their individual tax returns.[7]

Transferability

The partnership does not provide for the ready transfer of interest from one owner to another. Partners do not individually own or have a share in specific partnership property. Each partner has an interest in all partnership property, from the photocopier to the laptops to its intellectual property.

Agency and the Partnership Act

Partnership law is based in large part on contract law, agency law, and provincial partnership legislation, known in every jurisdiction as the *Partnership Act*.[8] The

---

7   J Anthony VanDuzer, *The Law of Partnerships and Corporations*, 3d ed (Toronto: Irwin Law, 2009) at 12.
8   Legislation is virtually identical across the common law provinces.

legislation in place in the common law provinces provides mandatory rules with respect to

- when a partnership exists.
- what the relationship of partners is to outsiders.

These acts have optional rules (i.e., the rules are subject to an agreement to the contrary) with respect to

- the relationship of partners to one another.
- how and why a partnership ends.

Some of these partnership concepts have already been introduced to give a sketch of how partnerships operate relative to other business vehicles. The following section describes partnerships from a more technical and detailed perspective.

When a Partnership Exists According to the *Partnership Act*, a partnership exists when two or more people "carry on business in common with a view towards profit." The definition excludes charitable and not-for-profit endeavours. It does not, however, exclude unprofitable ventures that otherwise meet the definition of partnership so long as an intention to make a profit is present.

The statutory definition of partnership covers people who expressly intend to be partners as well as people who may not necessarily intend to be partners but act as if they were. That is, a person who conducts himself as if he were a partner—by sharing in profits, managing the business, or contributing capital to establish a business—is a partner in the eyes of the law. Such a person, therefore, has all the rights and liabilities of a partner.

The *Partnership Act* also sets out a number of circumstances that point toward there being a partnership but not conclusively so.[9] For example, if two or more persons own property together, this does not of itself make them partners. However, if in addition to owning property together, the persons share profits associated with that property and restrict their ability to unilaterally sell their interest in the property, a court is likely to conclude that a partnership exists.[10] This would likely be the result even though the parties have indicated in their written agreement that their relationship is not a "partnership."[11] The court will look to the essence of the relationship rather than the labels used by the parties.

This means, for example, that if Roger wants to take an active part in the management of the business and share in the profits yet simultaneously avoid the joint, unlimited personal liability that goes with partnership, he is unlikely to succeed. If the business runs into financial difficulties, creditors can come after Roger for the liabilities, even if Roger has a document—signed by Luke and Raina—stating that Roger is not a partner. In classifying Roger's status, what matters is what Roger actually does in relation to the business, not what a document says.

---

9 *Supra* note 5 at s 3. The legislation provides that a number of situations do not by themselves create a partnership. A relationship is not necessarily a "partnership" in the following situations: the parties jointly own property; one party receives repayment of a debt out of profits; an employment contract where remuneration varies with profits; a loan where the lender's compensation is to be a share of profits; an annuity paid out of profits to a spouse or child of a deceased partner; and receipt of a share of profits of a business paid to a vendor as consideration for the sale of a business.

10 For a discussion of the difference between partnership and mere co-ownership, see *AE LePage Ltd v Kamex Developments Ltd* (1977), 16 OR (2d) 193, 78 DLR (3d) 223 (CA), aff'd [1979] 2 SCR 155, 105 DLR (3d) 84 (SCC).

11 *Lansing Building Supply (Ontario) Ltd v Ierullo*, (1989) CarswellOnt 2316, 71 OR (2d) 173 (Dist Ct).

THE LOTTERY PARTNERSHIP?

Nineteen employees of Bell Canada won a $50 million Lotto Max prize on New Year's Eve. A short time later, nine of their colleagues whose names were not on the group form—and who had not contributed to the purchase of the winning ticket—claimed a share of the prize. The nine claimants alleged that they had been part of a group of lottery players at the Bell Toronto office that constituted a partnership. They claimed that the rules of their partnership provided that each of the partners would contribute an agreed-upon weekly amount towards the purchase of lottery tickets, and that partners who failed to contribute on a specific occasion due to a temporary absence for any reason would be permitted and expected to make their required payment at a later time. They further claimed that the 19 winners withdrew from the partnership and formed their own group without any notice, either written or oral, of the unilateral dissolution or termination of the partnership arrangement.

The parties submitted their dispute to binding arbitration and ultimately, the arbitrator dismissed the claims of the nine co-workers. The lawyer, representing the Bell 19, said the arbitrator's ruling boils down to: "If you pay, you're

Is the relationship between the members of a group of lottery players a partnership?

in. If we bought a ticket together last March and I win (with another ticket) in December, you can't say because we were together in March, I'm a lifetime partner."[12]

Critical Analysis: Do you think this decision precludes a lottery group from being a partnership? How could the parties have prevented this dispute?

Source: Anna Mehler Paperny, "Nine Bell employees sue 19 co-workers over $50-million lottery jackpot", *The Globe and Mail* (22 May 2011) online: *The Globe and Mail* <http://www.theglobeandmail.com/news/national/toronto/nine-bell-employees-sue-colleagues-over-50-million-lotto-max-win/article1913556/>.

The Relationship of Partners to One Another If Luke, Raina, and Roger become partners, the *Partnership Act* provides that they also become one another's agents as well as the agents of the firm in matters relating to the partnership's business. This is significant because it imports the law concerning agency, discussed in Chapter 13. It also means that the partners owe fiduciary duties to one another, which require a partner to put the interests of her partners above her own interests.

Accordingly, Luke cannot set up a secret business that competes with the partnership he has formed with Raina and Roger. He cannot tell a client of the firm to buy a time management system from him "on the side" and then proceed to pocket the profits, or use the firm photocopier at night to run a duplicating service without his partners' permission. In short, the law does not allow a partner to make personal profit from the partnership property, to compete against the

12 Alyshah Hasham, "The Bell 19 get full $50 million Lotto Max jackpot after two-year dispute" *The Star* (13 November 2012) online: The Star <http://www.thestar.com/news/gta/2012/11/13/the_bell_19_get_full_50_million_lotto_max_jackpot_after_twoyear_dispute.html>.

FIGURE 14.2 Partnership Agreement Checklist

A partnership has been described as a "marriage without love" because many of the concerns that partners face are similar to the ones faced by spouses—sharing of work, financial matters, authority to make decisions, and resolution of disputes. And just as many marriages end in divorce, so too many partnerships fail. Just as a marriage contract cannot save a bad marriage, a partnership agreement cannot guarantee a successful partnership. An agreement can, however, help in avoiding costly litigation and personal animosity if a "divorce" proves necessary.

A partnership agreement should address the following issues:

Creation of the partnership—name and address of partners, partnership name, term of partnership, if any, description of firm's business

Capital contribution—description of contribution by each partner, how shortfalls are handled, how the accounts are managed

Decision making—description of the partners' duties, any limits on authority, dispute resolution mechanism

Profit distribution—description of how profits are to be shared, how and when they are to be distributed, rights of withdrawal

Changes to partnership—rules for changing the relationship, admission of new partners, retirement of partners, option to purchase partner's interest, valuation of interests

Dissolution of partnership—description of events that could trigger dissolution, how dissolution will be handled, valuation of assets

A partnership agreement should also be reviewed and updated periodically to reflect changes in circumstances.

partnership, or to use a partnership opportunity for exclusive personal gain. Luke is required by law to put the interests of the partnership ahead of his own.

Persons who wish to be associated in partnership should have a partnership agreement, preferably one drafted by a lawyer; Figure 14.2 summarizes the issues that the agreement should address. The partnership agreement provides the parties with significant freedom to define their relationship. For example, a partnership agreement can provide for the division of profits among Luke, Raina, and Roger in any proportion they see fit. If there is no agreement, the *Partnership Act* will dictate that Luke, Raina, and Roger will share in profits equally—a result that may be neither wanted nor intended.

As already noted, if the partners do not have a contract or if they have a contract that is silent on some points, the *Partnership Act* of the province in which the partners are residing will govern the relationship.

Relationship of Partners to Outsiders While partners are free to enter into a partnership agreement in order to set out the rights and obligations between them, this will not modify the relationship between partners and outsiders, which is governed specifically by the *Partnership Act* and generally by partnership law, including agency law.

First and foremost, a partner is an agent of the firm. She acts for herself as well as for her partners, who from the perspective of the agency relationship are her principals. For this reason, the firm is responsible for contracts she enters into with actual or apparent authority. For example, assume that Raina enters into a long-term contract with an advertising agency. Assume further that Luke and Roger are appalled, since it is not clear that advertising services are needed at this point, let alone for an extended period of time. They are still bound, however, because Raina—as a partner and therefore as their agent—has the apparent authority to enter into contracts for marketing services for the purpose of the partnership.

THE *PARTNERSHIP ACT:* THE RELATIONS BETWEEN PARTNERS

All of the common law provinces have a *Partnership Act* modelled on the British Act of the same name. These Acts are substantially similar from province to province and have been subject to little change since their original enactments.

The Acts have both mandatory and optional provisions. The mandatory provisions relate to the relationship between partners and outsiders. The optional rules with respect to the relationship between partners can therefore be varied by agreement.

In each province, the *Partnership Act* provides for the following optional rules:

1. All partners are to share equally in the capital and profits of the business and must contribute equally to the losses.

2. Property acquired for the partnership shall be used exclusively for the partnership and not for the private purposes of individual partners. Property purchased with partnership money is deemed to be partnership property.

3. A partner shall be indemnified by the other partners for any liability incurred on behalf of the partnership. This means that all partners are liable for partnership liabilities and that a partner who pays a debt is entitled to reimbursement from her partners.

4. A payment made by a partner for the purposes of the partnership in excess of his agreed subscription shall earn interest.

5. Each partner may take part in the management of the business.

6. No partner is entitled to remuneration for acting in the partnership business.

7. No new member shall be admitted to the partnership without the consent of all the partners.

8. Disputes regarding the partnership business may be decided by a majority, but the nature of the partnership may not be changed without the consent of all the members.

9. Partnership books shall be kept at the partnership's place of business, and all partners shall have access to them.

10. No simple majority may expel any partner.

Critical Analysis: When are the optional rules appropriate for partners?

Source: *Partnership Act*, RSNB 1973, c P-4, ss 21(1), 25, 26.

Between the disappointed principals (Luke and Roger) and the advertising agency that had no idea that Raina was entering into a contract unpopular with her partners, the law protects the advertising agency. This is because Raina's partners are in a better position to monitor and restrict her ability to do business on behalf of the firm, even to the point of voting her out of the partnership altogether. They must, therefore, absorb the risk of her "going astray."

Indeed, because the relationship between partners is based on agreement, Raina's authority to enter into contracts on behalf of the firm can be restricted. The parties can enter into an agreement whereby Raina promises not to enter into any long-term contract without first securing her partners' approval. Raina will presumably respect and abide by this restriction. However, should she enter into a contract that exceeds her actual authority, the firm will still be bound unless the outsider knows or should know that her authority has been limited in this way. The firm is obligated by virtue of the doctrine of apparent authority.

The *Partnership Act* and agency law also make partners responsible for one another's mistakes. For example, if Luke gives poor advice to an organization as to its time management needs and is sued for the tort of negligence, all the partners, not just Luke, are liable for any damages that result. This is because Luke was acting in the course of firm business and incurred a liability by committing a tort. He and his partners have **joint and several liability**.[13]

Each partner is individually as well as collectively responsible for the entire obligation. This means that the client can recover all of the damages from any partner or he can recover some of the damages from each. A partner who pays the debt may, however, have a right of contribution from the other partners.

Joint and several liability

Individual and collective liability for a debt. Each liable party is individually responsible for the entire debt as well as being collectively liable for the entire debt.

C A S E

Strother v 3464920 Canada Inc, 2007 SCC 24, [2007] 2 SCR 177

THE BUSINESS CONTEXT: This decision clarifies the fiduciary duties owed by law firms to their clients. It also explores the liability of a law firm for the actions of one lawyer.

FACTUAL BACKGROUND: In the early 1990s, Monarch Entertainment Inc. (now a numbered company, 3464920 Canada Inc.) retained Davis & Company, a Vancouver-based law firm. Robert Strother, a partner specializing in taxation, was responsible for a crucial aspect of Monarch's business—setting up tax-sheltered syndication deals to finance film productions. Effective October 1996, the retainer agreement between Davis and Monarch expressly prohibited Davis from acting for clients other than Monarch in relation to these tax schemes. Near the end of 1997, the federal government implemented new rules that appeared to effectively shut down the tax shelters. Strother informed Monarch that he had no "technical fix," and, acting on this advice, Monarch abandoned its tax-shelter business. The agreement prohibiting Davis from acting for competitors ended in December 1997; however Monarch continued as a firm client. Throughout 1998 and 1999, Davis did legal work for Monarch on outstanding matters related to the tax

schemes as well as unrelated general corporate work. In early 1998, Strother was approached by a former employee of Monarch, Paul Darc, who presented "a way around" the new rules. Strother agreed to prepare a tax ruling request in return for a share in the profits of the venture (called Sentinel Hill). Strother did not inform Monarch of his new client, nor did he inform Monarch that there might be a way around the new rules. Strother obtained a favourable tax ruling that allowed Sentinel Hill to sell tax-sheltered limited partnerships to finance film productions. Strother informed Davis's management committee about his possible conflict of interest with respect to acting for Monarch and Darc/Sentinel and was told that he would not be permitted to own any interest in Sentinel. In early 1999, Strother left Davis and joined Darc as a 50 percent shareholder of Sentinel Hill. The venture was extremely successful, and during the period from 1998 to June 2001, Strother earned more than $32 million from it. When Monarch discovered the Sentinel Hill tax ruling, it sued both Strother and Davis for breach of fiduciary duty. At trial, Strother and Davis were successful in arguing that any obligation to keep Monarch advised of tax shelters ended when the retainer agreement ended near the end of 1997. The Court of Appeal, however, held that Strother was

(Continued)

---

13 See, for example, *Partnership Act*, RSNB 1973, c P-4, s 13, which provides that every partner is liable jointly with co-partners and also severally for wrongful acts or omissions of a partner acting within the course of employment. The differences between joint liability and joint and several liability are subtle. They mainly affect the procedures for maintaining the right to sue a partner who was not originally included in a legal action. Except to this extent, the differences simply do not matter. Regardless of whether liability is joint or joint and several, partners are both individually and to the extent of the partnership assets accountable to third parties.

in breach of his fiduciary duty to Monarch and ordered him to disgorge his estimated $32 million profit from his involvement with Sentinel Hill. It also ordered Davis to disgorge the profits that it earned in legal fees from acting for Sentinel and to return to Monarch all fees it paid during the time Davis acted for both Sentinel and Monarch. Strother and Davis appealed.

THE LEGAL QUESTION: Had Strother breached his fiduciary obligations to Monarch by accepting Darc/Sentinel as a new client and accepting a financial interest in Sentinel? Had Davis breached its fiduciary obligations to Monarch by accepting Darc/Sentinel as a client? If the issues are resolved in favour of Monarch, what remedies lie against Strother and/or Davis?

RESOLUTION: In a 5–4 decision, the court held that Strother breached his fiduciary duty when he acquired a financial interest in a competitor of Monarch's and when he failed to advise Monarch how it could take advantage of a tax ruling. When a lawyer is retained by a client, the scope of his retainer will be governed by contract, which will determine the services he is to perform. However, this relationship is overlaid with fiduciary duties that may include obligations beyond what the parties expressed in their written retainer.

The fiduciary duty includes the duty of loyalty, of which an element is the avoidance of conflicts of interest. Strother was free to take on Darc and Sentinel as clients once the exclusivity arrangement with Monarch expired at the end of 1997. However, Strother was not free to take a personal financial interest in the Darc/Sentinel venture. The difficulty is not that Sentinel and Monarch were competitors, but that Strother aligned his personal interest with Darc/Sentinel's interest; Strother's personal interest was in conflict with his duty to Monarch. Taking a direct and significant interest in the potential profits of Monarch's competitor created a substantial risk that his representation of Monarch would be materially and adversely affected by consideration of his own interests.

With regard to the obligations of Davis, the court stated that Davis was free to take on Darc and Sentinel as new clients. Conflict of interest guidelines do not generally preclude a firm from acting concurrently for different clients who are in the same line of business or who compete with each other for business. Commercial conflicts between clients do not present a conflict problem if they do not impair a lawyer's ability to properly represent the legal interests of both clients. As Davis was not aware of Strother's personal financial interest in Sentinel and as the managing partner had forbidden Strother from taking an interest in Sentinel, it was not acting in a conflict of interest. Davis cannot be held to have breached a fiduciary duty on the basis of facts of which its partners are ignorant.

Strother was ordered to remit to Monarch the personal profit gained directly from his involvement in Sentinel and indirectly through his earnings as a Davis partner on account of billings to Monarch for the period of 1 January 1998 to 31 March 1999, when Strother resigned from Davis. (This amount is estimated to be about $1 million.) As Davis had not committed any breach of fiduciary duty to Monarch, its only liability was under section 12 of the *Partnership Act*, which deems partners liable for any wrongful act or omission of any partner acting in the ordinary course of the business of the firm. While the acceptance of personal financial benefits is not in the ordinary course of the firm's business, the wrongful act was "so connected" with Davis's ordinary business that it was not possible to hold that Strother was off "on a frolic of his own."

CRITICAL ANALYSIS: What are the implications of this decision for the Canadian legal profession and other professions such as those providing financial advisory services? This case represents a big win for Davis & Company because under the earlier appeal court ruling, it would have had to remit to Monarch several million dollars in fees that it earned from Strother's tax shelter business. Under the Supreme Court of Canada ruling, it will only have to pay if Strother defaults, which is unlikely. How should partnerships like Davis & Company manage the risk of liability for the actions of one of their partners? In other words, what more could the Davis partners have done to keep Strother out of trouble?

How and Why a Partnership Ends The *Partnership Act* provides for the termination of a partnership under certain circumstances:

- if entered into for a fixed term, by the expiration of the term.
- if entered into for a single venture or undertaking, by the termination of that venture or undertaking.
- by any partner giving notice to the others of her intention to dissolve the partnership.
- following the death, insanity, or bankruptcy of a partner.

Nevertheless, these provisions may be varied by agreement.[14] For example, many partnership agreements do in fact provide for the continuation of the business by the remaining partners even if the particular partnership entity is dissolved. For example, large professional partnerships—such as accounting firms and law firms—have partners joining or leaving every year. Their carefully drafted agreements generally call for an immediate transfer of all assets and liabilities from the old partnership to the new one.

On dissolution of a partnership, partnership legislation provides a process for dealing with partnership property. It must be applied in payment of the debts and liabilities of the partnership first and then to payment of what is due to the partners. In the event that the partnership property is insufficient to satisfy all of the firm's obligations, partners must individually contribute to the obligations in proportion to their entitlement to profits or in another agreed-upon proportion.

After all of the firm's debts are satisfied, any excess is applied, in the following order, to:

1. repayment of loans made to the firm by partners.

2. repayment of capital contributed by the partners.

3. payment of any surplus to partners according to their respective rights to profits.[15]

Regulations

As with sole proprietorships, there are no legal requirements for the establishment and conduct of a partnership. The partners simply begin their business activity. While a lawyer may be required to assist in the preparation of a partnership agreement, doing business through a partnership is reasonably simple and inexpensive.

The pros and cons of partnership are summarized in Figure 14.3.

Partnerships are bound by all rules of general application, including the obligation to comply with laws concerning licensing, employment, tax collection, and public health, for example. Additionally, most provinces require the filing of a declaration of partnership that contains information on the partners, the partnership name, and the duration of the partnership. Failure to file a declaration is not fatal, but it can impede legal actions filed in the name of the partnership and can result in fines.[16]

---

14 See Figure 14.2, Partnership Agreement Checklist, on page 329.
15 These provisions may be varied by agreement.
16 There are variations in this area from province to province.

FIGURE 14.3 Pros and Cons of the Partnership

Pros	Cons
Simplicity: There are few licensing and registration requirements for partnerships.	**Unlimited personal liability:** Each partner carries the entire risk of the business failing. If it does, both the partnership assets and each partner's personal assets are at risk.
Lower costs: The fees for provincial and municipal licences tend to be small. However, a lawyer may be required to assist in drafting the partnership agreement.	**Loss of speed and independence:** The partners must work together, and a consensus is not always achievable.
Greater access to capital: The capital available to the business includes the assets of each partner and the extent of each partner's credit.	**Limitations on transferability:** The partner's interest in the partnership is not freely transferable.
Profit motive: Any after-tax profits or other assets accrue to the partners, according to their partnership interest.	**Profit sharing:** The partners must share profits equally or according to their partnership agreement.
Tax benefits: Profits and losses are reported on each partner's personal income tax return, according to that person's share in the partnership. This may be favourable or unfavourable, depending on the taxpayer's circumstances.	**Tax disadvantages:** See tax benefits.

BUSINESS APPLICATION OF THE LAW

MANAGING PARTNERSHIP RISKS

The risks associated with the partnership form of doing business are not insignificant. First, each partner is the agent of the partnership, meaning that each of the partners may bind the partnership when acting in the usual course of the partnership business. Second, each partner is fully liable for partnership obligations, meaning that all his personal assets may be seized to satisfy them. In addition, a partner who leaves a partnership may be liable for partnership debts incurred after he leaves if creditors are unaware of the partner's departure. Partners have both legal and practical methods of addressing liability concerns. The partnership agreement may expressly limit and control a partner's ability to bind the partnership. For example, the agreement may provide that all expenditures above a certain amount require the approval of a majority of partners. Such a measure will not be effective against third parties who are unaware of the restrictions. It will, however, provide a basis for a contractual claim by the partners against the partner who exceeded his authority.

From a practical perspective, partnership risks can also be reduced by

- choosing partners with care (partner only with people who can be trusted).
- educating partners on their authority and limits, and the consequences of exceeding them.
- monitoring the activities of partners to help prevent partners from overreaching their authority or entering unwanted transactions.
- notifying clients and customers of the departure of partners so that the partnership cannot be held liable for debts contracted by the departed partners.
- insuring against liabilities that might result from a partner's wrongdoing.

Critical Analysis: How do the partnership variations discussed below reduce the risks associated with a general partnership?

Partnership Variations

There are two variations of the partnership: the limited partnership and the limited liability partnership.

Limited Partnership

A **limited partnership** is a partnership in which at least one partner has unlimited liability while others have limited liability. General partners have unlimited liability, whereas the limited partners have a liability limited to the amount that they have contributed to the partnership capital.

This vehicle has been used mostly as an investment device. Limited partners put money into a business, in such sectors as entertainment (e.g., Cineplex Entertainment), publishing (e.g., FP Canadian Newspapers), or real estate (e.g., Century 21 Canada), in return for tax breaks and profits. The general partner manages the investment for a fee and carries the responsibility—assuming that the limited partners have not made guarantees or commitments beyond their investment.

This type of business entity cannot be created informally. A limited partnership requires a written agreement that must be registered with the appropriate provincial body. Without this filing, the limited partnership does not exist. The registration of the agreement is also important because it provides public notice of the capital contribution of the limited partners and identifies the general partners. This, in effect, allows members of the public to decide whether they want to do business with the limited partnership.

General partners have substantially the same rights and powers as partners in ordinary partnerships; limited partners have more narrowly defined rights. They have the right to share in profits and the right to have their contribution returned on dissolution, but they cannot take part in the management of the partnership. If they do, they lose their status of limited partners and become general partners. This is a significant consequence, since it puts all their assets—not just the amount of their capital contribution—at risk should the enterprise fail. Furthermore, what constitutes partaking in management is difficult to define and can be a contentious issue. In the end, the question is resolved by courts assessing the extent and the nature of the limited partner's involvement and deciding whether, on the balance, the limited partner should lose protected status.

Because Roger wishes to protect his assets, he might want to suggest that Luke and Raina's product be marketed through a limited partnership. The advantage is that Roger's losses as a limited partner will be restricted to his capital investment. For example, creditors will not be able to come after his personal assets. The disadvantage is that Roger must not take part in management or he risks unlimited personal liability.

Limited Liability Partnership

A **limited liability partnership (LLP)** is a variation on the partnership form of business. It is designed to address concerns of professionals who are not permitted to use incorporation as a means of achieving limited liability.[17] All of the provinces and territories with the exceptions of Prince Edward Island, Yukon, and Nunavut have amended their *Partnership Acts* to allow for this variety of partnership.

An LLP has the characteristics of a general partnership, but with specific limitations on the liability of partners. The limitation on liability (the liability shield) varies depending on the jurisdiction.[18] Some jurisdictions (Alberta, Manitoba, Quebec, and Nova Scotia) provide a partial shield that protects a partner from liabilities arising

Limited partnership

A partnership in which the liability of some partners is limited to their capital contribution.

Limited liability partnership (LLP)

A partnership in which the partners have unlimited liability for their own malpractice but limited liability for other partners' malpractice.

17 Alberta Law Reform Institute, *Limited Liability Partnerships, Final Report No 77* (Edmonton: Alberta Law Reform Institute, 1999) at 5.

18 There are considerable differences in the application of the liability shield in each jurisdiction.

PART FOUR

from the negligent or wrongful acts of her partners or employees (so long as she is innocent or uninvolved in the negligence or wrongful acts), but continues to hold the partners liable for all other obligations of the partnership. Partners continue to be personally liable for their own acts and omissions, and the partnership assets continue to be available with respect to the acts and omissions of all partners.

In other jurisdictions (Saskatchewan, New Brunswick, British Columbia, Ontario, Newfoundland and Labrador, and the Northwest Territories), the legislation provides a full shield that not only protects a partner from the negligent or wrongful acts of her partners or employees (so long as she is innocent or uninvolved in the negligence or wrongful acts), but also protects the partners from the contractual obligations of the partnership, such as accounts payable and general debts. The liability shield means that partners' personal assets cannot be seized to satisfy these claims. Partners, however, continue to have liability for their own negligence,[19] and partnership assets continue to be available to satisfy claims against partners.

The LLP may be used for the purpose of practising a profession (e.g., accounting or law), provided the statute governing the profession expressly permits its members to practise using this vehicle.[20] An LLP must include the words "limited liability partnership," its abbreviation "LLP," or the French equivalents in the partnership name, and it must be registered as a limited liability partnership. Also, the legislation may require professionals to have liability insurance to help ensure victims will be compensated for losses from wrongful acts.

Most large accounting and law firms have registered as limited liability partnerships. What are the advantages of changing from a general partnership to an LLP?

The Corporation

The corporation is the most important form of business organization today. Chapters 15 and 16 explore the corporation in detail, including its formation, operation, and termination. The purpose of this section is to provide a brief account of the corporation for the purpose of contrasting it with the other business vehicles already discussed.

---

19 A partner may also be liable for the negligent acts and omissions of a person who is under her direct supervision and control, depending on the applicable law in each jurisdiction.
20 British Columbia does not restrict the use of the limited liability partnership to "eligible professions."

Financial Liability

The corporation is the safest vehicle that Luke, Raina, and Roger could choose to conduct their business because a corporation is a distinct legal entity in law and is therefore capable of assuming its own obligations. Luke, Raina, and Roger could each participate in the profits of the corporation as a **shareholder** and manage its operations as a **director**.

Consider the following examples.

- *The bank loan.* If Luke, Raina, and Roger form a corporation, the corporation has the legal capacity to borrow money. This means that the corporation promises to repay the loan with interest, making the corporation, and no other entity, the debtor.

If the corporation cannot repay the loan, the bank will take the necessary steps to recover as much as it can from the corporation to make up the full amount owing. The bank will be in a position to seize anything owned by the corporation. However, the bank will not be able to seize assets belonging to Luke, Raina, and Roger. Even though they have a close relationship to the corporation as its three shareholders, they did not promise to repay the loan. That commitment came from the corporation alone. Put another way, the corporation is the debtor, not the shareholders.

There is an important proviso to this analysis, which concerns guarantees.[21] When a corporation does not have an established track record of creditworthiness and perhaps holds few assets, the bank will seek personal guarantees from those involved in the corporation, such as the shareholders. There is a very strong possibility that when Luke, Raina, and Roger approach the bank for a loan to the corporation, the bank will agree only if the three provide personal guarantees. A personal guarantee means that if the corporation fails to meet its obligation to the bank, Luke, Raina, and Roger will be held responsible for that default. Then, as with a partnership or sole proprietorship, all their personal assets will be at risk. At such a point, it becomes irrelevant that a corporation is a separate legal entity capable of assuming its own obligations. Luke, Raina, and Roger would have no more protection than if they had proceeded by way of a partnership.

- *The breach of contract.* If the corporation supplies defective time management systems to a customer, it is the corporation and no other entity that is in breach of contract. It is the corporation that will be sued, and it is the corporate assets that are at risk.[22]

Again, recall the discussion of guarantees. Any entity that deals with a corporation may demand the personal guarantee of the corporation's shareholders or directors.

The key characteristic of a corporation is that it provides **limited liability** to its shareholders. That is, should the corporation's financial health take a bad turn, the shareholder's loss is limited to what she paid to purchase shares in the corporation. Unless, in addition, the shareholder provided a personal guarantee, she has no liability for the corporation's obligations, however they were incurred.[23]

Shareholder

A person who has an ownership interest in a corporation.

Director

A person elected by shareholders to manage a corporation.

Limited liability

Responsibility for obligations restricted to the amount of investment.

---

21 See Chapter 26 for a discussion of guarantees.

22 Of course, if an employee of the corporation misrepresented the product or committed a tort of some description, that employee would be liable. This is a matter distinct from the contractual liability of the corporation. See Chapter 16.

23 Only in rare situations, such as fraud on the creditors, will the courts hold the shareholders personally responsible for the corporation's actions. See Chapter 16.

Profit Sharing

Profits of the corporation are distributed to shareholders through dividends. That is, shareholders are paid a return on their investment in the corporation, but only if there is profit, and only if the directors declare a **dividend**.

The corporate form of business organization is inherently flexible from an investment perspective, because it permits varying degrees of ownership and various means for sharing profits.

Decision Making

The corporation is managed by a board of directors which, in turn, is elected by the shareholders.

In addition, officers—that is, high-ranking corporate employees—can be hired by the board to assist in running the corporation. This provides a broad management base that allows the corporation to benefit from specialized and top-level expertise. However, it can also result in layers of authority that can delay decision making.

Sources of Capital

A corporation can get its capital in two ways: it can borrow, or its directors can issue shares. The purchase price of the shares is an important and potentially large source of capital for the corporation. A share represents an equity position in the corporation and provides the shareholder with the chance of making a profit through the declaration of dividends, which it is hoped will be greater than the interest rate the shareholder would have received had he simply lent the money. The disadvantage is that if the corporation fails, the shareholder is left with nothing while the creditor technically retains the right to be repaid. However, if the corporation is insolvent, that right is of little value.

Because the principle of limited liability protects investors against unlimited losses, the corporation is well suited to raise large amounts of capital.

Corporations that offer their shares to the public must publish information concerning their finances; this makes the corporation subject to greater outside scrutiny than the partnership or sole proprietorship.

Taxation

Because it is a separate legal entity, a corporation pays its own taxes. In other words, the income of the corporation is subject to taxation quite apart from the taxation of its owners. A shareholder of a corporation will be taxed if she earns a salary from the corporation, receives a dividend from it, or realizes a capital gain from the sale of her shares. Advantages in the form of reduced or deferred taxes may sometimes be gained through the appropriate splitting of distributions to shareholders between dividend and salary payments. For example, Roger could take a salary from the corporation and his family could receive income through dividends. This may produce a more favourable tax treatment than if Roger took both a salary and dividend payments himself. The ultimate effect of this kind of income splitting depends on a variety of factors, including the corporate tax rate and the marginal tax rate of the shareholder and employee. It is significant that the partnership and sole proprietorship enjoy no such options, since all income from the business is taxed at personal rates.

Transferability

The fact that a corporation has a separate legal identity often allows for easy transference of an ownership interest represented by shares. A shareholder can sell or bequeath his shares with no interference from corporate creditors because the shareholder has no liability for corporate debts. The shares belong to him and he can do what he wants with them. Transferability is, however, subject to restrictions in the corporation's incorporating documents and may also be restricted by a shareholders' agreement.

Perpetual Existence

Because the corporation exists independently of its shareholders, the death or bankruptcy of one or more shareholders does not affect the existence of the corporation. The corporation continues in existence perpetually unless it is dissolved, either by order of a court for failure to comply with statutory regulations or through a voluntary surrender of its legal status to the government.

Regulations

Like sole proprietorships and partnerships, a corporation must comply with laws of general application.

Most significantly, however, the corporation comes into existence only if proper documents are submitted to the government and it issues, in return, a certificate of incorporation. Thus, it is almost always more expensive to organize a corporation than a sole proprietorship or partnership because there are legal bills and additional filing fees to pay. As well, there are extensive rules contained in corporation statutes that govern many corporate decisions and result in the need for considerable record keeping. These extra requirements and expenses, however, can be more than offset by the protection provided to investors by the principle of limited liability.

The pros and cons of the corporation are summarized in Figure 14.4, and a comparison of the major forms of business organization can be found in Figure 14.5.

FIGURE 14.4 Pros and Cons of the Corporation

Pros	Cons
Limited liability: Because it is a separate legal entity, a corporation can assume its own liabilities. The shareholder stands to lose the amount he invested in the corporation, but no more.	**Higher costs:** Creating a corporation incurs filing fees and legal costs.
Flexibility: A corporation permits differing degrees of ownership and sharing in profits.	**Public disclosure:** When a corporation offers shares to the public, the corporation must comply with strict disclosure and reporting requirements.
Greater access to capital: Limited liability makes the corporation a very suitable vehicle through which to raise capital.	**Greater regulation:** Corporation statutes govern many decisions, limiting management options and requiring specific kinds of record keeping.
Continuous existence: The life span of a corporation is not tied to its shareholders.	**Dissolution:** Ending a corporation's life can be complicated.
Tax benefits: Though this is a fact-specific issue, a corporation can facilitate greater tax planning, for example, by permitting income splitting.	**Tax disadvantages:** A corporation may be subject to double taxation, depending on the circumstances. This is a fact-specific issue.
Transferability: Ownership in a corporation is more easily transferable through shares.	**Possible loss of control:** A corporation has diminished control because it issues shares with voting rights.
Potentially broad management base: A corporation is managed by directors and officers, who can provide a level of specialized expertise to the corporation.	**Potential bureaucracy:** The many levels of authority in a corporation may impede decision making.

FIGURE 14.5 A Comparison of Major Forms of Business Organization

Characteristic	Sole Proprietorship	Partnership	Corporation
Creation	• at will of owner	• by agreement or conduct of the parties	• by incorporation documents
Duration	• limited by life of owner	• terminated by agreement, death	• perpetual unless dissolved
Liability of owners	• unlimited	• unlimited	• limited
Taxation	• net income taxed at personal rate	• net income taxed at personal rate	• income taxed to the corporation; dividends and salary taxed to shareholders
Transferability	• only assets may be transferred	• transferable by agreement	• transferable unless incorporating documents restrict transferability
Management	• owner manages	• all partners manage equally unless otherwise specified in agreement	• shareholders elect a board to manage the affairs of the corporation; officers can also be hired

* These are the legal differences between the major business forms. In practice, however, there are ways of minimizing the consequences of these differences. Whether one form of business organization or another is chosen will depend on individual circumstances. As with all other legal concerns, legal, accounting, and management advice should be sought in order to make an informed decision.

Business Arrangements

The preceding section introduced the basic forms of business organizations. Subject to some specialized exceptions, such as real estate investment trusts and mutual funds, every business will use one of these forms.

There are additional ways to carry on the business activity itself. These ways are not distinct business organizations but are, for the lack of a more accurate term, arrangements. These arrangements do not have any strict legal meaning as such; most commonly they refer to some sort of contractual commitment between two or more business organizations. These relationships are important from a legal perspective because they involve agency principles and fiduciary duties, in addition to contractual obligations.

Luke and Raina, for example, may not be able to raise the capital necessary to expand their business. They may then decide to license rights to their product or they may enter an arrangement with another business to sell their product. The business may be extremely successful and they may want to expand further. One option is to grow internally by opening new branches, expanding existing branches, and hiring new employees. They may, however, for many reasons decide to enter an arrangement with another entity. Luke and Raina may want to capitalize on the goodwill they have developed, or another organization may more easily be able to penetrate a market, or they may simply feel that they do not have the time and expertise needed to handle an internal expansion. The following section explores the range of options open to entrepreneurs like Luke and Raina.

The Franchise

A **franchise** is a contractual arrangement between a manufacturer, wholesaler, or service organization (franchisor) and an independent business (franchisee),

Franchise

An agreement whereby an owner of a trademark or trade name permits another to sell a product or service under that trademark or name.

What legal factors are important to the success of a franchise?

who buys the right to own and operate one or more units of the franchise system. Franchise organizations are normally based on some unique product, service, or method of doing business; on a trade name or patent; or on goodwill that the franchisor has developed.

Almost every kind of business has been franchised—motels, fast-food restaurants, dental centres, hair salons, maid services, and fitness centres, to name a few. Some familiar examples are Pizza Hut, Tim Hortons, McDonald's, Subway, Molly Maid, Magicuts, Shoppers Drug Mart, and Weight Watchers. Luke and Raina, too, could potentially franchise their business if it is successful.

Franchising involves a contract between the franchisor and the franchisee. Wide variations exist in franchise agreements, but they generally cover arrangements regarding such matters as how the business is to be run, where supplies may or must be purchased, royalty levels to be paid to the franchisor for sharing its business operation plan and other benefits, and charges for management, advertising, and other corporate services. The agreement negotiated depends on the relative bargaining power of the parties and the issues brought to the table. Usually, however, the franchisor, having a great deal more information about the business, is in the better position to negotiate an advantageous agreement.

The Franchise Relationship

The relationship between a franchisor and a franchisee is one of contract. The contractual relationship is governed by the general principles of contract. In Alberta,[24] Ontario,[25] Prince Edward Island,[26] New Brunswick,[27] and Manitoba,[28] the general principles are augmented by specific franchise legislation. The legislation is designed to provide protection for franchisees.

---

24 *Franchises Act*, RSA 2000, c F-23.
25 *Arthur Wishart Act (Franchise Disclosure)*, 2000, SO 2000, c 3.
26 *Franchises Act*, RSPEI 1998, c F-14.1.
27 *Franchises Act*, SNB 2007, c F-23.5.
28 The *Franchises Act*, CCSM c F156.

MANITOBA'S FRANCHISE LEGISLATION

Manitoba is the fifth province to enact franchise legislation, joining Alberta, Ontario, Prince Edward Island, and New Brunswick. British Columbia has studied the issue and although the government has not yet tabled a bill, the opposition has introduced a private member's bill.[29] The legislation in all provinces is similar in form and structure, but there are important differences in some details. The basic elements of the Manitoba statute are a definition of franchise, a duty of fair dealing on all parties to the franchise agreement, disclosure requirements of the franchisor, and a right of association for the franchisee.

Definition of Franchise: The definition of franchise includes both the "business format" franchises, such as fast-food outlets, and "product distribution" arrangements, such as vending machines. The elements common to the definition of a franchise are

- the granting of a right to conduct business under a trademark;
- the charging of some initial and/or ongoing fee for that right; and
- the exercising of substantial control over the franchise operations.

If one of these elements is not present in a business, then it is unlikely to be a franchise as defined by the legislation.

Fair Dealing: Parties to a franchise agreement have a duty of fair dealing in the performance and enforcement of the agreement. The duty of fair dealing includes a duty to act in good faith and in accordance with reasonable commercial standards. This means, in effect, that both the franchisor and the franchisee have at least the obligation to consider the interests of the other in making decisions and exercising discretion. The Act also establishes a right to sue for the breach of that duty.

Disclosure Requirements: Franchisors are required to deliver a disclosure document to prospective franchisees 14 days prior to the franchisee entering into binding agreements or paying money. Unique to Manitoba is that franchisors may provide disclosure information in sequential parts as opposed to one document. The 14-day disclosure period does not begin until all disclosure documents have been delivered. Also, the Act provides that substantially complete documents are acceptable. The disclosure requirements set out in the Act and regulations[30] require the franchisor to disclose all material facts relating to the franchise, including risk warning statements, background information on the franchise and franchisor (i.e., bankruptcy and insolvency history, expected costs of establishing a franchise, contact particulars for current and former franchisees), and financial statements.

Franchisees have the right to rescind or cancel the franchise agreement within certain time periods if the disclosure document is late or does not meet the requirements of the Act (60 days), or if they do not receive it at all (2 years). In such cases, they are entitled to receive everything they paid for the franchise, as well as compensation for any losses incurred. In addition, the franchisee has a right of action for damages where it suffers a loss because of a misrepresentation contained in the disclosure document or as a result of a franchisor's failure to comply with its disclosure obligations.

Right of Association: Franchisees have the right to associate with one another and form or join an organization of franchisees. Franchisors may not interfere, either directly or indirectly, with the exercise of this right. The franchisee has a right of action for damages for contravention of this section.

Critical Analysis: What are the advantages of franchise legislation? What are the problems, if any, with franchise legislation?

---

29 Bill M219, *Franchise Act,* 4th Sess, 40th Parl, British Columbia, 2015.
30 Man Reg 29/2012.

The relationship between a franchisor and a franchisee does not normally create fiduciary obligations.[31] However, the legislation imposes on the parties a duty of good faith and fair dealing in the performance and enforcement of the franchise agreement. The courts have also adopted this concept at common law.[32] The following case discusses the duty of good faith and fair dealing.

Fairview Donut Inc. v TDL Group Corp., 2012 ONSC 1252, [2012] OJ No. 834, aff'd 2012 ONCA 867, CarswellOnt 15496, leave to appeal refused (2013), CarswellOnt 6051, CanLII 26760 (SCC).

BUSINESS CONTEXT: Franchise legislation has made class action lawsuits very prevalent. Many of Canada's high profile franchises—Quiznos, Midas, Shoppers Drug Mart, Pet Valu, Sears, and Suncor—have all been involved in class action litigation.

FACTUAL BACKGROUND: A group of Tim Hortons franchisees complained that two changes introduced by the franchisor negatively affected their profitability. The "Always Fresh" model required franchisees to purchase par-baked (half baked and then flash frozen) goods from a central bakery rather than baking the products in-store from scratch. This, they argued, resulted in higher costs and reduced profit margins. The second change, the "Lunch Menu," required the franchisees to provide various meal options to supplement coffee and baked goods. The franchisees argued that the franchisor charged unreasonably high prices for the ingredients for these items and that the Lunch Menu diverted resources away from more profitable items. Again, they claimed their profit margins were reduced. In their statement of claim, the franchisees alleged, among other things, that the franchisor had breached express and implied terms of the franchise agreement and the duty of good faith and fair dealing. They claimed $1.95 billion in damages on behalf of a class of between 500 and 800 franchise owners. The franchisees

brought a motion to certify the class action and the franchisor brought a counter motion to dismiss the entire action.

THE LEGAL QUESTION: Did the franchisor breach express or implied terms in the franchise agreement? Did the franchisor breach the duty of good faith and fair dealing?

RESOLUTION: The Ontario Superior Court dismissed all claims against Tim Hortons. The court found that there was no breach of an express term as there was no requirement that a new product or model of doing business had to be profitable in its own right. The language of the franchise agreement provided Tim Hortons with wide discretion to make business decisions for the financial benefit of the franchise system as a whole. Evidence suggested that the Always Fresh model was beneficial to the franchisees and was a rational business decision by Tim Hortons as it addressed legitimate concerns about the long-term viability of the making from scratch method. The court also held that there was no implied term requiring Tim Hortons to supply ingredients to franchisees at lower prices than they could obtain on the open market. There was no evidence that franchisors in general, and Tim Hortons in particular, passed on to their franchisees the benefit of their purchasing power on every single item they supplied.

On the good faith and fair dealing argument, the court noted that the duty does not require the franchisor to consider the franchisees' interests at the expense of its own. Further, it does not create an obligation on the franchisor to ensure that a franchisee makes a profit on

(Continued)

31 *Jirna Ltd v Mister Donut of Canada Ltd*, [1975] 1 SCR 2, 40 DLR (3d) 303.
32 *Shelanu Inc v Print Three Franchising Corporation* (2003), 64 OR (3d) 533, 226 DLR (4th) 577 (CA).

every item that it sells. The franchisor's concern is for the system as a whole and since the system remained beneficial to the franchisees overall, there was no breach of the duty of good faith and fair dealing. The duty of good faith and fair dealing must be assessed in the context of the entire relationship, not to isolated incidents.

The appeal court endorsed the lower court decision and Tim Hortons was awarded costs of $1.85 million.[33] Leave to appeal to the Supreme Court of Canada has been dismissed.

CRITICAL ANALYSIS: Once the judge dismissed the action, the question of certification was moot. He did, however, indicate that if the claims had not been dismissed, he would have certified the class action. He also stated that franchise disputes are frequently suitable for certification. Why do you think franchise

Why are franchising companies a magnet for class action litigation?

disputes are suitable for class action certification? Once a certification is granted, the class action is most often settled and does not proceed to trial. Why do you think that happens?

Joint Venture

Joint venture

A grouping of two or more businesses to undertake a particular project.

A **joint venture** is an association of business entities—corporations, individuals, or partnerships—that unite for the purpose of carrying on a business venture. Normally, the parties agree to share profits and losses and management of the project. The key feature of a joint venture is that it is usually limited to a specific project or to a specific period of time. For example, several oil and gas companies may join for offshore exploration in a certain region, or a steel fabricator may combine with a construction company to refurbish a nuclear plant. Luke and Raina could conceivably enter into a joint venture with another entity for the purposes of marketing and selling their product to a particular event such as an international trade show.

The joint venture itself can take a variety of forms. The joint venture may be a partnership, in which case all the legal consequences associated with a partnership apply. It may also be what is known as an equity joint venture. This is when the parties incorporate a separate corporation for the project and each party holds shares in that corporation, in which case the consequences of incorporation apply. For example, Rogers Communications and Bell Canada formed Inukshuk Internet Inc. to build and operate a national wireless network. A joint venture may also simply be a contractual arrangement between the parties. In such a case, the contract may spell out the nature of the relationship between the parties. Also, the law can impose duties on the parties beyond those specified in the contract.[34] Most significantly, parties to a joint venture can be held to owe fiduciary duties to one another in relation to the activities of the joint venture.

---

33 2014 ONSC 776, [2014] OJ No 508.
34 *Supra* note 7 at 20.

What are the legal risks with joint ventures?

Strategic Alliance

A **strategic alliance** is a cooperative arrangement among businesses. It is an arrangement that may involve joint research, technology sharing, or joint use of production, for example.[35] Miranda Gold Corp. and its wholly owned Canadian subsidiary has an alliance with Agnico-Eagle Mines Limited for precious metal exploration in Colombia.[36] Luke and Raina could form a strategic alliance with another entity to do joint research into applications of their time management system.

Like a joint venture, a strategic alliance does not have a precise legal meaning. The underlying relationship between the parties is normally contractual. The contract or a series of contracts will spell out the parties' rights and obligations, including whether or not they are agents for each other. Whether the parties to a strategic alliance owe fiduciary obligations to each other is unclear.

Strategic alliance

An arrangement whereby two or more businesses agree to cooperate for some purpose.

Distributorship or Dealership

A product or service **distributorship** is very much like a franchise. A contract is entered into whereby a manufacturer agrees to provide products and the distributor or dealer agrees to carry products or perform services prescribed by the manufacturer. This kind of arrangement is often encountered in the automotive and computer industries. Rather than selling their system themselves, Luke and Raina could engage a distributor or dealer to sell their systems.

Distributorship

A contractual relationship where one business agrees to sell another's products.

---

35 The term "strategic alliance" is sometimes used to include joint ventures. There is little precision in terminology in this area. The key point is that terms usually describe a contractual arrangement between two or more parties.

36 Miranda Gold Corp, *JV Partners*, online: Miranda Gold Corp.<http://www.mirandagold.com/s/JVPartners .asp?ReportID=128106&_Title=Agnico-Eagle-Mines-Limited>.

The relationship between the parties is governed by the contract. There are no fiduciary obligations owed by the parties to each other beyond those spelled out in the contract. As well, a distributorship does not normally involve an agency relationship. In fact, the contract may specify that the distributorship is not an agency.

GOING GLOBAL

Strategic alliances are one of the leading business strategies of the twenty-first century. They take many forms, from simple market exchanges or cross-licensing agreements to complex cooperative-manufacturing arrangements or joint-equity ventures. Strategic alliances can help firms lower costs, exploit each other's specialized skills, fund costly research and development efforts, and expand into foreign markets. Using a strategic alliance to access a foreign market usually involves "partnering" with a "local" to take advantage of his familiarity with the social, cultural, legal, and other conditions in the market. There can also be a host of other advantages to this business arrangement, including sharing costs and risks with the local partner, avoiding import restrictions and other trade barriers, and meeting the host country's requirements for local ownership.

Critical Analysis: What are the risks associated with using a strategic alliance to access a foreign market? Why would a country require that a foreign business have local participation? Can you think of any legal reasons?

Sales Agency

Sales agency

An agreement in which a manufacturer or distributor allows another to sell products on its behalf.

A **sales agency** relationship is usually an arrangement whereby a manufacturer or distributor contracts with an agent to sell goods or services supplied by the manufacturer or distributor on a principal/agent basis.[37] The agent is not the actual vendor but acts on behalf of a principal, who is the owner of the goods or services. As this relationship is one of agency, fiduciary obligations are owed. This arrangement is often encountered in the travel, real estate, and insurance industries.

Product Licensing

Product licensing

An arrangement whereby the owner of a trademark or other proprietary right grants to another the right to manufacture or distribute products associated with the trademark or other proprietary right.

In a **product licensing** arrangement, the licensee is granted the right to manufacture and distribute products associated with the licensor's trademarks or other proprietary rights, usually within a defined geographic area. Licensing is common for many consumer goods such as clothing, sporting goods, and merchandise connected to the entertainment industry. Anne of Green Gables (images of Anne, Green Gables, and related trademarks), for example, is licensed to almost 100 businesses.[38] The relationship between the parties is contractual, and the agreement usually covers such matters as the granting of rights, the obligations of the parties, the term of the agreement, and fees and royalties. This arrangement is explored in more depth in Chapter 18.

---

37 See Chapter 13 for a discussion of the duties and liabilities of agents.
38 Anne of Green Gables Licensing Authority Inc, *Licensed Products*, online: Innovation PEI <http://www.innovationpei.com/ann_list.php3>.

BUSINESS LAW IN PRACTICE REVISITED

1. What forms of business organization are available for carrying on Luke and Raina's business?

Luke and Raina may carry on their business as a sole proprietorship, in partnership with others, or through a corporation.

2. What are the major considerations in choosing a particular form?

Roger is willing to invest in the business but is unwilling to accept risk beyond his investment. This consideration eliminates an ordinary partnership, as it would expose him to additional risk; a limited partnership is a possibility. However, Roger would not be able to partake in the management of the organization. If he did, he could lose his limited liability status. As Roger has a great deal of business experience, Luke and Raina might want to be able to seek his assistance. A sole proprietorship exposes only one person to unlimited liability; however, if the others participate in profits and management, there is a risk of an "unintended" partnership. Thus, it would seem that the most viable alternative is a corporation, with Roger investing his money in shares. This alternative limits his exposure to risk and allows for his potential participation in profits.

Both Luke and Raina are interested in taking a role in the management of the venture. This consideration could be accommodated within a partnership agreement, although it may be difficult to agree on the valuation of their time and expertise. As well, they may be averse to the risks associated with a partnership. The other option is a corporation, with both investing in shares. This would allow participation in profits as a means of compensation for services.

3. Which form is best for Luke and Raina's business?

For the reasons given above, a corporation may be the most appropriate, but the success of Luke and Raina's business is not dependent on the form chosen. Much more important is the viability of the idea and their ability to bring it to fruition.

CHAPTER SUMMARY

Most businesses are carried on using one of the basic forms—sole proprietorship, partnership (or one of its variations), or corporation. These forms have varying characteristics, most notably with respect to the exposure to liability. Sole proprietorships and partnerships expose their owners to personal liability for the business's obligations. A corporation, on the other hand, has the attraction of limited liability for the owners—their liability is limited to the amount of their investment. This characteristic, however, can be neutralized. For example, a sole proprietor can escape the effects of unlimited liability by transferring assets to a relative prior to commencing business. As well, the advantage of limited liability in the corporate form can become meaningless if creditors insist on a personal guarantee from the owners of the corporation.

Each form has other advantages and disadvantages. The form chosen for a business enterprise depends on an evaluation of numerous factors such as investors' aversion to risk, their desire to earn profits, and their wish to participate in decision making. In short, the best form for a particular situation depends on all the circumstances.

A partnership is the form most often found in the professions. This is due, in part, to prohibitions against some professionals incorporating. A partnership subjects the partners to unlimited liability. The other defining feature of a partnership is agency—a partner is an agent for other partners and for the partnership. The effects of agency between the partners can be modified by a partnership agreement; however, the effects of agency in relation to outsiders cannot, and are governed by the *Partnership Act*.

A business may also at some point enter into an arrangement with another entity for carrying out business activities. The various arrangements are all based on a contract negotiated between the parties. Regardless of the arrangement entered into, the business still needs to be carried on using one of the basic business forms.

It is important to remember that it is the viability of the business itself that is critical, not necessarily the form of the business or the particular arrangements made. Put another way, a business does not succeed because it chooses a franchise arrangement over a distributorship. The key to a successful business is having a solid business plan that is well executed.

CHAPTER STUDY

Key Terms and Concepts

director (p. 337)

distributorship (p. 345)

dividend (p. 338)

franchise (p. 340)

joint and several liability (p. 331)

joint liability (p. 325)

joint venture (p. 344)

limited liability (p. 337)

limited liability partnership (LLP) (p. 335)

limited partnership (p. 335)

partnership (p. 324)

product licensing (p. 346)

sales agency (p. 346)

shareholder (p. 337)

sole proprietorship (p. 321)

strategic alliance (p. 345)

unlimited liability (p. 322)

Questions for Review

1. Define sole proprietorship, partnership, and corporation.

2. What are the advantages and disadvantages of a sole proprietorship?

3. How is a sole proprietorship created?

4. What are the advantages and disadvantages of a partnership?

5. How can a partnership come into existence?

6. Does the sharing of profits result in the creation of a partnership? Explain.

7. How can a partnership come to an end?

8. How can the risks of the partnership form be managed?

9. What is the difference between a general and a limited partner?

10. Explain the difference between a limited partnership and a limited liability partnership.

11. What are the advantages and disadvantages of the corporate form?

12. How is a corporation created?

13. What is the difference between a business form and a business arrangement?

14. What is the basis of a franchise? What is the relationship between parties to a franchise agreement?

15. How does franchise legislation change the relationship between a franchisor and a franchisee?

16. Is a joint venture a partnership? Explain.

17. What is the difference between a joint venture and a strategic alliance?

18. Is a distributor an agent? Explain.

Questions for Critical Thinking

1. Franchising is a common method of doing business in Canada. The Canadian Franchise Association reports that there are over 78 000 franchise units in Canada directly employing over 1 000 000 people, and that franchise business accounts for 40 percent of all retail sales.[39] What are the benefits and risks of franchising?

2. Joint ventures are appropriate in situations where a complex project requires the combining of the expertise and resources of two or more entities for a limited period of time. From a legal perspective, what are the risks associated with joint ventures? How can the parties manage the risk?

3. The limited liability partnership is a response to concerns about professionals' exposure to liability for their partners' malpractice. What is the nature of the liability created by the partnership form? How does the creation of an LLP address this liability concern? Is it appropriate that accountants and lawyers, for example, enjoy limited liability? Is there a downside for a law or accounting firm to converting to an LLP?

4. What are the circumstances in which a partnership may be found to exist? What steps can be taken to avoid a finding of partnership? How can the consequences of being found a partner be minimized?

5. In the limited partnership form of carrying on business, the limited partner's liability is limited to her actual or agreed upon contribution to the partnership. To preserve this status, the limited partner must not participate in the management of the partnership business. What do you think is the reason for this prohibition? Can you think of situations where it would be useful for the limited partner to participate in management?

---

39 Canadian Franchise Association, *Fast Franchising Facts* online: Canadian Franchise Association <http://www.cfa.ca/tools_resources/franchise-research-facts/>.

6. The three basic business forms are sole proprietorship, partnership, and corporation. How is each formed? How is each owned? How does each form allocate the risk associated with doing business?

Situations for Discussion

1. Kennedy, Logan, and Morgan were avid hockey fans. They decided to put together an expression of interest for the purchase of a 50 percent interest in an NHL hockey team. They discussed some of the terms they wished to include in their proposal but did not come to an agreement as to the terms by which they were prepared to be bound. They also did not discuss the terms that would govern their relationship but all three understood that no member of the group could bind the others to any agreement during negotiations with the team owners. Over several months, the three put together a number of proposals but none were of interest to the owners. A short time later, Kennedy decided he no longer wished to pursue the joint acquisition and left the group. He did tell Logan and Morgan that he remained interested in acquiring a share in the team in the future should the opportunity arise. Logan and Morgan did not commit to including him as part of the group again and no conditions were imposed on any member of the group at the time of Kennedy's departure.

    Logan and Morgan developed a proposal based on a different ownership structure than that proposed before Kennedy's departure. It involved the purchase of a 75 percent interest in both the team and the arena. Negotiations based on this proposal did not progress significantly until Logan and Morgan offered to purchase 100 percent of the team and the arena. When Kennedy learned that Logan and Morgan were negotiating to acquire full ownership of the Canucks, he asked them whether he could participate in the deal. They said "no."

    Logan and Morgan continued to negotiate with the team owners but were unable to reach an agreement. Kennedy, without informing Logan and Morgan, entered into negotiations with the team owners and reached agreement to purchase 50 percent of the team and the arena with an option to purchase the remaining 50%. Ten days later, Logan and Morgan learned about the deal in the newspaper. They sued Kennedy, alleging they had formed a partnership or joint venture with Kennedy and as a result Kennedy owed them a fiduciary duty, which he breached by acquiring an interest in the team and arena while Logan and Morgan were attempting to do the same.[40] Was there a partnership or joint venture between Kennedy, Logan, and Morgan? Did Kennedy owe any duties to Logan and Morgan?

2. Edie, Alma, and Tim established a restaurant called EATs. Edie, a retired teacher, invested $20 000 in the venture, and Alma and Tim each invested $10 000. Edie, Alma, and Tim do not have a formal agreement concerning the allocation of responsibilities, but they each take turns doing the cooking. The serving and clean-up tasks are done by staff. One day, while Edie was doing the cooking, Juan got food poisoning from his meal. Juan intends to sue EATs, Edie, Alma, and Tim for damages of $100 000. If Juan is successful, how will the damages be allocated among the parties? If the restaurant were incorporated under EATs Inc. and Edie owned 50 percent of the shares, Alma owned 25 percent, and Tim owned 25 percent, how would the damages be allocated? What do these two situations illustrate about risk?

3. Regan, Riley, Madison, and Mackenzie were partners in a law firm. Regan gave the other partners written notice that he was leaving the partnership on March 31. The other partners purchased Regan's interest and agreed that he would not be liable for any future partnership debts. At the end of May, it was discovered that Riley had, during the previous month, made various investments on behalf of a couple of elderly clients. The investments were either unsecured or undersecured and the elderly clients lost over $250 000. None of the other partners were aware of Riley's activities although the law firm had occasionally invested funds on behalf of clients in the past.[41] Who is responsible for the elderly clients' losses? What precautions could the partners have taken to prevent this situation?

4. Review *Strother v 3464920 Canada Inc.* on page 331. At the time of the dispute between Monarch, Strother, and Davis & Company, Davis operated as a general partnership. It became possible for a British Columbia law firm to become a limited liability partnership (LLP) only in 2005. At that time, Davis, along with many other BC firms, became an LLP. Assume that Davis was an LLP at the time of the dispute with Monarch. How would being a member of an LLP affect Strother's personal liability to Monarch? How would Davis being an LLP affect the liability of the other partners? How might the LLP structure affect the relationship between a law firm and its clients? How might the LLP structure affect the relationship between lawyers within a law firm?

5. Jody Ingalls is a recent university graduate with a BSc in kinesiology. As she was having difficulty finding a job, Jody decided that she could create her own job by opening a fitness club. As luck would have it, she saw an advertisement in a Halifax newspaper featuring franchise opportunities in the fitness industry. Jody responded to the ad and the franchise owner showed her the financial statements for a "Fit for Life" fitness franchise in a Halifax suburb. The income statements indicated that the franchise had made $100 000 per year for the past several years. Jody was extremely excited and agreed to lease it for $50 000 per year for a five-year period. She signed the contract and started carrying on the business. Jody worked 12-hour days for a year but was not able to make a profit, and now she wants out of her contract. Can Jody get out of the agreement? Explain. Would your answer be different if the franchise was located in New Brunswick? Explain. What are the legal risks associated with "purchasing" a franchise? How can the risks be managed?

6. Ragini and Rajiv were co-owners of a number of properties located in the suburbs of Surrey, BC. They had acquired the properties for resale and planned to subdivide and sell them for a

---

40 Based on *Blue Line Hockey Acquisition Co., Inc. v Orca Bay Hockey Limited Partnership*, 2008 BCSC 27, 40 BLR (4th) 83, aff'd 2009 BCCA 34, [2009] 8 WWR 83.

41 *McDonic v Hetherington* (1997), 142 DLR. (4th) 648, 31 OR (3D) 577 (Ont CA), leave to appeal to SCC refused, [1997] SCCA No 119.

profit over the next few years. One property, known as "the Corner" was too small to meet the legal requirements for subdivision. Ragini and Rajiv hoped that they would be able to acquire adjacent property so that their subdivision plans could proceed. Rajiv did all of the work in the investigation of the surrounding properties while Ragini stayed in the background. She had recently been "downsized" out of her job and spent most of her time looking for alternative employment. Rajiv learned through his investigative skills that Ming, the owner of an adjacent property, would be willing to sell his property for the right price. Rajiv also knew that Ragini, because of her job loss, would not be able to raise her share of the purchase price, so he purchased Ming's property on his own behalf. Shortly thereafter, he offered to buy out Ragini's interest in "the Corner" for $15 000 more than the fair market value; Ragini accepted the offer. Rajiv consolidated "the Corner" and Ming's former property, subdivided them, and sold them for a $250 000 profit. When Ragini learned of Rajiv's purchase of Ming's property and the sale of the subdivided lots, she was very upset. Rajiv simply pointed out that she did not have the money or the means to share in the purchase of Ming's property, and he had paid a premium price for her interest in "the Corner." Besides, he argued, it was his investigative skills and hard work, not hers, that led to the profit on the subdivision sale. What is the nature of the relationship between Ragini and Rajiv? Does Rajiv have any legal liability in these circumstances? Explain.

7. Thomas, a young entrepreneur, started a construction business. Ari, who owned and operated a radio station, agreed to run some advertisements for him. Unfortunately, Thomas was unable to pay Ari for the services. In the hopes of making the business profitable so that he could get payment under the broadcasting contract, Ari, without remuneration, assisted Thomas in his business. In fact, on behalf of Thomas, Ari signed a contract with Lopez for plumbing and heating supplies. When payment for the supplies was not forthcoming, Lopez sued Ari, claiming that Ari was Thomas's partner and therefore was responsible for the debt. Ari claimed that, when he signed the contract, he was acting as Thomas's agent.[42] What difference does it make whether Ari is considered to be Thomas's agent or his partner? What factors are important in determining the nature of a relationship between individuals?

8. In *2038724 Ontario Ltd v Quizno's Canada Restaurant Corporation*,[43] the franchisees brought a national class action against Quiznos and its designated supplier, Gordon Food Services, over alleged overcharging on supplies. The defendants opposed certification primarily on the grounds that damages were not common among franchisees and would have to be established individually. Despite the defendants' arguments and a "class action waiver" clause in the franchise agreement purporting to prevent the franchisees from initiating or being part of any action, the Ontario Court of Appeal affirmed the certification of the class action. In certifying the class action lawsuit against the franchisor, the court strongly endorsed class actions as a means of resolving franchise disputes. What is it about franchising disputes that makes them suitable for resolution by class action? Why do you think the "class action waiver" failed to protect the franchisors from class action litigation?

---

42 Based, in part, on *Lampert Plumbing* (Danforth) Ltd v Agathos, [1972] 3 OR 11, 27 DLR (3d) 284 (Co Ct).

43 2010 ONCA 466, 100 OR (3d) 721; See also David Sterns, "Appeal rulings clear the path for franchise class actions," *The Lawyers Weekly* (3 September 2010) 12.

15

THE CORPORATE FORM: ORGANIZATIONAL MATTERS

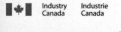

Industry Canada. *Guide to Federal Incorporation.* Reproduced with the permission of the Minister of Industry, 2015.

BUSINESS LAW IN PRACTICE

Luke, and Raina (introduced in Chapter 14) have been working with Sandra Higgins of Envision Business Labs to develop a business plan for their team management system. They are delighted that industry analysts have given a thumbs-up to their plan. Buoyed by favourable feedback, the team decided to engage the services of a marketing firm to assist with a detailed marketing strategy. Initial results from the marketing firm's consumer surveys indicate that there is, indeed, significant demand for the team management system in a wide range of industries.

Anxious to proceed with the plan, Luke and Raina have made an appointment with a lawyer to assist with incorporating a company with a head office in Calgary. They have a name, Time-in Team Management Incorporated (Time-in Inc., for short), and they plan to be equal shareholders given that they will both continue to be involved in the management and expansion of the business. However, Luke and Raina are unsure how to structure an investor's involvement in the business. Roger (introduced in Chapter 14) will not be participating in the day-to-day operations, but will be giving advice and contributing $200 000 in capital.

The only major problem revealed by the business plan—and it is a significant one—is that the business is underfunded. Sandra informs them that they will need an additional $350 000 to fund the expansion into other countries and markets. Luke is not too concerned about this news, in part because he has read an article in the *Globe and Mail* on ten of Canada's most successful crowdfunding campaigns.[1] "I can crowdfund. No problem." says Luke. "I'll make a short video on our team management system, upload it on the Internet, and have people purchase shares in the business. And if that does not work, I will simply sell some shares to friends and family."

1. How is a corporation formed, and what factors should Luke and Raina consider in forming a corporation?

2. What options are available for involving Roger in the business?

3. What factors should Luke and Raina consider in seeking to raise money by selling shares?

---

1   Katherine Scarrow, "Ten of Canada's most successful crowdfunding campaigns" *The Globe and Mail* (1 January 2014) online: The Globe and Mail <http://www.theglobeandmail.com/report-on-business/small-business/sb-money/business-funding/photos-the-years-top-crowdfunders/article16111603/>.

The Corporation Defined

The corporation[2] is the predominant business vehicle in modern commerce because it is a separate legal entity. For this reason, it is able to remedy many of the shortcomings associated with the other prevalent business forms—the sole proprietorship and the partnership.

The notion that the corporation possesses a legal identity separate and distinct from its owners has fundamental repercussions. It means that the corporation alone is responsible for its own debts and other liabilities. Should the corporation fail to make good on its obligations, the shareholders are not responsible for the default. The most that they stand to lose is the purchase price of their shares.

If Luke and Raina decide to run their team management business with Luke as a sole proprietor (and Raina as an employee), Luke is gambling his personal assets if the venture proves to be a financial disaster. Yet if they decide to run the identical business through a corporation, none of Luke's assets are at risk.

The law recognizes this different outcome as being perfectly legitimate and eminently just. As indicated in Chapter 14, the key question is this: who has incurred the obligation in question? Liability falls on that entity—be it an individual or a corporation—and that entity alone. Put another way, the creditor must decide with whom she is doing business and live with the consequences of that decision.

The concept of a corporation being a separate legal entity is complex.[3] It was established in 1897 in a case that remains at the centre of modern corporation law.

Since *Salomon v Salomon Ltd* (see Landmark Case below), the separate legal existence of the corporation has not been seriously challenged. Corporations, with few exceptions, continue to be treated as entities separate from their shareholders. The cornerstone of corporation law—limited liability—is secure.

LANDMARK CASE

Salomon v Salomon Ltd, [1897] AC 22 (HL)

THE HISTORICAL CONTEXT: When *Salomon* was decided, the corporate form was just coming into wider usage. At the time, it was unclear whether companies with few shareholders would be recognized as separate legal entities.

FACTUAL BACKGROUND: Aron Salomon carried on a profitable shoe-manufacturing business for many years as a sole proprietor. He decided to form an incorporated company—Aron Salomon and Company, Limited—as the vehicle through which to run his business. *The Companies Act*, which set out the rules for creating a company, required that a company have a minimum of seven shareholders. Therefore, Aron took one share and members of his family took the remaining six shares.

Aron became the managing director. Practically speaking, Aron Salomon and Company, Limited, was a "one-person company," since Aron entirely controlled the company. Put another way, the other participants in the company had no involvement in operations: any decision the company took was only because Aron wanted it to follow that particular course of action.

(Continued)

---

2   In British Columbia, a corporation is usually called a "company." Although, strictly speaking, the terms are not synonymous, they are used interchangeably in this text.

3   Most of the distinguishing characteristics of a corporation—limited liability for shareholders, perpetual existence, separation of ownership and management, ease of transferring ownership, and separate taxation—are a consequence of a corporation being a legal entity distinct from its shareholders. The characteristics of a corporation are discussed in Chapter 14.

Next, Aron Salomon and Company, Limited, agreed to purchase the assets of Aron's sole proprietorship. As the corporation had little cash, Aron was issued 20 000 shares and a mortgage secured by the shoe-business assets. In this way, Aron became a highly protected creditor of his own company.

The business suffered financial problems due to a series of strikes and the loss of government contracts. The company became insolvent, and a trustee was appointed to deal with its creditors and close down the business. Many creditors of Aron Salomon and Company, Limited, lined up for payment, but there were insufficient assets to satisfy them. In response, the trustee in bankruptcy took the position that Aron was personally responsible for all his company's debts.

THE LEGAL QUESTION: Was Aron liable for the debts of Aron Salomon and Company, Limited? Was Aron a legitimate creditor of the company?

RESOLUTION: A corporation—large or small—is a separate legal entity and, as such, is totally responsible for its own obligations. Indeed, one of the main reasons for creating a company is to limit liability in the event of bankruptcy. The court rejected the argument that there was something essentially improper about an individual conducting his business through a one-person corporation to secure the protection of limited liability. If a number of persons can limit their liability in this way, then why shouldn't a single person be able to do the same thing? After all, it should not make any difference to a creditor whether one or several shareholders limit their liability.

The House of Lords also confirmed that there is nothing wrong with a shareholder being a creditor of the corporation, even when that shareholder essentially controls the company in question. Furthermore, the creditors had chosen to deal with Aron's company—not with Aron, the individual—and had chosen to do so on an unsecured basis. They, in turn, would have to live with the adverse outcome of that business decision.

CRITICAL ANALYSIS: Do you think that the court went too far in giving independent existence to the corporation, especially when the interests of Aron and his company were virtually identical? Should the shareholder of a one-person company be entitled to limited liability? How could the creditors, other than Aron, have better protected themselves in this situation?

Stakeholders in the Corporation

The corporation has a legal existence and, as such, is treated in law as a person. That said, the corporation is an artificial entity whose activities are controlled entirely by human beings. A corporation not only comes into being through the actions of humans, but also can make decisions, formulate policy, and enter contracts only through the actions of humans. These individuals, or groups of individuals, are often referred to as the internal **stakeholders** of the corporation. In short, internal stakeholders are those who have either a direct or indirect role in governing the corporation and determining its mission and how it will be achieved. Shareholders are those persons who have invested in the corporation by buying shares in return for a potential share of the corporate profits and other benefits. Shareholders do not have any direct authority to manage the corporation. However, they do have the power to elect the board of directors and therefore can have a strong influence on the direction of the corporation. The board of directors is charged with management functions—including policy development—and is answerable to the shareholders since, should it perform poorly, the board runs the risk of being voted out of office. Corporate officers, such as the president, secretary, and treasurer, are another important internal group. They are hired by the board of directors and are charged with managing the day-to-day operations of the corporation.

Stakeholder

One who has an interest in a corporation.

Not surprisingly, the internal stakeholders may come into conflict with one another, as well as with the corporation itself. The bulk of corporation law seeks to regulate the relationships among the corporation's internal stakeholders. Chapter 16 will provide a more detailed account of internal stakeholders. They are introduced here to establish some of the basic vocabulary associated with the corporate form, as well as to identify its central players.

The internal stakeholders are not the only stakeholders. The corporation has a tremendous impact on much of society. External stakeholders are people who have dealings with or are affected by the corporation but do not have an explicit role in governing the corporation. Examples are government, the general public, employees, customers, and creditors. These groups, although external in the sense that they are generally not involved in corporate governance, nonetheless have an interest in the corporation, and their interests receive recognition in some circumstances. The relationship between the corporation and its external stakeholders is explored briefly in Chapter 16.

Pre-Incorporation Issues

Assuming Luke and Raina decide to do business through a corporation, they must make a number of decisions prior to preparing and filing incorporation documents. They must decide

- whether to incorporate federally or provincially.
- what type of shares will be available and to whom.
- what to name the corporation.

These decisions will be influenced by a host of factors, such as the kind of business they intend to operate, where they intend to operate, how they intend to manage the corporation, how they wish to accommodate future growth, and, in the case of a corporate name, its availability.

Provincial and Federal Incorporation

Luke and Raina have the choice between incorporating federally and incorporating provincially. They have this choice because jurisdiction over the incorporation of companies is divided between the federal government and the provincial governments. Both levels of government have passed legislation that provides for the incorporation of companies. These acts embody different models or prototypes as to how the corporation comes into existence.[4] Although the way in which the corporation is created varies, the different methods of incorporation have much in common. All methods allow for the creation of an entity that is recognized as a legal person, is owned by shareholders who enjoy limited liability for the debts of the entity,[5] and is managed by directors who owe fiduciary duties to the entity.

---

4 The different models currently in use are articles of incorporation, memorandum of association, and letters patent. The federal government, Alberta, Manitoba, New Brunswick, Newfoundland and Labrador, Ontario, and Saskatchewan follow the articles of incorporation model. See *Canada Business Corporations Act*, RSC 1985, c C-44; *Business Corporations Act*, RSA 2000, c B-9; *Corporations Act*, RSM 1987, CCSM c C-225; *Business Corporations Act*, SNB 1981, c B-9.1; *Business Corporations Act*, RSN 1990, c C-36; *Business Corporations Act*, RSO 1990, c B-16; and *Business Corporations Act*, RSS 1978, c B-10. Nova Scotia follows the memorandum of association model. See *Companies Act*, RSNS 1989, c 81. Prince Edward Island and Quebec follow the letters patent model. See *Companies Act*, RSPEI 1988, c C-14 and *Companies Act*, RSQ 1977, c C-38. British Columbia has features of both the articles of association and the memorandum of association models. See *Business Corporations Act*, SBC 2002, c 57.

5 Nova Scotia, Alberta, and British Columbia also provide for unlimited liability corporations (ULC).

When, then, should a business incorporate federally, and when would it be best advised to incorporate provincially? There is no hard-and-fast answer to this question. Federally incorporated corporations have a right to carry on business in each province, whereas provincially incorporated corporations have the right to carry on business only in the province in which they are incorporated. This difference has little practical significance, because each province has straightforward licensing procedures through which corporations incorporated in other provinces can do business in that province.[6]

For corporations that intend to operate in more than two provinces, federal incorporation may result in lower administrative costs. For corporations that intend to operate in only one or two provinces, provincial incorporation usually results in lower administrative costs.[7] Since Luke and Raina intend to operate nationally and even internationally, they should seriously consider incorporating under federal legislation.

Shares and Shareholders

As part of the preparation for incorporation, Luke and Raina must decide on a **share structure** for the corporation. This entails deciding on the class or classes of shares that the corporation will be authorized to issue, what rights and privileges attach to each class, and the number of each authorized for issuance. Luke and Raina must also consider how the shares will be available and to whom they will be available.

Classes of Shares
A share represents an ownership interest in the issuing corporation. It is, however, a unique kind of ownership interest. It does not give the owner or holder any right to use the assets of the corporation or any right to directly control or manage the corporation. It does, however, give the owner those rights that specifically attach to the share.

A corporation may simply have one type or class of shares with all the basic shareholder rights attached to it. In this case, the share must include the right to

- vote for the election of directors.
- receive dividends declared by the directors.
- share in the proceeds on dissolution of the corporation, after the creditors have been paid.

A one-person corporation with no plans or aspirations for growth may choose this option. However, to ensure that the corporation has the flexibility to meet future needs, it is prudent to establish different classes at the outset. Though different classes could be created when the need arises, this would require an amendment to the corporation's constitution—a potentially costly and complicated procedure.

There are many possibilities for creating shares with diverse rights (see Figure 15.1) so long as the basic rights mentioned above are distributed to one or more classes. For example, if Roger simply wants to be a passive investor in the business, shares without voting rights could be created to meet his needs. If he wants some qualified assurance of the return of his share capital when and

Share structure

The shares that a corporation is permitted to issue by its constitution.

---

6 Peter Hogg, *Constitutional Law of Canada*, 5th ed sup vol. 1, loose-leaf (consulted on 21 July 2014) (Toronto, ON: Carswell, 2007) at 23–7.
7 Kevin Patrick McGuinness, *Canadian Business Corporations Law*, 2d ed (Markham, ON: LexisNexis, 2007) at 178.

FIGURE 15.1 Creating Classes of Shares

A class of shares may include a combination of various rights and privileges. Examples of typical rights that may attach to a class of shares include the following:

- voting rights: the right to vote for election of directors.
- financial rights: the right to receive dividends when declared by directors or the right to receive fixed dividends on a regular basis.
- preference rights: the right to receive dividends before dividends may be paid to any other class of shareholders and/or the right, on dissolution, to receive investment before any payments are made to any other class of shareholders.
- cumulative rights: the right to have a dividend not paid in a particular year added to the amount payable the following year.
- redemption rights: the right to have the corporation buy back the shares at a set price.

if Time–in Inc. winds down, then shares with preference rights on dissolution could be created. The possibilities are almost limitless; however, careful consideration must be given to how management and financial rights are distributed among classes of shares.

Luke and Raina may limit the number of shares of each class that can be issued by stating a maximum number, or they can simply leave matters open-ended by indicating that the number is "unlimited."

Availability of Shares A corporation may issue shares to the general public. This type of corporation is usually referred to as a **widely held corporation** (or public corporation).[8] A corporation that issues shares to the public is subject to regulation pursuant to the relevant **securities legislation** in those provinces in which the securities are issued or traded. Securities legislation, discussed in more detail below, imposes registration and disclosure requirements on the issuers of the shares.

A corporation that does not issue its shares to the general public is usually known as a **closely held corporation** or private corporation.[9] The vast majority of Canadian corporations—including some very large enterprises, such as McCain Foods and the Irving companies in New Brunswick, the Paterson grain and food companies in Manitoba, and Holt Renfrew & Co. in Ontario—fall into this category. These corporations are generally exempt from most of the obligations of securities regulation so long as they meet the definition of a private corporation. For example, in Ontario, the *Securities Act*[10] says that a corporation qualifies as a private corporation if it has the following provisions in its incorporating documents:

- a restriction on the transfer of shares.
- a limit (with certain exceptions) on the number of shareholders in the corporation to no more than 50.
- a prohibition on any invitation to the public to subscribe for the corporation's shares.

Widely held corporation

A corporation whose shares are normally traded on a stock exchange.

Securities legislation

Laws designed to regulate transactions involving shares and bonds of a corporation.

Closely held corporation

A corporation that does not sell its shares to the public.

---

8 The term "widely held" is used interchangeably with "public" to denote a corporation that offers its shares for sale to the public. In some jurisdictions, the terms "offering" or "reporting" are also used.

9 The term "closely held" is used interchangeably with "private" to denote a corporation that does not offer its shares for sale to the public. In some jurisdictions, the terms "non-offering" or "non-reporting" are also used.

10 RSO 1990, c S-5, s 1(1) "private company".

What are the advantages of a private corporation?

An added advantage of private corporation status is the potential for a lower rate of income tax. *The Income Tax Act*[11] provides that a Canadian-controlled private corporation is entitled to a lower tax rate on its first $500 000 of business income earned in Canada in its fiscal year. In effect, a qualifying corporation pays about half the normal corporate income tax rate of approximately 50 percent on this income.

BUSINESS APPLICATION OF THE LAW

THE TRIALS OF LORD BLACK OF CROSSHARBOUR—CONTINUED

In 2007, Conrad Black (Lord Black of Crossharbour), former chief executive officer and chairman of Hollinger International, was convicted of one count of obstruction of justice and three counts of fraud. He was sentenced to six and a half years in prison, ordered to forfeit US $6.1 million (the estimated amount of the fraud), and fined $125 000. Through various legal challenges, his convictions were reduced to two and his sentence to 42 months. Black served 27 months at the Coleman Federal Correction Complex in Florida and was released in May 2012.

The Fraud Convictions: The criminal convictions stem from Black's involvement with Hollinger Inc. (a Canadian company), and Hollinger International (an American subsidiary of Hollinger Inc., now known as the

Lord Black of Crossharbour

Sun-Media Times group). During the 1980s and 1990s, Hollinger International gained control of several prominent newspapers including London's *Daily Telegraph*, the *Chicago Sun-Times*, the Southam newspaper chain, the *Financial Post,* and *Saturday Night*, as well as many small-town U.S. dailies. By the late

---

11 RSC 1985, c 1 (5th Supp), s 125.

1990s, Hollinger International's newspaper holdings comprised the world's third-largest group. It was publishing over 500 newspapers with a total daily circulation of nearly five million and was boasting revenues of more than $3 billion annually.

By 2000, however, the newspapers were heavily in debt and Hollinger International sold most of the Canadian newspapers to CanWest Global Communications for $3.2 billion. As part of the deal, Black and four other executives received $80 million in non-competition payments. A New York investment firm with an 18 percent stake in Hollinger International was outraged by the payments and insisted that Hollinger International investigate these and other payments to Black and his associates. Hollinger International created a special committee to review the payments, and Black resigned as CEO of Hollinger International after the committee reported US $32.15 million in unauthorized payments had been made to Black and the other officers. In 2004, Hollinger International ousted Black as its chairman and launched a US $200 million lawsuit against him and the others, seeking the return of management fees and other payments. Several months after the launch of the lawsuit, the Breeden Report (named after its author, Richard Breeden, a former SEC chief who was named special monitor of Hollinger International) was released. In the report, Black and his associates were accused of having run a "corporate kleptocracy" at Hollinger International. Black was accused of pillaging hundreds of millions of dollars from Hollinger International, violating his fiduciary obligations, and ignoring corporate governance principles.

The Ontario Securities Commission Action:

In the wake of the Breeden Report, several legal actions were brought against Black and his associates, including the criminal case referred to above. While the criminal trial was ongoing, charges filed by the Ontario Securities Commission (OSC) were put on hold. In 2014, the OSC restarted the case against Black and two other former Hollinger executives. The suit accused them of improperly diverting proceeds from Hollinger International to themselves through non-competition payments. Settlement was reached with one of the executives and, in February 2015, Black and the other executive were found guilty of the charges. Both were permanently banned from acting as a director or officer of a company that issues securities in Ontario. They were not, however, banned from trading securities in Ontario.

The saga of Lord Black raises interesting questions about how Black and his associates were able to defraud Hollinger International. Some of the answers may lie in the corporate governance structure of Hollinger International.

Dual-Class Structure: Hollinger International was, at the time of the wrongdoings outlined above, controlled by Hollinger Inc., a publicly traded holding company. Hollinger Inc. was, in turn, controlled by Ravelston, Black's private holding company. Hollinger Inc. was able to control Hollinger International through what is known as a dual-class structure—different classes of shares having different voting rights. Hollinger Inc. owned all of Hollinger International's Class B shares, which gave it 30 percent of the equity but 73 percent of the votes. The multiple-voting share structure allowed Hollinger Inc. to control the fate of Hollinger International while holding a fraction of the equity. This structure has been a favourite of Canadian corporate empire builders and remains entrenched despite criticism from shareholder activists. The structure, in essence, allowed Black to call the shots and to select Hollinger International's board of directors. Indeed, the board was largely filled with prominent, outside directors, hand-selected by Black and with whom he had a social, political, or business relationship. Apparently the "Black Board" functioned like a social club or public policy association, with extremely short meetings followed by a good lunch and a discussion of world affairs—actual operating results or corporate performance were rarely discussed. The board was often given false or misleading information, but it did not do much on its own about excessive management fees and non-compete payments. It took no steps and asked no questions.

Who May Own Shares A share is a piece of property and is freely transferable unless there is a restriction in place. In widely held corporations, shares are almost always freely transferable; otherwise the shares will not be accepted for listing on a stock exchange. In closely held corporations where shares are generally issued to family or friends, the shareholders have a strong interest in having control over who the other shareholders are. It is therefore common to have a provision in the incorporating documents that shares cannot be transferred without the agreement of the directors or a majority of the shareholders of the corporation. At the same time, shareholders require some flexibility in being able to transfer their shares; thus it is common to include "a right of first refusal" for directors or shareholders. When a right of first refusal is in place, it means that the shareholder wishing to sell must first offer her shares to the directors (or shareholders, as the case may be) at the same price she has negotiated with the outsider. This gives the insiders one last chance to acquire the shares for themselves instead of having to welcome a new investor to the company.

As an alternative to having a restriction in the corporation's constitution, the shareholders could have an agreement that covers transferring. Shareholder agreements are discussed in Chapter 16.

A Corporate Name

All jurisdictions require a company to be identified by a name or designated number. The selection and use of corporate names is subject to regulation by trademark law,[12] tort law,[13] and corporation law.

The basic requirements for a name are as follows:

- it must be distinctive (different from other existing names in the same field).
- it must not cause confusion with any existing name or trademark.
- it must include a legal element (e.g., Limited or Ltd., Incorporated or Inc., or Corporation or Corp., or the French equivalents). The purpose of the word is to distinguish a corporation from a partnership and a sole proprietorship and to signal to the public the fact of limited liability.

---

12 See Chapter 18.
13 The tort of passing off.

- it must not include any unacceptable terms (e.g., it must not suggest a connection that does not exist, falsely describe the business, or be obscene or scandalous).

On choosing a corporate name, entrepreneurs such as Luke and Raina are advised to be particularly careful. If the corporate registry inadvertently approves a name that is confusingly similar to the name of another business, the entrepreneurs can be sued for trademark infringement and the tort of passing off.[14] They will be liable for any damages that the other business has suffered and, perhaps even more problematically, be ordered to change the name of their corporation. This will require Luke and Raina to re-establish a corporate identity and reputation in the marketplace, as well as replace letterhead, invoices, business signs, and anything else bearing the former corporate name. This is obviously costly. The Business Application of the Law box below illustrates how such a dispute can arise.

BUSINESS APPLICATION OF THE LAW

THE TANGERINE NAME DISPUTE

In 2012, Scotiabank acquired ING Bank of Canada from its Dutch parent, ING Groep NV for $3.1 billion. As part of the terms of the sale, Scotiabank was required to change the name of ING Bank of Canada. After considering over 3000 possible names, Scotiabank settled on Tangerine. As reported in the *Toronto Star*, Peter Aceto, chief executive officer of ING Canada, stated, "...we wanted a name that speaks to the future."[15] In 2014, Scotiabank introduced its new name supported by a massive advertising campaign that included signage, promotional materials, and a television ad featuring a spokesperson hanging from the side of a moving train.

Shortly thereafter, a small financial institute filed an application to block the use of the name because it believes it owns the name and was using it first. The company, RSP Generation LP of Vancouver, alleges that in 2012, it bought the assets of a business called Tangerine Financial Projects LP, which had gone into receivership. This "Tangerine" company planned to market a financial strategy related to unused registered retirement savings plan contribution limits and had been using the name since 2008. A bid by Scotiabank to strike RSP's claim was dismissed

What are the basic requirements for a corporate name? Why is the name of a business important?

by the Supreme Court of British Columbia. However, the appeal court found RSP's application to be an abuse of process as the application was filed in receivership proceeedings against a non-party.

Critical Analysis: What is the problem with similar names for businesses?

Sources: Jeff Gray, "Tangerine Bank faces battle over name," *The Globe and Mail* (12 June 2014) B3; James Langton, "Application by Vancouver-based RSP Generation LP dismissed," *Investment Executive* (17 August 2015) online: Investment Executive <http://www.investmentexecutive.com/-/b-c-appeal-court-backs-scotiabank-in-tangerine-appeal>.

---

14   This is because Luke would be representing to the public—either intentionally or not—that there is a relationship between his business and the other business when no such relationship exists.

15   Dana Flavelle, "ING Direct renames itself Tangerine" *The Star* (15 June 2014) online: The Star <http://www.thestar.com/business/personal_finance/2013/11/05/ing_direct_renames_itself_tangerine.html>.

Assuming that Luke and Raina want to incorporate federally, they will have to send their proposed name—Time-in Team Management Inc.—to the federal corporate registry for approval. They will also have to have a Newly Upgraded Automated Name Search Report, or **NUANS Report**. This document lists those business names and trademarks—if any—that are similar to the name being proposed. A NUANS Report is prepared using a database containing existing and reserved business names, as well as trademarks. If some other business is using the name "Time-in Team Management Inc." or a name similar to it—such as "Time-out Team Management Inc."—the NUANS Report would presumably contain such information. In that case, Luke and Raina should avoid the name and come up with an alternative name for their fledgling business.

It is common for a company's legislation to permit a corporation to be assigned a numbered name. Under the federal legislation, for example, the corporation can be issued a designating number, followed by the word "Canada" and then a legal element—such as "Limited" or "Incorporated." A numbered company is useful when a corporation must be created quickly, when the incorporators are having difficulty coming up with a suitable name, or when there is a wish to create a **shelf company**. Shelf companies are often incorporated by law firms for the future use of their clients. The company does not engage in any active business. It simply sits "on the shelf" until a firm's client needs it.

The Process of Incorporation

All Canadian jurisdictions follow a similar procedure for the creation of a corporation, though precise requirements do vary. Assuming that Luke and Raina want to incorporate federally, they must submit the following to the federal corporate registry in Ottawa:[16]

- articles of incorporation.[17]
- notice of registered office.
- notice of directors.
- Newly Upgraded Automated Name Search (NUANS) Report.
- the filing fee, payable to the Receiver General for Canada.

The **articles of incorporation** set out the basic features of the corporation—name, place of the corporation's registered office, class and number of shares authorized to be issued, any restrictions on the transferring of shares, the number of directors, any restrictions on the business that can be carried on, and any other provisions that an **incorporator** requires to customize the corporation to meet his needs. For example, incorporators may include provisions that require directors to own at least one share in the corporation, provisions prescribing how shareholders will fill a vacancy in the board of directors, or provisions that limit the number of shareholders to a certain number. The

---

16   Federal incorporation is available online by accessing the Corporations Canada Online Filing Centre website at <https://www.ic.gc.ca/app/scr/cc/CorporationsCanada/hm.html?locale=en_CA>.

17   The term "articles of incorporation" is also used in Alberta, Manitoba, New Brunswick, Newfoundland and Labrador, Ontario, and Saskatchewan. The equivalent term in Nova Scotia is "memorandum of association"; in Prince Edward Island and Quebec, it is "letters patent"; and in British Columbia it is "notice of articles."

name or names of the incorporators must also be included in the articles of incorporation.

The Notice of Registered Office form is very brief because it has only one purpose: to provide a public record of the corporation's official address. This is the address that those having dealings with the company can use to communicate with the corporation, particularly with respect to formal matters, including lawsuits.

The Notice of Directors form contains the names and residential addresses of the directors and must correspond with the number of directors given in the articles of incorporation.

The completed forms, along with the requisite fee, are then submitted to the appropriate government office—the Corporations Directorate of Industry Canada. If the forms are in order, the directorate will issue a "birth certificate" for the corporation, known as the certificate of incorporation.

Provincial incorporation legislation has its own requirements, which are parallel but are not necessarily identical to the requirements and procedures under the *Canada Business Corporations Act*.

Organizing the Corporation

Following incorporation, the first directors will ordinarily undertake a number of tasks. Under federal legislation, for example, the directors are required to call an organizational meeting to

- make **bylaws**.[18]
- adopt forms of share certificates and corporate records.
- authorize the issue of shares and other securities.
- appoint officers.
- appoint an auditor to hold office until the first annual meeting of shareholders.
- make banking arrangements.
- transact any other business.[19]

Federal legislation also specifies that the directors named in the articles of incorporation hold office until the first meeting of the shareholders. That meeting must be called within 18 months of incorporation.[20] At that first meeting, shareholders elect the permanent directors, who hold office for the specified term.[21] The directors carry on the management of the corporation until the next annual meeting, at which time they report to the shareholders on the corporation's performance.

Financing the Corporation

Luke and Raina need to finance their company to have the funds to operate. They have two basic means of doing so: Time-in Team Management Inc. can borrow money (debt financing) or issue shares (equity financing).

Bylaws

Rules specifying the day-to-day operating procedures of a corporation.

---

18 "Bylaws" is the term used in the articles of incorporation and letters patent jurisdiction. In Nova Scotia, "articles of association"—the very general equivalent of bylaws—is the term used, and in British Columbia the term is "articles."

19 *Canada Business Corporations Act*, RSC 1985, c C-44, s 104 (1).

20 *Ibid* at s 133 (1) (a).

21 *Ibid* at s 106(3).

Debt Financing

Bond

A document evidencing a debt owed by the corporation, often used to refer to a secured debt.

A corporation may raise money by borrowing. The company may obtain a loan from shareholders, family or friends of shareholders, lending institutions, or, in some cases, the government. If it is borrowing a substantial sum of money on a long-term basis, the corporation may issue bonds or debentures. The terms **bond** and **debenture** are often used interchangeably and refer to a corporate IOU, which is either secured or unsecured. Note that the word "bond" is sometimes used to describe a secured debt, and "debenture" to refer to an unsecured debt, but the only way to know what is actually involved is to read the debt instrument itself.

Debenture

A document evidencing a debt owed by the corporation, often used to refer to an unsecured debt.

A bond or debenture does not represent any ownership interest in the corporation, and the holder does not have any right to participate in the management of the corporation.[22] However, these debts are often secured by a charge on the assets of the corporation. This means that if the debt is not repaid, the assets can be sold to repay the debt and the bondholder has a better chance of recovering his investment. Bonds and debentures—like shares—may have any number of features and are freely transferable, creating a secondary market for their purchase and sale.

The advantage of raising cash by issuing bonds is that Luke and Raina do not have to relinquish formal control. That is, they can raise money to run their operation without having to give management rights to their lenders. On the other hand, there is a requirement that the interest on the bonds be paid regardless of whether a profit is earned. In fact, if the interest is not paid on the debt, the corporation faces bankruptcy unless it can reach a new agreement with the bondholders.

Equity Financing

Shares are frequently used to raise money for the use of the corporation. This is done by issuing shares to investors in exchange for a purchase price.

Shares provide a flexible means of raising capital for a corporation because they can be created with different bundles of rights attached to them to appeal to different investors. Shares can be attractive to investors because, unlike debt, where the return is usually limited to a fixed amount, shares provide an opportunity to benefit from the corporation's growth. If the corporation prospers, the value of the shares will increase. Shares are advantageous to the issuer in that the money raised by selling shares does not have to be repaid in the way a loan must. On the other hand, the sale of shares may mean the relinquishing of management rights. Although it is possible to raise capital through the sale of shares that do not have any voting rights attached, investors may be interested only in shares that give them a say in the control and operation of the corporation.

Securities

Shares and bonds issued by a corporation.

Shares and bonds represent two very different ways of raising money for corporate activities. There are, however, many combinations of these two types of **securities**. Much depends on the features that investors are interested in purchasing. Most businesses, particularly large ones, use some combination of these various methods of raising funds, maintaining a reasonable balance

---

22   It is possible, however, for bondholders to obtain management rights if the company defaults on the loan. This depends on the terms of issuance.

FIGURE 15.2 Securities Compared

	Shareholder	Bondholder
Status of holder	Investor/owner	Investor/creditor
Participation in management	Elects directors (if voting rights); approves major activities	Does not participate (except in special circumstances)
Rights to income	Dividends, if declared	Interest payments
Security for the holder on insolvency of the corporation	Entitled to share in proceeds after all creditors paid	Entitled to payment from proceeds before general creditors, if secured, and before shareholders

between them. Furthermore, shares and bonds can come with a **conversion right**. A convertible bondholder, for example, is entitled to convert his debt interest into shares and thereby assume an equity position in the company instead of being a creditor.

Figure 15.2 shows a comparison of the preceding points regarding securities.

The issuance of securities including bonds, debentures, and shares to the general public is governed by securities legislation. This means that the issuer must follow a complicated and potentially costly procedure. Securities legislation seeks to ensure that the potential purchasers know what they are getting into before they make any decision.

Conversion right

The right to convert one type of security into another type.

BUSINESS AND LEGISLATION

CROWDFUNDING

Crowdfunding is the practice of funding a project or a business venture through soliciting small amounts of money from a large number of people, usually through the Internet. Entrepreneurs and others seeking financing can present the project—typically through a video—to the "crowd" using a website or portal and request small contributions. If successful, a large number of people will contribute and a sizeable sum of money will be raised. Canadian projects that have been funded in this manner include video games, waterproof toques, 3-D printers, and craft beer.

Crowdfunding Models: There are several models of crowdfunding. The donation model is where individuals make a contribution without expectation of anything in return, although they may receive a reward such as a sample product. The

The Peachy Printer is a 3-D printer made by a Saskatchewan company, Rinnovated Design, that raised $651 091 through a crowdfunding portal.

Courtesy of Peachy Printer

lending model is where individuals lend money with the expectation that it will be repaid at some point. The third model and most controversial is the investment or equity model. This is where an individual receives equity in return for financing. It is this model that attracts security regulation.

After much study and debate, and in response to pressure from entrepreneurs and owners of small and medium enterprises who wish to access capital, the securities commissions of six[23] provinces have implemented equity crowd funding exemptions. These rules allow issuers of securities to raise capital without having to undergo the expense of producing a prospectus or to comply with the dealer registration requirement.[24] Known as start-up exemptions, these exemptions are for companies in the very early stages of development and are not available to large companies that currently distribute securities as reporting issuers.[25] The exemptions allow a non-reporting issuer to raise up to $250 000 per offering with a limit of two offerings per year. Individual investors can only put in $1500 per year and the listing can remain open for a maximum of 90 days. The issuer's head office must be in one of the participating provinces. The funding portal does not have to register with a security regulator but must have a head office in a participating province.[26]

Ontario has indicated that it will implement its own broader, crowdfunding rules, which will apply to both startups and reporting issuers. The broader model will allow both reporting and non-reporting issuers to raise up to $1.5 million per year and will allow individual investors to put in $2500 per offering to a maximum of $10 000 per year. The model will also require the portal to register with the relevant securities regulator and meet strict standards, including minimum capital requirements, insurance, and record keeping.

Critical Analysis: What is driving the growth of crowdfunding? What are the pros and cons of crowdfunding?

Sources: Norman Snyder, "Crowdfunding exemptions adopted by Canadian securities regulators" *Taylor McCaffrey LLP* (8 July 2015) online: Taylor McCaffrey <http://www.tmlawyers.com/crowdfunding-exemptions-adopted-by-canadian-securities-regulators/>; Donalee Moulton "Regulators wrestle with crowdfunding" *The Lawyers Weekly* (29 November 2013) 12; Michael Yang & Mark Neighbour, "Canadian securities regulators propose crowdfunding exemption" *McMillan LLP* (5 April 2014) online: McMillan <http://www.mcmillan.ca/Canadian-Securities-Regulators-Propose-Crowdfunding-Exemption>; Tavia Grant, "To find seed money, Canadian startups follow the crowd" *The Globe and Mail* (24 March 2014) B1; Katherine Scarrow, "Ten of Canada's most successful crowdfunding campaigns" *The Globe and Mail* (1 January 2014) online: Globe and Mail <http://www.theglobeandmail.com/report-on-business/small-business/sb-money/business-funding/photos-the-years-top-crowdfunders/article16111603/>.

Securities Legislation

All provinces have enacted securities acts.[27] In very general terms, the aim of all securities legislation is to

- provide the mechanism for the transfer of securities.
- ensure that all investors have the ability to access adequate information in order to make informed decisions.
- ensure that the system is such that the public has confidence in the marketplace.
- regulate those engaged in the trading of securities.
- remove or punish those participants not complying with established rules.

With these objectives at the forefront, all securities regimes have three basic requirements: registration, disclosure, and insider-trading restrictions.

---

23 British Columbia, Saskatchewan, Manitoba, Quebec, New Brunswick, and Nova Scotia.
24 The registration exemption exempts a funding portal from having to register as a dealer.
25 Reporting issuers are companies whose securities are publicly traded.
26 Janet Mcfarland, "Crowdfunding approved in six provinces" *The Globe and Mail* (8 July 2015) B1.
27 The *Canada Business Corporations Act* also contains provisions that regulate securities that are issued or traded by CBCA corporations.

A CO-OPERATIVE NATIONAL SECURITIES REGULATOR

Canada is the only major, industrialized economy without a centralized, national body regulating securities. Instead, there are 13 different provincial and territorial securities regulators, with a corresponding multiplicity of statutes, regulations, policies, and interpretations.

Since the 1960s, there have been numerous calls for a national securities commission. In 2011, the federal finance minister, despite the vehement opposition of several provinces, unveiled draft legislation establishing a national body. However, the Supreme Court of Canada[28] unanimously held the legislation to be unconstitutional as provinces have jurisdiction over the day-to-day regulation of the securities market. The court did state that the federal government has a role in guarding against systemic risk and could seek a co-operative approach.

Heeding the Court's words, the federal government has reached an agreement, in principle, with British Columbia and Ontario to set up a co-operative securities regulator. Based in Toronto, the regulator would administer a single set of rules and regulations and be directed by a board of independent directors. Since the agreement, Saskatchewan, New Brunswick and Prince Edward Island have also signed on. The hope is that all provinces and territories will eventually join the cooperative regulatory system. Quebec has threatened to challenge the constitutionality of the agreement and Alberta and Manitoba have indicated that they will not give up their rights in the area of securities regulation.

Critical Analysis: What are the policy arguments in favour of a single securities regulator for all of Canada? What are the policy arguments against a single regulator?

Sources: Grant Cameron, "Feds reach securities regulator deal with Ontario, B.C." *The Lawyers Weekly* (1 November 2013) 26; Gordon Isfeld, "Joe Oliver says national securities regulator could become law by fall 2015" *The Financial Post* (9 June 2014) online: Financial Post <https://www.google.ca/#q=Joe+Oliver+says+national+securities +regulator+could+become+law+by+fall+2015>; Steven Chase, "Oliver gains new support on national regulator" *The Globe and Mail* (9 July 2014) B1; "PEI joins cooperative capital markets regulatory system" *Stikeman Elliott LLP* (16 October 2014) online: Mondaq <http://www.mondaq.com/canada/x/347512/Securities/PEI +Joins+Cooperative+Capital+Markets+Regulatory+System>.

Registration

Any company intending to sell securities to the public in a given province must be registered to do so with the relevant provincial securities commission. Furthermore, all persons engaged in advising on and selling securities to the public must be registered with the relevant securities commission. The definitions of those covered by the various statutes vary between provinces but generally extend to advisors, underwriters, dealers, salespeople, brokers, and securities issuers.

SECURITIES CLASS ACTIONS

The number of securities class action lawsuits against corporate Canada is steady. According to a recently published study by National Economic Research Associates Inc., 11 new securities class actions were filed during 2014, the same number as in 2013. Ten of the new filings in 2014 involved claims under the secondary market civil liability provisions (see Figure 15.3 on the next page) of the provincial securities acts. In total, 63 cases have been filed under these provisions since they

---

28 *Reference Re Securities Act*, 2011 SCC 66, [2011] 3 SCR 837.

came in force in 2005. The majority of new cases (8 of 11 in 2014) were filed in Ontario. There were settlements in six cases in 2014, the same number as in 2013, with defendants paying a total of $38.4 million. At the end of 2014, there were 60 active Canadian securities class actions representing approximately $35 billion in outstanding claims.

In order to proceed with a secondary market liability action, a judge must certify the class action and grant leave to proceed to trial. Leave is granted if (1) the claimants are acting in good faith (e.g. they have an honest belief that they have an arguable claim); and (2) the claimants have a reasonable possibility of success at trial.

Critical Analysis: What do you think is the purpose of the leave requirement?

Sources: Bradley A Heys, Mark L Berenblut, and Jacob Dwhytie, "Trends in Canadian securities class actions: 2014 update: The docket continues to grow as new filings outpace settlements," *NERA Economic Consulting* (10 February 2015) online: *NERA Economic Consulting* <http://www.nera.com/publications/archive/2015/trends-in-canadian-securities-class-actions-2014-update-the-do.html>; Bradley A Heys, Mark L Berenblut, and Jacob Dwhytie, "Trends in Canadian securities class actions: 2013 update: Filings steady, law in flux and settlements on rise," *NERA Economic Consulting* (19 February 2014) online: *NERA Economic Consulting* <http://www.nera.com/nera-files/PUB_Recent_Trends_Canada_2013_0214.pdf>.

Disclosure

Prospectus

The document a corporation must publish when offering securities to the public.

The company must comply with disclosure or **prospectus** provisions set forth in the securities legislation. With limited exceptions, this means that any sale or distribution of a security—in this case, meaning either debt (bonds) or equity (shares)—must be preceded by a prospectus that is accepted and approved by the appropriate securities commission. A prospectus is the statement by the issuing company of prescribed information. The list of information required to be in the prospectus is lengthy and ranges from financial information to biographical information about the directors. The overriding

FIGURE 15.3 **Number of Active Securities Class Action Cases in Canada**

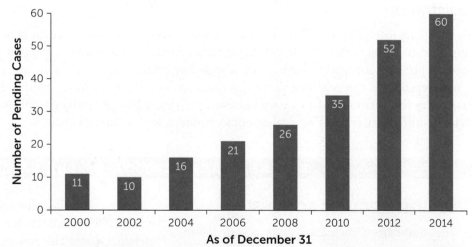

Note: Cases that are initially dismissed but subsequently overturned on appeal are shown as pending at each year end since the date of initial filing. Cases that have been dismissed are not included among the pending cases from the year of the initial dismissal decision even if they may still be subject to appeal.

Critical Analysis: *What factors may account for the increase in Canadian securities class action lawsuits?*

Bradley A Heys, Mark L Berenblut, and Jacob Dwhytie,"Trends in Canadian securities class actions: 2014 update: The docket continues to grow as new filings outpace settlements," *NERA Economic Consulting* (10 February 2015) online: *NERA Economic Consulting* <http://www.nera.com/publications/archive/2015/trends-in-canadian-securities-class-actions-2014-update-the-do.html>.

requirement is for "full, true, and plain" disclosure of all material facts, that is, facts that are likely to affect the price of the securities. The legislation assumes that prospective investors will rely on the prospectus in making investment decisions.

The issuer of securities has an obligation to continue to keep the public informed of its activities. In general terms, this means that it must notify the public of any material change in its affairs, first by issuing a press release and second by filing a report with the securities commission within 10 days of the change. A material change is defined as one that is likely to have a significant effect on the market value of the securities and is not known to the public in general.

SECURITIES LEGISLATION AND SECONDARY MARKET LIABILITY

All provinces and territories have amended their securities statutes[29] to provide a statutory right of action for misrepresentations contained in secondary market disclosures. The objective of these regimes is to create a meaningful civil remedy for secondary market investors and to facilitate class action lawsuits. As a result, there has been a marked increase in the number of security class actions (see: Business Application of the Law: Securities Class Actions, page 367).

Prior to the amendments, securities legislation provided only a statutory cause of action to investors who purchased securities in the primary market (i.e., purchased pursuant to a prospectus, offering memorandum, or securities exchange takeover bid circular). Investors in the secondary market[30] (i.e., purchasing from or selling to third parties) had to rely on a common law action for fraudulent or negligent misrepresentation. This meant that the secondary market purchasers had to establish that they relied on the defendants' misrepresentations in making their investment decisions. This requirement made it next to impossible to have a class action certified because of the individual issues of reliance. The amendments create the statutory cause of action "without regard to whether"

the purchaser or seller relied on the alleged misrepresentation. In other words, the investor is deemed to have relied on the disclosures and does not have to prove that she relied detrimentally on the misrepresentation. This amendment facilitates the certification of class actions by removing the issue of proof of individual class member reliance.

The key provisions of the amendments[31] are as follows:

- *cause of action.* Secondary market investors have a right to sue where they bought or sold securities during a period where there was an uncorrected misrepresentation made by or on behalf of an issuer in a document released by the company or in a public oral statement. The right to sue is also available where there was a failure to make timely disclosure of a material change in the issuer's business.

- *defendants.* The class of people that may be liable for a company's misrepresentation or failure to disclose is broad and includes the reporting issuer, its directors, officers, influential persons (including controlling shareholders, promoters, and insiders), and experts (including auditors and lawyers).

- *defences.* There are a number of defences available to defendants, including

29 See for example, *Securities Act* RSO 1990, c S-5, Part XXIII.1, s 138.3 (1).

30 It is estimated that secondary market trading accounts for more than 90 percent of all equity trading in Canada.

31 The discussion below is based on the Ontario legislative scheme. All the provinces and territories have similar provisions.

reasonable investigation (defendant had conducted a reasonable investigation and had no reason to believe the document or oral statement contained a misrepresentation), plaintiff's knowledge (defendant proves that the plaintiff knew there was a misrepresentation or failure to disclose at the relevant time), no involvement, and reasonable reliance on experts.

- *damages.* There is a complex formula for calculating damages, but generally a person who is found liable will be responsible for the losses the investor suffers (the difference between the price paid or received for a security and the average price in the 10-day period following the disclosure or public correction). If more than one person is liable, each defendant will be responsible only for the proportionate share of damages that corresponds to his responsibility unless he knowingly participated in the misrepresentation or failure to disclose. Also, liability for damage awards is capped except when a defendant knowingly participates in the misrepresentation or failure to disclose. Liability for individual defendants is the greater of $25 000 and 50 percent of their compensation from the issuer in the prior 12 months. The liability limits for corporate defendants are

Why did all provinces and territories amend their securities acts to create a statutory cause of action in the secondary market?

the greater of 5 percent of capitalization and $1 million.

- *leave.* A unique feature of the legislation is the requirement that the claimant obtain leave of the court before commencing a secondary market liability claim (see: Business Application of the Law: Securities Class Actions, for the test). To date, only a handful of secondary market cases have advanced beyond the leave stage.

Critical Analysis: How do the amendments enhance investor protection? Do the amendments do enough for investors?

Insider trading

Transactions in securities of a corporation by or on behalf of an insider on the basis of relevant material information concerning the corporation that is not known to the general public.

Insider

A person whose relationship with the issuer of securities is such that he is likely to have access to relevant material information concerning the issuer that is not known to the public.

Insider-Trading Restrictions

The objective of provisions against **insider trading** is to ensure that trading in securities takes place only on the basis of information available to the public at large. Securities legislation achieves this aim in two primary ways: first, it requires an **insider** to report any trading that he has engaged in, and second, it prohibits trading by certain insiders—such as directors, senior officers, employees, and the corporation itself—on the basis of information not publicly available.

The reason insiders must report any trade is simple: if someone in this capacity is either buying or selling large blocks of securities, this is critical information for the investing public. Even small trades can be relevant. Insiders are prohibited not only from trading on material information not publicly disclosed but also from passing on this information to a third party or **tippee**. This person is similarly prohibited from trading on such information.

Those who engage in insider trading are subject to both criminal and civil liability under securities legislation and under corporation legislation.[32] In addition, the *Criminal Code* has improper insider trading and tipping offences. The insider trading offence carries a penalty of up to 10 years in prison and the tipping offence is punishable by up to five years in prison.[33]

In considering whether to offer securities to the public through a stock exchange, Luke and Raina have a number of factors to consider. Although selling securities is a means of obtaining funds from a wide group of investors, it entails public disclosure of information that would otherwise not be known to competitors, and certainly requires costly compliance with regulations.[34]

Tippee

A person who acquires material information about an issuer of securities from an insider.

ETHICAL CONSIDERATIONS

BRE-X MINERALS: THE FINAL CHAPTER

In 1995, Bre-X Minerals burst from the ranks of Canada's junior mining companies to become the toast of markets across North America. It was considered a "can't miss" by gold analysts at many of the top brokerage firms on the strength of reports that it had discovered, at Busang, Indonesia, the biggest gold find the world had ever seen. By 1997, it was revealed that the Busang properties contained insignificant amounts of gold. An independent consultant hired to investigate various discrepancies reported that the core samples had been tampered with, resulting in the falsification of assay values (assaying is the process of subjecting the samples to specified testing procedures to determine what quantity of a given mineral is present). Billions of dollars in stock market value evaporated; shares that traded at about $286 fell to pennies and were delisted, leaving many people with huge losses.

The debacle spawned an array of police investigations, regulatory probes, and class action lawsuits in Canada and Texas. Sixteen years later, the lawsuits are over with investors recouping next to nothing. The Ontario class action recovered approximately $4.2 million. As this amounts to about two cents on the dollar for class members, they requested that it be donated to the Law Foundation of Ontario's Access to Justice Fund. An Ontario court dismissed all remaining

Bre-X share certificate

Courtesy of Barry E.C. Boothman, personal collection

Bre-X lawsuits and released the class action lawyers from their undertaking to continue the case. In Alberta, the trustee in bankruptcy for Bre-X pursued various avenues of recovery including litigation in the Cayman Islands, Bahamas, and Philippines. The trustee ultimately recouped about $5 million, which was divided between the Ontario and the Texas class actions with 67 percent going to the Ontario class and 33 percent to the Texas class. All remaining class action suits were dismissed as the bankruptcy trustee indicated that there was no reasonable prospect of any further recovery.

The only person ever charged in relation to Bre-X was John Felderhof, the chief geologist of Bre-X. He was charged with eight violations

---

32 *Supra* note 19 at s 131(4).
33 *Criminal Code*, RSC, 1995, c C-46, Part X, ss 382.1 (1) (2).
34 Edmund MA Kwaw, *The Law of Corporate Finance in Canada* (Toronto: Butterworths, 1997) at 121–22.

John Felderhof

Firdia Lisnawati/AP Photo/The Canadian Press

having information about the company that had not been publicly disclosed. After a lengthy and controversial trial, he was acquitted. The OSC was unable to prove beyond a reasonable doubt that Felderhof had knowledge of the fraud at the time he sold the shares.

Critical Analysis: After the dismissal of the remaining class actions, lawyer Clint Docken, who represented some of the investors, stated, "It's a sad day. . . We have arguably Canada's largest (ever) fraud and no accountability. There's no criminal accountability, there's no regulatory accountability and (now) there doesn't appear to be any civil liability."[35] What factors do you think contributed to the lack of accountability?

Sources: "Investors reach settlement in Bre-X mining fraud case" *The Montreal Gazette* (31 May 2013) A23; Paul Wildie, "Bre-X staggers to an end—but its mystery stands" *The Globe and Mail* (21 March 2013) 18; Jeff Gray, "Bre-X class actions to come to an end" *The Globe and Mail* (14 January 2014) online: *The Globe and Mail* <http://www.theglobeandmail.com/report-on-business/industry-news/the-law-page/bre-x-class-actions-to-come-to-an-end/article16318066/>; "Bre-X Summary" *Sutts, Strosberg* (23 April 2014) online: *Sutts, Strosberg* <https://www.strosbergco.com/brexcomp>; "Bre-X Minerals Ltd., in bankruptcy" *Deloitte* (11 March 2015) online: *Deloitte* <http://www.deloitte.com/view/en_CA/ca/specialsections/insolvencyandrestructuringproceedings/028d753c7717b310VgnVCM1000003256f70aRCRD.htm>.

of the Ontario *Securities Act*, including four based on insider trading. The Ontario Securities Commission (OSC) alleged that Felderhof sold $84 million of Bre-X stock in 1996 while

BUSINESS LAW IN PRACTICE REVISITED

1. How is a corporation formed, and what factors should Luke and Raina consider in forming a corporation?

A corporation is formed by an incorporator or incorporators making an application to the appropriate government body. The choice of the corporate form requires the consideration of a number of issues, including the cost of incorporation and where the corporation will conduct its business. Luke and Raina foresee rapid expansion nationally and internationally; thus a federal incorporation would probably be the logical choice.

Luke and Raina also need to consider such factors as whether the name they have chosen is already in use, what sort of capital structure they will employ, and how the corporation will be capitalized. In particular, Luke and Raina need to

---

35 Hugh McKenna, "Bre-X class action settlement approved; investors get fraction of losses" *National Post* (30 May 2013) online: National Post <http://business.financialpost.com/2013/05/30/bre-x-class-action-settlement-approved-investors-get-fraction-of-losses/>.

recognize that their proposed share structure—half the shares to Luke and half to Raina—may result in shareholder deadlock.

2. What options are available for involving Roger in the business?

Roger could invest as a shareholder, but a loan would give him priority over shareholders in the event of dissolution; however, a loan provides little opportunity to participate in profits unless the interest rate is tied to the profitability of the corporation. Shares offer profit opportunities but have greater risks of loss of investment should the company fail. Roger's investment—whether in shares or debt—can be tailored to address Roger's desire to participate in profits while avoiding risk.

3. What factors should Luke and Raina consider in seeking to raise money by selling shares?

In attempting to raise money by issuing shares, Luke and Raina need to consider a number of factors. Most importantly, both public and private sales involve a consideration from a financial perspective as to whether there is a market for the corporation's shares. As well, any issuance or sale of shares involves an assessment of the impact on the control of the corporation. Sales on the public market also involve requirements as specified by the relevant securities legislation. These requirements can be significant and costly. Selling shares through crowdfunding is not a viable option in Alberta (the proposed head office for the business) as Alberta has not yet implemented equity crowdfunding exemptions.

CHAPTER SUMMARY

The corporate form is prevalent and widespread. The characteristic that distinguishes it from the other basic forms for carrying on business is its separate legal status. This means that the owners are not liable for the debts and obligations of the corporation. It also means that those who are dealing with a corporation need to understand that the owner's risk is limited. Thus, if security is important, they should demand a personal guarantee.

A corporation may be incorporated federally or provincially. There are few distinct advantages of incorporating in one jurisdiction versus another. Prior to commencing the incorporation process, incorporators must decide on a share structure, that is, the classes and number of shares authorized for issuance. The share structure may be simple or complex depending on the needs of the investors.

The actual process of establishing a corporation is relatively simple, and essentially the same format is followed in all jurisdictions. It is a matter of completing and filing the correct forms with the appropriate government body. That said, the incorporation process is not without risks, such as the risk of choosing a name that is similar to that of another business. This risk can be substantially reduced by obtaining legal advice.

A corporation can be financed by equity or debt. Equity represents what the shareholders have invested in the corporation in return for shares. Debt consists of loans that have been made to the corporation. The issuance of shares and debt instruments such as bonds to the public is strictly regulated by securities laws.

CHAPTER STUDY

Key Terms and Concepts

articles of incorporation (p. 362)

bond (p. 364)

bylaws (p. 363)

closely held corporation (p. 357)

conversion right (p. 365)

debenture (p. 364)

incorporator (p. 362)

insider (p. 370)

insider trading (p. 370)

NUANS Report (p. 362)

prospectus (p. 368)

securities (p. 364)

securities legislation (p. 357)

share structure (p. 356)

shelf company (p. 362)

stakeholder (p. 354)

tippee (p. 371)

widely held corporation (p. 357)

Questions for Review

1. What does limited liability mean?

2. Who are the corporation's internal stakeholders? Who are the corporation's external stakeholders?

3. When should a business incorporate federally, and when should it incorporate provincially?

4. What basic rights must attach to at least one class of shares?

5. A class of shares may include a combination of various rights and privileges. Name three examples of typical rights that may attach to a class of shares.

6. What is the difference between a widely held and a closely held corporation?

7. How can a corporation qualify as a private corporation in Ontario? What are the advantages of a corporation qualifying as a private corporation?

8. What is a dual-class structure?

9. Are shares freely transferable? Explain.

10. What are the basic requirements for a corporate name?

11. What is a NUANS Report, and what is its purpose?

12. What is a shelf company, and what is its purpose?

13. Describe the process for incorporating a company.

14. What is crowdfunding? Is equity crowdfunding permissible in Canada?

15. Compare shares to bonds. Which is the more advantageous method of raising money?

16. What are the objectives of securities legislation? How are the objectives achieved?

17. All securities acts have been amended to provide a new statutory right of action for misrepresentations contained in secondary market disclosures. What is the difference between the primary market and the secondary market for securities? What is the statutory right of action for purchasers in the secondary market? Explain.

18. What is meant by insider trading? insider? tippee?

19. Is all insider trading prohibited? Explain.

20. What is a prospectus? What is its purpose?

Questions for Critical Thinking

1. *Salomon v Salomon* stands for the proposition that the corporation has a separate existence from its shareholders. This means that creditors of a corporation do not have recourse against the shareholders' assets. Is this fair? Is it fair that creditors of a sole proprietorship seek the sole proprietor's personal assets? What is the justification for the difference in treatment?

2. Nova Scotia, Alberta, and British Columbia permit a company to incorporate as an ULC, a vehicle whereby shareholders are, in certain circumstances, jointly and severally liable for

the debts and liabilities of the corporation. The ULC is most often used by American investors in Canadian ventures because of significant advantages under U.S. tax law for U.S. residents. This is because, although ULCs are generally subject to taxation in Canada on the same basis as any other Canadian corporation, under U.S. tax law they are treated for many purposes as a partnership. This treatment allows for the "flow-through" of certain income and expenses to U.S. shareholders, thus avoiding some of the double taxation that would otherwise exist. The U.S. owner of the ULC is allowed to consolidate the ULC's foreign income and losses and to claim a U.S. foreign tax credit for any Canadian income tax paid by the ULC. The problem of exposing shareholders of ULCs to unlimited liability can be addressed by interposing an appropriate limited liability entity between the U.S. shareholders and the ULC.

Why would governments amend their corporations legislation to allow for the incorporation of ULCs?

3. Dual-class share structures (more than one vote per share) are prevalent in Canada. There are roughly 80 companies listed on the Toronto Stock Exchange that use some form of dual-class, multiple-voting share structure. Included in this group are Bombardier Inc., Canadian Tire Corp., Power Corp., Rogers Communications Inc., Shaw Communications Inc., Tech Resources Ltd., and Telus Corp.[36] Why do you think dual-class structures have emerged in Canada?

4. The Internet has had a tremendous impact on the securities industry—it has spawned online brokerages, has emerged as the primary source of information for investors, and is the means by which businesses can distribute prospectuses, financial statements, news releases, and the like. It also poses considerable challenges as its global, invisible nature increases the likelihood of fraud. Because scam artists can anonymously and cheaply communicate with a vast number of people,

they can readily spread rumours that result in the manipulation of market prices, trade in securities without being registered to do so, and distribute securities in nonexistent entities. What is the rationale for regulating trade in securities? Do you think the rationale changes when the commercial activity is conducted over the Internet?

5. The Supreme Court of Canada ruled that the federal government's draft legislation for the creation of a single national securities regulatory body was unconstitutional. One of the strongest arguments for the establishment of a single national securities regulatory body is the need for effective enforcement of securities market conduct. How does a single national body, as opposed to 13 provincial and territorial bodies, improve enforcement?[37]

6. In 2012, the United States enacted the *Jumpstart Our Business Startup (JOBS) Act*.[38] The Act amends U.S. securities laws by introducing a crowdfunding exemption that allows entrepreneurs to raise funds and issue securities via an Internet portal. Once the Securities and Exchange Commission introduces rules governing the industry, equity crowdfunding will be available in the United States. Why is most of Canada (see Business and Legislation: Crowdfunding, page 365) behind the United States in permitting equity crowdfunding?

Situations for Discussion

1. In *Silver v IMAX Corp*, shareholders in a class action against IMAX Corporation and certain directors and officers are seeking $500 million in damages and an additional $100 million in punitives. The shareholders allege that IMAX misrepresented its 2005 earnings revenue in press releases and other disclosures for the period 9 March 2006 to 9 August 2006. It is alleged that 2005 revenues were overstated because IMAX recognized revenues from theatres that had yet to open and that this overstatement artificially inflated the trading

36 Janet McFarland, "Stronach move not expected to bury culture of dual-class ownership" *The Globe and Mail* (25 May 2010) online: The Globe and Mail <http://www.theglobeandmail.com/globe-investor/stronach-move-not-expected-to-bury-culture>.

37 Poonam Puri, "The case keeps growing for a national securities regulator," *The Lawyers Weekly* (3 December 2010) 5.
38 Pub L 112-106, 126 Stat 306.

price of IMAX securities. On 9 March, IMAX shares traded on the Toronto Stock Exchange (TSX) at $11.94. On 9 August, IMAX issued a press release stating that the U.S. Securities and Exchange Commission had made an informal inquiry about the company's timing of revenue recognition. On 10 August, the price of IMAX shares dropped to $6.44 on the TSX.[39] What will the plaintiffs have to prove at trial to be successful? How do the secondary market liability amendments in securities legislation assist the plaintiffs? If the plaintiffs are successful, how will damages be calculated?

2. Steering Clear Ltd. is a manufacturer of an expensive automatic helmsman that is used to navigate ocean cruisers. Perry Jones ordered such a helmsman on behalf of a company called Cruisin' Ltd. The helmsman was supplied, but Cruisin' Ltd. did not pay its account. Because of this delinquency, Steering Clear Ltd. decided to investigate the background of Cruisin' Ltd. and discovered that it has a grand total of two issued shares—one held by Perry and the other by his wife. Perry has advised Steering Clear that the debtor company has only $5 in the bank and may have to go out of business soon. Steering Clear wants to sue Perry personally for the debt.[40] Will Steering Clear be successful? On what basis? What is the largest obstacle facing Steering Clear's potential action against Perry? What should Steering Clear have done differently from a business perspective?

3. Sophie Smith has an opportunity to open a designer shoe store in a new mall. She believes that the shoe store will be quite lucrative because of the mall's location adjacent to a condominium development catering to young professionals. To exploit favourable tax laws, Sophie has decided to incorporate a company, and to save money she is going to do it herself. She knows that she will need a name for her corporation. Some of names that she is considering are Shoe Store Inc., Princess Sophie's Shoes Ltd., DownTown Shoes Inc., Sophie Smith Ltd., Nu Shuz Inc., Sophie Smith Clothing and Apparel Inc., and, simply, Sophie's

Shoes. Are there any problems with the names that Sophie is considering for her corporation? Explain. Assume that Sophie has XZONIC Shoes Inc. approved as the corporation's name. What rights does registration of a corporate name give Sophie?

4. Paws Pet Food & Accessories Ltd. (Paws Pet Food) was incorporated under the Alberta *Business Corporations Act*. Three years later, Paws & Shop Inc. (Paws & Shop) was created under the same piece of legislation. Both corporations operated in Calgary, and both were in the business of retailing pet food and accessories. Paws Pet Food was successful in getting a court order directing Paws & Shop to change its name even though the registrar had approved and registered its name. Why do you think Paws Pet Food was successful in getting the court order? What are the costs to Paws & Shop of a name change? The registrar made a mistake in registering Paws & Shop's name. Who should bear the cost of the mistake—the business itself or the taxpayers?

5. Globex Foreign Exchange Corporation (Globex) is an Edmonton-based currency trader. It entered into a contract with 3077860 Nova Scotia Limited (Numberco) for the purchase by Numberco of nearly 1.2 million British pounds. Carl Launt is the sole director and shareholder of Numberco. He funded Numberco with a deposit of $124 676 to effect the trade with Globex. Numberco failed to pay for the rest of the funds purchased and Globex incurred a loss of nearly $90 000 when it resold the currency. Globex commenced an action for breach of contract against Globex and discovered that it was a defunct company with no assets.[41] Is there any legal basis for holding Launt responsible for the unpaid debt of Numberco owed to Globex? Could Globex successfully argue that Numberco was Launt's agent? How could Globex have better protected itself in this situation?

6. In 2010, Frank Stronach relinquished control of auto parts giant Magna International. Since 1978, Magna has had a dual-class, multiple-vote share structure. Through this structure, Stronach was able to control the

---

39 John Jaffey, "Class action lawsuit to test new shareholder rights law," *The Lawyers Weekly* (22 September 2006) 1.

40 Based on *Henry Browne & Sons Ltd v Smith*, [1964] 2 Lloyd's Rep 477 (QB).

41 *Globex Foreign Exchange Corporation v Launt*, 2010 NSSC 229.

company despite owning just 0.6 percent of its 113 million shares because his 720 000 Class B shares each carried 300 votes, while the remaining 112 million Class A shares had one vote each. In return for cancelling the Class B shares, the Stronach family trust received US $300 million in cash and 9 million new Class A shares. In addition, Stronach received a four-year consulting contract and a 27 percent stake in Magna's electric car business. It is estimated that the deal was worth $1 billion—an 1800 percent premium on the value of Stronach's shares. Seventy-five percent of the Class A shareholders voted for the deal and subsequently the Ontario Superior Court[42] approved the deal. Market reaction to the deal was also favourable—on the day following the announcement of the deal, Magna shares closed up 14 percent on the Toronto Stock Exchange.[43] What are the problems with dual-class share structures? What are the advantages? Do you think the deal to eliminate the dual-class structure at Magna was fair?

7. Former RBC Dominion Securities investment banker Andrew Rankin was found guilty in Ontario provincial court of 10 counts of tipping a friend, Daniel Duic, about pending corporate deals. Duic used the tips to make a net profit of over $4.5 million in stock trades in a 12-month period. Insider-trading charges against Duic were dropped in return for his testimony against Rankin and the payment of a $1.9 million fine. Rankin was acquitted of 10 counts of the more serious offence of insider trading because he was apparently not aware of his friend's deals and he did not directly profit from them. Rankin was sentenced to six months in jail. Rankin's conviction, however, was overturned because of contradictory evidence (inconsistencies in Duic's evidence) and errors by the trial judge. Before a new criminal trial was to begin, the Ontario Securities Commission (OSC) agreed to withdraw criminal charges in return for an admission by Rankin that he engaged in illegal tipping. Rankin also agreed to a payment of $250 000 toward OSC's investigation costs, a lifetime ban from working in the securities industry or serving as a director or officer of a public company, and a 10-year ban on trading on securities in Ontario. What are the problems with insider trading? Why is it difficult to secure a conviction for improper insider trading? Do Rankin's penalties fit the "crime"? Why or why not?

8. Alimentation Couche-Tard Inc. is the Canadian leader in the convenience store industry. At 8:30 A.M. on 6 October 2003, Couche-Tard publicly announced a deal to purchase the 2013-store Circle K chain. Completion of the deal would make Couche-Tard the fourth largest convenience store operators in North America. When trading opened on the Toronto Stock Exchange at 9:30 A.M., the company's Class B stock was up 40 cents at $17.50. The price steadily gained all day and closed at $21, for a gain of $3.90. Within five minutes of the opening, Roger Longré, a Couche-Tard director, bought 1500 shares and by 10:30 he had bought a further 2500. At the end of the day, he had a one-day gain, on paper, of $11 372.[44] Did Longré breach any legal requirements? Did he breach any ethical requirements? Should insiders be prohibited from trading prior to earnings announcements and after major announcements? Should insiders be required to clear all proposed trades in the company's securities with a designated in-house trading monitor?

42 *Magna International Inc, (Re)* [2010] OJ No 3454.
43 Tony Van Alphen, "Vote would loosen Stronach's grip on Magna" *the star.com* (7 May 2010) online: the star.com <http://www.thestar.com/business/companies/magna/article/805365—vote-could-loosen-str>; Michael McKiernan, "$1-billion Magna deal's fairness scrutinized", *Canadian Lawyer Magazine* (21 March 2011) online: Canadian Lawyer Magazine <http://www.canadianlawyermag.com/$1-billion-magna-deals-fairness-scrutinized.html>.
44 "Insider trading: A special report," *The Globe and Mail* (18 December 2003) B6.

16

OBJECTIVES

After studying this chapter, you should have an understanding of

- the liabilities of a corporation
- the duties and liabilities of corporate directors and officers
- the rights and liabilities of shareholders and creditors
- how the corporation is terminated

THE CORPORATE FORM: OPERATIONAL MATTERS

BUSINESS LAW IN PRACTICE

Time-in Team Management Inc. (Time-in), incorporated under the *Canada Business Corporations Act*, has been in operation for over two years. Luke Bailey owns 55 percent of the common shares as he had the idea for the business, while Raina El Khoury owns the remaining 45 percent. Roger Wiley contributed $200 000 and was issued 100 preferred shares. An angel investor[1] loaned the company $350 000. Luke and Raina are directors and officers of the corporation, and Roger is an officer although not a director. He is the president of the corporation.

Because Time-in hired a number of employees, Luke and Raina were able to devote all their energy to sales and business development. Under their leadership, the company has done remarkably well, with $2 million in annual sales and excellent financial projections going forward. Not only do they have customers in all the major sports, but a broad range of organizations have also bought into their system. The company continues to field inquiries from abroad and is exploring an international launch. There is, however, a major problem confronting the company.

Several weeks ago, Raina approached Luke with the idea of Time-in purchasing a junior, semi-professional sports team. She told him that she had run the numbers and had concluded that such an investment was feasible, would be an excellent marketing ploy, *and* would be good for the image of the company in the community. Luke responded by telling Raina that buying a sports team was easily one of the worst ideas he had heard in a very long time. "Eventually, I would agree, that buying a team might well make some sense. But I'm not convinced that Time-in is currently big enough and profitable enough to own a sports team. I suggest giving your head a really good shake because you are losing your grip," he told her. Determined to have her way, Raina told Luke that if Time-in did not purchase the team, she would form her own company whose business purpose would be to buy a team and win a championship. "Then we'll see who is the smart one around here," she told him. Raina and Luke had been finding it increasingly difficult to get along given the pressures, tensions, and fatigue of

---

1 An affluent individual who provides funds for a business start-up usually in exchange for equity or a convertible debt.

running a rapidly expanding business. This particular disagreement had simply brought matters to a head.

In response, Luke decided to show Raina who was the boss. He called a shareholders' meeting and, exercising his rights as a majority shareholder, voted Raina off the board of directors. For good measure, Luke also excluded her from participating in the management of Time-in. Raina is devastated because Time-in was her whole life.

Roger does not want to get involved in the dispute at all because he has much more immediate concerns. Roger believes that Time-in is plagued by lax standards in its day-to-day operations. From Roger's perspective, this is what Luke and Raina should focus their attention on. For example, Roger has discovered that Time-in has not been deducting and remitting income tax on salary paid to certain employees. Roger not only finds this unacceptable from an accounting perspective, but also worries about Time-in's liability and fears that he may have personal liability for this "oversight."

1. What obligations do Luke, Raina, and Roger have as corporate officers and directors?

2. Are there any problems with Raina forming her own company to purchase a sports team?

3. Can Raina do anything about Luke voting her off the board and ousting her from management?

4. Is Time-in liable for the failure to deduct and remit income tax? Does Roger, as an officer of Time-in, have any personal liability for the failure to deduct and remit the taxes?

5. What are Roger's rights as a shareholder if he does not like how Time-in is being managed?

Corporate Liability

A corporation is a legal person in the eyes of the law. The corollary is that the corporation is responsible for its own actions. The responsibility of the corporation is, however, complicated by the necessity of corporations to act through human agents. The law has developed rules regarding how a corporation can be said to have committed a tort, committed a crime or regulatory offence, or entered a contract. These rules are particularly important to stakeholders such as Roger, because they determine the legal consequences of corporate behaviour. A summary of the rules regarding liability for corporate conduct can be found in Figure 16.3 on page 406.

Liability in Tort

A corporation can experience two distinct kinds of liability in tort: primary liability and vicarious liability.

A corporation has primary liability for a tort when, in law, it is regarded as the entity that actually committed the tort in question. The idea of a corporation having primary liability is inherently problematic since a corporation, as noted above, can work only through human agents. How can a corporation commit a tort when it does not have a mind of its own and does not have a physical existence?

Identification theory

A theory specifying that a corporation is liable when the person committing the wrong is the corporation's directing mind.

The courts have overcome this hurdle by developing what is known as the **identification theory** of corporate liability.[2] A corporation has liability—and could therefore be described as directly "at fault"—when the person committing the wrong was the corporation's "directing mind and will."

The theory seeks to determine which person or persons are the directing mind of the corporation. When that person or persons commit a tort related to the business enterprise, this conduct is identified with or attributed to the corporation itself. The liability of the corporation is thereby made direct—not vicarious—because in law, the conduct of the directing mind is the conduct of the corporation.

Generally, it is the highly placed corporate officers who are classified as "directing" minds, while low-level employees are not. Whether a mid-range employee would be a directing mind is a more complicated and fact-specific inquiry. A corporation may have more than one directing mind. Each may be responsible for a different aspect of the corporation's business. For example, the vice president for marketing may be the corporation's directing mind in relation to the marketing function, whereas the vice president for finance may be the directing mind in relation to finance.

A corporation has vicarious liability[3] when the tort has been committed by an agent or employee who is not a directing mind of the corporation. The law of vicarious liability does not distinguish between the natural employer/principal—that is, a living, breathing human being—and the artificial employer/principal—that is, a corporation. Instead, the same principle applies to both.

Liability in Contract

While there is no reason why the identification theory could not be used as a way of assessing a corporation's liability in contract, the courts generally have not followed this approach. Instead, agency law largely determines when a corporation is liable on a contract and when it is not.

A corporation is bound by the actions of the agent only if the agent is acting within his actual or apparent authority. For example, if Raina were to enter a contract on behalf of Time-in to purchase a sports team, Time-in would be bound to the contract so long as Raina had the actual or apparent authority to enter the contract. Historically, an agent's apparent authority could be limited by filing with the incorporation documents a specific limitation of the agent's authority. As these documents were publicly filed, outsiders were deemed to have notice of them and to have read their contents. This was known as the doctrine of constructive notice and produced commercial inconvenience, since the only way that an outsider could fully protect herself would be to go down to the registry office and review what the company had filed there. The doctrine has been abolished,[4] meaning that outsiders can now generally rely on the apparent authority of agents. In such a case, the corporation would be liable on the contract.

To avoid personal liability, the person signing a document on behalf of a corporation should ensure that the document contains a clause clearly indicating that the person is signing on behalf of the corporation and is not signing

---

2 *Lennard's Carrying Co v Asiatic Petroleum Co,* [1915] AC 705.
3 Vicarious liability is discussed in Chapters 10 and 20.
4 See, for example, *Canada Business Corporations Act,* RSC 1985, c C-44, s 17.

PART FOUR: STRUCTURING BUSINESS ACTIVITY   NEL

in her personal capacity. This precaution is equally important in the case of pre-incorporation contracts.

Pre-incorporation contracts are contracts that have been entered into by the company's promoters[5] on behalf of the corporation before it has even been created. Such contracts are governed by federal and provincial corporate law statutes, which permit the company to adopt the contract—something that was impossible to do at common law. When adoption occurs, the corporation assumes liability on the contract. The promoter can avoid liability so long as the pre-incorporation contract expressly indicates that the promoter was acting on behalf of the corporation.[6] Pre-incorporation contracts can be problematic if they do not indicate clearly who is intended to be liable[7] and if the corporation fails to come into existence.

From a risk management perspective, people would probably do well to avoid pre-incorporation contracts altogether. Although such contracts are sometimes necessary to take advantage of a valuable business opportunity that just cannot wait, it is usually possible to find a corporate vehicle quickly—such as through the purchase of a shelf company. In this way, the corporation is immediately in place and can enter the contemplated contract directly.

Criminal and Regulatory Liability

Criminal Liability

The criminal liability of a corporation poses the same conceptual problems as tort liability. As Baron Thurlow, L.C., observed in the eighteenth century, "Did you ever expect a corporation to have a conscience, when it has no soul to be damned and no body to be kicked?"

The judiciary solved this problem by adapting the identification theory to the criminal law scenario. The theory maintains that a corporation has committed a crime if the person who committed the crime was a directing mind of the corporation and he committed it in the course of his duties and did so mostly for the benefit of the corporation.[8] A directing mind of a corporation is an individual who exercises decision-making authority in matters of corporate policy. This approach to corporate criminal liability proved to be problematic because of the difficulty in proving beyond a reasonable doubt that the directing mind behaved in a criminal manner. This problem was highlighted by the lack of criminal convictions in the 1992 Westray mine explosion in Nova Scotia.[9] In response to the Westray public inquiry's findings, the federal government amended the *Criminal Code*.[10] The amendments increased the scope of

---

5 A promoter is someone who participates in setting up a corporation.

6 *Supra* note 4, s 14(4): "Exemption from personal liability—If expressly so provided in the written contract, a person who purported to act in the name of or on behalf of the corporation before it came into existence is not. . . bound by the contract."

7 The legislative provisions protecting the promoter from personal liability have been strictly construed by the courts. For example, in *Landmark Inns of Canada Ltd v Horeak* (1982), 18 Sask R 30, 2 WWR 377 (QB), the court held that merely naming the yet-to-be incorporated corporation as a party to the contract was insufficient to relieve the promoter of personal liability. The contract must also contain an express provision that specifically relieves him of liability.

8 A corporation is not liable for an offence committed by a "directing mind" that is totally unrelated to her corporate position. For example, a corporation is not liable for a break and enter committed by the president on her way home from the office.

9 On May 9, 1992, 26 miners died in an underground methane explosion at the Westray coal mine in Plymouth, Nova Scotia. The employees of the mine were working in unsafe conditions that were known to the corporation yet criminal proceedings against the corporation and the mine's managers were unsuccessful.

10 RSC 1985, c C-46.

potential criminal liability of corporations[11] by expanding the range of individuals whose actions can trigger liability, by broadening corporate responsibility for all criminal offences, and by increasing the penalties.

Prior to the amendments, a corporation could be liable for a criminal offence only if the directing mind of the corporation committed the offence. The amendments expand the range of individuals whose actions can trigger liability of the corporation to senior officers. These are individuals who play an important role in the establishment of the organization's policies or are responsible for managing an important aspect of the organization's activities. The definition focuses on the function of the individual, rather than any particular title.

The amendments also address both crimes requiring proof of knowledge or intent and crimes requiring proof of negligence. For offences that require intent,[12] an organization will be criminally liable if a senior officer, while acting in the scope of his or her authority and intending at least in part to benefit the organization, either actively engages in unsafe conduct, directs representatives[13] to do it, or knows about the unsafe conduct but does nothing or not enough to put a stop to it, and death or injury results. The effect of the changes is that it is no longer necessary that the intent and the guilty act of a criminal offence reside in the same person. Also, senior officers are now under a positive obligation to act when they have knowledge that an offence has been or will be committed; failure to act will result in corporate criminal liability. For offences based on negligence,[14] an organization can be convicted if any representative providing services for the organization causes injury or death by unsafe conduct and the senior officer or officers in charge of the activities of the representative depart markedly from the reasonable standard of care necessary to prevent the incident. These changes broaden negligence offences by allowing the combined conduct of two individuals, who individually may not be acting in a manner that is careless or reckless, to constitute the necessary elements of the crime.

The amendments provide for stiffer penalties and corporate probation orders. A less serious summary conviction offence carries a fine of up to $100 000 (an increase from $25 000) and fines for more serious indictable offences remain with no prescribed limits. The legislation also enumerates factors that the courts must consider when setting fines, including moral blameworthiness (i.e., the economic advantage gained by the organization by committing the crime), public interest (i.e., the cost of investigation and prosecution, the need to keep the organization in business), and the prospects of rehabilitation (remedial steps directed to preventing the likelihood of a subsequent offence). A corporate probation order may involve conditions such as providing restitution to victims, publishing the offence in the media, and implementing policies and procedures. Its purpose is to allow the court to oversee and regulate an organization's efforts to reform.

---

11 The amendments extended criminal liability to "organizations," which includes corporations, companies, partnerships, trade unions, and any association of persons that was created for a common purpose, has a structure, and holds itself out as an association of persons.

12 Most crimes in the *Criminal Code* fall within this category; examples include fraud, theft, and bribery.

13 A representative includes everyone working for or affiliated with an organization, such as a director, partner, employee, agent, or contractor.

14 Examples of negligence-based crimes include storing a firearm in a careless manner, operating a motor vehicle in a manner dangerous to the public, and showing wanton and reckless disregard for the lives or safety of others.

DEATH IN THE WORKPLACE

On Christmas Eve 2009, four construction workers who were repairing concrete balconies at an apartment building died when their swing stage scaffolding broke and they plummeted 13 storeys to the ground. A fifth worker suffered severe leg and spinal injuries and a sixth worker, who had attached himself to a lifeline, was uninjured. Since the accident, five parties have been found guilty of safety-related offences:

- In June 2012, Metron Construction Corporation pleaded guilty to one count of criminal negligence causing death and was fined $200 000. On appeal, the fine was quadrupled to $750 000.[15] Metron's *Criminal Code* liability resulted from the actions of its site supervisor, a "senior officer" of Metron. The site supervisor, who died in the accident, permitted six workers to work on the swing stage when there were only two harnesses and the usual practice is to have only two workers on a stage, and he permitted some workers to be under the influence of marijuana.

- A director of Metron was convicted of breaching the province's *Occupational Health* and *Safety Act* (*OHSA*) and fined $90 000. He failed to ensure that non-English speaking workers received written material in their native languages; failed to ensure that training records were maintained; failed to ensure that the swing stage was not defective or hazardous; and failed to ensure that the swing stage was not loaded in excess of the load that the platform was designed and constructed to bear.

- Swing N Scaff Inc., the company that supplied the swing stage platform, pleaded guilty to an occupational health and safety offence of failing to ensure that the

What is an appropriate punishment for a corporation convicted of criminal negligence causing death?

platform was in good condition and was fined $350 000.

- The director of Swing N Scaff pleaded guilty to failing to take all reasonable care to ensure the platform was in good condition and that a platform weighing more than 525 kilograms was designed by a professional engineer in accordance with good engineering practice. He was fined $50 000 under the *OHSA*.

- The project manager for Metron was convicted of four counts of criminal negligence causing death and one count of criminal negligence causing bodily harm. He oversaw the construction crew and allowed his workers to board the swing stage even though he was aware that fall protections were not in place. The court has not yet imposed a sentence.

Critical Analysis: What are the lessons for employers from this case?

Sources: "Deadly scaffold leads to $340K in penalties", *CBC News* (13 July 2012), online: *CBC News* <http://www.cbc.ca/news/canada/toronto/story/2012/07/13/toronto-metron-fine.html>; "Construction manager faces trial in employee deaths", *The Star* (4 February 2015), online: *The Star* <http://www.thestar.com/news/crime/2015/01/15/construction-manager-faces-trial-in-employee-deaths.html>.

15   *R. v. Metron Construction Corporation*, 2013 ONCA 541, [2013] 300 CCC (3d) 212.

Regulatory Offences

In addition to criminal liability under the *Criminal Code*, a corporation faces liability pursuant to a wide range of statutory enactments related to taxation, human rights, pay equity, employment standards, consumer protection, unfair or anticompetitive business practices, occupational health and safety, and environmental protection, to name a few. The relevant legislation often imposes penalties on the corporation, and sometimes on its directors and officers, including civil liability for damages.

Regulatory offence

An offence contrary to the public interest.

An offence like those alluded to above is known as a **regulatory offence**. Regulatory offences have a criminal aspect because they involve some kind of punishable conduct that is contrary to the public interest, such as polluting streams.

Owing to the large number of regulatory offences affecting business, as well as the expense and public relations problems associated with their commission, corporations are concerned with assessing and managing their exposure as they may be subject to large penalties. Consider, for example, the following:

- In 2014, Panasonic Corporation was fined $4.7 million for its participation in bid-rigging contrary to the *Competition Act*. Panasonic conspired with another Japanese motor vehicle components manufacturer when responding to requests for bids from Toyota Canada. The two companies both co-ordinated their responses and agreed on which party would win the bid to supply components such as turn switches, wiper switches, steering wheel switches, and steering angle sensors.[16]

- In 2014, Bloom Lake General Partner Ltd. was fined $7.5 million for offences under the federal *Fisheries Act* and the *Metal Mining Effluent Regulations*. Included in the infractions was a major breach of a tailings pond that released more than 200 000 cubic metres of tailings and water into fish bearing water in Quebec.[17]

- In 2013, Sinopec Shanghai Engineering Co. Ltd. was fined $1.5 million after pleading guilty to three charges under Alberta's *Occupational Health and Safety Act*. Two workers were killed and five injured after a tank at an oil sands site collapsed while under construction.[18]

- In 2010, Syncrude Canada Ltd. was fined $3 million after being found guilty of the deaths of 1606 birds on its tailings ponds. It had been charged under the *Alberta Environmental Protection and Enhancement Act* for storing a hazardous substance in a manner enabling it to contaminate wildlife, and under the federal *Migratory Bird Convention Act* for depositing substances harmful to migratory birds in areas that they frequent.[19]

Time-in's operations may be affected by many legislative provisions. For example, the *Income Tax Act*[20] requires that every person paying salary, wages, or other remuneration withhold a prescribed amount of income tax. Time-in is

---

16 "Panasonic fined $4.7 million for rigging bids", *Competition Bureau* (20 February 2014), online: Competition Bureau <http://www.competitionbureau.gc.ca/eic/site/cb-bc.nsf/eng/03669.html>.

17 Bertrand Marotte, "Cliffs' Bloom Lake mine hit with record $7.5 million environmental fine", *Globe and Mail* (25 December 2014), online: *Globe and Mail* <http://www.theglobeandmail.com/news/national/cliffs-bloom -lake-mine-hit-with-record-75-million-environmental-fine/article22210209/>.

18 Kelly Crydermann, "Sinopec unit fined $1.5-million over deaths at Alberta oil sands project", *The Globe and Mail* (24 January 2013), online: *The Globe and Mail* <http://www.theglobeandmail.com/report-on -business/industry-news/the-law-page/sinopec-unit-fined-15-million-over-deaths-at-alberta-oil-sands-project/ article7823202/>.

19 Josh Wingrove, "$3-million fine a drop in the barrel for Syncrude", *The Globe and Mail* (23 October 2010) A20.

20 RSC 1985, c 1 (5th Supp), s 153(1).

a person paying salary so it comes within the provisions of the legislation. Its failure to deduct and remit income taxes can trigger penalties including, for a first offence, a fine of 10 percent of the amount owing. Liability under this taxation legislation is strict,[21] and defences are therefore rare.[22]

What factors should the courts consider when fining a corporation that causes the death of wildlife?

Directors and Officers

The directors, who are elected by shareholders, manage or supervise the management of the business and the affairs of the corporation.[23] In addition to this general authority, directors have specific powers and obligations set out in legislation. For example, directors can declare dividends, call shareholder meetings, adopt bylaws, and issue shares. Directors are, however, not usually in a position to carry out the actual management themselves; generally they are authorized to appoint officers to carry out many of their duties and exercise most of their powers.[24] This power of delegation does not, however, relieve the directors of ultimate responsibility for the management of the corporation.

BUSINESS APPLICATION OF THE LAW

CORPORATE GOVERNANCE AND WOMEN ON BOARDS

The Canadian Securities Administrators (CSA)[25] have policies on corporate governance best practices[26] and the disclosure of corporate governance practices.[27] The best practices, which are not mandatory for companies listed on Canadian stock exchanges, include recommendations on the role of the board, the composition of the board, independence of directors, and the like.

---

21 The vast majority of regulatory offences are strict liability offences. This means that the accused may avoid liability if he can show that he acted with due diligence or took all reasonable care. Few offences impose absolute liability, that is, liability is imposed for doing the act, and it is not open to the accused to show he was without fault.

22 Vern Krishna, "Directors' liability for corporate taxes", *The Lawyers Weekly* (14 July 2000) 5.

23 This general power may be circumscribed by the bylaws or by a unanimous shareholder agreement.

24 Note that some matters, such as declaring dividends and approving the annual financial statements, may not be delegated.

25 A body composed of the 13 provincial and territorial securities regulators, whose role is to coordinate and harmonize securities regulation policy across Canada.

26 National Instrument 58-201 *Corporate Governance Guidelines*.

27 National Instrument 58-101 *Disclosure of Corporate Governance Practices*.

Why is it important to have more women on the boards of directors of companies?

Public companies are encouraged to follow these practices and are required to describe their practices. Where their practices are different from the recommendations, they must explain why they are not following the recommendations.

The Ontario Securities Commission (OSC) as well as the securities regulatory bodies in most other jurisdictions[28] has amended the rule on the disclosure of corporate governance practice to increase the representation of women on boards and in senior decision-making positions. The OSC reported that significant gender disparity persists on boards in the ranks of senior officials. Its survey of 1 000 companies listed on the Toronto Stock Exchange (TSX) in 2013 indicated that

- only 10.5 percent of directors of companies on the Standard & Poor's (S&P)/TSX Composite index were women.

- 57 percent of companies on the index did not have a woman on the board.
- 53 percent of the companies indicated that women held less than 10 percent of executive positions.

The amendment, which follows a "comply or explain" model, requires affected companies to publish annually a description of their diversity policies, including whether they have internal targets for promoting women to their boards of directors or to senior executive roles. Like other corporate governance rules, the amendment does not require companies to add women to their boards or adopt a diversity policy, but requires them to explain why they have opted not to comply with the recommendation.

Critical Analysis: What is the advantage of the "comply or explain" approach? Do you think mandatory quotas would be a better option?

Sources: "Canadian securities regulators finalize rule amendments regarding disclosure of women on boards and in senior management", *Ontario Securities Commission* (15 October 2014), online: OSC <http://www.osc.gov.on.ca/en/NewsEvents_nr_20141015_csa-regarding-disclosure-of-women.htm>; Allison Greene, "Comply or explain why", *The Lawyers Weekly* (6 September 2013) 17; Janet McFarland, "OSC proposes model to get more women in top jobs", *The Globe and Mail* (16 January 2014), online: *Globe and Mail* <http://www.theglobeandmail.com/report-on-business/osc-plans-reporting-rule-on-companies-efforts-to-add-women-to-boards/article16363857/>; "Women on boards: OSC proposes 'comply or explain' model over quotas", *Davies LLP* (17 January 2014), online: *Davies LLP* <http://www.dwpv.com/en/Resources/Publications/2014/Women-on-Boards-OSC-Proposes-Comply-or-Explain-Model-Over-Quotas>.

Duties of Directors and Officers

In exercising their management function, directors and officers have obligations contained in two broad categories: a fiduciary duty and a duty of competence.

The Fiduciary Duty

This duty requires directors and officers to act honestly and in good faith with a view to the best interests of the corporation. They cannot allow themselves to favour one particular group of shareholders, for example, because their duty is not to that group but rather to the corporation as a whole. One of the central

---

28 Securities regulators in all Canadian jurisdictions other than Alberta and British Columbia have approved the rule. Andrew MacDougall, "New disclosure rules regarding women on boards to be effective for 2015 proxy season", *Osler* (15 October 2014), online: Osler <http://www.osler.com/NewsResources/New-Disclosure-Rules-Regarding-Women-on-Boards-to-be-Effective-for-2015-Proxy-Season/>.

principles informing fiduciary duties in corporate law can be summarized as follows: directors and officers must not allow their personal interest to conflict with their duty to the corporation. Not surprisingly, then, the fiduciary principle arises in multiple circumstances, two of which are explored below.

The Self-Dealing Contract To understand how a **self-dealing contract** works, assume the following scenario. Time-in requires some office furniture, which Luke just so happens to be in a position to supply. He has several reasonably nice executive desks stored in his garage and is willing to sell them to the corporation. Luke is now in a conflict-of-interest situation.

As director of Time-in, Luke is obligated to try to buy the furniture at as low a price as possible. As vendor of the furniture, however, Luke may be motivated by self-interest to sell the furniture at as high a price as possible. In this way, his duty to the corporation and his self-interest may collide because Luke is on both sides of the contract. (See Figure 16.1.)

FIGURE 16.1 Self-Dealing Contract

Luke (the corporate director) ➡ buys from ➡ Luke (the individual)

In law, Luke is said to be in a self-dealing contract: he is dealing with himself in the purchase and sale of the office furniture.

Many jurisdictions have enacted procedures through which self-dealing contracts are permissible. The idea is to ensure that the corporation is not "ripped off" and, at the same time, to avoid a blanket prohibition on self-dealing contracts since some of them could be beneficial to the company. Under the *Canada Business Corporations Act*, for example, Luke's contract to sell furniture to his own company will be enforceable provided that

- Luke discloses the contract to the corporation in writing.
- Luke does not participate in any vote of the directors approving the contract.
- the contract is fair and reasonable to the corporation.[29]

Failure to follow these statutory provisions gives the corporation the right to ask a court for a remedy, including that the contract be set aside or "cancelled" on any terms the court sees fit.

Corporate Opportunities Another area in which conflicts of interest frequently arise concerns **corporate opportunity**. Directors and officers are often required to assess any number of projects in which their corporation could become involved. These projects are known in law as "corporate opportunities"— they are opportunities to do business that the company can pursue or decline. If the directors and officers were permitted to take up any of these opportunities for themselves, problems very much like the ones present in the self-dealing contract scenario would arise.

Assume that Time-in has been approached by an Ontario company that is in need of a program for scheduling, on a moment's notice, a large workforce with a variety of different skills located in many different parts of the world. That company would like to work with Time-in to create a scheduling system, the revenue potential of which appears to be very high. Luke is in a conflict-of-interest situation. As

29 Supra note 4, s 120.

a director, he is required to assess the corporate opportunity on its own merits. As an individual, however, because he is interested in the contract for himself, he is motivated by self-interest. Put another way, if Luke were permitted to pursue the opportunity himself, he would be tempted—in his capacity as director—to turn down the project, not because it was in the best interests of the corporation to do so but because he wanted to develop the scheduling system himself.

Given her fiduciary duty as a director, Raina must proceed cautiously to purchase the sports team. Provided that Raina secures Luke's and Roger's fully informed consent, perhaps in the form of a directors' resolution and a shareholders' resolution, there is no obvious legal impediment to her proceeding to purchase the team. She is being aboveboard and acting fairly vis-à-vis Time-in. Since Time-in does not want to pursue the opportunity, it would be highly unlikely that a court would decide that Raina was in breach of her fiduciary duty to Time-in by pursuing the opportunity for herself.

Canadian Aero Service Ltd v O'Malley, [1974] SCR 592, 40 DLR (3d) 371

THE HISTORICAL CONTEXT: The Supreme Court's decision in this case is the leading analysis of the principles underlying the corporate opportunity doctrine. The case is also important because of the court's recognition that officers may owe fiduciary duties to the corporation and a director or officer may be precluded from appropriating a business opportunity even after she resigns.

FACTUAL BACKGROUND: On behalf of their company, Canadian Aero Service Ltd. (Canaero), the president and executive vice president had been negotiating to win an aerial mapping contract in Guyana. Subsequently, both officers left Canaero and set up their own company, Terra Surveys Limited. Terra began to pursue the very same line of work as Canaero and successfully bid on the aerial mapping contract in Guyana. Canaero brought an action against Terra and Canaero's former executives for improperly taking Canaero's corporate opportunity.

THE LEGAL QUESTION: Were the former executives in breach of their fiduciary duty to Canaero? Did the fact that the two had resigned and then, some time later, acquired the opportunity for themselves mean that there was no liability?

RESOLUTION: The former executives were held liable to account to Canaero for the profits they made under the contract. They

had breached their fiduciary duties by taking something that belonged to the corporation. In determining whether the appropriation of an opportunity is a breach of fiduciary duty, the court suggested an examination of factors such as these:

- the position or office held by the directors and officers (the higher they are in the organization, the higher their duty).
- the nature of the corporate opportunity (how clearly was the opportunity identified by the corporation and how close was the corporation to acquiring the opportunity?).
- the director's or managerial officer's relation to the opportunity (was the opportunity one that the fiduciary worked on or had responsibility for?).
- the amount of knowledge the directors and officers possessed and the circumstances in which it was obtained.
- the time between when the opportunity arose and when the officers took the opportunity for themselves.
- the circumstances under which the employment relationship between the officers and the company terminated (was termination due to retirement, resignation, or discharge?).

Because the former officers violated their fiduciary duty, any profit gained—even if it was not at the expense of their former company—had to be given to the company.

That they had resigned before pursuing the opportunity did not change the analysis.

CRITICAL ANALYSIS: When do you think a director of a corporation should be able to take advantage of a business opportunity? In other words, when is a business opportunity her own and when does it belong to the company she serves as director?

ETHICAL CONSIDERATIONS

CORPORATE SOCIAL RESPONSIBILITY

"Corporate social responsibility" (CSR) is a term without a precise definition. It is usually defined as "voluntary activities undertaken by a corporation to operate in an economic, social, and environmentally sustainable manner." Typical examples of CSR are Royal Bank of Canada's "generator" fund, a $10 million pool of capital for investing in new business models that address social and environmental challenges; PepsiCo Inc.'s partnerships to provide access to safe drinking water to 3 million people in developing countries; Aventure plc's practice of diverting almost one-third of its procurement spending to small, minority- and women-owned businesses; and Best Buy Co. Inc.'s recycling program that gives customers the ability to safely recycle their end-of-life electronic products.

Not surprisingly, CSR has become a common item on the agendas of corporate boards. Evidence of CSR's prominence is *Maclean's* annual ranking of the top 50 socially responsible corporations. In partnership with Sustainalytics, they select the top "do-gooders" in an array of industries including banking, retailing, energy and utilities, and materials including mining.

Despite the emphasis on CSR and the laudable efforts of many businesses, there remain examples of Canadian corporate involvement in activities with undesirable and sometimes horrific outcomes. Two notable recent examples are the collapse of the Rana Plaza in Bangladesh (see page 14) where clothing was manufactured for Loblaw's Joe Fresh line, and the death of seven

© cglade/iStock

What can business gain from being socially responsible? What are the risks?

people searching for gold in waste rock from African Barrick's North Mara mine in northern Tanzania.[30] African Barrick is a majority-owned subsidiary of Canada's Barrick Gold Corp. These examples raise the question of whether social responsibilities should remain voluntary or be made legally enforceable, particularly with respect to activities in underdeveloped and developing countries. The most recent attempt at legislating corporate social responsibility—a private member's bill requiring Canadian mining firms to respect environmental and human rights standards abroad—was defeated.[31]

Critical Analysis: Should governments pass legislation requiring CSR? Why or why not?

30 Lisa Wright & Jocelyn Edwards, "Seven dead in clash at African Barrick mine", *The Star* (17 May 2011), online: *The Star* <http://www.thestar.com/business/2011/05/17/seven_dead_in_clash_at_african_barrick_mine.html>.
31 Bill Curry, "Ethical mining bill defeated after fierce lobbying", *The Globe and Mail* (28 October 2010), online: BNN <http://www.bnn.ca/News/2010/10/28/Ethical-mining-bill-defeated-after-fierce-lobbying.aspx>.

PART FOUR

The Duty of Competence

This duty requires directors and officers to exercise the care, diligence, and skill that a reasonably prudent person would exercise in comparable circumstances. Put more informally, directors and officers must meet a general standard of competence.

At one time, directors had very minimal obligations to act with care in exercising their responsibilities. In *Re City Equitable Fire Insurance Co,*[32] for example, the court held that "a director need not exhibit in the performance of his duties a greater degree of skill than may reasonably be expected from a person of his knowledge and experience." This meant that if the director were ill-informed and foolish, then little could be expected of her; she was required only to display the competence of an ill-informed and foolish person. The unfortunate outcome at common law was that the less qualified a director was for office, the less time and attention she devoted to her duties, and the greater the reliance she placed on others, the lower was the standard that she was required to meet in managing the business affairs of the company.

Recognizing that the common law standard of care was unduly low, legislatures have codified and upgraded what is expected of directors. The present standard contained in corporation legislation requires directors and officers to display the care, diligence, and skill that a reasonably prudent person would exercise in comparable circumstances. This is an objective standard, and, while directors are not expected to be perfect, they are to act prudently and on a reasonably informed basis.

Peoples Department Stores Inc (Trustee of) v Wise (2004), 2004 SCC 68, 3 SCR 461

THE BUSINESS CONTEXT: The *Canada Business Corporations Act* imposes a duty on directors and officers to act honestly and in good faith with a view to the best interests of the corporation (the fiduciary duty) and to exercise the care, diligence, and skill that a reasonably prudent person would exercise in comparable circumstances (a duty of care).[33] There have been questions about whether the duties of directors extend to creditors, particularly when the corporation is financially troubled.

FACTUAL BACKGROUND: Lionel, Ralph, and Harold Wise were majority shareholders and directors of Wise Stores Inc., a publicly traded company operating about 50 junior department stores in Quebec with annual sales of $100 million. In 1992, Wise Inc. acquired all of the shares of Peoples Department Stores Inc. from Marks & Spencer for $27 million. Peoples owned 81 stores and generated sales of $160 million annually. The Wise brothers became the sole directors of Peoples. The joint operation of Wise and Peoples did not function smoothly. In an effort to help the sagging fortunes of the companies, the Wise brothers implemented a joint inventory purchasing policy on the recommendation of the companies' vice president of administration and finance. The result of the policy was that Peoples purchased and paid for most of Wise Inc.'s inventory, subject to reimbursement by Wise Inc. Peoples ended up extending large amounts of trade credit to Wise and, by June 1994, Wise owed more than $18 million to Peoples. The financial situations of both companies

---

32 [1925] 1 Ch 407 at 428.
33 Most provincial corporate statutes provide for similar duties.

continued to deteriorate and both ended up bankrupt in January 1995. After the sale of the assets and the payment of secured creditors, approximately $21.5 million in trade debt went unpaid. The Peoples trustee in bankruptcy, representing the interests of the unpaid creditors, sued the Wise brothers, alleging that in implementing the joint inventory procurement program, they breached their duties as directors of Peoples.

THE LEGAL QUESTION: Did the Wise brothers as directors of Peoples owe duties to the creditors of Peoples? If so, did they breach these duties?

RESOLUTION: In a unanimous decision, the Supreme Court of Canada held that the Wise brothers did not owe a fiduciary duty to the creditors. While directors are entitled to have regard to the interests of various stakeholders—shareholders, employees, suppliers, creditors, consumers, government, and the environment—they owe their fiduciary duty only to the corporation. The directors' fiduciary duty does not change when the corporation is in the "vicinity of insolvency." The court further noted that stakeholders, like creditors, have other avenues of potential relief. The creditors can use the oppression remedy to protect their interests from the prejudicial conduct of directors.

The Court also held that creditors can pursue an action based on breach of the duty of care as the identity of the beneficiaries of this duty was "more open ended" and "obviously" included creditors (this marks the first time that the Supreme Court has extended the duty of care beyond the corporation). The Court stated that the duty of care is to be judged objectively. In analyzing whether particular conduct met the standard of care, the Court will consider the factual circumstances as well as the socioeconomic conditions. The Supreme Court (also for the first time) endorsed the "business judgment rule" in assessing whether directors have fulfilled the duty of care. The rule holds that the Court will not second-guess business judgments that are made honestly and on the basis of reasonable information. The Wise brothers did not breach their duty of care to creditors, as the inventory policy was a reasonable effort to address inventory management problems.

CRITICAL ANALYSIS: Is the decision in *Peoples v Wise* good news for directors of corporations? Is it good news for creditors?

Liabilities of Directors and Officers

Directors and officers are exposed to a broad range of liabilities relating to the business of the corporation, including liability in torts and contracts, and liability by statutory offences.

This section will discuss such liabilities in relation to directors, while recognizing that the same analysis usually also applies to officers.[34]

Liability in Tort and Contract

When a director is acting on behalf of a corporation and commits a tort, his actions may be attributed to the corporation itself by virtue of the identification theory. Similarly, when the director enters into a contract, as agent for his corporation, his actions make the corporation the other party to that contract and the director slips out of the equation altogether. There are times, however, when a director has personal liability for a tort he may have committed or a contract he may have entered into.

---

34 For example, particular legislation may impose liability on directors but not officers of the corporation.

Liability in Tort Traditionally, courts have been reluctant to say that a director is automatically liable just because he commits a tort on company time. The idea is to permit the director to conduct company business without risking personal, unlimited liability at every turn. Think of it this way: if Luke were personally liable for any tort he committed during the course of his business day, there would really be little benefit in incorporating Time-in from his perspective as a director. His liability would be the same whether he was running his business through a corporation or as a sole proprietorship, and the principle in *Salomon v Salomon* would fall by the wayside.

That said, courts have acknowledged that in some circumstances the actions of the director done in the course of carrying out their duties may result in personal liability. Courts disagree in their approach as to when that will occur, however. Some courts have ruled that directors are not personally liable provided that they were acting in furtherance of their duties to the corporation and their conduct was justifiable.[35] Other courts have opined that personal liability is confined to actions that are tortious in themselves or that "exhibit a separate identity or interest from that of the corporation so as to make the act or conduct complained of their own. . ."[36] Still other courts appear to suggest that directors and officers will almost always be responsible for their own tortious conduct even if they were acting in the best interests of the corporation.[37] With this in mind, prudent directors will take care not to commit torts and will thereby avoid having to establish what the law concerning the matter is in their jurisdiction.

Most certainly, where the director's conduct is extreme, she will be found liable for committing a tort regardless of the approach taken by the court in question. For example, assume that Luke is meeting in his office with a customer who has not paid his bill to Time-in. Things get a little out of hand and Luke bars the door for several hours, saying to the customer, "You're not getting out of here until you write a cheque for what you owe us." On these facts, Luke would face personal liability no matter what the legal test applied might be.

Liability in Contract The director does not generally attract liability for the corporation's contracts—the principles of agency operate in such a way that the corporation is liable to the outsider and the director who has acted as agent for the corporation drops out of the transaction.

Nonetheless, a director faces personal liability on a contract if the facts indicate that the director intended to assume personal liability, as when

- the director contracts on his own behalf, as well as on behalf of the company.
- the director guarantees the contractual performance of the company.

---

35 *McFadden v 481782 Ontario Ltd,* (1984), 47 OR (2d) 134, 27 BLR 173 (HC).

36 *Hogarth v Rocky Mountain Slate Inc,* 2013 ABCA 57, [2013] 5 WWR 457. See also: *Blacklaws v Morrow,* 2000 ABCA 175, 187 DLR (4th) 614, leave refused [2000] SCCA No 442, [2001] 1 SCR vii.

37 See, for example, *ADGA Systems International Ltd v Valcom Ltd* (1999), 43 OR (3d) 101, 168 DLR (4th) 351 (CA), leave to appeal to SCC refused, [1999] SCCA No 124. Also see Edward M Iacobucci, "Unfinished Business: An Analysis of Stones Unturned in *ADGA Systems International v Valcom Ltd*", (2001) 35 *Can Bus LJ* 39; Janis Sarra, "The Corporate Veil Lifted: Director and Officer Liability to Third Parties", (2001) 35 *Can Bus LJ* 55; and Christopher C Nicholls, "Liability of Corporate Officers and Directors to Third Parties", (2001) 35 *Can Bus LJ* 1.

Liability by Statute

In addition to the exposure that directors face for breaching their general management duties, dozens of pieces of legislation place obligations on them (see Figure 16.2 for examples of the range of legislation affecting directors). These statutes impose potentially serious penalties for failure to comply, including fines of up to $1 million and imprisonment for up to two years.[38]

For example, the failure of Time-in to withhold and remit income taxes can result in the directors being personally liable for the corporation's failure unless the directors can demonstrate that they acted in a reasonable and diligent manner.[39] Thus Luke and Raina, as directors of Time-in, face personal liability for Time-in's failure. Interestingly the *Income Tax Act* does not impose personal liability on officers—such as Roger—for this particular failure. While Roger owes duties as a corporate officer under the *Canada Business Corporations Act*, at common law, and under his employment contract, he does not have any direct personal liability for his company's failure to remit under the *Income Tax Act*. It is important to check the provisions of legislation to determine who may be potentially liable.

FIGURE 16.2 Directors' Statutory Liabilities: A Sampling

Statutory Breach	Type of Statute	Nature of Penalty
Failure to pay employee wages	Federal and provincial incorporation statutes	Liability for wages
Directing, authorizing, or permitting the release of a toxic substance into the environment	Federal and provincial environmental protection statute	Fines and/or imprisonment
Failure to remit required taxes	Provincial and federal revenue acts	Liability for amount outstanding and interest or penalties
Failure to maintain health and safety standards	Provincial workplace health and safety legislation	Fines and/or imprisonment
Insider trading—using confidential information in buying and selling shares	Provincial securities acts, federal and provincial incorporation statutes	Fines and/or imprisonment
Engaging in anticompetitive behaviour	Federal *Competition Act*	Criminal and civil liabilities
Paying a dividend when company is insolvent	Federal and provincial incorporation statutes	Personal repayment
Misrepresentation in a prospectus	Provincial securities legislation	Damages
Improperly transporting dangerous goods	Federal and provincial transportation of dangerous goods legislation	Fines and/or imprisonment

38 See, for example, the federal *Hazardous Products Act*, RSC 1985, c H-3, s 28(1).
39 *Supra* note 20, s 227.1 (1)(3).

THE LIABILITY OF DIRECTORS AND OFFICERS

In January 2005, General Chemical Canada closed its plant in Amherstburg, Ontario, leaving behind a badly contaminated lagoon, several environmental orders issued by the Ministry of the Environment (MOE), and estimated clean-up costs of over $60 million. As the company was on the verge of bankruptcy and unlikely to be in a position to pay the clean-up costs, the MOE issued clean-up orders against General Chemical's U.S. parent company and a number of directors and officers of both companies. The directors and officers appealed the MOE clean-up orders but ultimately agreed to pay more than $10 million to settle the case against them. This case highlights the potential liability of directors and officers for a corporation's environmental transgressions.

Both the *Canadian Environmental Protection Act, 1999*[40] (CEPA) and provincial environmental statutes have specific provisions imposing personal liability on directors and officers for the corporation's commission of an environmental offence.[41] In addition, directors and officers are subject to liability for a corporation's wrongdoing on the grounds that they aided or abetted the corporation. They may also be named in a variety of administrative orders issued by government agencies for the prevention, control, or clean-up of environmental contamination.

Specific Offences: The *CEPA* specifies that where a corporation commits an offence, any officer, director, or agent who directed, authorized, assented to, acquiesced in, or participated in the commission of the offence, regardless of whether the corporation has been prosecuted

General Chemical Plant in Amherstburg, Ontario

Tyler Brownbridge/The Windsor Star

or convicted, is guilty of the offence. In addition to this provision that imposes liability on the basis of participation, the legislation also imposes on directors and officers a duty to take all reasonable care to ensure that the corporation complies with the Act, its regulations, and environmental orders.[42]

Directors and officers have also been singled out in provincial legislation for personal liability in relation to corporate environmental practices. In Ontario, for example, the legislation imposes on directors and officers a positive duty to take all reasonable care to prevent the corporation from causing an unlawful discharge, contravening administrative orders, and contravening obligations with respect to approvals, notification of unlawful discharges, and hazardous waste management.[43] Failure to carry out that duty is an offence.

Defences: Environmental offences are generally of a strict liability[44] nature, meaning directors and officers have available the defence of due diligence.

---

40 SC 1999, c 33, s 280 (1).
41 Only New Brunswick's environmental legislation does not specifically address the liability of officers and directors.
42 *Supra* note 40, s 280.1(1).
43 *Environmental Protection Act*, RSO 1990, c E-19, s 194.
44 Offences are generally categorized as absolute or strict liability. An absolute liability offence is one where the prosecution need only prove the physical elements of the offence and the blameworthiness or negligence of the defendant is immaterial. There are few defences available for these offences. A strict liability offence requires the same proof but unlike absolute liability offence, the defence of due diligence is available. Most regulatory offences, including environmental offences, are strict liability.

A defendant is entitled to acquittal if he can show that he had "exercised all reasonable care by establishing a proper system to prevent commission of the offence and by taking reasonable steps to ensure the effective operation of the prevention system."[45] The defence of reasonable care and due diligence does not mean superhuman efforts, but it does mean a high standard of awareness and decisive, prompt, and continuing action.[46]

Penalties: Convictions for environmental offences can result in a range of penalties, including fines and/or imprisonment. For example, individuals convicted under Manitoba's *Environment Act* are subject to a fine of up to $50 000 for a first offence or a term of imprisonment up to six months, or both.[47] Penalties are doubled for a second offence. Under the CEPA, directors and officers are subject to fines ranging from a minimum of $5000 to a maximum of $1 million and prison terms up to three years, or both for the most serious offences.[48] In addition to these penalties, directors and officers face personal liability for the cost of preventative or remedial measures when they are named in an administrative order.

Critical Analysis: What can directors do to protect against environmental liability? What factors do you think are important in assessing whether directors and officers have been diligent?

Sources: Dianne Saxe, "General Chemical directors settle personal claim", (9 October 2009), online: Environmental Law and Litigation <http://envirolaw.com/general-chemical-directors-settle/>; Jamie Benidickson, *Environmental Law*, 3d ed (Toronto: Irwin Law, 2009) at 190–198.

Avoiding Liability

Directors have onerous duties to the corporation, and no one should agree to become a director without a sound understanding of the obligations involved. Most important is the recognition that service on a board of directors carries significant risk. Directors are exposed to the risk of criminal, civil, and regulatory liability, as well as reputational risk. The exposure to risk suggests that a risk management plan, as discussed in Chapter 3, is warranted. The basis for such a plan is provided in the Business Application of the Law box below.

BUSINESS APPLICATION OF THE LAW

AVOIDING THE RISK OF PERSONAL LIABILITY

Directors can reduce their exposure to personal liability by exercising care, diligence, and skill in the performance of their duties. Directors can meet the statutory standard of care by being attentive, active, and informed. In this regard, directors should

- regularly attend directors' meetings.
- read all relevant materials.
- ask questions and speak up at meetings.
- keep personal notes of meetings and review minutes of meetings.
- make all their decisions informed decisions.
- do what is necessary to learn about matters affecting the company.
- identify possible problems within the company.
- stay apprised of and alert to the corporation's financial and other affairs.

---

45 *R v Sault Ste Marie (City)*, [1978] 2 SCR 1299, 85 DLR (3d) 161.
46 *R v Courtaulds Fibres Canada* (1992), 9 CELR (NS) 304, 76 CCC (3d) 68 (Ont Div Ct). For general principles of a director's due diligence see: *R v Bata Industries Ltd*, [1992] OJ No 667, 7 CELR (NS) 245 (Ont Div Ct).
47 *Environment Act*, CCSM c E125, s 33 (1).
48 Supra note 40, s 272.

- ensure that they receive reliable professional advice.

Directors may also protect themselves by ensuring that an **indemnification** agreement with their company is in place. The purpose of such an agreement is to ensure that the corporation pays any costs or expenses that a director faces as a result of being sued because he is a director.

Directors should also ensure that the corporation carries adequate insurance. Directors'

and officers' liability (D&O) insurance provides coverage to the director who has a judgment or other claim against him. Directors should carefully review the policy's exclusion clauses to ensure that maximum protection is provided.

Source: Alex L MacFarlane & Alexandra North, "Canada: Directors' and Officers' Liability in the Shadow of Insolvency", *Mondaq Corporate/ Company Law* (11 April 2011), online: Mondaq <http://mondaq.com/canada/article.asp?articleid=128316>.

Indemnification

The corporate practice of paying the litigation expenses of officers and directors for lawsuits related to corporate affairs.

Shareholders and Creditors

Shareholders

A shareholder is someone who invests in a company by buying shares. As soon as Time-in was created, for example, the company—through the directors—issued shares in the company to Luke, Raina, and Roger. Another way of becoming a shareholder is by buying the shares from an existing shareholder or receiving the shares as a gift.

Regardless of how the shares are obtained, the shareholder has few responsibilities with respect to the corporation. Unlike directors and officers, the shareholder has no duty to act in the best interests of the corporation.[49] She can freely compete with the corporation in which she holds a share. She is not obligated to attend shareholder meetings, cast her vote, read the corporation's financial reports, or take any interest whatsoever in the progress of the corporation. And, of course, she is not generally liable for the debts and obligations of the corporation because of the principle in *Salomon*.

There are exceptions to this immunity, however, as the following section explores.

Shareholder Liability

Lifting the corporate veil

Determining that the corporation is not a separate legal entity from its shareholders.

Owners of the corporation are occasionally held responsible for debts and liabilities incurred by the corporation. In other words, the corporation is not considered a separate entity from its shareholders. This is known as piercing or **lifting the corporate veil**. Due to the *Salomon* principle, courts are generally reluctant to lift the corporate veil except when they are satisfied that a company is a "mere facade" concealing the true facts.[50] It must be shown that there is complete domination and control by the person or entity sought to be made liable, and that the corporate form must have been used as a shield for conduct akin to fraud that deprives claimants of their rights.[51]

---

49 There is an exception in some jurisdictions where an obligation can be imposed on shareholders if they hold enough shares to be classified as insiders, in which case they must not use insider information to their own benefit.

50 Kevin Patrick McGuiness, *Canadian Business Corporations Law*, 2d ed (Markham, ON: LexisNexis, 2007) at 49–60 points out a number of other situations where the veil will be lifted, including when it is required by statute, contract, or other documents, and when it can be established that the company is the agent of its controllers or shareholders.

51 *Gregorio v Intrans-Corp* (1994), 18 OR (3d) 527, 115 DLR (4th) 200 (CA).

For example, in *Big Bend Hotel Ltd v Security Mutual Casualty Co,*[52] the court ignored the separate existence of the corporation when the corporation was being used to hide the identity of the person behind the corporation. Vincent Kumar purchased insurance for his company, Big Bend Ltd., which owned a hotel. The hotel burned down, but the insurance company refused to pay because Kumar had failed to disclose on the application for insurance that he had been president and sole shareholder of another corporation whose hotel had burned down less than three years earlier. The court held that the insurance company should be able to disregard the separate existence of the corporation and treat the policy as if it had been applied for by Kumar himself.

Also, in *Wildman v Wildman,*[53] the Ontario Court of Appeal ignored the principle of a corporation as a separate entity and held a husband's corporation liable for spousal and child support. The court opined that the corporation as a separate legal entity was not an absolute principle and the principle should not be used to defeat the enforcement of family law orders. The court allowed the wife to look to the corporation to satisfy the obligations of the principal and sole shareholder—the husband.

PART FOUR

CASE

Chan v City Commercial Realty Group Ltd., 2011 ONSC 2854, 90 CCEL (3d) 235.

THE BUSINESS CONTEXT: A corporation is an entity separate from its owners, and the courts will not readily ignore the corporate form and hold the shareholders liable for the conduct of the corporation. However, the corporate veil may be lifted when incorporation occurs for a purpose that is illegal, fraudulent, or improper.

FACTUAL BACKGROUND: City Commercial Realty Services (Canada) Ltd. (City 1), a Toronto real estate brokerage company, sued Stephen Chan and others in respect of a real estate transaction. City 1 lost both at trial and on appeal. Costs were awarded against City 1, which were not paid. Shortly before the appeal was heard, City Commercial Realty Group Ltd. (City 2) was formed to continue the business of City 1. The principals of City 1 were two brothers, Samuel and Martin Wygodny. Martin resigned from City 1, transferred his shares in City 1 to Samuel, and became the sole officer, director, and shareholder of City 2.

City 1 became inactive and its brokerage registration lapsed. City 2 engaged in the same business as City 1, using the same premises, furniture, phone number, business name, and signage, and some of the same personnel. The plaintiffs requested that the court lift the corporate veil on the basis that City 2 was incorporated for an illegal, fraudulent, or improper purpose. The defendants argued that it was not unlawful or improper to let City 1 expire or to incorporate City 2, which was not burdened by City 1's liabilities.

THE LEGAL QUESTION: Are the brothers personally liable for the debts of City 1?

RESOLUTION: The court held that the rule that a corporation is a separate legal person is not inviolate and would not be applied if its result would be "too flagrantly opposed to justice." The court stated: "The alter ego theory is designed to prevent the use of a corporate vehicle to achieve an objective which offends a right minded person's sense of fairness. . . . Two elements must be proven by the plaintiffs in this case: first, that the activities of the companies were completely dominated by Martin and Samuel, and second, that they

(Continued)

---

52 (1980), 19 BCLR 102, ILR 1-1217 (SC).
53 (2006), 82 OR (3d) 401, 215 OAC 239.

engaged in improper conduct that unjustly deprived the plaintiffs of their rights." The brothers were responsible for City 1's cost award as the plaintiffs' inability to recover any amount was attributable to their improper conduct in "organizing their corporate affairs in a way which provided them with all the benefits of their real estate activities and none of its burdens."

CRITICAL ANALYSIS: Despite the success of the plaintiffs in having the court "lift the corporate veil," courts are generally reluctant to do so. Can you think of situations where it would be appropriate to lift the corporate veil?

Shareholder Rights

Shareholder rights fall into three broad categories: the right to vote, the right to information, and financial rights. How directors decide to allocate these rights when issuing different classes of shares is largely up to them, as there are few requirements in this area. One kind of share can have all three rights, while another kind of share may have only one of these rights. All that is normally required, in this regard, is that the voting and financial rights referred to above be allocated to at least one class of shares; however, all those rights are not required to be attached to only one particular class.

The idea behind having different classes of shares is to permit different levels of participation in the corporation. As noted earlier, if Roger does not want much of a role in the company, he may be content with nonvoting shares. A non-voting share is often called a **preferred share**.[54] A voting share is usually called a **common share**. Although nonvoting shares are normally called preferred and voting shares are normally called common, this is not always the case. The only way to know for certain what rights are attached to shares is to review the share certificate itself, as well as the articles of incorporation.

Right to Vote Corporation legislation requires that there be at least one class of voting shareholders in a corporation. The most significant voting right traditionally attached to common shares is the right to vote for the board of directors. Note that the number of votes that a particular shareholder may cast usually depends on the number of shares he holds. If Luke holds 1000 common shares, he has 1000 votes. As he holds a majority of the shares, he is in a position to elect at least a majority of the board of directors and therefore control the company.

As well, voting shareholders have the right to approve or disapprove of directors' actions since the last general meeting. This is because the right to vote brings with it other rights, including the right to

- hold a shareholder general meeting each year.
- be given notice of the meeting.
- attend the meeting.
- ask questions.
- introduce motions.

Preferred share

A share or stock that has a preference in the distribution of dividends and the proceeds on dissolution.

Common share

A share that generally has a right to vote, share in dividends, and share in proceeds on dissolution.

---

54 They are called preferred shares because ordinarily the holders of preferred shares get priority—or have a "preference"—on taking a slice of the corporation's assets if it is liquidated.

A shareholder who cannot attend a meeting can exercise her voting power through a **proxy**, which means granting formal permission to someone else to vote her shares on her behalf. The use of a proxy is important, particularly in large corporations when there is a dispute between competing groups of shareholders. Whichever group does the best job of soliciting proxies is most likely to carry the day. Nonvoting shareholders—usually preferred shareholders—have the right to vote in certain specialized matters. Under the *Canada Business Corporations Act*, for example, Roger—as the holder of preferred shares in Time-in—would have the right to vote on any proposal to sell all the corporation's assets.[55] The rationale is that even nonvoting shareholders should have a say when such a fundamental change in corporate direction is being put forward.

Proxy

A person who is authorized to exercise a shareholder's voting rights.

Right to Information

Shareholders have the right to certain fundamental information concerning the corporation. This includes the right to

- inspect the annual financial statement for the corporation.
- apply to the court to have an inspector appointed to look into the affairs of the corporation if it can be shown that there is a serious concern about mismanagement.
- inspect certain records, including minute books, the register of share transfers, incorporating documents, bylaws and special resolutions, and the registry of shareholders and directors.
- know whether directors have been purchasing shares of the corporation. This is to permit shareholders to determine whether directors have been using confidential information to make personal profits.[56]

Financial Rights

Shareholders generally buy shares with the hope or expectation that the corporation will prosper and generate financial rewards, in terms of either capital gains or income for them. In this respect, one of the fundamental rights of the shareholder is the right to receive any dividend declared by the corporation. The shareholder has no right to have dividends just because the corporation has earned large profits, since the declaration of dividends is done at the discretion of the board of directors. However, if the shareholders can show that the directors are abusing their discretion, they can consider bringing an oppression action, which is discussed later in this chapter.

Once dividends are declared, directors are bound to pay them in order of preference assigned to the classes of shares. As well, there cannot be any discrimination among shareholders belonging to the same class. If Luke and Raina both own the same class of shares, it is illegal for the directors to declare that Raina gets a certain dividend but Luke does not.

Shareholders have a right to share in the assets of a corporation on dissolution after creditors are paid. Again, the right is dependent on the priorities of each class of shares. Preferred shareholders are often given the right to be first in line for corporate assets once all the creditors have been paid.

Additionally, a shareholder may have what is known as a **pre-emptive right**. When this right exists, it requires the corporation to offer existing shareholders

Pre-emptive right

A shareholder's right to maintain a proportionate share of ownership by purchasing a proportionate share of any new stock issue.

---

55 *Supra* note 4, s 189(3).
56 See, for example, *Securities Act*, RSO 1990, c S-5, ss 106–9.

the chance to purchase a new issue of shares before these shares are offered to outsiders. This gives existing shareholders a chance to maintain their level of control or power in the corporation. For example, assume that Luke has 1000 common shares in Time-in., and because of other entrepreneurial interests, he has unwisely resigned as a director in the company for the time being. Assume Raina is the only corporate director left and she resolves to issue 2000 common shares to Roger. This issue would transform Luke's position from being a majority shareholder to being in the minority, but his pre-emptive right would allow him to maintain his proportional interest in the company if he could afford to purchase further shares.

Shareholder Remedies

A shareholder, such as Roger, who is dissatisfied with a corporation's performance or management has a number of remedies available to him.

Selling the Shares

Often the simplest and least costly remedy for a shareholder who is dissatisfied with the operation or performance of a corporation is simply to sell his shares.

This, of course, is an easily viable remedy only in the widely held or public corporation, where shares are traded on a stock exchange and there are no restrictions on their transferability.

The situation is quite different in the closely held or private corporation. In this case, there are usually restrictions on the transference of shares and—even where the restrictions are minimal—it may be difficult to find someone willing to buy such shares. Historically, this reality put the minority shareholder in the unenviable position of having little input into the operation of the corporation and no easy way to extricate his investment. In response, both the common law and the legislatures developed a number of remedies to protect a minority shareholder from abuse by the majority. The most important are the appraisal remedy, the derivative action, and the oppression remedy.[57]

Exercising Dissent and Appraisal Rights

In situations where shareholders, by a two-thirds majority vote, approve a fundamental change to the corporation, a dissenting shareholder may elect to have her shares bought by the corporation.[58] This **dissent and appraisal right** is limited to specific actions such as changes to the restrictions on share transfers or restrictions on the business a corporation may carry on; the amalgamation or merger with another corporation; or the sale, lease, or exchange of substantially all of the corporation's assets. The procedure for obtaining the remedy is complex, and the dissenter must strictly follow the prescribed steps.

Bringing a Derivative Action

Because of their managerial control, directors are well placed to rob the very corporation that they are charged with serving. For example, they could take a corporate opportunity and develop it for their own personal gain, they could vote that the corporation sell corporate assets to

Dissent and appraisal right

The right of shareholders who dissent from certain fundamental changes to the corporation to have their shares purchased by the corporation at a fair price.

---

57   Other remedies include winding up, which involves dissolution of the corporation and the return of surplus assets to the shareholders. The use of this remedy is uncommon.

58   See, for example, *Canada Business Corporations Act, supra* note 4, s 190.

one of them at a price ridiculously below market, or they could vote themselves outrageously high compensation packages. What can a minority shareholder do when the directors are breaching their duty to the corporation and causing it injury?

At common law, courts permitted minority shareholders to take action on behalf of the corporation against the directors, but the system was far from adequate. In response, corporate law statutes have created what is called the statutory **derivative action**.[59] This permits a shareholder to obtain leave from the court to bring an action on behalf of the corporation, where he can establish that

- directors will not bring an action.
- he is acting in good faith.
- it appears to be in the interests of the corporation that the action proceed.

This action means that directors cannot treat the corporation as their own personal fiefdom with impunity. They owe strict duties to the corporation. Even if they breach those duties with the support of the majority of the shareholders, the minority has recourse to the courts and can secure any number of remedies on behalf of the corporation. By virtue of the derivative action, if the directors have stolen a corporate opportunity, they can be forced by the court to account for that profit. If they have disposed of corporate assets at below market value, the court can order them to account for the difference between what the asset is actually worth and what was paid for it. If they have voted to overpay themselves, the court can order them to return their ill-gotten gains. The court even has the power to remove the directors from office and replace them. In fact, the legislation empowers the court to make any order it sees fit.

Bringing an Oppression Action The most widely used remedy by shareholders in Canada is called the **oppression remedy**. It applies when the actions or omissions of the corporation or its directors have oppressed or unfairly disregarded or prejudiced the interests of the shareholders. The remedy is available when the reasonable expectations of the shareholder about management conduct have not been met. Conduct that the courts have found to be oppressive usually falls into the following categories:

- lack of a valid corporate purpose for a transaction.
- lack of good faith on the part of the directors of the corporation.
- discrimination between shareholders with the effect of benefiting the majority shareholder to the exclusion or the detriment of the minority shareholder.
- lack of adequate and proper disclosure of material information to minority shareholders.
- conflict of interest between the interests of the corporation and the personal interests of one or more directors.[60]

Derivative action

A suit by a shareholder on behalf of the corporation to enforce a corporate cause of action.

Oppression remedy

A statutory remedy available to shareholders and other stakeholders to protect their corporate interests.

---

59 For a discussion of the jurisdictions that provide for such an action, see Bruce Welling, *Corporate Law in Canada: The Governing Principles*, 3d ed (London, ON: Scribblers, 2006) at 509ff.

60 Shelly Obal, ed *Corporate Governance in Canada: A Guide to the Responsibilities of Corporate Directors in Canada*, 5th ed (Toronto: Osler, Hoskin & Harcourt, 2009) at 15.

Raina may argue that Luke's actions in voting her off the board and ousting her from management for no good reason other than to show her who was boss were oppressive and against her reasonable expectations of continued involvement in Time-in.

The court is entitled to make such an order as it deems just and appropriate, including ordering the corporation to purchase the complainant's shares, ordering the improper conduct to cease, and, in extreme circumstances, ordering the company to be dissolved. The remedy is extremely flexible and has few attendant technicalities. Unlike a derivative action, which is brought on behalf of the corporation, the oppression remedy is a personal action, which can be brought by shareholders and specified stakeholders—security holders, creditors, directors, or officers.

Like all litigation, however, the process in securing a shareholder remedy is time consuming, costly, and unpredictable. Furthermore, the courts historically have been less than enthusiastic about getting involved in the internal affairs of corporations. Put another way, it is often a heavy and onerous burden to convince the court that the majority is in the wrong and has been oppressive.

As a way of avoiding litigation, shareholders may decide to enter into an agreement at the very beginning of their association in order to deal with potentially contentious areas and to streamline the procedure leading to the resolution of any conflict. Depending on the jurisdiction, there are two possibilities in this regard: a shareholders' agreement and a unanimous shareholders' agreement (also called a USA). Of course, such agreements do not guarantee that litigation will be avoided, since the meaning and enforceability of these agreements can themselves become the subject matter of litigation.

CASE

BCE Inc v 1976 Debentureholders, 2008 SCC 69, [2008] 3 SCR 560

THE BUSINESS CONTEXT: The following decision provides clarification of the duties of directors in the context of change-of-control transactions and in situations where stakeholder interests are in conflict. It also provides guidance on the application of the oppression remedy.

FACTUAL BACKGROUND: In June 2007, BCE Inc. announced an agreement with a consortium of investors led by the Ontario Teachers' Pension Plan Board. The agreement proposed the acquisition of all outstanding shares of BCE by a $52 billion highly leveraged plan of arrangement under the *Canada Business Corporations Act (CBCA)*. The purchase price of Cdn $42.75 per common share would provide a 40 percent premium for BCE's common shareholders but would require Bell Canada Inc., BCE's wholly owned

subsidiary, to provide guarantees of approximately $30 billion to support Teachers' borrowings. These guarantees would result in the loss of investment-grade status of Bell Canada's outstanding debentures and a reduction in their trading value. The debentureholders opposed the transaction on the basis that it was oppressive.

THE LEGAL QUESTION: Did the directors of BCE act in an oppressive manner toward the debentureholders of Bell Canada by approving the sale of BCE?

RESOLUTION: The trial court dismissed all of the bondholders' claims and approved the plan. The Court of Appeal reversed the decision, holding that BCE had failed to establish that the plan was fair and reasonable. The Supreme Court of Canada, in a unanimous decision, reversed the Court of Appeal's decision and allowed the transaction to proceed.

OPPRESSION REMEDY: The *CBCA* provides a remedy to a wide range of stakeholders whose legal and equitable interests have been affected by oppressive acts of a corporation or its directors. The remedy gives a broad jurisdiction to enforce not only just what is legal but also what is fair in the circumstances. What is just and equitable is judged by the reasonable expectations of the stakeholders in the context. In assessing a claim for oppression, the court must determine whether the evidence supports the reasonable expectation of the stakeholder and whether the reasonable expectation of the stakeholder was violated by oppressive conduct. To determine whether a reasonable expectation exists, courts must consider the following factors: general commercial practice; the nature of the corporation; the relationship between the parties; past practice; steps the claimant could take to protect itself; representations and agreements; and the resolution of conflicting interests between corporate stakeholders (see below for the court's discussion of this factor). For the second question, a claimant must show that the failure to meet reasonable expectations was the result of unfair conduct.

The debentureholders argued that they had a reasonable expectation that BCE would protect their economic interests by putting forward a plan that maintains the investment-grade trading value of their debentures. In the alternative, they argued that they had a reasonable expectation that the directors would consider their economic interests in maintaining the trading value of their debentures. The Supreme Court of Canada concluded that the debentureholders could not have reasonably expected that the directors of BCE would protect Bell Canada's investment-grade credit rating or the value of the debentures. The court noted that any statements by Bell Canada suggesting a commitment to retain investment-grade ratings were accompanied by warnings precluding such expectations. The Court did find that the debentureholders had a reasonable expectation that the BCE directors would consider their interests in the proposed transaction. However, the directors had considered the interests of debentureholders but reasonably concluded that while the contractual terms of the debentures would be honoured, no further commitments could be made.

DIRECTORS' FIDUCIARY DUTIES IN RESOLVING COMPETING STAKEHOLDER INTERESTS: In the context of a conflict between the interests of different corporate stakeholders (in this case, between shareholders and debentureholders), the Supreme Court of Canada restated its holding in *Peoples v Wise* that the directors' fiduciary duty is to act in the best interests of the corporation. It stated that "the fiduciary duty of the directors is a broad, contextual concept. It is not confined to short-term profit or share value. Where the corporation is an ongoing concern, it looks to the long-term interests of the corporation. The content of this duty varies with the situation at hand." The duty to act in the best interests of the corporation requires directors to consider the interests of all stakeholders and to treat individual stakeholders equitably and fairly. There are no absolute rules. "In each case, the question is whether, in all the circumstances, the directors acted in the best interests of the corporation, having regard to all relevant considerations, including, but not confined to, the need to treat affected stakeholders in a fair manner, commensurate with the corporation's duties as a responsible corporate citizen." The directors may look at the interests of shareholders, employees, creditors, consumers, governments, and the environment to inform their decision making, but in doing so, there is no principle that one set of interests must prevail over another. Thus the court conclusively rejected the "shareholder primacy" model according to which the directors' duty in a change-of-control situation is to maximize shareholder value. Instead, the directors should use business judgment to determine what is in the best interests of the corporation in the particular situation. In

(Continued)

this regard, a court should give appropriate deference to the business judgment of directors, so long as the directors' decision is in the range of reasonable alternatives.

CRITICAL ANALYSIS: The Supreme Court's decision rejects the view that directors have a duty to maximize shareholder value in the context of change-of-control transactions in favour of a director's duty to treat all affected stakeholders fairly, commensurate with the corporation's duties as a responsible citizen. Does this holding make it easier or harder for stakeholders to challenge directors' decisions?

POSTSCRIPT: The transaction did not proceed, as a solvency opinion that was required as a condition precedent to the agreement could not be obtained. Auditor KPMG said BCE would have been forced into bankruptcy by the debt burden it would have acquired.

Shareholders' agreement

An agreement that defines the relationship among people who have an ownership interest in a corporation.

Unanimous shareholders' agreement (USA)

An agreement among all shareholders that restricts the powers of the directors to manage the corporation.

Asserting a Remedy under a Shareholders' Agreement or a USA A **shareholders' agreement** is common, particularly in a small, closely held corporation. Shareholders' agreements serve a multitude of purposes, but in particular they allow shareholders to define their relationship in a manner that is different from that provided by the governing statute. Such agreements may address, for example, how the corporation is to be managed, how shares will be transferred, and how disputes will be resolved.

A **unanimous shareholders' agreement (USA)** is a specialized kind of shareholders' agreement among all shareholders that restricts, in whole or in part, the powers of the directors to manage the corporation. The purpose of a USA is to ensure that control over matters dealt with in the USA remains with the shareholders. When shareholders, through a USA, take management powers away from directors, those directors are relieved of their duties and liabilities to the same extent. This means that if the shareholders improperly manage the corporation, they may be successfully sued for negligence or breach of fiduciary duty, for example.

The objective of a shareholders' agreement is to comprehensively set out—by agreement and in advance of any conflict—what the shareholders' expectations are, how the company is to be managed, and how disputes will be addressed. Shareholders' agreements seek to confront the reality that disagreements are inevitable and can be resolved according to mechanisms set up during the "honeymoon" phase of a business relationship.

Luke, Raina, and Roger most definitely need a shareholders' agreement for the reasons given above.

BUSINESS APPLICATION OF THE LAW

MANAGING RISK THROUGH SHAREHOLDERS' AGREEMENTS

A shareholders' agreement allows the shareholders to define their relationship, now and in the future. It should, as well, provide mechanisms and procedures that can be employed when the relationship encounters difficulties, along with means for undoing the relationship if the need to do so arises. An agreement must be tailored to meet the requirements of the particular situation and should address the following issues:

1. *Management of the company.* Who will be responsible for management? What will their rights and obligations be? How will they be appointed or elected or hired? How will they be paid?

2. *Protection for the minority shareholder.* How will the minority be protected from domination by the majority? How will representation on the board of directors be achieved? How will fundamental issues, such as dividends, sale of assets, and the like, be handled?

3. *Control over who the other shareholders will be.* What are the qualifications needed for being a shareholder? What happens in the event of a shareholder's death, retirement, disability, or simple loss of interest in the company?

4. *Provision of a market for shares.*[61] What are the circumstances that require a shareholder to sell her shares? What happens if a shareholder dies? Who will buy the shares and for how much? How will the purchase be funded?

5. *Capital contribution.* What happens if the corporation needs more cash? Who will provide it, and how much? How will payment be compelled?

6. *Buy–sell arrangements in the event of a dispute.* What (e.g., death, retirement, insolvency) triggers a sale? How will the shares be valued? What method will be chosen for their valuation (i.e., independent third party, formula, value fixed in advance and updated annually)?

7. *Mechanism for terminating the agreement.* How can the agreement be terminated? Can it be terminated on notice? How much notice?

Critical Analysis: When should the shareholders of a corporation consider entering into a shareholders' agreement?

***

Source: James W. Carr, "Shareholder Agreements" in *Advising the Business Client* (Edmonton: The Legal Education Society of Alberta, 1995) at 14–16.

Creditor Protection

A corporation is responsible for its own liabilities, including its debts. As such, the shareholders/owners may be tempted to strip the entity of its assets in an attempt to defeat creditors, but doing so would be illegal. For example, if Time-in falls on hard financial times, Luke cannot clean out the entire inventory of supplies and bring it home with him to sell later. This is because the inventory belongs to the corporation, not to Luke, and the corporation's creditors have a prior claim on such property.

To help prevent abuses by shareholders, a number of legislative provisions have been enacted. For example, the *Canada Business Corporations Act*[62] forbids the corporation to pay a dividend to shareholders if doing so would jeopardize its ability to pay its own debts as they fall due (the liquidity test). The same section forbids such a dividend if that would make the company insolvent—that is, leave it without enough assets to cover its liabilities.[63] Directors who consent to

***

61 Common mechanisms in shareholders' agreements for selling shares include a right of first refusal and a shotgun clause. A right of first refusal involves a shareholder offering to sell shares to other shareholders; if they refuse to purchase, then, for a limited time, the shareholder may sell to someone else for the same price. A shotgun clause involves a shareholder offering to sell shares at a certain price to another shareholder, who must either buy all the shares at that price or sell all his shares at the same price.

62 *Supra* note 4, s 42.

63 Insolvency is discussed in Chapter 27.

a dividend under such circumstances are personally liable to restore to the corporation any amounts so paid.

The Supreme Court of Canada has also indicated that duty of care imposed on directors by the *CBCA*[64] is owed not only just to the corporation but also to the creditors.[65] Also, the same court stated that creditors can avail themselves of the oppression remedy as a means of protecting themselves from the prejudicial conduct of directors.

FIGURE 16.3 Summary of Liability for Corporate Conduct

	Liability in Tort Law	Liability in Contract Law	Liability in Criminal Law	Liability for Regulatory Offences
Corporation	Identification Theory: The corporation is liable when a directing mind commits the tort in the course of carrying out her duties. Vicarious Liability: A corporation is vicariously liable for the torts of employees (who are not directing minds) committed in the course of employment.	Agency Theory: The corporation is liable so long as the agent was acting within actual or apparent authority.	Identification Theory: The corporation is liable if a senior officer of the corporation committed the offence at least partially in the interests of the corporation. A senior officer is someone who plays an important role in the establishment of the corporation's policies or is responsible for managing an important aspect of the corporation's activities.	The legislation specifies liability but generally the corporation is liable when a person engages in the prohibited behaviour on behalf of the corporation.
Directors/ Officers	Law unclear and jurisdiction-specific. While formerly liable only for more extreme conduct, possibly liable for virtually any tort committed in the course of carrying out duties.	Agency Theory: No liability unless intended to assume liability.	Personally liable for the commission of criminal offences.	Statutes may impose liability on directors, officers, or both for a corporation's conduct.
Shareholders	Generally not liable for corporation's torts unless corporate veil lifted.	Generally not liable for corporation's contracts unless corporate veil lifted.	No liability for corporation's crimes.	No liability imposed on shareholders by statute.

Termination of the Corporation

When and if the time comes for Time-in to shut down, it can be dissolved in several ways. In most jurisdictions, provisions in companies legislation or a separate **winding up** act set out a process. The steps involved can be somewhat complicated, so in many instances it is more feasible simply to let the company lapse.

Winding up

The process of dissolving a corporation.

---

64 *Supra* note 4, s 122 (10 (b).
65 *Peoples Department Stores Inc (Trustee of) v Wise*, 2004 SCC 68, [2004] 3 SCR 461.

This is particularly the case with a small, closely held corporation. The principals may simply neglect to file their annual report or follow other reporting requirements; this will ultimately result in the company being struck from the corporate register.

A court has the authority to order a company to be terminated when a shareholder has been wrongfully treated and this is the only way to do justice between the parties. As well, a corporation whose debts exceed its assets may eventually go bankrupt. The result of bankruptcy is usually the dissolution of the corporation.

BUSINESS LAW IN PRACTICE REVISITED

1. What obligations do Luke, Raina, and Roger have as corporate officers and directors?

As corporate officers and directors, Luke, Raina, and Roger are obliged to competently manage the corporation and to act in the best interests of the corporation. This means, in effect, that they must not only apply their skills and knowledge to the operations of the corporation but also put the corporation's interests above their own personal interests.

2. Are there any problems with Raina forming her own company to purchase a sports team?

If Raina decides to incorporate a company to purchase a sports team, she needs to be mindful of her fiduciary obligations to Time-in. The law is somewhat unclear as to when a director may pursue an opportunity that came to her as a result of her position as director. However, as the company has rejected the opportunity, it would seem that Raina in the circumstances (she was in favour of Time-in pursuing the opportunity) is free to take it up on her own, particularly upon securing the informed consent of both Luke and Roger.

3. Can Raina do anything about Luke voting her off the board and ousting her from management?

Raina may bring an oppression action arguing that she has been wronged by the majority shareholder, Luke. In order to get relief, Raina needs to show that she had a reasonable expectation that Luke would not exercise his dominant position and vote her off the board of directors and oust her from management. Given her discussions with Luke about involvement in the management and expansion of the business, Raina had the reasonable expectation that she would have a presence in Time-in and participate in the company's future growth over the long term. Raina must show that her reasonable expectations were disappointed by Luke in a way that was oppressive, unfairly prejudicial, or unfairly disregarded her interests. Luke's conduct was oppressive because he removed Raina for a petty reason—simply to show her who was boss. If Raina's action is successful, the court has the discretion to make any order necessary to rectify the situation. If the parties can no longer work together, this may involve the compulsory buy-out of shares. Raina can also seek compensation for lost remuneration.

4. Is Time-in liable for the failure to deduct and remit income tax? Does Roger, as an officer of Time-in, have any personal liability for the failure to deduct and remit the taxes?

The *Income Tax Act* imposes liability on a person for failure to withhold and remit income taxes, and as Time-in is considered to be a person, it is liable for this failure. Additionally, the Act imposes liability on the directors of the corporation for the corporation's failure to withhold and remit taxes. Therefore, unless they have a valid defence, Luke and Raina are exposed to liability. The Act does not impose liability on officers, however; therefore, Roger is not exposed to personal liability on this front.

5. What are Roger's rights as a shareholder if he does not like how Time-in is being managed?

Roger could simply sell his shares, if he is permitted to do so and if he can find a buyer. Corporation legislation also provides for shareholder remedies; however, the remedies are not usually available simply because a shareholder dislikes how the corporation is being managed. There must be something more, such as oppressive conduct by the directors. Even if oppression can be proven, litigation can be costly and time consuming. Again, this issue should have been considered in advance and a remedy or alternative course of action should have been built into a shareholder agreement.

CHAPTER SUMMARY

Of particular concern to anyone launching a corporation is the potential liability, both civil and criminal, that the corporation and its stakeholders are exposed to. A corporation, as a distinct legal entity, may be liable in tort, in contract, and for criminal and regulatory offences. Likewise, directors and officers also may be liable in criminal, civil, and regulatory law for actions relating to the business of the corporation.

Directors and officers who are charged with the management of the corporation owe duties of competence and fiduciary duties to the corporation, and they may be liable to the corporation for breach of these duties.

Shareholders generally face few liabilities with respect to the actions of the corporation. There are, however, limited exceptions to this general rule—most importantly when the corporate form is being used to commit a fraud. Shareholders do, however, have certain statutory rights with respect to the operations of the corporation—the right to vote, the right to information, and financial rights. They also have remedies to enforce their rights. Shareholders can enter into agreements that define their relationships with one another and that provide mechanisms for resolving disputes and means for protecting their interests.

Creditors receive some specific protection under corporate law provisions. Also, the Supreme Court of Canada has indicated that directors owe creditors a duty of care and creditors can avail themselves of the oppression remedy. Creditors can also negotiate for other rights.[66]

A corporation can enjoy perpetual existence; however, it can also be dissolved. The most common methods of dissolution are winding-up procedures and simply letting the corporation lapse.

---

66 See Chapter 26 for a discussion of creditors' rights.

CHAPTER STUDY

Key Terms and Concepts

common share (p. 398)

corporate opportunity (p. 387)

derivative action (p. 401)

dissent and appraisal right (p. 400)

identification theory (p. 380)

indemnification (p. 396)

lifting the corporate veil (p. 396)

oppression remedy (p. 401)

pre-emptive right (p. 399)

preferred share (p. 398)

proxy (p. 399)

regulatory offence (p. 384)

self-dealing contract (p. 387)

shareholders' agreement (p. 404)

unanimous shareholders' agreement (USA) (p. 404)

winding up (p. 406)

Questions for Review

1. How can a corporation be liable in tort law? Explain.

2. How does a corporation enter a contract? Explain.

3. How is the criminal liability of a corporation determined?

4. When is a director personally liable for committing a tort?

5. To whom do directors owe duties?

6. What is a self-dealing contract?

7. What are the duties of directors and officers?

8. Do directors owe duties to the corporation's creditors? Explain.

9. Is a director liable for a corporation's contracts? Explain.

10. How may a director avoid personal liability when carrying out her corporate duties?

11. What is meant by the term "lifting the corporate veil?" When will courts "lift the corporate veil?"

12. What three main rights do shareholders have?

13. What rights to dividends do shareholders have?

14. When is the dissent and appraisal remedy appropriate?

15. What is the difference between a derivative action and an oppression action?

16. When is a shareholder agreement appropriate? What issues should a shareholder agreement address?

17. What protection do creditors have from shareholders stripping the corporation of its assets?

18. How is a corporation terminated?

Questions for Critical Thinking

1. What are the arguments for prosecuting, convicting, and punishing corporations? Does holding corporations criminally responsible serve any social purpose? What are the arguments against prosecuting, convicting, and punishing corporations?

2. The Canadian Democracy and Corporate Accountability Commission, an independent body designed to investigate corporate influence, has recommended that corporation laws should be amended to allow directors, at their discretion, to take into consideration the effect of their actions on the corporation's employees, customers, suppliers, and creditors, as well as the effects of their actions on the community in which the corporation resides.[67] How does the Supreme Court of Canada's decision in BCE account for stakeholders' interests? What is the problem with directors owing duties to all stakeholders?

3. There are literally dozens of statutes that impose personal liability on directors, and in many cases, officers. Directors and officers face liability, for example, under securities,

---

67 Canadian Democracy and Corporate Accountability Commission, *The New Balance Sheet: Corporate Profits and Responsibility in the 21st Century* (January 2002), online: University of Ottawa <http://aix1 .uottawa.ca/~cforcese/other/commissionfinalreport.pdf>.

environmental, employment, tax, and bankruptcy and insolvency legislation. Why do you think this has occurred? What are the problems associated with holding directors to higher standards? How can directors protect themselves in an increasingly litigious environment?

4. In *Canadian Aero Service Ltd. v O'Malley* (page 388) the court set out factors in determining whether the appropriation of an opportunity is a breach of a fiduciary duty. Do you see any problems with applying these factors? How can directors ensure that they have not breached a fiduciary duty if they take a corporate opportunity for themselves?

5. Several countries including the United States and the United Kingdom require public companies to hold annual shareholder votes on executive compensation (so called "say on pay" votes). In Canada, although such votes are proliferating, they are not mandatory. What is the purpose of such votes and should they be mandatory? Why or why not?

6. In 2010, Syncrude Canada Ltd. received the largest fine in Alberta history for the violation of environmental legislation that resulted in the death of 1606 birds (see page 384). Prosecutors hailed the $3 million fine as precedent-setting and sending a clear message that the province will react to protect the environment. Critics of the fine, however, complained that the fine was a mere "drop in the barrel" for Syncrude and would not solve the problem of toxic tailings ponds and dead birds. They pointed out that the fine represents about a half day's profit for the oil sands company.[68] Do you agree with the position of the prosecutors or the critics? Is fining corporations the best way to deal with environmental transgressions? Why or why not?

Situations for Discussion

1. Jerome Neeson is a shareholder in Gourmet Chefs Inc., a company that owns and operates a test kitchen in a large metropolitan area.

The company is involved in a number of businesses, including catering at high-end business functions, giving cooking lessons, and developing new recipes. Gourmet Chefs recently added to its staff a top chef who was trained at Le Cordon Bleu cooking school in France. Jerome anticipated that the company's profits would increase in the future, and he was very happy with the direction in which the company was moving. He was therefore very surprised to receive notice of a shareholders' meeting, where the directors proposed to sell the company's test kitchen. Jerome is opposed to the sale and does not want to be involved with Gourmet Chefs if the sale is completed. Advise Jerome.

2. Roland Roy, an employee of Goodnuff Used Cars Ltd., turned back the odometers on several cars that were sold to unsuspecting customers. Goodnuff Used Cars Ltd. was charged under the following provision of the Criminal Code:

> s 380. (1) Every one who, by deceit, falsehood or other fraudulent means, whether or not it is a false pretence within the meaning of this Act, defrauds the public or any person, whether ascertained or not, of any property, money or valuable security or any service,
>
> (a) is guilty of an indictable offence and liable to a term of imprisonment not exceeding fourteen years, where the subject-matter of the offence is a testamentary instrument or the value of the subject-matter of the offence exceeds five thousand dollars. . .

Is Goodnuff Used Cars Ltd. guilty of the crime of fraud? If Goodnuff Used Cars Ltd. is convicted of the crime, what factors will the court consider in imposing punishment?

3. Lennie purchased a quantity of pressure-treated lumber from GoodWood Building Ltd. (GoodWood) in the spring. Lennie used the wood to build a deck around the front of his house. By the fall, however, he found that the wood was starting to rot, and it appeared that the stain used to treat the wood was peeling away. When Lennie tried to contact GoodWood, he discovered that the store had closed and the

68 *Supra* note 19.

company was insolvent. Lennie managed to locate the salesman who had sold him the wood, and he agreed that the wood appeared to be defective. He also told Lennie that because the wood had been imported from Thailand, a lawsuit against the manufacturer would probably be long and expensive. He suggested that Lennie bring an action against the directors and shareholders of GoodWood. The shareholders and directors are Jim, Tim, and Tom. What are Lennie's chances of success against the shareholders and directors? Does your answer change if GoodWood is an unincorporated business in which Tim, Jim, and Tom are the owners and managers? What are Lennie's chances of success against them in this circumstance?

4. The board of directors of Gizmos & Widgets Inc., a manufacturer of computer components, has embraced the "green shift." It takes great pride in its decisions that have benefited both the corporation and the environment. Examples of these environmentally friendly decisions include replacing all light bulbs with lower wattage bulbs, replacing old delivery vehicles with low-emission vehicles, installing solar panels on the rooftop, and instituting a recycling program for obsolete computers. Recently, a member of the board suggested that Gizmos & Widgets purchase a large tract of land and have it preserved as a sanctuary for migrating birds. Other members of the board are in agreement, but a group of shareholder activists have gotten wind of the idea and have threatened to sue the directors. If the board approves the purchase, on what potential basis could the shareholders sue? Are they likely to be successful? Explain.

5. Ryan and Sean are shareholders and directors of Springfield Meadows Ltd. (Springfield), a company that has developed land for a large trailer park. Springfield has 20 other shareholders. Ryan and Sean are approached by Louise, who wants to create a company whose business will be to lease trailers. Ryan and Sean are interested in participating as directors and shareholders in this new company, since this would be a good way to fill up some of the vacant sites at Springfield's trailer park. The new company is a big success, and Sean and Ryan receive impressively high dividends on a regular basis. Eventually, the other shareholders in Springfield learn about Sean and Ryan's new company and sue them for breach of their fiduciary duty. The shareholders contend that Sean and Ryan should have developed the opportunity to get into the trailer-leasing business for the benefit of Springfield and should not have taken that opportunity for themselves. Are Sean and Ryan in breach of their duty to act in the best interest of Springfield?

6. Peter sold his barbershop business to Andy for $25 000. As part of the agreement of purchase and sale, Peter agreed to a restrictive covenant that prohibited him from providing barbering services in an area within a 10-kilometre radius of his former shop for a period of one year. Within a month of the sale, Peter incorporated a company and commenced cutting hair in violation of the restrictive covenant.[69] Can Andy do anything about this situation? Should he do anything?

7. In *Allen v Aspen Group Resources Corporation*,[70] a class action lawsuit was certified against a Yukon oil-and-gas firm for alleged misrepresentations and omissions in a takeover circular. Included among the defendants are WeirFoulds LLP, a prominent Toronto-based law firm that acted on behalf of Aspen and advised it in connection with the takeover bid, and one of the firm's partners, Wayne Egan. Egan acted as legal counsel for Aspen and had been a member of its board of directors. The plaintiffs argue that Egan's liability both for his work as a lawyer and in his capacity as a director extends to WeirFoulds. What are the problems with professionals, such as lawyers and accountants, serving as directors for corporate clients? What are the advantages for the professional? What are the advantages for the corporation?

---

69 Based on *Gilford Motors Co v Horne*, [1933] Ch 935 (CA).
70 (2009), 81 CPC (6th) 298, 67 BLR (4th) 99 (Ont Sup Ct).

8. Basil Dobbin was a director of Sports Villas Inc., a company that was incorporated to acquire a lodge and golf course about 220 kilometres west of St. John's, Newfoundland, at Port Blandford. The golf course catered primarily to golf vacationers and delegates to conferences. A large percentage of the clientele of the golf course came from the Avalon Peninsula (a large peninsula that makes up the southeast portion of Newfoundland; both St. John's and Port Blandford are on the peninsula) and a large majority of them from St. John's. Approximately three years after the incorporation of Sports Villa, Dobbin incorporated a company, Clovelly Golf Course Inc., for the purpose of the development of a golf course in St. John's. This golf course did not have a hotel and it catered to clientele interested in several hours of golf after work. The golf course at Clovelly was intent on fostering the new and beginner golfer as opposed to the more expert and experienced golfer.[71] Is Dobbin's position as director of both Sports Villas and Clovelly a breach of his fiduciary duty? Explain. There is a public or societal interest in ensuring that directors adhere to a strict code of conduct. What is the problem with holding directors to a strict code of conduct?

---

71 Based on *Pardy v Dobbin*, 2000 NFCA 11 (CanLII), 185 Nfld & PEIR 281.

PROPERTY

Most business activity involves the ownership or possession or use of various forms of property. Property consists of rights and interests in anything of value that can be owned or possessed in a way that is enforceable by law.

The law classifies property into distinct categories and provides for the protection of rights and interests in property. Historically, property has been categorized as either real property or personal property. Real property refers to land and anything attached to it. All other forms of property are included under personal property, which consists of tangible and intangible items. Tangible personal property has a physical substance from which it derives its value. Examples are trucks and appliances, which are sometimes called goods or chattels. Intangible personal property derives its value from legal rights rather than its physical form. Examples are the right to enforce a contract and copyright in a published work. A business is likely to own an interest in many different forms of property that are important to its operation and value. An appreciation of the distinctions is useful for applying the rules that govern ownership and possession of the various forms, and for understanding the legal options for using property and generating value from it.

Rights in property can also take various forms other than ownership. While ownership confers the broadest rights in property, the temporary possession or the right to use property may be sufficient for a business's needs. For example, while a business could purchase land or other property to use in its business, it might be more economical or practical to lease certain types of property. We also tend to think of possession of property as conferring particular rights to the holder of property, but possession can also create obligations for those who come into possession of property that is owned by others. For example, a business that repairs a customer's property might temporarily come into possession of a client's property and in doing so, may incur legal obligations relating to the care and protection of the property.

Knowledge of what the law recognizes as property, the various forms of property, and the types of legal interests in property and how the law protects those interests is an essential business asset.

17

INTRODUCTION TO PROPERTY LAW

OBJECTIVES

After studying this chapter, you should have an understanding of

- the meaning of property
- the different forms of property
- how property can be acquired
- the types of legal rights and obligations associated with property

BUSINESS LAW IN PRACTICE

Atlantic Storage Ltd. (ASL) operates a large warehouse facility in Moncton, New Brunswick, where it provides storage and safekeeping of customers' property. For the past 20 years, the customers were commercial enterprises who entrusted a wide variety of property to ASL for storage, including surplus equipment, inventory, and supplies; seasonal inventory and displays; and business records and files. ASL is situated in a suburban industrial park and owns the land on which the warehouse facility is located. Because storage requirements vary according to the needs of business customers, the warehouse is divided into sections that can provide variations in storage conditions such as temperature and humidity. The building also contains extensive dividers, containers, and shelving. ASL leases five delivery vehicles and three forklifts from local equipment dealers.

ASL has recently decided to share in the sharp growth in the self-storage industry by expanding its business to allow commercial and individual customers to rent lockers for storage of their property. ASL's current facility is already at capacity and the new venture into self-storage will require new space. To accommodate the new venture, ASL has entered into negotiations with the owners of an adjacent property. ASL is hoping to purchase the property but is also considering other options including leasing.

Other property of ASL includes accounts receivable, bank accounts, investments, and customer records. Of considerable value is the goodwill associated with the ASL business name, which has been recognized and respected in the community for 20 years. The ASL name and logo are registered trademarks.

Several problems have troubled ASL management recently. Some commercial customers have complained about improper storage of their property, resulting in damage from such causes as dampness or excessive heat. Although ASL contracts are clear that ASL accepts no responsibility for damage to customers' property and customers are urged to obtain their own insurance coverage, ASL has been involved in several disputes with customers about responsibility for loss. ASL also expects that from time to time its new self-storage customers will stop paying rental fees and abandon their property. Finally, although ASL's name and logo are trademarked, a new business in Moncton with a similar name—"Atlantic Store-it-All"—has recently sprung up and ASL is

Action Sports Photography/Shutterstock

concerned that potential customers might believe the new business to be associated with ASL.

1. What types of property are used in ASL's business?
2. How is real property acquired by ASL and what are ASL's rights in relation to that property?
3. How did ASL acquire the personal property used in its business?
4. What are ASL's rights and obligations in relation to the tangible personal property that it leases or that is being stored by its customers?
5. What are ASL's rights in relation to its name and logo and how can ASL protect these rights?[1]

Introduction to Property Law

Property law consists of rules and laws that govern our relationship with things that can be owned.

Defining Property

While we tend to think of property as consisting of tangible "things" such as equipment, inventory, and real estate, what the law counts as property is considerably broader than physical things that can be held and touched. Property might even consist of something as esoteric as the right to use a particular industrial process or the right to use a particular business name. Nor does the mere fact that something has value and is worthy of protection make it property for the purposes of property law. For example, the right of citizenship is unquestionably valuable but it is not a right that can be transferred or sold to others. One of the roles of property law is to determine what counts as property and thus can be owned. Property law also enables owners to protect their rights in relation to their property.

Categories of Property

Real Property

Historically, the law has evolved to place property into distinct categories. **Real property** (see Chapter 19) is sometimes called "immovable" property and refers to land, whatever is permanently attached to it, and the associated legal rights. Even a growing crop would constitute real property until it is harvested and is no longer attached to the land. Each province operates a comprehensive system for publicly registering title to land and legal interests related to land.[2]

ASL, as the owner of the land on which its business is located, also owns the building and any items such as light fixtures and the walls that divide the warehouse into sections. The parking lot and any improvements to its land such as light posts installed by ASL would be considered real property. ASL's real property may even include certain rights it may have pertaining to things below the surface of the

Real property

Land and whatever is permanently affixed to it or part of it, such as buildings, mines, and minerals and the legal rights associated with those things.

---

1   Intellectual property rights are discussed in greater detail in Chapter 18 and the issue of rights to a name is included here to illustrate the range of property issues applicable to a business.
2   See Chapter 19.

land, such as the right to mine for natural gas or minerals. If ASL were successful in negotiating a contract in order to use the neighbouring property, then ASL's rights in the neighbouring property would also constitute a form of real property.

Personal Property

Personal property

All property, other than land and what is attached to it.

Personal **property** includes everything other than what is included as real property. Personal property falls into two major categories—tangible and intangible.

Tangible property refers to property that is concrete or material. In its business, ASL uses trucks, forklifts, furniture, office supplies, and other portable items that are not attached to land or a building. In law, these kinds of personal property are known as "chattels" or "moveables."

Tangible property

Personal property that is mobile, the value of which comes from its physical form.

Intangible property derives its value from legal rights, rather than concrete, physical qualities. Examples of intangible property are insurance policies, accounts receivable, bank accounts, and customer records, as well as the various forms of intellectual property. Internet domain names have been recognized as a form of property.[3] For example, the value of the fire insurance that ASL may have on its warehouse is not based on the piece of paper itself, which describes the terms of the insurance coverage. Rather, the value inherent in the fire insurance is the right that the policy creates, namely, the *right* to be compensated in the event that a fire destroys the warehouse. ASL's registered trademarks are a form of intellectual property (see Chapter 18) protected by legislation. In law, these kinds of property are known as "choses in action." Seen in this light, intangible property is no less real or significant than tangible property—in fact, it drives much of our modern economy.

Intangible property

Personal property, the value of which comes from legal rights.

BUSINESS APPLICATION OF THE LAW

SHOULD EVERYTHING BE CAPABLE OF BEING PRIVATELY OWNED? OWNERSHIP OF WATER RIGHTS

Chapters 17, 18, and 19 describe forms of property that might be described as private property, that is, real property and personal property that may be held by individuals or businesses. This begs the question: should all things be capable of being owned privately by individuals or businesses?

What constitutes property capable of being owned by individuals or businesses can change over time based on what a society through its state decides.[4] One reason a society might decide to limit the ability of its citizens to own a particular thing is because it considers that the thing in question should be available to everyone and that if it can be owned privately, then its owner could limit access to something that is an essential human need or right. For example, most nations place limitations on the ability to privately own watercourses and bodies of water in the theory that the ability to use and access water must be preserved for the benefit of all abutting property owners and also for the general benefit of society as a whole that might rely on that water for transportation, consumption, or even recreation. In Canada, the ownership of most bodies of water is vested in the provincial Crown. In Alberta, for example, this is explicitly recognized in the *Water Act*,[5] which states: "[t]he property in and the right to the diversion and use of all water in the Province is vested in Her Majesty in right of Alberta except as provided for in the regulations."

---

3 *Tucows.com Co v Lojas Renner SA*, 2011 ONCA 548, leave to appeal to SCC dismissed, 2012 CanLII 28261 (SCC)
4 C.B. MacPherson (ed.), "The Meaning of Property", *Property: Mainstream and Critical Positions* (Toronto: University of Toronto Press, 1978), pp. 11–12.
5 *Water Act*, R.S.A. 2000, c. W-3, s. 3 (2).

However some have suggested that even the Crown's ownership is not true full and absolute ownership and that the fundamental importance of water to life necessarily means that this Crown ownership of water *in situ*,[6] whether reflected in statute or not, is more in the nature of "custodianship" than "ownership."[7]

Historically, western Canadian jurisdictions have managed the distribution of water rights by prioritizing uses and issuing licences to users.[8] British Columbia is one of the last jurisdictions to create a system to regulate the withdrawal of groundwater, although this is now coming to an end as the province modernizes its century-old water legislation.[9] The lack of regulation of British Columbia groundwater usage recently came to public attention when it was reported that Nestlé Waters Canada, a division of the large Swiss-based company Nestlé Group, was removing 265 million litres of fresh water every year from an aquifer near the town of Hope without payment because the province's laws do not require payment for or even measurement of groundwater removed from wells.[10]

Sheila Muxlow has concerns about Nestlé withdrawing millions of litres of water without payment. How can society best manage and ensure efficient use of its water resources?

Critical Analysis: Should water as a resource be made the subject of private property? Would private ownership of water rights promote more efficient use of water? Why is the issue of privatizing fresh water supplies controversial?

There is no comprehensive system for publicly registering title to personal property as there is with real property, although there are some specialized registries for items such as motor vehicles, patents, and trademarks. One reason for the difference concerns the mobility of personal property. There is little utility in having a provincial registration system for most personal property when goods are so easily transported to another province. In addition, the value of individual items of personal property may not justify the cost of administering a registration system or the cost to owners of registering. Interests in personal property are registered, however, when that property is used as security in its purchase on credit or later as collateral for a loan. Registration is considered economical because it protects the creditor's rights to the pledged property.[11]

---

6   Water in its natural place and state as opposed to water that has been removed and bottled, for instance.

7   Jane Matthews Glenn, "Crown Ownership of Water *in situ* in Common Law Canada: Public Trust, Classical Trusts and Fiduciary Duties", *Les Cahiers de droit*, Volume 51, numéro 3–4, septembre–décembre 2010, pp. 493–519.

8   David R. Percy, "The Framework of Western and Northern Water Legislation", *Resources*, 1986, No. 16, pp. 1–3.

9   Bill 18-2014 was passed in April 2014. The new *Water Sustainability Act* is expected to be brought into effect in 2016.

10 Dan Fumano, "Nestlé tapping B.C. water for free; Company takes 265 million litres annually" *The Province*, (August 14, 2013) online: <http://www.theprovince.com/news/bc/Nestlé+tapping+water+free+Company +takes+million+litres+annually/10175100/story.html>.

11 This system of registration is governed by legislation in each province and is discussed in Chapter 26.

Acquiring Property Rights

The most obvious way to acquire property is to bring something new into existence. But ownership of property can be acquired by a business in a variety of ways:

- land may be acquired through purchase or lease.
- the ownership of goods is acquired by purchasing or manufacturing them.[12]
- insurance coverage is bought by paying premiums and is described in the insurance policy that gives the customer the right to recover losses in specified circumstances.[13]
- accounts receivable are created by delivering goods or services to customers, who agree to pay at a later date. The supplier acquires the right to collect the accounts, which can be sold to other businesses.[14]
- while certain kinds of intellectual property, such as copyright, are owned as a result of being created, ownership of other forms—such as a trademark—is established through use, or registration, or both. Intellectual property can also be bought from other owners.[15]

Ownership can also be acquired by finding and taking possession of lost or abandoned personal property. In law, a finder of personal property can assert ownership rights over the found property against everyone except its true owner. This aspect of the law illustrates how one person's rights to property can vary relative to the rights others might have in the same property. For example, if a patron found a piece of jewellery in a restaurant restroom, the finder's right to claim ownership would likely supersede the right of the restaurant owner.[16] However, unless its original owner intentionally abandoned the jewellery, the finder could not assert her ownership rights over those of the original owner.

Ownership rights in relation to land can also be acquired by occupying land owned by someone else, such as by inadvertently misplacing a fence or building on someone else's land. These rights are sometimes referred to as "squatter's rights" and they can be acquired if the occupation or "adverse possession" persists for a lengthy period of time (usually 10 years). In most jurisdictions, the squatter's occupation of the lands must be exclusive, continuous, and obvious, and the fact that the owner and squatter are both mistaken about the location of the true boundary is irrelevant. Furthermore, merely reentering the property such as for recreational purposes or even offering to sell the land to the squatter may not be sufficient to interrupt the adverse possession, and the paper title-holder might have to take actual legal steps to remove the squatter in order to protect its ownership rights.[17]

---

12 See the sale of goods in Chapter 23. Ownership can also be created by gift or inheritance.
13 See Chapter 28.
14 Known as assignments of contractual rights (see Chapter 9).
15 See Chapter 18.
16 See *Parker v British Airways Board*, [1982] 1 Q.B. 1004 (C.A.), where a gold bracelet was found by a traveller on the floor of an executive lounge at the Heathrow Airport. He turned the bracelet over to the occupier of the airport so that its owner could be found. The airport claimed ownership of the bracelet as occupier of the property but the Court of Appeal found that the airport's ownership could only be asserted if it had manifest control over the area in which the bracelet was found. As the bracelet was found in a public area, the finder's rights prevailed over those of the airport.
17 *1215565 Alberta Ltd. v Canadian Wellhead Isolation Corp.*, 2012 ABQB 145.

CAN HUMAN TISSUE REMOVED FOR MEDICAL TESTS BECOME PROPERTY, AND IF SO, WHO OWNS IT?

In May 2008, Dr. Abraham performed a colonoscopy on Snezana Piljak during which he removed a polyp from Ms. Piljak's colon. In August 2009, Ms. Piljak underwent unrelated testing at the Sunnybrook Hospital that revealed lesions on her liver and colon where the colonoscopy had been performed. She was diagnosed with colorectal cancer and died two years later. After her death, her estate commenced a negligence action against Dr. Abraham and other medical professionals involved in her treatment. One of the allegations was that Dr. Abraham should have detected the cancer and failed to meet the standard of care. In his defence, Dr. Abraham argued that unrelated medical conditions caused his patient's death and he sought the court's permission to access the liver tissue that was still in the possession of the Sunnybrook Hospital in order to test for a genetic condition known as HNPCC or Lynch Syndrome, a condition that is often undetected during colonoscopy and which increases the risk of certain types of cancer and causes cancer to develop very rapidly.

One of the issues raised in the case was the possibility that the testing would also reveal genetic information about Ms. Piljak's family members, some of whom might not want the information and might therefore object to the testing. Ontario's procedural rules permit a court to make an order for the inspection of "real or personal property where it appears to be necessary for the proper determination of an issue in a proceeding." Therefore, a preliminary issue the court had to determine was whether the tissue that had been removed from Ms. Piljak at the Sunnybrook Hospital counted as personal property.[18] The court ultimately concluded that the tissue sample constituted

With the rise of stem cells and genetic pharmaceuticals, personal medical data is becoming more of a commodity. Why is the ownership of stem cells and genetic material controversial?

personal property, "a moveable," and that while it had been owned by Ms. Piljak before its removal, it became the property of the hospital after its removal. According to the court, once excised, its possession and ownership was transferred to the hospital by virtue of being part of the hospital's medical record.[19] As for the rights of the patient in regard to excised tissue, the court accepted that at best a patient is entitled to have "reasonable access" to the tissue sample.

Critical Analysis: Do you agree with the court's analysis? If excised tissue becomes the property of the hospital and the hospital uses the tissue to develop a profitable patent, should the hospital have sole right to those profits? Should the hospital's right to use Ms. Piljak's tissue be subject to any limits?

Sources: Richard Warnica, "Human tissue removed for medical tests is 'personal property' of institution, not person it came from: ruling", National Post (5 June 2014) online: <http://news.nationalpost.com/news/canada/human-tissue-removed-for-medical-tests-is-personal-property-of-institution-not-person-it-came-from-ruling>; Mayo Clinic, "Diseases and Conditions, Lynch Syndrome," <http://www.mayoclinic.org/diseases-conditions/lynch-syndrome/basics/definition/con-20025651>, accessed April 6, 2015.

18 *Piljak Estate v. Abraham*, 2014 ONSC 2893.
19 *Ibid* at p. 26.

PART FIVE

Legal Rights Associated with Property

Unlike the *Constitution* of the United States, Canada's *Charter of Rights and Freedoms* does not provide for the constitutional protection of property. However, this is not to say that Canadian law does not provide protections for property.[20] Alberta, for example, has enacted the *Alberta Personal Property Bill of Rights*,[21] which echoes the *Fifth Amendment* of the *Bill of Rights* of 1791 insomuch as it renders void any provincial law that authorizes the Crown to acquire permanent title in personal property unless the law incorporates a process for providing compensation for acquiring that title.[22] The Canadian *Bill of Rights*[23] also provides that Canadians have to right to "enjoyment of property, and the right not to be deprived thereof except by due process of law," although this statute applies only to federally regulated matters and can be overridden by any other act of Parliament, without legal consequence. Specialized legislation also exists to protect certain types of property. For example, intellectual property rights are protected by several federal statutes such as the *Patent Act*,[24] and privately owned land is protected from arbitrary expropriation by provincial statutes such as the *Ontario Expropriations Act*[25] which also require governments to meet basic requirements of procedural fairness when expropriating privately owned land. Many of our rights to protect our property exist in the common law. For example, the torts of trespass and nuisance protect a person's possession and enjoyment of land from interference, and the tort of passing off protects the goodwill attached to the products of a business.[26]

The Bundle of Rights

Bundle of rights

The set of legal rights associated with property, which usually includes the right to exclude, the right to possess and use, and the right to transfer to others or dispose of property.

The collection of legal rights associated with ownership of property is sometimes characterized as a **bundle of rights**, and included in this bundle are the right to exclude, the right to possession, use, and enjoyment of property, and the right to transfer or dispose of property.

The owner of property who is also in possession is entitled to deal with it essentially as she sees fit. Her options include:

- selling the property and transferring ownership and possession to the buyer.
- leasing the property to another business with the intent of regaining possession or selling it when the lease expires.
- using the property as security for a loan, thereby giving the lender the right to seize or sell the property if the borrower defaults on the loan.
- transferring possession of its chattels to another business for storage, repair, or transport with the corresponding right to regain possession.

The Right to Exclude

One of the most important rights associated with property is the right to exclude others from accessing or interfering with it. For example, the property rights

---

20 Bruce Ziff, "'Taking' Liberties: Protection for Private Property in Canada", *Modern Studies in Property Law, Vol. III*, (Oxford: Hart, 2005), p. 341.
21 R.S.A. 2000, c. A-31.
22 *Ibid* at s 2.
23 S.C.1960, c. 44.
24 R.S.C.1985, c. P-4
25 S.O. 1968-69 c.36.
26 These torts are discussed in Chapter 12.

associated with land normally include the right to exclude others from entering upon land or interfering with the owner's use of the land, and the property rights in a book that is subject to copyright include the right to prohibit others from copying or modifying the work in question. Most business activity involves the expenditure of energy and resources in order to create property or increase its holdings of property, and therefore the right to exclude is a fundamental and important right.[27]

ASL has the right to exclude individuals from entering its warehouse and may enforce that right by commencing a suit for the tort of trespass. ASL can also grant others the legal right to enter its property. For example, ASL might grant an **easement**[28] to the City of Moncton that permits the city to install a water line on ASL's property and enter onto the property in order to repair and maintain the water line. ASL also has the right to exclude others from using the trademarks it has registered and could enforce this right by suing for damages and seeking an injunction to prevent further unauthorized use.

Easement

The right to use the land of another for a particular purpose only.

Right to Possess and Use

Another right usually associated with property is the right of possession. While the ownership of property and right to possess it are normally held by the same person or entity, it is often possible to separate these rights so that ownership may rest with one party while the right of possession rests with someone else. This is essentially the nature of a **lease**,[29] which results in one party owning the property while someone else has the right to possess that property for a period of time, after which possession is ultimately returned to the owner.

Lease

A contract that transfers possession of land or personal property in exchange for a fee.

There are several examples of possession rights in the ASL scenario that are common in a business environment:

- ASL has chosen to lease trucks and forklifts rather than buy them.
- ASL's customers are using its facilities to store their property temporarily. There is no intention for ASL to become the owner of the stored property.
- ASL could lease warehouse space from the owner of the neighbouring property or in turn lease to another business a portion of the space that it owns.

What most often drives the temporary split of ownership and possession is that it meets the business needs of both parties in each situation. For instance, by leasing, ASL gets the benefit of using vehicles and equipment without a large capital outlay. By storing equipment with ASL, customers get the benefit of a valuable service without having to purchase or lease a building themselves for that purpose. When ASL expands into the self-storage industry, it may lease the neighbouring property rather than make the considerable capital outlay that would be required to purchase the property.

Some property cannot be physically possessed by its owner and its value lies in the right to control the use of the property. For instance, intangible property such as a specialized process that is protected by a patent has no physical existence that is capable of being possessed, but the right to use the process may be very valuable. An inventor who develops and patents a new product or process

---

27 For a general discussion on the right to exclude, see T.W. Merrill, in "Property and the Right to Exclude", *Nebraska Law Review*. 1998, Vol. 77, p. 730.
28 Easements are discussed in Chapter 19.
29 Leases are discussed in Chapter 19.

Licence

Consent given by the owner of rights to someone to do something that only the owner can do.

might choose to grant a **licence** to permit someone else to manufacture and sell the product or use the process in exchange for the right to receive royalties from the product's future sales. ASL could grant a business a licence to use its name and logo in another location.[30]

Right to Transfer or Dispose

Normally the rights associated with the ownership of property also include the right to dispose of the property or transfer the property (such as by selling it) to someone else. However, there are exceptions. For example, the title to most land in Canada incorporates the right to sell the property, but it is also possible to own land only for the duration of one's life, after which the title reverts back to its initial owner or her estate. The owner whose rights are limited to the duration of his life cannot sell the property or otherwise dispose of it such as by gifting it.[31]

The ownership of personal property usually includes right to sell or transfer the property. However, there are some situations in which the property rights in personal property do not include the right to sell or transfer the property. For example, a person who rents or borrows personal property only has a temporary interest in the property and cannot sell it or otherwise dispose of it.

Personal property and real property rights might also be subject to a **trust**. A trust arises when the owner of property transfers his or her rights in specific property to someone who holds the property (the "trustee") for the benefit of the trust's beneficiaries. Although a trustee has legal title to the trust property, he is normally prohibited from using the property for his own personal benefit and owes fiduciary duties to the beneficiaries of the trust. Trusts are often used in wills to control how property is used after the death of the testator, but trusts have many other purposes and business uses. For example, most pension plans are facilitated by use of the trust concept. A pension plan is usually administered by pension trustees who hold legal title to the pension fund assets and manage the funds for the benefit of the plan's members who have the legal right to benefit from the assets held in the fund. The law of trusts is complex and a more detailed explanation of trusts is beyond the scope of this book.

Trust

A legal arrangement that is characterized by one party holding legal title of property for the benefit of someone else.

ASL likely owns the warehouse and land on which its business is situated in "fee simple"[32] and thus ASL could sell or transfer its real property as it sees fit. If ASL were to borrow funds such as from a bank, as the owner of the property in "fee simple," the property could be pledged by ASL as security for the loan. The delivery vehicles and forklifts are rented and thus ASL's rights are only temporary and do not include the right to sell or pledge these assets.

Obligations Associated with Real Property Ownership

While we typically associate ownership of property with rights, ownership might also entail legal obligations. Most municipalities impose a tax on the ownership of real property in order to fund municipal services such as police and fire

---

30 See Chapter 18.

31 Most land in Canada is owned in "fee simple," which is the largest bundle of rights associated with land and includes the right to sell the property, but land can also be owned as a "life estate" which limits the holder's right to use the land to the duration of her life, after which the property reverts to the fee simple owner or his or her estate. These concepts are discussed further in Chapter 19.

32 *Supra* note 27.

protection, road maintenance, and infrastructure. Landowners may also have obligations under legislation to cooperate with certain intrusions on their land. For example, in British Columbia, where the province owns most subsurface oil and gas rights, a landowner can be required to grant a developer access to the property. As with several other provinces, British Columbia imposes mandatory arbitration in the event the resource developer and surface landowner cannot agree on fees and terms of access.[33] Similarly, landowners of environmentally sensitive property may have statutory obligations to protect the natural features of the property.[34] A municipality may also impose land use rules in order to regulate local development and bylaws that require property owners to provide proper upkeep of their property.

Obligations Associated with Personal Property

One of the unique features of personal property is portability. Because of this characteristic, owners are not always in constant possession of their personal property. A **bailment** is a temporary transfer of possession of personal property from the owner, known as a **bailor**, to another party, known as a **bailee**.

There are many examples of bailment in commercial transactions, including the following:

- the short-term rental of a vehicle.
- the long-term lease of a vehicle (e.g., ASL's leasing of trucks and forklifts).
- the delivery of property for repair.
- the transport of property by a commercial carrier.
- the storage of property in a warehouse (e.g., the main business of ASL).
- the shipping of an envelope by courier.
- leaving clothing at a dry cleaning shop.
- depositing a car at a garage for servicing.

Bailments are also common in the non-commercial context, as shown in these examples:

- lending a lawn mower to a neighbour.
- asking someone in a café to watch your laptop while you place your order.
- borrowing library books.

In each of the above situations, someone is in possession of someone else's property. The question that arises is: how much responsibility is entailed in possessing someone else's property? For example, should a neighbour who borrows your lawn mower and a stranger who agrees to watch your laptop for a few minutes owe the same amount of responsibility for your property? Or, does someone who pays a fee to use your lawn mower owe the same level of care toward it as someone who has been allowed to use it for free? In business, liability issues can arise when some mishap occurs in relation to the property while it is in the possession of the bailee.[35] For example, the property of ASL's

Bailment

Temporary transfer of possession of personal property from one person to another.

Bailor

The owner of property who transfers possession in a bailment.

Bailee

The person who receives possession in a bailment.

---

33 *Petroleum and Natural Gas Act*, R.S.B.C. 1996, c. 361, ss. 152, 159.
34 See for example *Municipal Government Act*, R.S.A. 2000, c. M-26, ss. 664(3).
35 The work of Professor Moe Litman of the Faculty of Law, University of Alberta, in this section is gratefully acknowledged.

customers might be lost, damaged, or destroyed while in ASL's warehouse; employees might drop valuable equipment while moving it around; a forklift might run into items in its path; customer property could be stolen from the warehouse; there might be damage from water or a fire in the warehouse; if the property is perishable, it could spoil if not properly stored. Ideally, the contract between ASL and its customers will specify the extent of ASL's liability for these events. ASL is likely to transfer risks to customers by placing significant limits on its legal liability through exclusion or limitation of liability clauses in its storage contracts.

Bailees may not escape their responsibilities by turning over a bailed chattel to employees. If the chattel is damaged, lost, or stolen as a result of employees' negligence, the employer as bailee is vicariously liable so long as the employees were acting within the ordinary course or scope of their employment, that is, the employees were engaged in the performance of their assigned duties. In addition, bailees are liable for the intentional wrongdoing of their employees. A bailee who entrusts bailed goods to an employee is personally (not vicariously) liable for the theft of the goods by the employee. Another basis of liability of a bailee for theft by an employee is the law of negligence. The employer has a duty to hire honest, responsible people. Accordingly, failure to engage in proper hiring practices may result in liability for the employer.

In general, the liability of a bailee for bailed property will be governed by the common law of bailment, statutory rules that may be imposed on special types of bailees (e.g., warehouses and innkeepers) and the specific contract terms between the parties.

Common Law Liability of Bailees

The common law obligations of bailees to care for the goods of their bailors have evolved through various stages. Initially, bailees were 100 percent liable for the return of bailed chattels as well as for any damage, whether the bailee caused the damage or not and even where the bailee exercised reasonable or even extreme diligence. Later, the burden of the bailee to care for the goods of the bailor was determined by the concept of "benefit of the relationship." If a bailment benefited the bailor exclusively, the bailee was required to exercise slight care and was liable only for "gross neglect." If the bailment benefited the bailee exclusively, the bailee was required to exercise great care and was liable for even "slight negligence." If there was reciprocal benefit, the bailee was required to exercise ordinary diligence and was liable for "ordinary neglect."

Today, in the absence of statutory rules or a formal agreement between the parties, all bailees are expected to exercise care toward the bailor's property, however the *degree* of care expected will vary with the circumstances, including whether payment is involved, which party is benefiting from the bailment, the nature of the property being bailed, and the expertise of the bailee.

Is Payment Involved?

Most commercial bailments are based on a contract requiring payment for the use of the property or as compensation for storage or another service. This is known as a **bailment for value**.

Possession of property may also be transferred without payment by virtue of a loan or a free service. This would occur when, for example, a prospective buyer

Bailment for value

Bailment involving payment or compensation.

takes a vehicle for a test drive or someone parks his car in his neighbour's garage for the winter. Because there is no compensation involved in such arrangements, such an instance is known as a **gratuitous bailment** in the sense of being free or "without reward."

Gratuitous bailment

Bailment that involves no payment.

In general, a bailee who receives a payment must show greater care than a gratuitous bailee. For example, because ASL receives payment from its customers in exchange for the right to store their property in ASL's warehouse, ASL is required to exercise a higher degree of care toward the owners' property than would someone who permits a friend to store her holiday trailer on his land free of charge.

For Whose Benefit Is the Bailment?

The question of who benefits from a gratuitous bailment is particularly important, since the answer helps later to determine the bailee's responsibility for the property. Gratuitous bailments can benefit the bailor or the bailee. If the bailment is gratuitous and for the benefit of the bailor, the standard of care is very low. If the bailment is gratuitous and for the benefit of the bailee, the standard is very high.

For example, when someone stores his car in a friend's garage for the winter at no charge, the bailee—the person who owns the garage—derives no advantage from the relationship, while the bailor—the person who owns the car—now has protection for his vehicle from harsh weather. It is the bailor, therefore, who gains from the bailment and the standard of care is low. Conversely, when a person borrows his neighbour's lawn mower, the owner of the lawn mower—the bailor—is simply doing a favour and does not derive any tangible benefit from the bailment. The borrower—the bailee—can now cut his grass without having to buy or lease a lawn mower from someone else and is therefore the party who profits from the relationship and the standard of care is very high.

Bailments that benefit both the bailor and the bailee are most common in the commercial world and usually involve bailments for value—that is, bailments in which one of the parties is paid for the provision of a service or other benefit. For example, the owner of the vehicles and forklifts leased by ASL benefits from the relationship since it is paid by ASL. ASL also benefits since it gains possession of delivery vehicles and forklifts. Similarly, ASL benefits from storing the property of its customers since it is paid to provide the service. ASL's customers benefit because their property is stored and protected by ASL. The obligation of ASL in these situations is to take the same care of the goods as a "prudent warehouseman acting reasonably" might be expected to take of his own goods.

The Nature and Value of the Bailed Property

The standard of care expected of a bailee will be higher for more valuable property, and the care provided by the bailee should be appropriate for the type of property. For example, a bailee of valuable and delicate property such as a rare antique book would be expected to exercise a higher degree of care toward the book and might be expected to store it in a dry and secure place. A jeweller making arrangements to ship a customer's valuable ring for repairs might be expected to make certain the ring is transported in the safest possible matter and that adequate insurance is in place in case of the ring's loss during its transportation.[36]

Special Circumstances in the Transaction

Where the bailee is instructed by the bailor as to the value of the goods or special storage requirements, for example, this increases the standard of care that the bailee must meet.

The Expertise of the Bailee

A bailee who specializes in a certain type of bailment (such as storage) is expected to take greater care than an ordinary person.

The Contract of Bailment

In bailments for value, the contract between the bailor and the bailee is central. For example, the contract may raise or lower the standard of care owed by the bailee, or may set the standard at ordinary care and diligence but limit the amount of damages for which the bailee may be held liable.

The parties are free to negotiate the details of their own agreement. A contract will normally include a description of these aspects:

- the services to be provided by the bailee.
- the price to be paid by the bailor and payment terms.
- the extent to which the bailee is liable for damage or loss.
- the remedies of the parties for failure to perform.

In a storage contract, for example, the focus is on the bailee's liability for loss to the chattels in question and the bailee's remedies for collecting storage charges. Because a warehouse operator deals with the property of many customers in similar circumstances and is under pressure to keep prices competitive, a business such as ASL is likely to have a standard form agreement that all customers are expected to sign. The main object from ASL's perspective is to minimize its responsibility for damage caused to property in its possession, in order to keep costs down. At the same time, it is important for ASL to maintain a good reputation in the industry. Limiting liability through standard form agreements is common in the storage industry, as in the following clauses:

Warehouseman

A bailee who stores personal property.

(a) The responsibility of a **warehouseman** in the absence of written provisions is the reasonable care and diligence required by the law.

(b) The warehouseman's liability on any one package is limited to $40 unless the holder has declared in writing a valuation in excess of $40 and paid the additional charge specified to cover warehouse liability.[37]

While clause (b) may seem unfair—after all, if the warehouseman's negligence causes more than $40 in damage, should it not have to pay the full tab?—its function is to signal which party should buy insurance on the item being stored: the bailor or the bailee. In this case, the onus is on the bailor (as the owner who

---

36 See *Punch v Savoy's Jewellers Ltd* (1986), 54 OR (2d) 383 (CA).
37 See *London Drugs Ltd v Kuehne & Nagel International Ltd*, [1992] 3 SCR 2 in Chapter 9.

Who is responsible for property damaged during delivery? Who is responsible for damage to a leased truck?

is limited to a claim for $40) to purchase insurance, since the item being stored is likely worth much more than that amount.

The other focus of a bailment contract is on the remedies that the bailee can use to obtain payment from delinquent customers. For example, the contract may provide that ASL is entitled to retain possession of stored items until payment is received and may also give ASL the right to sell stored items in order to apply the proceeds to the outstanding account. Of course, ASL's prime interest is timely payment from customers. It is interested in the right to keep customers' property only as a backup remedy.

The terms of ASL's bailment agreement for the leasing of vehicles are likely to be written by the owner of the vehicles, called the lessor, who is interested in protecting its property while that property is in ASL's possession. This is accomplished by inserting a clause in the contract making ASL responsible for any damage and by imposing limits on the extent to which ASL can use the vehicles (such as distance for the trucks and time for the forklifts). Again, insurance should be purchased to cover loss or damage, in this case by ASL. The owner of the vehicles should consider making it a term of the contract that it be named in the insurance policy as the party who is paid in the event of loss.

Specialized Bailments Impacted by Statute

Certain types of bailment may be subject to special regulations or rules that may set out the standard of care and other rights and obligations of parties to the bailment contract. Contracts to transport goods, for example, are subject to standard statutory terms that may set out the standard of care, and businesses that store or repair goods may have special statutory remedies in the event of a customer's non-payment.

Transportation

A bailee who receives property and transports it according to the owner's instructions is called a **carrier**. There are several categories of carriers, each with different obligations toward the property. The most relevant in business are common carriers—those who represent themselves to the public as carriers for reward, meaning they are prepared to transport any property for any owner so long as their facilities permit and they are paid for the service. Common carriers are held to a very high standard of care regarding the property they carry.

Carrier

A bailee who transports personal property.

If property is lost or damaged while in their possession, it is presumed that the carrier is liable. The owner is not required to prove fault by the carrier, mainly because it is difficult for the owner to know what happened to the property during the transport. Carriers are required to account for their treatment of the property and justify the application of one of the limited legal defences, which mainly relate to circumstances within the control of the owner or beyond the control of the carrier. For example, if the owner fails to pack fragile goods adequately or the goods are destroyed in a natural disaster, the carrier could be excused from liability.

As a result of this heavy responsibility based on legislation and the common law, carriers normally include provisions in their standard form agreements with customers that the carriers' liability will be severely limited should mishap occur with the property. These clauses typically limit liability to a low dollar amount. Customers are protected by legislation covering each form of transport—rail, road, sea, and air. Clauses used in contracts on international or interprovincial routes must be approved by the Canadian Transport Agency. The case below illustrates potential problems with the transport of goods.

Carriers do not have the same legislative remedies as those who repair or store property. Carriers have a common law lien against the property for transport charges, but enjoy no corresponding right to sell the property if the owner fails to pay.

Carling O'Keefe Breweries of Canada Ltd v CN Marine Inc, [1990] 1 FC 483 (CA)

THE BUSINESS CONTEXT: Deciding who is responsible for damaged goods and for how much requires a full investigation of the events that occurred and a detailed examination of the terms of the contract, any legislation, and applicable international rules.

FACTUAL BACKGROUND: Carling engaged CN to ship 4240 cases of beer from St. John's to Goose Bay. CN arranged shipping aboard a ship owned by Labrador Shipping. The beer was placed in three large containers and stowed on the deck of the ship with the edges of the containers protruding over the sides of the ship. The containers were washed overboard in heavy seas. Carling claimed the value of the beer ($32 000) from CN and the owners of the ship. The ship's owners became insolvent, leaving CN as the defendant able to pay a judgment. CN argued that it was acting only as agent for the ship's owners and therefore had no liability, and that in any event its liability

Transportation of goods involves many parties, contracts, and risks. What are some potential legal problems arising from this scene?

Chuck Stoody/The Canadian Press

should be limited to $500 per container (a total of $1500) by virtue of the applicable federal legislation.

THE LEGAL QUESTION: Did the contract relieve CN from liability as a carrier and limit damages to $500 for each container? Did the $500 limit apply to each of the three large shipping containers or to each of the 4240 cases of beer?

RESOLUTION: The contract was governed by federal legislation (the *Carriage of Goods by Water Act*), which incorporated the *Hague Rules* (an international convention providing for standardized terms in such transactions). The *Hague Rules* prevented a carrier from avoiding liability for improper storage of goods and also limited claims to $500 "per package." The court found that CN was the carrier (not just the agent of the ship's owners) because it had signed the contract in its personal capacity (becoming a "carrier" as defined in the *Hague Rules*) and because it had acted as a carrier in the loading and stowage of the cargo on board the vessel.

In terms of the number of "packages" on which Carling O'Keefe could recover up to $500, the court looked to the intention of the parties as revealed by the language of the documents, what they said, and what they did. The shipping documents listed 4240 packages. It was also noted that "it is common knowledge that beer is shipped in cases." On this basis, Carling recovered its full loss from CN.

CRITICAL ANALYSIS: Is the adoption of international rules an effective way to manage risk? How could CN have limited its liability to $1500 instead of $32 000? How could Carling have controlled its risk?

Storage

This type of bailment forms the core of ASL's business—storage of commercial customers' property. Customers entrust their property to ASL and have limited means for monitoring ASL's treatment of their property. As a result, the law imposes a high level of accountability on ASL for its treatment of customers' property. Of particular importance are any limits on what ASL can do with the property in terms of the type of storage or the possibility of moving it to other locations. For example, ASL must keep items that would be harmed by cold temperatures in an adequately heated space. ASL may need permission from customers to store property in any facilities other than its own. Customers expect their property to be returned in the same condition in which it was delivered, unlike in the case of ASL's leased vehicles, where the intent is for ASL to use them. If the property is lost, damaged, or destroyed, customers will look to ASL for compensation. The main concern from ASL's perspective is payment of the storage fees by customers and its ability to collect.

As indicated earlier, ASL's general responsibility toward its customers' property is to treat it as a "prudent warehouseman" would deal with its own property.[38] This imposes a standard of reasonableness that includes responsibility for all foreseeable risks. Because the standard is high and the potential losses are high, ASL is likely to limit its liability to its customers in its standard form agreements with them. A typical limitation clause is the one shown on page 426, where the contract limits the bailee's liability to $40.

The circumstances of the self-storage contracts are much different in the sense that customers essentially rent the storage space and control the contents and their access to them. ASL is naturally reluctant to accept the same degree of responsibility that it might toward commercial customers whose property ASL more actively controls.

The remedies of a storage bailee, or warehouseman, are contained in legislation in each province.[39] The bailee has a lien over the property until the owner

38 See also note 39.
39 See, for example, *Warehouse Lien Act*, RSBC 1996, c 480; *Warehouser's Lien Act*, RSNL 1990, c W-2; *Repair and Storage Liens Act*, RSO 1990, c R-25.

pays the storage fees. This means that ASL can keep its customers' property until payment is complete. If payment is not forthcoming, ASL also has the right to sell the property and apply the proceeds to the outstanding charges. Any surplus proceeds of the sale go to the owner. The legislation contains safeguards for the owner in that notice of the intended sale must be given and the bailee must deal with the property in a reasonable manner—for example, not sell valuable property for the amount of a relatively small storage bill. These limitations are of particular concern to ASL in self-storage situations, where ASL may have limited knowledge of the property that is stored. See the *Halloway* case below for discussion of these limits.

These rights and responsibilities relating to a storage bailment apply only if the arrangement meets the definition of a bailment—there must be a transfer of possession and control from the owner to another person. Otherwise, the responsibility for the property is much less and the remedies for collection are less effective. For example, leaving a vehicle in a parking lot and paying a parking fee does not amount to a bailment unless the keys are delivered to an attendant, thereby transferring control of the vehicle. If the owner keeps the keys, the parking lot is not in control of the vehicle and the transaction is likely one for the use of the parking space, with minimal responsibility for what is in the space.[40] Operators of parking lots commonly issue tickets that are meant to define the relationship (use of space rather than bailment) and either exclude liability completely or limit it to a small amount. As with any standard form contract, the customer must receive adequate notice of onerous and unexpected terms. ASL's relationship with its self-storage consumers could be similarly characterized, since ASL has access to the storage space only in exceptional circumstances, such as non-payment of fees or emergency.

Repairs

When the owner of property takes it to a repair shop, the main purpose of the transaction is the repair of the property. If the property is left at the shop, a storage bailment, which is incidental to the main purpose of the arrangement, is also created. At the appointed time for pickup, the owner—the bailor—expects to receive the property in a good state of repair and otherwise in the condition in which it was delivered. The bailee must provide reasonable safekeeping for the property and complete the repairs in a workmanlike manner, as a reasonably competent repairer of that sort of property would.

From a business perspective, it makes sense to agree on a price in advance, but if the parties do not agree on the price for storage and repairs at the outset, the repairer's compensation will be a reasonable amount for the service provided. The repairer cannot charge more than is reasonable, nor can the owner refuse to pay anything, just because no price was agreed in advance.

Lien

The right to retain possession of personal property until payment for service is received.

Most provinces have legislation[41] giving the bailee a **lien** against the property for the value of the repairs as long as the bailee has possession of the property.[42] As with the storage situation, the bailee also has the right to sell the property (subject to procedural requirements) to recover the repair charges.

---

40 Bruce H Ziff, *Principles of Property Law*, 5th ed (Toronto: Carswell, 2010) at 321–22.
41 See, for example, *Mechanics' Lien Act*, RSNL 1990, c M-3; *Builders' Lien Act*, RSNS 1989, c 277; *Repairers' Lien Act*, RSBC 1996, c 404; *Repair and Storage Liens Act*, RSO 1990, c R-25.
42 Some legislation also allows for non-possessory liens based on an acknowledgment of the debt. See *Repair and Storage Liens Act*, RSO 1990, c R-25.

Melrose v Halloway Holdings Ltd, 2004 CanLII 50135 (ONSC)

THE BUSINESS CONTEXT: This case illustrates the risk that a storage company faces in exercising its rights to recover storage fees as well as the risk that the user of a storage locker takes in leaving valuable property in the locker. The primacy of legislation over contracts is also explored.

FACTUAL BACKGROUND: Robert Melrose (RM) rented storage locker 1415 from Halloway Holdings Ltd. (HH) in September 2001. Teri Melrose (TM), RM's wife, was listed on the rental agreement as an "authorized user" of the locker. According to TM, most of the tools, furniture, and household goods in locker 1415 were hers. In November, RM rented another locker (13130) from HH. Both lease agreements exempted HH from ". . . loss or damage, however caused . . ."; stated that failure to pay rent might result in the goods stored being sold; and stated that the price obtained for the goods was deemed to be the best possible price. In March 2002, the Melroses separated. They cleared out locker 13130, moved TM's property to locker 1415, and provided a new address for RM. The locker rental fell into arrears. HH sent several notices to RM at his old address. No notice was sent to TM before the property was sold to an auction house for $800 in November. TM claimed the value of her property from HH, which she alleges was $60 000.

THE LEGAL QUESTION: Was TM protected by the *Repair and Storage Liens Act*, (*RSLA*)?[43] Was the sale of the property proper? Did the locker rental contract affect the rights provided in the *RSLA*? If not, what is the quantum of damages?

RESOLUTION: TM was found to be a person from whom property was received for storage and for which payment was made. Therefore, she was protected by the Act and entitled to her rights, even though she had no written

contract with HH. HH was required to follow the statutory requirements and also owed her a common law duty of care as a bailee for value to treat the property as a prudent owner would do.

The sale by HH to the auction house did not conform to the requirements of the *RSLA* because notice was not sent to RM's last known address as required, notice was never sent to TM as required, and the notice sent to RM's old address was deficient in several respects. It lacked a specific description of the goods, the details of payment, and how payment could be made before the sale. In terms of the actual sale, there was no publicity, no attempt to ascertain the value of the property, and a huge gap between the sale price and the value alleged by TM.

The attempt by HH to have renters contract out of the provisions of the *RSLA* failed because the contract language was legalistic and in small print on the reverse of the agreement. There was no evidence that the terms were brought to RM's attention and even if they had been, that he would have fully understood their significance. In addition,

> [HH] disposed of the goods in a fashion so cavalier and lacking in the care that one might reasonably expect a bailee to exercise in relation to goods over which it holds a lien that, in my view, it can fairly be said that [HH's] conduct amounted to a fundamental breach of the contract of bailment.

In the alternative, Justice Clark found the offending terms to be unfair and unreasonable and therefore unconscionable. Regarding the quantum of damages, he ordered a trial to determine the contents of the locker, their fair market value, and any related damages.

CRITICAL ANALYSIS: Should there be a subsequent trial to determine damages? How could the participants in this transaction have better managed the risks arising from the locker rental? What changes in its business should HH make as a result of this case?

PART FIVE

---

43 RSO 1990, c R.25.

DEFINING LIABILITY IN CONTRACTS OF BAILMENT

As demonstrated by the exclusion of liability in the *Halloway* case above and the limit of $40 in the *London Drugs* case in Chapter 9, a key aspect of a bailment contract is often limitation of the liability that the common law rules of bailment create. The terms of these contracts are normally written by the businesses whose livelihood is based on the bailment relationship. For example, in a bailment for services such as the ASL storage business, ASL as bailee will create the standard form agreement. In a leasing contract, the lessor as bailor will write the contract.

In the *London Drugs* case, the enforceability of the $40 clause between the customer and the warehouse company was not challenged. However, such clauses are vulnerable and can be challenged in various ways:

- failure to bring the standard terms to the attention of the customer. See the *Halloway* case above and the *Tilden* case in Chapter 7 for examples.

- failure of the language in the clause to exclude liability in the circumstances. See the *Carling O'Keefe* case earlier in this chapter for the meaning of "package."

- serious defect affecting the formation or performance of the contract such as fundamental breach or unconscionability.

See the *Halloway* case above and the *Tercon Contractors* case in Chapter 9.

Exemption and limitation clauses are also regulated by statute:

- New Brunswick consumer protection legislation[44] applies to consumer sales that include leases. Clauses that limit liability will not be enforced unless they are considered to be "fair and reasonable."

- Industry-specific legislation may set the terms. See the *Carling O'Keefe* case above.

The courts are inclined to apply differing standards to commercial and consumer contracts. This is an important consideration for ASL since it serves both types of customers. ASL may presume that a business customer is more likely to understand contract terms and intend to be obligated by them than a consumer. Courts may also consider the contract price in relation to potential losses in deciding whether it is reasonable to enforce a limitation.[45]

Critical Analysis: Do these contract terms indicate that some businesses are exploiting customers who are less knowledgeable, less aware, or weaker, or do these clauses illustrate effective risk management? Are courts and legislatures justified in injecting ethical standards into business by applying standards such as "unfair," "unreasonable," and "unconscionable"?

Lodging

Innkeeper

Someone who offers lodging to the public.

Someone who offers lodging to the public is known as an **innkeeper**. At common law, an innkeeper's responsibility for guests' property is similar to that of common carriers. They must take great care of guests' property and are responsible for loss or theft. There is an important practical distinction in the degree of control between carriers and innkeepers. Carriers have total control of the property when it is delivered for shipment, while guests share control over their property through their occupation of rooms.

In some provinces, innkeepers are permitted by legislation[46] to limit their liability to a specific amount ($40 to $150, depending on the province) if they

---

44 *Consumer Product Warranty and Liability Act*, SNB 1978, c C-18.1.
45 See *Fraser Jewellers (1982) Ltd v Dominion Electric Protection Co* (1997), 148 DLR (4th) 496 (ON CA).
46 See, for example, *Innkeepers' Act*, RSO 1990, c I-7; *Hotel Keepers Act*, CCSM c H150.

FIGURE 17.1 Summary of Specialized Bailments

Type of Bailment	Storage	Repair	Transport	Lodging
Specialized designation for the bailor	Customer	Customer	Shipper	Guest
Specialized designation for the bailee	Warehouse	Repairer	Carrier	Innkeeper
Bailee's standard of care	Reasonable	Reasonable	High	High
Liability normally limited	Contract	Contract	Contract	Legislation
Who gets paid for a service	Bailee	Bailee	Bailee	Bailee
Remedies for non-payment	Lien, sale	Lien, sale	Lien	Lien
Applicable legislation	Yes	Yes	No	Yes
Examples	*Halloway* case (Business Law in Practice)	Situation for Discussion #4	*Carling* case Situation for Discussion #8	Question for Critical Thinking #3

post the legislated limits in the establishment. Their protection is lost if the loss to property is due to a negligent or deliberate act of the innkeeper (or the inn's employees) or if the property has been deposited with the inn for safekeeping.

See Figure 17.1 for a summary of the specialized bailments discussed in this chapter.

Risk Management

The risks relating to property concern protection of ownership, rights to possession, and the preservation of economic value. With tangible property, the major concern is with responsibility for loss or damage to the property. In bailments for value, an additional risk is the failure of the customer to pay for services such as storage or repair.

Businesses subject to these risks can use the risk management model to minimize their impact on the success of the business. For example, ASL can decline to accept items for storage that are particularly susceptible to loss or unsuitable for ASL's facilities, thereby avoiding such risks. ASL will strive to reduce the remaining risks through well-developed and administered procedures within its storage facilities. In bailment transactions, the transfer of risk is prominent. Carefully negotiated contracts will indicate who bears the loss in a variety of circumstances. The contract will assign the loss and thereby indicate which party should seek to transfer its risk through appropriate insurance policies. As in most business situations, the risks that cannot be avoided, reduced, or transferred will be retained.

BUSINESS LAW IN PRACTICE REVISITED

1. What types of property are used in ASL's business?

ASL uses real property (its land, warehouse, and anything permanently attached to the land and warehouse), tangible personal property (shelving, dividers, vehicles, customers' property), and intangible personal property (trademarks, accounts receivable). A typical business would use a similar range of property, including examples of the major classifications of property.

2. How is real property acquired by ASL and what are ASL's rights in relation to that property?

ASL acquired its land by purchase and it has the right to permit others to enter the property and use its facilities. ASL also has the right to exclude non-customers from entering the storage facility. As the owner of the land and building, ASL could lease the property to another business or sell the property. If ASL sold the property, the new owner would assume title to the land and building, as well as any personal property that has been permanently affixed to the property such as light fixtures and plumbing fixtures. As owner of the land, ASL could grant the City of Moncton an easement to allow the city to install and maintain a water line on ASL's property.

3. How did ASL acquire the personal property used in its business?

ASL acquired its property by lease (vehicles), bailment (customers' property), creation and use (business name), and dealing with customers (accounts receivable, customer records).

4. What are ASL's rights and obligations in relation to the tangible personal property that it leases or that is being stored by its customers?

For property it does not own, but of which it has temporary possession, ASL has more limited rights. For example, ASL has the right (according to legislation) to hold customers' property until they pay the agreed storage fees. If customers don't pay, ASL can sell their property to recover the outstanding fees. It is important to emphasize these rights in the agreements with customers. For property it does not own, ASL's obligations arise from the nature of the transactions involving the property and the terms of the applicable contracts and legislation. For example, ASL has a duty to treat customers' property as a reasonably competent warehouse proprietor would treat its own property, subject to the protection for ASL contained in its standard form customer contracts. For example, where a customer's stored documents suffered water damage, ASL needs to improve its treatment of this type of property. This protection will relate to ASL's conduct and its level of liability in dollar terms. This duty is complicated in self-storage, since ASL is not aware of the contents of lockers. Customers should be advised about the types of property that are suitable for ASL's facilities. In addition, ASL must take reasonable care of the leased vehicles subject to normal wear and tear. The leases will likely set out ASL's obligations, including responsibility for repairs, in considerable detail.

5. What are ASL's rights in relation to its name and logo and how can ASL protect these rights?

ASL's name and logo are registered trademarks and are a form of intellectual property protected by legislation. As an owner, ASL could license another business to use its name and logo in another location. ASL also has the right to exclude others from using the trademarks it has registered and could enforce this right by suing for damages and seeking an injunction to prevent further unauthorized use.

CHAPTER SUMMARY

One of the roles of property law is to determine what counts as property and thus can be "owned." Another role of property law is to enable owners to protect their rights in relation to property.

Property can be divided into real and personal. There are two categories of personal property: tangible, which includes goods or chattels, and intangible, which includes various contractual and statutory rights.

Ownership is acquired by purchase or manufacture (goods); creation or purchase (intellectual property); or trading (accounts receivable). Typical rights associated with the ownership of property are the right to exclude others from interfering with the property, the right to possess and use the property, and the right to transfer or dispose of the property.

A bailment is the temporary transfer of possession with no change in ownership. Key issues in bailment are the standard of care that the bailee must observe in relation to the property and the remedies that the parties have for recovering fees. Standard form contracts are a common feature of commercial bailments.

The most common types of bailments are leasing, storage, repairs, transportation, and lodging. Each has somewhat different rules for liability and remedies.

CHAPTER STUDY

Key Terms and Concepts

bailee (p. 423)

bailment (p. 423)

bailment for value (p. 424)

bailor (p. 423)

bundle of rights (p. 420)

carrier (p. 427)

easement (p. 421)

gratuitous bailment (p. 425)

innkeeper (p. 432)

intangible property (p. 416)

lease (p. 421)

licence (p. 422)

lien (p. 430)

personal property (p. 416)

real property (p. 415)

tangible property (p. 416)

trust (p. 422)

warehouseman (p. 426)

Questions for Review

1. Are all things capable of being privately owned?

2. What are some examples of real property?

3. How is personal property different from real property?

4. What are some examples of personal property?

5. How is tangible property different from intangible property?

6. How is ownership of real property acquired?

7. How is ownership of personal property acquired?

8. What is the "bundle of rights?"

9. What can the owner of personal property do with it?

10. How is ownership of intangible property protected?

11. What is a bailment?

12. What are some examples of bailments?

13. How do bailments for value differ from gratuitous bailments?

14. What is the liability of a bailee for damage to the goods?

15. How can a bailee limit the liability for damage to the goods?

16. How can a bailee for value collect fees?

17. When are contractual limits on damages not enforced?

18. What role does insurance play in bailment?

Questions for Critical Thinking

1. Personal property in the form of chattels is portable. Proving and tracking ownership and possession are challenging. Should we establish a comprehensive system of registering all chattels as we do for motor vehicles? How would such a system help in verifying and tracking? Would the benefits justify the expense?

2. Intangible personal property includes legal rights, which may be contained in legal documents such as an insurance policy or an assignment of accounts receivable. Are these rights as difficult to control as chattels? Should those documents be available for examination in a public registry?

3. Legislation governing innkeepers' liability for their guests' property was developed to deal with an environment when guests were to a large extent at the mercy of innkeepers with regard to the safety of their property. Is this the case today where most hotels are professionally owned and managed? Are guests still at risk?

4. The standard of care in a bailment depends on the type of bailment and the particular circumstances of the transaction. Therefore, the obligations of the bailor and bailee may be difficult to define in a contract in advance of a dispute. Would legislation be an easier way to set the standard?

5. The self-storage industry is growing rapidly as businesses and individuals need extra space to store their excess property. Does the rental of a storage locker fit the definition of bailment? Are there specific issues in this type of transaction that require a different set of rules from those in place for other bailment-type situations?

6. Commercial bailees generally try to minimize their liability in a standard form contract. They justify these low limits as a means of controlling risk and keeping their prices competitive. Is there a market opportunity for more generous liability terms? For example, could a storage business increase market share by accepting a greater risk of liability than its competitors and charging a higher price?

Situations for Discussion

1. Green Acres Ltd. operates a greenhouse on a large lot in Calgary. The lot immediately adjacent to Green Acres is owned by a car dealership and the two properties are separated by a steel fence that was in place when Green Acres purchased its lot. While planning an expansion of its greenhouse, Green Acres Ltd. discovered that the steel fence between the properties intrudes onto Green Acres Ltd's property by nearly three metres. To make matters worse, the car dealership paved the area on its side of the fence over nine years ago and uses the space to park its fleet of used vehicles. When Green Acres approached the dealership about the problem, the owner suggested they wait until spring to deal with the problem. How should Green Acres proceed?[47]

2. Clancy's Cars Ltd. engaged Railco Ltd. to transport several motor vehicles from Montreal to Halifax. The vehicles were to be delivered to Clancy's on Wednesday, but they were delayed. On Saturday, an employee of Railco informed Clancy's that the vehicles had arrived at Railco's facilities in Halifax and would be delivered to Clancy's on Monday. Over the weekend, a violent storm hit Halifax. Although the vehicles were parked in an area for safekeeping, they were severely damaged in the storm. When Clancy's claimed damages, Railco argued that the storm was so severe it was an "act of God."[48] Who is responsible for the damage to the vehicles?

3. Black was looking to buy a quality used luxury vehicle. He found a 2014 Audi at Dexter's Audi that met his needs. He examined the car on several occasions and took it for a couple of test drives. Discussions with Dexter's salesperson,

---

47 Based, in part, on *1215565 Alberta Ltd. v. Canadian Wellhead Isolation Corp.*, 2012 ABQB 145.

48 Based, in part, on *Carroll Pontiac Buick Ltd v Searail Cargo Surveys Ltd*, 2005 NSSM 12.

White, were productive, and Black and White were close to making a deal. Black wanted to have the car inspected by an expert mechanic before finally agreeing to buy it, so he asked to have the car over a long weekend so he could drive it further and complete the inspection. White agreed, but required Black to sign a draft agreement and pay a deposit on the purchase price. Black signed the document "subject to satisfactory inspection." Black took the car, but before the inspection could be done, he encountered a deer on the highway. He swerved to avoid the deer, lost control, went off the road, and hit a tree at high speed. Black was not injured but the car was demolished.[49] Was this a bailment situation? Who is responsible for the vehicle?

4. Ying leased a machine to haul large logs in her lumbering business. The lease required Ying to keep the machine in good repair and fully insured, and to return it at the end of the lease in its original condition, subject to "normal wear and tear." The machine never worked very well. Ying ran up large repair bills and began to suspect the machine was not heavy enough for the needs of her business. When she contacted the leasing company, she was reminded that the lessor had made no promises about performance of the equipment. Ying is thinking about stopping her lease payments and insurance premiums and leasing a heavier machine from another dealer. She needs that heavier machine to maintain profitable levels of production. What factors should she consider? What would you advise her to do? Would your opinion be different if Ying had instead leased a truck for her personal use?

5. Ying took her logging machine in for repairs. A week later she got a call from the shop to tell her that the machine was fixed and the bill was $4500. Ying had left strict instructions with the shop that she must approve all work before it was done. What rules of contract determine whether Ying is obligated to pay the bill? If she refuses, what are the shop's remedies? What safeguards and risks are involved in those remedies for Ying? Would the result be different for a consumer contract?[50]

6. Roach owned a truck with a large crane attached. Roach took the truck to Vern's Auto to have the crane removed with the intention of mounting it on another vehicle in the future. Vern's allowed Roach to leave the crane in its yard, assuring him it would be safe. A few months later, Roach decided to sell the crane. When he went to get the crane, it was gone. Vern's had no idea what had happened to it, and because the company had charged nothing for storing the crane, it was not interested in finding out.[51] Is Vern's responsible for the missing crane? What are the determining factors? What information is missing? What steps should Roach and Vern's have taken to safeguard the crane?

7. Horst is a collector of hockey memorabilia. He is particularly interested in hockey sticks that have been autographed by well-known players in the National Hockey League. When Horst checked on eBay, he found many autographed hockey sticks for sale, including several signed by his favourite players. He is prepared to pay the going rate, but wants to be sure that the autographs are authentic and that the current owners acquired the sticks legitimately. Horst has heard of organizations that purport to authenticate autographs, but has also heard of many "fake" autographs that were authenticated. What legal issues should Horst consider? How should he manage the risks facing him?

8. Canfor hired B.C. Rail to transport wood pulp from the interior of British Columbia to a shipping terminal for eventual delivery to a customer in Scotland. The contract between Canfor and B.C. Rail specified that the railcars would be clean and the pulp delivered free from contamination. Canfor insisted on wood-lined boxcars and also routinely inspected and swept out the cars before loading bales of pulp. When the pulp arrived in Scotland, it was contaminated with wood splinters and rejected by the customer. Canfor had to compensate its customer and pay for transporting the pulp back to B.C.[52] Can Canfor recover its losses from B.C. Rail? Explain.

49 Based on *Black v Dexter's Autohaus*, 2008 NSSC 274.
50 Based, in part, on *Gary Auto Repair v Velk*, 2010 ONSC 3183.

51 Based on *Lowe (DJ) (1980) Ltd v Roach* (1994), 131 NSR (2d) 268 (SC), aff'd (1995), 138 NSR (2d) 79 (CA).
52 Based on *B.C. Rail Ltd v Canadian Forest Products Ltd*, 2005 BCCA 369.

18

OBJECTIVES

After studying this chapter, you should have an understanding of

- the nature of intellectual property
- the rights that attach to intellectual property
- how intellectual property is acquired
- how to protect the intellectual property assets of an organization

© David Pearson/Alamy

INTELLECTUAL PROPERTY

BUSINESS LAW IN PRACTICE

Since graduating from university three years ago, Estelle Perez has been employed in the engineering department of ELEX Technologies Inc., a small manufacturer of electronic products including sensors, mobile phones, and wireless routers. Estelle's main responsibility has been to devise better and more efficient production methods. Although she likes her job with ELEX, Estelle's ultimate goal is to start a company that would focus on her real passion, namely invention and design. Driven by this ambition, Estelle spends virtually every evening and weekend experimenting with her own highly innovative product ideas.

Though ELEX is a successful company, it faces many challenges. For example, last year alone, as much as 15 percent of its products malfunctioned and were returned by customers, resulting in lost sales and profits. ELEX confirmed that product breakdown was being caused by electrostatic discharge (ESD) during shipping, a huge problem for electronic manufacturers across the board. Estelle concluded that the main industry solution relied upon by ELEX, that of using plastic packaging to reduce ESD, had been neither efficient (witness ELEX's failure rate) nor environmentally friendly (because all that plastic simply ended up in landfills). Estelle has come up with a seemingly optimal solution. She has designed protective packaging made of recyclable conductive paper, which has the ability to absorb the damaging effects of static electricity.[1] Estelle's design called for the static protection to be woven into the fibre of the paper, which could, in turn, be converted into boxes, bags, and envelopes. She has even figured out how to add colour options to the packaging, thereby providing customization opportunities to suit the commercial customer's individual marketing requirements.

Estelle believes in her new product and would like to quit her job with ELEX in order to work full time on it. However, she also worries about her lack of experience on the business side of product development and how she could ever keep her invention a secret while exploring the possibility of funding. Also, assuming the product is successful, Estelle is concerned that she will be required to share the proceeds of her invention with ELEX.

---

1 The idea for this Business Law in Practice is based on patented technology developed by Yonghao Ni, a professor and director of the University of New Brunswick's Limerick Pulp and Paper Research Centre. See <www.knowcharge.com>.

Estelle knows that the future of her anticipated new product will depend, in part, on marketing and she has already come up with a catchy name for her product—"Chargeless." She does not think anyone else is using that name except a financial services company that deploys it as part of the slogan, "We charge less." As her name has a different spelling and is in an entirely different business sector, Estelle concludes that she will be okay in using "Chargeless" as her product moniker.

1. Is Estelle's idea a patentable invention?

2. Who owns the rights to Estelle's invention—Estelle or ELEX?

3. How can Estelle protect her idea while she seeks funding from potential lenders and investors?

4. Is Estelle entitled to use the name "Chargeless" for her product, and should she do anything to protect the name?

Introduction

Intellectual property is a term often used to describe the results of intellectual or creative processes.[2] Put another way, the term is used for describing ideas or ways of expressing ideas. Some common business examples of intellectual property are:

- recipes and formulas for making products.
- manufacturing processes.
- methods of extracting minerals.
- advertising jingles.
- business and marketing plans.
- the distinctive name given to a product or service.

Estelle's method of weaving static protection into the fibre of paper and the name for her product are also examples.

The term "intellectual property"[3] is also used to describe the "bundle of rights" that people have regarding their ideas or the ways in which they are expressed. These rights are rewards or incentives for creating and developing ideas. There are differing rights in intellectual property as the law gives varying types of protection to its many forms. The main categories of intellectual property laws are patents, trademarks, copyrights, industrial designs, and confidential (business) information.[4] (See Figure 18.1 on page 464 for a comparison of these forms.) There are other laws, however, that provide protection for specific types of intellectual property. For example, there are laws

Intellectual property

The results of the creative process, such as ideas, the expression of ideas, formulas, schemes, trademarks, and the like; also refers to the protection attached to ideas through patent, copyright, trademark, industrial design, and other similar laws.

---

2 The authors gratefully acknowledge the suggestions of Professor Wayne Renke of the Faculty of Law, University of Alberta, and Professor Peter Lown, director of the Alberta Law Reform Institute, in reviewing an earlier draft of this chapter.

3 The term "intellectual property" is used to refer to both intangibles—such as ideas and their expression, formulas, schemes, trademarks, and the like—and rights that may attach to these intangibles. However, not all intellectual property can be technically called "property," as the basis for protection is not always "property" principles but principles of contract and tort as well as specific statutory provisions.

4 The term "confidential information" includes a broad range of information, such as government secrets and private personal information. In this text, the term "confidential business information" is used to distinguish information of a commercial nature from other types of information.

that protect plant varieties,[5] integrated circuit topographies,[6] and personality rights.[7]

Intellectual property is a necessary and critical asset in many industries, as illustrated in these examples:

- patents protect inventions and are essential to businesses in the pharmaceutical, electronics, chemical, and manufacturing industries, as patents may be used to exclude others from using new technology.
- industrial designs protect the appearance of useful articles against copying and are relevant to businesses that offer goods to consumers.
- trademarks serve to distinguish the goods or services of one provider from those of another and are essential to all businesses that sell goods or services to the public.
- copyright prevents the copying of certain works and is the basis for businesses involved in art, publishing, music, communications, and software, as copyright provides the basis for a saleable product.
- the law governing confidentiality is the means of protecting such information as marketing plans, customer lists, databases, and price lists, and is crucial to all businesses.[8]

Intellectual property offers both opportunities and challenges to business. Businesses can gain a competitive advantage by developing new products, innovative business methods, and creative brand names. Also, they can exploit these things by assigning or licensing their use to other businesses. However, the development of various technologies, such as photocopiers, tape recorders, video cameras, and computers, has made it easier for others to "take" intellectual property.[9]

This chapter explores the creation, acquisition, and protection of intellectual property.

Creation of Intellectual Property Rights

Estelle's intellectual property comprises the method for weaving static protection into the fibre, the name of her product, and any written materials such as drawings, plans, and brochures. Various aspects of her intellectual property may qualify for protection under different legal regimes.

Patents

Patent

A monopoly to make, use, or sell an invention.

Estelle's method for protecting electronic products may qualify for **patent** protection. A patent is a statutory right[10] that provides protection for inventions.

---

5   *Plant Breeders' Rights Act*, SC 1990, c 20. This Act provides 18-year patent-like protection for distinct new plant varieties.

6   *Integrated Circuit Topography Act*, SC 1990, c 37. This act provides 10-year protection for layout designs embedded in semiconductor chips or circuit boards (e.g., microchips).

7   Personality rights, or the right not to have one's name or likeness appropriated for another's gain, are protected under tort actions, trademark legislation, and privacy legislation, such as British Columbia's *Privacy Act*, RSBC 1996, c 373.

8   Sheldon Burshtein, "Executives remain unaware of the value of intellectual property assets", *The Lawyers Weekly* (27 June 1997) 23.

9   In recognition of the difficulties in policing copyright infringement of music, there is a levy on blank tapes and compact discs. See *Copyright Act*, RSC 1985, c C-42, s 82 (1).

10   The federal government has jurisdiction to make laws concerning patents, copyrights, and trademarks. See *Constitution Act*, 1867, s 91.

Patents Defined

The *Patent Act*[11] defines an invention as "any new and useful art, process, machine, manufacture or composition of matter or any new and useful improvement[12] in any art, process, machine, manufacture or composition of matter." The definition is very broad and encompasses a number of different kinds of inventions such as

- processes or methods (e.g., a pay-per-use billing system, a system for applying a selective herbicide to improve crop yield, a method of cleaning carpets).
- machines or apparatuses (e.g., computer hardware, a hay rake, a vacuum cleaner).
- products or compositions of matter (e.g., pharmaceuticals, chemical compounds, microorganisms).

Estelle's invention may qualify for patent protection as a new and improved method for protecting electronic products from electrostatic discharge.

Substances intended for food or medicine, as well as the processes for producing them, are patentable. The question of whether new life forms created as the result of genetic engineering should be patentable has been the subject of much controversy.

CASE

Monsanto v Schmeiser, 2004 SCC 34, [2004] 1 SCR 902

THE BUSINESS CONTEXT: In 2002, in *Harvard College v Canada (Commissioner of Patents)*,[13] the Supreme Court of Canada held by a narrow 5-to-4 margin that higher life forms are not patentable. Although the process for genetically modifying cells was held to be patentable, the end result, a mouse susceptible to cancer, was not. The decision was a large disappointment to many in the biotechnology industry, as Canada's major trading partners, including the United States, Europe, Australia, and Japan, permit such patents. The decision also created uncertainty as to the scope of protection afforded to biotechnology-related inventions.

FACTUAL BACKGROUND: Percy Schmeiser is a Saskatchewan farmer who grows canola. Monsanto is a multinational firm specializing in biotechnologies used in agriculture. In the 1990s, Monsanto introduced Roundup Ready canola, a variety of canola containing genetically modified genes and cells patented by Monsanto. Roundup Ready canola is resistant to Roundup, a pesticide, which means that the canola plants can be sprayed with Roundup to kill weeds but not harm the crop. Monsanto licensed its Roundup Ready canola to farmers for a fee, provided the farmers purchased the canola seeds from an authorized Monsanto agent.

Schmeiser did not purchase Roundup Ready canola seeds, nor did he obtain a licence from Monsanto. By chance, he discovered some Roundup Ready canola growing on his property. It is unclear how the canola got onto his property, but it is possible that the seeds blew there from a neighbour's land. Schmeiser collected and cultivated the seeds and most of his 1998 canola crop comprised Roundup Ready canola. Once his activities were detected, Monsanto sued him for patent infringement.

(Continued)

---

11 RSC 1985, c P-4, s 2.
12 Ninety percent of all patents are for improvements to existing patented inventions. See Canadian Intellectual Property Office, *A Guide to Patents*, online: Canadian Intellectual Property Office <http://www.ic.gc .ca/eic/site/cipointernet-internetopic.nsf/eng/h_wr03652.html?Open&wt_src=cipo-patent-main&wt _cxt=learn>.
13 2002 SCC 76, [2002] 4 SCR 45.

THE LEGAL QUESTION: Had Schmeiser, by collecting and planting the seeds and harvesting and selling the plants, infringed Monsanto's patents relating to genetically modified canola?

RESOLUTION: By a narrow 5-to-4 margin, the Supreme Court of Canada held that Monsanto's patents were valid and that Schmeiser had infringed them. Schmeiser had argued that he had not "used" the invention by growing canola plants because the plants are not covered by Monsanto's patents, only the plant cells containing the modified gene. The majority disagreed. The court held that the plants were composed of modified plant cells containing the modified genes, and therefore growing the modified plants constituted use of the invention. The majority used the following analogy: "If an infringing use were alleged in building a structure with patented Lego blocks, it would be no bar to a finding of infringement that only the blocks were used and not the whole structure." In essence, the court confirmed the patentability of cells and genes, and held that the rights in patented genes and cells extend to plants containing them.

CRITICAL ANALYSIS: Are there any concerns with manipulating genes in order to obtain better weed control or higher yields? How does this decision support the Canadian biotechnology industry?

POSTSCRIPT: In 2005, more of the genetically modified canola appeared on Percy and Louise

What are the benefits of granting patents for life forms?

Schmeiser's farm. They pulled it out themselves and sent Monsanto a bill for $600. Monsanto agreed to pay provided the Schmeisers signed a release stating they would never talk about the agreement. The Schmeisers refused and sued in small-claims court. In 2008, the case settled with Monsanto paying the Schmeisers $660 but without the Schmeisers signing an agreement stopping them from talking about the terms of the settlement.

Source: Matt Hartley, "Grain farmer claims moral victory in seed battle", *The Globe and Mail* (20 March 2008) A3.

Exclusions from Patent Protection

There are also exclusions or exceptions to what may be patented. The most common are the following:

- *things that receive exclusive protection under other areas of the law.* For example, computer programs (i.e., software) are not patentable, as they receive protection under copyright law. They could, however, receive patent protection as part of a broader patent, as, for example, a computerized method of controlling the operation of a plant.[14]
- *things that do not meet the definition of a patent.* For example, scientific principles, natural phenomena, and abstract theorems are "discoveries"

---

14 David Vaver, *Intellectual Property Law: Copyrights, Patents, Trademarks*, 2d ed (Toronto: Irwin Law, 2011) at 314.

as opposed to inventions and are therefore not patentable. A practical application of a theory could, however, qualify for protection.

- *things that are, for policy reasons, not patentable.* For example, methods of medical or surgical treatment are not patentable; neither are illicit objects. Also, historically, business methods such as franchising arrangements, accounting methods, insurance schemes, tax loopholes, and protocols for interacting with customers have not been patentable.[15] However, the Canadian Intellectual Property Office guidelines state that business methods[16] are not automatically excluded from patent protection, and a number of business methods patents have been issued in Canada. The following case is the first legal decision in Canada upholding the validity of a business methods patent.

CASE

Canada (Attorney General) v Amazon.com Inc 2011 FCA 328, [2012] 2 FCR 459

BUSINESS CONTEXT: In both Canada and the United States, there has been much debate about the patentability of methods of conducting business.[17] The following decision provides some clarity on the law in Canada and brings it more in line with the law in the United States.

FACTUAL BACKGROUND: In 1998, Amazon.com applied for a patent for an invention entitled "Method and system for placing a purchase order via a communications network." The invention is a system that allows a purchaser to reduce the number of interactions when ordering over the Internet. A purchaser can visit a website, enter her user and payment information and then be given an identifier that can be stored as a cookie on her computer. On a subsequent visit to the website, a server will be able to recognize the customer's computer with the identifying cookie and retrieve the user and payment information. By using this system, a customer could purchase an item with a single click of the mouse. The Canadian Intellectual Property Office rejected Amazon's "one-click" patent application on the basis that "a claimed invention which in form or in substance amounts to a business method is excluded from patentability" or alternatively, the claimed subject matter did not fall within the meaning of "art" in the *Patent Act*. Amazon.com appealed to the Federal Court.

LEGAL QUESTION: Is a business method patentable?

RESOLUTION: The Federal Court held that there is no authority in Canadian law to exclude business methods from patentability. A business method can be patentable under appropriate circumstances. To be patentable, an invention must fall within one of the categories of art, process, machine, manufacture, or composition of matter. The category for business methods is "art." Relying on the Supreme Court of Canada's decision in *Shell Oil Co v Commissioner of Patents*,[18] the court stated that to be a patentable art, the subject matter of the claim (a) must not be a disembodied idea but have a method of practical application; (b) must be

(Continued)

---

15 Business-methods patents have been allowed in the United States. See *State Street Bank & Trust v Signature Financial Group*, 149 F (3d) 1368 (Fed Cir 1998). However, in 2010, the U.S. Supreme Court made it much more difficult to obtain such patents. See *In re Bilski*, 545 F (3d) 943 (Fed Cir 2008) aff'd sub nom *Bilski v Kappos*, 130 S Ct 3218; *Alice Corp v CLS Bank*, No 13-298, slip op, 134 S Ct 2347 (USSC June 19, 2014).

16 Canadian Intellectual Property Office, *Manual of Patent Office Practice*, at s 12.04. 02, online: Canadian Intellectual Property Office <http://www.cipo.ic.gc.ca/eic/site/cipoInternet-Internetopic.nsf/eng/h_wr00720.html>.

17 Alan Macek, "Courts wrestle with business method patents", *The Lawyers Weekly* (1 October 2010) 13.

18 [1982] 2 SCR 536, 67 CPR (2d) 1.

a new and inventive method of applying skill and knowledge; and (c) must have a commercially useful result. The court applied the test and held Amazon's one-click application to be patentable. The Commissioner of Patents appealed.

The Federal Court of Appeal largely affirmed the lower court's legal analysis. However, the Court granted the Commissioner's appeal and ordered that the one-click application be sent back to the Canadian Intellectual Property Office for reevaluation. The court ruled that the lower court had insufficient evidence to determine whether the one-click application constitutes patentable subject matter.

CRITICAL ANALYSIS: This decision affirms that there is no legal rationale for excluding business

methods from patent protection. What will be the likely impact of this decision on business sectors such as insurance, banking, financial services, and securities?

POSTSCRIPT: The Canadian Intellectual Property Office ultimately allowed Amazon's patent application.

Requirements for Patentability

Not all inventions, however wonderful, are patentable. A patent will be granted only for an invention that is new, useful, and unobvious.

New The invention must be new or novel. An invention, however, need not be absolutely new.[19] It is "new" if it has not been disclosed publicly. This means that any public disclosure, public use, or sale of the invention prior to filing for a patent renders the invention "old" and unpatentable.[20] For example, displaying the new product at a trade show, distributing marketing brochures that describe or display the product, or advertising the product in a way that reveals the invention[21] is a disclosure and a bar to obtaining a patent.

There is, however, a one-year grace period. If the inventor or someone who derived knowledge from the inventor makes a disclosure within the year preceding the filing of the application, this will not operate as public disclosure.

Estelle needs to determine whether her new and improved method of protecting electronic products from electrostatic discharge has been disclosed to the public in some manner. She can have a patent agent search relevant literature so that an opinion can be formed as to whether her invention is novel.

Useful An invention must solve some practical problem, and it must actually work—that is, it must do what it purports to do. An invention that does not work is useless and unpatentable. The invention must have industrial value, although it need not be commercially successful. The invention must have practical use as opposed to

---

19 *Supra* note 14 at 320.
20 Also of relevance to the issue of novelty are applications for patents filed in other countries. Canada is a signatory to both the Paris Convention for the Protection of Industrial Property and the Patent Cooperation Treaty. An applicant, by filing in a member country, can claim this date in other countries so long as the corresponding applications are filed within one year. This means that the earlier date becomes the disclosure date for purposes of establishing novelty.
21 Ronald Dimock, *Canadian Marketing Law* (Toronto: Richard DeBoo, 1991) at 3–4.

being a mere scientific curiosity. For example, a perpetual motion machine[22] lacks utility, as it does not have a practical use. Estelle's product meets the requirement of usefulness as it solves an identifiable, industry problem and it apparently works.

Unobvious The third requirement relates to "inventiveness." It means that there must be some ingenuity or inventive step involved in the invention.[23] Changes to something that would be obvious to someone skilled in the art to which the invention pertains would not be patentable. For example, simply using a different material for making a product would not be patentable, as it does not involve an inventive step.

The test is difficult to apply in practice because it involves ascertaining the state of the art or knowledge prior to the invention and analyzing whether the invention was merely the obvious, next step in the state of the knowledge or instead involves an inventive step.

The question of whether Estelle's new method is unobvious can be answered only by asking someone knowledgeable in the field of electrostatic discharge (ESD). The **patent agent** who searches the literature to determine whether an invention is novel will also express an opinion on whether the invention is obvious. That said, the industry's problems with ESD are indicative that Estelle's invention is unobvious and involves an inventive step.

Patent Protection and Application

Patent protection, unlike some other intellectual property rights, does not arise automatically. An application for a patent must be filed with the Canadian Intellectual Property Office.[24] Timing of the application is a critical concern because the patent regime is based on a first-to-file system.[25] This means, for example, that if more than one person has independently invented the same process, method, or machine, the Canadian Intellectual Property Office gives priority to the first person to file the application.

The inventor is generally the first owner of the invention and thus the person entitled to apply for a patent. The *Patent Act* does not contain specific provisions for the ownership of inventions created by employees in the course of employment; generally, however, an employee will be the owner unless (1) the employee was specifically hired to produce the invention and makes the invention in the course of employment, or (2) there is an express or implied agreement that precludes the employee from claiming ownership of inventions relating to and developed in the course of employment.[26] As Estelle has not been employed to produce a method to protect electronic products, and as she invented the method on her own time, she is the "inventor" and entitled to apply for a patent. Assuming she has not signed an agreement to the contrary, she has no obligation to share the invention and its proceeds with her employer. Employers should consider whether employment contracts, as well as contracts with consultants, address the ownership of all intellectual property including inventions produced in the course of employment.

The preparation of a patent application is a highly complex matter and is normally done by a patent agent, who has particular expertise in this area. The

Patent agent

A professional trained in patent law and practice who can assist in the preparation of a patent application.

---

22 *Supra* note 14 at 340.
23 See *Apotex Inc v Sanof Synthelabo Canada Inc*, 2008 SCC 61, [2008] 3 SCR 265 for the test for "obviousness."
24 The Canadian Intellectual Property Office's patent database can be accessed at <http://brevets-patents.ic.gc.ca/opic-cipo/cpd/eng/introduction.html>.
25 Until 1989, Canada's patent regime was based on a first-to-invent system.
26 *Supra* note 14 at 368–69.

application has two main parts: one part describes how the product is made or the best way to perform the process or method. This is known as the **specifications**. The other part is known as the **claims**.[27] These are the sequentially numbered, single-sentence definitions of the invention. This part in effect defines the exclusive rights enjoyed by the patent holder. In short, the specifications tell the reader how to put the invention into practice after the patent expires. The claims tell the reader what he cannot do prior to the expiry of the patent.

The application is examined[28] by the Canadian Intellectual Property Office to ensure that the invention has not already been invented and that the application complies with the *Patent Act*. If the application is successful, a patent is issued upon the payment of the required fee. The word "patented" and the patent number may be put on all manufactured goods. Marking is not mandatory, but it is legally useful, as it notifies others of the existence of a right and reduces the number of "innocent" infringers. Often manufacturers will put the term "patent pending" or "patent applied for" on their products before the patent is issued. This warns others that a patent may eventually be issued for these products and they could be liable to pay damages for infringing the patent once the patent is granted. A patent gives the inventor the right to exclude others from making, selling, or using the invention to which the patent relates for a period of 20 years from the date of filing the application so long as the appropriate maintenance fees[29] are paid.

Patents are national in nature in that they exist only in the country in which the applications are made and granted.[30] The rights under a Canadian patent do not apply elsewhere. For example, an owner of a Canadian patent cannot stop the use or sale of the invention in the United States, unless the owner also has a U.S. patent.

Estelle's method of weaving static protection into the fibre of paper qualifies for patent protection if the method is considered to be new, useful, and unobvious. If it is patentable, she will need to apply for a patent and pay the requisite fee. The patent process requires her to disclose (disclosure is discussed in the case below) her discovery to the world; in return, she receives a monopoly over the invention for 20 years. The patent process is costly and time consuming, so Estelle needs to evaluate the costs and benefits of pursuing this route.

CASE

Teva Canada Ltd. v Pfizer Canada Inc., 2012 SCC 60, [2012] 3 SCR 625.

BUSINESS CONTEXT: A pharmaceutical company can make millions of dollars per year from a single patented drug. It is not surprising that competitors, in an effort to enter the lucrative drug market, challenge the validity of drug patents.

FACTUAL BACKGROUND: Teva Canada wanted to market a generic version of the drug,

---

27 For an approach for interpreting and defining claims in patents, see *Free World Trust v Électro Santé Inc*, 2000 SCC 66, [2000] 2 SCR 1024; *Whirlpool Corp v Maytag Corp*, 2000 SCC 68, [2000] 2 SCR 1116; *Whirlpool Corp v Camco Inc*, 2000 SCC 67, [2000] 2 SCR 1067.

28 *Supra* note 11, s 35(1). An application for a patent is not automatically examined. The applicant must specifically request that an examination be done. Requests must be made within five years of filing the application, or the application will be deemed abandoned. The delay for requesting an examination gives the applicant a period of time to test the market for the invention.

29 Annual maintenance fees vary depending on how long a patent has been issued and whether the holder of the patent is a small or large entity. The amount paid by a large entity is usually double that paid by a small entity.

30 There is no such thing as an international patent. International treaties, however, have simplified the procedures for obtaining patents in different countries.

Viagra. In response, Pfizer, the owner of the Viagra patent, commenced an action called a patented Medicines Notice of Compliance, which stopped Teva from receiving approval to market generic Viagra until a court assessed the validity of the patent. In the lawsuit, Teva alleged, among other claims, that Pfizer's Viagra patent was invalid for insufficiency of disclosure. The *Patent Act* requires that a patent must correctly and fully describe the invention and its operation or use.

LEGAL QUESTION: Did Pfizer disclose its invention sufficiently in the patent?

RESOLUTION: Pfizer's patent indicated that four broad groups of compounds and an especially preferred group of compounds that included the compound sildenafil were effective in the treatment of erectile dysfunction. The Court, however, in examining Pfizer's actual work, found that Pfizer had only conducted tests that demonstrated that sildenafil was effective. None of the other compounds had been shown to be effective. The specifications in the patent, however, failed to indicate that sildenafil was the effective compound. The skilled person, having only the specifications, could not put the invention into practice without doing further research to determine the effective ingredient. The Court held

What is the effect on the patent holder when a patent is found to be invalid?

that the patent failed to meet the disclosure requirements of the *Patent Act* and was invalid. In reaching its conclusion, the court provided a warning to patentees to make full disclosure, ". . . Pfizer gained a benefit from the Act—exclusive monopoly rights—while withholding disclosure in spite of its disclosure obligations under the Act. As a matter of policy and sound statutory interpretation, patentees cannot be allowed to 'game' the system in this way."

CRITICAL ANALYSIS: What is the likely impact of this decision on future patent applications? Why is full disclosure so important in patents? What is the likely impact of this decision on patent-dominated industries?

PART FIVE

Industrial Designs

The *Industrial Design Act*[31] provides protection for the appearance of mass-produced (i.e., numbering more than 50) useful articles or objects.[32]

Industrial Designs Defined

The term **industrial design** is not defined in the Act. An industrial design is usually taken to mean a feature of shape, configuration, pattern, or ornament, or any combination of these, that in a finished article appeals to and is judged solely by the eye.[33] Put another way, an industrial design protects

Industrial design

The visual features of shape, configuration, pattern, ornamentation, or any combination of these applied to a finished article of manufacture.

31 RSC 1985, c I-9.

32 Works that qualify as industrial designs may also qualify for protection under the *Copyright Act*. To address the overlap, copyright protection is not given to designs applied to useful articles that are produced in quantities of more than 50. See *Copyright Act*, RSC 1985, c C-42, s 64(2), as am by *An Act to Amend the Copyright Act and Other Acts in Consequence Thereof*, SC 1988, c 65.

33 Martin PJ Kratz, *Canada's Intellectual Property Law in a Nutshell*, 2d ed (Scarborough, ON: Carswell, 2010) at 125.

What features of consumer goods may be protected by industrial design legislation?

the shapes or ornamental aspects of a product but does not protect the functional aspect.

Typical examples of industrial designs are the shape and ornamentations applied to toys, vehicles, furniture, and household utensils, and the patterns applied to wallpaper or fabric. Also, the electronic or computer-generated icons displayed on computer monitors, cellular telephones, radio pagers, home appliances, and the like may be registered as industrial designs.[34]

Requirements for Registration

To be registered, an industrial design must be original and novel. The originality standard is lower than the standard of inventiveness found in patents. A high degree of ingenuity or creativity is not necessary. That said, an industrial design must be substantially different from prior art, be more than a simple variation, and contain some spark of inspiration.[35]

An industrial design must be novel. Disclosure or use of the industrial design or of articles displaying, bearing, or embodying the industrial design is a bar to registration unless it was within the year prior to filing the application.[36]

Registration Process and Protection

As with patents, industrial design protection does not arise automatically. An application, usually drafted by a patent agent, must be submitted to the Canadian Intellectual Property Office.

The owner of the rights in the design is entitled to make the application. The designer is the owner unless the design was ordered and paid for by another. The application normally consists of a written description and a graphic depiction, photograph, or drawing. If the application meets the requirements of the Act, a certificate of registration will be issued.

The registration gives the owner the exclusive right to make, import, or sell any article in respect to which the design is registered. Also, the owner of the design can stop competitors from manufacturing and selling a design that looks confusingly similar. An industrial design registration lasts for 10 years.

---

34 Wing T Yan, "Screen display icons protectable as industrial designs", *The Lawyers Weekly* (17 November 2000) 14.
35 *Bodum USA, Inc. v Trudeau Coporation*, 2012 FC 1128, [2012] 105 CPR (4ᵗʰ) 88.
36 *Supra* note 33 at 68. International conventions also apply to the application for industrial designs.

It is not mandatory to mark the design to indicate that it is registered; however, doing so will enhance the owner's rights in a successful infringement action. If the product is marked, a court may award monetary damages for infringement. If there is no marking, the court is limited to awarding an injunction. The proper marking is a capital D inside a circle (Ⓓ), set next to the name of the design owner.

Trademarks

Estelle's intellectual property also includes the name of her product—Chargeless. This aspect of her intellectual property may qualify for protection under trademark law.

Trademark Defined

A **trademark**[37] is a word, symbol, design, or any combination of these used to distinguish a person's products or services from those of others. Its function is to indicate the source or origin of the goods or services.

Theoretically, a trademark could be anything, but it is usually one of the following:

- a word (e.g., Exxon, Xerox, Lego, Billabong).
- words (e.g., The Body Shop, The Pink Panther, Shake'n Bake).
- a slogan (e.g., "Just do it," "Mr. Christie, you make good cookies").
- a design (e.g., McDonald's golden arches, Disney's cartoon characters).
- a series of letters (e.g., ABC for a laundry detergent, BMW for a car).
- numbers (e.g., 6/49 for lottery services, 900 service for telephone operations).
- a symbol (e.g., a series of Chinese characters, Nike's "swoosh").
- a **distinguishing guise** (e.g., Coca-Cola bottle, Perrier bottle).
- any combination of the above (e.g., the words "London Fog" with a depiction of Big Ben for a brand of clothing).

A colour is not registrable as a trademark, but colour[38] (such as pink for insulation) may be claimed as part of a trademark. Smells or odours have not been registered as trademarks in Canada; sounds, however, are registrable.[39]

Trade Names

Closely related to trademarks are trade names, which also receive protection under trademark law. A **trade name** is the name under which a business is carried on. It may be the name of a corporation, a partnership, or a sole proprietorship.

Trademark

A word, symbol, design, or any combination of these used to distinguish the source of goods or services.

Distinguishing guise

A shaping of wares or their container, or a mode of wrapping or packaging wares.

Trade name

The name under which a sole proprietorship, a partnership, or a corporation does business.

---

37 In addition to the type of trademark used by a business to identify goods or services, another category of trademark is the certification mark. This mark is used to indicate that a product or service conforms to a particular standard. For example, the "Woolmark" is a certification mark used by the Wool Bureau of Canada to identify garments made from pure new wool, and the Canadian Standards Association uses "CSA Approved" to indicate products of a certain standard. Certification marks are not owned by producers; thus, they are not used to distinguish one producer from another. Instead, the mark certifies that a product meets a defined standard.

38 *Supra* note 14 at 469. The validity of registering smells as trademarks is uncertain.

39 Following a Federal Court order setting aside the Registrar of Trade-marks' refusal to grant Metro-Goldwyn-Mayer Lion Corp.'s trademark application for the sound of a lion roaring, the Canadian Intellectual Property Office published a notice indicating that it will accept applications for the registration of sound marks. See "Trade-mark consisting of a sound" CIPO, March 28, 2012, at <http://www.ic.gc.ca/eic/site/cipointernet -internetopic.nsf/eng/wr03439.html>.

An important connection between trade names and trademarks is that the adoption of a trademark may prevent the use of an identical or similar trade name, and vice versa—that is, the adoption of a trade name can prevent the adoption of a trademark. For example, if Estelle calls her business Chargeless, then her adoption of this as a trade name prevents others from using the name or a similar one as a trademark in the same line of business.

Common Law Trademarks

Trademarks may be registered or unregistered. If unregistered, they are often referred to as common law trademarks. Whether registered or unregistered, trademarks receive protection under both the common law and the *Trade-marks Act*.[40]

A common law trademark comes into existence when a business simply adopts and uses it. If Estelle simply starts using Chargeless to describe her product, then she has a common law trademark. Such a trademark is considered to be part of the goodwill of a company, and rights attach to it in much the same manner as they do to registered trademarks. Infringement of the trademark by a competitor using the same or a similar trademark can be addressed through the tort of passing off.

The rights that attach to common law trademarks, however, tend to be more restrictive, and there are certain advantages associated with registration. A common law trademark has rights only in the geographic areas in which it has been used and in areas into which the reputation of the owner has spread. For example, Estelle can prevent others from using her trademark or a similar one only in the areas where her reputation is known. A registered trademark enjoys protection throughout the country. Registration is also advantageous in that it creates a presumption of ownership and validity.

Trademarks and Domain Names

Domain name

The unique address of a website.

A **domain name** is essentially an Internet address. It consists of two or more elements divided into a hierarchical field separated by a "dot." To the right of the dot is an abbreviation describing the root identifier or a top-level domain (TLD). A TLD is either generic (such as .com, .org, or .net) or country-specific (such as .ca for Canada or .uk for the United Kingdom). To the left of the dot is the second-level domain, which is usually a business name, trademark, or other identifier. For example, in Nelson.com, "com" is the TLD and "Nelson" is the second-level domain.

Domain names are controlled by various organizations that act as registrars. Generic domain names such as .com, .org, .net, and .biz are controlled by the Internet Corporation for Assigned Names and Numbers (ICANN), a U.S. nonprofit corporation.[41] The country-specific domain names are assigned by national authorities. For example, in Canada, the Canadian Internet Registration Authority (CIRA)[42] is responsible for maintaining Canada's Internet domain names. The registrars issue names for a fee on a first-come, first-served basis.

Domain names come into conflict with trademarks when a domain name is issued that includes another's trademark. Sometime this occurs when two parties both have a legitimate interest in the trademark. For example, businesses such as Imperial Tobacco, Imperial Oil, and Imperial Margarine would all have a

---

40 RSC 1985, c T-13.

41 For more information, see <http://www.icann.org>. Over the next few years, over 1300 new top-level domain names or "strings" will be available. Soon to be available or already available are .homes, .autos, .guru, .buzz, .clothing, for examples.

42 For more information, see <http://www.cira.ca>.

legitimate interest in a domain name containing "Imperial." These disputes can be settled through litigation using the general law on the adoption and use of trademarks. Often, however, domain names are registered for illegitimate purposes, such as for the purpose of selling them to the trademark owners, or as a means of advertising the registrant's own services or products, or to redirect traffic to the registrant's own website, or to prevent the trademark owners from using them. These activities are generally known as **cyber-squatting**. In such cases, a complainant may negotiate the purchase of the domain name, institute court proceedings for trademark infringement, or use the dispute resolution procedures set up by the domain name provider. Both ICANN[43] and CIRA[44] provide a quick and cheap dispute resolution system to deal with bad-faith registration. To be successful, a complainant must prove that the domain name is identical or confusingly similar to the complainant's trademark, that the registrant has no legitimate interest in the domain name, and that the name is being used in bad faith by the registrant.[45] If the complainant is successful, the registrar can cancel the domain registration or transfer it to the trademark owner.

Requirements for Registration

To register a trademark, an applicant must demonstrate that he has title to the trademark (this requirement is sometimes simply referred to as use), that the trademark is distinctive or capable of becoming distinctive, and that the trademark is registrable.

Title An applicant may register only a trademark that he owns. Ownership or title is not established by inventing or selecting a mark. It comes from

- use of the trademark.
- filing an application to register a proposed trademark.
- making it known in Canada.

A trademark is deemed to be in "use" in Canada if the trademark is on the goods or the packaging at the time of any transfer in the ordinary course of business. With respect to services, a trademark is deemed to be in use if it is used or displayed in the performance or advertising of the services.

A trademark can be registered if it is not yet in use, as long as the registrant proposes to use it as a trademark in Canada and actual use commences prior to the grant of registration. Estelle may make an application to register "Chargeless" on this basis.

An application to register can be made on the basis that the mark, although not in use in Canada, is nonetheless well known in Canada. An applicant would need to demonstrate that the mark is, in fact, well known in Canada, that knowledge of the mark arose from advertisements that circulated in Canada, and that the applicant used the mark in another country.[46]

The following box indicates that several aspects of trademark law are about to change, most notably, the use requirement.

---

43 The dispute resolution policy is available at <http://www.icann.org/en/dndr/udrp/policy.htm>.
44 The dispute resolution policy is available at <http://www.cira.ca/assets/Documents/Legal/Dispute/CDRPpolicy.pdf>.
45 Also, to succeed under the CIRA dispute resolution procedure, the complainant must satisfy a Canadian presence requirement.
46 The foreign country must have been a country that is a member of the Paris Convention or the World Trade Organization.

AMENDMENTS TO THE
TRADE-MARKS ACT

On June 19, 2014, the federal government passed the *Economic Action Plan 2014 Act, No 1*.[47] Buried in the 350 plus pages of the Act are amendments to the *Trade-marks Act*. Among the amendments[48] are the following:

- the name of the Act is changed from *Trade-marks Act* to *Trademarks Act*.
- the definition of trademark is expanded to include signs permitting the registration of a word, a personal name, a design, a letter, a numeral, a colour, a figurative element, a three-dimensional shape, a hologram, a moving image, a mode of packaging goods, a sound, a scent, a taste, a texture, and the positioning of a sign, and the definition of distinguishing guise is deleted.
- the term of protection for new registrations is reduced from 15 years to 10 years.

- the registration requirements no longer require applicants to provide a declaration of use or a date of proposed use.

The last change is the most controversial. Rather than making the use of a trademark an essential condition for the creation of enforceable trademark rights, registration alone creates an enforceable right. The elimination of use as a requirement for registration is a fundamental departure from Canada's trademark system. The amendments will still allow a trademark to be attacked on the basis of non-use, but only three years after registration.

Critical Analysis: By doing away with the use requirements, the amendments may simplify the process of trademark registration. What are the concerns with the changes to use?

Source: Antonio Turco and Sheldon Burshtein, "Fundamental change to trade-mark law opposed by business and trade-mark professionals" *IP Osgoode* (13 June 2014), online: IP Osgoode <http://www.iposgoode.ca/2014/06/fundamental-change-to-trade-mark-law-opposed-by-business-and-trade-mark-professionals/>.

Distinctiveness The second general requirement goes to the heart of trademark law. The mark must be distinctive—in other words, it must actually distinguish the goods or services in association with which it is used. Invented words like "Lego," "Exxon," and "Kodak" are ideal candidates as they are inherently distinctive. Other, more descriptive words—such as "pleasant," "sudsy," and "shiny"—do not have the same quality of distinctiveness. They may gain this quality only through use in business and advertising.

Registrability The *Trade-marks Act* specifies that a mark must be "registrable." To be registrable, the trademark must *not* be

- primarily the name or surname of an individual who is living or has died within the preceding 30 years (e.g., "Smith" or "Joe Enman").
- descriptive[49] of the character or quality of the wares or services, or their place of origin (e.g., "sweet" for apples, "Ontario wines" for wines from Ontario, or "shredded wheat" for cereal[50]).
- deceptively misdescriptive of the character or quality of the wares or services, or their place of origin (e.g., "sugar sweet" for candy that is artificially sweetened, or "all-silk" for a cotton blouse).

---

47 SC 2014, c 20.
48 The amendments are expected to be in force sometime in 2016.
49 Note that descriptive words can be used as part of a trademark so long as the applicant includes a disclaimer that he does not claim exclusive rights to the descriptive words.
50 *Canadian Shredded Wheat Co Ltd v Kellogg Co of Canada Ltd*, [1938] 2 DLR 145, 55 RPC 125 (PC).

- the name in any language of any ware or service in connection with which it is used or proposed to be used (e.g., "avion" for airplanes, "wurst" for sausages).
- confusing with regard to another registered trademark (e.g., "Mego" for children's plastic building blocks; "Devlon" for hair care products)
- an official[51] or prohibited[52] mark.

CANADA GOOSE SUES FOR TRADEMARK INFRINGEMENT

Canada Goose Inc. is one of the world's leading makers of winter outerwear. Its high quality, fur-trimmed, down-filled parkas with the red, white, and blue circular patch on the left sleeve enjoy widespread consumer recognition both in Canada and abroad. It has indicated that it intends to protect its very valuable brand through litigation, if necessary.

Canada Goose has filed a lawsuit against Sears Canada in Federal Court alleging trademark infringement. It is alleging Sears is selling knock-offs of its highly distinctive coats and is intentionally trying to mislead consumers into believing they are buying a lower-end Canada Goose jacket. Canada Goose wants the Federal Court to order Sears to stop selling the coats. Sears has filed a defence claiming that Canada Goose is trying to claim the exclusive right to sell any winter coat with a fur collar and a circular logo on the sleeve. Further, Sears states that no consumer would confuse a Canada Goose jacket with Sears' Alpinetek coat. The *Globe and Mail* reports that Sears alleges "Canada Goose is simply attempting to bully Sears and others through demands, unfounded litigation,

statements in the press and the like, into ceasing activities that Canada Goose knows do not cause confusion or any harm to it."

Canada Goose previously sued International Clothiers for trademark infringement alleging it intentionally designed a logo and positioned it on the sleeves of jackets to confuse consumers into thinking the jackets were genuine Canada Goose product. The International Clothiers coats featured a white maple leaf on a red circular patch with three geese flying by and the words "Canada Weather Gear" and "Super Triple Goose" above and below the maple leaf. The Canada Goose patch has red trim on a blue background, a white silhouette of Antarctica in the middle, and the words "Canada Goose—Arctic program" around the edge. The matter has been settled out of court and the terms are confidential.

Critical Analysis: What is the harm in trademark infringement?

Source: Jonathan Mesiano-Crookston, "Trademark case hinges on confusion" *The Lawyers Weekly* (4 May 2012) 11; Allison Jones, "Sears accuses Canada Goose of bully tactics" *The Globe and Mail* (8 January 2014) B4; Jennifer Brown, "Canada Goose lawsuit heats up trademark concerns" *Canadian Lawyer Magazine* (28 February 2012), online: *Canadian Lawyer Magazine* <http://www.canadianlawyermag.com/legalfeeds/718/canada-goose-lawsuit-heats-up-trademark-concerns.html>.

Estelle's product name "Chargeless" may be registrable depending on the above factors. Although another business is using "charge less" in its slogan, this would not prevent the registration of Estelle's name, as "charge less" is not being used as a trademark, and it is being used in an entirely different business. A key concern,

---

51 Public authorities have the right to adopt an official mark and use that mark with respect to their wares or services. For example, The Official Island Store is an official mark of Gateway Village Development Inc. of Prince Edward Island.

52 Prohibited marks include marks that are likely to be mistaken for symbols or emblems of government, royalty, armed forces, or the Royal Canadian Mounted Police; the Red Cross, the Red Crescent, or the United Nations; flags and symbols of other countries; and symbols of public institutions. Also prohibited are scandalous, immoral, and obscene words, and anything that suggests a connection with a living or recently deceased individual.

however, will be whether the same or a similar trademark has been registered in the same industry and whether the mark is considered sufficiently distinctive.

Registration Process and Protection

The first person who uses or makes a trademark known in Canada is entitled to trademark registration. In the absence of use, the first to file a trademark application is entitled to registration.[53]

Prior to applying for registration, a trademark agent usually does a search of the trademarks office database[54] to ensure that the trademark or a similar one is not already registered. Federal and provincial business name registries and other sources such as trade journals, telephone directories, and specialty magazines are also consulted to determine whether there are common law rights.

The application must comply with all the provisions of the Act. In particular, applicants must provide a comprehensive list of products or services associated with the trademark. An examiner reviews the application, and if it is acceptable the trademarks office advertises the trademark in the trademark journal. Any interested members of the public can object to the registration on the grounds that they have a better title to the trademark than the applicant, that the trademark is not distinctive, or that the trademark does not meet the requirements of registrability. If, on the other hand, there is no opposition or the opposition is overcome, the registration will be issued on payment of the appropriate fee.

A trademark registration gives the owner the exclusive right to use the trademark in association with the wares and services specified in the registration. It also provides a right to prevent others from using a confusingly similar trademark. A trademark owner should clearly indicate its ownership of a trademark with the following marks:

® for registered trademarks.

™ for unregistered trademarks.

Registration provides protection across Canada for a period of 10 years.[55] The registration can be renewed for additional 10-year terms as long as the renewal fee is paid and the trademark continues in use.

Copyright

Estelle's intellectual property may also include promotional brochures, business plans, drawings, and other written material. All such works may qualify for **copyright** protection.

Copyright is governed almost entirely by the *Copyright Act*.[56] Copyright is intended to provide a right of exploitation to authors of certain works. As its name suggests, copyright is intended to prevent the copying of works. In other words, subject to certain exemptions, only the author (or the owner of the copyright) has the right to copy a work. Others are not entitled to copy the work

Copyright

The right to prevent others from copying or modifying certain works.

---

53 Canada is a signatory to the Paris Convention, which means that applicants from member countries have reciprocal rights with respect to filing in member countries. The date of filing in a convention country becomes the Canadian filing date, so long as the Canadian application is filed within six months of the date of the first filing in a convention country.

54 The Canadian Intellectual Property Office's trademark database can be accessed at <http://www.cipo.ic.gc.ca/eic/site/cipointernet-internetopic.nsf/eng/h_wr03082.html>.

55 *Supra* note 40, s 350.

56 RSC 1985, c C-42.

unless they fall within one of the exemption categories or have the author's permission to make a copy. This "right to copy" or "copyright," however, does not protect the author's underlying ideas or facts. For example, no one has copyright in the life story of Ken Thomson or K.C. Irving, but once the story is written, copyright resides in the expression of the life story.

Copyright Defined

Copyright applies to both traditional and non-traditional works. Copyright applies to every original literary, dramatic, musical, and artistic work, such as the following:

- *literary works*—books, pamphlets, compilations, translations, and computer programs.
- *dramatic works*—any piece for recitation, choreographic works, scenic arrangements, and cinematography productions such as plays, operas, mime, films, videos, and screenplays.
- *musical works*—any combination of melody and harmony, including sheet music.
- *artistic work*—paintings, drawings, maps, charts, plans, photographs, engravings, sculptures, works of artistic craftsmanship, and architectural works of art.

Does copyright apply to body art or tattoos?

In essence, copyright extends to almost anything written, composed, drawn, or shaped. Items not protected include facts, names, slogans, short phrases, and most titles. The examples of works included in each category are non-exhaustive, which means the categories can encompass new technologies and new forms of expression. Copyright also applies to non-traditional works such as sound recordings, performances, and broadcasts.[57]

There are many business examples of these various kinds of works. In fact, whole industries are founded on works of this nature, particularly the entertainment and publishing industries. Businesses that are not so directly affected still create many works that may attract copyright protection, such as advertising copy, photographs, manuals, memorandums, plans, sketches, and computer programs, to name a few common examples.

Requirements for Protection

To attract copyright protection, a work must meet requirements of originality and fixation.[58] Originality means that the work must "originate" from the author, not be copied from another, and involve the exercise of skill and judgment. In *CCH Canadian Ltd v Law Society of Upper Canada*,[59] the Supreme Court of Canada held that the headnotes (a short summary of a case and key words) of a legal decision are "original" works; however, the edited version of a court decision is not original because it involves only minor changes and additions—a mere mechanical exercise too trivial to warrant copyright protection.

---

57 *Ibid*, ss 15, 18, 21.
58 The nationality requirement is no longer very important, as Canada has implemented the Agreement on Trade-Related Aspects of Intellectual Property Rights (TRIPS). This agreement means that virtually every work qualifies for protection, regardless of the author's nationality.
59 2004 SCC 13, [2004] 1 SCR 339.

The requirement of fixation[60] means that the work must be expressed in some fixed form, such as paper or diskette. Works such as speeches, luncheon addresses, and interviews that do not exist in a fixed form do not attract copyright. The fixation requirement exists to separate unprotectable ideas from protectable expression and to provide a means of comparison for judging whether copyright has been infringed.

Registration Process and Protection

Copyright protection arises automatically on the creation of a work. There is an optional registration process that has an evidentiary advantage in that registration provides a presumption of ownership. The owner of a copyright may mark a work; however, there is no requirement to do so to enforce copyright in Canada. The mark can, however, enhance international protection of the work. The following is the typical form of a copyright notice:

© year of publication; name of owner.

Under the *Copyright Act*, the author[61] of a work is the copyright owner unless there is an agreement to the contrary. The major exception is for works created in the course of employment, in which case the employer is the owner. Copyright protection is generally for the life of the author or composer plus 50 years.[62]

Rights under Copyright

Copyright gives certain rights to the owner of the copyright (the rights may vary somewhat depending on the type of work). These rights include:

- *reproduction*—the right to reproduce the work or a substantial part of it in any material form.
- *public performance*—the right to perform the work or a substantial part of it.
- *publication*—the right, if the work is unpublished, to publish the work.
- *translation*—the right to produce, reproduce, perform, or publish any translation of the work.
- *adaptation*—the right to convert works into other formats (e.g., a book into a movie).
- *mechanical reproduction*—the right to make sound recordings or cinematographic recordings.
- *cinematographic presentation*—the right to reproduce, adapt, and publicly present the work by filming or videotaping.
- *communication*—the right to communicate the work to the public by telecommunication.
- *exhibition*—the right to present in public, for purposes other than sale or hire, an artistic work.[63]
- *rental*—the right to rent out sound recordings and computer programs.
- *authorization*—the right to "authorize" any of the other rights.

---

60 The fixation requirement is expressly found in the *Copyright Act* only for dramatic works and computer programs. The requirement in relation to other works has developed through the common law.
61 Copyright law recognizes the concept of joint authorship; however, contribution to a project does not in and of itself create joint authorship. The parties must intend to be joint authors. See *Neudorf v Nettwerk Productions*, [2000] 3 WWR 522, 71 BCLR (3d) 290 (SC).
62 For some works, such as sound recordings, the term of protection is 50 years.
63 This applies only to works created after 7 June 1988 and does not apply to charts, maps, and plans.

Copyright is infringed when anyone does, without the consent of the owner, anything only the owner can do. This includes, for example, copying *all or a substantial part* of a work.

The question of what is substantial is vexing. It is generally thought that *substantial* has both a qualitative and a quantitative aspect. The test seems to be whether the part that is taken is a key or distinctive part.[64]

Cinar Corporation v Robinson, 2013 SCC 73, [2013] 3 SCR 1168

BUSINESS CONTEXT: It is not uncommon for a new work such as an animated television program aimed at children to be based on or inspired by a work in the public domain. When two such works are created or produced, the issue of copyright infringement is likely to arise.

FACTUAL BACKGROUND: In 1982, Claude Robinson, an artist and cartoonist, prepared sketches, storyboards, scripts, synopses, and promotional material for a new children's television show titled *Robinson Curiosity* (*Curiosity*). He obtained copyright registration for his work in 1985. In an effort to find a producer, he contacted a number of companies including Cinar Corporation, a Montreal-based animation company. He was not successful. In 1995, a new television show titled *Robinson Sucroë* (*Sucroë*) and produced by Cinar aired in Quebec. Robinson brought an action for copyright infringement.

Curiosity and *Sucroë* were both inspired by the novel *Robinson Crusoe* written by Daniel Defoe in 1719. Both shows featured a protagonist who wore a beard, glasses, and a straw hat and lived on a tropical island interacting with characters who shared common personality traits. There were, however, also differences. The secondary characters in *Curiosity* were animals, whereas the secondary characters in *Sucroë* were mostly human and featured pirate villains. Also, the main personality trait of the protagonist in *Curiosity* was curiosity, whereas the protagonist in *Sucroë* was not particularly curious.

LEGAL QUESTION: Had Cinar infringed Robinson's copyright in *Robinson Curiosity* by copying a substantial part of his work?

Claude Robinson

Sun Media

RESOLUTION: Under the *Copyright Act*, copying all or a substantial part of a work without the copyright owner's permission is *prima facie* copyright infringement. The court noted that a substantial part of a work is a "flexible notion" and "a matter of degree" and that substantially is measured by the quality rather than the quantity of the original work. Further, infringement is not confined to a literal reproduction of a protected work but may also include non-literal copying. According to the court:

> A substantial part of a work is not limited to the words on the page or the brushstrokes on the canvas. The Act protects authors against both literal and non-literal copying, so long as the copied material forms a substantial part of the infringed work. As the House of Lords put it, . . . the "part" which is regarded as substantial can be a feature or combination of features of the work, abstracted from it rather than forming a discrete part . . . [T]he original elements in the plot of a play or novel may be a substantial part, so that copyright may be infringed by a work which does not reproduce a single sentence of the original.

(Continued)

---

64 *Supra* note 14 at 185–86.

The court also confirmed that the proper approach to determining infringement was qualitative and holistic, considering the cumulative effect of the copied features rather than dissecting the two works as a whole. Using this approach, the court held Cinar had "copied a number of features from *Curiosity*, including the visual appearance of the main protagonist, the personality traits of the main protagonist and the other characters, visual aspects of the setting, and recurring scenographic elements" and that "considered as a whole, the copied features constituted a substantial part of Robinson's work."

Robinson was awarded over $4 million, including $400 000 in non-pecuniary damages for psychological harm and $500 000 in punitive damages. He was also awarded costs including trial costs of $1.5 million.

CRITICAL ANALYSIS: Do you think the compensation awarded Robinson was generous? What does this case say about access to justice?

It is also infringement for anyone to authorize doing anything that only the copyright owner is allowed to do. Authorization means to "sanction, approve and countenance."[65] A person does not, however, authorize infringement by merely providing the means that could be used to infringe copyright. For example, the provision of photocopiers does not constitute authorization of the use of the copiers to infringe copyright, particularly in the case where the provider has little control over the user.

The enforcement of rights has been problematic, particularly the collection of fees and royalties for the use of copyrighted works. These problems have been addressed by provisions in the *Copyright Act* for the establishment of collectives that negotiate agreements with users on royalties and use. For example, Access Copyright (The Canadian Copyright Licensing Agency, formerly known as CanCopy) represents numerous publishers and authors and negotiates agreements with institutions such as universities, libraries, and copy shops, providing for the payment of royalties for photocopying from books. Similar collectives such as the Society of Composers, Authors and Music Publishers of Canada (SOCAN) operate in the music industry.

ETHICAL CONSIDERATIONS

THE BUSINESS OF COUNTERFEIT GOODS

The sale of counterfeit and pirated goods is big business. Phony Prada shoes, Chanel sunglasses, Louis Vuitton hand bags, Gucci scarves, North Face ski wear, and Canada Goose parkas can be purchased in street markets, boutiques, and malls in many parts of Canada. Counterfeit goods, however, are not limited to high-end designer goods. Increasingly less expensive items like toothpaste, medications, printer cartridges, batteries, toys, sporting goods, and car parts are being counterfeited, mass-produced, and sold. For example, police in Toronto charged 21 people in connection with the sale of knock-off versions of Viagra and Cialis, makeup, contact lenses, ice wine, and TTC tokens. The exact cost to economies of counterfeit and pirated goods is not known, however recent estimates value it at more than $30 billion per year in Canada. This estimate does not include the value of pirated software ($1.14 billion) or pirated movies ($118 million).[66]

---

65 Supra note 59.

66 Alex Boutilier, "Federal government studying $30 billion counterfeit market" *The Star* (29 May 2014) online: The Star <http://www.thestar.com/news/canada/2013/11/01/federal_government_studying_30_billion_counterfeit_market.html>.

Most of the knock-offs and fakes come from China and other parts of Asia and most enter Canada through the port of Vancouver. Some of the fakes, however, are produced in Canada. In 2007, the CBC reported that Canada had become a leader in producing pirated DVDs for worldwide distribution.[67] In 2013, police in Halton, Ontario, dismantled the largest counterfeit DVD manufacturing operation in Canadian history. Hundreds of thousands of illegal DVDs destined for sale around the world were seized. The prevalence of pirated goods leaving and entering Canada has not gone unnoticed. Each year the United States Trade Representative (USTR) publishes a report identifying the countries that inadequately protect intellectual property rights. Canada has become a fixture on its "watch list" and in 2009 was moved to the "priority watch list" where it remains. Among the USTR's concerns was Canada's need to improve its intellectual property enforcement systems so effective action can be taken against counterfeit and pirated products in Canada.

Canada has responded to the concerns by passing the *Combating Counterfeit Products Act*.[68] The Act amends the *Copyright Act* and the *Trademark Act* by strengthening the enforcement of intellectual property rights and curtailing commercial activity involving counterfeit and pirated goods. Amongst other provisions, the Act expands criminal provisions and penalties under the *Copyright Act*, introduces criminal offences and penalties under the *Trade-marks Act*, creates new civil causes of actions aimed at persons engaged in the sale or distribution of counterfeit goods, and improves customs and

What is the harm in knock-off versions of mass-produced goods?

border measures by increasing the power to detain suspected counterfeit goods.

Critical Analysis: What are the legal, ethical and economic problems posed by the manufacture and sale of counterfeit goods? Why do some people view counterfeiting to be a victimless crime? Do you agree with that view?

Source: "Vancouver: Canada's Counterfeit Capital", *The Vancouver Sun* (23 June 2007), online: canada.com <http://www.canada.com/vancouversun/story.html?id=3a272710-2f5e-42d9-ba86-5b814f-796c1f&k=34717>; John Cotter & Tara James, "Canada lands on U.S. trade rep's priority watch list", *The Lawyers Weekly* (7 August 2009) 11; Jeff Gray, "Fake purses, real money", *The Globe and Mail* (6 July 2011) B7; "USTR Releases Annual Special 301 Report on Intellectual Property Rights", *United States Trade Representative* (April 2012), online: USTR <http://www.ustr.gov/about-us/press-office/press-releases/2012/april/ustr-releases-annual-special-301-report-intellectual>; "Fake goods valued at $6.5M seized in Toronto" *CBC News* (9 November 2013), online: *CBC News* <http://www.cbc.ca/news/canada/toronto/fake-goods-valued-at-6-5m-seized-in-toronto-1.2444962>; "Police crack down on largest counterfeit DVD operation in Canadian history", *Global News* (29 April 2013), online: *Global News* <http://globalnews.ca/video/524295/police-crack-down-on-largest-counterfeit-dvd-operation-in-canadian-history/>.

Moral Rights

The author of a work has what are known as **moral rights**. Moral rights exist independently of copyright and provide authors with some control over how their works are used and exploited. Moral rights include the following:

- *paternity*. The author has the right to be associated with the work as its author by name or under a pseudonym and the right to remain anonymous if reasonable in the circumstances.

Moral rights

The author's rights to have work properly attributed and not prejudicially modified or associated with products.

---

67 "Counterfeit goods", *CBC News* (6 March 2007), online: CBC News <http://www.cbc.ca/news/background/consumers/counterfeit.html>.

68 SC 2014, c 32.

- *integrity.* The author has the right to object to dealings or uses of the work if they are prejudicial to the author's reputation or honour.
- *association.* The author has the right to object to the work being used in association with a product, service, cause, or institution.

Snow v The Eaton Centre Ltd (1982), 70 CPR (2d) 105 (Ont HC)

THE BUSINESS CONTEXT: Many works that receive copyright protection are created for the purpose of making a profit through a sale. However, the sale of a work does not extinguish all of the author's or creator's rights.

FACTUAL BACKGROUND: Michael Snow created a sculpture of geese known as *Flight Stop*, which was sold to the owners of the Eaton Centre in Toronto. In connection with a Christmas display, the Eaton Centre attached red ribbons to the necks of the 60 geese forming the sculpture. Snow claimed that his naturalistic composition had been made to look ridiculous by the addition. In short, he alleged that his moral rights in the sculpture had been infringed.

THE LEGAL QUESTION: Were the acts of the Eaton Centre a distortion or modification of Snow's work that would be prejudicial to his honour and reputation?

RESOLUTION: The court held that the ribbons distorted and modified Snow's work and that Snow's concern that this was prejudicial to his honour and reputation was reasonable in the circumstances. The Eaton Centre was required to remove the ribbons.

Michael Snow's Flight Stop

CRITICAL ANALYSIS: Since the Eaton Centre paid for the sculpture, why should it not be able to do as it wants with the sculpture? Would the outcome have been the same if the sculpture had been sent to the dump or otherwise destroyed?

Exemptions

There are a large number of exceptions or defences under the *Copyright Act*. Aside from specific exemptions for libraries, museums, archives, people with disabilities, and educational institutions, there are exemptions for copying for private purposes,[69] combining or using copyrighted material to create a "mash-up",[70] and making a

---

69 It is not an infringement of copyright to reproduce a work into another format (format shifting), to reproduce a work for later listing or viewing (time shifting), or to reproduce a work for backup purposes provided the source work is not an infringing work, the work was legally obtained (not borrowed or rented), and a Technological Protection Measure was not circumvented. *Supra* note 56 ss 29.22, 29.23.

70 It is not an infringement to create content by combining and using copyright material to create a "mashup" of clips, or to add music to a personal video provided the purpose is non-commercial, the source (where reasonable) is mentioned, the individual believed the source material was non-infringing, and there was no substantial adverse effect on the copyright holder's exploitation of his work. *Supra* note 56, s 29.21.

back-up and an adaptation copy of computer software.[71] In addition and most relevant to business is the **fair dealing** exemption. This exemption permits the copying of works for the purposes of private study, research, criticism, review, education, parody, or satire. The test for fair dealing involves a two-step analysis. First, the copying must be for one of the enumerated purposes. In *CCH Canadian Ltd v Law Society of Upper Canada*,[72] the Supreme Court ruled that research must be given a large and liberal interpretation and not be limited to non-commercial or private research. Further, research is not limited to creative purposes but can include consumer research for the purpose of purchasing goods or services.[73] Second, the dealing must also be fair. In assessing whether the dealing is fair, the following factors are considered:

- the purposes of the dealing.
- the character of the dealing.
- the amount of the dealing.
- alternatives to the dealing.
- the nature of the work.
- the effect of the dealing on the work.[74]

Fair dealing

A defence to copyright infringement that permits the copying of works for particular purposes.

Confidential Business Information

There is no specific statutory protection for **confidential business information**[75] and therefore no statutory definition for the term. Generally, however, the term refers to information that is used in a business or commercial context and is private or secret.

The general categories of business information that is used or is capable of being used in business are:

- strategic business information (e.g., customer lists, price lists, bookkeeping methods, presentation programs, advertising campaigns).
- products (e.g., recipes, formulas).
- compilations (e.g., databases).
- technological secrets (e.g., scientific processes, know-how).

Confidential business information

Information that provides a business advantage as a result of the fact that it is kept secret.

Requirements for Protection

A key requirement for protection is the secrecy or confidentiality of the information. A number of factors are considered in ascertaining whether the information is "confidential":

- *economic value as a result of not being generally known.* The information must have some commercial value to the company or its competitors. An indication of the commercial value of the information may be the efforts by others to obtain it. The value of the information derives in large measure from the fact that it is not known by some or is not generally known.

---

71 In addition to the back-up and adaptation exemption, there are provisions that specify that copying a computer program is not an infringement if it is to obtain information to make it or another program interoperable, to assess the vulnerability of or correct any security flaw in the computer or computer system, or to temporarily use the copy as part of a technological process to facilitate a use that is not infringing. *Supra* note 56, ss 30.61, 30.62, 30.63.

72 *Supra* note 59.

73 *Society of Composers, Authors and Music Publishers of Canada v Bell Canada* 2012 SCC 36, [2012] 2 SCR 326.

74 The Supreme Court of Canada endorsed these factors in *Alberta v Access* Copyright 2012 SCC 37, [2012] 2 SCR 345.

75 The term "trade secret" is also sometimes used either interchangeably with "confidential business information" or as a subset of "confidential information." The terms are used interchangeably in this text.

- *subject to efforts to keep it secret.* There must be efforts to keep the information secret. Thus, if a company is careless about information or fails to take steps to protect the confidentiality of information, the information may indeed lose its status of "confidential."
- *not generally known in the industry.* Information does not have to be absolutely confidential; it can be a compilation of readily available information from various sources. Also, information can be known by some and still maintain its status. In this regard, the extent to which the information is known within the company, as well as outside the company, is relevant.

Process and Scope of Protection

Confidential business information may be protected forever so long as the information is not disclosed to the general public. Recipes for well-known products such as Coca-Cola Classic, Hostess Twinkies, Mrs. Fields' Chocolate Chip Cookies, Listerine, and Kentucky Fried Chicken have been "secret" for many years. There are no application procedures for protection. Information receives protection through claims for breach of express terms, for breach of confidence, or through implied obligations.

Parties may have express obligations to keep information confidential. Non-disclosure agreements require recipients of information to respect its confidentiality by agreeing not to discuss, disclose, or use it. Estelle could require potential lenders and investors to sign a confidentiality agreement prior to discussing her invention with them. In the absence of an express provision regarding confidence, an obligation of confidence may be implied in a contract or arise by virtue of a fiduciary relationship. This is the case in the employment context, particularly in industries in which there is a lot of confidential information and the importance of confidentiality is stressed.

Finally, an obligation of confidence can exist when information was conveyed in circumstances suggesting a relationship of confidence. The following case is a leading decision on receipt of confidential information in circumstances of confidentiality.

LAC Minerals Ltd v International Corona Resources Ltd, [1989] 2 SCR 574, 61 DLR (4th) 14

THE HISTORICAL CONTEXT: In the negotiations preceding a contract, the parties may divulge a great deal of information, some of which is sensitive and confidential. This is often necessary in order to reach contractual consensus. This case explores the obligations of the recipient of the information to the revealer of the information, in the absence of a contract of confidentiality.

FACTUAL BACKGROUND: Corona was the owner of a group of mining claims that it was exploring. Being a junior company, it was eager to attract investors and had publicized certain information about its property. LAC Minerals, a major mining corporation, became interested, and a site visit was arranged. The LAC geologists were shown core samples and sections, and the parties discussed the geology of Corona's site as well as the property to the west, known as the Williams property. Another meeting was held a couple of days later in Toronto, during which it was again mentioned that Corona was attempting to purchase the Williams property. No mention was made of confidentiality. Following this meeting, there were further discussions and an exchange of joint venture ideas, as well as a full presentation by Corona of its results and its interest in the Williams property. A short time after these meetings, negotiations between LAC and Corona broke down. Subsequently, LAC made an offer to purchase the Williams property. The offer was accepted, and LAC proceeded to develop the property on its own. It turned out to be the biggest gold mine in Canada, and LAC made huge profits. Corona sued for breach of confidence and breach of fiduciary duty.

THE LEGAL QUESTION: Was LAC liable for breach of confidence or breach of fiduciary duty?

RESOLUTION: The Supreme Court of Canada unanimously found LAC liable on the grounds of breach of confidence. The court confirmed that there are three elements that must be established to impose liability on this ground:

- the information conveyed was confidential.
- it was communicated in circumstances in which a duty of confidence arises.
- it was misused by the party to whom it was communicated.

Although some of the information conveyed by Corona was not confidential, clearly most of it was, and LAC used it to acquire the Williams property. The court said the information was communicated with the mutual understanding that the parties were working toward a joint venture or some other arrangement. A reasonable person in the position of LAC would know that the information was being given in confidence. LAC used the information to its gain and at the expense of Corona. Although the court did not go so far as to find a breach of a fiduciary duty, there was a violation of confidence.

CRITICAL ANALYSIS: What is the importance of this case for business? How can a business determine whether information is confidential? Would it have been easier for Corona simply to have had LAC sign an express confidentiality agreement at the outset?

Limitations on Protection

Confidential business information loses the protection of the law when the information is no longer secret, either because the information has been divulged or because the information has been discovered by independent development using publicly available information, or by reverse engineering (i.e., finding the secret or confidential information by examining or dissecting a product). For example, if Estelle keeps her method a secret and at the same time manufactures and sells products using the method, she will not be able to prevent others who discover the method through reverse engineering from using it.

Information is also no longer confidential when it becomes part of the employee's personal knowledge, skill, or expertise (i.e., trade information). In distinguishing between information that is "confidential" and trade information, the courts attempt to strike a balance between the employee's right to use the skills, knowledge, and experience gained during the course of employment and the employer's right to protect its information.

Figure 18.1 compares the major forms of intellectual property.

Acquisition and Protection of Intellectual Property

Intellectual property rights can be extremely valuable to a business. Intellectual property is often created within the business in much the same manner as Estelle invented her method of protecting electronic products and chose her product name. The process of doing so can be time consuming and costly. This suggests that an effective intellectual property program should be put in place to ensure that intellectual assets are valid, enforceable, and effectively exploited. Such a

FIGURE 18.1 A Comparison of Major Forms of Intellectual Property

	Patents	Industrial Designs	Trademarks	Copyrights	Confidential Business Information[a]
Subject matter	Inventions	Shape, configuration, pattern, ornamentation	Word, symbol, design	Literary, dramatic, musical, and artistic works; sound recordings, performances, broadcasts	Business information (e.g., technology, product recipes, databases)
Requirements	New, useful, unobvious	Original, novel	Title, distinctiveness, registrable	Original, fixed	Economic value, efforts to keep secret, generally not known
Protects against	Use, sale, manufacture	Use, sale, manufacture	Use	Copying, modifying	Disclosure, use
Term of protection	20 years	10 years	15 + 15 + 15 years	Life + 50 years	Indefinite (until disclosure)
First owner[b]	Inventor	Designer	First person to use or apply	Author	Creator
Application process	Mandatory	Mandatory	Mandatory[c]	Optional	Not applicable
Example	Microwave oven	Design on the outside of oven	Name of the oven	User's manual	Ideas for improvement

a The term "confidential business information" is used interchangeably with "trade secrets."
b Ownership rights are subject to contracts that may specify other owners. This is particularly the case in employment.
c Registration is required for protection under the *Trade-marks Act*. Unregistered trademarks receive protection under the common law.

program should include the identification of all intellectual property assets; the determination of the nature, scope, and validity of the assets; and the evaluation of any potential risks and opportunities.

Assignments and Licences

Although intellectual property may be created in-house, it is also possible to purchase or receive an **assignment** of intellectual property rights or to receive a **licence** to use the intellectual property. By the same token, it is possible for a business to exploit its rights by assigning them or licensing their use. An assignment involves a change of ownership from the assignor to the assignee. As a general rule, all intellectual property rights are assignable in whole or in part. An exception to the general rule is that moral rights cannot be assigned, although they may be waived.

A business may also obtain a licence to use another's intellectual property. A licence is consent or permission to use the right on the terms specified in the licence. All intellectual property rights are capable of being licensed. This approach may be a viable way for Estelle to exploit her invention.

The process of getting an assignment or licence of intellectual property is not always easy. The process is often complicated by technological developments. Consider, for example, multimedia works that integrate text, graphics,

Assignment

The transfer of a right by an assignor to an assignee.

Licence

Consent given by the owner of rights to someone to do something that only the owner can do.

still images, sounds, music, animation, or video, and with which the user can interact. The product involves various forms of media working together and may rely on literally thousands of sources, including copyrighted text, images, and music, for its content. The developer of the multimedia work has to ensure that all the relevant rights to these copyrighted works have been obtained, either through ownership or some form of licence or other permission.

Intellectual rights are often subject to compulsory licensing. For example, the Canadian Intellectual Property Office may order a patent holder to grant a licence if the exclusive rights under the patent are deemed to be "abused." Examples of abuses are refusal by the patent holder to grant a licence on reasonable terms, thereby prejudicing trade or industry, and failure by the patent holder to meet local demand for a patented article.

Protection of Intellectual Property

Intellectual property is an asset in the same manner as other business assets. Just as an organization takes measures to protect its buildings, land, equipment, and personnel, so too must it take steps to protect its intellectual property. It is not sufficient for Estelle to simply "create" intellectual property rights. Her rights require continuous monitoring and protection.

Use

Intellectual property rights are subject to loss if they are not properly used and maintained, as is shown in the following examples:

- a patent may be considered abused if, among other things, insufficient quantities of the patented item are produced to meet demand in Canada. As a result, a licence to use the patent may be granted to another, or the patent may even be revoked.
- industrial design rights may be substantially reduced if the goods are not properly marked. A defence of innocent infringement is available unless proper notice (i.e., Ⓓ) is used on articles or their containers. The defence has the effect of limiting the owner's remedy for infringement to injunctive relief.
- a trademark can be subject to attacks for non-use or abandonment if it is not used continuously in association with the goods or services for which it is registered. A trademark may also be lost if it loses its distinctiveness, as when it slips into everyday usage. For example, nylon, kleenex, zipper, escalator, cellophane, and dry ice, once trademarks, lost their distinctiveness and thus their status as trademarks by falling into everyday usage and becoming generic terms.
- confidential business information is lost once it is disclosed. A business needs to be particularly vigilant in protecting confidential business information. A business can implement a program for maintaining security that includes restricting access to confidential information, implementing physical security measures (e.g., labelling documents "secret" or "confidential," locking areas where the information is kept, and changing computer passwords), and using confidentiality agreements that require others to maintain confidences.

CORPORATE ESPIONAGE AT COCA-COLA

In July 2006, three people, including Joya Williamson, an employee of Coca-Cola Co., were charged with stealing confidential information, including a sample of a new drink from Coca-Cola. A person identifying himself as "Dirk" wrote PepsiCo, claiming to be a high-level employee with Coca-Cola. He asked for $10 000 for trade secrets and $75 000 for a new product sample. PepsiCo informed Coca-Cola, which contacted the FBI. An undercover agent paid $30 000 for the documents, marked "classified and confidential," and the sample. He promised the balance after the sample was tested. The agent offered Dirk $1.5 million for other trade secrets. The suspects were arrested on the day that the exchange was to occur. The information and sample came from Williamson, an executive assistant to a high-level Coca-Cola executive at the company's Atlanta headquarters. Video surveillance showed her at her desk going through multiple files and stuffing documents into her bags.

After a seven-day federal trial, Williamson was found guilty of conspiracy to steal and sell Coca-Cola's trade secrets. She was sentenced to eight years in prison with three years of supervised probation after release and ordered to pay $40 000 in restitution. Her sentence was affirmed on appeal.[76] Her co-conspirators pleaded guilty. One was sentenced to five years

How does the law provide protection for trade secrets?

in prison. The other was given a lesser sentence of two years because he helped the government arrest Williamson. Both were ordered to pay $40 000 restitution, serve three years of supervised probation after release, and perform community service.

Critical Analysis: What steps should companies like Coca-Cola take to protect confidential business information?

Source: Kathleen Day, "3 accused in theft of Coke secrets", *The Washington Post* (6 July 2006) D1; Amy S Clark, "Two Plead Guilty in Coca-Cola Spy Case", (23 October 2006), online: CBS News <http://www.cbsnews.com/stories/2006/10/23/business/main2115712.shtml>; and "Former Coke Employee Guilty in Conspiracy to Steal, Sell Coca Cola Secrets", *The New York Times* (2 February 2007), online: The New York Times <http://www.nytimes.com/2007/02/02/business/worldbusiness/02iht-coke.4451443.html>.

Litigation

At some point it may be necessary to engage in litigation in order to protect intellectual property rights. Intellectual property litigation is complex and expensive, often requiring the services of experts.

In many intellectual property infringement cases, it is common for the plaintiff to seek an injunction before trial to prevent the infringer from continuing to damage the business of the plaintiff. An injunction is granted if the applicant can demonstrate that there is a serious issue to be tried, irreparable harm may be caused, and the balance of convenience favours the applicant. In addition, because infringers may flee and destroy evidence, the law provides for the seizure of property before judgment. An **Anton Pillar order** allows the plaintiff to access the defendant's premises to inspect and seize evidence of infringement.

Anton Pillar order

A pretrial order allowing the seizure of material, including material that infringes intellectual property rights.

---

76 *United States v Williams*, 2998 WL 731993 (11th Cir, 2008).

The most common intellectual property actions are as follows:

- *patent infringement*. Infringement is not defined in the *Patent Act*, but it is generally taken to mean an unlicensed intrusion on the patent holder's rights (i.e., making, selling, using, or constructing something that comes within the scope of the patent claims). There is no requirement to show that the infringer intended to infringe on the patent, nor is it a requirement that the infringer's action come within the precise language of the claims. As long as the infringer is taking the substance of the invention, that will suffice. A successful action for patent infringement may result in the infringer having to pay damages or turn profits over to the patent holder, also known as the patentee. The patentee may also be entitled to an injunction prior to trial or after trial to prevent further infringement, and a "delivering-up" of the infringing product.

- *copyright infringement*. Copyright is infringed whenever anyone, without the consent of the owner of the copyright, does anything that only the owner has the right to do. As noted above, this could involve various activities—copying, publishing, performing, translating, and the like. The copyright owner has a full range of remedies. An owner may also elect statutory damages of up to $5000 for non-commercial infringement and up to $20 000 for commercial infringement instead of damages and profits.[77] Also, the infringer is subject to criminal sanctions of fines up to $1 million and/or five years in jail.

- *industrial design infringement*. The *Industrial Design Act* prohibits anyone from applying a registered industrial design to the ornamentation of any article without the permission of the owner. The prohibition also includes applying a confusingly similar design. The traditional remedies for infringement are an injunction to restrain further use of the design, damages, and an accounting of profits made by the defendant in using the design. The Act also provides for nominal criminal sanctions.

- *trademark infringement*. Infringement of trademark is protected by both the *Trade-marks Act* and the tort of passing off. The action can be brought against a trader who misrepresents the source of goods or services so as to deceive the public. This may be done by using the same or a similar trademark. Remedies for trademark infringement include injunctions, damages or an accounting of profits, and the destruction or delivery of the offending goods or the means to produce them, as well as criminal sanctions.

- *confidential business information*. There is no statutory cause of action related to the misappropriation of confidential business information. There are, however, common law actions for breach of express and implied terms and breach of confidence, as discussed above. It must be shown that the information was confidential, that the information was disclosed under circumstances of confidence, and that the recipient misused the information to the detriment of the owner. Remedies available include injunctions, damages, an accounting, and/or a declaration of the entitlement to the information.

77 Supra note 56, s 38.1.

PROTECTING INTELLECTUAL PROPERTY ABROAD

It is difficult to protect intellectual property in a domestic setting; however, it is even more difficult to protect it in an international setting as, unlike tangible property, intellectual property is not bound by borders or geography. Protection is not just a question of designing and implementing rules for protection. There are very different perspectives on whether intellectual property should receive protection. Developing countries have little incentive to provide protection, as they need intellectual property to grow and prosper. Developed countries have a somewhat different perspective, as they consider intellectual property a valuable investment and worthy of protection.

Canada is a signatory to a number of treaties that give international protection to intellectual property rights. The major international conventions are these:

- *Paris Convention for the Protection of Industrial Property*. This convention provides national treatment and foreign filing priorities for patents, trademarks, and industrial designs.
- *Patent Cooperation Treaty*. This treaty is designed to facilitate the acquisition of patent protection in multiple countries around the world. Benefits are available only to nationals of contracting states.
- *Berne Convention*. This convention, which applies to literary and artistic works, provides for automatic copyright protection to nationals of member states without any requirement for formalities.
- *Universal Copyright Convention*. This convention provides national treatment for foreign copyrighted works provided the copyright symbol, the name of the copyright owner, and the date of publication are on the work.

- *Agreement on Trade-Related Aspects of Intellectual Property* (TRIPS). This is an agreement of the World Trade Organization (WTO) that establishes certain minimum standards of intellectual property protection for patents, trademarks, and copyrights. The agreement provides that a country should treat foreign nationals no less favourably than its own nationals with respect to intellectual property rights.
- *World Intellectual Property Organization's (WIPO's) Copyright Treaty* (WCT). Designed to bring copyright into the digital age, the WCT protects literary and artistic works. Signatories must prevent circumvention of encrypted information and the removal of digital tracking measures.
- *WIPO's Performances and Phonograms Treaty* (WPPT). This treaty protects performers and producers of sound recordings. It provides moral rights for performers and requires measures against decryption and the circumvention of digital tracking measures.

The latter two treaties came into force on August 13, 2014. The Canadian government has also tabled five other WIPO treaties to further harmonize Canada's patent, trademark, and industrial design law with its trading partners' laws.

The broad intent of the international agreements is to provide protection for foreign intellectual property. For example, works that have copyright protection in Canada have protection in countries that are signatories to the Berne Convention. By the same token, an author who is a citizen of a convention country receives copyright protection in Canada.

Critical Analysis: What is the justification for providing protection for foreign intellectual property? When intellectual property protection is extended in this manner, whose interests are curtailed?

BUSINESS LAW IN PRACTICE REVISITED

1. Is Estelle's idea a patentable invention?

Estelle's method for weaving static protection into the fibre of paper qualifies as an invention under the *Patent Act*. It is patentable if she can demonstrate that it is new, useful, and unobvious. Although there are currently methods of protecting products from electrostatic discharge, Estelle's method is new and an improvement over these methods. The very serious problems experienced by the electronic products industry indicate that Estelle's invention is useful and probably "unobvious." The cost of patenting is expensive but as the potential for the product is great, the investment is most likely to be worthwhile.

Keeping the method confidential or a trade secret is not really a feasible option for Estelle. Although secrecy does not cost anything in terms of filing fees, and secrecy can last forever, it hinders Estelle's ability to capitalize on her invention. As soon as she manufactures and sells a product utilizing her invention, other manufacturers, through the process of reverse engineering, may be able to discover her "secrets." In such a case, nothing prevents them from copying and using Estelle's invention.

2. Who owns the rights to Estelle's invention—Estelle or ELEX?

Estelle owns the rights to her invention. Although Estelle is employed as an engineer for a manufacturer of electronic products, she is entitled to ownership of her invention as she was not hired to invent a method of protecting products from electrostatic discharge, and she made the discovery on her own time. Only if she had signed an agreement regarding the ownership of inventions would she be required to transfer the patent (assuming a patent is granted) to her employer.

3. How can Estelle protect her idea while she seeks funding from potential lenders and investors?

Estelle can protect her idea while she seeks funding from potential investors and lenders by having them sign a confidentiality agreement. In the absence of an agreement, there may also be an implied obligation to keep the information confidential as the information would be conveyed in circumstances that suggest confidentiality.

4. Is Estelle entitled to use the name "Chargeless" for her product, and should she do anything to protect the name?

Estelle may start using the name "Chargeless" for her product so long as no one else has registered or is using the same or a similar name in the same line of business. By simply using a name and not registering it, however, she runs the risk of someone else adopting the same or a similar name in another part of the country. A common law (unregistered) trademark only provides protection in the area where a person's reputation has spread.

Estelle should register her name as a trademark to obtain national protection. To do so, she must meet requirements of use, distinctiveness, and registrability. Although another company in the financial services is using "charge less" as part of its slogan, this should not pose a problem because the use is in an entirely different industry. Estelle will have to have a trademark agent determine whether the name is in use as a trademark in the same industry and if it sufficiently distinctive.

CHAPTER SUMMARY

The term "intellectual property" is used to describe the results of an intellectual or creative process. The term is also used to describe the rights people have or acquire in ideas and in the ways they express those ideas. The main categories of intellectual property rights are patents, industrial designs, trademarks, copyrights, and confidential information. The rights that attach to each category vary but generally encompass the right to use and the right to exclude others from using.

There is considerable overlap between the various categories of intellectual property. It is possible for more than one area of intellectual property law to protect different aspects of a single product or process. Also, there may be alternatives for protecting a single product. For example, an invention may qualify for patent protection, or the invention can be kept secret through the mechanism of a trade secret. Patent protection provides a monopoly for a period of time, but the price of the monopoly is the requirement to disclose the invention. A trade secret is just that—a secret. Once disclosure occurs, there is no protection. The ornamentation of a product subject to patent protection may receive industrial design protection.

Businesses acquire intellectual property in a number of ways. A lot of intellectual property is created in-house by employees, but it can also be bought or acquired through a licensing agreement.

Intellectual property, like other business assets, must be protected. An effective intellectual property policy should encompass its acquisition and proper use. Failure to acquire and maintain intellectual property rights may result in missed opportunities and losses for the business. In some cases, intellectual property rights ultimately may need to be protected by bringing legal action against infringers.

CHAPTER STUDY

Key Terms and Concepts

Anton Pillar order (p. 466)

assignment (p. 464)

claims (p. 446)

confidential business information (p. 461)

copyright (p. 454)

cyber-squatting (p. 451)

distinguishing guise (p. 449)

domain name (p. 450)

fair dealing (p. 461)

industrial design (p. 447)

intellectual property (p. 439)

licence (p. 464)

moral rights (p. 459)

patent (p. 440)

patent agent (p. 445)

specifications (p. 446)

trade name (p. 449)

trademark (p. 449)

Questions for Review

1. What is intellectual property?

2. What are the major forms of intellectual property rights?

3. What is a patent? Give an example.

4. Are life forms patentable in Canada? Explain.

5. Are computer programs patentable in Canada? Explain.

6. What are the three requirements for patentability?

7. What is the difference between specifications and claims in a patent application?

8. How long does patent protection last?

9. What is an industrial design? What are the requirements for industrial design registration? How long does an industrial design *registration* last?

10. What is the advantage of marking an industrial design to indicate that the design is registered?

11. What is the purpose of a trademark?

12. What is the relationship between trademarks and trade names?

13. Must trademarks be registered to receive legal protection? Explain.

14. What is meant by the term "cyber-squatting"?

15. Who owns the copyright in a book? How long does copyright last?

16. What are the moral rights of an author? Give an example.

17. One of the exemptions under the *Copyright Act* is fair dealing. What is fair dealing?

18. What are the requirements for the protection of confidential business information?

19. What is the difference between an intellectual property assignment and a licence?

20. Give an example of how intellectual property rights may be lost if they are not properly used.

21. How is injunctive relief used in intellectual property disputes?

22. What are the penalties for copyright infringement?

Questions for Critical Thinking

1. Three-dimensional printers have the capacity to reproduce solid objects. Using computer modelling software, they can reproduce an object using materials such as rubber, plastics, ceramics, and metals. The potential is to reproduce everything from automobile parts to toys to household items.[78] How does this technology possibly impact intellectual property rights holders? How should companies deal with the risk posed by this technology?

2. When a major sporting event—the Grey Cup game, the Stanley Cup playoffs, the Olympics—occurs in a city, local businesses like to show their support of the home players. Often they decorate their businesses with the team logo, put signs of support in their display windows, or develop products named after their heroes. The official sponsors of an event who have paid for the right to be a sponsor are often not happy. They do not like to see other businesses capitalizing on the goodwill associated with the event without paying. For example, during the 2011 Stanley Cup playoffs, a Vancouver Honda dealership received a cease and desist letter from the National Hockey League after it displayed "Go Canucks Go!" above the words "honk if you're a fan" and the Canucks' stick-and-rink logo.[79] Do the actions of the dealership amount to trademark infringement? What intellectual property issues are raised when businesses try to benefit from the popularity and excitement of sporting events without paying for the right to be a sponsor? What is the risk to an organization in protecting its trademarks and sponsorship arrangements from violations?

3. Websites on the Internet offer powerful marketing opportunities for businesses. However, the websites, and the domain names that identify them, also present opportunities for others to take unfair advantage of the goodwill that a business has worked hard to establish. "Cyber-squatters" do this by registering domain names that include a business's trademark. How can a business, short of litigation, protect its portfolio of trademarks from cyber-squatters?

4. The United States Patent and Trademark Office has allowed patents for all manner of business methods, including, for example, Amazon's one-click method for purchasing goods on the Internet; Priceline's name-your-own price reverse-auction process; and Mattel's system that

78 Paul Banwatt & Ashlee Froese, "The practical and artistic sides of 3-D distinctiveness" *The Lawyers Weekly* (9 May 2014) 12; Paul Banwatt & Ashlee Froese, "The future in 3D" *The Lawyers Weekly* (3 May 2013) 10.

79 Sunny Dhillon, "Local businesses embrace Canucks—logos and all", *The Globe and Mail* (6 June 2011), online: The Globe and Mail <http://m .theglobeandmail.com/news/british-columbia/local-businesses-embrace -canucks—logos-and-all/article582434/?service=mobile>; David Spratley, "Team spirit—or IP infringement?", *The Lawyers Weekly* (1 July 2011) 10.

allows its customers to order personalized toys. Patents have even been granted for reserving office bathrooms, for enticing customers to order more food at fast-service restaurants, and for the process of obtaining a patent. The Federal Court of Appeal's decision in *Canada v Amazon* (see page 443) opens the door to similar patents being granted in Canada. Are business-method patents good for Canadian business? Some business-method patents have been criticized because they have covered subject matter that is old or obvious. What are other criticisms of allowing patents for business methods?

5. A "patent troll" is a person or company that holds patents for the sole purpose of extracting licence revenue or suing infringers. The troll does not make, use, or sell new products or technologies, but waits until a company has invested in, developed, and commercialized an idea and then it pounces—offering a licence in return for cash. The target company is often left with only two options: pay up or litigate.[80] How can companies manage the risk posed by patent trolls?

6. The intellectual property regimes of many countries, including all members of the European Union, contain *droit de suite* protection or artist resale rights. This right entitles artists for a term usually equal to copyright protection to a share of revenue (e.g., 5 percent of gross profit) when their art is resold. The artwork that carries this protection is generally visual artistic works such as paintings, photographs, engravings, sculptures, carvings, and the like.[81] Should Canadian copyright legislation contain a *droit de suite* right? What are the arguments for and against such a right?

Situations for Discussion

1. Masterpiece, an Alberta corporation, applied to register the trademark "MASTERPIECE LIVING" in relation to the retirement industry. The application was denied because Alavida, an Ontario company, had already been granted a registration for the same trademark for the same services. Masterpiece then applied to the Federal Court to expunge Alavida's trademark registration on the basis that Masterpiece had been using a confusingly similar trademark ("MASTERPIECE THE ART OF LIVING") prior to Alavida's application for trademark registration. Masterpiece failed at both the Federal Court and the Federal Court of Appeal but was successful at the Supreme Court of Canada.[82] What is the relationship between registered trademarks and common law trademarks? What are the most important business lessons to be learned from this decision? Is Masterpiece entitled to register "MASTERPIECE" for retirement services? Explain.

2. Duncan, a small town on Vancouver Island, is known as the "City of Totems." Almost 80 totem poles can be found spread throughout the city, both in its downtown core and on the Trans-Canada Highway. In 2007, the city council created a copyright policy to govern the use of images of the totem poles. The policy states that the city holds the copyright policy on the totem collection, that the use of the totem images requires approval from the city, and that the city reserves the right to levy a copyright charge.[83] On what basis could Duncan claim to own copyright in the various totem poles located in the town? If Duncan owns copyright in the totem poles, could people be prevented from taking pictures of the totem poles? Is existing copyright law suitable for the protection of Aboriginal cultural property, such as traditional legends, stories, songs, and knowledge?

3. Anne recently returned from a holiday in Ottawa. While there, she visited the National Gallery and was most impressed by a landscape painting by one of the Group of Seven artists. Anne believes that the scene depicted in the painting would provide a wonderful design for her housewares business. She would like to use it for wallpaper, dishes, and kitchen bric-a-brac. Does her plan have any implications in terms of intellectual property? Explain.

4. Tabatha Pelkey had worked at Physical Fitness Equipment Sales Ltd. as its manager for six years; she left following a pay dispute with the owner. A few weeks later, she opened her own store just

---

80 Sarah Chapin Columbia & Stacy L Blasberg, "Beware Patent Trolls", *Risk Management Magazine* 53 (April 2006) 22.
81 Bob Tarantino, "Forgotten corner of the copyright canvas", *The Lawyers Weekly* (20 January 2012) 13.

82 *Masterpiece Inc. v Alavida Lifestyles Inc.* 2011 SCC 27, [2011] 2 SCR 387.
83 David Spratley, "Copyright law offers poor protection for Aboriginal cultural property", *The Lawyers Weekly* (23 November 2007) 8.

18 blocks from Physical's site. She sold the same exercise equipment to the same market and featured an almost identical sign. Her business was instantly successful and had a serious negative impact on Physical's operations.[84] Could Physical successfully sue Pelkey for breach of confidence? What would Physical need to prove to be successful? How could Physical have protected itself from competition from Pelkey?

5. In 1995, Aldo Buccioni invented and patented a standup hockey bag with wheels, zippered storage compartments for each piece of a player's gear, and a strap on the outside to fasten a hockey stick. In 2004, he brought the design to Greg Collins, founder and owner of Grit Inc., an Ontario company. Collins refined the bag design, registered an industrial design for it, and concluded a royalty agreement between Grit Inc. and Buccioni. In 2013, Grit Inc. filed a case in federal court alleging that Sport Maska Inc., a subsidiary of Reebok-CCM Hockey Inc., infringed its intellectual property rights by marketing a hockey bag similar to Grit's. Grit's distinctive wedge-shaped bag called the Hockey Tower has sales of about $5 million annually. In 2010, Grit Inc. filed a similar claim against Travelway Group International Inc. and Hockey Canada over an upright hockey bag that was sold at Walmart stores. This case was settled out of court.[85]

    What does Grit have to prove for patent infringement? for industrial design infringement? What are the risks for Grit in taking on an industry giant like Reebok?

6. Coco Sharpe is a software developer specializing in online games and puzzles. He has developed a revolutionary new poker game aimed at enhancing the skills of would-be poker players. Coco believes that he can make a lot of money selling the game online. Coco calls his game Coco Cardsharp, and he has received a registered trademark for the name. However, when Coco applies to register the domain name, he discovers that <www.cococardsharp.com> is registered to Janet Rollins. When contacted by Coco, Janet claims that she knows nothing about Coco's game but that she is willing to sell the rights in the domain name to Coco for $50 000. What are Coco's options? How should Coco attempt to settle the dispute with Janet? What are the advantages and disadvantages of pursuing online dispute resolution? What are the advantages and disadvantages of pursuing litigation?

7. In 1969, Cynthia and Frederick Brick opened a high-end furniture store in Winnipeg. They called the store Brick's Fine Furniture. In 1988, Brick Warehouse Corp., a national chain of lower priced furniture, sent the Bricks a letter demanding that they stop using "Brick" as part of their business name. In 1977, Brick Warehouse had filed a number of trademark applications, which included the word "Brick." The Bricks had not registered the word "Brick" as a trademark. As they had used the same name for over 20 years, they refused to comply with Brick Warehouse's demand. The furniture chain sued and after a protracted legal battle that cost the Bricks $178 000 in legal fees, the case settled. The parties agreed to co-exist in Winnipeg.[86] What legal arguments were available to the Bricks? How could the Bricks have prevented this dispute?

8. For the past 15 years, Chuck Morrow has owned and operated Chuck's Grill House in Burnaby, British Columbia. His restaurant offers a selection of beef dishes including prime rib, steaks, burgers, and ribs. The most popular dish on the menu is Chuck's BBQ Ribs. The ribs are cured and smoked (using a secret method invented by Chuck), slow-roasted, and then finished on a grill. Chuck has recently developed a new and improved method of curing and smoking ribs using flavoured wood chips, and he wants to protect it so that others cannot use it. Chuck may be able to protect his new and improved method of curing and smoking ribs from being used by others through a patent or by keeping his recipe a trade secret. What are the requirements for patent protection? What are the advantages and disadvantages of patents versus trade secrets? What factors should be considered in making a choice between secrecy and patenting?

---

84 Based on *Physique Health Club Ltd v Carlsen* (1996), 193 AR 196, 141 DLR (4th) 64 (CA), leave to appeal dismissed, [1997] SCC No 40.
85 Janet McFarland, "Hockey bag maker goes toe to toe with Reebok over patent", *The Globe and Mail* (7 May 2013) B1.
86 Eric Swetsky, "Trademark law is a sleeping tiger", *In-House Counsel* (Fall 2010) 8; John Shmuel, "Tips on challenging the heavyweights", *Edmonton Journal* (18 May 2010) F4.

19

OBJECTIVES

After studying this chapter, you should have an understanding of

- the nature and ownership of real property
- the various ways to acquire and transfer ownership
- how a mortgage works
- the rights and duties of landlords and tenants

© Susan Van Etten/PhotoEdit

REAL PROPERTY

BUSINESS LAW IN PRACTICE

Ashley Bishop has operated a furniture store in Halifax, Nova Scotia, for a number of years. The store has been successful to the point where it has outgrown its current leased space. Ashley has recently discovered a newer strip mall for sale in what she considers to be an ideal location for her store. The strip mall was developed on land that was previously occupied by a gas station and grocery store. A business colleague, Andrew Doncaster, is interested in joining Ashley in the strip-mall venture. They will incorporate Alpha Developments Ltd. (Alpha) to purchase and operate the mall. Half of the space is currently occupied by a number of businesses leasing space from the current owner. The plan is for Ashley's store to occupy most of the vacant space and to find new tenants for the balance of the vacant space. The listing price for the mall is $2 million. Ashley and Andrew can raise $800 000 and plan to borrow the remainder. Before she and Andrew proceed further, Ashley wants to know how she can escape from her lease with her current landlord. She also wants to understand the implications of buying the mall, obtaining the necessary financing, and dealing with current and future tenants.

1. What are the legal issues for Ashley in the planned purchase of the mall?

2. What are the risks in borrowing 60 percent of the purchase price of the mall?

3. What does Ashley need to know about the rights and obligations of her current lease and leases for the mall?

Ownership

The legal concept of real property[1] refers to land or real estate.[2] When people own real property, they own a defined piece of land that includes not only the surface of the land but also everything above and below it—expressed in law as "the earth beneath and the air above." In practice, however, these broad ownership rights are limited by legal rules facilitating air travel above the surface and

---

1 See Chapter 17.
2 Bruce H Ziff, *Principles of Property Law,* 5th ed. (Toronto: Carswell, 2010) at 74.

mining and oil drilling below the surface, to name a few examples. The term "real estate" also includes structures on the land, such as fences and buildings, as well as anything attached to those structures. Items so attached are known as **fixtures** and include heating ducts, lights, and plumbing.[3]

Land has always been a valuable commodity, and therefore the rules governing real property have deep historical roots. Real property is largely governed by common law, and traditionally, the law was devoted to protecting rights to property, such as determining who owns a piece of land when more than one person is making a claim for it. Currently, however, public policy—in the areas of conservation and environmental protection, for example—means that statutes and administrative law are increasingly significant factors.

Interests in Land

The highest and most comprehensive level of ownership of land possible under our system of law is known as a **fee simple**.[4] An owner in fee simple essentially owns the land (subject to the limits described below) and can dispose of it in any way she sees fit. Ownership of land need not, however, be concentrated in one person or remain with that person in an uninterrupted fashion. In fact, ownership of land is easily divisible.

Division of Ownership

One piece of land can be owned by several people at once. For instance, rather than incorporating a new entity to buy the mall, Ashley and Andrew could choose to buy the mall themselves and share ownership. As co-owners they would each have an undivided interest in the entire building. Each owns a portion of the whole, but their respective shares cannot be singled out or identified in any distinct way.

Though Ashley and Andrew are the owners of the real estate, they are called tenants in this context. In ordinary usage, a tenant generally refers to someone who leases space rather than owns it outright; however, the legal use of the word "tenant" is much broader and includes someone who has any kind of right or title in land.

In the time leading up to purchase, Ashley and Andrew can negotiate either **tenancy in common** or joint tenancy. If they choose to be tenants in common, they each have an undivided interest in the land, meaning they can deal with their own interest in any way they see fit and without having to consult the other co-owner.[5] In a related fashion, if one of the tenants in common dies, that tenant's undivided interest in the real estate forms part of his personal estate and goes to his heirs.

A **joint tenancy** is also a form of undivided co-ownership but is distinguished by the right of survivorship. Should one of the joint tenants die, his undivided interest goes directly and automatically to the other joint tenants.[6] The heirs of the deceased co-owner would have no claim on the land co-owned with the other. Both forms of co-ownership require cooperation among the owners in order to use or sell the property.

Fixtures

Tangible personal property that is attached to land, buildings, or other structures.

Fee simple

The legal interest in real property that is closest to full ownership.

Tenancy in common

Co-ownership whereby each owner of an undivided interest can dispose of that interest.

Joint tenancy

Co-ownership whereby the survivor inherits the undivided interest of the deceased.

---

3   Bryan A Garner, ed, *Black's Law Dictionary*, 9th ed. (St. Paul, MN: West, 2009) at 713.
4   *Supra* note 1 at 422.
5   The parties can, of course, enter into a contract whereby they agree not to deal with their respective interests freely but to offer the other a right of first refusal, for example.
6   Many domestic couples own property as joint tenants because of this right of survivorship.

Limits on Ownership

There are numerous restrictions on land use imposed by statute law and common law, including the following:

- municipal governments have the authority to control land use through planning schemes and zoning regulations. For example, if an area of a town is zoned for residential use, it is normally not available for commercial development.
- environmental regulations affect the use of land by limiting or prohibiting the discharge of harmful substances and may even require owners to clean up environmental contamination caused by previous owners.
- the common law of nuisance limits any use of land that unduly interferes with other owners' enjoyment of their land. A landowner who produces smoke or noise is subject to being sued for the tort of nuisance.[7]
- family law may designate property as matrimonial—to be shared by both spouses—despite ownership registered in the name of one spouse. Both spouses must agree to the disposition of such property.
- many government agencies have the authority to expropriate land for particular purposes. For example, if a new highway is to be built, the government can assume ownership of the portions of land along the route after providing compensation to the owners according to specified procedures.
- in a similar fashion, government agencies can make use of privately owned land for a particular purpose, such as a pipeline.
- some jurisdictions also impose restrictions on foreign ownership of land, particularly agricultural land.[8]

Other limits on ownership result from contracts made by the landowner. In short, the landowner has the option to "sell" part or all of his rights to the land in exchange for a payment of money or other benefit. For example, the landowner may do the following:

- grant an adjoining landowner the right to use a portion of his land for a particular purpose. For instance, a landowner may give a neighbour the right to drive across his land to access her own, or give a cellphone company the right to erect a tower. In law, these are known as easements.[9]
- grant a lease to a tenant, thereby giving the tenant the right to occupy the land for the specified period in exchange for rent.
- grant an oil, gas, or mineral lease to occupy a portion of the land, access that portion, and remove materials.[10]
- grant a mortgage on the land as security for a loan. This makes ownership subject to repayment according to the agreed terms of the loan. The right of the lender to be repaid takes priority, and the "owner" then holds the land "subject to the mortgage."
- make the land subject to a **restrictive covenant**. Covenants are legally enforceable promises contained in the document transferring ownership.

Restrictive covenant

A restriction on the use of land as specified in the title document.

---

7   See Chapter 12.
8   See, for example, Alberta's Foreign Ownership of Land Regulations, Alta. Reg. 160/1979.
9   See Chapter 17.
10 The law governing oil, gas, and mineral rights is complex. For example, in Alberta and British Columbia, the government owns the rights and negotiates the leases.

For example, title documents to lots of land in a housing development may contain covenants that prohibit or restrict certain activities (such as cutting trees or erecting storage sheds) for the purpose of preserving the character of the development and thereby enhancing its value.

These various limits on ownership create a significant risk for businesspeople. Anyone contemplating the acquisition of any interest in land needs to do a thorough investigation of potential restrictions that could affect the rights to the particular piece of land. Otherwise, a buyer may end up owning land that cannot be used for its intended purpose.

Registration of Ownership

The provinces have constitutional jurisdiction over property rights.[11] A key aspect of this jurisdiction is the documentation and recording of interests in land. The value of land justifies a system in which those with an ownership interest are able to record or register their interests in a public fashion. The purposes of this type of system are twofold: first, to enable owners to give notice of the land they own and the extent of their ownership; and second, to enable anyone contemplating the acquisition of an interest in land to investigate the state of ownership in order to verify its status.

Because of the provincial control, the systems of registration vary from province to province, though historically there were only two general types.

A Registry System

The **registry system**, which originated in the eastern provinces,[12] provides the facilities for recording documents and maintaining the registrations. The public has access to the records and can examine or search the records to evaluate the state of ownership of a particular piece of land. This process is known as "searching the title" or investigating the "chain of title." Whenever a property is transferred or mortgaged, for example, a lawyer (or title searcher) must search for and examine the historical documents in order to confirm the ownership of the land, its location, and whether there are any claims against it. This must be done to assure the purchaser (or other interested party such as a bank) that the seller owns the land in question and that there are no conflicting claims to all or part of the land. If the investigation reveals that title is not "clear," then the parties will try to correct this situation. For example, if Alpha has negotiated to purchase the strip mall but a search reveals that there is an unregistered title document (known as a deed) in the chain, it may be possible to register the missing deed and perfect the registered record—that is, cure the defect in the current owner's registration. If the defect cannot be cured, Alpha may still decide to proceed with the deal but extract a price concession from the vendor. For example, if the search reveals a small encroachment on the property by an adjoining owner, Alpha may decide to proceed with the transaction at a reduced purchase price. If the defect is fundamental, the deal may collapse.

The administrators of a registry system take no responsibility for the validity of the documents that are filed and express no opinion on the state of the title of a particular piece of property. Lawyers retained by the buyer of property are

Registry system

The system of land registration whereby the records are available to be examined and evaluated by interested parties.

PART FIVE

---

11 *Constitution Act, 1867*, s. 92(13): "property and civil rights in the province."
12 Nova Scotia, New Brunswick, Prince Edward Island, Newfoundland and Labrador, and parts of Ontario and Manitoba. Quebec, a civil law jurisdiction, uses a form of registry known as the *cadastre* system.

responsible for the search and the evaluation of the results. If title problems emerge later, those who searched the title bear the potential liability.

The Land Titles System

Land titles system

The system of land registration whereby the administrators guarantee the title to land.

The **land titles system** originated in Australia and is used in the western provinces[13] and increasingly in the eastern provinces. The administrators of this system assume a much more active role, in that they evaluate each document presented for registration and maintain a record of the documents relating to each piece of property. They are also responsible for the accuracy of the information they provide, and they maintain an insurance fund to compensate those who suffer loss because of their errors. Transactions in a land titles system are less time consuming and costly because a person wishing to know the state of the title to a piece of land need only consult the certificate of title and is not ordinarily required to do a historical search. The certificate contains a legal description of the property and identifies the nature of and owners of the various interests in the land. Because the certificate itself is authoritative proof of title, there is less potential for competing claims. This enhanced certainty and reliability has caused several provinces that used the registry system, such as Ontario, New Brunswick, and Nova Scotia, to move toward the land titles system.[14]

The sequence of registration is crucial to both systems. If there are conflicting claims to the same piece of land, the person who registered his interest first has priority, regardless of which transaction was completed first. So long as the one who registers first is not engaged in fraud, has no knowledge of the earlier transaction, and has paid valuable consideration for the land in question, that person's interest in and claim to the land is fully protected. The party who registers second has no claim to the land but may have actions against those who assisted in the failed transaction or who made representations concerning the status of title.

TECHNOLOGY AND THE LAW

ELECTRONIC DEVELOPMENTS AFFECTING INTERESTS IN LAND

Technology has produced increased efficiency, accessibility, and communication in real estate law, especially in the registration of interests in land. All provinces, whether they are operating under the registry system, the land titles system, or in transition, are aggressively using technology to improve their systems of land registration.

There are several technology-based improvements that have been implemented to varying degrees in all provinces:

- *conversion of paper records to electronic records:* The savings in storage costs are huge.
- *creation of a central database in the province:* This is a vast improvement over a system where each county or district had its own separate registry of records.

---

13 Saskatchewan, Alberta, British Columbia, and parts of Manitoba and Ontario.

14 Some of the eastern provinces are in the process of converting to the land titles system. New Brunswick, for example, requires all new purchases and mortgages to convert and utilize its new land titles system. Nova Scotia began a conversion process in 2003 and according to Teranet, as of March 2011, approximately 99.9 percent of properties in Ontario were recorded under the Land Titles System, online: Teranet <http://www.teranet.ca/land-registration-system-ontario?popup=1>.

- *improved access:* For purposes of filing documents and searching the records, the central database can be accessed from any of the county or district offices and remotely from law offices and other locations with access to the system.

While historically government has managed registry or land titles systems, increasingly private enterprise is assuming this role. Manitoba and Ontario have entered into agreements with Teranet, a corporation specializing in electronic land registration systems, granting the corporation ownership and the right to operate the land registration systems in those provinces.[15]

Connectivity software now enables lawyers, lenders, title insurers, and land registries to communicate directly. Electronic funds transfers facilitate payments among buyers, sellers, lawyers, and lenders. This development poses additional challenges in terms of verification of identity and electronic signatures and is subject to the usual weaknesses of electronic databases—ensuring adequate capacity; controlling access; protection from viruses, crashes, and hacking; and the need for adequate backups.

Critical Analysis: Electronic systems are more vulnerable than paper systems in terms of issues such as documentation and security. Do the advantages in cost and efficiency compensate for these weaknesses? Who is responsible for the integrity of the electronic systems?

Sources: Dave Bilinsky, "Land registration systems in throes of change across Canada", *The Lawyers Weekly* (19 March 2004) 9; Christopher Guly, "A paperless world cuts both ways for property practitioners", *The Lawyers Weekly* (17 October 2008) 1; and Steven Pearlstein, "The next generation of conveyancing", *The Lawyers Weekly* (7 October 2011) 9.

The Purchasing Transaction

Buying land is a buyer-beware situation, expressed in law as *caveat emptor*. It is up to the buyer to investigate and evaluate the property in both financial and legal terms. The risks are significant and require careful management. The seller (known as the vendor) must not mislead the buyer but generally is under no obligation to disclose information about the property, even when that information might cause the buyer to hesitate. There are legal and ethical complications to this general rule, however. Misrepresentations may be oral or written false statements, but may also take the form of active attempts to hide defects in the property being sold. There is a positive duty to disclose significant latent defects (not easily visible) that are known to the seller, especially if the defects cause the property to be dangerous or uninhabitable. Where there is a misrepresentation, the seller cannot justify it by claiming that the buyer could have discovered the truth through investigation. However, the buyer must show that the misrepresentation is material—an important factor in the decision to buy.[16] Examples of misrepresentations in commercial transactions relate to revenue potential, uses permitted by zoning regulations, permission to subdivide, and adequacy of water supply.[17]

An important development in residential real estate transactions is the use of a property condition disclosure statement, which requires the seller to provide detailed information on many aspects of the property. This statement can then

15 Boyd Erman, "Teranet deal with Ontario likely first of many", *The Globe and Mail* (19 November 2010), online: The Globe and Mail <http://www.theglobeandmail.com/report-on-business/streetwise/teranet-deal-with-ontario-likely-first-of-many/article1461786/>.
16 See Luis Millan, "SCC clarifies real estate disclosure standards", *The Lawyers Weekly* (1 July 2011) 13 commenting on *Sharbern Holding Inc v. Vancouver Airport Centre*, 2011 SCC 23.
17 See Paul M Perell and Bruce H Engell, *Remedies and the Sale of Land*, 2d ed. (Toronto: Butterworths, 1998) at 97.

be incorporated into the agreement of purchase and sale and thereby eliminate much of the uncertainty surrounding potential defects. However, there remains some obligation of the buyer to verify the statements made. See the *Krawchuk v Scherbak* case[18] in Chapter 13 where the sellers and their real estate agent were found liable for negligent misrepresentation in the disclosure statement concerning the sinking of the house foundation which led to cracking of the walls and major plumbing problems.

Ashley and Andrew have already identified the property that Alpha will buy, but Alpha should have its legal advisor involved from the outset to identify, among other matters, the contractual significance of communication and documents used by Alpha and the current owner. The technical nature of real estate transactions makes the use of professional advice a practical necessity.

Participants in the Transaction

The main participants in a real estate transaction are the buyer and the seller. In a commercial deal, the parties to the contract of purchase and sale are likely to be corporations. In addition, each party may have a real estate agent, a property appraiser, a land surveyor, an engineer, and a lawyer providing expert advice and guidance. The seller, for example, will likely have engaged a real estate agent to find suitable buyers. For its part, Alpha might have engaged an agent to identify suitable properties. The lawyers on both sides will advise on the main agreement between the buyer and the seller. Appraisers may be hired to formally value the property, based on the structure and the current market. Surveyors may be retained to determine the physical boundaries of the property. Engineers and building inspectors may be retained to report on the structural integrity of the building and whether it is in compliance with building codes. Consultants may be involved to check for any environmental hazards.

From a legal point of view, Alpha's transaction is a complicated set of contracts revolving around the main contract for the transfer and sale of the property. Alpha must decide which professionals it requires and be clear regarding what services and advice each will provide. For example, a lawyer will normally do the investigation of title but is likely not in a position to place a value on the land.

In registry systems, lawyers have responsibility for evaluating the reliability of the title of the property their clients are buying. Lawyers search the title and give an opinion on its validity to clients and to the land registry if the property is in transition to the new system. They have professional liability insurance to cover negligence in providing this advice on title to property. In fact, a significant portion of claims made against lawyers arise from such situations. The cost of this insurance is reflected in the fees charged to clients in property transactions. In land titles systems, the administrators of the system accept responsibility for inaccuracies in recording interests in land.

Title insurance is also an important factor in real estate transactions. Title insurance is a type of coverage for buyers and lenders that covers title related issues (such as fraudulent transfers and mortgages, liens, boundary encroachments, issues related to government regulation, zoning problems, survey defects, and registration issues) but does not protect an insured from known defects with the property.

Title insurance

Insurance that covers title related issues such as fraudulent transfers and mortgages, liens, boundary encroachments, issues related to government regulation, zoning problems, survey defects, and registration issues.

---

18   2011 ONCA 352, 332 DLR (4th) 310.

The use of title insurance diverts some of the responsibility, work, and related fees from lawyers.[19] However, when clients choose to use title insurance along with a lawyer, part of the lawyer's duty is to explain the impact of the title insurance policy.[20] A title search is preventive in that it identifies problems before the transaction closes. Title insurance provides compensation if a problem is discovered later.

In addition to the buyer, the seller, and professionals, others are less directly involved, as illustrated in the following examples:

- if the property is currently mortgaged, that obligation must be discharged by the vendor, assumed by the purchaser, or otherwise addressed in the financial adjustments between the parties.
- if Alpha needs a loan to finance its purchase, a bank or some other lender must be brought into the transaction. Alpha will be required to grant the bank a mortgage on the property for the amount borrowed plus interest.
- since much of the strip mall is currently occupied by tenants, Alpha's ownership is subject to the rights of those tenants, depending on the jurisdiction involved and the length of the lease.

Stages in the Transaction

There are three stages in the transaction that will result in the transfer of the land to Alpha: the agreement of purchase and sale, the investigation, and the closing.

Agreement of Purchase and Sale

Of prime importance is the agreement of purchase and sale between Alpha and the seller. Though the content of this agreement is entirely as negotiated between the parties, normal elements would include provision for Alpha to conduct a full investigation of the property and the opportunity to bring matters of concern to the seller. This agreement can also be made conditional, for example, "subject to a satisfactory engineer's report" or "subject to financing." If Alpha makes good-faith efforts to secure financing but is unable to find a willing lender, it can terminate the agreement with the vendor because the condition of being able to secure financing has not been fulfilled.[21] In a commercial real estate transaction, it may be worthwhile to carry out some due diligence processes before entering into negotiations, such as confirming whether the property is subject to encumbrances such as restrictive covenants or leases that might be onerous for the purchaser or difficult to discharge, and confirming zoning and development agreements relating to the property.[22]

Alpha's agreement with the seller must contain all requirements or terms of importance to Alpha, such as those listed below. As with any contract, once this one is signed, it is difficult to change without the agreement of both parties.[23] An important legal requirement that affects this contract is that it must be in writing and signed by the parties.[24] This eliminates attempts to incorporate into the agreement items that may have been discussed but on which no formal agreement has been reached.

PART FIVE

What stages of a real estate transaction occurred before these signs appeared?

The contents of the agreement of purchase and sale depend on the nature of the property and the value of the transaction. The basic terms are these:

- the precise names of the parties.
- precise identification and description of the property, including reference to the registered title and sufficient detail so as to leave no doubt as to location, size, and boundaries.
- the purchase price, deposit, and method of payment.
- a statement of any conditions on which the agreement depends (such as financing, zoning approval, or environmental inspection).
- a list and description of exactly what is included in the price (e.g., equipment, fixtures).
- the date for closing and a list of what each party must deliver on that date.
- a statement of who is responsible for what during the period between signing and closing.
- any warranties relating to such matters as supply of water or soil contamination that continue after the closing.

Normally, Alpha would submit an offer to buy, and the seller would accept it or respond to it with a counteroffer, which Alpha would then accept or vary, and so on until they both agreed unconditionally on all the terms. Only then would a contract exist.[25]

The Investigation

The second stage consists of the investigation by the buyer and the seller's response to any problems the buyer may raise.

The buyer must thoroughly investigate all aspects of the property during the search period allowed in the contract. Normally, Alpha's lawyer will conduct various searches on Alpha's behalf.

Title search

Investigation of the registered ownership of land in a registry system.

Title to the Property Since this property is located in Nova Scotia, a **title search** in the local registry of deeds[26] may be needed. If this property has not been

---

25 See Chapter 6.
26 *Registry Act*, R.S.O. 1990, c. R-20; *Registry Act*, R.S.N.S. 1989, c. 392. See also *Land Registration Act*, S.N.S. 2001, c. 6.

converted to the new system, the search normally goes back 40 years to ensure clear title. Any problems that can be fixed, such as an unregistered deed, will be remedied. If there is a more serious problem (e.g., someone else owns part of the land), Alpha will have the option to renegotiate terms or pull out of the deal. In a commercial transaction, the buyer will usually want to pay particular attention to encumbrances that may restrict their use of the land such as easements and restrictive covenants. If the land has previously been converted to the new system in Nova Scotia (or if it were located in a land titles province), examination of the chain of title will not be necessary and Alpha can rely on the certificate of title from the land titles office as to who owns the property, the extent of that ownership (such as surface only or mines and minerals), and the encumbrances that are registered against the property as these will appear on the certificate of title.

Legal Claims against the Seller Searches should be done to establish what legal claims exist against the seller of the property in question. For example, judgments registered against the seller are valid for a number of years; the exact duration varies from jurisdiction to jurisdiction. Such a judgment can form the basis of a claim against any land owned by the seller—a matter that a prospective purchaser would want to know about. Alpha would not want to own a piece of land subject to such a claim because it would have a less than clear title.

Verification of Boundaries Alpha will retain a surveyor to confirm that the boundaries described in the registered title fit the physical boundaries of the land. For example, if the title provides for 1000 metres of road frontage but the surveyor finds only 800 metres, there is a problem to be addressed. The survey will also reveal the location of any buildings or other improvements in relation to the boundaries of the property and whether the property complies with local bylaws stipulating setbacks from the property boundary.

Physical Examination Alpha must confirm that the property is in the state it is expecting according to the agreement. Alpha must confirm the space occupied by the tenants currently in the mall. Alpha must also confirm the building's structural integrity, as provided for in the engineer or building inspector's report. Excessive dampness and mould, for example, are significant defects.

Environmental Audits and Site Assessments Environmental contamination is a *caveat emptor* situation as the legislation in most provinces provides that an owner can be issued a remediation order even if the contamination was caused by a prior owner.[27] For this reason, purchasers should investigate how the property was used in the past to ensure that there are no lingering or hidden environmental hazards. Because the property was formerly occupied by a gas station, Alpha must ensure that there is neither leaked fuel in the ground nor abandoned underground tanks that might leak and will want to ensure that its agreement to purchase the property is conditional upon a satisfactory environmental investigation (see the Environmental Perspective box below). Sellers who are aware of contamination also have a duty to inform potential buyers.

Taxes Alpha must be sure that the municipal property taxes and any other local charges related to the property are paid up to date. If they are not, they will be deducted from the total due to the seller at closing.

---

27 For example, see the *Environmental Protection Act*, R.S.O. 1990, c. E. 19, s. 157.1.

Local Bylaws Alpha must verify that the property can be used for its desired purpose. If Alpha were buying land on which to build or using an existing building for a new purpose, it would have to be especially careful that the zoning regulations permit that activity.

Any problems revealed by the various searches and investigations will be addressed according to the terms of the agreement. They will be fixed, or they will result in the renegotiation or termination of the agreement.

RESPONSIBILITY FOR CONTAMINATED LAND

The permanence of land facilitates the tracking of ownership because land cannot be moved or hidden. One of the negative features of this permanence concerns the long-term effects of commercial activities that may be harmful to the land itself and the surrounding community. In terms of pollution to the ground from toxic substances or the escape of harmful vapours from contaminants, the legal issue is liability for cleanup and for resulting harm to the environment and public health. Awarding damages for contamination is problematic since clean-up costs may well exceed the value of the land. Scientific advances have altered the public view of some activities; commercial activities that were once acceptable may not be any longer. The difficult issue is how to allocate responsibility for the harm already caused. There is a huge risk in buying property with a long history of use for industrial purposes (i.e., how should such "tainted" property be valued, and should the buyer purchase it or not?). A purchaser could face a large bill to clean up contamination caused by previous owners.

Liability for contaminated land has become such a barrier to development that all three levels of government are taking measures to encourage redevelopment of brownfields, the term for "abandoned, idle or under-utilized industrial or commercial facilities where expansion or redevelopment is complicated by real or perceived environmental contamination." For

The bankrupt AbitibiBowater plant in Newfoundland and Labrador draws a crowd.

example, Ontario legislation[28] provides limited immunity from certain clean-up orders after a site has been restored to specific standards and a Record of Site Condition has been filed. Municipalities are considering property tax relief for redevelopers. Environmental insurance is also available in such situations.

In the absence of these initiatives, the "polluter pays" principle is well established. The Supreme Court[29] has confirmed the right of a provincial regulatory authority to order further clean-up of a contaminated site that had been sold, cleaned up, and developed, only to exhibit subsequent effects of the earlier pollution. However, as the government of Newfoundland

---

28 *Environmental Protection Act*, R.S.O .1990, c. E-19, Part XV.1 (known as the *Brownfields Act*). But see Elaine Wiltshire, "Critics sound alarm over brownfields regulation" *The Lawyers Weekly* (26 February 2010) 11 for concern about higher standards.

29 *Imperial Oil Ltd v Quebec (Minister of the Environment)*, 2003 SCC 58, [2003] 2 SCR 624.

and Labrador recently learned, the "polluter pays" principle has its limitations, particularly where the polluter is no longer solvent. AbitibiBowater Inc. had carried out pulp and paper operations in Newfoundland and Labrador for over a century when it filed for creditor protection under the *Companies' Creditors Arrangement Act* (CCAA) in 2009.[30] After the company closed one of its mills, the province passed legislation permitting it to expropriate most of the company's assets including five sites that were later found to be contaminated. The province attempted to recover the estimated $50 million to $100 million in expected clean-up costs by issuing remediation orders against the company but the company argued that the orders were monetary claims and as such, were merely debts and therefore subject to its restructuring under CCAA. In a 7-to-2 ruling, the Supreme Court held that the remediation orders had no special priority and that the province had to stand in line along with other creditors to recover the clean-up costs.[31] Some have observed that the net effect of the decision is that taxpayers will ultimately be footing the bill for the clean-up. Concern has also been expressed that the ruling leaves the door open for companies to avoid their environmental responsibilities through insolvency protection proceedings.[32]

Given the practical limitations of the "polluter pays" principle, governments have looked for further ways to ensure that corporations meet their environmental obligations. In Alberta, for example, resource developers are required to make large security deposits at various stages of development to ensure that financial resources are in place to address future costs of remediation.[33] Another approach is to pursue directors and officers, particularly where the business itself is no longer solvent. For example, the Ontario Environmental Review Tribunal recently entered into a settlement with the former directors of the now bankrupt Northstar Aerospace Inc. that will see the directors of the helicopter parts manufacturing business personally pay $4.75 million toward clean-up of chemical contamination that affected more than 500 nearby homes.

Critical Analysis: Who should bear the cost of environmental protection and clean-up: the businesses that generate profits, directors and officers, or the public sector? Should a new owner who is unaware of prior contamination be legally responsible for its clean-up? What are the risks in encouraging redevelopment of land that may be contaminated?

Sources: Pamela Young, "Time (or money) heals urban wounds" *The Globe and Mail* (15 May 2007) B12; and Dianne Saxe, "Tribunal spurns 'polluter pays' principle" *The Lawyers Weekly* (22 January 2010) 14. Mike Blanchfield, "Supreme Court sides with Abitibi in environmental cleanup case" *The Globe and Mail* (7 December 2012), online: http://www.theglobeandmail.com/report-on-business/industry-news/energy-and-resources/supreme-court-sides-with-abitibi-in-environmental-cleanup-case/article6078535/. Charlotte Santry, "Will Director Liability Weaken Environmental Protection?" *The Law Times* (18 November 2013), online: http://www.lawtimesnews.com/201311183601/focus-on/focus-will-director-liability-weaken-environmental-protection.

The Closing

The third stage, the **closing**, occurs after all price adjustments have been made. At this point, final payment is made and a formal transfer of ownership occurs.

If any difficulties found during the various searches can be remedied and Alpha is able to get its mortgage, the closing will proceed after the price is

Closing

The final stage of a real estate transaction when final documentation and payment are exchanged.

---

30 R.S.C. 1985, c. C-36.

31 *Her Majesty the Queen in Right of the Province of Newfoundland and Labrador v AbitibiBowater Inc., et al.,* 2012 SCC 67.

32 Friends of the Earth/Ecojustice, "Supreme Court decision leaves taxpayers with the bill for cleaning up AbitibiBowater's pollution", (7 December 2012), online: Environmental Communication Options (ECO Strategy <http://huffstrategy.com/MediaManager/Includes/Print.php?ReleaseID=2674>.

33 For example, Alberta's Mine Financial Security Program (MFSP), online: Alberta Energy Regulator <https://www.aer.ca/abandonment-and-reclamation/liability-management/mfsp>.

PART FIVE

adjusted for such items as prepaid taxes (added to the price) or rent already received from tenants (deducted). Alpha will then make the final payment, and the seller will deliver the title document along with keys and other means of access to the property. It is likely that the agreement included a "state of repair" clause that required the seller to ensure the property remained in the same condition on possession day as it was at the time of the agreement. Alpha will then immediately register its title at the local registry office to ensure that no competing claims intervene to disrupt its ownership. If electronic registration is available, this risk is eliminated. At the moment of closing, Alpha becomes responsible for the property. Alpha must therefore arrange for insurance coverage and utilities to be transferred at that time as well.

Figure 19.1 summarizes the stages of a real estate transaction.

FIGURE 19.1 Summary of a Real Estate Transaction

FIRST STAGE: AGREEMENT OF PURCHASE AND SALE

Seller	Buyer
• decides to sell a piece of land	• decides to buy land
• determines the value of the land, possibly through a professional appraisal	• engages an agent to find suitable land
• engages a real estate agent to find a buyer and signs a listing agreement	• engages an appraiser to value the seller's land
• engages a lawyer to advise on the legal requirements	• engages a lawyer to advise on the legal requirements
• engages a surveyor to confirm boundaries	

Seller and Buyer
• negotiate, possibly with the assistance of their agents and lawyers
• reach agreement on all terms and conclude a formal written agreement

SECOND STAGE: INVESTIGATIONS

Seller	Buyer
• addresses any problems discovered through the buyer's investigation	• investigates all aspects of the property, including the seller's title and any outstanding claims
	• confirms the boundaries of the land by retaining a land surveyor
	• arranges for financing
	• has an engineer assess the structural soundness of the building
	• has a consultant investigate environmental soundness

FINAL STAGE: CLOSING

Seller	Buyer
• delivers the title document	• makes final payment
• delivers the keys to the property	• registers the title document
	• arranges for insurance and transfer of utilities
	• moves in

Incomplete Transactions

A deal may fall through for a number of reasons, some of which the agreement will anticipate. For example, if there is a title problem that cannot be fixed or the buyer is unable to arrange financing pursuant to a conditional agreement, the buyer normally has the right to bow out of the deal. In other situations, the buyer or the seller may find a better deal and simply refuse to complete the transaction as required by the agreement. Refusal to complete for a reason not contemplated by the agreement is a breach of contract and entitles the party not in breach to a remedy. If the buyer backs out, for example, the seller can keep the buyer's deposit. To claim further damages, the seller must try to mitigate by finding a replacement buyer. In such circumstances, the seller may experience costs in finding a new buyer and may end up selling the property for less than the defaulting buyer had agreed to. In such circumstances, the seller is entitled to recover the difference between these two prices from the defaulting buyer by way of damages for breach of contract.

If the seller refuses to complete, the buyer is entitled to the extra expense in acquiring a similar property. Historically, the buyer could claim for specific performance—a special remedy in which the seller is forced to complete the transaction.[34] However, in recent years the courts have been more reluctant to order specific performance unless a buyer shows that the property is unique and that an alternative property will not meet its needs.[35]

CASE

Covlin v Minhas, 2009 ABCA 404

THE BUSINESS CONTEXT: This case illustrates the legal process for buying and selling land and the complications that result if the transaction is not completed as planned.

FACTUAL BACKGROUND: In December 2004, Verna Covlin agreed to buy a residential property in Edmonton near the University of Alberta campus. She paid a deposit of $10 000 and agreed to pay the balance of $177 000 on the closing date of 17 January 2005. The agreement also required that the vendor bear the risk of loss or damage up to closing, that closing documents (including the transfer document) be delivered to the buyer in advance of closing, and that if either party failed to complete the transaction then the other could pursue all available remedies. Covlin along with her husband owned six other properties in the immediate area. She intended to renovate the property and rent it to students in the short

term, but planned a major residential and commercial development in the longer term. Before closing, a water pipe burst and caused damage eventually agreed to be $10 000. Covlin learned of the water damage only at closing. She agreed to close when the damage was assessed and rectified. The vendor refused to proceed. Covlin sued for specific performance or damages in lieu of $163 000 for the increase in market value since the closing date and $248 000 for loss of development value.

THE LEGAL QUESTION: Did the vendors breach the agreement? If so, is Covlin entitled to specific performance? If not, what damages should be awarded?

RESOLUTION: The trial judge found that the vendors were in default. No duly executed transfer document was ever delivered. Covlin was at all times ready, willing, and able to perform. Regarding specific performance, the court noted that while specific performance

(Continued)

---

34 See Chapter 9.
35 *Semelhago v Paramadevan*, [1996] 2 S.C.R. 415.

for breach of a real estate contract used to be granted as a matter of course on the basis that every piece of real estate is unique, alternative residential, business, and industrial properties are now widely available, and if a deal falls through for one property, another is frequently (though not always) readily available. Nevertheless, in the case before him, Justice Lutz concluded:

> While the Plaintiff could arguably develop six lots instead of seven, the addition of the seventh property provides her with an opportunity that cannot be reasonably duplicated. She cannot simply go out and purchase another property that would have the same value to her as the subject property.

Covlin was awarded specific performance plus $10 000 for the water damage. On appeal, the trial decision was upheld. The property was unique because it formed an integral part of a larger plan for redevelopment.

CRITICAL ANALYSIS: Could Covlin have negotiated terms in the agreement to prevent this dispute? This property was considered unique because it was part of a development scheme. What other aspects of land might make it unique?

The Real Estate Mortgage

How a Mortgage Works

Alpha requires further financing to purchase the land and has decided to borrow the needed $1 200 000. In this chapter, a mortgage on the land itself is discussed.[36] Alpha will approach potential lenders—usually banks or other financial institutions, but possibly private lenders. Assuming that Alpha has a good working relationship with its own bank and is creditworthy, the bank is likely to be the lender, provided that the parties can agree on such matters as the rate of interest and a repayment schedule.

Mortgage

A loan for real property that is secured by an interest in the property.

A mortgage transaction has two aspects. First, a **mortgage** is a contract for the extension of credit and is a debt owed by Alpha to its bank. The lender advances the principal sum to the borrower, who promises to repay the principal plus interest over the specified period. Alpha as a corporate borrower will likely be required to provide personal guarantees as well, probably from Ashley and Andrew.[37] Second, the mortgage transaction also involves the bank taking a security interest in the land purchased by Alpha. To attain this security protection, the bank must register the mortgage document, thereby giving notice to all subsequent creditors of Alpha—as well as anyone considering purchasing the property from Alpha—that the bank has first claim against the land. Registration gives the bank secured status, which will protect its claim against the land even if the borrower becomes bankrupt.

Any claims already registered against the land have priority over the new mortgage and will affect the bank's decision to grant the loan. The bank's mortgage does not forbid Alpha from attempting to borrow more money in the future using this land as security, but those subsequent lenders will be aware that the already registered mortgage forms a prior claim. Each subsequent mortgage against the same land involves significantly greater risk for its lender.

---

36 See corporate financing in Chapter 15 and personal property security in Chapter 26.
37 See Chapter 26.

Under the land titles system, registration of the mortgage creates a legal charge on the land. The registered mortgage amounts to a claim—or lien—on the land until repayment is complete. In provinces under the registry system, in contrast, the mortgage actually transfers ownership of the land to the lender for the duration of the lending period. The bank becomes the legal owner, but Alpha remains the equitable owner and has the right to have legal ownership restored to it upon repayment. This means that Alpha has the **equity of redemption**—the right to have legal ownership restored to it upon repayment. Alpha is the borrower, known as the **mortgagor**. The bank as the lender is known as the **mortgagee**.

Terms of the Mortgage

The focus of the mortgage is on preserving the value of the land in question. This protection is achieved by preventing the borrower from doing anything with the land that would lower its value and by giving the lender maximum flexibility in dealing with the borrower. For example, if the mortgagor does not adequately insure the property, the mortgagee (the bank) has the right to secure proper insurance and hold the borrower responsible for the cost. Recently the risk of fraud has become a major concern for lenders. They have developed practices to verify the identity of borrowers and to ensure that the necessary documentation is authentic. Provincial law societies also have regulations to guide lawyers in new client identification and verification.

Historically, the bank would not grant the loan unless it was confident of Alpha's ability to repay. As a precaution, however, the amount of the loan was likely to be less than the current value of the land, for two reasons. First, the mortgage is a long-term arrangement, so the bank will consider that market conditions might diminish the value of the security. Second, if Alpha defaults and the bank needs to use the security to recover its money, it is unlikely that the land will produce its full market value in a quick sale. A serious drop in the market could result in negative equity for the owner—that is, the amount owed on the mortgage could be more than the value of the property. This traditional approach was significantly altered in recent years (mainly in the United States) with the growth of subprime mortgages, which were granted to consumer borrowers with limited ability to pay and on the assumption of a continually rising real estate market. Borrowers were often enticed with low interest rates at the beginning of the mortgage term. As property values declined, the default rate became alarming, which contributed to widespread disaster in the financial sector. In an effort to prevent a similar situation from occurring in Canada, the government introduced a series of changes designed to tighten Canada's mortgage regulations. Since 2008, these changes include increasing minimum down payments, shortening allowable amortization periods, and tightening rules for home equity financed lines of credit.

Equity of redemption

The right to regain legal title to mortgaged land upon repayment of the debt.

Mortgagor

The party who borrows the money and signs the mortgage promising to repay the loan.

Mortgagee

The party who lends the money and receives the signed mortgage as security for repayment.

CASE

Scotia Mortgage Corporation v. Gutierrez, 2012 ABQB 683

THE BUSINESS CONTEXT: As with most jurisdictions, the Canadian real estate market has gone through cycles of boom and bust.

Inevitably, when the market takes a downturn, unscrupulous individuals find ways to capitalize on the plight of desperate homeowners who find themselves unable to meet their mortgage payments. In Alberta, a phenomenon known

(Continued)

as the "dollar dealer" appeared on the scene in the busts of the early 1970s and again in the early 1980s. The dollar dealer would offer to purchase a beleaguered homeowner's property for a dollar, assuring them they would be free of their obligations under the mortgage. The dollar dealer would then rent out the home and collect the rents, all while allowing the mortgage to fall further into default. Foreclosure proceedings, meanwhile, would take a considerable amount of time, and by the time of their conclusion, the dollar dealer had made a tidy profit. In response to the problem, the Alberta government changed the *Law of Property Act* to provide lenders with a speedier foreclosure process. After the financial crisis in 2008, a new version of the dollar dealer emerged.

FACTUAL BACKGROUND: In 2010, Sagrario and Roberto Gutierrez granted the Scotia Mortgage Corporation a mortgage on their Calgary home, where they lived with their children. The mortgage was a "high ratio" mortgage, meaning that it was granted without a down payment (0% down payment mortgages were possible until September 2012) or the down payment was very small relative to the value of the property. One of the features of a high ratio mortgage is that, in the event of default and foreclosure, the borrower can be sued personally in the event the proceeds from the sale of the property are insufficient to cover the outstanding debt. Unfortunately, Sagrario Gutierrez became ill and was no longer able to work and, as a result of losing her income, the Gutierrezes could no longer afford to pay their $1511 monthly mortgage and tax payments. With no other financial resources and wanting to stay in their home, they transferred their title to a numbered company owned by Derek Johnson, receiving nothing in return. The arrangement—which, the court noted, made no sense—was that they could remain on the property as renters, paying $1400 per month, and that Johnson's company would make up the difference plus pay the property taxes, and then after two years of losing money, would transfer the property back to the defendants. Of course, the numbered company did not

Andy Dean Photography/Shutterstock

make the mortgage payments. In the foreclosure proceedings, Johnson appeared in court and argued that his company would not pay up the arrears until he had "verified the mortgage," a position that the court noted was particularly absurd in Alberta's land titles system which guarantees the accuracy of registrations on certificates of title.

THE LEGAL QUESTION: Should the court grant the lender's request for an order to sell the property?

RESOLUTION: The court found that Johnson's intent was to delay the foreclosure so that Johnson's company could continue to collect rent from the Gutierrezes. The court noted the analogy to the dollar dealers of the 1970s and 1980s, observing that the new incarnation introduced a new twist:

> The new scoundrel, while collecting rent would appear in court and make outlandish statements to obfuscate and delay the proceedings. The scoundrel obtained a substantial cash flow from numerous desperate homeowners. While the homeowner was able to remain in the residence, the mortgage debts and legal costs increased substantially because of the activity of the scoundrel. Eventually the mortgage company would obtain title to the property and, in many cases, obtain a deficiency judgment against the homeowner.

The court noted that the company owned by Johnson had entered into similar arrangements with other unwary and desperate homeowners:

In many of these foreclosures, the mortgage company would also obtain judgment against the numbered Alberta corporation. It is clear that Mr. Johnson is a scoundrel for holding out hope to desperate homeowners in order to enrich himself. [The numbered company] has in many cases been added as a defendant and several judgments [have] been obtained against [it]. A search at the Personal Property Registry reveals that eight judgments have been assigned by the mortgage company to Canada Mortgage and Housing Corporation in the total amount of $624 655. Another insurer, Genworth Financial Mortgage Insurance Company, has six judgments assigned to it in the total amount of $729 920. Two other lenders have judgments against [the numbered company] totalling $157 083.

When Mr. Johnson advises the court that he has years of experience in the Calgary real estate market and that the Court has not kept up with and does not understand the current real estate practices, he makes a vexatious argument. My grandfather's generation would describe him as a snake oil salesman. There is no merit to any of his arguments. His appearances cause unnecessary costs and delay. He shows a lack of understanding of basic real estate and mortgage practice and procedures. His arguments have been rejected repeatedly by both Masters and Justices on appeal.

Unfortunately, with few other options, the court granted the bank's order for the sale of the home and found the Gutierrezes were liable to make up the deficiency.

CRITICAL ANALYSIS: The affidavit of default confirmed that the outstanding balance on the Gutierrez mortgage was $372 097.70 yet the appraised value of the home was only $360 000. Why are high ratio mortgages considered risky for both purchasers and lenders? As of September 2012, purchasers must come up with minimum down payments of at least 5 percent. Is this enough, or do you think that Canada's laws respecting high ratio mortgages should be changed further? Do you think the law does enough to protect desperate and unwary homeowners from unscrupulous dealers like the numbered company in this case?

Sources: *Scotia Mortgage Corporation v. Gutierrez*, 2012 ABQB 683, Mike Fotiou, "Dollar Dealer Scam Resurfacing in Calgary" Calgary Real Estate Review (19 November 2012), online: http://calgaryrealestater-eview.com/2012/11/19/dollar-dealer-scam-resurfacing-in-calgary/

The mortgage document is normally prepared by the lender. Though each bank has its own standard form of mortgage, all of them include the following as basic terms:

- amount of the loan (known as the principal).
- interest rate.
- date of renegotiation of the interest rate.
- period of repayment over which the loan is amortized.
- schedule of payments.
- provision for payment of property taxes.
- provision for full insurance coverage on the property, with the proceeds to be paid directly to the lender.
- borrower's obligation to keep the property in a good state of repair and refrain from any activity that would decrease its value.
- complete legal description of the land.
- provision for early repayment (possible penalty).
- acceleration clause, which provides that on default of payment by the borrower, the whole amount of the loan becomes due.

- remedies of the lender on default.
- discharge (release) of the mortgage at the end of the term when the full loan is repaid.

Of particular interest are the clauses dealing with taxes and insurance. The bank needs to be sure the taxes are paid because the appropriate municipal or provincial authorities have the right to sell the property to recover any unpaid taxes levied against the property. The land would then be owned by the purchaser at the tax sale and would not be available to the bank. The bank's interest in insurance is twofold. First, the bank needs full coverage on the property so that if a fire occurs, the proceeds from the insurance will essentially replace the portion of the security destroyed by the fire. Second, the bank needs direct access to those insurance proceeds and therefore the mortgage will contain a term assigning the insurance proceeds to the lender.

Life of a Mortgage

If the mortgage transaction proceeds as intended by both the borrower and the lender, the borrower will repay the loan as the mortgage requires and the lender's claim or charge against the land will cease. However, since a mortgage is a long-term arrangement, many events can occur that result in some change to the liability, such as the following:

- Alpha may choose to pay off the mortgage before it is due. The mortgagee will likely anticipate this possibility in the mortgage document and require Alpha to pay a "penalty" or extra charge.
- if the mall property that Alpha buys contains unused land, Alpha may choose to sell some of the excess. Since the mortgage forms a claim on all the land, Alpha needs to negotiate with the bank for a release of the piece to be sold. Only when this partial release is registered can Alpha transfer clear title to that piece.
- Alpha may need to renegotiate the mortgage for further financing. If the value of the land is well above the amount of the outstanding loan, the land could be used as security for an additional amount.
- Alpha may decide to sell all of the land. This requires that Alpha pay out the mortgage fully or negotiate with the buyer to take over or "assume" the mortgage if the terms are attractive. For example, if Alpha has a lower interest rate than the current market rate, the lower rate could be used as a selling point by Alpha. This "assumption" requires the agreement of the bank and likely entails a significant risk for Alpha. When a mortgage is assumed, the original borrower—Alpha—remains liable for payment in the event the new buyer defaults under the terms of the mortgage.[38]

Mortgagee's Remedies

Alpha's business may suffer to the point where cash flow no longer allows for payments to the bank. This is the situation that the bank most fears and that the mortgage is primarily designed to address in terms of remedies. The bank is likely to give Alpha some leeway in payment, especially if the bank is hopeful

---

38 However, see *Citadel General Assurance Co v Iaboni* (2004), 241 DLR (4th) 128 (Ont.C.A.) where the original mortgagors were not held responsible after they had sold their equity of redemption and the mortgage had been renewed without notice to them.

that Alpha's business may recover. If this fails, the bank will proceed to exercise its legal remedies pursuant to the mortgage and applicable legislation. The rights of the lender and the procedures to be followed vary from province to province,[39] but all involve a combination of four remedies—suing the borrower, taking possession of the land, selling the land or having it sold, and **foreclosure**.

Foreclosure refers to the lender's right to terminate the borrower's interest in the property to allow the lender to realize the value of the land by selling it directly pursuant to a power of sale or through a court-supervised sale. In some jurisdictions, the bank's recourse will be restricted to the land and the bank will not be able to pursue the borrower directly unless it is a high ratio mortgage.[40] Most provinces permit the lender to proceed against the borrower for the shortfall—known as the **deficiency**—between the outstanding amount and the proceeds from sale of the property.

At any point before the foreclosure process is complete, ownership of the land can be regained if the borrower is able to repay the loan (assuming of course that another source of financing becomes available). If Alpha cannot repay the loan, it loses the land and may be left owing a substantial debt. If there is more than one mortgage registered against the land, the remedies of the various mortgagees are more complicated. Each mortgagee's rights and remedies are determined in strict order of registration of the mortgages with mortgagees beyond the first less likely to recover than those that registered ahead of them.

The Real Estate Lease

The Landlord–Tenant Relationship

Ashley is currently in a landlord–tenant relationship because she is leasing her store space. Ashley is the **tenant**. The owner of the building that she occupies is the **landlord**. Since Alpha is intending to buy a partially leased mall, it will become an owner and landlord and will enter into further leases for the space not needed for Ashley's store.

A lease[41] is a contract between a landlord and a tenant. It records the rights and obligations of both parties. It is also an interest in land. Leases are of two general types—commercial and residential. The two types are significantly different in terms of the ability of the parties to negotiate their own terms, the rights and obligations in the lease, remedies, and enforcement mechanisms.

Residential leases are heavily regulated by provincial legislation[42] that

- prescribes the form and content of the lease.
- limits the amount of security deposits that can be required of residential tenants.
- defines the rights and obligations of the landlord and tenant, including tenant's security of tenure.
- requires the landlord to maintain the premises.

Foreclosure

The mortgagee's remedy to terminate the mortgagor's interest in the land.

Deficiency

The shortfall between the outstanding mortgage balance and the proceeds from sale of the land.

PART FIVE

Tenant

The party in possession of land that is leased.

Landlord

The owner of land who grants possession to the tenant.

---

39 Sale by the court is preferred in Alberta, Saskatchewan, and part of Manitoba, and is the only remedy in Nova Scotia. Otherwise, sale and foreclosure by the mortgagee is allowed.

40 In Alberta, Saskatchewan, and British Columbia, the mortgagee cannot personally sue individual borrowers and can sue only corporations that have waived their statutory protection. See for example, the *Law of Property Act*, R.S.A. 2000, C. L-7, s 44.

41 See Chapter 17.

42 See, for example, *Residential Tenancies Act*, R.S.N.S. 1989, c. 401; *Residential Tenancies Act*, 2006, S.O. 2006, c. 17; and *Residential Tenancies Act*, C.C.S.M. c. R119.

- provides remedies for breach of the terms of the lease.
- provides the procedures for resolving disputes.

Commercial leases are relatively unregulated.[43] The terms are negotiated solely by the landlord and tenant. They are free to agree on the format and content of the lease. If Alpha were the owner of an apartment complex and a commercial mall, the apartment lease would be under the residential regime and the mall lease governed by commercial rules. The discussion that follows is geared mainly to commercial situations.

A lease is a means of dividing ownership of property for a time. Its key feature is the idea of **exclusive possession**, which means the tenant has a high level of control over and responsibility for the premises during the term of the lease. This concept of exclusive possession is doubly important because first, it is the main factor in deciding whether a lease has been created to begin with and, second, it is the major consequence of the creation of a lease. For example, a five-year lease means that the tenant has the right to occupy and control the property for the full five years and cannot be legally evicted from the land unless the lease is violated by that tenant in a major way, even if the land is sold to another owner. If Alpha, as landlord, enters into a long-term lease with a tenant and later wrongfully terminates that lease, Alpha is in breach of contract and must pay damages to the tenant. Alpha may also be subject to an order for specific performance or an injunction preventing the eviction of the tenant.

As with any contract, the parties need to appreciate the point at which they have achieved sufficient consensus to form a legal relationship. Each party wants terms acceptable to it and wants to obligate the other party to them. An offer to lease or an agreement to lease becomes enforceable only if it contains all the key terms (identification of the parties, the premises to be occupied, the term, the rent, and the intent to grant exclusive possession to the tenant) and has been accepted by the other party.

Terms of the Lease

The complexity of the lease depends on the value, nature, and size of the property. A lease for an office tower is lengthy and complicated because there are many issues to address and a great deal is at stake. Conversely, a lease of a garage to store surplus equipment could be quite simple.

These are some basic terms in every commercial lease:

- identification of the parties.
- description of the premises.
- permitted alteration of the space by the tenant and what happens to the alteration when the lease ends.
- ownership of improvements to the space.
- calculation of rent (e.g., based on the amount of space and/or a percentage of gross sales).
- responsibility for repairs and maintenance to the leased space and any common areas.
- security and damage deposits.

Exclusive possession

The tenant's right to control land during the term of a lease.

---

43 But see legislation such as *Commercial Tenancies Act*, R.S.O. 1990, c. L.7; *Tenancies and Distress for Rent Act*, R.S.N.S. 1989, c. 464; and *Overholding Tenants Act*, R.S.N.S. 1989, c. 329 that deals with such issues as forfeiture, re-entry and distress in commercial tenancies.

What are some key negotiation points for the tenants leasing space in outlet malls?

- permitted uses of the space by the tenant.
- tenant's hours of operation.
- limits on the landlord's ability to lease other space to the tenant's competitors.
- time period of the lease (generally three to five years).
- provisions for renegotiation, renewal, or termination.
- provisions for assignment and subletting.
- remedies for either party if the other fails to comply with the lease.
- what happens in case of events such as fire or flood that damage the leased property and adjacent property owned by the landlord or others.
- protection of the landlord in the event of the tenant's bankruptcy.
- dispute resolution process.

Rights and Obligations

The rights and obligations contained in a commercial lease are formally known as covenants and consist largely of whatever the parties negotiate in the lease. Commercial leases vary significantly and must be reviewed closely in order to understand the rights and obligations of the parties. However, some covenants arise from the tenant's exclusive possession and corresponding responsibility:

- the tenant is responsible for repairs unless the lease imposes some obligation on the landlord.
- the tenant is entitled to exclusive and quiet possession of the premises for the full term. In return, the tenant must pay rent and observe the terms of the lease.
- the tenant cannot withhold rent, even if the landlord fails to meet a requirement in the lease. The tenant's remedy is to claim compensation from the landlord while continuing to pay rent.
- the tenant cannot terminate the lease and move out unless the landlord's breach of the lease has made the premises uninhabitable for normal purposes.

- ordinarily, the tenant can assign the lease or sublet the property to another tenant.[44] Assigning the lease transfers full rights (and the related obligations) for the remainder of the term. A sublease, in contrast, is an arrangement whereby the tenant permits someone else to occupy the leased premises for part of the time remaining in the lease. The original tenant remains fully liable under the lease but has rights against the subtenant—should the subtenant fail to pay the sub-rent, for example. It is common for the lease to require the landlord's consent for both of these arrangements. Such leases normally also provide that the landlord's consent may not be unreasonably withheld.

The landlord's basic obligations are to refrain from interfering with the tenant's use or enjoyment of the property and to provide any benefits or services promised in the lease. The landlord's goal is that the tenant pay rent, use the premises for acceptable purposes, and cause no damage to the property. The major risk for landlords is that the tenants may get into financial difficulties. Thus, remedies for landlords focus on collecting unpaid rent and evicting tenants for defaulting on payment or for other serious breaches. Unlike the usual contract situation, a commercial landlord has no obligation to mitigate damages if the tenant abandons the premises. Commercial landlords also have the remedy of **distress**: if a landlord follows proper procedures, she can seize the property of the tenant located in the leased premises, sell the property, and apply the proceeds to the unpaid rent. However, the landlord should be aware that electing to distrain for unpaid rent may have the effect of affirming the lease and the landlord may not be able to terminate the lease for the same breach—and may have to wait for a further default in order to terminate the lease.[45]

Distress

The right of a commercial landlord to seize the tenant's personal property for non-payment of rent.

CASE

Goodman Rosen Inc v Sobeys Groups Inc, 2003 NSCA 87

THE BUSINESS CONTEXT: This case illustrates the importance of the terms of a commercial lease, especially regarding the permitted activities of a tenant over the period of a long-term lease.

FACTUAL BACKGROUND: Sobeys signed a 25-year lease for space in a shopping mall in which to operate a supermarket. A clause in the lease stated, "[T]he Lessee shall use the Leased premises only for the purposes of the business of the retail sale of a complete line of food products, as well as general retail merchandising, as carried on by the rest of the majority of its stores." The lease also contained a covenant by the landlord not to permit any part of the mall

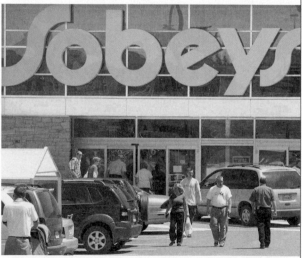

How can shopping mall leases deal with potential competition among tenants?

Ingrid Bulmer/Halifax Chronicle Herald/The Canadian Press

---

44 *See Gateway Realty Ltd v Arton Holdings Ltd* (1992), 112 NSR (2d) 180 in Chapter 7.
45 *Delane Industry Co. Limited v. PCI Properties Corp., PCI Waterfront Leasing Corp.,* 2014 BCCA 285.

to be used for the purpose of carrying on the business of the sale of food in any form. This non-competition covenant was a fundamental term of the lease that, if breached, would entitle Sobeys to terminate the lease. Shortly after Sobeys opened its store in the mall, Shoppers Drug Mart leased space for 20 years in which to operate a pharmacy. Shortly before the expiry of its lease, Sobeys opened a pharmacy within its supermarket as part of a corporate strategy to include a pharmacy in all of its stores. The landlord claimed that Sobeys' pharmacy was a violation of the lease and demanded that it be closed.

THE LEGAL QUESTION: Does the Sobeys pharmacy violate the lease? If so, what remedy is available to the landlord?

RESOLUTION: The court interpreted the clause in question to allow the retail sale of goods, but not the sale of services. The professional services offered by a pharmacy are outside the meaning of "general retail merchandising." The court also found that pharmacies were not yet part of the majority of Sobeys stores and therefore not permitted on that basis. The court granted an injunction to the landlord ordering Sobeys to cease the operation of its pharmacy.

CRITICAL ANALYSIS: How can the language of a long-term lease provide for developments in retail operations? What is likely to happen at the end of Sobeys' 25-year lease?

Termination of the Lease

The parties may be able to terminate their relationship if the terms of the lease are not followed. Normally, the lease runs its natural course and ends when the agreed period for the tenant's occupation expires.

There are two types of leases in terms of time. One identifies the exact duration of the lease. If Ashley's lease of her current space was for a fixed term of five years, which is about to expire, the lease will automatically end on the specified date. Similarly, the Sobeys lease in the case above will end when the 25-year term expires. Neither party is required to give any notice or obligated to negotiate a renewal or extension. Therefore the landlord should realize that Ashley is free to move, and she should realize that she has no right to stay beyond the specified date. If Ashley's current lease is not near its end, she will need to negotiate an early termination.

The other type is known as a **periodic tenancy** and automatically renews itself unless one party gives the required notice before the current term expires. For example, if Ashley has a lease from year to year, that lease will automatically be renewed for another full year unless either Ashley or the landlord gives sufficient notice (likely about three months). To avoid uncertainty, the parties should deal with termination in detail in the lease so that there is no doubt about the length, renewals, or the need for notice to terminate.

A lease as an interest in land is, in theory, not affected by the sale of the property by the landlord. The tenant is entitled to stay until the end of the lease, with the new owner as landlord. However, long-term leases must be registered in some provinces, and in any event should be registered to give those who are investigating title clear notice of their existence.

When Alpha buys the mall, it will inherit the existing leases for the duration of their remaining term. When deciding how much space to use for Ashley's store and therefore how much extra space to lease to new tenants, Alpha must be aware of the rigidity of long-term leases. Alpha could consider finding tenants who are prepared to enter a short-term tenancy or a periodic tenancy from month to

Periodic tenancy

A lease that is automatically renewed unless one party gives proper notice to terminate.

month. This would permit Alpha to regain full possession of the premises if the need arose. The disadvantage is that this may make the property less attractive to tenants unless their needs are short term ones as well.

Risk Management

The major risk relating to real property is the complexity of the law. A businessperson entering a transaction to buy, lease, or mortgage land needs to obtain competent legal advice to guide her through the complications and ensure that her interests are adequately protected. Real property is largely a buyer-beware proposition, in that those involved are expected to do their own thorough investigations before committing to a real estate transaction. Risk reduction is crucial.

Key commitments relate to contracts for the purchase or sale of land, the lease, or the mortgage. The language is complex, and it is crucial for those involved to understand the language in some detail as well as the broader implications of the transactions. A buyer of land must ensure that the agreement contains all terms of importance. A landlord and tenant need to understand the degree of control that the lease provides for the tenant. One who signs a mortgage should understand the far-reaching rights enjoyed by the lender in the event of default.

In many situations, the bargaining power of the businessperson may be limited by financial need, the challenges of dealing with large institutions, or the fluctuations of the market. The ability to avoid, reduce, or transfer risk may be limited. What cannot be bargained can at least be understood with the help of expert advice.

BUSINESS LAW IN PRACTICE REVISITED

1. What are the legal issues for Ashley in the planned purchase of the mall?

The major legal challenge in the purchase of the mall is the need to ensure that the agreement of purchase and sale is negotiated with legal assistance so that it provides adequate protection for Alpha, Ashley, and Andrew. They must realize that they have full responsibility to verify all aspects of the property, such as the title, zoning, and environmental condition, before proceeding to finalize the purchase.

2. What are the risks in borrowing 60 percent of the purchase price of the mall?

Ashley and Andrew need to appreciate the significance of signing a mortgage on behalf of Alpha for such a significant portion of the purchase price of the mall. They must be justifiably confident that the location and revenue from the mall will be ample to meet the mortgage payments. If Alpha defaults and they are unable to renegotiate more favourable terms, Alpha will lose ownership and possession of the mall. The lender may also require personal guarantees from Ashley and Andrew. If they agree to this condition, Ashley and Andrew's personal assets will be exposed.

3. What does Ashley need to know about the rights and obligations of her current lease and leases for the mall?

Ashley needs to understand the need to negotiate with her landlord for termination of her current lease. She and Andrew must understand that as purchasers of the mall through Alpha, they are obliged to honour the leases with the current tenants. They also need to appreciate the nature of the commitment to additional tenants for the space that will not be used for Ashley's store. Mall leases are complicated arrangements, so they need legal advice in drafting and negotiating.

CHAPTER SUMMARY

Real property is permanent and immovable, and the total quantity is fixed. The focus of the law is on the land itself rather than the buildings or fixtures attached to it. Ownership is called the fee simple and includes everything on, above, and below the land, subject to a wide variety of limits on use. The owner of land can transfer and divide ownership in a number of ways. Registration of any interest in land is required to preserve priority over other claimants. There were two systems of registration in Canada—registry and land titles—although all provinces are moving toward an electronic land titles system. The most common ways to acquire ownership are to purchase the fee simple through a real estate transaction or to become a tenant through a lease. Buying land involves considerable risk, which can be managed through investigation of all aspects of the land.

A mortgage is security for a loan that emphasizes the preservation of the value of the property. A mortgage gives the lender the right to sell the land or have it sold if the loan is not repaid.

The landlord transfers to the tenant the right of exclusive possession of the land for the term of the lease. In return, the landlord is entitled to rent and has the right to regain possession at the end of the lease or earlier if the tenant defaults. The lease will end when a specified term expires or when one party gives the required notice to the other.

The holder of the fee simple can dispose of her interest as she chooses: lease the land temporarily, sell it, or give it away while she is alive or in her will upon death.

CHAPTER STUDY

Key Terms and Concepts

closing (p. 485)

deficiency (p. 493)

distress (p. 496)

equity of redemption (p. 489)

exclusive possession (p. 494)

fee simple (p. 475)

fixtures (p. 475)

foreclosure (p. 493)

joint tenancy (p. 475)

landlord (p. 493)

land titles system (p. 478)

mortgage (p. 488)

mortgagee (p. 489)

mortgagor (p. 489)

periodic tenancy (p. 497)

registry system (p. 477)

restrictive covenant (p. 476)

tenancy in common (p. 475)

tenant (p. 493)

title insurance (p. 480)

title search (p. 482)

Questions for Review

1. What are the unique features of land as a form of property?

2. What is a fee simple?

3. What are the limits on an owner's use of his land?

4. How does a joint tenancy operate?

5. How can ownership of land be divided by time?

6. What is the purpose of registering title to land?

7. What is a restrictive covenant relating to land?

8. What are the benefits of an electronic registration system?

9. What are the three stages in a transaction for the purchase and sale of land?

10. What should a buyer of land investigate?

11. What is clear title?

12. What happens at the closing of a property transaction?

13. What are the key features of a mortgage?

14. What are a lender's remedies if the borrower fails to make mortgage payments?

15. What are the essential terms in a lease?

16. What is the remedy of distress?

17. What is a periodic tenancy?

18. How can the owner of land dispose of his interest?

Questions for Critical Thinking

1. Land registration determines property rights strictly according to the order of registration, unless there has been fraudulent activity. Should the system allow for late registration in exceptional circumstances, such as when a buyer either fails to consult a lawyer or the lawyer neglects to register the documents? Can you think of other exceptional circumstances?

2. Can a new owner be liable to clean up contamination that was caused by a previous property owner? What about the liability of the prior owner whose activities caused the contamination? Why are there practical limitations on the effectiveness of environmental protection remediation orders and what can be done about this situation?

3. Real property law originated as a means of protecting rights or resolving disputes between conflicting individual rights to property. Increasingly, broader uses of land in the public interest are coming into conflict with individual owners' rights. Some examples are wind turbines that produce noise; cell phone towers that are unsightly and may emit radiation; and oil or natural gas pipelines that entail environmental risks. What factors may help to resolve this friction between the public interest and individual ownership rights?

4. In most cases, a lender has more expertise and experience in credit transactions than the borrower. Do the rules of contracts and mortgages allow the mortgagee (lender) too much protection at the expense of the mortgagor (borrower)? Should the lender bear some responsibility for a decision to lend that turns out to be a bad one? Does it matter that the mortgage is a high ratio or subprime mortgage and the borrower has been enticed and persuaded by the lender to borrow the money?

5. The format and content of residential leases is largely dictated by legislation, while commercial leases are entirely negotiated by the parties, resulting in lengthy and complex documents. The difference is largely based on the assumption that commercial tenants can take care of themselves while residential tenants are vulnerable to exploitation by landlords. Is this a valid assumption? Should there be more similarity in the processes that create the two types of leases?

6. Covenants in commercial leases generally limit the landlord's ability to rent space to tenants whose businesses compete with those of existing tenants. In shopping malls, the anchor tenants have more bargaining power than smaller stores, so can better protect their business. In times of real estate downturn, small stores may fail at a higher rate. The covenants may limit the landlord's ability to fill the vacant space. What are the implications of this situation? Are there remedies to better promote the full use of mall space?

Situations for Discussion

1. The Mellicks owned a farm that the Haywards were interested in buying. During negotiations, the Mellicks told the Haywards that the farm contained a total of 94 acres, with 65 acres under cultivation. The offer to buy described the farm as containing 94 acres but made no mention of acres under cultivation. The agreement contained a clause indicating that there were no conditions, representations, or agreements other than those expressly contained in the offer. The deal closed, and several months later, the Haywards discovered that there were only 51.7 acres of land under cultivation.[46] Were the Haywards entitled to the 65 acres under cultivation?

2. Campbell's business is in financial difficulty. Technology is advancing quicker than Campbell can move. She is faced with a gradual reduction in business operations and a related need for less space. She has 20 years left in the lease of her business premises but cannot afford to pay the monthly rent. How should Campbell approach her landlord? What are her legal options? Is the situation different if Campbell owns her business premises subject to a mortgage on which she cannot make the payments? How should she approach her banker? What are her legal options?

3. Bayshore Trust granted a loan to Assam based on a mortgage for $210 000 with interest at 14 percent for a one-year term. The monthly payment was $2540. At the end of the term, Bayshore renewed the mortgage for another year at 14.5 percent. During that year, Assam defaulted and Bayshore sued Assam, who argued that Bayshore induced him into a state of financial disaster by granting a mortgage with monthly payments he could not possibly make. Assam alleged that Bayshore should never have lent him such a large sum of money. At the time of the mortgage, Assam's annual income was $28 000.[47] Who should decide whether a lender such as Assam can make payments on a loan? Should Bayshore be required to do anything more than protect its own interest in the mortgage? Would the outcome be different in today's subprime mortgage environment than when this case came to court in 1992?

4. Shoker engaged a real estate agent to find a property suitable for use as a trucking terminal. The agent found a property which was zoned "highway commercial." Its permitted uses included a retail store, car and truck sales agency, commercial garage, parking lot, and restaurant. Shoker signed an agreement to buy the property, which contained two conditions— the buyer would confirm the zoning with the municipality and the buyer would exercise due diligence to ensure that the property was suitable for his intended use. The agreement did not specify a trucking terminal as the intended use. Shoker discovered that the zoning would not permit the operation of a trucking terminal. He gave notice to terminate the agreement. The seller alleged breach of contract and kept the deposit of $50 000.[48] Is the agreement enforceable by the seller? How could the agreement have been more clearly written?

5. Bresson bought a piece of land for commercial development for $3 million. He was assured that it contained an unlimited supply of water from an existing well. When construction began, it was discovered that the water was unusable due to contamination in the soil caused by leakage of gasoline from underground tanks located on the adjacent property.[49] What investigation should Bresson have done before the deal closed? Was the seller obligated to disclose the state of the land? Is the owner of the adjacent property responsible?

6. Perkins leased space for two stores from Plazacorp. A few years ago, an awning across the front of the stores was removed, causing rain water to seep into one of the stores and damage carpets and inventory. Plazacorp fixed the leak after repeated complaints by Perkins over a period of time. The second store was affected by sewage backups that originated in the common area of the property. In an

---

46 Based on *Hayward v Mellick* (1984), 26 BLR 156 (Ont. C.A.).

47 Based on *Bayshore Trust Company v Assam*, [1992] OJ No 715 (Gen. Div.).

48 Based on *Shoker v Orchard Garden Markets Ltd* (2007), 62 RPR (4th) 81 (Ont. Sup. Ct. J.).

49 Based on *Bresson v Ward*, (1987) 79 NSR (2d) 156 (Co. Ct.) and *Edwards v. Boulderwood Development* (1984), 64 NSR (2d) 395 (C.A.).

attempt to prompt Plazacorp to remedy these situations, Perkins ceased paying rent. When Plazacorp sued for the rent arrears, Perkins counterclaimed for the cost of damage and repairs to the two stores.[50] Was Perkins entitled to stop paying rent? Is Perkins's counterclaim valid? On what does the answer depend?

7. Dewey entered into a commercial lease with defendant mall owner Pike. Dewey asserted an exclusive right to sell Canadian souvenirs under the terms of the lease and that Pike was permitting another tenant to sell souvenirs in breach of Dewey's rights. After Pike rejected Dewey's complaint, Dewey withheld rent for a period of time. Pike eventually demanded payment of approximately $100 000 for the unpaid rent and when Dewey failed to pay, Pike commenced distraint proceedings and sold some of Dewey's goods but realized only about $60 000 from the sale. Pike then served a notice of termination of the lease, relying on the balance of unpaid rent as the default. Was this recourse available to Pike? How should Pike proceed?[51]

8. Greenwood rented office space to Evergreen for five years with an option for renewal of three or five years. In the second year of the lease, Greenwood informed Evergreen that it could not comply with its obligations under the lease beyond the end of the current year; Greenwood planned to demolish the building and erect a 21-storey office tower. Greenwood offered Evergreen preferential treatment in the new building when it was completed. Evergreen refused to move, claiming that the current building had architectural value and should be preserved. The lease did not include clauses dealing with demolition or the landlord's right to resume possession during the term of the lease.[52] How does this situation illustrate rights of ownership and landlord–tenant relations? How could the dispute be resolved?

50 Based on *Plazacorp Retail Properties Ltd v. Perkins Health and Safety Ltd*, 2007 N.S.S.M. 30.

51 Based on *Delane Industry Co. Limited v. PCI Properties Corp., PCI Waterfront Leasing Corp.*, 2014 BCCA 285.

52 Based on *Evergreen Building Ltd v. IBI Leaseholds Ltd*, 2005 BCCA 583. See also Chris Atchison, "Tenants halt the wrecking ball's swing", *The Globe and Mail* (18 July 2011), online: The Globe and Mail <http://www.theglobeandmail.com/report-on-business/industry-news/property-report/tenants-halt-the-wrecking-balls-swing/article2101098/>.

EMPLOYMENT AND PROFESSIONAL RELATIONSHIPS

Employment and professional relationships are essential components of business. Without the skills, knowledge, and experience of others, businesses would be unable to function and compete effectively. Most businesses require a wide range of services, including managerial, clerical, administrative, and professional services, which they acquire by hiring employees or by contracting for the services as needed.

The employment of others, whether through the employment relationship or through an independent service contract, has been affected by significant social change: the entry of women in large numbers into the workforce; recognition of the disadvantaged position of minorities; greater awareness of the needs of people with disabilities; heightened public concern for the fair treatment of workers; adaptation to technological developments; and concern for job security. Not surprisingly, there has been much legal intervention to address these developments. In addition to the common law, a vast array of federal and provincial legislation affects all aspects of employment.

20

THE EMPLOYMENT RELATIONSHIP

OBJECTIVES

After studying this chapter, you should have an understanding of

- the basic elements of the employment relationship
- the ways in which the law affects recruitment practices
- the content of a typical employment contract
- the legal issues relating to the terms and conditions of employment

BUSINESS LAW IN PRACTICE

Hiram Dupuis owns and operates an independent weekly newspaper in southern Ontario. The newspaper has a circulation of 250 000 and focuses mainly on community news and human interest stories.

Several months ago, Hiram engaged the services of Jeong Nash to write a column as well as feature stories on the local sports scene. Hiram refers to all of the reporters as independent contractors and permits them to accept writing assignments from other newspapers as long as the assignments do not conflict with obligations to Hiram's newspaper. Hiram pays Jeong on the basis of a fee per published word, as well as a base monthly salary of $3000. Hiram provides Jeong with office space and a computer and gives Jeong the freedom to pursue whatever stories she likes as long as they have a sports angle.

Recently, Hiram learned that Jeong sent an email message to a local sports celebrity requesting an interview. When the hockey player declined the request, Jeong sent him a nasty reply. In addition, Jeong posted possibly defamatory remarks about the hockey player on a website dedicated to hockey.

1. Is Jeong an employee or an independent contractor?
2. Why is the distinction between an employee and an independent contractor important?
3. Is Hiram responsible for Jeong's conduct?

Employment Law

The employment relationship is a critical component of business activity. Engaging the services of others provide the means by which a business can carry out its mission. Employment is much more than an engine of business, however. It is a relationship that provides a livelihood for a large portion of society. Given the importance of this relationship to both the employer and the employee, it is not surprising that there is a vast body of law regulating employment.

Employment law in all Canadian jurisdictions, with the exception of Quebec, is rooted in the traditions of the English common law, with an overlay of legislation. Both the federal and provincial governments have jurisdiction to pass employment legislation, and both levels have been active in this area.

Ryan McVay/Photodisc

The federal government has jurisdiction to make laws that affect employees of the federal government and federally regulated industries, such as the banking, airline, broadcasting, railway, and shipping industries. It is estimated that about 10 percent of all employees are subject to federal regulation. The provincial governments have jurisdiction to make laws that affect all other employees, including provincial employees. For example, as the newspaper industry is not federally regulated, employees of newspapers come under provincial jurisdiction. An employee is subject to either federal or provincial jurisdiction, and it is not unusual for employees working in close proximity to be subject to different employment legislation.

Both levels of government have enacted human rights legislation and an array of employee welfare legislation, such as employment standards, occupational health and safety standards, and workers' compensation. In addition to legislation of general application, governments have passed legislation that affects employees in specific jobs. Public sector employees—such as police officers, teachers, medical personnel, and civil servants—are commonly affected by specific legislation.

Employees may also be unionized, in which case labour relations legislation is applicable to the employment relationship. The federal government and all of the provinces have enacted labour or industrial relations statutes that facilitate the unionization process.

This chapter focuses on laws that affect the employment process in the private, non-unionized sector, as the majority of employees fall within this category. At the end of the chapter, a note is provided on differences in the union environment.

The Employment Relationship

The **employment relationship** involves a contract whereby one party, the employer, provides remuneration to another, the employee, in return for work or services.[1] Not everyone who works for another or provides services to another is an employee, however. In some situations, someone who provides services is considered an agent[2] or **independent contractor**. Usually, doctors and lawyers, for example, provide services in the capacity of independent contractors, rather than as employees of their patients/clients. There is also an emerging trend to create a category of worker called a **dependent contractor**.[3] This is a person who is an independent contractor but has a relationship of economic dependency with the employer as a result of working exclusively or nearly exclusively for the employer for a long period.

Beginning in the 1980s with the advent of "downsizing" and "right-sizing," people who traditionally worked as employees increasingly worked as independent contractors. This trend has continued.[4] The benefits for independent contractors are tax savings, flexibility, and independence in arranging a work schedule. An employer may prefer to engage independent contractors because the relationship offers simplicity, fewer financial and legal obligations, and the ability to manage peak workloads.

Employment relationship

A contractual relationship whereby an employer provides remuneration to an employee in exchange for work or services.

Independent contractor

A person who is in a working relationship that does not meet the criteria of employment.

Dependent contractor

A person who is an independent contractor but has a relationship of economic dependency with the employer as a result of working exclusively or nearly exclusively for the employer for a long period.

PART SIX

---

1   The historical terms for employer and employee are "master" and "servant."
2   The law affecting agents is discussed in Chapter 13.
3   See: *Drew Oliphant Professional Corp. v Dr. Kelly Harrison*, 2011 ABQB 216, 56 Alta LR (5th) 233; *McKee v Reid's Heritage Homes Limited*, 2009 ONCA 916, 256 OAC 376 (CanLII)
4   See *1392644 Ontario Inc. (Connor Homes) v Canada (National Revenue)* 2013 FCA 85, 358 DLR (4th) 363; Adrianna Midence, "A risky new trend replacing employees with independent contractors", *Workforce* (13 November 2009), online: Workforce <http://www.workforce.com/articles/a-risky-new-trend-replacing -employees-with-independent-contractors>.

Employee versus Independent Contractor

The distinction between an employee and an independent contractor is not always readily apparent. It is common to think of independent contractors as being short-term and temporary, while employees are long-term and permanent. In practice, this might be the case, but it is not a distinction based in law. Historically, the courts have used a variety of tests to distinguish between the two relationships, including the following:

- *the degree of control exercised over the individual by the employer.* The more direction and supervision provided by the employer, the more likely that the relationship is employment. Hiram exercises little control over how Jeong carries out her work and permits her to pursue other assignments; this is indicative of an employer and independent contractor relationship.

- *the ownership of tools, chance of profit, and the risk of loss from performance of the requested service.*[5] Sharing profits and losses and the ownership of tools are indicative of an independent contractor. On this basis, it appears as if Jeong is an employee, because she does not own her own tools or share in the profits or losses of the business.

- *the degree of integration.* The nature of the work being performed is considered in relation to the business itself. The question is whether the work being performed is "integral" to the business, or is "adjunct" to the normal work of the business.[6] The more the work is integrated into the company's activities, the more likely it is that the individual is an employee. For example, Jeong's work is integral to the operation of a newspaper; based on this fact, she would appear to be an employee.

The Supreme Court of Canada in the following case has indicated that there is no one conclusive test that can be universally applied. The nature of a relationship is a question of fact and will vary with the situation.

CASE

671122 Ontario Ltd v Sagaz Industries Canada Inc, 2001 SCC 59, [2001] 2 SCR 983

THE BUSINESS CONTEXT: Changes in the workplace—corporate restructuring, globalization, and employee mobilization—have resulted in a shift away from traditional employment relationships. However, as relationships have grown more flexible, they have also grown more complex, and the question of whether a relationship is that of an employer and employee or that of an employer and independent contractor is receiving a great deal of attention.

FACTUAL BACKGROUND: A design company sold seat covers to Canadian Tire. However, it lost its contract with Canadian Tire to Sagaz because of the actions of American Independent Marketing (AIM), hired by Sagaz to assist in securing Canadian Tire business. AIM and its employee bribed an employee of Canadian Tire in order to induce Canadian Tire to buy from Sagaz. As a result, the design company lost a substantial amount of money and went into steep decline.

THE LEGAL QUESTION: Was Sagaz vicariously liable for the bribery scheme perpetrated by AIM?

---

5   *Montreal (City of) v Montreal Locomotive Works Ltd,* [1947] 1 DLR 161, [1946] 2 WWR 746 (PC).
6   *Co-operators Insurance Association v Kearney,* [1965] SCR 106, 48 DLR (2d) 1.

RESOLUTION: Vicarious liability is a theory that holds one person responsible for the misconduct of another because of the relationship between them. The most common relationship that attracts vicarious liability is the relationship between employers and employees. The relationship between employers and independent contractors, subject to limited exceptions, does not give rise to a claim for vicarious liability.

There is no one conclusive test that can be universally applied to determine whether a person is an employee or an independent contractor. What must always occur is a search for the total relationship of the parties. The central question is whether the person who has been engaged to perform the services is performing them as a person in business on his own account.

The contract designated AIM as an "independent contractor," but this classification is not always determinative for the purposes of vicarious liability. However, as AIM was in business on its own account, it is an independent contractor. This conclusion is supported by the following factors: AIM paid all of its own costs of conducting its business; AIM was free to carry on other activities and to represent other suppliers; Sagaz did not specify how much time AIM was to devote to representing Sagaz; AIM worked on commission on the sales of Sagaz's products; and AIM controlled how the work was to be done.

CRITICAL ANALYSIS: The determination of whether a worker is an employee or an independent contractor is critical, as employee status is the gateway to most employment protection under both the common law and employment-related legislation. What factors indicate the presence of an employer and employee relationship?

Recently the Federal Court of Appeal[7] suggested a two-part test for determining whether a worker is an employee or an independent contractor. First, is there a mutual understanding between the parties regarding their relationship? This may be answered by examining written contracts and the behaviour of the parties such as the issuance of an invoice, registration for GST, and income tax filings. Second, do the facts support the worker providing services as a business on her own account? The factors to consider in answering this question include the degree of control exercised over the work, provision of equipment, assumption of financial risk, hiring of helpers, and the opportunity for profit.

Implications of an Employment versus Independent (and Dependent) Contractor Relationship

Employees have certain statutory rights and benefits, such as paid holidays and paid overtime, which are not conferred on independent contractors. Employers have certain obligations with respect to employees, namely deduction of income taxes and Employment Insurance premiums, the payment of Canada (or Quebec) Pension Plan premiums, the provision of paid vacations, and the like, which they do not have with respect to independent contractors. The consequences of incorrectly characterizing a work relationship as an independent contractor arrangement can include retroactive responsibility for paying benefits as well as liability for penalties and interest charges.

Establishing the employment relationship is important to certain legal principles. For example, an employee can initiate an action for wrongful dismissal, but

---

7 *Supra* note 4.

this avenue is not available to an independent contractor. Also an employee is entitled to reasonable notice on termination whereas an independent contractor is not. A worker who is classified as a dependent contractor, however, is entitled to reasonable notice of termination. An employer is responsible for the torts of an employee committed in the ordinary course of employment, whereas an employer is not usually responsible for the torts of an independent contractor committed in the course of carrying out the contract.[8] An independent contractor may be an agent for the employer, in which case the employer can be vicariously liable for the acts of the agent under traditional agency principles.

Risks in Hiring

The hiring of workers is critical to business. Hiring well can be a boon to a business, and hiring poorly can result in low productivity and possibly a costly termination. From a business perspective, hiring the candidate who is best suited for the job results in the optimal use of resources. From a legal perspective, hiring well can reduce the risks associated with the employment relationship, in particular those associated with vicarious liability and negligent hiring.

Vicarious Liability

As previously stated, an employer is liable for the torts of an employee that are committed in the ordinary course or scope of employment. An employee's wrongful conduct is within the ordinary course or scope of employment if authorized by the employer. Thus, an employer is liable when an employee commits a wrong while carrying out assigned duties or authorized tasks. An employee's wrongful act is also within the ordinary course or scope of employment if it is an unauthorized mode of doing something that is authorized by the employer. Because the distinction between an unauthorized "mode" of performing an authorized act and an entirely independent act is difficult to discern, particularly in the case of intentional torts, the courts will consider whether the tortious conduct of the employee is significantly related or connected to conduct authorized by the employer. In other words, the employer will be vicariously liable if there is a significant connection between the wrongful acts of the employee and the creation or enhancement of the risk of the wrongful act by the employer. For example, when Jeong posted the possibly defamatory statement on the website, she was not carrying out assigned duties or authorized tasks; therefore, her employer will be liable for her acts only if there is a significant connection between her possibly wrongful conduct and the creation or enhancement of the risk of the wrongful conduct by the employer. Although the possibly defamatory statements are connected to conduct authorized by the employer—Jeong was authorized by her employer to write feature stories on the local sports scene—it is entirely possible that Jeong acted outside the employment relationship in that she was responding in a personal capacity to a perceived affront. An employer is not responsible for wrongs that occur completely outside the employment relationship.

---

8   The distinction between an employee and independent contractor for purposes of vicarious liability has been called into question. For example, in *Thiessen v Mutual Life Assurance*, 2002 BCCA 501, 6 BCLR (4th) 1 leave to appeal to SCC refused, [2002] SCCA No 454, the BC Court of Appeal imposed vicarious liability on an insurance company for the misconduct of a sales representative who was characterized as an independent contractor, not an employee.

The justifications for holding employers responsible for their employees' actions include that employers

- have the ability to control employees and therefore should be liable for the employee's conduct.
- benefit from the work of the employees and therefore should be responsible for liability incurred by employees.
- are usually in a better position than employees to pay damages. Imposing liability on employers helps ensure that an innocent victim is compensated.
- have an incentive to try to prevent torts from occurring in the first place.

The imposition of vicarious liability does not relieve the employee of liability. Both the employer and employee may be liable to the plaintiff. The employee may also be liable to the employer for breach of the employment contract; however, it is rare for an employer to pursue an action against an employee because of the inability of the employee to pay damages and the negative publicity associated with a legal action.

Negligent Hiring

Another potential risk for employers in the hiring process is in the area of "negligent hiring." An employer has a duty to use skill and care in hiring employees (the extent of the duty will vary according to the position the candidate is to fill).[9] Therefore, if an employee injures another employee or causes harm to a third party, there may be an action against the employer for being negligent in having hired that employee. This action differs from vicarious liability, which holds the employer strictly liable for the actions of the employee as long as the actions are sufficiently related to the employment. With vicarious liability, there is no requirement to prove that the employer was at fault. Negligent hiring, on the other hand, requires the plaintiff to prove that the employer was careless in, for example, hiring, training, or supervising.

The Hiring Process

The hiring process involves a number of steps. In hiring employees, employers would normally

- develop job descriptions.
- advertise the positions.
- have candidates complete an application form or submit a résumé.
- short-list candidates.
- check backgrounds or references.
- interview selected applicants.

All aspects of employment are affected by human rights legislation, and in some cases, by employment equity legislation. The legislation may affect the kind of advertising done, the form the application takes, the questions that are asked in the interview, and the decision as to who will ultimately be hired.

---

9 Stacey Ball, *Canadian Employment Law*, Student Edition (Toronto: Canada Law Book, 2012-2013) at 20.66.1.

Human Rights Requirements

The federal, provincial, and territorial governments have enacted human rights legislation[10] to provide equal access to employment opportunities for all. To this end, discrimination in employment is prohibited. The acts also provide for the establishment of a **human rights commission**, which is charged with administering the legislation and investigating and hearing complaints.

Prohibited Grounds of Discrimination

Human rights legislation does not prohibit all discrimination in employment, but only discrimination on certain prohibited grounds. There are variations from jurisdiction to jurisdiction as to what these prohibited grounds are, but generally the grounds are similar (see Figure 20.1).

If a particular ground of discrimination is not included in the human rights legislation, the exclusion may be challenged as a violation of the equality provisions of the *Canadian Charter of Rights and Freedoms*. If the challenge is successful, the courts may "read in" the ground. For example, alcohol dependency is included in physical disability; pregnancy[11] is included in sex.

FIGURE 20.1 Prohibited Grounds of Discrimination

> The following are prohibited grounds of discrimination under all Canadian legislation:
>
> ✘ marital status.
> ✘ race.
> ✘ colour.
> ✘ physical or mental disability.
> ✘ religion or creed.
> ✘ sex and sexual orientation.
> ✘ age.
>
> Examples of other common grounds that are expressly included in some jurisdictions are national or ethnic origin, family status, social condition, criminal record, ancestry, place of origin, political beliefs, and gender identity and expression.

Discrimination Defined

The human rights acts prohibit **discrimination** but do not generally define the term.[12] It usually means the act of treating someone differently on the basis of a prohibited ground. For example, to post an advertisement that says "Wanted: Malay workers for Malaysian restaurant" would be an act of discrimination, because it discriminates on the basis of national or ethnic origin. On the other hand, it is not discrimination to require job applicants to meet certain educational or training requirements.

Not only is direct or explicit discrimination prohibited, but adverse effects discrimination and systemic discrimination are also prohibited. **Adverse effects discrimination** involves the application of a rule that appears to be neutral but has discriminatory effects.[13] For example, a rule that requires all workers to wear hard hats and to work every second Saturday appears to be neutral, but its effect may be to discriminate against those whose religion requires them to wear a

---

Human rights commission

An administrative body that oversees the implementation and enforcement of human rights legislation.

Discrimination

The act of treating someone differently on the basis of a prohibited ground.

Adverse effects discrimination

Discrimination that occurs as a result of a rule that appears neutral but in its effects is discriminatory.

---

10 See, for example, *Canadian Human Rights Act*, RSC 1985, c H-6.
11 See Ball, *supra* note 9 at 33.76.
12 Only the Manitoba, Nova Scotia, Quebec, and Yukon acts offer statutory definitions of discrimination.
13 *Ontario (Human Rights Commission) v Simpson-Sears Ltd*, [1985] 2 SCR 536, 23 DLR (4th) 321 (SCC).

turban or to refrain from work on Saturdays. **Systemic discrimination** refers to the combined effects of many rules, practices, and policies that lead to a discriminatory outcome.[14] For example, if a workforce is overwhelmingly dominated by male workers, this may mean that there is systemic discrimination.

Defences to Discrimination

There are situations where it is permissible to discriminate on one of the prohibited grounds. Some defences to an allegation of discrimination include approved affirmative action or equity plans, and group insurance and pension plans. The most common defence to an allegation of discrimination is a *bona fide* occupational requirement (BFOR)—a discriminatory practice that is justified on the basis that it was adopted in good faith and for a legitimate business purpose. For example, a requirement that a person have a valid driver's licence discriminates against some persons with physical disabilities, but a valid driver's licence is a BFOR for the job of truck driver. Similarly, the requirement of wearing a hard hat discriminates against those whose religion requires them to wear a turban, but the hard hat requirement may be a BFOR for those working in construction. BFORs have been subject to much controversy, as there is little consensus on what constitutes legitimate, meaningful qualifications or requirements for job applicants. The Supreme Court of Canada in the *Meiorin* case described below set out a three-step test for determining whether a discriminatory standard qualifies as a BFOR.

Systemic discrimination

Discrimination that results from the combined effects of many rules, practices, and policies.

Bona fide occupational requirement (BFOR)

A defence that excuses discrimination on a prohibited ground when it is done in good faith and for a legitimate business reason.

CASE

British Columbia (Public Service Employee Relations Commission) v BCGEU (The Meiorin Case), [1999] 3 SCR 3, [1999] SCJ No 46

THE BUSINESS CONTEXT: Employers often implement physical performance standards or requirements for particular jobs. Standards are easy to apply and appear to be an objective or neutral basis for evaluating employees.

FACTUAL BACKGROUND: The province of British Columbia established a number of fitness standards for forest fire fighters. Among the standards, which included sit-up, pull-up, and push-up components, was an aerobic standard. The aerobic standard required a firefighter to run 2.5 km in 11 minutes. Tawney Meiorin, a three-year veteran of the service, was terminated from her job because she could not meet the standard. She needed an extra 49.4 seconds. Meiorin complained to the B.C. Human Rights Commission.

THE LEGAL QUESTION: Did the aerobic standard discriminate on the basis of sex?

RESOLUTION: The court held that the standard on its face was discriminatory, owing to physiological differences between males and females. Most women have a lower aerobic capacity than most men and cannot increase their aerobic capacity enough with training to meet the aerobic standard.

To justify the standard as a BFOR, the employer would have to show all of the following:

- the standard was adopted for a purpose rationally connected to the performance of the job.
- the standard was adopted in an honest and good-faith belief that it was necessary to fulfill a legitimate, work-related purpose.
- the standard was reasonably necessary to the accomplishment of that purpose. To show that a standard was reasonably

(Continued)

---

14 *Action Travail des Femmes v CNR Co*, [1987] 1 SCR 1114, 40 DLR (4th) 193 sub nom *Canadian National Railway Co v Canada (Canadian Human Rights Commission)*, [1985] 1 FC 96, 20 DLR (4th) 668 (FCA).

PART SIX

necessary, it must be demonstrated that it is impossible to accommodate individuals affected by the discriminatory standard without imposing undue hardship upon the employer.

Applying the approach, the court concluded that passing the aerobic standard was not reasonably necessary to the safe and efficient operation of the work of a forest fire fighter. The government had not established that it would experience undue hardship if a different standard were used. In other words, the employer failed to establish that the aerobic standard was reasonably necessary to identify those who are unable to perform the tasks of a forest fire fighter safely and efficiently.

CRITICAL ANALYSIS: The onus of proving that a standard, requirement, or qualification is a BFOR lies with the employer. What issues will the employer have to address in order to establish a BFOR?

Tawney Meiorin with lawyer John Brewin

Fred Chartrand/The Canadian Press

Duty to accommodate

The duty of an employer to modify work rules, practices, and requirements to meet the needs of individuals who would otherwise be subjected to unlawful discrimination.

The test in *Meiorin* incorporates a **duty to accommodate** the special needs of those who are negatively affected by a requirement, up to the point of undue hardship for the employer. In effect, this means that employers, when designing standards, requirements, and the like, must consider the need for individual accommodation. This does not mean that the employer must change working conditions in a fundamental way. Rather it means that the employer has a duty, if it can do so without undue hardship, to arrange the employee's workplace or duties to enable the employee to do his or her work.

CASE

Canada (Attorney General) v Johnstone, 2014 FCA 110, [2014] FCJ No 455.

THE BUSINESS CONTEXT: Many employees struggle with the demands of caring for both young children and elderly parents. The problem is exacerbated when both parents work variable, rotating shifts.

FACTUAL BACKGROUND: Fiona Johnstone and her husband worked with Canada Border Services Agency (CBSA) at Toronto's Pearson International Airport. Both were full-time employees

with rotating shift schedules that were irregular and unpredictable and overlapped about 60 percent of the time. After having children, Johnstone requested a move to fixed, full-time day shifts because the rotating shifts made it difficult to provide childcare on a reliable basis. Johnstone's request was denied on the basis that CBSA policy restricted fixed shifts to part-time employees even though some employees were given full-time fixed shifts for medical or religious reasons. Johnstone was offered part-time work on a fixed schedule, a result which would negatively affect her benefits, pension, and promotion opportunities. Johnstone filed a complaint with the Canadian Human Rights Commission.

THE LEGAL QUESTION: Had the CBSA discriminated against Johnstone on the ground of family status by refusing to accommodate her childcare needs through work scheduling arrangements?

RESOLUTION: The *Canadian Human Rights Act* prohibits discrimination on the basis of family status. The Canadian Human Rights Tribunal ruled and both the Federal Court and the Federal Court of Appeal agreed that "family status" extends to the needs and obligations that result from family relationships including parental legal obligations such as childcare. The tribunal held that the CBSA had discriminated against Johnstone on the basis of family status by failing to provide reasonable accommodation that would allow her to meet her childcare needs. The tribunal also held that the CBSA had failed to prove the undue hardship necessary to exempt it from its accommodation obligations. The Federal Court of Appeal upheld the decision and established a new four-part test that a claimant seeking accommodation must meet:

1. that a child is under his or her care or supervision;
2. that the childcare obligation at issue engages the individual's legal responsibility for that child, as opposed to a personal choice;

Fiona Johnstone helps her children Ethan, now 11, and Abigail, 9, with their homework at their home in Osgood, near Ottawa, last year.

3. that he or she has made reasonable but unsuccessful efforts to meet those childcare obligations through reasonable alternative solutions; and
4. that the workplace rule interferes with the fulfillment of the childcare obligations in a manner that is more than trivial or insubstantial.

CRITICAL ANALYSIS: As a result of this decision, do you think employers are required to accommodate an employee's childcare needs that result from participation in dance classes, sporting events, family trips, and the like? Must employers accommodate family care obligations involving family members other than young children?

What constitutes undue hardship and how far an employer must go to accommodate special needs is difficult to define. The Supreme Court of Canada[15] has indicated that undue hardship does not require the employer to show that it is impossible to accommodate the employee. It has also indicated that a measure that would require the employer to modify working conditions in a fundamental way or a measure that would completely alter the essence of the employment contract constitutes undue hardship. The court has declined to set strict guidelines, however, since every employee's condition and every workplace is unique. Factors such as the size of the organization,

---

15 *Hydro-Québec v Syndicat des employées de techniques professionnelles et de bureau d'Hydro-Québec*, 2008 SCC 43, [2008] 2 SCR 561 (CanLII).

its financial resources, the nature of operations, the cost of the accommodation measures, the risk the accommodation measures will pose to the health and safety of the employee and his colleagues and the public, and the effect of the accommodation measure on other employees and the productivity of the organization have all been taken into consideration in assessing the scope of the employer's duty.[16]

Penalties

Failure to avoid or eliminate discriminatory practices can result in a complaint to a human rights commission. This, in turn, can result in a board of inquiry investigating the complaint. If the board finds the complaint to be valid, it can order that the employer stop its practices, hire a particular individual, pay monetary compensation, write a letter of apology, reinstate an employee, or institute an affirmative action plan. Regardless of the outcome, a complaint may result in unwelcome publicity, expenditures of time and money to answer the complaint, and an unsettled work environment. To reduce the risk of a human rights complaint, an employer needs to review all aspects of the employment process.

BUSINESS APPLICATION OF THE LAW

AVOIDING DISCRIMINATION IN HIRING PRACTICES

A human rights complaint can be a costly and embarrassing situation for a company. Each step of the hiring process should be reviewed to ensure that the company is not discriminating.

Job Description: **Do** develop a list of job-related duties and responsibilities.

Don't describe job openings in terms of prohibited grounds (e.g., busboy, hostess, policeman, waitress).

Advertisements: **Do** advertise for qualifications related to ability to do the job.

Don't advertise for qualifications unrelated to ability to do the job (e.g., single, Canadian-born, young, tall, slim).

Application Forms: **Do** solicit information that is related to the applicant's ability to do the job.

Don't ask for information that suggests prohibited grounds are being considered (e.g., age, sex, photograph, or title [Miss, Ms., Mr., Mrs.]).

Interview: **Do** ask questions related to the applicant's suitability for the job.

Don't ask questions related to prohibited grounds (e.g., Are you planning to start a family? Do you have any physical disabilities? [unless the requirement not to have the disability is a *bona fide* occupational requirement] Have you ever been treated for a mental illness? How old are you? What church do you attend? What is your mother tongue? Have you ever received income assistance?).

An employer should provide human rights training for supervisors and other employees and develop policies prohibiting discrimination. Employees need to be made aware of the policies.

Critical Analysis: Why should employers be so constrained in the hiring process?

Source: "Pre-employment Inquiries Information Sheet", *Alberta Human Rights and Citizenship Commission* (February 2012) online: Alberta Human Rights and Citizenship Commission <http://www .albertahumanrights.ab.ca/preEmplinq.pdf>.

---

16 Ontario's *Human Rights Code,* RSO 1990, c H-19, s 17(2) restricts the criteria to the cost, outside sources of funding, and health and safety requirements.

Employment Equity

Employment equity may also affect hiring decisions. Employment equity attempts to achieve equality in the workplace by giving underrepresented groups special consideration in hiring. Human rights legislation prohibits discrimination; **employment equity legislation** requires employers to take positive steps to make the workplace more equitable.

The federal *Employment Equity Act*[17] targets the underrepresentation of women, Aboriginal peoples, people with disabilities, and visible minorities in the workforce. The Act, which is administered by the Canadian Human Rights Commission,[18] applies to businesses that have 100 or more employees and that are under the regulation of the federal government. It requires employers to

- consult with employee representatives regarding the implementation of employment equity.
- identify and eliminate barriers to the employment of the designated groups.
- institute policies and practices and make reasonable efforts at accommodation to ensure that the designated groups have a degree of representation in proportion to the workforce from which the employer can reasonably be expected to draw employees.
- prepare a plan that sets out the goals to be achieved and a timetable for implementation.

There has been much debate about whether such programs are a form of reverse discrimination. The equality provisions of the *Charter of Rights and Freedoms* specifically permit such programs; however, the programs are not insulated from claims of discrimination. The Supreme Court of Canada has stressed that government programs targeted at disadvantaged groups are not immune from challenges of being "underinclusive" or claims that they contravene the right of equality.[19]

None of the provincial jurisdictions has legislation in this area. However, many employers have their own voluntary employment equity programs. Also, the federal government has a non-legislated federal contractors program. This program seeks to ensure that all contractors who have 100 or more employees and are bidding on federal contracts worth more than $200 000 achieve and maintain a fair and representative workforce.

Employment equity legislation

Laws designed to improve the status of certain designated groups.

Formation of the Employment Contract

During the negotiations leading to an offer of employment, a lot of information is exchanged. In many cases, disputes have arisen upon termination, based on representations in the negotiations leading up to the offer. There may have been pre-hiring promises, or representations made concerning the nature of the employment that did not materialize. On termination, the employee may be able to allege breach of oral promises, as *Queen v Cognos* illustrates.

---

17 SC 1995, c 44.
18 For information on the Employment Equity Branch of the Commission, see: <http://www.chrc-ccdp.ca/eng/content/employment-equity>.
19 *Lovelace v Ontario*, 2000 SCC 37, [2000] 1 SCR 950.

Queen v Cognos Inc, [1993] 1 SCR 87, 99 DLR (4th) 626

THE BUSINESS CONTEXT: A company seeking to attract the most qualified candidate may sometimes oversell itself or the job. Promises and representations are often freely made.

FACTUAL BACKGROUND: Douglas Queen was hired by Cognos to help develop an accounting software package. Queen was told by an employee of Cognos that the project would run for a number of years and would be well funded. Based on these representations and a signed employment contract, Queen quit a secure job in Calgary and moved to Ottawa. About two weeks later, the company shifted funding into a different product. Queen was kept on for 18 months, during which time he had a number of fill-in jobs. After being dismissed, he brought an action against Cognos for negligent misrepresentation. He claimed that he would not have accepted the position had it not been for the representations about the scope and viability of the job.

THE LEGAL QUESTION: Does an interviewer owe a duty of care to a prospective employee?

RESOLUTION: The Supreme Court of Canada held that an interviewer has a duty to take reasonable care to avoid making misleading statements. Here, the interviewer failed by misrepresenting the security of the job. Although the contract Queen signed had a disclaimer that allowed the company to reassign or dismiss him, the disclaimer did not save the company from liability for making false promises about the job. Cognos was required to pay damages for Queen's loss of income, loss on the sale of his house in Calgary and the purchase of his house in Ottawa, emotional stress, and expenses incurred in finding a new job.

CRITICAL ANALYSIS: Promises and representations led to legal consequences for Cognos when the promises and representations failed to materialize. What if the promises and representations had been made by a recruiting firm rather than an employee of Cognos? What if the promises and representations had been made by an employee of Cognos who was not authorized to make them?

Offer of Employment

After employers have recruited job applicants, interviewed them, and checked their references, the next step is usually an offer of employment. The offer normally comes from the employer to the employee, but there is no legal requirement that it must.

Like offers in other types of contracts, the offer must be reasonably certain to constitute an "offer" in law. Thus, the statement, "We would like you to work for us" is not considered an offer, as it does not define the job, remuneration, or any of the other terms of employment. The offer, however, need not be in a particular form or in writing. As long as the statements are reasonably complete and certain, casual comments may be considered offers. Once made, the offer is capable of acceptance until it is terminated. Therefore, an offer of employment made to two candidates could result in two acceptances and two employment contracts for the one job. Offers should have time limits so that there are no problems with ascertaining when the offer expires.

Prior to making an offer, the employer should determine whether the candidate has any obligations to her most recent employer. These obligations may impede her ability to perform the job and could result in legal action against the new employer, such as in the following ways:

- *inducing breach of contract.* If the newly hired employee breaks an existing employment contract in order to accept an offer, the former employer may sue the new employer for the tort of "inducing a breach of contract."[20]

- *restrictive covenants*. It is also not uncommon for employment contracts to contain restrictive covenants limiting the former employee's ability to compete against the former employer or prohibiting the former employee from soliciting the customers or employees of the former employer. These restrictions are particularly common in industries in which businesses are highly dependent on customer contacts or skilled employees and there is a lot of confidential information and trade secrets. They are not, however, always enforceable.[21]

- *fiduciary obligations*. A potential employee may also be considered to be in a "fiduciary" relationship with his former employer. Whether or not an employee is a fiduciary will be determined by the position held by the employee, the employee's duties and responsibilities, the nature of the business, and the organizational structure. Historically, only senior employees were considered to be in this relationship, but junior employees who hold "key" positions may also be fiduciaries.[22] An employee may be in a fiduciary relationship with his employer without realizing it.[23] A finding of a fiduciary relationship may mean that such employees are prohibited from soliciting customers of their former employer and prohibited from taking advantage of business opportunities discovered through the former employer.[24]

C A S E

RBC Dominion Securities Inc v Merrill Lynch Canada Inc, 2008 SCC 54, [2008] 3 SCR 79

THE BUSINESS CONTEXT: This case clarifies the duties that departed employees owe their employer upon termination. It emphasizes that an employer, when recruiting from a competitor, must consider the express and implied duties that employees owe to their former employer.

FACTUAL BACKGROUND: The branch manager of the Cranbrook, B.C., office of RBC Dominion Securities orchestrated the departure of almost all of the investment advisors and assistants working under his supervision to join a competitor, Merrill Lynch. The employees did not give notice of their departure, and in the weeks preceding their exodus, they surreptitiously copied client records and transferred them to Merrill Lynch, which used the records to solicit RBC's clients. None of the employees had non-solicitation or non-competition clauses in their contracts. As a result of their actions, the RBC office lost approximately 85 percent of the client accounts serviced by the departed employees. RBC sued its former branch manager, its former investment advisors, and Merrill Lynch and its manager for damages. RBC based its action on the employees' failure

(Continued)

PART SIX

20 The tort of inducing breach of contract is discussed in Chapter 12.

21 See Chapter 8 for a detailed discussion of the enforceability of restrictive covenants in employment and other contracts.

22 *GasTOPS Ltd. v Forsyth*, 2012 ONCA 124, [2012] 99 CCEL (3d) 62; see also *Canadian Aero Service Ltd v O'Malley*, [1974] SCR 592, 40 DLR (3d) 371; *Imperial Sheet Metal Ltd v Landry*, 2006 NBQB 303, 308 NBR (2d) 42.

23 See *Adler Firestopping Ltd v Rea*, 2008 ABQB 95, [2008] AWLD 1436 where the Alberta Court of Appeal found that a senior employee who acted as a general manager, even though the title was not officially given to him and who was involved in discussions regarding business operations, was a fiduciary.

24 Confidential business information is discussed in Chapter 18.

to give notice, their solicitation of business away from the firm while in its employ, their unlawful removal of records, and their alleged breach of an implied duty to compete fairly following their employment, and on Merrill Lynch's conduct in inducing these events.

THE LEGAL QUESTIONS: Do employees have a duty not to compete post-employment? Do employees have a duty to give reasonable notice prior to resigning from their employment? To what extent are employees bound by duties of good faith and confidentiality?

RESOLUTION: The following is a summary of the court's findings.

Duty not to compete: Once the contract of employment is terminated by either the employer or employee, the employee's duty not to compete is at an end, in the absence of any written contractual provisions or a finding that the employee was a fiduciary. None of the former employees were deemed fiduciaries. Although some had some managerial duties, they did not occupy senior positions at RBC. They were primarily investment advisors.

Failure to give notice: The written employment contracts between RBC and their former employees did not contain terms requiring the employees to give advance notice. The employees, however, breached the implied duty to give reasonable notice of resignation, which was in this case held to be two-and-a-half weeks. A total of $40 000 was awarded based on the profits these investment advisors would have contributed during the notice period.

Duty of good faith: The RBC manager who orchestrated the mass exodus was also determined not to be a fiduciary. Although he was responsible for the day-to-day operations of the branch, he was not in a position to affect the economic interests of RBC at either the national

What duties do employees owe their employers?

or local level. He was, however, determined to have breached the implied duty of good faith owed by him to his then-current employer. He breached his duty by failing to make efforts to retain employees under his supervision and by orchestrating the mass departure. Damages of $1.5 million were awarded against him based on an estimate of lost profits to the Cranbrook branch over a five-year period.

Misuse of confidential information: Punitive damages were awarded against Merrill Lynch ($250 000), Merrill Lynch's branch manager ($10 000), the RBC manager ($10 000), and each of RBC's former investment advisers ($5000) on the basis of conversion relating to the removal and copying of RBC client records. Employees owe a duty of confidentiality to their employers and although the duty does not necessarily extend to preventing departing employees from taking client information, it does extend to the wrongful copying of confidential information.

CRITICAL ANALYSIS: Based on this decision, what are the duties of departing employees? What are the implications of this decision for businesses where competition by former employees is a concern?

Fixed- or definite-term contract

A contract for a specified period of time, which automatically ends on the expiry date.

The Employment Contract

The employment relationship is contractual. The contract may be for a specified period of time, in which case the contract is known as a **fixed- or definite-term contract**. The contract, however, need not specify any period of time; such a contract is known as an **indefinite-term contract**. The distinction is particularly important with respect to termination.[25] Historically, most employment contracts were indefinite, but term contracts are becoming more common. The contract may be oral or in writing,[26] but most commonly it is written.

Indefinite-term contract

A contract for no fixed period, which can end on giving reasonable notice.

Express and Implied Terms

Whether it is oral or written, the contract may include express terms and implied terms.[27] Express terms are those that have been actually agreed upon by the parties. They are included in the contract or incorporated by reference. Benefits packages, job descriptions, and company rules and policies are often in separate documents and included by reference. Implied terms are those that have not been specifically agreed upon by the parties but are what the courts believe the parties would have agreed to, had they sat down and negotiated the point. Employment is an area where traditionally there have been a great many implied terms. For example, if the parties do not specify the duration of the contract, it is implied that the contract is for an indefinite period of time. Therefore, the contract does not come to an end until one of the parties gives notice of termination. This term leads to another implied term that the notice of termination must be reasonable.[28]

Content of the Contract

Most employers and employees now see the need to introduce certainty into the employment relationship by putting their relationship into writing.

Besides the advantage of certainty, a written employment contract offers other advantages, including a forum for negotiating terms and conditions that are tailored to the situation—notice periods, restrictive covenants, and limitation of pre-contractual promises, to name a few (see Figure 20.2). Written terms will override terms that are implied at law.

FIGURE 20.2 Essential Content of an Employment Contract

An employment contract should contain the following information:

- ✓ names of the parties.
- ✓ date on which the contract begins.
- ✓ position and description of the work to be performed.
- ✓ compensation (i.e., salary, wages, bonuses).
- ✓ benefits (i.e., vacation, vacation pay, health and dental plans, pensions, etc.).
- ✓ probation period, if any.
- ✓ duration of the contract, if any.
- ✓ evaluation and discipline procedures.
- ✓ company policies or reference to employee policy manual.
- ✓ termination provisions (i.e., cause for dismissal, notice of termination, severance package).
- ✓ recital of management rights (i.e., employer has a right to make changes to job duties and responsibilities).
- ✓ confidentiality clause, if appropriate.
- ✓ ownership of intellectual property, if appropriate.
- ✓ restrictive covenants, if any.
- ✓ "entire agreement" clause (i.e., the written contract contains the whole agreement).

---

25 For example, if an employee's contract is classified as indefinite term, the employee is entitled to the common law protection of reasonable notice of termination. By contrast, if the contract is classified as fixed term, then the contract ends when the fixed term expires, without the requirement of notice.

26 Writing requirements are discussed in Chapter 8.

27 Implied terms in contracts are discussed in Chapter 7.

28 Notice and termination are discussed in Chapter 21.

Terms and Conditions

The ability of an employer and an employee to negotiate their contract has been abrogated to some extent by legislation designed to protect the employee. The terms of the employment contract are affected by legislation, and so are the conditions of employment.

Employee Welfare Issues

Employment Standards

Employment standards legislation

Laws that specify minimum standards in the workplace.

All the provinces and territories, as well as the federal government, have **employment standards legislation** (also sometimes called labour standards legislation) that sets out minimum standards in the workplace. An employer may provide greater benefits than those provided for in the legislation but not lesser. In short, any contractual provisions that provide lesser benefits than those set out in the legislation are not enforceable.

There are variations in the legislation from jurisdiction to jurisdiction. Most, however, cover the same general categories of benefits. A sampling of typical standards follows:

- hours of work and overtime. Hours of work that an employee can be asked to work vary from 40 to 48. Overtime is usually paid at one-and-a-half times the employee's regular wages. In some provinces, it is paid at one-and-a-half times the minimum wage.

- minimum wage. The minimum wage is usually set on an hourly basis. For example, in New Brunswick,[29] the minimum wage is $10.30 per hour.

- vacations and vacation pay. The length of paid vacation that an employee is entitled to usually depends on the amount of service. For example, in Alberta,[30] an employee is entitled to two weeks after one year of employment, and three weeks after five years.

- termination and severance. The legislation normally provides for notice and severance pay. For example, in British Columbia,[31] an employee is entitled to one week's notice after three months, two weeks' notice after 12 months, three weeks' notice after three years, and one additional week for each additional year of employment, to a maximum of eight weeks.

- statutory (paid) holidays. Every jurisdiction requires that employers pay employees for specific public holidays. For example, in Newfoundland and Labrador,[32] employees are entitled to New Year's Day, Good Friday, Memorial Day (July 1), Labour Day, Christmas Day, and Remembrance Day.

- bereavement and sick leave. All jurisdictions have provisions for leaves, either paid or unpaid, for various reasons. For example, the federal jurisdiction[33] provides for 17 weeks of sick leave after three months of employment.

---

29 NB Reg 2014-161.
30 *Employment Standards Code*, RSA 2000, c E-9, s 34.
31 *Employment Standards Act*, RSBC 1996, c 113, s 63 (3).
32 *Labour Standards Act*, RSNL 1990, c L-2, s 14(1).
33 *Canada Labour Code*, RSC 1985, c L-2, s 239(1).

- maternity and parental leave. Every jurisdiction provides for pregnancy leave after a minimum amount of service. For example, in Manitoba,[34] an eligible person is entitled to 17 weeks' maternity leave after seven months of service. All jurisdictions provide parental and child care leave for eligible persons.

Other typical standards include equal pay for equal work, prohibitions against sexual harassment, prohibitions against the employment of children, and various leave provisions such as for court duty and family emergencies.

Certain employees—such as doctors, lawyers, farmers, domestic workers, construction workers, and information technology professionals—may not be covered by the legislation or may be exempt from certain provisions, such as hours of work, minimum wages, and overtime pay.

The legislation also provides a mechanism for enforcing employment standards. In Ontario, for example, employment standards officers, employed by the Employment Standards Branch, investigate complaints, carry on general investigations, and, when necessary, issue orders requiring compliance with provisions of the *Employment Standards Act*.

BUSINESS APPLICATION OF THE LAW

UNPAID OVERTIME

Employment standards legislation in all jurisdictions requires employers to pay overtime to non-management employees after varying number of hours worked. In the federal jurisdiction, employers must pay employees who have worked more than eight hours in a day and 40 hours in a week.

In 2007, 10 000 employees (current and former) of the Canadian Imperial Bank of Commerce (CIBC) launched a $600 million class action lawsuit against their employer. The suit alleges that frontline employees regularly work overtime for which they do not get paid. The representative plaintiff in the suit is 34-year-old Dara Fresco, a personal banker and teller at a Toronto branch of the bank. She has worked for the bank for over 10 years and at the time of launching the lawsuit was paid an annual salary of $30 715. She calculates that she is owed $50 000 for unpaid overtime over the past decade and is required to work an average of two to five hours a week in unpaid overtime. Shortly after the CIBC employees launched their suit, a similar lawsuit was filed by Cindy Fulawka on behalf of 5000 current and former employees of

Dara Fresco and lawyer Louis Sokolov

Aaron Harris/The Canadian Press

the Bank of Nova Scotia (Scotiabank). They were seeking $350 million in damages for unpaid overtime.

In 2012, the Ontario Court of Appeal overturned[35] lower court rulings denying the CIBC certification and upheld[36] the lower court's certification of the Scotiabank case. The Court held that although there may be individual issues relating to damages (whether an individual worked overtime and how much), there was commonality as to the issue of liability (whether there was a systemic breach of contract by the banks).

---

34 *The Employment Standards Code*, CCSM, c E110, ss 53, 54(1).
35 *Fresco v Canadian Imperial Bank of Commerce*, 2012 ONCA 444, 100 CCEL (3d) 81.
36 *Fulawka v Bank of Nova Scotia*, 2012 ONCA 443, 352 DLR (4th) 1.

The Supreme Court of Canada denied leave to appeal in both cases on March 21, 2013.[37] In August 2014, the Scotiabank case settled for an estimated payout of $95 million. The CIBC case may now proceed to trial.

Critical Analysis: Managers and supervisors are not entitled to receive overtime pay under employment standards legislation. What is the distinction between a manager/supervisor and an employee entitled to overtime? If the class action lawsuit is ultimately successful, what will be the likely impact on employees working overtime? What should employers do to assess their exposure to similar class action lawsuits?

Sources: Madhavi Acharya and Tom Yew, "Ontario court approves settlement deal for unpaid overtime at Scotia bank" *Toronto Star* (12 August 2014) online: *Toronto Star* < http://www.thestar.com/business/economy/2014/08/12/ontario_court_approves_settlement_deal_for_unpaid_overtime_at_scotiabank.html> Shannon Kari, "Bank employee actions certified", *The Lawyers Weekly* (6 July 2012) 1.; Julius Melnitzer, "Overtime class actions: an endless maze of rulings and appeals", *The Law Times* (26 September 2010) online: Law Times <http://www.lawtimesnews.com/201009077484/Headline-News/Overtime-class-actions-an-endless-maze-of-rulings-and-appeals>; Virginia Galt & Janet McFarland, "CIBC faces massive overtime lawsuit", *The Globe and Mail* (6 June 2007) A1; Jacquie McNish, "Scotiabank hit with overtime suit", *The Globe and Mail* (11 December 2007) B14

ETHICAL CONSIDERATIONS

WORKING FOR FREE: THE UNPAID INTERNSHIP

In 2013, it was estimated that as many as 300 000 Canadians worked as unpaid interns.[38] While these programs are particularly popular in the publishing, broadcasting, journalism, and fashion industries, they are not limited to these fields. Unpaid internships have been advertised at communications giant Bell Mobility, Vancouver's Fairmont Waterfront Hotel, Rugby Canada, and Telico Networks (a communications and technology company). There may, however, be fewer unpaid internships in future as some provinces have begun to crack down on unpaid internships. For example, in March 2014, the Ontario Ministry of Labour told two Canadian magazines—*The Walrus* and *Toronto Life*—to end their unpaid internship programs as they contravened Ontario's *Employment Standards Act*.

The Law Whether an unpaid internship contravenes employment standards legislation may depend on the jurisdiction. In some jurisdictions, the employment standards legislation refers to interns and exempts them from the legislation

Who is harmed by the closure of unpaid internship programs?

Photo by Leslie Walker, *Ryersonian*

(and the entitlement to minimum wages) if they meet certain conditions. In Ontario, an internship must meet several conditions including: that the training is similar to that which is provided at a vocational school; that the training is for the benefit of the individual; and that the person providing the training derives little benefit from the activity of the individual being trained. Most unpaid internship programs do not meet these requirements and therefore would be in contravention of the legislation. In other jurisdictions, where there is no mention of interns in the legislation, the issue is whether the intern falls within the definition of employee in the legislation and is therefore entitled to the

37 *Canadian Imperial Bank of Commerce v Fresco*, [2012] SCCA No 379; *Bank of Nova Scotia v Fulawka* [2012] SCCA No 326.

38 Andrew Langille, "Why Canada needs better labour market data and the Canadian internship survey," *Youth and Work* (19 May 2014) online: Youth and Work <http://www.youthandwork.ca/2013/10/why-canada-needs-better-labour-market.html?q=unpaid+internships>.

protection of the legislation (i.e., entitlement to minimum wages). While the definitions vary, an employee is generally a person who receives or is entitled to receive wages in exchange for work. As it is unclear what "entitled to receive wages" means, it is uncertain whether interns fall within the legislation and the entitlement to minimum wages.

Regardless of the legal status of the internship programs, unpaid internships are unlikely to entirely disappear as many young people are not likely to make a complaint against an employer in an industry that they desire to enter.

Critical Analysis: What is the harm in unpaid internships?

Sources: Lee-Anne Goodman, "Study shines light on the dark side of internships", *The Canadian Press* (23 May 2014), online: Globe Advisor .com<https://secure.globeadvisor.com/servlet/ArticleNews/story/gam/20140523/RBCAINTERNSHIPS0522ATL>; Simon Houpt, "Unpaid internships at magazines new target of Ontario labour ministry", *The Globe and Mail* (27 March 2014), online: *The Globe and Mail* <http://www.theglobeandmail.com/arts/books-and-media/unpaid-internships-at-magazines-new-target-of-ontario-labour-ministry/article17694055/>; Christopher Munroe, "Are unpaid internships legal in Canada?", *Gowlings Knowledge Centre* (February 2014), online: Gowlings <http://www.gowlings.com/KnowledgeCentre/article.asp?pubID=3190>; Lee-Anne Goodman, "Unpaid internships appear to be on the rise as Canada's laws just a 'hodgepodge'", *The Star* (2 March 2014), online: *The Star* <http://www.thestar.com/news/canada/2014/03/02/unpaid_internships_appear_to_be_on_the_rise_as_canadas_laws_just_a_hodgepodge.html>; Lai-King Hum & Kristen Pennington, "Will work for free! Employers, beware of offers of free work by unpaid interns", *McMillan LLP* (24 July 2013), online: McMillan <http://www.mcmillan.ca/100152>; Canadian Intern Association (19 May 2014), online: <http://www.internassociation.ca/category/name-shame/>.

Safety and Compensation

Workers' compensation legislation is designed to address accidents and injuries in the workplace. It provides for a type of no-fault insurance scheme. Employers are required to pay into a fund, and workers who have job-related injuries, accidents, or illnesses are compensated from the fund, regardless of fault. Compensation covers lost wages, medical aid, and rehabilitation. The scheme prevents a civil suit by the employee against the employer relating to a workplace injury or accident. Not all employees, accidents, or illnesses are covered by the legislation, however. Illness must be job related, which is not always easy to determine, particularly as the causes of many illnesses are unclear and the illnesses themselves can take decades to develop.

All jurisdictions have enacted comprehensive occupational health and safety legislation that generally applies to all sectors of the economy. In addition to general provisions, there are industry-specific provisions and hazard-oriented provisions. The purpose of the legislation is to protect workers in the workplace by giving them a right to participate in safety issues, a right to know about hazards in the workplace, and a right to refuse to work in unsafe conditions.

Also, the *Criminal Code* [39] imposes a legal duty on organizations and individuals to protect the health and safety of workers. [40]

Employee Economic Safety

Two legislative schemes in the area of employee economic safety are Employment Insurance and the Canada and Quebec pension plans.

The *Employment Insurance Act* [41] is federal legislation that applies to both the federally and provincially regulated sectors. The basic concept of Employment

---

39 RSC 1985, c C-46, s 217.1 provides "Everyone who undertakes, or has the authority, to direct how another person does work or performs a task is under a legal duty to take reasonable steps to prevent bodily harm to that person, or any other person, arising from that work or task."
40 See Chapter 16 for further discussion.
41 SC 1996, c 23.

Insurance is that the employer and employee contribute to a fund that provides insurance against loss of income. The plan provides benefits for unemployment, maternity and parental leave, and sickness, as well as some retirement benefits. A limited number of employees are not covered by the scheme. The most common exclusions are casual workers, some part-time workers, and those employed in agriculture.

The Canada Pension Plan[42] (in Quebec, the Quebec Pension Plan) is an insurance plan designed to provide pensions or financial assistance in the case of retirement, disability, or death. Both the employer and the employee contribute to the plan.

Workplace Discrimination

Discrimination on certain grounds is prohibited in all aspects of employment, including promotions and terminations. One aspect of discrimination that has received a great deal of press is workplace harassment.

Workplace Harassment

Harassment is any unwanted physical or verbal behaviour that offends or humiliates the victim and detrimentally affects the work environment or leads to adverse job-related consequences for the victim. Such conduct can take many forms, including threats; intimidation; verbal abuse; unwelcome remarks or jokes about race, religion, sex, disability, or age; the display of sexist, racist, or other offensive pictures; sexually suggestive remarks or gestures; unnecessary physical contact, such as touching, patting, pinching, or punching; and physical assault, including sexual assault.[43]

Prohibitions against harassment in the workplace are found in an array of legislative provisions. Human rights legislation, in both the federal and provincial jurisdictions, prohibits harassment. For example, the *Canadian Human*

An anti-harassment policy addresses inappropriate behaviour in the workplace. What should the policy contain?

Fuse/Getty Images

---

42 RSC 1985, c C-8.
43 See the Canadian Human Rights Commission website at <http://www.chrc-ccdp.gc.ca/eng/content/what-harassment>.

Rights Act[44] provides "It is a discriminatory practice...(c) in matters related to employment, to harass an individual on a prohibited ground of discrimination." Employment standards legislation also often protects employees from harassment, particularly sexual harassment, and the *Criminal Code* protects people from physical and sexual assault. In addition, most jurisdictions have a provision in their occupational health and safety legislation that requires employers to take all reasonable precautions to protect the health and safety of employees. Some provinces have addressed the workplace harassment problem more directly (see the Business and Legislation: Workplace Bullying and Violence box).

BUSINESS AND LEGISLATION

WORKPLACE BULLYING AND VIOLENCE

In 2005, nurse Lori Dupont was stabbed to death at the Hotel-Dieu Grace Hospital in Windsor, Ontario, by her former boyfriend and co-worker, Dr. Marc Daniel. Although the hospital was aware of repeated and escalating harassment by Daniel, an anaesthesiologist, it failed to take steps to discipline him. Partly, in response to this tragic case of workplace violence, the government of Ontario introduced amendments[45] to the *Occupational Health and Safety Act*[46] to address workplace violence and harassment.

The amendments provide expansive definitions and a new right for employees. "Workplace harassment" is defined as engaging in a course of vexatious comment or conduct against a worker in a workplace that is known or ought reasonably to be known to be unwelcome. "Workplace violence" is defined to include threats of physical violence, attempts to exercise physical force, and the actual exercise of force. The definitions are such that the conduct can come from not only a fellow employee but also customers, suppliers, clients, patients, or the general public. Workers are entitled to refuse work where they have reason to believe that they are likely to be the target of workplace violence (the same right does not apply to workplace harassment).

The legislation places new, proactive obligations on employers. They are required to conduct a risk assessment for violence and harassment in the workplace. Following the assessment, they must develop policies to address the risks identified and provide training in respect to the policies. In addition, employers are required to take every reasonable precaution to address domestic violence in the workplace and they must disclose information about a person with a history of violent behaviour, where it is likely that a worker will be exposed to the person through the course of their work and that exposure creates a risk of physical injury.

The *Act* provides for fines of up to $500 000 for companies and up to $25 000 or 12 months' imprisonment for individuals for violations.

In 2012, British Columbia amended its *Workers Compensation Act* to allow workers to claim workers' compensation benefits if they become disabled due to workplace bullying and harassment. Also, employers are required to implement bullying and harassment policies and training.[47]

Critical Analysis: Human rights legislation prohibits harassment, so why are specific workplace anti-harassment and anti-violence rules needed?

Sources: Wallace Immen, "Keeping the bullies and brutes at bay", *The Globe and Mail* (12 June 2010) B16; Michael McKiernan, "Few ready for Bill 168", *Law Times News* (13 June 2010), online: Law Times <http://www.lawtimesnews.com>.

PART SIX

---

44 *Supra* note 10, s 14(1).
45 *Occupational Health & Safety Amendment Act (Violence and Harassment in the Workplace)* 2009, SO 2009 c 23.
46 RSO 1990 c O-1.
47 *Workers' Compensation Amendment Act, 2012*, SBC 2012 c23.

The prohibition against harassment in human rights legislation extends not only to employers but also to their employees. The employer is vicariously liable for any violations of human rights legislation committed by its employees.[48] Several jurisdictions modify this position by providing for a due diligence defence. For example, the Manitoba legislation[49] provides that an employer is responsible for any act of harassment committed by an employee or an agent of the employer in the course of employment unless it is established that the employer did not consent to the act and took all reasonable steps to prevent the act from being committed and, subsequently, took all reasonable steps to mitigate or avoid its consequences.

In order to fulfill their responsibilities under human rights legislation, it is incumbent on employers to develop and implement a workplace harassment policy. Although employers may still be liable for harassment, whether they knew of it or not, the penalties will be less or nonexistent for employers that not only respond quickly and effectively to instances of harassment but also take action to prevent the wrongful conduct from occurring in the first place.

Pay Equity

Discrimination in pay scales between men and women has led to legislation designed to ensure that female and male employees receive the same compensation for performing the same or substantially similar work. All jurisdictions provide for some type of equal pay in their human rights legislation.[50] In addition, some jurisdictions have equality of pay provisions in their employment standards law, and some have enacted specific **pay equity** statutes.[51]

Pay equity

Provisions designed to ensure that female and male employees receive the same compensation for performing similar or substantially similar work.

Pay equity provisions are designed to redress systemic discrimination in compensation for work performed. They require an employer to evaluate the work performed by employees in order to divide the workforce into job classes. The classes can then be considered to determine whether they are male or female dominated. Next, employers must value each of the job classes in terms of duties, responsibilities, and required qualifications; compare like classes; and endeavour to compensate each female job class with a wage rate comparable to the male job class performing work of equal value. This procedure, however, has been difficult to administer and apply. For example, a pay equity dispute between female postal workers and Canada Post took 28 years to resolve. It ended when the Supreme Court of Canada upheld a decision of the Canadian Human Rights Commission that awarded the workers $150 million.[52]

---

48 *Robichaud v The Queen*, [1987] 2 SCR 84, 40 DLR (4th) 577. The decision makes it clear that, subject to statutory provisions to the contrary, vicarious liability applies to human rights law.

49 *The Human Rights Code*, CCSM, c H175, s 10.

50 For example, the *Canadian Human Rights Act, supra* note 10, s 11 states "It is a discriminatory practice to establish or maintain differences in wage rates between male and female employees employed in the same establishment who are performing work of equal value."

51 The provinces of Manitoba, New Brunswick, Nova Scotia, Prince Edward Island, Ontario, and Quebec have specific pay equity legislation. Ontario and Quebec are the only provinces in which the legislation applies to the private sector. The other provinces limit the legislation's application to the public sector. See *Pay Equity Act*, RSO 1990, c P-7 and *Pay Equity* Act, CQLR c E-12.001.

52 Kathryn May, "After 28-year pay-equity fight, female postal workers awarded $150-million," *National Post* (17 November 2011), online: National Post <http://news.nationalpost.com/2011/11/17/after-28-year-pay-equity-fight-female-postal-workers-awarded-150-million/>.

Drug and Alcohol Testing

Employers have a legitimate interest in having a safe workplace. Sometimes they have attempted to achieve this goal through drug and alcohol testing of their employees. Such testing, however, is contentious as it is *prima facie* discriminatory. The following case provides some guidance to business on the legality of testing.

CASE

Communications, Energy and Paperworkers Union of Canada, Local 30 v Irving Pulp & Paper, Ltd., 2013 SCC 34, [2013] 2 SCR 458.

THE BUSINESS CONTEXT: In an effort to provide a safe workplace, employers have often implemented mandatory alcohol and drug testing for their employees. The imposition of any policy, however, must be balanced against the privacy rights of employees.

FACTUAL BACKGROUND: In 2006, Irving Pulp & Paper (Irving) adopted a new policy on alcohol and drug for use at its kraft paper mill in Saint John, New Brunswick. As part of the policy, Irving implemented a random alcohol testing program whereby 10 percent of employees in safety sensitive positions were to be randomly selected for unannounced breathalyser testing over the course of a year. Employee tests revealing a blood alcohol level concentration greater than 0.04 percent would warrant disciplinary action determined on a case-by-case basis. The mill is acknowledged to be a dangerous workplace with the potential for catastrophe. In the 15 years preceding the introduction of the policy, there were eight documented cases of alcohol consumption or impairment at the mill. There were no accidents, injuries, or near misses connected to alcohol.

Shortly after a mill employee was randomly selected to submit to the breathalyser test, the union challenged the random alcohol testing policy as an unreasonable exercise of management rights.

THE LEGAL QUESTION: Was Irving's random alcohol testing program unreasonable?

RESOLUTION: The Supreme Court of Canada held that to justify a random alcohol test in

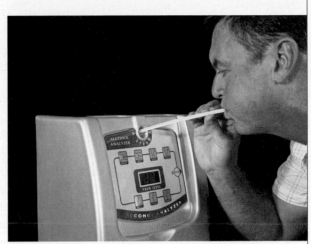

What evidence is necessary to establish the reasonableness of random alcohol testing in a dangerous workplace?

the workplace, the employer needs to prove that there is both a dangerous workplace and an enhanced risk such as a general substance abuse problem in the workplace. The Irving paper mill was acknowledged to be a dangerous workplace but there was insufficient evidence of an alcohol abuse problem in the workplace. Furthermore, the Court determined that while Irving's safety gains under the policy ranged from uncertain to minimal at best, the impact on the privacy of the employee was much more severe.

The Court confirmed that alcohol and drug testing of employees in safety sensitive jobs is generally permissible where the employer has reasonable cause to believe that the employee is impaired while on duty, where there has been an accident or near-miss and the employer has reasonable cause to believe the incident was related to impairment, and where the employee is subject to testing as part of a rehabilitation program.

CRITICAL ANALYSIS: When is alcohol testing permitted in the workplace?

Workplace Privacy

Privacy, particularly since technological developments have made it easier to "watch" or monitor employees, is a concern in the workplace. Issues centre on collecting and disseminating information about employees, watching and searching employees, and monitoring employees' electronic communications.

Collection and Dissemination of Information

Employers have the ability to collect and store, in hard copy or electronically, a great deal of employee data—performance reviews, work activity reports, medical records, disciplinary reports, credit ratings, and letters of recommendation. Employees, however, have rights to control the collection and use of information.

A wide array of legislation in the public sector, at both the federal and provincial levels, gives individuals the right to control personal information. For example, the federal *Privacy Act*[53] regulates the collection and use of personal information held by the federal government. The Act gives individuals the right to see information and to request corrections if it is inaccurate. Similar provincial legislation applies to information held by provincial governments. *The Personal Information Protection and Electronic Documents Act*[54] (*PIPEDA*) extends these rights to the private sector. *PIPEDA* applies to employee information in federal works, undertakings, and businesses. *PIPEDA* does not, however, apply to employee information in the provincial private sector as this information is regulated by similar provincial legislation. To date, Quebec,[55] Alberta,[56] British Columbia,[57] and Manitoba[58] have enacted similar legislation.

The basic principle of *PIPEDA* and its provincial counterparts is that personal information should not be collected, used, or disclosed without the prior knowledge and consent of the individual concerned. *PIPEDA* defines "personal information" as information about an identifiable individual.[59] The Act provides, however, that consent is not required for business contact information (name, title, and work address, telephone number, fax number, and electronic address) for the purpose of communicating in relation to employment.[60] The collection of all other types of employee information with limited exceptions requires the consent of the employee. One exception is that employers in federal works are able to collect, use and disclose employee information without consent if it is needed to "establish, manage or terminate" employment.[61]

The employer's obligations under *PIPEDA* and similar provincial legislation are set out in Figure 20.3.

---

53 RSC 1985, c P-21.
54 SC 2000, c 5.
55 *An Act Respecting the Protection of Personal Information in the Private Sector*, RSQ c P-39.1.
56 *Personal Information Protection Act*, SA 2003, c P-6.5.
57 *Personal Information Protection Act*, SBC 2003, c 63.
58 *The* Personal Information Protection and Identity Theft Prevention Act, CCSM, cP33-7. Assented to September 13, 2013, but not yet in force.
59 *Digital Privacy Act*, SC 2015, c 32, s 2(1). The Act, which amends PIPEDA, was passed on June 18, 2015, and although not all sections are in force at the time of writing, the sections relating to personal information and consent are in force.
60 *Ibid* s 4.
61 *Ibid* s 7.

FIGURE 20.3 Employers' Obligations Pursuant to Privacy Legislation

To meet their obligations under PIPEDA and similar provincial legislation, employers are required to

- identify and document the limited purposes for which personal information is collected, prior to collecting the information.
- communicate the identified purposes to the individual prior to obtaining the individual's consent.
- collect, use, and disclose the personal information only for the identified purposes.
- obtain the express consent of individuals for "sensitive" information such as health records and financial information (implied consent may be sufficient for less sensitive information).
- ensure individuals providing consent fully understand the potential consequences of providing personal information.[62]
- maintain responsibility for personal information under its possession or custody.
- designate a personal information supervisor.
- maintain the accuracy of personal information held by the organization.
- retain information only as long as required for the purposes identified.
- adopt security safeguards to protect personal information from loss and unauthorized use.
- provide access and the right to amend inaccurate information to each individual.

Penalties for breach of the Act include making public an organization's personal information policies, fines ranging from $10 000 to $100 000, and court orders to correct practices and to pay damages to the complainant.

Surveillance and Searches

Video cameras, Global Positioning Systems (GPS) tracking, and smartphones have made it possible for employers to closely monitor employees and their activities. Employers justify the use of technology on the basis of concerns about safety and security, productivity and efficiency, misappropriation of confidential or proprietary information, theft and other illegal activities, and liability.

The surveillance and monitoring of employees, however, may infringe the privacy rights of employees. Privacy protections for employees emanate from several sources: the terms of a collective agreement, the tort of invasion of privacy, and privacy legislation. Employees in the federally regulated sectors may challenge employers' practices pursuant to PIPEDA and employees in some provinces may challenge pursuant to privacy legislation governing the private sector.

Whether a specific monitoring practice is permissible or is an invasion of privacy depends on a host of factors including the method of surveillance, the purpose of surveillance, whether the surveillance was done openly, and the employee's reasonable expectation of privacy. The business interests of the employer are balanced against the employee's privacy rights and a determination is made as to whether the monitoring is reasonable in light of the balance.[63]

Intrusive searches of employees or their belongings are carefully scrutinized by the courts. An employer would need to have some particularly compelling reason, such as bomb threats being issued or thefts occurring, to undertake such practices. Additionally, the employer would need to demonstrate that all other alternatives for dealing with the threats had been exhausted. Employees should be informed in advance of any policy in this regard, and any searches would need to be conducted in a systematic and non-arbitrary manner; otherwise, the employer may be vulnerable to charges of discrimination.

---

62 *Ibid* s 5.
63 *Eastmond v Canadian Pacific Railway, 2004 FC 852, 254 FTR 169.*

PART SIX

Monitoring of Communications

Many employees, particularly those who work in an office, have access to email and the Internet, as well as traditional means of communication—telephone and facsimile. Employers have a legitimate interest in ensuring that employees are not spending excessive amounts of time on personal communication and are using company equipment for legitimate uses. Employees, on the other hand, have a legitimate expectation that their private and personal communications will not be monitored or intercepted. Currently, there is no comprehensive law in Canada prohibiting employers from monitoring their employees' email and Internet activities.

The *Criminal Code*[64] provides that it is an offence to intercept a private communication. The section, however, does not apply to communications that are not private or to interception that is consented to by one of the parties. A communication is private if the parties have an expectation that it will not be intercepted. There is judicial authority for the notion that email via the Internet ought to carry a reasonable expectation of privacy, although it is not to be accorded the same level of privacy protection as first-class mail.[65]

TECHNOLOGY AND THE LAW

PRIVACY OF PERSONAL INFORMATION ON WORK COMPUTERS

It is not uncommon for employees to store personal data on computers, laptops, and other devices that are supplied and owned by employers. Are employers entitled to monitor and access the personal content on these devices or do employees have a reasonable expectation of privacy?

The Supreme Court of Canada in *R v Cole*[66] provides valuable guidance in answering this question. The Court found that a high school teacher had a reasonable expectation of privacy in the information contained on his work-issued computer, particularly as the employer's policy and procedures allowed incidental personal use of the computer. The expectation of privacy, however, is not absolute. It is diminished by the fact that the employer owned the computer and had put into place policies and procedures governing its use. In particular, the policy specified that all data and messages were the employer's property and not that of the user, and that all work and email including that saved on the hard drive might be monitored. The Court held that an expectation of privacy must be determined from

Do employees have a right to privacy on workplace computers?

the totality of the circumstances. An employer that expressly allows personal use implies an increased expectation of privacy. A policy limiting or excluding personal use diminishes but does not totally eliminate the expectation of privacy.

Critical Analysis: The Supreme Court's finding that policies and procedures diminish an expectation of privacy demonstrates the importance of computer use policies in the workplace. What should a computer use policy contain?

---

64 RSC 1985, c C-46, s 184.
65 See *R v Weir*, 1998 ABQB 56, 59 Alta LR (3d) 319.
66 2012 SCC 53, 353 DLR (4th) 447.

The Union Context

Discussion in this chapter thus far has focused on the hiring and employment of non-unionized employees. It has also focused on private sector as opposed to public sector employees, as there is often specific legislation that affects public sector employees' employment.

In a unionized environment, many of the same employment issues that arise in a non-union environment are also relevant—recruiting, terms and conditions of employment, and so on. However, negotiating and entering into an employment contract is a much different process.

Both the federal and provincial governments have enacted labour or industrial relations legislation that guarantees the right of employees to join trade unions. The Acts apply to most employees, but certain employees—namely, managers and those in specific occupations, such as domestic workers and farm hands—are excluded. The legislative enactments provide for a **certification** process, by which the union is recognized as the bargaining agent for a group of employees. An employer, however, can voluntarily recognize the union as the bargaining agent for the employees without a certification process. The certification process is basically a method by which the **labour relations board** approves the union as the employees' representative upon the union being able to show that a majority of the employees in the bargaining unit want the union to represent them.

The legislation provides a mechanism known as **collective bargaining**, by which the parties enter a collective agreement or contract. The contract applies to all employees in the bargaining unit, regardless of whether they voted for the union representation. The union and the employer have a duty to bargain in good faith— that is, they must make a substantive effort to negotiate the agreement. The collective agreement, like an individual employment contract, sets out the terms and conditions of employment. The two types of contracts cover many of the same issues, such as wages, benefits, and the like, but a **collective agreement** is usually far more comprehensive. Also, a union bargaining on behalf of many employees generally has far more bargaining power than a single individual negotiating with an employer (although some highly skilled or specialized employees do have a lot of individual bargaining power). During the term of the collective agreement, there can be no legal strikes[67] by the employees or lockouts by the employer.

In return, the legislation provides a process involving grievance and arbitration procedures for resolving disputes. These procedures are discussed in Chapter 21.

BUSINESS LAW IN PRACTICE REVISITED

1. Is Jeong an employee or an independent contractor?

The distinction between an employee and an independent contractor is not always readily apparent. The label that the parties apply to their relationship is not conclusive, as the nature of the relationship is a question of fact. The courts have developed a number of tests to make the determination. Some factors, such as the lack of control, suggest that Jeong is an independent contractor. Other factors, such as the employer providing a computer, the method of payment, and the degree of integration, suggest that Jeong is an employee. In the final analysis, as Jeong does not appear to be in business for herself, it is likely that the courts will consider her an employee.

Certification

The process by which a union is recognized as a bargaining agent for a group of employees.

Labour relations board

A body that administers labour relations legislation.

Collective bargaining

A mechanism by which parties enter a collective agreement or contract.

Collective agreement

The employment agreement reached between the union and employer setting out the bargaining unit employees' terms and conditions of employment.

---

67 The right to strike is a constitutionally protected right. See: *Saskatchewan Federation of Labour v Saskatchewan*, 2015 SCC 4, [2015] 1 SCR 245.

2. Why is the distinction between an employee and an independent contractor important?

The distinction is important because an employer is responsible for torts committed by an employee in the course of employment, whereas the employer is not generally responsible for the torts of an independent contractor. In addition, the distinction is critical because common law, as well as statutory rights and obligations, in most cases applies only to employees and not to independent contractors.

3. Is Hiram responsible for Jeong's conduct?

If Jeong is considered an employee, then Hiram is responsible for the torts committed by Jeong in the course of employment. Hiram is not responsible for the torts committed by Jeong outside the course of her employment. Although the posting of the possibly defamatory statement on the hockey website is related to her work, it is likely that her actions will be considered to be outside the scope of employment because it appears that she was responding in a personal capacity to a perceived affront. Assuming this is the case, Hiram is not responsible.

CHAPTER SUMMARY

The employment relationship is one of the most fundamental relationships in business. The cornerstone of this relationship is a contract, either individual or collective, whereby one party provides services to another in return for remuneration. However, not everyone who provides services to another through a contract is an "employee." The distinction is crucial because common law, as well as statutory rights and obligations, in most cases applies only to employees and not to independent contractors.

The hiring process has a number of phases—advertising, application submission, interviewing, and reference checking. Legal issues such as discrimination and employment equity apply to each of these steps and provide the opportunity for potential liability for the unwary employer. Most of the costly mistakes made by employers who end up as the subject of a human rights investigation or the recipient of a wrongful dismissal suit can be avoided. Organizations need to be proactive by designing and implementing policies, practices, and procedures to address the legal issues at all stages of the employment relationship.

A well-drafted employment contract sets out the terms and conditions of employment. It describes the employment relationship and, at a minimum, sets out the job to be performed and the remuneration to be provided. The employment contract can be advantageous for both the employer and employee, as it contributes to certainty and clarity in the relationship.

The ability to freely negotiate an employment contract has been somewhat curtailed by a host of legislation designed to protect employees. This protection is provided not only with respect to the terms of employment, such as wages, vacation, and hours of work, but also with respect to the conditions of employment. There is a vast array of legislation affecting employee welfare, discrimination in the workplace, and privacy.

When a union is in place, negotiating and entering into an employment contract takes place through a process known as collective bargaining. The collective agreement that emerges from negotiations applies to all employees, regardless of whether they voted for union representation.

CHAPTER STUDY

Key Terms and Concepts

adverse effects discrimination (p. 510)

bona fide occupational requirement (BFOR) (p. 511)

certification (p. 531)

collective agreement (p. 531)

collective bargaining (p. 531)

dependent contractor (p. 505)

discrimination (p. 510)

duty to accommodate (p. 512)

employment equity legislation (p. 515)

employment relationship (p. 505)

employment standards legislation (p. 520)

fixed- or definite-term contract (p. 518)

human rights commission (p. 510)

indefinite-term contract (p. 519)

independent contractor (p. 505)

labour relations board (p. 531)

pay equity (p. 526)

systemic discrimination (p. 511)

Questions for Review

1. Which level of government has jurisdiction to make laws in the area of employment?

2. What are the tests for determining the difference between an employee and an independent contractor? Why is it important to distinguish between an employee and an independent contractor?

3. Define vicarious liability and negligent hiring. How do they differ?

4. The human rights acts attempt to prohibit discrimination in employment. What is meant by "discrimination?"

5. What is the difference between systemic and adverse effects discrimination?

6. What is a *bona fide* occupational requirement? Give an example.

7. What is the "duty to accommodate?"

8. What is the purpose of the federal Employment Equity Act?

9. Do employees have fiduciary obligations? Explain.

10. Do employment contracts need to be in writing to be enforceable? What are the advantages of a written employment contract? Can you think of any disadvantages?

11. What is the purpose of employment standards legislation? Give an example of an employment standard.

12. Explain how the freedom to contract in employment has been affected by legislation, and give examples.

13. What is the purpose of workers' compensation legislation?

14. Would displaying a picture of a nude person be an example of sexual harassment in the workplace? Explain.

15. What is the purpose of pay equity?

16. Is alcohol testing in the workplace permissible? Explain.

17. Do employees have a right to privacy? Explain.

18. Describe how unionized employees enter into employment contracts.

Questions for Critical Thinking

1. Recently, Yahoo Inc. changed its telecommuting policy that allowed employees to work from home. Employees are now required to be physically present at work. Employees have been told that they will be fired if they do not show up at the workplace. The change of policy provoked much debate among employees and the general public about working from home. What are the benefits associated with telecommuting? What are the problems with working from home? Are there any legal bases for Canadian employees to challenge Yahoo's actions? Explain.

2. Some employers such as Hooters bars require their female employees to be "slim and fit" or "skinny."[68] Is such a requirement discriminatory

---

68 Stuart Rudner "'The Look': The fine line between job description and discrimination," *The Lawyers Weekly* (4 November 2011) 9.

PART SIX

in Canada? On what basis? Could "looks" qualify as a *bona fide* occupational requirement? Do you think Canadian human rights statutes should be amended to prohibit discrimination on the basis of weight, height, or physical appearance?

3. The distinction between an independent contractor and an employee is not always clear. What steps can be taken by an employer who wishes to engage independent contractors in order to ensure that its workers will be classified as independent contractors? What are the risks associated with having "independent contractors" classified as employees?

4. Mandatory retirement requirements have been eliminated in all jurisdictions in Canada with the exception of *bona fide* occupational requirements and in some provinces *bona fide* retirement or pension plans. Is ending mandatory retirement good for business? What are the advantages and disadvantages of mandatory retirement policies? How might employers require their employees to retire at age 65 without breaching applicable human rights laws?

5. An employer has a duty to accommodate the special needs of a physically or mentally disabled employee unless the accommodation causes undue hardship. What is the duty to accommodate? What are some examples of accommodation? What is undue hardship? What are some factors to consider in determining undue hardship? What are some factors not to consider in determining undue hardship? Is accommodation "special treatment"? Is it fair that one person gets "special treatment" over another?

6. Social media sites such as Facebook, LinkedIn, and blogs provide a great deal of information about job candidates. Should employers access information on these sites in conducting background checks on job candidates? Should employers ask candidates to provide their log-in information? Why or why not?

Situations for Discussion

1. Connor Homes operated foster homes and group homes for children with behavioural problems. To carry out its services, Connor Homes hired a number of childcare workers including Marie Allaire. Prior to starting work with Connor Homes, Allaire signed a contract specifying that she was working as an independent contractor. Subsequently, she reported her income from the contract for income tax purposes as income earned as an independent contractor. A dispute arose as to whether Allaire was an independent contractor or employee. An investigation of Allaire's work showed that Connor Homes drafted and issued its own Policies and Procedures Manual, based on the requirements of the provincial legislation relating to child and family services. This manual defined and dictated the procedures to be followed by all childcare workers with respect to the provision of services within the homes. Connor Homes also controlled Allaire's duties on a day-to-day basis and provided guidance and instruction to her on how to manage difficult situations with clients. Allaire could adjust her pay through her hours of work, however Connor Homes scheduled the actual hours of work. She could also refuse certain schedules which were offered to her. She was required to have her own cell phone and have access to a computer. She was also expected to use her own motor vehicle to access the sites where her work was performed and to occasionally transport some of the children.[69]

Why does it matter if Allaire is classified as an employee or independent contractor? Is Allaire an independent contractor or an employee?

2. Silvia Cabrera is an account executive at a major bank. Over the past six months she has noticed that the performance of one of her loans officers, Jorge Rodriquez, has been declining. Jorge had always been an excellent employee who maintained great relationships with colleagues, performed his work on time, and rarely missed a day of work. However, in the past six months, he has had frequent absences from work, has had difficulty meeting deadlines, and is moody and distracted. When asked if he was having any problems, Jorge simply replied, "It's personal."

---

69 *Supra* note 4.

Last week, Silvia happened to be delivering some important bank documents to Jorge's office when she thought she saw some pornographic images on Jorge's computer before he switched screens to some graphs and tables. Silvia was not 100 percent sure of what she saw, so she did not say anything to Jorge. She decided to speak to the branch manager about her concerns.

The branch manager was quite taken aback and would like to search Jorge's computer, his email account, and his Internet usage.[70] Can the branch manager legally perform such a search? Discuss. Would it be appropriate and legal for the bank to install computer-surveillance technologies that target the use of information sources on all employees' computers?

3. Tom Mason was hired as a technical salesperson for Chem-Trend Limited Partnership, a chemical manufacturer that sold industrial chemicals worldwide. At the time of hiring, he signed a standard form contract that contained both a confidentiality clause and a non-competition clause. The confidentiality clause prohibited him from using or disclosing any trade secrets or confidential information after the termination of his employment. The non-competition clause prohibited him from engaging in any business or activity that could be deemed in competition with Chem-Trend for a period of one year following termination of his employment, regardless of whether he had been fired or quit. This prohibition included providing services or products to any business entity that was a client of Chem-Trend during the course of his employment.

Seventeen years later, Chem-Trend terminated Mason's employment. At the time of his termination, his sales territory spanned all of Canada and several U.S. states. As a result, he was familiar with some of Chem-Trend's clients that operated worldwide, and he had acquired extensive knowledge of Chem-Trend's products, operations, customers, and pricing.[71] Given this situation, are the confidentiality and non-competition clauses enforceable against Mason? What factors are relevant in determining the enforceability of the non-competition clause? How could Mason and Chem-Trend have better protected their interests?

4. In July 2012, Suncor Energy, Canada's largest oil producer, introduced a new drug and alcohol policy for union employees at two of its oil sands operations north of Fort McMurray. The policy required employees in safety sensitive positions to submit to random drug and alcohol testing. The selected employees were required to provide urine samples. In support of its policy, Suncor stated that there was an "out-of-control drug culture" in the Fort McMurray area and cited the following:

- in the nine year period between October 1, 2003, and December 31, 2012, there were 224 positive alcohol and drug tests of Suncor employees.

- there have been 20 fatalities at the two oil sands worksites, and alcohol or drugs were factors in three of them.

- between 2004 and August 2013, there were 2276 security incidents involving alcohol and drugs, including the discovery of devices used to defeat urine drug tests, such as whizzinators, bottles of urine, and urine testing kits.

- in 2009 through 2012, there were 115 positive employee alcohol and drug tests at the impugned workplace compared to only five positive alcohol tests and zero positive drug tests at all of Suncor's other operations in Canada.

Suncor also stated that it had tried other methods to address its concerns about alcohol and drug use, including the use of sniffer dogs and extensive safety training and education with respect to alcohol and drugs.[72] What are the competing interests involved in workplace alcohol and drug testing policies? Is Suncor's random drug and alcohol testing policy justified? Explain.

---

70 Source: Karen Sargeant, "Big brother is watching you", *The Lawyers Weekly* (28 September 2008) 9.

71 *Mason v Chem-Trend Limited Partnership*, 2011 ONCA 344, 106 OR (3d) 72.

72 *Communication, Energy and Paperworkers Union of Canada, Local 707 v Suncor Energy Inc*, 2012 ABCA 373, 84 Alta LR (5th) 181.

5. In January 2005, the CIBC launched a lawsuit against a number of its former employees and Genuity Capital Markets. CIBC is seeking damages in excess of $10 million. CIBC alleges a variety of transgressions, including the theft of client information and the solicitation of its employees. CIBC alleges that the former CEO of CIBC World Markets (CIBC terminated the CEO's employment in February 2004) and others set up a competitor, Genuity Capital, while still employed with CIBC. In less than a year, a total of over 20 senior employees of CIBC left to join Genuity. The allegations are supported by copies of numerous BlackBerry messages exchanged by the defendants in the summer of 2004. Since CIBC filed its suit, the defendants have counterclaimed for $14 million, alleging that the bank breached the privacy of the defendants by going through their email. Further, the former CEO has stated that he was not restricted by any agreement from competing with CIBC.[73] Assuming that the former CEO was not restricted by any agreement from competing with CIBC, does that exonerate him from liability? What can companies like CIBC do to avoid similar situations? What steps can an employer take to minimize the risks associated with the loss of employees and intellectual assets such as client lists, business strategies, and the like?

6. Melissa Antidormi was a successful 41-year-old working as a sales manager with BEA Systems Inc., a California-based software firm, when she left to join Blue Pumpkin Software Inc. At the time of her departure, her base salary was $90 000, and she was on target to earn approximately $300 000 in sales commissions. For 19 months, Blue Pumpkin had pursued her to lead its expansion into Canada and Latin America. She initially declined the offer as she had no interest in leaving her job at BEA Systems. However, Blue Pumpkin was persistent in selling its vision of a "New Canadian Team." Blue Pumpkin flew Antidormi to California, where the CEO indicated that

Melissa's new position would provide a long-term opportunity. With promises of better pay, greater responsibilities, and job security, she joined Blue Pumpkin. Six months later, Melissa was terminated when the company changed its business plans to concentrate on the U.S. market. The company offered her two weeks of severance; she sued for wrongful dismissal. After a two-year legal battle, the Ontario Superior Court awarded her $320 000—the equivalent of one year's salary, commission, and bonuses—plus her legal costs. The court ruled that Melissa deserved 10 months' notice because Blue Pumpkin had misrepresented certain facts—in particular, the job security that she would enjoy as long as she performed well.[74] How can employees protect against false promises and misrepresentations? How can employers protect against false promises and inflated expectations?

7. Jordan Wimmer, a blonde, 29-year-old financier employed by Nomos Capital Partners Ltd., is suing her supervisor because he allegedly sent her emails calling her a "dumb blonde" and "decorative." She is also claiming that he sent the following joke to her and her colleagues: "A blonde asks her boyfriend for help assembling a jigsaw puzzle. She struggles to match the pieces to the picture of a rooster on the box. Eventually the boyfriend calms her down and says 'Let's just put all the cornflakes back in the box.'"[75] What is the legal basis for Wimmer's lawsuit? What does she have to prove to be successful? Assuming the allegations are true, is she likely to be successful? Is Nomos Capital responsible for the supervisor's actions? How should companies deal with issues of "jokes" in the workplace?

8. Richard Evans was employed for six years by The Sports Corporation (TSC), as a sports agent. He was responsible for managing current and prospective NHL hockey players coming from the Czech Republic and Slovakia. Although Evans was neither a director nor a shareholder of TSC and had no power to

---

73 Patricia Best, "CIBC head invokes history in Genuity war", *The Globe and Mail* (6 December 2006) B2; Andrew Willis, "CIBC sues 6 former employees," *The Globe and Mail* (6 January 2005) B1; and Marjo Johne, "How to Cover Your Assets", *The Bay Street Bull* (August 2005), online: e2r Solutions <http://www.e2rsolutions.com/Libraries/Documents/How_to_Cover_Your_Assets.sflb.ashx>.

74 *Antidormi v Blue Pumpkin Software Inc*, 35 CCEL (3d) 247, 2004 CLLC 210-008 (Ont Sup Ct).

75 Dave McGinn, "Office blonde jokes no laughing matter," *The Globe and Mail* (24 November 2009) L3.

hire or promote employees, he had primary responsibility for TSC's eastern European operations and he developed close personal relationships with players. Evans's fixed-term employment contract contained the following non-solicitation clause:

> He will not, either during the continuance of his employment under this agreement or for a period of 24 months thereafter, directly or indirectly through others, call on, solicit, divert or take away or attempt to call on, solicit, divert or take away any client of the Company which has been a client of the Company or any other company to whom Evans provided any services related to the Company's business.

At the end of his fixed term contract, Evans left TSC and set up his own business. Prior to leaving TSC, he asked two TSC employees—Jaromir Henys and Peter Kadlecek, who were responsible for recruiting hockey players in the Czech Republic and Slovakia—to join him and they agreed. After setting up his business, Evans did not personally solicit TSC's clients but Henys and Kadlecek began directing TSC clients to Evans, who began representing those clients. TSC brought an action against Evans.[76] What are the potential cause(s) of action in this case? What would TSC need to prove to be successful? Is TSC likely to be successful? Explain.

76 *Evans v Sports Corporation*, 2013 ABCA 14, 358 DLR (4ᵗʰ) 428.

21

OBJECTIVES

After studying this chapter, you should have an understanding of

- how the employment relationship ends

- the differences among dismissals for just cause, dismissals with notice, constructive dismissals, and wrongful dismissals

- the issues arising from a wrongful dismissal suit

- the components of a termination settlement

TERMINATING THE EMPLOYMENT RELATIONSHIP

BUSINESS LAW IN PRACTICE

Hiram Dupuis, the owner and operator of an independent newspaper in southern Ontario, is reviewing his options in light of a dramatic drop in circulation. In recent years, the newspaper industry has changed significantly due to the merger of several large dailies and the advent of online sources of news. Hiram believes that there is still a role for the weekly community newspaper, but in order to survive he will have to downsize his workforce. He has come to the conclusion that Jeong Nash will have to go. Jeong, a staff reporter, is 32 years old and has been with the newspaper for a couple of years, but her stories are often controversial and Hiram has had to defend her on a couple of occasions. Most recently, a story she wrote about an aging basketball player has upset a number of advertisers, and they are threatening to take their business elsewhere.

The other change that Hiram is contemplating is the merger of two of the newspaper's departments—Community Homes & Gardens and Living in Our Community. The managers of the departments are 58-year-old Stella Blanchard, who has been with the newspaper for 25 years, and 37-year-old Josiah Rutgers, who has been with the newspaper for five years. As Stella is the older, more senior employee, Hiram wants to make her the manager of the new department. Josiah will retain his title and the same salary. The only difference is that, after the merger, he will report to Stella rather than to Hiram. The restructuring of the newspaper will give Hiram an opportunity to terminate the general manager, 56-year-old Levi Cameron. Although he has been with the newspaper for 15 years, he has, over the years, committed a number of infractions. He often tells off-colour jokes and sometimes makes comments about the appearance and dress of female colleagues. Recently, Hiram discovered inappropriate content on Levi's computer.

1. Is Hiram justified in terminating Jeong Nash and Levi Cameron?

2. Is Hiram entitled to change Josiah Rutgers's position?

3. What course of action would you advise Hiram to pursue?

Ending the Relationship

In many instances, the employment relationship ends in an amicable fashion. An employee resigns to pursue other interests, retires, or simply leaves at the end of a fixed-term employment contract.

The employment relationship can also come to an end through less pleasant means, as when the employer

- summarily dismisses, or fires, an employee.
- gives the employee notice of termination.
- acts in such a manner that the employment relationship becomes untenable.

It is an implied term of an employment contract that an employer may terminate the employment relationship without any notice if there is "just cause." This implied term is subject to collective agreements and individual employment contracts, which may specify the terms for ending the employment relationship. The term is also subject to legislation that may give to certain employees—such as teachers, police officers, and firefighters—special rights in the case of dismissal.

It is also an implied term that an employer may terminate the employment contract by giving the employee reasonable notice of the termination. In this case the employer is not required to have a reason or cause for the termination. The implied term is also subject to collective agreements and individual employment contracts that provide for notice periods and rights on dismissal. Also, provincial and federal employment standards legislation provides for notice periods and procedures on dismissal. The periods of notice provided by the legislation are only minimum periods, and often employees are entitled to more notice.

Dismissals for Just Cause

When there is **just cause**, an employer may dismiss an employee without notice. Just cause for dismissal means, in effect, that the employee has breached a fundamental term of the employment contract.

Just cause exists when the employee is guilty of one or more of the following:

- serious misconduct.
- habitual neglect of duty.
- incompetence.
- conduct incompatible with duties or prejudicial to the employer's business.
- willful disobedience in a matter of substance.[1]

The grounds for dismissal with cause are easy to articulate but difficult to apply in practice, because whether an employee's conduct justifies dismissal is a question of fact that requires an assessment of the context and circumstances of the conduct.[2] It is impossible to specify all of the conduct that may constitute just cause; however, it is possible to make some general comments about the various categories.

Just cause

Employee conduct that amounts to a fundamental breach of the employment contract.

1   *R v Arthurs, Ex parte Port Arthur Shipbuilding Co*, [1967] 2 OR 49, 62 DLR (2d) 342 (CA), reversed on other grounds, *Port Arthur Shipbuilding Co v Arthurs*, [1969] SCR 85, 70 DLR (2d) 693.
2   *McKinley v BC Tel*, 2001 SCC 38, [2001] 2 SCR 161.

Is using the company computer for personal use grounds for dismissal?

Serious Misconduct

A minor infraction by an employee is insufficient to justify dismissal, although the cumulative effect of many minor instances may be sufficient. The cumulative effect must be such that there is a serious impact on the employment relationship. For example, Levi's telling of an off-colour joke would not be sufficient grounds for dismissal. However, if the telling of the joke is combined with a number of other incidents, such as making inappropriate comments and having inappropriate content on his computer, then the cumulative effect of the incidents may be considered **serious misconduct**.

If Hiram wants to terminate on the basis of an accumulation of a number of minor incidents, he has a duty to warn the employee and give an opportunity to improve performance. This duty is particularly important in situations where there is a **progressive discipline policy** in place. This is a system whereby the employer applies discipline for relatively minor infractions on a progressive basis. Each step in the progression carries a more serious penalty, until the last step—dismissal—is reached. The warning may be oral[3] or in writing and should be clear and understood by the employee. The employee should be advised not just about the unacceptable conduct, but also about the consequences of failure to improve.

A single act of misconduct can justify dismissal if it is sufficiently serious. For example, a single act of dishonesty can be sufficient grounds for dismissal, as when an employee steals a large sum of money from the employer. However, an act of dishonesty, in and of itself, is not necessarily sufficient to warrant just cause for dismissal. The nature and context of any dishonesty must be considered.[4] Other examples of conduct that may constitute serious misconduct include lying to an employer, forging signatures and documents, and cheating. What constitutes serious misconduct may also be affected by workforce policies. For example, having an affair with a co-worker does not constitute just cause for dismissal unless the employer can prove that the conduct negatively affected the business or the employer has a policy against office romance.

Serious misconduct

Intentional, harmful conduct of the employee that permits the employer to dismiss without notice.

Progressive discipline policy

A system that follows a sequence of employee discipline from less to more severe punishment.

---

3 Warnings, especially oral warnings, need to be documented so that an employer can establish that the duty to warn was fulfilled.

4 *Supra* note 2.

An important principle with respect to any of the grounds for dismissal is **condonation**. Condonation occurs when an employer indicates through words or actions that behaviour constituting grounds for dismissal is being overlooked. For example, an employer who is aware of the harassing activities of an employee and who ignores or tolerates the activities will have difficulty arguing just cause for termination. Condonation occurs only if the employer is fully aware of the wrongful behaviour.

Condonation

Employer behaviour that indicates to the employee that misconduct is being overlooked.

Habitual Neglect of Duty

An employee may be terminated with cause for chronic absenteeism and lateness that are considered **habitual neglect of duty**. The absenteeism must be without the employer's permission or authorization and be more than an occasional absence. Important to this ground is whether warnings were issued, whether there was any excuse for the absence, and whether the absence occurred at a critical time for the employer.

Habitual neglect of duty

Persistent failure to perform employment duties.

BUSINESS APPLICATION OF THE LAW

FIRED DURING A MASS CONFERENCE CALL

One day after announcing hundreds of layoffs at Patch, the local news service run by AOL Inc., Tim Armstrong, chief executive officer of AOL called a conference call with more than 1000 employees of Patch. The call was meant to boost morale for the employees remaining with the news organization. In the middle of the call, Armstrong noticed someone taking pictures. According to media reports, he shouted, "Abel put that camera down right now! Abel, you're fired. Out!" Armstrong then proceeded with his message. The fired employee is Abel Lenz, Patch's creative director. According to Patch employees, he often snapped pictures during conference calls and staff meetings and would later post them to the company's internal website.

After a recording of the firing was leaked to news outlets and the story went viral, Armstrong issued a four-paragraph statement acknowledging that he had made a mistake. He stated that it was an emotional response at the start of a very difficult discussion. He further explained his reason for the firing was that confidential meetings should not be recorded and that Lenz had been warned previously not to make recordings.

Tim Armstrong, CEO of AOL Inc.

AOL stated that Lenz would not be hired back but that Armstrong had contacted him to apologize.

Critical Analysis: Did Armstrong have just cause to terminate Lenz's employment? What are the risks to AOL of Lenz's termination?

Sources: Peter daSilva, "AOL chief apologizes over firing of worker", *New York Times* (14 August 2013), online: NY Times.com <http://www.nytimes.com/2013/08/14/business/media/aols-armstrong-apologizes-to-staff-for-firing-of-employee.html?_r=0>; Edmund Lee, "AOL's Armstrong apologizes for openly firing employee at meeting", *Bloomberg* (14 August 2013), online: *Bloomberg* <http://www.bloomberg.com/news/2013-08-13/aol-s-tim-armstrong-apologizes-for-firing-employee-at-meeting.html>; Daniel Lubin, "Tips for the firing squad", *The Globe and Mail* (23 August 2013) B11; Steve Kovach, "Tim Armstrong: I made an emotional mistake firing that guy", *The Business Insider* (13 August 2013), online: *The Business Insider* <http://www.businessinsider.com/aol-ceo-apology-2013-8>.

Francois G. Durand/Getty Images

PART SIX

It is more difficult to establish lateness than absenteeism as grounds for dismissal. The courts will consider whether the employee had a valid excuse, whether there were warnings concerning lateness, and whether the time was ever made up.

Incompetence

To dismiss on the ground of **incompetence**, the employer must be more than merely dissatisfied with an employee's work. There must be actual incompetence. The substandard level of performance must be evident after the employee has been given a warning and an opportunity to improve. An employer must establish fair and reasonable performance standards against which to measure performance. An employee can raise a number of issues to explain poor performance—inadequate training, insufficient volume of business, inexperience, and condonation of performance problems.

A single act of incompetence is rarely grounds for dismissal, unless it shows a complete lack of skills that an employee claimed to have possessed.

Conduct Incompatible

An employer may be justified in terminating with cause for **conduct incompatible** with the employee's duties or prejudicial to the employer's business—for example, accepting lavish and inappropriate gifts from the employer's clients. The conduct complained of is not limited to conduct on the job—it can also apply to conduct outside working hours. For example, a school board was deemed justified in dismissing a school superintendent who was convicted of a petty fraud outside the performance of his duties.[5]

TECHNOLOGY AND THE LAW

THE FACEBOOK FIRINGS

Facebook, Twitter, blogs, and other social media are increasingly becoming part of the workplace. Employees are blogging, tweeting, and accessing social networking websites, and often, the conversation is work. Inappropriate social networking—whether done at work or outside of the workplace—can, however, be just cause for dismissal. Employers have the right to take disciplinary action including termination when employees post comments that expose confidential information or harm the interests of the employer including its reputation or harm the interests of other employees.

In *Lougheed Imports Ltd (West Coast Mazda) v United Food and Commercial Workers International*

Union, Local 1518,[6] the British Columbia Labour Relations Board upheld an employer's termination of two employees for posting inappropriate work-related comments on their personal Facebook profiles. The two employees, who worked at West Coast Mazda in Pitt Meadows, B.C., had been involved in the successful unionization of the workforce. During the unionization drive, they posted various derogatory and offensive comments in the statuses of their Facebook accounts. They openly called supervisors and managers offensive and insulting names and posted comments such as "don't spend your money at West Coast Mazda as they are crooks out to hose you and the shop ripped off a bunch of people I know." The comments increased in

---

5 *Cherniwchan v County of Two Hills No. 21* (1982), 21 Alta LR (2d) 353, 38 AR 125 (QB).
6 [2010] BCLRBD No 190, 186 CLRBR (2d) 82.

number and became increasingly angry once the union was certified. Among their 477 friends on Facebook were managers and co-workers, who were able to view every comment that was posted. When the comments included references to stabbing and TV's vigilante killer, Dexter, and homophobic slurs and threats, they were fired. The labour board found that despite the fact that the comments were off-site during non-work hours, they contributed to a hostile work environment and constituted insubordination.[7]

Critical Analysis: Do you think the outcome might have been different if the comments had been made to a few friends on a password-protected blog or if their privacy settings on Facebook only included a few friends? How can employers reduce the risk of their legitimate business interests being harmed by the social media activities of their employees?

When are the social media activities of employees grounds for dismissal?

THOMAS COEX/AFP/Getty Images

Closely related to incompatible conduct is the ground for dismissal pertaining to an employee's conflict of interest. For example, if an employee were to run a business that was in direct competition with the employer's business, it could be a breach of the employee's duty of loyalty and good faith to the employer.[8]

Willful Disobedience

An employer is entitled to expect an employee to carry out lawful and reasonable orders. Failure to do so is considered **willful disobedience**. A single act of disobedience would not ordinarily constitute grounds for dismissal, unless that act was very serious, such as not attending an important meeting or refusing to follow important safety rules. To rely on this ground, the employer would have to establish that the instructions or directions given to the employee were unambiguous and that the employee had no reasonable excuse for disobeying. Less serious instances of disobedience may justify dismissal when combined with other types of misconduct, such as insolence and insubordination.

An employer is entitled to expect an employee to carry out orders without extended debate and with respect. Whether an employer is justified in terminating an employee who fails to meet this standard depends on a number of factors, such as whether the employee was provoked, whether the employee was upset, and whether it was a moment of temporary anger.

Willful disobedience

Deliberate failure to carry out lawful and reasonable orders.

PART SIX

---

7 See also *Canada Post Corporation v Canadian Union of Postal Workers*, [2012] CLAD No 85, 216 LAC (4th) 202 where the dismissal of a postal worker with 31 years of experience for making comments on Facebook that maligned and threatened her supervisors was upheld.
8 Stacey Ball, *Canadian Employment Law*, Student Edition (Toronto: Canada Law Book, 2012-2013) at 11–24.

Should an office romance be just cause for dismissal?

Other Causes

In addition to the grounds discussed thus far, there can be other bases for termination without notice. Most may fit within the general category of misconduct; examples include harassment (including sexual harassment), disruption of corporate culture, consumption of alcohol or drugs in the workplace, and drug abuse.

The Supreme Court of Canada in the case below has indicated that whether an employer has just cause to terminate an employee in any situation depends on the nature and circumstances of the misconduct. The sanction imposed on an employee must be proportional—dismissal is only warranted if the misconduct strikes at the heart of the employment relationship.

CASE

McKinley v BC Tel, 2001 SCC 38, [2001] 2 SCR 161

THE BUSINESS CONTEXT: Employers often argue that a single act of dishonest conduct by an employee gives rise to just cause for dismissal. Employees contend that any act, including dishonesty, should be judged on its context and its entirety.

FACTUAL BACKGROUND: Martin McKinley, 48, was a chartered accountant who worked 17 years for BC Tel. He held various positions with the company, and in 1991 was promoted to controller. In May 1993, he began to experience high blood pressure, and in May of the following year, on the advice of his physician, he took a leave of absence. By July, his supervisor raised the issue of termination. McKinley indicated that he wished to return to work in a position that carried less responsibility. However, alternative positions were never offered to him, and in August his employment was terminated. BC Tel claimed that it had just cause to dismiss McKinley as he had been dishonest about his medical condition and treatments available for it. He had failed to clearly disclose that his doctor told him he could return to work if he took a beta-blocker, a medication with various side effects.

THE LEGAL QUESTION: Does an employee's dishonest conduct, in and of itself, give rise to just cause for dismissal?

RESOLUTION: The court noted that there were two approaches that have been adopted in various Canadian jurisdictions. One approach dictates that any dishonesty by an employee, however minor, is automatically considered just cause for dismissal. The other approach requires a determination of whether the nature and degree of the dishonesty warrants dismissal in the context of the entire employment relationship. The court adopted the "contextual" approach and restored the trial court's finding that McKinley had been wrongly dismissed. In other words, McKinley's conduct did not merit just cause for dismissal. The court did note, however, that in cases involving serious fraud, theft, or misappropriation, either approach would ultimately lead to a finding of just cause.

The court also went on to say that although less serious dishonesty may not merit firing without notice, "that is not to say that there cannot be lesser sanctions for less serious conduct. For example, an employer may be justified in docking an employee's pay for any loss incurred by a minor misuse of company property." The court indicated that this was one of several disciplinary measures that an employer might take in these circumstances.

CRITICAL ANALYSIS: Given that not all dishonesty is just cause, how big a lie must an employee tell before he can be fired for just cause? For example, could an employer fire an employee who left work early, saying he had a headache, and then went to the mall to shop?

Non-cause and Near Cause

There are many potential reasons or situations that may constitute just cause for dismissal. However, it is important to note that what might seem to be a good reason for terminating an employee is not necessarily just cause. For example, Hiram's newspaper has suffered economic setbacks, and although this is a good reason to scale back its workforce, it is not "just cause" for termination. Similarly, Jeong is a difficult employee, but although this may be a good reason to terminate her employment, again, it is not "just cause."

In the absence of just cause, the employer who wishes to terminate an employee is required to give notice or pay in lieu of notice. The period of notice will either be the term agreed upon in the employment contract, the period specified in employment standards legislation, or **reasonable notice**. What constitutes "reasonable" notice is to be determined in relation to factors such as age, length of service, availability of employment, and the status of the employee.

In some situations, an employer may have an employee who is neither particularly good nor bad. Is an employer entitled to give the "so-so" employee a lesser period of notice? In *Dowling v Halifax (City of)*,[9] a long-serving stationary engineer who would have been entitled to about 24-month notice of termination had the notice period reduced to six months by the employer because of inappropriate conduct—favouring one contractor over another and making work difficult for the competing contractor. The Supreme Court flatly refused to accept any argument by the employer that the reduction was justified because of near cause and sent the matter back to the trial judge for an assessment of reasonable notice. Thus, either an employer has just cause to dismiss an employee and the employee is not entitled to any notice, or the employer does not have just cause to dismiss and the employee is entitled to the full period of reasonable notice. There is no halfway position.

Reasonable notice

A period of time for an employee to find alternative employment prior to dismissal.

9 [1998] 1 SCR 22, 222 NR 1.

However, the Supreme Court of Canada in *McKinley* indicates that conduct that does not merit dismissal without notice can be addressed by lesser sanctions. The court gives the example of an employer docking an employee's pay for dishonest conduct that does not warrant firing. This approach opens the door to employers giving forms of discipline such as suspensions for "near cause" conduct.

Risks in Just Cause Dismissals

Since an employee is not entitled to any compensation when dismissed for cause, the employee is more likely to bring a suit against the employer. An employer should carefully consider all of the potential costs of dismissing for cause and consider a termination settlement.

An employer who determines that dismissal for cause is justified can reduce the risks considerably by ensuring that sound policies and procedures for dismissal with just cause are established and practised.

Dismissal with Notice

An employee who has been hired for an indefinite period of time may be dismissed at any time and without cause as long as the employer gives notice of the termination (or pay in lieu of notice).[10] While indefinite-term employment contracts are the norm in most industries, many individuals do work for fixed periods of time.[11] For those employees, their contracts end without any notice when the term expires. Termination of a fixed-term contract prior to its expiry is a breach of contract.

The period of notice required to terminate an indefinite-term employment contract involves the consideration of employment standards legislation, contractual provisions, if any, and the common law. At a minimum, employees are entitled to the period of notice set out in the applicable employment standards legislation. These provisions may not be abrogated by contract. The employment contract may provide for a period of notice but courts do not always uphold this period. This is particularly the case when the agreed-upon notice is considerably less than the reasonable notice implied by the common law. The courts may justify ignoring the contractual provisions on the basis that the circumstances of the employment contract have changed or that the contract was unfair and unconscionable. Therefore, as the statutory provisions are only a minimum and contractual provisions, if any, are not always enforceable, employees are often entitled to common law reasonable notice.[12] As Hiram is unlikely to establish just cause for terminating Jeong and possibly Levi, the better course of action is to give reasonable notice.

---

10 Note that employers cannot give effective notice or payment in lieu of notice to someone who is unable to work, since an employee who is disabled or on pregnancy or parental leave cannot take advantage of the notice period to look for other work.

11 Note that a series of fixed-term contracts may be interpreted as a contract for an indefinite term. For example, in *Ceccol v Ontario Gymnastic Federation*, 55 OR (3d) 614, [2001] OJ No 3488 (CA), the Ontario Court of Appeal held that a series of 15 one-year contracts was an indefinite-term contract and therefore the employee was entitled to reasonable notice of termination.

12 Typically, employment standards legislation provides one week of notice for each year of service up to a maximum of eight weeks, whereas reasonable notice for middle-level employees is, on average, more like one month of notice for each year of service up to a maximum of 24 months.

Reasonable Notice Periods

In theory, notice is a period of time to enable the soon-to-be terminated employee to find alternative employment. In determining how much notice, the primary factors to be considered are those set out in *Bardal v Globe & Mail Ltd*:[13]

- character of employment.
- length of service.
- age.
- availability of similar employment.

Character of Employment

This factor refers to whether the employee was at a high-status position in the organization. Generally, a senior, high-level, or management employee is entitled to more notice than a junior, non-management employee. For example, Levi occupies a higher position at the newspaper than Jeong, so on this basis Levi is entitled to more notice than Jeong. The rationale behind this factor is the assumption that it takes a higher-level employee a longer period of time to find alternative employment than it does a lower-level employee. However, this distinction has been called into question. Mr. Justice McPherson in *Cronk v Canadian General Insurance*[14] noted that those who are better educated or professionally trained are more likely to obtain employment after dismissal than individuals with fewer skills. His decision to grant a 55-year-old clerical worker with 35 years' experience 20-month reasonable notice, however, was reduced to 12 months on appeal.[15] The Court of Appeal decision in *Cronk* has been severely criticized as being repugnant to modern social values in contemporary Canada, and subsequent courts in Ontario and other jurisdictions have refused to assume that lower status jobs are in higher supply than high status jobs. These courts have held that all of the factors in *Bardal* must be appropriately weighted, and an inappropriate weight should not be given to "character of employment."[16]

Length of Service

A longer-term employee is entitled to more notice than a shorter-term employee. On this basis Levi, with 15 years' service, is entitled to more notice than Jeong, with a mere two years' service. The rationale is that a long-serving employee does not have the same degree or breadth of experience as an employee who has had several shorter-term jobs. In essence, a long-serving employee has a smaller range of comparable reemployment prospects.

Reasonable notice is not calculated by a rule of thumb of one month of notice for every year of service.[17] Short-term employees, in particular, have often received notice periods well above the one month per year of service benchmark.

---

13 [1960] OWN 253, 24 DLR (2d) 140 (Ont HC). These factors were endorsed by the Supreme Court of Canada in *Machtinger v HOJ Industries Ltd*, [1992] 1 SCR 986, 91 DLR (4th) 491.
14 (1994), 19 OR (3d) 515, 6 CCEL (2d) 15 (Gen Div).
15 (1995), 25 OR (3d) 505, 85 OAC 54 (CA).
16 *Supra* note 8 at 9–25.
17 *Supra* note 8 at 9–8.

Why are older employees generally entitled to more notice than younger employees?

Age

Older employees, particularly those over 50 years of age, are entitled to more notice than younger employees because they have more difficulty in finding employment. Many employers are unwilling to hire older persons. Levi, at 56 years of age, is entitled to more notice than 32-year-old Jeong.

Younger employees in their 20s and 30s are generally entitled only to short periods of notice despite high rates of unemployment among youth.

Availability of Similar Employment

The more employment opportunities available, the shorter the period of notice to which the employee will be entitled. The availability of employment opportunities may be gauged by expert opinion of job openings, advertisements, and other indicators of market conditions. From a practical perspective, the availability of job opportunities will be affected by an employee's experience, training, and qualifications.

Developments in Notice

Although the factors in *Bardal v Globe & Mail* remain of prime importance in determining reasonable notice, they are not an exhaustive list. Other factors that tend to lengthen notice are:

- a high degree of specialization.
- inducement to join an organization.
- company policy.
- custom and industry practice.
- personal characteristics.
- economic climate.[18]

Risks in Dismissal with Notice

The calculation of reasonable notice is a task fraught with uncertainty. Although the factors used in the calculation are well known, the weight to be given to each is uncertain; the only certainty is that each factor must be appropriately weighted. Most courts list the factors and then state a period of notice without indicating whether one factor has been given more weight than another. Notice periods have generally increased, and there have even been cases where the notice period has exceeded two years.[19] This development

---

18   See generally Ellen Mole & Marion J Stendon, *The Wrongful Dismissal Handbook*, 3d ed (Markham, Ontario: LexisNexis, 2004) at 255–281.

19   See, for example, *Baranowski v Binks Manufacturing Co* (2000), 49 CCEL (2d) 170, 93 ACWS (3d) 1033 (Ont SCJ), where the court awarded 30-month notice; and *UPM-Kymmene Miramichi Inc v Walsh*, 2003 NBCA 32, 257 NBR (2d) 331 where the court awarded 28-month notice.

suggests that there is not a general cap on notice, although in most provinces it is recognized that the maximum range for reasonable notice is between 18 and 24 months.[20]

How much notice would Levi and Jeong be entitled to? Levi is a 56-year-old management employee with 15 years' experience and unknown employment opportunities. He would be entitled to approximately 16- to 18-month notice. Jeong is a 32-year-old staff reporter with two years' experience and unknown employment opportunities. She would probably be entitled to notice of one to two months.

Constructive Dismissal

An employer has no entitlement to make a fundamental or substantial change to the employment contract without the employee's consent. The employee may accept the change and create a new employment contract or refuse to accept the change, quit, and sue for what is called **constructive dismissal**. The dismissal is not express—the employer has not said to the employee, "You're fired"—but changing a key aspect of the employment contract may be equivalent to dismissal.

Constructive dismissal

Unilateral employer conduct that amounts to a fundamental or substantial change to an employee's contract.

Fundamental or Substantial Changes

Constructive dismissal occurs when the employer unilaterally makes a significant change to a **fundamental term** (or substantial term) of the contract without the employee's consent. The test for determining whether a substantial change is made is an objective one; the basic question is whether at the time of the change the reasonable person would believe that essential terms of the employment contract were being changed.[21] A minor change will not generally trigger a constructive dismissal, although the cumulative effect of many minor changes may do so. As well, the employment contract may reserve for the employer the right to make certain unilateral changes without triggering a constructive dismissal. For example, geographical transfers are often provided for in the contract. The following case provides clarification of the test for constructive dismissal.

Fundamental term

A term that is considered to be essential to the contract.

CASE

Potter v New Brunswick Legal Aid Services Commission, [2015] 1 SCR 500, 2015 SCC 10

THE BUSINESS CONTEXT: Employers expose themselves to liability when they make decisions that affect important terms of employment such as duties, compensation, reporting structure and such.

FACTUAL BACKGROUND: David Potter was appointed Executive Director of New Brunswick Legal Aid Services Commission for a seven-year term. Partway through his term,

(Continued)

---

20 *Supra* note 8 at 9–11.
21 *Farber v Royal Trust Co,* [1997] 1 SCR 846, 145 DLR (4th) 1.

the relationship between Potter and the Commission deteriorated and the parties started negotiations on a buyout of the remainder of his contract. Before a settlement was reached, Potter took sick leave. While he was on sick leave, the Commission put him on indefinite administrative suspension with full pay and benefits and his powers and duties were assigned to another employee. Despite a request by Potter, no reasons for the suspension were given. At the same time and unbeknownst to Potter, the Commission recommended that the Minister of Justice terminate Potter's employment with cause. Eight weeks later, Potter sued for constructive dismissal.

THE LEGAL QUESTION: Was Potter constructively dismissed?

RESOLUTION: The Supreme Court of Canada stated that constructive dismissal can take two forms: a single unilateral act by the employee that breaches an essential term of the employment contract; or a series of acts by the employer that, taken together, show the employer no longer intends to be bound by the employment contract. The first form requires a determination of whether the employer unilaterally breached an express or implied term of the contract and if so, did the breach substantially alter an essential term of the contract? For the second form, the employee need not point to a specific substantial change, but rather the focus is on a course of conduct by the employer that evidences an intention not to be bound by the contract. As a particular act

(the suspension) was at issue, the first form applied to Potter.

In applying the first form to the facts, the Court found that there was no express term in the employment contract that provided for the non-disciplinary suspension of the employee. There was also no implied term to suspend because the employer had a duty to provide the employee with work. Even if the employer had an implied authority to relieve Potter of some or all of his duties, such authority is not unfettered and is subject to a requirement of business justification. The employer failed to establish that the suspension was reasonable or justified because it gave no reasons (let alone legitimate reasons) for the suspension and it failed to meet the basic requirement to be honest and forthright with the employee. Therefore, as there was not an express or an implied term giving the employer the authority to suspend, and as Potter did not consent or acquiesce to the suspension, the suspension is a breach of contract. The first step in the analysis is satisfied. With regard to the second step, it was reasonable for Potter to perceive that the decision to suspend for an indefinite time without reasons or explanation substantially changed essential terms of the contract. The Court held that Potter was constructively dismissed.

CRITICAL ANALYSIS: How can employees mitigate the risk of constructive dismissal claims?

Generally, the changes that are considered to be fundamental are adverse changes to salary or benefits, job content and function, responsibility, status and prestige, and the power/reporting structures, although other changes may be considered fundamental, depending on the circumstances. It is negative changes that usually trigger constructive dismissal, as employees normally readily accept positive changes. Hiram's contemplated merger of two departments with the result that Josiah reports to Stella rather than Hiram may trigger a constructive dismissal. Even though Josiah may have the same job title and may be earning the same money, changing the reporting structure is, in effect, a demotion.

"Bad" Behaviour

Although most constructive dismissal cases involve demotions and pay cuts, the doctrine is not limited to these kinds of factors. Unacceptable or unethical practices by an employer may amount to constructive dismissal. For example, the B.C. Supreme Court awarded constructive dismissal damages to an employee who quit when he discovered that his boss was sending out fraudulent bills.[22] Humiliating or abusive behaviour, such as shouting and swearing, and threats of dismissal can also constitute constructive dismissal.[23]

In *Shah v Xerox Canada Ltd*,[24] the Ontario Court of Appeal upheld an employee's claim of constructive dismissal where the employer's conduct, which included unjustified criticisms and unfair performance appraisals, created intolerable working conditions. The court indicated that it is unnecessary that an employee establish that the employer breached a specific term of the employment contract. It is sufficient that the employee prove a poisoned or intolerable work environment.

Risks in Constructive Dismissal

Before making changes that affect an employee's job, employers need to consider the nature of the change, whether the change is likely to be acceptable to the employee, why the change is being made, and whether there are any contractual provisions that permit the contemplated changes. An employer should also provide a "try-out" period during which the employee can assess the changes prior to being required to accept them. These actions can help minimize the risk of triggering a constructive dismissal because of a change to a substantial or fundamental term. In order to manage the risk of a constructive dismissal because of a poisoned work environment, employers should have policies that ensure the dignity of the workplace and promote interactions that are civil and respectful. These policies need to be uniformly enforced.

Wrongful Dismissal Suit

A wrongful dismissal suit may arise in several situations, such as when an employee has been dismissed for cause and the employee claims there was no just cause, or when an employee is given notice of dismissal and the employee claims the notice was inadequate. Wrongful dismissal can also arise from a constructive dismissal. An employee is not obligated to go to a court to claim wrongful dismissal; she may proceed by making a claim to an employment standards tribunal. This action would limit an employee's compensation to an amount equivalent to the statutory period of notice. It is the route most often used by low-level employees, as they are often entitled to no more than the statutory notice and this method is considerably less expensive.

---

22 *Nethery v Lindsey Morden Claim Services Ltd*, 1999 BCCA 340, 127 BCAC 237.
23 See *Lloyd v Imperial Parking Ltd* (1996), 192 AR 190, 46 Alta LR (3d) 220 (QB).
24 131 OAC 44, [2000] OJ No 849 (CA).

PART SIX

PROTECTION FOR WHISTLEBLOWERS IN CANADA AND THE UNITED STATES

Timothy Wallender, a trainmaster for Canadian National Railway Co. (CNR) in Memphis, Tennessee, has filed a lawsuit claiming he was fired after "blowing the whistle" on widespread fraud at CNR. Wallender alleges that he and other employees were asked to tamper with statistics to make it appear that CNR trains moved 20 to 30 percent more efficiently from the freight yards than competitors' trains. He also alleges that efficiency statistics were improved by moving trains onto "ghost" tracks and counting broken cars as having been delivered to customers. He claims these fraudulent practices inflated performance numbers and thereby increased company share prices. Wallender is seeking reinstatement, back pay with interest, damages, and costs.[25] CNR has denied the charges and states that Wallender was fired for repeatedly filing false data.

Assuming his allegations are true, Wallender is what is referred to as a whistleblower—an employee who reports wrongdoing involving his employers. The protection afforded a whistleblower is markedly different in the United States as compared to Canada.

U.S. Whistleblowing Protection. In the United States, legislation facilitates the ability of an employee to report misconduct of the employer. For example, the *Sarbanes-Oxley Act 2000*[26] prevents a publicly traded company from taking retaliatory action against an employee who reports fraud against shareholders. This legislation, which was enacted following the financial frauds at WorldCom and Enron Corp. in the late 1990s, has been amended[27] to provide financial incentives. The whistleblower may now claim between 10 and 39 percent of any penalty imposed by the U.S. Securities and Exchange Commission that exceeds US $1 million. Whistleblowers can also file a suit under the *U.S. False Claims Act*[28] if the federal government has been financially defrauded. A successful suit can result in large payments to the whistleblower and large fines for the wrongdoer.

Canada's Whistleblowing Protection. In Canada there is no similar legislation that both protects and rewards whistleblowers.[29] There are, however, a number of provisions that do attempt to protect whistleblowers in certain circumstances. The *Criminal Code of Canada*[30] makes it an offence for employers to retaliate against an employee who provides information to law enforcement about the commission of an offence by his employer. This is a protection that applies to both public and private sector whistleblowers. The *Public Servants Disclosure Act*[31] provides protection for whistleblowers in the federal public service, and legislation in Alberta, Manitoba, Saskatchewan, New Brunswick, and Ontario provides protection for provincial public service employees. Only Saskatchewan[32] and New Brunswick[33] provide protection for whistleblowers in the private sector. In these provinces, employers are not permitted to retaliate against an employee who reports or proposes to report to a lawful authority any activity that is or is likely to result in an offence. In addition to these

25 "Whistle blower complaint pursuant to 18 USC s1514A" *United States District Court for the Western District of Tennessee* (5 August 2013), online: <http://aptn.ca/pages/news/files/2013/09/CNUScomplaint.pdf>.
26 Pub L No 107-204, 2002 USCCAN (116 Stat) 745 s 1107.
27 *Dodd-Frank Wall Street Reform and Consumer Protection Act*, Pub L No 111-203, 124 Stat 1376 (2010) s 922.
28 31 USC s3729-3733.
29 Canada Revenue Agency, however, has a program that has incentives for reporting international tax evasion. See: Daniel Leblanc, "Whistleblowers in line for rewards as Ottawa cracks down on tax cheats," *The Globe and Mail* (21 March 2013), online: Globe and Mail <http://www.theglobeandmail.com/news/politics/budget/whistleblowers-in-line-for-rewards-as-ottawa-cracks-down-on-tax-cheats/article10083229/>; also, the Ontario Securities Commission is considering establishing incentives for reporting serious financial crimes. See: Janet Mcfarland, "OSC proposes plan to pay whistleblowers," *The Globe and Mail* (4 February 2015) B8.
30 RSC 1985, c C-46, s 425.1.
31 SC 2005, c46.
32 *The Saskatchewan Employment Act*, SS 2014, c S-15.1, s 2-42 (2).
33 *Employment Standards Act*, SNB 1982, cE-7.2, s 28.

Does whistleblowing by an employee conflict with the employee's duty of loyalty and good faith to the employer?

provisions, some legislation such as occupational health and safety and environmental acts provide protection against adverse employment consequences for reporting contraventions of these acts. As noted earlier, none of the whistleblowing protection provisions in Canada provide incentives for reporting wrongdoing.

Critical Analysis: Why do you think Canadian whistleblowing legislation is weak in comparison to U.S. whistleblowing legislation? Should there be financial incentives for reporting wrongdoing? Why or why not?

Sources: Jim Middlemiss, "Blowing the whistle on fraud", *The Canadian Lawyer* (27 January 2014), online: *The Canadian Lawyer* <http://www.canadianlawyermag.com/4972/Blowing-the-whistle-on-fraud.html>; Barbara Shecter, "Why Canada's whistleblower hotlines are staying silent", *The Financial Post* (24 May 2014), online: Financial Post <http://business.financialpost.com/2014/05/24/why-canadas-whistleblower-hotlines-are-staying-silent/>; Joseph Cohen-Lyons, "Whistleblowing in the public sector: A balance of rights and interests", *Public Sector Digest* (Spring 2012), online: *Public Sector Digest* <https://www.publicsectordigest.com/articles/view/977>; John Nicol & Dave Seglins, "Whistleblower lawsuit says CN is cooking its books", *CBC News* (24 October 2013), online: *CBC News* <http://www.cbc.ca/news/whistleblower-lawsuit-says-cn-is-cooking-its-books-1.2187724>.

Specific performance or reinstatement is rarely an option in the non-unionized sector.[34] The common law does not provide for this remedy, on the rationale that after a termination the employment relationship is usually irreparably damaged.

Wrongful Dismissal Damages

Once a court determines how many months' notice a successful claimant is entitled to, the general approach is to multiply this number by the salary and the benefits that the employee was entitled to for each month. In addition, the claimant may be entitled to other special damages for out of pocket losses associated with the termination. From the total, a deduction may be made for any money earned (income from a new job) or received (Employment Insurance) during the notice period. Also, a deduction may be made for a failure to mitigate damages by promptly seeking replacement employment. Figure 21.1 illustrates a typical damage award in a successful wrongful dismissal case.

Manner of Dismissal

An employee may be entitled to additional damages for the manner of dismissal. Compensation for such treatment may include aggravated damages including mental distress damages, and punitive damages. Aggravated damages are designed to compensate the victim by focusing on the victim's losses. Punitive damages are designed to punish the wrongdoer by focusing on the wrongdoer's conduct.

If the dismissal is conducted "in bad faith" or in an unfair manner, the employer may be responsible for these damages. The Supreme Court of Canada in

---

34 Human rights legislation, however, provides for reinstatement.

CHAPTER 21: TERMINATING THE EMPLOYMENT RELATIONSHIP

PART SIX

FIGURE 21.1 A Sample Damage Award for Wrongful Dismissal

Millyard Systems Manager, 53 years old, 20 years of service, $84 000 annual salary	
Base salary: ($7075.83 × 18 months[35])	$127 364.94
Bonus: ($910.00 × 18)	16 380.00
Commissions ($1500.00 × 18)	27 000.00
Employee share purchase plan ($140.00 × 18)	2 520.00
Health care spending account ($25.00 × 18)	450.00
Medical services plan ($90.00 × 18)	1 620.00
Extended medical and dental coverage ($99.00 × 18)	1 782.00
Long-term disability ($172.12 × 18)	3 098.16
Car allowance (includes a component for ongoing lease commitments)	15 600.00
Total damages	$195 815.10

Source: *Jamieson v Finning International Inc*, 2009 BCSC 861, [2009] BCWLD 5513.

Wallace v United Grain Growers[36] held that employees are entitled to an extension or "bump-up" (known as *Wallace* damages) to reasonable notice where the employer has breached the duty of good faith in terminating the employee. Examples of bad faith are alleging cause when there is none, refusing to provide a deserved letter of reference, terminating while on disability leave, failing to communicate a termination decision in a timely manner, and communicating false allegation to potential employers. In *Honda v Keays*, the Supreme Court indicated that damages for the manner of dismissal[37] must be based on the losses employees actually suffer and are no longer to be awarded by arbitrarily extending the notice period. If an employee can prove that the manner of dismissal caused mental distress, the damages are awarded through an award that reflects the actual damage.

Punitive damages, which focus on the employer's conduct, will be awarded only where there is a separate, actionable wrong, such as deceit, breach of fiduciary duty, abuse of power, or defamation. They are generally awarded only in very exceptional circumstances.

CASE

Honda Canada Inc v Keays, 2008 SCC 39, [2008] 2 SCR 362

THE BUSINESS CONTEXT: This case greatly clarifies for employers and employees how damages should be assessed in wrongful dismissal cases. It also outlines the circumstances warranting an award of punitive damages.

FACTUAL BACKGROUND: Kevin Keays began working at Honda's Alliston, Ontario, assembly plant in 1986. After 20 months on the production line, he moved to the Quality Engineering Department, where he became a specialist in implementing design changes in cars. His health deteriorated, and in 1996 he began receiving disability payments. Two years later the payments were terminated when the insurance company concluded that his claim could not be supported by "objective medical evidence." He returned to work, although his

---

35 The damages were based on a 19-month notice period, with a one-month deduction for the possibility of mitigation earnings, as the decision was handed down well in advance of the expiry of the notice period.

36 [1997] 3 SCR 701, [1997] SCJ No 94.

37 The Supreme Court of Canada confirmed the existence of the duty of good faith in the manner of termination in *Bhasin v Hrynew*, 2014 SCC 71. See Chapter 7, pages 148–149 for a summary of the case.

doctor had diagnosed him as suffering from chronic fatigue syndrome. Keays continued to experience work absences, and when he claimed that a disability caused his absences, Honda put him on a program that required him to produce a doctor's note every time he was absent. When Keays's absences exceeded his doctor's estimates, he was directed to the company doctor, who expressed reservations about his condition and suggested that he should be sent back to the production line. When Honda subsequently requested him to see an independent medical specialist, Keays refused to go unless the company clearly stated the purpose of the second medical assessment. The company refused and terminated Keays for insubordination. Keays was advised of his termination by a co-worker who phoned him at home to tell him that his dismissal had been announced to the department.

THE LEGAL QUESTION: Was Keays wrongfully terminated from his employment? If so, what is the appropriate remedy?

RESOLUTION: The trial court found that Keays had been wrongfully dismissed, and it awarded 15 months' salary in lieu of notice. The court concluded that Honda's request for Keays to see the independent medical specialist was not made in good faith but was made as a prelude to terminating him to avoid having to accommodate his disability. Keays, because of previous difficulties with his employer over his absences, had a reasonable basis for believing that Honda would continue to refuse to recognize the legitimacy of his disability. Therefore, Keays had good cause for his failure to follow the employer's direction. Honda's reaction to Keays's alleged insubordination was disproportionate. It was not just cause for dismissing Keays. The court also awarded an additional nine months of *Wallace* damages for the manner of dismissal and $500 000 in punitive damages for the discriminatory and highhanded treatment of Keays by Honda.

The Ontario Court of Appeal upheld the 15-month notice period and the nine-month *Wallace* extension, but reduced the punitive

When are employers required to pay punitive damages in wrongful dismissal cases?

damages to $100 000 on the basis that the trial judge relied on findings of fact that were not supported by the evidence and because the award did not meet the requirement of proportionality. In particular, the appeal court stated that the trial judge's finding that Honda's outrageous conduct had persisted over a period of five years was a gross distortion of the circumstances. The misconduct for which Honda was responsible took place over a seven-month period. Also, while the appeal court acknowledged the gravity of some of Honda's conduct, it could not be characterized as "malicious."

The Supreme Court of Canada agreed that 15 months was an appropriate period of notice for Keays's almost 14 years of service but eliminated the nine-month *Wallace* extension and the award of punitive damages.

With respect to the elimination of the nine-month *Wallace* extension, the court stated that damages for a bad-faith dismissal are available only if the employee can prove that the manner of dismissal actually caused mental distress and the distress suffered by the employee was in the contemplation of the parties at the time of entering the employment contract (the normal distress and hurt feelings resulting from dismissal are not compensable as it is not within the contemplation of the parties that these would be compensated). In other words, in order to receive damages for mental distress, the employee must show that the employer's behaviour in termination

(Continued)

was particularly egregious and its effect on the employee caused more harm than the normal impact of termination. The court also stated that awarding damages for bad-faith dismissal by an arbitrary increase to the period of reasonable notice is no longer the appropriate method. Damages are to be awarded through an award that reflects the actual damages. The Supreme Court concluded that Honda's conduct was "in no way an egregious display of bad faith justifying an award of damages for conduct in dismissal."

With respect to punitive damages, the court stated they must be awarded only in "exceptional cases" where the employer's bad faith acts "are so malicious and outrageous that they are deserving of punishment on their own." They are only recoverable if the conduct gives rise to an independent "actionable wrong." The court overturned the lower court's finding that a breach of human rights legislation can serve as an independent actionable wrong. Human rights claims are to be dealt with by human rights tribunals, not the courts.

CRITICAL ANALYSIS: What does this decision mean for employers?

Duty to Mitigate

Employees who have been terminated or constructively dismissed have a duty to mitigate their damages. The duty does not arise in all circumstances, however. The Ontario Court of Appeal[38] has held that when an employment contract stipulates the specific notice period to which an employee will be entitled on termination, and is silent on the duty to mitigate, the dismissed employee is not under an obligation to mitigate her damages. In other words, the employer is required to make all the payments specified in the contract without a deduction for failure to mitigate or for income earned from alternative employment during the notice period.

When the duty arises, it requires that an employee take reasonable steps to find comparable employment. What is required of an employee depends on the nature of the job, on the job market, and on the way that a job would normally be obtained in that market (e.g., by searching newspaper advertisements, registering at a human resource centre, searching the Internet, or engaging the services of an employment agency).

The duty requires the employee to look for comparable or similar employment. It does not require an employee to take or look for a lower-level job. It may, however, require an employee to accept an offer of re-employment with the same employer if the offer includes equivalent salary and working conditions and does not involve an acrimonious relationship.[39] Whether the duty to mitigate requires an employee to move to look for employment depends on a host of factors, including age of employee, family situation, attachment to the community, prospects of employment in the present area, and the housing market. A failure to mitigate will result in a deduction from the damages awarded. The amount of the reduction varies and depends on the circumstances.

---

38 *Bowes v Goss Power Products Ltd.* 2012 ONCA 425,351 DLR (4th) 219.
39 *Evans v Teamsters Local Union* [2008] 1 SCR 661, 2008 SCC 20.

Does mitigation require a terminated employee to accept any job?

Developments in Wrongful Dismissal Suits

In addition to wrongful dismissal suits, some employees have turned to other avenues to procure relief. In some situations the dismissed employee can sue for defamation. The advantage of this route is that damages for defamation are usually significantly higher than those for breach of the employment contract, as the amount of damages is not limited by the notice period. Also, the courts are usually more willing to award punitive damages pursuant to a defamation claim. A further claim that can be made by an employee is intentional infliction of mental suffering.[40] Litigants are also, in some jurisdictions, pursuing jury trials and are being rewarded by large damage awards as the box below illustrates.

BUSINESS APPLICATION OF THE LAW

PUNITIVE DAMAGES IN WRONGFUL DISMISSAL TRIALS

In *Higginson v Babine Forest Products*,[41] an employee with 34 years of service was terminated from his position as an electrical supervisor. Higginson alleged that his termination was part of a larger plan to eliminate long service employees and to avoid the costs of paying severance. He sued for wrongful dismissal and was successful in a jury trial. The jury awarded damages of approximately $809 000 including punitive damages of $573 000. An appeal has been settled confidentially.

---

40 The Ontario Court of Appeal has awarded damages for such a claim in the employment context. See *Prinzo v Baycrest Centre for Geriatric Care* (2002), 60 OR (3d) 474, 161 OAC 302 (CA).

41 The jury decision is not reported.

Should litigants have a right to jury trials in wrongful dismissal cases? Why or why not?

In *Boucher v Walmart and Jason Pinnock*,[42] a 10-year Walmart employee at the company's Windsor, Ontario, store resigned because of the behaviour of her manager. Boucher claimed that he engaged in belittling and demeaning conduct such as swearing at her and calling her an idiot and stupid. He also made her count wood skids in front of other employees to prove that she could count. Boucher sued for constructive dismissal. The jury, after deliberating for less than two hours, awarded her $1.4 million (20 weeks of salary, $200 000 in aggravated damages, $1 150 000 in punitive damages, and $100 000 for intentional infliction of mental suffering). On appeal, the Court upheld all aspects of the award except the amount of the punitive damage award. It was reduced to $110 000, still a large punitive damages award in an employment case.

Critical Analysis: Both of these cases are extraordinary because it is unusual to have a jury trial in civil matters and because of the amount of punitive damage awarded by the jury. Why are jury trials in employment cases uncommon? Are these cases likely to influence punitive damage awards in other wrongful dismissal cases? Why or why not?

Sources: Lyndsay A. Wasser, "Juries punish employers: Two recent cases highlight the risk of treating employees poorly", *McMillan LLP* (1 May 2013), online: McMillan <http://www.mcmillan.ca/juries-punish -employers-two-recent-cases-highlight-the-risk-of-treating -employees-poorly>; Ann Macaulay, "Settlement in wrongful dismissal case", *The Lawyers Weekly* (5 October 2012) 4; "Mistreated Wal-Mart employee gets $1.46 M" *The Star* (31 October 2012), online: *The Star* <http://www.thestar.com/business/personal_finance/2012/10/ 31/mistreated_walmart_employee_gets_146m.html>; Barry W. Kwasniewski, "Fired B.C. worker awarded over $800,000 by jury", *Charity Law Bulletin No. 289* (27 September 2012), online: Carters Professional Corporation <http://www.carters.ca/pub/bulletin/charity/ 2012/chylb289.htm>; Earl Phillips, "Wal-mart ordered to pay over 1 million in damages", *British Columbia Employment Advisor* (3 December 2012), online: McCarthy Tetrault <http://www .bcemployerlaw.com/2012/11/22/e-alert-wal-mart-ordered-to-pay -over-1-million-in-damages/>; Shane D. Todd & Samantha Seabrook, "Court of Appeal reduces $1.45 million award to constructively dismissed employee" *Hicks Morley* (23 May 2014), online: *Hicks Morley* <http:// hicks.com/index.php?name=News&file=article&sid=2176&catid=6>.

Termination Settlements

The costs associated with a wrongful dismissal suit can be high. Therefore, it may be incumbent on an employer to offer a termination settlement or severance package rather than dismiss for just cause.

Negotiation of the Settlement

Severance pay

An amount owed to a terminated employee under employment standards legislation.

The package offered should contain all monies due to the employee at the time of termination including statutory entitlements such as **severance pay**. The package may also include other items such as pension benefits, medical or dental coverage, disability insurance, tax-sheltered income, stock options, and financial or career counselling. An employer should also consider providing a factual letter

---

42 2014 ONCA 419, [2014] OJ No 2452.

of reference to assist the employee. An employee should be given a period of time (one to two weeks) to consider the termination settlement and should be encouraged to seek independent advice on the fairness of the offer.

The termination settlement may help the departed employee feel better about the termination. A fair offer and settlement may also help keep remaining employees motivated. A fair settlement may ultimately avoid a lawsuit and be less costly in the long run. It also helps maintain a positive corporate image.

The Release

When an employee accepts a termination package, it is customary to have the employee sign a **release**. The release normally indicates that the employee has been dismissed and paid a sum of money in return for giving up any right of action against the employer. The release form may include a stipulation that the employee will not pursue an action for wrongful dismissal, as well as a statement that the employee has not been discriminated against, and therefore will not pursue a claim under human rights legislation. It may also contain provisions to keep the settlement confidential and restrictions preventing the employee from competing against the former employer.

A release will normally be binding on the employee, provided that the settlement was fair and reasonable, the release was clear and unambiguous, and the employee had ample time to consider the package and obtain independent advice. On the other hand, a release will likely be unenforceable if the termination package was "unconscionable" and the employee did not obtain independent advice.

Release

A written or oral statement discharging another from an existing duty.

The Union Context

The provisions of a collective agreement will vary depending on the nature of the industry involved and the issues the parties bring to the negotiating table. The agreement will provide for a process for settling disputes arising from the agreement. This procedure is usually the only route a unionized employee has to challenge an employer's dismissal decision.[43] The final step in the procedure is arbitration, which is binding on the parties. Unlike the situation in the non-unionized sector, courts do not make the final decision.

In addition, most agreements will have specific provisions relating to termination.

Grievance and Arbitration

Regardless of the individual content of collective agreements, disputes about their interpretation, administration, or application are required to be submitted to a **grievance process**. The grievance procedure will vary widely from organization to organization. Some procedures involve only a couple of steps; others have several. All usually have time limits attached to the steps, and most begin with an informal consultation. The final step in almost all jurisdictions is third-party binding arbitration.[44] This step arises when the dispute cannot be resolved by less formal means and all the other steps in the grievance process have failed.

Grievance process

A procedure for resolving disputes contained in union contracts.

---

43 The existence of a collective agreement that applies to an employee and provides for final settlement of disputes bars a wrongful dismissal action. *Supra* note 18 at 128.
44 Saskatchewan is the exception.

The arbitration itself usually involves either a single arbitrator or a three-person panel that conducts a hearing of the grievance and renders a decision. The arbitrator may dismiss the grievance; order compensation for breach of the collective agreement; order reinstatement of the employee without loss of seniority and with back wages and benefits; or, in most jurisdictions, fashion a remedy somewhere between dismissal and full reinstatement. The arbitration award can be filed with the court and enforced in the same manner as a judicial decision.

Seniority

Most collective agreements contain an extensive clause dealing with seniority (the length of time the employee has been with the company). These clauses usually provide that an employer cannot promote, demote, transfer, lay off (usually defined as temporary suspension of the employment relationship), or recall without giving some consideration to the seniority of the employee. These clauses do not, however, affect the employer's ability to terminate the employment relationship (usually referred to as "discharge" in labour law).

Discipline and Discharge

The general rule in the union context is that an employer may not discipline or discharge an employee without justification or just cause.

The discipline and discharge of employees is the largest category of grievances carried to arbitration. In assessing whether the penalty imposed by the employer was appropriate in the circumstances, the arbitrator will look for evidence of progressive discipline. In other words, discipline should progress from warnings to suspensions and only finally to discharge. In upholding a particular penalty imposed by an employer, the arbitrator will consider many factors, including the following:

- the record and service of the employee.
- provocation.
- any special economic hardship imposed on the employee by the penalty.
- the seriousness of the offence.
- premeditation.
- uniform enforcement of policies and rules.
- circumstances negating intent.
- condonation.

The arbitrator has the authority to mitigate or soften the severity of the penalty imposed by the employer. In other words, the arbitrator may substitute his judgment for that of management (unless the collective agreement mandates a specific penalty for the infraction).

BUSINESS LAW IN PRACTICE REVISITED

1. Is Hiram justified in terminating Jeong Nash and Levi Cameron?

A dramatic drop in circulation that results in a genuine lack of work is a good reason for terminating employees, but it is not legal or just cause, which deprives employees of reasonable notice. Jeong's controversial stories do not amount to incompetence or misconduct, particularly in view of Hiram's apparent condonation. The cumulative effect of Levi's infractions—off-colour jokes, sexist comments, and inappropriate material on his computer—may constitute misconduct. However, prior to dismissal, the employer must consider the following questions: Was Levi's behaviour contrary to a company policy? Was Levi aware of the company policy? Was Levi given a warning about his behaviour? Did he understand that failure to improve could lead to termination? That said, a single incidence of bad conduct may be sufficient grounds for dismissal without notice. For example, if Levi downloaded truly offensive material onto his work computer, that could amount to grounds for dismissal.

2. Is Hiram entitled to change Josiah Rutgers's position?

The merger of two departments resulting in a change to the reporting structure may trigger a constructive dismissal. Although Josiah would receive the same pay and have the same title, reporting to Stella rather than Hiram is an obvious demotion. Hiram may want to consider whether Josiah is likely to accept the change and whether there are sufficient benefits to the change that, in the overall context, he will not view the change negatively. Also, Hiram may want to offer Josiah a period of time to try out the change to see if he likes it. An employer is entitled to make some changes without triggering a dismissal; Hiram should check Josiah's employment contract to see what is permissible.

3. What course of action would you advise Hiram to pursue?

As it is highly unlikely that Hiram has grounds to dismiss Jeong and, possibly, Levi, he needs to consider what a reasonable settlement would be. Levi is an older, long-serving, high-level employee, so he is probably entitled to notice somewhere in the 16- to 18-month range. For Jeong, a younger, shorter-term, low-level employee, reasonable notice would probably be somewhere in the one- to two-month range. The amount of notice for both employees is affected in either direction by the availability of alternative employment. Hiram should seek legal advice on this issue, as this area of the law is somewhat unpredictable and subject to rapid change.

Hiram should know that the proposed change in Josiah's position may trigger a constructive dismissal. He needs to consider whether Josiah is likely to view the change negatively. If that is likely, Hiram needs to reconsider the change or terminate Josiah's employment with reasonable notice. As a younger, short-term, middle-level employee, Josiah is likely entitled to notice in the two- to four-month range—depending, again, on alternative employment opportunities.

Hiram should carefully choose the manner of dismissal. The amount of damages payable to employees in the event of a wrongful dismissal action could be severely affected by any bad-faith conduct on his part, such as alleging cause when there is none, escorting the employee out the door, refusing to provide a fair reference, or otherwise acting in bad faith.

CHAPTER SUMMARY

Employment ends when an employee resigns or retires, or when the employer dismisses, gives notice, or otherwise terminates the relationship. An employer may, subject to contractual provisions, summarily terminate an employee if just cause exists. What constitutes just cause is a question of fact, but it must involve a situation where the employee has breached a fundamental term of the employment contract. In the absence of just cause, an employer must give notice of termination (or pay in lieu of notice). Notice is either what is specified in the employment contract or employment legislation, or reasonable notice. The latter is determined by reference to the employee's age, position within the organization, and length of service, and by the availability of alternative employment. When the employer breaches a fundamental term of the employment contract (i.e., demotes or cuts pay), the employee may treat the breach as a constructive dismissal. The termination of employment by the employer is often a traumatic event in the life of the employee. Courts have increasingly put an onus on the employer to act fairly and decently toward the terminated employee. In the event of a successful wrongful dismissal suit, an employer may be required to compensate for unfair and harsh conduct in the termination process. Wrongful dismissal suits can be costly, time consuming, and embarrassing. An employer may want to reduce the risks by considering a termination settlement that provides a measure of compensation to an employee. It may be much cheaper in the long run.

CHAPTER STUDY

Key Terms and Concepts

condonation (p. 541)

conduct incompatible (p. 542)

constructive dismissal (p. 549)

fundamental term (p. 549)

grievance process (p. 559)

habitual neglect of duty (p. 541)

incompetence (p. 542)

just cause (p. 539)

progressive discipline policy (p. 540)

reasonable notice (p. 545)

release (p. 559)

serious misconduct (p. 540)

severance pay (p. 558)

willful disobedience (p. 543)

Questions for Review

1. In what circumstances may an employee be terminated?

2. What is meant by "just cause?"

3. What is a progressive discipline policy? How does a progressive discipline policy affect the termination of employees?

4. When does incompetence amount to just cause for dismissal?

5. An employer may dismiss an employee for cause when the employee's conduct is prejudicial to the employer's business. Give an example of conduct that is prejudicial to the employer's business.

6. In the absence of just cause, how much notice of termination must an employee be given?

7. In the absence of just cause, how much notice must a superior-performing employee be given?

8. How is reasonable notice calculated?

9. In the calculation of reasonable notice, which factor is the most important? Explain.

10. In general, a longer-term employee is entitled to more notice than a shorter-term employee. What is the rationale for this distinction?

11. What is constructive dismissal? Give an example.

12. How can a wrongful dismissal suit arise? Name three ways.

13. Why is the manner of termination important?

14. When is a successful litigant entitled to punitive damages? Explain.

15. What is the duty to mitigate? When does it arise?

16. What should a termination settlement contain?

17. How does the process for termination differ between the union and non-union sectors?

18. What is the grievance process? When is it used?

Questions for Critical Thinking

1. On occasion, employers and employees have argued for a rule of thumb in calculating reasonable notice. Most frequently they have argued for a "month-per-year-of-service" rule. Courts have generally rejected such an approach. What are the advantages of such a rule? How is such a rule defective?

2. With the abolition of mandatory retirement, more people will work past the traditional retirement ages of 60 to 65. When there was mandatory retirement, employers often ignored performance issues with older employees because they would soon retire. With the abolition of mandatory retirement, employers will have to deal with aging workers who may not be able to keep up with the evolving demands of their occupations or companies. How should employers manage this challenge? What is the risk for employers who require older employees to acquire new skills?

3. Social media has become part of most people's lives. Many employees have a Facebook or LinkedIn account. Others post comments, pictures, and video on Twitter, YouTube, or Flickr. Still others keep a personal blog. What are the risks to the employer of employees using social media at work or at home? Should an employee's social media conduct be grounds for termination? Explain. How can employers reduce the risks posed by social media use by employees?

4. The Supreme Court of Canada[45] has indicated that in some circumstances, it is necessary for a dismissed employee to mitigate her damages by returning to work for the same employer. In what circumstances do you think a terminated employee should be required to return to work for her ex-employer? Do you see any problems for the terminated employee and the employer with the employee returning to work?

5. In *Honda v Keays*, the Supreme Court of Canada stated that if an employee can prove the manner of dismissal caused mental stress that was in the contemplation of the parties (mental distress over and above the normal impact of termination), the damages should be awarded through an award that reflects the actual damages, not through an arbitrary extension of the notice period. Is this approach beneficial to employees? Explain.

6. Office romances are exceedingly common. The long hours that co-workers often spend together coupled with minimal social contact outside the job can create the ideal conditions for love to flourish. What are the risks of office romances for employees? What are the risks for employers? Should companies have policies regarding workplace romances? If so, what should such a policy contain?

Situations for Discussion

1. Rhianne Dolman was an insurance adjuster who had worked for Dillman Adjusters for eight years. Her annual salary with Dillman was $60 000. Groger Adjusters persuaded Rhianne to work for it at a salary of $75 000 per year. Rhianne agreed and signed an employment contract. Several days later, Groger asked her to sign a non-solicitation agreement. Rhianne agreed.

   Three months later, Rhianne was having lunch with some colleagues when Rhianne asked one of them if he would be interested in opening an adjusting business to compete with Groger. She also asked another employee if, hypothetically, he would like to work for her someday in the adjusting business. The conversation was overheard by another employee of Groger, who informed senior management. Rhianne's employment was terminated immediately.[46] Did Groger have just cause to terminate Rhianne? What is the effect of the non-solicitation clause? If Groger does not have just cause to terminate Rhianne, to how much notice is she entitled?

45. *Supra* note 39.

46. Based on *Alishah v JD Collins Fire Protection Co*, [2006] OJ No 4634, 55 CCEL (3d) 116 (SC).

2. Debbie Hull, a licensed customs broker, was employed by Hercules Forward Inc. After about two years, she was promoted to manager of the customs department and became responsible for supervising two employees. Not all went well in the department under Hull's supervision. The employees who reported to Hull did not take criticism very well and, as a result, she was often at odds with them. Despite this animosity, she and her two employees often got together and used emails to criticize and belittle other employees at Hercules. However, matters came to a boiling point when, after returning from an appointment, she was ignored by the employee who filled in during her absence. Hull responded by swearing at her and threatening her with termination. When Hull tried to suspend the employee, she was overruled by her boss. Feeling betrayed and unable to discipline her staff, Hull left the workplace. A few days later, Hull sent a letter to Hercules complaining that the workplace was poisonous and that she would be unable to return unless the employee who had ignored her was dismissed. Hercules interpreted Hull's letter as a resignation. Hull sued for wrongful dismissal.[47] Has Hull been wrongfully dismissed? Explain.

3. Margaret Brien, 51, was terminated from her job as office manager at Niagara Motors Limited, a car dealership, after 23 years. Her termination came as a complete surprise to her as she had never been disciplined and had not received any warnings about her performance. At the time of her termination, the dealership told Brien that she was being terminated because her position was being eliminated. This was not correct. The dealership had secretly advertised her position and required Brien to train her replacement after her dismissal. She was offered eight weeks' pay in lieu of notice and 23 weeks of severance if she signed a release. Brien sued for wrongful dismissal. In response, the dealership alleged that Brien performed her duties incompetently and unprofessionally and that it had just cause for her termination. The dealership also refused to provide Brien with a letter of reference or to assist her in any way with her job search. Brien successfully sued Niagara Motors for wrongful dismissal.[48] What would be reasonable notice in this situation? What factors will the court consider in an award for damages?

4. Randal Martin joined International Maple Leaf Springs Water Corp. of Vancouver, B.C., in July 2004. He was hired to assist with the construction of a bottling plant at a spring near Chilliwack, B.C., and to develop markets in North America and Asia. He had been running a similar operation in Saskatchewan but left on the assurance that the B.C. company was viable and would be able to finance the new plant and fund the marketing initiatives. By March 2005, Martin had settled contracts with six companies and was close to three more, including a major deal with an American brewery that wanted to use its own brand name on Maple Leaf's products.

    In April 2005, the company fired Martin, accusing him of dishonesty and of coming to work drunk. Maple Leaf alleged that Martin was dishonest in registering trade names belonging to the company. Martin had registered the trade names personally, as the company did not have the funds to do this itself. The president of Maple Leaf knew about Martin registering the trade names and knew that the trade names would be transferred to the company as soon as Martin was repaid. There was no evidence of Martin's coming to work drunk. Martin successfully sued for wrongful dismissal.[49] What would be reasonable notice in this situation? What factors would the courts consider in awarding a period of notice?

5. Clyde Peters worked as a senior systems analyst for 17 years at NJ Industries. He had a good work record and a positive image throughout the company. Recently, he came under the supervision of the new controller, John Baxter, who quickly found himself dissatisfied with Peters's performance. Baxter believes that Peters failed to properly implement the company's new computerized financial system. As well, he feels that Peters has failed to design a strategic plan for his department.

---

47 Based on *Danielisz v Hercules Forwarding Inc.*, 2012 BCSC 1155, 1 CCEL (4th) 76.

48 Based on *Brien v Niagara Motors Limited*, 2009 ONCA 887, 78 CCEL (3d) 10.

49 Based on *Martin v International Maple Leaf Springs Water Corp*, [1998] BCJ No 1663, 38 CCEL (2d) 128 (SC).

These two matters have caused considerable problems between the two. Baxter is considering recommending Peters's termination.[50] How should the problem be resolved? Do grounds for termination exist?

6. Sandra Sigouin had worked at a Montreal branch of the National Bank for 20 years before being promoted to the position of special loans administrative officer. She was given the post even though she lacked the proper qualifications and training. The new job went badly. Sigouin made many mistakes, and the bank warned her in writing that if she did not improve she would be terminated. She asked to take courses and promised to improve but no further training was provided. A few months later, she was fired for incompetence after failing to renew a letter of credit. The mistake cost the bank $850 000.[51] What should Seguin do? Do you think the bank had grounds to terminate Seguin for just cause? Do you think the bank acted fairly? Should an employer be permitted to promote an employee to his level of incompetence and then fire him for incompetence? What are the risks for an employer that uses such a tactic?

7. Don Smith worked at a call centre as an accounts payable specialist for nine years. During a two month period, Smith received over a dozen pornographic emails from a friend. The pornography was legal adult pornography. These emails were not solicited, however, Smith did not tell his friend to stop sending them. When he received the emails, Smith either deleted them or sent them to his home email account. He did not share them with anyone at work. The employer became aware of the emails through its network monitoring system. Smith was immediately dismissed for cause on the basis that he breached company policy set out in the employee handbook. The policy prohibited "accessing, receiving, or storing any information that is discriminatory, profane, harassing, or defamatory in any way (e.g. sexually-explicit or racially discriminatory material)." Smith had no previous record of misconduct or disciplinary action. Smith sued his employer for wrongful dismissal.[52] Is he likely to be successful? What factors will the court consider in determining whether Smith was wrongfully dismissed?

8. Terry Schimp, 25, worked as a bartender for RCR Catering and Pubs. Although he was occasionally tardy, sometimes missed a staff meeting, and a few times was short on his cash, he was considered a productive employee. At the end of a private function that RCR was catering, one of Schimp's supervisors noticed an open water bottle on his bar. He took a drink and discovered that it was vodka, not water. Suspecting that Schimp had stolen the vodka, the supervisor immediately fired Schimp. He was escorted off the premises in front of about 50 other staff members, and he was banned for six months from returning to the hotel premises where RCR's offices were located. Schimp was extremely upset, but within a month he was able to get a new job with the same hourly rate of pay, only without tips. He sued for wrongful dismissal. At trial he was awarded $30 000 in damages. On appeal, the damages were reduced to $10 000, of which approximately $7000 was compensation for the humiliation and degradation he suffered.[53] Aside from the damages award, what costs did RCR incur as a result of this situation? How should RCR have acted differently?

50 Based on *Russell v Nova Scotia Power Inc* (1996), 150 NSR (2d) 271, 436 APR 271 (SC).

51 Paul Waldie, "Federal Court rules against placing employees in a Catch-22 situation," *The Globe and Mail* (17 April 2008) A3; and Wallace Immen, "Peter Principle meets legal principles," *The Globe and Mail* (18 April 2008) C2.

52 Based on *Asurion Canada Inc. v Brown and Cormier*, 2013 NBCA 13, 6 CCEL (4th) 99.

53 Based on *Schimp v RCR Catering Ltd*, 2004 NSCA 29, 221 NSR (2d) 379.

22

© Marcus Clackson/E+/Getty Images

PROFESSIONAL SERVICES

BUSINESS LAW IN PRACTICE

Ted Dalmo is the CEO of Dalmo Technology Ltd. (DT), a well established business that supplies components to large telecommunications companies. Ted and his management team (which included CFO Sandra Roberts, a professional accountant) decided to explore a major expansion of DT's business in order to take advantage of growth in the industry. DT engaged DRC Consultants Ltd. to do a feasibility study of the expansion plans. Ted indicated to DRC that the projected profitability of the expanded business would need to be favourable in order to attract lenders and investors.

DRC's report indicated that, based on DT's plans and projections, the expansion should produce sufficient cash flow to repay lenders and generate profits for a healthy return on equity for investors. To finance the expansion, DT borrowed money from the Provincial Bank and sold shares in DT to a group of local investors. A few months later, after the expansion had begun, one of DT's major customers moved to another supplier, putting DT's revenue projections in jeopardy. In addition, when DT's accounting firm Asher & Breem did its next audit, it was revealed that revenue had been inflated because of premature recognition of revenue from sales. The bank and the investors became nervous. They put pressure on Ted to deliver better financial results. Ted met with Sandra and told her that, to survive the current crisis and keep the business going, the company would continue to recognize revenue as early as possible.

Sandra was concerned about Ted's demand. In her opinion, current revenue recognition practices at DT were pushing the limit of what is acceptable under generally accepted accounting principles. She was reluctant to continue the practice of recognizing revenue early for the sole purpose of improving DT's bottom line. Sandra consulted Bill Caton, DT's in-house legal counsel, regarding her legal and ethical position. Bill thought it best to obtain independent legal advice, so he engaged DT's outside law firm, Holland & Hunt, to provide an opinion. Holland & Hunt advised Bill and Sandra to leave decisions regarding the recognition of revenue to DT's auditors. DT continued to operate in the same manner and its situation worsened. Within a year, the company was bankrupt.

1. Did the professionals fulfill their obligations to DT?

2. Can the bank and investors in DT recover their losses from the professionals?

3. Did the professionals act in accordance with their obligations to their professional governing bodies?

Businesses and Professional Services

This chapter discusses the relationship between professionals and business. The first part of the chapter focuses on the duty of professionals to their clients and others who rely on their work, including a discussion on the different ways that professionals manage risk. The second part of the chapter focuses on the obligations of professionals to their professional governing bodies.

It is important for businesspeople to understand the relationship between professionals and business so they can effectively use professional services, develop realistic expectations of professional services, and manage the risks involved. Also, students who intend to become professionals should have an understanding of professional relationships and how professionals are governed.

Relationships and Legal Obligations

Businesses depend on professional services, which can be either supplied in-house or provided by outside firms. Many mid-sized, and most large, businesses have professionals in-house. For example, DT employs a professional accountant, Sandra, as its CFO, and a practising lawyer, Bill, as its in-house legal counsel. Other professional services, such as those of engineers, architects, auditors, or consultants, are obtained from outside firms, if and when they are needed.

Whether the **professional** is an employee or an independent service provider, that person owes responsibilities to the business. Professionals who are employees are governed by the basic principles of employment law. Relationships with external professional service providers are defined by contract law. In addition, the professional–client relationship is a special relationship of trust and loyalty that goes beyond the protection normally provided by contract. Professionals are held to higher standards than other service providers.

Professional

Someone engaged in an occupation, usually governed by a professional body, requiring the exercise of specialized knowledge, education, and skill.

Ethical Obligations

Professionals have ethical obligations that other employees and service providers do not have. Professionals who are members of professional governing bodies are bound by rules of professional conduct and codes of ethics that are established and administered by the relevant governing bodies. These obligations bring a level of independence and judgment that distinguishes a professional from other employees and service providers.

Ethical issues tend to arise when a business is under stress. Ted pressured Sandra to adopt aggressive accounting practices that she believed may have been contrary to professional accounting practices. Although Ted's motives may have been honourable, Sandra has an obligation to comply with her professional obligations. If Sandra violates these rules, she risks disciplinary action by her governing professional body. She will also be placing DT at risk, because creditors and investors of DT will hold DT responsible for any harm that results from Sandra's improper behaviour.

Professionals may find themselves in a conflict of interest, where their obligations to one client are in conflict with their obligations to another client. Professionals must be careful to avoid conflicts of interest and must deal with them promptly and appropriately when they arise.

Hiring Professionals In-House

Deciding whether to obtain professional services on a contract basis from outside providers or to hire full-time professionals as employees is an important business decision. If the cost of outside professional services becomes significant, the business will likely consider hiring one or more professionals as employees. However, all relevant factors should be considered in making this decision. What level of experience is required? Is there a need for specialization? To what extent will the firm still need to obtain outside professional services? Will there be enough work to justify hiring the professional and, if not, is there other work that the person may perform?

Typically, a business will still require the services of outside professionals from time to time. However, in-house professionals can provide enhanced value through their knowledge of the organization, their skill in managing external professional services, and their ability to contribute to the development and implementation of risk management programs.[1]

The legal and ethical obligations that in-house professionals owe their employers vary according to the capacity in which they are hired. For example, some employed professionals perform purely managerial functions, so they become non-practising members of their professions. Others choose to retain their professional status and are hired in this capacity. Bill, who acts as in-house legal counsel for DT, is a practising lawyer and a member of the provincial bar. Sandra, the CFO for DT, holds a professional accounting designation and is a member of the relevant professional governing body.

Employed professionals who retain their professional status owe the same legal obligations to their employers as outside professionals: they are in a fiduciary relationship with their employers; they may be liable for negligence for their actions; and their employers may be vicariously liable to others for their actions.

Responsibilities of Professionals to Clients and Others Who Rely on Their Work

Professionals owe a range of responsibilities to their clients. These responsibilities can be grouped into three categories: contractual duties, tort duties, and fiduciary duties. For example, the professionals retained by DT—the consultants DRC, the accounting firm Asher & Breem, and the law firm Holland & Hunt—all owe these three duties to DT. They owe a duty to honour the contracts they have with DT. They owe a duty to DT not to act negligently. They owe a fiduciary duty to DT. These will be discussed in more detail below.

Responsibilities in Contract

Professional responsibilities in any given engagement are defined, in part, by contract. The nature of the service to be provided, the timeliness of the delivery of the service, and the way in which fees for service will be charged are established

---

1   See Christopher Guly, "Dealing with the storms," *In-House Counsel* (Spring 2010) 24 for examples of how legal counsel can be involved in all stages of crisis management.

by the terms of the contract between the professional and the client. The legal rules governing the contract are those described in Part Two of this text.

In practice, contractual terms are often presented by the professional, and only a well-prepared client might think to negotiate additional or alternative provisions. Clients may be unaware of provisions in the contract dealing with how work will be billed and how and when a **retainer** will be required. Clients should treat their contracts with professionals in the same careful and questioning manner as other contracts for goods and services.

Both the professional and the client must comply with the terms of the contract agreed upon. The most contentious issues in practice tend to be those relating to quality of service and fees. If a client is dissatisfied, most professional governing bodies have mechanisms for investigating complaints and helping to resolve disputes. Lawyer–client bills are subject to special provisions.[2] Clients may submit lawyers' bills to taxing officers for review. The officer determines whether the amount charged was fair and reasonable in the circumstances.

Retainer

An advance payment requested by a professional from a client to fund services to be provided to the client.

BUSINESS APPLICATION OF THE LAW

PROFESSIONAL SERVICE CONTRACTS

Prior to engaging a professional's services, a client needs to address the key terms of the contract. Of particular importance are the following:

- how will fees be charged? Fees may be determined by the amount of time expended, as a flat fee for the particular task, as a percentage of the value of the transaction, or on a contingency basis?[3] The charges should be appropriate for the nature of the services provided. Flat fees and percentage fees provide the client with greater certainty. Hourly rates can, with proper monitoring, provide control over costs. Clients may even seek to link fees to subjective factors such as the professional's demonstrated understanding of the client's affairs, responsiveness, predictive accuracy, and effectiveness. Particularly in the legal profession, there is a move toward value-based and fixed fee arrangements rather than fees based exclusively on time spent.[4] Increasingly, professionals are receptive

to alternative fee structures and terms of payment that fit the client's business structure and practices.[5]

- what expertise is required for the work? Does the professional fully understand the client's business needs?
- do both parties understand the nature of the work to be performed and the likely results? Are the client's expectations appropriate and reflected in the agreement?
- when is the project to be completed? How will changes to the schedule be addressed?
- how frequently and in what manner will the professional and client communicate? Various forms of instant communication have heightened the expectations of many clients in terms of ongoing communication.
- how will disputes about the engagement be handled? The agreement should contain a process acceptable to both parties.
- how will risk be allocated? The agreement should provide for unforeseen developments during the course of the contract.

---

2 For example, see the *Legal Profession Act*, SBC 1998, c 9, ss 69–74.
3 See Chapter 4 for discussion of contingency fees.
4 See Christopher Guly, "Alternative billing on the verge?", *The Lawyers Weekly* (7 October 2011) 21.
5 See Luis Millan, "Project management," *The Lawyers Weekly* (11 February 2011) 20.

If a contract price is not stated, the principle of *quantum meruit* applies—the professional provides an appropriate level of service, and the client pays a reasonable amount for that service. For small tasks performed by a familiar service provider, this situation is satisfactory because fee disputes are unlikely and there is little at risk. However, for larger engagements or contracts with a new service provider, such an arrangement leaves too many potential issues unresolved.

Critical Analysis: What are the risks if a formal professional service contract is not in place? How can a client properly assess a contract prepared and submitted to the client by its own lawyer?

Responsibilities in Tort

General Responsibility

Professionals have duties in tort similar to those of other service providers. While they can be responsible for a range of torts, negligence is most common. The professional must perform services in accordance with the standards of a reasonably competent member of that profession. Liability for negligence was introduced in Chapter 11. In order for a professional to be liable for negligence, the claimant must establish the basic elements of a negligence action:

- the professional owes the claimant a duty of care.
- the professional has breached the applicable standard of care.
- the professional's conduct has caused the claimant's loss.
- the claimant's loss is not too remote from the professional's actions.

In the context of professional services, negligence usually consists of careless or negligent advice, characterized in legal terms as negligent misstatement or negligent misrepresentation. The four elements of negligence listed above have been adapted into five requirements for proof of negligent misrepresentation:[6]

- there must be a duty of care based on a special relationship between the professional and the recipient of the advice.
- the representation made by the professional must be untrue, inaccurate, or misleading.
- the professional must have been negligent in making the representation.
- the recipient must have reasonably relied on the misrepresentation.
- the reliance by the recipient on the representation must have resulted in damages to the recipient.

These elements involve particular challenges in terms of defining the scope of a professional's special relationship, professional performance standards, and types of losses that can be claimed by recipients. The most difficult cases are those in which professionals give careless advice (misrepresentations) with negative economic consequences for claimants who are third parties (not clients). For example, DT's auditors and consultants have produced reports on which DT's bank and investors have relied. They may claim compensation for

---

6   See *Queen v Cognos Inc*, [1993] 1 SCR 87 (summarized in Chapter 20), confirmed in *Sharbern Holding Inc v Vancouver Airport Centre*, 2011 SCC 23.

Who is responsible for the losses and injuries resulting from this disaster?

their losses resulting from DT's bankruptcy. Why should this be any different from any other form of negligence liability? What is the difference between a negligently prepared appraisal or audit and a negligently manufactured widget? In cases of professional negligence, there is a risk of imposing liability "in an indeterminate amount for an indeterminate time to an indeterminate class."[7]

The remainder of this section will focus on this difficult issue in professional responsibility—the extent of the professional's duty of care.

Responsibility to Third Parties

Traditionally, the courts denied the claims of third parties (i.e., non-clients) who had relied on a professional's negligent misstatements. They refused to extend the duty of care beyond the client. Underlying these decisions was the public policy concern of maintaining the economic viability of those professions in the business of giving advice. For example, while a property appraiser can manage the risk exposure to the client, extending such risk to all subsequent purchasers of property may be economically oppressive. If all existing and potential investors could sue for negligence as a result of depending on a negligently prepared audit opinion for a public company, the delivery of audit services might no longer be economically feasible. Nonetheless, denying claims against the professionals in such situations does not necessarily leave the user without remedy. The purchaser of contaminated land can sue the vendor. Audit failures typically are uncovered because of some significant failure in the company itself. Shareholders can pursue their rights in corporate law and may also be able to sue the directors. The professions have been attractive targets for plaintiffs—to some extent because they have "deep pockets" and are typically covered by liability insurance. In the event of a business failure (such as DT in the Business Law in Practice), they may be the only persons left with the economic resources to meet claims.

The potential for third-party claims for economic loss resulting from negligent misrepresentations was first recognized in Britain in 1964.[8] In Canada,

---

7   This remains the best-known statement of this problem and comes from a U.S. case: *Ultramares Corp v Touche Niven & Co* (1931), 255 NY 170 (Ct App).
8   *Hedley Byrne & Co v Heller & Partners*, [1964] AC 465 (HL (Eng)). The court held that the bank *would* have been liable for its misrepresentation to the third party, but in the result an exclusion clause protected the bank from liability.

CHAPTER 22: PROFESSIONAL SERVICES

PART SIX

Haig v Bamford[9] was the key case in which the court found that auditors owed a duty of care where they had actual knowledge of the limited group that would use and rely on their statements. From the auditor's perspective of risk management, imposing liability in this context did not extend liability beyond that of most other providers of goods and services. The existence of the limited group of investors who might use the audit opinion was known at the time of the engagement.

The difficult question remaining after *Haig v Bamford* was whether liability should extend beyond this relatively narrow scope. Of critical importance was the question of whether liability would also exist in situations where third parties were neither known to the professional nor limited in number. Specifically, would a court apply the neighbour principle from *Donoghue v Stevenson*[10] in cases of negligent misrepresentation resulting in economic loss? In the context of auditing, would investors in a public company be entitled to make claims against the auditor if the audit opinion they relied on for their investment decision was negligently prepared?

These issues were eventually addressed by the Supreme Court of Canada in *Hercules Management Ltd v Ernst & Young*.[11] This case is summarized and discussed in detail under "Negligent Misstatement (or Negligent Misrepresentation)" in Chapter 11. In that case, shareholder investors in a company brought an action against the auditing firm Ernst & Young based on inaccurate financial statements produced as the result of an incompetent audit. To decide whether the auditors owed the investors a duty of care, the court applied a two-step test and found that the auditor did not owe the investors a duty of care.

The court held that, in the case of an audit, it was reasonably foreseeable that a large number of persons would use and rely on the audited statements. Applying the first stage of the test, a duty of care exists. However, in applying the second step of the test and evaluating possible policy considerations, the court held that there was no duty of care.

The court examined the limited purpose of the audited financial statements as set out in the relevant legislation—"to assist the collectivity of shareholders of the audited companies in their task of overseeing management." Because the shareholders were using the audited statements for investment decisions, and not the statutory purpose of the audit, they were owed no duty of care. The court held that to decide otherwise "would be to expose auditors to the possibility of indeterminate liability, since such a finding would imply that auditors owe a duty of care to any known class of potential plaintiffs regardless of the purpose to which they put the auditors' reports."

Since the court held that no duty of care was owed by the auditors to the investors, there was no need to consider the other elements of a negligent misrepresentation claim. The only remedy the investor plaintiffs had was the indirect right to bring a derivative action on behalf of the company, which they had not done.[12] The decision in *Hercules Management Ltd v Ernst & Young* has been criticized on the basis that it establishes too low a standard for the conduct of auditors and that its impact may be to effectively deny any remedy

---

9 [1977] 1 SCR 466.
10 [1932] AC 562 (HL (Eng)) in Chapter 11.
11 [1997] 2 SCR 165.
12 Derivative actions are discussed in Chapter 16.

to people who have honestly relied on negligently prepared audited financial statements.[13]

In the Business Law in Practice scenario, DT, Provincial Bank, and the investors may consider suing DRC Consultants, Asher & Breem, and Holland & Hunt for negligence. The cases would be decided by applying the five requirements for negligent misrepresentation as follows:

- all three professional firms owe their client (DT) a duty of care, but they will owe Provincial Bank and the investors, who are third-party claimants, a duty of care only if there exist no policy considerations that would limit the duty of care as in the *Hercules* case. This will depend on the stated purpose of their engagements. Did the professionals know that their advice would be relied upon by people other than DT?

- the claimants must prove that the professional firms provided untrue, inaccurate, or misleading reports.

- whether the firms were negligent will depend on whether they breached the standard of care in their respective professions. Did Asher & Breem comply with generally accepted auditing standards? Did Holland & Hunt do what a reasonably diligent and competent lawyer would have done?

- the claimants must establish that they relied on the reports. Did they actually use the reports in making their decisions?

- did the reliance of the claimants on the reports cause their losses? Or, did some of their losses result from some other cause?

Although the *Hercules* decision severely restricted auditors' duty of care to third-party investors, the second stage of the duty test invites analysis on a case by case basis.[14]

BUSINESS APPLICATION OF THE LAW

ACCOUNTABILITY FOR AUDITORS

Accounting firms and auditors, in particular, have long been subject to claims for compensation by clients and investors who allege they have suffered losses due to negligent work by members of the firm. These claims have normally been considered on a case-by-case basis. *Haig v Bamford* and *Hercules Management Ltd v Ernst & Young* are two examples discussed earlier in this chapter. Creditors and investors have rarely been successful in lawsuits against auditors of public companies. The following case represents one victory for creditors in such a case.

Livent was a theatre company that produced popular shows such as *Phantom of the Opera* and *Joseph and the Amazing Technicolor Dreamcoat*, and was involved in the construction and management of theatres. Following its initial success, Livent was ultimately found to have been an enormous accounting fraud. Creditors and investors lost millions of dollars after having been provided with audited financial statements which did not reveal fraudulent accounting practices that had been ongoing for years.

Livent sought bankruptcy protection in 1998, and its founders, Garth Drabinsky and Myron

13 See, for example, Al Rosen and Mark Rosen, *Swindlers* (Toronto: Madison Press Books, 2010).
14 See for example *Widdrington (Estate of) v Wightman*, 2011 QCCS 1788 where auditors were held liable to investors based on Quebec law. The court also examined the common law and focused on the auditors' knowledge of users of the audits and the various purposes for which they were prepared.

How should Deloitte have managed its legal risk?

Gottlieb, were convicted of fraud and sent to jail in 2009. In 2002, the receiver in the Livent bankruptcy sued Deloitte, who had been Livent's auditor for many years leading up to its collapse. The receiver claimed that Deloitte had failed in its duty as Livent's corporate auditor.

In April 2014, the Ontario Superior Court of Justice held that Deloitte was negligent and ordered the firm to pay $84.8 million to creditors of Livent. In July 2014, the court added $33 million of interest to that amount, for a total judgment of $118 million.

The court found that there were numerous warning signs of fraud that Deloitte failed to detect and the judge said he could not understand how Deloitte could have signed a clean audit opinion on Livent's financial statements.

Why were the creditors successful in this case when it would appear that their situation was similar to that of the claimants in the *Hercules* case? Livent had sought bankruptcy protection, so the receiver was now in the position of the company. As such, the receiver was owed a duty of care by Deloitte just like the company was owed a duty of care. And, since the receiver's role was to obtain value for the company's creditors, the receiver could successfully sue Deloitte for the losses that the creditors suffered. The creditors could not have successfully sued Deloitte directly, because of the principle set down by the Supreme Court of Canada in *Hercules*. But Livent's receiver, having stepped into the shoes of the defunct company, was able to successfully sue Deloitte.

Deloitte has appealed the decision to the Ontario Court of Appeal. In its appeal, Deloitte will argue that the trial court decision goes far beyond the principles established by the Supreme Court of Canada and will expose auditors to significant new liability.

Critical Analysis: How does the risk of litigation affect the viability of professional firms? Should public company auditors owe a duty of care to investors who rely on their audited financial statements? How can auditors manage this potential risk?

Sources: Drew Hasselback, "Livent auditor Deloitte ordered to pay $84.8 million for failing to detect fraud", *Financial Post* (6 April 2014); Janet McFarland, "Deloitte appeals Livent compensation ruling" *The Globe and Mail* (16 April 2014); Janet McFarland, "Deloitte ordered to pay another $33 million in Livent negligence case" *The Globe and Mail* (15 July 2014).

Fiduciary Responsibilities

The term "fiduciary" was introduced in Chapter 13, and further discussed in Chapters 14, 16, and 20. Agents owe fiduciary responsibilities to their principals; directors owe fiduciary responsibilities to the corporation; partners owe fiduciary responsibilities to one another; and senior or key employees owe fiduciary responsibilities to their employers. The essence of the professional–client relationship is also fiduciary. Professionals act in a fiduciary capacity and, as such, owe their clients duties of loyalty, trust, and confidence that go beyond the contractual or tort responsibilities that are owed by service providers who are not professionals.

A fiduciary must act primarily in the interest of the person to whom the responsibility is owed. This is a broad and overriding concept captured by the notions of loyalty and trust. It is also expressed in terms of specific obligations. The professional, as fiduciary, must

- avoid any conflict of interest between the client's affairs and those of the professional or the firm.

- refrain from using the relationship for personal profit beyond charging a reasonable fee for services provided.
- disclose all relevant information to the client.
- act honestly and in good faith.
- maintain confidentiality of client information.

CASE

Hodgkinson v Simms, [1994] 3 SCR 377

THE BUSINESS CONTEXT: Professionals sometimes blur their professional and business activities, raising questions of where the boundaries of the fiduciary obligations begin and end.

FACTUAL BACKGROUND: In 1980, Hodgkinson hired Simms, a chartered accountant, for independent advice about tax shelters. Simms recommended investment in multi-unit residential buildings (MURBs). Their relationship and Hodgkinson's confidence in Simms were such that Hodgkinson did not ask many questions regarding the investments. He trusted Simms to do the necessary analysis and believed that if Simms recommended a project, it was a good investment. Hodgkinson made substantial investments in four MURBs recommended by Simms. In 1981, the real estate market in British Columbia collapsed, and Hodgkinson lost most of his investment. His claim against Simms was based on breach of fiduciary duty. Specifically, by not advising Hodgkinson that he had a personal stake in the MURBs (the developers were also Simms's clients and, in addition to fees, Simms received a bonus for MURBs sold), Simms failed to provide the independent advice for which he was hired and thus breached his fiduciary duties to Hodgkinson.

THE LEGAL QUESTION: Did Simms owe a fiduciary responsibility to Hodgkinson? If so, did his actions amount to breach of that responsibility and what are the consequences of the breach?

RESOLUTION: Justice La Forest examined the nature of the relationship between Simms and Hodgkinson and found that a fiduciary duty was owed, based on "the elements of trust and confidence and reliance on skill and knowledge and advice." He also discussed the relationship between fiduciary responsibilities and the rules of the respective professions, stating that the rules of the accounting profession of which Simms was a member required that "all real and apparent conflicts of interest be fully disclosed to clients, particularly in the area of tax-related investment advice. The basis of this requirement is the maintenance of the independence and honesty which is the linchpin of the profession's credibility with the public."

Therefore, the fiduciary duties imposed by courts should be at least as stringent as those of a self-regulating profession. Simms had been in a clear conflict of interest. The court accepted Hodgkinson's evidence that he never would have purchased the MURBs had he been aware of Simms's interest in selling them. The breach of fiduciary obligation was deemed to be so serious that the court was prepared to place all risk of market failure on Simms and compensated Hodgkinson accordingly.

CRITICAL ANALYSIS: It could be argued that Hodgkinson's losses were caused by the failure of the real estate market in British Columbia. What is the justification for transferring the losses to Simms simply because he assisted in the selection of the particular MURBs? What is the message for professionals? For clients?

The fiduciary must comply with the *spirit* of the obligation and not merely the letter. This case illustrates the fiduciary obligation of an accountant. See the *Strother* case[15] in Chapter 14 for discussion of a law firm's fiduciary duty to its clients.

---

15 *Strother v 3464920 Canada Inc*, 2007 SCC 24.

PART SIX

The fiduciary obligation to give independent advice free from self-interest has a distinct meaning in the case of the audit. The auditor, besides acting without self-interest, must also act independently of any interest of the company, since she is fulfilling a public function—namely, providing assurance to shareholders (and, indirectly, to the financial markets, in the case of public companies) that the financial statements have been prepared according to established principles. Audit firms are prohibited from involvement in their clients' businesses and are increasingly limited in their ability to provide services other than the audit to their audit clients.[16]

Professionals owe a **duty of confidentiality** to their clients because of both fiduciary principles and professional rules of conduct.[17] For example, a rule of conduct for professional engineers is the following:

> Engineers, geoscientists, and members-in-training shall… not disclose information concerning the business affairs or technical processes of clients or employers without their consent.[18]

Related to confidentiality is the concept of **lawyer–client privilege**. When Bill seeks legal advice on behalf of DT, Holland & Hunt must not divulge the contents of that consultation to others. The basis for this principle is the overriding need of clients in specific circumstances to be able to put their entire trust in their lawyer. The only advice to which privilege attaches is legal advice. Privilege may extend to the advice given by other professionals only when they prepare documentation at a lawyer's request and only as part of the lawyer's advice to the client. Lawyer–client privilege belongs to the client—not the lawyer—and can only be waived by the client.

Professionals' Risk Management Practices

How professionals manage risk exposure arising from their responsibilities has a direct impact on the businesses that hire them. Clients need to be aware of the risk management strategies of professionals and plan their affairs accordingly. Three ways in which professionals can manage risk are through contracts, incorporation or limited liability partnerships, and insurance.

Professional Service Contracts

As discussed earlier, these contracts define the parameters of the work that professionals are engaged to do. Both parties benefit from a clear and carefully prepared agreement that includes all essential terms and clarifies expectations.

Incorporation and Limited Liability Partnerships

Historically, businesses have managed risk through corporations that provide limited liability for shareholders, while professional service providers have been

---

Duty of confidentiality

The obligation of a professional not to disclose any information provided by the client without the client's consent.

Lawyer–client privilege

The right of a client not to have communications between lawyer and client divulged to third parties.

---

16   See "Independence Standards—Harmonized Rule of Professional Conduct 204," online: Chartered Accountants of Canada <http://www.cica.ca/about-cica-and-the-profession/protecting-the-public-interest/item80092.pdf>.

17   In very limited circumstances, confidentiality must be violated, such as when a patient tells her doctor that she plans to seriously harm herself or others.

18   Association of Professional Engineers and Geoscientists of New Brunswick, *Engineering and Geoscience Professions Act: By-Laws and Code of Ethics* 2011, s 4, online: Engineers & Geoscientists New Brunswick <http://www.apegnb.com/site/media/APEGNB/2011_By_Laws.pdf>.

required to assume liability personally. There are now other models for managing professional liability.

Some professions may incorporate by establishing a **professional corporation**. Generally, professions may incorporate only if they are specifically permitted to do so by the legislation governing the particular profession in that province.[19] Even where incorporation is allowed, it typically does not protect the professional from the liability of greatest concern—namely, personal liability for negligence. For example, where accountants have been able to incorporate, the statute authorizing incorporation provides that the personal liability of the accountant for negligence will not be affected by reason only that the accountant's services are provided by a corporation.[20] From the client's perspective, the individual professional generally remains personally liable for negligent work, and the assets of the professional corporation may be used to satisfy any judgment obtained against the professional.

Partnerships may register as limited liability partnerships (LLPs) (see Chapter 14). The impetus for allowing this business form came from the large professional partnerships that considered it unfair, for example, that a partner in Vancouver should be responsible for the negligence of a partner in Ontario. LLPs have been introduced by amendments to the provincial *Partnership Acts*. Whether or not individual professions allow members to form LLPs is determined by the provincial legislation governing that profession.[21] LLPs protect individual partners from personal liability for negligence committed by another partner in the firm, so long as the partner did not know about the negligence or participate in the work that was done negligently. Individual partners remain liable for their own negligence. The firm itself remains liable for the negligence of all of its partners, and the firm's assets (and insurance) can be used to compensate for losses.

A new aspect of law firm organization coming under discussion is whether firms should be able to seek outside investors, or even offer shares to the public, in order to expand and compete more widely. Greater competition may improve the public's access to legal services, but there is concern that the fiduciary relationship between lawyers and clients may be clouded by obligations to investors.[22]

Insurance

Errors and omissions insurance is described in Chapter 28. It is a condition of practice in most professions that members carry some minimum amount of this professional liability insurance. For the claimant, guarantees of insurance coverage are essential. Insurance claims, however, can be a challenge for claimants. Professional insurers, such as the Canadian Medical Protection Association, are highly specialized and expert at defending claims. If the loss is significant, the claimant should not contemplate litigation without hiring a lawyer who has the necessary expertise. Where contingency fees are unavailable, the cost associated with hiring such lawyers may effectively prevent some claimants from pursuing litigation.

Professional corporation

A corporation authorized by statute to carry on a specific profession.

19 For example, *Business Corporations Act*, SNB 1981, c B-9.1, s 13(3)(d); *Business Corporations Act*, RSO 1990, c B.16, s 3(1).

20 For example, *Public Accountants Act*, RSNS 1989, c 369, s 22A(2).

21 For example, *Partnerships Act*, RSO 1990, c P.5, s 10(2); and *Partnership Act*, RSA 2000, c P-3. See also the *Law Society Act*, RSO 1990, c L.8.

22 Mitch Kowalski, "How to make a law firm float: Some lessons from the world's first publicly traded law firm on what the future may hold for Canadian firms," *CBA National* (January–February 2014).

PART S X

Governance Structures of Professions

Legislation

Professions are self-regulating—that is, there are provincial statutes that establish the rights of the professions to govern themselves. The statutes create the governing body for the profession and specify when individuals may represent themselves as being qualified to practise the profession in that province. The legislation gives autonomy and sometimes a monopoly over specific activities to professional bodies sanctioned by the legislation. For example, the *Legal Profession Act*,[23] which governs the practice of law in British Columbia:

- provides a very detailed definition of the "practice of law."
- defines members of the Law Society as those lawyers who hold a practising certificate for the current year.
- states that only members of the Law Society in good standing are allowed to engage in the practice of law.
- provides that the Law Society is governed by elected members of the profession (benchers), who determine whether or not a person is a member in good standing and establish and maintain a system of legal education and training.

Each profession is governed by similar legislation in each province. The provincial professional associations are often linked to federal associations.

The self-regulating model has come under attack for its alleged failure to protect the public interest. Critics say that the accountability of professions is sacrificed in favour of self-interest and protection of members. As a result, the legal profession in England, Wales, Australia, and New Zealand has lost much of its autonomy through the legislated imposition of public bodies to oversee the profession's disciplinary process, creating a consumer-oriented model of regulation based on competence and service.[24] These changes have attracted attention in Canada. The governing body in Ontario (Law Society of Upper Canada) has appointed an independent commissioner to oversee the discipline process.[25] The Competition Bureau is engaged in a multi-staged evaluation of the anti-competitive practices of several professions including accountants and lawyers.[26]

The regulation of the accounting profession in Canada is in transition. Historically, each province had three professional governing bodies for accountants. The three different designations were: Chartered Accountant (CA), Certified General Accountant (CGA), and Certified Management Accountant (CMA). Recently, there has been a concerted effort to establish one governing body in each province for all professional accountants. The new designation is Chartered Professional Accountant (CPA). During the first 10 years, a member will use the CPA designation in addition to the member's previous designation. After this period, CPA will be the only professional accounting designation in Canada. The status of unification varies by province, but it is expected that all the provinces

---

23 SBC 1998, c 9.
24 Alice Woolley, "Canada lags in regulating lawyers", *The Lawyers Weekly* (17 June 2011) 8.
25 Thomas Claridge, "Ontario Law Society watchdog sees more complaints", *The Lawyers Weekly* (5 June 2009) 1.
26 Competition Bureau of Canada, "Competition Bureau releases ex-post assessment of the self-regulated professions study" (2 September 2011), online: Competition Bureau Canada <http://www.competitionbureau .gc.ca/eic/site/cb-bc.nsf/eng/03406.html>.

will pass legislation to approve the merger and create one professional governing body for accounting in each province.[27]

Professional Practice

Professionals must belong to a provincial governing body in order to practise within the particular province. Some professionals are licensed to practise in more than one jurisdiction. More commonly, professionals choose to work in firms that operate regionally or nationally, so they can effectively offer services to clients across multiple jurisdictions.

From a business perspective, operating across several provinces may require professional assistance in different jurisdictions. If DT is sued in another province, for example, it may choose to employ the services of a regional or national law firm, or it can ask its local firm, Holland & Hunt, to hire a firm in the other jurisdiction on DT's behalf.

Increasingly, professional firms are choosing to operate internationally. Many large law and accounting firms are now organized internationally, with branches in various different countries. From the client's perspective, having a professional firm within an international network may offer increased convenience and better service.[28]

Disciplining Professionals

Each profession in Canada has established rules of professional conduct or codes of ethics that prescribe acceptable behaviour. Each has established mechanisms for enforcing those rules and disciplining any member who violates them.

Professional rules and codes are critical for the protection of the public. Most professional governing bodies have information available online[29] outlining the processes for people to follow if they have a complaint. In the disciplinary process itself, complainants are only witnesses and observers. For damages or other compensation, a client must sue the professional involved. Depending on the nature of the claim, the professional may have insurance coverage. The legal profession also has an indemnification or assurance fund to compensate clients whose money has been stolen by members of the profession, usually from funds held in trust.

To be effective, the investigatory and disciplinary process must protect the rights of complainants and professionals. Any investigation is a serious matter for the professional, who must participate and who will usually need legal representation. If the professional is found to have violated the rules, the consequences may range from a reprimand, to a fine, to withdrawal of the right to practise in very serious cases. In addition, the professional may be ordered to pay the costs incurred by the governing body in investigating and adjudicating the complaint. Although the disciplinary process is formal, there may be alternative dispute resolution options to resolve complaints before formal hearings are held.

Professionals are also subject to criminal prosecution if their misconduct constitutes a criminal offence. For example, lawyers have been implicated in cases of fraud, both as direct participants in the fraud or for not detecting the fraud committed

---

27 Canadian Chartered Professional Accountants, "A Framework for Uniting the Canadian Accounting Profession," <http://unification.cpacanada.ca/a-framework-for-uniting-the-canadian-accounting-profession/>.

28 Christopher Guly, "Global law firms look to Canada," *The Lawyers Weekly* (15 July 2011) 21.

29 For example, see the Institute of Chartered Accountants of Nova Scotia, online: <http://www.icans.ns.ca/about-icans/how-to-file-a-complaint/item68851.aspx> and The Law Society of Alberta, online: <http://www.lawsociety.ab.ca/lawyer_regulation/complaints/complaints_initiate.aspx>.

by others.[30] The following case arises from the same facts as the Livent situation discussed in the Business Application of the Law earlier in this chapter. This case illustrates the application of the disciplinary process in the accounting profession.

CASE

Barrington v The Institute of Chartered Accountants of Ontario, 2011 ONCA 409

THE BUSINESS CONTEXT: This case deals with the disciplinary process conducted by the professional governing body and the implications for its members who performed the audit.

FACTUAL BACKGROUND: Livent Inc. was a public company that promoted live entertainment and was involved in the construction and management of theatres. Deloitte & Touche LLP was Livent's auditor from 1989 to 1997. In April 1998, Deloitte provided an unqualified audit opinion of Livent's 1997 financial statements. Power, Russo, and Barrington were the senior members of the audit team. Later in 1998, serious irregularities were discovered in Livent's books. The statements for 1996 and 1997 were revised and criminal fraud charges were laid against Garth Drabinsky and Myron Gottlieb, Livent's major shareholders and senior officers.[31] The Professional Conduct Committee (PPC) of the Institute of Chartered Accountants of Ontario (ICAO) brought charges of professional misconduct against Power, Russo, and Barrington. They were charged with failure to follow generally accepted accounting principles (GAAP) and auditing standards (GAAS) in their decisions about the recognition of income, the transfer of receivables, and audit evidence and procedures. The ICAO's Discipline Committee (DC) conducted a hearing for 37 days and found all three members guilty. The DC formally reprimanded the members, ordered them to post notices of the decision, fined each of them $100 000, and ordered them collectively to pay the costs of the disciplinary process of $1 251 000. The members appealed to the ICAO's Appeal Committee (AC) who affirmed the decision of the DC. The members then sought review by the Divisional Court where they were partially successful. All parties appealed.

THE LEGAL QUESTION: Were the members treated fairly in the disciplinary process? Did they have adequate notice of the charges? Did the DC provide adequate reasons? Were the penalties authorized by legislation?

RESOLUTION: The Court of Appeal restored the decision of the DC in full. The court found that the DC process was procedurally fair. The members had adequate notice of the charges and evidence against them. The DC fairly considered the evidence of experts regarding accounting and auditing standards and the DC gave adequate reasons for its decision. Justice Karakatsanis commented:

> This case is important to the ICAO and the self-regulation of the accounting profession.... The hearing was the longest in the history of the Institute. More significantly, the issues of audit process and opinion go to the heart of the integrity of our commercial system. The public, shareholders, investors, lenders, and business partners of public companies depend upon the objectivity and professionalism of the auditors of financial statements.
>
> Obviously, this is also an important case for the professional members who have had successful and even distinguished careers.... While the ICAO did not revoke their professional designations, it reprimanded and fined them. They have a right to natural justice and procedural fairness in the defence of their reputations and to know the reasons for any finding of misconduct.

CRITICAL ANALYSIS: Does this process provide adequate protection of the public? Is it fair to the auditors?

30 Jeff Gray, "Alleged fraud victims come gunning for the lawyers," *The Globe and Mail* (22 June 2011) B11, online: Globe and Mail <http://www.theglobeandmail.com/report-on-business/industry-news/the-law-page/alleged-fraud-victims-come-looking-for-the-lawyers/article2069873/>.

31 See Janet McFarland, "Drabinsky loses appeal bid," *The Globe and Mail* (29 March 2012), online: Globe and Mail <http://www.theglobeandmail.com/globe-investor/drabinsky-loses-bid-to-appeal-fraud-conviction/article2385423/>.

BUSINESS LAW IN PRACTICE REVISITED

1. Did the professionals fulfill their obligations to DT?

DT is concerned with the quality of accounting and legal services received from employees (Sandra Roberts and Bill Caton) and the firms they have retained (Asher & Breem and Holland & Hunt, along with the consulting services provided by DRC Consulting). The obligations of Sandra and Bill to DT are largely a function of their employment—to perform their defined duties according to defined or reasonable standards. The outside firms have obligations to DT based on contract, tort, and fiduciary relationships. Contractual obligations are found in the express terms of the contract or implied as obligations to provide the services requested to the standard of a reasonably competent professional. The duties of the firms in tort are similarly based on the standard of reasonableness. Fiduciary obligations relate to the avoidance of conflicts of interest and placing DT's interests first. Their advice should be based primarily on what is in the business interest of their client.

2. Can the bank and investors in DT recover their losses from the professionals?

Provincial Bank and the investors can sue only for negligence, and their principal obstacle will be establishing that a duty of care was owed to them. The bank and investors were foreseeable users of the consulting report and audited financial statements, but they must establish that no policy considerations exist to limit this duty. This issue will depend on the stated purpose of the consulting and the audit which will depend on the discussions that were held when the provision of those services was agreed upon. Since DRC was told that its consulting report would be important for financing purposes, the limited group of third-party users would be owed a duty of care. If Ted failed to be this explicit, then a court, applying a policy analysis, would not likely find that a duty of care was owed.

Claimants will need to prove the other elements of negligent misrepresentation, including a failure to act reasonably in the circumstances. The claimants must prove that they relied on the reports and that this reliance caused their losses. Since the financiers had no other known source of information about the financial state of DT, these last elements in this particular case should be reasonably easy to prove. If the claim is successful, damages will include the amount lost on the loan and the investments.

The law firm, on the other hand, is unlikely to suffer any third-party liability. Its opinion was provided only to DT and not relied upon by any third parties.

3. Did the professionals act in accordance with their obligations to their professional governing bodies?

The accountants, consultants, and lawyers must act in accordance with the professional and ethical standards of their professional bodies. The in-house professionals must avoid conflicts between their professional and ethical duties and the wishes of their employer. Sandra has a conflict between the obligations she owes to her employer and the ethical obligations she owes to her profession, as well as possible conflicts with her own personal values. Professional obligations must prevail, even if that requires her to leave DT. There may be legitimate alternatives she can present to Ted that at least partially meet his objectives. Sandra cannot engage in any practices that violate the rules of professional conduct. To do so

PART SIX

would be ethically wrong, would expose her to professional discipline, and would create potential liability for herself, DT, and Ted.

CHAPTER SUMMARY

Professionals owe a range of duties to their clients. Professionals are governed by contract and tort law. They must deliver services as contracted for and in accordance with the requisite professional expertise. If they are negligent in performing their responsibilities, they may be responsible for damages. In addition, professionals are in a fiduciary relationship with their clients if the elements of trust and confidence and the reliance on skill, knowledge, and advice are present. In such situations, clients are owed a duty of loyalty and trust.

Professionals may also owe a duty of care to those who are not clients but who rely on their work and advice. Whether a duty is owed in a particular situation depends on foreseeability and the need to impose reasonable limits on potential liability.

Professional service providers manage risk for the same reasons as businesses in general. Insurance coverage is important, and many professions make such coverage mandatory. Some professionals can organize their practices as limited liability partnerships or corporations. New organizational forms of practice, such as national and international firms, offer other benefits.

The professions are governed by legislation that establishes them as self-regulating bodies. The professions create codes of conduct or rules of practice. These determine the standards that their members must meet, as well as providing a measure of the expected standard of care in contracts, torts, and fiduciary obligations.

Most professional bodies have created dispute resolution services or complaint procedures to assist clients. They also maintain a discipline process that provides assurance to users that professionals violating professional rules will be appropriately disciplined.

CHAPTER STUDY

Key Terms and Concepts

duty of confidentiality (p. 576)

lawyer–client privilege (p. 576)

professional (p. 567)

professional corporation (p. 577)

retainer (p. 569)

Questions for Review

1. Who is a professional?

2. What is the meaning of "fiduciary" in the context of professional–client relationships?

3. How may a professional be in a conflict of interest?

4. What should a professional services contract contain?

5. What are the options for setting professional fees?

6. What is a retainer?

7. What is the basis for determining the cost of professional services if there is no formal contractual term addressing the issue?

8. What are the three types of professional responsibility?

9. Why were accountants traditionally protected from third-party claims?

10. How did the Supreme Court of Canada limit the duty of care for negligent misstatements in the *Hercules* decision?

11. What is the meaning of "self-regulating profession"?

12. What are the key roles of the bodies created to oversee the professions?

13. During a disciplinary process, why is it important to protect the rights of the professional against whom a complaint has been made?

14. What are LLPs?

15. What rules establish who can be a member of a particular profession?

16. If a conflict between a professional's ethical obligations to the profession and those to the client cannot be resolved, what must the professional do?

17. What is a professional's duty of confidentiality?

18. How does the duty of confidentiality differ from lawyer–client privilege?

Questions for Critical Thinking

1. The following is an excerpt from an auditor's report:

   > An audit involves performing procedures to obtain audit evidence about the amounts and disclosures in the financial statements. The procedures selected depend on the auditor's judgment, including the assessment of the risks of material misstatement of the financial statements, whether due to fraud or error. In making those risk assessments, the auditor considers internal control relevant to the entity's preparation and fair presentation of the financial statements in order to design audit procedures that are appropriate in the circumstances, but not for the purpose of expressing an opinion on the effectiveness of the entity's internal control. An audit also includes evaluating the appropriateness of accounting policies used and the reasonableness of accounting estimates made by management, as well as evaluating the overall presentation of the financial statements.

   Is this description of an audit adequate for clients? Could it be written in such a way as to make the extent of auditors' responsibilities clearer to users?

2. If you are the manager in an organization responsible for finalizing contracts with professional service providers, what factors would you consider in deciding between fees based on an hourly basis versus flat fees on a per-job basis? What protection might you try to build into the contracts?

3. The *Hercules* decision was heavily criticized by some members of the business press as too lenient on auditors, but was received with great relief by auditors. Did the Supreme Court of Canada define the purpose of the audit too narrowly? What is the appropriate balance between fairly compensating those who suffer loss and discouraging professionals from providing needed services?

4. In an economic downturn, investors often look to their investment advisors to explain their losses. Investors may claim that their advisors were more interested in their own fees and commissions than their clients' portfolios, or that their advisors failed to fully explain the degree of risk in their investments. Are investment advisors "professionals"? Do they owe their clients fiduciary duties? What standards should advisors be required to meet?

5. Most professionals are required to maintain a minimum level of liability insurance in the event that claims are brought against them by those who rely on their advice. However, the cost of this insurance is passed on to clients through the fees they pay for services received. Does this system encourage professional responsibility? Is there a more effective method?

6. Professional organizations are authorized by legislation to regulate their own members in terms of controlling permission to practise, setting standards, and imposing discipline. Can the public expect to receive fair treatment from professional organizations that have a vested interest in protecting their own members? Should all the professions be self-regulated?

Situations for Discussion

1. Over the years of running a small business, Lan had acquired sizable savings. She wanted to get the best return on this money and discussed this with her lawyer, Harvey. He advised her that this was an excellent time to get into real estate; he had many clients who required financing. Lan could provide either first or second mortgages, depending on her desired level of risk and return. Harvey said he had some clients involved in a large townhouse development. Lan trusted him implicitly, as he had been her lawyer since she had first started her business. Thus, she lent the bulk of her savings—$200 000—as a second mortgage, which would earn interest at 19 percent per annum over 5 years.

   Within eight months the real estate market collapsed. The mortgagees defaulted on payment, and once the holders of the first mortgage had foreclosed, there was nothing left for Lan. When she complained to Harvey, he said that investments of any sort carry inherent risk. His personal investment company, for example, had been one of the partners in the townhouse development, and he too had lost his entire investment.

   Lan seeks advice about what she can do to recoup her losses. Identify Lan's options.

2. Good Property engaged the services of a professional real estate appraisal firm, McGee and McGee, prior to purchasing a large tract of property on the outskirts of town. When Dan, the CFO of Good Property, first discussed the appraisal with Andy McGee, he said the appraisal was required by 10 January. Andy said this was impossible owing to other commitments and proposed 26 January. It was agreed that Andy would be the appraiser. Dan said he would get back to Andy about the date.

   The project was more complex than either Good Property or the appraisers expected. The local water conservation authority was about to issue a report that seriously affected the land, so Andy waited for it. The appraisal was not handed to Good Property until 29 January. By this time, another purchaser had acquired the property. When Dan was handed the sizable

invoice for the work, he claimed that Andy had breached the contract by finishing the work late and had caused Dan to lose out on being able to buy the land. Furthermore, the invoice was for far more than he had expected to pay. How are these matters likely to be resolved? What arguments can Good Property and McGee raise? What would happen if McGee had not waited for the water report and Good Property had bought the land, which was later devalued by the report?

3. Maxine is a highly respected pharmacist and operates her own small pharmacy business in Alberta. For several years, Maxine has provided customers with a loyalty card, which accumulates points for each prescription or service purchased, ultimately enabling the holder to use the points to purchase other merchandise and obtain discounts. Recently, the Alberta College of Pharmacists has introduced legislation to prohibit pharmacists from offering incentives for purchasing pharmacy drugs, including loyalty and rewards programs. The College says that such incentives create conflicts of interest and are unprofessional. But critics of the new rule, such as the grocer Sobeys, say that studies have shown that such loyalty programs build the relationship between pharmacies and their patients, and encourage better use of medications. Many seniors and disabled people rely on loyalty and incentive programs to purchase items that they might otherwise not be able to afford. [32]

   Is prohibiting loyalty and incentive programs for the purchase of prescription drugs a good idea? Does it protect the public? What are Maxine's options if she is opposed to the rule?

4. Sino-Forest Corp. was an international forestry company. Between 2007 and 2011, the company raised $2.7 billion in the capital markets. In June 2011, allegations were made that Sino-Forest's forest holdings in China and other countries were grossly and fraudulently overstated. The share price plummeted from $26 to $1 and then the company applied for

---

32 "Grocer to fight rule targeting loyalty programs", *Edmonton Journal* (15 April 2014).

bankruptcy protection in Canada. Investors sued the company, its executives and directors, its auditors Ernst & Young, and a number of investment banks who acted as underwriters, for $9.18 billion in a class action lawsuit. The allegations against Ernst & Young consist of negligence in the audits which should have detected the overstatement of holdings and objections to the presence on the Sino-Forest board of directors of former Ernst & Young partners.[33] In 2013, an Ontario court approved a $117 million settlement in the case against Sino-Forest's auditors Ernst & Young. The auditing firm did not admit liability as part of the settlement agreement. Ernst & Young still faces allegations from the Ontario Securities Commission that it exercised a lack of diligence in regard to its audit of Sino-Forest.

Would the investors have been successful against Ernst & Young if they had proceeded to trial? What must the claimants have been able to prove in order to establish Ernst & Young's liability? If the forest holdings were overstated as alleged, should the audits have revealed the problem?

5. Yul is a CGA working as comptroller for Jones Manufacturing. He is concerned about the cash flow position of the company. Customers have placed large orders, but Andrew (the CEO) has insisted on an aggressive pricing policy, and prices charged do not cover costs.

Yul approaches Andrew with his concerns, but Andrew will not listen. Andrew is a high-profile member of the local community; the success of the company means that it can hire a large number of people in this economically depressed area, and it is inconceivable to him that booming sales could translate into losses. Yul explains that the auditors will be coming soon and, if he doesn't expose the current position, they will uncover it anyway. Andrew tells him that he understands, but that he wants Yul to do whatever it takes to get through this audit. Afterward, prices can be raised, since by then the company will be in a strong position

in the marketplace and this temporary hurdle will have been overcome.

Yul is trying to devise a strategy to reconcile his professional responsibilities and the survival of this company. It would be devastating to see the company close if he is unable to find a way of presenting the information to satisfy the auditors.

Discuss the pressures Yul faces. What should he do now?

6. Environmental Consultants Ltd. (ECL) was hired by Crass Developments Ltd. (CD) to evaluate a prospective development site for signs of pollution. The site had previously been used for a variety of industrial purposes, but was then vacant. CD was considering a number of possible sites and wanted to choose the one with the lowest environmental risk. At the time, ECL had plenty of work and wished to complete the evaluation for CD as quickly as possible. The senior partner at ECL assigned two junior employees to the CD job—one with two years' experience and the other just recently hired. They did a site inspection and conducted a few soil tests that were appropriate for a "clean" site, but not for one that had been used previously. They produced a positive report. The senior partner was out of the office for a few days, so the report was sent to CD without his approval. CD bought the land; a year later, signs of pollution began to emerge and CD was responsible for an expensive clean-up effort. To what degree are ECL and the three employees responsible for CD's clean-up costs?

7. Jonathan commenced a lawsuit against Randy for an alleged breach of contract, claiming $500 000 in damages plus interest and costs. Randy approached Smithson, a local lawyer, to provide her with legal advice regarding the lawsuit. Smithson spent many hours discussing the facts of the case with Randy, and reviewed all of the evidence that Randy had in her possession. At the end of the review, Smithson advised Randy that, in his opinion, Randy had an excellent likelihood of success defending the lawsuit and that he would be happy to assist her in doing so. Randy and Smithson then signed a retainer agreement, which

33 Jeff Gray, "Ontario court approves $117 million settlement with Sino-Forest auditors," *Globe and Mail* (20 March 2013).

provided for the engagement of Smithson as Randy's lawyer in connection with the lawsuit and the payment of legal fees based on the time expended by Smithson on the file. The lawsuit went to trial, and Randy lost. She was ordered to pay the full amount of $500 000, plus $40 000 in interest and $30 000 in costs. Following the trial, Smithson sent Randy a bill for $75 000 in fees, including the time that

he had spent prior to the retainer agreement having been signed. Randy feels that she did not receive competent legal advice from Smithson, and that she should not have to pay the entire bill.

How much should Randy have to pay? What are Smithson's obligations to Randy? What are Randy's options?

THE SALE OF GOODS, CONSUMER PROTECTION, AND COMPETITION LAW

Sale of goods transactions are critically important to business and the economy. Traditionally, these transactions were governed by the rules of contract law, as discussed in Part Two. However, the law sometimes modifies those principles in order to promote trade and commerce, to ensure fair competition, and to protect consumers.

Chapter 23 discusses the laws that govern the sale of goods. Chapter 24 focuses on the laws that protect consumers when they are involved in purchasing goods or services, and competition law. There is some overlap between consumer protection law and competition law because competition law, in addition to promoting a competitive marketplace, also seeks to protect consumers.

23

marylooo/Shutterstock

THE SALE OF GOODS

BUSINESS LAW IN PRACTICE

Skin Renew Limited (SRL) develops, manufactures, and sells various skin care products. SRL has developed a new moisturizing cream which is made entirely from natural ingredients. In preliminary testing, users of the new cream reported it being very effective in keeping their skin moist. Importantly, they also rated the cream very highly in terms of colour and scent. SRL believes that the new cream, which it intends to call "NaturalNew," will complement its existing product line and result in significant additional market share.

SRL intends to promote, distribute, and sell NaturalNew nationally. The cream will be sold in three different sizes with two different delivery mechanisms (pump bottle and squeeze tube). SRL will sell NaturalNew to national drug and grocery chains, who will resell the product to their retail customers. SRL currently sells its existing products through these same distribution channels, and SRL intends to leverage its existing business relationships in order to distribute NaturalNew.

SRL plans to begin manufacturing large quantities of NaturalNew, and wants to ensure that it has properly structured the purchase and sale contracts that it has with its customers. SRL also wants to properly manage the risks that are involved with the sale and delivery of its new product.

1. What legal issues arise in regard to the sale of NaturalNew to drug and grocery chains?

2. What should SRL be aware of when negotiating the contract of sale with drug and grocery chains?

3. What terms should SRL use in regard to the shipping of NaturalNew?

4. What happens if a shipment of NaturalNew is lost or damaged before it reaches the buyer?

Introduction

The sale of goods, like other aspects of business, is influenced by various laws and regulations. The fundamental laws affecting sales are the common law principles of contract and tort law explained in Parts Two and Three of this text. There are also a number of important statutes, both federal and provincial, that apply to the sale and marketing of goods. The main objectives of these laws are:

- to protect the parties to sale of goods transactions, particularly buyers.
- to protect consumers from physical harm.
- to promote a fair and competitive marketplace.
- to protect consumers from unfair selling and marketing practices.

The laws relating to the first of these objectives will be discussed in this chapter. The laws dealing with the other three objectives will be discussed in Chapter 24. There is some overlap, because the sale of goods, the protection of consumers, and the promotion of a fair and competitive marketplace are related concepts.

In regard to the sale of goods, several legal issues will be discussed in this chapter: the sale of goods contract, the impact of sale of goods legislation, the implied terms in a sale of goods contract, when ownership and the risk of loss are transferred from a seller of goods to the buyer, and the remedies available when a sale of goods contract is breached.

If a business sells its products internationally, or purchases goods from foreign sellers, the business may be subject to the laws of other countries and may also be affected by rules governing the international sale of goods.

The Sale of Goods

The sale of goods is very important to the overall Canadian economy. From the supply of oil and gas, to the resale of manufacturing and building materials, to the purchase of items such as automobiles and groceries by consumers, millions of dollars in goods are bought and sold every day in Canada. One of the purposes of business law is to promote trade and commerce—in order to achieve that goal, the law takes a role in transactions involving the sale of goods.

The Contract of Sale

The contract of sale is the legal foundation for every sale of goods transaction. Several key aspects of the contract of sale are worthy of particular attention—the terms of the contract relating to the sale, the transfer of ownership of the goods to the buyer, the terms relating to payment and delivery, and the remedies for a breach of the contract.

The Common Law

When buyers agree to purchase goods, they typically have expectations regarding the attributes and characteristics of the goods. Purchasers of NaturalNew, for example, will probably assume that the product is properly manufactured and safe for its intended use.

Whether such expectations are protected from a legal perspective is a different matter. The historic foundation of the common law concerning the sale of goods is reflected by the Latin phrase *caveat emptor,* which means "let the buyer beware" or "let the buyer take care." The common law required prospective purchasers to take care of themselves, to be aware of what they were purchasing, and to make appropriate investigations before buying. If the purchaser expected a product to have certain attributes or exhibit certain characteristics,

Caveat emptor

"Let the buyer beware" or "let the buyer take care."

the common law required those expectations to be contained in the contract. Otherwise, the purchaser would be left without a remedy if the product proved to be deficient.[1]

Because an unwavering application of the doctrine of *caveat emptor* often produced unfair results, judges began to create principles that would provide a measure of protection for purchasers of goods. Eventually, these principles were codified in sale of goods statutes.

Sale of Goods Legislation

Beginning in the 1800s, English judges generated the basic principles that inform the modern law concerning the sale of goods. In response to the harshness of *caveat emptor*, they developed common law rules that, among other matters, implied specific terms into contracts for the sale of goods, whether the parties had expressly agreed to those terms or not. In addition, rules evolved regarding the transfer of ownership from seller to buyer, which was particularly important because the owner of the goods was generally considered to bear the risk of any damage or loss in regard to the goods. On this basis, a reasonably predictable set of exceptions to the doctrine of *caveat emptor* was developed. For example, common law rules arose to the effect that goods sold would be reasonably suitable for the purpose for which they were intended to be used and would be of merchantable—or reasonable—quality.

In 1893, the English Parliament enacted the *Sale of Goods Act*,[2] an influential piece of legislation based on the common law principles which had developed. The Act summarized—rather than reformed—the common law of the time. The Act implied a set of terms into every transaction for the sale of goods unless it was contrary to the parties' intentions. The legislation also provided remedies if these statutory terms were breached. These implied terms operated in addition to any express terms or representations that were agreed upon by the parties at the time the contract of sale was made.

England's 1893 *Sale of Goods Act* forms the cornerstone of modern sale of goods legislation everywhere in Canada except Quebec.[3] The law governing the sale of goods is a specialized branch of contract law. This means that the sale of goods is governed by legislation and, where the legislation is not relevant, by the common law rules of contract. In some situations, such as business transactions where the parties have agreed to exclude the *Sale of Goods Act*, the Act will not apply. Otherwise, the Act applies to every contract for the sale of goods. Since all the provincial statutes are based on the original English legislation, they are all nearly identical.

The parties to a sale of goods transaction may agree to exclude, or vary, the terms implied by the *Sale of Goods Act*. This may be done expressly, or may be apparent from the manner in which the parties deal with each other. However, every province has passed legislation which prohibits the parties from excluding, or varying, these implied terms in consumer transactions. This aspect of consumer protection law will be discussed in the next chapter.

---

1   See Chapter 8 for a discussion of the law concerning mistake as well as negligent and fraudulent misrepresentation.

2   *Sale of Goods Act*, 1893, (56 & 57 Vict) c 71(a). The Act has been repealed and replaced by the *Sale of Goods Act 1979* (UK), c 54.

3   For example, *Sale of Goods Act*, RSO 1990, c S.1; *Sale of Goods Act*, RSA 2000, c S-2. Articles 1726–31 of Quebec's *Civil Code* contain warranties implied in sales transactions.

Goods and Services

The *Sale of Goods Act* applies only to the "sale of goods."

A "sale" means that money and ownership must be exchanged. The Act does not apply to loans, gifts, leases, or licences. Importantly, this means that generally the Act does not apply to the provision of commercial software, which is typically licensed to users rather than sold.

"Goods" means personal property in its tangible, portable form as well as items attached to land that can be severed. For example, the moisturizing cream supplied by SRL would be considered goods. Goods do not include the sale of land or buildings, or the provision of services. Goods also do not include intangible personal property, such as accounts receivable, intellectual property, or shares of a corporation.[4]

It may be difficult to distinguish a contract for the sale of goods from one for the provision of services. The distinction is important because it will determine whether or not the *Sale of Goods Act* applies. For example, in *Gee v. White Spot*,[5] the court held that a cooked meal served to a customer at a sit-down restaurant was a sale of goods, even though the transaction involved a significant provision of services, including setting the table, cooking the food, and clearing the dishes. In the case of *Borek v Hooper*,[6] a contract between a homeowner and an artist for a large custom painting was found not to be a sale of goods, although the artist did supply some goods, such as the canvas, the paint and the frame. The legal test is whether the contract was *primarily* for the sale of goods or *primarily* for the supply of services. Accordingly, when a contract involves both a sale of goods and a supply of services, whether or not the *Sale of Goods Act* applies will depend on the primary purpose of the contract.

Implied Terms—Conditions and Warranties

When the *Sale of Goods Act* applies to a contract for the sale of goods, the effect is that a number of terms are automatically implied into the contract. The legislation classifies these implied terms as either conditions or warranties.[7] The primary difference between implied conditions and implied warranties rests in the remedy that the innocent party will have upon a breach. In the event of breach of an implied condition, the buyer will be able to repudiate the contract of sale, return the goods (if they have been delivered), and obtain a return of the purchase price (if it has been paid). In the event of a breach of an implied warranty, the innocent party cannot repudiate the contract and may only sue for damages for breach of contract. When a condition has been breached, instead of repudiation the buyer has the option to proceed with the contract, treat the breach of condition as a breach of warranty, and sue for damages.

Conditions implied by the *Sale of Goods Act*:

- the seller has the right to sell the goods.
- the goods will be reasonably fit for their intended purpose where the buyer, expressly or by implication, makes it known what the intended purpose

---

4 See Chapter 17 for a discussion of the various types of personal property, including real and personal property, and tangible and intangible personal property.

5 (1986), 32 D.L.R. (4th) 238 (B.C.S.C.).

6 (1994), 114 D.L.R. (4th) 570 (Ont. Div. Ct.). In that case, the court found the *Sale of Goods Act* did not apply to the contract, but nevertheless implied certain terms into the contract under the common law, including terms relating to quality and suitability for the intended purpose.

7 This common law distinction, along with innominate terms that cannot be easily classified, is discussed in Chapter 9.

of the goods will be, in such a way as to show that he is relying on the skill and judgment of the seller (a buyer need not make the intended purpose known when goods are used for their ordinary purpose).

- the goods will be of merchantable quality ("merchantable quality" means the goods are of reasonable quality considering the price paid).
- where goods are sold by sample, the goods will correspond to the sample.
- where goods are sold by description, the goods will correspond with the description.

Warranties implied by the *Sale of Goods Act:*

- the buyer will enjoy quiet possession of the goods, which generally means that third parties will not claim rights against them.
- the goods are free from liens and encumbrances in favour of third parties that were not declared or known to the buyer when the contract was made.
- payment of the purchase price for the goods will be made within a reasonable time.
- delivery of the goods will be made within a reasonable time.

In order to understand how the *Sale of Goods Act* applies, consider the following examples.

Example 1 A major grocery chain ordered 24 000 cases of NaturalNew, and the written contract of sale states that the parties have agreed to exclude the application of the *Sale of Goods Act* to the transaction. Following delivery of the product, the buyer complains that the seller has breached an implied term of the contract of sale because the cream is not reasonably fit for its intended purpose. The buyer will not be able to rely on the implied terms of the *Sale of Goods Act* because the parties have agreed to exclude the application of the Act and the transaction is not a consumer transaction. The buyer will have to rely on the terms of the written contract for a remedy.

Example 2 A consumer purchased a tube of NaturalNew direct from SRL through SRL's website. The customer paid the purchase price when she placed the order, but the cream was not delivered to her for five months. The terms and conditions on SRL's website, to which the customer agreed, state that the terms of the *Sale of Goods Act* are excluded from all online sales. The late delivery constitutes a breach of the implied warranty that the goods will be delivered within a reasonable time. The exclusion of the *Sale of Goods Act* is ineffective, because the customer is a consumer and therefore the terms implied by the Act cannot be excluded or varied.[8] Since the breach of contract relates to a breach of warranty, rather than a breach of condition, the customer must keep the cream and cannot demand a refund, but she can sue SRL for damages.

Example 3 A drug store purchased 200 tubes of NaturalNew from SRL, to resell to its customers, after the manager of the store saw a description of the product on SRL's website. The website described NaturalNew as "hypoallergenic." However, after trying the cream, the manager developed a noticeable allergic reaction at the location where he had applied the cream. The contract of sale between the

---

8 This aspect of consumer protection law is discussed in Chapter 24.

drug store and SRL said nothing about implied terms or the *Sale of Goods Act*. The Act applies because the parties have not agreed to exclude its application. SRL has breached the implied condition that the goods will match their description, because the cream was described as hypoallergenic but is, in fact, not hypoallergenic. As a result, the drug store may return the product to SRL and obtain a refund of the purchase price paid.

CONTRACTS FOR THE INTERNATIONAL SALE OF GOODS

In international trade, it is important that shipping terms be standardized to ensure that there is a common understanding between jurisdictions. The International Chamber of Commerce has published a set of definitions for trade terms, known as INCOTERMS. These definitions do not have the force of law but are often adopted by contracting parties. They may differ from the terms outlined above. Businesspeople need to be familiar with the appropriate terms applying to their specific transaction.[9]

In 1980, the United Nations Commission on International Trade Law (UNCITRAL) produced a treaty, the *Convention on the International Sale of Goods (CISG)*. The treaty, signed in Vienna in 1980, came into force in 1988 and has been ratified by more than 80 countries, including Canada and the United States. The goal of the convention is to create a uniform body of international commercial law. The *CISG* applies to business-to-business contracts for the sale of goods. The convention automatically applies to the contract if the parties are from ratifying countries, unless they contract out of its provisions. It does not apply to contracts for services and technology, leases and licences, or goods bought for personal, family, or household use.

The convention provides a uniform set of rules for forming contracts and establishes the obligations of the buyer and seller. It addresses in a comprehensive manner such issues as the requirement of writing; offer and acceptance; implied terms; performance of the contract, including the buyer's and seller's obligations; and breach of contract. Because the rules constitute a compromise among differing rules in the various legal systems, Canadian buyers and sellers need to be aware of significant differences between the *CISG* and Canadian rules. For example, under Canadian law, contracts for the sale of goods worth more than a minimum amount must be in writing in order to be enforceable. The *CISG* states that such contracts need not be in writing or in any particular form.

Reservations have been expressed about the *CISG*:

> The crux of the problem with the *CISG* is its contradictions, its lack of rules around the validity of the contract, . . . the lack of its widespread use, and the domestic gloss it has been given by various courts, including those of Canada. All of these factors combine to suggest that despite the laudable objectives of the drafters of the convention itself, businesses may favour the continued use of tried and tested national sales laws.

Critical Analysis: The *CISG* is a compromise agreed to by many nations and encompassing aspects of many different legal systems. How useful is this convention to Canadian business?

Sources: *United Nations Convention on Contracts for the International Sale of Goods* (1980) [*CISG*], online: Pace Law School <http://www.cisg.law.pace.edu/cisg/text/treaty.html>; and Sheerin Kalia, *International Business Law for Canadians: A Practical Guide* (Toronto: LexisNexis Canada, 2010) at 109, 126 and 131.

---

9 International Chamber of Commerce, "INCOTERMS 2010", online: International Chamber of Commerce <http://www.iccwbo.org/incoterms/>.

Shipping Terms

Business has developed standardized terms for often used delivery and payment arrangements in contracts of sale. To illustrate these terms, assume that SRL has agreed to sell $10 000 worth of NaturalNew to Super Grocer, a Winnipeg-based grocery retailer, and the goods will be shipped from SRL's warehouse to Super Grocer's warehouse through a carrier called Custom Trucking.

Bill of Lading

Bill of lading

A shipping document that serves as a contract between the seller and the carrier.

The **bill of lading**, generically known as a "shipping document," is the contract between the seller (SRL) and the carrier (Custom Trucking). It specifies to whom the goods must be delivered and provides evidence that the goods have been transferred from the seller to the carrier. The bill of lading often also sets out the terms of the shipping arrangement, including fees, expenses, delivery times, and any agreed upon limitations of liability.

The time it takes for goods to reach their destination can be significant, particularly in international business transactions. What happens when, a few days after shipping the goods, SRL learns that Super Grocer is insolvent or bankrupt? In that case, SRL has the right to exercise **stoppage in transit**.[10] SRL can direct the carrier to return the goods to SRL, even though title may have transferred to Super Grocer. Provided Custom Trucking receives this direction before it has delivered the goods to Super Grocer, it must return them (at SRL's expense) to SRL.

Stoppage in transit

The right of a seller to demand that goods be returned by a shipper to the seller, provided the buyer is insolvent.

Cost, Insurance, and Freight

c.i.f.

A contractual term making the seller responsible for insurance and shipping.

The initials **c.i.f.** stand for "cost, insurance, freight." In a c.i.f. contract, the seller is responsible for arranging the insurance (in the buyer's name) and shipping. The purchase price includes the cost of the goods, insurance, and shipping. The seller must deliver the goods to the carrier and send copies of all documentation and a full statement of costs to the buyer.

Free on Board

f.o.b.

A contractual term whereby the buyer specifies the type of transportation and the seller arranges that transportation and delivery of goods to the carrier at the buyer's expense.

The initials **f.o.b.** stand for "free on board." In an f.o.b. contract, the buyer specifies the type of transportation to be used, and the seller arranges the shipping and delivers the goods to the carrier. The seller has completed its responsibilities when the goods are delivered to the carrier. The seller incurs the cost of delivering the goods to the carrier, and generally the buyer pays for shipping and insurance. For example, if the contract is "f.o.b. Winnipeg," Super Grocer will advise SRL how the goods are to be transported, and SRL will arrange for that transportation and ensure that the goods are delivered to the relevant carrier.

Cash on Delivery

c.o.d.

A contractual term requiring the purchaser to pay the carrier in cash upon delivery of the goods.

A **c.o.d.** or "cash on delivery" contract was once common with consumer orders, particularly before credit cards existed. The purchaser is obliged to pay for the goods upon delivery. This term was used to ensure that the carrier did not part with possession of the goods without the purchaser having paid for the goods.

---

10 See, for example, *Sale of Goods Act*, R.S.O. 1990 c S.1, s. 42.

Transfer of Title

The transfer of title, or ownership, from seller to buyer is an essential feature of every transaction involving the sale of goods.[11] The determination of when ownership is transferred is important because of the historic legal maxim that "risk follows title." This means that, generally, the risk of loss—theft, damage, or destruction—will be borne by the party who owns the goods. Accordingly, the risk of loss will transfer from seller to buyer when ownership of the goods passes from seller to buyer. Consider these examples:

- a truckload of goods is destroyed by fire in mid-delivery between seller and buyer. Who bears the risk of loss?
- the parties agree that certain goods will be paid for within 30 days of sale. Does the 30 days begin upon delivery of the goods or at some earlier point?
- a custom-built machine has been built but has not yet been delivered to the customer or paid for. If the seller goes bankrupt, who owns the machine?

Importantly, possession and ownership of goods can be held by different parties. Possessing goods without owning them (i.e., without having title) confers certain obligations and rights.[12] Ownership confers additional rights. Many people incorrectly assume that delivery and payment automatically result in the transfer of title from seller to buyer—while this may sometimes be the case, it is not always the case.

The best way for parties to ensure clarity as to when title, and therefore risk, will pass from seller to buyer is to write the contract of sale in a way that specifies delivery and payment terms and clearly indicates when and how title will pass from seller to buyer. The parties can then predict when responsibility for the goods will shift to the buyer and they can arrange matters such as insurance coverage accordingly. When the parties fail to agree on when title will transfer from seller to buyer, there are statutory provisions that resolve the issue.

The provincial *Sale of Goods* Act sets out a series of rules[13] that determine when title will pass from seller to buyer, in the absence of agreement by the parties. It is important to remember that these rules only take effect when the parties have failed, either in express terms of a written contract or through their conduct, to agree on when title will transfer. If the parties have agreed on the transfer of title, expressly or impliedly, their agreement will govern and these rules will not come into play. In this way, the rules function as a set of default principles that apply when it would otherwise be difficult or impossible to determine the intention of the parties as to the transfer of title.

The rules are stated below, along with an example of each. In broad terms, the acts address two contrasting sets of circumstances. The first four rules deal with **specific goods**, which are goods that are already in existence and can be clearly identified when the contract is formed. The fifth rule deals with unascertained goods and future goods. **Unascertained goods** are goods that are yet to be set aside and identified as being the subject matter of the contract. For example, when a customer walks into a department store, points to a television on display, and asks to purchase that television, the customer is really asking to buy a television *just like* the one on display. In that case, the television which the

Specific goods

Goods that are in existence and identifiable at the time a contract of sale is formed.

Unascertained goods

Goods that are not yet set aside and identifiable as the subject matter of the contract at the time a contract of sale is formed.

11 The concept of ownership of personal property in the form of goods is discussed in detail in Chapter 17.
12 This often constitutes a bailment, which is discussed in Chapter 17.
13 For example, *Sale of Goods Act*, RSO 1990, c S.1, s 19.

Future goods

Goods that are not yet in existence at the time a contract of sale is formed.

customer is purchasing is unascertained goods, because the specific television set that the customer will take home has not yet been set aside and identified. **Future goods** are goods that are not yet in existence at the time the contract is entered into. For example, a contract for 10 000 tubes of NaturalNew which have not yet been manufactured is a contract for future goods. It is important to determine whether the goods at issue are specific goods, unascertained goods, or future goods, so that the proper rule is applied.

Rule 1

Where there is an unconditional contract for the sale of specific goods in a deliverable state, the property in the goods passes to the buyer when the contract is made, and it is immaterial whether the time of payment or the time of delivery or both is postponed.

Example SRL had an inventory surplus at the end of the year and offered a special discount to bulk purchasers who would pay immediately. ABC Discounter went to SRL's warehouse, saw 500 cases of product that it wanted to purchase, and agreed to buy the product. ABC paid in full and the product was moved to a loading dock for pick-up. ABC and SRL agreed that ABC would pick up the product the following day. The contract said nothing about the transfer of title. Unfortunately, there was a fire at the warehouse that night, and all the product was destroyed. Title in the goods passed to ABC when the contract was made, since the goods were specific goods in a deliverable state (i.e., nothing needed to be done to them to make them ready for delivery). Rule 1 applies; since the goods belonged to ABC at the time of the fire, ABC was forced to bear the loss.

Rule 2

Where there is a contract for the sale of specific goods and the seller is bound to do something to the goods for the purpose of putting them in a deliverable state, the property does not pass until the thing is done and the buyer has received notice.

Example XYZ Retailer and SRL had a contract in which XYZ agreed to buy 5000 cases of NaturalNew, and SRL agreed to put custom-made private brand labels on each tube of product. The contract said nothing about the transfer of title. SRL finished placing the private brand labels on the product on the weekend, and planned to call XYZ the following day to tell them that the product was ready for pick-up. That night, however, SRL was the victim of a robbery and all of the product was stolen. Title in the goods had not passed to XYZ because although SRL had put the goods in a deliverable state, the buyer had not been notified. Rule 2 applies; since title had not passed, SRL would bear the loss.

Rule 3

Where there is a contract for the sale of specific goods in a deliverable state but the seller is bound to weigh, measure, test, or do some other act or thing with reference to the goods for the purpose of ascertaining their price, the property does not pass until such act or thing is done and the buyer has received notice.

Example SRL agreed to buy raw materials from DEF, with the purchase price to be determined by the weight of the materials. No intention was expressed regarding the transfer of title. The raw materials had been manufactured and set aside by DEF to fill SRL's order, but DEF had not yet weighed them. DEF wanted to fill another customer's order with the materials it had set aside for SRL, but was not sure whether that was allowed. Rule 3 applies; title had not yet passed to SRL because the goods had not been weighed (and SRL had not been notified). DEF was free to use the goods for another purpose provided, of course, that it obtained other materials to satisfy its contractual obligations to SRL.

Rule 4

Where goods are delivered to the buyer on approval or on "sale or return" or other similar terms, the property passes to the buyer:

a. when she signifies her approval or acceptance to the seller or does any other act adopting the transaction, or

b. if she does not signify her approval or acceptance to the seller but retains the goods without giving notice of rejection, when a time that has been fixed for the return of the goods expires, and if no time has been fixed, on the expiration of a reasonable time.

Example SRL had a standing contract with KLM which provided that SRL would ship a certain amount of product to KLM each month, and KLM would be permitted to return any product which it was not able to sell within 30 days. SRL shipped 25 000 cases of product to KLM on August 15. On September 7, there was a flood in KLM's warehouse, and all the product was destroyed. KLM did not signify approval or acceptance of the product, nor did it do anything to ratify the transaction. Since the time period agreed upon for return of the goods had not expired, title had not passed and the goods belonged to SRL. SLR must bear the loss.

Rule 5

Where there is a contract for the sale of unascertained or future goods by description and goods of that description and in a deliverable state are unconditionally appropriated to the contract, either by the seller with the assent of the buyer or by the buyer with the assent of the seller, the property passes to the buyer, and such assent may be express or implied and may be given either before or after the appropriation is made.

Example MNO placed an order with SRL for 500 cases of NaturalNew. The contract stated that SRL would notify MNO by email when the product was ready for pick-up. At the time the contract was formed, SRL had 12 500 cases of NaturalNew in its warehouse. The following day, a forklift truck operator in the SRL warehouse took 500 cases of NaturalNew and set it aside in the loading dock area. A label was affixed to the 500 cases stating that it was to be picked up by MNO. The shipping manager in the warehouse then emailed MNO to say that its product was ready to be picked up. After the email had been sent, the forklift truck operator accidentally dropped another shipment onto the 500 cases, seriously damaging the product. The goods in this situation were unascertained goods, because although they were in existence when the contract was formed, they had not been set aside for the contract, or unconditionally appropriated. As such, Rule 5 applies; title to the goods passed to MNO when the goods were set aside and marked specifically for MNO and the email was sent. MNO had expressly assented, in advance, to SRL unconditionally appropriating goods to

What are the legal issues raised in connection with shipping goods?

the contract. The product was the property of MNO when it was damaged and MNO must bear the risk of damage.

Although the *Sale of Goods Act* rules are important, they are complex. In practice, it is always preferable to avoid potential misunderstandings by drafting contracts that set out clearly when title and the corresponding risk will shift from the seller to the buyer.

Remedies

Whether or not title has passed from the seller to the buyer affects the compensation to which the seller is entitled in the event of a breach by the buyer. For example, if the buyer breaches the contract by cancelling an order, the seller is entitled to damages for that breach. If title has not passed to the buyer, the seller still owns the goods. The seller is therefore entitled to the normal measure of **damages for non-acceptance**, recognizing that the seller has an obligation to mitigate the loss. If title has passed to the buyer, the buyer owns the goods and must pay the full amount of its obligation under the contract (i.e., the purchase price). The seller's claim in that case is known as **action for the price**.

Generally, when a term of a contract of sale is breached, classification of the relevant term of the contract is essential to determining the remedy to which the innocent party is entitled. The breach of a condition by the seller will give the innocent party the right not only to claim damages but also to reject the goods and treat the contract as ended. This is known as the right of repudiation and means that the purchaser may choose not to comply with the rest of its obligations under the contract. For example, the drug store that received NaturalNew that did not correspond with the description on SRL's website was not obligated to accept further shipments from SRL. The drug store was entitled to terminate its contract with SRL, return the product, and find another supplier.

When a warranty is breached, the innocent party is entitled only to claim damages or, in the case of an innocent buyer, to ask the court to reduce the purchase price due to the breach. A buyer cannot return the goods as a result of a breach of warranty and must continue to perform its obligations under the contract. Similarly, a seller cannot refuse to supply goods as a result of a breach of warranty by the buyer, but may only claim for the damages it has suffered as a result of the breach. The following case demonstrates the importance of these rules in commercial transactions.

Damages for non-acceptance

Damages to which a seller is entitled if a buyer refuses to accept goods prior to the passing of title.

Action for the price

The seller's claim when the buyer has breached the contract and title to the goods has passed to the buyer.

Chalmers Suspensions International Ltd v B&B Automation Equipment Inc, [2008] OJ No 1394 (Sup Ct J), aff'd 2009 ONCA 360

THE BUSINESS CONTEXT: Two corporations dealing with highly technical equipment on relatively equal terms need to be aware of the implications of contract terms implied by the applicable *Sale of Goods Act*.

FACTUAL BACKGROUND: Chalmers manufactured automotive suspensions for large vehicles. In 2000, Chalmers converted from manual to robotic welding for its truck suspensions. B&B agreed to design and manufacture a robotic welding machine for Chalmers, to be delivered in 16 to 18 weeks, with payment of $198 000 in three installments. The machine was to complete the welding for each frame in 10 minutes. B&B completed the machine, but after repeated testing and inspection, it could not do welds of acceptable CSA quality within the specified time cycle. Negotiation and consultation went on at length, but eventually Chalmers declared the machine unacceptable and claimed the return of payments made. B&B counterclaimed for the balance plus additional costs and storage fees, alleging that the machine was fully operational and that the problem was with Chalmers's parts.

THE LEGAL QUESTION: Was there a condition implied in the contract that the robotic machine be suitable for the purpose specified by Chalmers? If so, was the condition breached? If the condition was breached, what was Chalmers's remedy?

RESOLUTION: Chalmers received the refund of payments made. B&B's counterclaim was dismissed. The court found that the condition was implied because B&B had previously designed and manufactured equipment for Chalmers and was therefore aware of Chalmers's business; B&B admitted that this type of contract was within its course of business; B&B had complete knowledge of Chalmers's intended purpose for the machine; Chalmers had relied on B&B's expertise in the past; and a reasonable person would have realized Chalmers's reliance in this contract. Expert evidence established that the machine failed to fit Chalmers's process and the welds failed to meet CSA standards. B&B's breach of the implied condition went to the root of the contract, justifying Chalmers's rejection of the machine and its claim for return of payments.

CRITICAL ANALYSIS: Commercial parties such as Chalmers and B&B are able to agree on their own terms and conditions by modifying or excluding the application of the applicable *Sale of Goods Act*. Why did B&B not transfer the risks to Chalmers in the contract?

Limitations of Sale of Goods Legislation

Sale of goods legislation provides buyers with relief from the harshness of the doctrine of *caveat emptor*, and provides greater certainty for buyers and sellers, but the legislation has limitations. For example, the *Sale of Goods Act*

- applies only to sales of goods, not land, intangibles, or services.
- requires that there be privity of contract between the customer and the "offending" party; breach of warranties by the manufacturer, for example, are not covered.
- permits contracting out of the implied terms (the buyer and seller can agree that some or all of the terms will not apply).
- does not address pre-contractual representations made by a seller.

In order to deal with these limitations, all the provinces have enacted consumer protection legislation. This legislation is discussed in detail in Chapter 24.

BUSINESS LAW IN PRACTICE REVISITED

1. What legal issues arise in regard to the sale of NaturalNew to drug and grocery chains?

The common law principles of contract and tort law will apply to the sale of goods by SRL. Accordingly, SRL must abide by its obligations as set out in the contract for the sale of its goods, and it must take reasonable care to avoid causing injury. In addition, unless the contract of sale modifies or excludes the terms implied by the *Sale of Goods Act,* SRL must also honour these implied terms, including the implied conditions that the goods will match their description, that the goods will match a sample provided, that the goods will be of reasonable quality, and that the goods will be reasonably suitable for the purpose for which they are intended. Finally, SRL will need to know when ownership of the goods will transfer from SRL to the buyer—if the contract does not make this clear, then the rules in the *Sale of Goods Act* will apply.

2. What should SRL be aware of when negotiating the contract of sale with drug and grocery chains?

SRL should ensure that the contract of sale is clear and comprehensive. The contract should provide specifications for the goods so the quality and attributes of the goods are clearly understood and agreed upon. SRL should decide whether it wants to exclude or modify the implied conditions and warranties contained in the *Sale of Goods Act.* If SRL decides to exclude or modify the implied terms, then that should be made clear in the contract of sale. SRL may want to describe in the contract precisely how and when ownership of the goods will shift from SRL to the buyer, so that confusion is avoided and recourse to the rules of the *Sale of Goods Act* is not required.

3. What terms should SRL use in regard to the shipping of NaturalNew?

SRL will have to decide which shipping terms are most appropriate for the way it conducts its business and the nature of the product being shipped. SRL may prefer to ship goods f.o.b., in order to reduce its shipping costs, but the purchaser may insist on the goods being shipped c.i.f. In any event, SRL should remain aware of the financial condition of its purchasers and, if one of them becomes insolvent after SRL has shipped goods, then SRL should consider its rights to stop the goods in transit in order to minimize any losses it may suffer.

4. What happens if a shipment of NaturalNew is lost or damaged before it reaches the buyer?

Risk generally follows title. Therefore, the goods will be at the risk of SRL until title to the goods shifts to the buyer. If the goods are lost or damaged before title has transferred to the buyer, then SRL will be responsible for the loss. If the loss or damage occurs after title has transferred to the buyer, then the buyer will be responsible. SRL should purchase insurance coverage that covers the goods up until the time that title transfers to the buyer, but not longer. The buyer should purchase insurance coverage to cover the goods from the point at which the buyer has title.

CHAPTER SUMMARY

The law that applies generally to the sale of goods is the law of contract and tort. However, these common law principles have been modified in every province by sale of goods legislation, which provides increased certainty and greater protection for buyers of goods.

The sale of goods legislation in each province implies conditions and warranties into contracts for the sale of goods, unless the transaction is a business transaction and the parties have agreed to exclude those implied terms. The legislation also provides rules to establish when title to the goods shifts from seller to buyer in a sale of goods transaction—this is important to determine who bears the risk if the goods are lost or damaged. Finally, the *Sale of Goods Act* provides remedies in the event of a breach of the sale of goods contract. All sellers of goods must be knowledgeable about the provisions of sale of goods legislation in order to properly and intelligently structure their sale of goods transactions.

Businesses often use standardized shipping terms in order to conveniently refer to a set of commonly used shipping and delivery terms. Shipping conventions include f.o.b., c.i.f., and c.o.d.

CHAPTER STUDY

Key Terms and Concepts

action for the price (p. 598)

bill of lading (p. 594)

caveat emptor **(p. 589)**

c.i.f. (p. 594)

c.o.d. (p. 594)

damages for non-acceptance (p. 598)

f.o.b. (p. 594)

future goods (p. 596)

specific goods (p. 595)

stoppage in transit (p. 594)

unascertained goods (p. 595)

Questions for Review

1. What is the general law that applies to the sale of goods?

2. How did sale of goods legislation originate?

3. What is the purpose of sale of goods legislation?

4. How does the law distinguish between a contract for the sale of goods and one for the supply of services?

5. Does the *Sale of Goods Act* apply to a meal served at a sit-down restaurant?

6. What is the difference between an implied condition and an implied warranty under the *Sale of Goods Act*?

7. What is an example of a condition implied by the *Sale of Goods Act* into a contract for the sale of goods?

8. What rules apply to a contract for the international sale of goods?

9. What is a bill of lading?

10. What does "f.o.b." mean?

11. What are "specific" goods?

12. What are "unascertained" goods?

13. When do the rules in the *Sale of Goods Act* regarding the transfer of title apply to a sale of goods transaction?

14. How do the rules in the *Sale of Goods Act* determine when ownership of goods passes from the seller to the buyer?

Questions for Critical Thinking

1. Why do we need sale of goods legislation? Why not simply rely on the free market to protect buyers and sellers of goods?

2. Why do businesses need to be familiar with the law relating to the sale of goods? How does a knowledge of this area of law relate to risk management?

3. When should a business exclude or modify the contractual terms that are implied by the *Sale of Goods Act*?

4. Should parties to a business transaction for the sale of goods be allowed to exclude or modify the terms implied by the *Sale of Goods Act*?

5. Why do we need statutory rules to determine the point at which ownership of goods transfers from seller to buyer? Why not simply rely on the express terms of the contract of sale?

6. Why does title not automatically transfer from seller to buyer when the goods are delivered and paid for? What is the purpose of Rule 1, which provides that title may transfer when the contract is made, even though the parties have agreed that delivery and payment will be made later?

Situations for Discussion

1. Ralph wanted a portrait of his whole family. Ralph had seen a family portrait at his friend's house which he liked very much. He was told that Margaret had painted the portrait based on a photograph the friend had provided to her. Ralph contacted Margaret, and they agreed that Margaret would paint a family portrait for Ralph, similar to the one she had painted for Ralph's friend, based on a photograph which Ralph supplied to her. When the painting was finished, Ralph was very upset. The painting was cartoonish compared to the more lifelike painting that he had seen at his friend's house, and it was much smaller. Ralph does not want to pay Margaret for the painting, and insists that she has breached their contract, including the terms implied by the *Sale of Goods Act*. Margaret insists that Ralph must pay for the painting, and argues that the provisions of the *Sale of Goods Act* do not apply to their transaction. How will this dispute be resolved? Does the *Sale of Goods Act* apply to the transaction? If so, what implied terms are relevant?

2. Ace Manufacturing Ltd. agreed to manufacture and sell 5000 chairs to a convention centre. The contract contained detailed specifications for the chairs, and provided that the purchase price of $200 000 would be paid in two equal installments: one-half when the contract was signed and the other one-half when the convention centre was notified that the chairs were ready to be picked up. The contract said nothing about when ownership of the chairs would transfer to the buyer. The convention centre paid the first installment when the contract was signed. The chairs were manufactured by Ace and were in Ace's warehouse when a serious fire destroyed the warehouse and all the chairs. Ace had not yet notified the convention centre that the chairs were ready for pick-up, because the person who ordinarily makes such phone calls had been away from work due to an illness. Ace has demanded payment in full for the chairs from the convention centre. The convention centre has refused to pay the balance and has asked for a refund of the first installment it had paid. Has title to the chairs passed from Ace to the convention centre? Does the convention centre have to pay the balance of the purchase price? Can the convention centre obtain a refund for the amount it has already paid?

3. Outdoor World sells new and used snowmobiles. Each January, Outdoor World has a major "blowout" sale that is heavily promoted and provides genuine savings. Morley was in the market for a used snowmobile. He told the salesperson at Outdoor World that he wanted "a basic machine" and as good a deal as he could get. The salesperson showed him three snowmobiles, started each one, and told Morley that they were roughly equivalent. Morley took a quick look and picked one based on colour, because he knew little about snowmobiles. Morley purchased the snowmobile for $3500. The contract of sale said nothing about implied

terms or the *Sale of Goods Act*. Two days later, there was a good snowfall and Morley took the snowmobile out for a run. Five kilometres from home, the snowmobile spluttered to a stop and Morley could not get it restarted. In the end, a friend of Morley's rescued him, and he had the snowmobile towed back to Outdoor World. What are Morley's rights under the common law? Do the provisions of the *Sale of Goods Act* help Morley?

4. McAsphalt Industries Ltd. is a supplier of asphalt and cement for use in road paving work. Chapman Bros. Ltd. is a road paving company. Chapman ordered some modified asphalt cement from McAsphalt, who assured Chapman that the material could be used with Chapman's conventional equipment. When Chapman used the material, it broke into chunks, requiring the removal of a filter and the alteration of its equipment. Much of the paving had to be redone. Chapman refused to pay McAsphalt for the material and claimed compensation for the cost of repaving and the profit lost on other jobs.[14] Who is responsible for the quality of the material and its suitability for Chapman's equipment? How will the conflicting claims be resolved?

5. Bravo Limited and Good Enough Inc. (GEI) agreed that Bravo would purchase a large amount of surplus construction materials from GEI. The contract of sale, signed by both parties, stated that "the materials are sold as is, where is," and further provided that "all statutory and implied warranties, including without limitation those contained in the *Sale of Goods Act*, are hereby excluded." After delivery of the materials to Bravo, Bravo realized that most of them were cracked and damaged, rendering them unusable and unsaleable. Bravo's owner tried to return the materials for a refund, but the representative for GEI told him that "a deal is a deal." The owner of Bravo feels taken advantage of and wants to know what Bravo's possible remedies against GEI are.

6. Marco and Sammy agreed that Sammy would purchase 300 barbecues from Marco for resale in Sammy's retail store. The specific barbecues that were to be the subject of the sale were identified at the time the contract was entered into and they were set aside from Marco's large inventory of barbecues. The contract of sale was entered into on April 15 and provided that Sammy would pay for the barbecues in full on or before June 15, and Marco would deliver the barbecues to Sammy's store between July 1 and July 10. The contract of sale also said that ownership of the barbecues would pass from Marco to Sammy when the goods had been paid for in full. Sammy paid Marco the full purchase price on June 10. On June 29, three days before Marco was intending to deliver the barbecues to Sammy, burglars broke into Marco's warehouse and stole all the barbecues. When did title to the barbecues pass from Marco to Sammy? Who will be responsible for the loss of the barbecues?

---

14 Based on *McAsphalt Industries Ltd v Chapman Bros Ltd*, 2008 NSSC 324.

24

CONSUMER PROTECTION AND COMPETITION LAW

OBJECTIVES

After studying this chapter, you should have an understanding of

- the laws that protect consumers when they are purchasing goods or services

- the obligations of manufacturers regarding product safety, and the packaging and labelling of products

- the scope of competition law and the various practices that are prohibited by competition legislation

marylooo/Shutterstock

BUSINESS LAW IN PRACTICE

Skin Renew Limited (SRL), which was introduced in the previous chapter, is continuing to develop its sales and marketing plan for NaturalNew, SRL's new moisturizing cream made entirely from natural ingredients.

SRL has decided that, in addition to selling NaturalNew through national drug and grocery retailers, it will also offer NaturalNew direct to consumers through its website.

The marketing campaign for NaturalNew will stress its natural ingredients, and will focus on the simplicity and safety of an all-natural product. In particular, SRL would like to advertise NaturalNew as being "all-natural" with "no artificial ingredients."

SRL will promote NaturalNew primarily through in-store displays, television, and print media, with a special focus on advertising in beauty and glamour magazines. NaturalNew will cost slightly more than competitive products. The premium pricing will reflect the strategy of selling to relatively affluent consumers who are willing to pay a little bit more for an all-natural product.

SRL plans to invest heavily in the launch of NaturalNew, and it wants to ensure that it has properly managed any risks that may arise in connection with the promotion and marketing of the product.

1. What legal issues arise in regard to the sale of NaturalNew directly to consumers?

2. What impact does the law have on the promotion of NaturalNew as an "all-natural" product with "no artificial ingredients"?

3. What product safety requirements, if any, apply to the manufacture and sale of NaturalNew?

4. How does the law affect SRL's intended marketing strategy?

Introduction

The previous chapter discussed the law as it applies to the sale of goods, and it was pointed out that the sale of goods legislation has certain limitations, particularly in respect to consumer transactions. This chapter begins with a discussion of how sale of goods legislation has been expanded to protect consumers. The discussion in the first part of this chapter then moves on to other aspects of consumer protection law, including laws that regulate unfair business practices, false and misleading advertising, direct marketing, product safety, packaging, and labelling. The second part of this chapter focuses on competition law, which is the area of law that aims to promote a fair and competitive marketplace, and prohibits business practices which are uncompetitive in nature.

There is some overlap between consumer protection law and competition law, because promoting a fair and competitive marketplace, to some degree, also protects consumers. Indeed, some aspects of competition law, such as laws against misleading advertising and false sale prices, are intended primarily to protect consumers.

The general theme that runs through both consumer protection law and competition law is that the law tries to achieve a balance between (1) the self-regulation inherent in the free market and (2) the protection of the marketplace as a whole along with its most vulnerable participants. The free market, when left completely unregulated, tends to lead to exploitative and monopolistic behaviour on the part of businesses, both of which frustrate the goal of promoting trade and commerce. Government regulation, on the other hand, increases the cost of doing business and creates barriers to entry. Where the balance between the free market and government regulation ought to be is a matter of some debate. The law tries to promote the free market while also imposing regulations on business in order to ensure fair competition and protect consumers.

Consumer Protection Law

Consumer protection law, as the name suggests, is primarily concerned with protecting the interests of consumers. The law recognizes that consumers are in need of greater protection than non-consumers, and this recognition is based on the assumption that consumers are at a disadvantage compared to businesses. Consumers may be at a disadvantage because they may have less bargaining power, they may not be as well informed, and they may not participate in transactions as frequently. However, the assumption that consumers are always in need of greater protection than businesses may not be true in every case. Nevertheless, consumer protection laws typically operate to protect only consumers, even if a particular consumer may be far more knowledgeable and experienced than a specific business.

As discussed in the previous chapter, all the provinces have recognized the need to address the limitations of the *Sale of Goods Act,* particularly as it affects consumers. However, consumer protection laws go much further and address a number of concerns, including: contracts for the provision of services (rather than goods), unfair trade practices (such as false or misleading advertising), particular types of consumer transactions (including direct sales and online agreements), consumer transactions in specific industries (such as time shares and fitness clubs), credit agreements, product safety standards, labelling and packaging requirements, and matters relating to remedies and enforcement.[1]

The goals of consumer protection laws are to protect consumers:

- in contracts for the purchase of goods and services.
- from unfair selling and marketing practices.
- from physical harm and injury.

Consumer

An individual who purchases goods or services primarily for personal, domestic or household purposes.

1 For example, *Consumer Protection Act,* SS 1996, c C-30.1, ss 39–75; *Consumer Product Warranty and Liability Act,* SNB 1978, c C-18.1; *Consumer Protection Act,* 2002, SO 2002, c 30, Schedule A.

PART SEVEN

It is also important to note that many businesses are regulated, largely for the benefit of consumers. Provincially regulated businesses include the sale of real estate, automobile repair, payday loans, funeral services, debt collection, and the sale of investment products. The methods used to ensure compliance vary, but typically involve registration and licensing (which often includes a mandatory education component and a minimum amount of experience), the posting of a performance bond which is forfeited in the event of non-compliance, and a set of standards which must be followed.

Expansion of Sale of Goods Law

Provincial consumer protection legislation supplements the *Sale of Goods Act* by effectively preventing the parties from excluding or modifying the implied conditions and warranties in consumer transactions. The approach in some provinces[2] has been to imply certain conditions and warranties similar to those contained in the *Sale of Goods Act* into all retail sales of consumer products and to prevent their exclusion. Other provinces[3] have adopted an approach that prevents the exclusion or modification of the *Sale of Goods Act* conditions and warranties in consumer transactions. For example, when SRL sells NaturalNew direct to consumers through its website, any attempt by SRL to exclude or modify the implied terms of the *Sale of Goods Act* will be unenforceable, even if the purchaser has agreed to exclude or modify those terms.

While there are some differences in the approaches various provinces have taken, overall the consumer protection statutes are quite similar. As a starting point, provincial consumer protection legislation has a broader scope than sale of goods laws because it applies to all forms of consumer transactions, not just the sale of goods. Protected transactions include leasing contracts, conditional sales contracts, and contracts for services. For example, in Ontario the law provides that there is an implied warranty, in any contract with a consumer for the provision of services, that the services supplied will be of reasonably acceptable quality.

In many provinces, privity of contract cannot be raised as a defence against the ultimate consumer. This means that a consumer may argue a breach of implied conditions and warranties against a manufacturer of goods, even though there is no contract in place between the manufacturer and consumer. Under the ordinary principles of common law, the doctrine of privity would deny the consumer a remedy unless negligence on the part of the manufacturer could be proven.

Unfair Practices

Provincial consumer protection legislation prohibits selling and marketing practices that are considered to be unfair, again on the assumption that consumers are in need of greater protection than businesses.[4] Unfairness typically arises in the context of unequal bargaining power. **Unfair practices** arise, for example, when a business intentionally

Unfair practices

Illegal business practices that exploit the unequal bargaining position of consumers.

- targets customers with physical infirmity, ignorance, illiteracy, inability to understand the language or the agreement, or other similar factors and who are therefore unable to understand the nature of the agreement.

---

2 *Consumer Protection Act*, CCSM c C200, s 58; *Consumer Protection Act*, RSNS 1989, c 92, ss 26, 28; *Consumer Protection Act*, RSNWT 1988, c C-17, s 70; *Consumer Protection Act*, RSY 2002, c 40, s 58.
3 *Sale of Goods Act*, RSBC 1996, c 410, s 20.
4 For example, *Business Practices and Consumer Protection Act*, SBC 2004, c 2; *Consumer Protection and Business Practices Act*, SNL 2009, c C-31.1; *Consumer Protection Act, 2002*, SO 2002, c 30, Schedule A; *Business Practices Act*, RSPEI 1988, c B-7; *Consumer Protection Act*, RSQ c P-40.1.

- sells at a price that grossly exceeds the price at which similar goods or services are readily available to similar consumers.
- engages in a calculated and cynical marketing scheme that subjects a consumer to undue pressure to enter into a transaction.
- persuades a consumer to buy where there is no reasonable probability of payment in full by the consumer.
- imposes terms and conditions on a proposed transaction which are so adverse to the consumer as to be inequitable.

An agreement with a consumer which results from an unfair practice may be rescinded by the consumer. If rescission is not possible, the consumer may recover damages or the amount by which the consumer's payment exceeds the value that the goods or services have to the consumer.

False or Misleading Claims—Provincial Laws

Every province prohibits the making of false, misleading, deceptive, or exaggerated claims in connection with a proposed sale to consumers. **False or misleading representation** may involve claims that

- goods or services are endorsed or sponsored, when they are not.
- goods or services have features, characteristics, or qualities that they do not have.
- goods are new, when they are used.
- goods are available or can be delivered, or services can be performed, when the person making the representation knows or ought to know that it is not true.
- a service or part is required, when it is not.
- a price constitutes a special price, when it does not.
- uses exaggeration, innuendo, or ambiguity as to a material fact, or fails to state a material fact, if such use or failure tends to deceive.

In most provinces, a consumer who has entered into a contract for a product or service as a result of a misrepresentation has the right to rescind the contract.[5]

In addition, the federal *Competition Act*[6] also prohibits the making of misleading representations to consumers. The *Competition Act* provisions on false and misleading claims will be dealt with in the second part of this chapter.

SRL will want to ensure that its promotional and advertising material does not contain representations which could be considered false, deceptive, or misleading. In addition, SRL should properly educate its salespeople regarding the features and attributes of its products, so that claims are not made to prospective buyers which would violate consumer protection laws.

Direct Marketing

Direct marketing is a broad concept that includes a variety of sales approaches. The common theme is that it is the seller who initiates contact with the prospective purchaser, rather than the other way around. Traditional techniques used in

False or misleading representation

A promotional statement made to a consumer that is false, deceptive, or misleading.

---

5 For example, in Ontario, the making of a false, misleading, or deceptive representation is deemed to be an unfair practice, with the result that the same remedies are available to an affected consumer.
6 RSC 1985, c C-34.

direct marketing include **door-to-door selling**, promotional letters, and telemarketing. Increasingly, electronic methods are being used for direct marketing, such as cell phone text messaging, emails, and interactive consumer oriented websites. Legislation traditionally focused on door-to-door selling. However, over time the law has evolved to address other types of direct sales.

The provinces take different approaches to regulating door-to-door selling. In many provinces, door-to-door salespeople must be registered and must post a performance bond which may be forfeited in the event of non-compliance with the law. In other provinces, consumers who sign contracts with door-to-door sellers are entitled to a statutory "cooling-off" period, during which they may cancel the contract for any reason without further obligation.[7] In addition, in most provinces direct sales contracts over a specific minimum amount must be in writing and the consumer must receive a copy of the written contract in order for it to be enforceable.

Telemarketing activities which are regulated by law include the making of unsolicited telephone calls to consumers. **Telemarketing** is regulated primarily by the *Competition Act,* but there are other federal and provincial laws[8] which also govern the making of unsolicited telephone calls.[9] Deceptive telemarketing will be discussed in the second part of this chapter.

Online Sales

Selling directly to consumers online is the fastest-growing area of retailing in Canada.[10] As would be expected, a number of legal issues are raised in connection with online sales. Generally, online retailers must comply with the laws that apply to traditional retailers: the provisions of the *Sale of Goods Act,* consumer protection legislation, the *Competition Act,* the new Canadian anti-spam legislation, and the principles of common law that apply to all business relationships such as contract law and tort law. However, there are some areas in which online sales raise legal issues that are different from those faced by traditional retailers. For example:

- websites come and go, and the physical location of the vendor is often unknown. Where will a consumer go to obtain a refund or complain about a defective product?

- online retailers typically collect and use more private information that is supplied by consumers. As a result, online vendors must be careful to comply with laws regarding the collection, use, storage, and disclosure of private or personal information.

- recently, there have been a number of well publicized breaches of security at major online retailers. Online retailers must be careful to ensure that the financial information of their customers, particularly credit card information, is safe and secure.

---

7 For example, *Fair Trading Act,* RSA 2000, c F-2; *Direct Sellers' Regulation Act,* RSNS 1989, c 129, *Consumer Protection Act,* S.O. 2002, c 30. In Alberta, Nova Scotia, and Ontario, the cooling-off period is 10 days. In Ontario, the cooling-off period has been expanded to apply to payments made in advance to join a gym or fitness club, payday loans, and the purchase of time shares.

8 For example, in British Columbia, the Telemarketer Licensing Regulation under the *Business Practices and Consumer Protection Act,* [SBC 2004], c 2.

9 Competition Bureau of Canada, "What you should know about telemarketing," online: Competition Bureau Canada <http://www.competitionbureau.gc.ca/eic/site/cb-bc.nsf/eng/03127.html>.

10 Brenda Bouw, "Pace of online sales growing five times more than traditional retail: report," *Yahoo! Finance Canada,* (8 July 2014) online: <https://ca.finance.yahoo.com/blogs/dashboard/pace-online-sales-growing-five-times-more-traditional-161549631.html>.

- it may be difficult to determine the jurisdiction in which an online retailer is actually carrying on its business. What happens if something goes wrong? Which laws apply? What court will have jurisdiction?

The challenge the law faces, similar to other areas of consumer protection law, is to provide sufficient security and regulation of online transactions without stifling the enormous commercial potential of ecommerce.

All the provinces have now adopted laws based on the *Internet Sales Contract Harmonization Template*, as discussed in Chapter 8. Ontario's *Consumer Protection Act*[11] has special provisions for Internet agreements and requires disclosure of specified information about the goods or services, dispute resolution limits, contract terms, an express opportunity to accept or decline the contract, a copy of the contract in written or electronic form, the right to cancel the contract within a specified time, and the right to refunds from sellers and credit card companies.

BUSINESS AND LEGISLATION

CANADA'S ANTI-SPAM LAW

On July 1, 2014, Canada's federal anti-spam law (CASL) came into effect.[12] The CASL is an ambitious attempt by the federal government to establish a regulatory framework to protect electronic commerce in Canada. The legislation prohibits unsolicited commercial electronic mail (spam) unless an exemption applies or the recipient has consented to receive the message. The CASL also regulates the unauthorized installation of computer programs.

The new law has serious ramifications for all organizations that do business in Canada or promote their goods and services in Canada. It is expected that the costs of compliance for organizations will be substantial. Generally, commercial electronic messages are not allowed unless the recipient has "opted in," or consented in advance to receive the message. In addition, all commercial electronic messages are required to have an unsubscribe link. The CASL is widely recognized as one of the strictest anti-spam regimes in the world. Businesses must now turn their minds to understanding, and complying with, the new rules.

The CASL also contains extensive anti-spyware and anti-malware provisions[13] because, as the government of Canada notes:[14]

Spam has become the primary vehicle for the delivery of online threats, such as spyware, malware and phishing. Spyware is software that collects information about a user and/or modifies the operation of a user's computer without the user's knowledge or consent. Malware is a general term for all forms of harmful and malicious content, especially hostile software such as viruses, worms and Trojan horses. Phishing involves impersonating a trusted person or organization in order to steal someone's personal information, generally for the purpose of identity theft.

Collectively, these online threats disrupt online commerce and reduce business and consumer confidence in the online marketplace; congest networks, imposing heavy costs on network operators and users, and threatening network reliability and security; and undermine personal privacy.

11 *Consumer Protection Act, 2002*, SO 2002, c 30, Schedule A. See Eva Chan, "*Consumer Protection Act* creates a major increase in consumer rights", The *Lawyers Weekly* (2 June 2006) 9.

12 S.C. 2010, c 23.

13 For discussion, see Barry Sookman, "Don't forget about the computer program 'malware' and 'spyware' provisions" (7 April 2014) online: Barry Sookman <http://www.barrysookman.com/tag/malware/>.

14 Industry Canada, "Government of Canada Introduces Anti-Spam Legislation (CASL)" (15 February 2013 date last modified) online: Government of Canada <https://www.ic.gc.ca/eic/site/ecic-ceac.nsf/eng/gv00521 .html#q3>.

PART SEVEN

The CASL will be enforced by three organizations: the CRTC, which will investigate and take action against the sending of spam and the installation of unauthorized computer programs; the Competition Bureau, which will address misleading and deceptive practices and representations online; and the Office of the Privacy Commissioner, which will take measures against the collection of personal information and the unauthorized compiling or supplying of lists of electronic addresses.

Violations of the new law may lead to penalties of up to $1 million for individuals and $10 million for others. In addition, the law provides for civil damages including personal liability for directors and officers of offending corporations.

The new law is not without critics. Some have argued that the costs of compliance will outweigh the benefits of reducing spam. Others have argued that the rules will not be able to be effectively enforced. Finally, it has been suggested that the burden of compliance with the complex regulations will disproportionately affect small and medium-sized businesses.

Critical Analysis: Is anti-spam legislation necessary? Are the benefits to be gained by prohibiting spam worth the significant costs to businesses? Can anti-spam laws really be enforced in the real world?

Sources: David Canton, "CASL Observations", *Slaw* (14 May 2014) online: Slaw <http://www.slaw.ca/2014/05/07/casl-observations>; Julius Melnitzer, "Canada's anti-spam law comes into effect in July, 2014", *Financial Post* (4 December 2013) online: *Financial Post* <http://business.financialpost.com/2013/12/04/canadas-anti-spam-law-comes-into-effect-in-july-2014>; Brenda Bouw, "New anti-spam law 'a big deal' for small businesses", *The Globe and Mail* (24 March 2014) online: Globe and Mail <http://www.theglobeandmail.com/report-on-business/small-business/sb-digital/biz-categories-technology/businesses-rush-to-comply-with-tough-new-anti-spam-law/article17609044/>.

Packaging and Labelling

Package design and labelling are important business concerns. Packaging should protect the product and should be convenient for shipping, storage, and display. Packaging and labelling are also used to attract customers. However, package design and labelling must comply with applicable laws and regulations. The information on package labels may be relevant in determining whether a manufacturer has breached the required standard of care for product liability. Trademark law[15] may also affect package design.[16]

Most packaging and labelling legislation is federal and therefore applies throughout the country.[17] Some legislation is industry specific—for example, the *Food and Drug Act*,[18] the *Textile Labelling Act*,[19] and the *Tobacco Act*.[20] Other legislation regulates consumer products generally. The most comprehensive legislation is the *Consumer Packaging and Labelling Act* (CPLA),[21] which sets out minimum packaging and labelling requirements for all prepackaged goods sold in

---

15 Trademarks are discussed in Chapter 18.
16 See Canadian Food Inspection Agency, "The Use of Trade-Marks in Labelling of Foods Sold in Canada" (27 April 2012), online: Canadian Food Inspection Agency <http://inspection.gc.ca/food/labelling/other-requirements/trade-marks/eng/1335544176482/1335544253720>.
17 The principal exception to this is the Quebec language legislation, most importantly that found in s 51 of the *Charter of the French Language*, RSQ c C-11. Otherwise, provincial legislation tends to apply to specialized industries such as alcohol, milk, and margarine.
18 RSC 1985, c F-27.
19 RSC 1985, c T-10. See Competition Bureau of Canada, *Guide to the Textile Labelling and Advertising Regulations* (September 2000), online: Competition Bureau Canada <http://www.competitionbureau.gc.ca/eic/site/cb-bc.nsf/eng/01249.html>.
20 SC 1997, c 13.
21 RSC 1985, c C-38. See also Competition Bureau of Canada, *Guide to the Consumer Products Labelling Act and Regulations: Enforcement Guidelines* (October 1999), online: Competition Bureau Canada <http://www.competitionbureau.gc.ca/eic/site/cb-bc.nsf/eng/01248.html>.

Canada (other than drugs, cosmetics, and medical devices, which are regulated by the *Food and Drug Act*).

The CPLA encourages fair competition between manufacturers and other sellers by ensuring that consumers can compare the price and quantity of products. The CPLA is enforced by Health Canada and the Canada Food Inspection Agency for food products and by the Competition Bureau for non-food products.

The CPLA requires manufacturers to provide consumers with certain essential information, including a generic description of the goods, the net quantity, and the identity of the manufacturer or importer of the goods. Manufacturers must also eliminate any misleading information about the nature or quantity of the product that might flow either from statements made on the container or from the shape or size of the container. For example, goods cannot be labelled "Made in Canada" or "Product of Canada" unless they meet specific requirements.[22]

Much of the information required by law must be disclosed in both French and English. In addition, the regulations can be very specific. For example, wrapping paper, aluminum foil, and paper towels (bi-dimensional products) must be described in appropriate units—square metres, or dimensions of roll, ply, and the number of perforated individual units for paper towels. All information must be prominently and clearly presented. Without this information, prospective purchasers may have to guess about the quantity being purchased, and a manufacturer might be tempted to make the product look bigger than it really is.

Some products are inherently hazardous, so the information related to the product should include sufficient warning of any hazards, special instructions for handling or using the product, and critical information about what to do if the product causes harm to the user. Examples of potentially hazardous or dangerous products are chemicals such as household cleaners or petroleum distillates and a wide range of goods, such as pressurized metal cans, flammable carpets, baby cribs, car seats, tents, cigarette lighters, and children's sleepwear. The potential danger to children of these products has major implications for packaging and labelling. Containers must be childproof or child-resistant and must be clearly labelled to warn adults of the dangers to children.

Product Safety

Consumer products may pose serious safety risks and there have been several incidents in recent years where consumers have suffered harm as a result of dangerous products, including children's toys painted with lead-based paint, prescription drugs with serious side effects, contaminated food, and defective car seats for babies and toddlers. In 2011, the *Consumer Product Safety Act* (CPSA)[23] came into force in order to address concerns over the safety of consumer products.

What is the purpose of the information on this container?

22 See Competition Bureau, "'Product of Canada' and 'Made in Canada' Claims", (22 December 2009) online: Competition Bureau Canada <http://www.competitionbureau.gc.ca/eic/site/cb-bc.nsf/eng/03169.html>.
23 SC 2010, c 21.

FEDERAL CONSUMER PRODUCT SAFETY LEGISLATION

Prior to the CPSA, there were standards for product safety, but manufacturers were left to monitor their own products. Importers were responsible for determining the safety and quality of the products they imported. Information provided to consumers through labels, warnings, or advertising claims was not vetted in advance, but merely subject to complaints of inaccuracy by consumers or competitors. Regulators had little authority to remove products from store shelves or issue recalls. Violators were rarely caught. Penalties for serious violations were seldom levied.

In June 2011, the *Consumer Product Safety Act (CPSA) came into force and replaced the previous law,* Part 1 of the *Hazardous Products Act.* The *CPSA* creates a new system to regulate consumer products that might pose a danger to human health and safety. The purpose of the CPSA is to protect the public by addressing or preventing dangers to human health or safety that are posed by consumer products in Canada. The CPSA:

- prohibits the manufacture, importation, advertisement, or sale of consumer products that constitute a danger to human health or safety.
- prohibits misleading claims on packages, labels, or advertising as they relate to health or safety.
- provides authority to order the testing and evaluation of consumer products to verify compliance.
- requires manufacturers, importers, and sellers to report dangerous incidents, product defects, inadequate labels, and product recalls.

- authorizes entrance to private property, inspection, and seizure of products to verify compliance or noncompliance.
- enables government to institute and enforce corrective measures, including product recalls.
- provides for criminal penalties up to $5 million and administrative penalties up to $25 000.

It is too early to determine whether the *CPSA* will achieve its goal of protecting the public from dangerous consumer products. It is also not yet clear whether the greater accountability required of manufacturers, importers, and sellers of consumer products will be enforced. Some questions are:

- is the CPSA comprehensible to the consumers who are meant to be protected, the businesses who are meant to comply with the rules, and the regulators who will enforce the rules?
- will businesses see sufficient benefit in complying with the new rules?
- will government devote adequate resources to enforcement?
- will consumer complaints be investigated and disposed of in a timely and appropriate manner?
- will the increased penalties for violators act as an effective deterrent?

Critical Analysis: How effective can the law be in dealing with dangerous and unsafe products? How does the growth of global trade make the problem more challenging?

Sources: Health Canada, *Canada Consumer Product Safety Act Quick Reference Guide* (2011), online: Health Canada <http://www.hc-sc.gc.ca/cps-spc/pubs/indust/ccpsa_ref-lcspc/index-eng.php#a8>; Luis Millan, "The new consumer safety law", *The Lawyers Weekly* (19 August 2011).

Product Design and Manufacture

There are laws that protect inventions and product design.[24] For example, if another business has obtained a patent in respect to the formulation of a product, or registered a particular industrial design, another business cannot manufacture

---

24 Patents and industrial designs are discussed in Chapter 18.

What legal challenges are presented by the design of this product?

or sell products which infringe those rights without a licence from the registered patent or industrial design owner.

In addition, organizations such as the Canadian Standards Association (CSA) develop voluntary guidelines for use by both producers and users of goods. Guidelines are developed with the assistance of a broad range of experts, including representatives from industry.[25] These guidelines may be adopted by regulators as mandatory standards, and they will typically represent the measure of the standard of care for tort liability.

All businesses should be familiar with the voluntary guidelines and mandatory standards that apply to the goods and services that they provide. Legislation imposes minimum standards for many goods and services where it is considered to be in the public interest to reduce the risk of harm. For example,

- the *Motor Vehicle Safety Act* regulates the manufacture and importation of motor vehicles and motor vehicle equipment.[26]
- broad categories of products such as food and drugs cannot be sold if they are unsafe or if they fail to meet approved standards.[27]
- it is now illegal under the CPSA to manufacture, import, advertise, or sell a consumer product which poses a danger to human health or safety as a result of normal or foreseeable use of the product.

Businesses may consider regulations and voluntary guidelines to be impediments, but they are better viewed as the collective opinion of specialists in risk assessment. Viewed in this light, they are a valuable resource for producers like SRL. Ignoring the standards would seriously compromise SRL's marketplace reputation and significantly increase its exposure to legal liability.

---

25 *The Standards Council of Canada Act*, RSC 1985, c S-16, s 3 creates a Standards Council, which, in turn, accredits bodies, including the CSA, online:<http://www.scc.ca> that create different standards. The CSA also provides testing and certification of products under its brand name CSA International. The international standard-setting body is the International Organization for Standardization (ISO).

26 SC 1993, c 16.

27 *Food and Drugs Act*, RSC 1985, c F-27 (*FDA*).

PART SEVEN

Advertising Standards

Most businesses promote their goods and services using some form of advertising. Advertising must not violate the prohibitions against false or misleading claims, as discussed elsewhere in this chapter. In addition, there are important voluntary standards with which most advertisers choose to comply. Advertising Standards Canada (ASC) is an organization established by the advertising community to promote public confidence in its products and services. The Canadian Broadcast Standards Council (CBSC) is a council supported by the Canadian Association of Broadcasters (CAB) with the approval of the Canadian Radio-television and Telecommunications Commission (CRTC).

The ASC addresses advertising in general and has a detailed code of industry guidelines. It provides a mechanism for public complaints concerning violations of that code, as well as business-to-business complaints. Complaints are investigated and, if found to be valid, result in a finding that the advertiser should change or remove the offending promotion. Since this is a voluntary process, enforcement relies on moral suasion. However, findings are publicized, and members of the advertising community generally have been reluctant to ignore a ruling made against them by their peers. For example, in 2011 the ASC ruled on a complaint concerning a billboard advertisement for a radio morning show that featured a close-up of a woman wearing a tight T-shirt. Printed across the chest of her T-shirt were the words "Pray For More Rain." The Council found "that this advertisement demeaned and denigrated women and encouraged, gratuitously and without merit, attitudes that offended standards of decency among a significant segment of the population."[28]

The CBSC has an equivalent code of ethics and complaints process, dealing specifically with promotion in broadcast media. In addition, it has developed more specialized codes, such as those related to sexual stereotyping and violence. The Television Bureau of Canada (TBC) is a self-regulating, not-for-profit association that acts as a resource centre for Canadian television broadcasters and approves television commercials before they are broadcast.

NaturalNew is a product involving inherent risks that need to be managed. People may have allergic or other harmful reactions to the product. Consumers may use the product for purposes for which it is not intended. A batch of product which is defective in some way may give rise to product liability claims in negligence. Competitors may claim that SRL has infringed their intellectual property rights in regard to a trademark, patent, or industrial design. However, if SRL ensures that NaturalNew is properly manufactured, and packages and labels it appropriately, they will have managed these risks and minimized the likelihood of encountering legal problems.

Competition Law

The goals of competition law are to

- promote a fair, competitive and efficient marketplace.
- strengthen businesses' ability to adapt and compete in global markets.
- give small and medium-sized businesses the ability to compete in the marketplace.
- provide consumers with competitive prices, product choices, and the information they need to make informed buying decisions.

---

28 Advertising Standards Council, "Recent Complaint Case Summaries," online: Advertising Standards Canada <http://www.adstandards.com/en/standards/adComplaintsreportscurrent.asp>.

Similar to consumer protection law, competition law seeks to achieve a balance between the interests of consumers and producers. Competition law also tries to achieve a balance between wholesalers and retailers, dominant market players and minor players, and public and private interests.

The primary source of competition law in Canada is the federal *Competition Act*,[29] which has its origins in antitrust legislation passed first in 1889.[30] The *Competition Act* is administered and enforced by the Commissioner of Competition, who is the head of the Competition Bureau, which in turn is a part of Industry Canada. The Commissioner publishes a wide range of bulletins and guidelines, along with an annual report that describes the Bureau's activities. The Commissioner is also responsible for administering and enforcing the *Consumer Packaging and Labelling Act*,[31] the *Textile Labelling Act*,[32] and the *Precious Metals Marking Act*.[33]

Practices that are regulated by the *Competition Act* are either criminal or civil in nature. Criminal matters are of a more serious nature than civil matters, which are also called "reviewable" matters. Examples of criminal offences are materially false or misleading representations made knowingly or recklessly, price fixing, and deceptive telemarketing. Under the criminal process, alleged offences are investigated by the Bureau, and evidence obtained in criminal matters can be referred by the Commissioner to the Attorney General of Canada, who may decide to prosecute, as is the normal practice with criminal matters. The accused may also consent to a course of action to avoid prosecution.

Examples of reviewable matters are misleading advertising, discriminatory practices, and abuse of dominant position. The civil process was developed to address concerns about the time required for and the difficulty of proving criminal cases. The primary purpose of the civil process is to stop the anticompetitive activity. The Competition Bureau will typically seek an order prohibiting the reviewable activity. Those found responsible may also be ordered to publish an information notice and pay an administrative penalty. Any violation of an order may itself be a criminal offence. While the penalties are not as severe as in criminal matters, civil reviewable matters are easier to resolve since proof of criminal intent is not necessary.

A recent example of a settlement under the *Competition Act* concerned misrepresentations by Bell Canada about the prices offered for services. The Competition Bureau found that for several years Bell had charged higher prices than advertised for home phone, Internet, TV, and wireless services by hiding additional mandatory fees in fine print disclaimers. Bell agreed to modify its non-compliant ads and pay the maximum administrative penalty of $10 million.[34]

For reviewable matters, the accused may defend by arguing that she exercised due diligence. **Due diligence** is what a reasonable person would have done in similar circumstances. If the accused reasonably believed in a mistaken set of facts which, if true, would render the act or omission innocent, or if the accused took all reasonable steps to avoid the particular event, then there will be no civil liability, because a civil duty does not require greater diligence than what would have been reasonable in the circumstances.[35]

Due diligence

A defence based on adopting reasonable steps to avoid the violation of a legal duty.

29 *Competition Act*, RSC 1985, c C-34.
30 *Act for the Prevention and Suppression of Combinations Formed in the Restraint of Trade*, SC 1889, c 41.
31 RSC 1985, c C-38.
32 RSC 1985, c T-10.
33 RSC 1985, c P-19.
34 Competition Bureau of Canada, "Competition Bureau reaches agreement with Bell Canada" (28 June 2011) online: Competition Bureau Canada <http://www.competitionbureau.gc.ca/eic/site/cb-bc.nsf/eng/03388 .html>.
35 *R v Sault Ste Marie (City)*, [1978] 2 SCR 1299 at para 60.

The *Competition Act* also allows for civil actions to be brought by individuals or commercial complainants who are harmed by the actions of competitors. In such cases, the complainant may seek an injunction in addition to any damages incurred.

Mergers, Acquisitions, and Takeovers

An important responsibility of the Competition Bureau is the review of proposed mergers, acquisitions, and takeovers. In Canada, it is recognized that there is a fine line between allowing business to expand through merger, acquisition, or takeover in order to operate profitably in what is a relatively small but geographically dispersed market, and avoiding the negative consequences of what might through these processes become harmful, monopolistic behaviour. Under the *Competition Act,* mergers of all sizes and in all sectors of the economy are subject to review by the Commissioner to determine whether they will likely result in a substantial lessening or prevention of competition. What is considered "substantial" by the Bureau is described in its guidelines[36] as the result of material increase in prices that is not likely to be offset by increased efficiency in the market.

If the size of a proposed merger exceeds the pre-notification threshold,[37] the businesses proposing the merger must notify the Commissioner of their intentions prior to the merger. If the Commissioner has concerns about the merger, the parties may be ordered to provide further information. Within a specified time the parties are provided with a determination as to whether the Commissioner considers that the merger will substantially lessen or prevent competition. The Commissioner then decides whether the merger can proceed as notified, only on specified conditions, or not at all.[38]

False or Misleading Claims—Federal Laws

The provincial laws regarding false or misleading claims were discussed in the first part of this chapter. This discussion focuses on the rules against the making of false or misleading claims that are found in the federal *Competition Act*.

The *Competition Act* defines a false or misleading claim as occurring when a person for the purpose of promoting, directly or indirectly, the supply or use of a product or for the purpose of promoting, directly or indirectly, any business interest, by any means whatever, makes a representation to the public that is false or misleading in a material respect.[39]

This provision is stated in broad terms so as to capture not only those who deliberately make false statements, but also those who push the limits of truth— intentionally or otherwise—in the impressions given to buyers.

Falsity is judged by an objective test. Whether or not a statement is misleading is measured by the impression that might be formed by an ordinary member of the group of persons to whom the statement is directed. What is important is the impression created by the advertisement in its entirety, including illustrations

---

36   Competition Bureau of Canada, "Merger Enforcement Guidelines" (6 October 2011), online: Competition Bureau Canada <http://www.competitionbureau.gc.ca/eic/site/cb-bc.nsf/eng/03420.html>.

37   As of 2014, the pre-merger notification threshold was $82 million, increased from $80 million in 2013. See Competition Bureau of Canada, "2014 Pre-Merger Notification Transaction Size-Threshold" (20 January 2014), online: Competition Bureau Canada <http://www.competitionbureau.gc.ca/eic/site/cb-bc.nsf/eng/03646.html>.

38   For an example of a ruling on a takeover, see Competition Bureau of Canada, "Competition Bureau Statement on Bell and Rogers' Acquisition of Maple Leaf Sports & Entertainment" (2 May 2012), online: Competition Bureau Canada <http://www.competitionbureau.gc.ca/eic/site/cb-bc.nsf/eng/03464.html>.

39   Other federal legislation tends to focus on specific issues. For example, the *Consumer Packaging and Labelling Act*, RSC 1985, c C-38, prohibits misleading advertising, specifically in the context of prepackaged goods; it would be misleading to describe the product box as "full" or "large" if this is not the case.

and disclaimers.[40] The misrepresentation must be "material"—that is, it must apply to statements that entice prospective purchasers to the place of business or that influence the customer's decision to purchase the particular item. For example, a fitness company admitted that by failing to disclose additional mandatory fees in its advertising of membership offers in newspapers, billboards, and storefront signs, it had led consumers to believe that the price of memberships was significantly less than the actual price.[41]

False or misleading claims may be treated as either criminal or civil matters, depending on whether the misrepresentations were made knowingly or recklessly.

There are more specific guidelines for particular types of advertising. One example is environmental or "green" advertising.

ETHICAL CONSIDERATIONS

ENVIRONMENTAL CLAIMS IN ADVERTISING

Consumers are becoming increasingly aware of the environmental consequences of their consumption of products. Accordingly, they are attracted to environmentally friendly products and producers. Marketers are keen to cater to this development in the marketplace and may be tempted to overstate the environmental features of their products. This has become known as "greenwashing."

The CSA has adopted international standards on environmental labelling. To assist business in interpreting this standard, the CSA and the Competition Bureau developed a best practices guide, *Environmental Claims: A Guide for Industry and Advertisers*.[42] It contains detailed advice regarding three aspects of environmental claims:

- claims that imply general environmental improvement are insufficient and should be avoided.
- claims should be clear, specific, and accurate, and contain no misleading information.
- claims must be verified and substantiated with supporting data that is accurate and available for scrutiny.

In terms of sustainability in the context of wood, for example, the statement "This wood comes from a forest that is certified to a sustainable forest management standard published by CSA" is preferred. The statement "This wood is sustainable" is discouraged.

Although the guide is not law, following its advice will help businesses avoid making misleading claims and the bureau will use the guide to assess environmental advertising. Potential penalties are the same as those for contravention of the misleading advertising provisions of the *Competition Act* under the criminal and civil regimes.

Applying the guidelines, the Bureau has taken action against a number of hot tub and spa retailers regarding claims that their products were eligible for ENERGY STAR certification, an international standard. In fact, no products of this type for sale in Canada are eligible for this certification. Two retailers signed a consent agreement, in which they agreed to cease the misleading misrepresentations, pay

---

40 For example, a Vancouver career management company made representations to prospective clients that created the false impression that they had an extensive network of personal contacts in the corporate world. See Competition Bureau of Canada, "Federal Court of Appeal rules that career management firm misled vulnerable job seekers" (16 October 2009), online: Competition Bureau Canada <http://www.competitionbureau.gc.ca/eic/site/cb-bc.nsf/eng/03144.html>.

41 Competition Bureau of Canada, "Premier Fitness undisclosed fees investigation successfully concluded" (27 November 2007), online: Competition Bureau Canada <http://www.competitionbureau.gc.ca/eic/site/cb-bc.nsf/eng/02518.html>.

42 Competition Bureau of Canada, "Environmental Claims: A Guide for Industry and Advertisers" (25 June 2008), online: Competition Bureau Canada <http://www.competitionbureau.gc.ca/eic/site/cb-bc.nsf/eng/02701.html>.

an administrative penalty of $130 000, publish corrective notices, and develop a corporate compliance program.

Companies must be careful when making environmental claims about their products, and the claims they make must be clear, specific, accurate, and not misleading.

Critical Analysis: Will business use these guidelines to improve the quality of environmental advertising? Are consumers likely to receive the information they need to make environmentally sensitive buying choices?

Sources: Tom Bruursema, "Environmental Claims: What does green really mean?" (22 August 2012), online: GreenGoPost <http://green gopost.com/environmental-claims-what-does-green-really-mean>; Competition Bureau of Canada, "Spa retailers required to stop making false ENERGY STAR claims" (17 January 2011), online: Competition Bureau Canada <http://www.competitionbureau.gc.ca/eic/site/cb-bc.nsf/eng/03342.html>.

In addition to the general prohibition against false or misleading claims, the *Competition Act* prohibits or regulates a number of specific marketing practices, many of which are related to false or misleading claims. Some of these are discussed below.

Deceptive Telemarketing

In 2008, the Canadian Radio-television and Telecommunications Commission (CRTC) launched the National Do Not Call List (DNCL). Telemarketers are prohibited from calling consumers who have registered their phone numbers on the DNCL. Some organizations are exempt from the DNCL, including registered charities raising funds, newspapers looking for subscriptions, political parties and candidates, and companies collecting survey data. The DNCL does not apply to calls made to businesses, and it does not apply to calls made to consumers who have conducted business with the caller during the previous 18 months. All telemarketers must be registered with the DNCL, even if they are exempt. Telemarketers must disclose the reason they are calling, on whose behalf the call is being made, and the type of product or business they are promoting. The penalties for violating the DNCL rules include fines of up to $1500 per violation for individuals and up to $15 000 per violation for corporations.

Telemarketing is not illegal, however, deceptive telemarketing is a criminal offence and offenders have been successfully prosecuted. For example, five Alberta individuals received significant prison sentences for their involvement in a deceptive scheme promoting business directories. Over three years, telemarketers used an "assumed sale" technique—convincing victims that they had already made a purchase and were obligated to pay. They defrauded as many as 10 000 businesses and organizations of an estimated $3.75 million. Charges were laid under the *Competition Act* and the *Criminal Code*. Sentences ranged from probation to two years in prison.[43]

In another case involving business directories, a Montreal man was sentenced to 18 months in prison for his involvement in a deceptive telemarketing scheme that targeted thousands of businesses and not-for-profit organizations across Canada and the United States.[44] The convicted business owner pleaded guilty to

---

43 Competition Bureau of Canada, "Five Alberta individuals sentenced in deceptive telemarketing scheme" (30 August 2011), online: Competition Bureau Canada <http://www.competitionbureau.gc.ca/eic/site/cb-bc.nsf/eng/03402.html>.

44 Competition Bureau of Canada, "Deceptive telemarketer receives 18-month prison sentence" (27 May 2014), online: Competition Bureau Canada <http://www.competitionbureau.gc.ca/eic/site/cb-bc.nsf/eng/03722.html>.

What are the legal issues raised in connection with telemarketing?

eight charges of misleading advertising and deceptive telemarketing under the *Competition Act* and one charge of possession of property obtained by crime under the *Criminal Code*. The scheme involved telemarketers contacting businesses and not-for-profit organizations, claiming that these organizations had previously ordered online business directory listings. By falsely implying a pre-existing business relationship, the telemarketers deceived the organizations into paying for listings they had not ordered.

Businesses may still choose to promote their goods and services through telemarketing which is not deceptive, but they must comply with the DNCL rules, which significantly limit the scope of promotional telemarketing activities.

False Sale or Bargain Prices

It is a reviewable offence for a seller to mislead consumers about the "ordinary" price of a product. Sellers must not advertise that a product is "on sale" when it is not. A seller may legitimately claim a price to be the regular price if either

- a substantial volume of the product has been sold at that regular price within a reasonable period of time before or after making the representation (volume test); or
- the product has been offered for sale in good faith at that regular price (or higher) for a substantial period of time before or immediately after making the representation (time test).

The Competition Bureau has taken the position that, for the volume test, a "substantial volume" means more than 50 percent of sales and a "reasonable period of time" means 12 months, and, for the time test, a "substantial period of time" means more than 50 percent of the six months before or after making the representation.

Stating that prices are "subject to error" provides protection only in the context of catalogue sales, since catalogues are not printed regularly and some protection is reasonable for the seller. Because this is a reviewable matter, the due diligence defence applies, and sellers should try to correct errors quickly and in a manner consistent with the original promotion.

Complaints regarding inflated "regular" prices have been common in recent years and have generated activity at the Competition Bureau. The *Sears* case was the first contested proceeding.

Canada (Commissioner of Competition) v Sears Canada Inc (2005), 37 CPR (4th) 65 (Competition Tribunal)

THE BUSINESS CONTEXT: Consumers are attracted by bargains. Retailers may be tempted to make their bargains appear as attractive as possible as they compete for consumer sales. The challenge for retailers is to fairly present the bargain price in comparison with the regular or ordinary price.

FACTUAL BACKGROUND: In 1999 Sears advertised five lines of all-season tires. The ads contained claims such as "save 40 percent" and "1/2 price" and drew comparisons between Sears's ordinary prices and its sale prices. During a lengthy investigation and hearing, Sears admitted that it failed to meet the volume test.

THE LEGAL QUESTION: Did Sears satisfy the time test in terms of good faith and substantial period of time?

RESOLUTION: The Tribunal concluded that good faith should be determined on a subjective basis—did Sears truly believe that its ordinary prices were genuine and *bona fide* prices, set with the expectation that the market would validate the prices as ordinary? Sears's claims of good faith were rejected based on its admission that it expected only 5–10 percent of the tires to be sold at the ordinary price; Sears's ordinary price was not competitive

What must this retailer ensure to avoid complaints about this sale?

in the market; and Sears could not track the number of tires sold at the ordinary price. In terms of substantial period of time, the Tribunal concluded that if a product is on sale more than half the time, then it has not been offered at its ordinary price for a substantial period of time.

Following the Tribunal's decision, Sears reached a settlement with the bureau regarding penalty. The Tribunal ordered Sears to pay an administrative penalty of $100 000 and costs in the amount of $387 000.

CRITICAL ANALYSIS: In other cases, prominent retailers agreed to pay substantial penalties, some in excess of $1 million. Have these high-profile cases altered the behaviour of retailers? Do consumers have confidence in advertised bargain prices?

Sale above Advertised Price

A civil provision of the Act prohibits the sale of a product at a price higher than advertised, unless the price was a mistake which was immediately corrected. Accordingly, sellers should take care to ensure that the prices charged for products are the same as the advertised prices. Note that this type of behaviour would not be an issue under contract law, because an advertised price is generally considered to be an invitation to treat rather than an offer to sell.

Double ticketing

The offence of failing to sell at the lower of the two or more prices marked on or otherwise appearing with regard to a product.

Double Ticketing

If there are two or more prices on a product, it must be sold at the lower of those prices. To do otherwise amounts to the criminal offence of **double ticketing**. Obligations extend to in-store promotions and displays, as well as prices listed in store computers. However, if consumers intentionally move the goods (or change pricing labels), they are committing fraud.

The Competition Bureau is particularly concerned about differentials between prices posted on store shelves and those stored in automatic price-scanning systems, since it is easy for customers to fail to notice an increased price at the checkout counter.

SCANNER PRICE ACCURACY VOLUNTARY CODE

In 2002, several Canadian retail associations launched this code to demonstrate their commitment to accurate scanner pricing. The associations involved are the Retail Council of Canada, the Canadian Association of Chain Drug Stores, the Canadian Association of Independent Grocers, and the Canadian Council of Grocery Distributors. The code acknowledges that incorrect prices can harm customer relations and attract legal sanctions. Its purposes are to demonstrate retailer commitment to scanner accuracy, provide retailers with a national framework, and provide a mechanism for consumer complaints. The code has been endorsed by the Competition Bureau. Over 5 000 retailers are voluntary participants.

Key aspects of the code are the following:

- the Item Free Scanner Policy, which states that, for claims that a scanned price exceeds the advertised or display price, the customer is entitled to the product free of charge where the correct price is less than $10; where the correct price is greater than $10, the customer is entitled to $10 off the correct price.

- retailers should correct errors as quickly as possible.

- retailers must establish appropriate internal policies, procedures, and training programs.

- clear and legible labels must be affixed to the shelf next to the product.

- clear and complete receipts must be provided to customers.

Scanning Code of Practice

If the scanned price of a non-price ticketed item is higher than the shelf price or any other displayed price, the customer is entitled to receive the first item free, up to a $10 maximum. If the item is more than $10 the customer is entitled to $10 off the lowest advertised or displayed price. If a Code of Practice problem cannot be resolved at the store level, please call 1-866-499-4599 to register your complaint.

Code de procédure d'application pour le balayage électronique

Dans le cas d'un article ne comportant pas d'étiquette de prix, si le prix affiché par le lecteur optique à la caisse est plus élevé que le prix sur les tablettes ou tout autre prix affiché, le client a le droit de recevoir le premier article gratuitement, si celui-ci ne coûte pas plus de 10 $. Si l'article en question coûte plus de 10 $, le client a droit à une remise de 10 $ sur le plus bas prix annoncé ou affiché. Si un problème relatif au Code volontaire sur la lecture optique des prix ne peut être réglé en magasin, veuillez composer (sans frais) le 1-866-499-4599 pour déposer une plainte.

Reprinted with permission of Competition Bureau Canada

Do people know that they have this type of protection?

- a Scanner Price Accuracy Committee is established to oversee the code.

- there is a multi-step consumer complaint process that culminates in arbitration.

There has been some criticism of the absence of accountability in the code. There is no effective way to discipline retailers that fail to follow the code and no independent review of how the code is working.

Critical Analysis: Do voluntary codes such as this one provide helpful strength to the provisions of the *Competition Act*? Can voluntary codes replace regulation and enforcement? Are you aware of this code?

Sources: Competition Bureau of Canada, "Consumers to be compensated for overcharged scanned purchases" (11 June 2002), online: Competition Bureau Canada <http://www.competitionbureau.gc.ca/eic/site/cb-bc.nsf/eng/03252.html>; Shauna Rempel, "Did the store overcharge you? No need to fume", *The Toronto Star* (14 October 2009), online: The Star <http://www.thestar.com/living/shopping/article/709716—did-the-store-overcharge-you-no-need-to-fume>.

Tests and Testimonials

Advertisers often promote products and services either by presenting supportive test results or by using the assurances of convincing spokespersons, either real or hypothetical. Tests must be carried out prior to the promotion. If conducted by a third

PART SEVEN

party, there must be permission to draw from the tests or they must already be in the public domain. Testimonials must be accurately stated and current, and the person providing the testimonial must have actually used or evaluated the product. Using a well-known personality to provide a testimonial will attract close scrutiny. If an advertiser uses an actor to represent a hypothetical product user, the statements made will be measured by the general provisions dealing with false or misleading claims.

Comparative Advertising

Comparative advertising is where providers of goods or services compare their offerings to those of their competitors, usually in terms of price, quality, features, or performance. Comparative advertising is not prohibited by the *Competition Act*, because when legitimately done it fosters competition. However, when comparative claims are made that are false or misleading, or when performance claims are made that cannot be substantiated, then it constitutes a violation of the Act. In addition, the Act allows for civil actions to be brought by individuals or commercial complainants who are harmed by the actions of competitors in the context of comparative advertising. Since stopping the advertising campaign is of primary importance, the complainant may seek an injunction in addition to any damages incurred. The Commissioner may also request a court to order restitution to those affected by false or misleading representations.

In recent years, there has been considerable litigation among telecommunications companies around claims about the speed and reliability of cellphone and Internet networks and services.[45]

Performance Claims

It is a reviewable matter under the *Competition Act* to make a performance claim that is not based on adequate and proper testing. This specific prohibition is in addition to the general prohibitions against false or misleading advertising described earlier. Tests must be conducted before the promotional statement is made, and the onus of proof that proper and adequate testing has been done rests with the person making the performance claim.

The Competition Bureau has set out a list of factors it will consider when determining whether testing has been "adequate and proper."[46] Performance claims are a frequent source of complaint to the Bureau.

BUSINESS APPLICATION OF THE LAW

UNJUSTIFIED PERFORMANCE CLAIMS

Optimistic claims about the performance of products are common, but the manufacturer cannot make claims about their effectiveness without proof of their truth. Here are three cases that involved claims relating to stress reduction, cancer treatment, and body slimming.

---

45 See Iain Marlow, "Bell Aliant sues Rogers over Internet ads", *The Globe and Mail* (15 February 2010), online: Globe and Mail <http://www.theglobeandmail.com/news/technology/bell-aliant-sues-rogers-over-internet -ads/article1468899/>; Simon Houpt, "Rogers ditching 'most-reliable' claim", *The Globe and Mail* (30 November 2009), online: Globe and Mail <http://www.theglobeandmail.com/globe-investor/rogers-ditching -most-reliable-claim/article1383253/>; and Bertrand Marotte and Simon Houpt, "Bell takes Videotron to court over 'fastest' claim", *The Globe and Mail* (30 April 2010), online: Globe and Mail <http://www.theglobeandmail .com/report-on-business/bell-takes-vidotron-to-court-over-fastest-claim/article1552315/>.
46 Competition Bureau of Canada, "Performance Representations not Based on Adequate and Proper Tests", online: Competition Bureau Canada <http://www.competitionbureau.gc.ca/eic/site/cb-bc.nsf/eng/00520.html>.

Lululemon Athletica, a manufacturer of yoga wear, claimed that its seaweed-based clothing would, upon contact with moisture, release minerals and vitamins into the skin to produce effects such as enhancing the blood supply to the skin, promoting skin cell regeneration, and reducing stress. Following complaints and investigation by the Bureau, Lululemon agreed to remove all claims alleging therapeutic benefits from its VitaSea line of clothing. The agreement included clothing tags, the company website, and information provided by store managers and employees. Lululemon also agreed to conduct a review of all of its promotional and marketing materials to ensure compliance with legal requirements.

In 2009, the Bureau took action against a number of advertisers as part of its education and enforcement initiative, Project False Hope, to target cancer-related health fraud online. Bioenergy Wellness Inc. was an Edmonton company that made claims online about magnetic pulse devices and infrared sauna treatments for cancer patients. The claims were not based on adequate and proper tests. The company and its director agreed to stop making the claims, offer refunds to customers, and post corrective notices.

Beiersdorf Canada is the Canadian distributor of Nivea products. The company misled consumers by claiming that its "My Silhouette" product would slim and reshape the body, causing a reduction of up to 3 centimetres on targeted body parts, and that use of the product would make skin more toned and elastic. Following investigation by the Bureau, Beiersdorf agreed to remove the product from stores, provide refunds to customers, pay an administrative penalty, and publish corrective notices. In the notice, Beiersdorf stated that "performance claims and testing related to Nivea 'My Silhouette' are supported by independent research, which has always complied with Canadian requirements and guidelines." The bureau objected to this statement as a violation of the agreement and it was removed.

Critical Analysis: Why are sellers tempted to make claims that they cannot support?

Sources: Competition Bureau of Canada, "Competition Bureau takes action against unproven cancer treatment sold online" (19 February 2009), online: Competition Bureau Canada <http://www.competitionbureau.gc.ca/eic/site/cb-bc.nsf/eng/02988.html>; Competition Bureau of Canada, "Competition Bureau requires maker of Nivea to correct inaccurate public statements related to Nivea consent agreement" (22 September 2011), online: Competition Bureau Canada <http://www.competitionbureau.gc.ca/eic/site/cb-bc.nsf/eng/03413.html>; Hollie Shaw, "Lululemon removes claims from VitaSea products" (16 November 2007), online: Financial Post < http://www.financialpost.com/story.html?id=f8a5fa39-bccb-4b13-80c1-fa073d703e6d>.

Bait and Switch

An unscrupulous promotional practice is "**bait and switch**". The product is advertised at a very low price (the bait) but the supply is insufficient to meet expected demand. When consumers ask for the product, they are informed that the product is "not in stock," "of poor quality," or "inferior to Product B." They are then persuaded to purchase the higher-priced or higher-margin Product B (the switch). It is, of course, Product B that the promoter intended to sell all along. This is a reviewable practice under the *Competition Act*. This is the reason that some advertised specials state the number of items that are available at the sale price.

Bait and switch

Advertising a product at a very low price to attract customers, then encouraging them to buy another product that is more expensive.

Deceptive Prize Notices

It is a criminal offence under the *Competition Act* to notify a person that they have won a prize, or give them the general impression that they have won a prize, and ask for payment before the person can collect the prize.

In a recent case, the Supreme Court awarded damages in a claim based on a misleading magazine subscription contest.[47] Mr. Richard received a letter from *Time*

47 *Richard v Time Inc*, 2012 SCC 8 and see Cristin Schmitz, "*Caveat venditor* for advertisers", *The Lawyers Weekly* (9 March 2012) 2.

PART SEVEN

magazine that stated in bold letters at the top of the page "OUR SWEEPSTAKES RESULTS ARE NOW FINAL: MR. JEAN MARC RICHARD HAS WON A CASH PRIZE OF $833,337.00!" However, in fine print above that statement the letter said "If you have and return the Grand Prize winning entry in time and correctly answer a skill-testing question, we will announce that..." The same technique was used several times throughout the letter. Mr. Richard believed that he had won the grand prize, and it was not until later that he discovered the letter was merely announcing the contest. Mr. Richard sued and the trial court awarded him $1000 in compensation and $100 000 in punitive damages. The Quebec Court of Appeal overturned the ruling and dismissed the case, but the Supreme Court of Canada reversed the Court of Appeal decision and reinstated the trial decision, but reduced the amount of punitive damages to $15 000. The Supreme Court of Canada held that the letter from *Time* was specifically designed to mislead, and did mislead, Mr. Richard.

Pricing Conspiracies

Price is one of the most competitive variables in the marketplace. In a fair and competitive environment, price plays a central role in allowing buyers to make informed buying decisions among different producers and competing products. However, some producers may collude with competitors, take advantage of their strength in the market, or attempt to control prices at the retail level. The *Competition Act* prohibits these pricing practices. The objective of the legislation is to promote a level playing field with respect to pricing—that is, prices ought to be freely negotiated at all levels of distribution. To this end, the Act includes the criminal offences of price fixing and bid rigging, and makes price maintenance a reviewable activity.

Price Fixing

One way for business to manipulate a market is through conspiring with direct competitors to control prices. For example, assume there are only three suppliers of the tubes that SRL uses to package NaturalNew. SRL observes that all three suppliers quote identical prices for equivalent orders. Each supplier likely faces similar costs, and all three may have similar profit expectations. It could be, however, that this is part of a conspiracy to control the cost of the tubes to major buyers such as SRL. If this can be proven, the tube suppliers will be guilty of a criminal offence under the *Competition Act*. The **price fixing** offence is defined in these terms:

> Every person commits an offence who, with a competitor of that person with respect to a product, conspires, agrees or arranges...to fix, maintain, increase or control the price for the supply of the product.

The penalties for conviction were increased in 2010 to a maximum of 14 years' imprisonment and/or a fine of $25 million.

For a criminal offence to be proven, it must be established not only that there was an agreement or a conspiracy to set prices, but also that the agreement lessened competition. This latter requirement relates to the market structure (factors such as number of competitors and barriers to entry) and the behaviour of the parties (implementation of their agreement combined with market power).[48]

Convictions for price fixing have occurred mostly as a consequence of guilty pleas. As of 2012, Air France, KLM, Martinair, Qantas, British Airways, Cargolux, and Korean Air had all pleaded guilty to fixing air cargo surcharges for

Price fixing

Conspiring with competitors to fix the prices charged for goods or services.

---

48 See *R. v Nova Scotia Pharmaceutical Society et al,* [1992] 2 SCR 606.

shipments on certain routes from Canada.[49] The fines as a result of these convictions totalled over $22.6 million. In announcing the convictions, the Competition Bureau stated:

> Price-fixing conspiracies are, because of their secret nature, very difficult to detect and prove. Suspicions and identical prices are not enough to establish an offence. There must be evidence that competitors have agreed to set those prices.

Twenty-seven individuals and seven companies pleaded guilty to fixing the price of gasoline at the pumps in several Quebec towns. Fines totalled $3 million and six individuals were sentenced to a total of 54 months' imprisonment. This case constituted the largest criminal investigation in the history of the Bureau. Investigators seized over 100 000 records, searched 90 locations, and intercepted thousands of phone conversations.[50]

In connection with price fixing and other anticompetitive conduct, there is a growing volume of litigation in the form of private competition class actions by the purchasers who purchased products for the "fixed" prices. Even indirect purchasers—those who did not buy directly from co-conspirators—may be able to recover damages.

CASE

How Sweet It ... Isn't

THE BUSINESS CONTEXT: The chocolate industry is a very competitive industry, at least it is supposed to be. When producers want to increase revenues, they may be tempted to conspire with their competitors to charge artificially high prices. As long as all of them are charging the same price, they all win—until they get caught.

FACTUAL BACKGROUND: Between 2001 and 2009, four of the largest chocolate producers in Canada—Cadbury, Hershey, Nestlé, and Mars—are alleged to have illegally fixed the prices for chocolate. Purchasers sued the four producers in a class-action lawsuit for damages. In addition, the Competition Bureau brought criminal charges against all four producers.

THE LEGAL QUESTION: Did the defendants conspire illegally to fix and maintain the price of chocolate? Did their actions amount to criminal behaviour?

RESOLUTION: In 2013, all four producers agreed to settle the class-action lawsuit without

How can price fixing be proven?

admitting liability. The four defendants paid a total of $23 million pursuant to the settlement agreement to people who purchased chocolate between October 1, 2005, and September 1, 2007. The purchasers included both consumers and commercial buyers. Consumer claims not supported by receipts were capped at $50. In addition, 10 percent of the settlement funds were to be distributed to several not-for-profit organizations for the purposes of promoting

(Continued)

49 Competition Bureau of Canada, "Korean Air pleads guilty to price-fixing conspiracy" (19 July 2012), online: Competition Bureau Canada <http://www.competitionbureau.gc.ca/eic/site/cb-bc.nsf/eng/03482.html>.
50 Competition Bureau of Canada, "Six guilty pleas for fixing gas prices in Victoriaville" (13 April 2012), online: Competition Bureau Canada <http://www.competitionbureau.gc.ca/eic/site/cb-bc.nsf/eng/03459.html>.

competition and consumer education and advocacy in Canada.

Shortly before the settlement was reached, Hershey Canada pleaded guilty to the crime of price fixing and was fined $4 million. Hershey admitted that it had conspired, agreed, or arranged to fix the price of chocolate confectionary products in Canada, and agreed to cooperate with federal prosecutors.

CRITICAL ANALYSIS: Will results like this simply force unscrupulous sellers to be more secretive in their dealings with competitors? Is it ever appropriate for competitors to agree on the prices they intend to charge?

Sources: Canadian Press, *"Canadian chocolate makers to pay $23.2-million in price-fixing lawsuit"* (16 September 2013), The Globe and Mail: <http://www.theglobeandmail.com/report-on-business/canadian-chocolate-makers-to-pay-232-million-in-price-fixing-lawsuit/article14361922/>; Armina Ligaya, *"Criminal charges laid against Nestlé Canada, other companies for chocolate price fixing"*, (6 June 2013), Financial Post: <http://business.financialpost.com/2013/06/06/criminal-charges-laid-against-nestle-canada-other-companies-for-chocolate-price-fixing/>.

Bid Rigging

Bid rigging

Conspiring to fix the bidding process to suit the collective needs of those submitting bids.

Bid rigging is a specialized form of conspiracy by producers or suppliers to manipulate a market through price. **Bid rigging** occurs when suppliers conspire to fix the bidding process in a manner that suits their collective needs or wishes. No market impact need be proven. It is a serious criminal offence, since it attacks the heart of the competitive process. Bid rigging can take many forms, such as agreements to submit bids on a rotating basis or to split a market geographically.

Bid rigging investigations are not uncommon. For example, an Ottawa-based consulting company pleaded guilty to rigging bids for the supply of real estate consultants and experts for the federal government. Similar bids were submitted by related firms.[51] A Quebec company admitted to its role in rigging bids for private sector ventilation contracts for residential high-rise buildings in Montreal.[52]

Abuse of Dominant Position

Abuse of dominant position

A dominant company or group of companies engaging in anticompetitive behaviour that unduly prevents or lessens competition.

There is no law prohibiting a business from becoming dominant in its industry, but the law is concerned if that dominant position is achieved or maintained through activities that stifle competition in the industry.

Abuse of dominant position is reviewable conduct consisting of anticompetitive acts by a dominant company or group of companies that substantially prevents or lessens competition. Anticompetitive acts include buying up products to prevent the erosion of price levels, requiring suppliers to sell only to certain customers, and selling products below acquisition cost in order to discipline or eliminate competitors.

Price discrimination is a reviewable practice whereby a seller provides different pricing terms and conditions to competing customers for equivalent volume sales at an equivalent time. This situation may arise either because a producer

---

51 Competition Bureau of Canada, "Company pleads guilty to bid-rigging of federal government contracts" (30 July 2012), online: Competition Bureau Canada <http://www.competitionbureau.gc.ca/eic/site/cb-bc.nsf/eng/03484.html>.
52 Competition Bureau of Canada, "Guilty plea and $425,000 fine for bid-rigging in Montreal" (19 July 2011), online: Competition Bureau Canada <http://www.competitionbureau.gc.ca/eic/site/cb-bc.nsf/eng/03391.html>.

offers discriminatory prices, or, more commonly, because the producer responds to a customer's pressure tactics. The producer may see this as the only way of maintaining its dominant position in the market. Differential discounts are permitted provided it can be shown that customers who were prepared to purchase under equivalent conditions were offered the same terms. Any difference must be a direct reflection of cost differentials—say, in terms of volume or delivery.

Predatory pricing is also a reviewable matter and occurs when a seller sets prices unreasonably low with the intent of driving out its competition. This activity can occur at different levels of the distribution chain. What amounts to unreasonably low prices and predatory effect is seldom clear-cut. Most intervention by the Competition Bureau follows complaints made by competitors or concerned suppliers.

In order to take action for abuse of dominant position, the Competition Tribunal must find that the company or group of companies substantially controls the market under investigation, that those under investigation have engaged in a practice of anticompetitive acts, and that the practice has the effect of substantially lessening or preventing competition in the market. The Tribunal applies the civil burden of proof and has the authority to make orders stopping the particular behaviour. If these orders are ignored, penalties can be imposed. The threat of civil action may lead to a voluntary agreement between the offending party and the Bureau. Otherwise, the Tribunal may order the offender to take corrective action and may impose administrative penalties up to $10 million.[53]

Two high profile cases involved real estate agents and listings. The first case involved the Canadian Real Estate Association (CREA) and its restrictions on the use of the Multiple Listing Service (MLS) system. After several years of negotiation, the Commissioner challenged CREA's anticompetitive rules before the Competition Tribunal. The challenge alleged that the CREA rules imposed exclusionary restrictions that enabled it to maintain substantial control of the market, denying consumers the ability to choose their desired real estate services. Following the application, CREA and the Bureau reached a 10-year agreement, in which CREA agreed to eliminate its anticompetitive rules that discriminate against agents who want to offer less than full service.[54] In a related case, the Bureau filed a similar application in 2011 against the Toronto Real Estate Board (TREB) and its restrictions on the use of information from the Toronto MLS system.[55] The Competition Tribunal dismissed that application in 2013, but the Bureau successfully appealed that decision before the Federal Court of Appeal, which ruled in 2014 that the Tribunal must reconsider the Bureau's case.

Price Maintenance

A producer engages in reviewable conduct known as **price maintenance** by attempting to drive upward the final retail price at which its goods are sold to the public. The producer might do this by exerting pressure on the retailer or by placing notice on the goods themselves.

Price maintenance

The attempt to drive the final retail price of goods upward and the imposition of recriminations upon noncompliant retailers.

---

53 Competition Bureau of Canada, *"The Abuse of Dominance Provisions: Enforcement Guidelines"* (20 September 2012), online: Competition Bureau Canada <http://www.competitionbureau.gc.ca/eic/site/cb-bc.nsf/eng/03497.html>.

54 Competition Bureau of Canada, "Final Agreement Paves Way for More Competition in Canada's Real Estate Market" (24 October 2010), online: Competition Bureau Canada <http://www.competitionbureau.gc.ca/eic/site/cb-bc.nsf/eng/03305.html>.

55 Competition Bureau of Canada, "Supreme Court Denies Toronto Real Estate Board's Application for Leave to Appeal Pro-Competitive Federal Court of Appeal Ruling" (24 July 2014) online: Competition Bureau Canada <http://www.competitionbureau.gc.ca/eic/site/cb-bc.nsf/eng/03781.html>.

A producer may become concerned that widely advertised low prices for its products will damage its product image. As a result, it may warn retailers to stop dropping prices. It may also print on the packaging the "recommended retail price" and refuse to sell to any retailer who sells below that price.

Two aspects of this strategy are reviewable: the attempt to influence the final retail price upward and the recriminations against noncompliant retailers. Both constitute anticompetitive behaviour. The producer can suggest a recommended retail price, but cannot insist on that price as a minimum selling price.

There are some circumstances that justify price maintenance. A producer may refuse to sell to retailers that are selling at unreasonably low prices, provided it can show that the retailers were using its products in any of the following ways:

- as loss leaders (typically, below cost price).
- for bait and switch selling.
- in misleading advertising.
- in sales where they fail to provide a reasonable level of service.

A recent case under the price maintenance provisions involves Visa and MasterCard. In response to complaints from retail merchants, the Bureau launched an inquiry and in 2010 filed an application with the Tribunal regarding restrictive and anticompetitive rules.[56] The rules under challenge prohibit merchants from encouraging customers to consider lower fee payment options, require merchants to accept all cards from a company, and prohibit merchants from applying surcharges on purchases made with high-cost cards. Visa and MasterCard control 90 percent of credit card transactions in Canada, which has among the highest credit card fees in the world. In July 2013, the Competition Tribunal dismissed the Commissioner's application, even though the Tribunal found that Visa and MasterCard's conduct was influencing the price of credit card services in Canada upwards and having an adverse effect on competition. The Tribunal was of the opinion that regulation of the industry was a more suitable approach.

Restrictive Distribution Practices

Distribution decisions determine whether products will be sold through retailers, wholesalers, a multi-level organization, employed salespeople, door-to-door salespeople, telemarketers, or online sales. Whatever structure or channels sellers choose, they should observe two key principles in order to avoid legal difficulties. First, they must resist the temptation to control their distribution scheme to the extent that competition for their products is adversely affected. Second, they should aim for full disclosure of terms and conditions at each selling stage.

A supplier is not permitted to require or induce a customer to deal only, or mostly, in certain products or require or induce a customer to buy a second product as a condition of supplying a particular product. In addition, a supplier cannot refuse to sell to a purchaser on the same terms as those offered to other purchasers. These are all reviewable matters under the *Competition Act*.

Suppose SRL's NaturalNew has become the dominant moisturizing cream in the market. SRL tells its distributors that it will continue to supply them with NaturalNew only if they agree to buy no other competing moisturizing creams. If this practice lessens competition substantially, it falls within the definition of

---

56 Competition Bureau of Canada, "Competition Bureau Will Not Appeal Credit Cards Decision" (30 September 2013), online: Competition Bureau Canada <http://www.competitionbureau.gc.ca/eic/site/cb-bc.nsf/eng/03614.html>.

exclusive dealing and is therefore reviewable. Exclusive dealing is different from the permissible practice of exclusive distributorship, where a seller distributes certain products to only one retailer.

SRL advises its retailers that they will only be permitted to purchase NaturalNew if they also agree to buy a number of less popular products from SRL. This practice may be **tied selling** and is reviewable provided, again, that the action substantially lessens or prevents competition.

If SRL refuses to sell NaturalNew to a particular retail chain, because the chain has a history of promoting products that are competitive with SRL's products, even though the chain is willing and able to meet SRL's usual conditions of sale, that may constitute **refusal to deal**. This conduct will be reviewable if SRL has an adequate inventory of product and its refusal to sell to the chain substantially lessens or prevents competition.

Multi-level Marketing

Multi-level marketing involves a product distribution structure that creates multiple levels of distributorships. Commissions are paid upward through the various levels of the sales structure. Multi-level marketing has become big business, especially for products that are sold directly through house parties or door-to-door. Multi-level marketing, when conducted within the parameters of the law, is a legal business activity, but this type of business must be distinguished from pyramid selling, which is a criminal offence.

Whether a scheme is multi-level marketing or pyramid selling will be determined by a number of factors. If a genuine business activity is not obvious, the scheme is likely an illegal pyramid scheme. Pyramid schemes are unstable and, inevitably, those joining at the late stages receive little or no value as the scheme collapses for lack of new participants.[57]

Pyramid selling is a criminal act under the *Competition Act* if

- participants pay money for the right to receive compensation for recruiting new participants.
- a participant is required to buy a specific quantity of products, other than at cost price, for the purpose of advertising, before the participant is allowed to join the plan or advance within the plan.
- participants are knowingly sold commercially unreasonable quantities of the product or products (this practice is called inventory loading).
- participants are not allowed to return products on reasonable commercial terms.

Promotional Contests

Promotional contests are regulated by the *Competition Act*, the *Criminal Code*, and provincial legislation in some provinces. Improper operation of a promotional contest may lead to civil or criminal liability, so businesses that wish to engage in contests should be aware of the various rules that apply. Generally, operating a lottery is a criminal offence. Contest operators will often require a skill-testing question, or ensure that contestants can enter with "no purchase necessary," in order to avoid the contest being considered a lottery under the *Criminal Code*. Even where a promotional contest is not a lottery, the *Competition Act* imposes

Exclusive dealing

When a seller agrees to sell to the purchaser only if the purchaser buys from it exclusively.

Tied selling

When a seller will sell to the purchaser only if the purchaser buys other, less desirable goods as well.

Refusal to deal

When a seller refuses to sell to a purchaser on the same terms as those that are offered to the purchaser's competitors.

Multi-level marketing

A scheme for distributing products or services that involves participants recruiting others to become involved in distribution.

Pyramid selling

A form of multi-level selling that is illegal under the *Competition Act*.

57 Competition Bureau of Canada, *"Multi-level Marketing and Pyramid Selling"*, online: Competition Bureau Canada <http://www.competitionbureau.gc.ca/eic/site/cb-bc.nsf/eng/01230.html>.

PART SEVEN

requirements of disclosure, including the number and approximate value of prizes, the geographical areas in which they may be won, and the odds of winning.

It is very important that contest rules be in compliance with the law and that the required statutory disclosure be drafted properly. In addition, there are many sophisticated contest entrants who will typically exploit any loophole or inadvertent omission in the contest rules, such as being able to enter thousands of ballots electronically. When this happens, the business purposes for which the contest is being held may fail to be achieved.

Risk Management

Risk management in regards to consumer protection and competition law requires consideration of the four-step legal risk management model presented in Chapter 3 and the business risks discussed in Parts Two and Three of this text. The products and services must be as advertised and must perform as intended. The manner in which the products and services are distributed and sold must not be misleading or deceptive. The packaging and labelling of products must conform to applicable laws. The design of the products themselves must not infringe on the intellectual property rights of others. Consumer products must be safe and foreseeable risks must be addressed. The pricing and distribution of products must not violate applicable competition laws.

BUSINESS LAW IN PRACTICE REVISITED

1. What legal issues arise in regard to the sale of NaturalNew directly to consumers?

When SRL sells NaturalNew directly to consumers, the implied conditions and warranties found in the *Sale of Goods Act* will apply to those sales, even if the parties agree to exclude such implied terms. Even if SRL sells to consumers through distributors or retailers, in many provinces the implied terms will still apply despite the lack of privity between SRL and consumers. SRL must ensure that it does not engage in advertising aimed at consumers which may be considered to be false or misleading.

2. What impact does the law have on the promotion of NaturalNew as an "all-natural" product with "no artificial ingredients"?

The claims made on NaturalNew labels will be subject to the general provincial and federal laws which prohibit false or misleading claims. In addition, if NaturalNew is a cosmetic, then the labelling requirements of the *Food and Drug Act* will apply. If NaturalNew is not a cosmetic, then the *Consumer Packaging and Labelling Act* will apply. In any case, SRL must ensure that it has conducted adequate testing to make the claim that the product is "all-natural" and contains "no artificial ingredients." In addition, the terms "natural" and "artificial" are not easily defined, so SRL must decide whether it wants to label its product with terms that may cause confusion in the minds of some consumers.

3. What product safety requirements, if any, apply to the manufacture and sale of NaturalNew?

The *Consumer Product Safety Act* will apply to the manufacture and sale of NaturalNew. As a result, SRL is required to report incidents relating to the safety of NaturalNew, including manufacturing defects and product recalls. SRL should keep adequate records regarding the testing and manufacture of NaturalNew so that it can demonstrate compliance with the Act if the need should arise.

4. How does the law affect SRL's intended marketing strategy?

SRL should take reasonable steps to ensure that neither it nor its distributors are making representations about NaturalNew which could be considered to be false or misleading. SRL should keep adequate records of the steps it has taken in case SRL needs to make a defence based on due diligence. When selling directly to consumers, SRL must be careful not to promote false sale or bargain prices. If SRL includes test results, testimonials, or performance claims in its promotion of NaturalNew, those claims must comply with the provisions of the *Competition Act*. When selling to distributors or retailers, SRL must not engage in pricing conspiracies, such as price fixing, price maintenance, or abuse of dominant position. Finally, SRL must be careful to avoid restrictive distribution practices with its customers, including exclusive dealing, tied selling, or refusal to deal.

CHAPTER SUMMARY

Consumer protection law assumes that consumers are in greater need of protection than businesses, and uses a variety of means to achieve the goal of protecting consumers. Consumer protection laws in all the provinces expand the application of sale of goods legislation, so that the legislation applies to all consumer transactions, and includes not only sales but leases, licences, and the provision of services. In addition, consumer protection laws prohibit exploitative business practices such as the making of false or misleading claims. Consumer protection laws regulate certain types of consumer transactions, including direct marketing, online sales, and transactions in specific industries such as debt collection, automobile repair, and fitness club memberships. Finally, provincial and federal laws regulate the packaging and labelling of consumer products and prescribe minimum standards for product safety.

Competition law seeks to promote a fair and competitive marketplace and prevent behaviour which is uncompetitive. Competition law also provides a measure of consumer protection, because many of the provisions in the federal *Competition Act* are aimed at protecting consumers. In addition, it is assumed that greater competition in the marketplace, and the greater degree of choice that a more competitive environment provides, is generally good for consumers.

The Competition Bureau reviews corporate mergers, acquisitions, and takeovers, and has the power to impose conditions on such transactions, or even prevent them from occurring, if the effect of such a transaction would be to substantially lessen competition.

The provisions in the *Competition Act* relating to false and misleading claims apply to all promotional commercial activities—not only to consumer transactions. In addition to the general prohibition against the making of false or misleading claims, there are specific provisions that deal with a variety of business practices, including deceptive telemarketing, misrepresentations regarding price, and representations such as test results and performance.

Finally, the *Competition Act* prohibits certain anticompetitive behaviours, such as price fixing, price maintenance, bid rigging, abuse of dominant position, and restrictive distribution practices.

Offences under the *Competition Act* are either criminal or civil in nature, and some may be treated in either manner, depending on the severity and the degree of intent.

CHAPTER STUDY

Key Terms and Concepts

abuse of dominant position (p. 626)

bait and switch (p. 623)

bid rigging (p. 626)

consumer (p. 605)

door-to-door selling (p. 608)

double ticketing (p. 620)

due diligence (p. 615)

exclusive dealing (p. 629)

false or misleading representation (p. 607)

multi-level marketing (p. 629)

price fixing (p. 624)

price maintenance (p. 627)

pyramid selling (p. 629)

refusal to deal (p. 629)

telemarketing (p. 608)

tied selling (p. 629)

unfair practices (p. 606)

Questions for Review

1. In what ways does consumer protection legislation expand the application of the *Sale of Goods Act?*

2. What is a consumer?

3. What is an unfair practice?

4. How are door-to-door sellers regulated?

5. Provide three examples of false or misleading advertising.

6. What are two primary concerns of consumers buying online?

7. What are the key provisions of the *Consumer Packaging and Labelling Act?*

8. What is the purpose of the *Consumer Products Safety Act?*

9. What does Advertising Standards Canada do?

10. What are the main purposes of competition law?

11. What is a due diligence defence?

12. What is deceptive telemarketing?

13. What is a conspiracy to fix prices?

14. What is abuse of dominant position?

15. When is it acceptable to state "recommended retail price" on a product?

16. What is bid rigging?

17. What is the meaning of "ordinary price" in evaluating the promotion of goods?

18. How can a corporation use the provisions of the *Competition Act* against a competitor?

19. What is the selling practice known as "bait and switch"?

20. What is the difference between legal multi-level selling and pyramid selling?

Questions for Critical Thinking

1. Why do we need consumer protection legislation? Are all consumers really in need of greater protection than all businesses?

2. Are businesses generally familiar with the laws relating to consumer protection and competition? Do most businesses comply with these laws?

3. Does consumer protection law place too great a burden on business? Is protecting consumers worth the additional regulation and the transaction costs that come with the additional regulation?

4. Why does the *Competition Act* focus on regulating the behaviour of businesses rather than providing remedies directly to consumers? Does provincial legislation serve consumers more effectively?

5. Compare the criminal and civil approaches relating to deceptive marketing practices in the *Competition Act*. What are the advantages of one process over the other?

6. Will Canada's new anti-spam law finally deter spammers? How will we know if it is working?

7. Internet shopping opens up a broad range of risks to consumers. What recommendations would you have for federal and provincial governments moving to improve regulation to enhance consumer confidence?

Situations for Discussion

1. Senior management of Superior Chemicals Ltd. has decided to revamp the marketing program for the company's line of household products, which includes kitchen, bathroom, furniture, flooring, and all-purpose cleaners. They want to promote these products as more environmentally friendly than those of their competitors. The marketing department has developed a large number of possible messages such as "natural," "nature clean," "renewable ingredients," "biodegradable," "the environmental choice," "the responsible choice," and "We care about the earth." What should management consider in developing the advertising campaign for their cleaning products?

   Which claims are appropriate? How must Superior be able to support its claims?

2. Hammer and Nails Hardware, a nationwide chain, has devised a new product line. It has discerned a growing niche in the market among older "empty nesters" who are moving from houses into apartments or condominiums. It has devised a "We meet all your basic needs" campaign that prepackages tools, home repair products, and decorating products. It intends to introduce a series of 10 different lines over a six-month period. They will be boxed in an attractive, uniform style of packaging that includes "how-to" books. The packages will include the basic items needed for particular household tasks.

   What must Hammer and Nails consider in terms of its choice of package contents, packaging, labelling, instructions, and promotion in order to comply with legal requirements and avoid creating inflated expectations from customers?

3. Softest Diapers is one of two leading producers of diapers for infants. It has spent several years researching and testing a new brand of super-absorbent diaper. It is now devising an advertising campaign that will make direct comparison with its competitor's products. The marketing team has spent months comparing the two lines of products and genuinely believes that the new Softest diapers absorb significantly more moisture than do the equivalently priced products of the competitor. The team has asked the scientists to confirm their results, and after several months of testing, the scientists report that there is, on average, a 10 percent increase in absorbency. The campaign is an immediate success.

   The competitor, recognizing the threat, immediately seeks an injunction to stop this campaign under section 36 of the *Competition Act*. What provisions of the Act and what arguments will the competitor rely upon? What will Softest use in its defence? What are the possible outcomes?

4. Great Buys Inc. imports a wide range of consumer goods from China for online resale in Canada. Some of its most popular products are cell phone and laptop replacement batteries, which use lithium ion technology. In recent discussions with its Chinese supplier, Great Buys has discovered that one shipment of batteries was inadvertently shipped to Canada before quality inspection was completed and, as a result, may not be compliant with CSA standards. Great Buys has already sold the batteries to dozens of customers and no complaints have been received. While most lithium batteries are safe, some, mostly counterfeit and no-brand batteries, have overheated and caught fire. These fires are difficult to extinguish and produce toxic fumes.

   What are the relevant rules for the import and sale of lithium ion batteries? What is Great Buys' potential legal liability? What should Great Buys do about the one possibly unsafe shipment?

5. Mega Goods Inc. is a major discount retailer operating throughout Canada. The Home Co-op is also a nationwide chain, but it is a cooperative buying group of smaller retailers that band together in order to achieve buying power. Both retailers buy large volumes of plastic food containers from the major manufacturer (PFC Inc.) in the market. The product line is an important customer draw and is often used in special promotions.

   Mega Goods is eager to increase its market share, particularly with the entry of a multinational, U.S.-based discounter into the Canadian market. It decides to attempt to eliminate the direct competition from Home Co-op in smaller centres. Mega Goods approaches PFC and requests changed conditions of purchase. Specifically, it asks for a significant drop in price in return for a reduced payment period. This change will place it at a distinct advantage over Home Co-op, as Home Co-op cannot pay quickly because of its membership structure. Mega Goods intends to approach all other major suppliers if this proposal works.

PFC management is quite concerned, as Home Co-op is a longstanding customer. Would supplying on Mega Goods' terms be legal? Is it a wise business practice?

6. There are three major suppliers of commercial diamond cutting equipment in Canada. They have all operated for many years, and they respect each other and the quality of their products. They recognize that the market, while profitable, is finite, and that for each company to survive, none of them can have a significantly greater market share than the share currently held. For many years, it has been accepted that when calls for commercial diamond cutting equipment are made by various customers, Western Cutting Ltd. will respond for Western Canada, Central Equipment Ltd. for Ontario, and East Coast Cutting Equipment Inc. for Quebec and the Maritimes. Recently, purchasers have been questioning why, of all the equipment that they regularly purchase, diamond cutting equipment seems to be subject to the least fluctuation in prices. The customers have made inquiries, and have learned from employees of the three companies of the arrangement that they have.

What are the legal implications for the three companies, their employees, and their customers? What are the possible outcomes?

7. Textiles Inc. is a major chain of fabric sellers. In this market, there are a few high-end sellers of fashion designer fabrics, some small independents, and three chains, with Textiles being the largest and most profitable. Textiles thrives on its ability to attract customers, often through discount pricing.

Every few weeks Textiles has a major promotion, with certain materials being sold at a reduced cost. The business sells both regular fabrics and fashion fabrics. Textiles tends to discount the regular fabrics while the prices of fashion fabrics retain their high markup. After a while, even though advertisements state that fabric prices are reduced by 30 percent and even 50 percent, regular customers have become so accustomed to these reductions that they seldom expect to pay the full price.

These practices are attracting the attention of competitors, who have notified the Competition Bureau. Why is the bureau likely to be interested in Textiles' pricing practices?

8. Two companies (WSI and CA) dominated the commercial waste collection service industry on Vancouver Island. Their customers were restaurants, schools, office complexes, and condominium developments. They jointly engaged in certain business practices to preserve their dominant position and discourage other small and medium-sized waste collection companies. These practices included the use of long-term contracts that locked in customers and contained highly restrictive terms such as automatic renewal clauses and significant penalties for early contract termination. One small competitor (UP) was frustrated by its difficulty in finding customers because it provided prices and services that were competitive with the two major players. UP eventually discovered the terms of the contracts used by WSI and CA. UP considered filing a complaint with the Competition Bureau.[58] How would such a complaint be dealt with?

9. Smart Sales Inc. is a big box retailer, specializing in consumer electronics. Smart Sales intends to advertise that it will "Match any competitor's price on all Orange brand computers." The fine print at the bottom of the ad states that the price match guarantee only applies to identical products offered for sale in Canada. Smart Sales has negotiated an exclusive distributor agreement with Orange, whereby Orange manufactures and sells three particular models of computer only to Smart Sales. These three models, which have slightly different combinations of features than other computer models which Orange sells to retailers other than Smart Sales, are the only models of Orange computers that Smart Sales offers for sale. As a result, Smart Sales never actually has to honour its price match guarantee, because there are no identical products offered for sale in Canada.

What legal issues are raised in regard to the exclusive distribution agreement between Smart Sales and Orange? In regard to Smart Sales' promise to match competitor's prices?

---

58 Based in part on Competition Bureau of Canada, "Competition Bureau cracks down on joint abuse of dominance by waste companies" (16 June 2009), online: Competition Bureau Canada <http://www .competitionbureau.gc.ca/eic/site/cb-bc.nsf/eng/03081.html>.

FINANCING THE BUSINESS

The decisions related to financing a business range from paying a supplier to financing an expansion of operations and dealing with financial difficulties. Virtually all financial aspects of starting, operating, and terminating a business have legal implications. As with other sectors of a business, an understanding of the legal aspects of finance can be used to structure activities in a way that minimizes unfavourable legal consequences. Part Eight presents the various aspects of financing a business—not simply as a list of legal topics, but rather as a businessperson might encounter them. The major chapter topics are dealing with banks, obtaining credit, and coping with business failure.

25

OBJECTIVES

After studying this chapter, you should have an understanding of

- the relationship between a business and its bank

- the legal issues involved in electronic banking

- the costs and benefits of various methods of payment

- the legal framework of negotiable instruments

- the rights and obligations of those connected with negotiable instruments

BUSINESS AND BANKING

BUSINESS LAW IN PRACTICE

Bill Ikeda and Martha Wong operate a building supply outlet in Timmins, Ontario. They also sell hardware, plumbing, and electrical supplies. Their customers are retail and commercial. They operate the business through a corporation, Hometown Hardware Ltd. (Hometown). Bill is the CEO and majority owner. He conducts most of the business apart from the operation of the store. Martha is the vice president and owns the remaining shares. She manages the store. The business has dealt with the local branch of the same bank for many years—the Full Service Bank (FSB). Both Bill and Martha have signing authority for Hometown.

Bill and Martha have recently begun to reconsider their relationship with FSB. The branch has a new manager. There have been other personnel changes, as well, so that Hometown's accounts and loans are now handled by unfamiliar employees who seem uninterested in Hometown's business and have recently been unhelpful. Bill is also not sure that Hometown has the appropriate types of bank accounts. He is concerned about high service fees on his accounts and rising interest rates on his loans. He wonders whether he should consider moving his business to another bank, or try to renegotiate his relationship with FSB. Martha has been advised by business acquaintances that banks are offering a vast array of financial services and that Hometown's banking can be done more easily and cheaply online.

Bill is also concerned about the growing number of cheques being returned to him by the bank because customers have insufficient funds in their accounts to cover them. He currently accepts payment by cash, cheque, debit card, and credit card. Hometown also extends credit to some commercial customers. Bill is interested in the cost and risk of various payment options.

1. What do Bill and Martha need to know about the legal aspects of the relationship between their business and a bank?

2. What are the risks and benefits of various payment options and banking electronically?

3. What are the risks and benefits of using cheques to pay bills and allowing customers to pay by cheque?

When operating a business, what financial decisions with legal consequences must the owners make?

Business and Banking

This chapter describes the relationship that a business has with its bank, including the financial services the bank provides and the agreements and duties involved in the relationship. Various forms of payment and the related risks are explored—traditional paper-based payments and the growing number of electronic options. The chapter begins with a brief look at the banking system.

The Regulation of Banks

Traditionally, the Canadian financial services industry had four distinct sectors: banks, trust companies, stock brokerages, and insurance companies. To ensure stability within each sector and to avoid conflicts of interest resulting from institutions providing services from several sectors, each was separately regulated, and institutions in one sector were prohibited from conducting business beyond that sector.

The internationalization of the financial services industry in the 1980s placed pressure on governments to deregulate and relax the strict separation of the four sectors. In 1987, Canadian legislation[1] allowed banks to go beyond traditional banking and participate in other sectors in their branches or through subsidiary firms. Banks have become financial marketplaces, offering services in cash management, payment services, investment advice, and business financing. Subsequent legislation[2] further blurred the distinctions between different types of financial institutions by allowing greater structural flexibility. Among many other changes, it provided for liberalized ownership rules for banks. The key remaining limit on banks' business is the prohibition against selling or promoting insurance products in their branches. Banks have responded by opening separate insurance branches and attempting to conduct

---

1 The *Office of the Superintendent of Financial Institutions Act*, RSC 1985, c 18 (3rd Supp) Part 1 created a single federal regulator (OSFI).
2 *Financial Consumer Agency of Canada Act*, SC 2001, c 9.

insurance business online.[3] The financial sector legislation is reviewed every five years.[4]

Bank regulation has become a topic of great interest since the world financial crisis began in 2008. During that crisis, Canadian banks fared much better than many banks in other countries, leading to the perception that Canadian banks are generally well capitalized, well managed, and well regulated.[5]

Banks are increasingly offering international banking services, such as letters of credit, cross-border transfers, and accounts in different currencies. These services are governed largely by voluntary rules created by international bodies, such as the Bank for International Settlements and the International Chamber of Commerce. Parties involved in international transactions frequently incorporate these rules into their agreements.

In Canada, banks are under federal jurisdiction and are regulated through the federal *Bank Act*.[6] The main purposes of the Act are to ensure the stability and liquidity of banks and to identify and regulate the types of business they are permitted to conduct. The relationship between a bank and its individual customers is not a primary concern of the Act. The terms and conditions of that relationship are, instead, found primarily in the agreements made between the bank and its customers, which are influenced by banking practice and common law rules. Contract law is the prime source of guidance in interpreting and enforcing the rights and obligations of the parties in this relationship.

The Bank—Customer Relationship

In its simplest form, the relationship between a business and its bank consists of one bank account into which the business deposits its cash receipts from customers and from which it makes payments to suppliers, employees, government, and owners. As a result of regulatory changes and decisions by banks to broaden their range of services, the relationship is now more comprehensive. It is a challenge for businesspeople like Bill and Martha to decide what banking services they need, which services they can afford, and who will do the best job of providing them.

The legal nature of the relationship is clear. In terms of the customer's money on deposit with the bank, the relationship is that of the bank as debtor and the customer as creditor. Normally, the bank is not obligated to give advice or to look out for the best interest of the customer, unless, for example, the bank provides services such as financial advice, which are outside the normal scope of traditional banking services. In that situation, a fiduciary

---

3   See *Regulations Amending the Insurance Business (Banks and Bank Holding Companies) Regulations*, SOR/2011–183, online: Canada Gazette <http://gazette.gc.ca/rp-pr/p2/2011/2011-10-12/html/sor-dors183-eng.html>.

4   The latest review culminated in the *Financial System Review Act*, SC 2012, c 5 which contains relatively minor changes. See Bill Curry and Tara Perkins, "New bill would increase minister's power over banks", *The Globe and Mail* (23 November 2011), online: Globe and Mail <http://www.theglobeandmail.com/report-on-business/new-bill-would-increase-finance-ministers-power-over-banks/article2246925/>.

5   The World Economic Forum ranked Canada's banks as the most sound in the world for seven years in a row. See "Global Banking Regulations and Banks in Canada," Canadian Bankers Association (13 March 2015), online: <http://www.cba.ca/en/media-room/50-backgrounders-on-banking-issues/667-global-banking-regulations-and-banks-in-canada>.

6   SC 1991, c 46.

relationship may exist, and the bank has several additional onerous duties, including to

- provide advice with care and skill.
- disclose any actual or potential conflicts of interest.
- consider the interests of the customer ahead of those of the bank.[7]

For example, if Bill has sought and received advice from his banker as to the amount and structure of the financing Hometown needs, he can expect to receive competent advice from the bank and should be encouraged to seek independent legal advice before agreeing to a financing arrangement which may operate heavily in the bank's favour.

The practical advice for customers is to appreciate the basic nature of the relationship and to understand that banks generally have no obligation to look beyond their own self-interest. However, banks are beginning to broaden their roles to remain competitive.[8] They are also under pressure to deal fairly with customers and to refrain from strict enforcement of agreements that are onerous for their customers. For example, financial services legislation[9] established the Financial Consumer Agency of Canada (FCAC)[10] to protect and educate consumers through the monitoring of institutions' business practices regarding such matters as account fees and credit card rates. In addition, the financial services industry, in cooperation with the federal government, has created the Centre for the Financial Services OmbudsNetwork (CFSON)[11] to provide a one-stop complaint procedure covering brokers, banks, insurance companies, and sellers of mutual funds in order to ensure fair and impartial complaint resolution for consumers.

Duties of the Bank and the Customer

The common law and banking practice imply legal duties on both parties in the banking relationship. For example, the bank must

- honour payment instructions and repay deposits.
- collect payments for the customer.
- provide account information to the customer on a regular basis.
- maintain secrecy of the customer's affairs.[12] This duty is qualified by legislation.

---

7 Alison R Manzer & Jordan S Bernamoff, *The Corporate Counsel Guide to Banking and Credit Relationships* (Aurora, ON: Canada Law Book, 1999) at 36.

8 See Tara Perkins, "Bankers evolve into advisory roles", *The Globe and Mail* (19 October 2010), online: Globe and Mail <http://www.theglobeandmail.com/report-on-business/small-business/sb-marketing/bankers-evolve-into-advisory-roles/article4258802/>.

9 *Supra* note 2.

10 See Financial Consumer Agency of Canada, online: <http://www.fcac-acfc.gc.ca>.

11 See Financial Services OmbudsNetwork, online: <http://www.fson.org> and the Ombudsman for Banking Services and Investments (OBSI), online: <http://www.obsi.ca>. However, some banks have opted out of the OBSI process. See Grant Robertson, "Opt-outs undermine dispute resolution: bank ombudsman", *The Globe and Mail* (24 February 2012), online: Globe and Mail <http://www.theglobeandmail.com/globe-investor/opt-outs-undermine-dispute-resolution-bank-ombudsman/article4171747/>. See also Department of Finance Canada, "Harper government imposes tough new pro-consumer oversight on banking complaints" (6 July 2012), online: Department of Finance Canada <http://www.fin.gc.ca/n12/12-079-eng.asp>.

12 *Supra* note 7 at 14.

CLIENT INFORMATION AND MONEY LAUNDERING

The bank's duty to maintain secrecy of customer information is subject to the law concerning **money laundering**—that is, the false reporting of income obtained through criminal activity as income gained through legitimate business enterprises. According to the United Nations, money laundering in Canada in 2011 was estimated to be between $5 billion and $15 billion. Since 1991, banks have been urged to verify the identity of individual and corporate customers and the validity of their business activities, and to determine the source of transfers exceeding $10 000.[13]

Legislation passed in 2000[14] was meant to enable Canada to meet its international obligations in combating money laundering. The legislation created a mandatory reporting system in which banks, trust companies, insurance companies, and professionals must report to a new independent body—the Financial Transactions and Reports Analysis Centre (FINTRAC)—suspicious financial transactions and large cross-border currency transfers. Suspicious transactions are not defined in the Act, but FINTRAC provides guidelines under headings such as "economic purpose" of the transaction. For example, if a transaction seems to be inconsistent with the client's apparent financial standing or usual pattern of activities, does not appear to be driven by normal commercial considerations, or is unnecessarily complex for its stated purpose, it should be considered suspicious.

FINTRAC is responsible for managing the information reported by the various organizations affected by the Act and deciding which transactions to refer to law enforcement agencies for investigation.

Subsequent regulatory changes have tightened the requirements by broadening the applicability and expanding the obligations of record keeping, reporting, and registration; increasing client identification requirements; requiring compliance regimes, employee training, and education; and establishing federal registration for money service and foreign exchange businesses.

Critical Analysis: To what extent should the confidentiality of individual client accounts be compromised to combat money laundering by a minority of clients? How is the effectiveness of this regime measured? Is the regulatory burden justified?

Sources: Department of Finance Canada, "Minister of Finance launches consultation to update anti-money laundering and anti-terrorist financing regime" (21 December 2011), online: Department of Finance Canada <http://www.fin.gc.ca/n11/11-142-eng.asp>; Christine Duhaime, "Push to expand money laundering law," *The Lawyers Weekly* (9 March 2012) 11.

Money laundering

The false reporting of income from criminal activity as income from legitimate business.

Customers also have implied duties to the bank. They must

- take reasonable steps to provide documentation as to who is authorized to give instructions to the bank, in order to prevent fraud and forgery.
- keep authorizations current.
- notify the bank of any suspected problems.
- provide safeguards for electronic communications.[15]

The Bank–Customer Agreement

Standard banking documents are designed primarily to protect the bank, not the customer. Large customers may have some bargaining power, but small businesses such as Hometown have little. Understanding the terms and conditions in

---

13   *Proceeds of Crime (Money Laundering) Act,* SC 1991, c 26.
14   *Proceeds of Crime (Money Laundering) and Terrorist Financing Act,* SC 2000, c 17. See also SC 2006, c 12.
15   *Supra* note 7 at 15.

the agreement will enable Bill and Martha to identify the risks arising from the banking aspects of their business. They can then establish practices to avoid incidents resulting in loss for which the banking agreement may make Hometown responsible.

The purposes of the **account agreement** are to

- specify who has the authority to issue instructions to the bank and sign cheques on behalf of the customer.
- allocate the risk of loss resulting from problems with verifying the customer's authority and carrying out the customer's instructions.
- describe the fees and other service charges which the bank may charge the customer.
- describe the manner in which cheques and other instruments will be handled by the bank.
- establish procedures and allocate risk for the security of accounts and confidential information.

The account agreement, or account operating agreement, is a standard form contract prepared by the bank. While some specific terms of the agreement may be negotiable—such as certain service charges and the interest rate to be charged on credit facilities—most of the terms are not negotiable, including terms which limit the bank's duties and liabilities. Accordingly, Bill and Martha must be cautious in their dealings with the bank. For example, a verification clause commonly found in account agreements gives the customer 30 days to detect and report any unauthorized payments that the bank makes from the customer's account. Beyond that period, the customer is responsible for the loss. Normally, the bank also has flexibility in dealing with all of the customer's accounts. For example, the bank can transfer funds from an account with a positive balance to one that is overdrawn.

Many business accounts have an **overdraft** feature which operates in a similar way to a line of credit and allows an account to temporarily have a negative balance in order to prevent cheques written on the account from being returned for insufficient funds. Usually, a high interest rate is charged on any overdraft balance, making it an unattractive source of funds on an ongoing basis.

Traditional banking transactions are increasingly done online.

Overdraft

An overdraft occurs when money is withdrawn from a bank account with the result that the balance in the account goes below zero.

Electronic Banking

Electronic banking includes a growing range and variety of transactions that previously required formal documentation. A wide variety of technological developments are changing the ways that businesses deal with banks, customers, and other businesses. Banks are encouraging customers to conduct their banking business through ATMs, telephone, or online, rather than through in-person transactions in bank branches. These methods can be more convenient for customers and significantly less expensive for the banks. Some new banks have no physical branches at all and conduct all their business online.

There are several legal issues arising from electronic transactions. Electronic storage means that data are subject to system crashes or hackers. Fraud has become a significant concern. Other potential problems are transmission failures or system crashes. As business comes to rely increasingly on instant payments, possibly at the last minute, the potential loss from a failed or delayed transfer is significant.

Electronic banking

Financial transactions carried out through the use of computers, telephones, or other electronic means.

PART EIGHT

What rules govern ATM transactions?

Identity theft

The fraudulent use of others' personal information to create a false identity.

Much of the legal uncertainty surrounding electronic banking is the result of the inapplicability of existing legislation to a paperless environment. The process and timing of electronic transactions do not fit with existing rules related to risk allocation for authentication, verification, and finalization of payments in paper-based transactions.

The gap in the rules governing electronic banking is being filled in several ways. First, account agreements now include provisions dealing with electronic transactions and related matters. Banks want to limit their liability through their agreements with customers, but they also want to reassure customers that their electronic banking environments are secure. The result is a balance, with the bank assuming some risks and the customer assuming others. For example, customers are generally required to report suspicious transactions to the bank. Provided they do so, the bank will often assume responsibility for a fraudulent transaction involving the customer's account. Customers are also required to choose personal identification numbers (PINs) that are not obvious, to change PINs regularly, and to safeguard those PINs from unauthorized use. If it fails to meet these requirements, the customer will be liable for any losses that result. Banks are also placing daily and weekly monetary limits on transactions in order to control the losses in the event of fraud. In addition, industry codes have been created to provide guidance. The *Code of Conduct for Credit and Debit Card Industry* was revised in 2010[16] and the Minister of Finance has formed a working group to develop a voluntary code for electronic funds transfers and electronic banking. There are also international rules, such as the UNCITRAL *Model Law on International Credit Transfers,*[17] since electronic transfers are often used for international business transactions. If the sending and receiving banks are in different countries, these international rules deal with the obligations of the parties, timing for payment, consequences for technical problems, and liability and damages.

BUSINESS AND LEGISLATION

IDENTITY THEFT

The Internet has increased the potential for fraudulent activities. In particular, **identity theft** has become a serious problem. Identity theft involves obtaining others' personal information through various means and using that information for fraudulent purposes such as accessing bank accounts or obtaining credit cards, loans, mortgages, or title to property. The victims can be individuals or businesses. Their entire financial situation may be compromised. One common method for initiating identity theft is through "phishing," whereby fraudsters send email messages that appear to be from reputable companies, such as banks, and direct recipients to websites that appear genuine, where victims are urged to disclose personal

16 (18 May 2010), online: Department of Finance Canada <http://www.fin.gc.ca/n10/data/10-049_1-eng.asp>.
17 *UNCITRAL Model Law on International Credit Transfers* (1992), 32 ILM 587, online: UNCITRAL <http://www.uncitral.org/uncitral/en/uncitral_texts/payments/1992Model_credit_transfers.html>.

information in order to verify their accounts and ensure their continued access. Visiting one of these websites may enable fraudsters to extract valuable information. The information is then used to steal the victim's identity. The danger of identity theft has increased with the advent of wireless technology, to the extent that identity theft has become an organized criminal activity.

To combat this increase in identity theft, the federal government passed legislation[18] to create several new criminal offences, including

- obtaining or possessing identity information with the intent to commit certain crimes.
- trafficking in identity information with knowledge of or recklessness as to its intended use.

- unlawfully possessing or trafficking in government-issued identity documents.

Identity information is broadly defined to include anything that is commonly used alone or in combination with other information to identify an individual, such as name, address, fingerprints, date of birth, signature, bank account number, and passport number. Penalties for violation of the law include imprisonment for up to five years. The challenge with such a law is to address the criminal activity without unduly restricting legitimate business.

Sources: Sharda Prashad, "Identity theft strikes small businesses", *The Globe and Mail* (23 August 2012), online: Globe and Mail <http://www.theglobeandmail.com/report-on-business/small-business/start/legal/identity-theft-strikes-small-businesses/article1433204/>; Christopher Guly, "Identity theft may target innocent acts", *The Lawyers Weekly* (18 December 2009) 17; and Eva Hoare, "Bank staff thwart identity thefts", *The Chronicle Herald* (20 March 2010) A3.

Although fraud and data security breaches are matters of concern, there is little evidence yet of significant legal problems arising from electronic transfers. Business customers of banks are interested in security, convenience, and low costs in terms of banking services. As long as banks can demonstrate to customers that their needs are being met without significant risks, the volume of electronic banking will increase.

Methods of Payment

When Bill and Martha pay an account to one of Hometown's suppliers, they have several options. They could use cash, but it is inconvenient, does not leave a paper trail, and may require keeping large amounts of cash on hand which may be unwise. Other options are to pay by cheque (a written order to the bank), by **credit card** (if the supplier accepts that form of payment), or by **electronic funds transfer**.

Electronic payments are expanding in terms of scope and volume.

Credit card

A card issued by a financial institution that allows the user to borrow funds on a short-term basis, usually to purchase goods or services.

Electronic funds transfer

The transfer of money from one bank account to another through computer-based systems and without the direct assistance of bank staff.

TECHNOLOGY AND THE LAW

DEVELOPMENTS IN ELECTRONIC PAYMENTS SYSTEMS

Customers are now offered a wide range of electronic options by their banks. Some examples are automatic payments from chequing accounts, direct deposit of cheques, automatic teller machines (ATMs), payment by telephone or computer, and point-of-sale transfers. Banks now offer smart phone apps for access to their accounts. ATMs are available for deposits,

18   *An Act to Amend the Criminal Code (Identity Theft and Related Misconduct)*, SC 2009, c 28 (in force 8 January 2010).

PART EIGHT

withdrawals, transfers between accounts, and bill payments. Telephone banking and online banking can be used for everything other than cash transactions, including applications for mortgages and loans.

There are many models for cashless transactions. Debit cards allow buyers to purchase goods and services and to transfer payment directly from a bank account to the seller. Prepaid money cards allow virtual money to be loaded on the card and transferred directly from the card to the seller. Mobile wallets allow cellphones to be waved or tapped in order to process credit card transactions or spend money which has been pre-loaded by computer onto the phone. Customers can now use their cellphone cameras to photograph cheques to be cashed and send the digital image to the bank. In Canada, the Interac e-Transfer system allows online banking customers to send money to an email address over a secured Internet connection. Payments can also be made through secure online commercial intermediaries such as PayPal.

Credit card transactions are processed electronically as well. Credit cards have evolved from manual processing to networks accessed with magnetic stripes, then to embedded microchips and PINs, and now to contactless payments using microchips and radio frequencies where the card is simply waved at a reader. They involve three contracts—one between the card issuer and the user, the second between the credit card company and the merchant, and the basic contract of sale between the user (buyer) and the merchant. The second contract has become contentious since merchants are largely at the mercy of card companies in terms of acceptance of cards from buyers and the associated fees. This imbalance of power has attracted the attention of the Competition Bureau.

Bitcoins are a digital form of money, sometimes called "cryptocurrency" or "the currency of the Internet." Bitcoins involve a mobile app or computer program that provides a user with a personal bitcoin wallet, thereby allowing the user to send and receive bitcoins over a decentralized peer-to-peer network. Bitcoins were introduced with much fanfare, but became enveloped in controversy after the collapse of the biggest bitcoin exchange and the resulting disappearance of bitcoins worth hundreds of millions of dollars.

Critical Analysis: The range of electronic payment mechanisms is continually expanding. Are the risks associated with these methods outweighed by the low cost, convenience, and customer demand? Can the developers of such methods and the lawmakers stay ahead of those who seek to breach security?

Sources: Ivor Tossell, "Enter the digital wallet", *The Globe and Mail* (7 November 2011), online: Globe and Mail <http://www.theglobeandmail.com/report-on-business/small-business/enter-the-digital-wallet/article2226181/>; Tara S Bernard and Claire C Miller, "Swiping is the easy part", *The New York Times* (23 March 2011), online: The New York Times <http://www.nytimes.com/2011/03/24/technology/24wallet.html>; Grant Robertson, "Say cheese! Photo chequing on its way to Canada", The Globe and Mail (26 March 2012), online: Globe and Mail <http://www.theglobeandmail.com/globe-investor/say-cheese-photo-chequing-on-its-way-to-canada/article2381965/>; and Competition Bureau of Canada, "Competition Bureau challenges Visa and Mastercard's Anti-competitive rules" (15 December 2010), online: Competition Bureau Canada <http://www.competitionbureau.gc.ca/eic/site/cb-bc.nsf/eng /03325.html>. Heidi Moore, "The Mt Gox bitcoin scandal is the best thing to happen to bitcoin in years", *The Guardian* (26 February 2014), online: <http://www.theguardian.com/money/us-money-blog/2014/feb/25/bitcoin-mt-gox-scandal-reputation-crime>.

Igor Vladimirovich Zhorov/Shutterstock • Family Business/Shutterstock • LDProd/iStock/Getty Images Plus

Do the same rules apply to various payment choices?

The rules governing payment by cheque are well defined and are part of the law of negotiable instruments.

Negotiable Instruments

A **negotiable instrument** is a signed document that promises payment of a specific sum of money. A **cheque** is the most common example of a negotiable instrument, but promissory notes and bills of exchange are also negotiable instruments. A **promissory note** is a written promise to pay another person a specific amount on demand or on a specified date. A **bill of exchange** is a written order by one person (the drawer) to a third party (the drawee) to pay money to another person (the payee). A cheque is a special type of bill of exchange, which is payable on demand and where the party instructed to pay is a bank. Negotiable instruments are "negotiable" in the sense that they may be transferred from one holder to another. Negotiable instruments are federally regulated by the *Bills of Exchange Act*.[19]

There are several requirements for an instrument to become negotiable (i.e., transferable) without the need to investigate its validity through reference to the circumstances of its creation or other documents:

- it must be in written form and be signed by the person making the promise or authorizing the payment.
- it must specify an amount of money to be paid on demand or on a specified date.
- the obligation to pay must be unconditional.

For example, if a promise is made to pay "the balance due" on a construction contract, the promise cannot be a negotiable instrument because the balance can be determined only by consulting the original contract and investigating the work done and payments already made. A negotiable instrument must be for a specific sum without conditions. When Hometown issues a cheque for $1000.00 to one of its suppliers, Hometown is giving a written order to its bank to pay a specified sum to the supplier. The cheque is therefore a negotiable instrument.

As illustrated in Figure 25.1, Hometown is the drawer of the instrument, because Hometown is ordering its bank to pay the supplier the amount of the cheque. The supplier is the payee. Hometown's bank, as the recipient of Hometown's instruction to pay, is the drawee.

The account agreement that Hometown has with its bank will describe the manner in which cheques written on Hometown's accounts will be handled. For

Negotiable instrument

A signed document containing an unconditional promise or order to pay a specific sum on demand or on a specified date to a specific person.

Cheque

A bill of exchange which is drawn on a bank and is payable on demand.

Promissory note

A written promise to pay another person a specific amount on demand or on a specified date.

Bill of exchange

A written order by one person (the drawer) to a third person (the drawee) to pay money to another person (the payee).

FIGURE 25.1 An Annotated Cheque

---

19 RSC 1985, c B-4.

PART EIGHT

FIGURE 25.2 Steps in the Cheque Circulation Process

> Hometown (Drawer) issues cheque to Supplier (Payee). Supplier deposits cheque in its bank.

> Supplier's bank places funds in Supplier's account. Through the cheque-clearing process, the cheque moves from the Supplier's bank to Hometown's bank (Drawee).

> Hometown's bank removes funds from Hometown's account and transfers to the Supplier's bank. Supplier's bank recovers its funds.

example, the agreement will typically provide that Hometown must keep adequate funds in its accounts to pay any cheques that are issued, and the bank must take reasonable care in honouring instructions to pay out the money.[20]

Hometown's supplier will likely take the cheque to its own bank for deposit. Through the centralized clearing process, the cheque will find its way from the supplier's bank to Hometown's bank, and the specified sum will be taken from Hometown's account (see Figure 25.2). As long as there are adequate funds in Hometown's account and there is no defect in the cheque, it will proceed smoothly through the steps.

If Hometown accepts cheques as payment from its customers, the customer is the drawer, the customer's bank is the drawee, and Hometown is the payee. The following sections describe the potential risks involved in issuing and accepting cheques.

Implications of Creating a Cheque

When Bill chooses to pay a supplier by cheque, he is discharging a debt that Hometown owes as debtor to the supplier as creditor. That debt has arisen through the contract between Hometown and the supplier for the provision of goods or services. Assuming that Hometown buys its supplies from a number of suppliers, it will have regular payment obligations arising from its contractual arrangements with those suppliers. If there are problems with the supplies (e.g., they are defective or not delivered), Hometown will have a valid complaint against the supplier (subject to the terms of their contract). Hometown can pursue that complaint as it would any breach of contract.

However, if Hometown has issued a cheque to the supplier, its claim for breach of contract is a totally different matter from its obligation to pay the cheque. By issuing the cheque, Hometown has made an unconditional promise to pay the specified sum not just to the supplier, but potentially to anyone (known as a **holder**) who presents the cheque to Hometown's bank for payment. The special

Holder

A person who has possession of a negotiable instrument.

---

20 *Supra* note 7 at 30.

status of the cheque and the holder are created by legislation[21] that deliberately places the holder in a strong position in terms of collecting on the cheque. If the holder has acted in good faith (meaning she has no reason to doubt the validity of the cheque), that person acquires the status of a **holder in due course**. There are limited arguments (e.g., a forged signature or an alteration of the cheque) that Hometown can use to justify refusing to pay a holder in due course. The rights of such a holder are not affected by any terms of Hometown's contract with its supplier. Hometown's bank will pay out the cheque to the holder and Hometown must seek compensation separately from its supplier.

A negotiable instrument (including a cheque) is markedly different from an ordinary assignment of contractual rights, where there can be any number of defences against paying. For example, if Hometown owes money to a supplier, that supplier can assign the right to collect to someone else (an assignee). In the absence of a negotiable instrument, the assignee's right to collect from Hometown is subject to any problems with the contract between Hometown and the supplier. Thus, if Hometown has a valid reason for refusing to pay the supplier, it can use the same reason to avoid paying the assignee. In law, this idea is captured in the expression "an assignee can have no better rights than the assignor."[22]

This important distinction between an assignment and a negotiable instrument is illustrated by the former practice in some sales to consumers where the separation of obligations arising from the negotiable instrument and the contract of sale was abused. If a consumer bought goods on credit, and signed a negotiable instrument such as a promissory note in favour of the seller, the seller could transfer the note to another party (such as a finance company). The legal result of the transfer of the note was that the financier became a holder in due course. The buyer's obligation to pay the financier was then nearly absolute and independent of problems with the quality of the purchased goods. Such problems could be pursued against the seller based on the contract of sale, but they did not affect the consumer's continuing obligation to make payments to the holder of the note (the finance company). These rules enabled collusion between unscrupulous sellers and financiers to sell substandard goods to consumers and require them to make all payments, even when the goods were clearly defective or even worthless.

The *Bills of Exchange Act*[23] now classifies a promissory note arising from a consumer credit sale as a **consumer note**. The holder of a consumer note is not accorded the special status of a holder in due course and is subject to claims arising from the original contract of sale. Thus, the consumer's obligation to pay the note is subject to remedies the consumer may have against the seller if the goods are defective. See Figure 25.3 for a comparison of the payment and collection arrangements discussed to this point.

Implications of Accepting a Cheque

The major risk involved in accepting a cheque relates to the financial health of the drawer of the cheque. The strong and secure legal position of a holder in due course is of no value if the drawer's account does not contain enough money to cover the cheque when it is presented for payment. The likelihood of that happening is the key consideration in Bill's decision about whether to accept payments by

Holder in due course

A holder in good faith without notice of defects, who acquires greater rights than the parties who dealt directly with each other as the drawer and payee.

Consumer note

A negotiable instrument signed by a consumer to buy goods or services on credit.

---

21   *Supra* note 19 at s 55.
22   See Chapter 9 for a more complete discussion of assignments.
23   *Supra* note 19 at s 191.

FIGURE 25.3 Comparison of Payment and Collection Arrangements

Type of Arrangement	Parties Involved	Enforcement Rights
Contract	Buyer (debtor) Seller (creditor)	Seller can collect subject to performance of its obligations.
Assignment of contractual right	Debtor Creditor (assignor) Assignee	Assignee's right to collect is subject to the debtor's obligation to pay the assignor.
Negotiable instrument (e.g., a cheque)	Drawer (debtor) Payee (creditor) Holder in due course	Holder in due course's right to collect is not tied to the original contract.
Consumer note	Consumer Seller Finance company	Finance company does not have status as a holder in due course—consumer's obligation to pay depends on the original contract.

cheque from customers. Deciding to accept cheques is similar to extending credit, because there is normally a gap of several days between handing over the goods and receiving payment from the cheque.

In larger transactions, a bank draft or certified cheque may be used to overcome the above risk. A **bank draft** is a cheque written by a bank on the request of its customer. The customer pays the bank the amount of the draft when the draft is created, so the bank bears no risk that its customer will not have sufficient funds to cover the draft. Since the draft is issued by the bank on its own account, the payee can be assured that it will be honoured when it is presented for payment. To make a **certified cheque**, the drawer or payee takes the cheque to the drawer's bank and has the bank certify it for payment. The bank immediately removes the money from the drawer's account and holds it in reserve until the cheque is presented for payment. This process removes the risk of there being insufficient funds in the drawer's account when the cheque is cashed.

Certifying a cheque usually prevents the drawer from putting a **stop payment** on the cheque. A stop payment means that the drawer has cancelled its instructions to pay the cheque and orders its bank to refuse payment when the cheque is presented. These instructions can be issued at any time before a cheque has been charged against the drawer's account. However, the banking contract will likely absolve the bank from responsibility if the cheque is cashed accidentally, despite the stop payment order. The drawer of a cheque may also postdate it, which makes it payable on the future specified date and not on the date of creation. Since the bank must follow the drawer's instructions, it cannot cash the cheque until that future date.

Despite the secure position of holders in due course, those who are called upon to accept the transfer of a cheque may be reluctant to do so without verification of the various endorsements on the cheque and some means of recovering funds advanced on a cheque that turns out to be invalid. Thus, banks are reluctant to cash cheques for people who are not their customers with significant balances on deposit with them. If the cheque comes back to the bank due to a lack of funds in the drawer's account, the amount can be deducted from the customer's account (likely in accordance with the account agreement). The bank, therefore,

Bank draft

A cheque written by a bank on the request (and payment) of its customer.

Certified cheque

A cheque on which the drawee bank has guaranteed payment.

Stop payment

When the drawer of a cheque orders its bank not to pay the holder who presents the cheque for payment.

will not suffer the ultimate loss on the cheque. If the bank cashes a cheque for someone who is not a customer, it will be more difficult to recover the funds if the cheque turns out to be worthless. If Hometown accepts a cheque from a customer, it bears the risk that the cheque will turn out to be worthless. Even though the cheque may be deposited into Hometown's bank account, and the updated balance may reflect the deposited amount, if the cheque is subsequently dishonoured by the customer's bank, Hometown's bank will deduct the amount of the cheque from Hometown's account.

Endorsement and Transfer of Negotiable Instruments

A cheque normally follows a relatively short route, as shown in Figure 25.2, but it may also be transferred many times from holder to holder. Eventually, it is presented by a holder to the drawer's bank for payment. The transfer process is known as negotiation—hence the name "negotiable instrument." However, negotiation in this context has a different meaning from its more common use as a process for resolving disputes. All that is needed for the negotiation of an instrument is for the current holder to **endorse**, or sign, the instrument over to a new holder, who then becomes entitled to either present the instrument for payment or transfer it to yet another holder. With cheques, endorsements are typically made by signing the back of the cheque.

Endorse

To sign a negotiable instrument (such as a cheque) in order to enable negotiation.

Although a bank or anyone else who gives money in return for a cheque runs the risk that the drawer is not able or obligated to honour it, anyone who has endorsed the cheque is also potentially liable for the amount of the cheque. This liability is a significant risk for anyone who endorses a negotiable instrument.

A bank's responsibility to carry out the instructions of its customers includes verifying a customer's signature on a cheque.[24] The bank and its customers both have obligations when forgery is involved. The bank has a duty to detect unauthorized instructions (such as a forged signature), and customers must take reasonable steps to prevent forgeries and immediately report any potential problems to the bank (see the case below). If a bank is left with liability for a forged cheque, it can look to prior endorsers of the cheque to recover its money. Therefore, anyone accepting a cheque should verify the authenticity of the endorsements on it.

CASE

SNS Industrial Products Limited v Bank of Montreal, 2010 ONCA 500

THE BUSINESS CONTEXT: There are situations where the bank fails to detect forged signatures and the customer does not immediately notice that the forged cheques have been cashed from its account. In these cases, the courts will look to the legislation and the bank–customer agreement.

FACTUAL BACKGROUND: Sanfillippo was the president of SNS Industrial Limited. In 1994, he opened an account at the Bank of Montreal and signed an agreement which included a verification clause: "Upon receipt of the... statement of account, the Corporation will check the debit and credit entries, examine the cheques and vouchers and notify the Bank in writing of any errors, irregularities or omissions. This notice will be provided to the Bank

(Continued)

---

24 However, it has been suggested that, due to the volume of cheques being processed, banks do not look at payee names, signatures, or endorsements on cheques deposited using ATMs. See Kathy Tomlinson, "Banks don't look at names, signatures on cheques," *CBC News* (03 May 2011), online: <http://www.cbc.ca/news/banks-don-t-look-at-names-signatures-on-cheques-1.978046>.

within 30 days…" Over a three-year period from 2003 to 2006, the office manager of SNS forged Sanfillippo's signature on a number of cheques worth $186 488. In May 2006, Sanfillippo noticed considerably less money in his account than he expected and inquired at the bank, where he was advised to begin telephone or online banking so that he could more easily monitor his account balance. At this time he signed a new agreement whose verification clause made explicit reference to forged cheques. Shortly afterward, Sanfillippo discovered the forgeries and claimed the value of the cheques from the bank.

THE LEGAL QUESTION: Who was responsible for detecting the forgeries—the customer or the bank?

RESOLUTION: The Court of Appeal relied primarily on the applicable legislation. The *Bills of Exchange Act* (s 48)[25] states: "where a signature on a bill of exchange is forged, or placed thereon without the authority of the person whose signature it purports to be, the forged or unauthorized signature is wholly inoperative…." It was open to the bank to transfer the risk to the customer, but in the 1994 agreement, the Verification Clause does not refer expressly to forged cheques or otherwise to cheques debited to a customer's account for improper purposes or by illegal means. Further, the terms "error," "irregularity," and "omission" are not defined in the Verification Clause. Nor is their meaning clear on a plain reading of the Verification Clause as a whole. Thus, the meaning of these terms is not apparent on the face of the Verification Clause. Certainly, the scope of these terms would not be self-evident to many, if any, customers of the bank without clarification or explanation. It is difficult to conceive, therefore, absent evidence to the contrary that does not exist in this case, that both parties intended, when the banking agreement was entered into, that the Verification Clause would extend to forged cheques honoured by the bank.

Therefore, the bank remained responsible for honouring the forged cheques.

CRITICAL ANALYSIS: Does the specific reference to forgery in the 2006 contract support the court's conclusion regarding the 1994 clause? The trial judge found that the forger did a good job on Sanfillippo's signature and that Sanfillippo did not have adequate controls in place. Are these findings relevant to the interpretation of the legislation and the agreement?

Endorsement in blank

Signing a cheque without any special instructions.

Restrictive endorsement

Signing a cheque for deposit only to a particular bank account.

Special endorsement

Signing a cheque and making it payable to a specific person.

Those in possession of cheques should take steps to safeguard them and transfer them by endorsing in a way that minimizes the risk that others may illegally obtain and cash them. Simply signing a cheque on the back is known as an **endorsement in blank**. This means that the signatures are complete and anyone who acquires the cheque can cash it (subject to a bank's willingness to do so). Holders should therefore take care with the form of endorsements. Businesses commonly endorse cheques "for deposit only." This is known as a **restrictive endorsement** and means that the cheques can be deposited only in the account of that business. Restrictive endorsements stop the circulation of cheques and remove the risk of anyone else acquiring and cashing them. If Hometown accepts cheques from customers, it should routinely endorse them in this manner as soon as possible. If a cheque received by a payee is to be transferred to someone other than a bank, it is wise to endorse it directly to that person (e.g., "Pay to Desmond Chu/signed Bill Ikeda"). This is known as a **special endorsement**; it ensures that only the designated person is able to deal with the cheque further.

Those accepting cheques should realize that there are financial and legal reasons why collection may be a problem. Apart from a bank draft or certified cheque,

---

25 *Supra* note 19.

there is no guarantee of payment. Bill must understand that if a customer's cheque is returned to him by Hometown's bank because of insufficient funds in the customer's account, Hometown will recover the funds only if it can collect from the customer. If the customer cannot be located or is unable to pay the amount, Hometown will bear the loss. However, if Hometown can locate the customer, the cheque is valuable evidence of the customer's contractual obligation to pay.

The Future of Payments

A negotiable instrument has a life of its own, quite separate from the contract that produced it. Liability for payment is independent of the original debtor–creditor relationship. The result is convenience and dependability in the commercial environment. The tradeoff is that the instruments must be honoured by their creators (or endorsers) even in situations where there is a good reason for liability to be borne by another party, such as someone who breached the originating contract through failure to deliver goods or services.

The basis of the well-established and comprehensive set of rules governing negotiable instruments is the instrument itself—the piece of paper. The information it contains and where it goes are the key features of any dispute. Electronic transfers present several challenges in relation to this set of rules. First, since there is no key piece of paper that circulates through the system, there is a limited paper trail in the event of a dispute. Second, electronic transfers are instantaneous, so there is no opportunity to change the instructions for payment (e.g., by issuing a stop payment). There is no need for the certification process because the transfer is unlikely to be effective unless the account from which the transfer is made has sufficient funds. Electronic deposits may result in problems if no one verifies the validity of the instruments being deposited. For example, if there is a serious defect in a cheque deposited electronically, the amount will initially be added to the customer's balance, but it will be deducted later when the defect is discovered. By this time, the customer may have already spent the money.

Electronic transfers are inexpensive, convenient, and efficient. There is no paper to track or store. Instructions can be issued by the customer to the bank instantly, and the funds are transferred to the recipient immediately. However, safeguarding the authority for such transfers can be a major challenge. Rather than verifying signatures on cheques, banks are looking for the necessary authorization codes in electronic messages. Potential methods for forgery and fraud are changed and expanded. Tracing the cause of an electronic loss may be difficult.

Commercial and consumer transactions are increasingly being conducted electronically and online. The volume of cheques is declining, and traditional paper cheques are increasingly being converted to digital images for processing. In practical and legal terms, the focus is shifting to electronic banking, although that transition will not be without its challenges. [26]

Risk Management

In determining how Hometown should conduct its banking, and what methods of payment Hometown will use and accept from customers, Bill and Martha must consider marketing and financial factors as well as legal issues. They must be

26 Benjamin Geva, "Is the Death of the Paper Cheque upon Us?", *Banking and Finance Law Review*, (November 2014) 30 B.F.L.R. 113.

PART EIGHT

responsive to the needs and demands of Hometown's customers and sensitive to the risk and cost of various payment options.

Bill and Martha must understand the relationship that Hometown has with its bank, and they should ensure that the account agreement properly describes that relationship. They should be clear on the fees that Hometown is required to pay the bank, and they should shop around to make sure they are not overpaying for the services they are receiving.

Making and accepting payments by cheque involves risk. Payment by cheque creates an unconditional obligation independent of the purchase for which the cheque is used as payment. Accepting cheques as payment requires careful endorsement to maximize security and creates the risk that there will not be sufficient funds in the customers' accounts to honour the cheques.

As long as Bill and Martha are the only ones with signing authority at the bank, authorization should not be a problem. When they reach the point at which they need to share that responsibility, they must make the terms of the arrangement clear to the persons receiving the authority and to the bank. Bill and Martha must also familiarize themselves with the practices of their bank related to authorization by phone, fax, or computer if they choose to use them.

Regarding debit cards and credit cards, Bill and Martha need to understand the agreements Hometown has with those service providers and the fees that Hometown will have to pay to accept payments in that form. Accepting debit cards means Hometown will get paid immediately, and credit cards provide an assurance of payment as long as Hometown complies with the requirements in its service agreements, such as verification of signatures.

Bill and Martha need to ask their bank what happens if an electronic transfer does not happen or the bank transfers funds without proper authorization. They need to ensure that the bank has anticipated potential problems and has a reasonable strategy of dealing with them. They need to evaluate the risks against the potential benefits of electronic banking.

Figure 25.4 summarizes the comparative risks of the various payment methods. The possibility of extending credit to customers is the subject of Chapter 26.

FIGURE 25.4 Comparative Risks of Methods of Accepting Payment

Form of Payment	Nature of Payment	Risk for Person Accepting Payment
Cash	Immediate	The money may be counterfeit or the proceeds of a crime.
Cheque	Deposited	There may be insufficient funds in the account on which the cheque was drawn; the signature may be forged.
Credit card	Guaranteed	Risk is borne largely by the card provider. Additional fees apply.
Debit card	Immediate transfer	Risk is borne largely by the payments system. Additional fees apply.
Electronic funds transfer	Immediate transfer	Risk is borne largely by the payments system.
Credit	Payment at a later date	The debtor may be unable or unwilling to pay.

BUSINESS LAW IN PRACTICE REVISITED

1. What do Bill and Martha need to know about the legal aspects of the relationship between their business and a bank?

Bill and Martha need to appreciate that their basic relationship with the bank is one in which the bank must safeguard their money and follow their payment instructions, but is otherwise not responsible for their interests, unless the bank is engaged to provide expert advice. Bill and Martha need to appreciate the importance of the contract with the bank and become familiar with its basic rights and obligations. They should understand that the contract is written largely to protect the bank and that their bargaining power is limited. Bill and Martha should, however, seek a level of service and comfort that meets their needs and allays their concerns with their current bank.

2. What are the risks and benefits of various payment options and banking electronically?

If Hometown engages in electronic banking, it will be cheaper and faster, but the risks include: transmission problems, difficulty cancelling electronic transactions because they are instantaneous, and a limited paper trail. Bill and Martha need to discuss these risks with the bank so that they are comfortable with their banking arrangements. Since Hometown accepts payments by credit card and debit card, they need to negotiate with the providers of those services and be prepared to pay the fees. Such arrangements are not typically part of the normal package of basic banking services.

3. What are the risks and benefits of using cheques to pay bills and allowing customers to pay by cheque?

The risk of paying by cheque is that Hometown cannot avoid its obligation to honour the cheque (apart from stopping payment) if there is a problem with the goods or services for which the cheque was used as payment. The risk of allowing customers to pay by cheque is that they may have insufficient funds in their accounts, they may be engaged in fraud or forgery, they might issue a stop payment, or there may be a technical defect in the cheque.

The benefits of paying by cheque are the relative security compared to paying with cash, the paper trail provided by the cheque, and the ability to issue a stop payment before the cheque is cashed. Accepting payments by cheque is more risky than taking only cash, but it is safer than credit.

CHAPTER SUMMARY

Customers should be knowledgeable about the relationship they have with their banks. The relationship between a customer and its bank is a contractual one and thus the rights and obligations of the parties are found in the contract. However, because these contracts are standard form contracts written by the banks, they tend to favour the banks' interests more than those of their customers.

Electronic banking is increasingly convenient and inexpensive. In addition, the instantaneous nature of electronic transactions greatly improves efficiency, but it also makes transfers irrevocable. The absence of paper and the inapplicability of the rules that govern paper transactions may create challenges for security and liability.

The legal framework for negotiable instruments focuses on the commercial convenience of instruments circulating freely, with little need for the various holders to be concerned about their validity as long as the requirements for negotiability are met. It is a paper-based system that places prime importance on the piece of paper and the secure status of those in possession of that paper.

The essential feature of a negotiable instrument is the ability of a holder in due course to collect from the person who originally promised to pay the specified amount, along with any holders who endorsed the instrument along the way.

CHAPTER STUDY

Key Terms and Concepts

account agreement (p. 641)

bank draft (p. 648)

bill of exchange (p. 645)

certified cheque (p. 648)

cheque (p. 645)

consumer note (p. 647)

credit card (p. 643)

electronic banking (p. 641)

electronic funds transfer (p. 643)

endorse (p. 649)

endorsement in blank (p. 650)

holder (p. 646)

holder in due course (p. 647)

identity theft (p. 642)

money laundering (p. 640)

negotiable instrument (p. 645)

overdraft (p. 641)

promissory note (p. 645)

restrictive endorsement (p. 650)

special endorsement (p. 650)

stop payment (p. 648)

Questions for Review

1. What is the basic nature of the bank–customer relationship?

2. How are banks regulated?

3. What are the key issues addressed in an account agreement?

4. What are the key duties of the customer and the bank?

5. What are the requirements for an instrument to be negotiable?

6. What is a cheque?

7. Why is the volume of cheques declining?

8. Why are electronic transfers not subject to the same regulations as paper transactions?

9. When a business issues a cheque to a supplier, who is the drawer, who is the drawee, and who is the payee of the cheque?

10. What is an electronic funds transfer?

11. What are the key risks for a business in accepting cheques from customers?

12. Why is a holder in due course in a stronger position to collect on a negotiable instrument than an assignee is to collect a debt?

13. What are the banks' obligations regarding suspected money laundering?

14. What is identity theft?

15. What are the benefits of electronic banking?

16. What are the legal uncertainties in electronic banking?

17. How can smart phones be used for banking?

18. What is "phishing"?

Questions for Critical Thinking

1. In banking relationships, customers are expected to take care of themselves and to negotiate and be aware of their rights and obligations. In practice, the terms of banking contracts are dictated by the banks and found in standard form agreements that are not open to negotiation. Should banking contracts be regulated to ensure a basic level of fairness for customers?

2. Retail merchants are caught between their customers and the credit card companies. Customers want their cards to be accepted, especially those offering attractive rewards to card users. Meanwhile, the card companies require merchants to accept all cards and pay whatever fees the companies choose to impose. How can merchants deal with this dilemma?

3. Electronic banking presents a regulatory challenge in that paper-based rules do not apply and the nature of electronic transactions produces a new set of potential problems. What are some of those problems? Are the regulations likely to be outpaced by developments in technology?

4. In 2015 it was discovered that 1859 individuals linked to Canada, including a number of prominent billionaires, had secretly been keeping money in HSBC's Swiss private bank, presumably in some cases to avoid the payment of Canadian income taxes. Largely through programs which provide leniency in exchange for voluntary disclosure, tax authorities have so far recovered $63 million in unpaid taxes, but no charges have been laid. What is the best way to deal with Canadians who use private banks to hide money for the purpose of evading taxes?[27]

5. The use of cheques is decreasing while various forms of electronic payments are on the rise. Is there any reason to maintain the paper-based cheque system and the legal framework in which it operates?

6. Electronic transactions can result in the creation and combination of databases containing sensitive business and personal information. Those who provide this information are naturally concerned about its security and their privacy. One way to deal with such concerns is to enable anonymous transactions through such means as encryption, which in turn creates concern for illicit activities such as money laundering. Which is more important—providing security or preventing fraud or crime?

Situations for Discussion

1. Grenville agreed to facilitate transfers of funds for a Taiwanese businessman whom he did not know. Grenville was to deposit cheques in his account and forward the funds to Asian accounts in exchange for a 5 percent commission. Without Grenville's knowledge, the first cheque (in the amount of $10 000) that he deposited in his credit union account had been altered and forged. Several months after the cheque cleared, the defects in the cheque were discovered. Grenville's credit union took the full balance in Grenville's account ($6000) and sued him for the remaining $4000.[28] Is the credit union entitled to recover the $10 000 from Grenville? What are the relevant rules?

2. Ken needed $100 000 to start his restaurant. He sought advice from W Bank. Pamela, the loans officer at the bank, suggested a working capital loan on certain specified terms. She assured Ken that he should have no problem being approved if he decided to apply for a loan. The approval process took longer than usual, but Ken went ahead and signed a lease for space for his restaurant and a contract for renovation of the space. Eventually, W Bank rejected Ken's application. Based on recent

27 Frederic Zalac, "HSBC's private bank in Switzerland used by several Canadian billionaires", *CBC News,* (12 February 2015), online: <http://www.cbc.ca/news/business/hsbc-s-private-bank-in-switzerland-used-by-several-canadian-billionaires-1.2955651>.

28 Based on *Meridian Credit Union Limited v Grenville-Wood Estate,* 2011 ONCA 512 (leave to appeal to SCC dismissed 8 March 2012).

experience, the bank decided that restaurants are too risky since most do not last beyond six months. Ken was unable to arrange alternative financing in time and suffered a large loss in his business.[29] Is this a typical banking relationship where Ken must look out for himself, or does the bank have some responsibility for his plight? What should Ken and the bank have done differently?

3. Rattray Publications wrote a cheque payable to LePage on its account at CIBC in payment for the first month's rent on an office lease. Rattray changed its mind about the lease and instructed CIBC to stop payment on the cheque. The following day, LePage got the cheque certified at another branch of CIBC and deposited the cheque in its account at TD Bank. When TD presented the cheque to CIBC for payment, CIBC refused to honour it.[30] Which prevails—the stop payment or the certification? Does the validity of the cheque depend on the lease agreement between Rattray and LePage? Which of the four parties should bear the loss?

4. Stephen, Eric, and the Kaptor Group were all customers of the same bank. Stephen was involved in a business arrangement with the Kaptor Group, pursuant to which he made regular payments to Kaptor by way of cheques. The bank discovered that Eric and the Kaptor Group were circulating worthless cheques in a fraudulent scheme known as "cheque kiting." As a result, the bank froze Kaptor's accounts, and discovered the accounts were overdrawn in the amount of $7 million. However, the bank did not tell Stephen that it had frozen Kaptor's accounts, nor of its suspicions that Kaptor was engaged in fraudulent behaviour, and continued to process cheques issued by Stephen and payable to Kaptor. In fact, the bank used the funds represented by those cheques to reduce the indebtedness owed by Kaptor to the bank.[31] What obligations does the bank owe to Stephen in this situation? Does the bank owe a duty of

confidentiality to Kaptor? If so, how far does that duty extend if it jeopardizes the interests of another customer of the bank?

5. Lauren and Peter installed devices on several ATM machines to obtain the debit and credit card information of people using the machines. The devices consisted of an overlay on the card reader which captured the data stored on the magnetic stripe of the card along with a pinhole video camera which secretly recorded PINs as they were entered. The information obtained was used to make counterfeit cards that were then used to make fraudulent purchases and cash withdrawals. In the end, Lauren and Peter committed hundreds of fraudulent transactions over many months using the illegally obtained information.[32] What does this reveal about the perils of electronic banking? Are these risks likely to be prevented by banking practices, contracts, or the law? Who should be responsible for the losses?

6. Rubin and Russell were partners in RRP Associates. They did their personal and business banking with Colossal Bank, where they arranged their accounts so that transfers from one to the other could be made by either partner online, by phone, or in person. Although the business prospered, Rubin and Russell had difficulty working together. Following a serious disagreement, Russell went online and transferred $50 000 from the RRP account to his personal account. When Rubin discovered this transaction, he complained to the bank and was told that the transfer was done in accordance with the agreement between RRP and the bank. How can partners best balance the risks arising from banking arrangements with the need for convenient banking? What action can Rubin take now?

7. Bob was the sole officer, director, and shareholder of 545012 Ltd. Bank of Montreal issued a bank card to Bob for the company's account. Bob entrusted an employee, Paul, with the corporate card and its PIN. Paul forged cheques payable to the company, deposited them in the corporate account, and then used the corporate card to withdraw cash and make

29 Based on *Royal Bank of Canada v Woloszyn* (1998), 170 NSR (2d) 122 (SC).
30 Based on *A.E. LePage Real Estate Services Ltd v Rattray Publications Ltd* (1994), 21 OR (3d) 164 (CA).
31 Based on *Grossman v. Toronto-Dominion Bank*, 2014 ONSC 3578 (Ont. S.C.J.).
32 Based on *R. v. Girdea*, 2014 ONCJ 128 (Ont. C.J.).

point-of-sale purchases, creating an overdraft of $60 000 on the corporate account. The bank sued 545012 Ltd. and Bob for the amount of the overdraft.[33] Who is responsible for the overdraft? What factors are relevant in analyzing this situation?

8. BMP Global Inc. (BMP) was a distributor of nonstick bakeware in British Columbia. BMP was a customer of the Bank of Nova Scotia (BNS) in Vancouver. Hashka and Backman were the two owners of BMP and had personal accounts in the same branch of BNS. BMP received a cheque for $902 563 drawn by First National Financial Corp. on the Royal Bank of Canada (RBC) in Toronto. Hashka deposited the cheque in the BMP account and informed the manager, Richards, that the cheque was a down payment on a distributorship contract with an American company. Richards placed a hold on the cheque for seven days. The cheque cleared and was paid by RBC to BNS and released to BMP. Hashka and Backman paid several creditors and transferred funds to their personal accounts. Ten days later RBC notified Richards that the signatures on the $902 563 cheque were forged. Richards froze the three accounts in his branch and returned the combined balance of $776 000 to RBC.[34] Was Richards justified in freezing and seizing the accounts of BMP, Hashka, and Backman? Can they take action against Richards and BNS? Is RBC responsible for accepting the cheque with the forged signatures?

---

33 Based on *Bank of Montreal v 545012 Ontario Limited*, 2009 CanLII 55127 (Ont Sup Ct J).

34 Based on *BMP Global Distribution Inc v Bank of Nova Scotia*, 2009 SCC 15.

26

OBJECTIVES

After studying this chapter, you should have an understanding of

- the legal significance of credit transactions in business
- methods used by creditors to reduce risk
- the difference between secured and unsecured creditors
- the ways that lenders and borrowers are protected
- the implications of guaranteeing a debt

THE LEGAL ASPECTS OF CREDIT

BUSINESS LAW IN PRACTICE

Hometown Hardware Ltd. (Hometown) and its owners, Bill Ikeda and Martha Wong, were introduced in Chapter 25. They operate a building supply store in Timmins, Ontario. Bill has become concerned about rumours that a big-box store will soon be arriving in Timmins. Bill is worried about the impact on Hometown and has decided that the only way Hometown can remain competitive is to expand and offer a broader range of supplies. Bill is confident that his customers will remain loyal to Hometown if they can obtain the same range of products from Hometown as will be available from the new big-box store. At the same time, Bill is concerned about the recent slowdown in housing construction.

In order to finance the planned expansion, Bill has determined that Hometown needs $250 000. Bill and Martha hope to have Hometown borrow that amount from the bank.

1. What is the bank likely to require before agreeing to loan money to Hometown?
2. What will the terms of the loan be?
3. What are the risks for Hometown in borrowing the money?
4. Will Bill and Martha be personally liable for the bank loan?

Introduction to Debt and Credit

A business participates on a daily basis in a variety of transactions that involve credit. Some credit arrangements are formal and deliberate, with carefully negotiated terms, while others are an incidental feature of routine transactions. A business like Hometown will be both a borrower, or debtor, and a lender, or creditor. When Hometown buys lumber from its suppliers, it is required to pay the invoice within 30 days, making it a debtor. When Hometown sells the lumber to its commercial customers, those customers are probably expected to pay on similar terms, making Hometown a creditor. Retail customers are likely expected to pay immediately, although Hometown may offer financing terms to some retail customers on large purchases.

Credit is a contractual relationship, with the lender agreeing to lend money in exchange for a promise by the borrower to repay the loan, usually with interest and within a certain time frame. There may be other terms and conditions which are agreed to

What legal risks arise in financing the expansion of a business?

by the parties. Since credit is a contractual relationship, all the fundamental principles of contract law apply. As well, there are legal regulations and principles which are specific to credit. The law of credit forms part of what is known as debtor and creditor law.

Credit can be either secured or unsecured. **Secured credit** means the creditor has an interest in all or some of the property of the debtor in order to secure payment of the debt. If the debtor defaults in repaying the loan, the secured creditor can seize the secured property and sell it to pay down the debt. **Unsecured credit** means that the creditor has only a contractual right to receive payment from the debtor. The unsecured creditor does not have an interest in the property of the debtor that it can enforce in the event of default by the debtor. If the debtor defaults, a secured creditor is in a much better position than an unsecured creditor.

When Hometown agrees to pay its suppliers within 30 days, or when Hometown's commercial customers agree to pay Hometown on similar terms, that is known as trade credit. Trade credit is usually unsecured. In most cases, payment is made within the designated time period and collection remedies are not needed. Since these transactions are unsecured, if a debtor fails to pay on time, the creditor may have to sue the debtor, obtain judgment, and then enforce that judgment. If the debtor has limited financial resources, the creditor may end up not being paid. For this reason, it is very important for creditors to exercise good judgment when deciding whether to extend credit. Trade credit can be very risky if the parties have not dealt with each other before, especially if the supplier and the customer are located in different countries. The following International Perspective box provides an example.

Secured credit

A debt where the creditor has an interest in the debtor's property to secure payment.

Unsecured credit

A debt where the creditor has only a contractual right to be repaid.

INTERNATIONAL PERSPECTIVE

CREDIT RISK IN INTERNATIONAL TRADE

Canadian companies import products from countries around the world to sell in Canada. For example, an international trade relationship might originate with a visit by representatives of the Canadian government and importers to a country that is identified as a potential source of trade. Assume that Star Clothing, based in Toronto, participates in such a trip to China and identifies a manufacturer, Beijing Clothing, which can supply high-quality clothing at a lower cost than Star's current supplier in

PART EIGHT

Canada. Representatives of Star negotiate with their counterparts in the Chinese company and eventually agree upon a contract worth $50 000 for clothing to be delivered in time for the spring fashion season in Canada. The contract includes terms dealing with quantity, price, delivery dates, and shipment of the goods from China to Canada.

Since these companies are dealing with each other for the first time, they are sensitive to the risks involved. Beijing wants payment before the goods are shipped because there is significant risk for Beijing if it ships the clothing to Canada with no means of ensuring payment. Beijing appreciates the difficulties involved in suing a Canadian company from its location in China. Star, on the other hand, is reluctant to pay for the clothing until it knows that the agreed upon quality and quantity of clothing has been manufactured and shipped to Canada. Star knows that suing a Chinese company for breach of contract will be difficult and expensive.

Letters of credit issued by international banks are a common means of dealing with these risks. A **letter of credit** is a written promise made by the importer's bank (on the importer's instructions) and given to the exporter's bank to make payment to the exporter when specified conditions are met. These conditions relate to the exporter's delivery of documents, such as an invoice, shipping receipt (bill of lading), proof of insurance, and customs declaration. These documents are presented and payment is made once the goods have been shipped, but before the importer receives the goods. The exporter ships the goods knowing that payment will be made upon presentation of the documents confirming shipment, and the importer allows payment to be made knowing the goods have been shipped and with confidence that the goods will arrive. In this way, both parties reduce some of the risks to which they are exposed.

Critical Analysis: Is the letter of credit a device that could be used to manage risk in domestic as well as international transactions? Can it take the place of reputation and experience in commercial dealings?

Source: Mary Jo Nicholson, *Legal Aspects of International Business: A Canadian Perspective*, 2d ed (Toronto: Emond Montgomery, 2007) at 236.

Letter of credit

A written promise by a buyer's bank to a seller's bank to pay the seller when specified conditions are met.

A business may also decide to raise a significant amount of capital by borrowing. These credit arrangements tend to be more formal and provide more security to the lender. Borrowing a large amount of money to purchase a major asset or to finance an expansion, as Hometown is planning to do, is an example of a credit transaction in which the rights and obligations of the parties are carefully negotiated. When Hometown applies to the bank for a loan of $250 000, the bank will probably require extensive documentation to support the loan application, such as a business plan, financial statements and cash-flow projections. The bank will then consider two major criteria in evaluating the loan application. First, the bank will focus on Hometown's financial health—in particular, the likelihood that the expansion plans will succeed and Hometown will be able to repay the loan within a reasonable time period. Second, the bank will investigate the security that Hometown can provide—if Hometown cannot repay the loan, the lender will want to ensure that it can seize Hometown's property and sell it for enough money to pay the outstanding loan. In this way, the lender ensures that it will be repaid, whether Hometown's business succeeds or fails.

In addition to the ability of the debtor to repay the loan and the value of the security that the debtor can provide, a lender will also consider the state of the economy, the particular industry in which the debtor carries on business, whether personal guarantees are available, and the state of the credit markets generally. Based on all of these considerations, the lender will decide whether to grant the loan and, if so, on what terms. The lender will set the interest rate at a level that corresponds to the riskiness of the loan from the lender's perspective.

If the borrower and the lender are able to agree on the terms of the loan, they will enter into a credit or loan agreement. The terms of this agreement are negotiated by the parties, and may include many different terms and conditions, including repayment terms, interest, security, fees, and **events of default**. In most cases, however, these terms are largely dictated by the lender. Normally, both the borrower and the lender will have their own lawyers to advise them on the credit agreement. In most cases, however, the legal and other fees of the lender must be paid by the borrower.

Methods Used to Reduce Risk in Credit Transactions

There are several ways that creditors can reduce the risk of non-payment by debtors.

First, creditors should employ good credit policies and procedures. This involves steps such as having debtors fill out credit applications and checking debtors' credit references. The easiest way to minimize the risk of default is by not lending money to people who will not pay it back. Although this is a relatively easy and inexpensive strategy, it is often overlooked.

Second, creditors may be able to change the structure of a transaction so that it is not a credit arrangement at all. For example, a supplier of equipment may choose to lease the equipment rather than sell it, so that the supplier retains ownership of the equipment. In the event of default, the lessor can usually repossess the equipment.

Third, creditors may insist on security, or **collateral**, to back up the borrower's promise to pay. If a creditor is able to seize property of the debtor and sell it to pay down the debt, the risk to the creditor is reduced.

Fourth, creditors may ask for assurances from other people that the debt will be repaid. If a creditor is able to obtain a guarantee of the debt from another creditworthy person, then the risk is lessened.

Finally, creditors often include terms in credit agreements which require debtors to carry on business in accordance with specific requirements. For example, a credit agreement may require the debtor to refrain from making significant capital expenditures or allowing certain financial ratios to fall below defined limits.

It is important for businesspeople to think of themselves as creditors any time they are extending credit. In many cases, suppliers will extend credit to customers but fail to take any measures to reduce the risk of not being paid. Banks and other sophisticated creditors employ the techniques described above in order to reduce their risk—businesspeople who extend credit would be wise to think along similar lines.

The Credit or Loan Agreement

In the case of trade credit, the agreement between the debtor and the creditor is usually informal and may even be verbal. If the terms of trade credit are written down, they will often be on a standard form document such as a purchase order or a set of terms and conditions provided by the supplier.

In the case of a large debt financing, however, the credit agreement is typically called a loan agreement and is much more comprehensive and carefully negotiated by the parties. The process of applying for a loan and formulating the terms of credit is much the same as for the negotiation of any other contract. Hometown's need for $250 000 is major in terms of its expansion plans, but it is a routine transaction for a large commercial lender such as a bank. When Hometown applies for the loan, the bank will demand whatever information it deems necessary in order to assess the risk and determine how much, if anything, it is prepared to lend to Hometown and on what terms. If the bank decides to grant the loan, it will usually provide a **letter of commitment** to Hometown, which will set out in a summary manner the basic terms on which the lender is prepared to make the loan. These terms may include:

- amount of the loan and how it will be disbursed.
- rate of interest, and whether it is floating or fixed.
- repayment terms, including the amount and frequency of payments.
- term of the loan and conditions for renewal (if the entire loan will not be paid out during the term).
- conditions that must be satisfied before the loan is made (e.g., guarantees, appraisals).
- security or collateral required by the lender.
- requirements for maintenance of the borrower's financial position.
- events that constitute default and the lender's remedies.
- fees to be paid by the borrower.

The borrower is free to try and negotiate the terms set out in the letter of commitment, or to try to negotiate with other potential lenders, but the final say over whether the loan will be made is that of the lender. Once the letter of commitment is signed by the borrower, the lender will prepare a more formal and comprehensive loan agreement. The loan agreement will cover all of the terms and conditions set out in the letter of commitment and will often be accompanied by other agreements, such as a mortgage, security agreement, or personal guarantee.

Security

In order to reduce the risk of non-payment, a lender may require that the borrower provide security or collateral. Collateral can be either real property, in which case it is accomplished through a mortgage (as discussed in Chapter 19), or personal property (discussed next). While the loan obligation is evidenced by the credit or loan agreement, the taking of security is normally covered by a separate security agreement.

Lenders will often try to match their security to the use of the loan proceeds. For example, if Hometown borrows money in order to buy a new piece of equipment, the security for the loan may be the equipment itself. Similarly, if Hometown negotiates a line of credit for working capital, the lender may take security in Hometown's inventory and accounts receivable. Generally, the most attractive collateral to a lender is that which is most liquid (i.e., can most easily be converted into cash).

If the bank decides to lend money to Hometown to fund its planned expansion, the bank will likely require a **general security agreement**, which will include as collateral all the personal property assets currently held by Hometown, as well as all **after-acquired property**, which are assets that are acquired by Hometown during the term of the loan. Hometown is free to carry on business and use its

Letter of commitment

A document that is provided by a lender to a borrower and sets out the terms of a loan.

General security agreement

A security agreement that includes all of the debtor's personal property assets as collateral.

After-acquired property

Collateral that includes personal property acquired by the debtor during the term of the loan.

assets as long as it makes the required payments on the loan and complies with its other obligations under the loan agreement. However, if Hometown defaults on the loan, the bank's security will include all of the assets held by Hometown at the time of default.

Some assets used as collateral are intended to be retained by the debtor. For example, if Hometown buys a forklift for use in its warehouse, the forklift is available as security for its entire useful life. Other assets, such as inventory and accounts receivable, are meant to circulate through the business on a regular basis. The security in those assets is their value at any given time. The security agreement will allow Hometown to sell inventory in the ordinary course of its business, but will probably prohibit Hometown from selling the forklift while the loan is outstanding. In addition, the security agreement will likely require Hometown to maintain adequate insurance on the forklift and its other assets, in order to protect the value of those assets as collateral.

The type and extent of security that a lender requires will depend on several factors, including the risk of default and the market value of the collateral. If Hometown borrows money to buy a piece of equipment and then defaults on the loan, the lender's security is a used piece of equipment. The lender knows that the proceeds from a quick sale of used equipment are likely to be much less than the original purchase price or its value to Hometown in its ongoing business. Similarly, if Hometown gives a general security agreement to the lender, the value of all of Hometown's assets in the event of the business failing is much less than it may have been when the loan was originally made. For these reasons, the lender will typically require security in an amount that exceeds the amount borrowed. Credit insurance may be available to lenders as an additional source of protection against the risk of uncollectible accounts.

Personal Property Security Legislation

When considering whether to grant secured credit, lenders must be confident as to their position with respect to the collateral. Every province and territory has legislation in place to provide an orderly system for recognizing interests in personal property collateral and setting out rules to determine priority disputes among competing claims to the same collateral. The personal property security systems allow lenders to grant credit, knowing where they will stand with respect to the collateral in the event of default by the debtor. The legislation in each province and territory (except Quebec) is called the *Personal Property Security Act* (PPSA).[1] Although the legislation varies somewhat by province and territory, there are a few basic concepts that are common to all the provinces and territories: attachment, perfection, registration, priorities, and remedies.

The *PPSA* applies to every transaction that in substance creates a **security interest**. Even if the transaction is called something else (e.g., a lease or a conditional sale), if its real purpose is to create an interest in personal property to secure payment or performance of an obligation (normally a debt), the transaction is a security interest and the *PPSA* applies. The *PPSA* also applies to some transactions that are not intended as security, such as leases for a term of more than one year, commercial consignments (except in Ontario), and absolute assignments (transfers) of accounts (such as accounts receivable).

Security interest

An interest in personal property that is intended to secure payment or performance of an obligation (usually a debt).

1 See, for example, *Personal Property Security Act*, RSO 1990, c P-10; and *Personal Property Security Act*, SNS 1995–96, c 13.

Attachment

Attachment occurs when three conditions are satisfied:

- the debtor has rights in the collateral (e.g., ownership).
- the secured party has provided value (e.g., granted a loan or extended credit).
- the debtor has signed a written security agreement.

Once attachment has occurred, the security interest is enforceable against the debtor. If Hometown grants a security interest to a lender over a piece of equipment and the three conditions necessary for attachment have been satisfied, then the lender can seize the equipment from Hometown and sell it if Hometown defaults on the loan.

Perfection

Registration

The registration of a financing statement to record a security interest.

Financing statement

The document registered as evidence of a security interest.

Perfection is the combination of (a) attachment, and (b) **registration** or possession of the collateral.[2] Once a security interest has been perfected, the secured party will have priority over security interests that have not been perfected, as well as judgment creditors and a trustee in bankruptcy. If the security interest in Hometown's equipment is perfected, then on default by Hometown the lender can seize the equipment, sell it, and apply the proceeds of the sale to the debt owed, even if Hometown has become bankrupt, a process which is discussed in the next chapter.

Registration involves filing a form called a **financing statement**. The financing statement discloses the name of the debtor and the type of collateral secured. The *PPSA* registration system is computerized and public and can be searched either by debtor name or, in the case of motor vehicles, by serial number.

Possession, for the purposes of perfection, occurs when the secured party physically takes possession of the collateral for the purposes of holding it as security. For example, if Hometown wanted to pledge a gold bar as security, the lender might take physical possession of the gold bar until the loan is repaid. In that case, assuming attachment has occurred, the lender will have a security interest perfected by possession.

The most common form of perfection is by registration. When a person searches the *PPSA* register and discovers a financing statement of interest to them, they can find out the details of the security interest to which that financing statement relates by making an inquiry to the secured party.

It is important to note that perfection is not "perfect" in the sense that it confers the best possible interest one can have in the collateral—it does not. The term "perfection" is simply a defined term in the *PPSA* and it has only the specific meaning given to it within that legislation.

It is also important to note that perfection may occur even if attachment occurs after registration (except when dealing with consumer goods). When Hometown applies for the loan, the bank may register a financing statement under the *PPSA*. If the loan has not yet been granted, there has been no attachment. However, once the conditions for attachment have been met, the security interest will immediately be perfected, because registration has already occurred.

---

2   In the case of collateral which is investment property, a security interest may also be perfected in some provinces by "control."

This concept becomes very important when we discover that, in a contest between two perfected security interests in the same collateral, the first to register—not the first to perfect—has priority.

Priority among Creditors

One of the most important functions of the *PPSA* is to determine who has priority when there are competing interests in the same collateral. The *PPSA* has rules to resolve such conflicts. The general policy behind the priority rules is that a security interest that has been made public (e.g., by registration) should have priority over a subsequent interest in the same collateral, except where specific policy objectives warrant a different outcome. The priority rules produce predictable outcomes, which promotes the extension of credit generally:

- when there are two unperfected security interests that have both attached, the first to attach has priority.
- when there is one unperfected security interest and one perfected security interest, the perfected security interest has priority.
- when there are two security interests perfected by registration, the first to register (not the first to perfect) has priority.

There are other priority rules dealing with specific types of collateral and security interests perfected otherwise than by registration.

The **purchase-money security interest (PMSI)** is a special type of security interest that gives the secured party priority over existing perfected security interests. In order to qualify for this "super priority," two conditions must be met: first, the credit advanced must allow the debtor to acquire the assets in which the security interest is taken; and second, the security interest must be registered within a specific period of time.[3] If these conditions are met, the PMSI holder will have priority over an existing perfected security interest in the collateral that was financed. Suppose Hometown has given a general security agreement to its bank securing all of its assets including after-acquired property, and the bank registers its security interest. Then, Hometown borrows $40 000 from a truck dealer to finance the purchase of a truck, and the dealer takes a security interest in the truck to secure repayment of the loan. If the dealer meets the PMSI conditions, the dealer will have priority over the bank with respect to the truck, even though the bank registered its security interest first. The purpose of the PMSI rule is to enable debtors to obtain financing after they have entered into a security agreement which confers an interest in after-acquired property. Without the PMSI rule, the truck dealer would not have priority over the bank and presumably would not extend the credit required by Hometown to purchase the truck.

Transfers of Collateral

Generally, perfected security interests follow the collateral and take priority over subsequent purchasers of the collateral. Why then is it not necessary to conduct a *PPSA* search every time an item is bought in a retail store? The reason is the exemption for goods sold in the ordinary course of business. The *PPSA* contains a provision which gives priority to a buyer who buys goods in the ordinary course

Purchase-money security interest (PMSI)

A security interest that enables the debtor to acquire assets and gives the secured party priority over existing perfected security interests.

PART EIGHT

---

3 For example, in Ontario, within 10 days of the debtor obtaining the collateral for non-inventory collateral, and before the debtor obtains the collateral for collateral which is inventory.

of the seller's business. If Hometown buys a car from a car dealer, it does not have to worry about a security interest in the car given by the car dealer (e.g., to its supplier). However, if Hometown buys a car from a person who does not sell cars in the ordinary course of its business, then the onus is on Hometown to conduct a *PPSA* search prior to purchasing the car, or Hometown will take the car subject to any existing perfected security interest given by the seller of the car.

The computerized and centralized system associated with the *PPSA* is a vast improvement over the earlier patchwork of different statutes and rules within each province dealing with personal property security interests. However, there remain inconsistencies among the various provincial statutes, and there is always the practical problem that personal property is portable and may be moved from one province to another. There are rules in the *PPSA* to deal with the relocation of collateral, but they are complicated and vary by jurisdiction. Lenders and borrowers must both be informed of the rules that apply in the jurisdictions in which they carry on business and in which collateral may be, or end up being, located.

The *PPSA* system provides potential creditors and buyers with a high level of protection. A lender can search the *PPSA* registry before granting credit to determine whether there are existing registrations against the borrower. The creditor can even register a financing statement in advance of granting credit, to ensure that its priority position will be undisturbed when it eventually grants the loan. Purchasers of goods can search the *PPSA* registry to determine whether the goods are subject to a security interest that would take priority over them. This knowledge allows creditors and buyers to make informed business decisions with the confidence of knowing where they will stand in the event of default by the debtor. The same assets can provide security for more than one credit arrangement, but the claims of competing lenders are subject to the priority rules described above. A lender may decide to grant a loan, even with the knowledge that there are existing security interests in the same collateral, but presumably the lender will tailor the terms of the loan, and in particular the interest rate, to suit the particular circumstances.

Other Security Legislation

The federal *Bank Act*[4] permits banks to take security in the inventory and other assets of certain business borrowers. *Bank Act* security is only available to banks that are regulated by the *Bank Act*. *Bank Act* security is registered, but the registration system is quite different from that of the *PPSA* system. Priority disputes between *Bank Act* security and *PPSA* security are complicated and have resulted in a great deal of litigation. In 2012, amendments were made to the *Bank Act* which may help resolve some of these priority disputes.[5]

Each province and territory has legislation which allows suppliers, building subcontractors, and workers to place liens on real property if they are not paid for work done, or materials supplied, to the property.[6] These liens are called construction or builders' liens and they remain in place until the supplier, subcontractor, or worker has been paid in full. The legislation requires property owners who enter into contracts with builders to hold back a portion of the contract price

---

4 SC 1991, c 46, s 427.

5 The question now appears to be answered by determining which security interest was perfected first. See James I. Reynolds, "The Odd Couple: Priorities Issues between the *Bank Act* and the *Personal Property Security Act*," *Priorities–2013*.

6 See, for example, *Builders' Lien Act*, RSA 2000, c B-7.

until the lien period has expired (usually between 30 and 60 days after the contract work is completed). This mechanism provides an incentive for contractors to pay their suppliers and subcontractors in a timely manner.

Remedies

A creditor's remedies in the event of the borrower's failure to pay are largely determined by whether the creditor is secured or unsecured. Unsecured creditors have the right to sue the debtor for the unpaid debt and may, at the end of that litigation process, obtain a judgment against the debtor. In most cases, the unsecured creditor will then be able to enforce its judgment against the assets of the debtor that are not already claimed by secured creditors. Secured creditors also have the right to sue the debtor but, in addition, they can immediately seize the collateral and sell it to pay down the debt owed. The ability to seize the personal property of the debtor without having to commence litigation places the secured creditor in a much better position than the unsecured creditor. Furthermore, if the debtor ends up bankrupt, the secured creditor will still be able to claim its collateral, while the unsecured creditor will have no remedy except under the bankruptcy proceedings (see Chapter 27).

Lenders' Remedies

If the borrower defaults on the loan, secured parties have a variety of remedies from two sources: the security agreement and the *PPSA*. The remedies provided for in security agreements are often broader than those permitted by the *PPSA*, in which case the secured party is generally limited to the remedies permitted by the *PPSA*.

Credit agreements normally contain an **acceleration clause**, which permits the creditor to call the entire loan if the debtor misses one payment. This gives the debtor an incentive to make timely payments and allows the creditor to sue for the entire debt immediately upon any default by the debtor.

A secured party can enter the borrower's premises and seize the collateral immediately upon default by the debtor, although the secured party must not break the law and is generally required to provide advance notice to the debtor. The secured party can then dispose of the collateral (or collect collateral such as accounts receivable). The proceeds are applied first to the expenses of the secured party in enforcing its security and then to the unpaid debt. The fees and expenses of the secured party in seizing and selling collateral can often be considerable.

If the amount received by the secured party in disposing of the collateral (less its costs) exceeds the amount owed by the debtor, the surplus must be paid to the next secured party in line, if there is one, and then to the debtor. If, on the other hand, the net proceeds are insufficient to pay the outstanding debt, then the secured party becomes an unsecured creditor for the deficiency, which is the balance still owing, and has the rights only of an unsecured creditor in respect to the deficiency.

If the security agreement permits, the secured party may appoint a **receiver** or receiver–manager to take possession of the collateral and manage the business of the debtor while a sale of the collateral can be arranged. If the security agreement is silent on whether or not a receiver may be appointed, the secured party can apply to a court for an order appointing a receiver or receiver–manager.

In some cases, the secured party may keep the collateral in satisfaction of the debt owed, however in most provinces doing so will extinguish any deficiency.

Acceleration clause

A term of a loan agreement that makes the entire loan due if one payment is missed.

Receiver

A person appointed by the secured party or by the court to seize, and usually sell, collateral.

Limits on Lenders' Remedies

When enforcing its security, the secured party must act in a commercially reasonable manner in every respect.[7] What is commercially reasonable will depend on the particular circumstances, but the secured party must take reasonable care of the collateral and obtain a reasonable price when disposing of the collateral. Creditors are not expected to obtain the highest possible price, but they must act reasonably. Creditors must also avoid conflicts of interest created by buying collateral themselves or selling to related businesses at a price less than fair market value. Typically, lenders will have the collateral valued by at least one independent appraiser to ensure that the price is reasonable, or they will sell the collateral at public auction where the price is set by the highest bidder.

The courts have held that secured parties must generally give the debtor reasonable notice before calling a loan or enforcing their security, even if the credit agreement does not require notice.[8] What is reasonable will depend on the particular circumstances, including the type of collateral and whether it is perishable, the relationship between the debtor and the creditor, and any industry norms or standards. In addition, the *PPSA* requires that debtors be notified of any intended sale of collateral and have the opportunity to pay off the debt and reclaim the collateral prior to the sale. This way, the debtor can monitor any sale and, if possible, bring the debt into good standing and avoid the sale of its assets.

If a secured party is enforcing a security interest against all or substantially all of the inventory, accounts receivable, or other assets of a business debtor, the *Bankruptcy and Insolvency Act*[9] requires that the secured party provide the debtor with 10 days' notice of its intention to enforce its security. The notice is in a prescribed form and is commonly known as a "Section 244 Notice." During the 10-day period, the secured party cannot take any steps to enforce its security.

The *PPSA* and other legislation provides special protection for consumer debtors. For example, secured parties may be prohibited from seizing collateral if a consumer debtor has already paid two-thirds of the loan, and in some provinces creditors are limited to the proceeds from the seized assets and may not sue the debtor for any deficiency.

Personal Guarantees

If the bank agrees to lend Hometown the money for its expansion, the bank will likely require personal guarantees from Hometown's shareholders. Guarantees reduce the bank's risk because the personal assets of the shareholders will ultimately be available to the bank if Hometown defaults on the loan. Bill and Martha are not normally liable for Hometown's debt, because as shareholders they enjoy limited liability. However, if they personally agree to guarantee the loan, then they lose their limited liability protection with respect to that debt. In such a case, their personal liability to the bank arises not from their position as shareholders of Hometown, but because they have agreed to be personally responsible for the debt. The scope of their personal liability will be determined by the guarantee contract. The relationship among the borrower, the lender, and the guarantor is shown in Figure 26.1.

---

7   For example, *Personal Property Security Act*, SNS 1995–96, c 13, s 66(2).
8   *R.E. Lister Ltd. v. Dunlop Canada Ltd.*, 1979 CanLII 75 (OCA).
9   RSC 1985, c B-3.

FIGURE 26.1 Relationships in Personal Guarantees

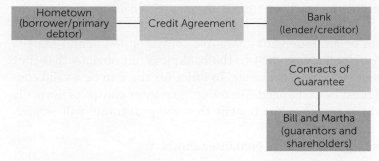

A **guarantee** is a contract between a creditor and a **guarantor**. The terms and conditions of the guarantee are set out in the guarantee contract and, since it is a contractual relationship, the fundamental principles of contract law apply. The essence of the guarantee is a promise by the guarantor to pay the debt if the debtor defaults. The guarantee promise is conditional or secondary to the primary obligation of the debtor. A guarantee must be distinguished from a contract of **indemnity**, in which the indemnifier is primarily and not conditionally liable for the obligation of the debtor.

The implications for those who give personal guarantees are significant. Guarantors lose their limited liability to the extent of their promises to the creditor and thereby put their personal assets at risk. If the debtor defaults, the creditor can pursue the guarantors for payment immediately and without the need to take any further legal action.

A continuing guarantee is one where the guarantor is liable for any past, present, and future obligations of the debtor. Bank guarantees usually apply to the total debt owed to the bank at any given time. When the initial loan is granted by the bank, Bill and Martha may be confident in Hometown's future and comfortable with the amount of the loan. As time passes, however, the amount of debt may increase, and Hometown's financial situation may deteriorate. The guarantees, however, are continuing. If Hometown eventually defaults, the guarantors will be required to pay the balance owing, whatever that might be at the time of default. If the guarantors are unable to pay, they may be forced into personal bankruptcy.

The Guarantee Agreement

A guarantee is one of few contracts that must be in writing and be signed by the guarantor in order to be enforceable.[10]

The guarantee is normally one component of a larger credit arrangement. The lender will require that the guarantor sign the lender's standard form guarantee agreement, which is designed to severely limit ways that the guarantors may avoid liability and provide the lender with maximum flexibility in dealing with the debtor. Guarantees may be required in order for Hometown to obtain the loan, but the shareholders of Hometown must consider these guarantees as an important factor in their decision to seek debt financing on behalf of Hometown.

The guarantee agreement is entered into between the guarantor and the creditor—not between guarantor and debtor—because the creditor wants to be able to enforce the contract without the cooperation of the debtor. If the guarantee

Guarantee

A conditional promise to a creditor to pay a debt if the debtor defaults.

Guarantor

A person who guarantees a debt.

Indemnity

A primary obligation to pay a debt owed by another person.

---

10 The in-writing requirement is in place in all provinces except Manitoba, generally in the *Statute of Frauds*.

contract was entered into between the guarantor and the debtor, privity of contract would prevent the creditor from enforcing the contract against the guarantor.

Consideration can be an issue with guarantee contracts. If Bill and Martha promise to guarantee Hometown's debt to the bank, it is not obvious that they are receiving anything of value in exchange. In order for there to be a valid contract, consideration must be exchanged. Therefore, guarantee contracts normally include language which describes the benefit that the guarantors will receive, even if that benefit is indirect.

The following are typical terms in a guarantee contract:

- guarantors are jointly liable for the entire debt. If Bill and Martha guarantee the $250 000 loan, they are each liable for the full $250 000 and the bank can recover that amount from either of them.

- the guarantee applies to all credit extended to the debtor while the guarantee is in force. Any limitation must be clearly stated in the guarantee contract.

- the guarantee is in force for an unlimited period. This may become a problem if one of the guarantors decides to sell its shares and leave the business—the creditor may not agree to release the guarantor.

- guarantees normally exclude any terms, conditions, statements, or representations that are not in the written agreement. Guarantors should ensure that any material assurances or assumptions are clearly stated in the guarantee contract.

- bank guarantees usually provide that the bank may deal with the debtor and the debt without affecting the guarantee (e.g., increasing the amount of the loan). This is a direct reversal of the common law rule that terminates the guarantee if the terms of the debt are changed without the guarantors' consent.

Subrogation

The right of a guarantor to recover from the debtor any payments made to the creditor.

If Hometown defaults on its loan, and Bill and Martha are required to honour their guarantees and pay the debt, they have a right of **subrogation** against Hometown. Of course, if the guarantors are called upon to pay, it is unlikely that Hometown will be able to repay them. Still, the right of subrogation extends to any rights that the creditor has against the debtor. For example, if the bank had a security interest or a judgment against Hometown, and Bill and Martha have paid Hometown's debt to the bank, then Bill and Martha would become entitled to the benefit of the bank's security interest or judgment against Hometown.

Defences Available to Guarantors

Guarantors have some common law defences available to them. First, the guarantee obligation is limited to the terms of the debt guaranteed. If the terms of that debt are changed in a way that increases the risk to the guarantors, the guarantee is terminated unless the guarantors have agreed to the changes. Such changes may include increasing the amount of the loan or the interest rate, extending the time for payment, or altering the collateral the debtor has provided. However, standard guarantee contracts usually eliminate this defence by authorizing the creditor to deal with the debtor and the debt in any manner the creditor sees fit without the consent of the guarantor.

Guarantors may argue they did not understand the terms of the guarantee contract or the risk of giving the guarantee. Spouses, friends, or other relatives of the debtor with little or no involvement in the debtor's business may sign guarantees under pressure. Sometimes, a court will relieve a guarantor from liability if it is satisfied that the guarantor did not appreciate the nature and consequences of the guarantee. For this reason, when guarantors are individuals who are not directly involved in the debtor's business, it is customary for them to obtain independent legal advice before signing the guarantee contract. If the bank requires Bill and Martha's spouses also to sign guarantees, the bank will likely insist that they receive independent legal advice before the bank will extend the loan. The bank does not want the guarantors to be able to avoid their obligations using such defences.

The written guarantee contract will normally take precedence over verbal reassurances or statements that contradict or modify its terms. However, courts tend to interpret guarantee terms strictly against the creditor who is relying on the guarantee. For example, if the guarantee contract provides a blanket authorization for the creditor to alter the debt contract without the guarantor's consent, that intention must be clearly stated in the guarantee contract. If there is doubt or ambiguity about the meaning or scope of language in the guarantee contract, that doubt or ambiguity will generally be resolved in favour of the guarantor.

Apart from the requirement that guarantees be in writing, the only regulation of guarantees in Canada is in Alberta.[11] The Alberta statute provides that, for a guarantee to be valid, a notary public must certify that the guarantors were aware of and understood the contents of the guarantee. The statute does not, however, place any limit on the actual content of the guarantee.

It may be argued that the terms of standard form guarantee contracts are so one-sided as to be unfair. Especially for small businesspeople, the language of guarantee contracts, and the legal principles involved, may well be beyond their grasp.

CASE

Royal Bank of Canada v Samson Management & Solutions Ltd., 2013 ONCA 313 (CanLII)

THE BUSINESS CONTEXT: Small business owners and their spouses are often required to sign standard form guarantee contracts as a condition of obtaining bank financing. When the underlying loan is changed in some significant way, a dispute may arise as to whether the guarantees remain enforceable.

FACTUAL BACKGROUND: Brasseur owned and operated a business called Samson Management & Solutions (Samson). When Samson applied for a business loan, the bank asked for personal guarantees from both Brasseur and his spouse, Cusack. In 2005, Brasseur and

Cusack both signed the bank's standard form guarantee contract, guaranteeing the debts of Samson to the bank up to $150 000. One year later, Cusack signed another guarantee for up to $250 000. The guarantee contracts were not tied to any specific loan, but rather applied to all amounts, present or future, owed by Samson to the bank. The guarantees also allowed the bank to take various actions in respect to the loan, including increasing the amount, extending the time for repayment, increasing the interest rate, and introducing new terms and conditions. Cusack never had any direct contact with the bank—the bank provided the guarantee contracts to Brasseur, who gave them to Cusack. Cusack obtained independent legal advice before signing each guarantee, signed

(Continued)

---

11 *Guarantees Acknowledgment Act*, RSA 2000, c G-11.

CHAPTER 26: THE LEGAL ASPECTS OF CREDIT

the guarantees, and returned them to Brasseur who gave them to the bank. Cusack never saw a loan agreement between Samson and the bank, but she did acknowledge that she had signed the guarantees in order to enable her husband to obtain a loan for his business. In 2008, the bank entered into a new loan agreement with Samson, replacing the earlier loan agreement and increasing the amount of the loan to $500 000. The new loan agreement also imposed new conditions on Samson, including increased reporting requirements. In 2009, yet another new loan agreement was entered into, replacing the 2008 loan agreement, and increasing the loan to $750 000. In 2011, Samson defaulted on the loan and the bank demanded payment from Cusack based on her 2006 guarantee in the amount of $250 000.

THE LEGAL QUESTION: Is the 2006 guarantee signed by Cusack enforceable in light of the subsequent changes to the loan agreement between Samson and the bank?

RESOLUTION: The trial court found that the guarantee was unenforceable and dismissed the bank's action against Cusack. The court found that the increase in the loan amount, and the new reporting requirements, changed Cusack's risk under the guarantee and made it more likely that she would have to pay under the guarantee. As these were material changes of which Cusack was not notified and to which she did not consent, she was relieved of liability under the guarantee.

The bank appealed the decision and the Ontario Court of Appeal unanimously allowed the appeal. The appeal court agreed with the trial court that there had been material changes in the credit arrangements between Samson and the bank to which Cusack had not consented and which increased her risk. However, the court held that Cusack had contracted out of the protection provided to her by the common law. The court held that the language in the guarantee was clear, unambiguous, and "plainly designed" to remove the protections that would otherwise be provided under the common law. The court held that the increased loan amounts were contemplated by the parties and permitted by the language of the guarantee contract. The guarantee was thus enforceable against Ms. Cusack.

CRITICAL ANALYSIS: Does this case illustrate the unfairness of standard form guarantee contracts? Did the court properly balance the interests of the bank and the guarantor?

Regulation of Credit

Consumer debt

A loan to an individual for a non-commercial purpose.

Government regulation of credit is largely restricted to **consumer debt**, where the borrower is a consumer rather than a business. Each province has legislation which attempts to protect consumers from the potentially unfair bargaining advantage that lenders enjoy. People with poor credit records are especially vulnerable, and their need for credit may be greater than those on more solid financial footing. However, if consumers are not aware of their legal rights or the legal processes by which they may enforce those rights, the legislative protection is of little practical value. This is a problem that some governments have addressed by providing consumer information and debt counselling.[12]

Within each province and territory, forms of protection are often scattered throughout a number of statutes, but generally they seek to regulate the provision of credit by licensing certain activities, prohibiting other activities, and requiring disclosure regarding the terms of credit transactions. As a result, there are many different rules that businesses must follow when extending credit to consumers.

---

12   For example, in Nova Scotia, through Service Nova Scotia and Municipal Relations.

The provincial and territorial legislation

- enables the courts to review and reverse transactions where "the cost of the loan is excessive and the transaction is harsh and unconscionable."[13]
- prohibits credit transactions where there is "no reasonable probability of making payment in full" or where there is no substantial benefit to the consumer.[14]
- prohibits lenders from making misleading statements in advertising dealing with credit transactions and during the loan application and negotiation process.[15]
- requires lenders to provide detailed disclosure regarding credit transactions, including the true cost of borrowing, the annual effective interest rate, and any other charges (such as registration fees or insurance) that the borrower must pay, and the total amount of the loan.[16]

If a lender fails to comply with these regulations, the borrower can file a complaint against the lender with a regulatory body, which may lead to fines, licence suspension or revocation, or orders prohibiting further violations. The borrower can also apply to the courts to have the terms of the loan adjusted or, in some cases, to obtain damages. However, in the case of consumer disputes, the courts are often not a realistic choice for consumers, due to factors such as cost, inconvenience, and the length of time it takes the courts to resolve disputes.

A **credit bureau** provides a service to lenders by compiling credit information on consumers and reporting on their credit history. Lenders use this information to evaluate loan applications. There are licensing regulations to ensure the respectability of credit bureaus, and to ensure the accuracy of the information that is compiled. Consumers have access to their credit reports and the opportunity to correct errors.[17] One valuable tool for consumers to protect themselves from identity theft is to obtain a copy of their credit report on a regular basis to ensure that it does not disclose any unauthorized credit transactions.

A **collection agency** assists lenders in recovering delinquent loans. These agencies are subject to licensing regulations and cannot harass, threaten, or exert undue pressure on defaulting borrowers. They are also prohibited from contacting anyone other than the borrower (such as a family member or business associate) even when the debtor is bankrupt or deceased.[18] Agencies that go beyond the permitted methods of collection risk the revocation of their operating licences.

In addition to the provincial legislation, there are also federal laws dealing with the regulation of credit.

There are regulations that apply to credit cards issued by federally regulated financial institutions,[19] in order "to make financial products more transparent for consumers" and to "protect Canadians and their families from unexpected costs and provide clear information to help them make better financial decisions."[20]

Credit bureau

An agency that compiles credit information on borrowers.

Collection agency

An agency that assists lenders in obtaining payment on outstanding loans.

---

13 *Unconscionable Transactions Relief Act*, RSNS 1989, c 481, s 3.
14 *Consumer Protection Act*, 2002, SO 2002, c 30, Schedule A, s 15. See also Chapter 24.
15 *Fair Trading Act*, RSA 2000, c F-2.
16 *Business Practices and Consumer Protection Act*, SBC 2004, c 2.
17 See, for example, *Consumer Reporting Act*, RSO 1990, c C-33, s 12.
18 *Collection Agencies Act*, RSO 1990, c C-14.
19 *Credit Business Practices*, SOR/2009-257.
20 Jim Flaherty, (Minister of Finance), News Release, Ottawa, "Regulations Come into Force to Protect Canadian Credit Card Users" (1 September 2010).

The regulations require

- a summary box on credit applications and contracts clearly indicating key features, such as interest rates and fees.
- express consent for credit limit increases.
- express consent for the provision of credit card cheques.
- restrictions on debt collection practices used by financial institutions.
- disclosure of the time to pay off the balance by making only minimum payments.
- notice of any interest rate increases.
- mandatory 21-day, interest-free grace period for new purchases.
- allocation of payments to the balance with the highest interest rate first.

In addition, the federal *Criminal Code*[21] prohibits lending at a rate of interest above 60 percent on an annual basis, although this provision has recently been amended to exclude most **payday loans**. Loans with an interest rate in excess of 60 percent are illegal and, as such, are generally unenforceable. In addition, lenders who receive such interest may be subject to fines and imprisonment.

The average payday loan is for $280 and is outstanding for 10 days.[22] Payday lenders typically extend credit until the borrower's next payday. The borrower provides the lender with a post-dated cheque or a pre-authorized withdrawal from a bank account for the amount of the loan plus interest and fees. In many cases, the annual effective interest rate exceeds 60 percent, and can be as high as 1200 percent![23]

Proponents of the payday loan industry argue that the loans fulfill an unmet need for short-term credit and convenience. Critics argue that the industry is rife with unscrupulous and abusive business practices (such as misleading advertising and hidden fees) and exploits people who are already financially vulnerable. Until recently, payday loans were largely unregulated in Canada.

The *Criminal Code* now excludes payday loans from its limitation on the rate of interest that may be charged, provided the loan is for $1500 or less, the term of the loan is for 62 days or fewer, and the province in which the loan is made has provincial regulations dealing with payday loans. The goal of the new federal legislation is to encourage the provinces to enact legislation which will protect borrowers and limit the total cost of borrowing. Every province except Quebec and Newfoundland have passed legislation regulating payday loans.[24] Quebec prohibits payday loans entirely and Newfoundland has opted not to pass payday loan legislation (meaning that the federal laws apply). Critics of the new regulations argue that delegating responsibility to the provincial governments will lead to a lack of consistency in the regulations and their enforcement.[25]

Provincial payday loan legislation generally prohibits a variety of unfair business practices (such as misleading advertising and "rollover" loans), imposes a limit on the total cost of borrowing, provides the borrower with a two-day "cooling off" period, and limits various collection practices.[26] In Ontario, for

Payday loans

Short-term loans for a relatively small amount of money, provided by a non-traditional lender to an individual.

---

21 RSC 1985, c C-46, s 347.

22 Bob Whitelaw, "$280 till payday: The short-term loan industry says it provides a service the (average) Canadian needs, wants and appreciates", *Vancouver Sun* (8 June 2005), A21.

23 Andrew Kitching and Sheena Starky, "Payday Loan Companies in Canada: Determining the Public Interest", PRB 05-81E, Parliamentary Information and Research Service, Library of Parliament, Ottawa (26 January 2006).

24 See, for example, *Payday Loans Act, 2008*, SO 2008, c 9.

25 Jacob Ziegel, "Pass the buck: Ottawa has paramount jurisdiction over interest rate regulation", *Financial Post* (10 November 2006) online: Financial Post <http://www.canada.com/nationalpost/news/story .html?id=b3efb360-60fc-4c86-8818-b579b31fcd63>.

26 *Supra* note 25.

Regulations in place for payday loans.

example, payday loan borrowers may not be charged more than $21 for each $100 borrowed. In Alberta, British Columbia, and Saskatchewan, the maximum charge is $23 for each $100 borrowed. Accordingly, in Alberta, a loan of $300 for 14 days, which is a typical payday loan, will require the borrower to repay a total of $369, for an annual effective interest rate of 599.64 percent.

ETHICAL CONSIDERATIONS

THE "NO INTEREST" OFFER

The local electronics store flyer advertises "No interest for 24 months on all purchases!" The offer is attractive, especially when the item being considered is a luxury item, such as a giant computer monitor for $299—something Susan would like to have, but does not really need. In Ontario, Susan would have to pay $337.87 including taxes to buy the monitor if she pays cash at the time of purchase. Instead, Susan is enticed by the offer of 24 equal payments without interest, or only $12.46 per month!

The problem is in the fine print. If Susan reads the fine print tucked away inside the flyer, she will see that there are terms and conditions attached to the "no interest" offer. First, there is an "administration fee" of $49.95, which must be paid at the time of purchase. Second, the sales taxes applicable to both the monitor and the administration fee must also be paid at the time of purchase. Finally, "Interest is charged on all accounts at the annual rate of 28.8 percent. Interest will be waived only if the customer makes all payments on or before the due date, failing which this offer will not apply."

Suppose Susan buys the monitor and makes all 24 payments when due. In that case, she pays $95.31 at the time of purchase (administration fee plus sales taxes on the monitor and the administration fee). She pays $12.46 per month for 24 months for a total of $299. Accordingly, Susan pays a total of $394.31, compared to the $337.87 that she would have paid if she had bought the monitor for cash. Some deal!

But things get worse—much worse—if Susan is late making a payment. Suppose now that Susan buys the monitor with the "no interest" offer, but because she goes away for a few days during spring break, she is late making one of the 24 monthly payments. Susan makes the other 23 payments on time. Unfortunately for Susan, the terms of the offer no longer apply because she did not comply with the conditions of the offer, which were clearly stated. Interest is now charged on the entire amount for the whole two-year period, even though Susan made 23 out of 24 payments on time. Susan now pays $95.31 at the time of purchase plus $12.46 per month for 24 months, as before,

PART EIGHT

but now Susan also pays interest at the rate of 28.8 percent for two years, amounting to an additional $130.23. Susan now pays a total of $524.54 for her $299 monitor! The total cost of borrowing is $186.67, or 62 percent of the original purchase price.

Critical Analysis: Is this type of credit offer fair? Should consumers be bound by such terms and conditions? Should the "administration fee" be included in the calculation of interest, with the result that the offer would violate the *Criminal Code*?

BUSINESS LAW IN PRACTICE REVISITED

1. What is the bank likely to require before agreeing to loan money to Hometown?

Hometown will be asked to provide a loan application together with detailed financial statements and a business plan to justify the expansion and the loan.

2. What will the terms of the loan be?

The bank will require Hometown to provide collateral with sufficient value to cover the loan. The interest rate on the loan will accord with the risk perceived by the bank. Hometown will be required to maintain minimum levels of accounts receivable and inventory, to stay within a specified debt/equity ratio, and to provide financial information to the lender at specified intervals. Hometown will need the lender's permission to deal with secured assets other than inventory, and will be required to maintain appropriate insurance coverage on the collateral.

3. What are the risks for Hometown in borrowing the money?

The major risk is the possibility that the business will be less profitable than anticipated and that Hometown will be unable to repay the loan. If Hometown fails to repay the loan, the collateral can be seized and sold by the bank. In many cases, this will mean the end of the business.

4. Will Bill and Martha be personally liable for the loan?

Bill and Martha will likely be required to personally guarantee the loan. If Hometown defaults, their personal assets will ultimately be available to the bank. Since the guarantees are probably unlimited in scope, the failure of Hometown to repay the loan could eventually result in personal bankruptcy for the guarantors.

CHAPTER SUMMARY

Credit transactions are an important and normal part of every business. A business can be a debtor or a creditor, depending on the transaction. Some arrangements are continuous and informal, such as between a customer and supplier. Others are major individual transactions and involve a formal credit agreement specifying the rights and obligations of the borrower and the lender. Unsecured creditors have a right to be repaid and can sue the debtor in the event of non-payment. Secured creditors have, in addition, the right to seize and sell the collateral to pay down the debt owed. When a debtor defaults, secured creditors are in a much better position than unsecured creditors.

Personal property security is mostly governed by the *PPSA* in each province. The important concepts of the *PPSA* are attachment, perfection, priorities, and lenders' remedies. Lenders and borrowers are protected by credit agreements and by the PPSA and other legislation.

Guarantors place their personal assets at risk when they provide a guarantee. Guarantors should be aware of the onerous terms in most guarantees and must ensure that they understand their obligations under standard form guarantee contracts.

CHAPTER STUDY

Key Terms and Concepts

acceleration clause (p. 667)

after-acquired property (p. 662)

collateral (p. 661)

collection agency (p. 673)

consumer debt (p. 672)

credit bureau (p. 673)

events of default (p. 661)

financing statement (p. 664)

general security agreement (p. 662)

guarantee (p. 669)

guarantor (p. 669)

indemnity (p. 669)

letter of commitment (p. 662)

letter of credit (p. 660)

payday loans (p. 674)

purchase-money security interest (PMSI) (p. 665)

receiver (p. 667)

registration (p. 664)

secured credit (p. 659)

security interest (p. 663)

subrogation (p. 670)

unsecured credit (p. 659)

Questions for Review

1. What are some examples of credit transactions?

2. What are some of the methods that creditors use to reduce risk in credit transactions?

3. What are the rights of an unsecured creditor on default by the debtor?

4. What are the key aspects of personal property security legislation?

5. What are the disclosure requirements for a consumer loan?

6. What is a criminal rate of interest?

7. Why are payday loans regulated differently than other loans?

8. Why is after-acquired property included as collateral in a general security agreement?

9. What is the role of a financing statement?

10. How are lenders' remedies limited by law?

11. What is a purchase-money security interest?

12. Why is a secured creditor in a better position than an unsecured creditor?

13. What is the role of a receiver?

14. What is a deficiency?

15. Who are the parties in a guarantee contract?

16. What are the issues with standard form guarantee contracts?

17. How does a guarantee affect the limited liability of a shareholder?

Questions for Critical Thinking

1. When a business fails, most of the assets may be claimed by secured creditors. Unsecured creditors may receive very little, if anything, and shareholders may be left with nothing. Is the protection accorded to secured creditors justified?

2. There is a complex web of rules governing consumer credit. Should commercial credit be regulated the way consumer credit is now or left to the lender and borrower to negotiate?

3. What factors affect the ability of a borrower to finance a business using debt? How does an economic downturn or credit freeze affect the ability of a business to borrow? How do these developments affect existing credit agreements?

4. Creditors holding general security agreements are required to give the borrower reasonable notice before appointing a receiver to take possession of the assets of the business. How should a secured creditor decide how much time to give a debtor?

5. The current legislative framework for payday loans varies from province to province, but essentially allows lenders to loan funds to consumers at interest rates that would otherwise be considered criminal. Do existing payday loan laws adequately balance the interests between lenders, borrowers, and the public? Should payday loans be allowed at all?

6. In light of this chapter, what factors would you advise Bill and Martha to consider in financing Hometown's expansion? Did they make the right decision in borrowing money from the bank? What provisions should Bill and Martha be concerned about when they review the loan commitment letter provided to them by the bank?

Situations for Discussion

1. Douglas Pools Inc. operates a pool company in Toronto. In order to finance the business, Douglas Pools negotiated a line of credit with the Bank of Montreal to a maximum indebtedness of $300 000. The line of credit was secured by a general security agreement in favour of the bank, in which the collateral is described as "all assets of Douglas Pools, all after-acquired property and proceeds thereof." The Bank registered its security interest under the *PPSA* on 10 January 2011. On 30 March 2011, Douglas Pools bought a 2009 Dodge Ram pick-up truck from London Dodge for $15 000. London Dodge agreed to accept payment for the truck over three years, with interest at 6 percent per year, and took a security interest in the truck in order to secure payment of the purchase price. London Dodge registered its security interest under the *PPSA* on 4 April 2011.

On 11 November 2011, Douglas Pools sold the truck to Fisher & Co. (a company owned by the same person that owns Douglas Pools) for $1.00. Douglas Pools defaulted on its obligations to both the bank and London Dodge and, on 28 November 2011, declared bankruptcy. At the time of the bankruptcy, Douglas Pools owed the bank $240 000 and London Dodge $12 000. Now, the bank, London Dodge, the trustee in bankruptcy, and Fisher & Co. all claim the truck. Whose claim to the truck has first priority? Whose claim has second priority?

2. The Weiss Brothers operated a successful business in Montreal for 30 years. They bought a bankrupt hardware business in Ottawa, even though they had no experience selling hardware. Their bank, TD, got nervous about their financial stability and suggested they seek financing elsewhere. The brothers contacted a former employee of TD who was with Aetna Financial Services and negotiated a new line of credit for up to $1 million. Security for the line was a general security agreement, pledge of accounts receivable, mortgage on land, and guarantees by the brothers. Six months later, the brothers defaulted on the line. Aetna demanded payment in full and appointed a receiver, who seized all the assets three hours later.[27] What can the Weiss Brothers do to save the business and their personal assets? What could they have done to prevent this disaster? Why did Aetna grant credit after TD had become reluctant to continue?

3. The bank agreed to lend money to Wilder Enterprises Ltd. and, in order to secure repayment of the loan, the company granted the bank a security interest in all of its assets. The loan was also personally guaranteed by members of the Wilder family, who owned the company. Periodically, the bank increased the company's credit limit as the company expanded its business. When the company experienced financial difficulty, however, the bank dishonoured two of the company's cheques. That prompted a meeting between the bank and the Wilders, the result of which was that the bank agreed to loan additional funds to the company, and refrain from demanding

---

27 Based on *Kavcar Investments v Aetna Financial Services* (1989), 62 DLR (4th) 277 (Ont CA).

payment on its loan, in exchange for additional guarantees from members of the Wilder family. Despite the agreement, and without warning, the bank stopped honouring the company's cheques and demanded payment of the loan in full. When the company was unable to pay, the bank appointed a receiver–manager and took control of the company. The receiver–manager refused the company's request to complete the projects that the company then had underway and, as a result, the company went bankrupt. The bank sued the Wilders for payment pursuant to the guarantees that the bank had, all of which permitted the bank to "deal with the customer as the bank may see fit."[28] Will the Wilders be obligated on their guarantees? How sympathetic are the courts likely to be? Could the Wilders have structured their affairs differently to avoid high personal risk for the escalating debts of their failing business?

4. Kyle owned and operated a retail sporting goods shop. A new ski resort was built in the area and, to take advantage of increased activity, Kyle decided to expand his shop. He borrowed money from the bank, who took a security interest in his present inventory and any after-acquired inventory. One year later, an avalanche destroyed the ski lodge. Kyle's business suffered, and he was left with twice as much inventory as he had when he first obtained the loan. When he defaulted on the loan payments, the bank seized all his inventory. Kyle claims the bank is entitled only to the value of the inventory at the time of the loan. How much inventory can the bank claim? Could Kyle have negotiated better terms at the outset?

5. Bruce was employed as a general labourer. With his pay of $1250 every two weeks, Bruce was barely making ends meet. In February of 2014, after making his car payment and paying his utility bills, Bruce did not have enough money left to pay his rent of $750. He had been late paying the rent three times in the previous six months, and his landlord had told him that if he was late one more time his apartment lease would be terminated. Desperate, Bruce went downtown to a payday loan store which was part of a national chain. The loan company did not conduct a credit check against Bruce—all he had to show was that he had a bank account and a job. Bruce borrowed $750 for two weeks and promised to repay the loan from his next paycheque, along with interest of 21% and an administration fee of $39. What is the cost of borrowing in this scenario? What is the annual effective interest rate? Is this a sensible strategy for Bruce given his short-term cash problems?

6. New Solutions Financial loaned Transport Express, a transport trucking company, $500 000 under a commercial lending agreement. The interest rate was 4 percent per month calculated daily and payable monthly. This arrangement produced an effective annual rate of 60.1 percent. Other clauses in the agreement specified other charges, including legal fees, a monitoring fee, a standby fee, royalty payments, and a commitment fee totalling 30.8 percent for a total effective annual rate of 90.9 percent. Transport Express found the terms of the agreement too onerous and refused to make the agreed payments.[29] Is this agreement enforceable? Why or why not? Should a commercial arrangement like this be treated differently from a payday loan?

7. RST Ltd. is an independent printing company in a medium-sized town in Saskatchewan. It was established 15 years ago by Ron, Sandra, and Tara, who each own one-third of the shares in the company. In 2015, RST revenues were $4 million, mainly from local contracts for such items as customized office stationery, business cards, advertising posters, calendars, and entertainment programs. Because the business is prospering, the owners are planning to expand their printing and sales space. They know that significant financing is required for the expanded facilities and the increased business. The current capital structure of RST is 60 percent owners' equity and 40 percent debt. Rather than issue shares to other investors, the owners are prepared to put more equity into the business by purchasing additional shares in order to maintain their debt/equity ratio. The expansion project will cost $1 million, so they need to borrow $400 000. Do you agree with the owners' financing decisions? What are the risks? How can the owners plan for uncertainty in their industry and the economy in general?

28 Based on *Bank of Montreal v Wilder* (1986), 32 DLR (4th) 9 (SCC).

29 Based on *Transport North American Express Inc v New Solutions Financial Corp*, [2004] 1 SCR 249.

27

BANKRUPTCY AND INSOLVENCY

OBJECTIVES

After studying this chapter, you should have an understanding of

- the legal aspects of business failure

- the rights and obligations of debtors and creditors when a business fails

- alternatives to bankruptcy

- the stages in the bankruptcy process

BUSINESS LAW IN PRACTICE

Hometown Hardware Ltd. (Hometown) and its owners, Bill Ikeda and Martha Wong, were introduced in Chapters 25 and 26. They have successfully operated a building supply outlet in Timmins, Ontario, for the past 35 years. Eighteen months ago, Bill and Martha became concerned about the imminent arrival of a big-box building supply store. They decided to expand Hometown's business in order to respond to the competitive threat. To finance the expansion, Hometown borrowed $250 000 from its bank. The loan was structured as a mortgage of $150 000 on Hometown's land and buildings, and a line of credit for up to $100 000 secured by Hometown's inventory and accounts receivable. Bill and Martha personally guaranteed the line of credit. The expansion strategy failed. Just after the large competitor opened, the housing market collapsed. Hometown experienced a 30 percent drop in sales and Bill does not expect the situation to improve.

When the big-box store first opened, Bill reacted with a costly promotional campaign. To cover this extra expense, Bill borrowed $10 000 from his brother, George. More recently, he was under pressure from a major supplier, Good Lumber, to pay Hometown's overdue account. Bill sold land that the company owned adjacent to the store. With the proceeds, Bill paid $20 000 to Good Lumber and repaid George.

Hometown's assets consist of the land and buildings (subject to the mortgage) on which the business is located, inventory, accounts receivable, and a few pieces of equipment. Hometown's liabilities include the mortgage, the line of credit, accounts payable, property taxes, and a shareholder loan of $70 000 owed to Bill. Hometown is also late in remitting its employee source deductions to the government.

Bill wants to keep Hometown in business as long as possible, but he fears that the store may no longer be viable and he is wondering what he should do.

Bill would like to continue to draw his regular salary for as long as possible, and he would also like to continue to pay Martha, the store manager. He is concerned that if Hometown stops making payments to the bank or suppliers, they will take some kind of legal action. He is also concerned about the personal guarantees that he and Martha have given to the bank.

1. What options does Hometown have in dealing with this financial crisis?

Frank Gunn/The Canadian Press

2. What rights do Hometown's creditors have?

3. What will happen to Hometown, its owners, its creditors, Bill, and Martha if Hometown goes bankrupt?

Business Failure

Business failure is often overlooked in the study of business, which tends to emphasize success and entrepreneurship. Even when the economy is strong, businesses fail or falter because of poor management, lack of adequate financing, death or illness of a principal, fraud, and other reasons. When an industry or the overall economy experiences a downturn, even strong businesses may run into financial difficulty. Hometown is caught in a declining economy, an industry collapse, and a changing market in which local stores are threatened by big-box retailers. Hometown must deal with cash-flow problems, persistent and competing creditors, and possible legal action. The manner in which Hometown responds to these threats affects many people in addition to the business owners. If Hometown fails, customers, suppliers, and employees will be harmed, and the local economy may suffer. How the law addresses the respective interests of creditors and others is of critical importance to a wide and diverse group of stakeholders.

In an attempt to ensure that all stakeholders are treated fairly, a body of law, generically called bankruptcy and insolvency law, has evolved. The two primary pieces of legislation that govern insolvency law in Canada are the *Bankruptcy and Insolvency Act*[1] *(BIA)* and the *Companies' Creditors Arrangement Act*[2] *(CCAA)*. In addition, there are a number of other statutes and common law rules that affect bankruptcy and insolvency.

If a business such as Hometown is no longer able to cope with a specific debt or its financial obligations in general, there are several options available, ranging from informal negotiations to bankruptcy.

Informal Steps

Before contemplating bankruptcy, Hometown may first try to solve its financial problems by way of a negotiated settlement. If Bill can convince Hometown's creditors that the business can be salvaged, they may be willing to make concessions in terms of payment. Bill can deal with creditors individually or as a group. A settlement can be more or less formal, depending on the circumstances. Creditors may agree to meet with Bill and, possibly using the services of a professional facilitator (an accountant, a lawyer, or a debt counsellor), they may be able to reach an agreement that is acceptable to all of them and either allows Hometown to continue operating or wind up its affairs without the need for expensive legal proceedings. In practice, the more creditors that Hometown has, the less likely it is that they will be able to reach such an agreement.

The key to negotiated settlements is ensuring that all creditors are in agreement. Creditors will agree to a settlement if they believe that it will likely produce better results for them in the long run than legal proceedings or bankruptcy. One possible danger is that some creditors will attempt to push through an agreement

---

1   RSC 1985, c B-3.
2   RSC 1985, c C-36.

that is unfair to others or that simply ignores them. The value of using facilitators with appropriate expertise is that they are trained to identify these risks and deal with them. Furthermore, the parties themselves may not recognize alternatives that would result in a better overall outcome. A skilled facilitator will raise these alternatives for consideration.

In some cases, especially when the business is in serious financial trouble, negotiations may not be a viable option or may fail after a reasonable attempt. Creditors may refuse to participate in negotiations, or they may decide that it is not in their best interests to facilitate the debtor continuing to carry on business. In that case, the debtor must look to other options.

Proceedings before Bankruptcy

If informal negotiations fail to produce a settlement with Hometown's creditors, and Hometown's financial situation does not improve, Bill will likely explore more formal proceedings. He should seek advice from a lawyer or accountant with insolvency expertise so that he understands all the available options. If Bill decides that bankruptcy is the best or only option, he will need the services of a **trustee in bankruptcy**.

Trustee in bankruptcy

The person who has legal responsibility under the *BIA* for administering bankruptcies and proposals.

Trustees in bankruptcy are professionals who are licensed by the Office of the Superintendent of Bankruptcy and have legal authority to administer the bankruptcy process. A trustee in bankruptcy will usually agree to take on a matter if there is no conflict of interest present and the debtor has sufficient assets to pay for the trustee's services. Sometimes the debtor is not able to pay for the trustee and, in that case, it may be very difficult for the debtor to find a trustee willing to assist.

Estate

The collective term for the assets of a bankrupt individual or corporation.

When Bill and the trustee first meet, the trustee will explain the options available to Hometown, the bankruptcy process, and the role of the trustee. The trustee will also begin to assess the **estate** and prepare a preliminary statement of assets and liabilities. Often, in the case of small businesses, this assessment requires the untangling of business and personal affairs. In Hometown's case, the pending bankruptcy is that of Hometown Hardware Ltd., since it is the legal entity that carries on the business. However, it is possible that Bill and Martha may also become bankrupt, or make a proposal to their creditors, as a result of their personal guarantees.

Following consultation with Bill, the trustee will prepare a statement such as the one shown in Figure 27.1.

Insolvent

Unable to meet financial obligations as they become due or having insufficient assets, if liquidated, to meet financial obligations.

From this initial assessment, it is apparent that Hometown is **insolvent** as that term is defined in the *BIA*.[3] That is, Hometown owes more than $1000 and

- is unable to meet its obligations as they become due, or
- has ceased paying its obligations as they become due, or
- has assets with a fair market value less than its liabilities.

It is important to note that insolvency and bankruptcy are not the same, although the two terms are often, incorrectly, used interchangeably. Insolvency is a factual matter relating to a person's assets and liabilities or his ability to pay his debts. Bankruptcy is a legal mechanism whereby the assets of an insolvent person are transferred to a trustee, liquidated, and the net proceeds are distributed to creditors in a manner determined by the *BIA*.

---

3 *Supra* note 1, s 2.

FIGURE 27.1 Preliminary Statement of Assets and Liabilities for Hometown Hardware Ltd.

Assets* at estimated cash value	
Cash	$ 1 000
Accounts receivable	11 000
Inventory of plumbing supplies	27 000
Land and building	125 000
Equipment	30 000
	$ 194 000

Liabilities	
Unremitted payroll deductions (due to Canada Revenue Agency)	$ 24 000
Accounts payable to suppliers	94 000
Mortgage on land and building	110 000
Line of credit at bank (secured by inventory and accounts receivable)	85 000
Shareholder loan	70 000
Municipal property taxes	10 000
	$ 393 000

* Leased property is not an asset of the estate but will revert to the lessors upon default.

Proposals and Arrangements

It may be possible for an insolvent debtor to avoid bankruptcy by making a proposal or entering into an arrangement with creditors. The general assumption that underlies proposals and arrangements is that a business is worth more to all of its varied stakeholders (e.g., creditors, employees, suppliers, customers, government, etc.) as a going concern than if it is forced to liquidate all of its assets. If Bill wants to keep the business of Hometown going, he should consider making a proposal to Hometown's creditors.

Proposals under the *BIA*

A proposal is a procedure governed by the *BIA* that allows a debtor to restructure its debt in order to avoid bankruptcy. When a debtor makes a proposal, the debtor offers creditors a percentage of what is owed to them, or to extend the time for payment of debts, or some combination of the two. The goal is to restructure the debts owed by the debtor so that the debtor is able to pay them. In many cases, creditors prefer that a debtor avoid bankruptcy, especially if it means that the creditor will receive more money than if the debtor were to become bankrupt.

There are two types of proposal under the *BIA:*

- Division I proposals[4] are available to individuals and corporations with no limit on the total amount of debt that is owed.
- Division II proposals[5] are available to individuals with total debts less than $250 000 (not including a mortgage on a principal residence). Division II proposals are known as "consumer proposals."

---

4 *Supra* note 1, s 50.
5 *Supra* note 1, s 66.11.

In either case, the debtor works with a trustee in bankruptcy to develop a proposal which is first filed with the Office of the Superintendent of Bankruptcy and is then sent to the creditors of the debtor. Once the proposal is filed, the debtor stops making payments to its unsecured creditors, salary garnishments stop, and lawsuits against the debtor by creditors are stayed (stopped). In the case of a Division I proposal, there will be a meeting of creditors to consider and vote on the proposal, at which time the trustee will provide an estimate to the creditors of the amount they are expected to receive under the proposal compared to the amount they could expect to receive under a bankruptcy. In the case of a Division II proposal, there may or may not be a meeting of creditors, depending on whether they request one.

Creditors vote on whether to accept or reject the proposal. With a Division I proposal, the proposal is approved if creditors representing two-thirds of the total amount owed and a majority in number vote to accept it. In addition, a Division I proposal must be approved by the court. With a Division II proposal, the proposal is approved if creditors representing a majority of the total amount owed vote to accept it. If the proposal is approved by the creditors in this manner, then it is legally binding on all unsecured creditors, whether they voted for or against it.

If the proposal is approved, the debtor will make payments as provided in the proposal and, if the debtor makes all the payments and complies with any other conditions in the proposal, then the debtor is released from those debts. With Division I proposals, this gives a business the opportunity to remain in business and ultimately be successful. With Division II proposals, the debtor must also attend two mandatory financial counselling sessions, and the proposal will be recorded on the debtor's credit record for several years. If the debtor does not make the payments set out in the proposal, or fails to comply with conditions contained in it, then the trustee or any creditor can apply to have the proposal annulled.

However, if the proposal is not approved by the creditors, the debtor is deemed to be bankrupt under a Division I proposal as of the date of the first meeting of creditors.[6] In the case of a corporation, this usually means that the corporation will cease to exist as of that date. In a Division II proposal, the debtor is free to resubmit an amended proposal, consider other options, or make an assignment into bankruptcy. There is no automatic bankruptcy when a Division II proposal is rejected, unlike the result when a Division I proposal is rejected.

Generally, secured creditors are not bound by *BIA* proposals, unless they elect to participate. Secured creditors can realize on their security before or after the debtor has filed a proposal, even if the unsecured creditors have voted to accept the proposal. For this reason, it may be very difficult for a business to make a viable Division I proposal if the business has a large amount of secured debt. In that case, the secured creditors can be expected to appoint a receiver to seize their collateral and, if the collateral constitutes a majority of the assets used to operate the business, then the business will be effectively shut down.

Bill and the trustee may meet to discuss the possibility of Hometown submitting a Division I proposal to its creditors. The trustee will explain to Bill that as soon as the proposal is filed, the bank can be expected to realize on its security, including the land and buildings, inventory, and accounts receivable. That will leave Hometown with insufficient assets to carry on its business. For that reason, a proposal under the *BIA* is not a viable option for Hometown.

---

6 *Supra* note 1, s 57.

Arrangements under the *CCAA*

Another option for an insolvent business to avoid bankruptcy is an arrangement under the *CCAA*. The *CCAA* may be used by corporations that have total debt exceeding $5 million. The *CCAA* is a federal statute that allows an insolvent company to obtain protection from its creditors while it tries to reorganize its financial affairs. Similar to the situation with a proposal under the *BIA*, once a company obtains a court order under the *CCAA*, the company's creditors are prevented from taking any action to collect money that is owed to them. Unlike the *BIA*, however, the protection afforded by the *CCAA* applies to secured as well as unsecured creditors, and even to lessors and critical suppliers. After the initial court order is obtained, the company continues to operate while attempting to negotiate an arrangement with its creditors. Canadian companies that have reorganized under the *CCAA* include Air Canada, AbitibiBowater, Canwest, Nortel, QuebecorWorld, and Stelco.

When the court grants the initial *CCAA* order staying the creditors, it will also appoint a monitor, usually a major accounting firm, that will oversee the operations of the company while it attempts to reorganize. The monitor reports to the court on any major events that might impact the viability of the company, assists the company with the preparation of its reorganization plan, and tabulates the votes at meetings of creditors.

There are no restrictions on what may be contained in a *CCAA* arrangement. Indeed, one of the most attractive features of the *CCAA* for large companies is its flexibility. Arrangements will often involve companies paying a percentage of the debt owed to creditors, either in a lump sum or over time, or exchanging specific debt for debt with higher interest and longer repayment terms. Sometimes, shares will be offered to creditors in place of existing debt, or a combination of cash and shares.

Eventually, the arrangement will be voted on by creditors, who are grouped together by class for voting purposes. If the arrangement is approved by creditors of a class representing two-thirds of the total amount owed and a majority in number, then the arrangement is binding on that class of creditors. Once all the classes of creditors have approved the arrangement, court approval is required.

If a *CCAA* plan of arrangement is not approved by the creditors, then the company is not automatically bankrupt, as is the case with a Division I proposal under the *BIA*, but the court ordered stay of creditors is lifted. At that point, creditors are free to pursue their claims and it is likely that the company will be pushed into receivership or bankruptcy.

While a company is reorganizing under the *BIA* or the *CCAA*, it will need to fund its business operations. This may be difficult, because the reorganization proceedings are obvious evidence of insolvency and creditors will be reluctant to lend money in such circumstances. However, creditors may be willing to provide funding if the debtor has sufficient assets to provide as collateral and the creditors are given priority over existing creditors. This type of financing is called **debtor in possession (DIP) financing** or interim financing. DIP financing places existing secured creditors behind new lenders, which can be controversial. Accordingly, when approving DIP financing and giving priority to new lenders over existing secured creditors, courts are careful to balance the competing interests of existing secured creditors, the company in need of funds, and other creditors as well as employees and other stakeholders. The *BIA* was recently amended to allow for DIP financing in connection with a Division I proposal,[7] however, DIP financing is very difficult for smaller companies to find when making a *BIA* proposal.

Debtor in possession (DIP) financing

Secured credit provided to companies during the reorganization process with priority over existing secured creditors.

---

7 *Supra* note 1, s 50.6.

PART EIGHT

The *CCAA* is often preferred over the proposal mechanism of the *BIA* because of its flexibility, the fact that it binds secured creditors, and the availability of DIP financing. However, the minimum debt threshold of $5 000 000 and the very high costs associated with a *CCAA* reorganization make it a viable option only for very large companies.

BANKRUPTCY PROTECTION AND CORPORATE REORGANIZATION

In March of 2013, Target opened its first store in Canada. By January of 2015, the United States–based discount department store had 133 stores operating in Canada. A few days later, Target announced that it would be closing all of its Canadian stores and applied for bankruptcy protection. During its brief tenure in Canada, called "a spectacular failure" and "an unmitigated disaster," Target lost over $2 billion.

When Target Canada sought bankruptcy protection, it did so under the *CCAA*, which is unusual for a company that intends to cease operations. Traditionally, the *CCAA* has been used to reorganize the debts of a company so that it can remain viable. In Target's case, however, the *CCAA* was used to shut down the entire business and liquidate all of the company's assets.

Target Canada's single largest creditor was Target U.S., owed $1.9 billion. As a result, Target Canada's parent company had the most to gain from a liquidation controlled by the retailer, which the *CCAA* allows. However, the use of the *CCAA* for liquidation purposes is controversial, and some of Target Canada's creditors felt that Target was using the statute for a purpose for which it was never intended. Some landlords and other creditors, collectively owed hundreds of millions of dollars, wanted Target to have to file under the *BIA*, which would apply stricter rules and time limits to the sale of Target's assets.

As a result of Target shutting down its Canadian operations, the employment of over 17 600 employees was terminated. Target announced that it would provide every employee with 16-week notice of termination, or pay in lieu of notice, which is more than what provincial

What happens when a business is no longer viable?

employment law required. However, some critics were skeptical of Target's largesse, especially when it was revealed that the severance package given to Gregg Steinhafel, Target U.S. CEO and architect of the Canadian expansion, totalled $61 million, or slightly more than the amount paid to all 17 600 Canadian employees combined!

Critical Analysis: Were the interests of stakeholders, including employees and the public, adequately protected by the process described above? Should large companies be treated differently from smaller companies in the bankruptcy regime? Should the *CCAA* be available for companies that have no intention of staying in business?

Sources: Marina Strauss, "Target's retreat tactics raise questions about *CCAA*", *The Globe and Mail* (3 April 2015) online: *Globe and Mail* <http://www.theglobeandmail.com/report-on-business/targets-tricky-retreat-tactics-are-an-example-of-ccaas-failings/article23793761/>; Francine Kopun, "Target's severance deal a unique win for employees", *The Star* (6 February 2015) online: *The Star* <http://www.thestar.com/business/2015/02/06/targets-severance-deal-a-unique-win-for-employees.html>; Paul Hodgson, "Target CEO's golden parachute: $61 million", *Fortune* (1 June 2015) online: *Fortune* <http://fortune.com/2014/05/21/target-ceos-golden-parachute-61-million/>.

Remedies for Creditors

A creditor whose payments are overdue has several options. The first step is to determine the reason for the debtor's failure to pay. If the default is temporary, the creditor may decide to continue doing business with the debtor. However, if the debtor is in serious financial difficulty, then the creditor will want to take action before it is too late. The creditor often has a difficult choice to make: allow the debtor additional time to pay, or take legal action for the recovery of the debt.

A secured creditor can seize its collateral and sell it to pay down its debt, or appoint a receiver to take control of the debtor's business, as discussed in Chapter 26. An unsecured creditor can sue the debtor and try to obtain judgment, which can then be enforced against the debtor. A creditor with a guarantee can pursue the guarantor for payment upon default by the primary debtor. A supplier can threaten to discontinue selling to the debtor, as Good Lumber did with Hometown. Any creditor can threaten to commence legal action in the hope that the threat will persuade the debtor to bring the debt into good standing.

If the business is in serious financial jeopardy and is unable to make a proposal or reach an arrangement with its creditors, bankruptcy may be the only remaining option.

Bankruptcy

Bankruptcy is the legal process by which the assets of the **bankrupt** are automatically transferred to a trustee in bankruptcy for liquidation and distribution to creditors. The bankruptcy process is governed by the *BIA*. The purposes of the *BIA* are:

- to preserve the assets of the bankrupt for the benefit of creditors.
- to ensure a fair and equitable distribution of the assets to creditors.
- in the case of personal bankruptcies, to allow the debtor a fresh financial start.

There are three methods by which a person may become bankrupt. An **assignment in bankruptcy** occurs when a person voluntarily assigns her assets to a trustee in bankruptcy. Creditors can also apply to the court for a **bankruptcy order** which, if granted, results in a person being declared bankrupt. The bankruptcy order will normally be granted if the creditor is owed at least $1000 and the debtor has committed an **act of bankruptcy**. Acts of bankruptcy include: defaulting on a proposal, making a fraudulent transfer of property, preferring one creditor over another, trying to avoid or deceive creditors, admitting insolvency, or not meeting financial obligations as they come due.[8] Lastly, bankruptcy occurs automatically if the creditors reject a proposal, or if the creditors accept a proposal but the court rejects it. Regardless of the method by which a person becomes bankrupt, the result is the same.

If Hometown makes an assignment in bankruptcy, Hometown will be bankrupt as of the date of the assignment to the trustee in bankruptcy. If creditors of Hometown decide to apply to the court for a bankruptcy order against Hometown, they will probably obtain the order, as Hometown has likely engaged in at least one act of bankruptcy and owes several creditors more than $1000.

Bankrupt

The legal status of a debtor who has made an assignment or against whom a bankruptcy order has been issued (also used to describe a debtor who is bankrupt).

Assignment in bankruptcy

The debtor's voluntary assignment to the trustee in bankruptcy of legal title to the debtor's property for the benefit of creditors.

Bankruptcy order

An order of the court resulting in a person being declared bankrupt.

Act of bankruptcy

One of a list of specified acts that the debtor must commit before the court will grant a bankruptcy order.

---

8 *Supra* note 1, s 42.

ORIGINS AND PURPOSES OF BANKRUPTCY LEGISLATION

The most famous observer of the miseries of insolvency was Charles Dickens. In the early 19th century, debtors' prisons still existed in most countries. The dubious logic of imprisoning debtors for failing to pay their debts was not lost on Dickens, whose own father was imprisoned in the Marshalsea Prison when Charles was 12.

Dickens's writings made a powerful impact on the reading public throughout the English-speaking world. Largely as a result of Dickens's writings, bankruptcy legislation was introduced in England and elsewhere. Canadian bankruptcy legislation tries to balance the interests of a diverse group of stakeholders when debtors are unable to pay their debts. On one hand, the legislation enables honest but unfortunate debtors to free themselves of their crushing debts and obtain a fresh start. On the other hand, the law establishes priorities between creditors so that assets are distributed fairly and equitably. In the case of dishonest debtors, the law imposes punishment for those who commit bankruptcy offences. Finally, the legislation creates a framework under which potentially viable, but insolvent, businesses may be reorganized so they can continue operating for the benefit of creditors, suppliers, customers, employees, and the broader communities in which they carry on business.

There have been many attempts to revise and update bankruptcy legislation in Canada over the years. It has proven very difficult to

Marshalsea Prison, the debtors' prison where Charles Dickens's father was incarcerated.

© Historical Picture Archive/CORBIS

achieve consensus on how best to accomplish that goal, however, in large part due to the diverse group of stakeholders affected by the legislation. In 2009, the *BIA* and the *CCAA* were amended to facilitate DIP financing, deal with collective bargaining agreements, create a process for appointing a national receiver where appropriate, and give the courts authority to remove obstructive corporate directors, among other things. In addition, the 2009 amendments revised the rules regarding preferences and replaced the rules regarding settlements and reviewable transactions with comprehensive new "transfers at undervalue" rules (discussed later in this chapter).

Critical Analysis: Should individuals who make bad financial decisions be able to start over? Should companies that fail as a result of poor management decision making be entitled to a second chance? Whose interests are being protected by these laws?

The Bankruptcy Process

Once a person is bankrupt, the assets of the person are transferred to the trustee in bankruptcy, who holds those assets in trust for the benefit of creditors. The trustee has legal authority and responsibility to deal with the assets in a manner which preserves their value. Ultimately, the trustee will dispose of the assets and distribute the proceeds to creditors of the bankrupt in the manner required by the *BIA*. Creditors may appoint an **inspector** to act on their behalf and supervise the actions of the trustee.[9]

Inspector

A person appointed by creditors to act on their behalf and supervise the actions of the trustee in bankruptcy.

9 *Supra* note 1, s 116.

Protection of Assets

Following an assignment in bankruptcy or bankruptcy order, the trustee gives public notice of the bankruptcy in order to identify and protect the assets of the estate and to identify all liabilities. Typically, the trustee will

- secure the business premises and storage facilities.
- conduct a detailed examination of assets.
- prepare the appropriate statements.
- ensure that assets are adequately protected, including insurance coverage.
- establish appropriate books and accounts.
- sell any perishable goods immediately.

In exceptional circumstances, the trustee may continue running the business for a period of time in order to perform the duties above.

The protection of assets requires a review not only of assets in possession of the debtor at the time of bankruptcy, but also of assets that were transferred by the debtor prior to bankruptcy. If the debtor made payments to creditors in the ordinary course of business, they will not be challenged. However, if payments were made to favour one creditor over another, assets were transferred for less than their fair value, or transactions have taken place with related parties, then the trustee will review those transactions to ensure that creditors are treated equitably and according to the priorities set out in the *BIA*. The 2009 amendments to the *BIA* revised the rules regarding preferences and removed the concepts of settlements and reviewable transactions and replaced them with new **transfers at undervalue** rules.[10] The simultaneous *CCAA* amendments incorporated identical rules.[11]

Transfers at Undervalue

A transfer at undervalue occurs when assets are transferred, a payment is made, or services are provided for conspicuously less than their fair market value. Where a transfer at undervalue is found, the court can declare the transfer to be void or can order that the other party to the transaction pay the bankrupt estate the amount by which the consideration for the transaction was less than fair market value.

In order for a transfer at undervalue to be found, specific conditions must be satisfied and the conditions differ depending on whether or not the transaction was at arm's length. Parties are at **arm's length** when they are independent and not related (there are extensive rules in the *BIA* to determine when parties are related[12]).

If the parties to the transaction are at arm's length, then a transaction is a transfer at undervalue if: (a) it took place within one year prior to bankruptcy; (b) the debtor is insolvent (or was rendered insolvent by the transaction); and (c) the debtor intended to defraud, defeat, or delay the interests of a creditor.

If the parties to the transaction are not at arm's length, then a transaction is a transfer at undervalue if it took place within one year prior to bankruptcy. In that case, there are no solvency or intent criteria. If a non-arm's length transaction took place within five years prior to bankruptcy, it is a transfer at undervalue if the solvency and intent criteria in (b) and (c) above are satisfied.

Transfers at undervalue

Transfers of property or provision of services for less than fair market value.

Arm's length

People who are independent of each other and not related.

PART EIGHT

---

10 *Supra* note 1, s 96.
11 *Supra* note 2, s 36.1.
12 *Supra* note 1, s 4.

For example, if Hometown transferred its inventory to Bill six months before bankruptcy, the transfer would be a transfer at undervalue and would be void.

There are no cases yet that illustrate the approach the courts will take in determining whether a party intended to defraud, defeat, or delay creditors pursuant to the new *BIA* rules. However, there are cases dealing with similar language in other statutes which suggest that the courts will look primarily to the value of the consideration for which property was transferred in determining intent. If a debtor transfers property to a third party and receives nothing or significantly less than its fair market value in consideration, there will be a presumption of fraudulent intent on the part of the debtor. The presumption will be stronger where the transfer was made in secret or in contemplation of impending bankruptcy or litigation. There may even be fraudulent intent where property is transferred for fair value, if the court finds that the intention of the debtor was fraudulent and the recipient of the property knew of the debtor's intention. The issue of fraudulent intent is always highly specific to the facts of each case.[13]

Preferences

A preference is a payment that benefits one creditor over another. With solvent companies, this is a common occurrence and not a concern. However, when a company is insolvent, the preference may result in the other creditor not being paid at all. One of the purposes of the *BIA* is to ensure that creditors are treated fairly and equitably. This means that ordinary unsecured creditors should be treated equally. When one such creditor receives payment and another does not, this goal is not achieved. If a payment is found to be a preference, the court can rule the payment void, meaning that the creditor in receipt of the payment would have to repay that amount to the bankrupt estate.

As with transfers at undervalue, there is a distinction with respect to preferences depending on whether the parties are dealing at arm's length. If the parties are dealing at arm's length, a payment is a preference if it is made within three months prior to bankruptcy and it is made with the intention of preferring one creditor over another. If the parties are not dealing at arm's length, then a payment is a preference if it is made within one year prior to bankruptcy and it has the effect of preferring one creditor over another. In this case, it need only be shown that the effect of the payment was to prefer one creditor over another. The intention of the debtor is irrelevant.

It may be difficult to determine whether the debtor intended to prefer one creditor over another when making a payment. However, the courts have held that there is a rebuttable presumption of that intent if the result of the payment is that one creditor gets paid and another does not. This presumption can be rebutted if it can be shown, for example, that the payment was made in the ordinary course of business, or was made to take advantage of favourable payment terms or to secure the continued supply of goods or services needed for the debtor to remain in business.

Suppose Hometown has made an assignment in bankruptcy. If Hometown's payment to Good Lumber was made within three months of bankruptcy, and the effect of the payment was that Good Lumber received payment while other

---

13 For example, see *Abakhan & Associates Inc v Braydon*, (2009) BCCA 521, leave to appeal to SCC refused [2010] SCCA No 26 (June 24, 2010).

creditors did not, then the payment is likely a preference, and Good Lumber will have to return the payment to the trustee. Good Lumber is only entitled to the same proportion of its debt as other unsecured creditors. Similarly, the payment to George will be a preference if it was made within one year of bankruptcy, since George is not at arm's length to Hometown. Provided the salaries paid to Bill and Martha were genuine payments for services given, and were paid in the ordinary course of business, they will probably not be considered preferences. Regular payments made to trade creditors that were made in the normal course of business would also not be considered preferences.

Hometown could argue that the payment to Good Lumber was made in good faith and was therefore not a preference. If the payment was made for goods supplied to Hometown, and was made with the intention of obtaining a continued supply of lumber so Hometown could remain in business, then the payment should be allowed to stand.

Fraudulent Conveyances

In addition to the *BIA* provisions dealing with preferences and transfers at under-value, there are provincial laws dealing with similar situations where creditors are unfairly prejudiced. In Ontario, the *Fraudulent Conveyances Act*[14] provides that every transfer of property that is made with the intent to defeat, hinder, delay, or defraud creditors is void. This provision may be used by creditors outside of a bankruptcy situation, or may be used by a trustee in a bankruptcy situation. Whether the debtor intended to defeat, hinder, delay, or defraud creditors is highly fact specific and will depend on the circumstances of each case.

Bankruptcy Offences

For the *BIA* to be respected, it must provide penalties for those who violate its provisions. These violations are known as **bankruptcy offences**. They are criminal acts and can be committed by any of the key participants, including debtors, creditors, and trustees.

The *BIA* contains an extensive list of bankruptcy offences.[15] The most common bankruptcy offences include: fraudulently transferring property before or after bankruptcy, refusing to answer questions truthfully, providing false information, hiding, falsifying, or destroying records, hiding or concealing assets, and obtaining credit through false representations.

Penalties for bankruptcy offences range from conditional discharges to fines up to $10 000 and prison terms up to three years.

Bankruptcy offences

Criminal acts defined by the *BIA* in relation to the bankruptcy process.

Identification of Debts

Creditors find out about the bankruptcy through a notice sent by the trustee in bankruptcy. The details of the bankrupt estate are provided at the first meeting of creditors.

Each creditor must file a **proof of claim** in respect to the amount that it is owed. The trustee examines each proof of claim and either accepts or rejects the claim. The trustee rejects claims of unsecured creditors if there is inadequate evidence of the debt. The trustee rejects claims of secured creditors if the security interest is not perfected. Creditors whose claims are rejected have the option to challenge the rejection in court.

Proof of claim

A formal notice provided by the creditor to the trustee of the amount owed and the nature of the debt.

---

14 RSO 1990, c F-29.
15 *Supra* note 1, Part VIII.

Distribution to Creditors

Once the trustee has liquidated the assets and determined the debts of the bankrupt estate, the trustee will turn to the distribution of the proceeds to creditors. The *BIA* contains a comprehensive set of priority rules that determine the order of payment. The three broad categories of creditors are: secured, preferred, and unsecured. In addition, unpaid suppliers have a right of repossession under the *BIA* and certain government debts are deemed to be statutory trusts and thus are paid before any creditors.

Unpaid Suppliers

Unpaid suppliers are given special protection under the *BIA*. They are allowed to recover any goods shipped in the past 30 days which were not paid for, provided the debtor is bankrupt and the goods are in the same condition as when shipped.

Deemed Statutory Trusts

The federal government has passed legislation which deems property to be held in trust in regard to unremitted payroll deductions[16] and GST/HST which has been collected but not remitted.[17] These amounts are considered not to be part of the bankrupt estate and as such are payable ahead of all creditors.

Secured Creditors

Secured creditors with properly perfected security interests are entitled to take possession of their collateral and dispose of it, regardless of bankruptcy. If there is a deficiency still owed to the secured creditor, after payment of the secured creditor's expenses and application of the proceeds of sale to the debt, then the secured creditor becomes an ordinary unsecured creditor for the deficiency. A secured creditor can waive its security and elect to proceed as an unsecured creditor for the entire debt owed—this is sometimes done if the collateral is of little value or if it would require undue effort or expense to seize and dispose of the collateral.

Preferred Creditors

Preferred creditors

Certain unsecured creditors who are given priority over other unsecured creditors in the bankruptcy distribution.

Preferred creditors are paid after secured creditors and before other unsecured creditors, in strict order of priority as set out in section 136 of the *BIA*. The list of preferred creditors reflects the legislative intent as to the creditors who should be paid first. Preferred creditors, in order of priority, include:

- funeral expenses.
- trustee fees and expenses, including legal fees.
- arrears in wages (up to $2000 per employee for the previous six months).[18]
- municipal taxes.
- arrears of rent and accelerated rent, in each case up to three months.

---

16 *Income Tax Act*, RSC 1985, c 1, s 227(4).
17 *Excise Tax Act*, RSC 1985, c E-15, s 222(3).
18 This amount is secured by a first charge on the employer's current assets pursuant to s 81.3 of the *BIA*.

FIGURE 27.2 Revised Statement of Assets and Liabilities for Hometown Hardware Ltd.

Assets at estimated cash value	
Cash	$ 31 000*
Accounts receivable	11 000
Inventory	20 000**
Land and building	125 000
Equipment	30 000
Cash available for distribution	$ 217 000

Liabilities at estimated cash value	
CRA payroll deductions	$ 24 000
Mortgage on land and building	110 000
Trustee's fees and expenses	4 000
Municipal property taxes	10 000
Accounts payable to suppliers	87 000
Amount owed Good Lumber	20 000
Amount owed George	10 000
Shareholder Loan owed to Bill	70 000
Line of credit at bank	85 000***
	$ 420 000

* Includes original balance ($1 000) plus monies recovered from George and GL ($10 000 + $20 000).

** Portion ($7 000) of original was taken back by suppliers (reducing accounts payable from $94 000 to $87 000).

*** Since Bill Ikeda and Martha Wong have provided personal guarantees for the line of credit, they will be personally liable for any outstanding balance, after distribution.

Preferred creditors are paid in full before anything is paid to other unsecured creditors.

Unsecured Creditors

The remaining funds in the bankrupt estate, if any, are paid to the ordinary unsecured creditors in proportion to the amounts they are owed. Secured creditors with deficiencies are unsecured creditors to the extent of those deficiencies. Good Lumber and George, to the extent that the payments to them by Hometown are found to be preferences and repaid to the trustee, are unsecured creditors for those amounts (see Figure 27.2).

Employees

Employees who are owed wages are deemed to be secured creditors, with a first charge on the current assets of their employer, for up to $2 000 per employee. In addition, the *Wage Earner Protection Program* allows employees to recover some unpaid wages when their employment is terminated as a result of bankruptcy or receivership. These provisions are intended to protect employees, who are particularly vulnerable in the event of business failure due to bankruptcy or insolvency.

In the final distribution of assets (see Figure 27.3),

- CRA is paid in full for the unremitted payroll deductions
- the bank is paid in full under its mortgage as a secured creditor
- the trustee's fees and municipal taxes are paid in full as preferred creditors
- the remaining claims of unsecured creditors are paid at the rate of $0.1577 for each dollar owed

PART EIGHT

FIGURE 27.3 Final Distribution of Assets of Hometown Hardware Ltd. by Class of Creditor

Schedule 1: Distribution of cash to secured and preferred creditors	
Opening balance available	$ 217 000
Pay CRA the payroll deductions	24 000
	193 000
Secured creditors	
Pay mortgage on land and building	110 000
Pay bank from inventory and accounts receivable	31 000
	$ 52 000
Preferred creditors	
Trustee's fees and expenses	$ 4 000
Pay municipal taxes	10 000
Balance available for unsecured creditors	$ 38 000

Schedule 2: Distribution of cash to unsecured creditors	
Balance available for unsecured creditors	$ 38 000
Balance due to unsecured creditors:	
Accounts payable to suppliers	87 000
Amount owed George	10 000
Amount owed Good Lumber	20 000
Shareholder Loan owed to Bill	70 000
Line of credit at bank ($31 000 already paid)	54 000
	$ 241 000

Amount to be paid per dollar of unsecured debt: $38 000/241 000 = 0.1577 or just under $0.16 for every dollar owed.

Payments to unsecured creditors (rounded)	
Accounts payable to suppliers	$ 13 718
George	1 577
Good Lumber	3 154
Bill (shareholder loan)	11 037
Line of credit at bank	8 514
Total payments to unsecured creditors	$ 38 000
Balance	0

Bill Ikeda and Martha Wong personally owe the bank the unpaid balance of the line of credit since they have guaranteed the debt: ($85 000 − (31 000 + 8 514) = $45 486).

Since Bill and Martha personally guaranteed the line of credit to the bank, they are personally liable to pay $45 486—the amount remaining on that debt—to the bank. If they cannot pay, they may have to explore their own options regarding insolvency or bankruptcy.

A discharge from bankruptcy is not available to a bankrupt corporation unless it has paid its debts in full. Hometown no longer exists as a corporation as of the date of its assignment in bankruptcy. It is the end of the road for Hometown.

Personal Bankruptcy

Personal bankruptcy is the last remaining option when an individual is unable to pay her debts and there are no alternatives to bankruptcy. People become insolvent for a wide variety of reasons, including loss of employment, medical or other expenses beyond their control, bad business investments, or poor financial planning. Personal bankruptcies differ from corporate bankruptcies in a number of important respects.

People in financial difficulty may attempt informal measures to address their financial situation, including altering their budget, consolidating their debts into a single loan with lower interest and easier payments, or negotiating directly with their creditors for lower payments or more time to pay.

Division II (consumer) proposals are available to individuals with debts (other than those secured by a principal residence) under $250 000, as discussed above. Some provinces[19] have systems for the "orderly payment of debts," which involve a consolidation of debts under the supervision of the courts.

If no other options are available, individuals may be forced into personal bankruptcy. Personal bankruptcy involves the assets of the bankrupt being assigned to a trustee in bankruptcy who holds those assets, and ultimately disposes of them, for the benefit of creditors. Personal bankruptcy can be voluntary, with the debtor making an assignment in bankruptcy, or involuntary, as the result of an application to the court by a creditor for a bankruptcy order.

In a personal bankruptcy, a debtor is entitled to retain certain assets to support herself and her family, along with any registered retirement savings (except deposits within one year of bankruptcy). The *BIA* provides that the property of the bankrupt transferred to the trustee excludes any property that would be exempt from seizure under provincial law. Accordingly, the property that will be exempt will vary by province. In Ontario, the *Execution Act* provides exemptions for items such as clothing up to $5650 in value, household furniture and utensils up to $11 300, tools of a trade up to $11 300, and one motor vehicle up to $5650.[20]

During the bankruptcy process, the debtor will usually be required to make payments to the trustee for the benefit of creditors. The amounts of the payments are determined by the trustee, taking into account the debtor's total income and living expenses. The bankrupt will also be examined under oath in regard to her assets and liabilities, the causes of bankruptcy, and the disposition of any property. The debtor must also attend two mandatory financial counselling sessions.

Provided the bankrupt has completed all of the steps described earlier, has not committed a bankruptcy offence, and is not required to make additional payments, a first time bankrupt will receive an automatic **discharge of bankruptcy** nine months following bankruptcy. For a second bankruptcy, automatic discharge takes place 24 months following bankruptcy. If an automatic discharge is not available for any reason, the bankrupt must apply to the court for a discharge and the court will conduct a hearing.

Once discharged, a bankrupt is released from most of her debts. Not all debts are released by the discharge. Fines, penalties, alimony and support payments, debts arising from fraud, and to some extent student loans[21] survive the discharge. Corporations are not discharged from bankruptcy unless they have paid their debts in full.

Following discharge from bankruptcy, a first bankruptcy remains on a person's credit record for six years. A second bankruptcy remains on the record for 14 years and a consumer proposal remains on the record for three years.

Discharge of bankruptcy

An order releasing the debtor from bankrupt status and from most remaining debts.

---

19 For example, Alberta, Saskatchewan, and Nova Scotia.
20 *Execution Act* RSO 1998, c E-24.
21 If it is less than seven years after ceasing to be a student. However, application may be made for release on the basis of hardship after 5 years.

PART EIGHT

The discharge may be opposed—by the Superintendent of Bankruptcy, the trustee, or a creditor—if a bankruptcy offence has been committed or where there is evidence of extravagance prior to the bankruptcy.

McRudden (Re), 2014 BCSC 217 (CanLII)

THE BUSINESS CONTEXT: Individuals who go bankrupt are eligible to be discharged from their debts at the end of the bankruptcy process. However, the discharge may be opposed by the trustee in bankruptcy or one or more creditors, in which case the court may refuse the discharge or impose conditions.

FACTUAL BACKGROUND: McRudden was a dentist who made an assignment into bankruptcy in 2008. At the time of his bankruptcy, McRudden owed more than $800 000 in unpaid taxes, plus penalties and interest. Some of the unpaid taxes were the result of Canada Revenue Agency (CRA) disallowing business expenses McRudden had claimed for his dental practice, including a hot tub, tanning bed, plastic surgery, a tractor lawn mower, and improvements to his personal residence. In the two years prior to bankruptcy, McRudden sold a building he owned for $636 728 and transferred $635 000 of that amount to his sister. McRudden did not disclose this transaction to the trustee in bankruptcy. When he went bankrupt, McRudden disclosed $3200 in assets and $1.15 million in debts, including over $900 000 to CRA, $200 000 to the College of Dental Surgeons (which was a fine and costs for assaulting a female tenant and other complaints), and $50 000 for arrears in child support. McRudden pled guilty to two counts under the *BIA* and one count under the *Criminal Code* in respect to the misinformation he provided when he went bankrupt. He was given a conditional sentence of 16 months, including six months of house arrest. McRudden lives in a waterfront home in Kelowna, B.C., worth $2.8 million, which he bought in 2000 and transferred to his sister in 2001. He pays no rent or property tax. McRudden drives a Corvette, which is also owned by his sister, and uses a boat, snowmobile, and Sea-Doo, all owned by his sister. He belongs to the Kelowna Yacht Club. In 2007, McRudden's licence to practise

dentistry was suspended indefinitely, and he claims to have earned no income since that time. According to his doctor, McRudden suffers from depression and self-medicates with alcohol. The trustee in bankruptcy opposed McRudden's application for a discharge.

THE LEGAL QUESTION: Is McRudden entitled to a discharge of his unpaid debts? If so, should the discharge be subject to conditions?

RESOLUTION: The judge found that McRudden was not entitled to an absolute discharge. The purpose of the *BIA* is to permit an honest but unfortunate debtor to obtain a discharge from his debts subject to reasonable conditions, and to permit the debtor to rehabilitate himself free from the overwhelming burden of debts. However, the judge found that McRudden was neither honest nor unfortunate:

> … his lifestyle has not been affected by this bankruptcy, and his creditors have not been paid a cent while he lives in a $2.8 million home, drives a Corvette, and belongs to a yacht club. This bankrupt might have overwhelming debt but he does not deserve an absolute discharge. This bankrupt has made no effort to rehabilitate himself. In fact, he has very obviously not changed his lifestyle, flaunting it in the face of the bankruptcy system. If ever a case cried out for deterrence, this is the one. Deterrence is not to punish the bankrupt for misconduct but is to send a message to others who might be tempted to evade income tax liability by conveniently using bankruptcy (or the hiding of assets) as a financial planning tool.

The judge ordered that McRudden be discharged conditional on paying $200 000 for the benefit of creditors and that he file income tax returns (and pay any resulting income tax) until that money is paid and for two years at a minimum.

CRITICAL ANALYSIS: Does this case preserve the integrity of the bankruptcy system? Did the judge adequately balance the interests of the debtor, the creditors, and the public?

BUSINESS LAW IN PRACTICE REVISITED

1. What options does Hometown have in dealing with this financial crisis?

Hometown can seek a voluntary negotiated settlement with creditors in order to continue the business or bring it to an end. Hometown can make a Division I proposal to creditors under the *BIA* that would allow the business to continue. As a last resort, Hometown can make an assignment in bankruptcy.

2. What rights do Hometown's creditors have?

Creditors can exert pressure on Hometown or threaten legal action in an attempt to persuade Hometown to pay. Secured creditors can seize and dispose of their collateral. Unsecured creditors can sue Hometown and try to obtain judgment. Finally, creditors can apply to a court for a bankruptcy order against Hometown.

3. What will happen to Hometown, its owners, its creditors, Bill, and Martha if Hometown goes bankrupt?

Bankruptcy will result in the transfer of all of Hometown's assets to the trustee, including payments made which constitute preferences. The trustee will dispose of the assets and distribute the proceeds to creditors. Secured creditors will likely realize on their security, leaving only the unsecured assets to be dealt with by the trustee. Preferred creditors will be paid in full before other unsecured creditors receive any payment. Ordinary unsecured creditors will receive a small fraction of what they are owed. Any unpaid debts that Bill and Martha have guaranteed will become their personal responsibility and may result in their personal bankruptcies. Hometown will cease to exist as a result of the bankruptcy.

CHAPTER SUMMARY

The *BIA* and *CCAA* govern situations where debtors become insolvent. The purposes of the legislation are to ensure that all stakeholders are treated fairly, including debtors, creditors, employees, government, and the broader community. It is, however, a very difficult task to try and reconcile all of these different interests.

Prior to bankruptcy, debtors may be able to take informal steps to address their financial situation. Creditors will usually be willing to negotiate if they believe that they will fare better through an informal process than through a formal process such as a proposal or bankruptcy.

If informal steps are not an option, an insolvent debtor can make a proposal to creditors under the *BIA*. Individuals with less than $250 000 in debt can make consumer proposals. Large companies with more than $5 000 000 in debt can reorganize under the *CCAA*. In order to be successful, the debtor will have to submit a plan of reorganization that creditors will approve.

Secured creditors are in a much better position than unsecured creditors in the event of insolvency or bankruptcy, because they can generally enforce their security regardless of bankruptcy proceedings. Secured creditors become unsecured creditors for any deficiency owed.

Bankruptcy is usually a last resort. Bankruptcy is the formal legal process by which the assets of the debtor are transferred to a trustee in bankruptcy for the benefit of creditors. Bankruptcy can be either voluntary, by the debtor, or involuntary, on an application by creditors. The *BIA* contains rules to ensure that creditors are treated fairly and that debtors conduct themselves appropriately both before and during the bankruptcy process. In a bankruptcy situation, secured creditors will usually realize on their security first, leaving only unsecured assets for the trustee to deal with. The trustee will dispose of the remaining assets and distribute the proceeds to creditors in the specific manner and order of priority set out in the *BIA*. Personal bankruptcy differs from business bankruptcy in a number of important respects, including the ability of the bankrupt to be discharged from most debts after a period of time.

CHAPTER STUDY

Key Terms and Concepts

act of bankruptcy (p. 687)

arm's length (p. 689)

assignment in bankruptcy (p. 687)

bankrupt (p. 687)

bankruptcy offences (p. 691)

bankruptcy order (p. 687)

debtor in possession (DIP) financing (p. 685)

discharge of bankruptcy (p. 695)

estate (p. 682)

insolvent (p. 682)

inspector (p. 688)

preferred creditors (p. 692)

proof of claim (p. 691)

transfers at undervalue (p. 689)

trustee in bankruptcy (p. 682)

Questions for Review

1. How can negotiated settlements be used when a business is in financial difficulty?

2. What is the difference between insolvency and bankruptcy?

3. What are the purposes of bankruptcy legislation?

4. What are the requirements for a creditor to obtain a bankruptcy order?

5. What are two examples of an act of bankruptcy?

6. What is a fraudulent conveyance?

7. Who can oppose a bankruptcy discharge?

8. Who are preferred creditors?

9. How are preferred creditors treated differently from secured and unsecured creditors?

10. How are employees protected in the bankruptcy of their employer?

11. Under what circumstances will a court place conditions on a discharge from bankruptcy?

12. What are the duties of the trustee in bankruptcy?

13. What debts are not released in a discharge from bankruptcy?

14. What is the purpose of a proposal?

15. What is the difference between a Division I proposal and a consumer proposal?

16. Why might a large company prefer reorganizing under the *CCAA* rather than making a proposal under the *BIA*?

17. What happens if unsecured creditors do not vote to approve a proposal?

18. What are the differences between an individual being bankrupt and a corporation being bankrupt?

Questions for Critical Thinking

1. Business decisions made prior to bankruptcy can be challenged by the trustee if they are found to be preferences or transfers at undervalue. What is the rationale for giving the trustee this authority? How does it relate to the purposes of bankruptcy legislation?

2. Current bankruptcy law bars graduates from being discharged from their outstanding student loans for seven years after the completion of their studies or 5 years in

cases of hardship. Why does the law deal with student loans in this way? Is it fair to treat student loans differently from other debts?

3. In 2009, Nortel Networks Corporation filed for protection from creditors under the *CCAA*. Nortel initially sought to emerge from bankruptcy protection as a viable business, but in June of 2009 Nortel announced that it would sell off all its assets and cease operations. Nortel's share price went to $0.185 after having been as high as $1 245. Ninety thousand people would lose their jobs as a result of Nortel's demise. In the end, the amount paid to lawyers, accountants, financial experts and consultants in connection with the bankruptcy of Nortel would surpass $1 billion. Is the *CCAA* an appropriate mechanism for companies to seek protection from creditors?

4. Proposals are an important part of the bankruptcy and insolvency legislation. However, despite the controls that exist, they can have the effect of delaying legal actions by creditors to protect their interests. Does the potential benefit of proposals in salvaging troubled businesses outweigh the potential losses to creditors?

5. The category of preferred creditor is not found in the bankruptcy legislation of many countries. What is the rationale for the protection afforded preferred creditors in Canadian law? Is this special treatment appropriate considering the interests of all creditors?

6. Why does the bankruptcy legislation treat individuals differently from corporations regarding a discharge from bankruptcy? Is this treatment appropriate?

Situations for Discussion

1. Before creditors can petition a debtor into bankruptcy, they must be able to show that at least one act of bankruptcy has been committed by the debtor. Review the events in the Hometown situation and identify any possible acts of bankruptcy. Do the various acts of bankruptcy have a common theme? Should it be obvious to a debtor such as Hometown that such conduct is inadvisable? When the debtor has committed an act of bankruptcy, at what point should the creditors act upon it?

2. Halifax Realty (HR) is a property developer based in Halifax. It is in the business of building office buildings and other commercial premises. Over the past several years, HR has overextended itself with the result that it now finds itself with more liabilities than assts. HR's debts are $150 million and its assets at today's values are worth $80 million. Two banks hold security for 90 percent of the debt. The balance of the debt is unsecured. The company is now unable to make regular payments on its loans and will not be able to make its regular payroll at the end of this month.

John, the CEO of HR, believes the company could remain viable as long as it could find a way to reduce its immediate cash flow requirements. His discussions with HR's two major creditors suggest that only one of them would be prepared to negotiate a more favourable payment scheme. John seeks advice from an insolvency practitioner about the pros and cons of making a proposal.

What advice is John likely to receive? What factors will the creditors consider in responding to HR's situation? What should John do?

3. Designer Shirts is a supplier to Classic Stores (Classic), a major national retail outlet. There are rumours that Classic is in trouble, but the company has been in trouble before and has managed to recover. Industry analysts say that there is too much at stake to allow the company to fail.

Classic has recently announced an infusion of cash from a major investor. On the strength of this news, Designer Shirts agrees to make deliveries, although it insists on a shorter payment period than normal. Designer makes the first delivery of summer stock at the end of March. It receives its payment within the specified 20 days. It then makes a second delivery, but this time payment is not forthcoming in 20 days. Based on further promises that the payment will be made within two days, Designer makes a third shipment. Within 10 days there is an announcement that Classic has made an assignment in bankruptcy. Designer has received payment for neither the second nor the third shipment and is owed $1.5 million.

What are Designer's options? Could Designer have better managed its risk in this situation?

4. Falcon Gypsum Ltd. is in the business of manufacturing wallboard, largely for the U.S. housing market, which has been growing for many years. In recent months, several developments have caused Falcon's management to become concerned. The U.S. housing industry has slowed considerably. This has caused wallboard prices to fall sharply. In addition, the Canadian dollar has risen in relation to the U.S. dollar, making Canadian manufacturers such as Falcon less competitive in export sales. Falcon currently employs 40 workers. The company owes $32 million to 90 different creditors. The major creditors are the bank and the provincial government, who hold secured loans. Management's strategy is to attempt to wait out the current adverse conditions and hopefully return to prosperity. In order to do that, Falcon needs some breathing room from creditors and some additional bridge financing.[22] What are Falcon's options? What should Falcon do? If Falcon makes a proposal, are creditors likely to approve the proposal?

5. Kim owns a family business that is experiencing serious difficulties because of changing economic circumstances. It operates as a sole proprietorship and has borrowed from a number of sources (originally commercial, but lately from friends and family) over the last three years to keep the business afloat. There are three employees, without whose services Kim could no longer run the business. He is beginning to feel overwhelmed and needs some basic advice as to what he can and cannot do. For example, should he create a corporation and sell the business assets to that corporation? Should he consolidate his loans and pay off as many as he can now by extending his borrowing with the bank? If he repays his friends and family, is there any risk in doing so? What should Kim do?

6. In 2011, DVD rental chain Blockbuster announced that it was going out of business. The success of video streaming and video-on-demand services such as Netflix was insurmountable competition for Blockbuster's traditional video rental business. Blockbuster initially tried to reorganize and reduce its debt but, ultimately, it was not able to obtain adequate DIP financing. Blockbuster closed its 400 Canadian stores and terminated all of its employees. What could Blockbuster have done differently to avoid bankruptcy? What can a company do if its business model becomes obsolete in the face of new competition?

7. Gaklis was the sole director, officer, and shareholder of Christy Crops Ltd. He controlled the company and made all major decisions. The company had financial difficulty and was placed in receivership. Gaklis had guaranteed substantial debts of the company and was unable to respond to demands for payment. He was forced into bankruptcy and eventually applied for discharge. The trustee and the creditors opposed his application for a discharge based on his conduct: Gaklis had disposed of land belonging to the company. He had given a security interest for $60 000 on an airplane and transferred ownership to his father. He had failed to cooperate with the trustee by refusing to disclose particulars of bank accounts and insurance policies.[23]

Should Gaklis be discharged from bankruptcy and released from his unpaid debts? If so, on what terms?

8. Gregor Grant was the president and sole shareholder of Grant's Contracting Ltd. On application by a major creditor, an order of bankruptcy was issued against the company. In the course of investigating the company's affairs prior to bankruptcy, the trustee discovered that a cheque received in payment from a supplier had not been deposited in the company's account but had been diverted to another company owned by Gregor's brother, Harper. Harper had kept some of the money for himself and returned the remainder in smaller amounts to Gregor.[24] What, if anything, can the trustee do about this situation? What could the impact be on the two companies, the two brothers, and the customer who sent the cheque?

---

22 Based on Bruce Erskine, "Plant shuts down for a bit", *The Chronicle Herald* (13 June 2008) at C1.

23 Based on *Re Gaklis* (1984), 62 NSR (2d) 52 (SCTD).

24 Based on *Grant Bros Contracting Ltd v Grant*, 2005 NSSC 358.

TRANSFERENCE OF RISK

CHAPTER 28
Insurance

Risk management is the process of establishing and maintaining procedures for identifying risks and reducing, avoiding, or retaining their consequences. Throughout the preceding chapters, the focus has been on identifying legal risks and the means for minimizing them through risk reduction strategies.

This part of the text explores the transference of risk through the use of various insurance products. It explores the general principles of a contract of insurance and discusses how insurance can protect against contractual, tortious, environmental, and other business and legal risks.

28

OBJECTIVES

After studying this chapter, you should have an understanding of

- the role of insurance in risk management
- the nature of an insurance contract, including the rights and obligations of the insurer and the insured
- the various kinds of insurance

Jim Wells/Calgary Sun

INSURANCE

BUSINESS LAW IN PRACTICE

Wire Experts and Company Ltd. (WEC) is a small business owned and operated by three shareholders. It produces wires used in the manufacture of tires. It buys metal, formulates the alloys, extrudes the necessary wires, and then sells them to tire manufacturers both in Canada and abroad. The manufacture of the wire creates some contaminated waste products that require special storage and disposal. WEC's business office is on the first floor of its manufacturing plant. Suppliers, sales personnel, and representatives of various purchasers are frequent visitors. WEC also owns several trucks, which its delivery personnel use to deliver wires to customers.

As there are considerable risks associated with its business, WEC has purchased a full range of insurance products, including comprehensive general liability, automobile, property, occupier's liability, errors and omissions, directors and officers, and business interruption insurance.

In 2013, WEC moved its operations to Alberta to be closer to its customer base. WEC closed its manufacturing plant in New Brunswick and opened a new facility in Red Deer. Three months later, the vacant plant was destroyed by fire. WEC brought a claim under its fire insurance policy. The insurance company denied the claim on the basis that WEC failed to inform it that the plant was vacant. Furthermore, the insurance company alleged that the fire was suspicious and that perhaps WEC was involved in the plant's destruction.

1. Was WEC under a duty to disclose the plant's vacancy to the insurance company? If so, what is the effect of a failure to disclose?

2. What risk does the insurance company run by making allegations of arson?

Introduction

A cornerstone of an effective risk management program is insurance coverage. As discussed in Chapter 3, insurance is the primary means of transferring the risk of various kinds of losses. It permits a business to shift the risk, because through an **insurance policy**, the **insurer** promises to compensate the person or business (known as the **insured**) should the contemplated loss actually occur. The insurer provides this protection in exchange for payment, known as an insurance **premium**, from the insured (see Figure 28.1).

FIGURE 28.1 The Insurance Relationship

| INSURER (provides protection against a specified loss) | → | INSURED (purchases protection against a specified loss) |

Insurance is not, however, a panacea for all risks, as insurance can be costly and is not always available (or is available only at an exorbitant cost). For example, disasters across North America—including flooding in Alberta and Ontario, a massive train derailment and explosion in Quebec, and ice storms from Ontario to the Maritimes—have resulted in billions of dollars in payouts by insurance companies. These events and likely future weather and climate disasters are resulting in higher premiums and changes in the extent of coverage.[1] For some companies, this has meant that the insurance is so expensive that it is essentially unobtainable. It is also important to remember that insurance does not prevent a loss from occurring, nor does it prevent the potential adverse publicity associated with a loss.

How does climate change affect insurance?

An insurance policy is a contract. By the terms of the contract, the parties agree to what kind of loss is covered, in what amount, under what circumstances, and at what cost. Insurance policies are also regulated by legislation in each of the provinces.

Insurance legislation serves a number of significant purposes, including the following:

- mandating the terms that must be found in insurance contracts.
- regulating the insurance industry generally by setting out licensing requirements for insurance companies, insurance brokers, and insurance adjusters.
- putting in place a system for monitoring insurance companies, particularly with respect to their financial operation.

---

1 Jacqueline Nelson, "One year after Alberta's floods, an altered landscape for insurers," *The Globe and Mail* (20 June 2014) B1.

Insurance policy
A contract of insurance.

Insurer
A company that sells insurance coverage.

Insured
One who buys insurance coverage.

Premium
The price paid for insurance coverage.

PART NINE

The main goal of insurance legislation is to protect the public from unscrupulous, financially unstable, and otherwise problematic insurance companies. It also provides working rules that create stability within the industry at large.

The three basic kinds of insurance are as follows:

- *life and disability insurance*: provides payments on the death or disability of the insured.
- *property insurance* (also known as *fire insurance*): provides payment when property of the insured is damaged or destroyed through accidents. It also can cover the costs of machine breakdown.
- *liability insurance* (also known as *casualty insurance*): provides payment in circumstances where the insured is held legally responsible for causing loss or damage to another, known as the third party.[2]

With the exception of life insurance contracts, insurance policies can be written so that the insured pays a **deductible**. This means that the insured is responsible for the first part of the loss, and the insurer has liability for the balance. Agreeing to a deductible generally reduces the premiums that the insured must pay for the coverage. For example, WEC agreed to a $100 deductible for windshield replacement on its delivery trucks. If a WEC vehicle windshield requires replacement and the cost is $600, WEC's insurers will pay $500. The $100 deductible is WEC's responsibility, and to that extent, WEC is self-insured.

The Insurance Contract
Duty to Disclose

Insurance contracts are of a special nature. They are known as contracts of utmost good faith. A key consequence is that the insured has a **duty to disclose** to the insurer all information relevant to the risk; if the insured fails in that duty, the insurer may choose not to honour the policy. For example, assume that WEC wants to change insurers in an effort to save on premiums. Max, one of WEC's employees, fills in an application for fire insurance. In response to the question, "Have you ever experienced a fire?" Max writes, "Yes—in 2006." Max does not mention that WEC also had a fire in 2005, because he is convinced that WEC will end up paying an outrageously high premium. Max has failed to disclose a fact that is germane to the insurer's decision to insure and relevant to what the premiums should be in light of the risk. For this reason, if WEC tries to claim for fire loss should another fire occur at the plant, the insurer could refuse to honour the policy based on Max's non-disclosure.

An insurance company can deny coverage for non-disclosure even if the loss has nothing to do with the matter that was left undisclosed. For example, since WEC has failed to disclose a previous fire loss, the insurer can deny a vandalism claim that WEC might make at some future time.

The law places a duty of disclosure on the insured for a straightforward reason: the insurer has to be in a position to fully assess the risk against which the insured wants protection. The only way the insurer can properly assess risk is if the insured is candid and forthcoming. In short, the insured is usually in the best position to provide the insurer with the information needed.

Deductible

The part of a loss for which the insured is responsible.

Duty to disclose

The obligation of the insured to provide to the insurer all information that relates to the risk being insured.

---

2   The person who is injured or otherwise suffers loss is the third party in relation to the contract of insurance. In the contract of insurance, the insurer and insured are the first and second parties.

GENETIC TESTING AND INSURANCE

Advances in medical science have revealed that many diseases—colon cancer, breast cancer, diabetes, cystic fibrosis, muscular dystrophy, and Huntington's disease, for example—are at least, in part, genetic diseases. And advances in medical technology have made it possible to test for many of these diseases at a low cost. People may take advantage of the testing out of concern about having children or for mitigating the risks of the disease by making lifestyle changes or taking prescribed drugs, or for the sake of aiding research into ailments and preventative therapies. There can, however, be an unintended consequence of accessing testing—the effect on insurance.

Insurance contracts are contracts of utmost good faith, requiring full disclosure of material facts that may affect insurability and the insurance premium. Disclosing a genetic predisposition to certain conditions may result in the denial of insurance coverage, higher insurance premiums or reduced insurance benefits. Failure to disclose may result in the insurance contract being voided. As a result of these consequences, many people may not access testing. This, according to Professor Elizabeth Adjin-Tettey, would "undermine the health benefits of genetic testing, with detrimental consequences for public health and quality of life and increased health care costs."

To address this troubling dilemma, some countries have banned reliance on genetic testing in insurance decisions. Other countries have adopted a two-tiered system where access to

How does genetic testing affect access to insurance?

basic insurance coverage is guaranteed without reference to genetic characteristics. Disclosure of genetic test results is only required for insurance coverage beyond the basic level. In Canada, neither approach has been adopted to date. Private member's bills to include genetic discrimination as a prohibited ground of discrimination in the Canadian[3] and Ontario[4] *Human Rights Acts* have been introduced but are not yet law.

Critical Analysis: What is the problem with an outright ban on insurance companies using genetic information in insurance decisions? Are there any concerns with the two-tiered approach?

Sources: Elizabeth Adjin-Tettey, "Time to write some rules for genetic risk", *The Lawyers Weekly* (8 June 2012) 10; Elizabeth Adjin-Tettey, "How genetic information affects access to insurance," *The Lawyers Weekly* (21 August 2009), online: *The Lawyers Weekly* <http://www.lawyersweekly.ca/index.php?section=article&articleid=977>.

However, the duty to disclose is not all encompassing. The law expects the insurer to be "worldly wise" and to show "personal judgment."[5] For this reason, there is no onus on the insured to inform the insurer of matters "not personal to the applicant." For example, assume that in the application for fire insurance Max notes that some welding occurs on the premises, but he does not go on to observe that welding causes sparks, which, in turn, can cause a fire. This is not a

---

3 Bill S-201 *An Act to Prohibit and Prevent Genetic Discrimination,* 2nd Sess, 41st Parl, 2013.
4 Bill 127, *Human Rights Code Amendment Act (Genetic Characteristics),* 2nd Sess, 40th Leg, Ontario, 2013.
5 Craig Brown & Thomas Donnelly, *Insurance Law in Canada,* Vol 1 loose-leaf, (consulted on July 21, 2014) (Toronto: Carswell, 2002), ch 5 at 5-6.1.

PART NINE

When does an insured have a duty to disclose?

failure to disclose—after all, the insurer is expected to be worldly wise. That said, the insured is much better to err on the side of disclosure, since a miscalculation on the insured's part can lead to the policy being void.

A duty to disclose exists not just at the time of applying for the insurance—it is an ongoing duty. The insurer must be notified about any change material to the risk. For example, if WEC decides to stop producing wire and turn its attention instead to manufacturing plastic cable, the insurer should be advised, in writing, of this change. In the same vein, when WEC leaves a building vacant, the insurer should be contacted so that necessary adjustments to the policy can be made.

CASE

Marche v Halifax Insurance Co, 2005 SCC 6, [2005] 1 SCR 47

THE BUSINESS CONTEXT: The duty of an insured to report material changes to the risk in a fire insurance policy is currently prescribed by statutory conditions in all Canadian common law provinces. This case concerns the ability of an insurance company to deny coverage on the basis of the insured's alleged breach of the statutory condition requiring an insured to report a material change.[6]

FACTUAL BACKGROUND: Theresa Marche and Gary Fitzgerald (the insureds) purchased a house, converted it into apartments, and insured it under a fire insurance policy issued by the Halifax Insurance Co. In September 1998, the insureds left Cape Breton Island to find work in British Columbia. The house remained vacant from September to early December, when Danny, a brother of one of the insureds, moved in. Danny fell behind in the rent but refused to vacate the premises. In an effort to induce Danny to move out, the insureds had the water and electrical power disconnected. On 7 February 1999, the house was destroyed by fire. At this time, Danny's possessions were still in the house.

Halifax denied liability on the grounds that the insureds had failed to notify Halifax of the vacancy between September and December 1998. The insurer alleged that this was a breach of Statutory Condition 4 of Part VII of Nova Scotia's *Insurance Act* that provides, in part, "Any change material to the risk and within the control and knowledge of the insured shall avoid the contract as to the part affected thereby, unless the change is promptly notified in writing to the insurer."

---

6 See also *Royal Bank of Canada v State Farm Fire and Casualty Co*, 2005 SCC 34, [2005] 1 SCR 779. This case deals with the statutory condition requiring reporting of a material change in relation to an insurance policy's standard mortgage clause.

The insured argued that, if their failure to report the vacancy constituted a breach, they should be relieved from the consequences of the breach by section 171(b) of the *Insurance Act* that provides in part, "Where a contract... contains any stipulation, condition or warranty that is or may be material to the risk... the exclusion, stipulation, condition, or warranty shall not be binding on the insured if it is held to be unjust or unreasonable."

THE LEGAL QUESTION: Does section 171(b) of the Nova Scotia *Insurance Act* apply to statutory conditions? Was there a breach of Statutory Condition 4?

RESOLUTION: The Supreme Court of Canada held that section 171(b) applies to both contractual and statutory conditions. In coming to this conclusion, the majority rejected the notion that statutory conditions by definition cannot be unnecessary or unjust. The court noted that as the purpose of section 171(b) is to provide relief from unjust or unreasonable insurance policy conditions, it should be given a broad interpretation. The word "condition" in section 171(b) is not qualified by a restrictive adjective and further, a reading of the entire Act does not support the contention that "condition" in section 171(b) refers only to contractual conditions. The court stated that section 171 (b) authorizes the court to not only relieve against conditions that are *prima facie* unjust but also to relieve against conditions that in their application lead to unjust or unreasonable results.

The court noted that while the insureds had failed to report the vacancy, it is unclear whether the failure constituted a breach of Statutory Condition 4 as the vacancy had been rectified prior to the loss occurring. In any event, if the insureds were in breach, section 171(b) should be applied to relieve the insureds from the consequences of this breach. It would be unjust to void the insurance policy when the vacancy had been rectified prior to the loss occurring and was not causally related to the loss.

CRITICAL ANALYSIS: The court rejected the insurance company's attempt to deny coverage based on an alleged breach of Statutory Condition 4. What is the uncertainty created by the decision for insurers?

Insurable Interest

The special nature of the insurance contract also means that its validity is contingent on the insured having an **insurable interest** in the thing insured.[7] The test for whether the insured has an insurable interest is whether he benefits from its existence and would be prejudiced from its destruction.[8] The rationale behind this rule is that allowing people to insure property they have no real interest in may, for example, lead them to intentionally destroy the property in order to make an insurance claim. If WEC's bank holds a mortgage on the WEC production plant, it can purchase insurance on the plant because the bank has an insurable interest in property that is being used as security for a loan. The bank benefits from the continued existence of the plant and would be prejudiced by its destruction. Once the mortgage is paid off, the insurable interest of the bank no longer exists, and the bank cannot file a claim.

Insurable interest

A financial stake in what is being insured.

---

7   Craig Brown & Andrew Mercer, *Introduction to Canadian Insurance Law* 3 ed (Markham, On: Lexis-Nexis, 2013), at 41. Note that the ordinary insurable interest test is typically altered by statute for life insurance. In life insurance, the statutes generally provide that certain dependants have an insurable interest in the life insured, as does anyone else who gets the written consent of the person whose life is being insured.

8   *Lucena v Craufurd* (1806), 2 Bos & Pul (NR) 269 at 301, 127 ER 630 (HL).

Indemnity

With the exception of life insurance contracts, insurance contracts are contracts of indemnity. This means that the insured is not supposed to profit from the happening of the insured-against event, but at most will come out even. For example, if WEC insured its manufacturing plant against the risk of fire with two different insurance companies, WEC, in the event of a loss, is entitled to collect only the amount of the loss. WEC cannot collect the loss from both insurance companies. However, WEC would be entitled to select the policy under which it will claim indemnity (subject to any conditions to the contrary). The insurer, in turn, would be entitled to contribution from the other insurer on a prorated basis.

Some policies, such as fire insurance policies, require the insured to have coverage for a specified minimum portion of the value of the property in order to fully recover from the insurer in the event of a fire. This requirement takes the form of a coinsurance clause, which is intended to discourage the insured from insuring the property for less than its value on the gamble that any loss is likely to be less than total. If such a clause is in place, and the insured carries less insurance than the amount specified in the clause, the insurer will pay only a specified portion of the loss, and the insured must absorb the remainder. In essence, the insured becomes a coinsurer for the amount of the deficiency (see Figure 28.2).

FIGURE 28.2 Example of the Application of a Coinsurance Clause

Building value	$500 000
Actual insurance coverage	$300 000
Amount of loss	$100 000
Coinsurance clause	80%

$$\frac{\text{Amount of insurance coverage purchased}}{\text{Minimum required under coinsurance clause}} \times \text{Actual loss} = \text{Insurer's liability*}$$

$$\frac{\$300\ 000}{(\$500\ 000 \times 80\%)} \times \$100\ 000 = \$75\ 000\ \text{(amount the insurer must pay)}$$

* Subject to policy limits

Subrogation

The insurer also has what is called a right of subrogation. This right means that when an insurer compensates the insured, it has the right to sue a third party—the wrongdoer—who caused the loss and to recover from that party what it has already paid out to its insured. In this sense, the right of subrogation permits the insurer to "step into the shoes" of the insured and sue the wrongdoer. Subject to the policy and applicable legislation, the insurer's right of subrogation arises only when the customer is fully indemnified for the loss. When the insurer has paid the full extent of the loss, the insurer gains control over any legal proceedings against a third party, although such proceedings are brought in the name of the insured. Because of the insurer's right of subrogation, WEC must act carefully in the face of a loss. For example, it should not admit liability for any accident that has occurred, since doing so might jeopardize any future action the insurer might commence against the wrongdoer. Instead,

WEC should immediately contact its insurer, as well as its legal counsel, for advice on how to proceed.

In addition to the right of subrogation, the insurance company will also have the right to rebuild, repair, or replace what is damaged so as to minimize its costs. It will also have the right of **salvage**. If, for example, stolen goods are recovered, the insurer can sell the goods to recover its costs.

An insured is also not permitted to profit from his willful misconduct. If he deliberately causes a loss, the **forfeiture rule** will prevent him from collecting on his insurance. For example, if an insured deliberately sets fire to his business, he cannot collect on his fire insurance.

The Policy

Insurance contracts are particularly technical documents. Their content is settled to some extent by legislation, which requires standard form policies for some types of insurance. Apart from standard form policies required by legislation, there is no requirement that a policy conform to a particular format. That said, a policy will normally contain terms that specify

- the subject matter of the insurance, the duration of coverage, the premium, monetary limits of coverage and the period against which insurance is provided.
- obligations that the customer must satisfy in order to preserve coverage.
- events or circumstances, known as exclusions, that result in there being no coverage.

Policies generally contain a number of exclusion clauses. For example, the standard fire policy excludes coverage when the insured building has been left unoccupied for more than 30 consecutive days. If a loss occurs after this point, the policy does not cover it. Other common exclusions in property insurance include damage caused by wear and tear or mould, and vandalism or malicious acts caused by the insured.

Changes in standard policy terms take the form of riders and endorsements. A **rider** adds to or alters the standard coverage and is part of the policy from the outset. An **endorsement** is an alteration to the coverage at some point during the time in which the policy is in force.

Salvage

An insurer's right to title of what remains of property after paying for a total loss.

Forfeiture rule

A rule that provides that a criminal should not be permitted to profit from a crime.

Rider

A clause altering or adding to coverage in a standard insurance policy.

Endorsement

Written evidence of a change to an existing insurance policy.

Canadian National Railway v Royal and Sun Alliance Insurance Co of Canada, 2008 SCC 66, [2008] 3 SCR 453

THE BUSINESS CONTEXT: Exclusions are common in insurance policies. For example, in standard property insurance policies, common exclusions include damage that arises from external sources such as pollution, arson, mould, vandalism, temperature changes, settlement, and earth movement. Property insurance policies also contain exclusions that preclude coverage from internal defects such as faulty materials, workmanship, or design. The following decision addresses the "faulty or improper design" exclusion in **all-risks property insurance**. Prior to this decision, there were two competing standards for interpreting "faulty or improper design." One standard held that a design was faulty if it simply failed to work for its intended purpose. The second standard held that a design was faulty if it failed to provide for, and withstand, all foreseeable risks.

FACTUAL BACKGROUND: In the early 1990s, Canadian National Railway (CNR) undertook to build a rail tunnel under the St. Clair River from Sarnia, Ontario, to Port Huron, Michigan. To do so, it commissioned the design of the world's largest tunnel boring machine (TBM). Prior to undertaking the project and in recognition of the risks inherent in developing such a machine, CNR purchased an all-risks insurance policy from Royal and Sun Alliance Insurance Co. of Canada (Royal). The policy insured all risks of direct physical loss or damage to all real and personal property including the TBM. There was also an exclusionary provision that stated "this Policy does not insure the cost of making good faulty or improper design."

The TBM, constructed in 1993 was 10 metres in diameter, 85 metres long, and designed to withstand 6000 metric tonnes of pressure from soil and water. A system of 26 independent lubricated seals prevented excavated material from getting into the main bearing. However, after two months of excavating with only 14 percent of the tunnel complete, dirt penetrated through to the bearing. During design,

Rail tunnel under the St. Clair River

Stephen C. Host/The Canadian Press

the engineers realized that dirt could penetrate and bypass the seals if the differential between key components was more or less than 3 mm, but were satisfied that the differential could be kept within the range. In operation, however, this was not possible and the sealing system failed. The project had to be stopped and, after a delay of 229 days and a cost of more than $20 million, the boring was restarted and completed. CNR attempted to collect on its insurance policy with Royal but it denied coverage based on the clause in the policy that excluded damages caused by "faulty or improper design."

THE LEGAL QUESTION: Did the design of the TBM fall within the "faulty or improper design" exclusion in the all-risks insurance policy?

RESOLUTION: In a 4 to 3 decision, the Supreme Court of Canada adopted a narrow interpretation of the "faulty or improper design" exclusion and found in favour of CNR. Binnie J. writing for the majority stated that, "the policy did not exclude all loss attributable to 'the design' but only loss attributable to a 'faulty or improper design.'" Simply because a design fails to achieve its intended purpose is not sufficient evidence that it is a "faulty or improper design." The term "faulty or improper design" implied a comparative standard and that the appropriate standard was the state of the art. If a design met the highest standards of the day and failure occurred simply because engineering knowledge was inadequate to the task, the design is not faulty or improper. As the TBM had been designed to state of the art specifications at the time, Royal was not entitled to the benefit of the exclusion simply because the state of the art fell short of perfection and omniscience. The damages caused by the design failure were, therefore, properly covered by the insurance policy.

CRITICAL ANALYSIS: How does this decision affect policy-holders who suffer a loss that the insurer attributes to a failed design?

Insurance Products

Insurance is broadly divisible into three categories—life, property, and liability. However, there are many specialized insurance policies or products available to meet the risk management needs of businesses. In order to secure optimal coverage, a businessperson should assess the business operation and identify the kinds of legal risks it may encounter. For example, in its business, WEC faces a number of possible kinds of liabilities and losses, including the following:

- *injury and property damage* related to the operation of WEC's delivery trucks. If WEC's delivery personnel drive negligently, they may be involved in traffic accidents that cause injury to other people, as well as property damage to other vehicles. Additionally, such negligence may cause injury to the WEC drivers themselves and damage to WEC vehicles.

- *personal injury* to suppliers, sales personnel, and purchasers who visit the manufacturing plant floor. Since WEC's business office is located in its manufacturing plant, many people who are not directly involved in production may visit the plant on business. Injuries—from tripping on a carpet to being burned by the extrusion process—can result. As well, WEC employees who work in the manufacturing process and elsewhere face the risk of being hurt on the job.

- *financial loss and injury* to others caused by defective wire that WEC produced. If WEC delivers defective wires that are later incorporated into tires produced by WEC customers, those tires may fail while being used or repaired, potentially causing both physical injury and financial loss to those involved.

- *financial loss and injury* caused by employees giving negligent advice to WEC customers concerning their wire needs. If an employee provides bad advice to WEC customers, they may end up with wire that is not appropriate for its intended use. This problem, in turn, may lead to physical injury and financial loss to WEC customers and to the ultimate consumers of the tires produced by WEC customers.

- *injury and property damage* caused by a fire or other disaster in the manufacturing plant. If WEC experiences a fire in its plant, there can be a significant financial loss, since the building, as well as the equipment and machinery, will have to be repaired or replaced before company operations can resume.

- *loss of profit* owing to business interruption as a result of a fire or other causes of a plant shutdown. In the event of a fire or other disaster, WEC may have to suspend business operations while it rebuilds. This loss of profit could cripple the company financially and even cause its demise.

- *environmental damage* caused by improper storage or disposal of waste products. Environmental protection legislation in all jurisdictions prohibits businesses from discharging or spilling contaminants into the

All-risks property insurance

Insurance coverage that protects property against all types of physical loss or injury arising from an external cause unless specifically excluded.

environment. Legislation may also permit the government to order the party responsible to clean up or otherwise repair the environmental damage that the contaminant caused.

This clean-up can be costly for the company involved. As well, WEC can face civil actions by those who are injured or who suffer loss because WEC has improperly stored or disposed of its waste products. Since WEC produces fabricated metal products—a process that is likely to have significant environmental implications—it needs to pay particular attention to this kind of potentially catastrophic liability.

- *Death* of one of the shareholders in WEC. Should one of the WEC shareholders die, the others will likely want to buy out that person's shares. Financing the buyout will be a challenge for WEC.

In order to address these risks, WEC has in place the following policies.

Auto Insurance

An automobile owner is required by law to have insurance for liability arising from its ownership, use, and operation. While each jurisdiction has its own scheme in place, a common aim of these schemes is to ensure that owners are financially responsible for the liabilities that arise through use of their vehicles. Most people do not have the assets on hand to pay off a large judgment against them; insurance provides the funds to fulfill that financial responsibility, should it arise.

There are several types of auto insurance coverage. In Alberta, for example, the Standard Automobile Policy provides the insured with coverage against liability for the injury or death of someone else (third-party liability) caused by the operation of the insured vehicle. It also provides benefits to the insured for injury or death caused by an accident arising from the use or operation of the insured automobile, as well as compensation for loss or damage to the insured automobile itself. The latter is known as collision coverage.

Some people decide not to get collision coverage because the car itself is not worth very much. Third-party liability insurance, however, is not an option, and its

What are the advantages and disadvantages of no-fault automobile insurance systems?

purchase is required by law. Since a car accident causing paraplegia, for example, can result in millions of dollars of damages, owners should not be content with purchasing the minimum amount required by law. The minimum amount is simply not enough to cover a catastrophic accident. If there is a deficiency between the amount of insurance coverage and the actual damages sustained by the plaintiff, the insured will be personally responsible for the difference.

Each province specifies through legislation the minimum amount of coverage an owner must obtain for third-party liability. In Ontario, for example, the statutory minimum is $200 000.[9] Since this amount is insufficient to pay damages to another who has been seriously injured, the owner should purchase additional coverage.

BUSINESS APPLICATION OF THE LAW

NO-FAULT INSURANCE SYSTEMS

Automobile insurance systems vary significantly from province to province. A major distinguishing feature is the extent to which they emphasize either a tort-based liability system or a "no-fault"[10] system for compensating claims for bodily injury or death. A no-fault system involves the diminution of the ability to sue a tort-feasor for compensation. In this system, the emphasis is on providing accident benefits without regard to the victim's fault. This is a marked departure from the traditional tort system with its emphasis on fault-based liability.

Quebec was the first Canadian jurisdiction to adopt a pure no-fault system for bodily injuries. Automobile accident victims have lost the right to sue for pain and suffering and other costs in return for a form of income replacement benefit, medical and funeral expenses, and a modest award for pain and suffering depending on the extent of the injury. Manitoba has adopted no-fault legislation similar to Quebec's. Manitoba has eliminated all tort actions for bodily injury or death resulting from automobile accidents. Victims are restricted to recovery of no-fault benefits provided by a universal bodily injury compensation scheme. Saskatchewan consumers can choose between no-fault (or tort-restricted) auto insurance and a tort option. The tort option provides reduced accident benefits, but claimants can sue to recover general damages for their non-economic losses. The no-fault option eliminates the right to sue to recover damages for pain and suffering.

Ontario has adopted a threshold no-fault scheme. Under this scheme, a person who is injured in an automobile accident is entitled to statutory accident benefits (e.g., income replacement, medical benefits, rehabilitation benefits, attendant care benefits, death and funeral benefits), regardless of fault. In order to make a claim for general damages caused by another, however, the injured person must have sustained injuries in excess of the threshold, which is defined as death, permanent serious disfigurement, permanent serious physical impairment, or impairment of important psychological and mental functions. If an accident victim is entitled to receive general damages, then a $30 000 deductible will be applied unless the general damages awarded are $100 000 or more. Also, an injured person may sue for economic losses, such as lost wages and medical expenses, and no threshold is applied to such a claim.

In the other provinces and territories, the automobile insurance systems are based on the tort-liability model. This means accident victims can sue an at-fault driver for compensation.

---

9 *Insurance Act*, RSO 1990, c I-8, s 251(1) provides: "Every contract evidenced by a motor vehicle liability policy insures, in respect of any one accident, to the limit of at least $200 000 exclusive of interest and costs, against liability resulting from bodily injury to or the death of one or more persons and loss of or damage to property."

10 "No-fault insurance" is a confusing term. It does not mean that no one is at fault. It means, in effect, that some or all of the insured person's loss is paid for regardless of who caused the loss. A person who is injured or whose property is damaged deals with her own insurance company regardless of fault.

However, as tort claims can take years to resolve, no-fault accident benefits are usually provided in the meantime. For example, in British Columbia, medical and rehabilitative, wage loss, and death benefits are available to the injured. In Newfoundland and Labrador, because accident benefits under automobile policies are optional, some accident victims have no choice but to rely on tort law for recovery of their bodily injury or death claims. Also, New Brunswick, Nova Scotia, Prince Edward Island, and Alberta have a cap on damage awards for minor personal injuries (usually defined as a strain, sprain, or whiplash injury that leaves no long term impairment or pain). The caps are adjusted annually for inflation and in 2015 were approximately $8400 in Nova Scotia, $7500 in New Brunswick and Prince Edward Island, and $4900 in Alberta.

Critical Analysis: What is the purpose of "pain and suffering" caps for minor injuries? Do you see any problems with imposing caps?

Sources: Craig Brown & Thomas Donnelly, *Insurance Law in Canada*, vol 1 loose-leaf, (consulted on 28 July 2014) (Toronto Carswell, 2002), at 17-1–17-19; Donna Ford, "Commentary: Has Ontario's no-fault system lost its way?", *The Lawyers Weekly* (12 January 2007) 7.

Employees injured in car accidents on the job may have coverage through workers' compensation legislation. Under such legislation, which is in place in every Canadian province, participating employers pay premiums into a fund administered by a tribunal. Employees who are injured in the workplace or who, for example, suffer from a disease as a result of exposure to a pollutant in the workplace, can then make a claim for benefits from this fund. When an employer participates in a workers' compensation board (WCB) plan, payment from the fund is usually the only compensation the employee is entitled to receive. The legislation makes participation mandatory for most industries and business activities[11] and prevents employees from suing the employer for losses that occur in the course of employment.

Occupiers' Liability Insurance

WEC, as a building owner and occupier, is liable for injuries suffered to people on its premises if the injuries are due to WEC's failure to ensure that the premises are safe. WEC's occupiers' liability insurance will compensate the injured person on behalf of WEC if unsafe conditions, such as improperly installed carpet, uneven walkways, wet floors, or the like, caused the injury. Although WEC has a program in place to prevent such accidents, the insurance will fill the gap when and if the system fails.

Comprehensive General Liability Insurance

The purpose of comprehensive general liability insurance (also known as CGL insurance) is to compensate enterprises like WEC, in a comprehensive way, for any liabilities they incur during the course of their business. For example, an important general risk faced by WEC is that its wires may fail in use and lead to some kind of loss. WEC's CGL insurance will respond by compensating WEC for property damages, personal injury, loss of profit, and related losses suffered by a third party when WEC is legally responsible for such losses.[12]

---

11 Participation is non-mandatory for some businesses. For example, in Ontario participation is optional for law offices, insurance companies, and call offices.
12 Note that coverage generally extends only to unintentional torts, rather than intentional acts.

The CGL does not respond, however, to losses directly suffered by WEC itself. For this latter type of loss, WEC would need a property policy with a defective product endorsement. The following examples reveal the important difference between these two kinds of policies.

Example 1 WEC produces wire that is seriously defective. When the customer incorporates that wire into its tire-manufacturing process, the tires fail and must be discarded. The customer loses about $50 000 in materials, time, and profit—all of which is attributable to WEC's defective product. WEC's CGL insurance policy will cover this loss.

Example 2 WEC produces wire that the customer notices is defective as soon as WEC attempts to deliver the shipment. Accordingly, the customer refuses to accept delivery, and WEC loses $50 000 in revenue. CGL insurance does not cover this loss because it is not a loss sustained by a WEC customer or other third party—it is a loss suffered directly by WEC itself. For coverage in this situation, WEC would need a property policy with a defective product endorsement. Since the cost of the endorsement is so high, WEC has not purchased it. From a business perspective, WEC has determined that it is better off establishing an effective quality assurance and testing program, thereby dealing with such risks in-house rather than looking to an insurance company for coverage.

Errors and Omissions Insurance

When WEC's engineers provide professional engineering advice to WEC customers, they are promising that they meet the standard of the reasonably competent person engaged in such activity. Although this implied promise does not amount to a guarantee of perfection, they will be responsible for losses resulting from negligent advice. Through errors and omissions insurance (also known as E&O insurance),[13] the insurer promises to pay on the engineers' behalf all the sums they are legally obligated to pay as damages resulting from the performance of their professional services. Investigation costs and legal expenses will also usually be covered by the policy. However, there may be limits. For example, the policy may only cover defence costs for actions brought in Canada.[14] Like all insurance policies, the engineers' coverage is subject to a number of conditions, such as the requirement that they give immediate notice to the insurer of a claim or potential claim. This notice allows the insurance company to carry out an investigation and otherwise gather facts associated with the alleged negligence. Failure to give prompt notice or to comply with any other condition can result in the insurance company successfully denying coverage.

Corporate directors and officers also face liability for their errors and omissions related to operating their company. This risk can be insured against through directors and officers (D&O) liability insurance. D&O insurance typically provides the following: coverage for directors and officers against losses that are not reimbursed by the corporation (Side A coverage); coverage for the corporation for amounts paid to indemnify directors and officers for their losses (Side B coverage); and/or coverage to protect the corporation from claims arising from securities litigation (Side C coverage).

---

13 See Scott J Hammel, "Insurance Pitfalls: Your errors and omission coverage may surprise you," *Canadian Consulting Engineer* (December 2004), online: Canadian Consulting Engineer <http://www .canadianconsultingengineer.com/news/insurance-pitfalls/1000191738/>.

14 *Ibid.*

Property Insurance

WEC has insured its manufacturing plant and equipment in order to fund any rebuilding or replacement that a fire or other disaster might occasion. One of the key choices WEC made was whether to insure for the replacement value of its property or for the property's actual cash value.

If WEC had chosen the second option, it would receive from the insurance company only the value of the property at the time it was destroyed; that is, not enough to purchase a replacement. WEC chose the first option; therefore, it will receive a higher level of compensation from the insurer—and also pay a higher premium—but the insurer has the right to require WEC to actually rebuild or otherwise replace its property before it will pay out on the claim. WEC also chose coverage for a number of losses, including loss caused by fire, falling aircraft, earthquake, hail, water damage, malicious damage, smoke damage, and impact by vehicles. Not surprisingly, the more perils WEC insures against, the higher the premiums it must pay.

Business Interruption Loss Insurance

This kind of coverage provides WEC with financial compensation should it have to temporarily shut down because of a fire or other insured peril. The following box describes this insurance.

BUSINESS APPLICATION OF THE LAW

BUSINESS INTERRUPTION INSURANCE EXPLAINED

Fire, theft, vandalism, flood, or other disaster can have a devastating effect on a business. In 2013, floods in Alberta affected over 1300 businesses. Water ruined mechanical equipment, electrical systems, vehicles, and inventory; damaged buildings and furnishings; and caused operations to cease. Commercial property insurance with an overland flooding[15] (damage caused by water that comes through doors and windows) option covers the cost of repairing or replacing the physical assets. However, even if insurance covers 100 percent of property losses, a business may still suffer. It may take months to repair a damaged building and replace equipment, inventory, and furnishings and in the meantime, the business may suffer

a substantial loss of income and profit. Also, the business may incur extra expenses such as renting temporary premises and equipment to use while the originals are being repaired. To address these risks, a business may need business interruption insurance, an optional add-on to the commercial property insurance policy.

There are many different forms of business interruption insurance but in general, they cover the loss of income suffered when an insured against peril occurs. Typical forms are:

- *gross earnings* (or *limited*), which insures for the earnings lost as a result of an insurable claim. Earnings are calculated as revenue minus the expenses that cease while the business is not in operation (i.e., utilities). The coverage usually ends

---

15 Most homeowner insurance policies exclude coverage for overland water damage; however, commercial property owners can opt for overland flooding insurance coverage.

when the business resumes operations regardless of whether or not the business has regained its previous level of earnings. There may also be limits on the time the business is covered and the amount paid by the insurer in any one month. This insurance is commonly used by manufacturers.

- *profits* (or *extended*), which covers loss of profits and ongoing fixed expenses. The coverage continues until the business resumes its normal, pre-interruption profit level subject to the period of indemnity listed in the policy. This coverage is commonly used by highly competitive businesses where an extended interruption could cost market share and client loyalty.

- *extra expense*, which covers the cost of getting a business operational. This policy is designed for businesses that must remain operational during the period affected by the damage. It covers the expenses (i.e., telephone, advertising, moving to other location, and outsourcing) incurred to carry on business at another location.

How can a business use insurance to manage the risk of a natural catastrophe?

Critical Analysis: When should a business not purchase business interruption insurance?

Sources: "The basics of business interruption and extra expense insurance", *Pro-form Sinclair Professional-Newsletter* (October 2012), online: Sinclair <http://proformsinclair.ca/docs/nov12newsletter.pdf>; Gordon Powers, "The Alberta flooding case for business interruption insurance", *MSN Money* (12 July 2013), online. *MSN Money* <http://money.ca.msn.com/insurance/insight/the-alberta-flooding-case-for-business-interruption-insurance>.

Environmental Impairment Insurance

Not only may WEC face substantial fines for failing to comply with environmental protection legislation and for any clean-up costs associated with a spill or other accident, but it can also be sued by its neighbours for polluting the soil or ground water. Furthermore, if a subsequent owner of WEC's plant can trace pollutants back to WEC, it has civil liability for the clean-up and other associated costs, even though it no longer owns the land.

The extensive nature of this type of liability explains why comprehensive general liability insurance policies usually contain pollution exclusion clauses[16] and why environmental impairment liability policies are very expensive. A more viable—though not foolproof—alternative is for WEC to ensure that it has an operational management policy in place to prevent environmental accidents from happening in the first place.[17]

---

16 Jonathan LS Hodes, "Pollution Exclusion Clauses in the CGL Policy", *Clark Wilson LLP (February, 2009)*, online: Clark Wilson LLP <http://www.cwilson.com/services/18-resource-centre/203-pollution-exclusion-clauses-in-the-cgl-policy.html>.
17 See Chapter 3 for a discussion of a risk management plan.

THE POLLUTION EXCLUSION IN COMMERCIAL GENERAL LIABILITY POLICIES

The cost of environmental clean-up can be enormous. Beginning in the 1970s, in an attempt to limit its exposure, the insurance industry started including a pollution exclusion clause in commercial general liability (CGL) policies. The wording of these clauses has changed considerably in response to court decisions that tended to limit their effect. By the mid-1980s, the "absolute pollution exclusion" became the standard used in most CLG policies. The clause is very broad and attempts to exclude from coverage all losses arising out of the discharge or escape of pollutants into the environment.

Interpreting the Pollution Exclusion: The effect and scope of absolute pollution exclusion clauses has also been the subject of much litigation. In *Zurich Insurance Co v 686234 Ontario Ltd*,[18] the Ontario Court of Appeal concluded that the exclusion clause did not apply to the escape of carbon monoxide from a negligently installed furnace in a high-rise apartment building. In reaching its decision, the court emphasized that insurance coverage should be interpreted broadly in favour of the insured and exclusion clauses strictly and narrowly construed against the insurer.

More recently, in *ING Insurance Company of Canada v Miracle (Mohawk Imperial Sales and Mohawk Liquidate)*,[19] the Ontario Court of Appeal appears to have taken a more expansive approach to pollution exclusion clauses. The court held that a pollution exclusion clause applied to a liability claim for the escape of gasoline from a service station.

Reconciling the Decisions: In *Zurich*, the Court found that although carbon monoxide was a pollutant within the meaning of the exclusion, the history of exclusion clauses shows that their purpose was to bar coverage for damages arising

Clean-up of Sydney tar sands is estimated to be $400 million.

Ray Fahey/Cape Breton Post/The Canadian Press

from environmental pollution, not damages where faulty equipment caused pollution. The pollution exclusion clause was meant to apply only to an insured whose regular business activities placed it in the category of an active industrial polluter of the natural environment. It was not intended to apply to a case where faulty equipment caused the pollution. Therefore, an improperly operating furnace that produced carbon monoxide in a residential building fell outside of the exclusion.

In *Miracle*, the court noted that the insured was engaged in an activity that carries an obvious and well-known risk of pollution and environmental damage. The business of the insured—the running of a gas station and the associated storage of gasoline in the ground for resale at the gas bar—was precisely the kind of activity that the exclusion was intended to address. The court stated that the phrase "active industrial polluter of the natural environment" should not be read to restrict the pollution exclusion clauses to situations where the insured is engaged in an activity that necessarily results in pollution. The exclusion was found to apply to activities that carry a known risk of pollution and environmental harm, such as storing gasoline in the ground for resale.

The Ontario Court of Appeal's decision in *Miracle* appears to have clarified the scope of

---

18 (2002), 62 OR (3d) 447, 222 DLR (4th) 655 (Ont CA).
19 2011 ONCA 321, 105 OR (3d) 241.

PART NINE: TRANSFERENCE OF RISK

its decision in *Zurich*. An exclusion clause's actual wording and its historical roots are important factors determining its effect and scope. However, an exclusion clause's application is also dependent on the nature of the business and the actual business activities of the insured.

Critical Analysis: Does giving effect to the pollution exclusion clause virtually nullify the insured's coverage? What are public policy considerations in upholding absolute pollution clauses?

Sources: Douglas McInnis & Aleksandra Zivanovic, "Clarifying pollution exclusions in commercial insurance policies", *The Lawyer's Weekly* (19 August 2011), online: *McCague Borlack LLP* <http://www.mccagueborlack.com/emails/articles/pollution_exclusions.html>; Daniel Kirby, John MacDonald & Dave Mollica, "Ontario Court of Appeal clarifies application of pollution exclusion clauses in commercial general liability policies," (5 July 2011), online: Mondaq <http://www.mondaq.com/canada/x/137682/Insurance/Ontario+Court+Of+Appeal+Clarifies+Application+Of+Pollution+Exclusion+Clauses+In+Commercial+General+Liability+Policies>

Key-Person Life Insurance

The partners in a firm or the shareholders of a small corporation likely wish their business to continue to be operated by the surviving owners if one of them dies. Their partnership agreement or shareholders' agreement will specify that the surviving owners have the right to buy the shares of the deceased owner. The effective exercise of that right requires a means of valuing the business and the shares of the deceased, as well as a means of financing the purchase of the shares by the survivors. Insurance on the lives of the owners is a means of financing the buyout. The owners need to agree on a method of evaluating the business when the insurance is purchased and at the time of death. They must then agree on how much insurance to purchase on the life of each key person. Key factors in this decision are the age of the key people, the extent of their ownership, and the payment method each prefers for their survivors.

The amount of life insurance purchased by the business for each key person will depend on the affordability of the premium, which will be higher for older owners. Because of their age or medical condition, key people may find that insurance is unobtainable. The owners must also decide whether to purchase enough coverage to provide a lump sum large enough to buy the shares of the deceased outright, or whether the insurance should provide a portion of the buyout price, with the remainder paid to the heirs by the business over a period of time.

Since WEC is owned by three shareholders, it would be prudent for there to be life insurance policies on each one of them. However, as this proved to be uneconomic for some of the shareholders, an agreement between them addresses how the deceased's shares will be purchased.

It may also be prudent for the main stakeholders in WEC to secure disability insurance, so that if one of them is unable to work—owing to serious illness, for example—insurance will fund at least part of that person's salary or other remuneration.

Remedies of the Insured

Against the Broker

It was crucial for WEC to establish a solid working relationship with an insurance broker[20] in order to secure proper advice as to what kind of insurance it required. The term "insurance broker" refers to the middle person between the insurance

---

20 See Chapter 13 for further discussion of insurance brokers and insurance agents.

companies and the insured. As the party who sought insurance, WEC needed the assistance of the broker in reviewing its business operations, assessing the risks it faces, and understanding the coverages available and the policy costs. If WEC did not spend sufficient time with the broker or if it chose a broker who was simply not up to the job, WEC may have ended up with the wrong coverage—or not enough coverage—and face a loss against which it has not been properly insured.

Should WEC face such a situation, it may have an action against its broker for negligence. If WEC is successful in its action, the broker will be required to reimburse WEC for any of its underinsured or uninsured losses or liabilities.

The term "insurance agent" usually refers to someone who acts on behalf of an insurer to sell insurance. An agent acting in that capacity is primarily obligated to the insurer as principal, and not usually to the third-party insured.

Against the Insurance Company

Insurance adjuster

One who investigates and evaluates insurance claims.

When an insured makes a claim under its policy, an **insurance adjuster** will likely investigate the events and evaluate the loss. On the adjuster's advice, the insurer will offer to settle the claim. There may be disagreements between the insured and the insurer as to the nature or amount of coverage. Should they be unable to resolve these differences, the insured may have to sue the insurer for breach of contract. The claim will be that the insurer has failed to honour its obligations under the policy.

In addition to the obligations specified in the insurance policy, an insurer owes the insured a duty of good faith, including a duty to deal with an insured's claim in good faith. Factors considered in determining whether an insurer has fulfilled its obligation to act in good faith include whether the insurer carried out an adequate investigation of a claim, whether the insurer properly evaluated the claim, whether the insurer fairly interpreted the policy, and whether the insurer handled and paid the claim in a timely manner.[21] When the duty of good faith has been breached, the court may award punitive damages, as was done in *Whiten v Pilot Insurance Co* discussed below.

CASE

Whiten v Pilot Insurance Co, 2002 SCC 18, [2002] 1 SCR 595

THE BUSINESS CONTEXT: An insurer's bad-faith conduct—alleging fraud when none exists or refusing to pay out under a policy, for example—can have a devastating effect on the insured. This kind of reprehensible conduct by the insurer can be addressed by an award of punitive damages. Prior to this decision, the highest punitive damage award handed down by a Canadian court against an insurance company had been $15 000.

FACTUAL BACKGROUND: In January 1994, the Whitens' family home burned down in the middle of the night, destroying all their possessions and

three family cats. Knowing that the family was in poor financial shape, the insurer, Pilot Insurance, made a single $5000 payment for living expenses and covered the rent on a cottage for a couple of months. Pilot then cut off the rent without telling the family, and thereafter it pursued a confrontational policy that ultimately led to a protracted trial. Pilot maintained that the Whitens had burned down the house, even though it had opinions from its adjuster, its expert engineer, an investigative agency retained by it, and the fire chief that the fire was accidental. After receiving a strong recommendation from its adjuster that the claim be paid, Pilot replaced the adjuster. Counsel for Pilot pressured

---

21 *Adams v Confederation Life Insurance*, 152 AR 121, [1994] 6 WWR 662 (Alta QB).

its experts to provide opinions supporting an arson defence, deliberately withheld relevant information from the experts, and provided them with misleading information to obtain opinions favourable to an arson theory. Pilot's position was wholly discredited at trial. The jury awarded compensatory damages and $1 million in punitive damages. The majority of the Court of Appeal allowed the appeal in part and reduced the punitive damages award to $100 000.

THE LEGAL QUESTION: Should the jury's punitive damages award be restored?

RESOLUTION: The court held that, although the jury's award of punitive damages was high, it was reasonable. Pilot's conduct had been exceptionally reprehensible. Its actions, which continued for over two years, were designed to force the Whitens to make an unfair settlement for less than what they were entitled to receive. The jury believed that Pilot knew its allegations of arson were not sustainable and yet it persisted. Insurance contracts are purchased for peace of mind. The more devastating the loss, the more the insured is at the financial mercy of the insurer, and the more difficult it may be to challenge a wrongful refusal to pay.

The jury decided that a strong message of denunciation, retribution, and deterrence needed to be sent to Pilot. The obligation of good-faith dealing requires that the insurer must respect the insured's vulnerability and reliance on the insurer. It was this relationship that was outrageously exploited by Pilot.

An award of punitive damages in a contract case is permissible if there is a separate actionable wrong. In addition to the contractual requirement to pay the claim, Pilot was under an obligation to deal with the insured in good faith. The breach of this separate obligation supports a claim for the punitive damages. The award of $1 million in punitive damages was more than the court would have awarded but was still within the high end of the range where juries are free to make their assessment.

CRITICAL ANALYSIS: The Insurance Council of Canada was an intervenor at the Supreme Court. It submitted that there should be a judicially imposed cap of $25 000 on punitive damages awards. What are the arguments for such a cap? What are the arguments against such a cap?

Since *Whiten*, it is invariably the case that litigation against an insurer will include allegations of bad faith and a claim for punitive damages. Appellate courts, however, following the Supreme Court of Canada decision in *Fidler v Sun Life Assurance Company of Canada*,[22] have exercised restraint and have only awarded punitive damages in exceptional cases.[23] In *Fidler*, the court stated that the duty of good faith requires an insurer to deal with the insured's claim fairly in both the manner of investigating and the decision whether to pay. An insurer must not deny coverage or delay payment in order to take advantage of an insured's economic vulnerability or to gain bargaining leverage in negotiating a settlement. However, a finding of lack of good faith does not lead inexorably to an award of punitive damages. While a lack of good faith is a precondition, a court will only award punitive damages if there has been malicious, oppressive, or high-handed misconduct that offends the court's sense of decency.

---

22 2006 SCC 30, [2006] 2 SCR 3.

23 A Saskatchewan court awarded a record $4.5 million punitive damage award against an insurer over their conduct in wrongly denying a disabled worker benefits for many years. See *Branco v American Home Insurance Company*, 2013 SKQB 98, 416 Sask. R. 77. The appeal court reduced the award to $675 000. See *Branco v American Home Insurance Company* [2015] SJ No 286, SKCA 71.

BUSINESS LAW IN PRACTICE REVISITED

1. Was WEC under a duty to disclose the plant's vacancy to the insurance company? If so, what is the effect of a failure to disclose?

A contract of insurance is a contract of good faith. This means that the insured has a duty to disclose all material facts to the insurer concerning the subject matter to be insured. Good faith on the part of the applicant is necessary for insurance firms to effectively assess risks and set premiums. The duty to disclose not only arises at the time of applying for insurance but also is a continuing obligation of disclosure. Leaving a building vacant for a period of time, particularly in excess of 30 days, would constitute a breach of the obligation to disclose. The effect of the breach would make the insurance contract null and void with respect to the loss suffered by WEC. In addition, it is probable that WEC's insurance policy contains a clause excluding coverage when the insured building has been left vacant for more than 30 consecutive days.

2. What risk does the insurance company run by making allegations of arson?

The insurer has a duty to deal with an insured's claim in good faith. An insurer's duty to act in good faith developed as a counterweight to the immense power that an insurer has over the insured during the claims process. An insurer may be in breach of its duty of good faith if, for example, it does not properly investigate a claim, does not properly evaluate the claim, and does not handle the claim in a timely manner. Making unfounded allegations of fraud and arson is a breach of the duty of good faith and could result in an award of punitive damages if the dispute between WEC and the insurer ends up in litigation.

CHAPTER SUMMARY

Insurance is one of the simplest and most cost-effective ways of managing risk in a business environment. It permits the business to shift such risks as fire, automobile accidents, and liability for defective products onto an insurance company in exchange for the payment of premiums by the business.

An insurance contract is a contract of utmost good faith. This means that the insured must make full disclosure at the time of applying for insurance, as well as during the life of the policy. Failure to do so may permit the insurer to deny coverage when a loss has occurred.

The insured must have an insurable interest in the item insured to prevent moral hazards. The test for insurable interest is whether the insured benefits from the existence of the thing insured and would be prejudiced from its destruction.

Insurance contracts are not intended to improve the position of the insured should the loss occur. Rather, they are contracts of indemnity and are intended to compensate the insured only up to the amount of the loss suffered.

When the insurer pays out under an insurance policy, it has the right of subrogation. This right permits the insurer to sue the wrongdoer as if it were the party that had been directly injured or otherwise sustained the loss.

A business needs to communicate effectively with its insurance broker, as well as its insurance company, in order to assess the kinds of risks its operation faces and the types of insurance coverage that can be purchased to address those risks. Though insurance policies can take a variety of forms, there are three basic kinds: life and disability insurance, property insurance, and liability insurance. More specific insurance policies are simply a variation on one of these types.

Insurance policies are technically worded and often contain exclusion clauses. These clauses identify circumstances or events for which coverage is denied. They may also identify people for whom coverage is denied.

If the insured ends up with insurance of the wrong type or in an inadequate amount, it may have an action against its broker for breach of contract and/or negligence. If the insurance company wrongly refuses to honour the policy, the insured may have to sue the insurer to obtain compensation for its losses.

CHAPTER STUDY

Key Terms and Concepts

all-risks property insurance (p. 711)

deductible (p. 704)

duty to disclose (p. 704)

endorsement (p. 709)

forfeiture rule (p. 709)

insurable interest (p. 707)

insurance adjuster (p. 720)

insurance policy (p. 703)

insured (p. 703)

insurer (p. 703)

premium (p. 703)

rider (p. 709)

salvage (p. 709)

Questions for Review

1. What is the purpose of an insurance contract?

2. What is a premium?

3. Every province has enacted insurance legislation. What are the purposes of insurance legislation?

4. What are the three main types of insurance?

5. What is a deductible? What effect does it have on insurance premiums?

6. What does it mean to say that an insured has a duty to disclose? What happens if the insured fails in this duty?

7. What is an insurable interest? Why is it important?

8. Why are contracts of insurance known as contracts of indemnity?

9. What is a coinsurance clause? What is its purpose?

10. What is the right of subrogation? When does the right of subrogation arise?

11. What is the difference between a rider and an endorsement in an insurance policy?

12. How do "no-fault" liability systems differ from tort-based liability systems?

13. Describe comprehensive general liability insurance. How does it differ from warranty insurance?

14. What is the purpose of errors and omissions insurance?

15. When should a business consider buying key-person life insurance?

16. What does an insurance broker do?

17. What is the purpose of an insurance adjuster?

18. Does the insurer have a duty of good faith? Explain.

Questions for Critical Thinking

1. A manufacturing business is in the process of applying for property insurance. What kind of information must the business disclose to the insurance company? Why can insurance companies deny coverage on the basis of non-disclosure or misrepresentation of information?

2. What does it take to establish an insurable interest? For example, does an employer have an insurable interest in an employee's life? A retired executive's life? Does a creditor have an insurable interest in a debtor's life? The owner of property has an insurable interest in the property. Do mortgagees and lien holders have an insurable interest in property? Does a tenant have an insurable interest in the landlord's property? Does a thief have an insurable interest in stolen property?

3. In many regions of the world, kidnapping for ransom has become a thriving business. The victims of this crime have included not only journalists, diplomats, and aid workers, but also business executives. What role, if any, should insurance play in addressing the risk of being kidnapped in a foreign country? Do you think that the presence of insurance might exacerbate the risk? Aside from having money to pay a ransom demand, what are the other advantages of having kidnapping insurance?

4. Serving on the board of directors of a corporation entails significant risks—particularly the risk of being sued. To mitigate the risk, corporate legislation in Canada generally allows corporations to indemnify directors for legal proceedings that arise out of actions taken by a corporation. In addition, a person who serves on the board may enter into an individual indemnification agreement with the corporation. If indemnification rights are contained in corporate bylaws or in an indemnification agreement, is there any need for directors and officers liability insurance? Explain.

5. In *Whiten v Pilot*, the court upheld an award of punitive damages against an insurer for breach of the insurer's duty of good faith. Should the courts award punitive damages against claimants who make fraudulent insurance claims? For example, there have been instances where a group of individuals have conspired to stage motor vehicle accidents and then submitted false property damage and personal injury claims.[24] What factors should the courts consider in awarding damages for insurance fraud?

6. In early 2014, cyber attackers broke into eBay's database and affected 145 million customers. The database included customers' names, encrypted passwords, email addresses, physical addresses, phone numbers, and dates of birth. What are the potential costs to eBay as a result of this hacking incident? What are the insurance issues?

Situations for Discussion

1. Athena Aristotle operates a retail clothing store in West Vancouver. The store is located on the bottom floor of a building owned by Athena. One of Athena's friends rents the top floor for a residence. Recently, Athena suffered major property damage when a three-alarm fire destroyed her building. The cause of the fire is not known, although faulty wiring is suspected. As a result of the fire, Athena was required to temporarily move her retail operations to a nearby location. Her friend had to find a new place to live.[25] What type of insurance coverage will respond to Athena's loss? Assume that Athena discovers that she is not covered for the full extent of her losses. Must Athena absorb the uninsured portion of the loss, or does Athena have any other options? Explain. What steps should Athena take to ensure that she has optimal insurance coverage?

2. In an increasing number of residential communities, dwellings are being used for marijuana grow operations. In many instances, a rented house is converted to a hothouse to cultivate the plants. The conversion causes extensive structural damage, a compromised electrical system, excessive condensation, and mould, and it is unlikely that the damage is covered under the homeowner's insurance policy. This is because it is common practice in the insurance industry to include a clause that excludes damage that results from illegal

---

24 Tara Perkins & Grant Robertson, "Staged car accidents on rise, insurers say", *The Globe and Mail* (27 November 2010) A17.

25 Based, in part, on Denise Deveau, "Lost: A workplace, and a living", *The Edmonton Journal* (6 October 2008) A14.

activity, whether the homeowner is aware of the illegal activity or not, and a clause that specifically excludes damage that arises from marijuana growing operations. How can a business that rents out real estate manage the risk posed by marijuana grow operations? What steps should the business take prior to renting out its property? What steps should the business take after the property has been rented out?

3. Dorothy is a sole proprietor who recently incorporated her business in order to take the benefits of limited liability. As part of this change, she transferred all her business assets over to her corporation, Dorothy Enterprises Ltd. Unfortunately, she forgot to change her insurance policies to name the company as the new insured. The property remains insured in Dorothy's name. Soon after the transfer, there was a break-in at Dorothy Enterprises Ltd.'s corporate offices, and much of the company's expensive computer equipment was stolen. Dorothy made a claim on her policy, but the insurance company took the position that she did not have an insurable interest in the corporate property.[26] Explain why the insurance company refused Dorothy's claim. What can she do now? What arguments can she make in support of her claim? What practical advice would Dorothy now give to other small-business owners?

4. Twelve-year-old Aaliyah Braybrook was babysitting two boys, aged three and five, when a fire broke out in their home. Braybrook was able to get the boys and the family pet out but the fire destroyed the home and damaged two neighbouring homes. It is alleged the fire was started by the five-year-old playing with a lighter in the bathroom. TD Insurance, the insurance company for the owners of one of the damaged neighbouring homes, filed on their behalf a $350 000 lawsuit against Braybrook and the father of the boys, who was the owner of the destroyed home. After a public outcry, including a speech by the local Member of Parliament in the House of Commons, TD

Insurance dropped the suit against Braybrook.[27] What was the likely basis of the lawsuit by the neighbours against Braybrook? On what basis could TD Insurance sue Braybrook on behalf of the neighbours? What do you think was the reason for TD Insurance naming Braybrook in the lawsuit? What was the risk to TD Insurance in naming Braybrook in the lawsuit?

5. Precision Machine Ltd. manufactures pistons and rings for draglines and excavators that are used in oil sands exploration. Demand for these components is unpredictable but critical, as machines cannot operate without them. In an effort to ensure that customers are satisfied, Precision keeps about $100 000 worth of components in inventory at all times. The value of the inventory is covered by property insurance from SPADE Insurance Ltd. The policy contains a coinsurance clause that requires Precision to hold 80 percent coverage. Precision, however, only carries $60 000 worth of coverage. An electrical fire destroys some of Precision's inventory and precision makes a claim of $30 000 on its policy. How much of the claim is Precision entitled to receive from SPADE? Why would Precision underinsure its inventory? How much is Precision entitled to receive from SPADE if its loss is $40 000?

6. Nathalie Blanchard took a medical leave for depression from her job as an IBM technician. Shortly thereafter, she began receiving monthly disability benefits from her insurer, Manulife Financial Corp. A year later, and without warning, the payments ceased. When Blanchard called Manulife to find out why her benefits were discontinued, she says she was told that her Facebook photos showed she was able to work. Investigators had discovered several pictures Blanchard posted on Facebook, including ones showing her drinking at a Chippendales bar show, at her birthday party, and frolicking on the beach during a sun holiday. Manulife would not comment on Blanchard's case but confirmed that it uses the social networking site to investigate clients. It also stated to CBC news: "We would not deny or terminate a valid

26 Based on *Kosmopoulos v Constitution Insurance Co of Canada*, [1987] 1 SCR 2, 34 DLR (4th) 208.

27 Florence Loyie, "'Hero' babysitter sued over fire", *Edmonton Journal* (6 May 2010) A12; Karen Kleiss, "Insurer drops lawsuit against hero babysitter", *Edmonton Journal* (8 May 2010) A3.

claim solely based on information published on websites such as Facebook."[28] Do insurers' use of social networks to check on people impinge on privacy rights? Should insurance companies be able to use information culled from sites such as Facebook to deny or terminate an insurance claim or to investigate fraud?

7. Thieves broke into the home of Paul and Judy Bronfman while they were out for the evening. They stole a safe that contained expensive jewellery, $50 000 in cash, and other valuables including two 1970s-era Montreal Canadiens Stanley Cup rings. The thieves were never found and the property was never recovered. The Bronfmans discovered, when making a claim, that their insurance policies only provided for $20 000 in coverage for jewellery and $1500 for cash. The Bronfmans sued their insurance broker for $3 million alleging the broker was negligent for failing to ensure that their policy reflected their standard of living. The broker countered that the Bronfmans were well aware of the coverage limits, which were spelled out in form letters sent to them.[29] How far must an insurance broker go to ensure a client's insurance policies are adequate?

8. In 1999, John Jacks signed a long-term car lease agreement, which was assigned by the dealership to GMAC Leaseco. On the same day, Jacks contacted a representative of the Wawanesa Mutual Insurance Company to insure the vehicle. The representative asked Jacks a few questions related to driving. In particular, the representative asked Jacks how many accidents he had had in the previous six years, whether he had ever been convicted of impaired driving, and whether his driver's licence had ever been revoked or suspended.

In 2002, Jacks had an accident and his car was destroyed. In response to his claim for compensation, Wawanesa conducted an investigation and discovered that the insured had been convicted of several crimes between 1980 and 1991, including break and enter, theft, possession of property obtained by crime, abetting in fraud, identity theft, fraud, and possession of drugs. Wawanesa refused to pay compensation on the basis that Jacks had failed in his duty to disclose.[30] What is the purpose of the insured's duty to disclose? What is the content of the duty to disclose? Who has the onus of proving whether the duty to disclose has been fulfilled? Did Jacks fulfill the duty to disclose? Discuss.

28 "Depressed woman loses benefits over Facebook photos", *CBC News* (21 November 2009), online: CBC News <http://www.cbc.ca/news/canada/montreal/story/2009/11/19/quebec-facebook-sick-leave-benefits.html>.

29 Jeff Gray, "Legal battle over Bronfman insurance policy headed for Court of Appeal", *The Globe and Mail* (14 March 2014), online: Globe and Mail <http://www.theglobeandmail.com/news/toronto/legal-battle-over-bronfman-insurance-policy-headed-for-court-of-appeal/article17624709/>.

30 Based on *Compagnie mutuelle d'assurances Wawanesa v GMAC location ltée*, 2005 QCCA 197, [2005] RRA 25 (Que CA).

GLOSSARY

Absolute privilege A defence to defamation in relation to parliamentary or judicial proceedings. (p. 282)

Abuse of dominant position A dominant company or group of companies engaging in anticompetitive behaviour that unduly prevents or lessens competition. (p. 626)

Acceleration clause A term of a loan agreement that makes the entire loan due if one payment is missed. (p. 667)

Acceptance An unqualified willingness to enter into a contract on the terms in the offer. (p. 120)

Account agreement A contract that specifies the rights and obligations of a bank and its customer. (p. 641)

Act of bankruptcy One of a list of specified acts that the debtor must commit before the court will grant a bankruptcy order. (p. 687)

Action for the price The seller's claim when the buyer has breached the contract and title to the goods has passed to the buyer. (p. 598)

Actual authority The power of an agent that derives from either express or implied agreement. (p. 298)

Administrative law Rules created and applied by those having governmental powers. (p. 38)

Adverse effects discrimination Discrimination that occurs as a result of a rule that appears neutral but in its effects is discriminatory. (p. 510)

After-acquired property Collateral that includes personal property acquired by the debtor during the term of the loan. (p. 662)

Age of majority The age at which a person becomes an adult for legal purposes. In Canada, this ranges from 18 to 19 years of age, depending on the province. (p. 8)

Agency by estoppel An agency relationship created when the principal acts such that third parties reasonably conclude that an agency relationship exists. (p. 300)

Agency by ratification An agency relationship created when one party adopts a contract entered into on his behalf by another who at the time acted without authority. (p. 302)

Agency A relationship that exists when one party represents another party in the formation of legal relations. (p. 295)

Agent A person who is authorized to act on behalf of another. (p. 295)

Aggravated damages Compensation for intangible injuries such as distress and humiliation caused by the defendant's reprehensible conduct. (p. 235)

All-risks property insurance Insurance coverage that protects property against all types of physical loss or injury arising from an external cause unless specifically excluded. (p. 710)

Alternative dispute resolution (ADR) A range of options for resolving disputes as an alternative to litigation. (p. 70)

Anticipatory breach A breach that occurs before the date for performance. (p. 207)

Anton Pillar order A pretrial order allowing the seizure of material, including material that infringes intellectual property rights. (p. 466)

Apparent authority The power that an agent appears to have to an outsider because of conduct or statements of the principal. (p. 299)

Appeal The process of arguing to a higher court that a court decision is wrong. (p. 86)

Appellant The party who begins or files an appeal. (p. 87)

Arbitration A process through which a neutral party makes a decision (usually binding) that resolves a dispute. (p. 11)

Arbitrator A person who listens to the parties to a dispute and makes a ruling that is usually binding on the parties. (p. 75)

Arm's length People who are independent of each other and not related. (p. 689)

Articles of incorporation The document that defines the basic characteristics of corporations incorporated in Newfoundland, New Brunswick, Ontario, Manitoba, Saskatchewan, Alberta, and the federal jurisdiction. (p. 362)

Assault Threat of imminent physical harm by disturbing someone's sense of security. (p. 275)

Assignment in bankruptcy The debtor's voluntary assignment to the trustee in bankruptcy of legal title to the debtor's property for the benefit of creditors. (p. 687)

Assignment The transfer of a right by an assignor to an assignee. (p. 198, 464)

Bailee The person who receives possession in a bailment. (p. 423)

Bailment for value Bailment involving payment or compensation. (p. 424)

Bailment Temporary transfer of possession of personal property from one person to another. (p. 423)

Bailor The owner of property who transfers possession in a bailment. (p. 423)

Bait and switch Advertising a product at a very low price to attract customers, then encouraging them to buy another product that is more expensive. (p. 623)

Balance of probabilities Proof that there is a better than 50 percent chance that the circumstances of the contract are as the plaintiff contends. (p. 202)

Bank draft A cheque written by a bank on the request (and payment) of its customer. (p. 648)

Bankrupt The legal status of a debtor who has made an assignment or against whom a bankruptcy order has been issued (also used to describe a debtor who is bankrupt). (p. 687)

Bankruptcy offences Criminal acts defined by the Bankruptcy and Insolvency Act (BIA) in relation to the bankruptcy process. (p. 691)

Bankruptcy order An order of the court resulting in a person being declared bankrupt. (p. 687)

Battery Intentional infliction of harmful or offensive physical contact. (p. 228, 275)

Bid rigging Conspiring to fix the bidding process to suit the collective needs of those submitting bids. (p. 626)

Bill Proposed legislation. (p. 33)

Bill of exchange A written order by one person (the drawer) to a third person (the drawee) to pay money to another person (the payee). (p. 645)

Bill of lading A shipping document that serves as a contract between the seller and the carrier. (p. 594)

Binding Final and enforceable in the courts. (p. 77)

Bona fide occupational requirement (BFOR) A defence that excuses discrimination on a prohibited ground when it is done in good faith and for a legitimate business reason. (p. 511)

Bond A document evidencing a debt owed by the corporation, often used to refer to a secured debt. (p. 364)

Breach of contract Failure to comply with a contractual promise. (p. 7)

Bundle of rights The set of legal rights associated with property, which usually includes the right to exclude, the right to possess and use, and the right to transfer to others or dispose of property. (p. 420)

Burden of proof The obligation of the plaintiff to prove its case. (p. 84)

Business ethics Moral principles and values that seek to determine right and wrong in the business world. (p. 13)

Business law A set of established rules governing commercial relationships, including the enforcement of rights. (p. 3)

Bylaws Laws made by the municipal level of government. (p. 27)

Bylaws Rules specifying the day-to-day operating procedures of a corporation. (p. 363)

c.i.f. A contractual term making the seller responsible for insurance and shipping. (p. 594)

c.o.d. A contractual term requiring the purchaser to pay the carrier in cash upon delivery of the goods. (p. 594)

Cabinet A body composed of all ministers heading government departments, as well as the prime minister or premier. (p. 28)

Canadian Charter of Rights and Freedoms A guarantee of specific rights and freedoms enshrined in the Constitution and enforceable by the judiciary. (p. 29)

Canadian legal system The machinery that comprises and governs the legislative, executive, and judicial branches of government. (p. 20)

Carrier A bailee who transports personal property. (p. 427)

Causation The relationship that exists between the defendant's conduct and the plaintiff's loss or injury. (p. 247)

Caveat emptor "Let the buyer beware" or "let the buyer take care." (p. 589)

Certification The process by which a union is recognized as a bargaining agent for a group of employees. (p. 531)

Certified cheque A cheque on which the drawee bank has guaranteed payment. (p. 648)

Cheque A bill of exchange which is drawn on a bank and is payable on demand. (p. 645)

Civil Code of Quebec The rules of private law that govern Quebec. (p. 37)

Claim The formal document that initiates litigation by setting out the plaintiff's allegations against the defendant. (p. 81)

Claims The exclusive rights of the patent holder. (p. 446)

Class action A lawsuit launched by one person who represents a class of persons having similar claims against the same defendant. (p. 79)

Closely held corporation A corporation that does not sell its shares to the public. (p. 357)

Closing The final stage of a real estate transaction when final documentation and payment are exchanged. (p. 485)

Collateral Property in which a creditor takes an interest as security for a borrower's promise to repay a loan. (p. 662)

Collection agency An agency that assists lenders in obtaining payment on outstanding loans. (p. 673)

Collective agreement The employment agreement reached between the union and employer setting out the bargaining unit employees' terms and conditions of employment. (p. 531)

Collective bargaining A mechanism by which parties enter a collective agreement or contract. (p. 531)

Common law Rules that are formulated in judgments. (p. 33)

Common mistake Both parties to the agreement share the same fundamental mistake. (p. 179)

Common share A share that generally has a right to vote, share in dividends, and share in proceeds on dissolution. (p. 398)

Concurrent jurisdiction Jurisdiction that is shared between levels of government. (p. 24)

Condition An important term that, if breached, gives the innocent party the right to terminate the contract and claim damages. (p. 204)

Condition precedent An event or circumstance that, until it occurs, suspends the parties' obligations to perform their contractual obligations. (p. 154)

Condition subsequent An event or circumstance that, when it occurs, brings an existing contract to an end. (p. 154)

Condonation Employer behaviour that indicates to the employee that misconduct is being overlooked. (p. 541)

Conduct incompatible Personal behaviour that is irreconcilable with employment duties or prejudicial to the employer's business. (p. 542)

Confidential business information Information that provides a business advantage as a result of the fact that it is kept secret. (p. 461)

Consideration The price paid for a promise. (p. 128)

Constitutional conventions Important rules that are not enforceable by a court of law but that practically determine how a given power is exercised by government. (p. 22)

Constitutional law The supreme law of Canada that constrains and controls how the branches of government exercise power. (p. 20)

Constructive dismissal Unilateral employer conduct that amounts to a fundamental or substantial change to an employee's contract. (p. 549)

Consumer debt A loan to an individual for a non-commercial purpose. (p. 672)

Consumer note A negotiable instrument signed by a consumer to buy goods or services on credit. (p. 647)

Consumer An individual who purchases goods or services primarily for personal, domestic or household purposes. (p. 605)

Contingency fee A fee based on a percentage of the judgment awarded, and paid by the client to the lawyer only if the action is successful. (p. 88)

Contract law Rules that make agreements binding and, therefore, facilitate planning and the enforcement of expectations. (p. 9)

Contract An agreement between two parties that is enforceable in a court of law. (p. 97)

Contractual entrant Any person who has paid (contracted) for the right to enter the premises. (p. 268)

Contractual quantum meruit Awarding one party a reasonable sum for the goods or services provided under a contract. (p. 148)

Contributory negligence A defence claiming that the plaintiff is at least partially responsible for the harm that has occurred. (p. 231)

Conversion right The right to convert one type of security into another type. (p. 365)

Copyright The right to prevent others from copying or modifying certain works. (p. 454)

Corporate opportunity A business opportunity in which the corporation has an interest. (p. 387)

Costs Legal expenses that a judge orders the loser to pay the winner. (p. 84)

Counterclaim A claim by the defendant against the plaintiff. (p. 82)

Counteroffer The rejection of one offer and proposal of a new one. (p. 120)

Credit bureau An agency that compiles credit information on borrowers. (p. 673)

Credit card A card issued by a financial institution that allows the user to borrow funds on a short-term basis, usually to purchase goods or services. (p. 643)

Cyber-squatting The bad-faith practice of registering trademarks or trade names of others as domain names for the purpose of selling the domain name to the rightful owner or preventing the rightful owner from obtaining the domain name. (p. 451)

Damages for non-acceptance Damages to which a seller is entitled if a buyer refuses to accept goods prior to the passing of title. (p. 598)

Damages Monetary compensation for breach of contract or other actionable wrong. (p. 207)

Debenture A document evidencing a debt owed by the corporation, often used to refer to an unsecured debt. (p. 364)

Debtor in possession (DIP) financing Secured credit provided to companies during the reorganization process with priority over existing secured creditors. (p. 685)

Deceit or fraud A false representation intentionally or recklessly made by one person to another that causes damage. (p. 225, 278)

Decision The judgment of the court that specifies which party is successful and why. (p. 84)

Deductible The part of a loss for which the insured is responsible. (p. 704)

Defamation The public utterance of a false statement of fact or opinion that harms another's reputation. (p. 281)

Defence The defendant's formal response to the plaintiff's allegations. (p. 82)

Defendant The party being sued. (p. 78)

Deficiency The shortfall between the outstanding mortgage balance and the proceeds from sale of the land. (p. 493)

Dependent contractor A person who is an independent contractor but has a relationship of economic dependency with the employer as a result of working exclusively or nearly exclusively for the employer for a long period. (p. 505)

Derivative action A suit by a shareholder on behalf of the corporation to enforce a corporate cause of action. (p. 401)

Director A person elected by shareholders to manage a corporation. (p. 337)

Discharge of bankruptcy An order releasing the debtor from bankrupt status and from most remaining debts. (p. 695)

Discovery The process of disclosing evidence to support the claims in a lawsuit. (p. 82)

Discrimination The act of treating someone differently on the basis of a prohibited ground. (p. 510)

Dissent and appraisal right The right of shareholders who dissent from certain fundamental changes to the corporation to have their shares purchased by the corporation at a fair price. (p. 400)

Distinguishing guise A shaping of wares or their container, or a mode of wrapping or packaging wares. (p. 449)

Distress The right of a commercial landlord to seize the tenant's personal property for non-payment of rent. (p. 496)

Distributorship A contractual relationship where one business agrees to sell another's products. (p. 435)

Dividend A division of profits payable to shareholders. (p. 338)

Domain name The unique address of a website. (p. 450)

Domestic law The internal law of a given country, which includes both statute and common law. (p. 36)

Door-to-door selling The act of selling in person directly, at a customer's residence. (p. 608)

Double ticketing The offence of failing to sell at the lower of the two or more prices marked on or otherwise appearing with regard to a product. (p. 620)

Due diligence A defence based on adopting reasonable steps to avoid the violation of a legal duty. (p. 615)

Duty of care The responsibility owed to avoid carelessness that causes harm to others. (p. 245)

Duty of confidentiality The obligation of a professional not to disclose any information provided by the client without the client's consent. (p. 576)

Duty to accommodate The duty of an employer to modify work rules, practices, and requirements to meet the needs of individuals who would otherwise be subjected to unlawful discrimination. (p. 512)

Duty to disclose The obligation of the insured to provide to the insurer all information that relates to the risk being insured. (p. 704)

Duty to mitigate The obligation to take reasonable steps to minimize the losses resulting from a breach of contract or other wrong. (p. 212)

Easement The right to use the land of another for a particular purpose only. (p. 421)

Economic duress The threat of economic harm that coerces the will of the other party and results in a contract. (p. 170)

Electronic banking Financial transactions carried out through the use of computers, telephones, or other electronic means. (p. 641)

Electronic funds transfer The transfer of money from one bank account to another through computer-based systems and without the direct assistance of bank staff. (p. 643)

Employment equity legislation Laws designed to improve the status of certain designated groups. (p. 515)

Employment relationship A contractual relationship whereby an employer provides remuneration to an employee in exchange for work or services. (p. 505)

Employment standards legislation Laws that specify minimum standards in the workplace. (p. 520)

Endorse To sign a negotiable instrument (such as a cheque) in order to enable negotiation. (p. 649)

Endorsement in blank Signing a cheque without any special instructions. (p. 650)

Endorsement Written evidence of a change to an existing insurance policy. (p. 709)

Enterprise risk management The process of identifying and managing all business risks. (p. 46)

Entire contract clause A term in a contract in which the parties agree that their contract is complete as written. (p. 148)

Equal bargaining power The legal assumption that parties to a contract are able to look out for their own interests. (p. 102)

Equity Rules that focus on what would be fair given the specific circumstances of the case, as opposed to what the strict rules of common law might dictate. (p. 35)

Equity of redemption The right to regain legal title to mortgaged land upon repayment of the debt. (p. 489)

Estate The collective term for the assets of a bankrupt individual or corporation. (p. 682)

Events of default Failure by the debtor to make required payments on a loan or to fulfill its other obligations under the credit agreement. (p. 661)

Evidence Proof presented in court to support a claim. (p. 84)

Exclusive dealing When a seller agrees to sell to the purchaser only if the purchaser buys from it exclusively. (p. 629)

Exclusive jurisdiction Jurisdiction that one level of government holds entirely on its own and not on a shared basis with another level. (p. 24)

Exclusive possession The tenant's right to control land during the term of a lease. (p. 494)

Exemption clause A term of a contract that identifies events causing loss for which there is no liability. (p. 156)

Expectation damages Damages which provide the plaintiff with the monetary equivalent of contractual performance. (p. 208)

Express term A provision of a contract that states a promise explicitly. (p. 141)

f.o.b. A contractual term whereby the buyer specifies the type of transportation and the seller arranges that transportation and delivery of goods to the carrier at the buyer's expense. (p. 594)

Fair comment A defence to defamation that is established when the plaintiff cannot show malice and the defendant can show that the comment concerned a matter of public interest, was factually based, and expressed a view that could honestly be held by anyone. (p. 281)

Fair dealing A defence to copyright infringement that permits the copying of works for particular purposes. (p. 461)

False imprisonment Unlawful detention or physical restraint or coercion by psychological means. (p. 227, 276)

False or misleading representation A promotional statement made to a consumer that is false, deceptive, or misleading. (p. 607)

Federal Court of Canada The court that deals with some types of litigation involving the federal government. (p. 29)

Fee simple The legal interest in real property that is closest to full ownership. (p. 475)

Fiduciary duty A duty imposed on a person who has a special relationship of trust with another. (p. 304)

Fiduciary A person who has a duty of good faith toward another because of their relationship. (p. 304)

Financing statement The document registered as evidence of a security interest. (p. 664)

Fixed- or definite-term contract A contract for a specified period of time, which automatically ends on the expiry date. (p. 518)

Fixtures Tangible personal property that is attached to land, buildings, or other structures. (p. 475)

Foreclosure The mortgagee's remedy to terminate the mortgagor's interest in the land. (p. 493)

Forfeiture rule A rule that provides that a criminal should not be permitted to profit from a crime. (p. 709)

Formal executive The branch of government responsible for the ceremonial features of government. (p. 27)

Franchise An agreement whereby an owner of a trademark or trade name permits another to sell a product or service under that trademark or name. (p. 340)

Frustration Termination of a contract upon the occurrence of an unforeseen catastrophic event which makes contractual performance impossible or prevents the contract from being performed in a manner at all similar to what the parties envisioned when they entered the contract. (p. 199)

Fundamental breach A breach of contract that affects the foundation of the contract. (p. 205)

Fundamental term A term that is considered to be essential to the contract. (p. 549)

Future goods Goods that are not yet in existence at the time a contract of sale is formed. (p. 596)

General security agreement A security agreement that includes all of the debtor's personal property assets as collateral. (p. 662)

Government policy The central ideas or principles that guide government in its work, including the kind of laws it passes. (p. 20)

Gratuitous bailment Bailment that involves no payment. (p. 425)

Gratuitous promise A promise for which no consideration is given. (p. 128)

Grievance process A procedure for resolving disputes contained in union contracts. (p. 559)

Guarantee A conditional promise to a creditor to pay a debt if the debtor defaults. (p. 669)

Guarantor A person who guarantees a debt. (p. 669)

Habitual neglect of duty Persistent failure to perform employment duties. (p. 541)

Holder in due course A holder in good faith without notice of defects, who acquires greater rights than the parties who dealt directly with each other as the drawer and payee. (p. 647)

Holder A person who has possession of a negotiable instrument. (p. 646)

Human rights commission An administrative body that oversees the implementation and enforcement of human rights legislation. (p. 510)

Identification theory A theory specifying that a corporation is liable when the person committing the wrong is the corporation's directing mind. (p. 380)

Identity theft The fraudulent use of others' personal information to create a false identity. (p. 642)

Illegal contract A contract that cannot be enforced because it is contrary to legislation or public policy. (p. 180)

Implied term A provision that is not expressly included in a contract but that is necessary to give effect to the parties' intention. (p. 143)

Incompetence Lack of ability, knowledge, or qualification to perform employment obligations. (p. 542)

Incorporator The person who sets the incorporation process in motion. (p. 362)

Indefinite-term contract A contract for no fixed period, which can end on giving reasonable notice. (p. 519)

Indemnification The corporate practice of paying the litigation expenses of officers and directors for lawsuits related to corporate affairs. (p. 396)

Indemnity A primary obligation to pay a debt owed by another person. (p. 669)

Independent contractor A person who is in a working relationship that does not meet the criteria of employment. (p. 505)

Industrial design The visual features of shape, configuration, pattern, ornamentation, or any combination of these applied to a finished article of manufacture. (p. 447)

Inferior court A court with limited financial jurisdiction whose judges are appointed by the provincial government. (p. 28)

Injurious or malicious falsehood The utterance of a false statement about another's goods or services that is harmful to the reputation of those goods or services. (p. 284)

Innkeeper Someone who offers lodging to the public. (p. 432)

Innominate term A term that cannot easily be classified as either a condition or a warranty. (p. 204)

Insider trading Transactions in securities of a corporation by or on behalf of an insider on the basis of relevant material information concerning the corporation that is not known to the general public. (p. 370)

Insider A person whose relationship with the issuer of securities is such that he is likely to have access to relevant material information concerning the issuer that is not known to the public. (p. 370)

Insolvent Unable to meet financial obligations as they become due or having insufficient assets, if liquidated, to meet financial obligations. (p. 682)

Inspector A person appointed by creditors to act on their behalf and supervise the actions of the trustee in bankruptcy. (p. 688)

Insurable interest A financial stake in what is being insured. (p. 707)

Insurance adjuster One who investigates and evaluates insurance claims. (p. 720)

Insurance broker An independent business that deals with several insurance companies and advises clients on the appropriate insurance coverage. (p. 308)

Insurance policy A contract of insurance. (p. 703)

Insured One who buys insurance coverage. (p. 703)

Insurer A company that sells insurance coverage. (p. 702)

Intangible property Personal property, the value of which comes from legal rights. (p. 416)

Intellectual property The results of the creative process, such as ideas, the expression of ideas, formulas, schemes, trademarks, and the like; also refers to the protection attached to ideas through patent, copyright, trademark, industrial design, and other similar laws. (p. 439)

Intentional tort A harmful act that is committed deliberately or on purpose. (p. 227)

Interference with contractual relations Incitement to break the contractual obligations of another. (p. 280)

Interlocutory injunction An order to refrain from doing something for a limited period of time. (p. 214)

International law Law that governs relations between states and other entities with international legal status. (p. 36)

Intrusion upon seclusion Intentional, offensive invasion of another's personal affairs without lawful justification. (p. 285)

Invitation to treat An expression of willingness to do business. (p. 112)

Invitee Any person who comes onto the property to provide the occupier with a benefit. (p. 268)

Joint and several liability Individual and collective liability for a debt. Each liable party is individually responsible for the entire debt as well as being collectively liable for the entire debt. (p. 331)

Joint liability Liability shared by two or more parties where each is personally liable for the full amount of the obligation. (p. 325)

Joint tenancy Co-ownership whereby the survivor inherits the undivided interest of the deceased. (p. 475)

Joint tort-feasors Two or more persons whom a court has held to be jointly responsible for the plaintiff's loss or injuries. (p. 231)

Joint venture A grouping of two or more businesses to undertake a particular project. (p. 344)

Judges Those appointed by federal or provincial governments to adjudicate on a variety of disputes, as well as to preside over criminal proceedings. (p. 28)

Judgment debtor The party ordered by the court to pay a specified amount to the winner of a lawsuit. (p. 86)

Judiciary A collective reference to judges. (p. 28)

Jurisdiction The power that a given level of government has to enact laws. (p. 23)

Just cause Employee conduct that amounts to a fundamental breach of the employment contract. (p. 539)

Justification A defence to defamation based on the defamatory statement being substantially true. (p. 281)

Labour relations board A body that administers labour relations legislation. (p. 531)

Land titles system The system of land registration whereby the administrators guarantee the title to land. (p. 478)

Landlord The owner of land who grants possession to the tenant. (p. 493)

Lapse The expiration of an offer after a specified or reasonable period. (p. 119)

Law firm A partnership formed by lawyers. (p. 61)

Law of agency The law governing the relationship where one party, the agent, acts on behalf of another, the principal. (p. 297)

Law The set of rules and principles guiding conduct in society. (p. 5)

Lawyer A person who is legally qualified to practise law. (p. 61)

Lawyer–client privilege The right of a client not to have communications between lawyer and client divulged to third parties. (p. 576)

Lease A contract that transfers possession of land or personal property in exchange for a fee. (p. 421)

Legal authority The authority by law to detain under section 494 of the *Criminal Code*. (p. 276)

Legal capacity The ability to make binding contracts. (p. 168)

Legal risk management plan A comprehensive action plan for dealing with the legal risks involved in operating a business. (p. 13)

Legal risk A business risk with legal implications. (p. 46)

Legislative branch The branch of government that creates statute law. (p. 22)

Letter of commitment A document that is provided by a lender to a borrower and sets out the terms of a loan. (p. 662)

Letter of credit A written promise by a buyer's bank to a seller's bank to pay the seller when specified conditions are met. (p. 660)

Liability Legal responsibility for the event or loss that has occurred. (p. 12)

Liberalism A political philosophy that emphasizes individual freedom as its key organizing value. (p. 20)

Licence Consent given by the owner of rights to someone to do something that only the owner can do. (p. 422, 464)

Licensee Any person whose presence is not a benefit to the occupier but to which the occupier has no objection. (p. 268)

Lien The right to retain possession of personal property until payment for service is received. (p. 430)

Lifting the corporate veil Determining that the corporation is not a separate legal entity from its shareholders. (p. 396)

Limitation of liability clause A term of a contract that limits liability for breach to something less than would otherwise be recoverable. (p. 156)

Limitation period The time period specified by legislation for commencing legal action. (p. 78)

Limited liability partnership (LLP) A partnership in which the partners have unlimited liability for their own malpractice but limited liability for other partners' malpractice. (p. 335)

Limited liability Responsibility for obligations restricted to the amount of investment. (p. 337)

Limited partnership A partnership in which the liability of some partners is limited to their capital contribution. (p. 335)

Liquidated damages clause A term of a contract that specifies how much one party must pay to the other in the event of breach. (p. 159)

Litigation The process involved when one person sues another. (p. 10)

Mediation A process through which the parties to a dispute endeavour to reach a resolution with the assistance of a neutral person. (p. 11)

Mediator A person who helps the parties resolve their dispute. (p. 74)

Misrepresentation A false statement of fact that causes someone to enter a contract. (p. 176)

Mistake An error made by one or both parties that seriously undermines a contract. (p. 178)

Money laundering The false reporting of income from criminal activity as income from legitimate business. (p. 640)

Moral rights The author's rights to have work properly attributed and not prejudicially modified or associated with products. (p. 459)

Mortgage A loan for real property that is secured by an interest in the property. (p. 488)

Mortgagee The party who lends the money and receives the signed mortgage as security for repayment. (p. 489)

Mortgagor The party who borrows the money and signs the mortgage promising to repay the loan. (p. 489)

Multi-level marketing A scheme for distributing products or services that involves participants recruiting others to become involved in distribution. (p. 629)

Negligence Unreasonable conduct, including a careless act or omission, that causes harm to another. (p. 225)

Negligent misstatement or negligent misrepresentation An incorrect statement made carelessly. (p. 254)

Negotiable instrument A signed document containing an unconditional promise or order to pay a specific sum on demand or on a specified date to a specific person. (p. 645)

Negotiation A process of deliberation and discussion intended to reach a mutually acceptable resolution to a dispute. (p. 70)

Neighbour Anyone who might reasonably be affected by the defendant's conduct. (p. 245)

Non-competition clause A clause forbidding competition for a certain period of time. (p. 182)

Non-pecuniary damages Compensation for pain and suffering, loss of enjoyment of life, and loss of life expectancy. (p. 232)

Non-solicitation clause A clause forbidding contact with the business's customers. (p. 182)

Novation The substitution of parties in a contract or the replacement of one contract with another. (p. 197)

NUANS Report A document that shows the result of a search for business names. (p. 362)

Nuisance Any activity on an occupier's property that unreasonably and substantially interferes with the neighbour's rights to enjoyment of the neighbour's own property. (p. 271)

Objective standard test A test based on how a "reasonable person" would view the matter. (p. 102)

Occupier Someone who has some degree of control over land or buildings on that land. (p. 267)

Offer A promise to perform specified acts on certain terms. (p. 111)

Offeree The person to whom an offer is made. (p. 116)

Offeror The person who makes an offer. (p. 116)

Oppression remedy A statutory remedy available to shareholders and other stakeholders to protect their corporate interests. (p. 401)

Option agreement An agreement where, in exchange for payment, an offeror is obligated to keep an offer open for a specified time. (p. 118)

Outsider The party with whom the agent does business on behalf of the principal. (p. 296)

Overdraft An overdraft occurs when money is withdrawn from a bank account with the result that the balance in the account goes below zero. (p. 641)

Paramountcy A doctrine that provides that federal laws prevail when there are conflicting or inconsistent federal and provincial laws. (p. 25)

Parol evidence rule A rule that limits the evidence a party can introduce concerning the contents of the contract. (p. 150)

Partnership A business carried on by two or more persons with the intention of making a profit. (p. 324)

Passing off Presenting another's goods or services as one's own. (p. 278)

Patent agent A professional trained in patent law and practice who can assist in the preparation of a patent application. (p. 445)

Patent A monopoly to make, use, or sell an invention. (p. 440)

Pay equity Provisions designed to ensure that female and male employees receive the same compensation for performing similar or substantially similar work. (p. 526)

Payday loans Short-term loans for a relatively small amount of money, provided by a non-traditional lender to an individual. (p. 674)

Pecuniary damages Compensation for out-of-pocket expenses, loss of future income, and cost of future care. (p. 233)

Penalty clause A term which is not enforceable because it sets an exorbitant amount that one party must pay to the other in event of breach. (p. 160)

Periodic tenancy A lease that is automatically renewed unless one party gives proper notice to terminate. (p. 497)

Personal property All property, other than land and what is attached to it. (p. 416)

Plaintiff The party that initiates a lawsuit against another party. (p. 78)

Pleadings The formal documents concerning the basis for a lawsuit. (p. 81)

Political executive The branch of government responsible for day-to-day operations, including formulating and executing government policy, as well as administering all departments of government. (p. 27)

Power of attorney An agency agreement in writing and under seal. (p. 298)

Precedent An earlier case used to resolve a current case because of its similarity. (p. 35)

Pre-emptive right A shareholder's right to maintain a proportionate share of ownership by purchasing a proportionate share of any new stock issue. (p. 399)

Pre-existing legal duty A legal obligation that a person already owes. (p. 129)

Preferred creditors Certain unsecured creditors who are given priority over other unsecured creditors in the bankruptcy distribution. (p. 692)

Preferred share A share or stock that has a preference in the distribution of dividends and the proceeds on dissolution. (p. 398)

Premium The price paid for insurance coverage. (p. 703)

Price fixing Conspiring with competitors to fix the prices charged for goods or services. (p. 624)

Price maintenance The attempt to drive the final retail price of goods upward and the imposition of recriminations upon noncompliant retailers. (p. 627)

Prima facie At first sight or on first appearances. (p. 246)

Principal A person who has permitted another to act on her behalf. (p. 295)

Private law Areas of law that concern dealings between persons. (p. 36)

Procedural law The law governing the procedure to enforce rights, duties, and liabilities. (p. 36)

Product liability Liability relating to the design, manufacture, or sale of the product. (p. 255)

Product licensing An arrangement whereby the owner of a trademark or other proprietary right grants to another the right to manufacture or distribute products associated with the trademark or other proprietary right. (p. 346)

Professional corporation A corporation authorized by statute to carry on a specific profession. (p. 577)

Professional Someone engaged in an occupation requiring the exercise of special knowledge, education, and skill. (p. 254, 567)

Progressive discipline policy A system that follows a sequence of employee discipline from less to more severe punishment. (p. 540)

Promissory estoppel A doctrine whereby someone who relies on a gratuitous promise may be able to enforce it. (p. 132)

Promissory note A written promise to pay another person a specific amount on demand or on a specified date. (p. 645)

Proof of claim A formal notice provided by the creditor to the trustee of the amount owed and the nature of the debt. (p. 691)

Prospectus The document a corporation must publish when offering securities to the public. (p. 368)

Proxy A person who is authorized to exercise a shareholder's voting rights. (p. 399)

Public law Areas of the law that relate to or regulate the relationship between persons and government at all levels. (p. 36)

Public policy The community's common sense and common conscience. (p. 181)

Punitive damages An award to the plaintiff to punish the defendant for malicious, oppressive, and high-handed conduct. (p. 208)

Purchase-money security interest (PMSI) A security interest that enables the debtor to acquire assets and gives the secured party priority over existing perfected security interests. (p. 665)

Pure economic loss Financial loss that results from a negligent act where there has been no accompanying property or personal injury damage to the person claiming the loss. (p. 251)

Pyramid selling A form of multi-level selling that is illegal under the *Competition Act*. (p. 629)

Qualified privilege A defence to defamation based on the defamatory statement being relevant, without malice, and communicated only to a party who has a legitimate interest in receiving it. (p. 281)

Ratify To authorize or approve. (p. 26)

Real property Land and whatever is permanently affixed to it or part of it, such as buildings, mines, and minerals and the legal rights associated with those things. (p. 415)

Reasonable care The care that a reasonable person would exhibit in a similar situation. (p. 244)

Reasonable notice A period of time for an employee to find alternative employment prior to dismissal. (p. 545)

Reasonable person The standard used to judge whether a person's conduct in a particular situation is negligent. (p. 247)

Rebuttable presumption A legal presumption in favour of one party that the other side can seek to rebut or dislodge by leading evidence to the contrary. (p. 135)

Receiver A person appointed by the secured party or by the court to seize, and usually sell, collateral. (p. 667)

Refusal to deal When a seller refuses to sell to a purchaser on the same terms as those that are offered to the purchaser's competitors. (p. 629)

Registration The registration of a financing statement to record a security interest. (p. 664)

Registry system The system of land registration whereby the records are available to be examined and evaluated by interested parties. (p. 477)

Regulations Rules created by the political executive that have the force of law. (p. 28)

Regulatory offence An offence contrary to the public interest. (p. 384)

Rejection The refusal to accept an offer. (p. 119)

Release A written or oral statement discharging another from an existing duty. (p. 559)

Release An agreement where a party agrees to relinquish past, present, and future claims arising from a certain event. (p. 72)

Remoteness of damage The absence of a sufficiently close relationship between the defendant's action and the plaintiff's injury. (p. 249)

Rescission The remedy that results in the parties being returned to their pre-contractual positions. (p. 176)

Respondent The party against whom an appeal is filed. (p. 87)

Responsible communication on matters of public interest Defence that applies where some facts are incorrectly reported but (1) the publication is on a matter of "public interest" and (2) the publisher was diligent in trying to verify the allegation. (p. 282)

Restitutionary quantum meruit An amount that is reasonable given the benefit the plaintiff has conferred. (p. 214)

Restrictive covenant A restriction on the use of land as specified in the title document. (p. 476)

Restrictive endorsement Signing a cheque for deposit only to a particular bank account. (p. 650)

Retainer An advance payment requested by a professional from a client to fund services to be provided to the client. (p. 569)

Revocation The withdrawal of an offer. (p. 116)

Rider A clause altering or adding to coverage in a standard insurance policy. (p. 709)

Risk avoidance Ceasing a business activity because the legal risk is too great. (p. 53)

Risk reduction Implementing practices in a business to lower the probability of loss and its severity. (p. 53)

Risk retention Absorbing the loss if a legal risk materializes. (p. 54)

Risk transference Shifting the risk to someone else through a contract. (p. 54)

Royal prerogative Historical rights and privileges of the Crown, including the right to conduct foreign affairs and to declare war. (p. 33)

Rules of construction Guiding principles for interpreting or "constructing" the terms of a contract. (p. 142)

Sales agency An agreement in which a manufacturer or distributor allows another to sell products on its behalf. (p. 346)

Salvage An insurer's right to title of what remains of property after paying for a total loss. (p. 709)

Secured credit A debt where the creditor has an interest in the debtor's property to secure payment. (p. 659)

Securities legislation Laws designed to regulate transactions involving shares and bonds of a corporation. (p. 357)

Securities Shares and bonds issued by a corporation. (p. 364)

Security interest An interest in personal property that is intended to secure payment or performance of an obligation (usually a debt). (p. 663)

Self-dealing contract A contract in which a fiduciary has a conflict of interest. (p. 387)

Serious misconduct Intentional, harmful conduct of the employee that permits the employer to dismiss without notice. (p. 540)

Severance pay An amount owed to a terminated employee under employment standards legislation. (p. 558)

Share structure The shares that a corporation is permitted to issue by its constitution. (p. 356)

Shareholder A person who has an ownership interest in a corporation. (p. 337)

Shareholders' agreement An agreement that defines the relationship among people who have an ownership interest in a corporation. (p. 404)

Shelf company A company that does not engage in active business. (p. 362)

Small claims court A court that deals with claims up to a specified amount. (p. 29)

Sole proprietorship An unincorporated business organization that has only one owner. (p. 321)

Special endorsement Signing a cheque and making it payable to a specific person. (p. 650)

Specific goods Goods that are in existence and identifiable at the time a contract of sale is formed. (p. 595)

Specifications The description of an invention contained in a patent. (p. 446)

Stakeholder One who has an interest in a corporation. (p. 354)

Standard form contract A "take it or leave it" contract, where the customer agrees to a standard set of terms that favours the other side. (p. 113)

Statute law Formal, written laws created or enacted by the legislative branch of government. (p. 22)

Stop payment When the drawer of a cheque orders its bank not to pay the holder who presents the cheque for payment. (p. 648)

Stoppage in transit The right of a seller to demand that goods be returned by a shipper to the seller, provided the buyer is insolvent. (p. 594)

Strategic alliance An arrangement whereby two or more businesses agree to cooperate for some purpose. (p. 345)

Strict liability The principle that liability will be imposed irrespective of proof of negligence. (p. 258)

Subrogation The right of a guarantor to recover from the debtor any payments made to the creditor. (p. 670)

Substantive law Law that defines rights, duties, and liabilities. (p. 36)

Superior courts Courts with unlimited financial jurisdiction whose judges are appointed by the federal government. (p. 29)

Supreme Court of Canada The final court for appeals in the country. (p. 29)

Systemic discrimination Discrimination that results from the combined effects of many rules, practices, and policies. (p. 511)

Tangible property Personal property that is mobile, the value of which comes from its physical form. (p. 416)

Telemarketing The use of unsolicited telephone calls to market goods and services to prospective customers. (p. 608)

Tenancy in common Co-ownership whereby each owner of an undivided interest can dispose of that interest. (p. 475)

Tenant The party in possession of land that is leased. (p. 493)

Thin skull rule The principle that a defendant is liable for the full extent of a plaintiff's injury even where a prior vulnerability makes the harm more serious than it otherwise might be. (p. 250)

Third party One who is not a party to an agreement. (p. 254)

Tied selling When a seller will sell to the purchaser only if the purchaser buys other, less desirable goods as well. (p. 629)

Tippee A person who acquires material information about an issuer of securities from an insider. (p. 371)

Title insurance Insurance that covers title related issues such as fraudulent transfers and mortgages, liens, boundary encroachments, issues related to government regulation, zoning problems, survey defects, and registration issues. (p. 480)

Title search Investigation of the registered ownership of land in a registry system. (p. 482)

Tort A harm caused by one person to another, other than through breach of contract, and for which the law provides a remedy. (p. 225)

Tort-feasor Person who commits a tort. (p. 231)

Trade name The name under which a sole proprietorship, a partnership, or a corporation does business. (p. 449)

Trademark A word, symbol, design, or any combination of these used to distinguish the source of goods or services. (p. 449)

Transfers at undervalue Transfers of property or provision of services for less than fair market value. (p. 689)

Treaty An agreement between two or more states that is governed by international law. (p. 26)

Trespass to land Wrongful interference with someone's possession of land. (p. 225, 273)

Trespasser Any person who is not invited onto the property and whose presence is either unknown to the occupier or is objected to by the occupier. (p. 269)

Trial A formal hearing before a judge that results in a binding decision. (p. 83)

Trust A legal arrangement that is characterized by one party holding legal title of property for the benefit of someone else. (p. 422)

Trustee in bankruptcy The person who has legal responsibility under the *BIA* for administering bankruptcies and proposals. (p. 682)

Unanimous shareholders' agreement (USA) An agreement among all shareholders that restricts the powers of the directors to manage the corporation. (p. 404)

Unascertained goods Goods that are not yet set aside and identifiable as the subject matter of the contract at the time a contract of sale is formed. (p. 595)

Unconscionable contract An unfair contract formed when one party takes advantage of the weakness of another. (p. 173)

Undisclosed principal A principal whose identity is unknown to a third party who has no knowledge that the agent is acting in an agency capacity. (p. 310)

Undue influence Unfair manipulation that compromises someone's free will or choice. (p. 171)

Unfair practices Illegal business practices that exploit the unequal bargaining position of consumers. (p. 606)

Unjust enrichment Occurs when one party has undeservedly or unjustly secured a benefit at the other party's expense. (p. 214)

Unlimited liability Unrestricted legal responsibility for obligations. (p. 322)

Unsecured credit A debt where the creditor has only a contractual right to be repaid. (p. 659)

Vicarious liability The liability that an employer has for the tortious acts of an employee committed in the ordinary course or scope of employment. (p. 230)

Vicarious performance Performance of contractual obligations through others. (p. 197)

Void contract A contract involving a defect so substantial that it is of no force or effect. (p. 168)

Voidable contract A contract that, in certain circumstances, an aggrieved party can choose to keep in force or bring to an end. (p. 168)

Voluntary assumption of risk The defence that no liability exists as the plaintiff agreed to accept the risk inherent in the activity. (p. 252)

Warehouseman A bailee who stores personal property. (p. 426)

Warranty of authority A representation of authority by a person who purports to be an agent. (p. 309)

Warranty A minor term that, if breached, gives the innocent party the right to claim damages only. (p. 204)

Widely held corporation A corporation whose shares are normally traded on a stock exchange. (p. 357)

Willful disobedience Deliberate failure to carry out lawful and reasonable orders. (p. 543)

Winding up The process of dissolving a corporation. (p. 406)

Workers' compensation legislation Legislation that provides no-fault compensation for injured employees in lieu of their right to sue in tort. (p. 232)

INDEX

Boldface page locators indicate terms that are defined in the text

A

Absenteeism, 541
Absolute pollution exclusions, 718–719
Absolute privilege, **282, 727**
Abuse of dominant position, **626**–627, **727**
Acceleration clauses, **667, 727**
Acceptance, **122**–127, **727**
Access Copyright, 458
Accommodation, duty of, **512**–514, 554–555
Account agreement, **641, 727**
Accountants, 577–578
Accounts receivable, 416
Accused, 229
Ace Manufacturing Ltd., 602
Acquisitions, 616
Actionable misrepresentation, 176–178
Action for the price, **598, 727**
Acts of bankruptcy, **687, 727**
Actual authority, **298**–299, **727**
Actual pressure, 171
Adaptation rights, 456
Adequate and proper tests, 622, 623
Administrative bodies and officials affecting business, 40
functions of, 39
Administrative law, 37, **38**–40, **727**
ADR. *See* Alternative dispute resolution (ADR)
ADR Institute of Canada, 74, 77
Adverse effects discrimination, **510, 727**
Advertising
comparative, 622
environmental claims in, 617–618
false or misleading advertising, 605, 622
injurious or malicious falsehoods, **284**

as invitation to treat, 112–113
spam, effects of, 113–115
standards, 614
Advertising Standards Canada (ASC), 614
After-acquired property, **662**–663, **727**
Agency, **295, 727**
actual authority, **298**–299
agent duties, 304–306
by agreement, 297–298, 304
apparent authority, **299**–300
authority under, 298
contract liability, 309–313
corporate liability and, 380–381
defined, **295**–297
by estoppel, **300**–302, **727**
overview, 295–296
principal duties, 307–308
by ratification, **302**–304, **727**
termination of, 314–315
tort liability, 313–314
undisclosed principals, **310**
warranty of authority, **309**, 311
Agents, **295,** 296, 303, 304–307, **727**
Age of majority, **8**, 9, **168**–169, **727**
Age of Majority and Accountability Act, 168
Aggravated damages, **235**–236, 553, 558, **727**
Agreement of purchase and sale, 481–482
Agreement on Trade-Related Aspects of Intellectual Property (TRIPS), 468
Agreements, 97, 111, 135. *See also* Contracts
account, **641, 727, 747**
business, 135
click-wrap, 158–159
collective, **531,** 559–560
conditional, 154–155
credit, 661–662
family, 135
general security, **662, 732**
guarantee, 669–670

loan, 662–661
non-disclosure, 462
option, **118**–119
partnership, 326
purchase and sale, 481–482
settlement, 72, 75
shareholders', 402, **404, 737**
Alberta Environmental Protection and Enhancement Act, 384
Alberta (Human Rights and Citizenship Commission) v Kellogg, Brown & Root, 514
Alberta Personal Property Bill of Rights, 420
Alcohol, and negligence, 256–258
Alcohol testing, 527
Alimentation Couche-Tard Inc., 377
Allen v Aspen Group Resources Corporation, 411
All-risks property insurance, **727**
Alternative dispute resolution (ADR), **70, 727**
arbitration, 75–78
mediation, **74**–75
negotiation, **70**–73
Amazon.com, 443
Ambiguous language/terms, 141–142
Anderson, James, 143–144
Animals, humane treatment of, 8
Anticipatory breach, **207, 727**
Anti-smoking treaty, 26
Anton Pillar order, **466, 727**
Apology legislation, 71, 72
Apparent authority, **299**–300, **727**
Appeals, **86**–87, **727**
Appellants, **87, 727**
Arbitration, **11**, 75–78, 89, 559–560, **727**
Arbitration clauses, 76, 77
Arbitration legislation, 76, 78
Arbitrators, **75, 727**
Arm's length, **689**–690, **727**
Arrangements, business, 340–346
Arrangements and proposals, 683–687
Arthur Andersen, 281

K

Kanitz v Rogers Cable Inc., 159
Kauffman v Toronto Transit Commission, 263
Kelley, Mark, 5
Key-person life insurance, 719
Kirby, Daniel, 24
Knock-off goods, 458–459
Kralik v Mount Seymour Resorts 2008, 252
Krawchuk v Scherbak, 312–313

L

Labelling and packaging, 610–611
Labour relations boards, **531, 733**
Labour standards legislation, **520**–521
LAC Minerals Ltd v International Corona Resources Ltd, 462–463
Land, 475
Land, electronic developments affecting interests in, 478–479
Landlords, **493, 733**
Landlord-tenant relationship, **493**–498
Land titles systems, **478, 733**
Lapse, **119, 733**
Larmer, Robert, 206
Law, **5, 733**. *See also* Canadian legal system
  business environment, 3–4
  business ethics and, **13**–14
  for dispute resolution, 10–12
  to facilitate interactions, 9–10
  functioning of, 12
  impacts of, 3–4
  knowledge of, as business asset, 2–3, 13
  to protect people and property, 5–9
  providing mechanisms for dispute resolution, 10–12
Law firms, **61, 733**
Law of agency, **297, 733**. *See also* Agency
Lawsuits
  class action, 79–81
  stages of, 81–86
Lawyer, **733**
Lawyer-client privilege, **576, 733**

Lawyers, **61**
  certificate of independent legal advice, 172
  fees, **90**, 569–570
  fiduciary duties, 331–332
  legislation for, 578–579
  managing services of, 60–62
  role in legal risk management, 62
  title searches by, 481
Lawyers Weekly, 104
Layoffs, 541
Leases, 414–415, **421**, 493–498, **733**
Leave, employment, 520
Leave applications for appeals, 89
Legal advice timing, 61
Legal authority, **276**–278, **733**
Legal capacity, **168**–169, **733**
Legal obligations, professionals, 567
Legal Profession Act, 578
Legal risk, **734**
Legal risk management, 62
Legal risk management plans, **13, 46, 733**. *See also* Dispute resolution
  crisis management, 59–60
  development of, **60–62**
  devising, 52–55
  evaluation of risks, 51
  identification of legal risks, 47–50
  implementation of, 56–59
  lawyers' role in, 62
  monitoring and revision of, 56–59
  overview, 46–47, 58
  reacting when prevention fails, 59
  who is responsible for, 46–47
Legal risks, **46**
Legal services management, 60–62
Legislative Assembly, 22
Legislative branch, **22, 734**
  constitutionality issues and, 39
  functions of, 23
  paramountcy doctrine and, **25**–26
  as part of legal system, 22–27
Letters of commitment, **662, 734**
Letters of credit, **660**–661, **734**
Liability, **12, 734**
  avoiding, 395–396

  in contract, 392
  in contracts of bailment, 432
  shareholder, 396–397
  by statute, 393
  strict, **258**–259
Liability clauses, limitation of, **156**, 205–207, 432
Liability for a stolen Ford Mustang, 211
Liability insurance, 704, 711, 712
Libel. *See* Defamation
Liberalism, **20, 734**
Licences, **422, 464**, 579, **734**
Licensees, **268**–269, **734**
Licensing, **346**, 464
Liebeck, Stella, 234
Liens, **430**, 666, **734**
Lieutenant governors, 27, 28
Life insurance, 704, 708, 711, 719
Life insurance brokers, compensation of, **308**–309
Lifting the corporate veil, 396–397, **734**
Limitation of liability clauses, **156**, 205–207, 410–411, **734**
Limitation periods, **78, 734**
Limited liability, **337, 734**
Limited liability partnerships (LLP), **335**–336 , 577, **734**
Limited partnerships, **335, 734**
Liquidated damages clauses, **159**–160, **734**
Liquidity test, 405
Literary works, 455, 463, 468
Litigation, **10**, 11, 89, **734**
  appeals, 89
  arbitration compared, 75, 77
  class actions, **83**
  enforcement of judgments, 89
  limitation periods, **78**
  overview, 78
  parties to cases, 78
  process, 78–81
  stages of, 81–86
  U.S. compared to Canada, 87–88
Litigation period, **78**–79
Livent, 573–574
LLP (limited liability partnerships), **335**–336, 577
Loan agreements, 662–661
Loans. *See* Credit
Loblaw, 14

How to Read a Citation

Citation for a Civil Case

Canadian Civil Liberties Assn	v	Toronto Dominion Bank	(1998),	163	DLR	(4th)	193	(FCA)
plaintiff	versus (Latin, "against")	defendant	year of decision	volume number	report listing case	series	page number	court

Citation for a Criminal Case

R	v	Fuel Base Industries Inc	(1992),	44	C.P.R.	(3d)	184	(Alta Prov Ct)
Rex or Regina (Latin, "King" or "Queen")	versus defendant or accused (Latin, "against")		year of decision	volume number	report listing case	series	page number	court

Abbreviations

References to the decisions of the courts, to statutes, and to legal periodicals are abbreviated throughout the text in case citations and footnotes. The list below shows the abbreviations for frequently cited source material.

Jurisdictions

Canada

Alta	Alberta
BC	British Columbia
Man	Manitoba
NB	New Brunswick
NS	Nova Scotia
NWT	Northwest Territories
Nfld	Newfoundland
Ont	Ontario
PEI	Prince Edward Island
Qc	Quebec
Sask	Saskatchewan
Y	Yukon Territory

United Kingdom

E	England

United States

Ohio	Ohio
Minn	Minnesota

Courts

Canada

CA	Court of Appeal
Co Ct	County Court
CS	Cour Supérieure
Cty Ct	County Court
Div Ct	Divisional Court
FCA	Federal Court of Appeal
FCTD	Federal Court (Trial Division)
HC	High Court
H Ct J	High Court of Justice
Gen Div	General Division
Prov Ct	Provincial Court
Prov Div	Provincial Division
QB	Court of Queen's Bench
SC	Supreme Court
SC (AD)	Supreme Court (Appellate Division)
SC (TD)	Supreme Court (Trial Division)
SCC	Supreme Court of Canada

United Kingdom

CA	Court of Appeal
Ch	Chancery Court
ChD	High Court: Chancery Division
HL	House of Lords
KB	Court of King's Bench
PC	Judicial Committee of the Privy Council
QB	Court of Queen's Bench